Problems and Materials on
DECEDENTS' ESTATES AND TRUSTS

Problems and Materials on
DECEDENTS' ESTATES AND TRUSTS

Fifth Edition

Eugene F. Scoles
Max L. Rowe Professor of Law, Emeritus
College of Law, University of Illinois
Distinguished Professor of Law, Emeritus
School of Law, University of Oregon

Edward C. Halbach, Jr.
Walter Perry Johnson Professor
School of Law, University of California, Berkeley

Little, Brown and Company
Boston   Toronto   London

Library of Congress Catalog Card No. 92-75496

ISBN 0-316-77649-1

Fifth Edition

MV-PA

Published simultaneously in Canada
by Little, Brown & Company (Canada) Limited

Printed in the United States of America

To our wives
who made this book possible
and
to our children
who made it necessary

Summary of Contents

Contents

3

Family Protection and Restrictions on Testation   90

4
Execution of Wills   129

5
Integration, Extrinsic Evidence, and Related Matters — 155

8
Will Substitutes and Introduction to Estate Planning   236

9
Introduction to Trusts: Their Nature, Use, and Classification   302

10
The Elements of a Trust   320

11
Creation of Trusts   350

12
The Nature of the Beneficiaries' Interests   423

15
Introduction to Fiduciary Administration   558

16
Probate and Contest of Wills   616

17
The Fiduciary Office   679

19
Matters of Accounting and Successive Enjoyment   **861**

20
Constructional Problems in Estate Distribution   950

Preface to the Fifth Edition

The continuing upsurge of legislative reform in probate and trust law is reflected throughout this fifth edition, as it was in the second through the fourth. The materials on decedents' estates are particularly and inevitably oriented to statutory law, with special attention to the Uniform Probate Code. The UPC was promulgated in 1969 by the National Conference of Commissioners on Uniform State Laws, was extensively revised and expanded in 1989 and 1990, and remains a subject of ongoing study and modification.

The major considerations in revising the materials in this book, beyond the inclusion of recent judicial and legislative developments, have been pedagogical. For example, some materials have been relocated and, in an effort to strengthen our offering of problems as major vehicles for class discussion, we have added problems on several topics and revised or relocated some others. We have also increased our use of secondary sources, seeking to deepen student understanding of policy considerations underlying both present doctrine and reform proposals. In addition, there has been some modest expansion of subject matter coverage, especially in Chapters 3 and 8.

We hope all of this will contribute to the pace of progress through the materials and facilitate choices between intensive study and summary treatment. The experience and observations of those who have used the first four editions are, we believe, reflected in pedagogical details as well as in content, especially with a view toward aiding the student's independent mastery of much of the course material in order both to protect classroom time and to advance the level of class discussion.

The general thrust of the book as originally described in the preface to the first edition has been continued, in both coverage and approach, with the materials designed for an integrated course of forty to sixty hours covering succession, trusts, and fiduciary administration. The slightly increased length of recent editions is largely attributable to modestly increased attention to tax law (including changes through 1992); expansion of secondary source materials, including those of a comparative and interdisciplinary nature, intended to enrich study and class discussion without necessarily requiring specific class coverage; and continuing efforts to reflect new or shifting areas of activity and concern in our fields. We hope the latest revisions, deletions, and additions are supportive of the mix of practical and theoretical approaches reported by teachers and students who have used the prior editions.

A major confession we ought to make (among many, no doubt) is that we continue to struggle with the question of where in these materials to place Chapter 20. Its present location can be justified only on grounds (1) of furnishing a jumping-off point for other and tougher construction problems if the book is followed by future interest materials in a combined course (but when we teach a more broadly integrated course we don't always do future interests at the end anyway) and (2) of there being no "right" time (or maybe there are 7.3 so-far-known right times) to study some or all of Chapter 20's contents. Therefore, the end is as convenient a place as any for that material, so it can readily be assigned at the desired time(s). We have as many conflicting suggestions for relocating that chapter as we have colleagues discerning enough to point out that it is now in the wrong place—and, agreeing with all, we teach the material ourselves at different times from year to year.

We acknowledge with appreciation the authors and publishers who have granted us permission to reprint portions of their work and the many helpful suggestions from teachers who have used the prior editions. We are particularly indebted in one or both of these ways to Professors Martin Begleiter (Drake), Richard Gould (New England School of Law), John Langbein (Yale), Michael Smith (Berkeley), and the late William Fratcher (Missouri-Columbia).

Eugene F. Scoles
Edward C. Halbach, Jr.

March 1993

Preface to the First Edition

This book is designed primarily for a combined course in Decedents' Estates and Trusts, including fiduciary administration, or for use, in conjunction with separate materials on future interests, in a more inclusive course encompassing the traditional subjects of Wills, Trusts, and Future Interests.

The organization of the book is not necessarily a "logical" one. The materials are presented in a sequence calculated to make the study of them more meaningful, and also more efficient when possible. For example, matters relating to the termination of trusts are not presented at the end but are taken up earlier, because certain characteristics of trusts and certain rights of beneficiaries relating to termination are relevant to a thorough consideration of many aspects of trust administration. It will also be noted that much of the book is built around problems. The order in which some topics are taken up is dictated by the objective of adequately preparing students to approach the problems with an understanding of the legal and practical considerations that are relevant to public policy or to private solution through planning. In most instances the cases and other materials have been prepared not simply to be studied as such, but to be considered for the purpose of attacking a particular problem. We have tended to reverse the typical casebook format of cases followed by notes; usually we have placed text before the related cases, especially where basic doctrine can satisfactorily and more easily be imparted in this fashion. This organization, together with the more extensive use of textual material, is intended to make the experience of working with cases and problems more valuable and more interesting than if they were approached without some background in the basic rules involved. In other words, text is used to "set up" the cases and problems. Because a student does not come to them blindly, cases and problems which are more challenging can be used, or at least a more sophisticated discussion of a given case or problem can be expected. We believe that more is gained by this technique than is lost by what some teachers will consider a giving away of too much too readily. We hope, frankly, that a higher level of performance and interest can be stimulated concerning selected issues by having their practical and legal context, as well as by having a certain amount of general subject matter coverage, provided by text.

It is our objective that both the content and emphases of this book reflect the realities of present-day practice in the field of estates and trusts, while also revealing that the field is very much alive with new (as well as old) problems in need of solution. For example, although we do not seek in this book to teach tax planning, we do feel that course emphasis should reflect the types of current questions being opened up by various dispositions and fiduciary practices that are prompted by considerations of legitimate tax minimization. You may also note an effort in appropriate parts of the book to shift attention from the abundant case experience which grew out of the depression of the thirties to the largely unexplored issues arising from long-term inflation.

In the over-all picture, however, a very important factor in determining the content, emphasis, and method of this book is a realization that growing demands upon lawyers, and hence upon law school curricula, require that significant features of this course area be covered in fewer classroom hours than in the past, without unduly sacrificing either depth of understanding in the field itself or fundamental insights which this course should offer concerning the law in general.

Finally, we wish to express our appreciation to the authors and publishers who have granted us permission to reprint portions of copyrighted texts and articles in this book.

Eugene F. Scoles
Edward C. Halbach, Jr.

1965

Acknowledgments

We are grateful to copyright holders for permission to reprint excerpts from the following items:

American Bar Association, Code of Professional Responsibility, EC 5-6, EC 9-5, DR 9-102; Model Rules of Professional Conduct, Rules 1.1, 1.3-1.4, 1.7-1.8, 1.14; Statement of Principles Regarding Probate Practices and Expenses; Report of the Fiduciary Accounting Standards Committee. Reprinted by permission of the American Bar Association. Copies of the Model Rules may be obtained from Order Fulfillment, American Bar Association, 750 North Lake Shore Drive, Chicago, Illinois 60611.

American Institute of Certified Public Accountants Committee on Accounting Procedure, Accounting Research Bulletin No. 43, ch. 7(B). Copyright © 1953. Reprinted by permission of the American Institute of Certified Public Accountants, Inc.

American Law Institute, Restatement (Second) of Trusts §§2, 23, 38, 42-43, 46, 50-51, 58, 60-62, 65, 88, 102, 106-107, 154-157, 167, 184, 186, 205, 239-240, 330, 337, 339, 342, 368, 374-375, 399, 400. Copyright © 1959. Restatement (Third) of Trusts §§171, 227. Copyright © 1992. Restatement of Property §242. Copyright © 1940. Restatement of Restitution §182. Copyright © 1936. Reprinted with the permission of the American Law Institute.

Atkinson, T., Wills (2d ed. 1953). Copyright © 1935. Reprinted by permission.

Berle, Our Problem of Financial Power?, Washington Post, Aug. 11, 1968. Copyright © 1968. Reprinted by permission of the Washington Post.

Bogert, G., Trusts (4th ed. 1963). Copyright © 1963. Reprinted by permission.

Calkins, The Role of the Philanthropic Foundation, 11 Foundation News 1-13 (1970). Copyright © 1970. Reprinted by permission.

Church and Snitzer, Diversification, Risk and Modern Portfolio Theory, 124 Trusts & Estates 32 (1985). Copyright © 1985. Reprinted by permission.

Comment, Wills, Undue Influence, 50 Michigan Law Review 748, 758-760 (1952). Copyright © 1952. Reprinted by permission of the Michigan Law Review Association.

Davis, K., Discretionary Justice: A Preliminary Inquiry (1969). Copyright © 1969. Reprinted by permission.

Durand, Retention of Decedents' Business, 95 Trusts & Estates 907 (1962). Copyright © 1962. Reprinted by permission.

Effland, Rights of Creditors in Nonprobate Assets, 48 Missouri Law Review 431 (1983). Copyright © 1983. Reprinted with permission of The Curators of the University of Mississippi.

Emmerich, V., Estate Practice in the United States and Europe: Report to the Conference of the International Bar Association 7-8, 17-18, 38-41 (1950). Copyright © 1950. Reprinted by permission of Martinus Nijhoff n.v.

Fratcher, Bequests for Purposes, 56 Iowa Law Review 773 (1971). Copyright © 1971. Reprinted by permission.

————, Fiduciary Administration in England, 40 New York University Law Review 12, 35-36 (1965). Copyright © 1965. Reprinted by permission.

————, Probate Can Be Quick and Cheap: Trusts and Estates in England 48, 52, 55, 102-104 (1968). Copyright © 1968. Reprinted by permission.

Friedrich, The Economics of Inheritance, in Social Meaning of Legal Concepts (No. 1): Inheritance and the Power of Testamentary Disposition 27-33 (Cahn ed. 1948). Copyright © 1948. Reprinted by permission of New York University School of Law.

Glasser, Trusts, Perpetuities, Accumulations and Powers under the Estates, Powers and Trusts Law, 33 Brooklyn Law Review 551, 562-563 (1967). Copyright © 1967 by Fred B. Rothman & Company. Reprinted by permission.

Goheen, Let's Remove Foundations from Second-Class Philanthropic Citizenship, Los Angeles Times, July 24, 1973. Copyright © 1973. Reprinted by permission.

Griswold, E., Spendthrift Trusts §§32, 552, 554-555 (2d ed. 1947). Copyright © 1947. Reprinted by permission.

Gulliver and Tilson, Classification by Gratuities Transfers, 51 Yale Law Journal 1, 2-10 (1941). Copyright © 1941. Reprinted by permission of The Yale Law Journal Company and Fred B. Rothman & Company.

Hallgring, The Uniform Trustee's Act and the Basic Principles of Fiduciary Responsibility, 41 Washington Law Review 801, 808-811 (1966). Copyright © 1966. Reprinted by permission.

Hopkins, Certain Uncertainties of Trusts and Powers, 29 Camb. L.J. 68 (1971). Reprinted by permission.

Hyde, Variation of Private Trusts in Response to Unforeseen Needs of Beneficiaries: Proposals for Reform, 47 Boston University Law Review 567, 600, 608 (1976). Copyright © 1967. Reprinted by permission.

Langbein, Crumbling of the Wills Act: Australians Point the Way, 65
American Bar Assocation Journal 1192 (1979). Copyright © 1979.
Excerpted with permission from the American Bar Association
Journal.

Langbein and Posner, The Revolution in Trusts Investment Law, 62
American Bar Association Journal 887 (1976). Copyright © 1976.
Excerpted with permission from the American Bar Association
Journal.

Langbein and Waggoner, Reformation of Wills on the Ground of Mistake: Change of Direction in American Law?, 130 University of
Pennsylvania Law Review 521-522, 577-580, 590 (1982). Copyright
© 1982. Reprinted by permission.

Mechem, The Requirement of Delivery in Gifts of Chattels and of
Choses in Action Evidenced by Commercial Instruments, 21 Illinois
Law Review 341, 341-342, 348-350 (1926). Copyright © 1926 by
Northwestern University School of Law, Vol. 21, No. 4. Reprinted
by special permission of Illinois Law Review.

Nathanson, The Ethics of Inheritance, in Social Meaning of Legal Concepts (No. 1): Inheritance and the Power of Testamentary Disposition 74, 76, 85-89 (Cahn ed. 1948). Copyright © 1948. Reprinted
by permission of New York University Law School.

National Commission on the Observance of International Women's
Year, To Form a More Perfect Union (1976). Copyright © 1976.
Reprinted by permission.

Nussbaum, Liberty of Testation, 23 American Bar Association Journal
183-186 (1937). Copyright © 1937. Excerpted by permission of the
American Bar Association Journal.

Phillips, Toward a Trust Settlement Option, 24 Chartered Life Under-
writers Journal 38-43 (1970). Copyright © 1970 by the American
Society of Chartered Life Underwriters, 270 Bryn Mawr Avenue,
Bryn Mawr, PA 19010. Reprinted with permission from the Journal
of the American Society of Chartered Life Underwriters, Vol. 24,
No. 4 (Oct. 1970).

Powell, The Rule Against Perpetuities and Spendthrift Trusts in New
York, 71 Columbia Law Review 688 (1971). Copyright © 1971.
Reprinted by permission.

Power, Wills: A Primer of Interpretation and Construction, 51 Iowa
Law Review 75 (1965). Copyright © 1965. Reprinted by
permission.

Provisions for Dependents: The English Inheritance Act of 1938 —
Notes and Legislation, 53 Harvard Law Review 465, 466-467
(1940). Copyright © 1940 by the Harvard Law Review Association.
Reprinted by permission.

Ross, Let's Not Fence In the Foundations, Fortune 148, 166-172 (June
1969). Copyright © 1969. Reprinted by permission.

Problems and Materials on
DECEDENTS' ESTATES AND TRUSTS

1

Introduction

A. *Terminology*

These first few paragraphs are not intended as a substitute for a dictionary. The definitions provided here are in part a cast of characters for the course. It is also hoped that these definitions, though not exhaustive, will help to prevent your carrying some misconceptions through the course. Even though it happens every year in possibly every law school, it never ceases to shock teachers to discover that some students in the middle of their second year in law school still believe that the heirs of a person who died testate are those who take under the will. This first section is calculated, among other things, to improve communication and to reduce the number of shocks experienced on both sides of the teaching rostrum.

A person who dies without a will is said to die *intestate*. A *testator* or *testatrix* is one who has died *testate* — i.e., leaving a will. A testator *devises* real property to a *devisee* and *bequeaths* personal property to a *legatee*. Strictly speaking, a *legacy* is a bequest of a sum of money, but you will regularly encounter the term used as broadly as *bequest*, the generic term for testamentary gifts of personalty. In fact, in statutes, opinions, and everyday usage you will find the real and personal property lines disregarded; thus, many statutes today use *devise* to refer to a bequest as well as a testamentary disposition of land. Persons who take or, but for a will, would have taken a decedent's personalty under the laws of intestacy are, traditionally, *next of kin*; intestate successors to realty are the decedent's *heirs*. Although the surviving spouse shares in the intestate property, the spouse may or may not be properly classified as an *heir*, depending on the local law. As real and personal property have come generally to be governed by a single statute of descent (referring to land) and distribution (personalty), it has become fully acceptable and usual to refer to the persons designated by statute to take intestate property, real and personal, as the decedent's *heirs*. A living person has no heirs.

The personal property of a decedent, whether testate or intestate, is generally supposed to pass through a court-supervised process of estate *administration*. Traditionally, real property has bypassed this process, descending directly to the devisees or heirs, but administration has been extended to realty by most statutes. Because the process of administration generally affects realty, even if not fully subject to administration, this distinction between real and personal property usually is disregarded for purposes of terminology. The term *probate* is often used interchangeably with *administration,* but the term strictly refers to the process of proving and deciding the validity of a will in the appropriate court. Probate, then, is a preliminary step in testate administration. The person appointed to handle an estate — to collect assets, pay creditors, and distribute the remaining property — is the *personal representative.* The personal representative appointed by the court to administer an intestate estate is an *administrator* or *administratrix*; if for any reason a successor is required in this office, that person is called an *administrator d.b.n.* (*de bonis non,* i.e., of goods not administered). Wills usually nominate someone to serve as a personal representative; this nominee, if appointed, is called an *executor* or *executrix* of the will. Should the nominee predecease the testator or for other reason not be appointed, an *administrator c.t.a.* (*cum testamento annexo,* i.e., with will annexed) is appointed. If an executor or administrator c.t.a. ceases to serve after commencing administration, an *administrator c.t.a., d.b.n.* is appointed to finish the job. Again, casual usage is such that the term *executor* or *administrator* may be encountered in reference to any personal representative.

A little genealogical terminology is also useful at the start. Relationship by blood is by *consanguinity*; relationship by marriage is by *affinity. Ascendants* or *lineal ascendants* are ancestors; *descendants* or *issue* are children, grandchildren, and others of all degrees in the descending line. *Collaterals* are relatives who are neither ascendants nor descendants but are related to the person in question through common ancestry; a sister (related through common parents), an uncle (via grandparents), a maternal cousin once removed, and the like are collateral relatives.

Throughout this course reference will be made to *trusts.* The term is commonly and almost meaninglessly used, especially in judicial opinions, to connote a vague range of relationships, particularly of a fiduciary character but extending all the way from guardianship to agency to bailment. In this course the term is used in the narrower sense. It would be ultrahazardous to attempt a definition specific enough to be of any real value to you, but the American Law Institute's definition of a trust is quoted on page 311 infra. At this preliminary stage an example is probably more useful to present the fundamental notion. *A* bequeaths certain securities to *T* "in trust to manage, invest, and reinvest and to pay *B* the net income for life, and on *B*'s death to distribute the principal to *C.*" *A* has created an *express trust* by which *T*, called the *trustee,* is obligated to perform a function with regard to the *trust property* (of which *T* is generally legal owner) exclusively for the benefit of *B* and *C*. The beneficiary is often called the *cestui que trust*; here the cestuis, *B* and *C,* would more specifically be called *income beneficiary* and *remainderman* respectively. *A* is usually called the *settlor* or *trustor.* The *subject matter of the trust*

2. Real Property

At the outset, the character of feudal land holding in England delayed the development of succession to land. Because the relationship of lord and tenant was essentially a personal one, the "heir" of a deceased tenant did not succeed to the land but had to seek a re-grant. Even after the Conquest there is evidence of lords refusing to re-grant to heirs of deceased tenants. Despite the absence of obligation, however, it became customary for the lord to accept the heir as tenant on the payment of a relief. Gradually inheritance by the heir became a matter of right, and the relief paid the lord is recognizable as a predecessor of our succession taxes. "By 1100 it therefore appears that the hereditary principle was admitted by the king in favour of his tenants in chief, and by them in favour of their sub-tenants. Having gone that far, it must rapidly have spread all through the feudal network." T. Plucknett, A Concise History of the Common Law 524 (5th ed. 1956).

The feudal influence is reflected in the common law Canons of Descent as developed in the king's courts. Under these rules male descendants excluded females of the same degree; among males of equal degree only the eldest inherited (primogeniture); absent surviving sons or issue of deceased sons (for, under the principle of representation, issue, male or female, stood in the place of a deceased decendant), daughters took equally as coparceners. In the absence of issue the land passed to collaterals, because by the mid-twelfth century ascendants were not allowed to inherit; among collateral relatives the principle of representation was also adhered to, in what is called a *parentelic* system, but males were generally preferred over females. Whole-blood collaterals were preferred to half bloods, and the doctrine of ancestral property limited inheritance among collaterals to those of the blood of the "first purchaser" (usually the ancestor from whom the decedent had inherited the land). These canons were occasionally modified by local custom but essentially endured until beyond 1776. The Inheritance Act, 3 & 4 Wm. IV, c. 106 (1833), restored inheritance by ancestors and ended the preference for whole bloods over half bloods, but not until the Administration of Estates Act, 15 Geo. V, c. 23 (1925), was primogeniture abolished.[1] Since 1925 the same rules have governed intestate succession to real and personal property in England, and the preference for males over females has been eliminated. In the United States ancestors are allowed to inherit, and neither primogeniture nor preference for males is recognized; nevertheless, peculiarities of the English history of descent are reflected in varying degrees in our statutes.

---

1. Primogeniture's primitive origin was based on its effectiveness in avoiding inefficient dispersal of family wealth, power, and responsibility. In feudal England, it was valued for this same quality, and also for the spur it provided younger sons to make their own fortunes and thereby to enrich society. Its evident unfairness, plus possible skepticism about its supposed justifications, led to the system's eventual rejection.

The widow was not an heir at common law. She was provided for by dower, of which we know little of the history. Very early, husbands voluntarily gave portions of their property to their wives on marriage. Although church authorities may then have come to require such gifts, it was not until the thirteenth century that common law dower had fully developed. Dower, which endured in England until 1925, entitled the widow to a life estate in one-third of the lands of which her husband was seised at any time during the marriage and that were inheritable by his issue. Dower protected the wife against the husband's inter vivos conveyances, as well as against his testamentary dispositions after the power to devise land was created. See Haskins, The Development of Common Law Dower, 62 Harv. L. Rev. 42 (1948); Note, The Defeasibility of Dower, 98 U. Pa. L. Rev. 826 (1960). Until 1833 dower did not apply to equitable interests. The husband's curtesy, unlike dower, applied to equitable interests and to all, rather than one-third, of the wife's inheritable freeholds. As an extension of the marital right, by which he acquired an estate for the period of the marriage, the husband's curtesy gave him an estate for his life on birth of issue. The dower concept represents an early step in the development of modern restrictions on testation but in this country has been generally abolished in favor of a statutory forced share for surviving spouses.

Even when land became inheritable under the feudal system, testamentary disposition was allowed only by occasional local custom. In general, freehold interests in land could not be devised until 1540. But the centuries of intestate succession, unaccompanied by a right of testation, gave rise to some interesting and revealing developments that have left a significant mark on Anglo-American legal systems. The desire to devise property at death, together with efforts to avoid feudal incidents and certain inflexible legal rules, led to the practice of conveying land to several persons (jointly with right of survivorship) to hold title "to the use of" others. The use concept cannot be clearly traced, but its development in the ecclesiastical courts and later in chancery may be explained by reference to several possible sources, each of which may have had its influence. We have already noted the experience of ecclesiastics with executorship under wills of personal property; and the feoffee to uses also had its counterpart in the Germanic salman. In addition, institutions analogous to the use existed in the Roman and canon law, which were familiar to the prominent churchmen who long served the king in the office of Chancellor. Soon after the establishment of inheritance throughout the feudal system, it appears that a leading purpose of the use was to permit what amounted to testamentary disposition of land. Initially, feoffments to uses prescribed a particular beneficiary who was to receive the property after the feoffor's death. Later, conveyances to the use of such persons as the grantor might designate by will, followed by testamentary directions to the feoffee to uses, became a widespread method of "devising" land. This arrangement was a forerunner of our inter vivos trust with testamentary power of appointment.

Although the technique is easy to comprehend, the recognition and enforcement of uses were by no means a foregone conclusion in the courts that dealt with land in England. This was so despite the analogies available in the legal systems of other countries and in the ecclesiastical courts in England. The history of the use before the fifteenth century is particularly obscure. It is clear that uses were employed, relying on the feoffee's good faith, long before they became enforceable in the courts. In fact, statutes reflect a concern over the employment of unenforceable uses to defraud creditors and to circumvent such policies as that of the mortmain acts. Effective pressure, reinforcing a feoffee's good faith, resulted from the church's interest in the feoffee's honesty and in the use as a device for accomplishing social and religious objectives. Even after the king's courts excluded the ecclesiastical courts from the handling of matters involving land, the church could exert its influence through informal pressures. Later the religious influence was felt through the Chancellor, to whom petitions addressed to the king came officially to be channeled. As chancery developed a body of equitable doctrine different from the inflexible substantive (as well as procedural) rules of the law courts, the use came and remained within the exclusive jurisdiction of equity. By the early fifteenth century the Chancellor would enforce uses not inconsistent with public policy, and the body of rights of the cestui que use gradually took on the character of equitable ownership. A declining feudal system offered inadequate reason to withhold approval from the feoffment to uses to be declared by will. Consequently, of the many reasons why most of the land in England was held to uses by the early sixteenth century, this means of "testation" was at least one of the most important.

The Statute of Uses, 27 Hen. VIII, c. 10 (1535), which became effective in 1536, was the combined product of Henry's desire to replenish the treasury and the desire of lawyers in Parliament to recapture land litigation from chancery. The Statute of Uses transformed certain equitable estates into legal estates by executing uses where a person was "seised of land to the use of" another. In your first-year property course you learned that this process created new methods of conveyancing and new legal future interests. We are particularly interested in two other effects ensuing from the enactment of the Statute of Uses. First, the statute upset the use device as a means of disposing of land at death. The immediate discontent among the landowning classes produced the Statute of Wills, 32 Hen. VIII, c. 1 (1540). The Statute of Wills created, subject to the usual feudal dues, the power to devise certain lands by a written will. Rather than following the administration process typical of succession to personalty in the ecclesiastical courts, lands passed directly. The validity of a devise was tested in a common law action of ejectment. A will operated only on land owned by the testator at the time the will was executed, and this disability survived the Statute of Frauds, 1677, which made wills ambulatory as to personal property.

A second result of the Statute of Uses was its spur to the development of the modern trust. The statute did not execute all uses, and the exceptions are extremely important. The three basic categories of unexecuted uses included the use on a use, the use in personal property, and the active use. The decision protecting a use on a use came a hundred years after the statute, when feudal dues had ceased to be significant as a source of the Crown's revenue. Because the statute operated only where the feoffee to uses was "seised," it had no application to a use raised on personal property, and personalty was constantly growing in importance as a form of wealth. Shortly after its enactment, the statute was held not to execute an active use; i.e., one in which the grantee was charged with affirmative duties such as managing the property and collecting and paying over the rents. Having done away with most of the uses at the time, particularly the more objectionable ones, the statute left chancery free to mold the unexecuted use or trust into an effective institution for the management and disposition of property. The Chancellor was in a position to develop a body of equitable doctrine applicable to this special type of fiduciary relationship. Thus, the Statute of Uses accelerated evolution of the modern trust.

The unexecuted use served numerous purposes in the centuries that followed the Statute of Wills. Although it no longer was necessary as a means of wealth transmission on death, it has continued to serve as a will substitute. In the more immediate aftermath of the Statute of Uses/Statute of Wills period but preceding the American Revolution, the use served as a device to avoid destructibility of contingent remainders and as an element of the ingenious strict settlement. Probably of greater significance, the trust served to counter the husband's right to exclusive possession and to the profits of the wife's property during their joint lives. A devise or inter vivos conveyance to a person to the sole and separate use of the married woman gave rise to a use that equity held unexecuted. The legal title was required to be held for the cestui's exclusive benefit and control, despite the fact that the husband's estate jure uxoris generally applied to the wife's equitable estates as well as to her legal estates. Under this institution of the married woman's separate estate, which continued until removal of the wife's disability in 1882, chancery acquired long experience in supervising the relations between legal and equitable owners of property. Objectionable and rigid rules of the English common law thus led to the growth of the virtually unique Anglo-American concept of the trust. It has continued and in fact matured since the development of modern laws providing for testate and intestate succession.

C. *The Modern Role of Succession and Trusts*

The most commonly expressed view regarding the source and constitutional standing of succession rights is typified by language found in Irving Trust v. Day, 314 U.S. 556, 562 (1942): "Rights of succession to the property of a deceased, whether by will or by intestacy, are of statutory creation, and the dead hand rules succession only by sufferance. Nothing in the Federal Constitution forbids the legislature of a state to limit, condition, or even abolish the power of testamentary disposition over property within its jurisdiction." See also Kornstein, Inheritance: A Constitutional Right?, 36 Rut. L. Rev. 741 (1984).

A different view is expressed in Nunnemacher v. State, 129 Wis. 190, 108 N.W. 627 (1906), which involved an action to recover inheritance taxes paid under protest. In challenging the constitutionality of the tax law, the taxpayer asserted, as the first of several propositions, that the right to take property by will or inheritance is constitutionally protected as a "natural right which cannot wholly be taken away or substantially impaired by the Legislature." In agreement, the court stated:

> We are fully aware that the contrary proposition has been stated by the great majority of courts of this country, including the Supreme Court of the United States. The unanimity with which it is stated is perhaps only equaled by the paucity of reasoning by which it is supported. In its simplest form it is thus stated: "The right to take property by devise or descent is the creature of the law and not a natural right." Magoun v. Bank, 170 U.S. 283. In Eyre v. Jacob, 14 Grat. (Va.) 422, 73 Am. Dec. 367, it is stated more sweepingly thus: "It [the Legislature] may tomorrow, if it pleases, absolutely repeal the statute of wills, and that of descents and distributions, and declare that, upon the death of a party, his property shall be applied to the payment of his debts and the residue appropriated to public uses." . . .
>
> That there are inherent rights existing in the people prior to the making of any of our Constitutions is a fact recognized and declared by the Declaration of Independence, and by substantially every state Constitution. Our own Constitution says in its very first article: "All men are born equally free and independent and have certain inherent rights; among these are life, liberty and the pursuit of happiness; to secure these rights governments are instituted among men deriving their just powers from the consent of the governed." Notice the language, "to secure these (inherent) rights governments are instituted"; not to manufacture new rights or to confer them on its citizens, but to conserve and secure to its citizens the exercise of pre-existing rights. It is true that the inherent rights here referred to are not defined but are included under the very general terms of "life, liberty and the pursuit of happiness." It is relatively easy to define "life and liberty," but it is apparent that the term "pursuit of happiness" is a very comprehensive expression which covers a broad field. Unquestionably this expression covers the idea of the acquisition of

private property; not that the possession of property is the supreme good, but that there is planted in the breast of every person the desire to possess something useful or something pleasing which will serve to render life enjoyable, which shall be his very own, and which he may dispose of as he chooses, or leave to his children or his dependents at his decease. To deny that there is such universal desire, or to deny that the fulfillment of this desire contributes in a large degree to the attainment of human happiness is to deny a fact as patent as the shining of the sun at noonday. . . . And so we also find that, from the very earliest times, men have been acquiring property, protecting it by their own strong arm if necessary, and leaving it for the enjoyment of their descendants; and we find also that the right of the descendants, or some of them, to succeed to the ownership has been recognized from the dawn of human history. The birthright of the first-born existed long before Esau sold his right to the wily Jacob, and the Mosaic law fairly bristles with provisions recognizing the right of inheritance as then long existing, and regulating its details. The most ancient known codes recognize it as a right already existing and Justice Brown was clearly right when he said, in U.S. v. Perkins, 163 U.S. 625: "The general consent of the most enlightened nations has from the earliest historical period recognized a natural right in children to inherit the property of their parents." . . .

So clear does it seem to us from the historical point of view that the right to take property by inheritance or will has existed in some form among civilized nations from the time when the memory of man runneth not to the contrary, and so conclusive seems the argument that these rights are a part of the inherent rights which governments, under our conception, are established to conserve, that we feel entirely justified in rejecting the dictum so frequently asserted by such a vast array of courts that these rights are purely statutory and may be wholly taken away by the Legislature. . . .

But, while we utterly reject the doctrine of Eyre v. Jacob, and hold the right to demand that property pass by inheritance or will is an inherent right subject only to reasonable regulation by the Legislature, we are not thereby brought to the conclusion that inheritance or succession taxes can not be levied. They do not depend upon the right to confiscate. . . .

So we arrive at the conclusion that the general principle of inheritance taxation may be justified under the power of reasonable regulation and taxation of transfers of property.

HODEL v. IRVING
481 U.S. 704 (1987)

O'CONNOR, J. The question presented is whether the original version of the "escheat" provision of the Indian Land Consolidation Act of 1983, Pub. L. 94-459, Tit. II, 96 Stat. 2519, effected a "taking" of appellees' decedents' property without just compensation. . . .

. . . [The statutory provision] here amounts to virtually the abrogation of the right to pass on a certain type of property — the small undivided interest — to one's heirs. In one form or another, the right to pass on property — to one's family in particular — has been part of the Anglo-American legal system since feudal times. . . . The fact that it may be possible for the owners of these interests to effectively control disposition upon death through complex inter vivos transactions such as revocable trusts is simply not an adequate substitute for the rights taken, given the nature of the property. Even the United States concedes that total abrogation of the right to pass property is unprecedented and likely unconstitutional. . . . Moreover, this statute effectively abolishes both descent and devise of these property interests even when the passing of the property to the heir might [advance the statutory objectives]. . . . [Thus], a *total* abrogation of these rights cannot be upheld. . . .

In holding that complete abolition of both the descent and devise of a particular class of property may be a taking [in this situation], we reaffirm the continuing vitality of the long line of cases recognizing the States', and where appropriate, the United States', broad authority to adjust the rules governing the descent and devise of property without implicating the guarantees of the Just Compensation Clause. See, e.g., Irving Trust Co. v. Day, 314 U.S. 556, 562 (1942). . . . The difference in this case is the fact that both descent and devise are completely abolished . . . [even] when the governmental purpose sought to be advanced, consolidation of ownership of Indian lands, does not conflict with the further descent of the property.

There is little doubt that the extreme fractionation of Indian lands is a serious public problem. It may well be appropriate for the United States to ameliorate fractionation by means of regulating the descent and devise of Indian lands. . . . What is certainly not appropriate is to take the extraordinary step of abolishing both descent and devise of these property interests even when the passing of the property to the heir might result in consolidation of property. Accordingly, we find that this regulation, in the words of Justice Holmes, "goes too far." . . .

Despite the prevailing view in the country that there is no natural or constitutional right of succession, it is recognized, with as near certainty as such matters permit, that succession in some form and in some types of property is virtually a universal institution of civilized societies, ancient and modern, including present and former communist nations.[2]

2. The institution of succession appears to reflect a basic human urge, and its development accompanied that of private property as civilization evolved from the food-gathering to the hunting-fishing, pastoral, and then gardening stages. See E. Hoebel, The Anthropology of Inheritance, in Social Meaning of Legal Concepts (No. 1): Inheritance of Property and The Power of Testation 5-26 (1948), concluding: "Within the scope of our anthropological survey, we may conclude that inheritance is a mechanism of greater significance in early and simple primitive society than most writers on legal history have been prone to allow." Also see Tay, The Law of Inheritance in the New Russian Civil Code of 1964, 17 Intl. & Comp. L.Q. 472 (1968); L. Schwartz, The Inheritance Law of the People's Republic of China, 28 Harv. Intl. L.J. 433 (1987).

On the other hand, there is no such universality of the right to dispose of property by will. We have just reviewed the struggle to establish testation in England. Modern civil and Anglo-American legal systems accept the right of testation in some form. Often expressed notions that the power of testation is justified as an encouragement to industry and thrift have by no means gone unquestioned, but the will may be seen as a means of making succession more meaningful and responsive to the individual wishes of property owners. Through the will, succession can be adapted to the needs and circumstances of the particular decedent's family. The existence of succession having been more or less accepted, however, legislative attention has largely focused on the nature and extent of the power of testation and on the priority of potential claimants to intestate property.

The modern tendency in this country is slightly in the direction of narrowing the class of relatives entitled to succeed to the property of an intestate and of expanding the occasions of escheat. More significant inroads on succession may be found in the form of estate and inheritance taxation in the United States, but succession taxes today reflect little of earlier notions that such taxes should serve as major instruments of social and economic policy, particularly so far as concentration of inheritable wealth is concerned. (This function is more effectively being performed by the income tax.) Because of the intimate relationships between testation and inter vivos giving, especially through the trust device, any serious social policy or revenue-raising function of succession taxes must be implemented in such a way as to deal with the whole area of gratuitous transfers. Thus, modern death taxes deal with inter vivos dispositions, which are in effect will substitutes, and such taxes are often supplemented by a gift tax. Countries urgently concerned with land reform or with redistribution of economic power and opportunity may come to rely heavily on partial abolition of succession rights, directly or through taxes. This method of attacking concentrations of wealth — and it might encounter less resistance than programs of more immediate change — would have to be accompanied by some provision for the property owner's family and by restriction on inter vivos transmission of wealth. Thus, any soul-searching about the proper role of succession in a modern society must concern itself with the whole of what we might call donative transactions in property.

The modest restrictions on testation and inter vivos giving in this country have largely dealt with such matters as protecting the family from disinheritance and restraining the dead hand. (Despite the historical background of the *use* as a means of "succession," you will see that nearly all but the most modern of statutes dealing with family protections have disregarded will substitutes.) Temptations to disinherit members of the immediate family or to tie up property in perpetuity are sufficiently rare that these restrictions represent no substantial impairment of the freedom of testation of most of our clients. For the most part the trust is a rather generous and flexible institution through which a property owner may extend his personality beyond his lifetime, either for the good or the detriment of his beneficiaries. Inter vivos and testamentary trusts today allow for the accomplishment of nearly any reasonable objective. It is fair to say that most of today's legislative efforts concerning testation and the use of trusts have been in the direction not of limitation but of making these institutions more effective as a means of accomplishing individually formulated objectives. You will see, however, that policy restrictions, along with certain formal safeguards, do sometimes upset improperly handled attempts to exercise the broad freedoms allowed.

On the private side, succession and trusts play a varied role in the affairs of individuals. Intestate succession provides a scheme of descent and distribution that is generally said to be calculated to approximate the probable wishes of most decedents. It is questionable how well this objective has been achieved. See Fellows, Simon, and Rau, Public Attitudes About Property Distribution at Death and Intestate Succession Laws in the United States, 1978 Am. B. Found. Res. J. 319; Plager, The Spouse's Nonbarrable Share, 33 U. Chi. L. Rev. 681, 710 (1966). A statutory scheme of intestate succession, or the so-called estate plan by operation of law, can hardly be expected to satisfy the needs of everyone. In fact, it is unlikely to satisfy completely the wishes of any individual. Nor can the simple outright gift satisfy the objectives of all persons desirous of making inter vivos gifts. Thus, lawyers are actively involved in making testamentary succession and inter vivos donation serve the diverse purposes of individual clients. The will, frequently including testamentary trust provisions, is called on to enable a client to tailor succession to his precise goals and to the best interests of his beneficiaries. The living trust is called on to fulfill the particular objectives of the donor or to fit a gift to the needs of the donee. It also can serve as a substitute for a will, avoiding some of the drawbacks of having property pass through estate administration proceedings. More specifically, inter vivos and testamentary trusts offer means of providing for successive enjoyment of property. The trust is also a vehicle for managing property while a donee or legatee is legally or practically unable to manage it. Individuals may also use trusts when they find it necessary or desirable to defer certain dispositive decisions concerning the property and to entrust these decisions to another as fiduciary or as holder of a power of appointment. Today, planned giving and tediously planned testamentary dispositions are widely used to reduce income and death taxation as far as the donor is concerned and, more frequently, as far as the beneficiaries are concerned.

The trust has been praised as a device for reform in the law, and it has been condemned as a device for evading legal policies. Historical and present-day usages reflect the role trusts can play in circumventing conscious policies of the law, such as early and modern fiscal policies and restrictions on testation. Some avoidance techniques have been eliminated by legislation, and some attempts have been thwarted by judicial decision. On the other hand, the trust has been notably successful and valuable as a device for escaping disabilities and limitations that are merely the product of rigidity of concept or outmoded "legal technicalities" that courts of equity are willing to undercut. See Scott, The Trust as an Instrument of Law Reform, 31 Yale L.J. 457 (1922). The flexibility of the trust is such that its modern purposes are nearly as unlimited as lawyers' imaginations.

Despite the reasons for disposing of one's property by will or even by trust, most Americans die intestate. In fact, probably 85 percent of the adult deaths do not result in any estate proceedings. See Dunham, The Method, Process and Frequency of Wealth Transmission at Death, 30 U. Chi. L. Rev. 241, 244 (1963). Recent surveys indicate, however, that over one-half (possibly 60 percent) of the estates requiring formal administration are testate estates. E.g., cf. M. Sussman, J. Cates, and D. Smith, The Family and Inheritance 62 (1970). An even higher — far higher — percentage of the total wealth passing through estate proceedings had been owned by persons who took advantage of the opportunity of making a will. Meaningful figures are not available showing the extent to which trusts are being used, but the dramatic recent increase in the amounts of property held in trust by corporate fiduciaries reflects a growing interest in the trust device.

Serious question can be and has been raised about the wisdom of preserving significant inequalities based on inherited wealth and of perpetuating economic power that significantly affects the lives of others even when it no longer reflects the qualifications and merit of the power holder. We are thus asked to consider the justification for a system that allows private wealth to pass from generation to generation, with some individuals, selected by accident of birth, enjoying comforts and power they have not personally earned. Reflecting on society's rationale for the institution of succession is also helpful in understanding and thinking about the taxation of gifts and inheritances, about "the dead hand" (including questions concerning the duration and the permissible purposes and characteristics of trusts), and about the appropriate extent, freedom, and nature of succession to private wealth. Essays dealing with these and associated topics are excerpted at length below. Others, together with the related report of an American Assembly held in 1976, are collected in Death, Taxes and Family Property (E. Halbach ed. 1977). Of particular relevance are Friedman, The Law of Succession in Social Perspective, id. at 9; Shaffer, Death, Property and Ideals, id. at 26; Jantscher, The Aims of Death Taxation, id. at 40; and Boskin, An

Economist's Perspective on Estate Taxation, id. at 56. The philosophical and economic crosscurrents are aptly highlighted by viewing the Boskin essay (supra) through an egalitarian's eyes. Professor Boskin argues that the goals of equality are retarded rather than advanced if we raise death taxes (the only meaningful vehicle through which our society restricts the amount of succession) to a level that induces the wealthy to increase consumption at the expense of the capital base, thereby diminishing productivity and employment opportunities for others. Despite disagreement as to the point at which this regression might occur — at best speculative given the present state of knowledge (e.g., about "elasticity of demand for bequests") — even egalitarian principles of income/wealth redistribution acknowledge this danger by accepting that degree of inequality that will, in the long run by reason of incentives to productivity, provide the most for the poorest in society. See, e.g., Rawls, A Theory of Justice 275 (1971). Also, see generally R. Chester, Inheritance, Wealth, and Society (1982); A. Okun, Further Thoughts on Equality and Efficiency (Brookings General Series, Reprint 325, 1977).

FRIEDRICH, THE ECONOMICS OF INHERITANCE

Social Meaning of Legal Concepts (No. 1): Inheritance and the
Power of Testamentary Disposition 27-53 (E. Cahn ed. 1948)

In regard to any institution, there is a personal or private as well as a social interest. Thus Aristotle, I believe, offered as part of his defense of private property the personal satisfactions and enjoyments an owner may derive from what he owns. . . . Similarly to bequeath and to inherit wealth provide many satisfactions of a most agreeable kind. To secure the members of one's family against want; to bestow generously upon some worthy cause; to perpetuate one's personal success, position, prestige, and fortune in the family name for future generations: all this must provide substantial rewards, intangible as they may be. . . .

The [economist's interest in the institution of inheritance relates to] that inherited wealth which affects the lives of others in some significant degree [as distinct from] that which is solely a matter of the private lives of the heirs. Some writers have drawn the distinction between property for use and property for power. . . . Although $50,000 is an agreeable sum to inherit, it would generally be regarded as a modest competence and not one to create many serious social issues. [According to certain statistics] the social and economic issues are therefore concentrated in the upper 7% of the probated estates. The issues concern the advantages accuring to the very few in relation to the great many. . . .

Discussion of the economic aspects of inheritance has been and still is largely concerned with the effects of inheritance upon the distribution of wealth and income and upon its production. . . .

At first glance it appears that the disposition of wealth according to the various rules of inheritance falls quite outside the area of productive income. . . . [On the other hand,] acquisition of property in the form of wages, salaries, fees, its accumulation by saving, and the receipt of interest or profit as a result of shrewd and enterprising investment, rests upon at least a presumption of a productive contribution to the economy. . . .

When an estate is set up in the form of a trust . . . the dissociation of property as a productive function from property as a source of income is sharply defined. In this instance the heirs are excluded from the responsibilities of ownership by prescription of the testator. . . . Moreover, the prescriptions of the will and laws governing trust investments are usually severely restrictive as to the type of investments which may be made. This may be a quite proper arrangement on many grounds, but the fact remains that it is not conductive to the capital requirements of a dynamic capitalism. . . . [G]rowth requires enterprising, daring businessmen who have access to capital bold enough to venture in new directions. Capital buried deep in the restrictions of trust management is not that kind of capital, whatever else it may be.

From the social-economic point of view, private property and the various forms in which it may be held and distributed are measured by their consequences in furthering the productive activities of the economy. Considered on these terms, it would seem clear that the productive value of the institution of inheritance is open to some doubt. But the issue is not closed; there are additional considerations.

It can be and is argued that inheritance has a productive function as an integral part of a system of private property. . . . Self-interest and the egoistic drives are the stronger and more enduring motives of human action. Motivated in part by family affection, in part by a desire to perpetuate personal prestige and success, the expectations of accumulating an estate with the right of bequest will induce men (or women) to work more industriously, save more persistently, and enterprise more daringly than they would if their estates were to escheat to the political state. A social-economic appraisal of the institution of inheritance is concerned also with the effect of inheritance upon the distribution of wealth. . . . Some measure of inequality [of wealth and of associated opportunities is] a natural consequence of a system of economics in which rewards are more or less proportionate to the importance of the individual and the work he does in the carrying on of economic activity. . . . Moreover, so long as the economy is dependent upon private savings to an appreciable extent for new capital, the conditions which facilitate accumulation have some measure of social justification. . . . If the inequality of income is greater than is necessary to inspire the superior to excel and the poor to emulate, then inequality loses its claims to social merit and becomes merely the expression of acquisitive license and unrestrained greed. If the inequality which is conducive to accumulation by the few imposes undue hardship upon the many, its beneficence may justly be questioned.

Equality is also a positive good. According to Jeremy Bentham the maximum happiness of society can best be realized, assuming that productivity would not be impaired, when income is equally distributed. We do not need to rest our case for equality upon the hedonistic premises of Bentham and the marginal utility school of economics. There are the ethical grounds; in addition there are social and political reasons for presuming that a society in which wealth, income, and opportunity are more or less evenly distributed is likely to be more stable and peaceable than one in which there are great extremes between the rich and the poor. . . .

The institution of inheritance is not the sole cause of inequality of wealth and opportunity. But the inheritance of property is of equal and perhaps even of greater importance than inherited abilities, environment, and opportunity in accounting for economic inequality. "Its influence," asserts F. W. Taussig . . . "is enormous. It is this which explains the perpetuation of the incomes derived from capital, land, income-yielding property of all sorts, and so explains the great continuing gulf between the haves and have-nots. It serves also to strengthen all the lines of social stratification and reinforce the influences of custom and habit. Persons who inherit property also inherit opportunity." . . .

In summary the social-economic interest in inheritance may be expressed as follows: (1) The institution of inheritance distributes wealth not in accord with productive performance and competence but according to family relationships and the interest and caprice of the testator. Wealth so distributed may in some cases, perhaps in many cases, and under some circumstances be generally at variance with the capital requirements of an expanding economy. (2) But in a society based on private property, the institution of inheritance may be the better, or if you will, the least bad alternative for disposing of property upon the death of the owners. (3) And the expectations of founding a family fortune and the right of bequest may offset, or outweigh, the disadvantages of inheritance by strengthening incentives for the accumulation of capital. (4) Yet the "continuing gulf between the haves and have-nots" not only violates the norms of social ethics but may exaggerate the divisive tendencies within society, thus leading to social discord and political instability, and, it should be added, may also weaken the incentives to produce on the part of the discontented many.

The relative importance which economists and social philosophers generally will attach to the above opposing considerations will depend upon their basic premises and ultimate values. Those who attach supreme importance to the ideal of economic and social equality will relegate the bearing of inheritance upon [incentives and upon] the formation of capital to a secondary position or will disregard it altogether. Those who regard private property as the more workable pattern of economic organization will stress the importance of inheritance as a factor in [productivity and in] the accumulation of capital. It may be, however, that the antithesis between productiveness and equality is not so sharp as it sounds when baldly stated. Conceivably, society under some circumstances may have an increasing measure of both. It may have its cake and eat it too.

Throughout the history of western civilization there have been two opposing trends of thought regarding the institution of property and inheritance. One may be called, rather loosely to be sure, the individualistic tradition. It has been skeptical of the extent to which men would put forth their best efforts for the common good. Sustained and efficient performance depended, according to this tradition, upon the self-interest of the producers. . . . The other is the equalitarian tradition which has ever been the hope and aspiration of social reformers. Its persistence as a social ideal, its persuasive appeal throughout the ages indicates that it, too, has deep roots in the constitution of man. This tradition has to a varying degree rejected both property and inheritance and has put its faith in a social order based upon men's willingness to work for the public good.

Let us consider briefly the equalitarian point of view which today is represented in socialist thinking. . . . However much the socialists may differ as to their semantics and spiritual invocations, or as to the methods of achieving their social ideal, they agree in condemning an economic system based upon the private ownership of the means of production. Poverty, crime, depression, mass unemployment, class conflicts, national rivalries, and wars can be eliminated, they argue, only if property is owned in common and economic enterprises are socialized. . . .

From [the Marxian] point of view, inequality, exploitation, class domination are attributes inherent in capitalist property. According to Marx, the concentration of property is an historical necessity, decided not on the basis of legal relations, but by the underlying methods of production. Inheritance obviously, therefore, does not have a primary causal significance in the historical process. Inheritance may perpetuate the capitalist status of particular families, it may sharpen and consolidate class stratification; but it does not determine the form or substance of capitalist distribution.

Not all socialists, of course, follow this sequence of reasoning, but they would all agree that in a socialist state, as ideally conceived, inheritance would be abolished. In a socialist economy, the state or some equivalent social authority, would own all the productive wealth of the community and would order, manage, and direct all productive activities. The formation of capital would under these arrangements be a managerial function of the state. Personal incomes would be equal to that amount necessary to absorb the total output of consumer goods. There would be no need for personal savings, in view of the fact that all contingencies of a personal kind, old age, care of dependent children, sickness, accident, would be taken care of by some method of social payment. . . . Inheritance, except with respect to articles of personal use, would disappear not because it would be abolished by law but because it would have no function to perform. . . .

The socialists visualize the inheritance tax, not as a source of revenue for the state, but as a means of achieving their ultimate purpose of socializing wealth. The graduated inheritance tax is presented as a method of expropriation after the death rather than during the lifetime of capitalist owners. This, it is presumed, would be a relatively painless method of socialization. The living would continue to enjoy the wealth their skill in the art of making money would bring them but the state would in due course, if it retained title to the property the tax would yield, be in possession of all the productive wealth.

That the abolition of private property with its attendant rights to bequeath and inherit will impair the incentives to produce is set aside as invalid. Once the formal organization of the economy is changed, the socialist believes that the psychological propensities of human beings would also fall into line. . . . "From each according to his ability, to each according to his need" would, so the socialists hope, become the ruling principle of distribution and production.

How matters would operate in fact as compared with how they could operate in theory is, of course, another question on which one can only speculate. A socialist economy may be confronted with inflation as has the Russian economy repeatedly. Thus the state may urge the individual to save, to buy government bonds, in order to reduce private spending. The socialist state may seek to maximize the rate of capital accumulation even beyond the planned totals and thus may urge its citizens to add to their savings. The socialist state may find that the self-regarding sentiments of its members must be catered to in order to secure efficient and energetic participation in production. Thus incomes may be unequally distributed and the extremes between the highest and the lowest, if Russia is our guide, may be very great. Some may accumulate bank accounts and bonds in considerable amounts.

Of course, accumulations in a socialist society would not represent property rights identified with particular enterprises. A government bond, however, is a claim against the aggregate flow of national income and perhaps for that reason is somewhat more secure than a bond which depends upon the fortunes of a particular enterprise. Thus an inheritance in a socialist society may have some of the advantages it offers in a capitalist society — a larger income than can be obtained by personal exertion alone, a superior command over the goods and services, perhaps greater freedom of action and movement, and more leisure. And it is possible also that the advantages of parents may be transferred to their children, not necessarily by disposition of property, but by disposition of privileged position, status, prestige and the opportunities for success and power which are associated therewith. All this would be at variance with socialist ethics, but is there any more reason to assume that there will be a closer identity between what men profess and what they do in a socialist society than in any other?

The individualist school of economic thought, like the socialist, was confronted with the contradictory claims of equality as an ideal of social justice and productivity. The primary emphasis, they believe, should be upon the conditions necessary to a productive economy. It was better, as they viewed it, that the total product should be larger with both the rich and the poor having more than that there should be equal division of wealth and income with all having less. . . .

The individualists, however, were not altogether at ease with the institution of inheritance. . . . We read that the British custom of primogeniture is an economically desirable practice, precisely because it denies inheritance to the younger sons of British landed families. Lacking an inheritance . . . they were compelled to make themselves useful in industry, trade and commerce. . . .

It is not surprising, therefore, that some [have] suggested that if it is an advantage for some to be disinherited, it might be an advantage to the economy to have all disinherited.

To a few rugged individualists who believed in the competitive system as a kind of arena in which everyone should have an equal opportunity to prove his mettle and to be rewarded in terms of his abilities, the institution of inheritance struck a dissonant chord. . . .

In the main, however, economists of the individualist school of thought defended the institution of inheritance. Taking it for granted that a system of private property must necessarily provide for succession of property to new generations of private owners, they defended the freedom of bequest as best suited to an individualistic system of economics. The owner of an estate would not willingly, they believed, contemplate the dissolution of the productive enterprises which he had founded. He would, they argued, be strongly inclined to transfer his property and its control to those who would be more likely to carry on the enterprise.

Perhaps even greater importance was attached to the role of inheritance as an incentive toward the accumulation and maintenance of capital. According to Professor Taussig, for example, "In a society organized on the basis of private property inheritance is essential to the maintenance of capital. . . . For sustained accumulation and permanent investment, the main motives are domestic affection and family ambition. . . . If we were to put an end to inheritance, decreeing that all estates should escheat to the public at death, the owner would commonly dissipate his property. One of the motives for its first acquisition would be gone, and certainly the chief motive for its maintenance. Why accumulate and invest for the benefit of the community at large?''

Admitting that the institution of inheritance tended to perpetuate inequalities, the individualist school of thought nevertheless contended that these evils were more than outweighed by the beneficial effects of the right to bequeath and to inherit. Abolish the institution or reduce inheritance by taxation to the point where it no longer acts to excite men to work and to save — the consequence would be a diminution in the aggregate flow of wealth. The shares which each of us would get might be more equal but the total of wealth produced would be less until in due course all would be equally deprived.

The rights of bequest and inheritance were not, however, to be considered as absolute rights. Where social desirability pointed the way, these rights might properly be regulated and limited. Thus Jeremy Bentham, concerned with the canons of just taxation, suggested that the estate of one who dies intestate should escheat to the state and that a distinction should be made for purposes of taxation between direct and collateral descendants. John Stuart Mill differentiated between the right to bequeath, which he regarded as a part of the idea of private property, and the right to inherit. Thus the state in his view might properly regulate and limit the right of inheritance. Collateral [relatives] did not merit the same consideration as direct heirs. In order to moderate the tendency toward inequality, the state might also limit the amounts which could be inherited. Moreover, a limitation on the amount which could be inherited would have the additional advantage of inducing heirs to enter actively into productive enterprise.

Thus it is a reasonable conclusion that while, in general, economists of the individualist school of thought defended the institution of inheritance as having social and economic merit, their defense did not represent a blind support of inherited privilege and economic inequality. Today, there is a general acceptance of the principle of graduated death duties and inheritance taxes. Differences of opinion are aimed not at the principle but at some specific schedule of rates. The issue is not whether estates and inheritances should be taxed, but how high the rates may go without impairing the incentive value of the right to bequeath or inherit. Moreover, as our later discussion will indicate, changes in industry and in the forms of business organization have to a large extent relegated to a lesser importance the role of inheritance in the maintenance and development of the productive resources of society. The aggregation of capital proceeds today from many sources other than personal accumulation for the purpose of founding a family fortune.

When we move from the realm of opinion and theoretical discussion to a consideration of the actual operations of inheritance in contemporary United States, we are confronted with a major difficulty, namely, the lack of quantitative data and research. . . .

With this apologetic introduction, I should nevertheless like to venture certain observations about the role of inheritance in the economic development of the United States. I offer two suggestions: (1) that inherited wealth has played a relatively minor role, when compared to older societies, in shaping the American economy and the distribution of its wealth and opportunities, and (2) that its importance is a progressively declining one under present circumstances. . . .

Combining the inheritance and income taxes, it becomes increasingly difficult not only to create large private fortunes but to maintain them. . . .

One of the fears of the nineteenth century was that impairment of inheritance might result in the break-up of aggregates of productive property and thus compel the use of less efficient forms of organization. It is true, that if the payment of inheritance taxes meant the liquidation of assets of going enterprises, the result in many cases might be disastrous. But today such is no longer the consequence. The aggregates of wealth used for productive purposes are largely the property of corporations, with individuals holding paper claims against the income of the corporations. The transfer of ownership of stocks and bonds, their dispersion or concentration does not affect the unity, the continuity, or the productiveness of the corporate assets. The corporate entity carries its productive assets forward from one year to another, from one generation to another without the interposition of inheritance. . . .

Another concern of the nineteenth century economists was the effect an impairment of inheritance might have upon the rate of capital formation. Private savings are still an important source of capital formation, but their contribution to new capital resources is a declining ratio. The corporations are a major source of new capital, and in this instance, the formation of capital is a managerial decision, not an act of thrift or ambition by an individual seeking to found a family fortune. Insurance companies have accumulated vast pools of capital from millions of small contractual payments by individuals whom they insure. The state also is a large accumulator of capital through the agency of taxation. Capital discharges its economic function by supporting an expansion of productive power. In part today the expansion of productive power is derived from technical invention. A new and superior machine replaces an old; it may be paid for out of corporate funds and involve no additional investment of capital.

Without accepting wholly the argument of those who claim that private thrift and savings are now obsolete, one may concede that under the present régime of the corporation private accumulation of capital is less significant than was the case in the early history of capitalist development. Whether managerial capitalism will prove to be a superior type of organization is beside the point. Even if it were not, we have no choice but to keep it.

NATHANSON, THE ETHICS OF INHERITANCE
Social Meaning of Legal Concepts (No. 1): Inheritance and the
Power of Testamentary Disposition 74, 76, 85-89
(E. Cahn ed. 1948)

Does the system of inheritance have any ethical value? The simplest answer is, "Yes, it does." For on its best level, it is an expression of deep family ties which are indispensable to a good life and a good society.

The problem confronting us, however, is not so simple as this. We are rather called upon to decide whether the value it has outweighs or is outweighed by its disvalue. No simple answer to this problem could be satisfying, since it involves a complex of social relations about which it would be foolhardy to be dogmatic and set of ethical criteria which are at best indemonstrable. . . .

What, then, are the ethical criteria which we bring to bear on this question? First, that every human being counts or ought to count as a person. Second, that in human relations, concern with eliciting the best possibilities in another is essential to the best development of oneself. Third, that this is as applicable in the relations of groups to groups as it is in individual relations. . . .

[T]he drive for money . . . is only one among the many drives existing side by side in each of us, of which one or another may be dominant at different stages in our lives or, for that matter, in different moods. In a competitive economy such as ours, where a person's security and status depend so much upon the accumulation of money and the outward display of its possession, it is not surprising that the pecuniary incentive should play a major role. It is true that this incentive often breeds remarkable ingenuity, initiative, and creative powers. It is also true that insofar as it encourages self-reliance, it develops a strong moral fiber within us. But it is not true that all persons are stimulated to do their best by the goad of competition. Nor is it true that any of us, at all times, finds competition the best stimulus to our best efforts.

There is a cooperative, as well as a competitive, need in us. There is that which we do seemingly at our own expense, as well as to our own benefit. There is that which we do hoping for the approval of those whose judgment we respect, regardless of what the world at large may think. There is all that we do for those we love, when not even love reciprocated is in our minds. There are the sacrifices we make for an idea or cause, finding what satisfactions we can in contributing our mite to the larger end.

It would be impossible validly to generalize about the relation of the pecuniary incentive to these and other tendencies in human beings. Nor have we settled the problem on the economic level, let alone in ethical terms, when, as some do, we observe that the Soviet Union, for all its overall objectives, has had to resort to vast differences in financial reward to get the most out of its people. What any or all societies have done up to now can never be conclusive demonstration of what any or all societies must do in the future. . . .

The positive case for inheritance, viewed individually, rests on the desire of an individual to provide for his family after his death. In any form of society, this concern with one's family is a virtue, and in a competitive society the attempt to make provision for them comes from understandable and ethically laudable motives. Now in this capitalist economy of ours, the desire to provide for one's family is regarded as a major stimulus to the efforts of the individual. The average healthy person does wish his family to live as comfortably as possible, and he has a strong desire, as well, to accumulate sufficient savings to deal with unemployment, old-age retirement, and emergencies due to sickness, accident, or death.

The fact is, however, that despite the normal desire to achieve such protection, a tremendous percentage of workers . . . have been unable to do so. . . . At least for these people, therefore, bequests and the system of inheritance as a whole are, in personal terms, academic matters.

How is it for those whose economic status is higher? Everyone with a sufficient sensitivity to family obligations would like to make provision for dependent wives, children, and parents. To make as sure as possible that one's widow will be able to maintain the way of life to which she has been accustomed, that one's children will have the educational and vocational opportunities which will give them the best start in adult life, that one's parents in their declining years will not suffer from the threat or actuality of destitution — all this is a normal desire. The attempt to realize this ambition is unquestionably as much a stimulus to individual effort as is the concern with a family's immediate well-being. Socially, it is desirable as far as it helps to strengthen the family unit. Ethically, it is one phase of a person's attempt to express his best in family relations. In a competitive society, the power to insure the well-being of those closest to oneself is of great practical and ethical value.

On the negative side, however, there are considerations of major importance. In the first place, the power to provide for one's family is not an unequivocal good. If it often stimulates the valuable desire of helping to protect those who need protection, it also, not infrequently, plays into the hands of an unhealthy ego interest. It is commonplace, in speaking of inheritance, to talk of the way in which the dead hand of the past so often controls the present and future. What is not so often considered is the ethically destructive part such a desire to exercise control over the future can play in an individual. It ought to be axiomatic that nothing can be more unethical than the attempt to play god in the lives of other people. The relation of a husband to a wife, of a parent to children, of a child to parents, should never be one of control or domination. It should be one of stimulating their best qualities, developing in ways which are unique and surpass our perception. This is a hard truth, and it is one evidence of how difficult it is to achieve a genuinely democratic way of life.

The authoritarian habit of mind is more widespread than we like to believe. And it manifests itself in a desire to control the lives of others. The parent who wishes to "provide" for children sometimes does so on conditions that can be emotional strait-jackets for them, telling them what they must or must not do about education, vocation, or marriage. In these, and other relations, the testator makes a club of his bequest. He makes a legacy, not a means of showing his generous concern with those he cares about, but a tool of reward or punishment. . . .

For the legatees themselves, in addition, there are often consequences which go directly counter to the claims that our prevailing system best stimulates individual effort. Insofar as that effort derives from the pecuniary incentive, then it is evident that it must be largely vitiated for those who inherit fortunes, or whatever amount they do inherit which is in excess of their needs. . . .

Nor is this all. It can be argued that fortunes are accumulated through the superior ability or shrewdness or creativeness or good fortune of individuals, and that such power as goes with this accumulation is a justifiable reward. But the accident of birth is no argument in its behalf. For all the attempts to do so, it is not easy to justify the possession of power through inheritance. On feudal grounds, it can be done; it seems to me impossible on democratic grounds.

Our entire discussion has been in terms of the inheritance of property which plays an important part in our overall system of economic and social relations. The same considerations do not apply to the more personal possessions — the keepsakes, the books, and objets d'art, the trophies, yes, even jewels having a special significance — which are so much the expression of a person's individuality. In any society, one should have the right to dispose of all such things as he desires, as tokens of genuine regard and affection. The manner in which they are handled does not basically affect the ways we live together.

D. *Preview: The Course Content and Its Central Problems*

You are about to undertake a step-by-step study of wills, trusts, and fiduciary administration. A bird's-eye view of the body of doctrine and its central problem areas should serve to make each phase of the course a

bit more meaningful to you — at least that is the objective of this preliminary summary of the subject matter of the course.

This book deals principally with the will and the trust, but it also deals
with other methods of making gratuitous transfers, with some of which
you are already more or less familiar. Although we examine certain
aspects of these other methods, in many matters you will be drawing
upon your existing knowledge and considering its relationship to the
whole of the wealth-transmission process. Dispositions of property for
family purposes will occupy most of our attention, particularly dispositions to provide for members of the family following the death of the
property owner. Not only do we study the methods of disposition but
also the processes through which these methods operate — the administration of a decedent's estate and the longer-range process of trust
administration. We are concerned with what happens when, for example, the head of a family dies and with what can be done in advance to
alleviate the common problems. The lawyer's role in these matters is varied. One significant role is that of estate planner, arranging in advance
for the passage of the client's estate. In this capacity the lawyer must evaluate the alternative forms of transfer, each of which has its purpose —
will, testamentary trust, gift, inter vivos trust, joint tenancy and the various options under insurance policies and employee benefit plans; then
the lawyer must consider the details of planning and drafting instruments to effectuate the decisions; and, of course, among the many com-
plicating factors is the almost ever-present matter of tax consequences
to the client and others. The lawyer may be involved later, at the stage
of administration, as fiduciary or as counsel for a personal representative or trustee; or the lawyer may be called upon to represent a transferor, the transferor's estate, an estate or trust beneficiary, a debtor or
creditor, or a disappointed heir in litigation having to do with an estate
or trust matter. In passing on the title to real estate, the attorney may be
called on to advise a prospective purchaser concerning the effect of
transfers or omissions during estate proceedings or trust administration.
In varying degrees, regardless of your specialty or the character of your
community or law firm, problems involved in this course will come to you
in your practice. To many of you, estate practice — planning or working
on estate and trust matters — will constitute a principal source of your
professional income. Throughout this course, you should consider how
particular problems under discussion might better have been handled
from the viewpoint of planning and drafting; also consider how the law
could better deal with matters you encounter in cases and how the existing law might better have been used to obtain the result desired by a particular litigant. In particular you should consider the approaches
embodied in the Uniform Probate Code. Ask yourself why the drafters
felt it worth stating the rules they did. About a third of the states have
adopted substantially all of the UPC, and the law of almost every other

state has been influenced by it either by legislative enactment or judicial decision. See, e.g., Andersen, The Influence of the Uniform Probate Code in Nonadopting States, 8 U. Puget Sound L. Rev. 599 (1985); Effland, Will Construction Under the Uniform Probate Code, 63 Or. L. Rev. 337 (1984).

We have already noted that most Americans die intestate. In Chapter 2 you will see that the rules governing succession to the estates of such persons follow a more or less common pattern. The statutes first make some provision, which most property owners would find inadequate, for the surviving spouse, if any. The rest of the estate passes to the decedent's issue or, if there are no surviving descendants, to ancestors or collateral relatives. In most states legislation requires that some minimum provision be made for the surviving spouse, and some states limit bequests and devises to charity. Otherwise a decedent is generally free to leave property by will to anyone and in any sensible form. Most of the rules protecting those who would take by intestacy are what might be called *procedural* or formal safeguards concerning testation. These may be calculated to prevent disinheritance by oversight, such as safeguards preventing omission of children born after a will is executed unless the intent to disinherit is clear. Also, largely in order to reduce the risks of perjury of falsification of a will or its provisions, wills (and supplements by codicil) must generally be written, signed, and attested by at least two independent witnesses. Formal execution of testamentary instruments is easily accomplished, but courts are sometimes strict and technical in their insistence on compliance with requirements of the applicable wills act. These matters are taken up in Chapters 3 and 4.

The next four chapters (Chapters 5 through 8) reveal that various matters not subjected to the formal process of execution can affect or modify testamentary dispositions or can themselves have the same effect as a will. The formal safeguards of execution are sometimes relaxed to admit certain extrinsic data to complete a will or to alter its effect. Under appropriate conditions this is true of writings already in existence when the will is executed and also of certain events or facts having importance aside from their effect on the will. You will be introduced to the process of interpretation and to the general principles opposing the use of extrinsic evidence in attempting to determine the meaning of a writing; some exceptions are made, usually where it is concluded that the written language is ambiguous. Certain physical acts performed on an existing will, as well as later wills, can operate to revoke a will in most states; occasionally, certain extrinsic evidence and circumstances are admissible to impeach or qualify an apparent revocation. Although a contract to bequeath or devise does not operate to create or revoke a will, under appropriate circumstances it will be so enforced as to have much the same effect, despite its failure to satisfy testamentary formalities. We shall see that conveyances in various forms, certain contract rights, and joint ownership with right of survivorship regularly serve as will substitutes; but these arrangements have their drawbacks as well as their advantages. Sometimes a particular will substitute fails altogether on the ground it is testamentary in character and was not executed as required by the wills act.

Chapters 9, 10, and 11 examine the nature of trusts and their creation. Generally a trust must be created by a completed transfer of specific property in accordance with the usual requirements of effective inter vivos or testamentary gifts; however, one can also declare oneself trustee of one's own property, or create enforceable rights by contracting to create a trust in the future. As the elements of trusts are considered, you will see that some terms and ingredients of an express trust — including the trustee — can be provided by an appropriate court if not supplied by the settlor. On the other hand, certain essentials of express trusts must be so manifested by the settlor as to satisfy whatever formal requirements are applicable. Thus, definite or ascertainable beneficiaries and the intention to create a trust by inter vivos conveyance must be shown in a manner not inconsistent with the statute of frauds and parol evidence rule; in the case of testamentary trusts, these essentials must be manifested in a manner satisfying the wills act. Oral promises — or alleged oral promises — by transferees under wills and deeds present difficult and unfortunately frequent problems for the courts, with diverse results. Important problem areas also include questions of (1) whether a revocable inter vivos trust is so testamentary in character as to be subject to the formal requirements or substantive restrictions applicable to wills and (2) whether testamentary assets can validly be bequeathed to an inter vivos trustee to be administered according to trust terms that do not appear in the will.

The characteristics of the interests of trust beneficiaries are considered in Chapters 12 and 13. The beneficiaries are entitled to have their rights enforced in court; it follows from the character of fiduciary relationships that even when a beneficiary is entitled to payments only in the discretion of the trustee, a court will intervene if the discretion is abused. Most states permit restraints on alienation of equitable interests in a trust, but otherwise most types of trust interests are freely assignable and subject to claims of the beneficiary's creditors. In most states, once a trust has been established, the settlor cannot take away or modify the beneficiaries' interests unless the power to revoke or amend has been expressly reserved. In the relatively rare case in which all beneficiaries of a trust are living and sui juris, they can under some circumstances terminate or modify the trust by unanimous action. Without consent of all affected beneficiaries, however, courts are generally powerless to change the beneficial interests initially created by the settlor of a private trust. On the other hand, courts do have power under limited circumstances to modify the administrative provisions of private trusts and to modify the purposes of charitable trusts (the doctrine of cy pres, to be studied in Chapter 14).

The next five chapters deal with estate and trust administration. Chapter 15 acquaints you with the reasons for having a decedent's estate formally administered and with the problems resulting from a failure to do so. It also examines special procedural problems incident to estate and trust proceedings. In Chapter 16 you will study one of the initial steps in testate administration, the probate of a will; you will also become acquainted with the grounds of contest, primarily fraud, undue influence, and lack of testamentary capacity. Chapters 17, 18, and 19 cover the heart of fiduciary administration. Except for trustees of inter vivos trusts, fiduciaries generally receive official appointment from the appropriate court, and even the inter vivos trustee is subject to removal on proper grounds. Fiduciaries are normally allowed reasonable compensation and also have a right to indemnification from the estate or trust as a counterpart of their personal liability for torts and contracts arising in the course of their duties; but this right is qualified by liability to surcharge for breach of fiduciary duty. The highest of these duties is the virtually unqualified duty of loyalty, which precludes direct and indirect self-dealing and conflict of interest; this duty is complicated, as you will see throughout the rest of the course, by its requirement of loyalty and impartiality to all beneficiaries, some of whose interests necessarily conflict in matters ranging from investment decisions to fiduciary elections under the tax laws. Fiduciaries must exercise reasonable care, skill, and prudence, each of which means something different from the others. They must be careful about delegation of their duties and are required to render accounts of their performance to the beneficiaries, and sometimes in court; in the process, the fiduciary must show that disbursements have been proper and authorized and that receipts and expenditures have been properly allocated between the principal and income accounts. Principal and income problems are numerous; one's ordinary business accounting "sense" for what is net income will sometimes have to take a back seat. Estate accounting among various types of bequests and devises, and even nonprobate assets, can also become complex, especially where tax payments are concerned. The duties of fiduciaries presuppose some powers of administration. The usual powers of personal representatives, who are primarily short-term liquidators, are essentially different from those of a trustee, who is primarily a long-term manager; and individual instruments differ considerably in the powers each confers on its fiduciaries. Most important of the trustee's powers is that associated with the investment function. The trustee must be concerned both with the types of investments authorized by the instrument or by law and with the choice from among those that are authorized. This concern is reinforced by the threat of surcharge.

The final chapter (20) focuses your attention specifically on construction, although you are involved in constructional problems throughout the course. Constructional problems typical of simple wills are emphasized in this chapter, which can be used also as introductory material for the study of future interests. These problems in simple, outright dispositions usually result from changes in a testator's property after execution of the will or from the death of a legatee or devisee before the testator, generally causing the gift to lapse (fail) unless the situation is covered by an antilapse statute.

Students should keep in mind that the subject area of "estates and trusts" is inextricably related to the subject of "future interests," which deals primarily with provisions of wills and trust agreements directing the disposition of principal on the termination of a trust. The two subjects are sometimes taught together as one course. For curricular convenience this book purports only to deal with the trust and decedent's estate aspects of gratuitous family property transactions, and is designed to be followed or accompanied by a treatment of future interests using materials such as E. Halbach and E. Scoles, Problems and Materials on Future Interests (1977).

Because each of you who pursue a career in the legal profession will be a fiduciary to your clients, appropriate professional conduct should be considered incident to your study of the transactions in which lawyers participate. In addition, throughout these materials you will encounter certain fundamental and pervasive legal issues about which insight can be gained through this course. As you proceed, a conscious awareness of these "central problems" of the field should enhance your learning experience. The first of these is the *extrinsic evidence* problem — the struggle to preserve, without harsh inflexibility, the integrity of writings that are essentially unilateral. In varied contexts, and for varied purposes, interested parties seek to introduce extrinsic data into estate and trust proceedings. You should study the handling of the constant tension between (1) the quest for "right" results by seeking uninhibitedly to discover a transferor's true intention and (2) the objective of encouraging formal expressions of intent and safeguarding them (also in the interest of true intent) from possible perjury or falsification, especially after the death of one whose act or intent is in question, and even from misinterpretation of reliable data that the deceased donor can no longer explain. A second and often related central problem area is the *process of construction* of donative instruments — the struggle to assign a meaning to the donor's uncertain language where actual intention would have governed if discovered, but where typically there is no admissible evidence that the donor actually thought of the question presented. It is important to try to understand what construction is all about and what it really seeks to do; that is, to recognize the ingredients and policies present in construction, beyond giving effect to probable desires of donors, and to acquire a feel for the conflict between decision by rule of construction and individualized decision on a case-by-case basis. The third of our pervasive problems involves procedures, private and judicial, for *adjusting rights and long-term relationships in property* that is subject to divided beneficial ownership. More is involved than the serious questions of dead-hand control over living relationships in property; many complications follow simply from the recognition of property rights in unborn beneficiaries. Living, changing needs of existing beneficiaries, not to mention objectives of economic efficiency, conflict with the desire to give effect to the donor's intention and with the protection of potential interests created in the unborn. Disputed beneficial rights and fiduciary obligations can be litigated, but judicial modification of relationships and nonjudicial settlements and changes are also valuable to the living (and often also to the unborn) for reasons of vital flexibility as well as economy and simplicity. The last of our central problems concerns *the fiduciary concept* — principles governing that class of fiduciaries whose ownership of property for the exclusive benefit of others is flavored by objectives of conservation and by the almost inevitable involvement of beneficiaries who are unborn or who are otherwise legally or practically unable to look after their own best interests. The general problem involves application of principles that reflect the conflict between (1) the flexibility needed to meet unanticipated, changing conditions and the competing demands of different beneficial interests and (2) an insistence on impartiality among beneficiaries plus a high standard of fidelity to the donor's purpose and to the beneficiaries. This standard is reinforced by rigid prohibitions calculated to remove the mere opportunity for misconduct because of the ease of concealment by a fiduciary and the difficulty of proof by an "absent" beneficiary.

These central problems illustrate the conflicting forces that social and economic policies bring to bear on problem-solving in this area of the law. Because all law reflects the social and economic policies relevant to a particular field, consideration of these policies throughout the course is important to understanding the rules governing disposition of property and the application of those rules to the property of the many individuals who own it. These policies are pertinent not only to the central problems discussed above but also to specific issues constantly confronting the attorneys in estates practice — issues that depend on doctrine and on the meaning and limitation of instruments. Without attempting to discuss the weight of different policies in different circumstances (for particular policies do not have the same force in all situations), there are here set out a few that should be borne in mind as we proceed through this course. Some of these policies have been mentioned previously in these introductory materials; they are by no means exhaustive but are representative of the more significant, pervasive forces that are commonly given effect in the resolution of matters involving estates and trusts.

1. Protection of the family as a productive and social unit is a fundamental policy influencing much of the law in this area. Economic and social protection for obvious reasons are related in our society. Thus, this policy is reflected in rules of intestate succession and in family protection devices such as the family allowance, forced heirship, and priority in appointment as administrator. It is also reflected in construction, through specific presumptions and through general constructional preferences, where an instrument's meaning is unclear. The related policy of imposing intrafamily support obligations is an aspect of protecting family unity. A common manifestation of this subpolicy is the husband's duty to support his wife and children, whereas common law dower and family allowances typify its postmortem extensions. A subpolicy of recognizing a presumed contribution to the family estate by husband and wife is reflected in some of our statutes. The community property system rests largely on this policy, and elsewhere protection of a surviving spouse beyond the necessities of life can be traced to it. As a by-product of promoting the family as a productive and social unit, the state receives a measure of protection from the burden of indigent persons and from a source of social instability.

2. A policy of promoting economy in the transmission of wealth is reflected in most of the transactions that will be studied in this course. Ideally, according to this policy, estates should be so administered that the maximum value is available to the next generation of owners or, in trust estates, for owners of the present and future beneficial interests. This requires not only that the transfer from one generation to the next be accomplished with a minimum of expense but also that it be done expeditiously so that the assets are promptly available to the successor. It also requires the security against loss or diversion that is provided by generally insisting on prudence and utmost fidelity on the part of fiduciaries. Economy requires that these objectives be supported by simplicity and certainty — values that are often perceptible in doctrines relating to estate and trust administration and to the interpretation and construction of instruments.

3. A policy of the law generally, which has its particular applications in this area, is that of providing for justice and fairness among the claimants who may participate in an estate. This essential concept of equity and fair play often conflicts with formal safeguards (as illustrated by cases involving oral promises to hold property in trust), and sometimes with freedom of disposition. An example of the latter is the persistent problem of protecting creditors who have relied on the reasonable expectation of repayment from the total wealth of an individual. The conflict of this policy with those favoring protection of the family and freedom of disposition is a recurring one in matters handled by lawyers in this field.

4. Of fundamental concern in this area of law is the policy favoring

freedom of testamentary and inter vivos disposition. This involves the objective of permitting property accumulations to be disposed of as the owner sees fit. Although this policy is reflected in the constantly expressed desire of courts to give effect to the transferor's intention, it is also reflected in the sometimes conflicting objective of protecting formal and written expressions of intention against other evidence of a transferor's intention. This policy fosters the many variations in dispositions that are necessary if the individuality of owners is to be accommodated. In the minds of many it is a fundamental value of a free society that the individual's privilege remain free from interference unless good cause is shown. Freedom of disposition represents both an opportunity for individual property owners to provide for the particular needs of their beneficiaries and a form of reward and satisfaction held out by society to its members.

5. One of the strong historic policies in property law has been to resist the tying up of assets, traditionally emphasizing the free alienability of land. It has long been believed that proper utilization of resources requires that property be freely transferable by its owner, and also that it be subject to the owner's power of decision, without undue influence by government or by other persons, even including those from whom the property was acquired. Much of the law of property has developed from efforts to reconcile this policy with concepts and devices designed for protection of the family. Reconciliation of competing policies is also necessary insofar as the donor's freedom of disposition conflicts with policies, reflected either in legal restrictions or in constructional preferences, favoring free alienability of property and freedom of decision and use by persons receiving beneficial interests in the property. It is essential to recognize that today's dead-hand problems deal with more than simply dangers that particular land or other things will be withdrawn from the channels of commerce. They are concerned as well with the access of beneficial owners to quantums of wealth that are held for their benefit and with their control over the opportunities this wealth represents. The trust device, for example, not only *separates* decision-making power from beneficial ownership of property. It also *limits* the extent and character of current decision-making power over wealth that previous owners have placed in trust, resulting at least in a hard-to-appraise reallocation of economic opportunities.

Underlying these policies is the objective of protecting the governmental and economic order in a vigorous society. A social structure providing both stability and progress is related to the form as well as the concentration of property holdings. Attitudes concerning freedom, incentives, and security dictate that neither too much nor too little power be placed in the hands of individuals or groups through their ownership and disposition of property. Thus, the law governing succession and particularly trusts has a significant impact in maintaining the desired governmental and economic order. In turn, policies reflecting popular values influence doctrines governing the character and operation of devices available for holding and transmitting property. An awareness of fundamental policy influences, such as those that have just been reviewed, is therefore indispensable to a thorough understanding of legal rules and their application to specific estate and trust problems. As the course progresses, there will be occasion to consider the force of these and other policies as applied to particular fact situations. For an overview of the tensions among competing social and economic policies in succession, see Friedman, Property, Succession and Society, 1966 Wis. L. Rev. 340.

E. The Setting: An Illustrative Case History

My name is Eugene Edwards. I practice with a small law firm in Willton, Calinois. Professors Scoles and Halbach have asked me to write up the story of an estate I handled a few years ago. As I understand it, the reason for this is to offer you a vicarious experience, enabling you to see the subject matter of your course in context, and also simply to provide some basic information about estate and trust administration. The state of Calinois has a fairly representative probate code, and our trust law is probably not much different from that of your state. Of course, there are always variations from state to state. The estate I am going to tell you about had the unusual quality of involving almost no real complications, which makes it an easy case to get you started in your course. Just don't get the idea that estates are normally this simple. Oh, yes, a little later I will set out the terms of the will I drew for the client. The authors have asked that I emphasize that this will is not a model. In fact, they had some downright uncomplimentary things to say about it. But maybe they are forgetting the difficulties under which some of us have to work, squeezing a will in between trying a personal injury action and negotiating a lease — and the client always seems to be in a hurry. Then as the client leaves the office, the last words of instruction are, "Keep it short and simple, will you, Mr. Edwards?"

1. Planning the Estate

Harry Elder called me at the office about making a will before his departure on a vacation. He also wanted to know what information to bring with him to my office — deeds and so on — and whether his wife, Wilma, needed a will, since she had little property of her own. I explained that Wilma should have a will; for example, if she outlives Harry, she may not get around to seeing a lawyer before she dies.

I knew the Elders were well into their sixties and that Harry was retired, but when they came to my office many matters remained to be discussed. I learned that, in addition to social security, Harry was receiving $2,900 a month under his company's retirement plan and that Wilma would receive $1,850 a month for life if she survived him. Their two children, Sam and Doris (now Doris Young), were both married; there were four grandchildren. Neither client had living parents. Wilma's property consisted simply of her personal effects and her joint interests with Harry in a fluctuating checking account, in the family home, and in a small farm in an adjoining state. I verified that the checking account provided a right of survivorship and that the deeds to the home and farm created joint tenancies. In addition to personal effects and an automobile, Harry had some $3,400 in a savings account and about $510,000 worth of securities in his own name. His life was insured for $150,000. The home and farm were worth about $125,000 and $160,000 (net) respectively. I will spare you the details, especially of the personal and financial circumstances of the children, but you will see in your course that these facts are important to developing an estate plan. Interviewing is partly a matter of "educating" your clients; you must lead them to formulate a sound and complete scheme of disposition, starting with their embryo of an idea about what they want done with their property. This part of your job cannot be overemphasized.

I asked Harry whom he wished to take his property on his death. He indicated that he would like to leave small bequests to his grandchildren but that he mainly wanted to benefit his wife and then the children. Next, I discussed the federal estate tax with the Elders and told them about the marital deduction, under which Harry could leave any property he wished to Wilma estate tax free (although a bit of Calinois inheritance tax would be incurred). I also explained that, if he left enough to Wilma under that deduction, he could leave the rest of his estate free of federal tax essentially to anyone and in any way he might choose, because of a so-called unified credit that exempts $600,000 worth of transfers at death or major transfers during life that would otherwise be subject to gift taxation. We decided that if Harry died first we could obtain enough marital deduction to eliminate any federal tax on his estate simply by bequeathing his car and other tangible personalty to Wilma, by letting the checking account and real estate pass to her by right of survivorship, and by having the insurance policies remain payable to her. The value of these assets would be comfortably below the amount her own unified credit would shelter from tax later at her death.

Except for the bequests to Wilma and the grandchildren, Harry decided to leave the residue of his estate to the Willton Bank in trust for Wilma for her lifetime (planned in such a way as to keep that property from being includible in her taxable estate at death), with the trust remainder thereafter to go to Sam and Doris. If Wilma predeceased

Harry, he would leave everything directly to the children. Similarly, if Wilma survived, she wanted to leave everything to the children; but if she died first, she would leave what little she has outright to Harry. The way things stood, however, if Wilma died first, Harry's property holdings were sufficient to exceed his unified credit and to cause a substantial estate tax. (I talked further to Harry about this at a later time and pointed out that the tax under these circumstances could be avoided if he roughly divided his estate with Wilma during life, which he could do under the gift tax marital deduction; then whoever died first could use his or her unified credit to exempt the estate and establish a tax-planned trust for the survivor, whose estate could thereby be expected to remain small enough that no tax would have to be paid at the second death because of the survivor's own unified credit — but Harry was never quite prepared to do this.)

It surprised Harry to learn that part of the joint tenancy property and, in his situation, all of the life insurances proceeds would be includible in his estate for estate tax purposes (we call that the *gross estate*), even though they would pass to Wilma outside of his probate estate. Like other assets, though, these types of properties passing outright to a surviving spouse qualify for the marital deduction (which is also available to property passing into trusts, if the trusts are in qualifying form). Thus, for this purpose, and to avoid the delays and costs of probate in the process, we left the land in joint tenancy and left the insurance payable to Wilma. The reason for Wilma's having the home and checking account are probably obvious enough to you. By leaving the farm to her via joint tenancy the need for ancillary administration in the situs state was eliminated. Also, Wilma knew quite a bit about the farm, and this arrangement seemed better than converting it from joint tenancy in order to have Harry devise it to his residuary trustee. The insurance proceeds would provide Wilma some ready funds, but you must remember that estates also may have their liquidity problems. By having the proceeds paid to a named beneficiary, rather than to the estate, however, we also took advantage of an insurance exemption under the Calinois inheritance tax.

Harry decided to name Wilma to serve as his executrix, and vice versa. I don't always like to advise naming elderly widows or widowers to serve as executors, but the probate estate here was so simple — practically all securities. Anyway, I often find I have to handle most matters myself as attorney for an executor, so I might as well save the estate some executor's fee by recommending the surviving spouse for the job.

Incidentally, if either Sam or Doris should fail to outlive the clients, some provision was needed for their families. Once the clients got interested in this problem, they thought of everything! We decided to give Wilma a testamentary special power of appointment over the trust remainder under Harry's will to deal with the possibility of changed conditions, like this very question of a predeceased child — guess I should use these powers more often. You will see what I ended up with when you read Harry's will.

2.   Harry Elder's Will

As you read Harry's will, consider where I could have done better. Look for planning as well as drafting deficiencies. I can now think of a number of things; others should occur to you. As you study particular problems during the course, look back to see what provision I made for them, if any, and try to understand why I used particular clauses. Oh well, at least Harry got his short, simple will. Again, I emphasize, this will is a sample, not a model. You can find many reasonably good "model" forms around. You may be able to obtain form books from local trust companies. I started out using a variety of recommended forms until I developed my own set, which I know in detail now and which I *think* I fully understand. Yet you can never rely on forms to do your thinking for you. Individualized tailoring is always required.

LAST WILL AND TESTAMENT OF
HARRY D. ELDER

I, Harry Dunwoodie Elder, of Willton, Calinois, hereby make this my last will, revoking all previous wills and codicils.

Article I

If my wife, Wilma, survives me, I bequeath to her all of my tangible personal property, but exclude intangible properties such as securities and bank accounts.

Article II

I bequeath the sum of one thousand dollars ($1,000) to each of my grandchildren who is living at the date of my death. At present my living grandchildren are Sam E. Elder, Jr., Amy X. Elder, Barbara Y. Young, and Charles Z. Young. All references in this will to children, grandchildren, or to other issue shall include persons who are adopted.

Article III

I bequeath and devise the residue of my estate, but excluding any property over which I hold a power of appointment, to the Willton Bank,

Willton, Calinois, in trust, to be held, administered, and distributed as follows:

1. If my wife, Wilma, survives me, the trustee shall
    a. distribute the net income of the trust estate to my wife for as long as she lives, payments to be made at times and intervals convenient to the trustee but not less frequently than quarterly, and
    b. distribute to my wife principal in whatever amounts the trustee, in its discretion, deems appropriate for her health, maintenance, and support.

2. On the death of my wife, Wilma, if she survives me, the trustee shall distribute the trust estate to or for any one or more of my descendants and the spouses of my descendants, and in whatever interests, legal or equitable, my wife shall designate by her last will and testament.

3. If my wife, Wilma, does not survive me, or on the death of my wife, if she survives me but fails in whole or in part effectively to exercise the foregoing power of appointment, the trustee shall divide the trust estate into as many equal shares as there are children of mine then living and children of mine then deceased leaving issue then living. The trustee shall then allocate one equal share to each then living child; and one equal share shall be allocated among the then living issue, per stirpes, of each child then deceased leaving issue then living. Each share thus determined and allocated shall be retained in trust or distributed as follows:
    a. Each share so allocated to a living child, grandchild, or other descendant of mine who is then over the age of twenty-one shall be distributed to that person free of trust.
    b. Each share so allocated to a living child, grandchild, or other descendant of mine who is then under the age of twenty-one shall be retained by the trustee in a separate trust for that person. The trustee shall apply so much of the income or principal or both as he may deem advisable for the education, health, and support of the beneficiary until the beneficiary reaches the age of twenty-one, at which time the trust estate should be distributed to the beneficiary; if the beneficiary should die before age twenty-one, the trust shall then terminate and the trust estate shall be distributed to his heirs at law.

4. If there are no issue of mine who are living at the time of my death or at the time of the death of my wife, Wilma, if she survives me, the trust estate shall then be distributed to those of my brothers and sisters who are then living and by right of representation to the issue then living of those of my brothers and sisters who are then deceased; and in the absence of these persons, the trust estate shall be distributed to the Regents of Blackstone University, White Rock, Calinois, the whole or any part of the principal and income to be expended for purposes that the Regents may designate from time to time.

Article IV

To carry out the trusts, if any, created by Article III, above, the trustee shall possess the following powers affecting the trust estate, in addition to powers now or hereafter created by law or otherwise granted by this will: to manage, improve, sell, sell on deferred payments, exchange, grant options, and lease for periods within or extending beyond the duration of this trust; to retain property and to invest and reinvest in property and in the manner that the trustee in its discretion deems appropriate (including common and mutual funds and investment company shares); to borrow and to mortgage and encumber trust property; to hold bonds, stocks, and other securities in bearer form or in the name of a nominee; to receive additions to this trust; to employ counsel, custodians, brokers, and agents: to institute, defend, and compromise actions, proceedings, and controversies, including but not limited to those relating to taxes; and in making any division or partial or final distribution, I authorize the trustee to divide or distribute in cash or in kind, to decide what constitutes a proper division, and to fix values unless a particular method of valuation is otherwise specified.

Article V

I hereby nominate my wife, Wilma, as executrix of this will, if she survives me. If she ceases, declines, or is unable to serve, I nominate my son, Sam, as my executor. I request that the above nominees, if appointed, be excused from bond; neither of these nominees shall be liable for his acts or omissions or for those of any agent, nor shall the trustee be under any obligation to contest the accounts of one of these nominees.

My personal representative shall have, with regard to my estate, the same powers as are conferred on the trustee under Article IV, above, in addition to those now or hereafter conferred by law. All powers conferred on my trustee under Articles III and IV, above, shall apply to substitute and successor trustees.

I, Harry D. Elder, on this fourteenth day of March, 1987, hereby subscribe my name, declaring this instrument to be my will.

Harry D. Elder /s/
Harry D. Elder

The foregoing instrument was, on this fourteenth day of March, 1987, declared by the testator, Harry D. Elder, to be his last will in our presence; we, at his request and in his presence, have subscribed our names hereto as witness to the execution thereof.

Carleton B. Adams /s/ of Willton, Calinois
Jasper I. Plankton /s/ of Willton, Calinois

3.   Administration of the Decedent's Estate

About a year later, Sam Elder phoned me to tell me that his father had died and that Wilma had asked him to get in touch with me. Sam would make the funeral arrangements, for which the estate would assume any reasonable costs and about which Harry's will made no special provision. Calinois has a statute providing for summary (informal) administration of very small estates, but Harry's estate was well beyond the limits of the statute. Wilma agreed to serve as executrix and asked me to act as her attorney.

I had retained Harry's will for safekeeping and proceeded, on behalf of Wilma, to petition for probate of the will and for issuance of letters testamentary. (In an intestate estate the petition would be for letters of administration.) The petition, reciting the jurisdictional facts and the names and addresses of the heirs and testate beneficiaries, was filed in the Probate Court of Marshall County. Administration is in the court of probate, whatever it may be called, in the county and state where the decedent resided. Because, in general, under many existing statutes, a personal representative's authority as an arm of the appointing court may not extend to other states, ancillary administration may be required wherever the decedent owned assets that are subject to administration. You may recall that we eliminated this problem as to the Elders' only out-of-state asset by having the farm held in joint tenancy, but ancillary administration may have been required for any equipment or personal property on the farm or if Harry had owned other chattels or even intangibles in another state. Determining the situs of intangibles may pose problems. If ancillary administration is required, it usually helps to have the same person act as personal representative in all states. Statutes often impose restrictions on nonresidents in these positions; however, most statutes permit the domiciliary personal representative to serve as ancillary administrator or allow a person named in a will to serve as executor. After filing our petition, I saw to the giving of the prescribed notice to all interested parties of the time and place of the hearing on the petition, which was scheduled for some two weeks later. We have a typical provision for appointment of a special administrator for the period prior to the appointment of an executor or administrator, but this was unnecessary because Harry left no properties requiring prompt attention and there would be no will contest to unduly delay probate of the will.

In the meantime, I helped Wilma start the collection of insurance proceeds — the company's local agent took over and was most helpful. We also obtained the Calinois inheritance tax release to have the joint checking account transferred to Wilma's name individually. Joint accounts, like other bank accounts and safe-deposit boxes, are frozen in most states following an owner's death, but usually clearances for transfer to the proper person are readily obtained through a local office of the state tax collection agency as long as payment of any taxes appears assured. I advised Wilma to go ahead and pay current bills and to keep receipts, but that any large or questionable debts of Harry's were to be filed and proved in the estate proceedings.

When the time arrived for proving the will in court, our witnesses were readily available. After some routine questions by the judge the will was admitted to probate. As you will later learn, unless someone immediately wishes to contest, some states allow proceedings more informal than ours for prompt admission of a will to probate. Even under statutes like ours, providing for notice before the hearing, a period is allowed for subsequently setting aside the will. At the time of the hearing, Wilma also filed a petition requesting a family allowance so that estate funds could be distributed to her periodically during administration in amounts set by the judge on the basis of her needs and the size of the estate. Once it is apparent that an estate is solvent, our courts will authorize limited preliminary distributions, but otherwise estate assets are in general tied up during administration. As you will learn in your tax course, the timing of distributions is complicated by income tax considerations. In addition, prior to the probate hearing, we had prepared a tentative inventory estimating the value of Harry's estate, and the judge set the amount of Wilma's bond as executrix on this basis. You may recall that Harry's will purported to excuse bond; the effect of this in Calinois is merely to dispense with the sureties on the bond, but this may represent a worthwhile saving. Wilma filed her bond — a promise to pay a stated sum to the court, subject to cancellation if she properly performs her duties — and qualified as executrix. The court then issued letters testamentary, evidencing to others Wilma's authority to represent and act on behalf of the estate. For example, a copy of the letters accompanied Wilma's requests for reissuance of stock certificates standing in Harry's name at his death. The letters also enabled Wilma, on obtaining inheritance tax clearance, to have Harry's savings account placed in her name *as executrix.*

Promptly after Wilma's appointment, notice to creditors was published, as prescribed by statute, to commence the running of the period within which creditors must file their claims or have them barred by the nonclaim statute, a special statute of limitations. In Calinois the period is four months. Proof of a claim is submitted when it is filed. The personal representative passes on these claims but usually does not pay them until later in the administration. A disallowed claim may have to be litigated. Disputed claims against a decedent's estate can be litigated in the probate courts in Calinois, but in some states these claims are tried in courts of general jurisdiction. Incidentally, even in Calinois, actions by the personal representative against a debtor of the estate and against others to recover or determine ownership of property must be brought in courts of general jurisdiction. Probate courts will authorize compromise of claims by or against the estate.

Wilma encountered no serious problems in collecting and preserving the assets of the estate. She opened up a separate checking account in her name as executrix. I will not bother you now with matters you will later study having to do with investing, preserving, and accounting for estate assets. We had to prepare an inventory within sixty days showing the appraised values of probate assets, i.e., assets subject to estate administration. Inventory appraisals provide the basis of the personal representative's accounting and also are a factor in determining her compensation. Although these appraisals are not binding determinations of value, we had careful appraisals made (including non-probate assets such as the farm and home) to serve our needs for estate tax reporting. I will not go into the details of federal estate tax returns or the audit by the Internal Revenue Service, but I will just observe that we were concerned with valuations at the date of death and that we had to file a detailed estate tax return within nine months of Harry's death. We also had to take care of state inheritance tax matters and to file fiduciary income tax returns and an income tax return for the year of Harry's death. I might add further that the valuations were necessary for purposes of estate accounting. We had to file interim accounts, and Wilma's entire stewardship was subject to review at the final accounting.

Somewhat more than a year after Harry's death, we were ready to close the estate. Pursuant to a court order authorizing sale, Wilma had liquidated some securities and had paid the few creditors of the estate. Sufficient cash was also raised to meet the estate's tax liabilities and to set aside a fund for the eventual payment of legacies and expenses of administration. Where any doubt exists concerning the solvency of an estate, payments to unsecured creditors would be deferred until the time of termination of administration because the family allowance, funeral and administration expenses (including fiduciary commissions and attorney's fees), federal and state taxes, and sometimes claims for rent and wages are accorded priorities. The exact order of priorities varies from state to state.

In the final accounting at time of distribution, Wilma's administration was open to detailed examination through her accounts and reports. The Willton Bank, on behalf of the trust beneficiaries, was the party most interested in reviewing the accounts. In Calinois notice of the final accounting and petition for distribution of the estate is given to all interested parties. Hearing practices on these matters vary from county to county within the state, depending on the probate judge. The finality of final accountings and the res judicata effect of decrees discharging the personal representative or ordering distribution vary from state to state depending on statutory provisions. Our petition for distribution set forth Wilma's proposed distribution of the estate and requested the court to approve and decree distribution accordingly. You may recall that Harry's will included legacies of $1,000 to each of his grandchildren. Under Calinois statute it was not necessary to have a legal guardian of the property appointed for the minor distributees since the bequest was less than $2,500. The court authorized the sums, with interest at 6 percent from one year after Harry's death, to be paid over to the legatees' parents, the natural guardians of their persons. The court approved the distributions as proposed, and the Willton Bank receipted for the residue of the estate.

Oh, yes, I suppose you are interested to know that the court approved my fee in the amount of $18,400 for services as attorney for the executrix. Most of this fee was computed on the basis of the time I spent working on the estate coming into the control of the executrix and accounted for by her. Had Wilma not waived her commission, she would have been entitled to slightly less than the amount of my fee, computed in the same manner but without the compensation I was awarded for extra services. My fee did not include the fee paid me by Wilma individually for my work in clearing the title to her home and in assisting an out-of-state firm in clearing title to the farm. When title to joint tenancy property passes by right of survivorship, administration is avoided, but it is necessary to clear land titles and to have stock certificates reissued in the name of the survivor. This usually involves obtaining certificates of death and tax releases and then placing these on record or submitting them to transfer agents when the outstanding stock certificates are surrendered.

4.   The Testamentary Trust

Traditionally the administration of trusts, unlike that of decedents' estates, proceeds without any general involvement of the courts. If necessary for some reason, the procedure still used in some states is to invoke the jurisdiction of a court of equity by commencement of a suit in the usual manner. In Calinois, as in some other states, our courts of probate retain continuing jurisdiction and supervision of testamentary trusts. Yet the law of trusts, not of decedents' estates, applies. Such trusts are commonly called *court trusts,* to be distinguished from noncourt trusts such as those created inter vivos. Controversy continues among Calinois practitioners concerning the pros and cons of continuing jurisdiction — does this provision for court intervention and supervision result in harassment and greater expense in the long run, or are its disadvantages outweighed by the informality and simplicity of proceedings and the ready access to a court for instructions and periodic settlement of accounts? It must be obvious that the merits and impact of court involvement vary with the circumstances. But keep this question in mind during the course, because one can often control the character of a particular trust. In any event, Harry Elder's residuary trust was subject to the continuing jurisdiction of the Probate Court of Marshall County.

In Calinois, a testamentary trustee must qualify and be confirmed before a probate court will authorize distribution to him by an executor. As you might have assumed, the Willton Bank had no problem in this regard. During estate administration, notices were sent to the trustee, and the bank kept informed by careful examination of Wilma's reports and accounts. (This watching by one fiduciary over the shoulder of another is eliminated in the common situation in which a trust company is named both as executor and as trustee.) When Harry's estate was being closed and the residue distributed, the trustee sought and obtained instructions to determine (1) whether certain earnings of the estate during administration were allocable to trust principal or constituted trust income distributable to Wilma as the life beneficiary and (2) whether the discretionary power of investment under Article IV of Harry's will enlarged the class of permissible investments beyond those normally authorized for trustees under Calinois law. (I am sorry to confess that another provision of the will had to be construed later, but I leave it for you to guess which one.)

Following distribution of the residue of the estate to the Willton Bank, Wilma was invited to visit one of the trust officers of the bank, and later Sam and Doris also dropped in for a brief conference with him. At these conferences, the handling of trust affairs was explained to the beneficiaries, and the discussions also concerned the circumstances, wishes, and expectations of the beneficiaries. Most of the income that had accumulated during estate administration was promptly paid over to Wilma. Thereafter the trustee so scheduled its income payments to provide her with monthly checks in nearly constant amounts. A balanced investment portfolio was maintained, consisting of stocks and bonds. From time to time some of the trust's investments were changed, reflecting the current views of the trustee's investment division concerning various securities. Unlike executors in Calinois, trustees exercise their powers of sale and investment without court order. The trust produced an average yield over the period of Wilma's life of about 6 percent, showing some growth in the principal of the trust estate as well.

In accordance with her more or less customary practice, our local probate judge directed submission of accounts annually by the trustee, accompanied by notice to the beneficiaries. The frequency of accountings by testamentary trustees and the hearing procedures rests largely in the discretion of the probate courts in Calinois, unless a beneficiary exercises the right to compel accounting in court under various circumstances. At each of the accountings the bank asked and was granted reasonable compensation for its service as trustee. (These fees averaged about three-fourths of 1 percent of the principal each year.) In addition to submitting reports and accounts to the court, with copies to the beneficiaries, the trustee filed state and federal fiduciary income tax returns each year.

When Wilma died last year, without having exercised her power of appointment, the trustee filed its final account and requested the court's approval of its proposed distribution of the trust estate then in its hands, less commissions, attorney's fees, and expenses of termination. Because the persons beneficially interested in Wilma's individual estate (which, by the way, is still under administration) were the same as those entitled to the trust estate, the trust administration was smoothly concluded and the property was distributed promptly. Termination was also facilitated by the fact that the trustee had regularly accounted for its management of the trust estate in prior periods. Any questions concerning the binding effect of the court's decree, approving the final accounts, and discharging the trustee were for practical purposes rendered moot by the receipts and releases executed by the remainder beneficiaries, Sam Elder and Doris Young. The involvement of none but readily ascertained, adult beneficiaries certainly simplifies matters. Unfortunately, as you will see, all estate and trust administrations are not as trouble free, nor are all family situations as harmonious as in the case history I have just described for you.

2

Intestate Succession

When a person dies without having made a valid will, or if a will fails to make a complete disposition of the estate, the person is said to have died intestate or partially intestate. Statutes in each of the states provide a scheme of intestate succession under which intestate property will pass.

Intestate laws of various states tend to follow a common pattern, having been derived mainly from the English Statute of Distribution, 1670, 22 & 23 Car. II, c. 10. Nevertheless, in each state it is necessary to examine the statutory language and its interpretation because there will be significant local variations.

The Statute of Distribution applied only to personal property in England. Subject to local custom, the descent of land, until the Administration of Estates Act, 1925, 15 Geo. V, c. 23, was principally characterized by its preference of males over females, the doctrine of primogeniture, and its exclusion of ancestors. See generally 2 W. Blackstone, Commentaries on the Laws of England 208-234 (1761). Although in many states the law of decedents' estates continues to distinguish between real and personal property for some purposes, the statutes of distribution in this country treat both types of property alike with the rare exceptions.

STATUTE OF DISTRIBUTION, 1670
22 & 23 Car. II, c. 10

V. Provided Always, and Be It Enacted by the Authority Aforesaid, That all ordinaries and every other person who by this act is enabled to make distribution of the surplusage of the estate of any person dying intestate, shall distribute the whole surplusage of such estate or estates in manner and form following; that is to say, (2) one third part of the said surplusage to the wife of the intestate, and all the residue by equal portions, to and amongst the children of such persons dying intestate, and such persons as legally represent such children, in case any of the said children be then dead, other than such child or children (not being heir at law) who shall have any estate by the settlement of the intestate, or shall be advanced by the intestate in his life-time, by portion or portions equal to the share which shall by such distribution be allotted to the other children to whom such distribution is to be made: (3) and in case any child, other than the heir at law, who shall have any estate by settlement from the said intestate, or shall be advanced by the said intestate in his life-time by portion not equal to the share which will be due to the other children by such distribution as aforesaid; then so much of the surplusage of the estate of such intestate, to be distributed to such child or children as shall have any land by settlement from the intestate, or were advanced in the life-time of the intestate, as shall make the estate of all the said children to be equal as near as can be estimated: (4) but the heir at law, notwithstanding any land that he shall have by descent or otherwise from the intestate, is to have an equal part in the distribution with the rest of the children, without any consideration of the value of the land which he hath by descent, or otherwise from the intestate.

VI. AND IN CASE THERE BE NO CHILDREN NOR Any legal representatives of them, then one moiety of the said estate to be allowed to the wife of the intestate, the residue of the estate to be distributed equally to every of the next of kindred of the intestate, who are in equal degree and those who legally represent them.

VII. PROVIDED, That there be no representations admitted among collaterals after brothers' and sisters' children; (2) and in case there be no wife, then all the said estate to be distributed equally to and amongst the children; (3) and in case there be no child, then to the next of kindred in equal degree of or unto the intestate, and their legal representatives as aforesaid, and in no other manner whatsoever.

A. *General Patterns of Intestate Succession*

There is a basic similarity in the patterns of intestate succession in all of the states, but there are also significant differences in these statutory schemes. Consequently the rights of individuals may be different depending on which statutory scheme is applicable to a given estate. As a general guide, the traditional rules for deciding which state's intestacy law is to be applied may be summarized as follows: the law of the decedent's domicile at death governs questions of succession to personal property or, perhaps, more precisely, movables; the law of the situs of property governs such questions in relation to land or immovables. In recent years, however, there has developed an increasing acceptance of the view that the law of the decedent's domicile should determine succession to land as well as to personalty. Frequently expressed concerns with respect to land title records and land use appear, for the most part, to be unwarranted.

These choice of law rules must not be confused with the rule that a decedent's property is administered where it is located. Thus, if the decedent lives in State *A* but owns certain chattels situated in State *B*, this property will be administered in State *B*, but under its conflict of laws rule State *B* will determine who is entitled to succeed to the chattels by looking to the laws of State *A*.

In addition to the general textual survey and other contents of this chapter, meaningful study of intestate succession requires careful examination of statutory materials — and preferably an attempt to master some specific jurisdiction's legislation as a living unit. The materials that follow include illustrative and proposed statutes. Nevertheless, the legislation of your own or some other selected states should also be examined, using the materials in this chapter for guidance and comparison.

UNIFORM PROBATE CODE

§2-101. *Intestate Estate.*

(a) Any part of a decedent's estate not effectively disposed of by will passes by intestate succession to the decedent's heirs as prescribed in this Code, except as modified by the decedent's will.

(b) A decedent by will may expressly exclude or limit the right of an individual or class to succeed to property of the decedent passing by intestate succession. If that individual or a member of that class survives the decedent, the share of the decedent's intestate estate to which that individual or class would have succeeded passes as if that individual or each member of that class had disclaimed his [or her] intestate share.

§2-102. *Share of Spouse.*[1] The intestate share of a decedent's surviving spouse is:

(1) the entire intestate estate if:

(i) no descendant or parent of the decedent survives the decedent; or

(ii) all of the decedent's surviving descendants are also descendants of the surviving spouse and there is no other descendant of the surviving spouse who survives the decedent;

(2) the first [$200,000], plus three-fourths of any balance of the intestate estate, if no descendant of the decedent survives the decedent, but a parent of the decedent survives the decedent;

(3) the first [$150,000], plus one-half of any balance of the intestate estate, if all of the decedent's surviving descendants are also

1. For community property states this section is adapted so that these provisions for the spouse apply to separate property, while another subparagraph provides for inheritance of the decedent's share of community property, with the suggestion that this share pass to the surviving spouse. — EDS.

descendants of the surviving spouse and the surviving spouse has one or more surviving descendants who are not descendants of the decedent;

(4) the first [$100,000], plus one-half of any balance of the intestate estate, if one or more of the decedent's surviving descendants are not descendants of the surviving spouse.

§2-103. *Share of Heirs Other Than Surviving Spouse.*   Any part of the intestate estate not passing to the decedent's surviving spouse under Section 2-102, or the entire intestate estate if there is no surviving spouse, passes in the following order to the individuals designated below who survive the decedent:

(1) to the decedent's descendants by representation;

(2) if there is no surviving descendant, to the decedent's parents equally if both survive, or to the surviving parent;

(3) if there is no surviving descendant or parent, to the descendants of the decedent's parents or either of them by representation;

(4) if there is no surviving descendant, parent, or descendant of a parent, but the decedent is survived by one or more grandparents or descendants of grandparents, half of the estate passes to the decedent's paternal grandparents equally if both survive, or to the surviving paternal grandparent, or to the descendants of the decedent's paternal grandparents or either of them if both are deceased, the descendants taking by representation; and the other half passes to the decedent's maternal relatives in the same manner; but if there is no surviving grandparent or descendant of a grandparent on either the paternal or the maternal side, the entire estate passes to the decedent's relatives on the other side in the same manner as the half.

§2-105. *No Taker.*   If there is no taker under the provisions of this Article, the intestate estate passes to the [state].

Compare California Probate Code §6402(e), which, after setting out the substance of Uniform Probate Code §2-103, provides: "If there is no surviving issue, parent or issue of a parent, grandparent or issue of a grandparent, but the decedent is survived by the issue of a predeceased spouse, [then] to such issue. . . ." Absent these or other prior takers, §6402(f) provides that the decedent's "next of kin" take (under the modified civil law method, infra). And if this also fails, §6402(g) provides for the property to pass to certain of the decedent's in-laws, specifically to the parents or the issue of the parents of the decedent's predeceased spouse, before escheat to the state will occur. These provisions for a spouse's issue and other relatives by affinity are most unusual.

1. Share of Surviving Spouse

The provisions for the surviving spouse under the various state intestacy statutes differ considerably in detail.

One basic criticism leveled at most statutes is that the provision for a surviving spouse is grossly inadequate in the case of a small estate. The trend of reform is in the direction of increasing the surviving spouse's share, and this is reflected in Uniform Probate Code §2-102, under which the spouse receives at least a lump sum and half of the net estate of an intestate decedent. Despite this trend, it is still not unusual to find that a surviving spouse takes only one-third of the estate. Sometimes this share is enlarged when the decedent has left no descendants surviving, with the increase taking the form of a larger fraction (e.g., half instead of a third) or of a specific dollar amount plus a fraction of the net estate in excess of that amount.

In community property states, the intestate statutes generally provide a different treatment for separate and community property. Thus, it is common for the deceased spouse's separate estate to pass under provisions of the type described in the preceding paragraph, while the community property interest of the deceased spouse receives a different treatment. For example, in some states, if no testamentary disposition is made of the decedent's one-half interest, the survivor is entitled to both halves of the community property. E.g., Cal. Prob. Code §6401. At the other extreme, in some states it is provided that, if issue survive, the survivor does not participate in the intestate's half. E.g., Tex. Prob. Code Ann. §45.

NATIONAL COMMISSION ON THE OBSERVANCE OF INTERNATIONAL WOMEN'S YEAR, TO FORM A MORE PERFECT UNION — JUSTICE FOR AMERICAN WOMEN
(1976)

When the decedent's only surviving children are those of the marriage to the surviving spouse, the committee believes the surviving spouse should receive the entire estate. If the children are minors or unable to earn a living, the surviving spouse will be responsible for their support. When they are able-bodied and grown, they are no longer dependent, and the surviving spouse is likely to be at least approaching old age.

The provision on disposition of an estate when there are surviving parents but no children is arbitrary and may result in great inequity. . . . Suppose the parent or parents of a decedent husband have been dependent completely on the couple for a number of years and the marriage is of long duration; shouldn't the wife receive everything? On the other hand, if the decedent husband is young and the marriage has been of short duration and the parents have been partially supporting the couple, shouldn't the parents receive all the estate?

The "forced share" provision [see Chapter 3, infra] of one-third may be equitable in some circumstances but not in many. Suppose a farm wife has worked along with her husband for 30 years to make the farm a success, and he becomes senile and tries to leave her out of his will. Shouldn't she be entitled to the whole estate? Any wife who has had a long marriage and has contributed to her husband's success is certainly entitled to at least the amount she would have received if he had died intestate. On the other hand, if a young woman has been married to a wealthy man for only a few years and has squandered his wealth during that period, contributing nothing to his welfare or to acquisition of the money, should she receive as much as one-third? Here again the committee believes that the law should be redrafted to recognize a variety of circumstances.

How much variation can a statute of general application accommodate? An early draft of the original Uniform Probate Code attempted to distinguish among spouses of differing "merit" and circumstances but met with widespread resistance. The justifications and content of that early effort are discussed in Fratcher, Toward Uniform Succession Legislation, 41 N.Y.U.L. Rev. 1037, 1047 (1966).

M. SUSSMAN, J. CATES, AND D. SMITH, THE FAMILY AND INHERITANCE
83, 89-90, 143-144 (1970)

In this chapter, the testate disposition of property is compared with the distribution that would have occurred if the testator were intestate. . . .

[In the most significant deviation from the intestate pattern, the survey revealed that, even where issue survived, the] large majority of testators altered the distribution by bequeathing all to the surviving spouse. . . . Male and female testators differed very little in this pattern of willing the entire estate to the spouse. . . .

Testators who deviated from the norm of bequeathing their entire estates to their spouses generally had higher incomes or larger estates than those who followed the norm. They could afford to remember other relatives or friends in their wills. . . . In large estates, tax considerations may be an important factor affecting the pattern of distribution. . . .

[In intestate situations] where the statute prescribed a division between spouse and lineal kin, there were a large number of deviations. . . . [A]dult children usually signed over their shares to the surviving parent. . . . Where the children could not [do so] because they were not of legal age, parents may actually have been hamstrung in caring for their children. Parents were universally chagrined at the position they were in. . . .

An exception to the spouse-all pattern occurred in the case of remarriage. In both testate and intestate cases, the estates were more likely to be divided between spouse and children than were those in which the spouse was the parent of the surviving children.

2. Share of Issue

Whatever property remains after the spouse's share, or the entire net estate if there is no surviving spouse, passes to the descendants of the intestate. Although the term *issue* includes descendants of all degrees, remote descendants do not compete with their own living ancestors who are also descendants of the intestate. Thus *G*, a *grandchild* of the decedent, will not share in the estate so long as *G*'s parent, *C*, a *child* of the decedent, is still living. However, more remote descendants do share in the estate if they have no living ancestor who is also a descendant of the intestate. Thus, if *C* had predeceased the intestate, then *G* would participate in the intestate's property, even though he would thus share with the intestate's living children (*C*'s brothers and sisters).

Statutory or judicially established methods for determining the intestate shares of descendants under various circumstances differ from state to state, and some statutes are unclear on this matter. The question is often stated in terms of whether issue take per capita (by head) or per stirpes (by stocks).[2] The question does not arise when all children of the intestate survive because they receive equal shares whether the local rule follows a per capita or per stirpes pattern. Also, the result of granting the right of representation to issue is that, as long as any child of the intestate survives, the result is the same under a basically per capita rule or under a per stirpes rule.

PROBLEM

2-A. The intestate was predeceased by her spouse and both of her children, *S* who left a single child and *D* who left two children. Do the three grandchildren take equal one-third interests in the estate? Or does

---

2. It must not be assumed that these terms have the same meaning and application in all jurisdictions. See Kraemer v. Hook, 168 Ohio St. 221, 152 N.E.2d 430 (1958).

S's child take half, while *D*'s children take a quarter of the estate by dividing (under the principle of representation) the share *D* would have taken had she lived? (1) Can you answer this question under the statutes of your state? (2) Under the Uniform Probate Code §2-106(b) (below)? (3) Under the English Statute of Distribution?

See In re Ross' Trusts, L.R. 13 Eq. 286 (1871): "[I]t is difficult, I think, to resist the conclusion that, if there are descendants but no children living to share the estate, it is to be divided into as many shares as there are children who have left living descendants, and that the descendants of each such child are to take as representing the child. . . . The Statute of Distributions was drawn by a civilian, Sir Walter Walker, and seems to have been intended to introduce the rules of the Roman civil law into this branch of English law. It is, therefore, perhaps not irrelevant to remark that [this] view of the [statute] makes it conformable to the Roman law."

But cf. In re Martin's Estate, 96 Vt. 455, 120 Atl. 862 (1923): "In common with many if not all the American states, we get our law of descent largely from the English statute of distributions . . . under which it became settled at a very early day that the doctrine of representation applied only when the claimants were related to the intestate in unequal degrees; and that when they were equally related to him, they took directly and per capita — not by representation and per stirpes. . . . Such equality of benefit is the unmistakable spirit of our statute [and we hold] that grandchildren, who alone survive the ancestor, should take equally . . . — the clause providing for representation applying only when inequality of relationship exists."

Even where distribution would be made per capita among the grandchildren in the above problem, the issue of a deceased grandchild would take by right of representation the share that grandchild would have taken. Thus, if one of *D*'s two children had also predeceased the intestate and had left three children (great-grandchildren of the intestate), they would divide the one-third interest their parent would have taken; each would thus receive one-ninth of the estate. Of course, the living grandchildren would each take one-third.

Further questions on Problem 2-A: Consider next how distribution should be made if *S*'s child, as well as one of *D*'s children, had predeceased the intestate, *S*'s child leaving one child and *D*'s deceased child leaving the three children mentioned above. If in Problem 2-A the three grandchildren had taken the shares of their respective parents by representation (*S*'s child half and *D*'s children one-quarter each, as they would, e.g., under Iowa Probate Code tit. 32, §633.219(1)), the result here with respect to the great-grandchildren is obvious, is it not? If, however, the three grandchildren in Problem 2-A had taken equally (one-third apiece), how would "representation" operate with respect to the four great-grandchildren?

Prior to 1990, Uniform Probate Code §2-106, as originally promulgated in 1969, provided: "If representation is called for by this Code, the estate is divided into as many shares as there are surviving heirs in the nearest degree of kinship and deceased persons in the same degree who left issue who survive the decedent, each surviving heir in the nearest degree receiving one share and the share of each deceased person in the same degree being divided among his issue in the same manner." The 1969 provision reflects the concept of representation still prevalent in the United States, sometimes established by judicial decision and frequently by statutory enactment. The result is often now referred to as "conventional per capita with representation." The 1990 amendments to the UPC (below) provide for per capita distribution with per capita representation, often called "per capita at each generation." See UPC §2-106 cmt.; Waggoner, A Proposed Alternative to the [1969] Uniform Probate Code System for Intestate Distribution, 66 Nw. L. Rev. 626 (1971). See also Me. Rev. Stat. Ann. tit. 18-A, §§2-103, 2-106; N.C. Gen. Stat. §§29-15, 29-16. The California Probate Code continues the earlier UPC concept of representation for intestacy in §240 but also seeks to facilitate testator selection of alternative patterns of distribution among issue in §§245-247, including the testamentary option of distributing per capita at each generation (§247).

UNIFORM PROBATE CODE

§2-106. *Representation.*

(a) [Definitions.] In this section:

(1) "Deceased descendant," "deceased parent," or "deceased grandparent" means a descendant, parent, or grandparent who either predeceased the decedent or is deemed to have predeceased the decedent under Section 2-104.

(2) "Surviving descendant" means a descendant who neither predeceased the decedent nor is deemed to have predeceased the decedent under Section 2-104.

(b) [Decedent's Descendants.] If, under Section 2-103(1), a decedent's intestate estate or a part thereof passes "by representation" to the decedent's descendants, the estate or part thereof is divided into as many equal shares as there are (i) surviving descendants in the generation nearest to the decedent which contains one or more surviving descendants and (ii) deceased descendants in the same generation who left surviving descendants, if any. Each surviving descendant in the nearest generation is allocated one share. The remaining shares, if any, are combined and then divided in the same manner among the surviving descendants of the deceased descendants as if the surviving descendants who were allocated a share and their surviving descendants had predeceased the decedent.

(c) [Descendants of Parents or Grandparents.] If, under Section 2-103(3) or (4), a decedent's intestate estate or a part thereof passes "by representation" to the descendants of the decedent's deceased parents or either of them or to the descendants of the decedent's deceased paternal or maternal grandparents or either of them, the estate or part thereof is divided into as many equal shares as there are (i) surviving descendants in the generation nearest the deceased parents or either of them, or the deceased grandparents or either of them, that contains one or more surviving descendants and (ii) deceased descendants in the same generation who left surviving descendants, if any. Each surviving descendant in the nearest generation is allocated one share. The remaining shares, if any, are combined and then divided in the same manner among the surviving descendants of the deceased descendants as if the surviving descendants who were allocated a share and their surviving descendants had predeceased the decedent.

3. Shares of Ascendant and Collateral Relatives

American statutes typically provide that, in the absence of issue and subject to the share of the surviving spouse, intestate property passes to the parents or to the surviving parent of the decedent. In a few states brothers and sisters (and the issue of any who are deceased) share with parents, while some others allow them to share with a parent if but one parent survives. If neither parent survives the intestate, the property is divided among living brothers and sisters and the issue of any who are deceased, the brothers and sisters taking equal shares and the issue taking by right of representation.

The above-described shares of parents and the issue of parents are generally expressed in specific provisions of the statute. Occasionally legislation will also spell out the rights of grandparents and their descendants, but this is rare. Usually this "inner circle" of specifically mentioned relatives does not extend beyond parents and their descendants. Statutes typically provide that beyond this inner circle the property in question goes to the *next of kin* of the intestate. Frequently some method of determining the next of kin is indicated. If no method is prescribed, the so-called civil law method of computation is used. The classic methods of determining degrees of kinship are given below, but it must be kept in mind that the degree of kinship does not become relevant until it is determined that the property is not disposed of under the specific terms of the statute. Thus, even though an uncle is only three degrees removed from the decedent under the civil law count, usually the uncle would not share with the decedent's niece (also three degrees removed) because the latter is typically provided for either by the expressed terms of the statute, specifically referring to the intestate's nieces and nephews, or by specific reference to the children of brothers and sisters or to the issue of parents.

Under the civil law system of computation, used by the ecclesiastical courts in England and adopted by the Statute of Distribution in 1670, a claimant's degree of kinship is the total of (1) the number of the steps, counting one for each generation, from the decedent up to the nearest common ancestor of the decedent and the claimant, and (2) the number of steps from the common ancestor down to the claimant. The claimant having the lowest degree count (i.e., the nearest or next of kin) is entitled to the property. If there are two or more claimants who stand in equal degree of kinship to the decedent, they share per capita. However, under a widespread modification of this system, a statute may provide that, when there are several claimants of equal degree but claiming through different ancestors, those claiming through the ancestor nearest the decedent take to the exclusion of those who claim through a more remote ancestor. The civil law system of computation and its modified form have been widely adopted by statute in the United States.

The canon law (sometimes called the common law) method of computation also involved counting the steps in the line from the claimant to the nearest common ancestor of the claimant and the decedent and then counting the steps in the line from that ancestor to the decedent. The number of steps in the *longer* of these two lines was the relevant degree of kinship. The claimant or claimants having the *lowest* degree of kinship thus determined took as next of kin. This system was used by the canon law to determine whether a marriage between relatives was prohibited and by the common law in limiting successive donees in frankmarriage.

A number of statutes have enacted a form of parentelic system, resembling in part the rules for descent of land in England under the common law. Rather than mentioning certain near relatives and then providing that next of kin take in the absence of the specified relatives, these statutes require a determination of the nearest ancestors who either are alive or have issue living, and it is provided that the property goes to these nearest ancestors or their issue. These statutes do not involve the usual concept of next of kin. Universal representation eliminates the necessity of counting degrees of kinship. Statutes of this basic type vary in wording and detail.

Beyond that inner circle of relatives who are specifically designated, the right to take by representation often is not recognized in states using the civil law methods. Under these statutes when it becomes necessary to determine intestate succession by counting degrees of kinship, representation ceases. See also Statute of Distribution, ¶VII, supra page 47.

With but occasional and limited exceptions, intestate succession is confined to the surviving spouse and persons related to the decedent by consanguinity and adoption. If none of the relatives provided for in the statute are available to take the property, escheat will occur, and the property will go to the state or some subdivision or agency thereof. As a last resort prior to escheat, a few jurisdictions allow intestate property to pass to relatives by affinity. In a few other states certain property acquired by the decedent from a predeceased spouse passes to relatives of that spouse under various circumstances, and a few statutes provide for stepchildren in certain circumstances. The modern trend, however, exemplified by the Uniform Probate Code, is to confine intestate succession to near relatives of the decedent and to increase the occasions of escheat.

PROBLEMS

2-B.   *D* died intestate, survived only by the issue of two deceased brothers and of one deceased sister. Altogether there were five nephews and nieces, one of whom predeceased *D* leaving issue. The petition filed in this case avers that the living nephews and nieces should take equal shares of the estate and that one equal share should be divided among the issue of the deceased niece, or, in other words, that the number of primary shares is five. The appearing respondents contend that the nephews and nieces should also take by representation, so that the number of primary shares should be three.

The pertinent statute provides: "(3) If there be no issue or parent, then in equal shares to his brothers and sisters, and to the descendants of any deceased brother or sister by right of representation." Paragraph (4) continues: "If there is no brother or sister or issue of such, then to the next of kin of equal degree and the lawful issue of such next of kin by right of representation."

(a) What argument should be advanced for the petitioners? For the respondents? On what facts, language, and authorities do you rely?

(b) What result would be reached under the Uniform Probate Code? Your local statute?

(c) If the pertinent provisions are not adequate in the problem statute, what amendment would you suggest?

2-C.   Consider the chart that follows on page 58 and decide which of the three underlined (living) collateral claimants would receive the decedent's intestate property under (a) the civil law system, (b) the modified civil law system, (c) the canon law system, (d) the parentelic system, and (e) your local statute.

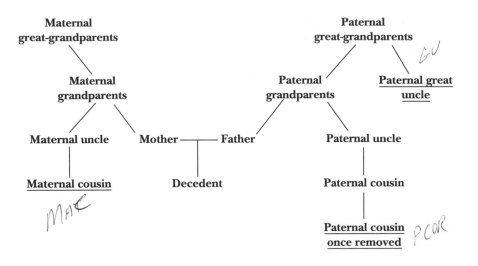

4.   A Comparison

WARREN, THE LAW OF PROPERTY ACT, 1922
21 Mich. L. Rev. 245, 263-267 (1923)

Amendment of the [English] law of intestacy is collateral to the main object of the act, but broadly within its spirit. The assimilation of real to personal property naturally meant a total change in the rules of descent. But to adopt for land the existing rules as to personal property would mean a discrimination between the sexes which the influence of women in Parliament would soon eradicate. This has been anticipated, not only by abolishing primogeniture as to land except in estate tail in equity, but also be placing the two sexes on an equality as to both realty and personalty by a thorough overhauling of the laws of descent and intestacy. All such laws are abolished, including descent to the heir, curtesy, dower, and escheat.

Upon the death of a person intestate as to any real or personal property, such property passes to his personal representatives upon trust to sell (with power to postpone sale), to pay funeral expenses, expenses of administration and debts, and then to hold on trust for distribution. This trust for sale lets in all power of management and of over-riding of equities given by the Act generally to trustees for sale. After payment of expenses and debts, the residuary estate is held on trust for the surviving spouse, whether there are issue or not, to the extent of the personal chattels [which are defined to exclude money, securities, and chattels acquired for business purposes] and £1,000; and as to the balance of the estate, if there are no issue, for the surviving spouse for life to the extent of the whole; if there are issue, for the surviving spouse for life to the extent of one-half, and subject thereto for the issue. If there are no issue, the statutory trusts are, subject to the interests as above of the surviving spouse, if any, for the following persons, who take in the order named in the absence of a member of the preceding class taking an absolute interest: (1) parents; (2) brothers and sisters of the whole blood; (3) brothers and sisters of the half blood; (4) grandparents; (5) uncles and aunts of the whole blood; (6) uncles and aunts of the half blood; (7) the surviving spouse absolutely; (8) the Crown.

When the statutory trust is for the issue of the intestate (and here is the provision perhaps the most interesting to the American lawyer), the trusts are: in trust "in equal shares (if more than one) for all or any of the children or child of the intestate, living at the death of the intestate, who attain the age of twenty-one years or marry under that age, and for all or any of the issue living at the death of the intestate who attain the age of twenty-one years or marry under that age of any child of the intestate, who predeceases the intestate, leaving issue living at the death of the intestate, such issue to take through all degrees according to their stocks in equal shares (if more than one) the share which their parent would have taken if living at the death of the intestate, and so that no issue shall take whose parent is living at the death of the intestate and so capable of taking."

Statutory power of advancement by trustees and provisions for maintenance during minority and for accumulation of surplus income are applicable. Accounting by the children of the intestate for money paid them by their father during his life must under certain conditions be made. Youthful heirs are not, by reason of their interest being contingent, deprived of the use of the family motor, for the personal representatives "may permit any infant contingently interested to have the use and enjoyment of any personal chattels" in a manner which the personal representative may consider reasonable without being liable to account for consequential loss. . . .

. . . Searches in Somerset House show that in about ninety-seven percent of the small wills the surviving spouse takes the whole or a life or other substantial interest. We may well copy the measure so far as personal chattels are concerned. Every well-drawn American will gives them to the spouse, and waste of time and money results in their going to tenants in common or joint tenants. But some may feel that the other provisions unduly favor the surviving husband or wife, particularly in the case of second marriages. Yet the original bill was attacked as not going far enough, and was altered in favor of the present provisions.

We cannot too highly commend the statutory trusts in favor of the issue of the testator and other classes of relatives. With some modification in regard to partition and over-riding equities to suit the varying public opinion in different states, they are well worth our experimentation. The beneficiaries are given contingent interests until twenty-one or marriage, with maintenance in the interval. This insures their subsistence and education during minority and prevents the cost of new letters of administration if they die before their shares vest in possession. . . .

ADMINISTRATION OF ESTATES ACT, 1925
15 & 16 Geo. V, c. 23, as amended by the Intestate Estates Act of
1952 and the Family Provisions Act of 1966

§46 . . . If the intestate [who leaves a husband or wife] —

(1) leaves no issue and no parent, or brother or sister of the whole blood, or issue of brother and sister of the whole blood, the residuary estate shall be held in trust for the surviving husband or wife absolutely;

(2) leaves issue (whether or not [others mentioned] above also survive), the surviving husband or wife shall take the personal chattels absolutely and, in addition, the residuary estate . . . shall stand charged with the payment of a fixed sum [as provided by the Family Provision Act*], free of death duties and costs, to the surviving husband or wife with interest thereon from the date of death at [rate set by order] per annum until paid, [and the remaining residuary estate] shall be held (a) as to one half upon trust for the surviving husband or wife during his life, and subject to such life interest, on the statutory trusts for the issue of the intestate, and (b) as to the other half, on the statutory trusts for the issue of the intestate;

(3) leaves one or more of the following, that is to say, a parent, a brother or sister of the whole blood, or the issue of a brother or sister of the whole blood, but leaves no issue, the surviving husband or wife shall take the personal chattels absolutely and, in addition, the residuary estate . . . shall stand charged with the payment of a fixed sum,* free of death duties and costs, to the surviving husband or wife [with interest], and the [remaining residuary estate] shall be held (a) as to one half in trust for the surviving husband absolutely, and (b) as to other half [in trust for the surviving parent or parents absolutely or for the whole-blood brothers and sisters and their issue].

Section 46 continues with provisions for others, mostly as described in the preceding Warren article, if no spouse survives. The statute provides for the spouse's fixed sum payment (at * above) to be determined by reference to the Family Provision Act of 1966. Under the original 1925 act the spouse was entitled to £1,000, and the 1952 act increased the amount to £5,000 under paragraph (2) and £20,000 under paragraph (3). The 1987 order of the Lord Chancellor increased the sums to £75,000 and £125,000, respectively. Section 47 describes the terms of the statutory trusts for children and other relatives, while Section 47A entitles the spouse to elect to receive outright the actuarial value of the life interest in lieu of the trust for life. 17 Halsbury's Stat. 290 (1991 Supp.). No American state has yet ventured nearly so far afield from the original English 1670 Statute of Distribution.

B. Questions of Definition and Status

1. In General

Posthumous heirs. The common law rule that a child in gestation at the death of the intestate is deemed to be in being, and thus entitled to inherit if subsequently born alive, has generally been codified in the United States. In cases involving collateral heirs conceived before the intestate's death, inheritance is also permitted, although statutory language may fail to provide for this situation.

Simultaneous and near-simultaneous death. Where two or more persons die in a common disaster, evidence of the order of death is usually lacking. Problems of this sort are not confined to intestate succession, of course, and must be resolved in some fashion. At common law the result usually turned simply on the inability of a claimant to carry his burden of proving that one through whom he claims survived the decedent. The Uniform Simultaneous Death Act, enacted in most states, provides that, absent contrary provision in the controlling instrument, where "title to property or the devolution thereof depends upon priority of death and there is no sufficient evidence that the persons have died otherwise than simultaneously, the property of each person shall be disposed of as if he had survived, except as otherwise provided by this Act." Specific provisions then deal with life insurance (providing for distribution as if the insured had survived the beneficiary), joint tenancy or tenancy by the entirety (treating each owner as the survivor with respect to half or other appropriate proportion of the property), and situations involving beneficiaries "designated to take successively by reason of survivorship under another person's disposition." Uniform Probate Code §2-104 requires that a relative survive the decedent by five days in order to inherit. Do you see the reasons for this innovation?

Aliens. Treaties or statutes frequently alter the alien's common law right to receive and dispose of personal property and his disability with regard to land. Despite serious doubt at the present time concerning their constitutionality, see Zschernig v. Miller, 389 U.S. 429 (1968), and Gorun v. Fall, 393 U.S. 398 (1969), some state statutes make this ability or disability depend on reciprocity or on the rights the alien will have with regard to the inheritance or both; these questions may pose legal questions that go to the very essence of property rights and concepts under the foreign law in question.

Half-blood relatives. Generally in the United States, relatives of the half blood inherit equally with those of the whole, and it appears that this is the rule in the absence of statute covering the question. However, it is necessary to determine whether, when the applicable statute does discriminate against half bloods, the latter take a smaller share, are postponed to whole-blood relatives of the same degree, or are postponed in favor of whole-blood relatives only in the case of "ancestral property." Half-blood problems exist, of course, only in the case of collateral relatives.

Ancestral property. In the descent of land under the common law in England, inheritance was limited to relatives of the blood of the ancestor who was the "first purchaser." The original doctrine is not applicable to personal property and is generally not recognized in the United States even as to land. Where the doctrine of ancestral property has been preserved by statute (and in several states this has been done by a statute applicable only to the passage of ancestral property where the claimants include half-blood relatives who are not of the blood of the ancestor), it is necessary to examine the statute carefully, and also the decisions construing it. The tendency has been to construe such statutes narrowly.

2. Adoption

Statutes typically create inheritance rights in adopted persons. The tendency is to treat the adopted child as if he or she had been born into the adopting family. See Uniform Probate Code §2-114. However, such statutes are often unclear in many respects. In examining a given statute it is necessary to consider the question of inheritance *from* as well as *by* an adopted person and particularly to consider the adoptee's status with regard to the natural relatives as well as to the adoptive relatives. See Binavince, Adoption and the Law of Descent, 51 Cornell L.Q. 152 (1966).

The need to examine statutes carefully and the adoptee's long, uphill struggle against narrow construction by courts of legislation in this area are aptly illustrated by In re Hewett's Estate, 153 Fla. 137, 13 So. 2d 904 (1943), involving the possible right of an adoptee to inherit *through* the adopting parents from other members of the adoptive family. In that case, the intestate's nearest relatives were two first cousins and the adopted daughter of a deceased first cousin. Applicable statutes provided (1) that intestate property should pass under these circumstances "to the uncles and aunts and the descendants of such of them as may be deceased" and (2) that an adopted child "shall be an heir at law and for the purpose of inheritance be regarded as a lineal descendant of its adopting parents." The court stated that "the statute says nothing about the adopting parents' ancestors" and that "we cannot add anything to the statute which is not expressly stated therein or which is not necessarily implied by the language used." It further stated:

> This statute is very liberal in its provisions in behalf of the adopted child. Such child inherits from its adopting parents as if it were their own natural child, and likewise inherits from its natural parents. Why should the legislature be *construed* to have gone further and intended by court-imposed implication, to give the adopted child the right to inherit from the adopting parents' ancestors or other blood kin? The legislature should not be construed to have intended this unless the language of the statute makes it plain that such was the legislative intent — which we do not think it does.

The opinion then refers to other cases indicating "that a statute which interrupts the natural course of the descent of property should be strictly construed" and that "to allow an adopted child to inherit from the ancestors of the adopter would often put property into the hands of unheard of adopted children, contrary to the wishes and expectations of such ancestors." 153 Fla. at 140-143, 13 So. 2d at 906-907.

Most statutes today have expressly and clearly expanded the rights of adoptees to include inheritance "through" the adoptive parents as well as from them, as in the statute in the problem below. See also Uniform Probate Code §2-114.

PROBLEM

2-D.   *H* and *W* were married and had a child, *C*. *H* and *W* were later divorced and *W* was awarded custody of *C*, with *H* being granted extensive visitation rights. Thereafter *W* married *S*, who subsequently and with *H*'s consent adopted *C*, then age 11. *S*, *W*, and *C* have enjoyed a happy family relationship. Through the years *C* also continued to spend considerable time with *H*, but a week ago *H* died intestate survived by his wife, *X*, and their daughter, *D*. (1) *C*, now age 24, asks you about his possible interest in *H*'s estate. How would you respond under the law of your state? Under the Uniform Probate Code? Or in a jurisdiction that has the statute set out below (Oregon R.S. §112.175)? Cf. Estate of Daigle, 642 P.2d 527 (Colo. App. 1982). (2) After *H*'s death, *G* (*H*'s widowed mother) died intestate; *H* was her only child. Does *C* have an interest in her estate under the law of your state? Under the UPC? Under the statute below?

> (1) An adopted person, his issue and kindred shall take by intestate succession from his adoptive parents, their issue and kindred, and his adoptive parents, their issue and kindred shall take by intestate succession from the adopted person, his issue and kindred, as though the adopted person were the natural child of his adoptive parents.
> (2) An adopted person shall cease to be treated as the child of his natural

parents for all purposes of intestate succession by the adopted person, his issue and kindred and his natural parents, their issue and kindred, except:

(a) If a natural parent of a person marries or remarries and the person is adopted by his stepparent, the adopted person shall continue also to be treated, for all purposes of intestate succession, as the child of the natural parent who is the spouse of the adoptive parent.

(b) If a natural parent of a person dies, the other natural parent remarries and the person is adopted by his stepparent, the adopted person shall continue also to be treated, for all purposes of intestate succession by any person through the deceased natural parent, as the child of the deceased natural parent. . . .

Even though legislation in most states has now clarified the more frequent of the intestacy problems involving adoptees, lawyers must still be conscious of analogous questions in drafting, for intestate succession statutes as such are not always controlling for purposes of ascertaining the meaning of class terminology such as *children* and *issue* in wills and trust agreements. For example, with respect to a testate counterpart of situation (2) in Problem 2-D, above, compare In re Tracy, 464 Pa. 300, 346 A.2d 750 (1975), with First National Bank v. Schwerin, 54 Or. App. 460, 635 P.2d 388 (1981). See also Lockwood v. Adamson, 409 Mass. 325, 566 N.E.2d 96 (1991) (concluding that the testator's gift to the "issue" of another included that other person's blood descendant who had been "adopted out" of the family, despite an *intestate* succession statute providing in relevant part that a "person shall by adoption lose his right to inherit" from the biological family; the court also noted that "[e]ven if we assume that a devise or bequest to an adoptee somehow undermines the adoptive family relationship, . . . where the child's relationship to his natural parents is ordinarily known to all concerned," it is unlikely that the right to take as a class member in the biological family would have an "adverse effect on the family relationship" or otherwise "undermine the policy goals of integrating children as fully as possible into their adoptive families"). Consider the problems that follow.

PROBLEMS

2-E.   Under *A*'s will Blackacre was devised to *A*'s daughter, *D*, for life, remainder to such of *D*'s issue as survive her. At *D*'s death she is survived by two children, one of whom was adopted. In determining the adopted child's rights under *A*'s will, what is the relevance, if any, of a statute in the state in which Blackacre is situated providing that adopted children shall be treated the same as natural children for purposes of inheritance by, from, and through the adopting parent? For the traditional view, still adhered to in some states, see Restatement of Property §287 (1940); but see Restatement (Second) of Property §25.4 (1987); In re Trusts under Agreement with Harrington, 311 Minn. 403, 250 N.W.2d 163 (1977); and In re Coe's Estate, 42 N.J. 485, 201 A.2d 571 (1964).[3] See also Uniform Probate Code §2-705. Should it be relevant whether the adoption occurred after *A*'s death, before it, or before execution of the will? See generally Halbach, Rights of Adopted Children Under Class Gifts, 50 Iowa L. Rev. 971 (1965).

3. In rejecting the traditional rule and in deciding that a person should take as a member of the class into which he has been adopted, the New Jersey court stated:

> [I]t is not important whether the adoption statute directly controls the interpretation of instruments. The important point is that the statute reflects the feeling and attitude of the average man and hence its policy should be followed unless the benefactor explicitly reveals a contrary purpose. . . . Hence even if the quoted provisions of the adoption statute . . . speak only of intestacy, they should nonetheless be accepted as a reflection of a common expectation and wish and hence as a guide to proper interpretation of a gift. . . .
>
> The trouble in our State began [with] an unwarranted assumption that when one who is not a party to the adoption makes a gift to a class consisting of children of the adopting parent, he probably intends to benefit only natural children. . . . We cannot believe it probable that strangers to the adoption would differentiate between the natural child and the adopted child of another. Rather we believe it more likely that they accept the relationships established by the parent whether the bond be natural or by adoption and seek to advance those relationships precisely as their parent would. . . .
>
> Finally, it is suggested that to depart from the stranger-to-the-adoption view would invite fraud by permitting a person to adopt someone solely to enable him to take under the will of another. . . . It seems to us that the prospect of fraud is quite remote and can be dealt with upon equitable principles if the circumstances are truly compelling.

42 N.J. 489-492, 201 A.2d 574-576. In Estate of Nicol, 74 N.J. 312, 372 A.2d 1201 (1977), the court did as suggested in *Coe* and found, on the basis of probable intent, that adult adoptees were not included as recipients of a future-interest class gift.

See also Elliott v. Hiddleson, 303 N.W.2d 140, 144 (Iowa 1981): "In rejecting the [stranger-to-the-adoption] rule, we do not preclude the right of a testator to distinguish between natural and adopted children as objects of his bounty. We merely require that such intent be shown. Unless a contrary intent appears, we will presume that a testator intended to treat adopted children in the same manner as natural children. In so doing, however, we will not permit the conscious use of adoption as a means of upsetting a transferor's normal expectations."

This flexibility to deal with manipulative adoptions, however, may not be available under simple but explicit will provisions and statutes calling for the inclusion of adoptees in class gifts. See, e.g., Lehman v. Corpus Christi Natl. Bank, 668 S.W.2d 687 (Tex. 1984) (both will clause and statutory language). Cf. Evans v. McCoy, 291 Md. 562, 436 A.2d 436 (1981) (elderly widow adopted adult neighbor, defeating her uncles' interests conditioned on her death without issue); Solomon v. Central Trust Co., 63 Ohio St. 3d 35, 584 N.E.2d 1185 (1992) (allowing a person adopted at age 44, long after settlor's death, to share with a biological child as "issue" of settlor's brother, the court expressly rejecting and seeking to remove the last vestiges of the "stranger-to-the-adoption" rule in Ohio); and the all-time shocker, Bedinger v. Graybill's Estate, 302 S.W.2d 594 (Ky. 1957) (life beneficiary adopted his wife, displacing other claimants under a remainder to his "heirs at law"), not followed in Minary's Estate, 419 S.W.2d 340 (Ky. App. 1967).

Do recent construction statutes apply to class gifts under preexisting documents? See, e.g., New England Merchants Natl. Bank v. Groswold, 387 Mass. 822, 444 N.E.2d 359 (1983).

2-F.   *A*'s will also left $500,000 in trust for his son. *S*, for life, remainder to such of *S*'s issue as survive him. *S* also had a small estate of his own. *S* died intestate survived by *X*, whom *S* had raised from infancy. It was generally believed, and believed by *S* and *X*, that *S* had adopted *X*, but the purported adoption was void. For the last ten years of *S*'s life he was a widower, and *Y* lived in *S*'s home, keeping house for him and generally caring for his needs. Out of gratitude, and with his father's trust in mind, *S* adopted *Y*. What are the rights of *X* and *Y* in *S*'s estate and in the trust?

MATTER OF HEIRS OF HODGE
470 So. 2d 740 (Fla. App. 1985)

DAUKSCH, J. . . .

This case involves the rarity, "virtual adoption." When someone gives his or her natural child to another with an agreement that the other will adopt the child then the child will be deemed to have an enforceable contractual right. . . .

[A]n oral or written promise to adopt may be enforced by the child in an intestacy proceeding to establish rights of inheritance. The elements to be proved include:

1. An agreement between the natural and adoptive parents;
2. Performance by the natural parents . . . in giving up custody;
3. Performance by the child by living [with] the adoptive parents;
4. Partial performance by the foster parents in taking the child into the home and treating the child as their child; and
5. Intestacy of the foster parents.

Appellee was three years old when her mother died and her father gave her to the Hodges. Although there was no one to testify directly that they heard or read an agreement to adopt, there was sufficient evidence in the record for the trial judge to conclude that there was an agreement to adopt. When [Appellee] was nine the Hodges told her she was not their natural daughter but was adopted. She lived with the Hodges until she married at age seventeen and was always called Hodge, loved as a daughter and responded in kind. Mr. Hodge was the president of her P.T.A. when she was in school, he signed her report cards, she paid his funeral expenses and attended his funeral. . . .

We agree with the trial judge that all elements were established. . . .

In considering whether a child raised but not formally adopted by testator's niece could take under a trust provision for the niece's "child or children," the court in Wheeling Dollar Savings & Trust Co. v. Singer, 250 S.E.2d 369, 372-374 (W. Va. 1978), stated:

> [W]e do not hesitate to hold that the concept of equitable adoption should be a viable theory for relief from injustice in West Virginia, as long as adequate care is taken to protect the tradition of our ancient law of future interests and inheritance. The status of adopted children long plagued this and other courts, but our holding in Wheeling Dollar Sav. & Trust Co. v. Hanes, 237 S.E.2d 499 (W. Va. 1977) . . . settled the controversy in West Virginia. In *Hanes* we set the law by saying:

>> It appears to the Court that most testators and trustors establish trusts for the benefit of those persons they love and for the benefit of those persons yet unknown and yet unborn whom such testators and trustors infer that their loved ones will eventually love. While there may be testators and trustors who are so concerned with medieval concepts of "bloodline" and "heirs of the body" that they would truly be upset at the thought that their hard-won assets would one day pass into the hands of persons not of their blood, we cannot formulate general rules of law for the benefit of eccentrics.

> Id. at 503. Since *Hanes* clearly establishes the right of adopted children to be treated as natural children, the only remaining question presented in the case before us is whether adherence to formal adoption procedures, W. Va. Code, 48-4-1 [1969] et seq. is the exclusive method by which a person may be accorded the protections of adoptive status in West Virginia. We find that it is not.

> While formal adoption is the only safe route, in many instances a child will be raised by persons not his parents from an age of tender years, treated as a natural child, and represented to others as a natural or adopted child. In many instances, the child will believe himself to be the natural or formally "adopted" child of the "adoptive" parents only to be treated as an outcast upon their death. We cannot ascertain any reasonable distinction between a child treated in all regards as an adopted child but who has been led to rely to his detriment upon the existence of formal legal paperwork imagined but never accomplished, and a formally adopted child. Our family centered society presumes that bonds of love and loyalty will prevail in the distribution of family wealth along family lines, and only by affirmative action, i.e., writing a will, may this presumption be overcome. An equitably adopted child in practical terms is as much a family member as a formally adopted child and should not be the subject of discrimination. He will be as loyal to his adoptive parents, take as faithful care of them in their old age, and provide them with as much financial and emotional support in their vicissitudes, as any natural or formally adopted child.

> However, the equitably adopted child and the formally adopted child are not without differences. The formally adopted child need only produce his adoption papers to guarantee his treatment as an adopted child. The equitably adopted child in any private property dispute such as the case under consideration involving the laws of *inheritance* or *private trusts* must prove by clear, cogent and convincing evidence that he has stood

from an age of tender years in a position *exactly* equivalent to a formally
adopted child. Circumstances which tend to show the existence of an equitable adoption include: the benefits of love and affection accruing to the
adopting party; the performances of services by the child; the surrender
of ties by the natural parent; the society, companionship and filial obedi-
ence of the child; an invalid or ineffectual adoption proceeding; reliance
by the adopted person upon the existence of his adoptive status; the representation to all the world that the child is a natural or adopted child; and
the rearing of the child from an age of tender years by the adopting parents. Of course, evidence can be presented which tends to negate an equitable adoption. . . .

Most of the cited cases predicate the finding of an equitable adoption
on the proof of an expressed or implied contract of adoption. While the
existence of an express contract of adoption is very convincing evidence,
an implied contract of adoption is an unnecessary fiction created by courts
as a protection from fraudulent claims. We find that if a claimant can, by
clear, cogent and convincing evidence, prove sufficient facts to convince
the trier of fact that his status is identical to that of a formally adopted
child, except only for the absence of a formal order of adoption, a finding
of an equitable adoption is proper without proof of an adoption contract.

In the case before us, appellant Singer alleges that she was taken from
an orphanage when she was eight or nine by the Whartons; that she was
given the surname of the Whartons; that she was raised as their child and
that, until this action, she believed herself to be the adopted child of the
Whartons. Furthermore it appears that Lyda Wharton [testator's niece]
devised and bequeathed her residuary estate to "my daughter, Ada Bell
Singer." If the appellant Singer can prove these allegations at the hearing
below, she has a strong case for equitable adoption, and one of the most
important elements in her proof is that she was held out to all the world
as a natural or adopted child. . . .

Many factors relevant to proof of equitable adoption are also relevant
in proving acknowledgment in paternity actions. But, as you will see, the
Constitution appears not to require a state to consider evidence that is
less "trustworthy" than a paternity judgment in giving a nonmarital
child an intestate share of the father's estate. The result in some states is
that a court will not consider such factors unless the father is alive to
defend (thus also apprising him of the possible desirability from his viewpoint of making a will).

Are there any circumstances in which it might be desirable for legislation to provide that stepchildren or foster children receive treatment
similar to that accorded adoptees? Such statutes are almost nonexistent,
but see California Probate Code §6408(b).

3. Nonmarital Children

Statutes vary widely in clarity and coverage concerning the rights of
persons born out of wedlock. Claims by unadopted, nonmarital children

to share in intestate estates of or class gifts by members of the natural families, maternal and paternal, arise in contexts as varied as those involving adoptees — and each of these groups of issues are frequent sources of litigation in the probate and trust field today. The causes of controversy include bad lawyer work and inadequately considered legislation and judicial opinions. In addition to this, the volume and seriousness of the litigation are reflections of the numbers of potential claimants of uncertain status. The demographic data will be startling to most of you: nearly one-quarter of American babies are born out of wedlock, with the percentage given up for adoption declining. Although such births remain highest among teenagers, recent increases are greatest among women ages 20 to 24, reflecting both living-together arrangements and women wishing to raise children without a long-term relationship with a man.

The law's primary traditional line of distinction has been between relationships on the maternal side and those on the paternal side. The latter seem to raise the specter of the nonmarital offspring's surprise appearance at the natural father's funeral. Clearly the circumstances of a person's birth will not affect inheritance from or by that person's own spouse and issue. In addition, an unadopted child born out of wedlock inherits from the mother, and statutes or decisions in many jurisdictions allow inheritance from maternal relatives; typical legislation also allows the mother, and now usually her relatives, to inherit from the child. The traditional rules, however, almost universally precluded inheritance from or by the father and his relatives, except that the subsequent marriage of the parents or the father's acknowledgment (often requiring a writing), and sometimes a judicial decree of paternity, have typically opened the lincs of inheritance between child and father, and sometimes paternal relatives.

Uniform Probate Code §2-114 and the Uniform Parentage Act represent recent efforts to broaden the inheritance rights of these children. Meanwhile, new problems in this area are being created by artificial insemination and surrogate parenting. Are "test-tube children" illegitimate for purposes of intestate succession? Cf. Gursky v. Gursky, 39 Misc. 2d 1083, 242 N.Y.S.2d 406 (1963). At the present time, however, many of the traditional lines and distinctions in this entire area are giving way to reform and constitutional pressure, although the specifics of constitutional requirements remain unsettled.

Without holding that legislative classifications based on illegitimacy are strictly suspect, the United States Supreme Court decided in Trimble v. Gordon, 430 U.S. 762 (1977), that such classifications are invalid under the fourteenth amendment if they are not substantially related to permissible state interests. Accordingly, by a five-to-four vote the Court invalidated an Illinois inheritance statute requiring not only acknowledgment by the father but also the marriage of the parents in order for the child born out of wedlock to inherit from the father. Writing for the

Court, Justice Powell rejected encouragement of legitimate family relationships as a purpose to be achieved by disadvantaging the child, but he
recognized as permissible the aim of maintaining an accurate and efficient system for the transfer of intestate property. He conceded that the
often difficult problem of proving paternity and the related danger of
spurious claims "might justify a more demanding standard for illegitimate children claiming under their father's estates than that required
either for illegitimate children claiming under their mother's estates or
for legitimate children generally." In requiring the marriage of the parents, however, the statute excluded "at least some significant categories
of illegitimate children of intestate men [whose] inheritance rights can
be recognized without jeopardizing the orderly settlement of estates or
the dependability of titles." The Court stated that the statute must be
more "carefully tuned to alternative considerations" than were the
broad rules of disqualification in the Illinois law. 430 U.S. at 770-772.
An argument that the statute was justifiable as a reflection of the probable intention of decedents was not considered by the Court because it
was procedurally improper, not having been raised and examined in the
state proceedings.

Soon thereafter, in Lalli v. Lalli, 439 U.S. 259 (1978), the Supreme
Court was confronted with New York's Estates, Powers, and Trusts Law
§4-1.2, enacted in 1965. The statute allowed, as usual, "an illegitimate
child and his issue [to] inherit from his mother and from his maternal
kindred" but provided that "he and his issue inherit from his father
[only] if a court of competent jurisdiction has, during the lifetime of the
father, made an order of filiation, declaring paternity." (A further time
limitation was not in issue in the case.) The statute also stated that "an
agreement obligating the father to support the illegitimate child does
not qualify such child or his issue to inherit from the father" in the
absence of the prescribed order of filiation. Following the father's death,
the nonmarital claimant offered evidence of his relationship to and with
the decedent, including a notarized document in which the latter gave
his consent to the marriage of "my son" and several affidavits by persons
who stated that the decedent had acknowledged his son openly and
often. The New York Court of Appeals in In re Lalli, 43 N.Y.2d 65, 371
N.E.2d 481 (1977), had found the statute sufficiently related to the
state's interest in "the orderly settlement of estates and dependability of
titles" to satisfy the dictates of equal protection.

By another five-to-four vote, the United States Supreme Court this
time upheld the statute. In a plurality opinion, Justice Powell found the
statute sufficiently related to its main purpose of providing "for the just
and orderly disposition of property at death." The statute, he wrote,
enhanced the accuracy of judicial fact-finding in paternity disputes,
facilitated the administration of estates by making "the entitlement of
an illegitimate child to notice and participation a matter of judicial rec-

ord before the administration commences," and reduces the frequency of "fraudulent assertions of paternity." Incidentally, it also permitted a man "to defend his reputation against 'unjust accusations in paternity claims.'" Justice Powell sought to distinguish his opinion in *Trimble* by stressing that the legislative history disavowed any New York intention to "discourage illegitimacy, to mold human conduct or to set societal norms" and that under the New York statute "the marital status of the parents is irrelevant." He also emphasized that the statute had been enacted mainly "to soften the rigors of previous law which permitted illegitimate children to inherit only from their mothers," was the product of a comprehensive and balanced study by individuals "experienced in the practical problems of estate administration," and had been interpreted "liberally" by the New York courts. 439 U.S. at 269-276. Petitioners argued that the New York law, like the Illinois law, denied inheritance to children who could provide convincing proof of paternity by other means than those prescribed in the statute, such as by formal written acknowledgment of paternity. Justice Powell recognized that this was so but responded that the New York statute did not disinherit as many deserving heirs as the Illinois statute.

Justice Blackmun, in a brief concurring opinion, found the distinctions between the two cases unconvincing, believed "the Court today gratifyingly reverts to [pre-*Trimble*] principles," and concluded: "I therefore must regard *Trimble* as a derelict . . . offering little precedent for constitutional analysis of State intestate succession laws. If *Trimble* is not a derelict, the corresponding statutes of other States will be of questionable validity until this court passes them, one by one, as being on the *Trimble* side of the line or the . . . *Lalli* side." 439 U.S. at 277.

A four-justice dissent notes a particular irony in the results of these two cases, for the probabilities of intention (on which intestate law is largely based) are most likely to favor the very nonmarital children the New York law excludes. This opinion states: "[A]s a practical matter, by requiring judicial filiation orders entered during the lifetime of the father, the New York statute makes it virtually impossible for acknowledged and freely supported illegitimate children to inherit intestate." 439 U.S. at 278.

Reed v. Campbell, 476 U.S. 859 (1986), made clear that application of an unjustifiably discriminatory Texas statute to bar a nonmarital child's claim as a pretermitted heir (see Chapter 3, section C, infra) was constitutionally impermissible, even though the father died before the *Trimble* decision.

"A distinction between rights to inherit from a natural father and . . . a natural mother may properly be based on the greater difficulty of proving paternity than of proving maternity." But the alleged greater difficulty of an administrator in "identifying and giving notice to the illegitimate children of a man" was not a justification for the distinction, especially given that "notice by publication should be adequate" for unknown claimants. The *state* constitution was thus held to be violated by a classification that denied an *openly admitted* illegitimate child the right to inherit from the father because it went beyond what would be necessary to "serve the State's interest in avoiding fraudulent claims" in Lowell v. Kowalski, 380 Mass. 663, 405 N.E.2d 135 (1980).

On evidentiary and related aspects of these cases, see Proof of Heirship of Illegitimate Children of the Father — Estate of Daniel Finigan (a Mock Trial), 13 Real Prop., Prob. & Tr. J. 733 (1978).

Even less certainty, and much less experimentation and development, is reflected in decisions and legislation on the construction of class gift terminology with respect to the rights of nonmarital descendants. (Incidentally, what is the effect of a formbook provision stating: "For purposes of this will, the term 'issue' refers to lawful descendants of all degree"?) Strikingly lacking in recent decisions is any discussion of a state's interests in effectuating decedents' probable intentions as a permissible justification for state-drawn distinctions in this area. Compare earlier recognition of that interest in Estate of Pakarinen, 287 Minn. 330, 336-337, 178 N.W.2d 714, 717-718 (1970). Estate of Dulles, 494 Pa. 180, 431 A.2d 208 (1981), is a post-*Lalli* case involving a rule of construction. It held a statutory presumption unconstitutional when the canon of construction flatly allowed, absent contrary intention, a nonmarital child to hold class membership through the mother but not through the father. The particular presumption then before the court would not have passed even a more lenient test, but in relying heavily on *Trimble* the opinion addressed *Lalli* only in a superficial note denying that it might be more permissive. Of broader significance, however, is the opinion's generally negative view of the permissibility of a purpose based on an attempt to effectuate probable or typical, rather than universal, intentions of transferors.

MATTER OF ESTATE OF HENDREN
459 N.E.2d 437 (Ind. App. 1984)

[This is an appeal from the award of a family allowance to the alleged minor, nonmarital child of the decedent. The child's mother had initiated a paternity action during decedent's lifetime seeking an award of child support. The parties reached an agreement, but the proposed order embodying that agreement was not approved by the court prior to the decedent's death. The statute now in question provides:

> For the purpose of inheritance to, through and from an illegitimate child, such child shall be treated the same as if he were the legitimate child of his

father if, but only if, (1) the paternity of such child has been established by law, during the father's lifetime or (2) if the putative father marries the mother . . . and acknowledges the child to be his own. . . . Such child shall also be treated the same as if he were a legitimate child of his father for the purpose of determining homestead rights, and the making of family allowances.]

GARRARD, J. . . .

The executors ask us to determine whether [a family] allowance can be awarded to an illegitimate in the absence of a legal determination of paternity during the father's lifetime. . . . The paternity determination was not completed during the putative father's lifetime. . . .

We have reviewed the case law in this area in some detail in an effort to discern the reasons for requiring a paternity determination during the putative father's lifetime as a condition precedent to intestate inheritance in IC 29-1-2-7(b). It appears the requirement is an evidentiary one intended to promote accuracy and fairness by insuring the determination takes place in an adversarial context. We now consider whether that requirement was satisfied in the present case. . . . Nothing in our present decision is to be construed as applying to a situation in which no effort was made to commence a paternity action until after the reputed father's death. We hold the lower court did not err in awarding the infant [a family] allowance. . . .

Needless to say, it is our obligation to construe the acts of the legislature to operate constitutionally where that may fairly be done under the language of the statute. In so doing, our courts will typically look through form to the substance of the provision in question. . . .

In the case before us a formal judicial proceeding was commenced during the putative father's lifetime. In addition, the putative father, by an executed written agreement submitted to the court in that proceeding acknowledged that he was the father of the child. Under these circumstances we have no hesitation in concluding the provisions of IC 29-1-2-7(b) were sufficiently complied with. . . .

HOFFMAN, J. . . .

I respectfully dissent. . . .

The majority concludes that the statutory requirements have been satisfied, and it implies that a more restrictive construction of the statute would render it unconstitutional. . . .

Assuming this issue was properly raised, the United States Supreme Court has upheld the constitutionality of a similar statute, requiring that legitimacy be declared by a court order during the lifetime of the father. . . . The *Lalli* Court specifically held that: "[F]ew statutory classifications are entirely free from the criticism that they sometimes produce inequitable results. . . . [The statute's] requirement [is not one] that inevitably disqualifies an unnecessarily large number of children born out of wedlock.''

There is no reason now to conclude that IC §29-1-2-7(b) would not be similarly construed. . . .

————————

With the above case, compare the almost inverse statutory interpretation issue with a similarly favorable outcome for the nonmarital claimant in Beck v. Golliff, 489 N.E.2d 825 (Ohio App. 1984). Other cases continue with a more restrictive treatment of nonmarital children, however, and are less expansive in their interpretation of current legislation. See, e.g., Mills v. Edwards, 665 S.W.2d 153 (Tex. App. 1983).

4. Disqualification for Misconduct

As a general matter the misconduct of an heir is not a basis for disqualification.[4] Under a few U.S. statutes, adultery or desertion by a spouse or abandonment by a parent may disqualify the offender from inheriting from the offended spouse or child. The English common law forfeiture of property rights by felons does not exist in the United States, and therefore inheritance rights are usually unaffected by the criminal activities of an heir. However, the right of one who commits homicide to take from the victim by will or inheritance, or under the terms of a life insurance policy or the survivorship provision of a deed, has been the subject of widespread legislation and litigation. See generally McGovern, Homicide and Succession to Property, 68 Mich. L. Rev. 65 (1969).

BRADLEY v. FOX
7 Ill. 2d 106, 129 N.E.2d 699 (1955)

Davis, J. . . .

[The] administrator of the estate of Matilda Fox, deceased, and Alice E. Bradley, daughter of the decedent, have appealed directly to this court from a judgment of the circuit court of Winnebago County, dismissing their claims for damages for the unlawful killing of Matilda Fox by her husband, defendant Lawrence Fox, and for the imposition of a constructive trust on property formerly held in joint tenancy by the decedent and defendant Lawrence Fox. . . .

The operative facts are not in dispute. It appears from the pleadings that Lawrence Fox and Matilda Fox were married on May 6, 1949, and resided near Rockford, in Winnebago County. On April 18, 1950, they

———

4. For example, a mother's abandonment of her child (who died at age 15) for a thirteen-year period following her divorce did not bar her right to share in the child's estate (absent formal termination of her parental rights) in Hotarek v. Benson, 211 Conn. 121, 557 A.2d 1259 (1989).

purchased with their individual funds the property in controversy, which they held in joint tenancy. Lawrence Fox murdered his wife on September 14, 1954, and three days later conveyed the premises, then valued at $20,000, to his attorney. Fox was convicted of murder . . . and sentenced to the State Penitentiary. . . .

The issue of whether a murderer may acquire or increase his property rights by the fruits of his crime is not a novel legal question. It has arisen in three principal categories of cases: where the beneficiary . . . under a life insurance policy murders the assured to acquire the proceeds of the policy; or where a devisee or distributee feloniously kills the testator or intestate ancestor; and, as in the instant case, where one joint tenant murders the other and thus creates survivorship rights.

In the insurance cases the courts, practically with unanimity, construe the insurance policy in the light of the fundamental common-law maxim originating in English law that no man shall profit by his own wrong, and follow the approach of the early United States Supreme Court case of New York, Mut. Life Ins. Co. v. Armstrong, 117 U.S. 591, which held that a person who procured a policy upon the life of another, payable to himself, and then murdered the assured could not recover thereon. Mr. Justice Field stated: "It would be a reproach to the jurisprudence of the country if one could recover insurance money payable on the death of a party whose life he had feloniously taken." In comformity therewith, the Illinois courts . . . construed insurance contracts as though the public policy and this common-law maxim were part of the contract, and denied recovery on the policy to the murderer or his heirs.

There has not been the same unanimity in the case law, however, with reference to the right of a devisee or distributee who feloniously kills his ancestor to inherit from the decedent in the absence of a statute. 30 Harv. L. Rev. 622; 39 A.L.R.2d 498. The New York courts have consistently followed the case of Riggs v. Palmer, 115 N.Y. 506, 22 N.E. 188, 5 L.R.A. 340, and have construed the statutes of descent to preclude the murderer from inheriting from his victim . . . on the ground that all laws, as well as contracts, may be controlled in their operation and effect by the fundamental maxims of the common law that no one shall be permitted to acquire property by his own crime or iniquity, which maxims, the court stated, were founded "in universal law administered by all civilized countries and have nowhere been superseded by statutes."

There is imposing precedent in conformity with the views of the New York court, wherein the courts deem it their duty to read the inheritance laws in conjunction with the common-law maxims incorporating moral and equitable principles. . . .

The Illinois court, however, in Wall v. Pfanschmidt [265 Ill. 180, 106 N.E. 785], felt constrained to ignore these maxims in construing the statutes of descent, and allowed a murderer to inherit from his victim on the theory that the statutes contain explicit provisions for the descent of property and for annulling wills, but did not preclude murderers from inheriting property, therefore the legal title which passed to the murderer must be deemed indefeasible.

The Illinois statute of descent, however, was modified in 1939, and provides in substance that a person who is convicted of the murder of another shall not inherit from the murdered person or acquire as surviving spouse any interest in the estate of the decedent by reason of the death. (Ill. Rev. Stat. 1939, 1953, chap. 3, par. 167.) Similar statutes have been enacted in most States, incorporating in effect the aforementioned common-law maxim as to the devolution of property. Wade, Acquisition of Property by Wilfully Killing Another — A Statutory Solution, 44 Harv. L. Rev. 715.

Defendants have questioned the constitutionality of the Illinois statute on the ground that it offends the constitutional prohibition against forfeiture of estate. Inasmuch as similar statutes in other States having identical constitutional mandates have been uniformly sustained on the theory that they do not deprive the murderer of his property, but merely prevent him from acquiring additional property in an unauthorized and unlawful way, . . . there is ample authority for sustaining the validity of the Illinois Law, and defendant's argument must be rejected.

However, the validity of that statutory provision is not determinative of the issue in the instant case, but at most indicates the broad policy of the State to prohibit a murderer from enjoying by descent the fruits of his crime, since at the time of the commission of the murder defendant held, not merely an expectation of an inheritance, but a joint tenancy with the deceased, and his rights arise largely from the original instrument under which he had a right of survivorship, rather than by descent.

In this category of cases the courts have differed as to whether the murderer should be allowed his survivorship rights. Those courts which hold that he is entitled to the entire property as surviving joint tenant predicate their conclusion on the legal fiction incident to the concept of joint tenancy, whereby each tenant is deemed to hold the entire estate from the time of the original investiture, and reason that the murderer acquired no additional interest by virtue of the felonious destruction of his joint tenant, of which he can be deprived. . . . Other courts, however, concerned with the equitable principles prohibiting a person from profiting from his own wrong, and with the realities of the situation, have abandoned the common-law fictions, and have either divested the killer of the entire estate; . . . or have deprived him of half the property; . . . or have imposed a constructive trust on the entire estate held by the murderer for the benefit of the heirs of the victim; . . . or a constructive trust modified by a life interest in half the property. . . .

The imposition of a constructive trust in the class of cases has been urged by legal scholars and is advocated by the Restatement of Restitution. Section 188b thereof provides in substance that when there are two joint tenants, and one of them murders the other, the murderer takes by survivorship the whole legal interest in the property, but he can be compelled to hold the entire interest upon a constructive trust for the estate of his cotenant, except that he is entitled to one half the income for life.

From the foregoing analysis of the entire issue as considered in the related insurance policy and descent cases, and in the analogous joint tenancy cases, as well as by legal scholars and lawmakers, certain conclusions follow. Contracts and other instruments creating rights should properly be construed in the light of prevailing public policy evidenced in the statutes. . . . The Illinois statute prohibiting the devolution of property to a convicted murderer from his victim, while not determinative of the rights of the parties in this situation, does evince a legislative policy to deny the convicted murderer the fruits of his crime. That policy would be thwarted by a blind adherence to the legal fiction that a joint tenant holds the entire property at the date of the original conveyance, and acquires no additional interest by virtue of the felonious death of his cotenant, since that rationale sanctions in effect the enhancement of property rights through murder. For legal fictions cannot obscure the fact that before the murder defendant, as a joint tenant, had to share the profits of the property, and his right to complete ownership, unfettered by the interests of a joint tenant, was contingent upon surviving his wife; whereas, after, and because of, his felonious act that contingency was removed, and he became the sole owner of the property, no longer sharing the profits with any one nor fearing the loss of his interest. . . .

In joint tenancy the contract that the survivors will take the whole necessarily presupposes that the death of either will be in the natural course of events and that it will not be generated by either tenant murdering the other. One of the implied conditions of the contract is that neither party will acquire the interest of the other by murder. It is fundamental that four coexisting unities are necessary and requisite to the creation and continuance of a joint tenancy; namely, unity of interest, unity of title, unity of time, and unity of possession. Any act of a joint tenant which destroys any of these unities operates as a severance of the joint tenancy and extinguishes the right of survivorship. . . . It is our conclusion that Fox by his felonious act destroyed all rights of survivorship and lawfully retained only the title to his undivided one-half interest in the property in dispute as a tenant in common with the heir-at-law of Matilda Fox, deceased. . . .

PROBLEMS

2-G. Consider the effect of the following statute: "No person convicted of the murder or voluntary manslaughter of the decedent may succeed to any portion of the estate; but the portion hereof to which he would otherwise be entitled to succeed goes to the other persons entitled thereto under the statutes of intestate succession."

(a) *D* is murdered by his son, *S*. In addition to *S*, *D* is survived by a daughter and by a grandchild, *G,* who is the child of *S.* Under the statute does *G* take anything, or does everything pass to the daughter, if *S* is convicted of murdering *D?*

(b) Can *S*'s right to inherit be questioned if *S* commits suicide before he can be tried? If *S* had been convicted, could the question of his guilt be relitigated in an action by *S* to collect insurance proceeds on *D*'s life?

(c) What if *S* were a juvenile, found to be "delinquent" by the juvenile court, but not tried as an adult? (See *Josephsons* case below.)

2-H.   In a state that has the Uniform Probate Code, *H* was killed by his wife, *W.* He left no will and was survived only by *W* and their two adult children. The district attorney has not and will not prosecute *W* because *H* had been terminally ill and begging for a "death with dignity."

(a) As administrator of *H*'s estate, should you bring this matter to the attention of the probate court? Does the position of the children matter? Would the situation be different if the children were minors?

(b) If you do not raise the issue, should the court raise it on its own motion?

(c) If *W*'s right to inherit is challenged, what result should the court reach?

(d) If *W* had accepted a plea bargain, pleading guilty or nolo contendere to involuntary homicide, would that alter the result? Cf. Matter of Estate of Safran, 102 Wis. 2d 79, 306 N.W.2d 27 (1981). What if *W* had been charged with murder and acquitted?

UNIFORM PROBATE CODE

§2-803.   *Effect of Homicide on Intestate Succession,*
          Wills, Trusts, Joint Assets, Life Insurance, and
          Beneficiary Designations.

(a) [Definitions.] In this section:

(1) "Disposition or appointment of property" includes a transfer of an item of property or any other benefit to a beneficiary designated in a governing instrument.

(2) "Governing instrument" means a governing instrument executed by the decedent.

(3) "Revocable," with respect to a disposition, appointment, provision, or nomination, means one under which the decedent, at the time of or immediately before death, was alone empowered, by law or under the governing instrument, to cancel the designation in favor of the killer, whether or not the decedent was then empowered to designate himself [or herself] in place of his [or her] killer and/or the decedent then had capacity to exercise the power.

(b) [Forfeiture of Statutory Benefits.] An individual who feloniously and intentionally kills the decedent forfeits all benefits under this Article with respect to the decedent's estate, including an intestate share, an elective share, an omitted spouse's or child's share, a homestead allowance, exempt property, and a family allowance. If the decedent died intestate, the decedent's intestate estate passes as if the killer disclaimed his [or her] intestate share.

(c) [Revocation of Benefits Under Governing Instruments.] The felonious and intentional killing of the decedent:

(1) revokes any revocable (i) disposition or appointment of property made by the decedent to the killer in a governing instrument, (ii) provision in a governing instrument conferring a general or non-general power of appointment on the killer, and (iii) nomination of the killer in a governing instrument, nominating or appointing the killer to serve in any fiduciary or representative capacity, including a personal representative, executor, trustee, or agent; and

(2) severs the interests of the decedent and killer in property held by them at the time of the killing as joint tenants with the right of survivorship [or as community property with the right of survivorship], transforming the interests of the decedent and killer into tenancies in common.

(d) [Effect of Severance.] A severance under subsection (c)(2) does not affect any third-party interest in property acquired for value and in good faith reliance on an apparent title by survivorship in the killer unless a writing declaring the severance has been noted, registered, filed, or recorded in records appropriate to the kind and location of the property which are relied upon, in the ordinary course of transactions involving such property, as evidence of ownership.

(e) [Effect of Revocation.] Provisions of a governing instrument that are not revoked by this section are given effect as if the killer disclaimed all revoked provisions or, in the case of a revoked nomination in a fiduciary or representative capacity, as if the killer predeceased the decedent.

(f) [Wrongful Acquisition of Property.] A wrongful acquisition of property or interest by a killer not covered by this section must be treated in accordance with the principle that a killer cannot profit from his [or her] wrong.

(g) [Felonious and Intentional Killing; How Determined.] After all right to appeal has been exhausted, a judgment of conviction establishing criminal accountability for the felonious and intentional killing of the decedent conclusively establishes the convicted individual as the decedent's killer for purposes of this section. In the absence of a conviction, the court, upon the petition of an interested person, must determine whether, under the preponderance of evidence standard, the individual would be found criminally accountable for the felonious and intentional killing of the decedent. If the court determines that, under that standard, the individual would be found criminally accountable for the felonious and intentional killing of the decedent, the determination conclusively establishes that individual as the decedent's killer for purposes of this section.

(h) [Protection of Payors and Other Third Parties.]

(1) A payor or other third party is not liable for having made a payment or transferred an item of property or any other benefit to a beneficiary designated in a governing instrument affected by an intentional and felonious killing, or for having taken any other action in good faith reliance on the validity of the governing instrument, upon request and satisfactory proof of the decedent's death, before the payor or other third party received written notice of a claimed forfeiture or revocation under this section. A payor or other third party is liable for a payment made or other action taken after the payor or other third party received written notice of a claimed forfeiture or revocation under this section.

(2) Written notice of a claimed forfeiture or revocation under paragraph (1) must be mailed to the payor's or other third party's main office or home by registered or certified mail, return receipt requested, or served upon the payor or other third party in the same manner as a summons in a civil action. Upon receipt of written notice of a claimed forfeiture or revocation under this section, a payor or other third party may pay any amount owed or transfer or deposit any item of property held by it to or with the court having jurisdiction of the probate proceedings relating to the decedent's estate, or if no proceedings have been commenced, to or with the court having jurisdiction of probate proceedings relating to decedents' estates located in the county of the decedent's residence. The court shall hold the funds or item of property and, upon its determination under this section, shall order disbursement in accordance with the determination. Payments, transfers, or deposits made to or with the court discharge the payor or other third party from all claims for the value of amounts paid to or items of property transferred to or deposited with the court.

(i) [Protection of Bona Fide Purchasers; Personal Liability of Recipient.]

(1) A person who purchases property for value and without notice, or who receives a payment or other item of property in partial or full satisfaction of a legally enforceable obligation, is neither obligated under this section to return the payment, item of property, or benefit nor is liable under this section for the amount of the payment or the value of the item of property or benefit. But a person who, not for value, receives a payment, item of property, or any other benefit to which the person is not entitled under this section is obligated to return the payment, item of property, or benefit, or is personally liable

for the amount of the payment or the value of the item of property or benefit, to the person who is entitled to it under this section.

(2) If this section or any part of this section is preempted by federal law with respect to a payment, an item of property, or any other benefit covered by this section, a person who, not for value, receives the payment, item of property, or any other benefit to which the person is not entitled under this section is obligated to return the payment, item of property, or benefit, or is personally liable for the amount of the payment or the value of the item of property or benefit, to the person who would have been entitled to it were this section or part of this section not preempted.

MATTER OF ESTATES OF JOSEPHSONS
297 N.W.2d 444 (N.D. 1980)

[Russell and Robbyn Josephson died of gunshot wounds. During county court proceedings in their estates, the administrator and the guardians ad litem for their three daughters raised the issue of whether son Michael was entitled to inherit from the intestate estates. The court determined that he was not because he had caused the deaths of his parents by felonious means. On appeal Michael alleged that a juvenile in North Dakota could not commit a felonious act. N.D.C.C. §30.1-10-03 was enacted in the 1973 adoption of the 1969 Uniform Probate Code. N.D.C.C. §27-20-30, however, provides that an order of disposition in a juvenile court proceeding "is not a conviction of crime and does not impose any civil disability ordinarily resulting from a conviction" and that the disposition and evidence in juvenile court may not be used against a child in proceedings in other courts.]

VANDE WALLE, J. . . .

Michael argues that [§27-20-30 is] exclusive and prohibits the operation of Section 30.1-10-03(1) against a minor who, if it were not for his age, would be guilty of a felony. . . . We do not agree. . . .

Although Section 30.1-10-03(1) may be considered the imposition of a civil disability it does not arise from any order or adjudication in a juvenile court proceeding. Rather, it is a civil disability imposed by statute separate and apart from any juvenile court proceedings. . . .

[Section 30.1-10-03(5)] makes it abundantly clear that, although a final judgment of conviction of felonious and intentional killing is conclusive for the purpose of determining whether or not an heir may receive benefits from the estate of the decedent, the final judgment of conviction is not the only basis for implementation of the prohibition. Subsection 5 specifically provides that in the absence of a conviction of felonious and intentional killing, the court may determine by a preponderance of evidence whether the killing was felonious and intentional. . . .

A comparison of this provision [with our prior statute] which was repealed by Chapter 257 of the 1973 Session Laws . . . seems to indicate that [previously] a final conviction of feloniously causing the death of the testator was required before the prohibition against inheritance became operative, whereas under the current status the felonious and intentional killing of the decedent may be proved by a preponderance of the evidence in a civil proceeding in the absence of a final judgment of conviction.

Michael's interpretation . . . [is] contrary to the expressed legislative intent in subsection 5 of Section 30.1-10-03 which clearly does not require conviction of a felony before an heir may be barred from receiving benefits from the decedent's estate. Subsection 5 . . . , in fact, prevents a person acquitted of a felony charge from inheriting if the court finds by a preponderance of the evidence that the killing was felonious and intentional. . . .

The manner in which a term is defined in one instance will not necessarily control the definition to be applied in a different situation. Rosenberger v. Northwestern Mutual Life Ins. Co., 176 F. Supp. 379 (D. Kan. 1959). Many of the cases we have examined concern the issue of whether or not the killing must be intentional or if negligence, which may also result in conviction of a felony, is sufficient. We have no such problem in this instance because Section 30.1-10-03(1) specifically requires that the killing be intentional as well as felonious. Subsection 5 of Section 30.1-10-03 provides not only that a conviction of a felonious and intentional killing is conclusive for the operation of the statute but that in the absence of a conviction the court may nevertheless determine by a preponderance of the evidence whether or not the killing was felonious and intentional. We agree with the district court that the term "feloniously," as used in Section 30.1-10-03(1), N.D.C.C., refers to a killing that is wrongful, that is without legal excuse or justification. In addition, of course, the statute requires that the killing be intentional. Although a minor adjudicated to be delinquent under the provisions of Chapter 27-20 is not, because of the provisions of Section 27-20-33(1), convicted of a crime, that does not mean the minor has not committed the wrongful act. . . .

Under the Uniform Juvenile Court Act Michael may be insulated from a criminal conviction for the felonious killing of his parents, but the terms of that Act do not require or permit us to extend that protection to a civil proceeding. . . . We do not deem it in the public interest to permit any person, including a minor, who intentionally and feloniously causes the death of a decedent, to inherit from that decedent. The dangers of a construction that permits a minor who intentionally and feloniously causes the death of his parents to inherit from those parents is obvious. The purpose of the Uniform Juvenile Court Act is to prevent that minor from being treated as a criminal in the hope of rehabilitation of the minor. The Act does not authorize us to relieve the minor from civil disabilities that result not from his adjudication as a delinquent but from the performance of the act itself. The determination by the county and district courts that Michael feloniously and intentionally caused the death of his parents is obviously not a conviction of a felony. It is a determination made in a civil proceeding and a determination which must be supported by only a preponderance of the evidence, not evidence beyond a reasonable doubt as in a criminal prosecution. That determination carries with it none of the consequences which flow from an adjudication of a child as delinquent. The protection afforded in Section 27-20-33(1) from any civil disability ordinarily resulting from a conviction does not protect Michael because the disability in this instance does not result from a criminal conviction but from a separate determination by the county court that Michael had, at age 13, feloniously and intentionally caused the death of his parents.

Michael also argues that because he is entitled to receive Federal Social Security benefits he is entitled to receive benefits from his parents' estates. He points out that although Federal regulations do not permit a person who has been finally convicted of the felonious and intentional homicide of a wage earner to receive benefits based on the earnings record of that wage earner, minors can be entitled to benefits if the jurisdiction does not consider homicide by a minor as felonious. Michael is receiving Federal Social Security benefits. Although the fact that Michael is receiving Federal Social Security benefits might be a factor to consider if our statutes on this matter were ambiguous, we cannot conclude there is any ambiguity and therefore the position of the Federal Government with regard to the payment of Federal Social Security benefits is of no significance to the issues before us. . . .

Finally, Michael argues that if we conclude he is not entitled to benefits from his parents' estates, the estates are nevertheless required to support him until he reaches eighteen years of age, the age of majority. In support of his position, Michael relies upon Section 14-09-08, N.D.C.C., which requires a parent to support a child, and Section 14-09-12, N.D.C.C., which provides that if a parent required to support a child dies leaving an estate sufficient for the child's support, the county may claim support from the estate. These are general provisions which have no application to the factual situation in this instance. The controlling statute is Section 30.1-10-03(1), N.D.C.C., which provides that an heir who feloniously and intentionally kills the decedent "is not entitled to any benefits. . . ." Support payments from the estate, even until the age of majority, would constitute "benefits" from the estate and would be directly contrary to statute.

The order of the district court is affirmed. . . .
[Now compare UPC §2-803(g).]

C. Effect of Prior Transactions on Inheritance Rights

The preceding materials show how certain events prior to a decedent's death may affect succession and related matters. The material that follows deals with other types of activity that can affect succession: the concepts of advancement, release, and assignment. In Chapter 3 we shall examine some protections for family members and shall see that these protections may also be relinquished prior to a decedent's death. For example, a spouse may forgo the protection of a statutory "forced share" by contract entered into while both spouses are alive or even before they are married.

Advancements. Nearly every state has a statutory provision relating to advancements. Despite differences in the terms of these statutes, the tendency of courts has been to construe them in a manner that eliminates potential differences in their application. The doctrine typically relates to instances of total intestacy. The related doctrine of satisfaction of testamentary disposition is taken up later.

Nobles v. Davenport, 183 N.C. 207, 209-210, 111 S.E. 180, 181 (1922), states:

> In its legal sense an advancement is an irrevocable gift in praesenti of money or property, real or personal, to a child by a parent, to enable the donee to anticipate his inheritance to the extent of the gift; or, as somewhat differently defined, a perfect and irrevocable gift, not required by law, made by a parent during his lifetime to his child, with the intention on the part of the donor that such gift shall represent a part or the whole of the donor's estate that the donee would be entitled to on the death of the donor intestate. . . . The doctrine of advancements was the subject of statutory enactment in England as early as the reign of Charles II (22 and 23 Car. II, 1682-1683), and in this jurisdiction it is set forth as to both real and personal property in sections 138 and 1654(2) of Consolidated Statutes. This doctrine is based on the presumption that a parent who dies intestate intends equality among his children in the division of his property, but such presumption is subject to rebuttal by parol evidence. . . . In the determination of the question whether a transfer of property from parent to child is a gift, a sale, or an advancement, the intention of the grantor is the controlling element. . . . And only such intention as exists at the time of the transaction is to be considered. Therefore a parent's transfer of property to his child may constitute in part an advancement and in part a gift or a sale. . . . In endeavoring to discover the donor's intention, we must consider the circumstances surrounding the interested parties at the time the property is transferred; for the circumstances may

be such as to create a presumption of advancement. Thus a substantial gift of property by a parent to his child, or a conveyance of land in consideration of love and affection, or a nominal sum, is ordinarily presumed to be an advancement. . . . But if the transfer is made for a valuable and adequate consideration there is no presumption of an advancement, but rather the contrary. . . . Nor is the doctrine of presumptions affected by the reservation of a life estate.

The doctrine of advancements is based on the "intention" of the intestate, but the major difficulty is in determining that intent. The presumption that a substantial gift to a child (and to other descendants under some applications of the common law rule) is intended as an advancement is a rebuttable one, but it is difficult to know what facts will serve to rebut the presumption.

The intestate's intent may be shown by his records, even informal ones, and by his declarations, even declarations subsequent to the alleged advancement if something of his state of mind at the time of the transfer may be inferred from them. Inferences as to intention may be drawn from the surrounding circumstances, the purpose, nature, and amount of the gift, and generally any factors that may be deemed persuasive as to the probable intent of the decedent at the time of making the gift.[5] The use of language of gift does not tend to rebut the presumption of advancement in an appropriate case, as an advancement is by its nature an irrevocable gift and merely attributes certain consequences to that gift.

The legislative trend is seen in a number of states that have modified the general advancement rule by statutes that require a writing, such as prescribed by the Uniform Probate Code. Is such a requirement desirable? See Fellows, Concealing Legislative Reform in the Common-Law Tradition: The Advancements Doctrine and the Uniform Probate Code, 37 Vand. L. Rev. 671 (1984).

What if a person is incompetent to form an intent? In Guardianship of Hudelson, 18 Cal. 2d 401, 115 P.2d 805 (1941), a court had granted a daughter a living allowance out of her incompetent father's estate but provided that all amounts paid to her would be considered advancements when he died. The California Supreme Court affirmed, holding that a court acts for an incompetent as it supposes the incompetent would have acted had he been competent; if a court can find that the ward would have provided his child with an allowance, it can also find that he would have imposed conditions on the payments.

Unlike a loan, an advancement does not create an obligation on the part of the recipient, and it is not subject to statutes of limitations. It

---

5. Subsequent intent may be relevant, however. If originally the gift was *not* intended as an advancement, a change of intent will not alter the result, but what was originally intended as an advancement may by subsequent intent be converted into an outright gift.

merely requires that before participating in the estate the recipient must bring the advancement into *hotchpot*. That is, the value of the advancement is added to the estate for purposes of computation, and the shares of the heirs in the mathematically "enlarged" estate are then determined. The recipient is then allowed to take from the estate the excess of that share over the advancement. If the advancement would exceed the share, the recipient would refuse to come into hotchpot, retaining the gift property without sharing in the estate.

The doctrine of advancements is generally said to apply to, and in favor of, children of the intestate. Statutes sometimes extend these rules to other heirs and to the surviving spouse. In the absence of such an extension of the doctrine, the share of the surviving spouse is not enlarged by the advancement (again, unlike a loan) to a child, nor is it diminished by inter vivos gifts to the spouse.

When an advancee predeceases the intestate, his or her issue are charged with the amount of the advancement in many states either by judicial decision or by statute (but cf. UPC §2-109, infra). Advancements are generally valued as described in the UPC, infra. Under some statutes, however, the valuation will be that of like property as of the intestate's death. The value may be liquidated by agreement between the intestate and the donee.

UNIFORM PROBATE CODE

§2-109. *Advancements.*

(a) If an individual dies intestate as to all or a portion of his [or her] estate, property the decedent gave during the decedent's lifetime to an individual who, at the decedent's death, is an heir is treated as an advancement against the heir's intestate share only if (i) the decedent declared in a contemporaneous writing or the heir acknowledged in writing that the gift is an advancement or (ii) the decedent's contemporaneous writing or the heir's written acknowledgment otherwise indicates that the gift is to be taken into account in computing the division and distribution of the decedent's intestate estate.

(b) For purposes of subsection (a), property advanced is valued as of the time the heir came into possession or enjoyment of the property or as of the time of the decedent's death, whichever first occurs.

(c) If the recipient of the property fails to survive the decedent, the property is not taken into account in computing the division and distribution of the decedent's intestate estate, unless the decedent's contemporaneous writing provides otherwise.

PROBLEMS

2-I. *D* died intestate survived by his widow, *W*, and three children of a prior marriage, *A*, *B*, and *C*. His net estate is valued at $200,000. *W* had no children. Advancements were made to *A* in the amount of $50,000 and to *B* in the amount of $10,000. How should *D*'s net estate be distributed (a) under a statute like the English Statute of Distribution, 1670, (b) under the Uniform Probate Code, and (c) under the law of your state (assuming community property is not involved)?

2-J. *D*, an elderly bachelor, sent a check for $10,000 to *N*, his nephew. An accompanying letter stated in part: "That is a little down payment on your legacy. I know you need it now, and there will be more in my will for you." *D*, however, died intestate, survived only by nieces and nephews.

(a) Does the above check change the normal distribution of *D*'s estate under the Statute of Distribution, 1670? Under the Uniform Probate Code? Under the law of your state?

(b) How would you argue (i) for the nieces and nephews other than *N*, and then (ii) for *N*, under a statute that merely declares: "An advancement to any heir shall be charged against his share of the estate and to the extent of that share shall be included in the estate to be distributed"?

(c) Would it matter if *N*'s father (*D*'s brother) had been living at the date of the gift? Would the check affect the share of *N*'s child if *N* predeceased *D*? In the latter case would it matter if, in return for the check, *N* had executed a release of all his interest in *D*'s estate?

Releases and Assignments. Somewhat analogous to the problem of advancements is that of the *release* of an expectancy by a potential heir, devisee, or legatee. The general rule is that when one who subsequently turns out to be an heir has released an expectant interest to the source (the intestate) before the latter's death, the release is binding on the heir if supported by a "fair and adequate consideration." It is also generally held that a purported *assignment* of an expectancy (to someone other than the source) for a fair and adequate consideration is binding on an heir or a beneficiary under a will.

An expectancy, being but a hope of succeeding to the property of another living person, is not treated as an existing property interest and therefore cannot be assigned gratuitously. Thus, in a true sense no present transfer of an expectancy is possible. Statutes in some states expressly codify these common law principles. Consequently, releases and "assignments" of expectancies can be made binding only under some theory other than that of a present transfer. In appropriate transactions, the doctrine of estoppel by deed may apply; or a court of equity may label the purported assignment an *equitable assignment* or a specifically enforceable *contract to assign*. In the case of a release, it may be best to analyze the transactions as an advancement, the effect of which is fixed by agreement, and some courts have done so — possibly to avoid the necessity of a writing in certain factual situations.

Reference is made to *fair and adequate* considerations in the release and assignment cases. This requirement is not necessarily satisfied by the consideration that will support a contract. Equity requires, before salvaging such a legally defective transfer, a greater showing of fairness and looks to the circumstances to discover any overreaching or bad faith. In the case of a release of an expectancy to the source, however, it is possible that a court would enforce the release without adequate consideration if it finds the basis of an estoppel in the release and in the reliance of the source in failing to make a will.

DONOUGH v. GARLAND
269 Ill. 565, 109 N.E. 1015 (1915)

[Thomas Garland died intestate, leaving a widow, Mary, and five children, Margaret Donough and Edward, Katherine, Mary Jane, and Lizzie Garland, as his heirs. Later, Mary Jane and Lizzie died, leaving their mother, brother, and sisters as heirs; thereafter Margaret quitclaimed to Edward and Katherine "all interest I now have or may hereafter acquire" in any lands owned by Thomas Garland at death or by Mary (his widow) at the date of the deed. After the deaths of Margaret and then Mary, Margaret's children sought to partition the lands Thomas and Mary had owned; the answer disputed their alleged title on the ground that Margaret had conveyed her interests in the lands to the defendants, who now appeal from a chancellor's decree in favor of Margaret's children. Clearly, Margaret conveyed all interests she had as a result of the deaths of her father and her sisters. The question was whether she also conveyed (and with what effect) her expectancy as heir of her mother, which on her mother's death, Margaret's children argue, passed to them.]

CARTWRIGHT, J. . . .

The expectancy of a prospective heir of a living person may be released to the ancestor or assigned to a stranger. In the case of a release to the ancestor a court of equity will enforce the contract for the benefit of the other heirs, and an assignment or transfer of an expectancy operates in equity as a contract by the assignor to convey the legal estate or interest when it vests in him, which will be enforced in equity when the expectancy has changed into a vested interest. 3 Pomeroy's Eq. Jur. §1287. . . .

. . . [Thus] a release by an heir presumptive of his expectancy operates as an extinguishment of the right of inheritance, cutting it off at its source. The line of inheritance is ended by the release made by the one having the expectancy at the time, and the release is binding not only upon him, but upon those who take as heirs in his place; otherwise a release would often be ineffective. That would always be the case where the one executing the release does not survive the one to whom the release is made, although he has himself received the consideration for the expectancy. If, however, the expectancy is assigned to another, the right of inheritance is not extinguished, but still exists, and the assignment is enforced as a contract to convey the legal estate or interest when it . . . becomes a vested estate. The assignee is regarded as bargaining for a legal interest depending on a future, uncertain, and contingent event. The assignee acquires a right to the legal estate if it ever vests in the assignor, but if it does not, he acquires nothing. In this case Edward Garland and Katherine Garland by the conveyance to them became entitled to enforce in equity a right to an interest in lands in case the interest should ever vest in Margaret Donough. The estate or interest did not vest in the grantor, and the chancellor did not err. . . .

As indicated by the result of the above case, one who takes by representation takes as a matter of personal right rather than through the person represented. As a result, a grandchild who takes in the place of a predeceased child of the intestate does not take subject to that child's assignments or the claims of the child's creditors. Can you explain why a release should be different in this regard from a purported assignment, as the above case indicates it would be?

3

Family Protection and Restrictions on Testation

Many of the policy conflicts in the area of decedents' estates and trusts concern the policies favoring freedom of property disposition as opposed to the policies favoring protection of the family and, incidentally, protection of the state from the burden of indigent families. Legislatures, reflecting general attitudes in society, often restrict the power of a person to dispose of property after death by requiring or encouraging some minimum provision for certain family members. The most common of these restrictions are considered in this chapter and raise the question whether a person should be able to dispose of property after death, by will or will substitute, without regard to the needs and expectations of spouse and children.

There are two basic types of protective provisions for family members. Some provisions might be classified as *substantive* limitations on testamentary power. Others are *formal* restrictions in that they are not really prohibitions but merely provide that certain results must be accomplished in a way that tends to protect against oversight. In addition, there are temporary allowances during administration of a decedent's estate to assist the family through the period of administration.

A. Allowances, Homesteads, and Exemptions

The statutory law of every state makes some provision to protect the family of a decedent against testamentary omission, the decedent's creditors, and the delays of administration. One or more and usually all of the following provisions exist in each state: (1) a support allowance for the families of the decedents, or sometimes just for widows and widowers, during a part or all of the period of estate administration; (2) a statutory or constitutional right of homestead in residential real estate; and (3) an exemption of certain personal property. These provisions are typically, but not always, in addition to the intestate share or other statutory rights of the family. In most jurisdictions it is presumed that any rights under the decedent's will are in addition to such provisions, although the terms of a will, particularly express disposition of the home or exempt property, may require a beneficiary to elect between an interest under the will and one or more of these statutory provisions.

UNIFORM PROBATE CODE

§2-404.   *Family Allowance.*

(a) In addition to the right to homestead allowance and exempt property, the decedent's surviving spouse and minor children whom the decedent was obligated to support and children who were in fact being supported by the decedent are entitled to a reasonable allowance in money out of the estate for their maintenance during the period of administration, which allowance may not continue for longer than one year if the estate is inadequate to discharge allowed claims. The allowance may be paid as a lump sum or in periodic installments. It is payable to the surviving spouse, if living, for the use of the surviving spouse and minor and dependent children; otherwise to the children, or persons having their care and custody. If a minor child or dependent child is not living with the surviving spouse, the allowance may be made partially to the child or his [or her] guardian or other person having the child's care and custody, and partially to the spouse, as their needs may appear. The family allowance is exempt from and has priority over all claims except the homestead allowance.

(b) The family allowance is not chargeable against any benefit or share passing to the surviving spouse or children by the will of the decedent, unless otherwise provided, by intestate succession or by way of elective share. The death of any person entitled to family allowance terminates the right to allowances not yet paid.

B.   *Minimum Rights of the Surviving Spouse*

1.   Dower, Forced Shares, and Community Property

Because protections afforded spouses vary from state to state, it is useful to note the choice of law rules governing these matters. With regard to land (immovables), the surviving spouse's protective rights in some states are still determined by the law of the situs, whereas these rights in all other property (movables) are based on the law of the decedent's domicile at death. Thus, in domiciliary administration, local law applies to real and personal property alike; in ancillary administration the court often applies its own law to land but ascertains and applies domiciliary law to any personalty in the state. The application of situs law to land has been widely criticized, and many states now provide, as does Uniform Probate Code §2-201, that, for decedents domiciled elsewhere, the situs state will determine the survivor's rights in immovables as well as movables according to domiciliary law.

At common law the widow had an inchoate interest in all lands of which her husband was seised at any time during the marriage. As a result of this *dower* right she was entitled, if she survived her husband, to a life estate in one-third of such property. Dower could not be defeated by the husband's will, the claims of his creditors, or even by his inter vivos conveyances in the absence of the wife's consent. Comparable to dower, but conditioned on birth of issue and relating to all of the wife's land, was the husband's common law *curtesy*. See generally R. Chused, Married Women's Property Law, 1800-1850, 71 Geo. L.J. 1359 (1983); H. Hartog, Marital Exits and Marital Expectations in Nineteenth Century America, 80 Geo. L.J. 95 (1991).

In the United States today a few jurisdictions still have statutes, relating to both husband and wife, that perpetuate the dower concept by granting a spouse a right in all lands owned by the other spouse during the marriage. Nearly all of these interests ripen into fee interests in a third of such lands. For a comprehensive treatment of spousal protection, see Committee Report, Spouse's Elective Share, 12 Real Prop., Prob. & Tr. J. 323 (1977); MacDonald, Fraud on the Widow's Share (1960).

In all of the non-community property states, surviving spouses are protected by a form of statutory forced heirship under which they are entitled to a share of the estate regardless of the deceased spouse's will. This nonbarrable right is generally a portion of the decedent's net estate, personal as well as real, subject to the debts and inter vivos transfers of the decedent. The forced share may be the same as the intestate share, but in many states it is less.

Where the community property system prevails, the main protection afforded spouses is their shared ownership of their community property. This system has long existed in eight states, Arizona, California, Idaho, Louisiana, Nevada, New Mexico, Texas, and Washington, and has now been adopted in a ninth state, Wisconsin, at least if we ignore differences in terminology and modest modifications in substance. It is important to note that there are also substantive differences among the traditional community property states. The Wisconsin legislation was based on the Uniform Marital Property Act, promulgated in 1983. In brief, in community property states, all property owned before the marriage or acquired during marriage by gift or by testate or intestate succession, including the proceeds and, in most but not all of these states, the income therefrom, is separate property. All other property acquired during the marriage is community property. In most, but not all, of these states the spouses acting together are free to convert community property to separate, and vice versa, and sometimes with startling informality. With limited exceptions, the community property rights of husband and wife are present and equal, although until recent years the husband generally had the management rights. As a result of this equal ownership, half of the community property belongs to the survivor and cannot be disposed of by the deceased spouse's will. Under earlier systems, vestiges of which may remain today (e.g., with respect to pre-1923 community property in California), the husband was entitled to all of such property if he survived, the wife having no power of testamentary disposition over it.

In community property states dower and its counterparts are nonexistent, and generally there are no forced share provisions applicable to separate property. Something in the general nature of a forced share of limited application, however, has been adopted in two community property states. Its purpose is to fill a gap that would otherwise exist in the protection of spouses who move from a common law state to a community property state, especially late in life. Quasi-community property, as this form of ownership is popularly known, is designed to give the survivor, at the deceased spouse's death, rights equivalent to community property rights in property (and in assets traceable to property) the decedent acquired during the marriage that would have been community property if the spouses had lived in a community property state at the time of the acquisition. See Cal. Prob. Code §§66, 101, 102; Idaho Code §§15-2-201 to 15-2-209 (1978). A comparable "deferred marital property" regime exists now in Wisconsin but broadened also to deal with problems of transition from the former common law to the new marital property system (which became effective on January 1, 1986). See Wis. Stat. Ann. c. 766, §§851.055, 861.02. (By other statutory provisions in these states, and by statutes and decisions in the other community and non-community property states, rules analogous to quasi-community property apply to the division of marital property on divorce.) Are inverse problems created by the removal of spouses from community property states to other jurisdictions? Are the laws of non-community property states equipped to handle these problems? The Uniform Disposition of Community Property at Death Act has been promulgated to offer a legislative solution to some of these problems in common law states.

The statutory rights of spouses may be modified or extinguished by antenuptial agreement and, in most states, by postnuptial agreement. In order to be valid these contracts generally must be either substantively fair and reasonable or based on full disclosure. In some states all interspousal contracts are presumed to result from undue influence if one party obtains an "advantage" over the other. Uniform Probate Code §2-204, allowing waiver of elective rights either before or after marriage, focuses on fairness in the formation of the contract and the absence of unconscionability. Compare Uniform Marital Property Act §10 (1983) and Uniform Pre-Marital Agreements Act §6 (1983). See generally Haskell, The Premarital Estate Contract and Social Policy, 57 N.C.L. Rev. 415, 416-418, 437 (1979), in which it is urged that premarital contracts not be enforceable if "financial hardship" would result because the survivor's property and earning capacity are insufficient to maintain a "reasonable approximation" of the spouse's "accustomed standard" of living.

In In re Estate of Loftin, 285 N.C. 717, 208 S.E.2d 670 (1974), the court stated:

> It is well settled in this jurisdiction that a man and woman contemplating marriage may enter into a valid contract with respect to the property and property rights of each after the marriage, and such contracts will be enforced as written. . . . After the marriage the persons may release and quit claim any rights as they might respectively acquire or may have acquired by marriage in the property of the other. G.S. §52-10. Such transactions between husband and wife are, however, subject to the provisions of G.S. §52-6, which provides that "no contract between husband and wife made during their coverture shall be valid to affect or change any part of the real estate of the wife . . . unless such contract . . . is in writing, and is acknowledged before a certifying officer who shall make a private examination of the wife according to the requirements formerly prevailing for conveyance of land."
>
> Antenuptial contracts, when properly executed and acknowledged, are not against public policy and may act as a bar to the wife's right to dissent and to petition for a year's allowance.

The *Loftin* court found that the wife had been examined in the manner called for by the statute even though it did not, by its terms, apply to antenuptial contracts. Finding the contract not unreasonable or injurious to her and that she had not proved she had been subjected to fraud, duress, or undue influence, the court enforced the contract and the will. See Oldham, Premarital Contracts Are Now Enforceable, Unless . . . , 21 Hous. L. Rev. 757 (1984).

Federal law requires certain tax-favored retirement plans to provide for surviving spouses unless provision is specifically waived by the spouse. 29 U.S.C. §§1001 et seq. (ERISA), as amended by the Retirement Equity Act of 1984, 98 Stat. 1426 (1984).

2.   Election by the Surviving Spouse

As already indicated, rights in the nature of dower, forced heirship provisions, and community property interests cannot be defeated by will. However, a testator can require the spouse to choose between these rights and whatever provision is made for the spouse in the will — i.e., to elect whether to take under the will or to take (or retain) the statutory rights. Furthermore, in asserting statutory rights, the spouse may be required to choose between dower rights and some or all of the forced share.

The concept of election is one of long standing in equity and is relevant in many estate matters. For example, assume that *A* owns Blackacre, appraised at $100,000, and that *B* owns Whiteacre, worth $50,000. *A* dies and his will devises Blackacre to *B* and purports to devise Whiteacre to *C*. What are *B*'s rights? See Havens v. Sackett, 15 N.Y. 365, 369 (1857): "One who accepts the benefit under a deed or will must adopt the whole contents of the instrument." "He is driven to a choice between the assumption of the burden and the rejection of the bounty, and this though the burden, unaccompanied by the bounty, would be an officious intermeddling with the concerns or interests of another. . . . The legacies and devises were acts of bounty merely. The testator was free to withhold them altogether, or to subject them to conditions, whether sensible or futile. The gift is to be taken as it is made or not at all." Oliver v. Wells, 254 N.Y. 451, 458, 173 N.E. 676, 679 (1930).

Today it is usually made clear by statute, or by judicial decision construing the statute, that the spouse cannot take dower or a forced share and also take under the will of the decedent, unless the contrary appears expressly or by clear implication from the will. At common law it was presumed that any testamentary provision for the spouse was in addition to dower unless the will provisions were inconsistent with this result: generally, a like rule still prevails in regard to community property. Uniform Probate Code §2-207 resolves this issue by crediting any testate provision for the spouse against the forced share.

To illustrate, assume that *H*'s will provides, "All of my property shall go to my wife, *W*, for life and on her death to my issue per stirpes." *W* must elect to take the life estate in all of *H*'s property or to take only her dower or forced share. But where community property is involved, this language in *H*'s will would normally not require an election, and *W* would take a life estate in *H*'s separate property and in his half of the community property, while keeping her half of the community property as well.

Statutes often prescribe the time and method of making an election. The right of election is generally deemed personal to the surviving spouse. If the spouse dies without having made an election (expressly or impliedly by conduct) the right expires, and the spouse is deemed to have accepted the terms of the will. A few states, however, have adopted the view that a spouse takes the statutory share automatically unless "divested" by an election. The guardian of an incompetent spouse cannot make the election in absence of statute, but the election can generally be made in behalf of the incompetent spouse by the court that has jurisdiction over the estate.[1]

_____

1. An interesting pair of cases illustrating the principles stated in this paragraph are Kinnett v. Hood, 25 Ill. 2d 600, 185 N.E.2d 888 (1962) (conservator denied authorization to renounce on behalf of incompetent widow where only her prospective heirs, not the widow herself, would gain by the election), and Rock Island Bank & Trust Co. v. First Natl. Bank, 26 Ill. 2d 47, 185 N.E.2d 890 (1962) (right of election died with widow despite her incompetence ever since husband's death).

PROBLEM²

3-A.   W died survived by H, her spouse of thirty years, and two children of that marriage. Her estate consisted of $100,000 cash and marketable securities, Blackacre appraised at $200,000, and Whiteacre appraised at $300,000. W had no debts. Her will bequeathed $50,000 to H, devised Blackacre to her oldest child, and left the residue of her estate to her children in equal shares.

(a) What course of action would you recommend H take if his statutory rights permitted him to take against the will either an interest like common law dower or a one-third forced share? What are H's rights under the law of your state?

(b) Would your advice differ if W left debts amounting to $500,000?

(c) What additional significance would you find in the fact that W also had $500,000 worth of life insurance payable to H?

(d) What if H were independently wealthy? How would this question be affected if the Uniform Probate Code sections set out below were in effect in your state?

UNIFORM PROBATE CODE

Elective Share of Surviving Spouse

GENERAL COMMENT

The elective share of the surviving spouse is substantially revised. The revised elective share has been endorsed by the Assembly of the National Association of Women Lawyers (NAWL), on the unanimous recommendation of NAWL's Executive Board.

The main purpose of the revisions is to bring elective-share law into line with the contemporary view of marriage as an economic partnership. The economic partnership theory of marriage is already implemented under the equitable-distribution system applied in both the common-law and community-property states when a marriage ends in divorce. When a marriage ends in death, that theory is also already implemented under the community-property system and under the system promulgated in the Uniform Marital Property Act. In the common-

2. In addition to, or instead of, Problem 3-A, students from community property states should consider whether, under the law of your state, the following facts require the surviving spouse, S, to make an election and if so what the alternatives are:

D's will leaves "all of my estate to T in trust for S for life, remainder to our issue by right of representation." The properties involved are $200,000 of assets traceable to D's recent inheritance; $400,000 of securities traceable to D's earnings during marriage, half being traceable to a period when D and S lived in a non-community property jurisdiction; pension benefits in annuity form payable to S; $200,000 worth of life insurance proceeds payable to "the trustee named in my will"; and $200,000 of assets held by D and S as joint tenants.

law states, however, elective-share law has not caught up to the partnership theory of marriage.

The general effect of implementing the partnership theory in elective-share law is to increase the entitlement of a surviving spouse in a long-term marriage in cases in which the marital assets were disproportionately titled in the decedent's name; and to decrease or even eliminate the entitlement of a surviving spouse in a long-term marriage in cases in which the marital assets were more or less equally titled or disproportionately titled in the surviving spouse's name. A further general effect is to decrease or even eliminate the entitlement of a surviving spouse in a short-term, later-in-life marriage in which neither spouse contributed much, if anything, to the acquisition of the other's wealth, except that a special supplemental elective-share amount is provided in cases in which the surviving spouse would otherwise be left without sufficient funds for support.

§2-201. *Elective Share.*

(a) [Elective-Share Amount.] The surviving spouse of a decedent who dies domiciled in this State has a right of election, under the limitations and conditions stated in this Part, to take an elective-share amount equal to the value of the elective-share percentage of the augmented estate, determined by the length of time the spouse and the decedent were married to each other, in accordance with the following schedule:

If the decedent and the spouse were married to each other:	*The elective-share percentage is:*
Less than 1 year	Supplemental Amount Only.
1 year but less than 2 years	3% of the augmented estate.
2 years but less than 3 years	6% of the augmented estate.
3 years but less than 4 years	9% of the augmented estate.
4 years but less than 5 years	12% of the augmented estate.
5 years but less than 6 years	15% of the augmented estate.
6 years but less than 7 years	18% of the augmented estate.
7 years but less than 8 years	21% of the augmented estate.
8 years but less than 9 years	24% of the augmented estate.
9 years but less than 10 years	27% of the augmented estate.
10 years but less than 11 years	30% of the augmented estate.
11 years but less than 12 years	34% of the augmented estate.
12 years but less than 13 years	38% of the augmented estate.
13 years but less than 14 years	42% of the augmented estate.
14 years but less than 15 years	46% of the augmented estate.
15 years or more	50% of the augmented estate.

(b) [Supplemental Elective-Share Amount.] If the sum of the amounts described in Sections 2-202(b)(3) and (4), 2-207(a)(1) and (3), and that part of the elective-share amount payable from the decedent's probate and reclaimable estates under Sections 2-207(b) and (c) is less than [$50,000], the surviving spouse is entitled to a supplemental elective-share amount equal to [$50,000], minus the sum of the amounts described in those sections. The supplemental elective-share amount is payable from the decedent's probate estate and from recipients of the decedent's reclaimable estate in the order of priority set forth in Sections 2-207(b) and (c).

(c) [Non-Domiciliary.] The right, if any, of the surviving spouse of a decedent who dies domiciled outside this State to take an elective share in property in this State is governed by the law of the decedent's domicile at death.

§2-202.   *Augmented Estate.*

(a) [Definitions.]
   (1) In this section:
      (i) "Bona fide purchaser" means a purchaser for value in good faith and without notice of an adverse claim. The notation of a state documentary fee on a recorded instrument pursuant to [insert appropriate reference] is prima facie evidence that the transfer described therein was made to a bona fide purchaser.
      (ii) "Nonadverse party" means a person who does not have a substantial beneficial interest in the trust or other property arrangement that would be adversely affected by the exercise or nonexercise of the power that he [or she] possesses respecting the trust or other property arrangement. A person having a general power of appointment over property is deemed to have a beneficial interest in the property.
      (iii) "Presently exercisable general power of appointment" means a power of appointment under which, at the time in question, the decedent by an exercise of the power could have created an interest, present or future, in himself [or herself] or his [or her] creditors.
      (iv) "Probate estate" means property, whether real or personal, movable or immovable, wherever situated, that would pass by intestate succession if the decedent died without a valid will.
      (v) "Right to income" includes a right to payments under an annuity or similar contractual arrangement.
      (vi) "Value of property owned by the surviving spouse at the decedent's death" and "value of property to which the surviving spouse succeeds by reason of the decedent's death" include the commuted value of any present or future interest then held by the surviving spouse and the commuted value of amounts payable

to the surviving spouse after the decedent's death under any trust, life insurance settlement option, annuity contract, public or private pension, disability compensation, death benefit or retirement plan, or any similar arrangement, exclusive of the federal Social Security system.

(2) In subsections (b)(2)(iii) and (iv), "transfer" includes an exercise or release of a power of appointment, but does not include a lapse of a power of appointment.

(b) [Property Included in Augmented Estate.] The augmented estate consists of the sum of:

(1) the value of the decedent's probate estate, reduced by funeral and administration expenses, homestead allowance, family allowances and exemptions, and enforceable claims;

(2) the value of the decedent's reclaimable estate. The decedent's reclaimable estate is composed of all property, whether real or personal, movable or immovable, wherever situated, not included in the decedent's probate estate, of any of the following types:

(i) property to the extent the passing of the principal thereof to or for the benefit of any person, other than the decedent's surviving spouse, was subject to a presently exercisable general power of appointment held by the decedent alone, if the decedent held that power immediately before his [or her] death or if and to the extent the decedent, while married to his [or her] surviving spouse and during the two-year period next preceding the decedent's death, released that power or exercised that power in favor of any person other than the decedent or the decedent's estate, spouse, or surviving spouse;

(ii) property, to the extent of the decedent's unilaterally severable interest therein, held by the decedent and any other person, except the decedent's surviving spouse, with right of survivorship, if the decedent held that interest immediately before his [or her] death or if and to the extent the decedent, while married to his [or her] surviving spouse and during the two-year period preceding the decedent's death, transferred that interest to any person other than the decedent's surviving spouse;

(iii) proceeds of insurance, including accidental death benefits, on the life of the decedent payable to any person other than the decedent's surviving spouse, if the decedent owned the insurance policy, had the power to change the beneficiary of the insurance policy, or the insurance policy was subject to a presently exercisable general power of appointment held by the decedent alone immediately before his [or her] death or if and to the extent the decedent, while married to his [or her] surviving spouse and during the two-year period next preceding the decedent's death, transferred that policy to any person other than the decedent's surviving spouse; and

(iv) property transferred by the decedent to any person other than a bona fide purchaser at any time during the decedent's marriage to the surviving spouse, to or for the benefit or any person, other than the decedent's surviving spouse, if the transfer is of any of the following types:

(A) any transfer to the extent that the decedent retained at the time of or during the two-year period next preceding his [or her] death the possession or enjoyment of, or right to income from, the property;

(B) any transfer to the extent that, at the time of or during the two-year period next preceding the decedent's death, the income or principal was subject to a power, exercisable by the decedent alone or in conjunction with any other person or exercisable by a nonadverse party, for the benefit of the decedent or the decedent's estate;

(C) any transfer of property, to the extent the decedent's contribution to it, as a percentage of the whole, was made within two years before the decedent's death, by which the property is held, at the time of or during the two-year period next preceding the decedent's death, by the decedent and another, other than the decedent's surviving spouse, with right of survivorship; or

(D) any transfer made to a donee within two years before the decedent's death to the extent that the aggregate transfers to any one donee in either of the years exceed $10,000.00;

(3) the value of property to which the surviving spouse succeeds by reason of the decedent's death, other than by homestead allowance, exempt property, family allowance, testate succession, or intestate succession, including the proceeds of insurance, including accidental death benefits, on the life of the decedent and benefits payable under a retirement plan in which the decedent was a participant, exclusive of the federal Social Security system; and

(4) the value of property owned by the surviving spouse at the decedent's death, reduced by enforceable claims against that property or that spouse, plus the value of amounts that would have been includible in the surviving spouse's reclaimable estate had the spouse predeceased the decedent. But amounts that would have been includible in the surviving spouse's reclaimable estate under subsection (b)(2)(iii) are not valued as if he [or she] were deceased.

(c) [Exclusions.] Any transfer or exercise or release of a power of appointment is excluded from the decedent's reclaimable estate (i) to the extent the decedent received adequate and full consideration in money or money's worth for the transfer, exercise, or release or (ii) if irrevocably made with the written consent or joinder of the surviving spouse.

(d) [Valuation.] Property is valued as of the decedent's death, but property irrevocably transferred during the two-year period next preceding the decedent's death which is included in the decedent's reclaimable estate under subsection (b)(2)(i), (ii), and (iv) is valued as of the time of the transfer. If the terms of more than one of the subparagraphs or sub-subparagraphs of subsection (b)(2) apply, the property is included in the augmented estate under the subparagraph or sub-subparagraph that yields the highest value. For the purposes of this subsection, an "irrevocable transfer of property" includes an irrevocable exercise or release of a power of appointment.

(e) [Protection of Payors and Other Third Parties.]

(1) Although under this section a payment, item of property, or other benefit is included in the decedent's reclaimable estate, a payor or other third party is not liable for having made a payment or transferred an item of property or other benefit to a beneficiary designated in a governing instrument, or for having taken any other action in good faith reliance on the validity of a governing instrument, upon request and satisfactory proof of the decedent's death, before the payor or other third party received written notice from the surviving spouse or spouse's representative of an intention to file a petition for the elective share or that a petition for the elective share has been filed. A payor or other third party is liable for payments made or other actions taken after the payor or other third party received written notice of an intention to file a petition for the elective share or that a petition for the elective share has been filed.

(2) The written notice of intention to file a petition for the elective share or that a petition for the elective share has been filed must be mailed to the payor's or other third party's main office or home by registered or certified mail, return receipt requested, or served upon the payor or other third party in the same manner as a summons in a civil action. Upon receipt of written notice of intention to file a petition for the elective share or that a petition for the elective share has been filed, a payor or other third party may pay any amount owed or transfer or deposit any item of property held by it to or with the court having jurisdiction of the probate proceedings relating to the decedent's estate, or if no proceedings have been commenced, to or with the court having jurisdiction of probate proceedings relating to decedents' estates located in the county of the decedent's residence. The court shall hold the funds or item of property and, upon its determination under Section 2-205(d), shall order disbursement in accordance with the determination. If no petition is filed in the court within the specified time under Section 2-205(a) or, if filed, the demand for an elective share is withdrawn under Section 2-205(c), the court shall order disbursement to the designated beneficiary. Payments, transfers, or deposits made to or with the court discharge the payor or other third party from all claims for the value of amounts paid to or items of property transferred to or deposited with the Court.

(3) Upon petition to the probate court by the beneficiary desig-

nated in a governing instrument, the court may order that all or part of the property be paid to the beneficiary in an amount and subject to conditions consistent with this section.

(f) [Protection of Bona Fide Purchasers; Personal Liability of Recipient.]

(1) A person who purchases property from a recipient for value and without notice, or who receives a payment or other item of property in partial or full satisfaction of a legally enforceable obligation, is neither obligated under this Part to return the payment, item of property, or benefit nor is liable under this Part for the amount of the payment or the value of the item of property or benefit. But a person who, not for value, receives a payment, item of property, or any other benefit included in the decedent's reclaimable estate is obligated to return the payment, item of property, or benefit, or is personally liable for the amount of the payment or the value of the item of property or benefit, as provided in Section 2-207.

(2) If any section or part of any section of this Part is preempted by federal law with respect to a payment, an item of property, or any other benefit included in the decedent's reclaimable estate, a person who, not for value, receives the payment, item of property, or any other benefit is obligated to return that payment, item of property, or benefit, or is personally liable for the amount of that payment or the value of that item of property or benefit, as provided in Section 2-207, to the person who would have been entitled to it were that section or part of that section not preempted.

§2-205. *Proceeding for Elective Share; Time Limit.*

. . . (d) After notice and hearing, the court shall determine the elective-share and supplemental elective-share amounts, and shall order its payment from the assets of the augmented estate or by contribution as appears appropriate under Section 2-207. If it appears that a fund or property included in the augmented estate has not come into the possession of the personal representative, or has been distributed by the personal representative, the court nevertheless shall fix the liability of any person who has any interest in the fund or property or who has possession thereof, whether as trustee or otherwise. The proceeding may be maintained against fewer than all persons against whom relief could be sought, but no person is subject to contribution in any greater amount than he [or she] would have been under Section 2-207 had relief been secured against all persons subject to contribution.

(e) An order or judgment of the court may be enforced as necessary in suit for contribution or payment in other courts of this State or other jurisdictions.

§2-206. *Effect of Election on Statutory Benefits.*   If the right of election is exercised by or on behalf of the surviving spouse, the surviving spouse's homestead allowance, exempt property, and family allowance, if any, are not charged against but are in addition to the elective-share and supplemental elective-share amounts.

§2-207.   *Charging Spouse with Owned Assets and Gifts*
          Received; Liability of Others for Balance of
          Elective Share.

(a) [Elective-Share Amount Only.] In a proceeding for an elective share, the following are applied first to satisfy the elective-share amount and to reduce or eliminate any contributions due from the decedent's probate estate and recipients of the decedent's reclaimable estate:

(1) amounts included in the augmented estate which pass or have passed to the surviving spouse by testate or intestate succession;

(2) amounts included in the augmented estate under Section 2-202(b)(3);

(3) amounts included in the augmented estate which would have passed to the spouse but were disclaimed; and

(4) amounts included in the augmented estate under Section 2-202(b)(4) up to the applicable percentage thereof. For the purposes of this subsection, the "applicable percentage" is twice the elective-share percentage set forth in the schedule in Section 2-201(a) appropriate to the length of time the spouse and the decedent were married to each other.

(b) [Unsatisfied Balance of Elective-Share Amount; Supplemental Elective-Share Amount.] If, after the application of subsection (a), the elective-share amount is not fully satisfied or the surviving spouse is entitled to a supplemental elective-share amount, amounts included in the decedent's probate estate and that portion of the decedent's reclaimable estate other than amounts irrevocably transferred within two years before the decedent's death are applied first to satisfy the unsatisfied balance of the elective-share amount or the supplemental elective-share amount. The decedent's probate estate and that portion of the decedent's reclaimable estate are so applied that liability for the unsatisfied balance of the elective-share amount or for the supplemental elective-share amount is equitably apportioned among the recipients of the decedent's probate estate and that portion of the decedent's reclaimable estate in proportion to the value of their interests therein.

(c) [Unsatisfied Balance of Elective-Share and Supplemental Elective-Share Amounts.] If, after the application of subsections (a) and (b), the elective-share or supplemental elective-share amount is not fully satisfied, the remaining portion of the decedent's reclaimable estate is so applied that liability for the unsatisfied balance of the elective-share or supplemental elective-share amount is equitably apportioned among the recipients of that portion of the decedent's reclaimable estate in proportion to the value of their interests therein.

Whether or not one approves of the terms of Uniform Probate Code §§2-202 to 2-207, at least their general policy and underlying objectives are rather obvious. Is the policy of §2-201(a) similarly apparent? Compare the equal "sharing" of marital earnings in the spousal "partnership" concept implicit in a community property system, regardless of the actual division of labor between the spouses. Also see the Uniform Marital Property Act (1983) excerpts in subsection 5, infra. What was the policy basis for setting the elective share in §2-201(a) of the original (1969) UPC at one-third, a fraction that has been and remains fairly typical of forced share statutes across the country? Can it be derived from some notion of support requirements? Is it based on an assumed contribution of the survivor to the deceased spouse's estate during the marriage? In short, what rationale could support allocating $25,000 out of a $75,000 estate to a 65-year-old survivor of a 45-year marriage, while also allocating a third of a $10 million estate to a surviving spouse after a three-year marriage? Contrast the "reasonable provision" approach of the English legislation discussed in section E of this chapter.

3. Effect of Spouse's Election

A variety of problems may arise when an election is required, particularly if the will in question fails to make a complete disposition of the decedent's estate, or under any circumstances if the spouse elects *against* the will.

Assume that *W*'s estate, after payment of debts, taxes, and expenses, consisted of Blackacre, Whiteacre, and $50,000 worth of securities and that her will devised Blackacre to her husband, *H*, and Whiteacre to her brother, *B*, but contained no residuary clause. Assume further that *H* elects to take Blackacre under *W*'s will, rather than to assert his forced share. *H* now argues that he is also entitled to half of the securities as his share of intestate property. Should his claim be upheld under the statutory provisions of your state? Compare Ness v. Lunde, 394 Ill. 286, 68 N.E.2d 458 (1946) (the will provided: "In lieu of dower, homestead, widow's award and of any and all rights or interest she might have or claim in my estate, as heir, widow, or otherwise. I make the following provision for my wife . . ." but failed to dispose of all the testator's realty; the wife elected to take under the will; the court held she was also entitled to an intestate share in the intestate property), and Waring v. Loring, 399 Mass. 419, 504 N.E.2d 644 (1987), with Trafton v. Trafton, 96 N.H. 188, 72 A.2d 457 (1950) (the widow failed to elect before her death and was thus deemed to take under the will; the statute provided: "Every devise or bequest [to the spouse] shall be holden to be in lieu of the rights which [the spouse] has by law . . . , unless it shall appear by will that such was not the intention"; the court held that the widow's estate was not entitled to share in the intestate property, since the statute "is not limited to cases of total testacy").

PROBLEM

3-B.   *H*'s will bequeaths a general legacy of $60,000 to The Brotherhood Orphanage and the residue of his estate to his son, *S*, and his daughter, *D*, in equal shares. *H*'s wife, *W*, elects to take her forced share, which is one-third of *H*'s net estate of $150,000.

(a) How should the remaining $100,000 be distributed as among *S*, *D*, and the orphanage in the absence of a statute in point? Under statutory provisions like those of your state (but assuming the above forced interest)? Cf. T. Atkinson, Wills §136 (2d ed. 1953), which states:

> "Abatement" is the reduction of legacies on account of the insufficiency of the estate to pay testator's debts and other legacies. Intestate property should be first applied for these purposes. In absence of testamentary indication as to order of abatement, legacies ordinarily abate in the following order: (1) residuary legacies, (2) general legacies, (3) specific and demonstrative legacies, which give way together ratably.

See also Uniform Probate Code §2-207. In absence of statutory provision in point, the general order of abatement has usually been followed. See Sellick v. Sellick, infra. Assuming no statute directly in point but that your state has a pretermitted heir statute like the Illinois statute on page 114, infra, how would you decide this case? See generally Traynor, Statutes Revolving in Common-Law Orbits. 17 Cath. U.L. Rev. 401 (1968); Williams, Statutes as Sources of Law Beyond Their Terms in Common-Law Cases, 50 Geo. Wash. L. Rev. 554 (1982).

(b) It is usual for a will to make provision for the most important objects of the testator's bounty by way of the residuary clause. What does this suggest about drafting? About judicial and legislative actions? Cf. Leach, Lessons from the Depression in Drafting Wills and Trusts, 27 Vt. B.A. Rep. 109 (1933).

SELLICK v. SELLICK
207 Mich. 194, 173 N.W. 609 (1919)

[William Sellick's will left $25,000 for life to his widow, remainder to the defendants, his niece and nephew. He also bequeathed $5,000 apiece to the defendants, $15,000 to other collateral relatives, and the residue of his estate (a bit over $130,000) to the plaintiff, his son by a prior marriage. The widow elected to take her one-third forced share (about $60,000) against the will.]

FELLOWS, J.

. . . [Plaintiff contends] that . . . we should not apply the doctrine of acceleration of remainders [as contended by defendants], but that [the] life estate [in the $25,000] given to the widow by the will should be sequestered to reimburse the plaintiff in part for the depletion of his bequest occasioned by the payment out of it of the sums necessary to make up the widow's statutory share. In short, that he is known in the law as a disappointed legatee, and that the doctrine of acceleration of remainders should not be adopted at the expense of disappointed legatees. . . .

That the determination of the life estate by act other than the death of the life tenant is as effective to let the remainderman into possession as the death of the life tenant, that the time of taking possession is accelerated by such act, is generally recognized in this country and in England. Thus in Jull v. Jacobs, 35 L.T.R. 153, the testator gave a life estate to his daughter, with remainder over to her children on their becoming of age. The daughter witnessed the will, thus incapacitating her from taking the life estate. The life estate having failed from this fact, it was held that the children who took the fee should be let into possession at once. . . .

In the case of Lainson v. Lainson, 18 Beav. 1, the testator gave an estate for life to A., and on his decease to B. in tail. By a codicil he revoked the devise to A. It was held that the estate of B. was accelerated, and that he took at once. . . .

This court has recognized the doctrine of acceleration of remainders upon the termination of the life estate of the widow by her election to take under the statute. In re Schulz's Estate, 113 Mich. 592, 71 N.W. 1079. But that was a case where none of the legatees were in any way harmed by the application of the doctrine. By the election of the widow to take under the statute their bequests were proportionately diminished, and by the acceleration of their remainders they were proportionately reimbursed. . . .

So likewise the Court of Appeals of Maryland recognized the doctrine of acceleration of remainders (Randall v. Randall, 85 Md. 430, 37 Atl. 209), but declined to apply it in a case somewhat similar to the instant case (Hinkley v. House of Refuge, 40 Md. 461, 17 Am. Rep. 617). . . .

We are persuaded that under the great weight of authority the contention of plaintiff's counsel in this regard must prevail. While the doctrine of acceleration of the time of taking effect of the remainder upon the termination of the life estate by act other than the death of the life tenant (i.e., by the election of the widow to take under the statute) must be recognized and applied in proper cases, such doctrine should not be applied where by the election a portion only of the legacies are diminished in order to make up the amount required by the statute to satisfy the widow's statutory rights. And that this should be true whether the legacy diminished be a specific or a residuary one. Under such circumstances the disappointed legatee may in a court of equity compel the sequestration of the legacy to the refractory legatee for the purpose of diminishing the amount of his disappointment.

. . . To adopt defendants' claim would give to them the $25,000 many years before the time fixed by the testator for its payment. They would not only receive the amount given them by the will, but they would also receive the widow's life estate renounced by her to the disadvantage of the plaintiff. Equitable principles do not require that this should be done.

We are asked to fix the present worth of the widow's life use of the $25,000 with a view of finally closing the estate and disposing of all matters at once. The parties interested are all of age, and may make such adjustments as they may desire, but we do not feel empowered to fix the present worth of the widow's use and direct its present payment. We see no occasion, however, to longer hold the estate open. A trustee may be appointed to handle this fund of $25,000. He shall annually pay the income thereon to the plaintiff during the life of the widow, and upon her death pay the corpus to defendants in equal shares. . . .

Can one who elects against a deceased spouse's will take an intestate share of property thereby renounced? Generally spouses cannot claim to benefit by "intestacies" of their own making, and typically there would be no actual intestacy because the renounced property should be sequestered for the benefit of those beneficiaries whose interests were impaired by the election. Even on this point, however, there is possible disagreement. In Estate of King, 19 Cal. 2d 354, 121 P.2d 716 (1942), *H*'s will clearly attempted to dispose of his wife's interest in the community property as well as his own, devising Ranch 1 to his widow, *W*, and Ranches 2 and 3 to his son, *S*. *W* elected to retain her half interest in each ranch against the will, thereby renouncing her right to take *H*'s half of Ranch 1. Instead of sequestering it to compensate *S* for the loss of other property intended for him under the will, *H*'s interest in Ranch 1 was treated as intestate property, there being no residuary clause to dispose of it. As intestate community property that half of Ranch 1 passed to *W*.

4. Attempts to Defeat Spouse's Statutory Rights

Because statutory rights in the nature of dower, as distinguished from forced heirship provisions, give rise to inchoate interests in lands owned during coverture, such rights cannot be defeated by conveyance after marriage without the spouse's consent. Persons who wish to deprive their spouses of dower rights may attempt to do so by conveyances *prior to marriage*. Where such a transfer of land is found to have been intended to "defraud" the prospective spouse, it is generally held not to defeat the latter's rights, even though land disposed of before marriage is normally not subject to dower.

Greater difficulty is encountered where the surviving spouse has merely a statutory forced share. These rights are generally subject to inter vivos transfers, applying only to the deceased spouse's estate at death. Nevertheless, transfers that appear to be will substitutes have been the subject of considerable litigation with varied results. Observe that these problems concern forced shares, not dower or community property rights, assuming the transfer in question is beyond the community "managerial" powers of the transferor.

PROBLEM

3-C.   Five years ago, following twenty years of marital strife, *H* began making gifts to his brother and sister. This year, at age 78, *H* died in the hospital following a sudden illness. His will left everything to his sister. His wife, *W*, elects to take her statutory rights. Consider what *W*'s rights may be under the law of your state with regard to the following transfers by *H*; consider also the effects of these transfers under other typical forms of legislation protecting the surviving spouse.

(a) Four years before his death *H* gave his sister, *S*, $50,000 in cash and securities, openly declaring his intent to leave as little as possible for his wife.

(b) Two years before his death, accompanied by similar declarations, *H* deeded Blackacre (worth $100,000) to his brother, *B*, in return for *B*'s cancellation of a note secured by a mortgage on Blackacre. The note ($40,000) represented the unpaid balance of a loan *B* had made to *H* to purchase Blackacre ten years earlier.

(c) In the hospital several days before his death, *H*, being aware that death was near, had the beneficiary designation on his insurance policies changed from *W* to *B*. Immediately thereafter *H* sent for *S* and made a gift to her of a large savings account, saying, "I won't be needing this any more."

Gillette v. Madden, 280 App. Div. 161, 162, 112 N.Y.S. 2d 543, 544 (1952), stated: "A married man has the right to make any disposition of his property he chooses even though he is motivated by a purpose to destroy an estate to which the survivor of the marriage might make claim under statute law. A purpose to defeat such a right by divestiture of the estate is not treated as a fraud invalidating the transfer." In re Montague's Estate, 403 Pa. 558, 170 A.2d 103 (1961).

In Allender v. Allender, 199 Md. 541, 550-551, 87 A.2d 608, 611-612 (1952), it is stated:

> The doctrine of fraud on marital rights represents an effort to balance the social and practical undesirability of restricting the free alienation of personal property against the desire to protect the legal share of a spouse. It has always been recognized that a husband, in the absence of statutory regulation like that in the case of dower, has an unqualified right to give away his personal property during his lifetime, even though the effect is to deprive the wife of her statutory share. But if the gift is not absolute and unconditional and the donor retains dominion and control over the property during his lifetime, the courts have held that the gift is colorable and may be set aside. . . .
>
> In the instant case it is clear that the donor retained no legal control over the devolution of the joint interest [with right of survivorship] at his death and no power to revoke or undo what he had done, a factor stressed in many of the cases. It is not necessary to decide whether the mere retention of a life estate would of itself amount to a violation of marital rights. In the instant case the donor retained nothing but a joint interest, and we think his practical, but unlawful, retention of benefits, without the knowledge or consent of the donees, does not render the transactions so colorable or illusory as to justify the setting aside of the transfers.
>
> Without relying solely on the test of degree, we may say that we think the fact that the joint interest in the Key stock of the decedent and his children was by law severable . . . was not such a reservation of dominion or title to the Key stock as amounted to a violation of the widow's rights.

Related problems involving the use of revocable trusts to avoid a spouse's forced share are covered in depth in Chapter 11, section C, infra.

5. Marital Property Reform in Common Law States

Changing patterns of spousal relationships in our society have resulted in considerable legislative action in recent years. Policy considerations leading to legislative changes involving property rights on termination of marriage during life are beginning to be reflected in legislative treatment of property on marital termination at death. Common law states allow courts to redistribute individual property on lifetime dissolution of marriage and now have rules prescribing treatment comparable to community property on divorce. The Uniform Marriage and Divorce Act (UMDA), enacted in nine states, is illustrative and addresses spousal property rights on separation and dissolution, as well as treating the formation of marriages and the support and custody of children. Section 306 provides that "In a proceeding for dissolution of marriage . . . the terms of the separation agreement [except those pertaining to children] are binding on the court unless it finds . . . that the separation agreement is unconscionable." Section 307(A) (Alternative A) provides that "the court, without regard to marital misconduct, shall finally equitably apportion between the parties the property and assets belonging to either or both. . . . "

Section 308 provides that "the court may grant a maintenance order for either spouse only if it finds that the spouse seeking maintenance (1) lacks sufficient property to provide for reasonable needs; and (2) is unable to support himself." It adds that maintenance "shall be in amounts and for periods of time the court deems just . . . considering all the relevant factors," which specifically include "the financial resources of the party seeking maintenance, including marital property apportioned to him." UMDA does not affect property rights during the ongoing marriage or on death. Does not the now unanimous acceptance of "equitable distribution" of property on divorce suggest (see 1990 UPC revisions, pages 96 to 104, supra) that spouses that stay with their marriage "until death do us part" should have the benefit of rules generally similar to those applicable to spouses who give up and dissolve the marriage during life?

The Uniform Marital Property Act (UMPA) does deal with property rights during the marriage and at death as well as on dissolution during life. It purports to be a comprehensive regime similar to a community property system. The following excerpt is from UMPA's Prefatory Note:

> . . . Beginning with California at the end of the 60's and promulgation of the Uniform Marriage and Divorce Act in the early 70's, no-fault divorce has swept the statute books. . . . "Equitable distribution" of property became the handmaiden of no-fault divorce in the Uniform Marriage and Divorce Act and in most other reforms. . . . [T]raditional common law jurisdictions now use some form of *property division* as a principal means of resolving economic dilemmas on dissolution. . . . [In] community property jurisdictions . . . such a division is an inherent aspect of spousal property. . . . These property division developments address and typically adopt sharing concepts and bring . . . common law jurisdictions close to a deferred community property approach to divorce. . . .
>
> The Uniform Marital Property Act makes its appearance on that stage to offer a means of establishing present shared property rights of spouses *during* the marriage. . . .
>
> What are the root concepts?
>
> FIRST: Property acquired during marriage by the effort of spouses is shared and is something the couple can truly style as "ours" . . . as a result of a present, vested ownership right which each spouse has in all property acquired by the personal efforts of either during the marriage. That property is "marital property." (Section 4).

Except for its income, property brought into the marriage or acquired afterward by gift or devise is not marital but "individual property." Its *appreciation* remains individual property. However, the *income* of that property becomes marital property, so that *all* income of a couple is marital property. (Section 4).

SECOND: . . . [M]anagement and control rights flow from the form in which title to property is held. If only one spouse holds property there is no requirement for the other spouse to participate in management and control functions. If both spouses hold property they must both participate in management and control unless the holding is in an alternative ("A *or* B") form. Couples can select their own options as they deem appropriate. (Sections 3, 5, 10, and 11). Management control is *different* from ownership. Ownership rights are not lost by relinquishing or even neglecting management and control rights. In essence, the Act's management and control system is substantially similar to the existing procedures of title based management in common law states. (Section 5).

To guard against possible abuses by a spouse with sole title, a court can implement the addition of the name of the other spouse to marital property so that it is held, managed and controlled by both spouses. (Section 15). . . .

THIRD: The varying patterns of today's marriages are accommodated by an opportunity to create custom systems by "marital property management." . . .

FOURTH: On dissolution, the structure of the Act as a *property statute* comes into full play. The Act takes the parties "to the door of the divorce court" only. It leaves to existing dissolution procedures in the several states the selection of the appropriate procedures for dividing property. On the other hand the Act has the function of confirming the *ownership* of property as the couple enters the process. Thus reallocation of property derived from the effort of both spouses during the marriage starts from a basis of the equal undivided ownership that the spouses share in their marital property. A given state's equitable distribution or other property division procedures could mean that the ownership will end that way, or that it could be substantially altered, but that will depend on other applicable state law and judicial determinations. An analogous situation obtains at death, with the Act operating primarily as a property statute rather than a probate statute. . . .

See J. Oldham, Should the Surviving Spouse's Forced Share Be Retained?, 38 Case W. Res. L. Rev. 223 (1987). The English Inheritance (Provision for Family and Dependents) Act 1975, §3 provides that in determining provisions for the surviving spouse, the court shall "have regard to the provision which the applicant might reasonably have expected to receive if on the day on which the deceased died the marriage, instead of being terminated by death, had been terminated by a decree of divorce."

C.   Protection of Issue from Disinheritance

McKAMEY v. WATKINS
257 Ind. 195, 273 N.E.2d 542 (1971)

[Appellant is the former wife of John Watkins, whose will left his entire estate to his mother and made no provision for his minor child whom he was required to support by divorce court order.]

GIVAN, J. . . .

[A]n examination of the briefs and record in this case discloses a very simple proposition of law with which we can readily deal.

. . . Appellant readily concedes the present law in Indiana to be that upon the death of a parent, his obligation to support his minor children terminates, and that any claims against the estate of the deceased made for support after decedent's death are not obligations of the estate, citing authority of Sorin v. Olinger, Administrator (1859), 12 Ind. 29. However, appellant urges this Court to adopt the reasoning of the Ohio Court of Common Pleas in Silberman v. Brown (1946 C.P.), 34 Ohio Op. 295, 72 N.E.2d 267, wherein it was held that the obligation to support as provided in a divorce decree was not discharged by the death of the father, and that his estate remained responsible for such payments.

Appellant points out that a specific statute found in Burns' Ind. Stat., 1968 Repl., §3-629, IC 1971, 31-4-1-7, specifically provides [that] the obligation of support by the father of a child born out of wedlock, whose paternity has been established, does not cease upon the father's death, and that his estate remains liable for such support. Appellant argues that if the legislature has seen fit to so provide by statute so far as illegitimate children are concerned, this Court should adopt the same philosophy so far as legitimate children are concerned. This argument, though grounded in reason, is not an argument to be presented to this Court but would properly be the subject for legislation. As recognized by the appellant the law as found by the trial court is well established in Indiana. We hold the trial court did not err in finding that the responsibility for support of the minor child ceased upon the death of the parent.

Unfortunately, the only striking things about the above case are that it was brought at all and that the appellant could find even a lower court decision to cite.

The statutory law of nearly all states includes a provision intended to diminish the risk of inadvertent disinheritance of descendants. These "pretermitted heir statutes" do not create forced shares for the protected issue. In but one state is there a form of forced heirship for descendants. La. Civ. Code, art. 1493; cf. Cal. Civ. Code §205 (if a dependent child would become a charge of the county, the county may assert a claim against the estate for the child's support). Thus, as a general rule, a child may be disinherited if the intention to do so is expressed and if the entire estate is otherwise disposed of. As a practical matter, the exclusion of a child may invite a successful contest of a will.

Pretermitted heir statutes are designed to avoid unintentional failure of a testator's natural and probable intention. In studying the following material, consider what kind of statute is best suited to accomplish this purpose and what kinds may breed litigation or even defeat intent. In examining your local statute it is important to look for certain details in which these statutes differ from state to state. For example, consider who may be a pretermitted heir.[3] Does your statute apply to all descendants who would take by intestacy, or just to children? Even if the statute merely refers to children, by judicial decision the issue of a deceased child may be allowed the protection of the statute as representatives of the child. Does the statute apply to such persons whenever born or only to those born after execution of the will? Consider also the conditions under which the statute does not operate. Must an intent to disinherit appear on the face of the will? Does a nontestamentary provision that is less than a full advancement of the intestate share prevent the statute's operation? Under many statutes one or more of these questions will not be clearly answered, and judicial decisions must be consulted.

PROBLEMS

3-D. *D*'s will provides: "Because my only son, *S*, has neglected me in my declining years and has led a life of sin, I leave him nothing at all. Everything I own I give to my friend, *F*." *F* predeceased *D*, and the provision for him fails under the lapse doctrine (which is taken up in Chapter 20). *D*'s only brother claims *D*'s estate as his next of kin after *S*. Who takes? See Estate of Baxter, 827 P.2d 184 (Okla. App. 1992). Cf. Note, The Intestate Claims of Heirs Excluded by Will: Should "Negative Wills" Be Enforced?, 52 U. Chi. L. Rev. 177 (1985); UPC §2-101(b).

3-E. *A*'s will provides: "I leave everything I own to my wife, *W*; I intentionally leave nothing to any other persons who may be my heirs." After the execution of the will a child, *C*, was born to *A* and *W*. Thereafter *A* died, and his will has been admitted to probate. Does *C* take as a pretermitted heir under the statute of your state? Under the statute set out below? How would you argue for *W*? For *C*? If *W* offers to prove by testimony and other evidence that *A* actually intended to leave everything to her and assumed she would later make provision for any children if she thought appropriate, how would you argue for and against admission of the evidence under these statutes?

---

3. See Estate of Frizzel, 156 So. 2d 558 (Fla. App. 1963), analyzing conflicting authorities and deciding that the pretermitted heir statute protected a child adopted after the will was executed.

If *C* had been born prior to the execution of the will, what result would be reached under the New Mexico statute in the case below?

Is it a good idea to insert a provision such as that quoted from *A*'s will as a routine matter in drawing wills? Explain.

ILLINOIS REVISED STATUTES

Chapter 110 ½, §4-10.   Unless provision is made in the will for a child of the testator born after the will is executed or unless it appears by the will that it was the intention of the testator to disinherit the child, the child is entitled to receive the portion of the estate to which he would be entitled if the testator had died intestate, and all legacies shall abate proportionately therefor.

MATTER OF ESTATE OF HILTON
98 N.M. 420, 649 P.2d 488 (1982)

[Testator had four children by his first marriage, the three daughters, appellees, and a son who died prior to the execution of testator's will and whose two children are the appellants. Testator had no children from his second marriage. Article V of his will left his residuary estate "to my three daughters, share and share alike. If any one or more of them should predecease me, then it is my will that the share of said deceased [daughters] shall go to their surviving children. If any one of them should predecease me, leaving no children, it is my will that my entire residuary estate shall go to the surviving residuary devisees hereunder." His will further declared that the three daughters were his only children and that "if any other person claims to be a child or heir of mine and establishes such claim in a Court of competent jurisdiction, I give to such person the sum of One Dollar."]

DONNELLY, J. . . .

[A]ppellants argue that the provisions of §45-2-302(A) [UPC §2-302, except for the New Mexico legislature's additions shown in brackets below] providing for pretermitted children supports their claim to a portion of their grandfather's estate. This section provides in pertinent part:

A. If a testator fails *to [name or]* provide in his will for any of his children born or adopted [*before or*] after the execution of his will, the omitted child [*or his issue*] receives a share in the estate equal in value to that which he would have received if the testator had died intestate unless:

(1) *it appears from the will that the omission was intentional;*

(2) when the will was executed, the testator had one or more children and devised substantially all his estate to the other parent of the omitted child; or

(3) the testator provided for the child by transfer outside the will and the intent that the transfer be in lieu of a testamentary provision is shown by statements of the testator or from the amount of the transfer or other evidence.

B. If at the time of the execution of the will the testator fails to provide in his will for a living child solely because he believes the child to be dead, the child receives a share in the estate equal in value to that which he would have received if the testator had died intestate.

(Emphasis supplied.) . . .

[T]he Probate Code controls the interpretation and construction of testator's will even though the document was executed prior to the code's adoption. . . .

Prior to the adoption of the code in New Mexico and at the time of the execution of decedent's will, §30-1-7, N.M.S.A. 1953, dealt with pretermitted children. This statute was copied from the statute in force in Missouri in 1901. . . . [It was] "adopted in response to the common law rule that an omission of a child from a will was presumed to be a deliberate omission. It was designed to change the common law rule and to provide that the omission of a child would be presumed to be unintentional."

. . . [U]nder §30-1-17, (the statute adopted from Missouri), the question whether a child was intentionally omitted from a testator's will could be answered only by reference to the will itself, and not through recourse to extrinsic evidence.

As noted in T. Atkinson, Law of Wills, ch. 3, §36, at 142 (2d ed. 1953): "Under the Missouri type of statute parol evidence is not admissible to show that the testator had not forgotten his omitted child — the question is simply whether the child was named or provided for in the will, and if not he takes his intestate share under the statute." A different rule evolved in states which adopted the Massachusetts type statute. The Massachusetts type statute provides that a child omitted from a testator's will may take his intestate share "unless it appears that the omission was intentional and not occasioned by accident or mistake." T. Atkinson, supra, at 141. Atkinson further states that, under the Massachusetts rule, "where the statute provides that the child takes unless it appears that the omission was intentional, parol evidence is usually admissible to show that intent." Id. at 143. . . .

Both the Missouri and Massachusetts type statutes are based upon the theory that if a testator failed to name or mention a child, he overlooked or forgot to provide for the child, and presumptively the parent did not wish to disinherit his children. T. Atkinson, supra, at 141. . . .

The framers of the Uniform Probate Code in drafting §2-302 adhered to the presumption that a testator who omitted or failed to mention in his will a child born after the will was executed did not wish to disinherit such a child, but materially departed from the provisions of the Missouri type statute by expressly providing that under certain situations set out in the statute, the presumption against disinheritance could be rebutted, and permitting the testator's intention to be shown by extrinsic evidence under the situations arising under §45-2-302, subsections (A)(2) and (3) and (B), supra. As noted in comment, The Uniform Probate Code in Utah, B.Y.U. Rev. 425, 434: "The UPC provision [§2-302] is based on the presumption that if the testator failed to mention a child born or adopted *prior* to the execution of the will, he intended to disinherit him."

Notably, although both New Mexico and Utah adopted the UPC, both amended §2-302 relating to pretermitted children and chose to add to this section additional language expanding the presumption against disinheritance to cover children born both *before* as well as *after* the date the testator executed his will. Because of the insertion of additional language in §45-2-302(A), supra, New Mexico's version of this section of the UPC is a hybrid.

This difference in wording between §2-302 of the UPC and §45-2-302(A), supra, negates the presumption that if a child or the child's issue *born before* execution of a will are not mentioned in the will of a testator, it is presumed that the testator intended to disinherit them. As stated in comment, The Uniform Probate Code in Utah, supra, at 433:

> The UPC [§2-302] provides that the section applies only to children born or adopted *after* the execution of the will; the UUPC [Uniform Utah Probate Code], however, contains no such restriction. The UUPC, then, requires the testator to satisfy one of the . . . requirements [stated in §2-302] in order to disinherit *even* children born or adopted *before* the execution of the will.

[Emphasis added.] . . .

In light of the peculiar language of the New Mexico statute relating to pretermitted children, we must therefore look to the will of decedent to determine if the document itself indicates any intention on the part of the testator to disinherit appellants as the heirs of his deceased son under §45-2-302(A)(1).

In T. Atkinson, supra, at 143, the rule is stated that "grandchildren are usually within the express provisions of the [pretermitted heir] statute if their parent is predeceased. . . . "

Appellees contend that the provisions of paragraph VII of testator's will constitutes a declaration of the decedent that he did not intend for appellants to take under his will and that it amounted to an express disinheritance of all other children or heirs except for those expressly named therein.

The question whether a clause in a will leaving a nominal sum to anyone who claims to be an heir or contests the will is sufficient to disinherit issue of one's child under the New Mexico Probate Code is a matter of first impression.

The courts of other jurisdictions are not in accord as to whether a "no contest clause" in a will constitutes an adequate statement of the testator's intention to disinherit children of heirs not specifically otherwise mentioned in the will.

[P]aragraph VII of decedent's will was more than a "no-contest clause." In it, testator designated a *class* of persons who might either contest his will *or* claim to be an heir to any part of his estate and establish such fact in a court of competent jurisdiction. Since an omitted child or heir does not assert his rights by contesting the will but by claiming an intestate share of decedent's estate, for language of a will to meet the requirements of §45-2-302(A)(1), supra, the clause must either mention the claimant by name *or* fairly and clearly express an intention on the part of the testator to exclude claimant as a group or class.

As noted in 8 Hastings L.J. 342 (1957), under the California Probate Code . . . [former] §90:

> The California Courts in interpreting this statute . . . in the past have evolved certain rules and principles which they now seem to use as guides. For example, it appears that it is not essential that the claimant be named or identified specifically by the will. The use by the testator of a word which describes a class of persons, such as "children" or "relatives" is generally considered sufficient to exclude the application of the pretermitted heir statute. Also, *the use of the word "heirs" in a will to describe the class of persons who are not to participate in the testator's estate has been held sufficient to show the intention of the testator to exclude his children from participating in the estate.*

[Emphasis supplied.]

In the case at bar, the language contained in paragraph VII of testator's will stating that if any person claims to be an "heir of mine and establishes such a claim in a court of competent jurisdiction" amounts to an expression by the testator of an intention to exclude appellants as *heirs* from taking under his will as a class.

As noted in 45 Cal. L. Rev. 220 (1957):

> The ordinary no-contest clause, disinheriting or leaving a nominal sum to "any other person or persons" or "anyone who may contest this will," has been held insufficient to show the required intent to exclude. On the other hand, clauses excluding or making nominal provisions for "heirs" or "persons claiming to be heirs" have been held specific enough to prevent descendants from claiming under the [pretermitted heir] statute.

. . . The court in [Estate of] Szekely [104 Cal. App. 3d 236, 163 Cal. Rptr. 506 (1980)] stated:

> The law is clear . . . that a disinheritance clause expressly omitting heirs indicates an intent to bar children or grandchildren and such clause overcomes any statement that he had no such relatives.
>
> Absent any evidence of testator's intent *not* to omit the claimant herein

. . . the disinheritance clause prevents the distribution of . . . [decedent's] estate to her as that clause does reveal a clear intent to omit any heirs not named.

Applying the above rationale to the instant case, we conclude that the language of paragraph VII of testator's will was a disinheritance clause whereby the testator effectively expressed his intention to disinherit any *heirs* of the testator, including appellants, not otherwise provided for in the will. Since testator's son had predeceased him, and was not living when testator made his will, it was not necessary for him to expressly mention his son in his will and the deceased son was not an "heir" within the meaning of the New Mexico Probate Code. See §45-1-201(17), N.M.S.A. 1978. We hold therefore, that the provisions of paragraph VII of testator's will satisfied the requirements of §45-2-302(A)(1), supra, and that the trial court's decision denying appellants' claim to an intestate portion of testator's estate was not error.

The judgment of the trial court is affirmed.

The pretermitted spouse. A number of states, because forced share protection is lacking or is significantly less than a spouse's intestate share, have pretermitted spouse statutes. This type of legislation protects spouses from the effects of wills executed prior to the marriage by granting the survivor an intestate share (or some modification of that share) of the deceased spouse's estate. These statutes do not apply if the will shows (or possibly if extrinsic evidence discloses) that it was executed in contemplation of the marriage or with an intention to exclude the subsequent spouse. Nor do they apply if the will, or maybe some other arrangement, makes provision for the testator's spouse — and cases usually require that the provision be for the survivor "as a spouse."

These statutes have many of the problems of pretermitted heir statutes. For example, when does a general anticontest or nonpretermission clause show the requisite intention to exclude the subsequent spouse or to limit the spouse's rights to those already provided (e.g., as friend) in the will? See generally Note, Premarital Wills and Pretermitted Children: West Virginia Law v. Revised Uniform Probate Code, 93 W. Va. L. Rev. 197 (1990).

D.   *Extent and Limits of Testamentary Power:
       Other Aspects*

Despite the unusual breadth of testamentary freedom typical of the states in this country, a testator's authority is subject to limitations, qualifications, and uncertainties that vary from jurisdiction to jurisdiction and that go beyond the widespread substantive and procedural safe-guards we have just examined. Even today relatively novel issues, evo-lutionary developments, and distinct changes of policy are observable. In this section we look at several such aspects of the limits of our powers of testation — special prohibitions, disabilities, and the nature of per-sonal and economic rights that may or may not be exercised by wills. It also might be worth pointing out briefly that many of the world's soci-eties tolerate far less freedom of testation and particularly object to "substitutions," thus refusing to recognize future interests and trusts as they are known and taken for granted in this country. Even the common law world's acceptance of these forms of "dead hand control" is not unlimited — hence rules regulating "perpetuities" (see, e.g., E. Halbach and E. Scoles, Problems and Materials on Future Interests (1977), Chap-ter 8), public policy restrictions on trust purposes and conditions (see Chapter 10, section E, and Chapter 14, infra), and the like.

Restrictions on charitable dispositions. In a shrinking minority of states testamentary gifts to charity are subject to some limitation, generally in order to minimize the possible consequences of a dying person's fear of the hereafter. These restrictions may take several forms, and each statute must be studied to determine the type of limitation involved and the cir-cumstances under which it operates.

Some statutes limit the amount that can be left to charity, and some others invalidate charitable bequests and devises by a will executed within a specified period prior to death. Still others embody both of these forms of limitation.

Typically these statutes apply only if the testator is survived by certain designated near relatives, and sometimes then only if and to the extent an objecting relative would take but for the charitable gift. See, e.g., Estate of Eckart, 39 N.Y.2d 493, 348 N.E.2d 905 (1976) (statute since repealed). In some states this has led to drafting practices that have — sucessfully — protected "prohibited" charitable bequests by providing substitute bequests to friends or others outside the protected class in the event the charitable bequest is invalidated.

SHRINERS' HOSPITAL v. HESTER
23 Ohio St. 3d 198, 492 N.E.2d 153 (1986)

SWEENEY, J. . . .
We believe that the protection of a testator's issue from disinheri-tance, as a result of the testator's unsound judgment or the undue influ-ence of third parties upon the testator, is a legitimate state objective. Our [equal protection] analysis narrows, therefore, to the question of whether R.C. 2107.06 is rationally related to the accomplishment of that objective.

It is apparent that R.C. 2107.06 will accomplish its objective in some cases — i.e., those in which the testator, having acted under the belief that his death was near, executed a will within the six months prior to his death, making bequests therein for . . . charitable purposes on the basis of unsound judgment or as the result of undue influence. Unfortunately, a large number of cases falling within the scope of R.C. 2107.06 involve the estates of testators who did *not* execute their last will under the belief that their death was near. Furthermore, out of the remaining cases impacted by the statute in which the testator did believe that he was near death, it is reasonable to assume that few involved bequests that were based upon unsound judgment or the result of undue influence. . . .

Thus, by operation of R.C. 2107.06, a select class of beneficiaries is deprived of testamentary bequests, even though in the vast majority of cases such bequests are entirely legitimate and not within the scope of the statute's objective. Additionally, R.C. 2107.06 effectively creates an irrebuttable presumption that a testator . . . acted with unsound judgment or under undue influence. Such "'irrebuttable presumptions have long been disfavored under the Due Process Clauses of the Fifth and Fourteenth Amendments,' especially when they are 'not necessarily or universally true in fact, and when the state has reasonable alternative means of making the crucial determination.'" . . .

The imprecise nature of R.C. 2107.06 is further borne out by its failure to address inter-vivos death-bed transfers that are made to the prejudice of the grantor's issue and bequests made by terminally ill testators *more* than six months before their death. . . .

Based upon all of the foregoing, we cannot conclude that former R.C. 2107.06 is *rationally related* to the accomplishment of a legitimate state objective. . . .

Extramarital relationships. A few states still have statutes that bar or limit testamentary gifts to participants in adulterous relationships with testators. These restrictions may or may not depend on whether certain family members or favored relatives would take the challenged disposition. See Ray v. Tate, 252 S.E.2d 568 (S.C. 1979), involving a statute invalidating bequests in excess of 25 percent of an estate to one with whom a testator "lived in adultery." Cf. E. Kandoian, Cohabitation, Common Law Marriage and the Possibility of a Shared Moral Life, 75 Geo. L.J. 1829 (1987).

A news story in The Advocate, Jan. 7, 1986, at 15, 16, reported on a New Orleans court battle between, inter alia, a son adopted at age 41 by the decedent in the same year decedent executed a will in that son's favor, and Danny, a lover to whom decedent purportedly left his estate by subsequent handwritten will. The judge ruled the latter will valid but that Danny was entitled only to 10 percent of decedent's personal property, the remaining estate going to the son under a statute limiting what persons living in "open concubinage" can leave to each other if the testator leaves issue. After noting the decision's "devastating impact on every gay couple in Louisiana," Danny's lawyer was quoted as stating that this ruling, based on a statute rooted "in the Puritan ethic of trying to make sure that everybody lives monogamous lives, . . . makes no sense in this situation because . . . there is no rational basis for punishing parties who are not married" when, under the state's law, "they could not be married if they wanted to."

"Rights of publicity" as estate assets. "Unlike the right of privacy, which has been recognized as a personal right in that it protects a person's 'right to be let alone,' the right of publicity has been recognized as a property right, in that ' . . . a celebrity has a legitimate proprietary interest in his public personality.'" Southeast Bank v. Lawrence, 483 N.Y.S.2d 218, 221 (App. Div. 1984). The opinion continues: "Some cases have held that, in order for the right of publicity to descend, the celebrity must have exploited that right during his or her lifetime. . . . Although we find that [Tennessee] Williams exploited his right of publicity when he was alive, we hold that there was no prerequisite" in New York that he have done so in order "to preserve [it for his] heirs." Id. at 222. "A number of courts have recognized the common law right of publicity," and the Appellate Division saw "no logical reason to terminate this right upon death of the person protected . . . , presumably [the reason] this right has been deemed a 'property right.'" Id. at 223. The New York Court of Appeals opinion follows.

SOUTHEAST BANK v. LAWRENCE
66 N.Y.2d 910, 489 N.W.2d 744 (1985)

MEMORANDUM [OPINION]. . . .

Plaintiff, a Florida-based bank acting as personal representative of the estate of the late playwright Tennessee Williams, a Florida domiciliary at the time of his death, commenced this action to enjoin defendants . . . from naming [their Manhattan] theatre the "Tennessee Williams." . . .

Special Term granted plaintiff's motion for a preliminary injunction and [was] affirmed by the Appellate Division. . . . We now reverse.

The parties have assumed that the substantive law of New York is dispositive of the appeal and have addressed Florida law only tangentially. Both Special Term and the Appellate Division . . . have overlooked the applicable choice of law principle, followed by both New York and Florida, that questions concerning personal property rights are to be determined by reference to the substantive law of the decedent's domicile.

Under Florida law, only one to whom a license has been issued during decedent's lifetime and the decedent's surviving spouse and children possess a descendible right of publicity, which is extremely limited and which Florida courts have reduced to extend beyond the contours of the statute. Since Tennessee Williams did not have a surviving spouse or child and did not issue a license during his lifetime, plaintiff possesses no enforceable property right. In light of this holding, we do not pass upon the question of whether a common-law descendible right of publicity exists in this State. . . .

Testamentary guardianships. Typical state legislation authorizes the will of the last surviving parent of a minor child to designate or nominate a guardian of the person (or whatever the local terminology may be) for the child. The effect of such a nomination varies from state to state, and in some jurisdictions appointing judges are required only to give the nomination consideration along with other factors relevant to their determination of a child's "best interests." On the other hand, in many states a guardian (or appropriate fiduciary) for the estate or property of a minor beneficiary may be named by any testator for property passing under the will, and this nominee is entitled to serve in the absence on some legally disqualifying characteristic.

PROBLEM

3-F.   *M* was granted custody of her child, *C,* on her divorce six years ago from *C*'s father, *F.* For the last four years *M* and *C* have lived with *M*'s widowed sister, *S,* and her two children, sharing expenses and financial, household, and some parental responsibilities. *M* has come to you to have a will drawn, and she tells you that one of her greatest fears is that, if she were to die, *C* (now eight years of age) "would be returned to *F.*" *M* believes it would be ideal for *C* to remain in *S*'s home with *S* and her children. What advice would you give to *M* under the laws of your state? What further facts do you need to ascertain as relevant to this question? Is there anything *M* might do now to improve the chances of attaining her desired result in the event of her death while *C* is still a minor? What are your duties in this matter?

UNIFORM PROBATE CODE

§5-202.   *[Parental Appointment of Guardian for Minor.]*

(a) The parent of an unmarried minor may appoint a guardian for the minor by will, or other writing signed by the parent and attested by at least 2 witnesses.

(b) Subject to the right of the minor under Section 5-203, if both parents are dead or incapacitated or the surviving parent has no parental rights or has been adjudged to be incapacitated, a parental appointment becomes effective when the guardian's acceptance is filed in the Court in which a nominating instrument is probated, or, in the case of a non-testamentary nominating instrument, in the Court at the place where the minor resides or is present. If both parents are dead, an effective appointment by the parent who died later has priority.

(c) A parental appointment effected by filing the guardian's acceptance under a will probated in the state of the testator's domicile is effective in this State.

(d) Upon acceptance of appointment, the guardian shall give written notice of acceptance to the minor and to the person having the minor's care or the minor's nearest adult relative.

In Louisiana, LSA-C.C. art. 257 provides: "The right of appointing a tutor . . . belongs exclusively to the father or mother dying last. . . . This is called tutorship by will, because generally it is given by testament but it may likewise be given by [declaration] before a notary and two witnesses." But LSA-C.C. art. 258 provides: "If the parents are divorced or judicially separated, only the one to whom the court has entrusted care and custody of the children has a right to appoint a tutor for them as provided in the preceding article." On problems that arose when a custodial parent died without exercising her power under article 258, see Tutorship of Stanfield, 404 So. 2d 522 (La. App. 1981).

In the absence of a rare statutory provision like article 258, above, consider the implications of general doctrine concerning parental custody as expressed in Matter of Adoption of L., 61 N.Y.2d 420, 425, 462 N.E.2d 1165, 1168-1169 (1984): "It has long been the law of this State that a parent has 'a right to the care and custody of a child superior to that of all others, unless he or she has abandoned that right or is proved unfit to assume the duties and privileges of parenthood.' . . . The state may not deprive a natural parent of her child's custody merely because a court or social agency believes . . . it has found someone better to raise the child. So long as the parental rights have not been forfeited . . . the question of best interests is not reached. For once it is found that the parent is fit, and has neither abandoned, surrendered, nor otherwise forfeited parental rights, the inquiry ends."

In In re Adoption of Markham, 414 N.E.2d 1351 (Ill. App. 1981), following the death of the mother (the custodial parent under a divorce decree), the appellate court granted "permanent custody and control" to the child's paternal aunt and uncle but refused to authorize adoption by them. The contesting father was not found to be "an unfit person" or to have forfeited his rights to visitation and to prevent an adoption, but the court reversed the trial court's finding in favor of the father on the custody issue because it had failed to recognize the children's best interests, particularly based on the important continuity of environment offered by the aunt and uncle. The court also granted the father "reasonable visitation privileges . . . to foster the love and affection which should exist between parent and children." But cf. In re Custody of Peterson, 491 N.E.2d 1150 (Ill. 1986), severely restricting the circumstances under which a nonparent may petition for custody if a parent is alive.

See also the Report of the Governor's Commission on the Family, 4 J. of Calif. Assembly 8061 (1969 Reg. Session), on the basis of which Cal. Civil Code §4600 was enacted:

> [I]n the occasional case where the child's interests would be served best by giving custody to a non-parent — a stepparent or relative for example — the court can not presently achieve this without an affirmative finding that the [parent or] parents are wholly unfit. This doctrine is designed to secure the rights of the parents, which is surely a fit goal. Unfortunately, it sometimes loses sight, we believe, of the right of the child to an award of custody which will promote the stability of his life and best permit him to grow up as a happy and productive member of society.
>
> We have no intention of undermining parents' rights to the custody of their children, and we believe that the primacy of those rights must be preserved. We are convinced, however, that no useful purpose can be served by forcing a formalized finding of unfitness. The cases in which the child's best interest would require a custodial award to a third person may be rare, but are nonetheless serious. To take the most common example, if the custodial parent dies and the Court should specifically find that the child's welfare would be best served by awarding custody to the stepparent, with whom the child has been living and with whom he has formed a warm and stable relationship, should not the Court be able to so order without having to find a long-absent or minimally-interested parent judicially unfit? We believe that it should. . . .
>
> However, before custody can be awarded to one other than a parent, the court must specifically find that an award of custody to a parent would be detrimental to the child, and that the award to a non-parent is required to serve the best interests of the child. What is "detrimental" has not been set forth [in the proposed statute] with particularity. It is a nearly impossible task to devise detailed standards which will leave the courts sufficient flexibility to make the proper judgment in all circumstances.

Living wills. The popular reference to a "living will" is not to a will at all but to a document by which one may direct (or attempt to direct) providers of health care not to use extraordinary means to prolong one's life in the event of terminal illness. Some form of so-called death-with-dignity statutes have now been enacted in nearly all states and the District of Columbia. Without aid of statute several courts have authorized patients' or (if the patient is disabled) family members' instructions to be implemented in these matters. Cf. Matter of Guardianship of L.W., 482 N.W.2d 60 (Wis. 1992) (guardian may consent to withdrawal of life-sustaining treatment for patient in persistent vegetative state). Durable powers of attorney (agencies that commence or that do not terminate on the principal's loss of capacity) are generally available for dealing with these matters in the various states (see, e.g., UPC §5-501) and may be preferable or complementary to living wills or other forms of patient directives to health care providers. In these matters, the applicable statutes or cases must be carefully examined for details, limitations, and formal and substantive requirements.

The ethical concerns for life and for the private decisions of the terminally ill culminated in Cruzan v. Director, Missouri Dept. of Health, 110 S. Ct. 2841 (1990). Nancy Cruzan had been in a persistent vegetative state for six years as the result of an automobile accident. Her parents requested the state hospital to terminate artificial nutrition and hydration in the belief that this was in accordance with her wishes and best interests. The hospital employees refused and litigation followed. The state probate court authorized the termination but the state supreme court reversed, reasoning that, absent compliance with the Missouri living will statute, clear and convincing evidence of Nancy's preferences was required but had not been presented at trial. 760 S.W.2d 408 (Mo. banc 1988). On certiorari, the United States Supreme Court affirmed the state supreme court and held that the state need not adhere to the directions of close family members but could constitutionally require clear and convincing evidence of the patient's preference. In subsequent proceedings in Missouri, the probate court found additional evidence sufficiently clear and convincing to support a finding that the patient did not want to live like a vegetable and ordered tubal feeding terminated. Nancy Cruzan died twelve days later on December 26, 1990. The Supreme Court's five-to-three decision generated several opinions, leaving most issues to the states to resolve, although analysis of the opinions suggests that a majority of the present Court views a patient's right of "liberty" as imposing some obligation on the states to honor a reliable writing executed by a patient in anticipation of incapacity when issues concerning life-prolonging treatment later arise.

Legislative activity has increased in recent years concerning the resolution of these and related health care issues. In an aging population, with the medical profession's ability to extend "life" at rapidly increasing social and economic costs, the problems incident to euthanasia and long-term health care are accumulating at a rapid pace. At some point the emphasis in estate planning often shifts from planning for the risk of an early death to planning for a life that lasts longer than may have been foreseen.

E. Testamentary Restrictions: Some Reflections and Comparisons

PROVISION FOR DEPENDENTS: THE ENGLISH INHERITANCE ACT OF 1938
Notes and Legislation, 53 Harv. L. Rev. 465, 466-467 (1940)

. . . The British statute of 1938 [Inheritance (Family Provision) Act, 1938, 1 & 2 Geo. VI, c. 45], based upon earlier legislation in the Dominions, attempts to solve the problem of providing a scheme sufficiently elastic to allow disinheritance of the undeserving, yet sufficiently rigid to prevent an unjust testator from disinheriting the worthy in another fashion. Instead of the characteristic civil-law provision for a fixed portion beyond the power of a testator to disturb, and a provision for disinheritance of heirs for specified offenses, the English act gives probate courts the power to order reasonable provision for maintenance out of the income of the estate of any testator who does not make reasonable provision for his or her spouse, unmarried or disabled daughters, and minor or disabled sons. If the testator leaves property of less than £2000, recourse may be had to the principal. The income is to stop on remarriage of the spouse, the marriage of daughters, the majority of sons, and the end of disability of infirm children. The court is to look to the nature of the property in the estate, the claims of other dependents, the reasons for the testator's failure to provide, and the conduct of the dependents towards the testator. Where a testator bequeaths at least two-thirds of the income of the net estate to his surviving spouse, and the only dependents are the latter's children, no order can be made. . . .

———————————

Again, pioneering and imaginative English legislation! This law has been most recently revised in the Inheritance (Provision for Family and Dependents) Act, 1975. Now, any child of the decedent may apply for maintenance. The court is also empowered to award maintenance to one who was treated by the decedent as a child of the decedent, or to a person who was in fact "maintained" by the decedent. See Re Beaumont, [1980] 1 All Eng. Rep. (Ch.) 266. There is even some provision for unremarried former spouses. Gratuitous transfers made by the decedent to defeat the maintenance provisions can in effect be revoked. In addition, the current statute no longer precludes a maintenance order where the spouse received "not less than two-thirds of the income of the net estate" and the only other dependents are the surviving spouse's children. Finally, the "periodical payments" are no longer payable only from income; resort to principal is no longer dependent on the testator's estate being under £2,000. If the court "sees fit," it can order "maintenance, in whole or in part, by way of a lump sum payment."

The Oregon Probate Code provides that the court shall make "necessary and reasonable provision" from the estate for the support for the decedent's spouse and dependent children, in a manner that is not detailed. See Note, Protection of the Surviving Spouse Under the Oregon Probate Code, 57 Or. L. Rev. 135 (1977). The provisions for support may be by periodic payments to continue for no more than two years or by outright transfers of real or personal property. In some cases the entire estate may be set aside for the support of the widow and dependent children. Or. Rev. Stat. §§114.015-114.085 (1983). Cf. Maine legislation as construed in In re Perkins, 141 Me. 137, 141, 39 A.2d 855, 857 (1944).

NUSSBAUM, LIBERTY OF TESTATION
23 A.B.A.J. 183-186 (1937)

The transmission from generation to generation of vast fortunes by will, inheritance, or gift is not consistent with the ideals and sentiments of the American people. The desire to provide security for one's self and one's family is natural and wholesome, but it is adequately served by a reasonable inheritance. Great accumulations of wealth cannot be justified on the basis of personal and family security. In the last analysis such accumulations amount to the perpetuation of great and undesirable concentration of control in a relatively few individuals over the employment and welfare of many, many others. Such inherited economic power is as inconsistent with the ideals of this generation as inherited political power was inconsistent with the ideals of the generation which established our Government.

This is the language used by President Roosevelt in his message to Congress of June 19, 1935. The immediate objective of the sentences quoted was the recommendation, by the President, of a progressive inheritance tax. But the legal philosophy behind it is of a broader scope. It touches upon basic principles of Anglo-American inheritance law which permit, to a much greater extent than does foreign law, the undivided transfer of the decedent's estate to a single individual heir. . . .

Associating liberty of testation with the spirit of pioneering seems to be a plausible hypothesis. This liberty indeed is quite in line with "rugged individualism." And it is equally true that liberty of testation at the same time favors the maintenance of aristocracy and is particularly valuable to an industrial aristocracy of the American type. The Roman aristocracy performed its social duties by military services, the English by political ones, the American by granting large gifts and legacies for humanitarian, educational and other "charitable" purposes. . . .

The question arises whether the common law countries will in the long run continue to maintain unrestricted liberty of testation. There are distinct symptoms to the contrary within the English empire. . . .

As to the United States there has not yet appeared a similar distinct and general counteraction against liberty of testation. But there are indications of a slow, almost unconscious change in the mind of the community. . . . A certain preference for the spouse over the children might be in harmony with prevailing human sentiment, as appears from the great majority of wills. Yet the contrast between the amplitude of the spouse's protection on the one hand and the entire absence of the children's protection on the other hand may be regarded as unsatisfactory in the long run. Thus from various sources pressure is going to be brought upon the time-honoured Anglo-American system for the institution of something like a legitime. Such an evolution might be considered as a weakening of the pioneer spirit. This process, however, seems to be inevitable due to the fact that the territorial prerequisites of American pioneering no longer exist. Rugged individualism probably is doomed. The fight for the maintenance of familial property will have to be conducted upon different fronts.

4

Execution of Wills

Although the original English Statute of Wills, 32 Hen. VIII, c. 1, was enacted in 1540, modern developments date from the English Statute of Frauds, 29 Car. II. c. 3 (1677), which prescribed certain formal requirements for wills disposing of land. It also imposed formalities on wills disposing of personalty, but these did not include a requirement of an attested writing. Over a century and a half later the English Wills Act, 7 Wm. IV & I Vict., c. 26 (1837), was enacted and set out formalities required for writings disposing of personal as well as real property on death. Legislation in all of the states of the United States followed the general pattern of the Statute of Frauds except that all American statutes, like the English Wills Act, treat real and personal property alike so far as attested wills are concerned. Certain formal details of the Wills Act also have commonly been put into wills acts in this country. Wholly new formalities have occasionally been introduced by American acts; for example, a requirement of publication is found in some statutes, requiring the testator to declare to the witnesses that the instrument is the testator's will.

STATUTE OF FRAUDS
29 Car. II, c. 3, §V (1677)

[A]ll devises and bequests of any lands or tenements, devisable either by force of the statute of wills, or by this statute, or by force of the custom of Kent, or the custom of any borough, or any other particular custom, shall be in writing, and signed by the party so devising the same, or by some other person in his presence and by his express directions, and shall be attested and subscribed in the presence of the said devisor by three or four credible witnesses, or else they shall be utterly void of non effect. . . .

WILLS ACT
7 Wm. IV & 1 Vict., c. 26, §IX (1837)

[N]o will shall be valid unless it shall be in Writing and Executed in manner hereinafter mentioned; (that is to say) it shall be signed at the

Foot or End thereof by the Testator, or by some other Person in his Presence and by his Direction; and such signature shall be made or acknowledged by the Testator in the Presence of Two or More Witnesses present at the same Time, and such Witnesses shall attest and shall subscribe the Will in the Presence of the Testator, but no Form of Attestation shall be necessary. . . .

MODEL PROBATE CODE

§47. *Execution.*   The execution of a will, other than a holographic or nuncupative will, must be by the signature of the testator and of at least two witnesses as follows:

(a) *Testator.* The testator shall signify to the attesting witnesses that the instrument is his will and either

(1) Himself sign, or

(2) Acknowledge his signature already made, or

(3) At his direction and in his presence have someone else sign his name for him, and

(4) In any of the above cases the act must be done in the presence of two or more attesting witnesses.

(b) *Witnesses.* The attesting witnesses must sign

(1) In the presence of the testator, and

(2) In the presence of each other.

UNIFORM PROBATE CODE

§2-502.   *Execution; Witnessed Wills; Holographic Wills.*

(a) Except as provided in subsection (b) and in Sections 2-503, 2-506, and 2-513, a will must be:

(1) in writing;

(2) signed by the testator or in the testator's name by some other individual in the testator's conscious presence and by the testator's direction; and

(3) signed by at least two individuals, each of whom signed within a reasonable time after he [or she] witnessed either the signing of the will as described in paragraph (2) or the testator's acknowledgment of that signature or acknowledgment of the will.

(b) A will that does not comply with subsection (a) is valid as a holographic will, whether or not witnessed, if the signature and material portions of the document are in the testator's handwriting.

(c) Intent that the document constitute the testator's will can be established by extrinsic evidence, including, for holographic wills, portions of the document that are not in the testator's handwriting.

§2-503. *Writings Intended as Wills, etc.* Although a document or writing added upon a document was not executed in compliance with Section 2-502, the document or writing is treated as if it had been executed in compliance with that section if the proponent of the document or writing establishes by clear and convincing evidence that the decedent intended the document or writing to constitute (i) the decedent's will, (ii) a partial or complete revocation of the will, (iii) an addition to or an alteration of the will, or (iv) a partial or complete revival of his [or her] formerly revoked will or of a formerly revoked portion of the will.

§2-504. *Self-Proved Will.*

(a) A will may be simultaneously executed, attested, and made self-proved, by acknowledgment thereof by the testator and affidavits of the witnesses, each made before an officer authorized to administer oaths under the laws of the state in which execution occurs and evidenced by the officer's certificate, under official seal, in substantially the following form:

I, _____, the testator, sign my name to this instrument this _____ day of _____, and being first duly sworn, do hereby declare to the undersigned authority that I sign and execute this instrument as my will and that I sign it willingly (or willingly direct another to sign for me), that I execute it as my free and voluntary act for the purposes therein expressed, and that I am eighteen years of age or older, of sound mind, and under no constraint or undue influence.

_____
Testator

We, _____, _____, the witnesses, sign our names to this instrument, being first duly sworn, and do hereby declare to the undersigned authority that the testator signs and executes this instrument as [his] [her] will and that [he] [she] signs it willingly (or willingly directs another to sign for [him] [her]), and that each of us, in the presence and hearing of the testator, hereby signs this will as witness to the testator's signing, and that to the best of our knowledge the testator is eighteen years of age or older, of sound mind, and under no constraint or undue influence.

_____
Witness

_____
Witness

The State of _____
County of _____

    Subscribed, sworn to and acknowledged before me by _____,
the testator, and subscribed and sworn to before me by _____,
and _____, witness, this _____ day of _____.

(Seal)

                         (Signed) _____

                         _____
                         (Official capacity of officer)

    (b) An attested will may be made self-proved at any time after its exe-
cution by the acknowledgment thereof by the testator and the affidavits
of the witnesses, each made before an officer authorized to administer
oaths under the laws of the state in which the acknowledgment occurs
and evidenced by the officer's certificate, under the official seal, attached
or annexed to the will in substantially the following form:

The State of _____
County of _____

    We, _____, _____, and _____, the testator
and the witnesses, respectively, whose names are signed to the attached or
foregoing instrument, being first duly sworn, do hereby declare to the
undersigned authority that the testator signed and executed the instrument as the testator's will and that [he] [she] had signed willingly (or willingly directed another to sign for [him] [her]), and that [he] [she]
executed it as [his] [her] free and voluntary act for the purposes therein
expressed, and that each of the witnesses, in the presence and hearing of
the testator, signed the will as witness and that to the best of [his] [her]
knowledge the testator was at that time eighteen years of age or older, of
sound mind, and under no constraint or undue influence.

                         _____
                         Testator

                         _____
                         Witness

                         _____
                         Witness

    Subscribed, sworn to and acknowledged before me by _____,
the testator, and subscribed and sworn to before me by _____,
and _____, witnesses, this _____ of _____.

(Seal)

                         (Signed) _____

                         _____
                         (Official capacity of officer)

(c) A signature affixed to a self-proving affidavit attached to a will is considered a signature affixed to the will, if necessary to prove the will's due execution.

§2-505. *Who May Witness.*

(a) An individual generally competent to be a witness may act as a witness to a will.

(b) The signing of a will by an interested witness does not invalidate the will or any provision of it.

§2-506. *Choice of Law as to Execution.* A written will is valid if executed in compliance with Section 2-502 or 2-503 or if its execution complies with the law at the time of execution of the place where the will is executed, or of the law of the place where at the time of execution or at the time of death the testator is domiciled, has a place of abode, or is a national.

GULLIVER AND TILSON, CLASSIFICATION OF GRATUITOUS TRANSFERS
51 Yale L.J. 1, 2-10 (1941)

[U]nder a legal system recognizing the individualistic institution of private property and granting to the owner the power to determine his successors in ownership, the general philosophy of the courts should favor giving effect to an intentional exercise of that power. This is commonplace enough, but it needs constant emphasis, for it may be obscured or neglected in inordinate preoccupation with detail or dialectic. A court absorbed in purely doctrinal arguments may lose sight of the important and desirable objective of sanctioning what the transferor wanted to do, even though it is convinced that he wanted to do it.

If this objective is primary, the requirements of execution, which concern only the form of the transfer — what the transferor or others must do to make it legally effective — seem justifiable only as implements for its accomplishment, and should be so interpreted by the courts in these cases. They surely should not be revered as ends in themselves, enthroning formality over frustrated intent. Why do these requirements exist and what functions may they usefully perform? . . . The fact that our judicial agencies are remote from the actual or fictitious occurrences relied on by the various claimants to the property, and so must accept second hand information, perhaps ambiguous, perhaps innocently misleading, perhaps deliberately falsified, seems to furnish the chief justification for requirements of transfer beyond evidence of oral statements of intent.

In the first place, the court needs to be convinced that the statements of the transferor were deliberately intended to effectuate a transfer. People are often careless in conversation and in informal writings. Even if the witnesses are entirely truthful and accurate, what is the court to conclude from testimony showing only that a father once stated that he wanted to give certain bonds to his son, John? Does this remark indicate finality of intention to transfer, or rambling meditation about some possible future disposition? Perhaps he meant that he would like to give the bonds to John later if John turned out to be a respectable and industrious citizen or perhaps that he would like to give them to John but could not because of his greater obligations to some other person. Possibly, the remark was inadvertent, or made in jest. Or suppose that the evidence shows, without more, that a writing containing dispositive language was found among the papers of the deceased at the time of his death? Does this demonstrate a deliberate transfer, or was it merely a tentative draft of some contemplated instrument, or perhaps random scribbling? Neither case would amount to an effective transfer, under the generally prevailing law. The court is far removed from the context of the statements, and the situation is so charged with uncertainty that even a judgment of probabilities is hazardous. Casual language, whether oral or written, is not intended to be legally operative, however appropriate its purely verbal content may be for that purpose. Dispositive effect should not be given to statements which were not intended to have that effect. The formalities of transfer therefore generally require the performance of some ceremonial for the purpose of impressing the transferor with the significance of his statements and thus justifying the court in reaching the conclusion if the ceremonial is performed, that they were deliberately intended to be operative. This purpose of the requirements of transfer may conveniently be termed their ritual function.

Secondly, the requirements of transfer may increase the reliability of the proof presented to the court. The extent to which the quantity and effect of available evidence should be restricted by qualitative standards is, of course, a controversial matter. Perhaps any and all evidence should be freely admitted in reliance on such safeguards as cross-examination, the oath, the proficiency of handwriting experts, and the discriminating judgment of courts and juries. On the other hand, the inaccuracies of oral testimony owing to lapse of memory, in misinterpretation of the statements of others, and the more or less unconscious coloring of recollection in the light of the personal interest of the witness or of those with whom he is friendly, are very prevalent; and the possibilities of perjury and forgery cannot be disregarded. These difficulties are entitled to especially serious consideration in prescribing requirements for gratuitous transfers, because the issue of the validity of the transfer is almost always raised after the alleged transferor is dead, and therefore the main actor is usually unavailable to testify, or to clarify or contradict other evidence concerning his all-important intention. At any rate, whatever the ideal solution may be, it seems quite clear that the existing requirements of transfer emphasize the purpose of supplying satisfactory evidence to the court. This purpose may conveniently be termed their evidentiary function.

Thirdly, some of the requirements of the statutes of wills have the stated prophylactic purpose of safeguarding the testator, at the time of the execution of the will, against undue influence or other forms of imposition. As indicated below, the value of this objective and the extent of its accomplishment are both doubtful. It may conveniently be termed the protective function.

The Functions of the Statutes of Wills . . .

Ritual Function. Compliance with the total combination of requirements for the execution of formal attested wills has a marked ritual value, since the general ceremonial precludes the possibility that the testator was acting in a casual or haphazard fashion. The ritual function is also specifically emphasized in individual requirements. It furnishes one justification for the provision that the will be signed by the testator himself or for him by some other person. Under the English Statute of Wills of 1540, specifying a will "in writing," no signature was expressly required. In construing this statute, the courts gave effect to various informal writings of the testator or others, even though the circumstances furnished no assurance that the testator intended them to be finally operative. These decisions are said to have been influential in the enactment of the provisions of the Statute of Frauds, which were the first to require a signature. The signature tends to show that the instrument was finally adopted by the testator as his will and to militate against the inference that the writing was merely a preliminary draft, an incomplete disposition, or haphazard scribbling. The requirement existing in some states that the signature of the testator be at the end of the will has also been justified in terms of this function; since it is the ordinary human practice to sign documents at the end, a will not so signed does not give the impression of being fully executed. The occasional provisions that the testator publish the will or that he request the witnesses to sign also seem chiefly attributable to this purpose, since such actions indicate finality of intention.

Evidentiary Function. The absence of any procedure for determining the validity of a will before the death of the testator has two important consequences relevant to this function. First, as has already been stated, the testator will inevitably be dead and therefore unable to testify when the issue is tried. Secondly, an extended lapse of time, during which the recollection of witnesses may fade considerably, may occur between a statement of testamentary intent and the probate proceedings. Both factors tend to make oral testimony even less trustworthy than it is in cases where there is some likelihood of the adverse party being an available witness and where the statute of limitations compels relative promptness in litigation. . . .

The important requirement that this type of will be attested obviously has great evidentiary significance. It affords some opportunity to secure proof of the facts of execution, which may have occurred long before probate, as contrasted with the difficulties that might otherwise arise if an unattested paper purporting to be a will executed, according to its date, thirty or forty years before, were found among the papers of the testator after his death. Of course, this purpose is not accomplished in every case, since all of the attesting witnesses may become unavailable to testify because of death or some other reason, and their unavailability will not defeat the probate of a will. . . .

The provision existing in some states that the will be signed or acknowledged by the testator in the presence of the attesting witnesses may be justified as having some evidentiary purpose in requiring a definitive act of the testator to be done before the witnesses, thus enabling them to testify with greater assurance that the will was intended to be operative.

Protective Function. Some of the requirements of the statutes of wills have the objective, according to judicial interpretation, of protecting the testator against imposition at the time of execution. This is difficult to justify under modern conditions. First, it must be reiterated that any requirement of transfer should have a clearly demonstrable affirmative value since it always presents the possibility of invalidating perfectly genuine and equitable transfers that fail to comply with it. . . . Secondly, there are appropriate independent remedies for the various forms of imposition, and these prophylactic provisions are therefore not, in the long run, of any essential utility except in instances where the imposition might not be detected. Thirdly, as indicated below, it is extremely doubtful that these provisions effectively accomplish any important purpose. Fourthly, they are atypical; no similar purpose is indicated in the requirements for inter vivos dispositions. Why should there be a differentiation between inter vivos and testamentary transfers in this respect? The purely legal elements of the two categories suggest no justification; in fact, the automatic revocability of a will presents a simpler and more uniformly prevalent means of nullifying the effect of imposition than exists for inter vivos transfers. In spite of the benevolent paternalism expressed in some of the decisions interpreting these requirements, the makers of wills are not a feeble or oppressed group of people needing unusual protection as a class; on the contrary, as the owners of property, earned or inherited, they are likely to be among the more capable and dominant members of our society. . . .

See also Fuller, Consideration and Form, 41 Colum. L. Rev. 800 (1941).

A. *The Formal Requirements of Attested Wills*

Although a lawyer must know the formal requirements for executing a will in his or her state, this is by no means sufficient. A will may come before the courts of other states and be judged on the basis of the requirements of a foreign law. To avoid invalidity, or at least costly litigation, an attorney drafting a will should assume that it may be offered for probate anywhere. Many states have less liberal rules on foreign execution than those prescribed in Uniform Probate Code §2-506, supra. The traditional rule, now modified in nearly all states by validating statutes like UPC §2-506, has been that the validity of a will was judged by the law of the situs as to immovables and by the law of the decedent's domicile at death as to movables. A lawyer should develop a simple set of execution procedures that will satisfy the laws of all states. See Scoles and Rheinstein, Conflict Avoidance in Succession Planning, 21 Law & Contemp. Probs. 499, 503-504 (1956). Consider what that procedure should be as the following materials are studied. The Uniform International Wills Act, promulgated in 1977 to facilitate implementation in this country of the Washington Convention of 1973, has been adopted in a number of states; compliance with special form and execution requirements, which must be certified by a qualified attorney or other "authorized person," assures validity as to form in all countries joining the convention. See Kearney, The International Wills Convention, 18 Intl. Law. 613 (1984). The Hague Convention on the Law Applicable to Succession to the Estates of Deceased Persons (1988) provides a choice of law guide for international estates in signatory nations.

Courts generally require at least substantial compliance with each of the formalities prescribed by statute, but they do not impose additional formal requirements, nor do they object to unnecessary formalities.

1. Requirement of a Writing

The requirement of a writing may be satisfied by typing or by any reasonably permanent writing. Valid wills have been written in foreign languages, handwritten in pencil, and even scratched on hard surfaces.[1]

1. The following item appeared in the Boston Globe, and undoubtedly other papers, on December 4, 1962, under an Associated Press dateline from Meadville, Pa.:

> A will that a dying man scribbled on a dresser top with yellow chalk at a Pymatuning Lake cottage was revealed by authorities yesterday.
> They said Michael P. Pusateri of Pittsburgh apparently made the will last Thursday just before dying of a heart attack at his cottage near Epsyville.
> The will was signed and dated, and left property to relatives, they said.
> The dresser is now in possession of county authorities.

2. Testator's Signature and Acknowledgment

The universal requirement that a formal will contain the testator's signature is accompanied in nearly all statutes by express provision allowing someone else to sign for him. The proxy signing by another person must be in the presence of the testator, and generally it must be at his "request" or "direction." In a number of states it is provided that the person so signing for the testator shall also sign his own name, but some of these statutes make it clear that failure to do so does not render the will invalid.

By judicial decision or statutory provision a signature is generally sufficient if it is the complete act intended by the testator to serve as his signature.[2] Thus, a will may validly be "signed" by initials, mark, or nickname; and partial and even typewritten names have been held to satisfy the requirement, although certainly a lawyer should not encourage his client to become a test case.

Many American statutes follow the English Statute of Frauds in not specifying where the signature of the testator is to be placed on the will, but many others, following the English Wills Act, do require that the will be "subscribed," signed "at the end," or so signed "as to make it manifest that the name is intended as a signature."

Statutes vary on the relationship of the witnessing process to the testator's act of authentication. Some require the testator to sign in the presence of the witnesses. As an alternative to his signing in their presence, many statutes allow the testator to acknowledge his signature to the witnesses, and still others provide that he may simply acknowledge in their presence that the instrument is his will. The law of some states requires the act (signing or acknowledgment) to be done in the presence of all of the witnesses at one time, rather than permitting it to be done before each witness separately. A substantial minority of states require "publication" by the testator, although most states impose no such requirement. Publication is the testator's declaration to the witnesses that the instrument is his will; this does not require that the contents of the will be disclosed.

As might be expected, numerous problems arise in connection with the requirements relating to the testator's signature. Matter of Winters, 277 A.D. 24, 98 N.Y.S.2d 312 (1950), is illustrative, invalidating a will because the testator's signature was followed by a clause appointing executors. New York Estates, Powers and Trust Law §3-2.1 still requires wills to be signed at the end but now provides that matter following the testator's signature at execution shall not invalidate matter preceding the signature, unless "in the discretion of the surrogate [the will without the omitted matter] is so incomplete as not to be readily comprehensible [or] would subvert the testator's general plan for the disposition or

2. See generally Mechem, The Rule in *Lemayne v. Stanley,* 29 Mich. L. Rev. 685 (1936).

administration of his estate." See also Clark v. National Bank of Commerce, 802 S.W.2d 452 (Ark. 1991) (addition was "non-dispositive," so document was "signed at the end").

Potter v. Ritchardson, 360 Mo. 661, 230 S.W.2d 672 (1950), noted in 16 Mo. L. Rev. 79 (1951), involved the question of whether a statute that does not expressly require signing at the end is satisfied by a signature elsewhere in the instrument. The court referred to the classic rule in Lemayne v. Stanley, 3 Lev. 1 (1691), that where a statute "does not appoint where a will shall be signed, . . . a signing in any part is sufficient." The court stated "that the ultimate fact is whether a testator's name was written with an intention . . . to make the document effective as his will; that the location of the name is an evidentiary fact relating to that intent; and that the name was not 'subscribed' is not conclusive that the required intent was not present." 360 Mo. at 668, 230 S.W.2d at 676.

Matter of Pulvermacher, 305 N.Y. 378, 113 N.E.2d 525 (1953), involved a statute requiring a testator to "declare the instrument . . . to be his last will and testament" at the time he signs or acknowledges it. The witnesses emphatically testified that they were not informed, nor did they know, that the instrument was intended to be a will and that they could not read any part of the instrument as it was placed before them. The court, in denying the instrument probate, stated: "While 'no particular form of words' is necessary, the courts have held the minimum statutory prescription to be some kind of communication that the instrument . . . is testamentary in character. . . . 'It must appear that, as between the testator and the witnesses there was some meeting of the minds' . . . derived, one court has written, 'from some unequivocal act or saying of the testator.'" The court added that the reason "for requiring publication is twofold: first, to furnish proof that the testator is under no misapprehension . . . as to the nature and identity of the instrument, and second, to impress upon the witnesses the fact that, since the document is a will, they are expected 'to remember what has occurred at its execution and be ready to vouch for its validity in court'" and that "if the result appears to be harsh . . . such consequence is compelled by legislative pronouncement." 305 N.Y. at 383, 385, 113 N.E.2d at 526, 528. Would the *Pulvermacher* case have been decided differently if the witnesses had known from another source, such as the testator's lawyer, that the instrument was intended as a will?

3.   Attestation by Witnesses

Formal or attested wills must be witnessed by two or more persons in most of the states, but three or more witnesses are required in several states. However, in all of the states presently requiring more than two witnesses, a written will that was signed by the testator is valid if it complies with law of the place of execution; in several of these states compliance with the law of the testator's domicile would also satisfy the local requirements under provisions similar to Uniform Probate Code §2-506. See Rees, American Wills Statutes, 46 Va. L. Rev. 613, 624-625, 906 (1960).

Whether by express statutory provision or by judicial interpretation of the attestation requirement, witnesses are required to sign the will in all but one state.[3] In that state apparently a will may be "proved" by the witnesses without their having signed it. Estate of Dawson, 277 Pa. 168, 120 A. 828 (1923). The signatures of witnesses may have to be "subscribed," but in many states a will is valid regardless of the location of the signatures. Some statutes also require that the witnesses be "requested" to act as such by the testator. A witness is occasionally directed by statute to write the witness's place of residence, but failure to do so is not fatal to the validity of the will.

The attestation requirement strongly suggests that the witnesses not sign the will until after the testator has performed the act of authentication to which they are to attest. It has frequently been held, however, that the order of signing is not critical as long as the testator and the witnesses all sign as a part of a "single transaction." The opposite conclusion has also been reached. Clearly, if an essential witness signs first and the testator signs on another occasion, the attestation is fatally defective.

Litigation has often resulted from the almost universal requirement that the witnesses sign "in the presence" of the testator or from the occasional requirement that they sign in the presence of each other.

CUNNINGHAM v. CUNNINGHAM
80 Minn. 180, 83 N.W. 58 (1900)

[The applicable statute required attested wills to be "in writing, and signed at the end thereof, by the testator . . . and attested and subscribed in his presence, by two or more competent witnesses."]

3. The statute in Estate of Peters, 107 N.J. 263, 526 A.2d 1005 (1987), simply required that a will be "signed by at least two persons who witnessed either (a) the signing or (b) the testator's acknowledgment of" the signing of the will. The opinion stated: "There may indeed be cases in which the affixation of witnesses' signatures after the testator's death would be reasonable, particularly if the witnesses were somehow precluded from signing before the testator died. This case, however, does not present such a situation. Even if one accepts the testimony that the emotional trauma of the moment prevented the witnesses from signing the will while the testator was hospitalized, there is simply no adequate explanation of the failure to have obtained their signatures in the extended fifteen-month interval prior to his death. If the Legislature's retention of the signing requirement is to be at all effectual, signing must occur within a reasonable time of observation to assure that the signature attests to what was actually observed, and not to what is vaguely remembered." Compare revised UPC §2-502(a)(3), supra.

COLLINS, J.

[T]he only question in issue on this appeal is whether the alleged will was attested and subscribed in the presence of the testator, Cunningham, by the two persons whose names were attached as witnesses. The testator had been confined to his room for some time. It was a small bedroom with a doorway which led into a large room upon the north, the head of his bed being near the partition between the two. There was no door, but a curtain had been hung in the doorway, which was drawn to the west side at the time in question. Three days before the signing the testator sent for his attending physician, Dr. Adams, to come to his house, and draw his will. At the same time he sent for Dr. Dugan to be present as a witness. The draft of a will made by Dr. Adams as dictated by Cunningham was unsatisfactory, and both of the physicians went away. They were again summoned November 12, 1899, and went to the house in the forenoon. Dr. Adams drew a new will as instructed by Cunningham, the latter remaining in his bed. When the document was fully written, both men stepped to the bedside, and Dr. Adams read it to the sick man. Having heard it read through, Cunningham pronounced it satisfactory, and then signed it. When so signing he sat on the edge of the bed, and used as a place for the paper a large book which was lying upon a chair. Drs. Adams and Dugan were then requested to sign as witnesses. For this purpose they stepped to a table in the sitting room, which stood about 10 feet from where Cunningham sat, and there affixed their signatures. The time occupied in so signing did not exceed two minutes, and immediately thereafter Dr. Adams returned to the bedside with the paper. Dr. Dugan stepped to the doorway, about three feet from Cunningham, and then Adams showed the signatures of the witnesses to him as he sat on the edge of the bed. Cunningham took the paper, looked it over, and said, in effect, that it was all right. From where he sat he could not see the table which was used by the witnesses when signing. He could have seen it by moving two or three feet. While they were signing he leaned forward, and inquired if the instrument needed a revenue stamp, to which Dr. Adams replied that he did not know, the reply being audible to Cunningham. These are the salient and controlling facts found by the court below, on which it based an ultimate finding that the instrument so witnessed was attested and subscribed in the presence of the testator, and then affirmed the order of the probate court admitting it to probate as the last will and testament of the deceased.

The appellants (contestants below) insist that the attestation and subscription by the witnesses was insufficient, because Mr. Cunningham did not and could not see the witnesses subscribe their names from where he sat, and their contention has an abundance of authority in support of it from jurisdictions in which statutes copied from the English law on the subject, and exactly like our own, are in force. The rule laid down in these authorities is that the attesting and subscribing by the witnesses must take place within the testator's range of vision, so that he may see the act of subscribing, if he wishes, without a material change in his position; and that he must be mentally observant of the act while in progress. . . . In brief, the courts have, almost without exception, construed a statute requiring an attestation of a will to be in the "presence" of the testator to mean that there must not only be a consciousness on the part of the latter as to the act of the witnesses while it is being performed, but a contiguity of persons, with an opportunity for the testator to see the actual subscribing of the names of the witnesses, if he chooses, without any material change of position on his part. And yet . . . it has been held almost universally that an attestation in the same room with the testator is good, without regard to intervening objects which might or did intercept the view; and also that an attestation outside the room or place where the testator sat or lay is valid if actually within his range of vision. And no court seems to have doubted that a man unable to see at all could properly make a will under the statute, if the witnesses attested within his "conscious" presence, whatever that means. . . . Take the case at bar. The testator sat on the edge of his bed when the witnesses signed at the table in the adjoining room, a few feet distant, and within easy sound of his voice. If he could have seen them by leaning forward, the authorities in favor of upholding the will are abundant. Physically he was capable of stepping two or three feet forward, and from this point the witnesses would have been within his range of vision. It is extremely difficult to distinguish between the two cases, and yet it has been done again and again in applying the rule. . . . To say that this was not a sufficient attestation within a statute which requires such attestation to be in the "presence" of the testator, simply because the witnesses actually signed a few feet out of the range of his vision, is to be extremely technical without the slightest reason for being so. The signing was within the sound of the testator's voice; he knew what was being done; the act occupied not more than two minutes; the witnesses returned at once to the testator; their signatures were pointed out to him; he took the instrument into his own hands, looked it over, and pronounced it satisfactory. The whole affair, from the time he signed the will himself down to and including his expression of approval, was a single and entire transaction; and no narrow construction of this statute, even if it has met the approval of the courts, should be allowed to stand in the way of right and justice, or be permitted to defeat a testator's disposition of his own property. . . .

In Matter of Will of Jefferson, 349 So. 2d 1032 (Miss. 1977), the intended will was signed by the testator and then as an attesting witness by his lawyer, who thereafter returned alone to his office and requested his partner to serve as a second witness. After telephoning the testator and receiving confirmation that the instrument was his will, the partner subscribed as requested. The chancellor concluded "that the telephone call constituted presence" and admitted the will to probate. On appeal, the court reversed for the partner's failure to attest "in the presence of the testator" and observed that the purposes of the presence requirement include avoidance of "imposition or fraud on either the testator or the witnesses by substitution of another will in place of that signed by the testator; and that the witnesses will be reasonably satisfied that the testator is of sound and disposing mind and capable of making a will."

Many cases have rejected the so-called conscious presence test, requiring that the decedent be able to see the writing by the witness if the decedent had looked. In re Beggan's Will, 69 N.J. Eq. 572, 59 A. 874 (1905), 3 Mich. L. Rev. 591, involved facts generally similar to *Cunningham*. Because of the conflicting evidence on the question of actual visibility had the testator turned in the proper direction, which the court considered to be the test, the evidence failed to rebut the presumption that a signing is out of the decedent's presence if it occurs in a room other than that where the decedent was at the time. Denial of probate was affirmed.

PROBLEM

4-A.   John Deaux was survived by his son and daughter. He left a net estate of $60,000. The following is his will:

> I, John Deaux, hereby make my last will. I bequeath $40,000 to my daughter, Doris, and leave the residue of my estate to my son, Sidney. I appoint Beth Green as my executor.
>
> *John Deaux*
>
> *Henry White,* Witness [daughter Doris's husband]
> *Robert Black,* Witness [a neighbor]
> *Beth Green,* Witness [nominated as executor]

Is the will valid? If so, how much do Doris and Sidney receive? Consider these questions under Model Probate Code §46(b), page 144, infra, under your local statute, and under the Uniform Probate Code. Would it matter if Black had predeceased Deaux? If Black had not been a witness?

American statutes generally require witnesses to be "competent," while in a number of states the term *credible* is used. In general these requirements are the same regardless of the terminology used, since a witness need not actually be worthy of belief but must be competent to testify in court.

Courts have generally construed the requirement of competence as relating to the time of execution, and this rule has been codified in nearly half the states. Thus, if an essential witness is competent when the will is executed but subsequently becomes incompetent, the will is valid. In support of this position it has been observed that witnesses who are competent at the time of execution serve the statutory purpose of preventing fraud at that critical time and also that to relate the requirement of competence to the time of probate would prevent the proving of a will whenever an essential witness "should become insane, infamous, or otherwise disqualified, which would be opposed to current authorities; for I take it to be well settled that in such cases the handwriting of the witnesses may be proved, and the will thereupon allowed." Bruce v. Shuler, 108 Va. 670, 673, 62 S.E. 973, 975 (1908).

At common law an interested party was incompetent as a witness, and therefore a legatee was not competent to serve as an attesting witness. If an essential witness to a will had an economic interest in it, probate was denied. Generally today, however, interested parties are competent to testify in court. Does this change in procedural law alter the meaning of *competence,* or does this requirement still have the meaning it had under the Statute of Frauds or under the state legislation when it was enacted? Different conclusions have been reached. The usual rule is represented by Hudson v. Flood, 28 Del. (5 Boyce) 450, 94 A. 760 (1915), where the wills statute required "two or more credible witnesses" and the evidence statute provided that no person was incompetent to "testify in a civil action" because he is "interested" in the litigation. The court concluded that, absent specific language dealing with wills, under the enabling act "persons taking an interest under a will are competent witnesses to prove its execution." A dissenting opinion argued that the Wills Act is unaffected by a change in the procedural law and that a beneficiary is still not a "credible" attesting witness.

In many states today this question has been resolved by legislation requiring "disinterested" witnesses. Under a few of these statutes, probate may still be denied if an essential witness would benefit from the will. Others are basically like Model Probate Code §46(b): "No will is invalidated because attested by an interested witness; but an interested witness shall, unless the will is also attested by two disinterested witnesses forfeit so much of the provisions therein made for him as in the aggregate exceeds in value, as of the date of the testator's death, what he would have received had the testator died intestate." (Do you see why some variations of this language refer to "what he would have received but for the will in question"?)

Uniform Probate Code §2-505 does not require witnesses to be disinterested and eliminates the forfeiture of benefits by interested witnesses, concluding that sufficient other safeguards exist in this area to permit doing away with penalties for the rare, innocent use of beneficiary-witnesses in home-drawn wills. Yale, Witnessing Wills and Losing Legacies, 100 Law Q. Rev. 453 (1984), notes that the English Wills Act provides that "the witness who subscribes a will (and his or her spouse) loses any benefit conferred by that will," and adds: "The attestation is good but the legacy is bad. So much is common knowledge, not only among lawyers, though by lawyers not invariably remembered. In Ross v. Caunters [1980] Ch. 297, the solicitor who forgot found himself making good the lost legacy." In criticizing the rule, the author quotes the comment to UPC §2-505, above, which states that a substantial gift to a witness "would itself be a suspicious circumstance, and the gift could be challenged on grounds of undue influence."

A rare American statute that, like the English act, goes so far as to void not only a gift to an essential witness but also one to the spouse of such a witness was held constitutional in Dorfman v. Allen, 386 Mass. 136, 434 N.E.2d 1012 (1982), as a reasonable means of achieving the objectives of lessening the likelihood of perjury by a subscribing witness and of protecting the testator from undue pressure or influence.

4. Testamentary Intent

Probably the most fundamental requisite of a valid will is testamentary intent. There is normally a rather forceful inference that an instrument that has been executed with proper formalities, appearing on its face to be a will, was executed with the intent that it operate as a will. Some courts have refused to receive evidence of a contrary intent, while others have permitted such an instrument to be denied probate if shown by clear and convincing evidence to have been executed as a joke or otherwise without testamentary intent.

If it appears by the terms of an instrument that the decedent intended it to operate as his will only under certain circumstances, this intent will be given effect. A few statutes specifically authorize conditional wills. Intent to condition cannot be shown by extrinsic evidence. Even the terms of the will itself are generally interpreted as a mere statement of motive rather than condition if they admit of such interpretation. See, e.g., Estate of Taylor, 119 Cal. App. 2d 574, 259 P.2d 1014 (1953), in which the words "in case Davie Jones gets me out in the Pacific" were held not to condition the will but only to explain why it was made.

PROBLEM

4-B. About a year before her death *D* filled out a standard deed form by which she might convey her farm, Blackacre, to her son, *S*. *D* had two friends sign next to her signature as witnesses, but it is conceded by all that she did not deliver the instrument to *S* and that there was no effective gift. *S* offers the instrument for probate as *D*'s will, *D* being otherwise intestate. Can *S* succeed under your local statute? Under any of the common statutes prescribing the formal requirements of an attested will? See, e.g., In re Estate of Ike, 7 Ohio App. 3d 87, 454 N.E.2d 577 (1982).

5. Attestation Clauses and Procedures for Execution

Although not required by the law of any state, it is desirable to include an attestation clause, certified by the witnesses and reciting the events of execution and other facts to which it is desired that the witnesses attest:

SPECIMEN ATTESTATION CLAUSE

The foregoing instrument (consisting of seven pages including this one) was on July 1, 1993, signed and declared to be his last will by John C. Doe in our joint presence; we, at his request and in his presence and in the presence of each other, subscribe our names as witnesses to the execution of this will, declaring our belief that he is of sound mind and memory and under no constraint or undue influence whatsoever.

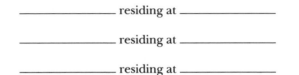

————————— residing at —————————

————————— residing at —————————

————————— residing at —————————

Compliance with the formalities recited in this clause would result in a valid execution of an attested will in any state, and the inclusion of an attestation clause generally creates a presumption of the events recited, at least if the signatures of the witnesses are identified. Although the presumption is, of course, a rebuttable one, the clause is useful for many purposes, as the following problem may suggest. The clause also serves as a guide for execution, facilitating compliance with required formalities that might otherwise be overlooked. Statutes that provide for self-proved wills go beyond the recognition of attestation clauses and use affidavits to preserve evidence. See Uniform Probate Code §2-504, supra.

PROBLEM

4-C. At *D*'s death a document is offered for probate as her will. Below her signature are the signatures of three witnesses. In the following cases, consider the will's admissibility to probate if it does and then if it does not contain an attestation clause.

(a) All witnesses to the execution predecease *D*, but their signatures are identified.

(b) One of the witnesses surviving *D* is *X*, who is a former secretary of *D*'s lawyer and who recognizes her own signature but understandably cannot recall this particular execution, its circumstances, or the identity of *D*.

(c) The only other surviving witness is *Y*, who also identifies his signature but denies that he actually saw *D* sign or hear *D* acknowledge the will or signature, and *Y* testifies that *D* lacked testamentary capacity. Compare In re Velie's Estate, 25 Ill. 2d 188, 183 N.E.2d 515 (1962), with Munster v. Marcrum, 393 N.E.2d 256 (Ind. App. 1979).

MATTER OF ESTATE OF COLLINS
60 N.Y.2d 466, 458 N.E.2d 797 (1983)

KAYE, J. . . .

Appellant [offered for probate a 1977 will containing] a printed form attestation clause, beneath which appeared the signatures of two witnesses, Mary Pedaci and Richard H. Skellen. . . .

Appellant produced five witnesses: the two attesting witnesses, a physician [who testified to the good mental and physical condition of the testatrix, his patient] and two persons supporting the authenticity of [her] signature on the will. Mary Pedaci testified that, in January, 1977, she was the assistant manager of the Ransomville branch of Marine Midland Bank. Shown the 1977 will, she identified both her signature and that of Richard Skellen, but had no recollection of the circumstances surrounding the execution of the will. Richard Skellen, the branch manager, testified that he recalled signing his name to the document, that both of the attesting witnesses "were right there," and that he had in his mind "an older lady." Skellen, who had witnessed a number of wills previously, further recalled that he had read the heading on the instrument, "Will and Testament." Otherwise he had no recollection of the event. . . .

Respondents moved to dismiss appellant's petition to probate the 1977 will on the ground that he had not presented prima facie proof of due execution. The court denied the motion, holding that the formalities of due execution can be established despite the imperfect memory of both attesting witnesses. Relying on the attestation clause, the genuineness of the three signatures, and the testimony of the physician, the court found that the 1977 will had been duly executed. The Appellate Division, 91 A.D.2d 1167, 459 N.Y.S.2d 132, reversed and dismissed appellant's petition, holding that [N.Y. Surr. Ct. Proc. Act §1405] (subd. 3) requires that at least one of the attesting witnesses confirm that the testatrix signed the instrument and intended it to be her will.

This appeal focuses on the import of SCPA 1405 (subd. 3), which . . .

provides: "Where an attesting witness has forgotten the occurrence or testifies against the execution of the will and at least 1 other attesting witness has been examined the will may be admitted to probate upon the testimony of the other witness or witnesses and such other facts as would be sufficient to prove the will." The issue of first impression which is presented is whether, given SCPA 1405 (subd. 3), a will may be admitted to probate where *both* attesting witnesses do not recollect the events surrounding execution of the will but the court is otherwise satisfied from all of the evidence that the will was properly executed. We conclude that the Legislature by this section did not intend the radical departure from prior statutory and decisional law urged upon us by respondents, and that a will may be admitted to probate even if both attesting witnesses cannot recall the will execution. . . .

For more than a century, the courts have consistently interpreted [predecessor] section 142 of the Surrogate's Court Act and its forbears to permit probate even where the attesting witnesses did not recall the event or testified against the will. "If the attestation clause is full and the signatures genuine and the circumstances corroborative of due execution, and no evidence disproving a compliance in any particular, the presumption may be lawfully indulged that all the provisions of the statute were complied with, although the witnesses are unable to recollect the execution or what took place at the time." (Matter of Kellum, 52 N.Y. 517, 519). . . .

To be sure, the testimony of the attesting witnesses is entitled to great weight. . . . A failure of their recollection intensifies the care and vigilance that must be exercised in examining the remaining evidence. . . .

Here, given the evidence, we cannot say that the Surrogate erred as a matter of law in admitting the will to probate. Accordingly, the order of the Appellate Division should be reversed and the case remitted to that court for a determination of whether the evidence is sufficient to prove the will.

B. Unattested Wills

There are several forms of wills that do not involve the formal safeguards of attested wills and that are likely to be used by persons unfamiliar with the law, particularly in haste or in ignorance. Of course, such wills have at least one basic requirement in common with attested wills: testamentary intent.

Even in the states that do not recognize unattested wills, they may be admitted to probate under statutes admitting foreign-executed wills or wills of foreign domiciliaries if certain minimum requirements are met, typically a writing signed (or subscribed) by the testator.

1. Holographic Wills

The statutes of most states authorize holographic wills, which are entirely in the handwriting of the testator. Where holographic wills are valid as such there is no requirement that they be witnessed, although a few states still impose special requirements concerning the place of keeping or the method of proving such wills.

Many of the statutes authorizing holographic wills require them to be dated. Why this requirement, which does not exist in any state for attested wills?

Although all holographic wills must be signed, only a few states require signing at the end. It is common, even among jurisdictions requiring attested wills to be subscribed, that a signature anywhere on a holographic will is sufficient if it adequately appears that the testator's name was written with an intent that it serve as his or her signature.

PROBLEMS

For purposes of the following recurring types of holographic will problems, assume that the following representative statute is in effect: "A holographic will is one that is entirely written, dated, and signed by the hand of the testator himself, and is subject to no other formality and need not be witnessed." Consider also how these problems might be resolved under the Uniform Probate Code and under your local statute if holographic wills are authorized.

4-D.   Can the instrument below be probated as the will of Abner Hatfield, who wrote all of it by hand except the italicized portions, which were printed parts of a will form?

LAST WILL AND TESTAMENT
Know all Men by These Presents: That I, Abner Hatfield *of* Piney Creek, *North Carolina, do make and publish this as my Last Will and Testament, in manner and form following.*
(1) To Ginny McCoy $5,000.
(2) My house and grounds to Clem Hatfield, because part of it's his anyway.
(3) To Maw all the rest of what's mine.

Signed this 13 *day of* June 1973. Abner Hatfield

Contrast In re Will of Parsons, 207 N.C. 584, 178 S.E. 78 (1935),[4] and Succession of Burke, 365 So. 2d 858 (La. App. 1979), with Estate of Thorn, 183 Cal. 512, 192 P. 19 (1920).

4. On the back of the document probated in the Parsons case appeared the following unexplained statement: "I want my sister-in-law, Effie King, to have J. O. Parsons."

4-E.   The following handwritten paper is offered for probate. Should it be admitted?

3-10-90

   I, Mary Jones, declare it to be my will that on my death all of my property shall go to my husband.

4-F.   In In re Richardson's Estate, 94 Cal. 63, 29 P. 484 (1892), the following handwritten letter was offered for probate by the deceased's sister, Nina. Should it have been probated?

Los Angeles
October 1, 1890

Nina:
   I wrote you yesterday, hastily. Answer my letter at once. I want to know everything about mother, and all about you, — your children. I have reached the point of perfect independence, pecuniarily. My health is probably ruined, and I want to anticipate possibilities. You and your children get everything. Your boy I want given the best of educations. I would like him to go to Harvard. I would like to have him a lawyer. Don't bring him up a prejudiced southerner, but teach honor, — make it clearer than life, and he must, with the blood in his veins, be a man. Write me. As soon as I possibly can, I will be in Savannah.

Brother

   In 1981 a cassette recording was admitted to probate as a holographic will in Alameda County, California, without contest and based on testimony identifying the decedent's voice. Cf. Nash, A Videowill: Safe and Sure, 70 A.B.A.J. 81 (Oct. 1984): "Lawyers diligently and awkwardly compile evidence of due execution where a contest is anticipated. . . . This procedure is unnecessarily difficult. One neat, compact, videocassette can contain not only the testator's dispositive scheme but also all the evidence required for it to be probated. . . . There have not yet been any cases reported of a videotape being offered for probate as a will, although the value of videotaping a will execution ceremony as supplementary evidence is being recognized. . . . It is time for the law to take the next logical step. The videotape will (or videowill) can easily fulfill the statutory requirements, protect the testator and preserve evidence better than a will." The article makes an interesting case for new legislation taking "the next logical step" — but certainly not for setting the client up as a test case under existing statutes.

ESTATE OF REED
672 P.2d 829 (Wyo. 1983)

BROWN, J. . . .

The issue here is whether a tape recorded statement made by a deceased person can be admitted to probate as a will. We agree with the trial court that it cannot. . . .

According to appellant the major difference in magnetic tape recording and hand print is that in the former writing is done through voice print while the latter is done through hand print. Appellant reasons, therefore, that in this age of advanced electronics and circuitry the tape recorder should be a method of "writing" which conforms with the holographic will statute. . . .

Where the language of a statute is plain and unambiguous and conveys a clear and definite meaning, . . . the court has no right to look for and impose another meaning. . . . We are not aware of any definition of "handwriting" [or] any authority . . . that "handwriting" includes voice prints. It seems to be stating the obvious that a voice print is not handwriting; therefore, the requirement that a holographic will be "entirely in the handwriting of the testator" has not been met in this case.

Appellant directs our attention to §2-6-105, W.S. 1977 [and to cases to the effect that] "the Intention of the testator as expressed in his will controls the legal effect of his disposition. . . . "

Section 2-6-105, supra, and the cases cited by appellant are pertinent to construction of language within a valid will. . . . We can not consider the testator's intent to justify the probate of a recorded statement that is not a valid will. An otherwise deficient will can not be made valid by showing the intent of the testator. . . .

Our attention is directed to Darley v. Ward, 28 Cal. 3d 257, 168 Cal. Rptr. 481, 617 P.2d 1113, 1115 (1980), where the court stated: "Tape recordings, properly authenticated, are admissable as 'writings.'" . . . Darley was not a will or probate case. . . .

There is [also] no indication that the definition of "handwritings" contained in Rule 1001(1) [Wyoming Rules of Evidence] was designed to change the plain meaning of handwriting in the holographic will statute. Were we to expand or modify the meaning of handwriting as required in the holographic will statute to include a tape recording, we would judicially amend the statute. This we refuse to do.

Affirmed.

2. Oral Wills

Oral wills are of two basic types: the nuncupative will, under which a person in peril of death may dispose of limited amounts of personal property; and soldiers' and sailors' wills, which also are typically restricted to personal property and sometimes to limited amounts thereof. A number of states make some provision for the probate of oral wills of one or both of these varieties.

Nuncupative wills generally must be made during the testator's last illness, before a certain number of witnesses at least one of whom was requested to bear witness to the will, and in the testator's home or place of death. In addition, some requirement usually exists regarding the time within which the will must be probated and regarding prompt reduction of the will to writing.

The typical requirements that soldiers be "in actual military service" and that sailors be "at sea" have been, as might be expected, sources of litigation in soldiers' and sailors' wills. See Page on Wills §§20.13 et seq. (Bowe-Parker rev. 1970).

C. Commentary and Comparison

LANGBEIN, THE CRUMBLING OF THE WILLS ACT: AUSTRALIANS POINT THE WAY
65 A.B.A.J. 1192 (1979)

. . . In dealing with . . . botched wills, Anglo-American courts have produced one of the cruelest chapters that survives in the common law. Purely technical violations that could in no way cast doubt on the authenticity or finality of wills are held to invalidate the offending instrument. . . .

Because this rule of strict compliance with wills act formalities produces results so harsh, sympathetic courts have . . . enabled themselves to find literal compliance in cases that in fact show defective compliance. . . .

Not surprisingly, this state of affairs has provoked discontent. Recent law school casebooks in the field have prodded students to ask whether the purposes of wills acts compel the result inflicted under the rule of literal compliance. The Uniform Probate Code of 1969 has made a contribution toward reducing the dimensions of the problem — at least, in those states that have enacted it — by reducing the number and complexity of formalities. . . . Signature and attestation are still required, but the rules about placement of signatures and presence of witnesses have been abolished.

Finally, the rule of literal compliance came under attack. Within a few months in 1974-1975, literature appeared in England, Australia, and the United States calling for the development of a purposive standard for evaluating defectively executed wills. . . .

[In 1974], the official Law Reform Committee of South Australia took

up the theme. . . . "It would seem to us that in all cases where there is a
technical failure to comply with the wills act, there should be a power
given to the court or a judge to declare that the will in question is a good
and valid testamentary document if he is satisfied that the document
does in fact represent the last will and testament of the testator." . . .

My position was summed up in the title [of my article at 88 Harv. L.
Rev. 489 (1975)]: there should be a rule of "Substantial Compliance
with the Wills Act" that would permit the proponents of a defectively
executed will to prove that the particular defect was harmless to the purposes of the wills act. Drawing on a rich literature devoted to identifying
the functions of the wills act formalities, I made the following points:

1. The wills act is meant to assure the implementation of the decedent's testamentary intention at a time when, by definition, he can no
longer be on hand to express himself. The requirement of written terms
forces the testator to leave permanent evidence of the substance of his
wishes. Signature and attestation provide evidence of the genuineness
of the instrument, and they caution the testator about the seriousness
and finality of his act. The attestation ceremony also has a protective
function: disinterested observers are supposed to prevent crooks from
deceiving or coercing the testator into making a disposition that does not
represent his true intentions. Taken together, these evidentiary, cau-
tionary and protective functions serve another end, the channeling function: when the formalities are complied with, they make testation
routine, eliminate contest, reduce probate costs and court time, and
facilitate good estate planning.

2. When, however, there has been a mechanical blunder, it does not
follow that the purposes of the wills act have been disserved. For example, if the statute calls for signature "at the end" in order to prevent
subsequent interpolation, it does not follow that in every case of misplaced signature such an event has occurred.

3. Accordingly, we could obtain all of the benefits of the wills act formal system and yet avoid so much of the hardship if the presumption of
invalidity applied to defectively executed wills were reduced from a conclusive to a rebuttable one. The proponents of a defectively executed will
should be allowed to prove what they are now entitled to presume in
cases of due execution — that the will in question expresses the decedent's true testamentary intent. They should be allowed to prove that the
defect is harmless to the purposes of the formality. In the example just
given of a misplaced signature, the proponents would bear the burden
of proving (on an ordinary preponderance-of-proof standard) that subsequent interpolation had not occurred.

4. Although the substantial compliance rule is a litigation doctrine, it
should not be feared as a potential litigation breeder. Precisely because
it is a litigation rule, it would have no place in professional estate planning. Nor would the substantial compliance doctrine attract the reliance

of amateurs. Every incentive for due execution would remain, for no testator sets out to throw his estate into litigation.

Other factors would operate to diminish the incidence and the difficulty of the litigation that would arise under the substantial compliance rule. By no means would every defectively executed instrument result in a contest. On many issues the proponents' burden of proof would be so onerous that they would forgo the trouble and expense of hopeless litigation. On certain other issues the proponents' burden would be so easy to discharge that potential contestants would not bother to litigate. . . . Indeed, it seems plausible that the substantial compliance doctrine might actually decrease the levels of probate litigation. In numerous situations, such as the "at-the-end" cases, the literal compliance rule has produced a large and contradictory case law. . . . By substituting a purposive analysis for a formal one, the substantial compliance doctrine would make the standard more predictable, and contestants would lose their incentive to prove harmless defects.

5. An equivalent substantial compliance doctrine has been working smoothly for decades in the functionally identical sphere of the major will substitute, life insurance, in those situations in which there are technical violations of the testament-like formalities for change-of-beneficiary designations. . . .

Section 9 of the Wills Act Amendment Act (No. 2) which came into effect in January, 1976, amends the South Australian Wills act to provide:

> A document purporting to embody the testamentary intentions of a deceased person shall, notwithstanding that it has not been executed with the formalities required by this Act, be deemed to be a will of the deceased person if the [court] . . . is satisfied that there can be no reasonable doubt that the deceased intended the document to constitute his will. . . .

[T]he first important lesson of the South Australian experiment appears to be — as proponents of the substantial compliance doctrine predicted — that the probate process functions well without the strict compliance rule. Future case loads may mount as potential schemers and contestants explore their new license, but the experience to date certainly is to the contrary. . . .

See also Langbein, Excusing Harmless Errors in the Execution of Wills: A Report on Australia's Tranquil Revolution in Probate Law, 87 Colum. L. Rev. 1 (1987), and Will of Ranney, 124 N.J. 1, 589 A.2d 1339 (1991), adopting a "substantial compliance" approach based on UPC §2-503 and the American Law Institute's 1990 approval of Restatement Second, Property §33.1 cmt. g (tent. draft).

5

Integration, Extrinsic Evidence, and Related Matters

Growing out of the requirements of execution are a variety of problems relating to the admissibility to probate of independent documents or separate sheets of paper not themselves displaying the signs of execution. What other writings or external facts are sufficiently "safeguarded" to be carried through the probate process by the protective formalities performed on an attested or holographic page? What are the *consequences* of permitting the "blessing" of one document's formal execution to be extended to another instrument, sometimes one that had itself been previously executed? To what extent may extrinsic evidence be introduced to clarify the meaning, or even to alter the effect, of a formally executed will? The principal problems involving the above questions are considered in this chapter: integration of separate pages into a single executed will; republication by codicil, which brings separate testamentary instruments together as a unit for at least some purposes; foreign documents being referred to and thereby incorporated into an executed instrument; independent facts that in some way affect the operation of a will; and the use of extrinsic evidence in interpreting or attacking the provisions of a will.

A. *Integration of Wills*

A will usually consists of several pages, all of which are admitted to probate as a single testamentary instrument. Occasionally a court is confronted with the question of whether several sheets of paper are to be probated together as the decedent's will. It must decide whether the pages were present at the time of execution and were then intended to be a part of the will. Integration problems are especially likely in the case of holographic wills. If a particular paper was not present at the execution or was not then intended to be part of the will, it cannot be integrated into the will for purposes of probate.

Typically the pages of a will are admitted to probate on the basis of a presumption of intent and presence resulting from their being physically fastened together. Consequently the average will presents no problem of integration. Lawyers often have their clients, and sometimes the witnesses, initial each consecutively numbered page for identification. Even in the case of unattached sheets of paper, integration may be predicated on the inference that naturally arises from the internal coherence of the provisions. Thus, a sentence may be begun at the bottom of one sheet and completed at the top of another, and the sheets may reveal a sensible pattern of disposition throughout. In such cases, then, it may readily be shown from the face of the alleged will that the separate sheets are to be integrated as a single instrument.

A more difficult problem is presented when separate sheets are offered for probate as a single will without physical attachment or coherent connection between the pages. Can the court rely on extrinsic evidence offered to prove that all of the pages were intended to be part of the will and were present at the execution? If so, how convincing must that extrinsic evidence be? Should courts be more liberal in the case of a holographic document?

In the leading case of Cole v. Webb, 220 Ky. 817, 205 S.W. 1035 (1927), two detached sheets of paper were offered for probate. The first contained dispositive provisions and named an executor, not leaving enough room for subscription and attestation. At the top of the other sheet was an attestation clause followed by the signatures of the testatrix and witnesses. Two attesting witnesses and a reputable attorney who prepared the alleged will identified the two sheets as those present before the testatrix at execution and intended as her will. On the basis of this uncontradicted testimony, the court admitted the papers to probate, observing that by the weight of authority in this country extrinsic evidence as well as internal coherence could support the integration of unattached sheets with one bearing the indicia of formal execution.

PROBLEM

5-A.   On D's death an envelope was found in his desk. On the envelope was written "Will of D," and in it were ten unattached, typewritten sheets of paper folded together lengthwise and numbered from 1 to 10 in what appears to be the same ink as that used for the testator's signature on the last page. These sheets were not all typed on the same typewriter, and on each of the first nine sheets was typed but a single, self-contained provision, the ninth being a disposition of the residue of the estate. Page 10 was signed by D and three witnesses, each of whom, after identifying his own signature and D's, now offers to testify (1) that he observed the facts of a proper execution and the signing of the sheet numbered 10 and (2) that a stack of papers like the one in question was before D at the time and was declared by D to be his will. No specific identification of pages 1 through 9 is possible. How would you argue for and against the admission of the testimony of these witnesses? If this evidence is admitted, how would you argue against the probate of these papers? In connection with this problem, consider the *Maginn* cases, infra; if these were the only integration cases in your jurisdiction, how would you argue in behalf of the proponents of the alleged will? Would a statutory provision like UPC §2-503 be helpful?

Should it matter in the decision of this problem that, instead of being typed, the pages in question were all written in the handwriting of *D* but with different colored ink appearing on different pages? See Re Sleeper, 129 Me. 194, 151 A. 150 (1930), 71 A.L.R. 518, 29 Mich. L. Rev. 266, 40 Yale L.J. 144.

MAGINN'S ESTATE
278 Pa. 89, 122 A. 264 (1923)

KEPHART, J. . . .

In the present case we have seven loose pages [found in an envelope], fastened by a sliding clip, physically laid together as a will. The testator's name appeared on the [top] page in signature, with those of the subscribing witnesses. The other pages followed. [The bottom sheet appeared to be an intended first page, beginning the will.] One might take any of the pages, after what may be called the proper first page, and omit it from the collection, and the balance would make a complete will. Or one might substitute, interpolate, or entirely withdraw pages, without in the least destroying the symmetry of the remaining papers. Held together as they were, the leaves could be slipped out without leaving the slightest mark on them. There was absolutely nothing in them, no relation or recital, by which to indicate they were connected one to the other, except possibly two of the smaller nondispositive papers, and they in very minor matters. Standing alone, the pages contained no words of a testamentary character, except the last, and the same pages could be used in any other will, and it would be just as logical. . . .

To sustain as a will this collection of papers not only opens the door to fraud of the most aggravated character, but strikes down every protection thrown about a decedent's estate. It would encourage heirs or persons evilly inclined to employ every available means to get possession of a will and (acting under our decision, if these papers are found as a will) proceed to adjust it to their satisfaction. As stated by Mr. Chief Justice Mitchell in Swire's Estate, 225 Pa. 188, 191, 192, 73 A. 1110, 1111, reviewing Heise v. Heise, 31 Pa. 246, and other cases:

> "Nor should we lose sight of the mischiefs which existed at the time when it (the statute) was enacted; mischiefs which it was designed to remedy. Among these, none was more serious than the facility with which

unfinished papers, mere inchoate expressions of intention, were admitted to probate as valid wills of decedents. Letters, memoranda, mere notes unsigned, which were entirely consistent with a half formed purpose, and which may have been thrown aside, and never intended to be operative, were rescued from their abandonment, proven as wills, and allowed to prevail as dispositions of property which there was much reason to believe the decedent never intended. It was to remedy this mischief that the act of 1893 provided that every will should be signed at the 'end thereof,' that thus, by his signature in that place, the testator should show that his testamentary purpose was consummated, and that the instrument was complete." . . . The purposes of the act of 1893 were accuracy in the transmission of the testator's wishes, the authentication of the instrument transmitting them, the identification of the testator, and certainty as to his completed testamentary purpose. . . .

As stated at the beginning of this opinion, it might have been testator's intention to write some sort of a will, but he has not complied with the law. As all the pages between the beginning and the end may have been, so far as we know, written after attestation, and as they are not connected by their internal sense, the papers cannot be sustained as a will. . . .

MAGINN'S ESTATE
281 Pa. 514, 127 A. 79 (1924)

WALLING, J.

This appeal is from a decree of the orphans' court setting aside the probate of three separate typewritten sheets or pages as the last will of the late Daniel Maginn of Pittsburgh. The three pages so rejected are a part of seven, the probate of which was set aside by this court in Maginn's Estate, 278 Pa. 89. . . .

To entitle separate loose sheets of paper to be probated as a will they must be identified by their internal sense. As stated in Seiter's Estate, 265 Pa. 202, 108 A. 614:

A will may be made on separate pieces of paper, but when so made they must be connected by their internal sense, by coherence or adaptation of parts, to constitute a will. The order of connection must appear upon the face of the will, it cannot be established by extrinsic evidence; and it must be a will executed as directed by the act of assembly. . . .

Here appellant's case fails, for there is no internal sense connecting the first sheet with the second, or the second with the third, or the first with the third. There is no reference or recital to indicate they are connected the one with the other. The sheets are not numbered, and it is reasonably certain the second of the three sheets did not originally join the third, for, as found after Maginn's death, four sheets came between them. How then can the three, having no internal connection, be probated as a will? At best they express but a fragment of the testamentary intent, while one omitted page entirely modifies a $5,000 bequest contained in those probated. The three pages do not disclose the testator's completed testamentary purpose. . . . The will on its face would be just as complete with the second page omitted and that page would fit just as well in any other will. . . .

It would be unsafe to probate a single page of a will, which on its face disclosed other pages, as the one might be modified by the others. For example, a clause appointing executors might be modified by another requiring them to give bond or serve without compensation.

Undoubtedly there may be a case where certain provisions of a will are valid and others invalid, in which the former may be probated and the latter not (40 Cyc. 1080); but here . . . it was purely arbitrary to drop out some and offer the others for probate. To permit this to be done would expose estates to all the perils which our former decision is intended to guard against. . . .

The decree is affirmed, and appeal dismissed, at the costs of the estate.

KEPHART, J. (dissenting).

Without undue discussion, it is my opinion that at least the first and last pages offered for probate were so connected by their internal sense as to express and constitute the last will of Daniel Maginn. For this reason I would probate these two pages.

SCHAFFER, J. I join in this dissent.

B. Republication by Codicil

Typically, a codicil is executed for the purpose of adding to or modifying an existing will without entirely revoking it. Thus, a codicil is normally a supplement to a will. The codicil itself must be executed with the statutory formalities of a will. A codicil may, rather than merely supplementing an effective will, serve to revive a revoked will or to validate an instrument that had been defectively executed. The revival of revoked wills is considered in Chapter 6, and the effect of a codicil on a defective instrument or on a defective addition to a will is considered as an aspect of incorporation by reference later in this chapter. The latter is properly a problem of incorporation by reference rather than one of republication, despite the tendency of courts to confuse them.

The effect of a codicil on the operation of a valid and subsisting will should be considered in light of the English law under the Statute of Wills, 1540, under which a will operated only on lands owned at its execution. Land acquired after execution of a will would not pass thereunder, but if a codicil were subsequently executed it was said to "republish" the will as of the date of the codicil. Thus, the will would speak as of the date of the codicil, and a residuary clause or a clause devising "all of my lands" would operate on land acquired between the execution of the will and the codicil.

Today, wills are clearly ambulatory in character in that they operate on the testator's property as it exists at his death without regard to when it was acquired. Thus, wills are said to speak as of the date of death. On the other hand, in *interpreting* a will, it is generally to be read as of the date of execution. Therefore, although a will speaks at the date of death, the meaning of what is spoken is generally judged on the basis of conditions existing at the time of execution. Under the doctrine of republication a codicil is seen as updating the will, which is normally deemed to have been executed anew at the date of the codicil. For many purposes, then, a will and its codicils are a testamentary unit brought together or "republished" under the latest execution. This process of updating may affect the interpretation or even the validity of portions of the will or prior codicils.

How literally is republication to be taken? Mechanical application of such a concept would be destructive of intention in certain cases, although in other contexts the effect of republication would be salutary. Consider the proper limits of the doctrine of republication by codicil as you examine the following problems.

PROBLEMS

5-B.   *T* and his brother, *B,* were the sole and equal shareholders of B&T Company. When *T* executed his will five years ago, his daughter, *D,* was already a successful physician, and his son, *S,* was finishing college with the intention of going to work for the B&T Company. *T*'s will provided: "All of the stock I now own in B&T Company I leave to *S.*" A bequest of $100,000 was made to *D,* and the residue of the estate was left to *T*'s wife, *W. B* was named executor.

Two years ago *B* died, and *T* purchased the entire interest of *B*'s estate in B&T Company for $130,000. About three months ago, *T* was hospitalized. Realizing that a new executor should be named to replace *B, T* executed a codicil naming *X* Bank & Trust Company executor and died two weeks later leaving a net estate of $500,000. To what is *S* entitled?

5-C.   Assume that, in addition to the facts in the above problem, *T*'s original will contained a bequest of $25,000 to *Y* church. Assume further that in the three years before *T*'s death a child, *C,* had been born to *T* and *W.* The relevant statutes include a restriction against all charitable bequests in wills executed within one month of death and a pretermitted heir provision protecting issue born after the execution of a will. How should the estate be distributed? On the pretermitted heir issue, see Azcunce v. Estate of Azcunce, 586 So. 2d 1216 (Fla. App. 1991), and ensuing action by unsuccessful "pretermission" claimant and personal representative against the drafting attorneys for malpractice (recovering only fees paid by testator) in Espinosa v. Sparber, Shevin, et al., 586 So. 2d 1221 (Fla. App. 1991).

C. *Incorporation by Reference*

Papers that cannot be "integrated" into a will because they were not present at the execution may, in most states, be given effect as a part of the will of a testator under the doctrine of incorporation by reference under appropriate circumstances. A few states refuse to permit incorporation by reference on the general ground that the incorporated instrument lacks the required formal safeguards against fraud.

The requirements for incorporating unexecuted writings by reference are thought to replace the safeguards of execution. These requirements are generally stated by the courts to be, in substance:

1. The extrinsic writing must in fact be in existence when the will is executed;
2. The will must refer to it as being in existence when the will is executed;
3. The intent to incorporate must appear in the will; and
4. The extrinsic writing must be identified with reasonable certainty and must conform to the description in the will.

How strictly these requirements are adhered to is quite a different question. The attitudes of courts have varied from case to case, even within a single jurisdiction. For example, In re Young's Estate, 123 Cal. 337, 342, 55 P. 1011, 1012 (1899), states that before "an extrinsic document may be so incorporated, the description of it in the will itself must be so clear, explicit, and unambiguous as to leave its identity free from doubt." With this, compare Clark v. Greenhalge, infra.

PROBLEM

5-D. On August 8, 1990, Howard Elliston executed a typewritten instrument purporting to be a will bequeathing all of his estate equally to Jones and Smith. However, at probate it has been proven that the execution of the instrument was fatally defective. Also offered for probate is a valid holographic instrument, which appears as follows:

Codicil to My Last Will and Testament. I hereby bequeath $10,000 to the Eastside Orphanage and $2,000 to my housekeeper, Nellie Wolf.

Howard Elliston
Campville, Sept. 18, 1992

Can anything be done in behalf of Jones and Smith, who are not Elliston's heirs at law? Cf. Estate of Erbach, 41 Wis. 2d 335, 164 N.W.2d 238 (1969). But cf. Estate of Norton, 330 N.C. 378, 410 S.E.2d 484 (1991).

UNIFORM PROBATE CODE

§2-510. *Incorporation by Reference.*   A writing in existence when a will is executed may be incorporated by reference if the language of the will manifests this intent and describes the writing sufficiently to permit its identification.

CLARK v. GREENHALGE
411 Mass. 410, 582 N.E.2d 949 (1991)

[Helen Nesmith's 1977 will named her cousin, F.T. Greenhalge, as executor and as recipient of all her tangible personal property, except that he is to "distribute such of the tangible property to and among such persons as I may designate by a memorandum left by me and known to him, or in accordance with my known wishes." With Greenhalge's assistance, Nesmith had earlier drafted a dated document, entitled "MEMORANDUM," listing 49 specific bequests of her tangible personal property. In 1976 she had modified that list by interlineations, additions, and deletions. Ms. Nesmith also made a later series of entries in a notebook under the title "List to be given, Helen Nesmith 1979." In 1980 she executed two codicils to her 1977 will, amending certain bequests, deleting others, and ratifying the will in all other respects. Following her death in 1986, Greenhalge, as executor, distributed Ms. Nesmith's property in accordance with the will and codicils and the 1972 memorandum as amended in 1976. He refused, however, to comply with a 1979 provision in the notebook purporting to bequeath a valuable painting to Virginia Clark, who commenced an action seeking to compel him to do so.]

NOLAN, J. . . .

The probate judge found that . . . [the] notebook qualified as a "memorandum" . . . within the meaning of Article Fifth of Helen Nesmith's will . . . [and that it] was in existence at the time of the execution of the 1980 codicils, which ratified the language of Article Fifth in its entirety. Based on these findings, the judge ruled that the notebook was incorporated by reference into the terms of the will . . . [and] awarded the painting to Ms. Clark. . . .

A properly executed will may incorporate by reference into its provisions any "document or paper not so executed . . . if it was in existence at the time of the execution of the will, and is identified by clear and satisfactory proof as the paper referred to therein." . . . The parties agree that the document entitled "memorandum," dated 1972 and amended in 1976, was . . . incorporated by reference into the terms of the will. . . .

The parties do not agree, however, as to whether the documentation contained in the notebook, dated 1979, similarly was incorporated into the will. . . . First, Greenhalge contends that the judge wrongly concluded that the notebook could be considered a "memorandum" within the meaning of Article Fifth, because it is not specifically identified as a "memorandum." Such a literal interpretation of the language and meaning of Article Fifth is not appropriate.

"The 'cardinal rule of the interpretation of wills, to which all other rules must bend, is that the intention of the testator shall prevail, provided it is consistent with the rules of law.'" . . . The intention of the testator is ascertained through consideration of the [language of the will] . . . as well as the circumstances existing at the time of the execution of the will. . . . The circumstances existing at the time of the execution of a codicil to a will are equally relevant, because the codicil serves to ratify the language in the will which has not been altered or affected by the terms of the codicil.

. . . The appellant argues, however, that the notebook cannot take effect . . . because the language of Article Fifth limits its application to "a" memorandum, or the 1972 memorandum. We reject this strict construction of Article Fifth. The language of Article Fifth does not preclude the existence of more than one memorandum which serves the intended purpose of that article. . . . To construe narrowly Article Fifth and to exclude the possibility that Helen Nesmith drafted the notebook contents as "a memorandum" under that article, would undermine our long-standing policy of interpreting wills in a manner which best carries out the known wishes of the testatrix. . . . [The testimony of witnesses also] supports the conclusion that Helen Nesmith intended that the bequests in her notebook be accorded the same power and effect as those contained in the 1972 memorandum. . . .

The appellant also contends that . . . the evidence established, at most, that [Nesmith] intended to bequeath the painting to Clark, and not that she intended to incorporate the notebook into her will. . . . The judge found that Helen Nesmith drafted the notebook contents with the expectation that Greenhalge would distribute the property accordingly. . . . It is clear that the judge fairly construed the evidence in reaching the determination that Helen Nesmith intended the notebook to serve as a memorandum of her wishes as contemplated under Article Fifth of her will. . . .

Judgment affirmed.

Was the notebook in the above case actually "in existence" at the time the will was executed? The court's implicit conclusion that it was is not novel. See, e.g., Simon v. Grayson, 15 Cal. 2d 531, 102 P.2d 1081 (1940), which involved a letter that was not in existence when the will was executed and bore a date subsequent to that of the will. The court noted, however, that "the letter was in existence at the time the codicil to the will was executed" and that "the execution of a codicil has the effect of republishing the will" so that the "letter was an 'existing document' within the incorporation rule [if it] can be satisfactorily identified as the one referred to in the will." See also Smith v. Weitzal, 338 S.W.2d 628 (Tenn. App. 1960).

Compare, however, Kellom v. Beverstock, 100 N.H. 329, 126 A.2d 127 (1956), where the court refused to apply the doctrine of incorporation by reference because "words of futurity" were used in referring to a list made up before the execution of a codicil but after the execution of the will, which stated: "I shall leave a list of [property], indicating to whom I wish to leave those items." And see the English statement of the rule: "[A] document will not be incorporated if the will refers to it in future terms, e.g., 'as I shall direct in a small memorandum' . . . even though the document is in fact in existence at the time of the will." Tiley, A Casebook on Equity and Succession 414-415 (1968).

Does an incorporated writing become a "physical" part of the incorporating instrument by analogy to integration? Courts are not in agreement whether the incorporated document is itself to be probated, thereby becoming a part of the public record, possibly contrary to the purpose of its incorporation. Can a nonholographic writing be incorporated into a holographic will? Again the courts are not in agreement. The modern trend seems to be against treating the incorporated writing as a physical part of the will. See, e.g., Johnson v. Johnson, 279 P.2d 928 (Okla. 1954) (valid incorporation of nonholographic writings into holographic will).

The primary present-day interest in incorporation by reference is in the area of "pouring over" from a will into an inter vivos trust. This subject is taken up in a subsequent chapter. Section D of this chapter is also relevant for purposes of the later study of "pour-overs."

D. *Reference to Facts of Independent Significance*

It is common — in fact generally accepted without question — that certain details of a will are to be supplied by looking outside the will. Descriptions of persons or property often require resort to extrinsic facts. When these facts are peculiarly within the control of the testator it is possible that a reference to them may be challenged as permitting unexecuted completion or variation of his will. Under many circumstances reference to extrinsic facts is not only quite safe but borders on sheer necessity if wills are to have an ambulatory character. Today no one would question the formal sufficiency of a disposition of the residue of an estate in equal shares to the testator's children who survive him. Yet the content of the "residue" depends on events, including acts of the testator, that occur unaccompanied by testamentary formalities after the will has been executed. The same is true of determining the testator's surviving children in the above disposition.

Basically, the identity of persons and property may be determined by reference to events and to acts of the testator and others, provided these events and acts have "independent significance." It is generally required that such events or acts have a *substantial significance apart from their impact on the will;* that is, that they be the kind of thing that would occur without regard to their effect on the will. Of course, many cases will be difficult to resolve by this basic rule.

In First National Bank v. Klein, 255 Ala. 505, 234 So. 2d 42 (1970), the testatrix left property to her son, providing that if he predeceased her the property should go to the beneficiaries of "his last will." Recognizing that incorporation by reference was not appropriate when the testatrix referred to any will the son might leave, the court upheld the disposition on the ground that the effect of the son's will on his own estate gave it a substantial significance independent of the will of the testatrix. The court also noted that the fact that another will was involved was an adequate safeguard for the mother's bequest.

PROBLEMS

5-E.   What is the effect of the following provisions?
"I bequeath $5,000 to
(a) "each person who may be a son-in-law or daughter-in-law of mine at my death."
(b) "the person who is my housekeeper at my death."
(c) "each of the persons listed on the paper I shall place with this will."
"I bequeath to *X*
(a) "all of the household furnishings in my apartment at my death."
(b) "the contents of my personal checking account."
(c) "all of the securities in my safe-deposit box."
(d) "the contents of the top drawer of my desk, and I bequeath the contents of the bottom drawer to *Y*."
5-F.   The temptation is great, especially for persons not trained in the law, to try to dispose of tools, kitchen utensils, personal effects, and the family floor clock to friends and relatives by casual promises or informally drawn and revised lists. How might you handle the problem of elderly clients who cannot make up their minds about the division of their personal effects, even after you have drawn their wills? Assume

these personally meaningful items have little monetary value — probably less than the time expected of you in keeping the wills up to date. The list of items and recipients is a long one. The clients telephone you frequently, possibly several times during a particularly thoughtful month, to make changes. What do you suggest? Do you approve of the novel provision of Uniform Probate Code §2-513?

UNIFORM PROBATE CODE

§2-512. *Events of Independent Significance.* A will may dispose of property by reference to acts and events that have significance apart from their effect upon the dispositions made by the will, whether they occur before or after the execution of the will or before or after the testator's death. The execution or revocation of another individual's will is such an event.

§2-513. *Separate Writing Identifying Devise of Certain Types of Tangible Personal Property.* Whether or not the provisions relating to holographic wills apply, a will may refer to a written statement or list to dispose of items of tangible personal property not otherwise specifically disposed of by the will, other than money. To be admissible under this section as evidence of the intended disposition, the writing must be signed by the testator and must describe the items and the devisees with reasonable certainty. The writing may be referred to as one to be in existence at the time of the testator's death; it may be prepared before or after the execution of the will; it may be altered by the testator after its preparation; and it may be a writing that has no significance apart from its effect on the dispositions made by the will.

E.   *Extrinsic Evidence*

1.   **Introduction to Interpretation**

The Restatement of Property, in §241, comment e, rejects the traditional distinction between *interpretation* and *construction*. Nevertheless, the distinction is often made and is often useful, even though it is unrealistic to view the two as separate or isolated processes. "Interpretation . . . seems to be used to denote the process of ascertaining the meaning of language used through a search for the intent of the parties to the instrument. Interpretation, therefore, is essentially a factual, as distinguished from a legal, concept. A rule of construction is defined as a rule that attaches a given legal consequence to the words employed 'unless a contrary intent is shown by admissible evidence.'" Note, 72 Harv. L.

Rev. 1154, 1155 (1959). Thus, it is sometimes said that construction supplies a meaning where interpretation has failed to discover an intended meaning through examination of admissible evidence.

A variety of "rules" are regularly encountered in statutes and judicial opinions purporting to govern the process of interpretation. We start with the often repeated principle that the ultimate object of the process is to discover the intent of the testator and that all rules of construction yield to that intent when it can be discovered. This quest for intention, however, must be considered in light of other widely recognized principles. It is often stated, for example, that courts are seeking the meaning of what is said in the will rather than the subjective intent of the testator. Consider the often quoted dictum of Judge Learned Hand in Boal v. Metropolitan Museum of Art, 292 F. 303, 304 (S.D.N.Y. 1923): "[I]t is the court's duty to find out the legal effect of documents and to construe the language of the testator, without regard to his unexpressed intent. . . . I have to do with a situation quite outside of anything which the testator had in contemplation, and it is therefore obvious that any solution is bound to be verbal and indeed formal. Yet while it is idle to speculate upon what he personally would have done had he been able to look ahead, courts have always permitted themselves, within limits, to impute to testators an intent which they could not foresee."

Before studying specific problem areas, examine the following representative quotations and keep them in mind as you study the problems and cases in the rest of this chapter.

"A testator's intent, unless unlawful, shall prevail; that intent shall be ascertained from a consideration of (a) all the language contained in his will, and (b) his scheme of distribution, and (c) the circumstances surrounding him at the time he made his will, and (d) the existing facts; and (e) canons of construction will be resorted to only if the language is ambiguous or conflicting or the testator's intent is for any reason uncertain." In re Carter's Estate, 435 Pa. 492, 496, 257 A.2d 843, 845 (1969).

"The will must be considered in its entirety to determine the testator's intent and, to the extent possible, that construction should be adopted which will give effect to all language employed; no technical rule of construction, however, will be permitted to interfere with ascertaining the testator's real intention." Landmark Trust Co. v. Aitken, 587 N.E.2d 1076, 1082 (Ill. App. 1992). Compare In re Gulbenkian's Will, 9 N.Y.2d 363, 370, 173 N.E.2d 481, 483 (1961): "[W]e may . . . glean the testator's dominant purpose 'from a sympathetic reading of the will *as an entirety* and in view of all the facts and circumstances under which the provisions of the will were framed' . . . and this purpose must prevail regardless of the fact that a literal interpretation might yield an inconsistent meaning because of the language and format employed."

"In determining the testator's intention, if no uncertainty or ambiguity exists, his meaning must be ascertained from the language of his will: it is not what the Court thinks he might or would have said in the existing circumstances, or even what the Court thinks he meant to say, but what is the meaning of his words." In re Ginter's Estate, 398 Pa. 440, 445, 158 A.2d 789, 792 (1960). "In determining the true intent and meaning of the testator we must look first to the will, and if the language therein is ambiguous we may look to surrounding facts and circumstances." Schubel v. Bonacker, 331 S.W.2d 552, 554 (Mo. 1960).

"[W]here a will is clear, definite and free from ambiguity, its provisions cannot be limited, extended or explained by resort to parol testimony." In re Bridge's Estate, 41 Wash. 916, 925, 253 P.2d 394, 399 (1953). "Extrinsic evidence is not admissible to determine the intent of the testator as expressed in his will unless there is a latent ambiguity. Such evidence is not admissible to determine the intent of the testator where the ambiguity is patent and not latent. A patent ambiguity is one which appears upon the face of the instrument. It must be removed by construction according to settled principles and not by evidence, and the intention of the testator is to be determined from the four corners of the will itself. . . . [If] 'nothing appears within its four corners to resolve or clarify the ambiguity, the words must be given their generally accepted literal and grammatical meaning.'" Jacobsen v. Farnham, 155 Neb. 776, 780, 54 N.W.2d 917, 920 (1952). Similarly, with respect to the terms of inter vivos trusts, it has been stated: "Long-settled rules of construction preclude an attempt to divine a settlor's intention by looking first to extrinsic evidence. . . . Rather, the trust instrument is to be construed as written and the settlor's intention determined solely from the unambiguous language of the instrument itself. . . . It is only where the court determines the words of the trust instrument to be ambiguous that it may properly resort to extrinsic evidence. . . . The rationale underlying this basic rule of construction is that the words used in the instrument itself are the best evidence of the intention of the drafter of the document." Mercury Bay Boating v. San Diego Yacht Club, 76 N.Y.2d 256, 267, 557 N.E.2d 87, 93 (1990).

It is stated in 3 Restatement of Property §242: "The judicially ascertained intent . . . is normally determined by the language employed . . . read as an entirety and in the light of the circumstances of its formulation." But see also Comment c: "The necessity for the reading of a deed or will as a whole does not, however, justify a construction which relies solely on its language and excludes evidence as to the circumstances of its formulation. Such an exclusion is often the result of the so-called 'single plain meaning rule,' which unduly stresses the controlling force of the ordinary meanings of the words employed. This rule, in so far as it causes such exclusion, is disapproved, since language is so colored by the circumstances of its formulation that the exclusion of otherwise admissible evidence as to such circumstances is never justified."

4 Page on Wills §32.9 (Bowe-Parker, 1961): "With the exception of cases in which language is used which seems intelligible and consistent, but which applies equally to two or more persons or things [called 'equivocations'], evidence of a testator's direct declarations of intent [is] inadmissible to show testator's actual intention, apart from . . . language which is used by him in the will itself." In re Fries' Estate, 221 Cal. App. 2d 725, 730, 34 Cal. Rptr. 749, 753 (1963): "[But this] proscription does not apply to oral declarations of a testator which are offered for the purpose of showing his state of mind with respect to the meaning of particular language used by him in a will which is ambiguous." See also Estate of Taff, 63 Cal. App. 3d 319, 326-327, 133 Cal. Rptr. 737, 741 (1976), in which a statute authorized various uncertainties of meaning to be clarified by extrinsic evidence, expressly "excluding the oral declarations of the testator as to his intentions." Yet the court noted that "it has long been held that oral declarations made by a testator to the scrivener of the will are admissible to resolve a latent ambiguity" because this statutory prohibition applies to mere incidental fugitive utterances or declarations of intent as distinguished from specific instructions as to testamentary disposition.

When it was argued in the *Taff* case, supra, that another section and case law "require a trial court to interpret technical words used in a will drawn by an attorney in their technical sense" and that "technical words in a will are to be taken in their technical sense, unless the context clearly indicates a contrary intention, or unless it satisfactorily appears that the will was drawn solely by the testator, and that he was unacquainted with such technical sense," the court responded that the "presumption of technical meaning . . . is subordinate to the dominant purpose of finding and effecting the intent of the testator; the presumption is an aid to be used in ascertaining that intent, not a tool by which the court frustrates the testator's objectives." Compare: "[N]ontechnical words are to be taken in their ordinary, proper, and grammatical sense unless it clearly appears that the testator intended to use them in another sense and that sense can be ascertained . . . ; technical words are to be given their correct meaning unless the contrary appears from the context . . . , although in determining whether such words were used in their technical sense the knowledge and skill of the draftsman in the use of such terms may be considered." Grace v. Continental Trust Co., 169 Md. 653, 657, 182 A. 573, 575 (1936).

"[A] construction of a will leading to a partial intestacy is not favored and will not be adopted unless plainly required by the language." Holmes v. Welch, 314 Mass. 106, 109, 49 N.E.2d 461, 463 (1943).

"Where a will contains provisions which are apparently inconsistent or repugnant, every effort must be made so to construe the instrument as to harmonize the conflicting words, phrases, or clauses." Wigglesworth v. Smith, 311 Ky. 366, 370, 224 S.W.2d 177, 179 (1949). "[W]hen there is an irreconcilable conflict between two clauses of a will pertaining to the same subject matter, the latter clause will prevail." In re Smith's Estate, 75 So. 2d 686, 688 (Fla. 1954). However, "[w]here an estate or interest is given in one clause of a will in clear and decisive terms, the interest so given cannot be taken away or cut down by . . . any subsequent words that are not so clear and decisive as the words of the clause giving the interest or estate." Springer v. Vickers, 259 Ala. 465, 469, 66 So. 2d 740, 744 (1953).

In re Helfman's Estate, 193 Cal. App. 2d 652, 655, 14 Cal. Rptr. 482, 484 (1961): "[W]here no extrinsic evidence is introduced or where there is no conflict in such evidence, the construction of an uncertain provision in a will is a question of law on which the independent judgment of the appellate court is to be exercised. Under such circumstances, there is no issue of fact and it is the duty of an appellate court to make the final determination in accordance with the applicable principles of law. . . .

"One of the most basic of all the rules relating to interpretation is that a 'will is to be construed according to the intention of the testator.' In arriving at such construction, each case ordinarily must depend upon its own particular set of facts. While respondent suggests application of the rule that unless a different intention finds expression in the will it should be construed as applying to and disposing of the estate in its condition at the time of the death of the testator, it is also true that a testator's intent is to be determined as of the date of the execution of the instrument. Thus both rules must be applied together. The court in applying the will as of the date of the testator's death, attempts to ascertain the intent of the testator by the language of the will as understood by the testator at the time he wrote it, related to the circumstances then present."

For a comprehensive analysis of some related issues, see Henderson, Mistake and Fraud in Wills, 47 B.U.L. Rev. 309, 461 (1967).

PROBLEM

5-G.   T's will bequeaths: "(1) All of my property to my wife, W, without bond to do with as she pleases, to sell or transfer any or all of it. (2) If there is anything left at her death it is to go equally to my brother B and sister S."

What are the rights of W in T's property, and how would you argue the case for her? What might B and S claim, and how would you argue their case? See the quotations from Wigglesworth v. Smith, In re Smith's Estate, and Springer v. Vickers, supra. On this much-litigated question, contrast Gardner v. Worrell, 201 Va. 355, 111 S.E.2d 285 (1959) (finding interests like those of B and S repugnant to and ineffective to cut down an "absolute" interest comparable to W's), and In re Wilson's Estate, 367 Mich. 143, 116 N.E.2d 215 (1962) (first bequest absolute), with Frederick v. Frederick, 355 Mass. 662, 247 N.E.2d 361 (1969) (upholding remainder), and Johnson v. Waldrop, 256 S.C. 372, 182 S.E.2d 730 (1971) (finding life estate and power to consume, followed by a valid remainder). A classic in the area is Fox v. Snow, 6 N.J. 12, 76 A.2d 877 (1950) (remainder impermissible), with widely noted dissenting opinion by Chief Justice Vanderbilt.

2. Mistake: Misdescription and Omission

It is generally accepted doctrine that mistakes resulting in an omission are without remedy because a court will neither probate what is not in the will nor reform the will to supply what has been omitted. A constructive trust might conceivably be imposed in a particularly appealing case, but at present in most states the only real hope of the omitted beneficiary is through *construction.* Although it has also been said that an omitted provision cannot be supplied by construction, this statement goes too far. For example, there is the common case of the implied remainder to the issue of *A* where property is devised "to *A* for life and if he die without issue, to *B.*" See L. Simes, Future Interests §100 (2d ed. 1966). If it is possible to "imply" a provision solely from what is in the will, authority exists under which a court might provide the remedy and call it construction. Cf. Leach, Perpetuities: Cy Pres on the March, in Perspectives of Law: Essays for Austin W. Scott 215 (1964). Contrast, for example, two cases decided the same day and reported almost simultaneously from the Surrogate's Court, New York County: In re Calabi's Estate, 196 N.Y.S.2d 443 (1959) (refusing even to admit evidence of the purpose of trusts *C* and *D* where the residue of the estate was to be divided into four lettered trusts but with terms supplied only for trusts *A* and *B*); In re Dorson's Estate, 196 N.Y.S.2d 344 (1959) (inadvertent omission of several lines of a will remedied by "construction" where the terms of residuary trusts Fund *A* and Fund *B* were identical but for three lines of dispositive provisions omitted regarding Fund *B*).

Far more common are mistakes in the description of property or persons. In studying the following material, consider *under what circumstances* and then *by what evidence* such mistakes may be shown. Keep in mind (1) the "established proposition" that a description that accurately applies to persons or property cannot be shown to have been intended to apply to persons or property not accurately described and (2) the common dicta — occasionally codified — that even when extrinsic evidence may be admitted, the testator's own oral, direct declarations of intention are not admissible for most purposes.

PROBLEMS

5-H.   Mrs. A. L. Gilkey's holographic will has been admitted to probate and appears as follows:

> My brother-in-law T. O. Gilkey owns a half interest in all of my livestock, and at my death I will him all of my interests in them, and also all my personal property. This is my will. T. O. Gilkey executor without bond. 8-17-90.

> (Sig.) *Mrs. A. L. Gilkey*

Mrs. Gilkey, a widow, left an estate consisting of a modest farm, machinery, livestock, some cash, and personal effects. Her sole heir at law was her sister, Bertha Chambers. T. O. Gilkey claims all the property of Mrs. Gilkey, including the farm. Bertha believes that the farm goes to her. How would you argue on behalf of each? Cf. Gilkey v. Chambers, 146 Tex. 355, 207 S.W.2d 70 (1948). For an extreme case holding "monies" to include real estate, see Estate of Breckenridge, 56 Ill. App. 3d 128, 371 N.E.2d 286 (1978). See also Sandy v. Mouhot, 1 Ohio St. 3d 143, 438 N.E.2d 117 (1982), holding "all of my personal property and household goods" to include *intangible* personal property even though the will also contained a residuary clause referring to "the rest, residue and remainder of my property, real, personal, and mixed."

5-I.   Effie Smith's will, executed five years before her death, has just been admitted to probate. The provision in dispute is Article II, which reads: "I bequeath to Al Jones my 100 shares of General Dynamics stock, as an expression of the very great appreciation I feel for the kindness shown to me by Al and his wife since the death of my husband seven years ago. They have been like son and daughter to me."

The residue of her estate was left "to my beloved son, John," who has been a successful lawyer in a distant state since graduating from law school thirty years ago. Jones was named executor.

Jones has come to you for assistance. He calls your attention to the fact that General Dynamics stock is now selling for about $60 a share, and that he is certain Effie meant to leave him 100 shares of General Ceramics stock.

Jones tells you that when he returned from military service he wanted to start a ceramics business. His neighbor, George Smith (Effie Smith's husband), seeing a promising future for Jones and wishing to help him, bought 100 shares of the $100 par value stock in General Ceramics, a corporation formed by Jones. In order to acquire control of the business Jones had borrowed money from other sources to buy the other 101 shares that his corporation was to issue. Today the General Ceramics stock has a value of about $500 a share. Jones insists that Effie intended to leave him this General Ceramics stock, which she had inherited from her husband.

Effie's net estate is valued at slightly over $175,000. Included in her estate are the 100 shares of General Ceramics (inventoried at $50,000), a house valued at $75,000, some personal effects, and about $45,000 in listed securities, among which are included 120 shares of General Dynamics (inventoried at $7,200).

Jones tells you that Effie, who died at age 78, had been somewhat senile in her late years, although no one questions her testamentary capacity or suggests the existence of undue influence. He also states that Effie had lived on a pension and had paid almost no attention to business or investment matters either before or after George's death, relying almost completely on her accountant and Jones to handle her affairs since her husband's death. George Smith's will is brought to your attention by Jones; it provided that, if Effie (who took everything under the will) had failed to survive George, the General Ceramics stock would go to Jones, while everything else was to go to George's son, John. Effie's accountant also tells you that Effie had stated she intended to leave Jones "all the bonds I own in his [Jones's] company." At no time did Effie actually own any *bonds* of General Ceramics.

How would you argue and try to prove the case in behalf of Jones? What additional facts would you want to determine in your investigation, and why? Would you advise him to accept John Smith's settlement offer of $30,000? Why? As to the manner in which the expenses of construction proceedings would be borne, see 4 Page on Wills §31.13 (Bowe-Parker, 1961).

BRECKHEIMER v. KRAFT
133 Ill. App. 2d 410, 273 N.E.2d 468 (1971)

[Clara Johnson's will, executed in April 1965, nine days before her death, bequeathed her residuary estate equally to her "nephew Raymond Schneikert and Mabel Schneikert his wife." At the time the will was executed, Raymond's wife's name was Evelyn, and his former wife, then named Mabel Reihs, had remarried. Relatives of Clara claimed the residue on the ground that the residuary bequest was invalid for misnomer; Raymond and Evelyn claimed the residue; and Mabel claimed half of the residue.]

DEMPSEY, J. . . .

Since the ambiguity is disclosed by extrinsic evidence it may be removed by such evidence. To assist the court in ascertaining what the language in the will means, it is proper in such an inquiry to take into consideration the facts and circumstances surrounding the testator at the time the will was executed and his relation with his family and the beneficiaries named in the will. . . .

At the hearing Mabel Reihs testified that . . . [f]rom 1952 until 1964 she neither saw nor corresponded with Mrs. Johnson and did not know of her death until two years after she passed away. . . . Evelyn Schneikert testified that she [first met Mrs. Johnson] in 1964. In their subsequent correspondence Mrs. Johnson addressed her as "Dear Evelyn"; she never referred to her as Mabel. They also spoke over the telephone. . . .

Mrs. Johnson's pastor and the attorney who drew her will also testified. . . . They said that the will was prepared at the hospital. After satisfying himself as to her competency, the attorney inquired who was to receive her estate and she informed him she wanted an old friend to have $1,000 and the balance was to go to her nephew and his wife. The attorney asked the nephew's name and she replied "Raymond Schneikert." The attorney then requested the wife's name. Mrs. Johnson thought a second or two and said "Mabel." . . .

From this evidence and the language of the will, the trial court concluded that Mrs. Johnson intended to bequeath her estate to Raymond Schneikert and "his present wife." . . .

If a bequest is made to the wife of a certain person, and there is nothing in the will indicating the contrary, the term "wife" will apply to the person who answers that description on the date of the will. . . . There was no one who answered to the name "Mabel Schneikert" but there was a person who answered the description "his wife, of Plymouth, Wisconsin." Alternatively, if the name "Schneikert" is ignored and only the name "Mabel" considered, the description, and the surrounding circumstances as well, point to Evelyn as the intended legatee. . . .

A mistake in description may be corrected by rejecting that which is shown to be false, but no words may be inserted in place of those stricken and no words may be supplied. . . .

Complaint is made that the court erred in admitting, over objection, the testimony of the pastor and attorney and further erred in permitting them to testify concerning questions asked of, and answers made by, Mrs. Johnson. Declarations of a testatrix as to what she intended are not admissible in interpreting a will. Neither witness, however, testified to any declaration by Mrs. Johnson that differed from the words in her will; in fact, what she told them was identical to the language found in the instrument. Where there is no ambiguity in a will, the testimony of the draftsman is inadmissible to show the testator's intention. But the rule excluding the draftsman's testimony does not supersede the rule that parol evidence is admissible to explain a latent ambiguity. The testimony of the draftsman or a witness to a will is not in a special class, distinguishable from other permissible parol evidence. . . .

The judgment of the Circuit Court is affirmed.

Breckheimer is a classic misdescription case. Consider how it would differ if Raymond's divorce from Mabel and his remarriage to Evelyn had occurred *after* the will was executed.

SIEGLEY v. SIMPSON
73 Wash. 69, 131 P. 479 (1913)

[M. J. Heney's will left $6,000 to "my good friend Richard H. Simpson." The legacy was claimed by Richard H. Simpson and Hamilton Ross Simpson. The lower court held for Hamilton Ross, and Richard H. has appealed, arguing that parol evidence was not admissible to oppose his claim.]

MOUNT, J. . . .

It is well settled that parol evidence is not admissible to add to, vary, or contradict the words of a written will, not only because the will itself is the best evidence of the testator's intention, but also because wills are required by the statute of frauds to be in writing.

30 Am. & Eng. Ency. Law (2d Ed.) p. 673.

It may be stated generally that, where the beneficiary under a will is not designated with precision, parol evidence is admissible to show who was intended. Thus, where a latent ambiguity results from the fact that the description of the legatee or devisee is perfectly answered by two or more persons, or is applicable in part to two or more persons, parol evidence to identify the person intended is admissible. But where there is no ambiguity, and the object of the testator's bounty is sufficiently designated by plain language, so that it is clear who was intended, the construction is for the court, and parol evidence is inadmissible, although it might be thereby shown that the testator's intention was entirely different from that expressed in the will.

30 Am. & Eng. Ency. Law (2d Ed.) pp. 682, 683. . . .

In cases of equivocation, as where the will or a provision thereof applies equally as well to two or more objects or persons, evidence of statements or declarations made by the testator at the time of the execution or about the time of the execution of his will is admissible for the purpose of identifying the person. . . .

40 Cyc. p. 1435. Necessarily extrinsic evidence is admissible to prove the identity of the beneficiary named in a will, especially when two or more persons are claiming to be the beneficiary named — not for the purpose of varying the terms of the will, but to determine the person meant by the testator. . . .

In Woman's Foreign Missionary Society v. Mitchell, 93 Md. 199, 48 A. 737, 53 L.R.A. 711, the court said: "It is the identity of the individual, natural or artificial, that is material, and not the name, for that is simply one of the numerous means by which the identity is ascertained. The identity being established, the name is of no importance." In Hockensmith v. Slusher, 26 Mo. 237, the court said: "The general rule is that parol evidence cannot be admitted to supply or contradict, enlarge, or vary the words of a will, nor to explain the intention of the testator, except in two specified cases: (1) Where there is a latent ambiguity, arising dehors the will, as to the person or subject meant to be described; and (2) to rebut a resulting trust." See also Reformed Presbyterian Church v. McMillan, 31 Wash. 643, 72 P. 502.

In this case if there had been two different persons by the name of Richard H. Simpson, and who in other respects answered the description in the will, and these two persons were claiming as legatees, clearly extrinsic evidence would be admissible to determine the identity of the person named in the will. For the same reason and upon the same principle, where there are two persons each claiming to be the beneficiary because they are each described in the will, the court must decide from extrinsic evidence if need be which is the person intended. And that is what was done in this case. The evidence is plain that by the words, "I give . . . unto my friend Richard H. Simpson the sum of six thousand dollars," the testator referred to his friend Hamilton Ross Simpson, the respondent here, for the latter was his employe, and had been so for several years in Alaska, and assisted the testator in railway work where the testator accumulated his estate. Hamilton Ross Simpson was the testator's personal associate much of the time in Alaska, and the testator had told different persons that he had made provision for him in his will. The testator, while he was intimate with H. R. Simpson, the respondent, did not in fact know his given name or the order of his initials, and always addressed him as "Mr. Simpson" or "Bill" or "Rotary Bill," as he was commonly known on account of his ability to handle a railroad rotary snowplow. Richard H. Simpson, the appellant, was not a friend of the testator, had met him only once in 20 years, and then merely spoke to him as they passed by. These and other facts not necessary to recount led the trial court to conclude that the testator used the name Richard H. Simpson when he referred to and really intended the person and name of Hamilton Ross Simpson as his beneficiary. Under the rule as above stated, where the beneficiary is not precisely described, extrinsic evidence was proper, and we are satisfied that the trial court correctly interpreted the intent of the testator and the meaning of the will.

The judgment is therefore affirmed.

CROW, C.J., and PARKER and GOSE, J.J., concur.

CHADWICK, J.

A most familiar rule of interpretation of wills is that effect should be given to every word contained therein. The testator, Heney, undertook to designate an object of his bounty. He did not do it by name alone. He said, "I give to my friend." The word "friend" is a word of weight and meaning. In the light of all the evidence it fits Hamilton Ross Simpson, and it does not fit Richard H. Simpson. The record shows, as is said in the majority opinion, that Richard H. Simpson was never the friend of the testator. It is not shown that he was more than a casual acquaintance, and there is no independent evidence of that fact. Hamilton Ross Simpson was Heney's friend. . . . This creates an uncertainty or ambiguity, and parol testimony is admissible to clear the doubt. . . . If there had been no qualifying word, there might be no room for construction; but when it is shown that Mr. Heney had but one friend Simpson, and that friend was known to him as "H.R." or "R.H." and by no familiar name other than "Bill," I have no hesitancy in holding that this case falls without the general rule quoted in the majority opinion.

MATTER OF SNIDE
52 N.Y.2d 193, 418 N.E.2d 656 (1981)

WACHTLER, J. . . .

This case involves the admissibility of a will to probate. The facts are simply stated and are not in dispute. Harvey Snide, the decedent, and his wife, Rose Snide, intending to execute mutual wills at a common execution ceremony, each executed by mistake the will intended for the other. . . .

Harvey Snide is survived by his widow [the sole beneficiary of his will] and three children, two of whom have reached the age of majority. These elder children have executed waivers and have consented to the admission of the instrument to probate. The minor child, however, is represented by a guardian ad litem who refuses to make such a concession. . . .

The gist of the objectant's argument is that Harvey Snide lacked the required testamentary intent because he never intended to execute the document he actually signed. This argument is not novel, and in the few American cases on point it has been the basis for the denial of probate. However, cases from other common-law jurisdictions have taken a different view of the matter and we think the view they espouse is more sound. . . .

[W]e decline the formalistic view that this intent attaches irrevocably to the document prepared, rather than the testamentary scheme it reflects. . . .

Moreover, the significance of the only variance between the two instruments is fully explained by consideration of the documents together, as well as in the undisputed surrounding circumstances. Under such facts it would indeed be ironic — if not perverse — to state that because what has occurred is so obvious, and what was intended so clear, we must act to nullify rather than sustain this testamentary scheme. . . .

There is absolutely no danger of fraud, and the refusal to read these wills together would serve merely to unnecessarily expand formalism, without any corresponding benefit. On these narrow facts we decline this unjust course.

Nor can we share the fears of the dissent that our holding will be the first step in the exercise of judicial imagination relating to the reformation of wills. . . .

[Reversed, four to three.]

JONES, J. (dissenting).

I . . . am of the conviction that the willingness of the majority in an appealing case to depart from what has been consistent precedent in the courts of the United States and England will prove troublesome in the future. This is indeed an instance of the old adage that hard cases make bad law. . . .

On the basis of commendably thorough world-wide research, counsel for appellant has uncovered a total of 17 available reported cases involving mutual wills mistakenly signed by the wrong testator. . . . Relief was granted in the six cases from the British Commonwealth. In these cases it appears that the court has been moved by the transparency of the obvious error and the egregious frustration of undisputed intention which would ensue from failure to correct that error. . . .

I fear an inability to contain the logical consequences of this decision in the future. Thus, why should the result be any different where, although the two wills are markedly different in content, it is equally clear that there has been an erroneous contemporaneous cross-signing by the two would-be testators, or where the scrivener has prepared several drafts for a single client and it is established beyond all doubt that the wrong draft has been mistakenly signed? Nor need imagination stop there. . . .

CONNECTICUT JUNIOR REPUBLIC v. SHARON HOSPITAL
181 Conn. 1, 448 A.2d 190 (1982)

HEALEY, J. . . .

The sole issue presented in this case is whether extrinsic evidence of a mistake by a scrivener of a testamentary instrument is admissible in a proceeding to determine the validity of the testamentary instrument. . . .

Contained in the decedent's will are three articles which set up trusts for the distribution of part of the decedent's estate and designate, as remaindermen, seven named charitable organizations (1960 charities), the defendants in this case. In the first codicil to his will, the decedent deleted the seven 1960 charities and substituted another group of eleven charitable organizations (1969 charities) as remaindermen, which are plaintiffs in this case. . . .

Subsequently, in 1975, the decedent instructed the trust officer of the Third National Bank of Hampden County to make changes in his will, as amended by the first codicil, so as to qualify the trusts as charitable annuity trusts under the Tax Reform Act of 1969, so that the charitable remainder interests would be allowable as federal estate tax deductions. The trust officer, thereafter, similarly instructed the decedent's attorney. The attorney, however, in drafting the second codicil, not only made the requested changes but also mistakenly reinstated the 1960 charities. . . . The decedent, who had never requested or authorized this change, signed the second codicil apparently without realizing the change in beneficiaries.

At the hearing on the application for the admission of the will and the two codicils, the Probate Court heard evidence on the matter and ruled that Connecticut law does not permit the introduction of extrinsic evidence on the issue of mistake, and found that in the absence of such evidence the presumption of the validity of a testamentary instrument mandated the admission of the entire second codicil to probate. . . . From this judgment, the plaintiffs have appealed to this court. . . .

The plaintiffs' first argument states . . . that courts which have considered the question have made a distinction between proceedings to admit a will to probate and will construction proceedings, holding or recognizing that extrinsic evidence showing a scrivener's error is admissible in the former but not in the latter proceeding, absent an ambiguity. . . .

> [C]ourts must weigh the desirability of [attempting to effectuate] the testator's true intention . . . against the danger of invalidating upon parole evidence an instrument executed in compliance with statutory requirements, the danger of relying on parole evidence being greater in cases of wills than in cases involving other instruments because the testator's testimony is not available.

Annot., 90 A.L.R.2d 924, 928, §2.

In Connecticut, our cases have not, on this point, distinguished between the two types of proceedings. . . . While it is obvious that the purpose behind each type of proceeding may be different, we are not inclined to establish a rule which would effectuate such a distinction . . . because a litigant, knowing that more favorable evidentiary rules await those with claims of mistake due to scrivener's error will always try to phrase his argument in a way so to state such a claim. . . .

This would tend to produce needless litigation by transforming a simple will construction proceeding into an admission to probate problem where no problem may have actually existed. . . .

We now turn to the major issue presented by this case. The trial court held that "parol evidence may not be admitted in the instant case to show that the scrivener erred in drafting the codicil or that the testator mistakenly signed it. Connecticut law does not allow extrinsic evidence of a testator's intent to be admitted in cases dealing with either will construction or cases challenging the probate of an instrument. While there is an exception to this rule when there is ambiguity on the face of the will or codicil itself, this exception is not applicable in the instant case." We agree with the trial court. . . .

The principle of law, which we reiterate today, has been viable for many years and we have not been given nor do we glean any persuasive reason that justice, experience or logic requires it be changed.

Finally, the plaintiffs contend that even if the proffered extrinsic evidence would not be admissible to show the scrivener's error, there exist . . . inconsistencies and ambiguities in the second codicil which would justify the admission of such evidence under the "ambiguity" exception to which we have previously referred. In claiming that the circumstances of this case make it an "especially appropriate one" in which to admit extrinsic evidence, they also argue that this is so because the evidence of mistake does not come "entirely from outside the will." The plaintiffs [state]:

> The last numbered paragraph of the second codicil, labelled "III E," states the testator's reason for executing it: "It is my intent to create charitable remainder annuity trusts within the meaning of Section 664(d)(1) and the provisions of these trusts shall be interpreted in accordance with this intent." The very next sentence negates any intention to alter the dispositive provisions of the will: "*In all other respects* I do hereby ratify, confirm and republish my said will executed by me on May 19, 1960 and my first codicil dated December 4, 1969." (Emphasis added.) This statement conflicts with the earlier provisions of the second codicil, which alter the beneficiaries.

(Emphasis in original.) . . .

We agree with the trial court that no ambiguity is presented by these two sentences in the last article of the second codicil. The provision beginning with "In all other respects . . . " is obviously separable from the rest of the codicil. Its purpose is clearly intended to demonstrate that all prior testamentary instruments remain unchanged except for those changes outlined in the new testamentary instrument. It creates no ambiguity or inconsistency in the present case. . . .

[T]he intent of the testator as expressed in the language he used is clear. The question is not what he meant to say, but what is meant by what he did say. . . .

There is no error.

ARMENTANO and SPONZO, J.J., concur.

PETERS, J. (dissenting). . . .

[T]he issue is even narrower than stated by the majority since the present aim of the proponents of the evidence of mistake is only to delete provisions from, rather than add provisions to, disputed testamentary disposition. . . . [This] surely [presents] a less problematical confrontation with the policy of the Statute of Wills. . . .

The risk of subversion of the intent of the testator, who can not personally defend his testamentary bequests, is without doubt a serious concern. Balanced against that concern is the risk of blindly enforcing a testamentary disposition that substantially misstates the testator's true intent. We have long ago resolved this balance in favor of admitting extrinsic evidence when the testator's intent is undermined by fraud, undue influence or incapacity. . . . Under the modern law of misrepresentation, innocent misrepresentation is treated as generally equivalent to fraud in terms of its legal consequences. . . . The Statute of Wills does not compel enforcement of testamentary dispositions that a testator never intended to make. . . . Wills that do not reflect the true intent of the testator should be refused probate.

SHEA, J., concurs.

ESTATE OF KREMLICK
417 Mich. 237, 331 N.W.2d 228 (1983)

[Part of the residue of the testator's estate was left to "the Michigan Cancer Society." In a per curiam opinion the court of appeals upheld that Society's claim to the devise, finding no ambiguity. Further appeal was taken to the Michigan Supreme Court by the American Cancer Society, Michigan Division.]

PER CURIAM. . . .

We agree with the Court of Appeals that the designation "Michigan Cancer Society" is not a patent ambiguity. Determining the presence of a latent ambiguity, however, is more difficult. This Court has held that in interpreting contracts where an ambiguity *may exist,* extrinsic evidence is admissible: (1) to prove the existence of ambiguity; (2) to indicate the actual intent of the parties; (3) to indicate the actual intent of the parties as an aid in construction.

These rules are equally applicable to interpreting wills. Thus, not only may extrinsic evidence be used to clarify the meaning of a latent ambiguity, but it may be used to demonstrate that an ambiguity exists in the first place and to establish intent.

In this case, appellants produced an affidavit from the executrix of Mr. Kremlick's estate in which she asserted that the intended beneficiary was the American Cancer Society, Michigan Division, instead of the Michigan Cancer Society, an affiliate of the Michigan Cancer Foundation. The executrix stated that she had discussed the provisions of Mr. Kremlick's will with him on many occasions and that he frequently had mentioned that the American Cancer Society was to be a beneficiary. Appellants also sought to establish that Mr. Kremlick previously had made substantial contributions to the American Cancer Society, that the Society had helped his wife when she was dying of cancer, and that at the time of her death he requested memorials to the American Cancer Society.

This is the very kind of information that may be used both to establish an ambiguity and to help resolve it. Appellants should have been given the opportunity to do that. . . .

In two other states, California and New Jersey, particularly noteworthy lines of cases are developing — possibly more noteworthy in their willingness to attempt to articulate openly what is being done than in the actual novelty of their use of evidence.

The California developments were largely fostered by Estate of Russell, 69 Cal. 2d 200, 70 Cal. Rptr. 561, 444 P.2d 353 (1968), which emphasized that whether or not a will is "ambiguous" cannot always be determined "until the surrounding circumstances are first considered." The court also noted, however, that if "in light of such extrinsic evidence" the terms of the will are not "reasonably susceptible of two or more meanings," evidence is not admissible to show "an intention *different* from that expressed by the words" — that is, to show a meaning of which the words are not "reasonably susceptible."

In New Jersey a greater departure from the traditional dicta has been acknowledged, as summarized recently in Engle v. Siegel, 74 N.J. 287, 290-291, 377 A.2d 892, 893-894 (1977): "The generally accepted method of determining testamentary intent was once described by this Court [as recently as 1953] in these words: 'It is elementary . . . that the controlling consideration is the effect of the words as actually written rather than the actual intention independently of the written words . . . [not] what he was minded to say, but rather the meaning of the terms chosen. . . . ' This statement can no longer be said accurately to express the law of our state. . . . [Under] what has come to be known as the doctrine of probable intent . . . a court not only examines 'the entire will' but also studies 'competent extrinsic evidence'; it attributes to the testator 'common human impulses' and seeks to find what he would *subjectively* have desired had he in fact actually addressed the contingency which has arisen."

3. Mistake in the Inducement

Mistakes that give rise to problems of interpretation and mistakes concerning the document executed or the contents included in it have just been considered. Quite different is the situation in which all or part of a will is contested on the ground that it is the product of a mistake in the inducement — that is, that although the document was as intended, the motivation underlying the will or provision in question was based on a mistaken belief.

UNION PLANTERS NATIONAL BANK v. INMAN
588 S.W.2d 757 (Tenn. App. 1979)

[The decedent's 1965 will, after a charitable bequest, would have left about a quarter of his estate outright to his wife and the residue equally to his three children. The will in question, executed in 1971, contained similar provisions except that the shares of the wife and children were left in trust rather than outright. The wife was given a power to appoint the remainder of her trust by will; the remainder interest in the children's trust was eventually to go to decedent's grandchildren; and both trusts contained spendthrift provisions (see Chapter 12, section B2, infra) to protect the beneficiaries from creditors. The 1971 will was contested by two of the children, who alleged that the decedent's lawyer falsely led the decedent to believe that one son was heavily in debt and another "had large exposure through real estate ventures" and encouraged the decedent to include the trust arrangements in his will as a protection against the sons' creditors (with trusts also for the wife and daughter in order not to single out and embarrass the sons). It was further alleged that the first son had paid off his debts before the 1971 will was planned and that, but for the attorney's misrepresentations, the decedent would not have changed his 1965 will. The evidence in the case could not support the contestants' allegations of fraud and undue influence, but there was conflicting evidence as to the financial circumstances of the sons. The trial judge, however, found "no genuine issue as to a material fact" and granted proponent's motion for summary judgment.]

EWELL, J. . . .

Taking the facts before us in the light most favorable to the contestants, we find that, at most, this is a case where the draftsman of the will was mistakenly informed as to the financial condition of a son of the testator and in the course of his conference with the testator related to him erroneous information. . . . In the final analysis the only substantial insistence of the contestants is that a portion of the testator's will is invalid because it was made under a mistake and misapprehension of the facts as they existed at the time of the execution of the will. The Supreme Court of this State in the case of Anderson v. Anderson, 220 Tenn. 496, 419 S.W.2d 166 (1967) affirmed the 1917 case of Bowerman v. Burris, 138 Tenn. 220, 197 S.W. 490 and quoted the following statement therefrom: "Moreover, if the evidence [of mistake] could be at all effective, under our system, two points would have to be established: Firstly, that the testator was laboring under a mistake as to the fact; and, secondly, that if the truth had been known he would have made a different disposition, *and we think these facts should appear in the will itself.*" (Emphasis supplied.)

We have been unable to find a Tennessee case wherein the mistake and misapprehension was brought about by statement of counsel. . . . The Missouri case of Elam v. Phariss, 289 Mo. 209, 232 S.W. 693 (1921) is based upon facts not substantially dissimilar to the case before us. In that case the Supreme Court of Missouri quoted with approval language from the case of Couch v. Easthan, 27 W. Va. 796, 55 Am. Rep. 346 as follows: "The mistake which will avail to set aside a will is a mistake as to what it contains, or as to the paper itself, not a mistake either of law or fact in the mind of the testator, as to the effect of what he actually and intentionally did."

We find the foregoing to be the majority view, and the Tennessee cases of *Bowerman,* supra and *Anderson,* supra are not inconsistent therewith. In this case it does not appear within the will itself that Inman was laboring under a mistake as to the facts and that if the erroneous statements had not been made by Martin, he would have made a different disposition. . . .

[A]ffirmed.

The frequently cited case of Bowerman v. Burris, quoted in the opinion above, involved a will allegedly executed under a mistaken belief that the testator's only son was dead. The court held that evidence of the testator's belief "was not competent" and observed that it would be "contrary to sound policy to admit evidence of conversations . . . as to his purposes or his reasons for making a disposition." To do so "would open the door wide to fraud" when the testator "cannot give his version of the matter." The court then stated the requirement that the will itself must disclose both the mistaken belief and that a different disposition would have been made if the truth were known.

Would *Bowerman* have been differently decided if, prior to execution of the will, one of the beneficiaries under the will had, knowing the contrary to be true, told the testator that his son was dead?

Would the case be affected if the will had begun: "Because my only son is dead, I therefore leave my estate as follows:"? Cf. Uniform Probate Code §2-302(c).

An even stronger stand against reformation of a will based on mistake in the inducement can be found in Carpenter v. Tinney, 420 S.W.2d 241, 244 (Tex. Civ. App. 1967), stating: "Generally a mistake of fact or law, in the absence of fraud or undue influence, will not defeat the probate of a will, even though the testator might have made a different will if there had been no such mistake inducing the testator to make the will. It is also the general rule that courts have no right to vary or modify the terms of a will or to reform it even on grounds of mistake. . . . It has been held that if the testator labors under no mistake in identity of the document executed, a mistake of fact or law, there being no fraud or undue influence, will not defeat probate of a will.''

PROBLEMS

5-J.   *T*'s will, executed shortly before death, left his estate in equal shares to *A* and *B,* two of his three children. The will also declared *T*'s desire to treat all of his children alike and that he had "advanced" his son, *C,* an amount roughly equal to his share of the estate. *C* offers testimony intended to prove that *T* was mistaken and that he had not made any such "advancement." How would you argue for admission of this evidence? Against it? If you were the court, would you grant *C* relief? Cf. Estate of Baum, 4 Utah 2d 375, 294 P.2d 711 (1956).

5-K.   The arguments and decision — the whole "feel" of the case — might be different in the above set of facts if *C* offered in evidence a large, uncleared check to him from his father. Why? If your decision with this evidence would differ from your decision without it, can you articulate a principled basis for these results for the guidance of other courts in other cases that might be somewhat analogous?

F.   *Further Explanation, Comments, and Comparison*

V. EMMERICH, ESTATE PRACTICE IN THE UNITED STATES AND EUROPE
10-11 (1950)

In Anglo-American law, documents must be explicit, detailed and unequivocal. Courts will not make [wills]. This and often antiquated legal diction have led to a very technical legal language and more lengthy and complicated documents than found in continental practice.

The German Code contains in article 242 the rule that contracts are construed according to the requirements of good faith. Judicial practice has given most extended application to this rule. German legal documents of the twentieth century, especially wills, show the tendency to shortness and simple wording, sometimes in an exaggerated degree. Courts are not reluctant to construe ambiguous provisions, to fill in gaps and even to amend or change provisions according to the good faith rule.

The situation in the French and Western-European countries is intermediate between the Anglo-American and Germanic one. A rule like that of article 242 of the German Civil Code has not been formulated and [is] even sometimes denied by the courts, but their practice was often a similar one. Legal documents are also here generally simpler and shorter than in the Anglo-American countries, even if not to the same degree as in Germany.

POWER, WILLS: A PRIMER OF INTERPRETATION AND CONSTRUCTION
51 Iowa L. Rev. 75, 76-87, 103-106 (1965)

Directions as to the disposition of property after death will be given effect only to the extent they are expressed in a valid will. To the extent that testamentary directions are clearly and unambiguously expressed they will be given effect even if [someone seeks to show] that the words of the will do not express the testator's wishes. These two propositions suggest the truism that there are many instances of mistake for which there is no relief. . . .

In the nature of things it is always necessary to look outside the will in order to identify persons and property described in it. Though the use of extrinsic evidence in the existing system extends substantially beyond this, "the policies embodied in the . . . Statute of Wills, and the necessities implicit in an orderly and expeditious administration of justice, require that inquiries as to the meaning of language be kept within reasonable limits." One could imagine a legal system, however, in which nothing in a will could ever be explained by extrinsic evidence so as to make effective a provision as to which [of] the testator's words are unclear. Such a system would treat ambiguities and unconventional usages as it treats total failures of expression, requiring that an adequate testamentary expression of a gift be stated so that no resort need be made to extrinsic evidence to resolve a doubt as to what was intended. Though litigation might be reduced, the will would become such a risky means of transmitting property because of the likelihood of failure resulting from inadequate expression that its usefulness would be seriously reduced. The law has properly rejected such an overly rigorous and impractical solution.

Troublesome problems arise in determining whether the will offers anything to interpret: is there merely a blurring of meaning which might be clarified by other parts of the will or by extrinsic evidence, or is there a total failure in expression, a hole? If the latter, there is nothing that may be clarified. Such is the case when the testator has written, "I give Blackacre to _____." Even if the testator had in his mind fixed upon a person to take Blackacre, such intention is not expressed in a witnessed writing as required by the Statute of Wills; hence, no extrinsic evidence is admissible and the words are without effect.[1] . . .

At the other end of the spectrum the question of whether the testator's intention can be determined by resorting to extrinsic evidence arises as to whether a "single plain meaning" can be disturbed. Instead of no expression of a testamentary wish, there is here a testamentary provision which may be given effect as it stands; there is an accurate, adequate description of some person or thing. . . . Can it be shown that some person or thing less well described was intended by the testator? A gift of property by will to Harry A. Waldo would be an adequate description to pass the property to Harry B. Waldo if there was no other person who could reasonably claim under such a description. The erroneous part of the description, the initial *A*, could be ignored. . . . Suppose, however, that there is a person Harry A. Waldo with whom the testator was acquainted; [can] Harry B. Waldo introduce extrinsic evidence to show he was intended? The view which is gaining acceptance today is that while there is a strong presumption that the better-described person or thing was the one intended, the "rule" against disturbing a clear meaning does not render extrinsic evidence inadmissible to show that the apparently clear words are in fact ambiguous and to show further that the words were intended to and do identify some less well described person or thing.[2] The objection to admitting extrinsic evidence to fill a hole (the objection being that the testamentary wish must find expression in

1. . . . In England the omission from probate of mistaken *insertions* resulting in misdescriptions in a will is established as a means of giving relief at the probate stage. In re Goods of Boehm, [1891] P. 247. . . .

2. . . . [I]n National Society for Prevention of Cruelty to Children v. Scottish National Society for Prevention of Cruelty to Children, [1915] A.C. 207, [a Scotsman] made a bequest to the "National Society for Prevention of Cruelty to Children." Such an institution existed in London (its activities did not extend to Scotland), but so far as the evidence revealed, the testator had never known of its existence, though he had known of an activity of the respondent Scottish National Society for Prevention of Cruelty to Children. The House of Lords [held the evidence did not] raise an ambiguity. . . . This regrettable decision [seems] to leave the plain meaning rule intact and to retreat from the earlier intimation in In re Jodrell, 44 Ch. D. 590 (1890), that the rule . . . is not so much a canon of construction as a counsel of caution. In . . . Estate of Gibbs, 14 Wis. 2d 490, 111 N.W.2d 413 (1961), the testator apparently intended his employee, Robert W. Krause of 2325 North Sherman Boulevard, Milwaukee, but erroneously designated him (probably as a result of picking the wrong name from the telephone directory) as Robert J. Krause of 4708 North 46th Street, where there lived a person named Robert J. Krause, a stranger to the testator so far as the evidence revealed. The Court, taking the view that there was no ambiguity, still permitted the intended beneficiary to take, saying:

> We conclude that details of identification, particularly such matters as middle initials, street addresses, and the like, which are highly susceptible to mistake, particularly in metropolitan areas, should not be accorded such sanctity as to frustrate an otherwise clearly demonstrable intent. Where such details of identification are involved, courts should receive evidence tending to show that a mistake has been made and should disregard the details when the proof establishes to the highest degree of certainty that a mistake was, in fact, made.

Id. at 499, 111 N.W.2d at 418.

the will) does not exist when a clear meaning is sought to be varied if the range of less well described persons or things is limited to those which would be adequately described were it not for the existence of the person or thing which is more adequately described. Hence, in jurisdictions where a rule against disturbing a clear meaning exists, it does not rest directly on the principle that all testamentary dispositions must be expressed in writing, but on the compatible and supplementary propositions that the person or thing better described was probably what the testator intended and that the benefits of not provoking litigation overbalance the benefits of [attempting to carry] out the testator's wishes by permitting a showing that a less well-described person or thing was intended. . . . Thus, traditionally the hole in the will and the clearly expressed meaning, symmetrically opposite situations, have been treated alike in that in both situations no extrinsic evidence was admissible. . . .

Between the extremes of no expression in a will and a clear expression lies the area of ambiguities [earlier defined as doubt occasioned when words admit a plurality of possible meanings] and uncertainties [doubt where there is no such plurality of possible meanings]. . . . When litigation occurs . . . it is sometimes clear that an ambiguity exists, and the issues involve only the admissibility and evaluation of extrinsic evidence. Often, however, one party is seeking to stretch the area of ambiguities to include what the other party contends is (1) a plain meaning . . . or (2) in cases at the other extreme, a failure of expression in the will. . . . An attempt to vary a "clear" meaning necessarily involves an attempt to create an ambiguity. Because ambiguity and other concepts used for analysis in this area are inherently elastic concepts, it is often extremely difficult to define these boundaries.

In some cases of ambiguities, called equivocations, the description of a person or thing is not erroneous so far as it goes but does not distinguish among two or more other persons or things. Thus, if the testator leaves his gold watch to his nephew George and it turns out he has two nephews named George, an ambiguity has been established[3] and extrin-

---

3. Bacon first enunciated the distinction, now repudiated by writers, e.g., 9 Wigmore, Evidence §2472; Restatement, Property §242, Comment j (1940), between patent and latent ambiguities. The former, being ambiguous on its face, "is never holpen by averment." A latent ambiguity, being revealed by "some collateral matter out of the deed that breedeth the ambiguity," may be removed by extrinsic evidence; that is, may be "holpen by averment." Bacon, Maxims of the Law, Regula XXIII, in The Elements of the Common Lawes of England 192 (1630). It is fair to say that this classification has proved more of a deterrent than an aid to courts in reaching sound results, having given rise to the seductive premise that as an ambiguity has been disclosed by extrinsic evidence, it thus may be removed by extrinsic evidence. What Bacon probably had in mind when he spoke of patent ambiguity was an obvious failure to express a gift sufficiently. Since some courts today still make this classification, it cannot be completely ignored as a practical matter.

sic evidence would be admissible to show which one was intended.[4] In some cases the description applies in part to one person or thing and in part to another, as when the testator had no nephew George but a cousin George and one nephew, Alfred. . . . The erroneous portion of the description may then be ignored, the portion remaining sufficiently identifying the intended beneficiary. Thus, . . . a gift may be saved if it is sufficiently expressed to be capable of clarification and if the extrinsic evidence makes clear the intended meaning. . . .

In cases where an uncertainty rather than a true ambiguity exists, extrinsic evidence is likewise admissible for the purpose of removing the doubt as to the identity of the intended person or object. . . .

There is yet another frequently found type of ambiguity: the description clearly applies to some person or thing, but it is not clear whether it applies to other persons or things as well, thus fitting the definition of a plurality of possible meanings. Such is the situation when the testator has written, "I give Blackacre to my grandchildren," and one of his children has an adopted child. Is the adopted child within the term "grandchildren"? The word has been used by the testator (1) with the intent of including the adopted child or (2) with the intent of excluding him or (3) without any intent as to the adopted child. . . . [A]n intended meaning can be sought from examination of the entire will and from extrinsic evidence of the circumstances, including such matters as the testator's habits of speech and relations with his family. Finally, should such attempts at interpretation not resolve the ambiguity, reference may be had to judicial definitions or rules of authoritative explanation as to what the unclear word will be taken to include. . . . It is to be noticed that in applying such a definition, however, the court is not interpreting the will as is the case when the court seeks to discover the intended meanings of the testator's words by extrinsic evidence; rather, the court is supplementing the will: after a search in vain for the testator's meaning of a word which is in the circumstances capable of more than one meaning, the court then ascribes to it a legal dictionary meaning. . . . In some cases in which the ambiguity does not involve words which have been judicially defined, a broader maxim of construction may save the provision when the sources of interpretation yield no answer. In other situations a maxim of

---

4. A significant distinction between equivocations and other kinds of ambiguities and uncertainties is the admissibility of direct evidence in cases of equivocation. Direct evidence is described by Wigmore as the testator's "declarations of intention." 9 Wigmore, Evidence §2471 (3d ed. 1940). Such evidence should be excluded because of the "rule which prohibits setting up any extrinsic utterance to compete with and overthrow the words of a document." Ibid. Though such evidence might be used for a proper purpose, that is, to explain and not to compete with, the words of the will, the risks of misuse militate against its admission except in cases of equivocation. In equivocations it may be said to clarify rather than compete, inasmuch as the description in the will is not erroneous but merely incomplete. . . .

construction might be used to avoid the judicial definition of a word or another maxim of construction which would lead to a different result. In applying broader maxims of construction it is obvious that again the court is not carrying out a provision according to what has been found to be the testator's expressed or inferable desires, but is supplementing the writing to give it the effect he probably wanted or would have wanted had the matter occurred to him, or the effect which is favored by some public policy in regard to property interests. If, however, the case involves not this sort of ambiguity but an incomprehensible or meaningless provision in which the testator purports to describe property or persons by words which do not clearly identify any likely beneficiaries or any property owned by him, the gift of necessity fails for indefiniteness if extrinsic evidence does not clarify it. Of course, the testator is not bound to usual linguistic conventions, and a seemingly incomprehensible word or symbol may often be readily explained by evidence of the testator's peculiar usages.

As a practical matter it often cannot be established with what intended meaning an ambiguous word was used, or whether it was used without thinking of its meaning. In such situations resorting to rules of authoritative explanation and other maxims of construction is justified as a means of giving some effect to a provision, even though in so doing there is a slight intrusion upon the principle that testamentary dispositions must be expressed in writing. . . .

. . . Though perhaps not true a century ago, today a judge usually wants to be liberal in giving effect to most testamentary wishes if this can be done within the limitations of the system. How ready should he be to find from the circumstances that the testator has deviated from the accepted meaning of a word? Would there be a sacrifice of some competing interest of the law if a court were given power to effect what it believes the testator wanted or would have wanted though nothing be stated in the will or though it be different from what is there stated? An answer is suggested by frequently quoted words of a New Jersey court:

> [I]t is against sound public policy to permit a pure mistake to defeat [a] competent testamentary act. But it is more important that the probate of the wills of dead people be effectively shielded from the attacks of a multitude of fictitious mistakes than that it be purged of wills containing a few real ones. The latter a testator may, by due care, avoid in his lifetime. Against the former he would be helpless.

Words and other graphic symbols are the only means of communicating complicated ideas. It is a worthy, even vital, objective for the law to preserve the instrumentality which enables such communication. . . . To the extent that words are said to mean something other than that which is established by conventional usage, absent an acceptable basis for finding an unconventional usage, communication of complicated ideas becomes uncertain and hence more difficult. . . . It is never claimed today that there exist infallible guides to determine a meaning, but that is not to say that basic sources of ascribing meaning may be ignored unless the context or circumstances permit. Neither can a sound interpretive process entail a commitment to inflexible adherence to a plain meaning, for, as Ogden and Richards have pointed out, words have meaning only as they are connected with objects and ideas through the writer's or reader's (or speaker's or hearer's) mental apparatus. An artificial limitation on the meaning to be derived from those arbitrary symbols, words, is as inimical to effective communication as is finding that words can mean something they do not ordinarily mean in the absence of an explanatory context or circumstance. . . .

A predictable result of a general discretion to repair would be a great increase in the incidence of litigation. . . . Judicial remaking of wills, whether avowed or under the guise of interpretation and construction, involves abandonment of the rationale of the Statute of Wills. The will, a unilateral act, has no existence apart from the writing which the testator executes. He is the only person whose intention is relevant, and his intention is relevant only to the extent it finds expression in the will. The fact that the owner of property has died (and consequently his unavailability as a witness) creates opportunity for fraud, and explains the limitations on relief for mistakes, epitomized in the frequent statement that equity will not reform a will. . . . Such limitations, which include restrictions on the sort of evidence which is admissible to show the meaning of the testator's words, are logical ramifications of the requirement of the Statute of Wills that testamentary dispositions be expressed in a witnessed writing and of the concomitant judicial reluctance or refusal to vary a clear meaning. It is tempting to think that judges are so skilled that they can best function freed from the restrictions of an elaborate system; that broad principles of justice and morality will alone suffice. . . . Though no one doubts that disharmony of the law and popular expectations in some particular often signals a need for change, a source of further reflection . . . is Ihering's discussion of the disadvantages of form:

> I begin with [the disadvantages of form] because without being sought out they are at once apparent to the unsophisticated, while the advantages of form require a conscious effort of research, and, I must add, demand for their discovery a juristic eye. It stands with formalism as with so many other arrangements — everyone feels its pinch, no one its benefits, because the latter are purely negative in nature, that is to say, consist in avoiding evil. A single case in which the disadvantages of form are presented in dramatic form to the public (as for example when a testament is declared void for a defect in form . . .) causes more talk than the thousands of cases in which the course of events was a normal one, and

form fulfilled its beneficial purpose. Small wonder that the judgment of the uninformed is so adverse to formalism.

[2 Ihering, Geist des Römischen Rechts 480 (7th ed. 1923).]

What predictability the law has achieved in this area, based on standardization of the meaning of symbols, should not be forfeited to get the "right" result in an occasional hardship case, with the concomitant invitation to ill-founded claims and litigation. It is not sound to maintain that a system of rules can or should achieve the fair result or "justice" in every case. The law has achieved all that can be expected if it has sought to channel transactions into forms which people can reasonably be expected to utilize with high probability of attaining the desired legal result, and which must therefore be as free as possible of traps that reasonably acting people might fall victim to. . . . Perhaps it is [not sufficiently] recognized that the will fails when it produces litigation even if the testator's wishes are not ultimately frustrated. . . . Occasional failures, hopefully statistically rare, are the inevitable concomitant of any function subject to human fallibility, and in the case of wills this price is not unreasonable for the easily overlooked benefits of formalities.

LANGBEIN AND WAGGONER, REFORMATION OF WILLS ON THE GROUND OF MISTAKE: CHANGE OF DIRECTION IN AMERICAN LAW?
130 U. Pa. L. Rev. 521, 522, 577-580, 590 (1982)

Although it has been "axiomatic" that our courts do not entertain suits to reform wills on the ground of mistake, appellate courts in California, New Jersey, and New York have decided cases within the last five years that may presage the abandonment of the ancient "no-reformation" rule. The new cases do not purport to make this fundamental doctrinal change. . . . What each court actually did was to prefer the extrinsic evidence of the testator's intent over the contrary but mistaken language in the will.

The inclination of modern courts to prevent injustice despite a long tradition of refusing to remedy mistakes in wills is, in our view, laudable. We do not, however, believe that courts should continue to reach such results by doctrinal sleight-of-hand. Rather, we take the position in the present Article that the time has come for forthright judicial reconsideration of the no-reformation rule. We believe that a reformation doctrine shaped and limited according to criteria that we identify has the capacity to prevent much of the hardship associated with the former rule, while effectively dealing with the concerns that motivated the rule.

The impulse to relieve against mistake is strongly felt in modern courts. . . . Yet because the black letter law has seemed so hostile, courts have often given remedy in specious or unreasoned theories of decision. We think that with the no-extrinsic-evidence rule now undergoing abrogation and with the Wills Act formal requirements understood to be not an obstacle, a principled reformation doctrine can be formulated that will strike the proper balance between the concerns that underlie the old no-reformation rule and the factors that have made that rule ever more unpalatable. . . .

The three elements of the [reformation] doctrine are already to be observed in the various situations where courts have been able to remedy mistake without affronting older notions of the force of the Wills Act. These elements . . . we label the (1) materiality, (2) particularity, and (3) burden-of-proof requirements. Each is directly responsive to the evidentiary concerns that were so prominent in discussions of the old no-reformation rule.

As with other remedial doctrines in the law of wills, for example the fraud and undue influence rules, the reformation doctrine will require that the error be shown to have affected specific terms in the will. Materiality is usually self evident in the proofs that establish the mistake, as in [Snide, supra]. . . . But cases can be found in which materiality is lacking even though the mistake be proved, [as in an] old Rhode Island case . . . where the court found it "very apparent . . . that the testatrix would have made the same will had she known" that she was mistaken. . . .

In cases of fraud and undue influence, materiality is usually presumed on account of the wrongdoer's conduct; the burden is shifted to him to disprove it, which he can virtually never do. In ordinary mistake cases, . . . the burden of proving materiality remains on the proponent of a mistake claim. . . .

[A] threshhold requirement [is] that a mistake claim be sufficiently circumscribed to be susceptible of proof. . . . Accordingly, the reformation doctrine will confine relief to situations where the alleged mistake involves a fact or event of particularity — for example, . . . the scrivener's misunderstanding of the import of the term "heirs"; . . . the scrivener's failure to provide a lapse clause appropriate to the testators' wishes; in Snide the mistaken execution of the spouse's will pursuant to the lawyer's direction. . . .

The essential safeguard for a reformation doctrine in the law of wills is a standard of proof effective to deal with the evidentiary concerns to which the former no-reformation rule was addressed. Although that rule has been found too harsh, it did respond to the difficulty and the danger of proving that a testator now dead made a mistake in his duly executed will. . . . [A] modern reformation doctrine for wills must follow the law of non-probate transfers by placing upon the proponent of a mistake claim the burden of proving it by evidence of exceptional quality. The clear-and-convincing-evidence standard is pitched above the ordinary preponderance-of-the-evidence test of most civil litigation, but below the beyond-reasonable-doubt rule of the criminal law. . . .

[Do] statutory gap-filling rules take precedence over reformation in a well-proven case of mistake[?] The answer is no. . . . Because reformation puts the language back in the will, there is no gap for the gap-filling statutes to fill. Reformation is based upon the testator's actual intent and his actual language, whereas a statutory rule of construction is a device of subsidiary rank. . . .

So long as it is human to err, instances of mistaken terms in wills are inevitable. The impulse to remedy these mistaken terms in order to prevent unjust enrichment is also deeply rooted in our sense of justice, which is why the simplistic rule forbidding relief against mistake is dissolving. . . . We think that a principled reformation doctrine has all the advantages over the patchwork of inconsistency and injustice that characterizes the present law. . . .

6

Revocation and Revival

Revocation may occur by operation of law, by some physical act performed on the will with intent to revoke, or expressly or impliedly by a subsequent instrument meeting the statutory requirements. A will may be revoked in whole or in part. All states recognize that wills are revocable, this being an aspect of a will's ambulatory character. A will that has been revoked may be restored to testamentary life or "revived" under various circumstances. Also, under the doctrine of dependent relative revocation, a will that was assumed to have been revoked may be held not to have lost its validity.

Problems of revocation and revival often turn on the precise wording of a statute or on fine distinctions tediously drawn by courts. Sometimes cases turn on the elusive intention of the testator, either in executing an instrument or in performing some act. However, it must always be kept in mind that both the requirement of an authorized act or instrument of revocation and the requirement of an accompanying intent to revoke must be satisfied. In addition to providing for revocation by subsequent, formally executed writings, most American statutes have employed some or all of the terms of the English Statute of Frauds (authorizing revocation by "burning, cancelling, tearing, or obliterating"), while a few statutes resemble somewhat the English Wills Act ("burning, tearing, or otherwise destroying"). In any close case it is necessary to consult the exact statutory language describing the methods of revocation.

In a sense, a revocation may occur by *ademption* (or *ademption by extinction*) when property specifically bequeathed or devised is not a part of the estate at the testator's death, or by *satisfaction* (or *ademption by satisfaction*) when a legatee receives an inter vivos gift of all or part of the legacy provided in the will. These matters are discussed elsewhere as problems of distribution rather than problems of revocation.

UNIFORM PROBATE CODE

§2-507. *Revocation by Writing or by Act.*

(a) A will or any part thereof is revoked:
    (1) by executing a subsequent will that revokes the previous will or part expressly or by inconsistency; or

(2) by performing a revocatory act on the will, if the testator performed the act with the intent and for the purpose of revoking the will or part or if another individual performed the act in the testator's conscious presence and by the testator's direction. For purposes of this paragraph, "revocatory act on the will" includes burning, tearing, canceling, obliterating, or destroying the will or any part of it. A burning, tearing, or canceling is a "revocatory act on the will," whether or not the burn, tear, or cancellation touched any of the words on the will.

(b) If a subsequent will does not expressly revoke a previous will, the execution of the subsequent will wholly revokes the previous will by inconsistency if the testator intended the subsequent will to replace rather than supplement the previous will.

(c) The testator is presumed to have intended a subsequent will to replace rather than supplement a previous will if the subsequent will makes a complete disposition of the testator's estate. If this presumption arises and is not rebutted by clear and convincing evidence, the previous will is revoked; only the subsequent will is operative on the testator's death.

(d) The testator is presumed to have intended a subsequent will to supplement rather than replace a previous will if the subsequent will does not make a complete disposition of the testator's estate. If this presumption arises and is not rebutted by clear and convincing evidence, the subsequent will revokes the previous will only to the extent the subsequent will is inconsistent with the previous will; each will is fully operative on the testator's death to the extent they are not inconsistent.

A. Revocation by Physical Act

Because revocation almost universally may be accomplished by an appropriate physical act, and because of what seems a natural temptation of laypersons to use such methods, litigation often is required to determine whether an apparent attempt to revoke satisfies the local statute. Obviously, physical acts performed on the will may be vulnerable to questions of (1) whether the necessary present intention to revoke accompanied the alleged act of revocation and (2) whether the act in question was done by the testator (or by another at the direction and in the presence of the testator, as is generally authorized by statute). Often, though, it is the sufficiency of the act itself that is questioned under the statute. Is a large cross-mark on one of the pages or on the cover of the will sufficient? Is a will "burned" if its edges are singed? What of a notation on the face or the back of the will? What if some or even all dispositive provisions, or the testator's signature, are lined out? The cases are numerous and the results are varied. Decisions are often highly technical in their interpretation of the statutory requirements. The common "cancellation" requirement is generally held to require defacing of the writ-ing,[1] not just of blank portions of the will, while a slight "tearing" or "burning" is usually deemed sufficient if accompanied by the requisite intention.

Partial revocations are also a recurrent source of difficulty. Although numerous courts have refused to recognize partial revocations by phys-ical act,[2] statutory language (such as "no will or any part thereof may be revoked except . . . ") is frequently construed to permit such revoca-tions, and a few courts have allowed partial revocation in the absence of any such statutory suggestion. Where a will can be revoked in part, dif-ficulties arise when a testator fails to make clear whether the intent was to revoke the entire will or only the mutilated provisions. Of course, the form of the act frequently leaves little doubt, such as where a particular bequest is distinctly and thoroughly lined out.

A few statutes expressly provide that revocation of a will also revokes all codicils thereto. Even in the absence of such a statutory provision it is generally held that, if so intended, a physical act performed upon the will also revokes its codicils. However, revocation of a codicil does not normally revoke a will.

While intensive study of dubious attempts to revoke is of little value except with reference to a particular problem about to be litigated, the materials following the problem below illustrate the possible attitudes of courts in these situations.

PROBLEM

6-A.   Three years ago Thomas properly executed a will dividing his estate among his wife and cousins. Ten days ago he told his lawyer, Addi-son, that he wanted to increase his wife's share and perhaps leave her the entire estate. Addison set an appointment to review the will, but before that date arrived he received a telephone call from Thomas in a distant state where Thomas was hospitalized after becoming ill while traveling. After learning that his wife would take all of his intestate property, Thomas told Addison that he wanted to revoke his will and directed Addison to get it from the file. Jane, Addison's secretary, brought the will and then picked up an extension phone in the office as the following conversation ensued:

Thomas: Addy, do you have the will?
Addison: Yes, Tom; Jane just brought it to me.

---

1. In Estate of Dickson, 590 So. 2d 471 (Fla. App. 1991), the testator sufficiently "defaced" the will to revoke it when he wrote "void" over the notarial in the self-proving affidavit to the will, and his entire handwritten statement on open parts of the document was admissible to establish the necessary accompanying intent to revoke by the act of defacement.
2. E.g., In re Minsinger's Estate, 228 Or. 218, 364 P.2d 615 (1961).

Thomas: Jane, are you there?

Jane: Yes, and we have the will I witnessed three years ago.

Thomas: Addy, tear it up. I want to revoke it. See that he does what I
   say, Jane.

Jane: I will. He's tearing it in two.

Thomas: I hear him tearing it. Is it done, Addy?

Addison: Yes, all done.

Thomas: Good, I want to die without a will.

This morning, Addison received word from the hospital that Thomas
had died during the night. Addison retrieved the fragments of the torn
will from the wastebasket and put them in an envelope in Thomas's file
with a memorandum of these facts. Will Thomas's estate be administered
testate or intestate under the Uniform Probate Code? Why? Under statutes like those in *Fox's Will* (page 201 infra)? Under the law of your state?
Matter of Will of Jefferson, 349 So. 2d 1032 (Miss. 1977).

THOMPSON v. ROYALL
163 Va. 492, 175 S.E. 748 (1934)

[Mrs. Kroll executed a will and a few days later a codicil amending the
will. Soon thereafter, in the presence of two friends, she requested her
lawyer to destroy both documents, but at his suggestion she decided to
preserve them for future reference. The following was then written on
the back of the manuscript cover of the will by the lawyer and signed by
Mrs. Kroll: "This will null and void and to be only held by H. P. Brittain
instead of being destroyed as a memorandum for another will if I desire
to make same. This 19 Sept. 1932. s/M. Lou Bowen Kroll." A similar
notation was made on the back of the sheet on which the codicil was written. Two weeks later Mrs. Kroll died. This is an appeal from the order
admitting the will and codicil to probate. The applicable statute provides: "No will or codicil, or any part thereof, shall be revoked, unless
. . . by a subsequent will or codicil, or by some writing declaring an intention to revoke the same, and executed in the manner in which a will is
required to be executed, or by the testator, or some person in his presence and by his direction, cutting, tearing, burning, obliterating, canceling, or destroying the same, or the signature thereto, with the intent
to revoke."]

HUDGKINS, J. . . .

The notations, dated September 19, 1932, are not wholly in the handwriting of the testatrix, nor are her signatures thereto attached attested
by subscribing witnesses; hence under the statute they are ineffectual as
"some writing declaring an intention to revoke." The faces of the two
instruments bear no physical evidence of any cutting, tearing, burning,
obliterating, canceling, or destroying. The only contention made by

appellants is that the notation written in the presence, and with the approval, of Mrs. Kroll, on the back of the manuscript cover in the one instance, and on the back of the sheet containing the codicil in the other, constitute "canceling" within the meaning of the statute.

Both parties concede that to effect revocation of a duly executed will, in any of the methods prescribed by statute, two things are necessary: (1) The doing of one of the acts specified, (2) accompanied by the intent to revoke — the animo revocandi. Proof of either, without proof of the other, is insufficient. Malone v. Hobbs, 1 Rob. (40 Va.) 346, 39 Am. Dec. 263; 2 Minor Ins. 925.

The proof established the intention to revoke. The entire controversy is confined to the acts used in carrying out that purpose. . . .

The [relevant authorities] hold that revocation of a will by cancellation within the meaning of the statute contemplates marks or lines across the written parts of the instrument, or a physical defacement, or some mutilation of the writing itself, with the intent to revoke. If written words are used for the purpose, they must be so placed as to physically affect the written portion of the will, not merely on blank parts of the paper on which the will is written. If the writing intended to be the act of canceling does not mutilate, or erase, or deface, or otherwise physically come in contact with, any part of written words of the will, it cannot be given any greater weight than a similar writing on a separate sheet of paper, which identifies the will referred to, just as definitely as does the writing on the back. . . .

For the reasons stated, the judgment of the trial court is affirmed.

What are the responsibilities and liabilities of the attorney for the testatrix in such a case as this? See Lucas v. Hamm, 56 Cal. 2d 583, 364 P.2d 685, 15 Cal. Rptr. 821 (1961); Heyer v. Flaig, 70 Cal. 2d 223, 449 P.2d 161 (1969); McAbee v. Edwards, 340 So. 2d 1169 (Fla. App. 1976); Ward v. Arnold, 52 Wash. 2d 581, 328 P.2d 164 (1958); Oglev V, Fuitan, 112 Ill. App. 3d 1048, 445 N.E.2d 1344 (1983); G. Johnston, Avoiding Legal Malpractice in Estate Planning, 43 U.S.C. Inst. on Fed. Tax 17.1 (1991).

KELLY v. DONALDSON
456 So. 2d 30 (Ala. 1984)

[Proponent offered her deceased aunt's will for probate, and decedent's sister and various nieces and nephews contested, alleging (inter alia) revocation. Proponent was the sole beneficiary of the will, and the sole evidence in support of the will was her testimony, including testimony that the decedent executed the lawyer-drawn will in duplicate originals, retained one copy, and gave the other to proponent. After the

decedent's death her retained copy could not be found by the proponent. From a jury verdict in favor of the proponent, contestants appeal.]
   BEATTY, J. . . .
   We affirm. . . .
   In Summerhill v. Craft, 425 So. 2d 1055, 1057 (Ala. 1982), this Court
stated: "If a testatrix keeps one of two duplicate original wills and gives
the other to another person, and no will is found in her possession at her
death, 'the presumption arises that [s]he destroyed it for the purpose of
revocation.' Stiles v. Brown, 380 So. 2d 792, 796 (Ala. 1980)." While this
presumption is rebuttable, the burden of rebutting the presumption
rests with the proponent of the will.
   Evidence offered by the proponent which merely shows "that a will
contestant had access to the will after the testatrix's death is not enough
to overcome the presumption [of revocation]." Summerhill, 425 So. 2d
at 1057. In Lovell v. Lovell, 272 Ala. 409, 412, 132 So. 2d 382, 384
(1961), it was held that the presumption was not overcome by evidence
showing that a contestant not only had opportunity to destroy the will,
but also told the proponent, who had a copy of the will, "that she would
have 'to find the original will and it has got to be signed and the date has
got to be right.'" Here, however, the proponent's testimony, taken as a
whole, tends to show much more than the evidence in Lovell. Her
account of the disordered condition of the house and her testimony that
Minnie had several times reaffirmed the existence of the will, the last
time being less than a month before her death, are factors to be considered. Cf. Stiles, supra (presumption rebutted by fact that attorney told
testator he must, to revoke the will, destroy both the copy retained by
the attorney and the copy retained by the testator, and with the fact that
the testator never attempted to destroy the copy retained by the attorney, coupled with the fact that a contestant had access to the will after
the testator's death).
   Where, as here, the proponent's evidence is contradicted by evidence
presented by the contestants, this Court cannot find that as a matter of
law the proponent has "over[come] the presumption of revocation raised
by the failure to find [the testatrix's] copy of the will." Summerhill, 425
So. 2d at 1057. However, a jury question on this issue was clearly presented, see Summerhill, supra, and the proponent's testimony, if believed,
was sufficient to support the verdict. Cf. New York Life Ins. Co. v. Turner,
213 Ala. 286, 288, 104 So. 643, 644 (1925) ("When a presumption [in a
civil case] is to be overcome, the jury, giving due weight to the presumption in the light of judgment and experience, and in connection with the
whole evidence, must be reasonably satisfied."). . . .
   Affirmed.

   _____

   When a will is traced to the testator's possession but cannot be found
at death, it is generally said that there is a presumption, and sometimes

"a strong presumption," that the will was destroyed with the intent to revoke. See generally T. Atkinson, Wills §86 (2d ed. 1953); Estate of Haynes, 25 Ohio St. 3d 101, 495 N.E.2d 23 (1986). In a few states such facts merely permit an *inference* of revocation. Scope v. Lynch, 132 Ind. App. 673, 176 N.E.2d 897 (1961). The testator's oral declarations and acts up to the date of death are generally admissible to rebut the presumption or counter the inference. Mimms v. Hunt, 458 S.W.2d 759 (Ky. App. 1970).

Assuming the presumption of revocation is rebutted, a lost or destroyed will may be probated in most states on satisfactory proof of its contents. Some statutes appear severely to restrict the probate of lost or destroyed wills, however, and in these states the requirements for an effective revocation may conflict with statutory provisions governing probate of lost or destroyed wills.

An example of this potential conflict is In re Fox's Will, 9 N.Y.2d 400, 174 N.E.2d 499 (1961). The decedent, Albert Fox, was an American citizen who lived in Germany for many years preceding his death in 1946. The question before the court was whether a will duly executed by him in Germany in 1939 and destroyed in the bombing of a Berlin building in 1944 could be admitted to probate in New York to exercise Fox's power of appointment over the remainder of a New York trust. Fox's son testified, over objection, that shortly after the war's end Fox learned of the destruction of his will and indicated that the will "had become without object" and that he intended to return to the United States and exercise the power of appointment in favor of his wife. Fox, however, made no new will during the ten months that elapsed between that time and his death. At all stages of the litigation the judges agreed that the will was not revoked; Decedent Estate Law §34 required destruction "with the intent and for the purpose of revoking the same," and subsequent "oral adoption" of the destruction could not constitute a revocation. The opponents of the will contended, however, that the case was controlled by §143 of the Surrogate's Court Procedure Act, which provides that a "lost or destroyed will" can be probated *only* if "the will was in existence at the time of the testator's death, or was fraudulently destroyed in his lifetime, and its provisions are clearly and distinctly proved by at least two credible witnesses, a correct copy or draft being equivalent to one witness." This contention was accepted by the Appellate Division and by the three dissenting judges of the Court of Appeals, but the four-judge majority reinstated the Surrogate's Court's granting of probate. Judge Fuld, writing for the majority, stated that, "even if admissible, the [son's] testimony did not negate a 'fraudulent destruction' within the meaning of the relevant statute," and continued:

> By requiring proof that a lost or destroyed will was either "in existence at the time of the testator's death, or was fraudulently destroyed in his lifetime," the Legislature merely intended to require proof that either the will

had not been destroyed during the testator's lifetime or that, if destroyed during his lifetime, it had not been destroyed by him or by his authority. In other words, all that section 143 requires is proof that the testator himself had not revoked the lost or destroyed will, proof that would overcome the common-law presumption of revocation. . . .

[T]he court in [Schultz v. Schultz, 35 N.Y. 653 (1886)] reasoned that the fact that the will had not been revoked by the testator necessarily implied compliance with the statutory requirement that the will either had been in existence at the time of death or had been "fraudulently destroyed." All that was intended by the words "fraudulently destroyed," said the court, was that the will "had been destroyed in [the testator's] lifetime, without his knowledge, consent or procurement, or accidentally lost." The phrase "fraudulently destroyed" has nothing to do with the question of the motive for destruction, but solely with the question of the agency of destruction. A will is considered to be "fraudulently destroyed" if it simply appears that it was destroyed by someone other than the testator and without his authorizing or directing the destruction.

The court below has distinguished Schultz v. Schultz, supra, on the ground that the testator in that case never learned of the destruction of his will and never "orally adopted" it. But, as is clear from an analysis of section 143 and from a reading of the Schultz opinion, the design of the section is solely to require proof that the lost or destroyed will offered for probate was not destroyed by the testator animo revocandi. Proof that the testator subsequently learned of the destruction of his will shows, if anything, that he himself did not destroy it and, therefore, such proof far from implying that the will was not "fraudulently destroyed," actually establishes that it was. . . .

Where a will is "clearly and distinctly proved" as required under section 143, the legal effect of refusing to admit it to probate on the ground that its destruction was subsequently "orally adopted" is to allow a will to be revoked without the formalities required by section 34 of the Decedent Estate Law. If a prior destruction of a will without "the intent and . . . the purpose of revoking the same" may subsequently be "orally adopted," with the effect of preventing its probate, our courts will again be forced, as the Appellate Division was in this case, to rely on parol evidence to defeat or sustain a writing executed with all the formalities required by law. This is precisely the condition found obnoxious at common law and which was sought to be avoided by the enactment of section 34 of our Decedent Estate Law.

However sophisticated the reasoning may appear, to speak of a destroyed will which is valid and unrevoked but which may not be admitted to probate is legal sophistry unless the refusal to admit it is based on reasonable doubt as to whether the will was really the testator's will. Here, there is no doubt whatsoever that the will offered for probate was the testator's will. Nor is there any question that it was not revoked with the formality required by law. There is, under the circumstances, no reason for denying it to probate.[3]

_____

3. 9 N.Y.2d 400, 408-410, 174 N.E.2d 499, 504-505 (1961).

Chief Judge Desmond, speaking for the minority, said that "section 143 is the only source of a Surrogate's power to probate a will destroyed during the testator's lifetime" and that the "plain language" of the section precluded probate, concluding:

> In a proper case constructive fraud or "fraud in law" as to a will's destruction may come within the terms and meaning of the statute so as to permit probate but the only likely instances are those where the testator dies without knowing that his will had been lost or obliterated. A testator who knows that his testament has been annihilated and accepts the fact and does nothing about it despite a reasonable opportunity to make a new will has not been the victim of a fraud, actual or constructive. It is not important whether we say with the Appellate Division that what happened here amounted to a post factum adoption of the prior destruction or say that the words "fraudulently destroyed" cannot be stretched to reach a case like this one. There is no decision anywhere allowing probate on such facts.[4]

Under a similar statute, the court In re Havel's Estate, 156 Minn. 253, 194 N.W. 633 (1923), focused on the language requiring that the will be in "existence" at the testator's death and concluded that this requirement refers not to physical existence but to legal existence, and that a will can lose its legal existence only by a valid revocation. Is such a theory tenable in light of the accompanying expressed exception for fraudulently destroyed wills?

See also Note, 39 Cal. L. Rev. 156 (1951), reviewing the experience under a comparable lost will statute.

Before passing too harsh a judgment on decisions that refuse to find a revocation for seemingly technical reasons and in apparent contravention of the decedent's intention, consider on what basis you formed your belief concerning the intent of the decedent, such as Mr. Fox. Such results are obviously unfortunate if we *assume* the decedent intended to revoke, but *did* he so intend? Is the evidence of his intent reliable — or is it representative of the very type of dangerous evidence that wills acts seek to exclude after the death of the person in question? If some danger exists in evidence of this type, is it not the legislature's prerogative to refuse to allow a jury to act on it? But are these arguments satisfying or sufficiently persuasive to render such results acceptable? Are they persuasive in relation to a case like Thompson v. Royall, supra, strictly limiting the meaning of *canceling*, as long as something as susceptible of falsification as marks on the face of a will would suffice as a revocation? And in *Fox,* had not the legislature exercised its "prerogative" of excluding risky evidence in lost will cases, only to be disregarded by the court? Cases testing the sufficiency of compliance with statutory formalities raise fundamental issues concerning all of the processes prescribed for executing and revoking wills.

4. 9 N.Y.2d at 413, 174 N.E.2d at 507.

Concerning the problem of the lost will statute in the *Fox* and *Havel* cases, consider whether the approach of these courts to the meaning of *existence* and *fraudulent destruction* can be squared with the rigid adherence to the literal wording of revocation statutes, as seen in Thompson v. Royall and in the revocation question in *Fox*. Have the courts in *Fox* and *Havel* refused to recognize the superiority of the legislature in lawmaking, or have they assisted their legislatures by finding workable solutions to difficult, unanticipated problems in accordance with a probable legislative purpose?

B. Revocation by Subsequent Instrument

A will may be revoked by a subsequent will or codicil. Although a few courts require that, in order effectively to revoke a prior will, the revoking instrument must make disposition of the testator's estate, typically a writing executed with the prescribed testamentary formalities is a sufficient revocation if it merely declares the prior will revoked.

When the testator's intent is to revoke prior wills, this should be clearly expressed in the will. If this is not the intent, the codicil should so state, refer to the other wills and codicils, and indicate its intended effect on their provisions (partial revocation being also permissible). In the latter case the instrument should be given the label of codicil, but merely designating a later instrument a "Last Will and Testament" is not conclusive that it is intended to revoke prior instruments.

The primary problem created by subsequent testamentary instruments is whether or to what extent revocation occurs when the intent of the testator regarding prior instruments is not expressed. A later instrument controls over an earlier one, and the earlier will is generally said to be revoked in whole or in part by implication to the extent the instruments are inconsistent; it might, however, be more accurate in partial inconsistency situations to say that the later provision "supersedes" the earlier, at least for as long as the later remains in effect. In a number of jurisdictions, statutes derived from early New York legislation provide essentially that "a will is not revoked by a subsequent will unless the latter contains an express revocation or terms wholly inconsistent with terms of the prior will" and that the prior will otherwise "remains effective so far as consistent with the provisions of the subsequent will." The difficulty, of course, is in determining what constitutes an inconsistency and the extent thereof. Contrast UPC §2-507.

C. Revocation by Operation of Law

Statutes prescribing the methods of revocation often fail to mention revocation by operation of law. Such statutes, even though purporting to make the recited methods exclusive, are often construed not to preclude revocation by operation of law; that is, the exclusive provisions of the statute may be deemed to refer only to revocation by the testator and thus to permit a court to hold a will revoked by operation of law under certain circumstances.

Unless otherwise provided by statute, divorce alone is generally not sufficient to revoke a will or even the provisions for the divorced spouse. If the divorce is accompanied by a property settlement, however, it is commonly provided by statute, or held by courts in the absence of a statute, that all provisions for the divorced spouse in a preexisting will are revoked. Some states have refused to recognize revocation even in this situation, either because of a general refusal to recognize revocation by operation of law (based on strict interpretation of statutes prescribing the exclusive methods of revocation) or because of a statutory provision dealing with revocation by operation of law without mention of this situation. A growing number of statutes now expressly provide that divorce revokes all provision for the spouse in a preexisting will. Some cases hold that in that event the affected property passes as if the former spouse had failed to survive the testator. E.g., Jones v. Brown, 219 Va. 599, 248 S.E.2d 812 (1978). But see, e.g., Davis v. Davis, 24 Ohio Misc. 17, 258 N.E.2d 277 (1970). Uniform Probate Code §2-804 revokes provision for a spouse or relative of a spouse in the event of subsequent divorce or annulment and declares that the property passes as if the former spouse or relative were dead. It also declares that revocation results from no change of circumstances other than divorce, annulment, or homicide.

To what extent do policies underlying revocation by operation of law on divorce also apply to will substitutes, such as joint tenancies and revocable trusts? (This question should be considered as you study Chapter 8 and Chapter 11, section A3.) Except as provided by the governing instrument, contract, or court orders, 1990 Uniform Probate Code §2-804 revokes any revocable disposition previously made to the divorced spouse or relative of the divorced spouse and severs the spouses' interests in joint and survivorship property. Illinois Revised Statutes, c. 148, §301, provides that unless the governing instrument and judgment "expressly provide otherwise, judicial termination of the marriage of the settlor of a trust revokes every provision which is revocable by the settlor pertaining to the settlor's former spouse in a trust instrument or amendment thereto, executed by the settlor before the entry" of that judgment, and that the trust is to be administered as if the former spouse had died.

The other situation that in some states may cause a revocation by operation of law is the subsequent marriage of the testator followed by birth of issue. This method of revocation existed at common law in England and was often recognized in this country by statute or common law, based on a presumed intent resulting from a fundamental change in the testator's situation. Modern statutes, however, generally deal with these problems solely through the pretermitted heir and omitted spouse statutes discussed in Chapter 3, section C.

MATTER OF ESTATE OF MARUCCIA
54 N.Y.2d 196, 429 N.E.2d 751 (1981)

[The issue on this appeal is whether the provisions of the separation agreement entered into between the decedent and his wife caused a revocation of provisions for her under his earlier will. EPTL 3-4.3 provides: "A conveyence, settlement or other act of a testator . . . which is wholly inconsistent with [a] previous testamentary disposition revokes it." Decedent transferred certain properties to petitioner pursuant to the separation agreement, which contained a general release stating that "each party hereby waives and releases to the other party the right to share in any of the property or estate of such other which has arisen or may hereafter arise by operation of the law or otherwise."]

JASEN, J. . . .

The Surrogate . . . found the language employed in the separation agreement to be "wholly inconsistent" with the testamentary disposition in petitioner's favor and held such provisions revoked. . . .

The Legislature has adopted an elaborate scheme [for] the revocation of a will . . . [and] may be said to have expressed its approval of [prior] narrow construction by the courts of waiver clauses in separation agreements. . . . Indeed, the statute itself, by employing the term "*wholly inconsistent*," supports a strict approach to implied revocations. . . .

With this in mind, we hold that in order for a separation agreement to have the effect of revoking a prior devise or bequest pursuant to EPTL 3-4.3, the agreement must either contain a provision whereby the spouse explicitly renounces any testamentary disposition in his or her favor made prior to the date of the separation agreement or employ language which clearly and unequivocally manifests an intent on the part of the spouses that they are no longer beneficiaries under each other's wills. . . .

In this case, the separation agreement does not contain any provision whereby petitioner renounced the *voluntary* bequests [but] merely provides for a relinquishment by petitioner of statutory rights arising from the marital relationship. . . . The ambiguous phrases whereby petitioner waived and released all right to share in the decedent's estate " . . . by operation of law or otherwise" and in which she gave up "all right to administer the estate" are alone insufficient. . . . [A] far clearer indication of decedent's intent is required before it can be concluded that he desired to revoke a prior devise or bequest to his wife. . . .

[I]t should be noted that . . . where execution of the separation agreement is followed by divorce or dissolution of the marriage, all prior testamentary dispositions to the former spouse will be revoked automatically by operation of law, unless the will provides otherwise. . . .

> [S]ound practice would indicate that whenever parties are legally separated or divorced, the client's will should be amended to reflect the changed circumstances and revised plan of testamentary dispositions.

(Rohan, Practice Comentary, McKinney's Cons. Laws of N.Y., Book 17B, p. 526.) . . .

D. Reestablishing Revoked or Apparently Revoked Wills

A lawyer may be called on to salvage the apparent intent of a decedent by attempting to probate a "revoked" will. The lawyer may find it necessary to urge that a *revoked will* has been revived, or may have to contend that a will is not revoked even though the testator has, with *actual* intent to revoke, performed upon it one of the physical acts of revocation authorized by statute or despite the valid execution of a subsequent writing declaring or implying that the will is revoked. The following problem presents such a case. With this problem situation in mind, study the text, cases, and shorter problems on revival and dependent relative revocation in the remainder of this chapter for possible solutions and for obstacles to be overcome.

PROBLEM

6-B. *X* comes to your office with three sheets of paper discovered among the papers of *T*, who has recently died leaving a net estate of $500,000. *T*'s next of kin are five nieces and nephews, *V, W, X, Y,* and *Z*, each of whom will take one-fifth of the estate if *T* is held to have died intestate. One of these papers is a will, which you have since determined was properly executed in 1976. This will purportedly leaves *T*'s estate in equal shares to *X, Y,* and *Z*. The second is a validly executed 1981 will, which provides in relevant part: "Because *Z* has recently been left a fortune by his Uncle *U*, I hereby leave my entire estate in equal shares to *X* and *Y*." No mention is made of the earlier will. Across the written side of this 1981 will is a large, red cross, which also shows the date February 1, 1986, in red. The third paper is also an attested writing. It is dated February 4, 1986, and merely recites: "I hereby revoke my 1981 will." *X* asks what can be done to secure for him and his brother, *Y*, their just shares of *T*'s estate.

On further inquiry you learn that the 1976 and 1986 papers were found folded together in a large envelope in *T*'s desk in a top drawer that contained various important papers and an insurance policy (the payees of which were *X*, *Y*, and *Z* under a beneficiary designation executed in 1987). The 1981 paper was found among some of *T*'s old bank statements, canceled checks, and other personal and financial records in a large drawer under that in which the other papers were found.

X also reveals that, as many of *T*'s friends can assure you is true, *T* greatly favored *X*, *Y*, and *Z*, over their cousins, *V* and *W*. This feeling had existed for many years because *V* and *W* had long ago moved far away from the city in which *T*, *X*, *Y*, and *Z* resided, although *T* did feel some fondness for *V* and *W* as well. *T* openly stated, and with *Z*'s concurrence, that, when *Z* inherited his fortune from *U*, *Z* should not expect more from *T*. However, *X* further informs you that in late 1985 *Z* lost nearly his entire fortune because of an adverse personal injury judgment. *Y* can testify that *T* thereafter stated to *Z*, in *Y*'s presence, that he would see to it that *Z* was provided for.

Would you take *X*'s case? On what basis and theories would you proceed? What added information would you look for? What obstacles and arguments would you expect to encounter, and how would you meet them? You have a lead suggesting that the 1986 instrument was defectively executed; will this sufficiently improve your case to justify pursuing this lead?

In the jurisdiction involved you encounter the following statute, patterned after early New York legislation and virtually identical to that enacted in about one-quarter of the states: "If, after making a will, the testator makes a second will, the destruction or other revocation of the second will does not revive the first will unless it appears by the terms of such revocation that the testator intended to revive and give effect to the first will, or unless the first will is duly republished." Consider the materials that follow. Consider also the statute of your state and the provisions of the Uniform Probate Code noted infra.

1. Revival of Revoked Wills

Assuming that a second will (no. 2) has revoked an earlier will (no. 1) either expressly or by implication, and that will no. 1 has not been destroyed, what methods are available for the testator to revoke will no. 2 and also revive will no. 1 so that it would be operative at death? It would be appropriate and desirable to draft and execute a new will following the terms of will no. 1. Instead, the testator might formally execute another instrument expressly revoking will no. 2, while expressly incorporating will no. 1 by reference or declaring his intent to republish it. All too often, however, a testator yields to the natural temptation merely to revoke will no. 2, usually by some physical act, intending will no. 1 to be effective. The problem then created is whether the prior, revoked will has been revived by this revocation of the subsequent will. Because this action is equally consistent with an intention to be intestate, the uncertainties of speculating about the testator's intent and the dangers of accepting available evidence of that intent are apparent.

The early English law furnishes a valuable background for considering the various American rules on revival. Under the English common law will no. 1 was revived automatically by the revocation of will no. 2, regardless of the testator's intent, on the theory that a will is ambulatory and therefore has no effect until the testator's death. Consequently, will no. 2 "never actually revoked" will no. 1. The English ecclesiastical courts took a quite different view. In their conception of the process through which wills and revocations operated, revocation took effect immediately when the revoking instrument was executed; nevertheless, the revoked will would be revived if the testator so intended when the subsequent will was revoked. English legislation (the Wills Act, 1837) resolves the matter by requiring reexecution to restore the effectiveness of a previously revoked will.

The American courts and legislatures have adopted a variety of views on the question of revival. Numerous courts have considered the revocation of will no. 2 to revive will no. 1, regardless of the testator's intent, following the English common law view; a few of these cases have indicated that this rule applies only when will no. 2 had revoked will no. 1 by inconsistency and that this rule would be inapplicable if will no. 1 had been expressly revoked. Many other courts have followed a form of the ecclesiastical rule that revival depends on the testator's intent. These courts have been liberal in regard to the types of evidence to be considered in establishing the intent to revive. Some decisions indicate no presumption as to this intention. Others presume the intent to revive did not exist, placing the burden of proof on those asserting such intent, while still others presume the existence of an intent to revive unless the contrary is shown. Finally, by statute in a great number of American jurisdictions (as in England since the Wills Act, 1837), and by judicial decision in a few states, the rule is that will no. 1 cannot be revived by the mere revocation of will no. 2; depending upon construction of the statute, republication of will no. 1 may be necessary to revive the first will. The commonest form of statute is quoted in Problem 6-B, supra. Courts may disagree about whether this type of statute applies to a partial revocation of will no. 1, and about what constitutes a revocation of a will by total inconsistency. Under statutes based on the original (now superseded) Uniform Probate Code §2-509, will no. 1 is revived by revocation of will no. 2 only (1) if the intent to do so "appears from the terms of" a subsequent revoking instrument or (2) if, in a revocation of will no. 2 by physical act, the intent to revive will no. 1 "is evident" from the circumstances or from the testator's contemporaneous or subsequent declarations.

Under any of the basic positions indicated above, a court might distinguish (1) *express* revocation of the earlier will by the later will from (2) an implied revocation of the earlier will *by inconsistency;* and in particular a court may distinguish complete revocation by either of these two methods from (3) a *partial* revocation of the earlier will by inconsistency of some of these provisions with the terms of the subsequent instrument, or possibly even by express revocation of only certain provisions of the earlier will.

UNIFORM PROBATE CODE

§2-509.   *Revival of Revoked Will.*

(a) If a subsequent will that wholly revoked a previous will is thereafter revoked by a revocatory act under Section 2-507(a)(2), the previous will remains revoked unless it is revived. The previous will is revived if it is evident from the circumstances of the revocation of the subsequent will or from the testator's contemporary or subsequent declarations that the testator intended the previous will to take effect as executed.

(b) If a subsequent will that partly revoked a previous will is thereafter revoked by a revocatory act under Section 2-507(a)(2), a revoked part of the previous will is revived unless it is evident from the circumstances of the revocation of the subsequent will or from the testator's contemporary or subsequent declarations that the testator did not intend the revoked part to take effect as executed.

(c) If a subsequent will that revoked a previous will in whole or in part is thereafter revoked by another, later, will, the previous will remains revoked in whole or in part, unless it or its revoked part is revived. The previous will or its revoked part is revived to the extent it appears from the terms of the later will that the testator intended the previous will to take effect.

PROBLEMS

6-C.   Ten years ago *T* executed a will devising Blackacre to *A* and giving the residue to *B*. Five years later *T* executed a new will expressly revoking the old one and giving his entire estate to *B*. A year ago *T* burned the second will. On *T*'s death how does his estate pass, assuming his nearest relative is *B*? Does it matter if evidence is offered that *T* declared to *W*, as he burned the later will: "Now *A* can have Blackacre"? How would the case be decided under a statute of the type in Problem 6-B, supra?

6-D.   Ten years ago *T* executed a will devising Blackacre to *A* and leaving the residue to *B*. Five years later *T* executed an instrument entitled "Codicil to My Will," devising Blackacre to *C* but not otherwise mentioning the prior will. Last year *T* burned the codicil and thereafter died. Result? What would be the result of destroying the later instrument if it had contained no heading and no reference to the earlier will, but had simply devised Blackacre to *C* and left the residue to *B*? Cf. Baily v. McElroy, 186 N.E.2d 219 (Ohio Prob. Ct. 1962); but see Estate of Schnoor, 4 Cal. 2d 590, 51 P.2d 424 (1935).

2. Dependent Relative Revocation

In studying the following cases and text, give particular attention to when, for what purposes, and to what extent extrinsic evidence may and should be admitted for the purpose of establishing a mistake and then to establish the "probable intent" on which the application of the doctrine of dependent relative revocation is generally predicated.

The doctrine of dependent relative revocation has been described as "a fictional process which consists of disregarding revocation brought about by mistake on the ground that the revocation was conditional." T. Atkinson, Wills §88 (2d ed. 1953). In general see Henderson, Mistake and Fraud in Wills, 47 B.U.L. Rev. 304, 330 (1967). Compare Palmer, Dependent Relative Revocation and Its Relation to Relief for Mistake, 69 Mich. L. Rev. 989 (1971), to the effect that the doctrine is neither applicable to all mistakes nor limited to mistake situations, but asserting that it should be confined to cases in which the "conditional" intent relates to another plan of disposition that fails.

The doctrine can best be introduced by a simple example of its operation. Assume that *T* had executed a valid will. Thereafter she had another instrument drawn and executed, intending and believing it to be her will. *T* canceled the old will, but on her death the new will is determined to be invalid. Assuming it is concluded that *T* would not have revoked the prior will but for her belief that the second will rendered it useless, a court would normally apply the doctrine to permit probate of the first will. In fact, once the mistake is established, a few courts might apply the doctrine mechanically, even without a finding that *T* would have preferred the first will over intestacy.

Although decisions are too few to be certain, at least a purist would say (with supporting authority) that the doctrine does not apply to the case of a testator whose will was revoked by cancelation with the intent to execute another very soon but who died without doing so. Of course, refusal to apply the doctrine can be explained on the ground that the testator did not act under a "mistake." Even if this result is sound, however, does the doctrine always require a mistake as distinguished from an expectation or hope that does not materialize? As you read, consider whether you find any case authority that supports the view of Palmer, supra, that it does not.

How is the mistake, and then the basis for a legally attributed intention, to be proved when extrinsic evidence is not generally allowed to impair the integrity of testamentary transactions? The answer often given is that the evidence is admissible in cases of apparent revocation by physical act because such acts performed on wills are inherently ambiguous and that parol evidence is therefore necessary to show the character of an alleged act of revocation. Then, courts have generally been willing to go a step further and receive extrinsic evidence to clarify the nature of the intent, or more precisely to show a motivating mistake on which that intent is based. This is so even though courts usually refuse to correct, or even to receive evidence of, a mistake in the inducement of a will.

Although some courts have flatly refused to apply the doctrine of a dependent relative revocation when confronted by an express revocation contained in a will — a distinction rejected in most modern decisions — the true source of difficulty in such cases may be the problem of introducing extrinsic evidence when a testamentary instrument is clear and unambiguous on its face. Should parol evidence be admitted to contradict or to qualify a formal writing declaring or clearly implying the revocation of a prior will?

PROBLEM

6-E.   What result would you expect in the following situations?

(a) Erroneously believing a favorite nephew to be dead, *T* destroys her will, which would have left everything to that nephew.

(b) Under the same erroneous belief, *T* executes a second will expressly revoking the first and leaving everything "in equal shares to all of my nieces and nephews who survive me."

(c) Under the same erroneous belief, *T* executes a second will reciting: "Because my nephew, *N,* is dead, I hereby revoke my prior will and bequeath and devise my property in equal shares to all of my nieces and nephews who survive me."

In re KAUFMAN'S ESTATE
25 Cal. 2d 854, 155 P.2d 831 (1945)

TRAYNOR, J.

On March 18, 1940, Samuel B. Kaufman executed a will in New York. He subsequently moved to California where he executed a new will on April 30, 1941, containing the clause "I, Samuel B. Kaufman, do hereby make and declare this to be my Last Will and Testament, revoking all former wills." Both wills named identical persons for identical cash bequests and the Second Church of Christ, Scientist, of New York City, as residuary legatee. The 1941 will named a new executor. . . . The testator died on May 2, 1941. On petition of one of the executors, the 1941 will was admitted to probate. [The charitable bequest in the 1941 will violated a then-existing statutory prohibition against charitable bequests executed within thirty days of death, so appellant] thereafter filed a petition to have the 1940 will admitted to probate, to which respondent filed a contest. The present appeal is taken from the judgment denying the 1940 will admission to probate.

The respondent contends that there is substantial evidence to support the finding of the trial court that it was the intention of the testator in executing the 1941 will to revoke the 1940 will unconditionally. The appellant contends that the 1940 will should be admitted to probate under the doctrine of dependent relative revocation, on the ground that the testator did not intend to destroy the testamentary effect of the 1940 will unless the 1941 will would become wholly effective. . . .

Under the doctrine of dependent relative revocation, an earlier will, revoked only to give effect to a later one on the supposition that the later one will become effective, remains in effect to the extent that the latter proves ineffective. The doctrine is designed to carry out the probable intention of the testator when there is no reason to suppose that he intended to revoke his earlier will if the later will became inoperative. The doctrine has been invoked in California and is sustained by the weight of authority. . . .

The doctrine is clearly applicable to the facts of the present case. . . . Since the second will was virtually identical with the first in the disposition of the testator's estate, it is clear that the first will was revoked only because the second duplicated its purpose and the testator would have preferred the first will to intestacy as to a substantial part of his estate. [A] testator who repeats his purpose intends to confirm and not revoke it, and does not intend to have the new will operate as a revocation independently of its operation as a will. . . .

The trial court's finding that the testator intended to revoke the 1940 will unconditionally is not supported by the evidence. All the testimony, including the testimony of Trust Officer Seaman and of Attorney Fogel and his secretary, shows that the testator wanted no change in his will except for the naming of a California executor. Any conclusion as to the testator's intention must be considered in the light of his knowledge at the time he executed the will. The testator was not advised that he might provide in his 1941 will that the revocation of the charitable bequest by the revocation clause in the 1941 will was dependent upon the legal effectiveness of the 1941 will to carry out his bequest, nor was he advised that the same result would follow under the doctrine of dependent relative revocation. . . . It does not follow from the fact that he was advised that the new will would not be effective unless he lived for thirty days that he intended that the charitable bequest should fail if he died within that period. To so hold would be to read into the charitable bequest an intentional condition precedent that the testator should live for more than thirty days. There is no evidence that the testator had any such intention.

The judgment is reversed with directions to admit the 1940 will to probate with the 1941 will. . . .

Newman v. Newman, 199 N.E.2d 904 (Ohio Prob. Ct. 1964), discussed but refused to follow *Kaufman* in an analogous situation.

Note the use of oral testimony in the *Kaufman* case. Was it essential to the result? Although such evidence is admissible under the modern view, some courts would refuse to receive it. Should a court that is more strict about extrinsic evidence consider the prior will for what it may suggest concerning what the testator probably would have desired?

With the above case, contrast the following: *T*'s will left the residue of his estate to charity *A*, but his provision is invalid as in *Kaufman*; a prior will, executed before the statutory period, had provided for the residue to go to charity *B*, the other provisions being identical to those of the later will. If the court will "admit extrinsic evidence only if a will is ambiguous," how would one argue for consideration of the prior will? Would the two wills alone satisfy a court that *T* would prefer to leave his property to charity *B* rather than die intestate, as they well might have under *Kaufman* facts? If not, what arguments are there for considering other evidence? What evidence would be persuasive? If the earlier will is admitted in evidence but its proponents can produce no other evidence from which to deduce what *T* would have wished if he had known of the defect in the second will, how would this case be decided? Consider the case that follows.

WOLF v. BOLLINGER
62 Ill. 368 (1872)

SHELDON, J. . . .

On the 2d day of February, 1868, Jacob Bizer duly executed his last will and testament, wherein Catharine Bollinger, the appellee, was made the devisee of a certain forty acres of land. A few weeks afterward, the testator sent for Frederick T. Krafft, the executor named in the will, and informed him that he wished to alter the will so that Christina Wolf, the appellant, should take the forty acres instead of Catharine Bollinger; and at his instance, Krafft cancelled the name of Catharine Bollinger in the will, by drawing lines through it with a pen, leaving the name still legible, and interlined over it the name of Christina Wolf, so as to make the will

read as a devise of the forty acres to her. . . . After the death of Jacob
Bizer, the will, in its altered condition, was admitted to probate. . . .

We come now to the main question in this case — the effect of this
alteration of the will. [For want of proper execution, the interlineations]
did not operate as a disposing will as to Christina Wolf. Had the alteration any legal effects as to Catharine Bollinger?

Before the alteration, the will contained a valid devise to her of this
forty acres of land. It is the rule that a valid will, once existing, must continue in force, unless revoked in the mode prescribed by statute; which,
by the fifteenth section of our Chapter of Wills, is as follows:

> No will, testament, or codicil shall be revoked, otherwise than by burning,
> cancelling, tearing, or obliterating the same by the testator himself, or in
> his presence, by his direction and consent, or by some other will, testament
> or codicil. . . .

The only mode of revocation of this devise to Catharine Bollinger, that
can be claimed in this case, is by cancellation or obliteration. Lines were
drawn with a pen through her name as devisee, leaving it still legible, and
the name of Christina Wolf was interlined above it. It has been often
determined, in the construction of similar statutes, that the mere acts
named, of cancellation or obliteration, will not constitute a valid revocation, unless done with the intent to revoke. And although every act of
cancelling imports prima facie that it is done with the intent to revoke,
it is but a presumption, which may be repelled by accompanying circumstances.

The intent of the testator, as expressed by himself, when he directed
the cancellation to be made, was, "that Christina Wolf should inherit the
forty acres instead of Catharine Bollinger." The cancellation was not
made with intent to revoke the devise to the complainant simply, but with
intent to substitute in her stead the defendant, Christina Wolf, as a devisee. The cancellation of the name of Catharine Bollinger was but as a
means toward the effecting of the end of such substitution; and the ultimate object of substitution having failed of accomplishment, the cancelling, which was done only in the view of, and in order to effect, that
object, should be esteemed for nothing, and be considered, not as having been made absolutely, but only conditionally, upon the attempted
substitution being made effectual. To give it effect under the circumstances, would seem to be to thwart the intention of the testator, and
make him intestate as to this piece of land, when he manifested the contrary intent by his will. It can by no means be said to have been the intent
of the testator, that in case Christina Wolf was not substituted as devisee,
Catharine Bollinger should not take the devise, or that as between the
latter and his heirs-at-law, he preferred that they should have the land.
The original intention of the will certainly was to make her a devisee; it

appears to have been changed no further than in order to effect the substitution of another devisee in her place; that purpose having failed to become perfected, the original intention to devise to Catharine Bollinger must be considered as remaining unchanged.

It is believed to be the doctrine, as laid down in Redfield on Wills, 314, 325, 327, and well settled by the authorities, that where the testator makes an alteration in his will, by erasure and interlineation, or in any other mode, without authenticating such alteration by a new attestation in the presence of witnesses, or other form required by the statute, it is presumed that the erasure was intended to be dependent upon the alteration going into effect as a substitute; and such alteration not being so made as to take effect, the will, therefore, stands in legal force, the same as it did before, so far as it is legible after the attempted alteration. Short v. Smith, 4 East, 417; Jackson v. Holloway, 7 J.R. 394; Laughton v. Atkins, 1 Pick, 535.

The award of costs against Christina Wolf, which is complained of, was a matter of discretion with the court, with the exercise of which we see no reason for interference.

Perceiving no error in the record, the decree of the court below is affirmed.

Is it apparent in the above case, even in light of the evidence of the testator's statement to Krafft, that the revocation of the devise to Catharine Bollinger was dependent on the validity of the devise to Christina Wolf? Would the decedent have desired the result reached by the court? Should this matter? Or does this particular court, when such a mistake appears, simply presume the fictitious intent to condition the revocation, at least if the contrary is not shown? Would it proceed differently if the revocation were by writing rather than by act?

Contrast (1) the obvious propriety of applying the doctrine of dependent relative revocation when the requisite intent is convincingly apparent in the alleged act of revocation performed upon the face of the will, as in the following invalid alteration:

$15,000
I bequeath $~~10,000~~ to my niece, Joan.

with (2) the *Wolf* case and with (3) the following:

$2,000
I bequeath $~~10,000~~ to my niece, Joan.

In the latter case would the testator prefer the larger legacy to stand rather than permit the legacy to fail? See Ruel v. Hardy, 90 N.H. 240, 6

A.2d 753 (1939), which acknowledged that the doctrine is based on probable intent — that is, on what the testator would have preferred if informed of the available choices. The court held that, although a presumption existed in favor of the doctrine's application, the nature and amount of the attempted change in the gift was sufficient to rebut the presumption absent other evidence of the decedent's intent. Thus, the court found the doctrine inapplicable under the evidence before it, while also indicating that "pertinent oral declarations" of the testator and other extrinsic evidence should be received in such cases.

7

Will Contracts

A surprising amount of litigation results from the attempts of persons to contract with regard to the disposition of property on the death of one or both of the parties. The problems are complicated in some cases by failure of the parties to reduce their "agreement" to writing or by failure to make the writing clear. Further complications sometimes result from confused intermingling of contract law with the law of wills in litigating these problems.

Two types of will contracts are particularly common. One arises from the situation in which one person, usually an elderly person, wishes to induce another to provide care and agrees to compensate the latter by bequeathing all or part of the promisor's estate. The other arises when two people — typically husband and wife — wish the survivor to receive the property of the first to die and then wish to assure by contract that on the survivor's death the property will pass in a certain fashion. Such arrangements are often thought useful where the natural objects of the bounty of each party are different persons.

UNIFORM PROBATE CODE

§2-514. *Contracts Concerning Succession.* A contract to make a will or devise, or not to revoke a will or devise, or to die intestate, if executed after the effective date of this Article, may be established only by (i) provisions of a will stating material provisions of the contract, (ii) an express reference in a will to a contract and extrinsic evidence proving the terms of the contract, or (iii) a writing signed by the decedent evidencing the contract. The execution of a joint will or mutual wills does not create a presumption of a contract not to revoke the will or wills.

A. *Contract to Bequeath or Devise*

Assuming the usual requirements for a valid contract and any special statutory requirements are met, a contract to make, not to make, or not to revoke a will, or to bequeath or devise certain property, is valid. It is

218

valid as a contract, however, and not as a will. The contract cannot be probated, for example, if the will is not made; nor can a revoked will be probated even if its revocation was in violation of a contract. Also, a contract generally cannot be used to oppose probate of an inconsistent will because the remedy for breach is not at probate. (Probate proceedings, however, should not be totally ignored. See Chapter 15 concerning timely filing of claims against estates.) If not performed, an enforceable promise gives rise to a cause of action against the estate or beneficiaries of the promisor. The problems of enforcement are basically those of enforcing any contract of a deceased person.

Contracts to make wills need not be executed with the formalities of wills, but there is frequently a requirement that such contracts be in writing. This requirement in some states stems from a statute specifically applicable to contracts to make wills. In other states typical statute of frauds provisions require a writing for many situations. For example, a contract to devise land is almost universally held to come within the statute; and generally when a contract relates to both real and personal property, it is held that the statute applies to the entire promise. Where land is not involved in the promise, there is a difference of opinion whether the provision relating to sale of goods is applicable, but usually the specific requirements of this section will be found satisfied as a result of the promisee's performance even if the section is deemed applicable. The section relating to contracts not to be performed within a year does not apply because the promise *may* be fully performed within that period.

If the promisor fails to perform and dies, the promisee *may* bring an action at law for damages. As an alternative, the promisee generally may obtain equitable relief under such labels as specific performance, quasi-specific performance, relief in the nature of specific performance, or constructive trust. In such cases — with the remedy generally sought in equity — the question of adequacy of the remedy at law is often not raised and is rarely given careful discussion. For the bases of equitable jurisdiction, see B. Sparks, Contracts to Make Wills 146-151 (1956). A third possible remedy is quantum meruit for the value of the services rendered or the support or other consideration furnished. This remedy is generally important as a means of obtaining relief when the requirement of a writing is found applicable and is neither satisfied nor removed on any of the usual grounds, although the presumption that the services of a relative are gratuitous presents difficulties for a plaintiff in such a proceeding. The niceties of the contracts and remedies problems need not be examined here, but the intricacies of local procedural rules should be considered in bringing an action on a breached will contract. The fundamental problems inherent in contracts to bequeath and devise should become apparent as the chapter is studied.

The problem that follows raises some of the commonly encountered difficulties in the context of a typical situation for which will contracts are employed. Consider this problem in light of your local statutes and your general knowledge from other sources.

PROBLEM

7-A.   *A* has come to you for advice and relates the following facts to you. Ten years ago *T, A*'s 68-year-old mother, requested *A* and her husband, *H,* to live in *T*'s home and to look after her in her late years when she was plagued by illness and loneliness. In return *T* promised orally to leave her house and at least half of the rest of her estate to *A.* As soon thereafter as *A* and *H* could terminate the lease on their apartment, they moved into *T*'s home. They resided with her until she died two months ago and cared for her through this difficult period at considerable inconvenience to themselves. Just after *A* and *H* moved into *T*'s house, *T* executed a will that read in relevant part: "As an expression of my gratitude to my daughter, *A,* I leave her my home and personal effects and one-half of the rest of my property. The rest I leave equally to my other children *B, C,* and *D.*" For about the last year of *T*'s life she was irritable and felt that, because she was deaf and unable to get around well, she was neither needed nor appreciated by her children. When she died the only traces of her will were the torn pieces of it in her desk drawer, with a notation on one piece reading "canceled." No one wishes to question *T*'s mental capacity to revoke or to make a will right up to the date of her death, but *A* asks whether she can take more than the $44,000 worth of property that she has determined would constitute her intestate share of *T*'s estate. (a) What are *A*'s rights? How should she proceed? (b) Would her case be different if she had not been related to *T*? (c) Would it matter if, instead of the above promise, *T* had merely said: "I shall reward you in my will"? See Restaino v. Vannah, 483 N.E.2d 847 (Mass. App. 1985).

B.   *Joint and Mutual Wills*

A joint will is a single instrument executed by two persons as the will of each. Mutual wills are separate wills of different persons, containing similar or reciprocal provisions.

At one time joint wills were invalid. Today it is generally accepted that such a will is valid unless it appears that the will was to operate only on the death of the survivor of the cotestators. A valid joint will, then, operates and is probated on the death of each cotestator as if there were two separate documents.

Joint or mutual wills are revocable in the same manner as other wills. Sometimes, however, such wills are executed pursuant to a contract in which it is agreed that the property of the testators will be disposed of according to the present wills or that the wills will not be revoked. Here it is essential, in order to avoid the confusion found in some cases, to distinguish between the wills and the contract. Properly analyzed, wills executed pursuant to a contract are revocable, but the *power* to revoke and alter a will is not the *right* to do so and does not preclude liability on the *contract*. Thus, it is generally recognized that in the probate of a will the court is not concerned with whether the will is executed pursuant to or in violation of a contract.

Because rights would be created by a contract, the existence or nonexistence of an underlying obligation is important in these will cases. Major problems therefore arise in determining whether a contract exists and in determining its terms, particularly with respect to the rights of the survivor. Essentially the problems of proving the contract are the same as in other types of contracts.

Mutual or joint will contracts are commonly employed in two types of cases. One is where a husband and wife have had no children, and each promises to leave everything to the survivor, who in turn promises to leave the property in agreed shares to certain collateral relatives of each. The other is where a husband or wife or both had children by a previous marriage, and the contract is arranged to assure that, on the survivor's death, certain provision will be made for the children of the first spouse to die. Of course, these are not the only cases in which it might be tempting to contract for the execution and nonrevocation of mutual or joint wills. The usual advice of those who have studied the multitude of problems created by contractual wills is not to use them; but before this advice can be followed without disservice to one's client, one must decide what alternative arrangements are available to accomplish the desired purpose and to eliminate the risks inherent in the uncertain order of the clients' deaths. As the problems and cases hereafter are studied, consider (1) how the wills and the alleged contracts could have been used and drafted without creating the issues in question and (2) what other arrangement you might have suggested to accomplish the apparent purposes of the parties. Also, we might simply note that contractual wills may give rise to a number of serious tax problems that should not be disregarded, particularly where the estates of the parties are substantial.

B. SPARKS, CONTRACTS TO MAKE WILLS
27-28 (1956)

The clear weight of authority, and certainly the sounder view, is that the mere presence of either joint or mutual wills does not raise any presumption that they were executed in pursuance of a contract. Nor is this rule altered by evidence that the parties had "agreed" to the making of such wills. Of course they had so agreed. The mere presence of such wills reveals that the parties must have talked the matter over and must have arrived at an understanding or agreement concerning their testamentary dispositions. Such discussions and such understandings between persons of close affinities, especially between husbands and wives, are not unusual and the fact that they have taken place is no indication that there has been any thought of a binding contract.

CUMMINGS v. SHERMAN
16 Wash. 2d 88, 132 P.2d 998 (1943)

[Homer and Phoebe Shinn executed mutual wills in 1931. Homer died later that year, willing his residuary estate to Phoebe "with full and exclusive right of disposition," providing that had she not survived half the residue would go to her relatives and half to his. The will was admitted to probate and Phoebe acted as executrix. When she died in 1934, however, she had executed a new will, which was admitted to probate. This will made no provision for Homer's relatives (respondents), who sought and were awarded half of Phoebe's estate based on a contract by the Shinns to make and not revoke the 1931 wills. Some of Phoebe's relatives appeal.]

SIMPSON, J. . . .

Allen v. Dillard, Wash., 129 P.2d 813, 817, . . . stated "contracts to make mutual wills are recognized under our law as valid and . . . may be specifically enforced. . . . Because, however, of the great opportunity for fraud, and because of reluctance on the part of courts to render ineffective a subsequent will of a testator, the contract to make mutual wills must be established by clear and convincing evidence."

The question first to be decided is whether or not the testimony introduced in this case was sufficient to prove the making of the oral contract under the rule to which we have just referred.

The proof of the oral agreement was supplied by Fred J. Cunningham, a member of the Spokane bar. Mr. Cunningham stated that he drew the wills in 1931 at the request of Mr. and Mrs. Shinn. His testimony relative to the oral agreement is as follows:

> Q. Now, the first time that they consulted you together, state what the conversation was . . . in regard to executing wills. . . .
>
> The Witness: They came in by appointment, and Mr. Shinn stated that they had now reached an agreement as to making wills, or the substance of the statement, and he asked that I explain to Mrs. Shinn the difference between mutual wills and individual wills, which I attempted to do.
>
> By Mr. Grant: Q. State what you said to them in response to that question.

A. As I recall, I stated that if they wanted to deal with their own share, each one's own share of the community property, they could make individual wills which could be changed at any time they wanted to, up until their death. If they wanted to deal with their community property by some agreement between them as to the character of their wills, and they entered into such wills, then when one of the parties died and that will was probated, their rights became fixed and the survivor could not change the will, at his option, in any way to violate their agreement. Then, as I recall, I asked Mr. Shinn what the substance of their agreement was as to their wills, and he said that they wanted to make identical wills. . . .

They stated briefly, that they wanted [the residue to go to the] survivor, with the right to use that property in any way they saw fit during their lifetime, and that any residue left should be willed or divided between the parties, and each one's share should go to each one's named relatives. Then I asked her if she had talked this over with him, and if that was her understanding, in general, of this arrangement for the disposal of their property, and she said it was.

Then he produced a roll of papers, documents, most of which I had seen before. They were typewritten copies of a draft of a will or wills, and there were a number of pencil notations and different writings that apparently he had made, and some other notes that I had given him at different times in our conversation before. I asked her if she was familiar with these, and she said, "Well, I think I am with most of them. We have talked this over enough" or some expression of that kind.

Then I went over those briefly, and . . . asked them if that was their understanding, and they both said it was.

In speaking of the 1931 will, Mr. Cunningham testified further:

In one of these sections of this draft there was some provision to the effect that they might each make wills — that the survivor might make wills, or something like that, but in making these wills, or in making a will they would have to observe the provisions or the spirit of this will, and he had pencil marks through that, and I asked him about that, and he said, "Well, now, we hope this is a final arrangement as to our property, and I don't want any suggestion that if I live the longest that I will make any will changing our property arrangement here, and if I should die first, I don't want my wife to feel, or to be encouraged to make such a will."

I remember at that time that Mrs. Shinn stated that, "Well, we have been worrying over this — " I can't remember her language, but it was to this effect, that "we have been worrying over this for several months, and I don't want — I think that we should have it settled, and these arrangements — that is satisfactory with me. I don't want to make any more wills, or I don't expect to change my will, when I make it," or words to that effect.

Appellants argue that the trial court was in error in allowing Mr. Cunningham to testify concerning the statements made by Mr. and Mrs.

Shinn for the reason that the conversations were prohibited under Rem. Rev. Stat. §1214, which reads: . . .

> 2. An attorney or counselor shall not, without the consent of his client, be examined as to any communication made by the client to him, or his advice given thereon in the course of the professional employment.

They also cite many authorities supporting this statute which is common to most jurisdictions. There are, however, many situations in which the statute does not and cannot apply.

The general rule is stated in 28 R.C.L. 566 §156, as follows:

> When two or more clients employ the same attorney in the same matter, communications made by them in relation thereto are not privileged . . . in any controversy between them or their personal representatives or successors in interest.

70 C.J. 438, §587, says:

> It is generally considered that the rule of privilege does not apply in litigation, after the client's death, between parties, all of whom claim under the client; and, so, where the controversy is to determine who shall take by succession the property of a deceased person and both parties claim under him, neither can set up a claim of privilege against the other as regards the communications of deceased with his attorney. . . .

In the present case, the statements concerning which Mr. Cunningham testified were made when both Mr. and Mrs. Shinn were present. The statements of the attorney which brought forth the ideas of the makers of the wills were given them in the presence of both. That advice given to them collectively concerned their community property rights and their obligations should they make mutual wills. The court did not err in admitting the testimony of Mr. Cunningham.

The next objection urged by appellants is that the facts and circumstances surrounding the making of prior wills by the Shinns demonstrated that they did not intend to make mutual wills in 1931. In support of this contention, counsel bring to our attention excerpts from wills made by Mr. and Mrs. Shinn in 1929 [which recited the terms of a contract limiting the rights of the survivor]. . . .

From the difference in the provisions of the 1929 and 1931 wills, it is argued that the 1929 wills were mutual and identical as shown by their contents and that having used different language in the 1931 wills it must be assumed that the 1931 wills did not express an intention on the part of the testators to make mutual identical wills.

We are unable to agree with this reasoning. The manifest intent in all of the wills was to see to it that each spouse should have his or her chosen individuals receive certain interests in the community property after the death of the makers of the wills.

Appellants next urge that the decree in the Homer J. Shinn estate forecloses the claims now made. They argue that the decree is an adjudication that Phoebe Shinn took the entire estate without restriction and that it cannot be contended she took a mere life estate with the right to use it during her lifetime. . . . The . . . decree [states]: . . .

> 4. That Phoebe Shinn is entitled to receive, and there is hereby distributed to her the entire residue of said estate. . . .

In the instant case the probate court neither attempted to interpret the provisions of the will pertaining to the mutual obligations of the parties nor to adjudicate respondents' equitable rights under the contract between the Shinns. . . .

Nor do we consider the distribution to Mrs. Shinn to be anything more than a distribution in accordance with the words and terms of the will and in no way inconsistent to respondents' claims. This is not a construction of the will, Martin v. Barger, 62 Wash. 672, 114 P. 505, and the failure to mention the restriction of disposition after death did not vest absolute title. . . .

Appellants take the position that the contract between Mr. and Mrs. Shinn was void since it was not drawn in conformity with Rem. Rev. Stat. §6894. . . .

> This court has definitely held that an agreement to make mutual wills is within the statute of frauds, if real property is involved, or real and personal property. We have also held that the making of mutual wills is not sufficient part performance to take the agreement without the statute of frauds, in the absence of any other consideration. We have also definitely fixed the quantum of proof required to establish such a contract.

Allen v. Dillard, Wash., 129 P.2d 813, 820.

The oral contract made by Mr. and Mrs. Shinn was within the provisions of the above statute and in itself unenforceable. However, mutual wills were made by the Shinns in conformity with their oral agreement. Thereafter, Mrs. Shinn probated her husband's estate and took his estate given to her by his will executed in 1931. The actions of the parties were sufficient part performance to take the contract from the statute of frauds.

Upon the death of Mr. Shinn, Mrs. Shinn filed his will for probate and accepted the benefits . . . of the contract and will, and could not thereafter free herself of her obligation. . . .

The judgment is affirmed.

What ethical problems do you see for the attorney advising the husband and wife in these cases?

A few decisions have held the mere execution of joint or mutual wills to be part performance, removing the contract from the statute of frauds, e.g., In re Fischer's Estate, 196 Wash. 41, 81 P.2d 836 (1938); and a few others have held that such wills constitute sufficient memorandum to satisfy the statute, even without reciting the existence of a contract, e.g., Estate of Beerenk, 429 Pa. 415, 241 A.2d 755 (1968). These positions have generally been rejected, however. More, of course, occurred than mere execution of the wills in Cummings v. Sherman, and the part performance doctrine has been widely applied to like facts. On the basis of your understanding of the part performance doctrine, is there anything questionable about its application to these facts? Another rationale for the same solution to the recurrent problem of mutual wills executed pursuant to an alleged oral contract is found in Notten v. Mensing, 3 Cal. 2d 469, 473-474, 45 P.2d 198, 200-201 (1935):

> In this state . . . oral agreements to leave property by will . . . are unenforceable. [Cases] hold that the execution of a will in accordance with the oral agreement, which does not expressly refer to the contract, does not constitute a note or memorandum sufficient to satisfy the statute of frauds. The same cases also indicate that the execution of mutual wills, the death of one of the makers, and the acceptance of the benefits under such a will by the other, does not constitute a sufficient part performance to take the case out of the statute of frauds. This is contrary to the rule in some states.
>
> However, the fact that the instant case does not come within one of the above two exceptions to the operation of the statute of frauds is not sufficient to dispose of the issues raised. There is a long line of authorities in this state to the effect that under the proper circumstances a party may be estopped to plead the statute of frauds. . . . [When] two parties execute reciprocal wills pursuant to an oral agreement, and one of the parties dies before either will is revoked, and the other party accepts the benefit of the decedent's will, and then revokes, a constructive fraud sufficient to raise an estoppel has been practiced on the decedent and on the beneficiaries of the oral agreement.

In recent years it appears that many courts have seemed increasingly willing to imply a contract merely from the jointness or similarity of the wills of spouses, with little or no extrinsic evidence of contractual intention. See, e.g., Pruitt v. Moss, 271 S.C. 305, 247 S.E.2d 324 (1978), Fisher v. Capp, 597 S.W.2d 393 (Tex. Civ. App. 1980), and Estate of Maloney v. Carsten, 65 Ind. Dec. 287, 381 N.E.2d 1263 (1978), all involving joint wills; and Woelke v. Calfee, 45 Ore. App. 459, 608 P.2d 606 (1980), involving separate wills. And compare open and explicit recognition that, if spouses' wills are "joint *and* mutual," they constitute "prima facie evidence of a contract not to revoke" in Larison v. Record, 489 N.E.2d 925, 927 (Ill. App. 1986). See also the novel cases of Northern Trust Co. v. Tarre, 404 N.E.2d 882 (Ill. App. 1980), and Reznik v. McKee, 216 Kan. 659, 534 P.2d 243 (1975), involving revocable inter vivos trusts that were held to become irrevocable and unamendable after the first spouse's death based on findings of unwritten agreements. If there is a growing inclination on the part of courts to find contractual obligations by implication in this area of the law, is there policy justification for this? Is such a trend desirable?

On the matter of remedies, Levis v. Hammond, 251 Iowa 567, 573-576, 100 N.W.2d 638, 642-644 (1960), states:

> [A] suit for specific performance against the survivor of an agreement to make mutual wills [requires] good consideration for the agreement, acceptance by the survivor of the property under the will of the first to die and reasonableness of the agreement. . . .
>
> Although the mutual promises may have amounted to technical consideration . . . there was a great inequality of consideration moving from the two makers. Thus the agreement was not sufficiently fair and reasonable to entitle plaintiff to the relief asked. . . .
>
> A suit for specific performance of an agreement is always addressed to the sound judicial discretion of the chancellor, guided by the general principles of equity. Relief is not a matter of absolute right but is granted or withheld according to the circumstances of each case.

Compare Rauch v. Rauch, 445 N.E.2d 77, 81 (Ill. App. 1983) ("on the death of the first testator" there is, in effect, "a life estate in the surviving testator, and the third-party beneficiaries receive a gift over"), and Halper v. Froula, 148 Cal. App. 3d 1000, 1005, 196 Cal. Rptr. 727, 730 (1983) (although survivor "had the right to use the [property] for her comfort and support during her lifetime, giving away the property is not a proper use and enjoyment . . . by the life tenant").

PROBLEM

7-B.   H and W entered into a written contract calling for irrevocable mutual wills under which the first to die was to leave his or her entire estate to the survivor, and the survivor was to leave everything to certain relatives of each. Wills were executed accordingly. H died recently, but by a later will he left W only her minimum statutory rights and the rest to his brother, B. W consults you to determine her rights. She informs you that shortly before his death, H told her he was going to change his will, and he did so despite her protests. What advice would you give W?

Incidentally, what if H had died leaving his will in the agreed form and, promptly after his death, W wished to assert her statutory one-third forced share by electing against his will? Cf. Estate of Edington, 489 N.E.2d 612 (Ind. App. 1986). Can she do so? Would it matter if W had advised H of her intentions while he was still competent a week or so before his death? Consider, as you study the rest of this chapter, why and under what circumstances she might wish to elect against H's will.

In considering the above problem, note the frequently cited case of Stone v. Hoskins, [1905] L.R.P. 194, 197, the holding of which is adequately reflected in its concluding dictum:

> If these two people had made wills which were standing at the death of the first to die, and the survivor had taken a benefit by that death, the view is perfectly well founded that the survivor cannot depart from the arrangement on his part, because . . . the will of that party and the arrangement have become irrevocable; but that case is entirely different from the present, where the first to die has not stood by the bargain and her "mutual" will has in consequence not become irrevocable. The only object of notice is to enable the other party to the bargain to alter his or her will also, but the survivor in the present case is not in any way prejudiced. He has notice as from the death. . . . [He] must, I think, fail to obtain the declaration which he seeks.

Dicta of similar effect are abundant in American cases, but it is usually observed also that for one of the parties to "revoke" during their joint lifetimes notice must be given to the other. Is it not a peculiar notion of contract that revocation of the promised will is permitted without liability — that is, in effect, a "rescission" without the *assent* of the other party? If the purported "agreement" is considered merely an offer of a unilateral contract, why must notice be given before the promisor's death rather than before performance by the promisee? Or is this in reality a problem of construing the contract and finding it to include an implied right to revoke by either party on notice to the other during their joint lives? If so, one must ask whether the contract in question allows of this construction when such a provision is not expressed. Today, possibly an implied power to "revoke" by giving timely notice can be justified by the widespread belief of lawyers, based on dicta in many cases, that Stone v. Hoskins represents the law of their states, especially if it can be shown that the parties were so advised by their lawyer. Where the precise question is presented, however, as in Problem 7-B, supra, the above-mentioned dicta have not necessarily been followed. See Estate of Johnson, 781 S.W.2d 390 (Tex. App. 1989); Brown v. Webster, 90 Neb. 591, 134 N.W. 185 (1912); In re Fischer's Estate, 196 Wash. 41, 81 P.2d 836 (1938); Note, 48 Calif. L. Rev. 858, 862-863 (1960). For a more recent look at the English view and at Stone v. Hoskins, see Rickett, Extending Equity's Reach Through the Mutual Wills Doctrine, 54 Mod. L. Rev. 581 (1991).

PROBLEMS

7-C.   *H* and *W* owned Blackacre as joint tenants. They contracted to execute a joint will under which the survivor would be entitled to a life estate in all of the property of both parties, with remainder on the death of the survivor to *A* and *B* equally. The parties executed a joint will reciting the terms of this agreement, adding that "the survivor shall not sell, encumber or give away any of the property without the consent of *A* and *B*." On *W*'s death five years ago her will was admitted to probate. Several months ago *H* executed a deed purporting to convey Blackacre to *X* for a fair consideration. *H* has invested the proceeds in a speculative venture and has suffered a great loss. *A* and *B* ask you what their rights are. How would you advise them? Is there anything *A* and *B* could have done to have prevented this problem?

7-D.   In 1980 *H* and *W* executed a written contract not to revoke their mutual wills. *H* died in 1985 leaving everything he owned to *W*, as agreed, and now *W* has just died. In accordance with the contract, her will provides for the estate to pass one-half to *H*'s nephew, *A*, and one-sixth to each of *W* 's nieces and nephews, *X*, *Y*, and *Z*. However, *A* predeceased *W*, although he was alive at *H*'s death. A typical statute in the state provides that if a named beneficiary dies before the testator his interest fails, except that if the bequest or devise is to "kindred" of the testator and if the beneficiary is also survived by issue, the bequest or devise passes to the issue of the beneficiary. *A*'s will left his entire estate to *B*, his widow. *A* is also survived by a child, *C*. *X*, *Y*, and *Z* are *W*'s sole heirs at law and claim the entire estate. Based on the materials that follow in this chapter, how would you argue their case? *C*'s? *B*'s? See Ruchert v. Boyd, 165 Wash. 2d 278, 352 P.2d 216 (1960); Rauch v. Rauch, 445 N.E.2d 77 (Ill. App. 1983). Contrast Keasey v. Engles, 259 Mich. 176, 242 N.W. 878 (1932), with Chadwick v. Bristow, 146 Tex. 481, 208 S.W.2d 888 (1948). Compare Haile v. Holtzclaw, 400 S.W.2d 603 (Tex. Civ. App. 1966).

LAWRENCE v. ASHBA
115 Ind. App. 485, 59 N.E.2d 568 (1945)

DRAPER, C.J.

The appellees, who are the three sons by her first marriage of Sarah E. Lawrence, deceased, brought this action . . . for the specific performance of a contract; for an accounting; to set aside the conveyance of real estate; and for a judgment declaring a trust. . . .

It appears that the father of appellees died in 1905 and in 1907 their mother married the appellant William T. Lawrence, who never had any children. In 1942 Mrs. Lawrence died. On July 1, 1937, Mr. and Mrs. Lawrence held some real estate by the entireties which they had been able to acquire largely as the result of her industry and thrift and a pension received by her because of the fact that the father of appellees was a Civil War veteran. On that day they each made a will. Items II and III of the will of Mrs. Lawrence read as follows:

> Item II. I will, bequeath and devise all my property, both personal and real, to my husband William T. Lawrence, absolutely and in fee simple.
>
> Item III. In the event my husband, William T. Lawrence, should predecease me, I then will, bequeath and devise all my property, both personal and real, to John J. Ashba, James A. Ashba and Charles R. Ashba, share and share alike.

The same clauses, but substituting the name of Sarah Lawrence for that of William T. Lawrence, appeared in the will of William T. Lawrence. There was no other [significant] difference in the wills. . . .

After making these wills they disposed of the real estate then held by them and acquired other real estate, taking title thereto by the entireties, and that real estate was so held when she died, and is the real estate involved in this case.

A few hours after her death William T. Lawrence, alone and unaccompanied by anyone, emptied their safety deposit box and by inference it appears he took therefrom cash and other personal property of considerable value, all of which he still retains. On October 13, 1942, her will was probated and he was appointed executor.

He married again on September 20, 1942, and eight days later made and caused to be made, conveyances intended to vest title to the real estate in his then wife, the appellant Iva B. Lawrence, said conveyances being intended to prevent appellees from ever acquiring the properties. Thereafter Mr. Lawrence stated to others that he had everything fixed and the boys wouldn't get a cent. There is no contention that Iva B. Lawrence furnished any consideration for the conveyances to her, or that she took without notice.

A will is generally ambulatory until the death of the testator, and mutual and reciprocal wills, unless founded on or embodying a binding contract, may be revoked at pleasure. 69 C.J. 1299, §2719.

The burden of proving that mutual and reciprocal wills were made pursuant to a valid and enforceable contract is upon those who assert such to be true, and the evidence thereof must be full and satisfactory. Indeed, the rule requires the agreement to be established by evidence clear, definite, convincing, unequivocal and satisfactory, and to be valid and enforceable the contract must be fair and just, definite and certain in its terms and as to the subject matter, and based upon a sufficient consideration.

The mere fact that the wills under consideration contain identical provisions and that they were drawn by the same scrivener, executed at the same time and before the same witnesses, with full knowledge on the part of each testator of the contents of both wills, and were clearly made for the accomplishment of a common purpose, is not sufficient evidence of a contract to make wills to remain unrevoked at the deaths of the testators, although such circumstances are to be regarded as some evidence that they were made pursuant to an agreement. But where the contract does not appear in the language of the wills, and so the wills, unaided, are not sufficient to show the contract, the agreement may be proven by the testimony of witnesses who know the facts, by admissions of the parties and by the acts and conduct of the parties and other circumstances surrounding the making of the wills.

With these rules in mind we examine the evidence. It reveals that at the time of the making of the wills Mr. and Mrs. Lawrence called at a lawyer's office. It was there discussed that the funds that had gone into their property held as tenants by the entireties had in a major part been the funds of Mrs. Lawrence before she married Mr. Lawrence. There was conversation that they might want to sell that property and invest in other property. They seemed in accord and harmony and wanted to execute such deeds, wills or other instruments as would effectuate their intentions, which were that their property should be held intact as long as each of them lived, and when both were gone, they wanted the property to go to the three boys. Both agreed to make disposition of their property in that fashion. No request was made that a provision be included in the wills making them irrevocable during the lifetime of both or after the death of either. They left it to the lawyer to prepare whatever papers were necessary to carry out their wishes and accomplish their purpose, and he prepared the wills above mentioned, he said, in conformity with their desires.

Before the death of Mrs. Lawrence she and Mr. Lawrence told one of the witnesses that they had made a will; that

> it was to be a joint will while if she outlived him everything should be hers for lifetime then it was to be the boys'; and if he outlived her why it should be the same way; her life earnings were in there and most of the money was hers and they decided that it was for the boys when they were gone.

The evidence above recited was in no way contradicted by either of the appellants or any other witness, nor in any manner questioned or impeached.

In our opinion this evidence, taken with the fact that the wills contain substantially identical provisions, were drawn by the same lawyer and were executed at the same time before the same witnesses with full knowledge by each testator of the contents of the other's will, was sufficient to meet the requirements of the rule and sustain a finding that the wills were mutual and reciprocal wills made pursuant to a valid and enforceable contract.

It is true the parties did not request that a provision be included making the wills irrevocable, but they did not in any respect suggest or dictate the kind of terms of the instruments to be used to accomplish their purpose. They apparently knew nothing of such things and so left every-thing to the lawyer. It is apparent however that their minds did meet on a particular testamentary disposition of the property to accomplish a particular purpose, and that they intended the wills made pursuant thereto to remain unrevoked at their death. The mutual agreement of the makers of the wills was sufficient consideration to bind the promi-sors. Equity will enforce such an agreement when well and fairly founded, and will not suffer one of the contracting parties to defraud and defeat his obligation, but will fasten a trust upon the property involved.

We agree with appellants that upon the death of a wife the husband takes all of their real estate held by entireties regardless of any attempt by the wife to make any disposition of it by testamentary devise [citations omitted], and so in this case it must be held that he took title to the real estate by operation of law and not as any result of the will. But we do not agree that the contract under consideration could not operate upon real estate so acquired by Mr. Lawrence. . . . Mr. Lawrence did not agree to leave to the appellees only the property he would take under the will of his wife. His agreement was that if his wife died before he did, he would leave to appellees *all* of his property.

[I]t seems clear the parties intended that the survivor should have the use and benefit of the property for life, he to have the right to dispose of any or all of the corpus of the estate for his reasonable needs in the event the income should be inadequate for that purpose, but he could not dispose of it to defraud and defeat his obligation.

No question concerning the statute of frauds was raised in this case. . . .

Judgment affirmed.

MATTER OF ESTATE OF JUD
238 Kan. 268, 710 P.2d 1241 (1985)

[John and Jean Jud each had two children by a prior marriage and executed a contractual joint will by which, on the death of the survivor, "we mutually give . . . the entire residue of our property" equally to the four children. On the husband's death, his children brought this action and appeal certain unfavorable determinations by the lower court.]

HERD, J. . . .

The first issue on appeal is whether the contractual provisions of the joint and mutual will apply to property acquired by Jean Jud after the death of John Jud. . . .

The contract is effective from the date of execution, while the wills are effective from the date of death of each testator. This means that once the will is executed by both parties it becomes a binding contract incapable of unilateral revocation and, after the death of one of the parties, it is irrevocable. . . .

[A] joint, mutual and contractual will speaks to the property of each testator at the time of his or her respective death and includes all after-acquired property of the survivor unless a different intention appears from the will. . . .

Appellants next argue the trial court erred in holding . . . the contractual will . . . did not sever the joint tenancies, under which ownership the Juds held much of their property. In light of our holding in the foregoing issue . . . this issue is moot. . . .

The trial court ruled Mrs. Jud's interest cannot be termed that of a "life tenant." We find this holding to be incorrect. . . . Accordingly our [earlier cases] relating to the duties of a life tenant to the remainderman are applicable here. . . .

Appellants argue Mrs. Jud, as a "trustee" of the residue of the estate, should be required to file periodic accountings of her administration of the trust or post a bond to protect the remainderman . . . since the bulk of the Jud's estate is composed of cash and personal property. . . . In the absence of an express provision in the will [so requiring], the survivor is not required to furnish bond and an accounting absent a showing of bad faith or waste. The issue is without merit. . . .

[A]ffirmed in part and reversed in part. . . .

On the line between gifts that are and are not permissible by the survivor in such cases, Dickson v. Seaman, 1983 N.Y.2d 18, 25, 85 N.E.2d 818, 820 (1908), states: "That line is to be drawn where the courts always draw it when they can, along the boundary of good faith. . . . [The plaintiff's] theory is that any gift, or at least any substantial gift . . . was unauthorized and void. We do not so read the contract. Any gift made with actual intent to defraud would be void, but none made without such intent, unless so out of proportion to the rest of his estate as to attack the integrity of the contract, when it would be fraudulent as a matter of law. The gift may be so large that, independent of intent or motive, fraud upon the contract would be imputed, or arise constructively by operation of law. Reasonable gifts were impliedly authorized. Unreasonable gifts were not. . . . [T]he question is one of degree, and depends upon the proportion that the value of the gift bears to the amounts of the donor's estate."

The surviving spouse who remarries sometimes places property in joint tenancy with the second spouse despite the binding promise to leave the property by will to others. In such a case the transfer may be set aside, or the property in the hands of the joint owners or the survivor may be impressed with a constructive trust for the contract beneficiaries. See Estate of Chayka, 47 Wis. 2d 102, 176 N.W.2d 561 (1970). But cf. Blackmon v. Estate of Battcock, 78 N.Y.2d 735, 587 N.E.2d 280 (1991).

Where the person whose property is subject to such a contractual obligation subsequently marries, does the right of the third-party beneficiaries also prevail over the forced heirship rights of the new spouse? Should it matter whether the spouse knows or does not know of the previous agreement? The position of the promisor who has taken under the will of the promisee is often described as a constructive trustee or analogized for a variety of purposes to the position of a life tenant with a limited power to consume principal. (An interesting example is Estate of Rath, 10 Cal. 2d 399, 67 P.2d 1073 (1937), treating contractual mutual wills as in effect creating, on the death of the first spouse, a life interest in the survivor and a remainder interest in the beneficiaries for inheritance tax purposes, so that the latter did not "inherit" from the surviving spouse on her later death.) What bearing do such analogies or descriptions have on the rights of the survivor's subsequent spouse?

This problem arises with some frequency. See, e.g., Estate of Beerenk, 429 Pa. 415, 241 A.2d 755 (1968), subordinating the widow's forced share to the rights of the contract beneficiaries who took as "creditors," not as mere legatees.

See also Rubinstein v. Mueller, 19 N.Y.2d 228, 233, 225 N.E.2d 540, 542-543 (1967), where the majority opinion stated:

> There is unanimity of opinion in this court that [Mueller's] final will was ineffective to alter the testamentary arrangement provided for in the joint will, but we are divided over the question of whether the decedent's earlier covenant with his first wife [takes] precedence over the claim of the widow to [an elective forced share]. . . . [W]e are of the opinion that the named beneficiaries under the joint will are entitled to prevail, and a constructive trust in their favor was properly impressed upon the widow under the later will.
>
> As to the property received by Mueller under the joint will there can be no question but that upon his acceptance of such benefits under that instrument a trust was impressed in favor of the beneficiaries. . . . As to such property Mueller really took but an interest during his life with a power to use or otherwise dispose of principal, and the named beneficiaries took the interest which remained. Under such circumstances he had no property interest in these assets against which the widow's right of election could operate.

The dissenting opinion stated: "The husband, after the death of the first wife . . . , had complete title [and] could have given the property away or consumed it without any fiduciary accountability. . . . [P]laintiff had no [enforceable] interest [in] such property during his lifetime, and at his death [plaintiff had only a contract right] subject to the right of election of the surviving wife." Id. at 236, 225 N.E.2d at 545. Can this be squared with the quotation from the same court's earlier Dickson v. Seaman decision, and with other authorities you have read?

Compare the interesting approach to protection of the later spouse in Re Marsland, [1939] 1 Ch. 820, where the English court construed a covenant not to revoke as extending only to acts of revocation and not to revocation by operation of law through later marriage, after Re Marsland, 4 All E.R. 279 (1938), had decided that a covenant that cannot be so construed is void as an impermissible restraint on marriage.

Among the American cases protecting the subsequent spouse in such cases is Patecky v. Friend, 220 Or. 612, 350 P.2d 170 (1960), where Samuel had contracted with his wife, Emma, that the survivor would leave everything to their only child, Blanche. Mutual wills were executed pursuant to the contract, and Emma later died. Samuel accepted the benefits of her will and subsequently remarried. On death he left the bulk of his estate to his second wife, Lillian. Blanche sued in equity to enforce the contract and was awarded the entire estate. On appeal, the court modified the decree, stating: "There is no evidence that Lillian, prior to Samuel's death, had knowledge of the contract between Samuel and Emma, nor of their wills. . . . Specific performance of a contract is not a matter of right in equity." Id. at 624, 350 P.2d at 175. Under the circumstances, the court deemed it equitable to allow Lillian only her statutory rights as widow, with Blanche entitled to the rest of the estate by contract. See also Shimp v. Huff, 315 Md. 624, 556 A.2d 252 (1989).

Compare McKinnon v. White, 698 P.2d 94 (Wash. App. 1985), protecting the children of a second marriage from a divorce-settlement contract calling for the father's estate to be left to the children of the first marriage.

8

Will Substitutes and Introduction to Estate Planning

Although we are inclined to think of the will as the primary means of providing for postmortem disposition of property, there are several well-developed and commonly used alternatives by which similar results can be reached. These include such devices as gifts causa mortis, joint and survivorship interests, bonds payable on death to another, life insurance, and employee benefit plans. One of the important alternative means of disposition is the inter vivos trust, which is treated in detail subsequently. All of these alternatives are useful to the estate planner but none, alone, will fit every client's needs. Indeed, scarcely will one alone satisfy the needs of any one person. Consequently, the lawyer must be familiar with all forms of gratuitous transfers; yet all are subject to abuse and offer traps for the unwary and unadvised.

Because most will substitutes are somewhat familiar to you from other courses, this chapter attempts mainly to orient your thinking toward the problems and uses of these devices in estates practice. Note how the issues in the cases differ: some ask whether, granted that the requirements of a valid life insurance contract (or whatever) are met, this is so close to a will that wills act requirements should be met (e.g., the *Rainey* case, page 239 infra); others focus on whether the requirements of an effective transfer or survivorship form (joint tenancy or whatever) are met (e.g., the *Wilson* case, page 244 infra) and at least initially do not raise issues about wills act requirements. Also, as each case or problem is studied, consider why the particular arrangement in question was used and how the parties' needs might better have been served. Finally, as this chapter and the next are read, including the materials on taxation, consider the following fairly common situation and questions.

Suppose *W* and *H* are retired and live on fairly generous pensions and income from investments. They own their home in joint tenancy, and their bank accounts are joint as well. Their life insurance is payable to one another or to their children outright; their investments are represented by joint stock certificates or payable-on-death bonds, and their car is rented. Their combined taxable estates could approximate $1 million, and the probate estate of the first to die would essentially consist of the change in the decedent's possession, some personal effects, household furniture, and the like. If debts and taxes are paid, along with funeral and last illness expenses, by the survivor, what need is there for probate — or at least for more than the summary proceedings allowed for "small estates" as defined by local probate law? On the other hand, are there other costs and risks in setting up an estate in this fashion, and in assuming that all significant assets should be handled in similar ways?

A. *Survivorship Rights via Contract and Joint Ownership*

1. Life Insurance, Annuities, and Related Arrangements

It is well settled that the usual selection of a beneficiary to receive the proceeds of a life insurance policy on the death of the insured is not a testamentary disposition. Thus, when the insured dies, the proceeds are payable directly to the designated beneficiary under the policy, if living, and are not subject to administration as assets of the insured's estate. Proceeds payable to a named beneficiary normally are not subject to the terms of the insured's will, even if inconsistent with the policy, because the terms of the contract are controlling. Generally these proceeds pass free of the claims of the deceased insured's creditors and are not part of the estate for purposes of the forced share of a surviving spouse. These results are not affected by the fact that the insured has paid the premiums and has retained incidents of ownership such as the rights to surrender, assign, and borrow against the policy, and the usual right during life to change the beneficiaries and select among the optional modes of settlement. Can you see any reasons why the insured might find it desirable to designate the insured's *estate* as the recipient of the insurance? Aside from tax considerations,[1] can you see the disadvantages? Can you see any alternatives, then, for accomplishing the purposes for which one might make the proceeds payable to the estate?

In addition to the right to designate beneficiaries, life insurance policies offer the insured or other policy owner the right to select either a lump sum payment or one of a fairly standard set of optional modes of settlement for the beneficiaries. If a settlement option has not been selected, so that at the death of the insured the payee is entitled to receive the proceeds in a lump sum, the privilege will remain open to the

---

1. Payment to the estate has state inheritance tax disadvantages in many states, but insurance proceeds are included in the insured's gross estate on death for purposes of the federal estate tax even though payable to a named beneficiary if the insured retained any of the *incidents of ownership* in the policies.

payee to select one of the options. These typical options are: (1) an *interest option,* under which the company retains the proceeds, paying interest periodically to the beneficiary (often accompanied by withdrawal privileges and sometimes by the later right to choose a different option); (2) a *fixed period option,* under which amounts are paid at regular intervals over a set period of years (the amount of the installment being based on interest plus liquidation of principal); (3) a *fixed amount option,* with periodic payments (comprised of interest and principal) in the fixed amount being paid until the proceeds are exhausted; and (4) a variety of *life income options,* with installments paid over the beneficiary's lifetime on the basis of a straight life annuity, a joint and survivor annuity, a life annuity with a term certain (i.e., with a minimum number of payments), or a refund annuity. The considerations pertinent to the selection of a form of settlement are varied and sometimes complex, ranging from tax factors (e.g., the Internal Revenue Code §101(d)(1)(B) exclusion) to a beneficiary's need of a guaranteed income for life, and including also considerations of estate liquidity and flexibility of expenditures and investment. As we shall see later, proceeds are sometimes made payable to trustees.

A significant modern development is the growth of pension and employee benefit programs, most of which provide some form of death benefits that pass outside estate administration procedures. Most widespread of these, of course, is the federal social security system, but there are an infinite number and variety of other public and private programs. See, e.g., Report, Federal Death Benefits, 5 Real Prop., Prob. & Tr. J. 248 (1970) (reviewing veterans, railroad retirement, social security, foreign service, and civil service benefits). See also Dunham, Sixty Different Succession Laws in Illinois, 46 Ill. B.J. 741 (1958), finding forty different state programs, plus twenty under federal statutes, all operating in one state. With few exceptions, survivor provisions offer little dispositive flexibility. Social security death benefits are paid in a prescribed pattern only for an overage or disabled spouse, underage (age 18, or 21 if a full-time student) or disabled children, and parents under some circumstances. Other plans typically confine payments to the employee's immediate family or certain near relatives, with limited freedom, if any, to select beneficiaries or modes of settlement — and then generally not by will. The rights under such public and private plans may constitute the primary wealth of a given client, so the lawyer must consider them carefully in planning a client's affairs and integrate them as much as possible into the overall scheme of disposition.

In addition, a client may dispose of some wealth through the purchase of annuities, and lawyers are sometimes called on to advise in such matters. Detailed study of these and the other diverse arrangements just surveyed is beyond the scope of this course, but they are regularly an aspect of estate situations and are occasionally a source of litigation. The following case and problem are illustrative of questions that are central to this course and arise in various forms.

KANSAS CITY LIFE INSURANCE CO. v. RAINEY
353 Mo. 477, 182 S.W.2d 624 (1944)

DOUGLAS, J.

In 1925 Jessie A. Rainey became Herbert F. Hall's secretary and continued as such until his death. In 1931 Hall, aged 72, purchased an "Investment Annuity Policy" from the Kansas City Life Insurance Company for $50,000, the income payable to him, the principal payable to his wife at his death. After his wife died he named Miss Rainey beneficiary in the policy. Hall died in 1941. . . .

After Hall's death Miss Rainey . . . claimed the [insurance] proceeds . . . from the insurance company. The executor of Hall's estate also claimed the proceeds. . . .

The question for decision is whether the policy is invalid as a testamentary disposition not in the form prescribed by the statute of wills.

The executor concedes a life insurance policy is generally considered as not testamentary in character. But he argues this policy is not an insurance policy because there is no element of risk involved. Hall paid the company $50,000 and received quarterly interest for four percent under the term annuity. The insurance company, upon Hall's death, was obligated to pay out only the same amount it originally received, namely $50,000. . . . Thus, the executor asserts the policy is merely a certificate of deposit to take effect upon Hall's death and is testamentary in character. . . .

An insurance policy is a contract. A policy payable to a third person is a contract for the benefit of the third person.

The policy we are considering is a contract between Hall and the insurance company for the benefit of Miss Rainey. This is true regardless of the element of risk. It still would be a contract for the benefit of a third person if made with a bank, a corporation of any other sort, or an individual. In the policy Miss Rainey is a third-party donee-beneficiary. Restatement of Contracts, §133. She is entitled to enforce the contract even though she is a stranger to both the contract and to the consideration. 12 Am. Jur. Contracts, §277.

The policy is not testamentary because it became effective before Hall's death. It was a contract made and in force during Hall's lifetime. Hence there would be no reason to surround it with formalities which safeguard a will. See Krell v. Codman, 154 Mass. 454, 28 N.E. 578, 14 L.R.A. 860, 26 Am. St. Rep. 260.

The policy became effective upon its execution and the payment of the consideration of $50,000, all done during Hall's lifetime. The payment of the consideration was an immediate disposition of the $50,000. The money became the property of the insurance company. Upon Hall's death the money to be paid to the beneficiary constituted no part of Hall's estate. So far as Miss Rainey is concerned, any disposition as to her was effected at the time she was designated as beneficiary. Her enjoyment of the fund was merely postponed until Hall's death, subject to the right of revocation retained by Hall.

The mere fact a note, bond or other instrument for the payment of money is not payable until or after death is not sufficient to make such an instrument testamentary in character and invalid for that reason.

The reservation of the right by Hall to change the beneficiary or to cash in the policy does not make it testamentary. These are but methods of revocation. We see no reason why there should be any distinction between the effect of reserving a right of revocation as was done in the policy and reserving one in a living trust. . . .

The [judgment is] affirmed.

PROBLEM

8-A. *H* owned a life insurance policy in the amount of $50,000, and under the policy his wife of twenty years, *W,* was designated to receive the full amount on his death. *H* also owned land and securities valued at $200,000. On *H*'s death without issue, his will was admitted to probate. The will made specific reference to the above-mentioned insurance and directed that *W* should receive one-half of the proceeds of the policy and that *B, H*'s brother, should receive the other half of the proceeds. The will further provided that all of *H*'s lands, securities, and other property were to be held by *T* Trust Company in trust to pay *W* the income and as much principal as required for her generous support, and on her death to pay the remaining principal to *B* or his issue then living by right of representation. What are *B*'s rights? Assuming *W* has no independently owned assets, as *W*'s lawyer what would you advise her? See Hartwig v. Schiefer, 147 Ind. 64, 46 N.E. 75 (1897); 5 Page on Wills §47.10 (Bowe-Parker, 1962). Cf. In re Estate of Smith, 108 Cal. 115, 40 P. 1037 (1895) (community property involved); Thurlow v. Thurlow, 317 Mass. 126, 56 N.E.2d 902 (1944) (joint tenancy property involved); Kentucky Trust Co. v. Kessell, 464 S.W.2d 275 (Ky. App. 1971) (tenancy by entirety involved).

2. Other Contract Rights and Joint Ownership

Under the joint tenancy form of ownership, on the death of one of the owners the property passes to the surviving owner or owners without administration and without regard to the deceased owner's will. The same is true of property held by husband and wife as tenants by the entirety, but it is not true of tenancy in common. The latter lacks the right of survivorship, which is the salient characteristic of the other two forms. Presumably you are acquainted with these forms of ownership, at least as they apply to real property, and this chapter does not examine extensively the nature of the various forms of concurrent ownership. These forms of ownership are in widespread use, particularly in the case of land owned by husband and wife. Of course, the joint tenancy form, unlike tenancy by the entirety, may be used by persons who are not husband and wife, and in most of the states that recognize one or both of these forms of ownership, they are available for personal as well as real property.

Because in most cases the client will not have given serious thought to the form in which title to property is held, the lawyer who is consulted for estate planning will find it necessary to go over such matters with the client. Certainly the lawyer cannot adequately plan a will without knowing the form in which the client's property is held, because, for example, wills do not operate on property subject to a right of survivorship. Furthermore, tax considerations may enter into the choice of ownership form. The creation or severance of a joint tenancy may have gift tax consequences, and such decisions also involve income tax and estate tax factors that should not be ignored.

At this point, consider what purposes are served by joint ownership with right of survivorship. Also consider what problems may arise from the careless creation of joint rights with regard to various properties, such as bank accounts and securities and valuables kept in safe-deposit boxes. In a great number of states these problems are affected by varying forms of legislation. A lawyer should become familiar with the terms of local statutes and with the case law thereunder. Uncertainty may also be created by various arrangements providing for payment to one person on the death of another. See Sheard, Avoiding Probate of Decedents' Estates, 36 U. Cin. L. Rev. 70 (1967). The following cases are illustrative of the handling of recurrent controversies.

MATTER OF GUARDIANSHIP OF WALTERS
460 N.E.2d 1011 (Ind. App. 1984)

[Martha and John Walters each had children from a previous marriage. They opened a joint savings account with right of survivorship, to which Martha contributed most of the funds. An injury later rendered her comatose, and her daughter Dorothy was appointed guardian of her estate, initially without the knowledge of John who was later appointed guardian of Martha's person; that court authorized either Dorothy or John to make withdrawals from the savings account after first obtaining a court order. When Martha died, the trial court held that her estate and John shared the balance of the account equally. John appealed, contending that his right of survivorship entitled him to the entire balance.]

STATON, P.J. . . .

In non-probate transfer cases we look to case law, statutory law and the third-party beneficiary contract principles which govern the interpretation of the signature card [which] reads in pertinent part:

> Walters, Martha [and John] as joint tenants with right of survivorship and not as tenants in common. . . . You are directed to act pursuant to any one or more of the joint tenants' signatures, . . . [and it] is agreed . . . that any funds placed in or added to the account by any one of the parties are and shall be conclusively intended to be a gift. . . .

The contractual terms agreed to in the Walters's signature card unambiguously created a joint account with right of survivorship. Without any showing of a contrary intent by either Martha or John the Walters's signature evidenced that upon the death of one, the survivor would acquire the deceased tenant's share in the joint account. Therefore, as Martha's survivor John is entitled to the entire balance of the joint savings account.

The statutory law compels [this] determination. . . . Section 4 of the Indiana Non-Probate Transfers Act provides that the balance of a joint account at the death of one of the parties belongs to the survivor(s) unless there is clear and convincing evidence of a different intention. . . .

[T]the court in Rogers v. Rogers (1982), Ind. App., 437 N.E.2d 92, 96 stated that if joint tenants owning by the half and by the whole do not dispose of their individual interests, during their lives the entire amount in the account passes to the survivor. The Court quoted the Commission of the Indiana Probate Code Study to support this decision:

> The theory of these sections is that the basic relationship of the parties is that of individual ownership of values attributable to their respective deposits and withdrawals; the right of survivorship which attaches unless negated by the form of the account really is a right to the values theretofore owned by another which the survivor receives for the first time at the death of the owner. That is to say, the account operates as a valid disposition at death rather than as a present joint tenancy.

Id. We agree with the rationale in *Rogers*, supra, that there exists an underlying assumption that most persons who use joint accounts want the survivor to take the balance. Id. at 96-7. This logic is particularly persuasive when the signature card provides for this result. Therefore, the trial court was incorrect to divide the balance of the Walters's joint savings account. . . .

The restrictions on the joint account during Martha's guardianship did not alter the terms of the signature card. . . .

Reversed.

FRANKLIN v. ANNA NATIONAL BANK
488 N.E.2d 1117 (Ill. App. 1986)

[Mrs. Franklin, as executor, commenced this action against defendant bank, alleging that funds in a joint savings account were property of the estate. The bank interpleaded Mrs. Goddard, who claimed the funds as surviving joint owner.]

WELCH, J. . . .

[T]he circuit court entered judgment for Mrs. Goddard. Mrs. Franklin appeals. We reverse. . . .

Decedent had eye surgery [and] was losing his eye sight in 1978. [His sister-in-law] Mrs. Goddard moved to Union City to help decedent and lived with him. [Soon thereafter they went together] to the bank, according to Mrs. Goddard, to have his money put in both their names so she could get money when they needed it, "and he wanted me to have this money if I outlived him."

A bank employee prepared a signature card [and both decedent and] Mrs. Goddard signed it. . . . The front of the card states that one signature is required for withdrawals. The back of the card states that all funds deposited are owned by the signatories as joint tenants with right of survivorship.

Mrs. Goddard testified that she did not deposit any of the money in the savings account [and she] made no withdrawals. . . . According to Mrs. Goddard, on the day she signed the signature card decedent "asked me . . . if I needed any more money at that time and I said, no, and I said, just leave it in here and I will get it out whenever I need it." . . . Asked whether she ever had the passbook . . . in her possession, Mrs. Goddard answered "Only while I was at [decedent's]. It was there." . . .

The instrument creating a joint tenancy account presumably speaks the whole truth. In order to go behind the terms of the agreement, the one claiming adversely thereto has the burden of establishing by clear and convincing evidence that a gift was not intended. Each case involving a joint tenancy account must be evaluated on its own facts and circumstances. The form of the agreement is not conclusive. . . . The decision of the donor, made subsequent to the creation of the joint tenancy, that he did not want the proceeds to pass to the survivor, would not, in itself, be sufficient to sever the tenancy. However, it is proper to consider events occurring after creation of the joint account in determining whether the donor actually intended [at the time of creating the account] to transfer his interest in the account at his death to the surviving joint tenant.

We must examine the instant facts in light of the above principles: [Testimony indicated that] just nine months after adding Mrs. Goddard's name to [the account] decedent attempted to remove Mrs. Goddard's name and substitute Mrs. Franklin's. The second of decedent's hand written letters to the bank [indicates his concern] that he might lose his sight and be unable to transact his own banking business. These facts show that decedent made Mrs. Goddard . . . a signatory for his own convenience . . . and not with intent to effect a present gift. It does not appear that Mrs. Goddard ever exercised any authority or control over the joint account. While decedent's statement that he wanted Mrs. Goddard to have the money in the account if she outlived him suggests decedent's donative intent, taken literally decedent's statement is inconsistent with intent to donate any interest during the decedent's lifetime. Mrs. Goddard does not argue that there was a valid testamentary disposition in her favor, nor do we so find on the instant facts. . . .

[D]ecedent's attempts to change the account show his consistent view of the account as his own. The surrounding circumstances show decedent's concern for his health and his . . . use of Mrs. Goddard . . . to assure his access to his funds. The money in account 316 should have been found to be the property of the estate. . . .

Where donative intent and survivorship rights are presumed in cases of this type, some courts treat the presumption as a weak one. In general, litigation of this type is appallingly abundant. In Johnson v. Herrin, 272 S.C. 224, 250 S.E.2d 334 (1978), the presumption of gift was found rebutted by the terms of a roughly contemporaneous will under which the testamentary scheme would have been rendered meaningless if a gift of the account funds had been intended. Four joint accounts were found to have been created for convenience only and with no donative intent in In re Estate of Fischer, 443 Pa. 419, 279 A.2d 754 (1971), where a court footnote says there is no reason for banks not to provide alternative forms, one of which is clearly marked for "convenience" only.

Compare Estate of Wilson, 404 Ill. 207, 88 N.E.2d 662 (1949), involving a controversy over money and bearer bonds found at decedent's death in a bank safe-deposit box. The card for the box showed the decedent and his wife as "joint tenants with right of survivorship and not as tenants in common." The assets in question had been decedent's property initially, and his will left his estate half to his wife and half to his children of a prior marriage. In denying the spouse's right to the assets by survivorship, the court's opinion referred both to "reason and logic" and to decisions "of other jurisdictions . . . that renting a lockbox in a bank in the name of two or more persons, as joint tenants with right of survivorship, does not on the death of one vest the personal property in the box in the survivor." But for a contrary decision holding that a printed form (signed during his life by the decedent and his sister-in-law, leasing a safe-deposit box and declaring the contents held "as joint tenants with right of survivorship") entitled the sister-in-law as survivor to cash that originally belonged to decedent but that was found in the box after his death, see Steinhauser v. Repko, 28 Ohio App. 2d 251, 277 N.E.2d 73 (1972).

Other issues about joint accounts and joint safe-deposit boxes also cause difficulty and are not consistently handled by the laws of the various states. See Judge Fuchsberg's concurring opinion in Kleinberg v. Heller, 38 N.Y.2d 836, 839, 345 N.E.2d 592, 594 (1976):

> Literally tens of thousands of our citizens are parties to joint savings accounts. . . . Experience indicates that most people who open such accounts, though lacking legal or business sophistication, do understand and intend some ultimate survivorship incident to a joint tenancy, at least with regard to funds remaining in such an account at the time of death. But they do not usually itend the perhaps more crucial fact that, from the moment of the creation of a joint account, a present unconditional property interest in an undivided one half of the moneys deposited devolves upon each tenant. Even when one of them is the sole donor of the fund, once such a moiety comes into existence it cannot be canceled unilaterally. . . . The niece's half interest . . . was as much hers as the remaining half was the aunt's, the latter's being no greater because she was the donor. Since half of the account was her property, the niece had the right and power to alienate it . . . [and] destroy her aunt's right of survivorship in it. . . . [W]here a joint tenant withdraws more than his or her moiety [in New York], there is an absolute right in the other tenant, during the lifetime of both, to recover such excess.

With this opinion, contrast Uniform Probate Code §6-211, infra.

Analogous problems frequently arise with regard to land and securities ostensibly held in joint tenancy. This is especially true in those community property states that permit free conversion of community property to separate or joint ownership, and vice versa. Where a deed or stock certificate reads in joint tenancy form but has a community property source, what is the true ownership form? Was the instrument taken in apparent joint tenancy form "purely for the convenience of the parties" without adequate understanding, or was there an "intent" to convert? Often the apparent or record form is presumed to reflect the intention of the parties but is readily rebuttable, even by oral evidence of their contrary, informal understanding. The results affect tax consequences as well as the rights of claimants. Related issues arise elsewhere and with regard to separate property, and then they are usually aggravated by more serious problems of gift, estate, and income taxation. Furthermore, for estate planning or other reasons, parties often desire or are counseled to sever joint tenancies, and questions arise concerning the intentions of the parties or the legal effectiveness of steps taken to convert to another form of ownership. Oversight, neglect, and even misunderstanding of the law (with respect to the rights of the parties to act unilaterally or with respect to techniques for exercising those rights) are surprisingly common in the work of lawyers in this area of vital matters that should be relatively simple from a planning viewpoint.

RIDDLE v. HARMON
102 Cal. App. 3d 524, 162 Cal. Rptr. 530 (1980)

POCHE, J.

We must decide whether Frances Riddle, now deceased, unilaterally terminated a joint tenancy by conveying her interest from herself as joint tenant to herself as tenant in common. The trial court determined, via summary judgment quieting title to her widower, that she did not. The facts follow.

Mr. and Mrs. Riddle purchased a parcel of real estate, taking title as joint tenants. Several months before her death, Mrs. Riddle retained an attorney to plan her estate. After reviewing pertinent documents, he advised her that the property was held in joint tenancy and that, upon her death, the property would pass to her husband. Distressed upon learning this, she requested that the joint tenancy be terminated so that she could dispose of her interest by will. As a result, the attorney prepared a grant deed whereby Mrs. Riddle granted to herself an undivided one-half interest in the subject property. . . .

This court is now asked to reexamine whether a strawman is required to *terminate* a joint tenancy.

Twelve years ago, in Clark v. Carter (1968) 265 Cal. App. 2d 291, 295, 70 Cal. Rptr. 923, the Court of Appeal considered the same question and found the strawman to be indispensable. . . .

That "two-to-transfer" notion stems from the English common law feoffment ceremony with livery of seisin. (Swenson and Degnan, Severance of Joint Tenancies (1954) 38 Minn. L. Rev. 466, 467.) If the ceremony took place upon the land being conveyed, the grantor (feoffor) would hand a symbol of the land, such as a lump of earth or a twig, to the grantee (feoffee). In order to complete the investiture of seisin it was necessary that the feoffor completely relinquish possession of the land to the feoffee. It is apparent from the requirement of livery of seisin that one could not enfeoff oneself — that is, one could not be both grantor and grantee in a single transaction. Handing oneself a dirt clod is ungainly. Just as livery of seisin has become obsolete, so should ancient vestiges of that ceremony give way to modern conveyancing realities. . . .

The most familiar technique for unilateral termination is the use of an intermediary "strawman." . . .

Another creative method of terminating a joint tenancy appears in Reiss v. Reiss (1941) 45 Cal. App. 2d 740, 114 P.2d 718. There a trust [with a right of reconveyance] was used. . . .

In view of the rituals that are available to unilaterally terminate a joint tenancy, there is little virtue in steadfastly adhering to cumbersome feudal law requirements.

> It is revolting to have no better reason for a rule of law than that so it was laid down in the time of Henry IV. It is still more revolting if the grounds

upon which it was laid down have vanished long since, and the rule simply persists from blind imitation of the past.

(Justice Oliver Wendell Holmes, Collected Legal Papers 187 (1920)). Common sense as well as legal efficiency dictate that a joint tenant should be able to accomplish directly what he or she could otherwise achieve indirectly by use of elaborate legal fictions. . . .

We discard the archaic rule that one cannot enfeoff oneself, which, if applied, would defeat the clear intention of the grantor. There is no question but that the decedent here could have accomplished her objective — termination of the joint tenancy — by one of a variety of circuitous processes. We reject the rationale of the *Clark* case because it rests on a common law notion whose reason for existence vanished about the time that grant deeds and title companies replaced colorful dirt clod ceremonies as the way to transfer title to real property. One joint tenant may unilaterally sever the joint tenancy without the use of an intermediary device.

The judgment is reversed.

Riddle was followed in Minonk State Bank v. Grassman, 95 Ill. 2d 392, 447 N.E.2d 822 (1983).

Contrast Veterans' Agent v. Rinaldi, 483 N.E.2d 829 (Mass. App. 1985), in which the decedent applied for state benefits as the dependent father of a veteran and, on approval of his application, allowed a lien under the benefits statute to be executed and filed at the registry of deeds on real property then held by the decedent and his wife as tenants by the entirety. On his death, his wife "became the sole owner of the property 'free and clear of [his] debts.' . . . Therefore, because [she] did not receive any of the benefits that gave rise to the lien and was the surviving tenant . . . the lien was extinguished." The court distinguished an earlier decision to the contrary where the survivor had been the recipient of the benefits; it also noted in a footnote that the present case is stronger than one involving a joint tenancy because each tenant by the entirety "has an indefeasible right of survivorship in the entire tenancy which can not be defeated by any act taken individually by either spouse during his or her lifetime." Id. at 831.

Government bonds are frequently held in the names of "*A* or *B*" and "*A* payable on his death to *B.*" Do you — do the parties — know the rights of *A* and *B* during their joint lives under each of these forms? Or *B*'s rights if *A* dies? Treasury Regulations and recent decisions provide that after *A*'s death payment is to be made to *B*. Where the purchaser's intention is to the contrary, however, it is still possible to conclude that the regulations permitting payment to *B* are for the convenience and protection of the government but do not necessarily establish the rights as between *A* and *B*. See Byer v. Byer, 180 Kan. 258, 303 P.2d 137 (1956); Decker v. Flower, 199 Wash. 549, 92 P.2d 254 (1939). But cf. United States v. Chandler, 410 U.S. 257 (1973).

In re Estate of Tonsik, 13 Ohio App. 2d 195, 235 N.E.2d 239 (1968), involved several "P.O.D." bank accounts (i.e., accounts in the name of the depositor, payable on death to another). The court upheld the P.O.D. provisions on the basis of legislation that had been enacted several years earlier, the opinion stating (at 196-197, 235 N.E.2d at 240-241) that but for the statute

> we would have had no difficulty in determining that this attempt to transfer title to the money in the bank was completely ineffective, either on the basis of an attempted testamentary transfer, or as a gift inter vivos or causa mortis that was incomplete. A gift . . . requires that the donor, during his lifetime divest himself of all dominion of the gift and invest the donee therewith. There was no present right on the part of the donees to withdraw any money from the bank, and, in that respect, the accounts cannot be considered joint and survivorship accounts.
>
> The contract . . . between the bank and the depositor . . . is clearly a testamentary disposition [but] the statute herein expressly exempts such a gift from the statute on wills.

Accord, Estate of Schwendenman v. State Savings & Loan Association, 112 Ill. App. 2d 273, 251 N.E.2d 99 (1969), applying a similar modern statute. For a consideration of the bank's responsibility to the parties when a P.O.D. provision is invalid, see Blais v. Colebrook Guaranty Savings Bank, 107 N.H. 300, 220 A.2d 763 (1966); Robinson v. Colebrook Guaranty Savings Bank, 109 N.H. 382, 254 A.2d 837 (1969).

In the case that follows, was the court confused by the intermingling of gift and contract concepts? What would you want to know of the terms of the obligation and extension agreement, in addition to those stated by the court? Also, if another court would decide the case differently, should it distinguish the present facts from a situation in which, instead of a revised agreement by the debtor and creditor, the latter attempted to create rights in others merely by written direction to the debtor to pay the debt to those others if the creditor should die before receiving payment?

McCARTHY v. PIERET
281 N.Y. 407, 24 N.E.2d 102 (1939)

CRANE, C.J.

On or about the 7th day of March, 1932, the defendant Thomas Pieret executed a bond and mortgage in the sum of $3,000 to Catherine McCarthy Jackman. Subsequently, and on the 18th day of December, 1934, Catherine McCarthy Jackman entered into an extension agreement of the aforesaid bond and mortgage wherein and whereby the due date of payment of the bond and mortgage was extended to March 7, 1940. The extension agreement contained the following unusual provision:

> And in the event of the death of the party of the first part prior to the 7th day of March, 1940, the interest is to be paid one-half to Daniel McCarthy, brother of the party of the first part and one-half to the heirs of Ellen Buckley, deceased sister of the party of the first part and the principal paid the same at time of maturity.

[Mrs. Jackman died on March 15, 1935, and the right to future payments is claimed by her husband as her administrator and also by her nieces, nephews, and brother.]

The judgments below have held this extension agreement to be a valid disposition in the nature of a gift, and not an attempted testamentary disposition in violation of section 21 of the Decedent Estate Law (Consol. Laws, ch. 13). It is not always easy to determine whether a transaction is a gift or is testamentary in character. It depends upon the intention of the donor.

A concise statement of the rule, easy of expression but difficult in application, is to be found in 28 C.J. (p. 624 ¶11-e):

> Where a gift is made effective in the lifetime of the decedent and he has divested himself of all power to recall it, such transaction is a gift inter vivos, and not testamentary in its nature. If the gift does not take effect as an executed and completed transfer to the donee, either legally or equitably, during the life of the donor, it is a testamentary disposition, good only when made by a valid will. . . . The test is whether the maker intended the instrument to have no effect until after the maker's death, or whether he intended it to transfer some present interest.

If this question of intention of the testator is the deciding factor we must, I think, draw the inference that the mortgagee never intended to transfer a vested interest in the mortgage to the brother and the heirs of her sister. Neither did she divest herself of all control or interest in the mortgage. After March 7, 1940, the principal and interest were to be paid to her if she were alive, likewise the interest and principal were to be paid to her any time during her lifetime up to March 7, 1940. She could have satisfied the mortgage and taken the principal at any time during her life. Had the mortgagor desired to pay the mortgage he could have paid it to the mortgagee. Surely if this had been done these collateral relatives would have had no interest by reason of the extension. Their rights, at best, only arose on the death of the mortgagee prior to March 7, 1940. Suppose there had been default in the payment of taxes and interest and foreclosure was necessary. Could the mortgagee have foreclosed or would it have been necessary to join these collateral relatives? To put the question is to answer it. These collaterals had no present interest. Nothing was transferred to them. The mortgagee never intended to divest herself of all rights and control in and over this mortgage until her death. . . .

I do not say that the passing of property at death may not be provided for by contract or by deed, but the donor in such cases divests himself of all interest and vests it in the beneficiary. His intention is to establish present rights and not postpone them until death. He retains no further control over the transaction but, for a consideration or else because of relationship, establishes a present enforceable interest, postponed in enjoyment perhaps until death. . . .

For the reasons here stated the judgment should be reversed and the complaint dismissed, with costs in all courts.

The *McCarthy* case was severely criticized in Mutual Benefit Insurance Co. v. Ellis, 125 F.2d 127 (2d Cir.), *cert. denied,* 316 U.S. 665 (1942), in Note, 53 Harv. L. Rev. 1060 (1940), and by Gulliver and Tillson, Classification of Gratuitous Transfers, 51 Yale L.J. 1, 30 (1941). Compare Note, Joint Bank Accounts: The Survivor's Right to Payments Due to the Account, 1968 Ill. L.F. 410. Following a proposal by the New York Law Revision Commission in 1950, legislation (now N.Y. EPTL §13-3.2) was enacted permitting contract designation of survivor beneficiaries by persons entitled to receive payment under formal pension, death benefit, bonus or profit sharing plans or annuities or insurance, but family or other noninstitutional agreements, like that in *McCarthy,* were not expressly covered. Does this recognition of institutionalized business practice merely reflect the weight of the insurance lobby, or are there other justifications for these distinctions?

In re ESTATE OF HILLOWITZ
22 N.Y.2d 107, 238 N.E.2d 723 (1968)

FULD, C.J.

This appeal stems from a discovery proceeding brought in the Surrogate's Court by the executors of the estate of Abraham Hillowitz against his widow, the appellant herein. The husband had been a partner in an "investment club" and, after his death, the club, pursuant to a provision of the partnership agreement, paid the widow the sum of $2,800, representing his interest in the partnership. "In the event of the death of any partner," the agreement recited, "his share will be transferred to his wife, with no termination of the partnership." The executors contend in their petition that the above provision was an invalid attempt to make a testamentary disposition of property and that the proceeds should pass under the decedent's will as an asset of his estate. The widow maintains that it was a valid and enforceable contract. Although the Surrogate agreed with her, the Appellate Division held that the agreement was invalid as "an attempted testamentary disposition" (24 A.D.2d 891, 264 N.Y.S.2d 868).

A partnership agreement which provides that, upon the death of one partner, his interest shall pass to the surviving partner or partners, resting as it does in contract, is unquestionably valid and may not be defeated by labeling it a testamentary disposition. We are unable to perceive a difference in principle between an agreement of this character and one, such as that before us, providing for a deceased partner's widow, rather than a surviving partner, to succeed to the decedent's interest in the partnership.

These partnership undertakings are, in effect, nothing more or less than third-party beneficiary contracts, performable at death. Like many similar instruments, contractual in nature, which provide for the disposition of property after death, they need not conform to the requirements of the statute of wills. Examples of such instruments include (1) a contract to make a will; (2) an inter vivos trust in which the settlor reserves a life estate; and (3) an insurance policy.

In short, members of a partnership may provide, without fear of running afoul of our statute of wills, that, upon the death of a partner, his widow shall be entitled to his interest in the firm. This type of third-party beneficiary contract is not invalid as an attempted testamentary disposition.

The executors may derive little satisfaction from McCarthy v. Pieret (281 N.Y. 407, 24 N.E.2d 102), upon which they heavily rely. In the first place, it is our considered judgment that the decision should be limited to its facts. And, in the second place, the case is clearly distinguishable from the one now before us in that the court expressly noted that the "facts . . . indicate a mere intention on the part of the mortgagee to make a testamentary disposition of the property and not an intention to convey an immediate interest" and, in addition, that the named beneficiaries "knew nothing of the provisions of the extension agreement" (p. 413, 24 N.E.2d p. 104).

The order of the Appellate Division should be reversed, with costs in this court and in the Appellate Division, and the order of the Surrogate's Court reinstated.

UNIFORM PROBATE CODE

Provisions Relating to Effect of Death

§6-101. *Nonprobate Transfers on Death.*

(a) A provision for a nonprobate transfer on death in an insurance policy, contract of employment, bond, mortgage, promissory note, certificated or uncertificated security, account agreement, custodial agreement, deposit agreement, compensation plan, pension plan, individual retirement plan, employee benefit plan, trust, conveyance, deed of gift, marital property agreement, or other written instrument of a similar nature is nontestamentary. This subsection includes a written provision that:

(1) money or other benefits due to, controlled by, or owned by a decedent before death must be paid after the decedent's death to a person whom the decedent designates either in the instrument or in a separate writing, including a will, executed either before or at the same time as the instrument, or later;

(2) money due or to become due under the instrument ceases to be payable in the event of death of the promisee or the promisor before payment or demand; or

(3) any property controlled by or owned by the decedent before death which is the subject of the instrument passes to a person the decedent designates either in the instrument or in a separate writing, including a will, executed either before or at the same time as the instrument, or later.

(b) This section does not limit rights of creditors under other laws of this State.

Multiple-Person Accounts

OWNERSHIP AS BETWEEN PARTIES AND OTHERS

§6-211. *Ownership During Lifetime.*

(a) In this section, "net contribution" of a party means the sum of all deposits to an account made by or for the party, less all payments from the account made to or for the party which have not been paid to or applied to the use of another party and a proportionate share of any charges deducted from the account, plus a proportionate share of any interest or dividends earned, whether or not included in the current balance. The term includes deposit life insurance proceeds added to the account by reason of death of the party whose net contribution is in question.

(b) During the lifetime of all parties, an account belongs to the parties in proportion to the net contribution of each to the sums on deposit, unless there is clear and convincing evidence of a different intent. As between parties married to each other, in the absence of proof otherwise, the net contribution of each is presumed to be an equal amount.

(c) A beneficiary in an account having a POD designation has no right to sums on deposit during the lifetime of any party.

(d) An agent in an account with an agency designation has no beneficial right to sums on deposit.

§6-212.   *Rights at Death.*

(a) Except as otherwise provided in this section, on death of a party sums on deposit in a multiple-party account belong to the surviving party or parties. If two or more parties survive and one is the surviving spouse of the decedent, the amount to which the decedent, immediately before death, was beneficially entitled under Section 6-211 belongs to the surviving spouse. If two or more parties survive and none is the surviving spouse of the decedent, the amount to which the decedent, immediately before death, was beneficially entitled under Section 6-211 belongs to the surviving parties in equal shares, and augments the proportion to which each survivor, immediately before the decedent's death, was beneficially entitled under Section 6-211, and the right of survivorship continues between the surviving parties.

(b) In an account with a POD designation:

(1) On death of one of two or more parties, the rights in sums on deposit are governed by subsection (a).

(2) On death of the sole party or the last survivor of two or more parties, sums on deposit belong to the surviving beneficiary or beneficiaries. If two or more beneficiaries survive, sums on deposit belong to them in equal and undivided shares, and there is no right of survivorship in the event of death of a beneficiary thereafter. If no beneficiary survives, sums on deposit belong to the estate of the last surviving party.

(c) Sums on deposit in a single-party account without a POD designation, or in a multiple-party account that, by the terms of the account, is without right of survivorship, are not affected by death of a party, but the amount to which the decedent, immediately before death, was beneficially entitled under Section 6-211 is transferred as part of the decedent's estate. A POD designation in a multiple-party account without right of survivorship is ineffective. For purposes of this section, designation of an account as a tenancy in common establishes that the account is without right of survivorship.

(d) The ownership right of a surviving party or beneficiary, or of the decedent's estate, in sums on deposit is subject to requests for payment made by a party before the party's death, whether paid by the financial institution before or after death, or unpaid. The surviving party or beneficiary, or the decedent's estate, is liable to the payee of an unpaid request for payment. The liability is limited to a proportionate share of the amount transferred under this section, to the extent necessary to discharge the request for payment.

§6-213.   *Alteration of Rights.*

(a) Rights at death under Section 6-212 are determined by the type of account at the death of a party. The type of account may be altered by written notice given by a party to the financial institution to change the type of account or to stop or vary payment under the terms of the account. The notice must be signed by a party and received by the financial institution during the party's lifetime.

(b) A right of survivorship arising from the express terms of the account, Section 6-212, or a POD designation, may not be altered by will.

§6-214. *Accounts and Transfers Nontestamentary.*   Except as provided in Part 2 of Article II (elective share of surviving spouse) or as a consequence of, and to the extent directed by, Section 6-215, a transfer resulting from the application of Section 6-212 is effective by reason of the terms of the account involved and this part and is not testamentary or subject to Articles I through IV (estate administration).

§6-215.   *Rights of Creditors and Others.*

(a) If other assets of the estate are insufficient, a transfer resulting from a right of survivorship or POD designation under this part is not effective against the estate of a deceased party to the extent needed to pay claims against the estate and statutory allowances to the surviving spouse and children.

(b) A surviving party or beneficiary who receives payment from an account after death of a party is liable to account to the personal representative of the decedent for a proportionate share of the amount received to the extent necessary to discharge the claims and allowances described in subsection (a) remaining unpaid after application of the decedent's estate. A proceeding to assert the liability may not be commenced unless the personal representative has received a written demand by the surviving spouse, a creditor, a child, or a person acting for a child of the decedent. The proceeding must be commenced within one year after death of the decedent.

(c) A surviving party or beneficiary against whom a proceeding to account is brought may join as a party to the proceeding a surviving party or beneficiary of any other account of the decedent.

(d) Sums recovered by the personal representative must be administered as part of the decedent's estate. This section does not affect the protection from claims of the personal representative or estate of a deceased party provided in Section 6-226 for a financial institution that makes payment in accordance with the terms of the account.

§6-216.   *Community Property and Tenancy by the Entireties.*

(a) A deposit of community property in an account does not alter the community character of the property or community rights in the property, but a right of survivorship between parties married to each other arising from the express terms of the account or Section 6-212 may not be altered by will.

(b) This part does not affect the law governing tenancy by the entireties.

B.   Inter Vivos Gifts of Personal Property

It is only too obvious that gifts made by a person during his or her lifetime may be a substitute for transmission on death. The temptation, at least on the part of persons without law training, to use gifts as a substitute for testamentary disposition is a constant source of litigation. Quite clearly, inept attempts to make such disposition result not only in wasteful litigation but also in defeat of the donor's intention in some cases.

1.   Gifts, Gifts Causa Mortis, and the Requirement of Delivery

PROBLEMS

8-B.   A few days before *D*'s death, she wrote several checks to *M* in the total amount of $65,000 and handed these to *M*, who had been *D*'s housekeeper and maid for seven years. Then *F*, a friend of both *D* and *M*, visited *D* at her home. In *D*'s presence, *M* endorsed the checks and handed them over to *F*, who agreed to arrange investment of the funds. At about the same time *D* told her physician, in *M*'s presence, that she wanted *M* to have $100,000. Then, at the hospital two days before her death, *D* told her physician that he need not bother to inform *D*'s niece, *N*, of *D*'s illness or death, because funeral arrangements would be taken care of by *M* and "*N* never paid any attention to me anyway." *D* died before the checks to *M* were presented and paid. She left no will, an estate of somewhat over $1 million, and *N* and a nephew as her sole heirs. *M* claims that *D* promised her $100,000 and that the $65,000 in checks was part payment of that amount. *N*, as administratrix, has denied the claim. How would you support *M*'s claim? How would you resist it if you represented *N*? What result do you anticipate and why? See Estate of Grizzard, N.Y.L.J., June 7, 1982, at 13.

8-C.   For many years *A*, a childless widower, has been a close friend of *B*. Taken seriously ill, *A* sent for *B* and, according to the testimony of two private nurses in attendance when *B* came to *A*'s hospital room, *A* said the following: "I sent for you, *B*, because my time has come. I have seen to everything and am ready to go. I have all my affairs in order except for giving you this ring, which I've always wanted you to have." *A* thereupon handed *B* a valuable ring and continued: "I am ready to die;

my affairs are now arranged." Thereafter A recovered from his illness and lived for nearly five years. At A's death, B still had the ring and A's executor brings suit to recover it as an asset of the estate.

(a) How would you classify this transaction as attorney for the executor?

(b) What classification would you urge if you represented B? How would you argue for this position?

(c) What functions of the statute of wills are satisfied?

(d) If A had given the ring to one of his nurses and said, "I know I'm going to die; give this ring to B if I die," would the result differ?

8-D.   Advise A on each of the following questions:

(a) How should he proceed in making a gift to B of C's debt to A if that debt is not represented by a written instrument? Cf. Dinslage v. Stratman, 105 Neb. 274, 180 N.W. 81 (1920).

(b) How should he make a gift to X of a valuable painting that, with A's permission, is already hanging in X's home?

(c) How should he make a gift to X of another valuable painting that is now in A's home and that A wishes to retain in his home as long as he lives?

GRUEN v. GRUEN
68 N.Y.2d 48, 496 N.E.2d 869 (1986)

SIMONS, J. . . .

Plaintiff commenced this action seeking a declaration that he is the rightful owner of a painting which he alleges his father, now deceased, gave to him. He concedes that he has never had possession of the painting but asserts that his father made a valid gift of the title in 1963 reserving a life estate for himself. His father retained possession of the painting until he died in 1980. Defendant, plaintiff's stepmother, has the painting now and has refused plaintiff's requests that she turn it over to him. . . .

The subject of the dispute is a work entitled "Schloss Kammer am Attersee II" painted by a noted Austrian modernist, Gustav Klimt. It was purchased by plaintiff's father, Victor Gruen, in 1959 for $8,000. On April 1, 1963 the elder Gruen . . . wrote a letter to plaintiff . . . stating that he was giving him the Klimt painting for his birthday but that he wished to retain the possession of it for his lifetime. This letter is not in evidence, apparently because plaintiff destroyed it on instructions from his father. Two other letters were received, however, one dated May 22, 1963 and the other April 1, 1963. Both had been dictated by Victor Gruen and sent together to plaintiff on or about May 22, 1963. The letter dated May 22, 1963 reads as follows:

Dear Michael:

I wrote you at the time of your birthday about the gift of the painting by Klimt.

Now my lawyer tells me that because of the existing tax laws, it was wrong to mention in that letter that I want to use the painting as long as I live. Though I still want to use it, this should not appear in the letter. I am enclosing, therefore, a new letter and I ask you to send the old one back to me so that it can be destroyed.

I know this is all very silly, but the lawyer and our accountant insist that they must have in their possession copies of a letter which will serve the purpose of making it possible for you, once I die, to get this picture without having to pay inheritance taxes on it.

Love,
s/*Victor*

Enclosed with this letter was a substitute gift letter, dated April 1, 1963, which stated:

Dear Michael:

The 21st birthday, being an important event in life, should be celebrated accordingly. I therefore wish to give you as a present the oil painting by Gustav Klimt of Schloss Kammer which now hangs in the New York living room. You know that Lazette and I bought it some 5 or 6 years ago, and you always told us how much you liked it.

Happy birthday again.

Love,
s/*Victor*

. . . The issues framed for appeal are whether a valid inter vivos gift of a chattel may be made where the donor has reserved a life estate in the chattel and the donee never has had physical possession of it before the donor's death and, if it may, which factual findings on the elements of a valid inter vivos gift more nearly comport with the weight of the evidence in this case, those of Special Term or those of the Appellate Division. The latter issue requires application of two general rules. First, to make a valid inter vivos gift there must exist the intent on the part of the donor to make a present transfer; delivery of the gift, either actual or constructive to the donee; and acceptance by the donee. . . . Second, the proponent of a gift has the burden of proving each of these elements by clear and convincing evidence. . . .

[*Donative Intent.*] There is an important distinction between the intent with which an inter vivos gift is made and the intent to make a gift by will. An inter vivos gift requires that the donor intend to make an irrevocable present transfer of ownership; if the intention is to make a testamentary disposition effective only after death, the gift is invalid unless made by will. . . .

Defendant contends that the trial court was correct in finding that Victor did not intend to transfer any present interest in the painting to plaintiff in 1963 but only expressed an intention that plaintiff was to get the painting upon his death. The evidence is all but conclusive, however, that Victor intended to transfer ownership of the painting to plaintiff in 1963 but to retain a life estate in it and that he did, therefore, effectively transfer a remainder interest in the painting to plaintiff at that time. Although the original letter was not in evidence, testimony of its contents was received along with the substitute gift letter and its covering letter dated May 22, 1963. The three letters should be considered together as a single instrument . . . and when they are they unambiguously establish that Victor Gruen intended to make a present gift of title to the painting at that time. But there was other evidence for after 1963 Victor made several statements orally and in writing indicating that he had previously given plaintiff the painting and that plaintiff owned it. . . . Victor's failure to file a gift tax return on the transaction was partially explained by allegedly erroneous legal advice he received, and while that omission sometimes may indicate that the donor had no intention of making a present gift, it does not necessarily do so and it is not dispositive in this case.

Defendant contends that even if a present gift was intended, Victor's reservation of a lifetime interest in the painting defeated it. . . .

Defendant recognizes that a valid inter vivos gift of a remainder interest can be made not only of real property but also of such intangibles as stocks and bonds. Indeed, several of the cases she cites so hold. That being so, it is difficult to perceive any legal basis for the distinction she urges which would permit gifts of remainder interests in those properties but not of remainder interests in chattels such as the Klimt painting here. . . . Insofar as some of our cases purport to require that the donor intend to transfer both title and possession immediately to have a valid inter vivos gift (see Gannon v. McGuire, 160 N.Y. 476, 481, 55 N.E. 7; Young v. Young, 80 N.Y. 422, 430), they state the rule too broadly and confuse the effectiveness of a gift with the transfer of the possession of the subject of that gift. . . . As long as the evidence establishes an intent to make a present and irrevocable transfer of title or the right of ownership, there is a present transfer of some interest and the gift is effective immediately. . . .

. . . Once the gift is made it is irrevocable and the donor is limited to the rights of a life tenant not an owner. Moreover, with the gift of a remainder title vests immediately in the donee and any possession is postponed until the donor's death whereas under a will neither title nor possession vests immediately. Finally, the postponement of enjoyment of the gift is produced by the express terms of the gift not by the nature of the instrument as it is with a will. . . .

[*Delivery.*] In order to have a valid inter vivos gift, there must be a delivery of the gift, either by a physical delivery of the subject of the gift or a constructive or symbolic delivery such as by an instrument of gift, sufficient to divest the donor of dominion and control over the property. . . . As the statement of the rule suggests, the requirement of delivery is not rigid or inflexible, but is to be applied in light of its purpose to avoid mistakes by donors and fraudulent claims by donees. . . . Accordingly, what is sufficient to constitute delivery "must be tailored to suit the circumstances of the case." . . .

Nor is there any reason to require a donor making a gift of a remainder interest in a chattel to physically deliver the chattel into the donee's hands only to have the donee redeliver it to the donor. . . . [I]n the absence of witnesses to the event or any written confirmation of the gift it would provide less protection against fraudulent claims than have the written instruments of gift delivered in this case.

[*Acceptance.*] Acceptance by the donee is essential to the validity of an inter vivos gift, but when a gift is of value to the donee, as it is here, the law will presume an acceptance. . . . [Here there is also] clear and convincing proof of his acceptance of a remainder interest in the Klimt painting by evidence that he had made several contemporaneous statements acknowledging the gift to his friends and associates, even showing some of them his father's gift letter, and that he had retained both letters for over 17 years. . . .

Ridden v. Thrall, 125 N.Y. 572, 575, 26 N.E. 627, 629 (1891), states: "In the case of gifts inter vivos, the moment the gift [is] consummated it becomes absolute and irrevocable. But in case of gifts causa mortis more is needed. The gift must be made under apprehension of death from some present disease, or some other impending peril, and it becomes void by recovery from the disease or escape from the peril. It is also revocable at any time by the donor, and becomes void by the death of the donee in the life-time of the donor. It is not needful that the gift be made in etremis [with] no time or opportunity to make a will. In many of the reported cases the gift was made weeks, and even months, before the death of the donor, when there was abundant time and opportunity for him to have made a will."

The court, rejecting dicta of other cases, went on to hold that there is no further requirement that the donor die from the particular disease or peril he had in mind, so long as the death occurs, even from another cause, before the danger is removed. Also, the court decided that by handing the donee a box containing the passbooks the donor had made adequate delivery of various deposits in savings banks. "The decisions are not entirely harmonious [but] the general rule . . . is that any delivery of property which transfers legal or equitable title is sufficient to effectuate a gift; and hence it has been held that the mere delivery of nonnegotiable notes, bonds, mortgages, or certificates of stock is sufficient."

Drew v. Haggerty, 81 Me. 231, 17 A. 63 (1889), faced the question "whether the gift of a savings-bank book, from husband to wife, causa mortis, is valid without delivery, provided the book is at the time of the alleged gift already in the possession of the wife." In deciding that it was not, the court noted that the purpose of delivery is not only to invest the donee with possession. It is "also important as evidence of deliberation and intention. It is a test of sincerity and distinguishes idle talk from serious purposes. And it makes fraud and perjury more difficult. Mere words are easily misrepresented. Even the change of an emphasis may make them convey a meaning different from what the speaker intended. Not so an act of delivery." The court then added:

> Gifts, causa mortis, are not to be encouraged. They are often sustained by fraud and perjury. [It] is far better that occasionally a gift of this kind should fail than that the rules of law be so relaxed as to encourage fraud and perjury.
>
> We are aware that some text writers have assumed that when the property is already in the possession of the donee, a delivery is not necessary. But the cases cited in support of the doctrine nearly all relate to gifts, inter vivos, not to gifts causa mortis. . . . It is the opinion of the court that the gift of a savings-bank book, causa mortis, to be valid, must be accompanied by an actual delivery of the book from the donor to the donee, or to someone for the donee.

In Waite v. Grubbe, 43 Or. 406, 408, 73 P. 206, 207 (1903), the court said: "It is not necessary that there be a manual delivery, or an actual tradition from hand to hand. The delivery may be constructive or symbolical, but the general rule is that it must be as perfect and complete as the nature of the property and the attendant circumstances and conditions will permit. . . . 'The title does not pass unless possession, or the means of obtaining it, are conferred by the donor.'" The court then mentioned a case in which a bedridden donor made a valid gift of the contents of some trunks by handing the keys to the donee. In upholding a gift causa mortis in the peculiar facts before it, the court stated: "The places of deposit [burial of money] were known only to him, and the secret was his protection from plunder. Being barely able to walk to the garden, a place apart from all other persons, he there imparted to his daughter the information as to the whereabouts of the money by pointing out to her definitely and particularly the several localities in which it was concealed, with a positive [declaration] that it was hers, cautioning her not to let any one else know where it was, and advising her to leave it there until the place was rented, or until she needed it. The delivery was as complete as the circumstances of the case would permit. He was physically unable to disinter the coins, and it was not advisable for the daughter to attempt to do so. . . . By imparting [the secret to her] he, in effect, gave her the key to his safety vault."

SCHERER v. HYLAND
75 N.J. 127, 380 A.2d 698 (1977)

PER CURIAM.

Defendant, the Administrator ad litem of the Estate of Catherine Wagner, appeals from an Appellate Division decision, one judge dissenting, affirming a summary judgment by the trial court holding that Ms. Wagner had made a valid gift causa mortis of a check to plaintiff. We affirm.

The facts are not in dispute. Catherine Wagner and the plaintiff, Robert Scherer, lived together for approximately fifteen years prior to Ms. Wagner's death in January 1974. In 1970, the decedent and plaintiff were involved in an automobile accident in which decedent suffered facial wounds and a broken hip. Because of the hip injury, decedent's physical mobility was substantially impaired. She was forced to give up her job and to restrict her activities. After the accident, plaintiff cared for her and assumed the sole financial responsibility for maintaining their household. During the weeks preceding her death, Ms. Wagner was acutely depressed. On one occasion, she attempted suicide by slashing her wrists. On January 23, 1974, she commited suicide by jumping from the roof of the apartment building in which they lived.

On the morning of the day of her death, Ms. Wagner received a check for $17,400 drawn by a Pennsylvania attorney who had represented her in a claim arising out of the automobile accident. The check represented settlement of the claim. Plaintiff telephoned Ms. Wagner at around 11:30 A.M. that day and was told that the check had arrived. Plaintiff noticed nothing unusual in Ms. Wagner's voice. At about 3:20 P.M., decedent left the apartment building and jumped to her death. The police, as part of their investigation of the suicide, asked the building superintendent to admit them to the apartment. On the kitchen table they found the check, endorsed in blank, and two notes handwritten by the decedent. In one, she described her depression over her physical condition, expressed her love for Scherer, and asked him to forgive her "for taking the easy way out." In the other, she indicated that she "bequeathed" to plaintiff all of her possessions, including "the check for $17,400.00. . . ." The police took possession of the check, which was eventually placed in an interest-bearing account pending disposition of this action.

Under our wills statute it is clear that Ms. Wagner's note bequeathing all her possessions to Mr. Scherer cannot take effect as a testamentary disposition. N.J.S.A. 3A:3-2. A donatio causa mortis has been traditionally defined as a gift of personal property made by a party in expectation of death, then imminent, subject to the condition that the donor die as anticipated. Establishment of the gift has uniformly called for proof of delivery.

The primary issue here is whether Ms. Wagner's acts of endorsing the settlement check, placing it on the kitchen table in the apartment she shared with Scherer, next to a writing clearly evidencing her intent to transfer the check to Scherer, and abandoning the apartment with a clear expectation of imminent death constituted delivery sufficient to sustain a gift causa mortis of the check. Defendant relying on the principles established in Foster v. Reiss, 18 N.J. 41, 112 A.2d 553 (1955), argues that there was no delivery because the donor did not unequivocally relinquish control of the check before her death. Central to this argument is the contention that suicide, the perceived peril, was one which decedent herself created and one which was completely within her control. According to this contention, the donor at any time before she jumped from the apartment roof could have changed her mind, reentered the apartment, and reclaimed the check. Defendant therefore reasons that decedent did not make an effective transfer of the check during her lifetime, as is required for a valid gift causa mortis. . . .

There is general agreement that the major purpose of the delivery requirement is evidentiary. Proof of delivery reduces the possibility that the evidence of intent has been fabricated or that a mere donative impulse, not consummated by action, has been mistaken for a completed gift. Since "these gifts come into question only after death has closed the lips of the donor," the delivery requirement provides a substantial safeguard against fraud and perjury. See Keepers v. Fidelity Title and Deposit Co., 56 N.J.L. 302, 308, 28 A. 585 (E. & A. 1893). In *Foster,* the majority concluded that these policies could best be fulfilled by a strict rule requiring actual manual tradition of the subject-matter of the gift except in a very narrow class of cases where "there can be no actual delivery" or where "the situation is incompatible with the performance of such ceremony." 18 N.J. at 50, 112 A.2d at 559. Justice Jacobs, in his dissenting opinion (joined by Justices Brennan and Wachenfeld) questioned the reasonableness of requiring direct physical delivery in cases where donative intent is "freely and clearly expressed in a written instrument." Id. at 56, 112 A.2d at 562. He observed that a more flexible approach to the delivery requirement had been taken by other jurisdictions and quoted approvingly from Devol v. Dye, 123 Ind. 321, 24 N.E. 246, 7 L.R.A. 439 (Sup. Ct. 1890). That case stated:

> [G]ifts causa mortis . . . are not to be held contrary to public policy, nor do they rest under the disfavor of the law, when the facts are clearly and satisfactorily shown which make it appear that they were freely and intelligently made. . . . The rule requiring delivery, either actual or symbolical, must be maintained, but its application is to be militated and applied according to the relative importance of the subject of the gift and the con-

dition of the donor. The intention of a donor in peril of death, when clearly ascertained and fairly consummated within the meaning of well-established rules, is not to be thwarted by a narrow and illiberal construction of what may have been intended for and deemed by him a sufficient delivery. . . .

In essence, this approach takes into account the purposes served by the requirement of delivery in determining whether that requirement has been met. It would find a constructive delivery adequate to support the gift when the evidence of donative intent is concrete and undisputed, when there is every indication that the donor intended to make a present transfer of the subject-matter of the gift, and when the steps taken by the donor to effect such a transfer must have been deemed by the donor as sufficient to pass the donor's interest to the donee. We are persuaded that this approach, which does not minimize the need for evidentiary safeguards to prevent frauds upon the estates of the deceased, reflects the realities which attend transfers of this kind.

In this case, the evidence of decedent's intent to transfer the check to Robert Scherer is concrete, unequivocal, and undisputed. The circumstances definitely rule out any possibility of fraud. The sole question, then, is whether the steps taken by the decedent, independent of her writing of the suicide notes, were sufficient to support a finding that she effected a lifetime transfer of the check to Scherer. We think that they were. First, the act of endorsing a check represents, in common experience and understanding, the only act needed (short of actual delivery) to render a check negotiable. The significance of such an act is universally understood. Accordingly, we have no trouble in viewing Ms. Wagner's endorsement of the settlement check as a substantial step taken by her for the purpose of effecting a transfer to Scherer of her right to the check proceeds. Second, we note that the only person other than the decedent who had routine access to the apartment was Robert Scherer. Indeed, the apartment was leased in his name. It is clear that Ms. Wagner before leaving the apartment placed the check in a place where Scherer could not fail to see it and fully expected that he would take actual possession of the check when he entered. And, although Ms. Wagner's subsequent suicide does not itself constitute a component of the delivery of this gift, it does provide persuasive evidence that when Ms. Wagner locked the door of the apartment she did so with no expectation of returning. When we consider her state of mind as it must have been upon leaving the apartment, her surrender of possession at that moment was complete. We find, therefore, that when she left the apartment she completed a constructive delivery of the check to Robert Scherer. In light of her resolve to take her own life and of her obvious desire not to be deterred from that purpose, Ms. Wagner's failure manually to transfer the check to Scherer is understandable. She clearly did all that she could do or thought necessary to do to surrender the check. Her donative intent has been conclusively demonstrated by independent evidence. The law should effectuate that intent rather than indulge in nice distinctions which would thwart her purpose. Upon these facts, we find that the constructive delivery she made was adequate to support a gift causa mortis.

Defendant's assertion that suicide is not the sort of peril that will sustain a gift causa mortis finds some support in precedents from other jurisdictions. . . . [D]eath is no less impending because of a resolve to commit suicide. . . . And, the notion that one in a state of mental depression serious enough to lead to suicide is somehow "freer" to renounce the depression and thus the danger than one suffering from a physical illness, although it has a certain augustinian appeal, has long since been replaced by more enlightened views of human psychology. . . . We also observe that an argument that the donor of a causa mortis gift might have changed his or her mind loses much of its force when one recalls that a causa mortis gift, by definition, can be revoked at any time before the donor dies and is automatically revoked if the donor recovers.

Finally, defendant asserts that this gift must fail because there was no acceptance prior to the donor's death. Although the issue of acceptance is rarely litigated, the authority that does exist indicates that, given a valid delivery, acceptance will be implied if the gift is unconditional and beneficial to the donee. . . . The presumption of acceptance may apply even if the donee does not learn of the gift until after the donor's death. . . .

Judgment affirmed.

CALIFORNIA CIVIL CODE

§5702.   *"Gift in view of impending death."*

(a) A gift in view of impending death is one which is made in contemplation, fear, or peril of impending death, whether from illness or other cause, and with intent that it shall be revoked if the giver recovers from the illness or escapes from the peril.

(b) A reference in a statute to a gift in view of death means a gift in view of impending death.

§5703. *Presumption regarding gifts made during final illness of giver.* A gift made during the last illness of the giver, or under circumstances which would naturally impress the giver with an expectation of speedy death, is presumed to be a gift in view of impending death.

§5704.   *Revocation of gift in view of impending death.*

(a) A gift in view of impending death is revoked by:

(1) The giver's recovery from the illness, or escape from the peril, under the presence of which it was made.

(2) The death of the donee before the death of the giver.

(b) A gift in view of impending death may be revoked by:

(1) The giver at any time.

(2) The giver's will if the will expresses an intention to revoke the gift.

(c) A gift in view of impending death is not affected by a previous will of the giver.

(d) Notwithstanding subdivisions (a) and (b), when the gift has been delivered to the donee, the rights of a purchaser or encumbrancer, acting before the revocation in good faith, for a valuable consideration, and without knowledge of the conditional nature of the gift, are not affected by the revocation.

MECHEM, THE REQUIREMENT OF DELIVERY IN GIFTS OF CHATTELS
21 Ill. L. Rev. 341, 341-342, 348-350 (1926)

It is well settled that delivery is essential to the validity of a parol gift of a chattel. This rule appears to be as old as the common law. After being doubted by certain English authorities in the latter part of the last century it was authoritatively reaffirmed in 1890 by the case of Cochrane v. Moore [(1890) 25 Q.B.D. 57].

It would be inaccurate in the extreme, however, to say that it is well settled just *what* amounts to delivery of a chattel. Courts have differed widely on that problem and an unfortunate confusion of the authorities has resulted. The doctrine of "constructive" or "symbolical" delivery, so-called, has been largely invoked, without, however, any very exact or analytical attempts being made to define just what is meant by such delivery, or just what acts or facts may constitute it. In some cases the doctrine has been so liberally and undiscriminatingly applied as practically to nullify the general rule. In others, narrow and technical distinctions have been drawn, tending to make the rule the cause of unnecessary hardship.

Considering the great and growing importance of the subject, it has seemed desirable to attempt some analysis of the situation. Obviously the focal point of attack must be this: exactly what *is* delivery, why is it required, and why (if at all) *should* it be required? An apparently plausible first step might be to define delivery in the abstract, as well as may be, in terms of possession. This would prove, in fact, fruitless, for two reasons, first, because it may be shown that in many cases the rule is satisfied by a "delivery" which involves no change of possession and, second, because the only sound and useful approach to a problem such as this is the pragmatic approach, i.e., the approach which defines a thing in terms of its functions. If we should succeed in defining delivery in terms of possession we should still have accomplished little, both because the definition would be unworkable in many cases, and because being made, it would still throw no light on the real root question, to wit, what is the logical connection between a change of possession and that complex group of changes in legal rights and relations compendiously described as "a gift."

The pragmatic approach, on the other hand, begins with what we have just described as the "root question." What is gained, we ask, by demanding that a gift be valid only when accompanied by a change of possession? Or, to phrase it differently, since we have seen that occasionally a change of possession seems not to be required: what are the legal desiderata which are deemed satisfied by a change in possession, or, under certain circumstances, by something else?

An examination of the question might lead to the belief that the requirement of delivery, however that word is to be defined, is an arbitrary and unnecessary one. In such a case further investigation would seem to be beside the point. One could only hope that such a requirement might be discarded as fast as judicial conventions and precedents permit. The examination, on the other hand, might lead to the discovery that some well founded (though possibly incompletely realized) considerations of policy lie behind the requirement. In such a case, the discovery of those considerations would seem to make possible the establishment of satisfactory criteria for applying the rule. . . .

In the first place, the delivery makes vivid and concrete to the donor the significance of the act he is doing. Any one can realize the psychological difference between a man's saying he gives something, yet retaining it, and saying he gives it and seeing it pass irrevocably out of his control. The *wrench* of delivery, if the expression be understood and permissible, the little mental twinge at seeing his property pass from his hands into those of another, is an important element to the protection of the donor. If he is uncertain, if he hardly understands himself just what he means or (which is perhaps even more important) what he is understood to mean, he cannot fail to understand (and be understood) when he hands over the property. It gives him a locus penitentiae. It forces upon the most thoughtless and hasty at least a moment's acute consideration of the effects of what he is proposing to do. Where valuable property is being passed without consideration, perhaps in the agony of a dying moment, it does not seem unwise to insist upon this simple and automatic safeguard.

Secondly, the act of manual tradition is as unequivocal to actual witnesses of the transaction as to the donor himself. Here normality is a big factor. What did the donor say? What did he mean? Perhaps he spoke under his breath, or was unable to speak clearly. Perhaps he hesitated and contradicted himself so that the outcome of his thought was not readily to be ascertained by witnesses in the flurry of the moment. If he hands over the property, he has done an act that will settle many doubts, an act perhaps capable of more than one interpretation, yet readily and naturally susceptible of but one.

Thirdly, and lastly, the fact of delivery gives the donee, subsequently to the act, at least prima facie evidence in favor of the alleged gift. The law does not presume unlawful acts. Possession is ordinarily rightful. The evidence is of course at best presumptive, yet better than none. If the donee comes out of the sick room and says the bonds have been given to him he will be more credited, and more reasonable, if he has them in his possession. It is easier to fabricate a story than to abstract the property.

The considerations just enumerated seem to the writer on the whole both to justify the rule as a salutary requirement, and to furnish criteria for its proper application. A study of the cases shows clearly enough the fear of judges that gifts will be fraudulently claimed, and clearly enough, too, that those fears are not without foundation. The policy that has led to the Statutes of Frauds and of Wills seems here to demand with added force that some kind of safeguards be set against fraudulent claims of gift. It is important to notice that the safeguard here advocated is neither arbitrary nor unreasonable. It arises automatically from the nature of the transaction. Cases where it is not spontaneously complied with are the exception and not the rule.

The impression appears to prevail in some quarters that the rule requiring delivery is an arbitrary and unnecessary formality. This arises, it is believed, both from the sentimental considerations always aroused by individual hard cases, and from the difficulty encountered in the cases where special circumstances make delivery difficult or impossible. An attempt will be made to handle this latter class of cases presently. As to the former, no greater hardship arises than frequently does in cases of wills imperfectly executed through ignorance of the law, and it has never been thought wise to sweep aside the salutary provisions of the Wills Act on account of individual hard cases. The situations, it seems, are markedly analogous. . . .

2.   Gifts to Minors

Parents and grandparents often wish to make gifts to minors. Generally, a minor's ownership of property that requires any amount of management supervision or business dealings will create a variety of problems, resulting in the necessity of obtaining formal appointment of a legal guardian or conservator of the minor's estate. For a variety of reasons a donor may find a guardianship or conservatorship arrangement unattractive. (See Chapter 9, section C.) The trust is, of course, an alternative and is taken up in subsequent chapters. For some purposes, especially where large amounts or special complications are involved, the flexible trust device will prove highly desirable. Often, however, the cost and nuisance of establishing a formal trust cause the donor to seek something less elaborate. Frequently, then, informal and purely oral trusts are employed, although the donor and "trustee" may not be aware of the significance or responsibilities of the arrangement — or even realize they are creating a trust.

In quest of another solution and to make readily available certain advantages under the federal gift tax law, all states have now enacted legislation based on the Uniform Gifts to Minors Act, the Model Gifts of Securities to Minors Act, or the more recent Uniform Transfers to Minors Act. Provided a qualified form of property is given in a qualified manner, donors today may conveniently utilize these statutes to create a statutory form of "canned" trusts, commonly referred to as *custodianships*. All that is required is that the act be invoked by a clear reference to it. Usually the property is simply registered or transferred, for example, to "[name] as custodian for [name] under the [state] Uniform Gifts to Minors Act." There is no need to prepare a complex document or to specify the details of the arrangement, for the statutory custodianship carries with it what amounts to a full set of beneficial provisions and managerial powers akin to an express private trust for an individual lasting for the period of his minority. The income and principal may be expended for the donee's benefit for as long as he is a minor; then the unexpended property is paid over to him or to his estate if he dies before coming of age.

The earlier versions of these acts, unfortunately, usually were limited to gifts of money and securities and could not be used for testamentary giving. The 1983 Uniform Transfers to Minors Act, however, addresses these matters and applies to all types of property and all forms of transfers, including those under powers of appointment, life insurance and pension beneficiary designations, and the like. Although these statutes usually call for the custodianship to terminate at the age of majority, some statutes continue it until age 21. One state, however, has provided greater flexibility in this matter; California Probate Code §§3900-3925 allow testators and, for the most part, other transferors to set a termination age as high as age 25 by simply inserting additional words indicating, for example, that the custodianship is "for [name] until age 25."

The Uniform Custodial Trust Act, promulgated in 1987, has been enacted in Hawaii, Idaho, Minnesota, Rhode Island, and Virginia. Under this act, the type of "canned" trust found in the Transfers to Minors Act is adapted to the needs of older adults. A simple designation in an instrument of transfer or registration creates a revocable custodial trust that becomes a discretionary trust on the beneficiary's incompetence, with the assets passing to the named successor on the beneficiary's death.

C.   *Testamentary Nature of Deeds*

NOBLE v. TIPTON
219 Ill. 182, 76 N.E. 151 (1905)

[John Noble died in 1904, survived by three sons and six daughters. His will, executed in 1898, disposed of all of his estate except the home farm, as the land in controversy was known. The will stated that the farm had previously been deeded to his son, Thomas. In 1897 a deed to this farm was executed, attested by two witnesses, and acknowledged. In 1898 John Noble placed the will, the deed in question, and another deed in the hands of a custodian, who put the documents in an envelope on the outside of which is written: "The deeds within to be delivered to grantees after death of grantor. . . . All of said property to be held subject to the order of John Noble." Thomas managed the farm and borrowed $3,000 from his father to make valuable improvements. They resided together on the farm until the latter's death. In a suit initiated by two of the daughters, the court below declared the deed null and void for want of delivery and ordered partition of the farm as intestate property. Thomas appealed.]

CARTWRIGHT, C.J. . . .

A delivery is essential to the validity of a deed, and to constitute a delivery the grantor must part with control over it and retain no right to reclaim or recall it. (Hawes v. Hawes, 177 Ill. 409; Spacy v. Ritter, 214 id. 266.) This deed was not delivered but was held by the custodian subject to the order of the grantor, who did not part with all control over it but retained the right to reclaim or recall it. The deed was intended as a testamentary disposition of the farm to take effect at the death of the grantor, and such a disposition can only be effected by an instrument in writing executed in conformity with the Statute of Wills. The instrument was not operative as a deed.

Counsel for appellant contends that if the deed was not operative as a conveyance the property was devised by the following clause of the will:

Fifth — The remainder of my estate, both real and personal, excepting the home farm, containing 503½ acres, which I have heretofore deeded to my son Thomas Noble, I give, devise and bequeath to my sons Robert Noble, Thomas Noble and John W. Noble, share and share alike.

By previous provisions of the will he had disposed of his household goods and furniture and farm implements and made certain bequests to his children. The argument is, that the testator could not be presumed to intend to die intestate as to any part of his property, and that by the will he evinced an intention to devise the farm to his son Thomas, who would therefore take it by implication under the will. The rule on that subject is, that where a recital in a will is to the effect that the testator has devised something in another part of the will when in fact he has not done so, the erroneous recital may operate as a devise by implication of the same property, for the reason that it shows an intention to devise the property by the will; but where the recital is to the effect that the testator has by some other instrument given to a certain person named in the recital, property, when in fact he has not done so, such a recital does not disclose an intention to give by the will . . . and the courts cannot give that recital the effect of a devise. Nor does the recital aid in establishing that there had been a valid delivery of the deed so as to make it operative as such. Lange v. Cullinan, 205 Ill. 365.

The deed did not operate as a conveyance of the property, and whether it must fail as a testamentary disposition of the farm is a question not involved under the pleadings in this case. . . . At any rate, the instrument could not be effective as a devise until admitted to probate, and the county court has exclusive jurisdiction for that purpose. (Beatty v. Clegg, 214 Ill. 34.) Where a disposition of property made by a written instrument is not to take effect until the death of the maker it is testamentary in character, and will remain subject to revocation or change during his life. (Massey v. Huntington, 118 Ill. 80.) And it is sufficient for the decision of this case that the deed was not delivered and did not take effect in the lifetime of the grantor.

Noble v. Fickes, 230 Ill. 594, 82 N.E. 950 (1907), 21 Harv. L. Rev. 451, affirmed the subsequent denial of probate of the instrument that was in issue as a deed in Noble v. Tipton. In affirming, the court (at 606-607, 82 N.E. at 953-954) stated:

Upon the general proposition that a valid will may be made in the form of an ordinary deed of bargain and sale, we entertain not the slightest doubt, where the formalities of the statute are properly observed, and it clearly appears on the face of the instrument that it is not to take effect until the death of the maker. The inherent difficulty with the instrument involved in this case is that there is nothing in the writing itself which imparts to it a testamentary character. To give it this character a resort must be had to extrinsic facts depending on parol evidence. . . . [But our] statute requires wills to be in writing. If an unambiguous deed, which on its face purports to convey a present interest, can be converted into a will by proving an animo testandi in the maker by parol evidence, the effect is not only to change the legal character of the instrument, but to engraft upon it one of the essentials of a will by parol, in the face of our statute, which requires all wills to be in writing.

This case is clearly distinguishable . . . [from] the case between these parties decided in 219 Ill., where the question at issue was whether a deed had been delivered. Delivery is largely a question of intention and may be shown by any competent evidence. Evidence on that point does not contradict or vary the terms of the instrument, but bears on the question whether the instrument, in fact, ever had a legal existence. It would be a strange result if the same evidence which destroyed the instrument as a deed should bring it to life as a will.

Our conclusion is that it would be an unsafe rule to hold that an undelivered deed, which by chance happened to be attested by two witnesses, could be converted into a will by parol evidence.

The dissenting opinion (Cartwright and Carter, J.J.) stated: "We do not see how it can consistently be said that the instrument amounts to a testamentary disposition of the property described in it and yet that it is not a testament, although it was executed with all the formalities required in the case of a will." Id. at 607-608, 82 N.E. at 954.

TENNANT v. JOHN TENNANT MEMORIAL HOME
167 Cal. 570, 140 P. 242 (1914)

SHAW, J.

On the seventh day of May, 1901, Margaret Tennant executed to the defendant, John Tennant Memorial Home, a deed purporting to grant and convey to it certain real property, "subject to the exceptions and reservations" thereinafter mentioned. Afterward she died and her heirs began and are prosecuting this action to quiet their title to the land and recover possession thereof, claiming that said deed is void. The administrator of her estate intervened and filed a complaint asking the same relief on behalf of her estate. The court below gave judgment for the defendant, from which the plaintiffs and the intervener appeal.

The exceptions and reservations mentioned in the opening clause of the deed are inserted therein immediately following the description of the property. They are as follows:

Excepting, however, and reserving to said grantor the exclusive possession and the use and enjoyment in her own right, of the rents, issues and profits of said lots and each of them for and during the term of her natural life.

And further reserving to the said grantor the right to revoke this deed as to the said property above described or as to any portion thereof, and further reserving to her, the said grantor, the right during her natural life to sell any of the above described property, and to sign and execute deeds therefor in her own individual name and to convey by any such deed a full, perfect and absolute title to the purchaser thereof, and with right to use the proceeds arising from such sale or sales to her own use, without any liability for her or her estate to account therefor. In case of such revocation being made, it shall be made and can only be made in writing, duly acknowledged and recorded.

Margaret Tennant did not exercise, or attempt to exercise the power to revoke the deed, nor the power to sell and convey the property, or any part thereof. The decision of the case depends on the validity of the deed. If it is valid, the judgment below was correct; if invalid, the judgment must be reversed. . . .

The effect of the reservation of a life estate is that the deed conveys a future interest, only, to the grantee. . . . The main contention of the appellants is that the deed in question is not a present grant of property, so far as the remainder is concerned, but is an instrument testamentary in character and therefore invalid as a disposition of the property, because it is not executed with the formalities necessary to the execution of a will. . . .

[T]he fact that in this case there is also reserved a power to revoke the deed and to sell the remainder, is of no consequence in the argument upon the question whether it is or is not testamentary. The power of revocation being valid, its exercise would at once revest the title in the grantor and she would then have absolute power to dispose of it by deed or otherwise. The power of sale reserved is therefore of no consequence, since it was necessarily included in the power to revoke. The reservation of the power to revoke did not operate to destroy, or in anywise restrict the effect of the deed as a present conveyance of a future vested interest. It merely afforded a means whereby such vested future estate could be defeated and divested before it ripened into an estate in possession. . . .

Another argument presented in favor of the proposition that this deed is testamentary in nature is founded upon the circumstance that the disposition which the grantor thereby made of the property conveyed was substantially the same as she might have made by a will, so far as her enjoyment of the property and her control over the fee is concerned. This circumstance does not determine the effect of the deed and has but little bearing on the question. An instrument is declared to be testamentary in nature only when, and because, it appears from its terms that the intention of the maker thereof was that it should not be operative as a conveyance or disposition of the property, or of any interest, present or future, therein, until his death. This is always essential. If the instrument, according to its proper legal effect under the rules of conveyancing, passes at the time of its execution a present interest or title in the property to a third person, although it may be only an interest in a future estate and may be subject to defeat on the happening or nonoccurrence of a future event, it is a present conveyance and not a will. . . .

The judgment is affirmed.

D. *Claims of Creditors*

PROBLEM

8-E. After working for a large manufacturer for years, *D*, an electrical engineer, decided to go into business for herself to manufacture and market an automobile antitheft device. It was designed to alert the owner by radio signal of any tampering and to broadcast a continuous signal that police could follow to locate the vehicle if moved. To finance this venture, *D* used her savings and $100,000 borrowed at a modest rate of interest from her uncle *U*. The business prospered and *D* continued to pay interest to *U* for over ten years. During this time she invested most of her surplus income through her stockbroker, *B*, under an agreement the pertinent part of which provided the following:

1. Account title: *D* or *S*, joint with right of survivorship.
2. All funds held pending investment or distribution subject to and payable on order of *D*.
3. All shares purchased shall be in name of "*D* or *S* or the survivor of them" and the certificates delivered to or held subject to order of *D*.
4. On death of either party, *D* or *S*, the net balance in the account after brokerage charges shall be paid to the survivor.

D, a widow, died unexpectedly as the result of an accident. It appeared that, about five years ago, she had given most of her business assets to *S*, her son. *D*'s probate estate is substantially insolvent. *S*, who was executor and sole devisee of *D*'s will, did not inventory the $650,000 dollars worth of securities held by *B* under the above agreement. *S* has declined to pay any more than $20,000 on *D*'s unsecured $100,000 note to *U*, as the probate assets will allow only a 20 percent payment on creditor's claims. Surprised and hurt, *U* has consulted you on this matter. How would you advise him under the law of your state? Under the Uniform Probate Code?

EFFLAND, RIGHTS OF CREDITORS IN NONPROBATE ASSETS
48 Mo. L. Rev. 431 (1983)

. . . Increasingly, a major portion of decedents' wealth is being transmitted to others not through the probate process but through a variety of devices which have acquired the label "nontestamentary." Some of these devices, like joint tenancy and gifts causa mortis, have long been legally accepted. Others, like revocable living trusts . . . and contractual benefits payable on death to designated beneficiaries, are developments of relatively recent origin.

At the outset, one must wonder why creditor groups have not been vocal about the drain of available assets from the probate estate. One possible explanation is that concern for creditors is misplaced. Contract creditors rely on security arrangements; retail organizations protect themselves by purchasing insurance against the risk of death of debtors or are content to write losses off on income tax returns; tort creditors sue primarily for the amount of insurance coverage. Interesting is the fact that during the preparation of the Uniform Probate Code (the Code) no credit organization voiced any comments on proposed claims procedures with the single exception of the American Association of Trial Lawyers, which was concerned only with tort liability. With regard to nonprobate assets, joint tenancy has long been a device that defeats unsecured creditors of the joint tenant who dies first; yet the one state which had legislation to protect such creditors has repealed the statute. Of course, one major creditor at death, the United States Government, has enacted its own procedure to reach taxable will substitutes if the probate estate is insufficient to pay estate taxes.

Institutional creditors therefore are likely to be able to protect themselves. It is the individual creditor who may be hurt most and who has no organization to speak on his behalf. The cases that are likely to occur with increasing frequency involve the divorced wife or child who has a claim by reason of a property settlement, separation agreement, or divorce decree. . . .

Still another explanation for the lack of creditor interest may be that in the majority of decedents' estates there are sufficient probate assets to meet claims of unsecured creditors. Only if the probate estate is inadequate for creditors is there a problem. A system that permits nonprobate assets to pass free of creditor claims therefore may be tolerable to creditors. Unfortunately, we have no empirical data to assess the validity of this explanation. . . .

. . . [P]robate, used in the broad sense of administration of a decedent's estate, serves other purposes than assuring succession to the persons intended by the decedent. Protecting the family against disinheritance is one; providing a convenient forum for creditors is another. Removing assets from the probate estate by will substitutes has posed a problem for the surviving spouse in those states where marital rights at death are defined in terms of an elective share in the probate estate. Significantly, the trend toward transmitting wealth by will substitutes led first to frequent litigation . . . and later in many states to legislation defining the share in terms of both the probate estate and the nonprobate assets passing by will substitutes. Lack of extensive creditor litigation may therefore mean that there is no corresponding need for creditor protection.

One subsidiary problem relates to the effect of nonclaim statutes on the right of creditors to pursue nonprobate assets. For example, section

3-803 of the Uniform Probate Code bars unpresented claims "against the estate, the personal representative, and the heirs and devisees of the decedent." There is no bar against the takers of nonprobate assets unless the courts would extend the statute by analogy. Some practicing lawyers therefore recommend against use of will substitutes where potential claims may be outstanding after death, as use of probate serves to cut off such claims if they are not presented in the administration of the estate and thus insulates the probate assets when distributed to the successors. . . .

There are two options. One is to do nothing and leave the law in its present uncertain and unsatisfactory state, in hope that courts will eventually work out a theory along the lines suggested in this Article: that effect should be given to the realities of nonprobate arrangements rather than to technical property doctrine; that realistically these arrangements shift economic benefits at death and a transfer therefore takes effect at that time; and that any such transfer is necessarily fraudulent as to creditors if the probate estate is insufficient to meet their claims.

The other option is to construct and enact a statutory solution along the lines of section 6-107 of the Uniform Probate Code [relating to multiparty accounts], with a delineation of nonprobate assets which should be available to the personal representative to satisfy presented claims if estate assets are insufficient. This would require appointment of a personal representative even if there are no probate assets to administer. In this latter case the lack of probate assets to pay administration expenses means that these in turn must be recovered from nonprobate assets. The statute should include either some system for equitable apportionment among recipients of nonprobate assets or a statutory scheme like abatement to determine the order in which nonprobate assets can be reached.

Joint tenancies pose special problems, because the original contribution for the purchase of the property may have come from the decedent, from the surviving joint tenant, or partly from each. Whether to treat the transfer at death as a transfer of a half interest or of the interest attributable to the decedent's contribution is the same issue involved in estate taxation. There is much to be said for the simple rule that a transfer at death involves in reality a half interest (or the appropriate fraction if there are more than two joint tenants) regardless of contribution, because that is the interest the creditor could reach immediately prior to the death of the debtor, unless the joint tenancy itself was a fraudulent conveyance. . . .

On Professor Effland's suggestion for treating the shift of economic benefits at death as a fraudulent conveyance if the estate thereby becomes insolvent, see In re Granwell, 20 N.Y.2d 91, 228 N.E.2d 779 (1967). See generally Andrews, Creditors' Rights Against Nonprobate Assets in Washington: Time for Reform, 65 Wash. L. Rev. 73 (1990).

E.   *Wills, Will Substitutes, and Will Supplements: A Peek at Integrated Planning*

At this point it should be useful to think in an overall way about the role of will substitutes and their effect on the role of wills in typical family situations. This is also a good time to look ahead to the trust and anticipate where it fits in. All of these things, along with tax considerations, especially in larger estates, are elements of an integrated process called estate planning. This process involves not only the drawing of wills, or even of wills and trusts; it involves decisions about ownership forms and about rights under the wide variety of wealth items the nature of which has been suggested in part at the outset of this chapter. The process also involves client education through proper interviewing — education about the client's own estate and about how personal and family objectives relate to it.

A lawyer does not merely ascertain a client's intention and then use legal craftsmanship to implement that intention. The lawyer must help the client to *develop* that intent in the light of all the relevant considerations. The client must be led both to broaden and sharpen the nucleus of an idea that is initially brought to the lawyer and yet to develop a plan that *is* the client's own. When the planning and execution process is complete, the client should understand the will reasonably well, the properties and property arrangements involved, and the reasons for the estate's being planned as it is. This understanding can be of great help to a client in avoiding subsequent mistakes that might undo the estate planning that has been done. It will also enable the client to understand what the lawyer has done and to know when it is important to return for further counsel.

The following excerpt should help to accomplish this pulling together, and maybe some putting in perspective as well, particularly for those who mistakenly think of estate planning — either favorably or unfavorably — as merely dealing with the tax concerns of the wealthy.

SHAFFER, NONESTATE PLANNING
106 Tr. & Est. 319-322 (1967)

This article proposes and explains a will form for the young and promising, but presently impecunious, Calvin Knox. He is called a "junior executive" by appliance dealers, and his property is called an "estate" by his flatterers. He is really a middle-class, white-collar worker, and what he really has is a nonestate of children and debts. . . .

He is married and the father of two preschool children. Employed as an engineer for an automobile body manufacturer, Mr. Knox earns $9,200 annually before taxes, and expects his salary to increase. His employer provides a retirement plan and hospital and life insurance — the latter in the face amount of $10,000. He also has privately obtained life insurance in additional face amounts totaling $30,000. He has as much as $1,800 in his checking account, a disappearing equity in an automobile, some beat-up furniture, and a fishing rod or two. He and his wife and children are in good health. He owns no real property but will probably "buy" a residential site within the next few years. . . .

Distilling what is found in bar-association pamphlets on wills, the writer sees three reasons for Calvin John Knox to have a will. First, the intestacy statute may give some of his property to his children. This reason is the weakest of the three and is inserted mainly to give a cumulative effect to the others. It is true that a good many intestacy statutes would give one-half or more to his children, thus invoking cumbersome, expensive guardianship protection against victimization by their mother. However, Knox has all his cash in a survivorship account, and if he buys residential real estate, it will probably be held by survivorship also. Almost all of the cash available to support his family after his death will be life insurance payable to his wife. What probate property there is will probably be eliminated by the widow's allowance or taken under a small-estate procedure. Knox's children stand to inherit a half interest in his automobile and fishing rods, if he does not make a will.

The second reason for a will assumes that Knox will not predecease his wife, or that they will die at about the same time. If Knox dies intestate, his and his wife's property will be available to their children, but it will undoubtedly be placed in guardianship. Included will be all Knox's life insurance, either by inheritance from Knox's wife or through secondary beneficiary designations on the policies. A guardianship is cumbersome, expensive, inflexible, and unnecessary, whereas a trust arrangement is less expensive, more flexible, and more likely to work if Knox's children are being cared for out of state. It is amenable to the settlor's express restrictions and directions. Knox, therefore, needs a will if he wants to see that his small wealth is used to maximum efficiency for his orphaned children. . . .

The trust arrangement, however, will not entirely eliminate a need for guardianship; it will only confine the guardianship to its proper and necessary ambit — the physical care of the children. If Knox and his wife die at about the same time, somebody will have to take the children, and that somebody will be best advised to do so pursuant to appointment as guardian of their persons. The third reason for a will, then, is that Knox can designate in it who this guardian is to be. The great value of this argument is not that it causes Knox to make a will, but that it causes him to consider who is available to take care of his children and to discuss it with the persons he and his wife choose to be guardians.

When the first of these three reasons, which is the least potent, is discounted, it is apparent that the reasons for Knox to make a will bear almost no resemblance to the reasons for a person with a quarter of a million dollars to make a will. This project, in other words, is not a compact version of a "big" will. Knox is no patriarch dispensing his largesse evenly or capriciously to waiting relatives and friends. Disposition is the least of his problems. After his death, he must provide exactly what he is providing now — bare support for his children. It is not a matter of "estate planning," but a matter of planning without an estate, of doing what he can to relieve a thoroughly horrible situation for his family. . . .

Knox will need . . . to appoint a guardian for his children, to establish a trust for property management, and to add whatever he leaves in his probate estate to that trust. [His will need not be used] to establish the family-support trust. [It is now generally safe to use] unfunded, contingent life-insurance trusts which do not go into operation until the insured dies and the insurance proceeds are collected by the trustee. Bank trust departments in most communities will accept these trusts without fee during the settlor-insured's life. The wills of both parents can be made to "pour over" into them. They are easily amended and are probably more flexible than testamentary trusts. Moreover, they go into operation immediately, so that insurance and any other funds made payable to them — even survivor benefits under employer-provided retirement plans — are available to the family without the delay and expense of probate. Assuming state law favors this sort of disposition and that the trust and will involved are drawn in reference to the tenor of state law, employing a "pour over insurance trust" is a useful primary device for providing a family-support trust. It does not, of course, eliminate the need for a will.

The payment of life insurance proceeds to testamentary trustees is an even more attractive alternative, eliminating the need for an inter vivos trustee and concentrating all economic resources in the testamentary trust. The insurance proceeds themselves, and the retirement-plan benefits, would not be subject to probate. In most cases, the only delay the device would entail is the delay before testamentary trustees are qualified to serve.

But the payment of insurance to testamentary trustees is a less fully sanctioned and less common alternative, carrying several risks with it. . . .

Joint ownership is another alternative, one that probably does not even need to be reduced to advice since Knox already holds his cash in survivorship. He may or may not own his automobile that way, but any residential real estate he obtains will probably be held by survivorship.

Many of the experts in "estate planning" would apparently urge Knox's lawyer to advise Knox to dissolve these survivorship arrangements in favor of sole ownership or tenancies in common; however, these commentators obviously are not writing for people like Knox. There seems to be no convincing reason against survivorship ownership for two people who are harmoniously married and who have no federal estate-tax problems. The device may even carry with it substantial state death-tax advantages, as well as some amount of immunity from the creditors of either spouse.

Knox should keep his bank account as it is, although a look at the signature card and an inquiry into the circumstances of its execution to make certain that it is what it appears to be is advisable. He should probably buy his residential real estate by the entirety or in joint tenancy, purchase his car in joint tenancy, and hold his securities if he ever buys any, in joint tenancy.

Survivorship ownership, insurance designations in favor of his wife and contingently to the trust, and the widow's allowance or small-estate statute will probably avoid probate in the traditional sense, if Knox's wife survives him. His will is a formality in that case. If his wife does not survive him, or if they die at about the same time, the will becomes essential — and that reflection implies, of course, that his wife ought to have the same sort of will he has. What is suggested for Knox (and his wife) is a children-centered will. The "poor man's will" of survivorship ownership and life insurance will just about take care of everything else. . . .

F. *An Introduction to Taxation and Tax Planning of Decedents' Estates, Trusts, Gifts, and Will Substitutes*

Now that you are familiar with much of the law governing wills and will substitutes, including various property ownership forms, and are ready to undertake a fairly detailed study of the law of trusts and fiduciary administration, it is useful to become somewhat acquainted with some of the more important areas of tax law affecting probate and trust practice and estate planning. Often tax considerations lead us into the more complex and challenging forms of estate planning, and particularly planning and drafting problems that involve the use of trusts. The material in the next few pages is not intended to describe our estate and gifts tax system or related income tax matters in detail or to explain tax planning techniques at a level of any sophistication. This brief summary of law and basic planning concepts attempts merely to present an overview of the federal system for taxing donative transfers, of selected features of the income tax, and of the tax system's influence on counseling with respect to the ownership and disposition of family wealth.

1.   Estate, Gift, and Related Transfer Taxes

A gift tax and estate tax, now supplemented by a generation-skipping transfer tax, make up the federal transfer tax system, applying to donative transfers of wealth during life and at death. An *estate tax* is an excise tax levied on the privilege of *transferring* property at death, with tax liability being measured essentially by the size of the decedent's estate. In contrast, most (but not all) state taxes take the form of an *inheritance tax,* imposed on the privilege of *receiving* property from a decedent; the tax is geared to the inheritance of each recipient, with the amount of the levy usually being based on a structure of rates and exemptions that vary with the closeness of the recipient's relationship to the decedent. As we shall later see, the federal estate and gift taxes were integrated by 1976 changes that made them cumulative and subject to a common scale of graduated rates, with a *unified credit* equivalent to an exemption of about $175,000. As a result of the Economic Recovery Tax Act of 1981, the unified credit was increased in stages so that the effective exemption level rose gradually to the present figure of $600,000.

Subject to limited but significant exceptions, the estate tax on a particular estate is unaffected by who takes the decedent's property, how many beneficiaries there are, and in what shares or forms those people take. The important exceptions include provisions to exempt qualified charitable dispositions and qualified interspousal transfers (the so-called marital deduction, which is now unlimited in amount). Under the estate tax format, the individual beneficiaries are not the taxpayers; they do not separately report the amounts of their individual inheritances as they would under an inheritance tax system of the type employed by many of the states. Thus, an estate tax looks at, and taxes, the amount the decedent is transferring rather than the amount the successor is inheriting. Our federal law is not concerned with the relationship of a beneficiary to the decedent, unless the recipient is the decedent's or donor's spouse.

a.   The Integrated or Unified Tax Structure

Historically the federal system for taxing family wealth transfers in this country has been a dual structure consisting of independent gift and estate taxes, each with its own separate exemption and rate structure. Gifts were cumulated over the donor's lifetime for purposes of the gift tax, but the amount of gifts had no effect on the size of the taxable estate at death or on the rates applicable to that estate. Consequently, lifetime giving offered enormous tax advantages. Taxpayers who were similarly situated would end up with significantly different overall tax burdens depending on whether substantial gift programs had been undertaken during life or whether the individual's wealth was retained and transferred at death. The Tax Reform Act of 1976 integrated the estate and gift taxes into what is commonly called a *unified transfer tax* under our present Internal Revenue Code (I.R.C.), although in form the statutes still appear as two taxes in separate chapters of the Code. The dual system's greatest avoidance opportunities were closed, but substantial incentives for carefully planned inter vivos giving remain. (The operation of the present unified system is described in subsection e at page 289 infra.)

b. Taxable Transfers: Gifts

The federal gift tax is intended to reach gratuitous transmission of wealth during the donor's lifetime. In order to avoid subjective questions concerning donative intent, the tax applies to all transfers of property "for less than adequate and full consideration in money or money's worth." Judicially developed exceptions exclude from gift taxation (a) legitimate, arm's-length business transactions and (b) transfers that are "incomplete" in the sense that the donor retains power to revoke the transfer or to modify the rights of the beneficiaries. The tax is imposed not on the donee but on the donor, who must report all included transfers annually.

The gift tax contains an important exemption that excludes many modest gifts from the transfers that must be reported by a donor. Each year a donor is entitled to an *annual exclusion* of $10,000 for gifts (unless disqualified as a gift of a *future interest*) to each donee, without limitation as to the number of donees. Only to the extent that more than the excludable amount is given to a single donee in any one year must the gift be reported by the donor. This annual exclusion is enhanced by a *gift-splitting privilege* that allows a gift of separate property by a married person to be treated as if it had been made one-half by each spouse — an accommodation to problems posed by differences in laws of our community and non-community property states.

c. Taxable Transfers: The Gross Estate at Death

The first step in applying the federal estate tax is to construct the *gross estate,* which is defined to include not only property owned by a decedent and passing at death to others but also to include ownership equivalents and a variety of property ownership forms or arrangements that serve as will substitutes.

Property owned at death (I.R.C. §2033). A general section provides for inclusion in the gross estate of all "property owned at death." It has traditionally been said that this section includes all probate assets — that is, all property of the decedent that is subject to estate administration. With increasing variations in the detail of the probate requirements of the various states, however, the inclusions under this section can more precisely be described as encompassing all property of the decedent that is subject to disposition by will or, in the absence of testamentary disposition, by the laws of intestate succession, even including property that is subject to some testamentary restriction by reason of the forced share or dower rights of a surviving spouse. This means that this basic section includes all separate property owned by a decedent (including the decedent's interest in any property held with others in undivided interests as tenants in common) and, if applicable, the decedent's one-half interest in community property, the other half of which is excluded as property of the surviving spouse. The section thus encompasses a broad array of property, whether real or personal, tangible or intangible.

If *D* owned a future interest (such as a trust remainder) that did not fail by reason of his death, or if he owned an interest of limited duration (such as a right to property for a fixed term, say ten years) that did not terminate at his death, these property interests are included in *D*'s gross estate for tax purposes. Interests that expire at his death, however, leaving nothing to pass from *D* to others (such as a legal life estate or his equitable interest as life beneficiary of a trust) are not transmissible property interests included under this basic section.

This latter point concerning interests that are terminable at death is a very important one, as we shall see, for it becomes the focus of our planning efforts when clients wish to provide beneficiaries with the benefit and enjoyment of property but at the same time wish to avoid having that property eventually included in the beneficiaries' gross estates at death.

Powers as virtual ownership (I.R.C. §2041). A special section of the estate tax law attempts to deal with situations in which a person holds, by virtue of a power to demand or consume property (usually trust property) or a power to dispose of the property, authority that might be considered the economic or substantial equivalent of either ownership or of free testamentary disposition. Property that is subject to such a power, referred to as a *general power of appointment,* is included in the gross estate of the decedent under many circumstances. Also, the exercise or release of such a power during life will usually constitute a taxable transfer for gift tax purposes. The Code defines general powers as powers by which the power holder may appoint "to himself, his creditors, his estate or the creditors of his estate."

On the other hand, even broad powers by which the decedent may benefit only others are generally not a basis for inclusion in the gross estate, nor are powers held by others (such as a trustee) to benefit the decedent. An understanding of these concepts is vitally important because lawyers and their clients work with powers that are not "general," as well as interests that are terminable at death (see §2033 above), to establish trusts and other arrangements that confer protection, enjoyment, and often very broad benefits, without the adverse estate or gift tax consequences that outright ownership would have for the beneficiaries or their estates.

An aside on terminable interests and planning. Let us for a moment pursue the concluding observations in the preceding discussions in order to illustrate the significance of these rules and associated planning principles in the dispositions of relatively wealthy property owners. To summarize, the basic point is that, as long as the interests that are conferred on a beneficiary end at death, and as long as the powers of that beneficiary to take the property during life or to dispose of it at death are so limited in the beneficiary's hands (or in the hands of others) as not to constitute general powers of appointment, the beneficiary may be given extensive benefits — not far different from the advantages of ownership in many situations — without the property being subjected to tax at the beneficiary's death.

If *W* dies leaving an estate of $1 million and the transfer of that estate is in large measure subjected to tax at her death, it is understandable that she would wish the remaining (after tax) amounts of the same property not again to be subjected to taxation at the death of *H,* her widower. If she left all her property outright to him, as many clients are inclined to do in the absence of persuasive tax considerations, that property would be taxed at *H*'s death for the second time in a single generation — and at the upper brackets on top of *H*'s own property. Our system does provide a temporary credit for successive taxation, but that credit declines 20 percent every two years and expires after ten.

The end result is likely to be that *W* will ask her lawyer just how much benefit and authority she can confer on her husband without this adverse result — that is, without the properties being later included in *H*'s gross estate when he dies. She will learn from a competent lawyer that she can place this property in trust with an independent trustee (such as a bank) who will pay the income to *H* for as long as he lives and who is authorized to pay him very liberal additional amounts of principal for whatever purposes the trustee deems appropriate. In addition, *H* may have the right to demand certain additional amounts of principal under some exceptions to the general power of appointment rule, as long as the amounts he can take under this power are limited in certain ways, the most important of which is called "an ascertainable standard relating to his health, education, support, and maintenance." Beyond this he may be given, within generous limits, power to decide who is to take the property on his death; thus, he may have almost full power to dispose of the property at death, as long as he is precluded from appointing to his estate or to its creditors and as long as he personally could not (but for the previously mentioned exceptions) have appointed to himself during his lifetime. In fact, with minor reductions in the trustee's authority, *W* could allow *H* to serve as trustee and to manage all of the property himself.

At this point your reaction may be like that of most tax policymakers — that this all sounds rather silly but that, so far at least, it is not really particularly disturbing in terms of its policy implications. This is because an important objective of our transfer tax system is that significant wealth be taxed under such a system once each generation but not more frequently than that; and it probably should not be taxed twice in the one generation of *W* and *H*. In fact, an understandable reaction might be simply that it is most unfortunate that we even have to use the trust under our system to avoid double taxation in a single generation; the taxes should be designed to work this out without the necessity of a trust. Proposals to bring about such a result have been made from time to time, and, as we shall see later, by reason of the marital deduction qualifying property can be left outright from the first spouse to the second with only a single tax in their generation. But this is only to the extent that the marital deduction exempts such property from tax at the first death, essentially on the condition that it be subject to tax at the second death. Nevertheless, a great deal of our estate planning (that is, beyond planning for the marital deduction) is designed to avoid unnecessary estate taxation through trusts as just described.

When the benefit-conferring, tax-avoiding trust concept is extended beyond the surviving spouse to its use in provisions for the lifetimes of the testator's children and subsequent generations, many in Congress and others concerned with tax policy feel quite differently and are quite troubled over the use of trusts by the wealthy as a means of continuous tax avoidance. Not only is there concern over the revenue loss but also over the inequitably disparate treatment of people who share substantially comparable economic circumstances, some through outright enjoyment and others with virtually equivalent enjoyment through the trust device.

The generation-skipping transfer tax (I.R.C. ch. 13). This concern eventually led to the second (recall our earlier discussion of unification of the gift and estate taxes) major revision of the transfer tax system in the 1976 Tax Reform Act. That legislation enacted, as a new Chapter 13 of the Code, a generation-skipping transfer tax. Then, the Internal Revenue Code of 1986 effectively replaced this much-criticized statute with a revised tax. As revised in 1986, Chapter 13 preserved many of the principles and provision of the 1976 tax but also made fundamental changes.

Without descending into the considerable complexities of the 1976 legislation, it provided in essence (but subject to important qualifications) for property held in trust or trust equivalents to be taxed at the death of a younger-generation beneficiary in much the same manner and rates as if that beneficiary had owned the property. Thus, originally, the tax was usually imposed at the marginal rates of an appropriate deceased life beneficiary. Under the 1986 legislation, however, the revised tax is imposed at a single rate: the same rate as the maximum federal estate tax rate, now 50 percent. The tax is usually payable from the trust property.

The original statute taxed only termination of enjoyment, usually treating the enjoyed property much as if it had been owned by the deceased beneficiary; if enjoyment terminated by distribution or otherwise during life, the termination was treated much like a gift by the beneficiary. The tax also did not (and still ordinarily does not) apply if the beneficiary was of the same generation as (or of an older generation than) the person who established the trust. Thus, in our earlier planning example, the tax would not apply to a trust that W established for the present benefit only of H, or of only her parents or brothers and sisters. You can see, then, that the 1976 statute was intended merely to limit the extent to which trusts could be used to avoid taxes while conferring economic rights on persons belonging to generations below that of the transferor. To illustrate with a basic, typical example, if A deeds to child B for life, remainder to B's child (A's grandchild) C, the 1976 tax usually applied in much the same manner as if B had owned the property and left it to C. In short, a tax was not imposed if a generation was totally skipped but only if a generation was partially skipped, in the sense that some one or more members of that younger generation enjoyed the property (through benefits or powers) before the property or its enjoyment passed to a subsequent generation.

The current tax is no longer this narrow; and, as we have seen, its rates are no longer tied to a beneficiary. The 1986 tax potentially applies as well to total (or *direct*) skips — most obviously when a testator leaves property directly to grandchildren, completely bypassing the children. An important exception provides that, if a child of the transferor (or of the transferor's spouse) is dead at the time the transfer is made by the donor or decedent, the child's issue move up a generation, so that a direct transfer to grandchildren in that line will not constitute a generation-skipping transfer.

Even with respect to what are clearly defined as generation-skipping transfers under this act, however, there are limited but potentially significant advantages to be achieved through the use of trusts and other generation-skipping transfers. Most significantly, the 1986 flat-rate tax is subject to an exemption of $1 million per transferor, with spouses allowed to "split" inter vivos transfers so that a nondonor spouse may elect to be treated as having made half of any gift made by the donor spouse.

All in all, the terminable interest trust arrangements discussed earlier continue to be of widespread importance from a tax-planning viewpoint. Chapter 13 does not impair the utility of (but may require care in drafting) trusts for the benefit even of spouses or others of the transferor's generation or higher. Trusts are also of continued importance in tax planning for children and others of younger generations to the extent of $1 million per transferor and under some circumstances even beyond that amount.

Lifetime transfers included as will substitutes (I.R.C. §§2035-2038). Let us now turn our attention to a second major category of rules concerning the contents of a decedent's gross estate. This category includes a variety of inter vivos transfers the decedent had made under circumstances in which it might be fair to say that the lifetime disposition or arrangement served as a will substitute, or more or less as a rough substitute for retaining the property until death.

One such rule (I.R.C. §2035) has traditionally required, in ways that have varied from time to time, inclusion in the decedent's gross estate of most property transferred within three years of death. This rule became less important and was modified following the unification of the transfer taxes in 1976 and finally, in 1981, was virtually abolished, with continued application only to transfers involving life insurance and several other highly specialized situations.

A second set of rules (I.R.C. §§2036-2038), in effect, says to a transferor, "If you do not wish the property you are transferring to be included in your gross estate at death, you had better make the transfer with almost no strings attached." More specifically, these rules say that property is to be included in the gross estate despite the decedent's transfer of it during life if the decedent retained for life either (a) significant rights to receive economic benefits from that property (usually by way of trust) or (b) significant rights to determine what persons (even persons other than the transferor) are to receive the present or future benefits of that property, or in what way. Note that lifetime benefits and nongeneral powers that would have been harmless for *other* beneficiaries (see above discussion of terminable interest planning) are, under this special set of rules, a source of tax dangers only to those who create trusts or similar arrangements during life.

Joint tenancies, life insurance, and annuities (I.R.C. §§2039-2040, 2042). Finally, the Code contains a set of rules designed to deal with certain common types of property or property ownership forms that are not adequately covered by the basic provisions applicable to property owned at death and general powers of appointment.

A special section (I.R.C. §2040) deals specifically with joint tenancies, tenancies by the entirety, and counterparts thereof. It provides for some or all of such properties to be included in the estates of decedents under most circumstances, often including more than the actual interest owned by the decedent during life. Essentially, this section provides a contribution-tracing test that directs inclusion in the gross estate of a portion of the property (even all of it) that corresponds to the portion of the consideration furnished by the decedent in purchasing (and improving) the property. An exception applies to survivorship arrangements exclusively between spouses: Under this simplified rule, enacted in 1981, half the property is included in the gross estate of the spouse who is the first to die, regardless of the source of the consideration. Incidentally, to the surprise of many taxpayers, the creation of joint tenancies and the like often (but not always) results in the making of taxable gifts.

A second section (I.R.C. §2042) deals specifically with insurance on the life of the decedent. (Insurance policies owned by a decedent on the life of *another* are covered by the basic section encompassing property owned at death.) The proceeds of insurance on the life of the decedent are included in the decedent's estate either (a) if those proceeds are payable to the decedent's estate or (b) if any of the "incidents of ownership" in the policy were held by the decedent at the time of death, even though the proceeds are payable directly to named beneficiaries. Incidents of ownership include such rights as the power to choose or change the beneficiaries, to select settlement options, to turn in a policy and receive its cash value, or to obtain loans from the insurance company against the policy.

Still another section (I.R.C. §2039) deals with annuities, pensions, and employee benefits that offer some form of postdeath payment or payments. This section often provides for inclusion of all or part of these benefits in the estate of a decedent. For many years this section contained a general and then limited exemption for payments under "qualified" (and certain counterpart) plans. Legislation in 1982, effective generally for decedents dying in 1983 or later, abolished this exemption entirely, so that a portion or all of the survivor or other death benefits under retirement plans are includible in the gross estate if the basic requirements of §2039 are met.

d. Deductions from Includible Transfers by Gift or at Death

In calculating the taxable gifts of a donor and the taxable estate of a decedent, the included transfers are reduced by allowable deductions. These fall into two major categories: (a) deductions for the purpose of arriving at what might be called a decedent's *net* transferable wealth — that is, deductions for such items as debts, expenses of estate administration, and casualty losses (I.R.C. §§2053-2054); and (b) deductions for qualified transfers to privileged recipients — that is, transfers eligible for the charitable and marital deductions. The first category can present a number of troublesome problems for practitioners but merit no more than this casual mention for our present purposes. The deductions in category (b), however, justify closer examination.

The charitable deduction (I.R.C. §§2055, 2522). Although their income tax counterpart is subject to specific percentage limitations, the federal estate and gift tax charitable deductions are unlimited in amount or percentage of the estate. One can leave an entire multimillion dollar estate tax free to or in trust for organizations or purposes that qualify as charitable under Internal Revenue Code definitions. In order to be deductible, gifts, bequests, or devises to charity must be outright or in other qualifying form. Illustrative of forms that pose both policy issues for the system and planning problems for the profession are "split interest" gifts, such as a transfer in trust for the life benefit of a private individual with remainder thereafter to charity. Is the value of the charitable remainder deductible? Traditionally, this type of issue has revolved around general questions of whether the interest is sufficiently certain and susceptible of reliable valuation to justify a particular deduction. Today these split interest issues are governed by detailed rules and requirements specified in the Code. Deductions can be lost for minor noncompliance with these provisions.

The marital deduction (I.R.C. §§2056, 2523). The most important and troublesome of the deductions is the marital deduction. In planning, lawyers are concerned initially with how much of the allowable marital deduction, if any, the client should utilize and then with the forms of interspousal transfers that should be used to qualify for that intended deduction.

Traditionally the maximum allowable deduction (designed originally to offer separate property a treatment similar to the split inherent in community property) was an amount equal to approximately one-half the value of the separate property in the decedent's gross estate and, for gift tax purposes, half the amount of a gift of separate property. Following a short-lived modification of this limit in 1976, the present law was enacted in 1981, allowing an unlimited marital deduction. Thus, if the client chooses, the entire tax (if any) for the spouses' generation can be paid at the survivor's death.

From a planning viewpoint, it is necessary to consider what amount of deduction is likely to be most advantageous for each particular client, recognizing that deductibility requires that the property pass to the surviving spouse in a form susceptible to estate or gift taxation on the spouse's later death or on later disposition of the property inter vivos. There are two main objectives in the use of the marital deduction: (a) estate splitting (under a graduated tax, two estates of equal size being taxed less overall than one large estate and one small) and (b) tax deferral. The two objectives reinforce each other up to the point at which deductible transfers could be expected to cause the spouses' estates to reach the same marginal tax brackets, but they conflict to the extent one is considering deductible transfers in excess of that level.

The marital deduction also involves a rigorously drawn, interpreted, and enforced set of rules specifying the form of disposition — that is, the types of interests — that qualify for the deduction. Present policy generally requires that deductible property pass in the form of "nonterminable interests" so that the property will not escape gift or estate taxation again when the survivor's ownership ends during life or at death. Inheritances or gifts received outright and unconditionally by the surviving spouse obviously qualify, but a variety of highly technical and often treacherous rules determine what other transfers (such as in trust) will qualify as exceptions to the terminable interest rule. Prior to 1982 these special qualifying forms required that the survivor have complete power to dispose of the marital deduction property during life or at death, or both. Legislation enacted in 1981, however, now allows certain *qualified terminable interest property* (so-called QTIP trusts or properties) to qualify for the deduction on the election of the donor, if alive, or of the transferor's personal representative. Detailed examination of these requirements and their problems is not worthwhile for our purposes here; suffice it to say that the planning or evaluation of possible marital deduction dispositions requires the careful attention of qualified counsel.

e.   Computing the Tax

The tax base. Traditionally the federal estate and gift taxes have each had a separate and independent tax base. Reportable gifts — essentially those in excess of $10,000 (formerly $3,000) per donee per year — have been and still are reported annually or more frequently over the lifetime of the donor, but on a cumulative basis so that in any given year all of the recognized gifts over the donor's lifetime are reported and a tax is paid on the difference between the tax for the total of these gifts and the tax for the gifts of prior years. In other words, the tax for each year is computed at marginal rates where the prior year's tax left off. Actual gift tax liability did not begin under pre-1976 law until the total of reportable gifts exceeded the donor's lifetime gift exemption of $30,000. Then, at death, the pre-1976 estate tax was separately applied without regard to the donor's past record of gift tax liability. The estate tax had its own separate (and higher) rate structure and an independent $60,000 exemption, after which the graduated rate table was applied beginning with the bottom brackets regardless of prior giving.

The essence of the unification of the two taxes under the current law, as revised in 1976, is that all transfers, both during life and at death, are cumulated and taxed on a single scale. The gift tax functions in essentially the same manner as before, but transfers at death are now treated rather like one large, last round of gifts to be reported and added on top of all lifetime gifts. The estate is taxed beginning at the marginal rate where the last gift tax return had left off. Thus, the estate tax return reports not only the taxable estate but also the taxable gifts over a lifetime and computes the tax on the aggregate amount, and the resulting transfer tax liability figure is reduced by the total amount of tax attributable to all prior gifts over the decedent's lifetime, with the difference being the estate tax liability.

Amounts exempted. The current law provides for a single *unified credit* to offset against one's transfer tax liability, either the gift tax or the estate tax or partially against each. Actually, it is easiest to understand the workings of this credit by thinking of it as equivalent to an exemption (replacing the old separate gift and estate exemptions) in the amount of $600,000. This means that no gift tax will be paid until *reportable* gifts over a lifetime exceed the $600,000 that is effectively exempted by the unified credit. If any of this "exemption" remains unused at death, it, in effect, reduces the decedent's estate that is subject to taxation.

Rates. With technical qualifications that are not significant for our purposes, the effective rate structure for the transfer tax system begins at 37 percent. (The actual rate table begins with rates below that, but for practical purposes the lower brackets are eliminated by the unified credit, which, with that in mind, we are then able to call an exemption.) Rates reach a maximum of 50 percent at the level of $2.5 million of reportable gift and estate transfers.

2. Selected Aspects of Federal Income Taxation

Income tax considerations are important in nearly all estate situations, even those for which estate and gift taxation is of little or no significance. Of particular importance for purposes of the subject matter of this course are rules affecting the income tax basis of estate and gift property and the income taxation of estates, trusts, beneficiaries, and settlors.

a. Tax Basis of Property Acquired from a Decedent or Donor (I.R.C. §§1014, 1015)

For purposes of computing taxable gain or loss on the sale of inherited property and, if applicable, determining its depreciation base for income tax purposes, the property's basis is its value on the estate tax valuation date — that is, the date of the decedent's death or (if available and elected) the alternate valuation date, which is generally six months later. This may result in either a *stepped-up* or *stepped-down basis,* depending on whether the adjusted basis in the hands of the decedent had been lower or higher than the estate tax value. With two potentially important exceptions, this so-called new basis applies to all property interests includible in the decedent's gross estate, whether or not a tax return was actually required for the particular estate. One exception is for community property, with respect to which the interest of the survivor as well as that of the decedent receives a new basis on the death of the first to die; the other is that assets that are classified as "income in respect of a decedent" (I.R.C. §691) receive no new basis at death.

In the case of property received by gift, the donee's federal income tax basis is the donor's basis adjusted for part of the gift taxes, if any, paid on the gift. For purposes of subsequently reporting a *loss*, however, the basis of the donee (other than the donor's spouse) is limited to the fair market value of the property at the time of the gift.

These basis rules can be quite significant from a planning perspective. For example, in selecting the subject matter of inter vivos giving programs, they tend to encourage lawyers to counsel donors to retain low-basis properties (in order to obtain a new basis at death) and to give their children, grandchildren, and other younger donees high-basis assets but generally not assets that have a basis in excess of value. (The latter can be sold in order to realize a loss that would be wasted either by giving the property away or by retaining it until death.) Basis considerations, along with other factors, also influence how spouses should hold title to their properties. There tends, for example, to be a rule of thumb in community property states that appreciated properties should be held in community form (to maximize the basis step up) and that potential loss properties be held as tenants in common (to minimize the step down of basis), at least in the latter case if it is desirable to avoid the survivorship feature of joint tenancy. Do you see, from the estate tax discussion above, why joint tenancy is usually to be avoided in tax planned estates?

b. Income Taxation of Estates, Trusts, and Beneficiaries

Decedents' estates and trusts are treated as separate tax entities for purposes of reporting and paying income taxes. Estates are allowed an exemption of $600, and trusts either $300 or $100 depending on the circumstances; their taxable income is computed like that of an individual with some exceptions, most importantly (a) the absence of a *zero bracket amount* and (b) the allowance of a special deduction for income that is taxable to beneficiaries or grantors. The applicable tax rates are on a dramatically compressed bracket structure, the rates applicable to individuals (for example, the 15 percent bracket of an estate or trust currently applies to less than $4,000 of taxable income).

The grantor rules (I.R.C. §§671-677). In the case of an inter vivos trust,

the first question that must be determined is whether the settlor continues to be taxable on any or all of the trust's income. Rather strict *grantor
rules* make the settlor accountable for trust income under certain circumstances, even if that income is in fact accumulated in the trust or
distributed to others. With limited exceptions, under these rules the settlor is treated as substantial owner of the trust property and is taxable
on its income if the settlor (and sometimes even another close to the settlor) retains either (1) certain beneficial rights under the trust or (2) certain significant powers over its administration or over the interests of the
beneficiaries. The specially privileged *Clifford* (or short-term) *trust* was
eliminated by the 1986 reform package.

Taxing estates and trusts and their beneficiaries (I.R.C. §663). In the case
of a decedent's estate, a testamentary trust, or a living trust under which
the income is not taxable to the settlor, the focus of concern is the allocation of tax accountability as between the estate or trust and its various
beneficiaries. The fundamental rule is that income is to be reported by
a beneficiary to whom it is actually or constructively (that is, "required
to be") distributed. Then the estate or trust is taxable as a separate entity
on the remaining income — on the income from estate or trust property
less the deduction for income distributions. That is, the entity is taxed
on income that is accumulated currently and that is not taxable to a beneficiary (or settlor). In the case of a trust, however, the taxation of
income to it is generally temporary because of the throwback rule
(below).

The "draw-out" and proration principles. When is a payment by an executor or trustee deemed to be a distribution of *income*? The answer is
important but regrettably complex. It involves what might be called the
draw-out principle, which applies to all interests that are not sheltered by
the limited "§663(a)(1) exceptions" for testamentary gifts of specific
property (such as a devise of Blackacre to *X*) or of specific sums (such as
a legacy of $5,000 to *Y*). Thus, its main application is to residuary and
intestate interests. Under this principle, all distributions from a decedent's estate or trust are treated as distributions of *income* as long as the
distributable net income of the entire[2] estate or trust has not been
exhausted. (Distributable net income, or DNI, is a concept roughly corresponding to current ordinary income and generally excludes, for
example, capital gain income.) Thus, regardless of accounting rules

---

2. In the case of *trusts,* however, if the trust consists of "substantially separate and independent shares" these are treated as separate trusts solely for purposes of the draw-out
principle and throwback rule (not, for example, for purposes of taxing accumulations in
the trust). In other trusts and in all decedents' estates, the draw-out principle (and the
throwback rule for trusts) apply to distributees without being limited to what one might
think of as the particular distributee's share of the income — there being no general concept for tax purposes of distinct shares of DNI or of accumulations.

under applicable state trust law, for tax purposes distributions are generally deemed to draw out (and the distributees are required to report) income only, unless the distributions for the year exceed the DNI of that year. Principal is deemed to come out only to the extent DNI (and, in some trust situations (see below), prior years' accumulated income) has been exhausted. In any year during which distributions do exceed DNI, the allocation of income (of all classes) and principal is generally governed by a system of proration, again regardless of the fiduciary's accounting for these items; subject to limited exceptions, all distributees in a given year share pro rata in the income and principal distributions of the year.

The throwback rule (I.R.C. §§665-668). In order that trust beneficiaries not be insulated permanently from tax liability by the trust device, the so-called *throwback rule* was enacted in 1965 and, in one form or another, has been a part of our tax law ever since. (It has no application to decedents' estates.) Under this highly complicated rule, trust distributions that exceed the current year's DNI are deemed to be distributions of prior years' accumulated income rather than principal until all income accumulations in the trust have been exhausted. The income that is deemed to be paid out by such *accumulation distributions* is then, in some manner that has varied from time to time under our changing legislation, taxed to the distributee(s) with a credit being allowed for taxes already paid by the trust. The throwback rule may be short-lived; with the slight tax savings now available through accumulations since the 1986 legislation, the rule (which has been at best sporadically enforced in any event) is hardly worth the cost and complexity to government and taxpayer alike.

To summarize briefly the allocation of income as between a trust and its distributees: regardless of trust accounting for distributions under local law, for income tax purposes current income (DNI) comes out first, accumulated income of prior years next, and principal comes out last; but any time more than DNI is thus deemed to have been distributed, the distributed items are allocated ratably among the distributees (except under special *tier system* rules that can be ignored for present purposes).

The *grantor rules* of the income tax, together with the analogous yet significantly different will-substitute rules of the estate tax (I.R.C. §§2035-2038), make the use of irrevocable inter vivos trusts a very complicated, if nevertheless an often attractive, part of substantial giving programs undertaken during life. Of more widespread importance, however, are the implications of the rules allocating income tax accountability between estates or trusts and their beneficiaries, and among the various beneficiaries. In estate administration, the applicable principles (including the lack of throwback and separate share rules for estates) significantly influence the use and timing of preliminary distributions and the preparation for and handling of final distribution, with sometimes extraordinary opportunities or risks being involved. In the planning of trusts, the rules are exploited through the use of discretionary trusts that may accumulate or pay out income and that are often designed to allow the trustee in making distributions to "sprinkle" income among a rather flexible class of beneficiaries — such as the testator's surviving spouse, children, and other descendants. This enables the testator to provide for a spouse or adult children, or some combination of both, in ways that are potentially generous but that (a) avoid burdening well-to-do primary beneficiaries with income of which they have no need and on which they would merely pay tax at unnecessarily high rates and (b) allow either distributions to low-bracket beneficiaries in the family (such as grandchildren) or limited accumulations in the trust. Even the traditional benefits of distributions to grandchildren or others under age 14 are undermined now by the 1986 enactment of the so-called kiddie tax, often causing unearned income of children to be taxed at the marginal rates of their parents.

3. Some Concluding Observations

Students at this point may well have come to suspect that the portions of the federal tax system discussed here are more complex and costly to live with than necessary, and more vulnerable than desirable to exploitation by competent counsel. A good case can certainly be made for that proposition, and a substantial part of the reason is simply legislative neglect. Some of the complexity, of course, reflects the presence of some problems of inherent conceptual and practical difficulty. Regardless of the cause, the complexities and burdens of the tax law in this field make both planning and administration hazardous — and create risks of professional oversight and error that have strikingly boosted the cost of malpractice insurance, for which the client public as well as practitioners are paying. Yet, taxation is a fact of life in this and most other fields. This discussion should at least provide you with some sense of the nature of our transfer taxes and of some closely related aspects of income taxation, and also an awareness of some fascinating even if challenging planning problems and opportunities. As you proceed into the study of trust law, this background may help you to appreciate that the trust device is significantly responsible for many of the complexities of our income and transfer taxes. Nevertheless, the trust is also valued as one of the most flexible tools American lawyers have to meet the personal and family needs of clients and to protect clients and their beneficiaries from unnecessary taxes.

G.   *Introduction to the Lawyer's Role and Responsibility in Estate Planning*

AMERICAN BAR ASSOCIATION, MODEL RULES OF PROFESSIONAL CONDUCT
(1983)

Rule 1.1 *Competence.*   A lawyer shall provide competent representation to a client. Competent representation requires the legal knowledge, skill, thoroughness and preparation reasonably necessary for the representation.

Rule 1.3 *Diligence.*   A lawyer shall act with reasonable diligence and promptness in representing a client.

Rule 1.4   *Communication.*

(a) A lawyer shall keep a client reasonably informed about the status of a matter and promptly comply with reasonable requests for information.

(b) A lawyer shall explain a matter to the extent reasonably necessary to permit the client to make informed decisions regarding the representation.

Rule 1.7   *Conflict of Interest: General Rule.*

(a) A lawyer shall not represent a client if the representation of that client will be directly adverse to another client, unless:

(1) the lawyer reasonably believes the representation will not adversely affect the relationship with the other client; and

(2) each client consents after consultation.

(b) A lawyer shall not represent a client if the representation of that client may be materially limited by the lawyer's responsibilities to another client or to a third person, or by the lawyer's own interests, unless:

(1) the lawyer reasonably believes the representation will not be adversely affected; and

(2) the client consents after consultation. When representation of multiple clients in a single matter is undertaken, the consultation shall include explanation of the implications of the common representation and the advantages and risks involved.

Comment: . . . Conflicts of interest in contexts other than litigation sometimes may be difficult to assess. Relevant factors in determining whether there is potential for adverse effect include the duration and intimacy of the lawyer's relationship with the client or clients involved, the functions being performed by the lawyer, the likelihood that actual conflict will arise and the likely prejudice to the client from the conflict if it does arise. The question is often one of proximity and degree. . . .

Conflict questions may also arise in estate planning and administration. A lawyer may be called upon to prepare wills for several family members, such as husband and wife, and, depending upon the circumstances, a conflict of interest may arise. In estate administration the identity of the client may be unclear under the law of a particular jurisdiction. Under one view, the client is the fiduciary; under another view the client is the estate or trust, including its beneficiaries. The lawyer should make clear the relationship to the parties involved. . . .

Rule 1.8   *Conflict of Interest: Prohibited Transactions.* . . .

(c) A lawyer shall not prepare an instrument giving the lawyer or a person related to the lawyer as parent, child, sibling, or spouse any substantial gift from a client, including a testamentary gift, except where the client is related to the donee.

Comment: . . . A lawyer may accept a gift from a client, if the transaction meets general standards of fairness. For example, a simple gift such as a present given at a holiday or as a token of appreciation is permitted. If effectuation of a substantial gift requires preparing a legal instrument, such as a will or conveyance, however, the client should have the detached advice that another lawyer can provide. Paragraph (c) recognizes an exception where the client is a relative of the donee or the gift is not substantial.

Rule 1.14   *Client Under a Disability.*

(a) When a client's ability to make adequately considered decisions in connection with the representation is impaired, whether because of minority, mental disability or for some other reason, the lawyer shall, as far as reasonably possible, maintain a normal client-lawyer relationship with the client.

(b) A lawyer may seek the appointment of a guardian or take other protective action with respect to a client, only when the lawyer reasonably believes that the client cannot adequately act in the client's own interest.

R. Link, Professional Responsibility of the Estate Planning (Part 1) and Estate Administration (Part 2) Lawyer: The Effect of the Model Rules of Professional Conduct, 22 Real Prop., Prob. & Trust J. 1 (1987) and 26 Id. 1 (1991).

PROBLEM

8-F.   *S* and *D* inform you that their father, *F*, has just died, leaving a recent will devising his entire estate in trust for *W* (the stepmother of *S* and *D*) for life, remainder essentially to *S* and *D* or their respective issue. Apparently, however, the probate estate consists only of trivial amounts of personal property, while substantial amounts of land and securities are held in the names of *F* and *W* as joint tenants. *S* and *D* tell you that, in the presence of two hospital staff members, *F* told them that he had just made a will that was in the custody of his lawyer. He further told them his will would assure that *W* had what she needed for as long as she lives and that thereafter they "would receive everything." How would you advise them concerning the courses of action that might be available to them?

LORRAINE v. GROVER, CIMENT, WEINSTEIN
467 So. 2d 315 (Fla. App. 1985)

NESBITT, J. . . .

Prior to his death, Johnson shared his residence with his mother, the plaintiff, and his minor son. [His] will contained a provision which left his mother a life estate in the residence with the remainder going to his sons. In the probate proceedings, however, it was determined that the residence was Johnson's homestead and consequently was not subject to devise. See Art. X, §4, Fla. Const.; §732.401-.4015, Fla. Stat. (1981). It therefore passed directly to Johnson's children [because his spouse predeceased him] pursuant to section 732.401, Florida Statutes (1981).

The plaintiff, Johnson's mother, instituted the suit against Weinstein, his law firm, and their insurer. The complaint alleges that due to Weinstein's negligence and lack of skill in drafting the will, the devise of the life estate in the residence to the plaintiff failed. Upon motion, the trial court entered a summary final judgment in favor of the defendants. This appeal followed.

Generally, in a negligence action against an attorney, the plaintiff must prove: (1) the attorney's employment by the plaintiff (privity); (2) the attorney's neglect of a reasonable duty owed to the plaintiff; and (3) that such negligence resulted in and was the proximate cause of loss to the plaintiff. Florida courts have recognized, however, that an attorney preparing a will has a duty not only to the testator-client, but also to the testator's intended beneficiaries. In limited circumstances, therefore, an intended beneficiary under a will may maintain a legal malpractice action against the attorney who prepared the will, if through the attorney's negligence a devise to that beneficiary fails. Although it is generally stated that the action can be grounded in theories of either tort (negligence) or contract (third-party beneficiary), the contractual theory is "conceptually superfluous since the crux of the action must lie in tort in any case; there can be no recovery without negligence." In effect, [Florida cases] have established a limited exception in the area of will drafting to the requirement of the first element (the privity requirement) in a legal malpractice action.

On this appeal, the plaintiff argues that Weinstein was negligent in not advising Johnson of the prohibition against devising homestead property and of possible alternatives. As the plaintiff suggests, it may have been possible to structure a conveyance to avoid the constitutional provision by having Johnson make an inter vivos transfer of a vested interest in the residence to her. It is also possible that Johnson might have wanted to devise some other comparable property interest to his mother if he had known of the constitutional prohibition or that the devise might fail. . . .

With regard to the first possibility, there is no indication in the record of any desire on the part of Johnson to make a transfer of any interest in the residence prior to his death. Even if such a desire did exist, however, any alleged negligence attributable to Weinstein's failure to advise Johnson concerning the possibility of an inter vivos transfer falls outside the limited exception . . . to the privity requirement in legal malpractice actions. Generally, an attorney is not liable to third parties for negligence or misadvice given to a client concerning an inter vivos transfer of property. . . .

The holding in DeMaris [v. Asti, 426 So. 2d 1153], encompasses two concepts. First, for an action to fall within the exception, the testamentary intent that has allegedly been frustrated must be "expressed in the will." Second, the beneficiary's loss must be a "direct result of," or proximately caused by the attorney's alleged negligence.

In the present case, there is no indication that Johnson wished or intended any alternative property interest to pass to his mother under the will if the devise of the life estate in the residence failed. An intent to devise a comparable interest in other property upon the failure of the primary devise cannot reasonably be extrapolated from any of the provisions in Johnson's will. Furthermore, a disappointed beneficiary may not prove, by evidence extrinsic to the will, that the testator's testamentary intent was other than that expressed in the will. *DeMaris.* In the instant case, Johnson's only testamentary intent expressed in the will that has been frustrated is his wish that his mother, the plaintiff, receive a life estate in his residence upon his death.

An attorney will be liable to an intended beneficiary under a will only if the attorney's negligence in drafting the will or having it properly executed directly results in the plaintiff-beneficiary's loss. *DeMaris,* 426 So. 2d at 1154. In the case at bar, the plaintiff alleges in her complaint, as she must to fit within the exception to the privity requirement, that the devise of the life estate failed and, thus, Johnson's testamentary intent was frustrated, due to Weinstein's negligence in drafting the will. The probate court, however, determined that . . . Johnson was survived by a minor child [and] the homestead was not subject to devise. . . . Johnson's testamentary intent was not frustrated by Weinstein's professional negligence, but rather by Florida's constitution and statutes. Summary judgment for the defendants was therefore proper since any alleged negligence on the part of Weinstein in drafting the will could not have been the cause of the plaintiff's claimed loss.

Upon the foregoing analysis, the summary final judgment is affirmed.

PEARSON, J., dissenting.

As I understand it, the majority opinion is bottomed on the legal premise that an attorney can be liable to an intended beneficiary under a will *only* if the beneficiary's loss resulted from the attorney's negligence in either drafting the will or seeing to its proper execution. Since here the will was indisputably composed in complete accordance with the testator's expressed wishes, and, of course, properly executed, it obviously follows, says the majority, that the appellant has no cause of action against the obedient scrivener. In other words, the majority declares the attorney to be immune from liability so long as, robot-like, he puts down on paper what the testator tells him to put down. And, according to the majority, if some law which was known or should have been known to the attorney prevents the testator's correctly recorded wishes from being carried out, it is the law, not the attorney, which has frustrated the testamentary intent.

I think it utterly indefensible to say that an attorney's failure to advise a testator that his desired devise is a nullity is any less negligent than an attorney's faulty draftsmanship or improper execution of a will. Whether a defendant can "be held liable to a third person not in privity is a matter of policy and involves the balancing of various factors, among which are the extent to which the transaction was intended to affect the plaintiff, the foreseeability of harm to him, the degree of certainty that the plaintiff suffered injury, the closeness of the connection between the defendant's conduct and the injury suffered, the moral blame attached to the defendant's conduct, and the policy of preventing future harm." The liability of an attorney to an intended beneficiary under a will exists because:

> [w]hen an attorney undertakes to fulfill the testamentary instructions of his client, he realistically and in fact assumes a relationship not only with the client but also with the client's intended beneficiaries. The attorney's actions and omissions will affect the success of the client's testamentary scheme; and thus the possibility of thwarting the testator's wishes immediately becomes foreseeable. Equally foreseeable is the possibility of injury to an intended beneficiary. In some ways, the beneficiary's interests loom

greater than those of the client. After the latter's death, a failure in his testamentary scheme works no practical effect except to deprive his intended beneficiaries of the intended bequests. Indeed, the executor of an estate has no standing to bring an action for the amount of the bequest against an attorney who negligently prepared the estate plan, since in the normal case the estate is not injured by such negligence except to the extent of the fees paid; only the beneficiaries suffer the real loss. . . . [U]nless the beneficiary could recover against the attorney in such a case, no one could do so and the social policy of preventing future harm would be frustrated.

Heyer v. Flaig, 70 Cal. 2d 223, 228, 74 Cal. Rptr. 225, 228-29, 449 P.2d 161, 164-65 (1969).

Not until today has any court suggested that an attorney's liability to an intended beneficiary of a will is limited to cases in which the attorney forgets or ignores the testator's specific instruction. Certainly, no important public policy is served by distinguishing between the negligence of an attorney who fails to do what the client has told him to do, and the negligence of an attorney who does what the client has told him to do in a negligent manner, or, as here, does what the client has told him to do, but fails to advise the client that what the client wants done cannot legally be done. Indeed, these latter forms of negligence are, as they should be, unhesitatingly recognized as actionable when brought by intended beneficiaries. See . . . Lucas v. Hamm, 56 Cal. 2d 583, 15 Cal. Rptr. 821, 364 P.2d 685 (1961) (doctrine of privity no bar to cause of action against attorney by intended beneficiaries under will where testamentary trust created therein was declared invalid as violating rule against perpetuities; cause of action barred, however, because confusion surrounding rule against perpetuities prevents finding of negligence); . . . Bucquet v. Livingston, 57 Cal. App. 2d 914, 129 Cal. Rptr. 514 (1976) (beneficiaries of inter-vivos trust have cause of action against attorney who failed to advise settlor that provision giving power of revocation to settlor's wife rendered nonmarital half of trust includable in wife's estate resulting in adverse tax consequences and ultimate financial loss to beneficiaries); McAbee v. Edwards, 340 So. 2d 1167 (daughter, intended sole beneficiary of estate, has cause of action against attorney who allegedly misadvised testator that it was unnecessary to change will in order to pretermit husband, whom testator married after will was executed).

I am equally, if not more, disturbed by the majority's conclusion that because there is no expression in the will as to what is to happen upon the failure of the "primary" devise "expressed in the will," that therefore Mr. Johnson had no intent to provide for his mother if a life estate in the homestead could not be devised. The majority's insistence that the appellant is an intended beneficiary of the will only if she could receive a life estate in the homestead is unfounded. Plainly, Mr. Johnson's intent to make his mother a substantial beneficiary of his estate is discernible from the will, and the reason, of course, that the will contains no secondary or alternative devise to the mother is that the testator allegedly was never informed that any was necessary.

In Ogle v. Fuiten, 102 Ill. 2d 356, 80 Ill. Dec. 772, 466 N.E.2d 224 (1984), the reciprocal wills of Alma and Oscar Smith gave the survivor the estate of the other, if the survivor survived more than thirty days, and, in a separate clause, gave their nephews, the Ogles, the entire estates in the event that the Smiths died in a common disaster. Alma Smith died of cancer fifteen days after her husband died of a stroke. Since the wills contained no other dispositive provisions, the estates passed by intestacy to persons other than the Ogles. The Ogles sued the attorney who prepared the wills, asserting, inter alia, that it was the testator's intention that their property go to the Ogles if, as happened, neither of the Smiths survived the other by thirty days.

The attorney argued that the Ogles could not prevail "because the testators' intent . . . shows that plaintiffs were to benefit only under certain circumstances [common disaster] which did not occur" and that therefore, "the intent of the testators to benefit plaintiffs is not, as required, . . . 'clearly evident.'" Id. at 774, 466 N.E.2d at 226. He further argued that [cases] permitting a cause of action by the intended beneficiary were distinguishable on the ground that in each of those cases, "the intent of the testator was expressly shown by the will." Id. at 775, 466 N.E.2d at 227. The court, finding no authority supporting the rule urged by the attorney, rejected the attorney's argument.

The only possible justification for the requirement that the testamentary intent be "expressed in the will," see DeMaris v. Asti, 426 So. 2d 1153, 1154 (Fla. 3d DCA 1983), is to guard against the onslaught of fraudulent claims. But where, as here, the . . . will on its face shows an intent by the testator to provide shelter or its equivalent for his mother during her lifetime in the event of his death, the envisioned horribles are of no concern, and there is thus no justification whatsoever to preclude the mother's action.

Although it may be said that to permit a finding of liability in this case is to contribute to the progressive "assault upon the citadel of privity," it seems to me that to absolve the attorney is to take a giant step backwards. . . .

According to Heyer v. Flaig, quoted in the dissenting opinion above, the statute of limitations in a testamentary malpractice action starts to run from the date of the testator's death because the intended beneficiary acquires no legal entitlement and has no standing to sue as an injured party until that time.

9

Introduction to Trusts: Their Nature, Use, and Classification

The trust is a device, nearly unique to the Anglo-American legal system,[1] under which property is held by one or more persons for the benefit of others, the management powers and the beneficial interests being separated. The one who holds the property is referred to as the *trustee*. That person usually has legal title to the property interests held in the trust,[2] and as to third parties is considered the owner of the trust property for most purposes. A person for whose benefit the property is held is a *beneficiary* or *cestui que trust*. The trustee is said to be in a fiduciary relationship with the beneficiary. Under this relationship a very high standard of conduct is required of the trustee in handling the property for the beneficiary. A trust is usually created by a transfer of the property to the trustee from the owner, whom we call the *settlor, trustor,* or *grantor*. The transfer may be made while the settlor is alive (that is, an *inter vivos* or *living trust*) or it may be by will (that is, a *testamentary trust*). In some situations the owner of property may declare that henceforth the property is held in trust for another, and by so doing the owner or settlor becomes a trustee without a transfer to another. This is referred to as a *declaration of trust*.

A. Classification of Trusts

The trust with which this course is most concerned is the *express trust*. This is a trust created, either by declaration or through inter vivos or

1. Efforts are currently under way to provide international recognition of trusts under certain circumstances, especially by nations that do not have trusts as a part of their domestic law. In 1984 the fifteenth Session of the Hague Conference on Private International Law approved the Convention on the Law Applicable to Trusts and on Their Recognition, with thirty-three nations, including the United States, participating. (The first signatories were Italy, Luxembourg, and the Netherlands, July 1, 1985, and the United Kingdom of Great Britain and Northern Ireland on January 10, 1986.) See generally Trautman and Gaillard, The Hague Conference Adopts a Convention for Trusts, 124 Tr. & Est. 23 (1985).

2. As will subsequently be seen, equitable interests in property may be held in trust, and in that case legal title will not be in the trustee.

testamentary disposition, by the express and intended direction of the settlor. It is a most flexible and valuable device in that the beneficiaries may be relieved of management responsibilities and liabilities while yet receiving the benefits from the property held in the trust. In this deliberate separation of the managerial and beneficial aspects of the ownership of property, the trustee may be chosen for his specialized managerial ability. This has advantages in many different areas, including some other than those we will presently study. For example, the business trust, the investment trust, and the trust deed as a security device all use trust concepts.

The purposes for which trusts may be created are many. The terms of the trust and the choice of trustees will be greatly affected by the purposes of the arrangement. We are concerned primarily with the usual family purposes of providing an income for life or for minority to immediate members of the family, particularly surviving spouses and children, while postponing distribution of principal to others at a later time — that is, in remainder. In this way a family may be assured means of support over an extended period of time. The main purpose of some trusts is to minimize estate and income taxation. Trusts are also created for charitable purposes whereby interests of the public in different endeavors are furthered through a nongovernmental device. The broad scope of charity includes the alleviation of poverty, support of religion or education, and, today, public recreation, as well as certain governmental matters. In short, most things of general interest and benefit to the public are broadly classified as charitable. We will see that there are some instances in which charitable trusts, their creation and administration, differ from the private trust with which we are most concerned. There are, of course, some limitations on the purposes for which a trust may be created. A trust will not be enforced, for example, if it is created to carry out a purpose that is contrary to law or so opposed to public policy that it should not receive the support of the government or of the public. Examples of illegal purposes include trusts for the operation of an illegal business or the operation of a business in an illegal fashion; and trusts in restraint of marriage are often contrary to public policy.

Trusts are not only classified in the manner noted above but also as regards the intention of the parties involved. The express trust, for example, is controlled by and is the product of the actual intention of the settlor. On the other hand, there are trusts that are said to arise by *operation of law,* without any expressed intention of the parties. For example, the resulting trust arises out of the inferred intention of the parties although unexpressed. Another so-called trust arising by operation of law is the *constructive trust.* This is a remedial or restitutionary device under which a person who has obtained the title to property by reason of fraud or overreaching or some other unlawful or improper means is considered as holding the property for the person who has been wrongfully deprived of its ownership. Here, obtaining property by fraud is a typical example; however, there are other instances in which the device is used. For example, we have seen that the murderer who receives property by reason of the victim's death may be required to hold the property on constructive trust for the persons to whom the property probably would have gone but for the wrongful action. Among other examples considered later in this course are situations in which a person obtains a devise or bequest based on a promise to dispose of it in a particular fashion, and the owner dies relying on this promise.

Still another classification of trusts has to do with the nature of the trust administration and the functions of the trustee. If the trustee is solely to hold title to the property without any affirmative obligations, we say the trust is *passive*. On the other hand, if the trustee is under an affirmative duty to manage the property in some way for the benefit of the beneficiaries, then we say the trust is *active*. Nearly all of our attention will be directed toward the active trust that is created by an expression of intention and for a valid purpose.

1. Trusts Arising by Operation of Law

a. Resulting Trusts

The doctrine, antedating the Statute of Uses, 27 Hen. VIII, c. 10 (1536), that when *A* gratuitously conveyed to *B*, a resulting use for *A* presumptively arose, is virtually extinct today. With the enactment of the Statute of Uses, the application of such a rule would render the conveyance an idle act, although it did take some time for the law to recognize that the rule no longer made sense.

A variety of situations today, however, still produce resulting trusts. Basically, they may be grouped under two headings: (1) purchase money resulting trusts and (2) resulting trusts that arise because an express trust fails or makes an incomplete disposition of the trust property — that is, simply equitable reversionary interests. Much will be seen of the second of these types of resulting trusts as the course progresses, but in general it might be noted here that the presumption of a resulting trust in such cases is calculated to effectuate the probable wishes of settlors. The law presumes, if no particular indication of the contrary is found, that the settlor did not intend to confer a beneficial interest on the trustee. If for some reason an express trust fails, in whole or in part, the trustee holds the property or appropriate portions thereof subject to a duty to reconvey to the settlor or to the settlor's estate or successors in interest. So, too, if the property placed in an express trust is excessive for the trust purposes, it is presumed that the excess is to be returned to the settlor or the settlor's successor. Throughout this course you will observe that trusts are frequently attacked by persons whose claims are predicated on assertions of resulting trust.

The purchase money resulting trust also merits some explanation at this point because it sometimes appears in family transactions. It arises, presumptively, when one person pays the purchase price for property but title is taken in the name of another. The titleholder is presumed to hold the property on resulting trust for the person who furnished the consideration. In some states this presumption has been abolished with but limited exceptions. In the others there is an important exception to the resulting trust presumption in this type of situation. The presumption does not arise — or maybe it is rebutted absent other showings of intent — where the person taking title is a natural object of payor's bounty: the overriding inference then is one of gift.[3] One might question whether the real scope of this exception, by which a gift is presumed, is properly defined by the "natural object" standard. Some cases continue to apply the resulting trust presumption where the one taking title is the spouse or parent of the person who paid the purchase price. See generally V W. Fratcher, Scott on Trusts §442 (4th ed. 1989).

Facts or circumstances may overcome the presumption of a purchase money resulting trust, or the reverse presumption that the transaction was a gift because of the relationship of the parties. If an intent to make a gift can be proven, this intent controls. It is also permissible to show and give effect to an agreement that is contrary to the resulting trust presumption. For example, if A pays money to B, who conveys title to C, it may be shown that A's payment was arranged as a loan to C. C then does not hold title for A but is indebted to A.

Courts generally admit evidence of intent quite freely without discussion in these cases, in what might appear to be violations of rules excluding parol evidence. Why is a claim of resulting trust in land not precluded by the Statute of Frauds, which requires trusts of land to be proved by a signed writing? Why is parol evidence admissible in these cases to rebut or reinforce a presumption of resulting trust or gift, as the case may be?

STATUTE OF FRAUDS
29 Car. II, c. 3 (1676)

VII. And be it further enacted by the authority aforesaid, that from and after the said four and twentieth day of June [1677] all declarations or creations of trusts or confidences of any lands, tenements or heredit-

---

3. In many states a gift has traditionally been presumed when a husband paid for property deeded to his wife, but a resulting trust was presumed when a wife furnished consideration for a deed in the husband's name. But see, e.g., Mims v. Mims, 305 N.C. 41, 286 S.E.2d 779 (1982), expressly overruling contrary cases and establishing a rebuttable presumption of gift in either case on a gender-neutral basis.

aments, shall be manifested and proved by some writing, signed by the party who is by law enabled to declare such trust, or by his last will in writing, or else they shall be utterly void and of none effect.

VIII. Provided always, that where any conveyance shall be made of any lands or tenements by which a trust or confidence shall or may arise or result by the implication or construction of law, or be transferred or extinguished by an act or operation of law, then and in every such case, such trust or confidence shall be of the like force and effect as the same would have been if this statute had not been made; anything hereinbefore contained to the contrary notwithstanding.

b. Constructive Trusts

POPE v. GARRETT
147 Tex. 18, 211 S.W.2d 559 (1948)

[Suit by Claytonia Garrett against the heirs of Carrie Simons to impress a constructive trust on property that passed to the heirs by intestacy. It was alleged, and found by the jury, that "by physical force or by creating a disturbance" two of the heirs had prevented Carrie Simons, shortly before her death, from executing a will solely in favor of the plaintiff. The trial court entered judgment for the plaintiff as to the whole of the property. The Court of Civil Appeals reversed in part, holding that a trust should not be impressed on the interests of those heirs who had not participated in the wrongdoing.]

SMEDLEY, J. . . .

The case is a typical one for the intervention of equity to prevent a wrongdoer, who by his fraudulent or otherwise wrongful act has acquired title to property, from retaining and enjoying the beneficial interest therein, by impressing a constructive trust on the property in favor of the one who is truly and equitably entitled to the same. . . .

It has been said that "[t]he specific instances in which equity impresses a constructive trust are numberless — as numberless as the modes by which property may be obtained through bad faith and unconscientious acts." Pomeroy's Equity Jurisprudence, 5th Ed., Vol. 4, p. 97, Sec. 1045. . . .

Citing Hutchins v. Hutchins, 7 Hill, N.Y., 104, the defendants, Pope et al., make the contention that plaintiff, Claytonia Garrett, is not entitled to any relief because she had no existing right in the property of Carrie Simons and thus was deprived by the acts of the defendants of nothing but an expectancy or hope to become a devisee. That case was an action at law for damages, the plaintiff alleging that the defendants, by false and fraudulent representations, induced his father to revoke a will in his favor and to execute a new one by which he was excluded from all participation in his father's estate. It was held that the plaintiff had no cause of action for damages because, according to the allegations of his declaration, he had no interest in the property beyond a mere naked possibility. Mr. Scott, citing the *Hutchins* case and two other like decisions and several decisions to the contrary, recognizes the conflict of authority on the question whether an action at law will lie against the heir for tort, but expresses his opinion that clearly a court of equity should prevent the heir from keeping the property which he has acquired by the result of his wrongful conduct and that the heir should be compelled to surrender the property to the intended legatee, since but for the wrong he would have received the property, and this even though the intended legatee had no interest in the property of the testator but only an expectancy. Scott on Trusts, Vol. 3, pp. 2371, 2372, Sec. 489.4. This opinion is supported by the authorities above cited and by many others.

The argument is often made that the imposition of the constructive trust in a case like this contravenes or circumvents the statute of descent and distribution, the statute of wills, the statute of frauds, or particularly a statute which prohibits the creation of a trust unless it is declared by an instrument in writing. It is generally held, however, that the constructive trust is not within such statutes or is an exception to them. It is the creature of equity. It does not arise out of the parol agreement of the parties. It is imposed irrespective of and even contrary to the intention of the parties. Resort is had to it in order that a statute enacted for the purpose of preventing fraud may not be used as an instrument for perpetrating or protecting a fraud.

In this case Claytonia Garrett does not acquire title through the will. The trust does not owe its validity to the will. The statute of descent and distribution is untouched. The legal title passed to the heirs of Carrie Simons when she died intestate, but equity deals with the holder of the legal title for the wrong done in preventing the execution of the will and impresses a trust on the property in favor of the one who is in good conscience entitled to it.

The second question is more difficult. Shall the trust in favor of Claytonia Garrett extend to the interests of the heirs who had no part in the wrongful acts? From the viewpoint of those heirs, it seems that they should be permitted to retain and enjoy the interests that vested in them as heirs, no will having been executed, and they not being responsible for the failure of Carrie Simons to execute it. On the other hand, from the viewpoint of Claytonia Garrett, it appears that a court of equity should extend the trust to all of the interests in the property in order that complete relief may be afforded her and that none of the heirs may profit as the result of the wrongful acts.

There are few decisions in point, and they are conflicting. . . .

The texts of Scott, Bogert and Perry seem to support [the view that a constructive trust] should be impressed even though the wrongful conduct because of which the title was acquired is that of a third person. Scott on Trusts, Vol. 3, pp. 2374-2376, Secs. 489.5, 489.6; Bogert's Trusts and Trustees, Vol. 3, p. 1467, Sec. 473; Perry on Trusts, 3d Ed., Vol. 1, pp. 260, 261, Sec. 211. The same is true of the Restatement. See illustrations 17 and 18, under Sec. 184, p. 754, Restatement of the Law of Restitution.

The policy against unjust enrichment argues in favor of the judgment rendered herein by the district court rather than that of the Court of Civil Appeals. But for the wrongful acts the innocent defendants would not have inherited interests in the property. Dean Roscoe Pound speaks of the constructive trust as a remedial institution and says that it is sometimes used "to develop a new field of equitable interposition, as in what we have come to think the typical case of constructive trust, namely, specific restitution of a received benefit in order to prevent unjust enrichment." 33 Harvard Law Review, pp. 420, 421. . . .

We realize that a constructive trust does not arise on every moral wrong and that it cannot correct every injustice. 54 Am. Jur., p. 169, Sec. 218. It must be used with caution, especially where as here proof of the wrongful act rests in parol, in order that it may not defeat the purposes of the statute of wills, the statute of descent and distribution, or the statute of frauds.

In the instant case the findings of the jury are well supported by the testimony of four disinterested, unimpeached witnesses, although their testimony is contradicted by that of two of the defendants. The will devising the property to the plaintiff, Claytonia Garrett, which Carrie Simons was prevented from executing, was introduced in evidence. In view of the authorities and equitable principles which have been cited and discussed, it is our opinion that the judgment of the district court should be affirmed in order that complete justice may be done.

The judgment of the Court of Civil Appeals is reversed and the judgment of the district court is affirmed.

See also Rogers v. Rogers, 63 N.Y.2d 582, 473 N.W.2d 226 (1984) (imposing a constructive trust on life insurance proceeds paid in violation of separation agreement, regardless of whether the designated recipient was innocent and without notice).

2. Active and Passive Trusts

STATUTE OF USES
27 Hen. VIII. c. 10 (1536)

That where any person or persons stand or be seised, or at any time hereafter shall happen to be seised, of . . . lands . . . to the use, confidence or trust of any person or persons, or of any body politick, . . . in every such case, all and every such person and persons, shall from henceforce stand and be seised . . . of . . . the same . . . lands . . . in such like estates as they had or shall have in use, trust or confidence. . . .

How, despite this statute, did the modern trust as we know it develop in England and in the American states that treat the Statute of Uses as a part of their common law? Obviously the statute does not execute all uses, and the typical trust of today must be an unexecuted use that is not within the scope of the statute for some reason. In drawing a trust instrument it is certainly not necessary to create a use on a use, or to transfer the property "to *T* to his own use to the use of *B*," the beneficiary, as in Doe v. Passingham, 6 B. & C. 305 (1827).

To what extent do procedures or the rights of interested parties vary depending on whether particular interests are legal or equitable?

Craig v. Kimsey, 370 Ill. 321, 324-325, 18 N.E.2d 895, 896 (1938), states:

> In construing the Statute of Uses three rules are applied whereby conveyances are excepted from its operation, viz: (1) Where a use was limited upon a use; (2) where a copyhold or leasehold estate or personal property was limited to uses; (3) where such powers or duties were imposed, with the estate, upon a donee to uses that it was necessary that he should continue to hold the legal title in order to perform his duty or execute the power. . . .
>
> It is true, as argued, that the [beneficiary] is permitted to collect the rents of the real estate and to have possession and control of the personal property. Nevertheless, the trust is far from passive. The duty is cast upon the trustees to determine if it is in the best interest of the [beneficiary] to sell the real estate and otherwise invest it. In such case it is their duty to sell, to determine whether the sale shall be public or private, to make the necessary conveyances and, in that event, to control and manage the property applying the income therefrom to the support and maintenance of the [beneficiary]. Where a trustee is required to make a conveyance he will take such title as will enable him to perform his duty and that, in this case, would be a fee simple.

HOOPER v. FELGNER
80 Md. 262, 30 A. 911 (1894)

ROBINSON, C.J. . . .

Where an estate is given to trustees and their heirs, upon trust to receive and pay the net income thereof to one for life, and, upon his death, in trust for all and singular his children and the issue of such children living at the death of the life tenant, the trust ceases upon the death of such life tenant, for the reason that it remains no longer an active trust. In such cases the statute of uses executes the use in those who are limited to take upon the expiration of the life estate, or, in other words, the statute transfers the use into possession, by converting the estate or interest of the cestui que trust into a legal estate, thereby determining the intermediate estate of the trustee. As to the real estate, it is clear, therefore, that . . . the trust was thereby at an end.

Now, as to the personal property, though it has been said that the object of the statute was to abolish all uses and trusts, yet, as the language of the statute was, "whenever any person is seised" etc., the English courts, by a strict construction, held that it did not apply to personal property, for the reason that one could not be said to be "seised" of a mere chattel interest. At the same time, however, it may be considered settled that a trust in regard to personal property will continue so long and no longer than the purposes of the trust require; and that, when all the objects of the trust have been accomplished, the person entitled to the beneficial use is regarded as the absolute owner, and as such entitled to the possession of the property. . . . Nor can we agree . . . that . . . the minority of one of the cestuis que trustent is any reason why the trust should continue until she is sui juris. . . . There can be no reason why the trust should continue merely to allow the trustees to receive the income, and pay it over to her guardians. . . .

RESTATEMENT (SECOND) OF TRUSTS

§88.   *Extent of trustee's estate.*

(1) Unless a different intention is manifested, the trustee of an interest in land takes such an estate, and only such an estate, as is necessary to enable him to perform the trust by the exercise of such powers as are incident to ownership of the estate.

(2) Unless a different intention is manifested, the trustee of personal property takes an interest of unlimited duration and not an interest limited to the duration of the trust.

B.   Nature of Trusts

It might be helpful to look briefly at the American Law Institute's definition of a trust and then to see what things are said not to be trusts. To state what classes of relationships are not trusts is a relatively simple matter, but to decide whether a particular set of facts gives rise to one of these classes of nontrust relationships or to a trust is another matter. Yet the determination of whether an arrangement is a trust or something else may materially affect the substantive rights of the persons involved and the procedure by which those rights are enforced.

RESTATEMENT (SECOND) OF TRUSTS

§2. . . . A trust, as the term is used in the Restatement of this Subject, when not qualified by the word "charitable," "resulting" or "constructive," is a fiduciary relationship with respect to property, subjecting the person by whom the title to the property is held to equitable duties to deal with the property for the benefit of another person, which arises as a result of a manifestation of an intention to create it.

———————

The Restatement then goes on to indicate, by way of distinction, what things are *not* trusts. It lists: a bailment (§5); an executorship or administratorship (§6); a guardianship (§7); an agency (§8); a mortgage, pledge, or lien (§9); an equitable charge (§10); an interest merely subject to a condition (§11); a debt (§12); a contract, whether or not specifically enforceable (§13); a contract for the benefit of a third party (§14); a relationship of assignor to assignee when a chose in action is assigned in whole (§15) or in part (§16); a position of corporate officer or director (§16A); a receivership (§16B); successive legal estates (such as life estate and remainder in different persons); and a custodianship under gifts to minors legislation (§16C).

How does a court go about deciding cases in which the outcome is affected by its characterization of an unclear relationship as a trust or something else? Does it look for an "appropriate result" between the parties and then find that relationship which supports the desired result? Or does it look at the facts, somehow decide what relationship exists, and let the chips fall as they may? Throughout the course, as well as in the cases that follow, watch for ways in which these characterizations matter. Even in counseling, the choice of the type of relationship to be created may be affected by these differences — and, of course, in a lawyer-planned transaction no uncertainty should be left about the intended relationship.

As you read the two cases that follow, consider specifically:

(1) *Why* was there no trust in *McLaughlin*? In *McKee*?

(2) What *difference* would a trust have made in *McLaughlin*? In *McKee*? Then consider whether, from the viewpoint of one claiming against another, a trust is preferable to a debt. When would it not be?

McLAUGHLIN v. EQUITABLE LIFE ASSURANCE CO.
112 N.J. Eq. 344, 164 A. 579 (1933)

[The defendant company issued an insurance policy on the life of the father of John F. McLaughlin, the minor complainant. The terms of the contract provided that in the event of the insured's death before his son attained age 18, the insurance proceeds ($2,000) should be held by the defendant until the son reached that age and should then be payable in equal annual installments over a period of four years. Prior to the son's reaching age 18, the defendant was to pay 3 percent interest annually on the retained proceeds to the wife of the insured as trustee for the son. The insured died when his son was 10 years of age. The bill of complaint asked permission to use so much of the corpus of the proceeds of the policy as the court might determine necessary for the support and education of the minor complainant. The court below directed the defendant to pay to the complainant's guardian $25 per week from the principal of the proceeds until further order.]

KAYS, J. . . .

The Vice Chancellor seemed to have based his conclusions on the supposition that the fund was a trust and on what the father would have done under the circumstances if he were alive. . . . The defendant below appeals to this Court on the ground that the policy of insurance and the claim which resulted thereunder by reason of the death of the insured did not create a trust and that the relation of the parties to the suit was not that of trustee and cestui que trust, and also for the reason that there was no evidence before the Vice Chancellor which justified him in decreeing that the defendant should pay the guardian of the infant $25 a week. We are of the opinion that the court below erred in respect to the construction which it placed upon the contract of insurance. The policy of insurance was a contract, and under its terms the insurance company was bound to carry out its provisions. The intention of the insured was to provide a fund for the education, support, and maintenance of his son, John F. McLaughlin, in the event that the insured died before his son attained the age of eighteen years and that he should not have access to such fund except as provided in the contract of insurance until he attained the designated age. This fund, therefore, did not become a trust fund until it was paid over by the insurance company under the term of the contract of insurance to the trustee. . . . We are of the opinion that the court could not change the terms of this contract and that the insurance company cannot be compelled to agree to any other terms than the terms set forth therein. It is, therefore, not necessary to consider the other point raised by the appellant.

The decree below is, therefore, reversed. [All justices concurred.]

McKEE v. PARADISE
299 U.S. 119 (1936)

[Certiorari to review the propriety of a preference allowed in a bankruptcy proceeding on the ground of a trust.]

MR. CHIEF JUSTICE HUGHES delivered the opinion of the Court. . . .

The facts were stipulated. The bankrupt, Grigsby-Grunow, Inc., maintained an unincorporated welfare association, known as the Majestic Employees Welfare Association, to provide life, health and accident insurance for its employees. The association was governed by its own officers and had its own bank account. The funds of the association were invested in United States securities and the earnings and increment of these investments were used for the contemplated insurance benefits. The initial membership fee of one dollar and weekly dues of twenty-five cents were "automatically deducted" from the wages of each employee who had been employed for the required period. Before February 4, 1933, the bankrupt regularly paid to the association the accumulations of each payroll deduction, less such expenses of the association as were paid by the bankrupt. From the date above-mentioned, the bankrupt fell into arrears and until November 24, 1933, when receivers in equity were appointed, there was always an unpaid balance to the credit of the association. That balance at the time of the receivership amounted to $14,607.51. The deductions from wages were made by charging the employee's account on the payroll records of the bankrupt and crediting the aggregate of all such deductions to the account of the association on the books of the bankrupt. "No actual money was taken from the pay envelopes of the employees and deposited in any account of the bankrupt, but to the contrary the matter was handled as a mere bookkeeping entry" and at no time did the bankrupt "segregate" any money due the association or "deposit any money in any separate trust account or bank account." The practice of the bankrupt was to deposit all its incoming revenue in its general bank account, from which it would from time to time withdraw moneys and establish various special accounts. The bankrupt was accustomed to withdraw from its general account or special accounts as the convenience of the situation required, and the payroll was drawn from the various accounts, both general and special, indiscriminately. . . .

We think that the facts afforded no adequate basis for the conclusion that a trust existed. The underlying relation was that of employer and employee. With respect to wages that the employee earned, the relation was that of debtor and creditor. By agreement, a part of the amounts thus becoming due as wages was to be paid to the association. What would otherwise be a debt to the employee was to become a debt to the association. Whether the agreement be viewed as an assignment by the employee to the association of the claim to the part of the wages as the latter became due, or as a novation, the result was that the bankrupt owed the association the agreed sums. The book entries of debits on the payroll records and credits to the association evidenced that understanding.

It does not appear that it was contemplated that the bankrupt should accumulate or hold any fund. On the contrary, the practice prior to February, 1933, was that the bankrupt regularly paid to the association the agreed amounts. The later failure to pay did not alter the nature of the transaction. The bankrupt was a debtor which had failed to pay its debt. We know of no principle upon which that failure can be treated as a conversion of property held in trust. At no time throughout the whole period was there a trust fund or res. No fund was segregated or set up by special deposit or in any manner. When the wages became due, there was no such fund but only the general assets of the employer and its obligation to pay a debt. The agreement of the employer to pay the association instead of the employee did not give to the employee or the association equitable title to or lien upon any part of the employer's property. The assets of the employer remained, as they were before, general assets. It would be impossible to state all the circumstances in which equity will fasten a constructive trust upon property in order to frustrate a violation of fiduciary duty. . . . The fact that the failure to pay the association was an acute disappointment and was especially regrettable as the claimant was an association of employees, cannot avail to change the debtor into a trustee or enable the creditor to obtain a preference over the claims against a bankrupt estate. . . .

C. *Reasons for Using Trusts*

Although trusts may be established for any of a great variety of reasons, certain particularly common reasons are mentioned at this point. Obviously the list is far from complete.

1. Testamentary Trusts

Property management. Of potential importance in planning the testamentary affairs of virtually every individual is the problem of providing for the management of property that may be given to persons who are legally or practically unable to manage it for themselves. Most frequently this problem arises with regard to minor beneficiaries and persons who are elderly or inexperienced in business matters. Even where both spouses are able and willing to manage their own property and all children are adults, the client should be led to consider the possible need to provide property management for grandchildren in the event an adult child should predecease the client. Rarely are management problems wholly absent, but they may be met in a variety of ways. For example, a legally competent but inexperienced individual may employ investment counsel and agents, and the property of a minor or incompetent may be handled by a conservator or other legally appointed fiduciary, whatever the local terminology. Often, however, trust arrangements will be considered preferable by the client when the matter is fully discussed with a lawyer. Agencies traditionally terminate in the event of subsequent incompetency; and regardless of the availability of investment counsel, property in the hands of an elderly or inexperienced person is exposed to possible neglect or imprudence. For minors, guardianship is typically cumbersome, inflexible, and costly and complicated by uncertainty. By contrast the trustees make most of their decisions without the cost and delay of court proceedings for orders or instructions. Trust flexibility is almost as unlimited as the combined imaginations of settlor and lawyer; and unnecessary uncertainties can be removed by proper planning and drafting. In general, then, the trust device can be personally tailored — much like the rest of the will itself — while the guardianship device provided by law necessarily lacks this advantage — somewhat as does the law of intestacy.

Providing for successive, concurrent, and limited enjoyment. The trust offers numerous advantages over arrangements involving successive legal estates, such as the incessantly troublesome life estate and remainder situation. Normally the trust offers greater assurance of the protection of the future interest, and there is generally a greater certainty regarding the rights of the parties. Although the legal life tenant may be granted powers similar to those of a trustee, the drafting problems are increased by the very nature of successive legal estates and divided ownership, particularly where some of the remainder beneficiaries are under age or unascertained. Certain managerial powers inhere in the office of trustee, and considerable advantage follows from the mere fact that a trustee generally holds full legal title to the subject matter of the trust. Furthermore, greater flexibility and judicial assistance are usually available to deal with unanticipated situations and problems not covered by the terms of the trust. Particular difficulties are encountered with regard to successive legal interests in certain types of personal property, such as chattels that are normally consumed in their use. On the other hand, other types of personalty, such as art objects, may satisfactorily be the subject matter of legal life interests and remainders.

Trust flexibility also permits the rights of intended beneficiaries to be tailored to the precise wishes of the testator. The interest of beneficiaries can be limited or adjusted to changed circumstances, and contingent or other special provisions can be made for persons who are not primary beneficiaries of the property owner. Again, the trust for a surviving spouse and the trust for minor children provide ready examples — applicable even to the young family with only a life insurance estate. In these and other cases, dispositive flexibility, although often overlooked, is likely to be more important than management considerations. Assume a young client, *C*, who is married and has three small children. *C* would leave everything to his or her spouse, *S*, if *S* survives, except for a concern that, should *S* remarry, the property is likely to be left later to the second spouse or, in part at least, to the children of the second marriage. If *C* has sufficient insurance or other assets to make these concerns and a trust realistic, the trust can be used to provide for *S*, and even in a limited way (such as for emergencies) for *S*'s second family if *C* wishes, while still assuring that *C*'s property (or what remains) will eventually go to *C*'s own children or their families. We must also plan for the possibility that *S* will predecease *C* or that they will die of a common disaster while their children are still small. This requires an alternative plan for the benefit of orphaned minors, plus naming a personal guardian. The usual equal shares left outright to the children, by will or intestacy, will be held in three separate guardianship estates. Because of the inevitably different needs (such as medical and dental expenses) of the children over their different periods of minority, the results are apt to be very different from the type of equality envisaged by the parents. In fact, the share of one child may prove inadequate for that child's needs, while the other children receive tidy sums as they enter their adult lives. And the smaller the estate the more serious these problems tend to be. If *C* prefers, however, the trust offers a variety of other solutions. For example, a single family trust can provide flexibly for the needs of all the children, with the corpus to be divided equally among them when the youngest reaches maturity or some specified age. If *C* wishes, the trusts for *S* and the children can be designed to provide also for emergency needs of *C*'s parents or others, such as the family of the children's personal guardian, maybe on the condition that such payments will not jeopardize the security of the primary beneficiaries during their minorities. The foregoing are but suggestive of the many ways in which trusts can usefully be employed to permit concurrent and successive enjoyment of even limited family wealth.

Tax purposes. Where substantial amounts are involved, as we observed in the material on taxation at the end of the previous chapter, trusts can be used to reduce or eliminate taxation of property later in the hands of the beneficiaries or in their estates.

First, trusts have been employed traditionally to prevent additional estate and inheritance taxation on the death of the testator's primary beneficiary or beneficiaries, while still conferring on them the protection and many of the benefits of the trust property. These opportunities under federal law were reduced but not eliminated by the enactment of the generation-skipping transfer tax first in 1976 and then in revised form in 1986. The trust's potential tax benefits to younger generation beneficiaries are still significant; and its benefits in planning for a surviving spouse and others not of "younger generations" were not impaired by that legislation. For example, *A* may leave her estate to *T* in trust to pay income to her husband, *H,* for life, and then to pay income to their child, *C,* for life, with the remainder to be distributed thereafter to *C*'s then living issue. Death taxation of the trust principal will be avoided on

H's death and can again be avoided (to the extent of up to $1 million of original corpus) on *C*'s death; this will be so, you may recall, even though *T* has broad authority to invade principal for the benefit of *H* and *C*, and even though *H* or *C* has power, subject to slight limitation, to decide how the property is to pass on the survivor's death (a special power of appointment).

Second, the testator may reduce the beneficiaries' income tax burdens by use of trusts. Even the trust just described offers some saving of income taxes because capital gains are normally taxable to the trust as a separate entity. Significant income tax savings can be achieved, however, through the proper use of discretionary trusts under which the trustee holds some power to select the recipients of the trust's income. Modest savings may also result from trusts that authorize distribution or accumulation of income in the trustee's discretion.

These and other tax-saving opportunities were alluded to in the prior chapter and can be studied thoroughly in other courses. The subsequent materials in this book do not cover tax law or tax aspects of estate planning specifically, but they do attempt to reflect new and special problems of trust law and fiduciary administration that are created by current tax laws or that arise out of tax-motivated behavior.

2. Inter Vivos Trusts

Living trusts may be subdivided, basically, into those that are revocable and those that are irrevocable. Which of these types will be used depends on the purposes the settlor has in mind. Some of the more common purposes of living trusts are indicated in the following paragraphs.

Avoidance of probate. One of the important uses of the *revocable* trust is as a will substitute, to dispose of property without its being subjected to estate administration on the settlor's death. Estate administration involves delays, sometimes of several years, and significant expenses that are, in large measure, dependent on the size of the probate estate. These costs and delays may be reduced through the use of a revocable trust, although the ultimate distribution of a living trust may, in part at least, have to await completion of certain phases of estate proceedings, particularly the handling of tax matters. Also, trustee's fees will be incurred when a corporate or professional trustee is employed; however, a family member may be better able to cope as trustee with the problems of trust administration than as executor with those of a decedent's estate. The inter vivos trust also offers continuity, which may be important in the case of "sensitive" assets (such as a business interest) held in trust and for purpose of maintaining income flow to persons who would not qualify for a family allowance under local probate law. Like joint tenancy, trusts of property located outside the domicile are sometimes used to avoid ancillary estate administration proceedings. Living trusts also permit privacy to be preserved, in contrast to the public nature of proceedings in the administration of estates. All of the reasons for — and shortcomings of — using revocable trusts to avoid probate cannot be fully developed at this point, but as the course progresses the student should watch for the problems and opportunities inherent in such planning. It will also be important for you to become acquainted with the ways in which fees of executors and trustees, and their attorneys, are generally determined in your community, so that these matters may be seen in a realistic context. (See generally Chapter 17, section B.)

Property management. Revocable living trusts are often superior to agency arrangements as methods of obtaining qualified supervision and handling of one's property. A revocable trust may be appropriate for one who is preoccupied with other affairs, unskilled in property management, fearful of senility, or merely likely to be absent at inconvenient times. In the event of legal incapacity, under traditional principles an agency terminates. Distasteful legal proceedings may be required to establish incompetency in order to vest managerial powers in an appropriate person, who then operates under the handicaps of the legal machinery provided for administering the estates of incompetents. (In quite recent years, the so-called durable power of attorney has been introduced through the Uniform Probate Code or its counterparts, allowing the agency relation to survive incompetency, if desired, but not death.) Under like situations, an inter vivos trust would normally continue uninterrupted in accordance with its presumably convenient provisions. In addition, living trusts offer a measure of protection against one's own imprudence, although interests retained by the settlor even in an irrevocable trust cannot be immunized from the claims of the settlor's creditors, at least under federal bankruptcy law.

Tax purposes. Gifts, whether outright or in trust, are of advantage particularly to the wealthy as a means of shifting income from property to persons in lower tax brackets and as a means of removing assets from the taxable estate of the donor at death. The same reasons that encourage the use of a testamentary trust in lieu of outright bequests also encourage the use of gifts in trust as replacements for outright gifts inter vivos. In addition, gifts in trust may be made in a manner that will assure the accomplishment of certain objectives of the settlor, but here care must be exercised to avoid retention of interests or powers that may jeopardize the tax objectives. The use of trusts as means of making gifts also gives rise to special gift tax problems, but these tend to be relatively minor and can sometimes be avoided by proper planning. Generally, then, tax-motivated gifts may be made in a form more suitable to the donor's objectives through the use of trusts, especially in the case of gifts to minors; and occasionally trusts may be used for income tax advantages where the donor could not afford to make an outright gift. Because of the strict "grantor rules" of the income and estate tax laws (see pages 286 and 291-292, above), great care is required in the planning and drafting of inter vivos trusts that are intended to shift income tax burdens or to reduce the settlor's taxable estate at death or both. Inter vivos trusts that are tax motivated are necessarily *irrevocable*. Basically, wholly revocable trusts offer no tax advantages, and irrevocable inter vivos trusts are rarely used for any but tax reasons.

"Devious" objectives. Trusts have, historically and in modern times, been used to circumvent or to attempt to circumvent legal policies. In the hands of resourceful lawyers and judges, the trust device has been an effective tool of avoidance — sometimes of outmoded rules, rigid concepts of technical disabilities, and sometimes of legitimate fiscal and social policies. It has been a constructive force for justice in individual cases and for innovation and progress in the law. As in feudal times, however, it continues to confound tax administrators and reformers. One of the most obvious illustrations of its role in policy avoidance is the use of revocable trusts to circumvent the forced heirship rights of a surviving spouse. This problem and others will be taken up in subsequent chapters.

10

The Elements of a Trust

RESTATEMENT (SECOND) OF TRUSTS

§23. . . . A trust is created only if the settlor properly manifests an intention to create a trust.

§2. . . . *Comment h.* . . . [A] trust involves three elements, namely, (1) a trustee . . . ; (2) a beneficiary . . . ; (3) trust property. . . . Although all three elements are present in a complete trust, one or more of them may be temporarily absent without destroying the trust or even without preventing the creation of the trust.

A. *Intention to Create a Trust*

A manifestation of the settlor's intention to create a trust is essential to the existence of an express trust. Normally the creating instrument leaves no doubt about this intent, but an unfortunate amount of litigation is caused by precatory language in wills, particularly those drawn by laymen. Are such words intended to be binding and to create a trust, or are they mere suggestions for the legatee or devisee to follow or disregard as he wishes? Although the presence or absence of trust language is likely to be persuasive, the use of the word "trust" does not *compel* a finding of intent to create a trust; nor does the failure to use the word *prevent* it.

PROBLEM

10-A. *A*'s will bequeathed $50,000 "to my son, *B,* with the request that he use whatever he thinks appropriate to provide for the welfare of my sister, *C.*"

(a) Does *B* take the money outright, or is he obligated to make provision for *C*? What other information would you want to know?

(b) Would the problem be different if *A* had left the money "with the request that *B* make such use of it for my family and friends as he thinks I would deem appropriate"? Why?

(c) How do these dispositions differ from a bequest by *A* to "*B* for life, remainder to such of *B*'s issue as *B* shall appoint by deed or will"; or a bequest to "*B* for life, remainder to such person or persons as *B* shall appoint by deed or will"?

COMFORD v. CANTRELL
177 Tenn. 553, 151 S.W.2d 1076 (1941)

GREEN, C.J. . . .

James G. Cantrell was the owner of valuable property on Fifth Avenue in Nashville which he devised to his wife. She was advised that she took an estate in fee under her husband's will and proceeded to dispose of the property by her will. Certain relatives of the husband, mentioned by his will in a connection that will hereafter appear, insist that Mrs. Cantrell took the property impressed with a trust in their favor at her death.

After certain provisions not here material, Cantrell's will continued:

> Third: I give, devise and bequeath all the rest, residue and remainder of my estate and property of whatsoever kind and nature, wherever situated, both real and personal, to which I am entitled, or which I may have the power to dispose of at my death, to my wife, Clara Augusta Cantrell, to be her absolute estate forever; but if said Clara Augusta Cantrell dies in my lifetime, I then bequeath the property described in the next succeeding paragraph to the persons and in accordance with the request therein contained.
>
> Fourth: It is my request that upon her death my said wife, Clara Augusta Cantrell, shall give, devise and bequeath my interest in the following described property in Nashville, Tennessee, to-wit; (Description follows)
>
> One quarter interest in my interest of the property described in the fourth section of this will to each of my brothers, Harvey W. Cantrell, Lee Cantrell and Julian W. Cantrell, or their heirs, and one quarter interest in my interest in said property to Charles E. Boisseau, Jr., and his sister Marguerite Boisseau, to be held by them jointly during the life of said Marguerite Boisseau, and at her death, the interest of said Marguerite Boisseau to revert to said Charles E. Boisseau or his heirs.

As observed by the chancellor, the testator used strong language in describing the character of the estate conferred upon his wife under his will. He said it was "to be her absolute estate forever." Absolute means without limitation or restriction. The word forever is almost invariably used in an instrument which creates an estate in fee simple. Forever is said to be an adjunct of a fee-simple estate. This will was obviously prepared by a lawyer and it is hard to conceive of words more clearly designed to pass a fee-simple estate than those quoted above.

Such being the will before us, we think the case falls under the authority of Smith v. Reynolds, 173 Tenn. 579, 121 S.W.2d 572, 574. In that case the court reviewed earlier decisions and re-affirmed the rule that a

clear and certain devise of a fee, about which the testamentary intention
was obvious, would not be cut down or lessened by subsequent words
which are ambiguous or of doubtful meaning. Although the will said that
the estate devised to his wife "is by my wish returned to my nearest blood
kin" at her death, the court held that the wife took the fee, it having been
clearly and without ambiguity given to her previously in the instrument.
The court said that the testator did not use the word wish as a command.
And further that a trust would not be declared on the basis of precatory
words where the will showed an intention to leave property absolutely.

In Smith v. Reynolds the court noted the change in the trend of
authority as to the force of precatory words. . . .

In 1 Bogert on Trusts and Trustees, §48, it is said:

> The words "request," "desire," and the like, do not naturally import a
> legal obligation. But the early view in England was that such words, when
> used in a will, were to be given an unnatural meaning, and were to be held
> to be courteous and softened means of creating duties enforceable by the
> courts. According to that opinion words of request prima facie created a
> trust. But since the beginning of the nineteenth century the English courts
> have changed their stand upon this question, and now hold that the nat-
> ural significance of precatory words is not a trust, but that such an obli-
> gation may be shown by other portions of the instrument or by extrinsic
> circumstances. The American courts have adopted this natural construc-
> tion of precatory expressions. . . .

Counsel for defendants rely on Daly v. Daly, 142 Tenn. 242, 218 S.W.
213, in which precatory words were treated as imperative. There, however, the court analyzed the whole will and showed that throughout the
testator used such words as expressing a command rather than a mere
desire. In Daly v. Daly our earlier cases were all set out and need not here
be considered. In none of these cases was a trust held to exist where the
recipient of the gift was to take it as an "absolute estate forever." These
words are just incompatible with any other interest in the estate. . . .

[T]he decree of the chancellor must be affirmed.

The outcome of a case of this type will be influenced by a variety of
factors. Courts tend to favor a "natural result" and are thus interested
in the relationship and circumstances of the parties. The case for a trust
would be strengthened by the fact that the bequest and suggestion are
made to a fiduciary, such as the executor, or that clear and detailed
instructions have been provided in the will. See generally G. Bogert,
Trusts and Trustees §48 (rev. 2d ed. 1984). For one of the recent but
increasingly rare cases of a trust based on precatory language ("and I
hereby request"), see Trustees of First Methodist Church v. Attorney
General, 270 N.E.2d 905 (Mass. 1971).

With these trust problems compare that of the nontrust "precatory remainder": *A* left his residuary estate to *B,* adding that "upon *B*'s death, it is my desire that the property be divided among *C, D,* and *E.*" See In re Wilson's Estate, 367 Mich. 143, 116 N.W.2d 215 (1962) (bequest to *B* absolute). See also Page v. Buchfinck, 202 Neb. 411, 275 N.W.2d 826 (1980) (bequest "upon the hope, desire and belief that . . . "). Such cases pose other issues than that of intention. See Problem 5-G in Chapter 5. See also the classic dissent of Chief Justice Vanderbilt in Fox v. Snow, 6 N.J. 12, 76 A.2d 877 (1950) (no remainder due to so-called doctrine of repugnancy applied as a rule of law, not of intent).

Where a client wishes to leave property to another "with the suggestion, but without requiring" that he use it for a particular purpose, the lawyer should consider whether from a tax viewpoint it might be preferable to create a trust or otherwise to impose a legal duty on the recipient. Cf. Delaney v. Gardner, 204 F.2d 855 (1st Cir. 1953).

B. The Trustee

1. Necessity of Trustee

Because of the very nature of a trust, its operation requires that there be a trustee. It is a well-settled and basic principle, however, that once a trust is established it will not fail merely because of the trustee's death, incapacity, resignation, or removal. A successor will be appointed unless it quite clearly appears that the trust was to continue only so long as the designated trustee continues to act. Thus, the rule is stated: *A trust will not fail for want of a trustee.*

Where the trustee named in a will predeceases the testator or disclaims, it is clear that a trustee will be appointed unless a contrary intention is manifested. In Hailes v. Garrison, 70 N.J. Eq. 605, 62 A. 865 (1906), the will left "all my property [to] be put in trust, and the income be divided between my brother, [my] sister, . . . and my wife." Once the court concluded that the intent to create a trust existed, it readily concluded that the failure to name a trustee "will not prevent the execution of the trust, for the court will always appoint a trustee wherever necessary to sustain the trust." 70 N.J. Eq. at 607, 62 A. at 865.

At the stage of trust creation, however, the absence of a trustee sometimes poses other complications because of its effect on the requirement, to be studied later, that a trust be created by a transfer of trust property. The preceding discussion involved wills, and an effective testamentary transfer requires only that the testator die with a will in force. Different issues arise when one attempts to create a trust by inter vivos transfer to a would-be trustee who is dead, undetermined, or legally incapable of taking title. In Frost v. Frost, 202 Mass. 100, 88 N.E. 446

(1909), the insured purported to assign his life insurance policies to "the trustees to be named in my will." The court found that the quoted language referred to the trustees under whatever will might finally be admitted to probate on the insured's death. The court then stated: "Upon the facts of this case these assignments never took effect within the lifetime of the assignor, for want of assignees, and never took effect after his death for want of proper attestation. There was therefore nothing upon which to base the contemplated trust, and it was never perfected." 202 Mass. at 103, 88 N.E. at 448. But cf. Wittmeier v. Heiligenstein, 308 Ill. 434, 139 N.E. 871 (1923), in Chapter 11, section A.

2.   Successor and Substitute Trustees

On the death of one of several cotrustees, the surviving trustee or trustees normally hold title to the trust property by survivorship because cotrustees hold title as joint tenants unless otherwise provided by the terms of the trust. A successor to the deceased cotrustee generally will not be appointed unless the settlor manifested such an intention or unless the court considers the appointment to be in the interest of proper administration.

On the death of a sole trustee, in the absence of trust provision or one of the commonly enacted statutes to the contrary, the title to the trust property passes, subject to the trust, to the trustee's heirs, devisee, legatee, or personal representative, depending on the passage of title to individually owned property of the same type under state law. Such persons are not authorized to administer the trust, however, and the proper court will appoint a new trustee. The court order will vest title in the new trustee, or it will require the holder of the title to transfer the property if that is necessary under applicable law and the circumstances.

In the event of the death, resignation, or removal of a sole trustee, or when the position of one of several trustees becomes vacant and the appointment of a successor is appropriate, in the absence of a trust provision naming a successor, a new trustee will be appointed by the appropriate court on the application of an interested person. In making such an appointment the court will usually consider the desires of the beneficiaries as well as the settlor's intent and the furtherance of sound administration. Frequently, however, trust instruments contain provisions naming successor trustees. Where this is the case, the terms of the trust will be followed in the absence of grounds for removal or grounds for refusing to confirm the appointment. Trust instruments sometimes provide procedures for the selection of successor trustees; for example, the trust may provide for the appointment of new trustees by the settlor of a living trust, by one or more adult beneficiaries, by a surviving

trustee, or by some other person. Where a person is empowered to select
a new trustee, it is generally said that courts will not disapprove a selection merely because it is one the court itself would not have made, but
that such a selection is not entitled to the same respect as an appointment by the settlor. If a life beneficiary is given power, for any reason
and with no express restriction, to remove the trustee and to appoint
successors, should self-appointment by the beneficiary be permitted?
The answer to this question may have significant tax implications, as well
as posing questions of practical desirability: see, e.g., Treasury Regulations §20.2041-1(b)(1).

Other matters, involving qualification, appointment, and removal of
trustees, are taken up in Chapter 17.

C. The Trust Property

"A trust requires a specific res, and where there is no specific res, there
can be no trust." Cahill v. Monahan, 58 N.J. Super. 54, 66, 155 A.2d
282, 288 (1959).

Note that the American Law Institute's definition of a trust, quoted
supra page 311, describes a trust as a fiduciary relationship with respect
to property. Also in the preceding chapter a pair of cases was encountered in which it was held that the arrangements in question were not
trusts, and the holdings were at least aided by the fact that no specific
res existed. In McKee v. Paradise, supra page 312, for example, the
United States Supreme Court emphasized that no fund had been segregated for the purpose in question and that no identifiable trust fund
or res had been established. McLaughlin v. Equitable Life Assurance
Co., supra page 311, involved an insurance contract, with the standard
result that retention of the proceeds by the company pursuant to a settlement option did not constitute a trust. This result is explained in IA
W. Fratcher, Scott on Trusts §87.1 (4th ed. 1987), as follows:

> . . . If, as is almost universally the case, the insurance company is not
> required to and does not segregate the proceeds but merely undertakes to
> make the required payments out of its general funds, the company is not
> a trustee. There is certainly no trust in the technical sense of the term, for
> nothing is held by one person for another. It is immaterial that the agree-
> ment between the company and the insured person is called a trust agree-
> ment . . . if it is also agreed that the proceeds shall not be segregated from
> the other assets of the company. There is no trust . . . as long as the pro-
> ceeds are not segregated.

The trust property may consist of virtually any property interests,
whether real or personal, tangible or intangible, legal or equitable. This
would include such properties as patents and even the goodwill of a busi-

ness. In general, then, any type of existing property interest that is transferable may be placed in trust, and even an interest that is not transferable can be held in trust. For example, where a tort claim is not assignable it cannot be *placed* in trust; but such a claim may comprise part of the subject matter of a trust and can be *held* in trust, as when it arises originally through tortious destruction of an asset held in the trust. Even property that is clearly transferable must be definite, or at least ascertainable, to be placed in trust. While the problem of trust property usually causes no difficulty when the intent presently to create a trust is clear, occasionally litigation arises in which there is a problem as to the identification of an "existing" property interest as the trust res.

PROBLEM

10-B.   *A* is a prosperous business executive whose father, *F*, died some years ago. By *F*'s will most of his estate was placed in trust for *M*, *A*'s mother, for life, remainder to *A*. *M* also has a substantial estate of her own, which she plans to leave to *A*. *A* has decided that for tax reasons it will not be advisable to enlarge his estate or to increase his income. He therefore decided that his remainder interest in the trust created by *F*, and also anything he receives from *M*, should be placed in a trust for his issue. *A* then executed a deed purporting presently to transfer to *T*, as trustee, his remainder interest and any property he may receive from the estate of *M*. Is a trust created? If so, of what? If you had been advising *A*, what would you have recommended to accomplish his purpose?

Would your answer be different if, under *F*'s trust, the remainder had been to *A* if living at *M*'s death and otherwise to *C* Church?

Would your answer be different if *M* had died before *A*'s deed to *T* was executed and delivered?

D.   The Beneficiaries

Except for charitable trusts and what are sometimes called "honorary trusts," a valid trust requires a beneficiary or beneficiaries who have a right to enforce it. Occasional cases present the question of whether a particular instrument satisfies the requirement that there be definite beneficiaries, or at least beneficiaries who will be definitely ascertainable within the period during which all interests must vest under the applicable law relating to perpetuities.

If a person has capacity to hold title to property, even though he cannot administer it, he can be the beneficiary of a trust. In fact, the inability of a beneficiary to manage his property is often the primary reason for creating a trust. In general, the ability to take and hold title to property is considered essential to the capacity to be a trust beneficiary. Thus, in some jurisdictions and under some circumstances, corporations may be precluded from receiving a beneficial interest in a trust, such as when the trust in question is created by will and the corporation could not have taken title to property directly by bequest or devise. Nevertheless, it is generally held that an unincorporated association can be the beneficiary of a trust even though the association is not an entity and is not able to hold title to property under applicable state law. This is so even though the settlor intended to benefit the continuing association rather than the individual members as of the date of the trust's creation. (This assumes that local rules relating to perpetuities are not violated.) The requirement that such a trust be enforceable is satisfied because suit may be brought by a member of the association, or even by the association where it is treated as an entity in equity though not at law. See generally II W. Fratcher, Scott on Trusts §§116-119 (4th ed. 1987).

It is clear that a valid trust can be created under which some of the beneficiaries are unborn at the time. In fact, such trusts are not at all unusual. Can a valid trust be created in which none of the described beneficiaries are in existence at the time? Can a person create a trust solely for his unborn children? Contrast G. Bogert, Trusts and Trustees §163 (rev. 2d ed. 1979), with II W. Fratcher, Scott on Trusts §112.1 (4th ed. 1987). See Fratcher, Trustor as Sole Trustee and Only Ascertainable Beneficiary, 47 Mich. L. Rev. 907 (1949). How could such a trust be enforced? Consider the following case summaries.

In Morsman v. Commissioner of Internal Revenue, 90 F.2d 18 (8th Cir.), *cert. denied,* 302 U.S. 701 (1937), *A,* a bachelor, declared himself trustee of certain property, providing that a trust company should succeed him as trustee within ten years. The terms of the declaration were that income was to be accumulated for five years and thereafter was to be paid to *A* for life and then for twenty years to his issue, at which time the principal was to be distributed to them; if *A* left no issue, the trust property was to pass to his widow, if any, and otherwise to his heirs. Soon after declaring himself trustee, *A* sold some of the securities at a profit and then turned the property over to the trust company, which reported the profit as income taxable to the trustee rather than to *A* individually. The court held the income taxable to *A* individually, on the theory that no trust had been created because there were no beneficiaries other than *A* himself. The court stated that if *A* had "sought to dissipate the property, there is no person in being who has such an interest that he may go into a court of equity and prevent the dissipation." The dissenting opinion pointed out that *A*'s brother, as a prospective heir, was a contingent beneficiary who could enforce the terms of the trust.

With *Morsman* compare Lane v. Taylor, 287 Ky. 116, 152 S.W.2d 271 (1941), in which *A* conveyed land to *B* in trust for *A* for life, and at *A*'s death, or in the event of an attempt to subject the land to *A*'s debts, the land was to go to *A*'s children. Thereafter *A*'s only child died, and all of

his property passed to *A* and his wife, *W. A* and *W* purported to convey
the land to *X,* who contracted to sell it to *Y. Y,* objecting to *X*'s title,
declined to accept the deed tendered by *X* in fulfillment of the contract.
In a suit by *X* against *Y* for declaratory relief, *X*'s title was held defective
in that *A,* who was still living, might have children in the future.

NICHOLS v. ALLEN
130 Mass. 211, 39 Am. Rep. 445 (1881)

[Testatrix bequeathed the residue of her estate to her executors and
their successors "to be distributed to such persons, societies or institutions as they may think most deserving."]

GRAY, C.J.

Two general rules are well settled: 1st. When a gift or bequest is made
in terms clearly manifesting an intention that it shall be taken in trust,
and the trust is not sufficiently defined to be carried into effect, the
donee or legatee takes the legal title only, and a trust results by implication of law to the donor and his representatives, or to the testator's
residuary legatees or next of kin. . . . 2d. A trust which by its terms may
be applied to objects which are not charitable in the legal sense, and to
persons not defined, by name or by class, is too indefinite to be carried
out. . . .

The terms of this bequest clearly manifest the intention of the testatrix
to create a trust. The bequest contains no words tending to show that
the executors are to take the property, or any part of it, absolutely or for
their own benefit; and by our law no such intention is to be implied. . . .
The bequest is not to the executors by name, but is to them and the survivor of them, and to their successors in the administration of the
estate. . . .

The strongest case in favor of the defendants is Gibbs v. Rumsey, 2 V.
& B. 294, in which a bequest to the executors named in the will, "to be
disposed of unto such person and persons, and in such manner and
form, and in such sum and sums of money, as they in their discretion
shall think proper and expedient," was held by Sir William Grant to give
the executors a purely arbitrary power of disposition, and consequently
a beneficial interest. That case differs from the present one in at least
three important particulars: 1st. The bequest was only to the executors
named. 2d. Much stress was laid on the fact that the words "in trust" had
been used in many other places in the will, and were omitted in this
clause. 3d. An authority to those, to whom the legal title is given, "to
dispose of" the property "in such manner and in such sums and to such
persons as they may think proper," is more consistent with an arbitrary
power of disposition than is a direction "to distribute" the property "to
such persons, societies or institutions as they may think most deserving."

And the decision in Gibbs v. Rumsey has always been treated by the English courts as not to be extended beyond its special circumstances. . . .

The omission of the words "in trust" is unimportant where, as in the case before us, an intention is clearly manifested that the whole property shall be applied by the legatees for the benefit of others than themselves. . . .

Upon a review of the authorities, we find nothing in them to control the conclusion, based upon the intention which appears to us to be clearly manifested on the face of this will, that the executors take the estate, not beneficially, but in trust; and that the beneficiaries not being described by name or by class, the trust cannot be upheld unless its purposes are such as the law deems charitable.

The trust declared cannot be sustained as a charity. There is no restriction as to the objects of the trust, except that they must be "such persons, societies or institutions as they" (the trustees) "may consider most deserving." "Deserving" denotes worth or merit, without regard to condition or circumstances, and is in no sense of the word limited to persons in need of assistance, or to objects which come within the class of charitable uses. . . .

A gift to charitable or public purposes is good. Dolan v. Macdermot, L.R., 3 Ch. 676. But if the trustees are authorized to apply or distribute it to other purposes or persons, it is void. . . .

The conclusion of the whole matter is, that the testatrix having given the residue of her property to her executors in trust, and not having defined the trust sufficiently to enable the court to execute it, the plaintiff, being her next of kin, is entitled to the residue by way of resulting trust.

Demurrer overruled.

Do you see why the intended trust in the above case was not upheld on the ground that the beneficiaries, though not ascertained, *will become ascertainable* within the period of the rule against perpetuities?

In the leading case of Morice v. Bishop of Durham, 10 Vex. 521 (Ch. 1805), the testatrix bequeathed her personal estate to the Bishop of Durham on trust to pay her debts and legacies and "to dispose of the ultimate residue to such objects of benevolence and liberality" as he "shall most approve of." Although the bishop disclaimed any beneficial interest and was ready to carry out the intended purposes of the testatrix, the trust failed for want of anyone to enforce it, its purpose being too broad to be enforceable as a charitable trust by the Attorney General. Lord Eldon held that the bishop should not be allowed to carry out the intended trust but held the property on a resulting trust for the next of kin of the testatrix.

An aside on powers of appointment. According to L. Simes, Future Interests §55 (2d ed. 1966),

> A power of appointment may be defined as a kind of power created by a person (called the donor) who owns or has the power to dispose of property, whereby a person (called the donee) can, subject to the restrictions of the creating instrument, designate the transferees of the property (called the appointees) or the shares or interests which they are to take. This definition may be supplemented by pointing out two important characteristics of a power of appointment: (a) the exercise of the power has a dual character; sometimes it is thought of as an event relating back to the instrument creating the power, and sometimes as a transfer of property; (b) the power is essentially personal to the donee.

Unlike the trust's requirement of definite beneficiaries, a valid power of appointment may have a definite class of beneficiaries or it may not. In fact, in general powers of appointment the permissible appointees, or "objects," are not limited. In marginal cases, such as those in this section, courts distinguish powers from trusts and try to decide whether something is a trust or a power. Yet powers are not incompatible with trusts; quite the contrary, for the typical power of appointment arises in conjunction with a trust and is but a part or provision thereof. The power is intended to give flexibility to the trust and usually to provide a beneficiary of a limited interest some broader power to dispose of trust property or of some interest in it, often by will but sometimes by inter vivos appointment.

A fairly typical illustration is the following: *A* leaves his estate to *B* Bank in trust to pay the income to *C* (who is likely to be *A*'s spouse or adult child) for life; on *C*'s death *B* is to distribute the principal to such of *C*'s issue as *C* may appoint by will, remainder in default of appointment to *C*'s then living issue by right of representation. *C* (as "donee") has a testamentary special power of appointment. Incidentally, in addition to its managerial powers, *B* Bank too may have a power over the beneficial interests, most frequently in the form of a power to invade principal for *C*'s needs but sometimes in other forms, such as a power to divert income from *C* and distribute it among other beneficiaries. The power in *B* is a *fiduciary power,* and *B* must behave in a "fiduciary manner" with regard to it, as distinct from *C*'s power of appointment that may be exercised arbitrarily, or it may be left unexercised, as long as none but permissible appointees are benefited. What if *A* had failed to specify takers in default of appointment and *C* died intestate or otherwise leaving the power unexercised? Here, even with a power of appointment, it becomes important to determine whether there is a definite class of objects. If there is *not,* subject to very specialized exceptions, it will be held that *A* made an incomplete disposition of the property and that there is a reversion (or "resulting trust") under which the property belongs to the settlor or his (not *C*'s) successors in interest. On the other hand, if there *is* a definite class of objects, the property passes to that class. Most classes, such as *children,* then take in equal shares, but some classes, such as *issue* (and maybe *relatives* where such terms are considered definite enough), may take in the pattern of the local intestacy statutes. Where distribution is thus made to a definite class of objects, a remainder or gift in default of appointment is being *implied.* It is sometimes said that the gift was to the class, subject to *C*'s power to exclude some and to vary the shares; or more often, to the unfortunate confusion of our terminology, it is said that the power is a *trust power,* or a *power in trust,* or the like. Aside from the trust, therefore, it may be worthwhile for present purposes (despite judicial mixing of terms and concepts) to keep in mind as separate creatures to watch for: the fiduciary power; the power of appointment either with an expressed gift in default or in favor of indefinite objects; and the power of appointment for which takers in default will be implied and to which some "trust" label will probably be attached.

In Hopkins, Certain Uncertainties of Trusts and Powers, 29 Camb. L.J. 68, 68-71 (1971), it is stated:

> The traditional account of the distinction between a trust and a power runs thus. A trust imposes a duty upon a trustee; a power confers a discretion upon a donee. The former is imperative; the latter is discretionary. Thus, should a trustee fail to discharge his duty, the court will see to it that the duty is performed and will compel performance. If, on the other hand, a donee fails to execute a power, the property subject to the power will devolve on default of appointment. The court will seldom interfere in the case of the non-exercise of any power and, generally, will do so only if an improper purpose underlying the non-exercise is proved. And in the case of a power of appointment the court will normally interfere in an exercise of the power only on the ground of fraud, or excessive or defective execution, whilst as to non-exercise of the power, it will do so [only] to provide that the property subject to the power shall devolve on default of appointment.
>
> From such elementary principles of law, certain obvious consequences appear to flow. In the case of a trust, all the potential beneficiaries need to be ascertained — or to be ascertainable — since "the Court of Chancery, which acts in default of trustees, must know with sufficient certainty the objects of the beneficence of the donor so as to execute the trust," presumably upon the basis of equality being equity. Possibly for this reason, a number of non-charitable purpose trusts have been held to be void for uncertainty. On the other hand, as to a mere power of appointment, the full range of beneficiaries need not be known; no difficulty will be encountered although the power "is exercisable in favour of an indefinite class" [so long as the donee and the court can] determine whether or not a given person is or is not within the class. It is immaterial that all the class cannot be ascertained since the donee does not have to ascertain them in order to exercise the power and since the court will not have to order equal division between the several members of the class.

Apparently somewhere midway between trusts and powers, however, is a *tertium quid,* the so-called "power in the nature of a trust," the classic description of which is Lord Eldon's: "a power which the party to whom it is given is intrusted with and required to execute; if the person who has the duty imposed upon him does not discharge it, the court will, *to a certain extent,* discharge the duty in his room and place." . . . [T]he so-called power in the nature of a trust is regarded really as a trust, which masquerades under the guise of a power . . . partaking of the characteristics of a trust to such an extent that, as in the case of a trust, all the objects [have to] be ascertainable — presumably in order that the court might be able to divide the property between all members of the class in the event of the donee's failure to do so. . . .

The reasoning in the cases does have a certain logical charm. A trust is indeed mandatory and must be capable of execution by the court. The court normally will not substitute its own discretion for that of the trustees but will simply divide the property equally between the members of the class; if all the members of the class cannot be ascertained at the outset, the property cannot be distributed and the trust will accordingly fail for uncertainty. Yet the conclusion reached in these cases can be avoided and, henceforth, following Re Baden [discussed later in this section] should be [in England], in view of the court's expressed willingness to provide for an execution on a basis other than equality.

The case of Morice v. Bishop of Durham was criticized by Professor Ames in his classic article prompted by the failure of a provision of another famous will. See Ames, The Failure of the *"Tilden* Trust," 5 Harv. L. Rev. 389, 395-399 (1892):

It may be said that there can be no trust without a definite cestui que trust. This must be admitted. . . . But it does not follow from this admission that such a gift is void. Even though there be no express trust, there is a plain duty imposed upon *A* [one in the position of the Bishop of Durham] to act, and his act runs counter to no principle of public policy. Why then seek to nullify his act? The only objection that has ever been urged against such a gift is that the court cannot compel *A* to act if he is unwilling. Is it not a monstrous non sequitur to say that therefore the court will not permit him to act when he is willing?

It may be objected that a devise might in this way become "the mere equivalent of a general power of attorney"; but this objection seems purely rhetorical. Suppose a testator to give *A* a purely optional power of appointment in favor of any person in the world except himself, with a provision that in default of the exercise of the power the property shall go to the testator's representatives — or this provision may be omitted altogether, the effect being the same. Such a will is obviously nothing if not the mere equivalent of a general power of attorney. And yet the validity of the power would go unquestioned. If the power is exercised, the appointee takes. If it is not exercised, the testator's representative takes.

Now vary the case by supposing that the testator imposes upon the donee of the power the *duty* to exercise it. Can the imposition of this duty furnish any reason for a different result? In fact, A, the donee of the power has in this case also the option of appointing or not, since, although he ought to appoint, no one can compel him to do so. Does it not seem a mockery of legal reasoning to say that the court will sanction the exercise of the power where the donee was under no obligation to act at all, but will not sanction the appointment when the donee was in honor bound to make it?

It is time enough for the court to interfere when A proves false to his duty and sets up for himself. Then, indeed, a court of equity ought to turn him into a constructive trustee for the donor or his representative. This contingent right of the heir or next of kin may be safely trusted to secure the performance of his duty by the trustee. And its existence is a full answer to the suggestion . . . in Morice v. Bishop of Durham . . . that the trustee could keep the property without accountability to anyone, if the beneficial interests were not given to the heir or next of kin immediately upon the testator's death. The position of the heir or next of kin is, in substance, the same as in the cases where property is given to them subject to a purely optional power of appointment in another to be exercised, if at all, within a reasonable time. . . .

Although Morice v. Bishop of Durham has never been directly impeached, either in England or this country, there are several groups of cases, undistinguishable from it in principle, in which equity judges have declined to interfere, at the suit of the next kin, to prevent the performance of a purely honorary trust.

Mussett v. Bingle [W.N. (1876) 170] is one illustration. The testator bequeathed £300 upon trust for the erection of a monument to his wife's first husband. It was objected that the trust was purely honorary [and it was not charitable]; that is, there was no beneficiary to compel its performance. But the trustees being willing to perform, Hall, V.C., sustained the bequest. . . . There are many American cases to the same effect. . . .

The most conspicuous illustration of the doctrine which is here advocated is to be found in the recent English case of Cooper-Dean v. Stevens [41 Ch. D. 552]. There was in that case a bequest of £750 for the maintenance of the testator's horses and dogs. It was urged by the residuary legatee, on the authority of Morice v. Bishop of Durham, that this trust must fail, although the trustees desired to perform it. But the trust was upheld.

Professor Ames's theory has apparently been adopted by a very small number of decisions. E.g., Feinberg v. Feinberg, 36 Del. Ch. 438, 131 A.2d 658 (1957). See also Restatement (Second) of Trusts §§122, 123 (1959), reversing the position of its first edition. The clear weight of authority follows the rule of Nichols v. Allen. Nevertheless, as noted by Ames, the validity of "honorary (unenforceable) trusts" for limited types of definite, noncharitable purposes has become quite widely accepted. The case of trust for specific animals, too restrictive to be a charitable purpose, is a ready illustration. See Uniform Probate Code §2-907.

Bequests for the care of graves have generally been upheld and are now usually provided for by statute, as are employees' benefit trusts. A major hazard in the case of honorary trusts is the rule against perpetuities, except where specific statutory immunity has been granted to certain of such dispositions, such as perpetual upkeep of graves. See generally Fratcher, Bequests for Purposes, 56 Iowa L. Rev. 773 (1971), excerpts of which are included in Chapter 14 on charitable trusts.

Although Morice v. Bishop of Durham seems firmly a part of American trust doctrine, England's apparent recent escape from it is not. Nor does the modest impact that the Ames argument has had offer much encouragement that courts here will follow the more drastic approach of In re Baden's Deed Trust (McPhail v. Doulton), [1970] 2 All E.R. 228. The donation and trust deed in question were for the benefit of a large corporation's employees and their families, giving the trustees "absolute discretion" to make distributions to or for such beneficiaries as they may select. The opinion of Lord Wilberforce (id. at 246-247), despite its mild protestation to the contrary, seems quite clearly to indicate a reversal of direction in this area:

> The conclusion I would reach, implicit in the previous discussion, is that the whole distinction between the validity test for powers and that for trust powers, is unfortunate and wrong, that the rule [that a trust is void where the class of beneficiaries is "incapable of ascertainment"] ought to be discarded, and that the test . . . ought to be similar to that accepted by this House for powers, namely that the trust is valid if it can be said with certainty that any given individual is or is not a member of the class. . . .
>
> [T]he court, if called on to execute the trust power, will do so in the manner best calculated to give effect to the settlor's or testator's intentions. It may do so by appointing new trustees, or by authorizing or directing representative persons of the classes of beneficiaries to prepare a scheme of distribution, or even, should the proper basis for distribution appear, by itself directing the trustees to so distribute. . . . Then as to the trustees' duty of enquiry or ascertainment, in each case the trustees ought to make such a survey of the range of objects or possible beneficiaries as will enable them to carry out their fiduciary duty. A wider, more comprehensive range of enquiry is called for in the case of trust powers than in the case of powers. . . .
>
> There may be [cases] where the meaning of the words used is clear but the definition of beneficiaries is so hopelessly wide as not to form "anything like a class" so that the trust is administratively unworkable or in Lord Eldon LC's words one that cannot be executed (Morice v. Bishop of Durham). I hesitate to give examples for they may prejudice future cases.

A trust for a definite class, such as children, issue, or nieces and nephews, is sufficiently definite to be valid. Trusts have been upheld where the beneficiaries were described only by such terms as *employees* and *family*, although there are cases in which each of these designations has been held too indefinite to support a trust. The term *family,* of course, presents a question of construction, but it is one the courts have generally been willing to resolve. Many courts have been less willing to treat the word *relatives* as describing a sufficiently definite class to permit enforcement of a trust. Even this designation, however, has often been upheld by construing the terms as applying only to next of kin.

In most of the cases involving vague "class" designations, the description of the potential beneficiaries is accompanied by a power in the trustee to select from among persons fitting the description. In such cases, assuming the class is sufficiently definite to escape the holdings of Nichols v. Allen and Morice v. Bishop of Durham, as is — or at least may be — the case with the terms mentioned in the preceding paragraph, then certain additional problems are likely to arise. The trustee who holds a power to distribute to such of a testator's "relatives" as he may select may decide to make a distribution to a relative who is not among the testator's next of kin. Such a selection may be held permissible. Although the definiteness of the "class" in this case is sustained, for purpose of the initial validity of the trust, on the basis that "relatives" without a further method of ascertainment would be deemed to refer to next of kin, if necessary, the trustee's power of selection need not be so narrowly restricted. Another problem that might be posed by the same trust is that the trustee may die without having made a selection, or he might simply refuse to exercise his power of selection. In the absence of some standard to serve as a guide in the selection or a fairly clear indication of intention that a successor trustee should be appointed to exercise the power, the inference seems to be that the power was personal to the trustee chosen by the settlor. The court then would hold the rights of the beneficiaries to be the same as they would have been had the same class designation been employed without a power of selection. The property might thus be distributed equally among the class members. In a situation involving the term *relatives,* distribution would be made to those relatives who are the next of kin of the person in question, rather than attempting to make distribution among all relatives of all degrees. Then the shares of these kindred will be determined on the basis of the relevant rules of intestate succession.

Where the trustee has power to select beneficiaries from within a definite class, the required power to enjoin or redress a breach of trust resides in any of the members of the class, even though his individual right to take has not been established. See generally 2 A. Scott, Trusts §120 (3d ed. 1967).

Where the terms of a bequest to a person in trust provide that the trustee is to select and make payment to the person or persons who satisfy a particular description, the trust will be valid if the standards for selection are sufficiently certain to permit the court to exercise the power, if necessary, and to judge the propriety of the trustee's exercise,

on the basis of ascertainable facts. Thus, the beneficiaries are identified
on the basis of facts of independent significance. See Moss v. Axford,
246 Mich. 288, 224 N.W. 425 (1929), infra page 352.

PROBLEM

10-C.   Study the case of Clark v. Campbell, which follows. Assume
that the opinion is that of an intermediate appellate court of your state.
Assume also that Nichols v. Allen, supra, was decided by the highest
court of your state. On what theories might you seek reversal of the decision of the intermediate court, and how would you argue the case? After
considering the possibilities would you advise your client to pursue the
matter on the basis of these theories? How would you argue the case for
affirmance?

CLARK v. CAMPBELL

82 N.H. 281, 133 A. 166 (1926)

SNOW, J.
The ninth clause of the will of deceased reads:

> My estate will comprise so many and such a variety of articles of personal
> property such as books, photographic albums, pictures, statuary, bronzes,
> bric-a-brac, hunting and fishing equipment, antiques, rugs, scrap books,
> canes and masonic jewels, that probably I shall not distribute all, and per-
> haps no great part thereof during my life by gift among my friends. Each
> of my trustees is competent by reason of familiarity with the property, my
> wishes and friendships, to wisely distribute some portion at least of said
> property. I therefore give and bequeath to my trustees all my property
> embraced within the classification aforesaid in trust to make disposal by
> the way of a memento from myself, of such articles to such of my friends
> as they, my trustees, shall select. All of said property, not so disposed of
> by them, my trustees are directed to sell and the proceeds of such sale or
> sales to become and be disposed of as a part of the residue of my estate.

The question here reserved is whether or not the enumeration of chattels in this clause was intended to be restrictive or merely indicative of
the variety of the personal property bequeathed. The question is immaterial, if the bequest for the benefit of the testator's "friends" must fail
for the want of certainty of the beneficiaries.

By the common law there cannot be a valid bequest to an indefinite
person. There must be a beneficiary or a class of beneficiaries indicated
in the will capable of coming into court and claiming the benefit of the
bequest. Adye v. Smith, 44 Conn. 60, 26 Am. Rep. 424, 425. This principle applies to private but not to public trusts and charities. Harrington
v. Pier, 105 Wis. 485, 82 N.W. 345, 50 L.R.A. 307, 320, 76 Am. St. Rep.

924; 28 R.C.L. 339, 340; Morice v. Bishop of Durham, 9 Ves. 399, 10 Ves. 521.

The basis assigned for this distinction is the difference in the enforce-ability of the two classes of trusts. In the former, there being no definite cestui que trust to assert his right, there is no one who can compel per-formance, with the consequent unjust enrichment of the trustee; while, in the case of the latter, performance is considered to be sufficiently secured by the authority of the Attorney General to invoke the power of the courts. The soundness of this distinction and the grounds upon which it rests, as applied to cases where the trustee is willing to act, has been questioned by distinguished authorities (5 Harvard Law Review, 390, 394, 395; 65 University of Pennsylvania Law Review, 538, 540; 37 Harvard Law Review, 687, 688) and has been supported by other authorities of equal note (15 Harvard Law Review, 510, 513-515, 530). It is, however, conceded by the former that, since the doctrine was first stated in Morice v. Bishop of Durham, supra, more than a century ago, it has remained unchallenged, and has been followed by the courts in a practically unbroken line of decisions. Although it be conceded that the doctrine is not a legal necessity (15 Harvard Law Review, 515), the fact that it has never been impeached affords strong evidence that in its prac-tical application it has been generally found just and reasonable. This is a sufficient ground for continued adherence to the rule. . . .

That the foregoing is the established doctrine seems to be conceded, but it is contended in argument that it was not the intention of the tes-tator by the ninth clause to create a trust, at least as respects the selected articles, but to make an absolute gift thereof to the trustees individually. It is suggested that the recital of the qualifications of the trustees may be considered as investing them with personal and nonofficial character, and that the word "trustees" is merely descriptive of the persons who had been earlier named as trustees, and was not intended to limit the capacity in which they were to act here. . . . It is a sufficient answer to this contention that the language of the ninth clause does not warrant the assumed construction. The assertion of the competency of the trust-ees to wisely distribute the articles in question by reason of their famil-iarity with the testator's property, wishes and friendships seems quite as consistent with a design to clothe them with a trusteeship as with an intention to impose upon them a moral obligation only. . . .

The clause under consideration (ninth) expressly provides for the dis-posal of only a portion of the classified articles, and imposes upon the trustees the duty of selling the balance thereof and adding the proceeds to the residue which they are to continue to hold, and administer in their capacity as trustees. The proceeds thus accruing under this clause are expressly referred to in the eleventh clause in the enumeration of the ultimate funds to be distributed by them as trustees "in and among such charitable . . . institutions" as they shall select and designate. The conclusion is inescapable that there was no intention to bestow any part of the property enumerated in the ninth clause upon the trustees for their own benefit. This necessarily follows, since the direction to make disposal is clearly as broad as the gift.

It is further sought to sustain the bequest as a power. The distinction apparently relied upon is that a power, unlike a trust (Goodale v. Mooney, 60 N.H. 528, 534, 49 Am. Rep. 334), is not imperative and leaves the act to be done at the will of the donee of the power (21 R.C.L. 773; 26 R.C.L. 1169). But the ninth clause by its terms imposes upon the trustees the imperative duty to dispose of the selected articles among the testator's friends. If, therefore, the authority bestowed by the testator by the use of a loose terminology may be called a power, it is not an optional power, but a power coupled with a trust, to which the principles incident to a trust so far as here involved clearly apply.

We must therefore conclude that this clause presents the case of an attempt to create a private trust, and clearly falls within the principle of well-considered authorities. Nichols v. Allen, 130 Mass. 211, 212, 39 Am. Rep. 445; Blunt v. Taylor, 119 N.E. 954, 230 Mass. 303, 305. In so far as the cases cited by the petitioners upon this phase of the case are not readily distinguishable from the case at bar, they are in conflict with the great weight of authority. The question presented, therefore, is whether or not the ninth clause provides for definite and ascertainable beneficiaries, so that the bequest therein can be sustained as a private trust.

In this state the identity of a beneficiary is a question of fact to be found from the language of the will, construed in the light of all the competent evidence rather than by the application of arbitrary rules of law. It is believed that in no other jurisdiction is there greater liberality shown in seeking the intention of the testator in this, as in other particulars. We find, however, no case in which our courts have sustained a gift where the testator has attempted to delegate to a trustee the arbitrary selection of the beneficiaries of his bounty through means of a private trust.

Like the direct legatees in a will, the beneficiaries under a trust may be designated by class. But in such case the class must be capable of delimitation, as "brothers and sisters," "children," "issue," "nephews and nieces." . . . [Similarly,] the words "relatives" or "relations," to prevent gifts from being void for uncertainty, are commonly construed to mean those who would take under statutes of distribution or descent.

In the case now under consideration the cestuis que trust are designated as the "friends" of the testator. The word "friends," unlike "relations," has no accepted statutory or other controlling limitations, and in fact has no precise sense at all. Friendship is a word of broad and varied application. . . . There is no express evidence that the word is used in any restricted sense. The only implied limitation of the class is that fixed by the boundaries of the familiarity of the testator's trustees with his friendships. If such familiarity could be held to constitute such a line of demarcation as to define an ascertainable group, it is to be noted that the gift is not to such group as a class, the members of which are to take in some definite proportion (1 Jarman on Wills, 534; 2 Schouler, §1011), or according to their needs, but the disposition is to "such of my friends as they, my trustees, may select." No sufficient criterion is furnished to govern the selection of the individuals from the class. The assertion of the testator's confidence in the competency of his trustees "to wisely distribute some portion" of the enumerated articles "by reason of familiarity with the property, my wishes and friendships" does not furnish such a criterion. . . .

It was the evident purpose of the testator to invest his trustees with the power after his death to make disposition of the enumerated articles among an undefined class with practically the same freedom and irresponsibility that he himself would have exercised if living: that is, to substitute for the will of the testator the will and discretion of the trustees. Such a purpose is in contravention of the policy of the statute which [prescribes formalities of execution].

Where a gift is impressed with a trust, ineffectively declared, and incapable of taking effect because of the indefiniteness of the cestui que trust, the donee will hold the property in trust for the next taker under the will, or for the next of kin by way of a resulting trust. . . .

Case discharged.

All concurred.

E. *Trust Purposes*

Except in those few states in which statutes have attempted to enumerate the purposes for which trusts may be established, it is generally said, and in a sense it is true, that a trust may be created for any purpose that is not contrary to public policy. Thus, in some states it is provided by statute that a trust may be created "for any purpose or purposes for which a contract may be made" or for any purpose "which is not illegal."

This apparent liberality in describing trust purposes may be misleading. A purpose in the trust law may be "contrary to public policy" when it would not be in other contexts. The dead hand does not have all of the privileges of the living property owner. We have already seen that an express trust must either be for a charitable purpose or else for a private purpose with acceptably definite beneficiaries. Furthermore, the individual property owner does not determine what is or is not charitable, and private purposes are not allowed to endure in perpetuity. See generally Fratcher, Bequests for Purposes, 56 Iowa L. Rev. 773 (1971). What may be thrift for an individual may be an unlawful accumulation in a trust following death or an inter vivos conveyance. Unlike the private property of the living, the property of a trust cannot be devoted even to a quite harmless capricious purpose,[1] nor has the dead hand the freedom of the living in the use of wealth to influence the lives and behavior of others.

RESTATEMENT (SECOND) OF TRUSTS

§60. . . . An intended trust or a provision in the terms of a trust is invalid if illegal.

§61. . . . An intended trust or a provision in the terms of a trust is invalid if the performance of the trust or of the provision involves the commission of a criminal or tortious act by the trustee.

§62. . . . A trust or a provision in the terms of a trust is invalid if the enforcement of the trust or provision would be against public policy, even though its performance does not involve the commission of a criminal or tortious act by the trustee.

§65. . . . If a provision in the terms of the trust is illegal, the trust fails altogether if, but only if, the illegal provision cannot be separated from the other provisions without defeating the purpose of the settlor in creating the trust. . . .

Comment to §65: . . .

e. *Illegal conditions subsequent.* If . . . a trust is created by the terms of which the trustee is directed to pay the income to a man for life, but it is provided that if he should support his infant children the payments should cease, he is entitled to the income whether or not he supports his children.

f. *Illegal conditions precedent.* . . . Where, as is ordinarily the case, the settlor has made no provision as to what should happen if the condition should be held illegal, the beneficiary is entitled to the interest whether or not the event happens, unless it appears from properly admitted evidence that it would probably have been the intention of the settlor that if the condition should be illegal the interest of the beneficiary should fail altogether. . . .

PROBLEM

10-D. *A,* a wealthy client, has come to you to have his will planned and drawn. In the course of your interview he informs you that his daughter, *D,* has married a man, *X,* who is "a no-good bum." *D* and *X* "seem to be holding their marriage together well enough, but it has by

1. Compare the matter of waste, which "a well-ordered society cannot tolerate," in Eyerman v. Mercantile Tr. Co., 524 S.W.2d 210 (Mo. App. 1975), invalidating a testamentary direction that decedent's residence be razed.

no means been an easy life for *D.*" *A* would like to see the marriage come to an end. He wishes to leave half of his property to his son, *S,* and half in trust to pay *D* as much income as she may need as long as her marriage lasts. He wishes to give her all of her share outright only if she divorces *X.* If she does not divorce *X, A* would like the half of his estate that is held in trust for *D* to be distributed to *S* or *S*'s issue on the death of *D. A* wants to know if such a trust is valid. How would you advise him?

Can you establish a trust that will have the desired effect and still be upheld? How might you word the provisions of such a trust? Would it be ethical for you to create such a trust if you think you could do so in a way that would withstand attack? Assume that the cases that follow are decisions of courts in your state.

Would your response differ if Ind. Ann. Code §30-4-2-12 were applicable? It states that the terms of a trust "may not require the trustee to commit a criminal or tortious act or an act which is contrary to public policy" and adds: "A trust with terms which violate . . . this section is invalid unless the prohibited term is separable," in which case only that term is invalid "and the remainder of the trust is valid."

If the originally suggested trust had been created and the provision encouraging divorce were held invalid, what disposition would be made of the property involved?

FINEMAN v. CENTRAL NATIONAL BANK
161 N.E.2d 557 (Ohio Prob. Ct. 1959)

[Action for construction of the will of Saul I. Fineman and for a declaratory judgment. The relevant provisions of the will provide for the creation of a trust for the testator's daughter, Lillian, for her life and then provide for continuation of the trust for the purpose of making payments of $300 per month to testator's son, Roland, for as long as he remains married to his present wife, Ray. The trust is to terminate "at such time as my son, Roland, shall be divorced from his present wife, Ray Fineman, or at such time as his present wife shall be deceased"; and then, after paying $5,000 to a niece, distribution of the balance of the trust estate is to be made to Roland.]

MERRICK, J. . . .

It has been stipulated that there was no divorce action pending between the testator's son and his wife at the time of the making of this will, or at any time thereafter. The estate is substantial and the amount which might pass into the trust might exceed $100,000.

Any effort to interpret or construe the language of this will would necessarily lead to the conclusion that a divorce of the son from his wife would cause a vesting of a large sum of money in and for the taking by the son.

It has long been the established law in the State of Ohio, that a condition in a will by which an inducement is offered to a married person to
obtain a divorce, or to live separate and apart from the other spouse, is
contrary to public policy, and held to be invalid. Page on Wills, Lifetime
Edition, Volume 3, page 812. . . .

Whether such provision in a will is void is to be determined by the circumstances existing at the time of its execution. The primary reason
such a clause is void is that it is against public policy, because it places a
reward, benefit or price upon divorce or domestic separation. Under
some circumstances the surrounding facts might very well warrant a testator in placing such a contingency in his will. By carefully wording the
language, it could be made apparent that the testator was making some
provision or establishing some safeguard against the [possibility] of
divorce. Certainly a man could provide that a certain allowance should
be increased or a payment accelerated in the event that a daughter
should be divorced and lose some means of support; or in the event a
pending divorce case resulted in a final disposition that might be a hand-
icap to the future support or well being of the devisee. The test seems to
be whether the provision in the will provides a premium or reward in the
event of divorce. If it appears from the whole will that it was the purpose
of the testator to provide some support or maintenance for one who
might suffer economically from the divorce, then no divorce has been
encouraged and the clause would be valid. 40 Cyc. 1703.

A case in point is . . . Pickering v. Cleveland Trust Co., etc., 3 Ohio
Law Abs. 243, [where] the court distinguishes between clauses reward-
ing separation or divorce and those affording protection and sustenance
in the event of such an eventuality.

The plain language of the will in the instant case places a premium
upon the marital separation. There being no language which could in
any way change or modify this interpretation, the judgment of this Court
is that the clause in question is void as against public policy. [Therefore]
the remainder shall vest in Roland H. Fineman subject to the life interest
of Lillian Fineman.

[The judgment was later modified by the Court of Appeals to require
that Roland survive Lillian for the remainder to vest in him.]

How should a court treat a condition tending to *discourage* divorce,
such as a forfeiture of rights by any child who obtains a divorce?

During life parents sometimes use their wealth to attempt to influence
their children's lives; or an *outright bequest at death* may favor one child
over another, or even disinherit a child, dependent on certain aspects of
life-style or behavior at the time. Are these matters different in any significant way from the use of trusts for such purposes?

In re ESTATE OF HELLER
39 Wis. 2d 318, 159 N.W.2d 82 (1968)

[Lena Heller's will made no provision for her daughter, Katie Mau, "unless at the time of my death, she is married to and living with her husband, Willard Mau," in which case she "shall be included with my other daughters . . . and share equally with them." Katie divorced Willard before Lena's death.]

WILKIE, J. . . .

The trial court noted this was the first time he had been confronted with a question about a provision in a will "in which a legacy is conditioned on the continuance of a marriage." We find no Wisconsin cases on the validity of such a provision. . . .

The Restatement of the Law on Property surveys the law of testamentary provisions affecting marriage. It points out the following general rules.

(1) A condition rendering a gift contingent upon not marrying anyone is void unless clearly motivated by an intention to provide support until a marriage takes place. This invalidation results from the court's unwillingness to penalize a legatee for his failure to respect the socially undesirable attempt of the testator to use his property as a means of coercing abstention from marriage.

(2) Restraints limited as to person, group or time are valid unless the remaining sphere of permissible marriage is so small that a permitted marriage is not likely to occur. These partial restraints are valid upon the theory that guidance by parents or other donors with respect to a particular marriage is not unreasonable.

(3) Restraints on remarriage may be liberally imposed.

(4) Finally, attempts by testators to break up an already existing marriage, by conditioning a gift on divorce or separation, are invalid. If the dominant motive of the testator, however, is merely to provide support in the event of separation or marriage, the condition is valid.

Thus the Restatement does not deal directly with a situation such as that presented by the instant case. Appellant has not directed the court to any authority that has held a provision such as those before us invalid. Appellant's argument that the provision in Article V in effect discourages divorce, which has been declared to be good public policy (viz., public policy demands an end to intolerable marriages) regarding the marriage of Katie Mau, is not persuasive. The Restatement points out that the existence of statutes which permit divorce or separation of married persons is not an indication of public policy favoring provisions that encourage divorce. Likewise, statutes allowing divorce should not be indicative of a public policy that would attempt to prohibit restraints on the seeking of a divorce.

It is a familiar and well-settled principle of law that a will speaks as of the time of the death of the testator. Therefore, it would not be unreasonable to conclude that a will cannot contravene public policy until it begins to speak. Upon the death of the testatrix, there was nothing Katie Mau could do to increase or diminish the amount she was to receive under the will. Her portion (if any) was fixed absolutely as of the date of the death of the testatrix. It was Katie's status then that determined whether she was a beneficiary.

Katie Mau testified that until the death of her mother she was unaware of the questioned provision in the will. Therefore, irrespective of the true purpose of those provisions, it is difficult to understand how they could have had any restraining effect, one way or another, on Katie's marriage. Public policy regarding restraints on marriage should only be concerned with continuing inducements and not with a provision, as here, which could never truly be a restraint. A will written and executed is merely the expression of an intention to dispose of one's property in a certain way in the future, provided one does not have a change of mind. Only when death ensues, thus making a change of mind impossible, will these expressions of future intention bring rights into existence. When, as here, those rights become absolutely fixed at death, without a continuing inducement to either do or refrain from doing some act, it is difficult to imagine how a restraint in the true sense of the word could ever arise. . . .

Appellants contend that the Heller will attempts to penalize [Katie] for prosecuting a cause of action which a court found to be valid [and is therefore against public policy]. If appellant is correct then almost all conditional bequests would be void as against public policy because many donees are forced to forego the exercise of legal rights as a valid condition to taking under a will. The widow whose gift is conditioned on not remarrying is giving up a legal right in exchange for that gift. Yet, the widow's condition would not ordinarily be considered violative of public policy.

Judgment affirmed.

GEORGIA CODE

19-3-6. Marriage is encouraged by the law. Every effort to restrain or discourage marriage by contract, condition, limitation, or otherwise shall be invalid and void, provided that prohibitions against marriage to a particular person or persons or before a certain reasonable age or other prudential provisions looking only to the interest of the person to be benefited and not in general restraint of marriage will be allowed and held valid.

UNITED STATES NATIONAL BANK v.
SNODGRASS
202 Or. 530, 275 P.2d 860 (1954)

[The trustee brought suit for a declaratory judgment to establish the validity and interpretation of a trust created by the will of C. A. Rinehart, who died in 1932. The terms of the trust provided that certain monthly payments were to be made to the testator's daughter, Merle, who was age 13 at the time of his death, until she reached age 25, then all of the income was to be paid to her until age 32, when the trustee was directed to distribute the trust estate to the daughter

> provided she has proved conclusively to my trustee . . . that she has not embraced, nor become a member of, the Catholic faith nor ever married to a man of such faith. In the event my daughter . . . becomes ineligible to receive the trust fund then I direct the principal of such trust fund to be divided as follows,

specifying certain other relatives who, along with the daughter, are made defendants in this action. It was stipulated that the daughter reached age 32 in 1951, that she had married a member of the Catholic faith, and that at the time she knew of the above provisions of her father's will. The lower court upheld the provisions of the will and decreed the forfeiture of the daughter's interest in the trust estate.]

WARNER, J. . . .

The appellant asserts that the court erred in holding as valid that provision of the will which disinherited her because of her marriage to a member of the Catholic faith before she was 32 years old. She leans heavily upon the proposition that such a provision violates public policy.

Mrs. Snodgrass did not join the Catholic church and therefore the clause restraining membership in that faith is not before us. Her loss, if any, accrues by reason of the restriction on her marriage to a Catholic within the time limitation. If the provision is valid, then the defendants-respondents take the entire corpus of the trust set up in the contested paragraph 7, and testator's daughter takes nothing.

The problem here is one of the validity of testamentary restraints upon marriage. While there is an abundance of law on the subject from other jurisdictions, the question and its solution are one of first impression in this court. . . .

Litigation springing from religious differences, tincturing, as here, every part and parcel of this appeal, tenders to any court problems of an extremely delicate nature. This very delicacy, together with the novelty of the legal questions in this jurisdiction, warrants pausing before proceeding further and reorienting our thinking in terms of the real legal problem which we must resolve. As a first step we rid ourselves of some erroneous definitions and the smug acceptance of conclusions arising from the too-frequent and inept employment of such terms as "religious freedom," "religious intolerance" and "religious bigotry." We also disassociate ourselves from the erstwhile disposition of many persons to treat any opposition to a religious faith as a prima facie manifestation of religious bigotry, requiring legal condemnation.

The testamentary pattern of Mr. Rinehart may offend the sense of fair play of some in what appears as an ungracious and determined effort to bend the will of another to an acceptance of the testator's concept of the superiority of his own viewpoint. . . .

While one may personally and loudly condemn a species of "intolerance" as socially outrageous, a court on the other hand must guard against being judicially intolerant of such an "intolerance," unless the court can say the act of intolerance is in a form not sanctioned by the law. We are mindful that there are many places where a bigot may safely express himself and manifest his intolerance of the viewpoint of others without fear of legal restraint or punishment. With certain limitations, one of those areas with a wide latitude of sufferance is found in the construction of the pattern of one's last will and testament. It is a field wherein neither this court nor any other court will question the correctness of a testator's religious views or prejudices. In re Lesser's Estate, 158 Misc. 895, 287 N.Y.S. 209, 216.

Our exalted religious freedom is buttressed by another freedom of coordinate importance. In condemning what may appear to one as words of offensive religious intolerance, we must not forget that the offending expression may enjoy the protection of another public policy — the freedom of speech. . . .

We therefore have no intention or disposition to disturb the provisions of Mr. Rinehart's will unless it can be demonstrated that they do violence to some legal rule or precept. Two general and cardinal propositions give direction and limitation to our consideration. One is the traditionally great freedom that the law confers on the individual with respect to the disposition of his property, both before and after death. The other is that greater freedom, the freedom of opinion and right to expression in political and religious matters, together with the incidental and corollary right to implement the attainment of the ultimate and favored objectives of the religious teaching and social or political philosophy to which an individual subscribes. We do not intend to imply hereby that the right to devise or bequeath property is in any way dependent upon or related to the constitutional guarantees of freedom of speech. . . .

Although the appellant rests her appeal primarily upon the premise that paragraph 7 of the will violates public policy, she brings to us no precise statute or judicial pronouncement in support of this contention; but before examining and demonstrating that the authorities cited by appellant are inapplicable, we think it is proper to observe here that it has long been a firmly-established policy in Oregon to give great latitude to a testator in the final disposition of his estate, notwithstanding that the right to make a testamentary disposition is not an inherent, natural or constitutional right but is purely a creation of statute and within legislative control. . . . No one has had the temerity to suggest that Mr. Rinehart in his lifetime could not have accomplished the equivalent of what he sought to accomplish by his will. It was within his power, with or without assigning any reason therefor, to have completely disinherited his daughter and left her in a state of impecunious circumstances. He could have gone even further and given all his fortune to some institution or persons with directions to propagandize his views adverse to any certain religion or creed for which he harbored antipathies. . . .

To sustain the contention that the contested provision of the will is against the public policy of the United States, the appellant depends upon the First and Fourteenth Amendments to the United States Constitution: 42 U.S.C.A. §§1981-83, relating to civil rights . . . ; and Shelley v. Kraemer, 334 U.S. 1.

The First Amendment prohibits Congress from making any law respecting the establishment of a religion. Everson v. Board of Education, 330 U.S. 1, 15. That amendment is a limitation upon the power of Congress. It has no effect upon the transactions of individual citizens and has been so interpreted. McIntire v. Wm. Penn Broadcasting Co. of Philadelphia, 3 Cir., 151 F.2d 597, 601, *certiorari denied*, 327 U.S. 779; In re Kempf's Will, 252 App. Div. 28, 297 N.Y.S. 307, 312, *affirmed*, 278 N.Y. 613, 16 N.E.2d 123. Neither does the Fourteenth Amendment relate to individual conduct. The strictures there found circumscribe state action in the particulars mentioned and in no way bear on a transaction of the character now before us. In re Civil Rights Cases, 1883, 109 U.S. 3. . . . Shelley v. Kraemer, supra, is authority only for the proposition that the enforcement by state courts of a covenant in a deed restricting the use and occupancy of real property to persons of the Caucasian race falls within the purview of the Fourteenth Amendment as a violation of the equal protection clause, but, said the court, "That Amendment [Fourteenth] erects no shield against merely private conduct, however discriminatory or wrongful." 334 U.S. 1.

It is not clear to us from appellant's argument whether she reads the offending provision of the will as an invasion of her constitutional right or religious freedom or views it as an unconstitutional act of discrimination; but whether one or the other, we are content that it does no violence to public policy resting upon different grounds from those here urged by appellant.

We are not unmindful that even though no positive law can be found in Oregon limiting a testator as appellant would have us do here, we should, nevertheless, look into the decisions of the courts of other states to discover, if we can, the prevailing rule applied elsewhere when a testator attempts to limit or restrain the marriage of a beneficiary in the manner that the late C. A. Rinehart attempted to do.

The general rule seems to be well settled that conditions and limitations in partial restraint of marriage will be upheld if they do not unreasonably restrict the freedom of the beneficiary's choice. In 35 Am. Jur. 357-358, Marriage, §256, we find:

> . . . where the restraint is not general but is merely partial or temporary, or otherwise limited in effect, then the condition may or may not be void, according to whether it is considered reasonable or otherwise, and does not operate merely in terrorem. . . .
>
> Among the restrictions which have been held reasonable are: Conditions to marry or not to marry . . . a person of a particular . . . religion. . . .

Of the same tenor is 1 Restatement, Trusts, 194, §62(g), reading so far as pertinent:

> . . . such a provision is not invalid if it does not impose an undue restraint on marriage. Thus, a provision divesting the interest of the beneficiary if he or she should marry . . . a person of a particular religious faith or one of a different faith from that of the beneficiary, is not ordinarily invalid. . . .

We turn to an examination of the controverted provision and note that the condition is not one of complete restraint, in which character it might well be abhorrent to the law. It is merely partial and temporary and, as we shall show later, is not in terrorem. Mr. Rinehart's daughter is not thereby restrained from ever marrying a Catholic. This inhibition as a condition to taking under the will at the age of 32 lasts only 11 years, that is, from the legal marriageable age without parental consent (in this state, 21 years). After the age of 32 she is free to marry a Catholic or become a Catholic if she so pleases and have her estate, too. Moreover, the condition imposed does not restrict the beneficiary from enjoying marital status either before or after attaining the age of 32. Here, unfortunately, appellant would eat her cake and have it too. . . . So far as we are able to ascertain, only two states — Pennsylvania and Virginia — have invalidated testamentary provisions committing the beneficiary to adhere to the doctrines of a particular religion. This departure from the majority rule is reflected by Drace v. Klinedinst, 1922, 275 Pa. 266, 118 A. 907, 25 A.L.R. 1520; and Maddox v. Maddox's Admr., 1854, 11 Grat., Va., 804. . . . In the *Maddox* case the condition was that the testator's daughter should marry a member of the Society of Friends. There were only five or six marriageable males of that faith within the circle of her acquaintances, and under the circumstances peculiar to that case the court held that the condition was an unreasonable restraint on marriage.

The last contention of Mrs. Snodgrass requiring consideration is that the offending provision is in terrorem and therefore invalid. . . .

Generally, conditions in restraint of marriage are said to be in terrorem and therefore invalid when the subject of the gift is personal property and *there is no gift over;* but such a condition is not void as being in terrorem when there is a gift over. It is the absence of a gift over which supplies the quality of a coercive threat necessary to bring the condition under the in terrorem rule. 35 Am. Jur. 367, Marriage, §266. . . .

Affirmed. Neither party will recover costs.

BRAND, J., dissents.

If the validity of a restraint on marriage depends on the "reasonableness of its breadth and duration," how should a court treat provisions conditioned on the beneficiary's marrying someone "of Greek blood and descent and of Orthodox religion"? Kefflalas Estate, 426 Pa. 432, 233 A.2d 248 (1967), upheld the condition; the opinion also asserted that the probable effect, not subjective motivation, should determine the validity of a condition.

It is well accepted generally that a provision that tends to discourage marriage is valid as applied to the remarriage of a transferor's surviving spouse. Thus, it is common, and valid, for a testator's will to create a trust for a widow or widower, terminable in favor of the children if the spouse should remarry.

11

Creation of Trusts

Most present-day trusts are testamentary trusts created by will. Inter vivos or living trusts are also quite common, usually being created by a transfer from the settlor during lifetime to another person or corporation as trustee. Sometimes the settlor may create a trust by procuring a transfer from a third party to the trustee or by the exercise of a power of appointment. In each of these cases it can be seen that the trust comes about as the result of some kind of a *transfer,* whether by will, deed, or some other method by which a transfer of the property can be effectuated.

All trusts are not created by transfer, at least not in the normal sense of that word. A trust of specific property can be created by a present declaration of trust by the owner of that property. Thus, for example, "one may create a trust in securities standing on one's name by a simple declaration to that effect, without the necessity of any further act of transfer or delivery." Bourgeois v. Hurley, 392 N.E.2d 1061, 1065 (Mass. App. 1980). To one who already owns the property, an act of transfer would often seem unnecessary or even "unnatural" and is apparently viewed as an inappropriate requirement for such cases. The owner-settlor's manifestation of *present* intention to create a trust therefore suffices, and the normal transfer requirement is excused. Or, we might say, there *is* a "transfer" of the property, from the owner as an *individual* to the owner as *trustee* (or we might see it as a transfer of *equitable* title from the settlor to the beneficiaries), with simply the requirement of "delivery" being excused as an unwarranted formality under the circumstances. Regardless of how creation of a trust by declaration is conceptualized, the declaration normally must satisfy any formal requirements for the transfer of an interest in the particular property; thus, for example, if land is involved the local statute of frauds requirement of a writing would apply to the declaration; but such a requirement would typically not apply to a declaration creating a trust of personal property. The law does, however, insist strictly on a manifestation of present intent, so that an owner's gratuitous promise or expression of future intention will not suffice.

350

Just as valid and enforceable nontrust rights can be created by contract, enforceable rights may be created in intended trust beneficiaries by a person's *binding* promise to establish a trust, either by transfer or declaration. Here, the requirements of contract law must be met. Again, however, the trust concepts may not be clear. We might say that the promissory right is a property interest (a chose in action) presently held in trust; or we might view the situation as one in which there is no trust now but merely an enforceable obligation of the promissor to make a transfer in the future, with the trust coming into being at that later time. Analogous uncertainties of concept arise in connection with the creation of life insurance trusts, especially if (as usual) the policies are not actually assigned to the trustee.

Among the major problems relating to the creation of inter vivos trusts by transfer are questions concerning the effectiveness of the alleged transfer. These are problems of compliance with the formalities required for impressing the essential elements of the trust on the transferred property and problems of whether the creation of a given trust is subject to the formal requirements and substantive restrictions governing inter vivos transfer or to those applicable to testamentary dispositions.

Because an effective transfer is required to create a trust other than by declaration or contract, a preliminary requirement is that the settlor have capacity to make an effective transfer. The capacity to create a trust is the same as the capacity to transfer the property involved free of trust. For example, a person who can make a valid will can create a testamentary trust. If a person can transfer property by way of gift, that person can create a voluntary living trust. The test of capacity to transfer property inter vivos is also the test of a person's capacity to create a trust by declaration; and one who has capacity to contract can create a trust of a promise if it otherwise satisfies the requirements of an enforceable promise under applicable law.

A. *Trusts Created by Will*

When a testator intends to transfer property by will to another person or to a corporation to be held in trust, there must be compliance with the applicable wills act. The intended express trust fails if the trust intent and the essential terms of the trust are not manifested by means satisfying the statutory requirements. This is so even though the property is effectively transferred by a valid will. Two questions basically are presented: what constitutes sufficient compliance with the requirements of the wills acts, and what happens when an intended trust fails to satisfy these requirements?

MOSS v. AXFORD
246 Mich. 288, 224 N.W. 425 (1929)

[The will of Caroline Girard left the residue of her estate to Henry Axford, her executor, "to pay the same to the person who has given me the best care in my declining years and who in his opinion is the most worthy of my said property. I make him the sole judge. . . . " Mrs. Girard's heirs contended that the intended trust was invalid because no beneficiary was designated in the will. The testimony clearly established that Axford's selection of defendant Mary Piers was proper if the intended bequest was valid.]

FEAD, J. . . .

We do not read the will as conferring on Mr. Axford unrestrained discretion or right of personal opinion in the designation of a beneficiary. The unmistakable intention of the testatrix, apparent upon the face of the will, was that the residue of her estate should go to the person who should have given her the best care in her declining years. This was to be the basis of selection of the beneficiary as "most worthy" of her property. The duty of designation conferred upon Mr. Axford was a quasi judicial power or discretion to pass upon conflicting claims. It arose out of her confidence in him and his interest in her welfare, but was confined to ascertaining and naming the person who had given testatrix the best care.

The purpose of Mrs. Girard was lawful and should be carried out, "unless there is such an uncertainty that the law is fairly baffled." Tuxbury v. French, 41 Mich. 7, 1 N.W. 904. It is not necessary that a beneficiary be designated by name, or by a description which makes identification automatic. . . . Nor that the testator have in mind the particular individual upon whom his bounty may fall. . . . It is enough if the testator used language which is sufficiently clear to enable the court by extrinsic evidence to identify the beneficiary. . . .

The ascertainment of testatrix's beneficiary by Mr. Axford was an imperative duty. The test and method were prescribed by the will. He was bound to exercise good faith in the determination, and the honesty of his decision would be reviewable in equity. . . . Upon his failure or inability to perform the duty, the court could from extraneous evidence ascertain and declare the beneficiary to fully carry out the intention of the testatrix. We think the clause a valid devise in trust, and that the designation of Mrs. Piers by Mr. Axford constituted her the residuary legatee. . . .

PROBLEM

11-A.   A's will provided for certain legacies and left "the residue of my estate to my executor to pay the sums in her hands in her sole discretion to the persons I have previously indicated to her. I nominate *B* as my executor." *B,* who is also the attorney who drew the will, testified that, before calling in two witnesses and having the will executed, she had received oral instructions from *A* relating to the disposition of the residue. What result? Should the court allow *B* to testify to the nature of her instructions? See In re Liginger's Estate, 14 Wis. 2d 577, 111 N.W.2d 407 (1961). If the heirs of *A* succeed in obtaining the residuary property by way of resulting trust, is *B* liable to the intended beneficiaries for her handling of this matter? See Ogle v. Fuitan, 112 Ill. App. 3d 1048, 445 N.E.2d 1344 (1983); Committee on Professional Ethics v. Behnke, 276 N.W.2d 838 (Iowa 1979), *appeal dismissed,* 444 U.S. 805 (1979); Johnston, An Ethical Analysis of Common Estate Planning Practices, 45 Ohio St. L.J. 57 (1984). Cf. Lucas v. Hamm, 56 Cal. 2d 583, 364 P.2d 685, 15 Cal. Rptr. 821 (1961). Also see American Bar Association Code of Professional Responsibility, EC 5-5, 5-6; American Bar Association Model Rules of Professional Conduct, Rule 1.8(c).

In Wagner v. Clauson, 399 Ill. 403, 78 N.E.2d 203 (1948), the testatrix left the residue of her estate "to Katherine Clauson, as trustee, for the purpose of converting into cash and making distribution thereof in accordance with a memorandum of instructions prepared by me and delivered to her . . . so that only Katherine Clauson and the distributee shall know of its disposition." At the death of the testatrix a sealed envelope and the will were found together in a safe-deposit box. The envelope contained an unattested letter written by the testatrix and bearing a date several days later than the date the will was executed. Evidence disclosed that Clauson had placed both the will and the envelope in the safe-deposit box at the request of the testatrix but knew nothing of the contents of the envelope until after probate of the will. The intended trust was held invalid because the requirements for incorporation by reference were not met. (See Chapter 5.) The court held that, the intended express trust failing, there was a resulting trust for the heirs of the testatrix because it was apparent from the will that Clauson was not to take beneficially but as trustee.

How could the testatrix in Wagner v. Clauson have accomplished the purpose of secrecy expressed in her will? Would the result have been different if Clauson had promised to hold the property for the intended purpose?

Cases are abundant in which a bequest or devise, absolute on its face, is made to someone who has either expressly or impliedly agreed to administer the property for a specific purpose or to transfer it inter vivos or by will to another person. This is the so-called secret trust. Frequently the promise of the legatee or devisee is oral. The disposition may even be induced by the acquiescence implied from the legatee's silence when informed of the intended purpose of the bequest. What is the result of such cases? A few courts have taken the position that, unless actual fraud, duress, undue influence, or confidential relationship is shown, the recipient of an absolute bequest or devise takes the property free of obligation. The clear weight of authority, however, is represented by the statement in Olsen v. First National Bank, 76 S.D. 605, 611, 83 N.W.2d 842, 846 (1957):

> The general proposition is well settled that where a testator devises his property in reliance upon an agreement or understanding with a devisee or legatee that the latter hold it in trust, the devisee or legatee holds the property upon a constructive trust for the person for whom he agreed to hold it. Restatement, Trusts, §55; see also Annotations in 66 A.L.R. 156 and 155 A.L.R. 106. The principle rests on the basis that though the acquiring of the property was not wrongful the testator having relied on the agreements and made a disposition of his property accordingly the devisee or legatee would be unjustly enriched if he were permitted to retain the property. It is immaterial whether the agreement was made at the time of or after execution of the will. An agreement which induces the testator to refrain from revoking his will is as effective as an agreement which induced him to make a will. See comments, Restatement, Trusts, §55 and Restatement, Restitution, §186. The trust in other words arises not from the will, but from operation of equities. The will takes effect as written and proved, but to prevent injustice the court imposes a constructive trust to compel the devisee or legatee to apply the property obtained in accordance with his promise and good conscience.

See generally G. Bogert, Trusts and Trustees §§498-501 (3d ed. 1960); IA W. Fratcher, Scott on Trusts §§55.1-55.5 (4th ed. 1987); Levine and Holton, Enforcement of Secret and Semi-Secret Trusts, 5 Probate L.J. 7 (1985). Rarely is the rationale of this rule thoroughly discussed in the cases. Most courts consider the problem one of the wills acts, but some opinions treat the problem as one of contract law involving the statute of frauds. Which is it, or is it both? Should it matter whether the subject matter is land? Why, if the legatee is not to be unjustly enriched, is it not preferable to restore the property to the testator's estate? Compare the secret trust situation with the following often cited case involving what might be called a "semi-secret trust."

OLLIFFE v. WELLS
130 Mass. 221 (1881)

[Bill in equity by the heirs of Ellen Donovan, whose duly probated will left the residue of her estate "to the Rev. Eleazer M.P. Wells . . . to distribute the same in such manner as in his discretion shall appear best to carry out the wishes which I have expressed to him or may express to him." The bill sought distribution of the residue to the heirs, alleging that the bequest to Wells had failed. The defendant Wells, who had been appointed executor, answered, and all parties stipulated, that the testatrix had, before and after executing her will, expressed her intention and directed that Wells dispose of the residue for charitable purposes benefiting the aged, poor, and infirm. The answer also stated that Wells had agreed and desired to carry out these directions, but he died while the case was pending.]

GRAY, C.J.

Upon the face of this will the residuary bequest to the defendant gives him no beneficial interest. It expressly requires him to distribute all the property bequeathed to him, giving him no discretion upon the question whether he shall or shall not distribute it, or shall or shall not carry out the intentions of the testatrix, but allowing him a discretionary authority as to the manner only in which the property shall be distributed pursuant to her intentions. The will declares a trust too indefinite to be carried out, and the next of kin of the testatrix must take by way of resulting trust, unless the facts agreed show such a trust for the benefit of others as the court can execute. Nichols v. Allen, [130 Mass.] 211. . . .

It has been held in England and in other States, although the question has never arisen in this Commonwealth, that, if a person procures an absolute devise or bequest to himself by orally promising the testator that he will convey the property to or hold it for the benefit of third persons, and afterward refuses to perform his promise, a trust arises out of the confidence reposed in him by the testator and of his own fraud, which a court of equity, upon clear and satisfactory proof of the facts, will enforce against him at the suit of such third persons.

Upon like grounds, it has been held in England that, if a testator devises or bequeaths property to his executors upon trusts not defined in the will, but which, as he states in the will, he has communicated to them before its execution, such trusts, if for lawful purposes, may be proved by the admission of the executors, or by oral evidence, and enforced against them [and also] against the heirs or next of kin of the testator. . . . But these cases appear to us to have overlooked or disregarded a fundamental distinction.

Where a trust not declared in the will is established by a court of chancery against the devisee, it is by reason of the obligation resting upon the conscience of the devisee, and not as a valid testamentary disposition by the deceased. . . . Where the bequest is outright upon its face, the setting up of a trust, while it diminishes the right of the devisee, does not impair any right of the heirs or next of kin, in any aspect of the case; for if the trust were not set up, the whole property would go to the devisee by force of the devise; if the trust set up is a lawful one, it enures to the benefit of the cestuis que trust; and if the trust set up is unlawful, the heirs or next of kin take by way of resulting trust. . . .

Where the bequest is declared upon its face to be upon such trusts as the testator has otherwise signified to the devisee, it is equally clear that the devisee takes no beneficial interest; and, as between him and the beneficiaries intended, there is as much ground for establishing the trust as if the bequest to him were absolute on its face. But as between the devisee and the heirs or next of kin, the case stands differently. They are not excluded by the will itself. The will upon its face showing that the devisee takes the legal title only and not the beneficial interest, and the trust not being sufficiently defined by the will to take effect, the equitable interest goes, by way of resulting trust, to the heirs or next of kin, as property of the deceased, not disposed of by his will. . . . They cannot be deprived of that equitable interest, which accrues to them directly from the deceased, by any conduct of the devisee; nor by any intention of the deceased, unless signified in those forms which the law makes essential to every testamentary disposition. A trust not sufficiently declared on the face of the will cannot therefore be set up by extrinsic evidence to defeat the rights of the heirs at law or next of kin. . . .

Decree for the plaintiffs.

Where secret trusts are given effect by constructive trust, the trust is generally not considered testamentary, and it comes about through intervention of equity, not via probate. The fact that secret trusts generally escape the purely formal restrictions applicable to trusts created by will, however, does not mean that these trusts can also be used to escape substantive restrictions on testamentary freedom, such as limitations on charitable giving. See IA W. Fratcher, Scott on Trusts §55.6 (4th ed. 1987).

B.   Inter Vivos Trusts

1.   The Requirement of a Present Transfer or Declaration

Except in the case of a present declaration of trust or a binding promise made to a person as trustee, the creation of a trust requires a transfer. The trust and the equitable interests thereunder are created by a transfer, just as the rights of donees, legatees, and devisees are the result of a transfer either by inter vivos gift or by will. The problems of transfer in the creation of trusts are the same as in the transfers free of trust.

Essentially, the *transfer* requirement in testamentary trusts poses no difficulties other than those that relate to the validity of the will itself. If the will is valid, the required transfer will take place when the settlor dies.

The typical living trust situation, in which *A* transfers to *B* in trust for the designated beneficiaries, requires a *present transfer*. Clearly a mere promise by *A* to create a trust does not give rise to a trust unless the promise is enforceable. On the other hand, if a completed transfer in trust has been made in a manner sufficient to transfer like property free of trust, the result is enforceable without further consideration. The interests are created by gift in such cases. The typical inter vivos trust is the product of a donative transfer for the benefit of the transferor or family members. Consequently, if such a trust is to be established, a completed transfer must be shown. Present doctrine in this area is discussed and criticized in Love, Imperfect Gifts as Declarations of Trust: An Unapologetic Anomaly, 67 Ky. L. Rev. 309 (1979).

A declaration of trust is also enforceable even though gratuitous. Again, however, the declaration must be intended to be presently effective. It cannot be a mere unenforceable promise to hold in trust.

PROBLEM

11-B. *A* executed a deed of Blackacre to *T* as trustee for *B* for life, remainder to *R*. Before the deed was delivered, *T* died. *A* then talked to *X* about becoming trustee and gave *X* a photocopy of the deed that had been intended for *T*. *X* later wrote *A* that she would act as trustee. *A* wrote back immediately stating that he was having the deed redrawn with the same terms; *A* enclosed his personal promissory note for $25,000 payable on demand to *X* or order, stating in the letter that he also wanted the trust to start out with some cash. Nothing further was done by either *A* or *X* until *A*'s death three weeks later. Copies of this correspondence, along with a deed to *X* in terms identical to the deed to *T*, are found in a folder in *A*'s desk. On the front of the folder is written "My trust for *B* and *R*." Is there a trust? Would a trust be created if the deed to *X* had been executed and mailed by *A* but received by *X* after *A*'s death? In this latter situation, would it matter if *X* promptly renounced and declined to act as trustee?

Ex parte PYE
18 Ves. Jr. 140 (Ch. 1811)

[Petitioner Pye was administrator d.b.n. of the estate of the testator, William Mowbray, who had by letter authorized Christopher Dubost in Paris to purchase in France an annuity for the benefit of testator's mistress, Marie. This Dubost did, but because Marie was married and deranged, the annuity was purchased in the testator's name; therefore, the testator sent Dubost a power of attorney authorizing him to transfer the annuity to Marie. The testator died in June 1809, but Dubost did not learn of the death until November 1809 and in the meantime exercised the power of attorney to transfer the annuity to Marie. Pursuant to procedures for ascertaining foreign law, a Master was appointed, and he reported, inter alia, that by French law, the exercise of a power of attorney in ignorance of the principal's death is valid.]

The first petition prayed that so much of the Report as certifies the French annuity to be no part of the testator's personal estate may be set aside; and that it may be declared, that the annuity is part of his personal estate. . . . [The following is argued] in support of the first Petition. The French annuity being purchased in the testator's name, and no third person interposed as a trustee, the interest could not be transferred from him without certain acts, which were not done at the time of his death. It was therefore competent to him during his life to change his purpose, and to make some other provision for this lady by funds in this country; conceiving perhaps, that she might return here. . . .

The other question involves . . . whether the power of attorney amounts here to a declaration of trust? It is clear that this Court will not assist a volunteer yet, if the act is completed, though voluntary, the Court will act upon it. It has been decided, that upon an agreement to transfer stock this Court will not interpose; but if the party had declared himself to be the trustee of that stock, it becomes the property of the cestui que trust without more; and the Court will act upon it. (18 Ves. 99.)

THE LORD CHANCELLOR [ELDON]. These petitions call for the decision of points of more importance and difficulty that I should wish to decide in this way, if the case was not pressed upon the Court. With regard to the French annuity, the Master has stated his opinion as to the French law perhaps without sufficient authority, or sufficient inquiry into the effect of it, as applicable to the precise circumstances of this case; but it is not necessary to pursue that; as upon the documents before me it does appear, that, though in one sense this may be represented as the testator's personal estate, yet he has committed to writing what seems to me a sufficient declaration, that he held this part of the estate in trust for the annuitant.

[First petition dismissed.]

FARMERS' LOAN & TRUST CO. v. WINTHROP
238 N.Y. 477, 144 N.E. 686 (1924)

CARDOZO, J.

On February 3, 1920, Helen C. Bostwick executed her deed of trust to the Farmers' Loan and Trust Company as trustee. It is described as the 1920 deed, to distinguish it from an earlier one, made in 1918, which is the subject of another action. By the later of the two deeds she gave to her trustee $5,000, "the said sum, and all other property hereafter delivered to said trustee as hereinafter provided," to be held upon the trusts and limitations therein set forth. The income was to be paid to her own use during life, and the principal on her death was to be divided into two parts — one for the benefit of the children of a deceased son, Albert; and the other for the benefit of a daughter, Fannie, and the children of said daughter. The donor reserved "the right, at any time and from time to time during the continuance of the trusts, . . . to deliver to said trustee additional property to be held by it" thereunder. She reserved also a power of revocation.

At the date of the execution of this deed, a proceeding was pending in the Surrogate's Court for the settlement of the accounts of the United States Trust Company as trustee of a trust under the will of Jabez A. Bostwick. The effect of the decree, when entered, would be to transfer to Mrs. Bostwick money, shares of stock, and other property of the value of upwards of $2,300,000. The plan was that this property, when ready to be transferred, should be delivered to the trustee, and held subject to the trust. On February 3, 1920, simultaneously with the execution of the trust deed, three other documents, intended to effectuate this plan, were signed by the donor. One is a power of attorney whereby she authorized the Farmers' Loan & Trust Company as her attorney "to collect and receive any and all cash, shares of stock and other property" to which she might "be entitled under any decree or order made or entered" in the proceeding above mentioned. A second is a power of attorney authorizing the Farmers' Loan & Trust Company to transfer and sell any and all shares of stock then or thereafter standing in her name. A third is a letter to the Farmers' Loan & Trust Company, in which she states that she hands to the company the powers of attorney just described, and in which she gives instructions in respect of the action to be taken thereunder:

> My desire is and I hereby authorize you to receive from the United States Trust Company of New York all securities and property coming to me under the decree or order on the settlement of its account and to transfer such securities and property to yourself as trustee under agreement of trust bearing even date herewith executed by me to you.

The decree in the accounting proceeding [in Jabez Bostwick's estate] was entered March 16, 1920. It established the right of Helen C. Bostwick to the payment or transfer of shares of stock and other property of the market value (then or shortly thereafter) of $2,327,353.70. On April 27, 1920, a representative of the Farmers' Loan & Trust Company presented the power of attorney to the United States Trust Company and stated that he was authorized to receive such securities as were ready for delivery. Shares of stock having a market value of $856,880 were handed to him then and there. No question is made that these became subject to the provisions of the deed of trust. The controversy arises in respect of the rest of the securities, $1,470,473.70 in value, which were retained in the custody of the United States Trust Company, apparently for the reason that they were not yet ready for delivery. During the night of April

27, 1920, Helen C. Bostwick died. She left a will, appointing the Farmers' Loan & Trust Company executor, and disposing of an estate of the
value of over $20,000,000. The securities retained as we have seen, in
the custody of the United States Trust Company, were delivered on or
about July 13, 1920, to the executor under the will. Conflicting claims
of ownership are made by the legatees under the will and the remaindermen under the deed.

We think with the majority of the Appellate Division, that the gift
remained inchoate at the death of the donor. There is no occasion to
deny that in the setting of other circumstances a power of attorney,
authorizing a donee to reduce to possession the subject of a gift, may be
significant as evidence of a symbolical delivery. We assume, without
deciding, that such effect will be allowed if, apart from the power, there
is established an intention that the title of the donor shall be presently
divested and presently transferred. The assumption ignores difficulties
not to be underestimated . . . , but we pass them over for the purpose of
the argument, and treat them as surmounted. Even so, the basic obstacle
remains that there is here no expression of a purpose to effectuate a
present gift. The power of attorney, standing by itself, results, as all concede, in the creation of a revocable agency.

If some more was intended, if what was meant was a gift that was to be
operative at once, the expression of the meaning will have to be found
elsewhere, in the deed of trust or in the letter. Neither in the one, however, nor in the other, can such a purpose be discerned. Deed and letter
alike are framed on the assumption that the gift is executory and future,
and this though the addition of a few words would have established it
beyond cavil as executed and present. In the deed there is a present
transfer of $5,000 and no more. This wrought, there is merely the res-
ervation of a privilege to augment to the subject-matter of the trust by
deliveries thereafter. The absence of words of present assignment is
emphasized when we consider with what simplicity an assignment could
have been stated. All that was needed was to expand the description by
a phrase:

> The right, title, and interest of the grantor in the securities and other
> property due or to become due from the United States Trust Company as
> trustee under the will.

The deed and the other documents, we must remember, were not separated in time. They were parts of a single plan, and were executed
together. In these circumstances, a present transfer, if intended, would
naturally have found its place in the description of the deed itself. If
omitted for some reason there, the least we should expect would be to
find it in the letter. Again words of present transfer are conspicuously
absent. What we have instead is a request, or at best a mandate, incompetent without more to divest title, or transfer it, serving no other pur-

pose than a memorandum of instructions from principal to agent as a guide to future action. Deed and documents were prepared by counsel learned in the law. With industrious iteration, they rejected the familiar formulas that would have given unmistakable expression to the transfer of a present title. With like iteration, they chose the words and methods appropriate to a gift that was conceived of as executory and future. We must take the transfer as they made it. The very facility with which they could have made it something else is a warning that we are not at liberty, under the guise of construction, to make it other than it is. Matter of Van Alstyne, 207 N.Y. 298, 309, 310, 100 N.E. 802. They were willing to leave open what they might readily have closed. Death overtook the signer before the gap was filled.

Viewed thus as a gift, the transaction was inchoate. An intention may be assumed, and indeed is not disputed, that what was incomplete at the moment should be completed in the future. The difficulty is that the intention was never carried out. Mrs. Bostwick remained free (apart from any power of revocation reserved in the deed of trust) to revoke the executory mandate, and keep the property as her own. Very likely different forms and instrumentalities would have been utilized, if she or her counsel had supposed that death was to come so swiftly. We might say as much if she had left in her desk a letter or memorandum expressing her resolutions for the morrow. With appropriate forms and instrumentalities available, she chose what the course of events has proved to be the wrong one. The court is without power to substitute another.

The transaction, failing as a gift, because inchoate or incomplete, is not to be sustained as the declaration of a trust. The donor had no intention of becoming a trustee herself. The donee never got title, and so could not hold it for another.

There was no equitable assignment. Equity does not enforce a voluntary promise to make a gift thereafter. . . .

WITTMEIER v. HEILIGENSTEIN
308 Ill. 434, 139 N.E. 871 (1923)

Carter, J.

Certain issues in this case were decided in Heiligenstein v. Schlotterbeck, 300 Ill. 206, 133 N.E. 188. The issue here relates to rights claimed to arise under an invalid deed executed by Josephine Wittmeier to the St. Clare's Roman Catholic Church of Altamont seeking to convey to that church a 60-acre farm and part of two lots in Altamont. The deed was for the consideration of $1, and contained a provision that the church —

> shall pay to Charles Wittmeier the sum of $50 per month, beginning one
> month after my death, for and during his life, and shall pay the doctor's

and hospital bill, if any, and upon his death provide him with a Christian burial and pay his funeral expenses and inter his body on the lot owned by me in the cemetery at Altamont, Illinois.

Wittmeier was married to Josephine in 1880, but they separated in 1895, and she subsequently obtained a divorce.

We have already held in Heiligenstein v. Schlotterbeck, supra, that the deed made to the St. Clare's Roman Catholic Church of Altamont is void because an unincorporated religious society is incapable, in law, of taking by deed. . . .

The single issue here involved is whether the deed to the St. Clare's Church, void for want of a lawful grantee, can have the effect of impressing a trust upon the property in favor of Charles Wittmeier. Although void as a deed, does the instrument create a valid trust? Had the church been competent to take the property, words were used adequate to establish his rights. Does the incapacity of the church to take the property destroy the rights sought to be created in favor of Wittmeier? It is held by the standard works on trusts that no particular form of words to create a trust need be used in the instrument; that the word "trust" need not be used. It is a rule of equitable construction that there is no magic in particular words. Any expression which shows unequivocally the intention to create a trust will have that effect. . . .

The inability of the trustee to take will not invalidate a deed, where the settlor and the cestui que trust are both competent, and the property is of such a nature that it can be legally placed in trust.

Clearly, Josephine Wittmeier did everything necessary under the law to create a trust in favor of Charles Wittmeier except to choose a competent grantee. The deed was executed by the grantor with the intention to part with the title, subject to provision made for Charles. There were words sufficient to accomplish her purpose. There was a beneficiary capable of taking but no lawful grantee. The void deed did not transfer title to the property from Josephine, and title remained in her, notwithstanding the deed, from the date of its execution, August 21, 1919, until the date of her death, August 25, 1919. If the void deed impresses a trust upon the property in the hands of her heirs, it must have had the effect to impress a trust from the date of its execution. It is true as often said, that equity does not allow a trust to fail for want of a lawful grantee; and this statement applies, even though the grantor fails in one of her purposes — that of devoting the property to religious uses.

Somewhat related to the issue here involved was that in Childs v. Waite, 102 Me. 451, 67 A. 311, which involved a will leaving certain property to a school district for the purpose of building and supporting a church. The school district had no legal power to act, and it was held not to succeed to the title of the trust fund; but the court ordered the appointment of a trustee. In that case, however, the property was to be devoted to a single purpose, and the preservation of the trust completely carried out that purpose. While this is not exactly the situation here, the principle involved in that case is identical with the one involved here. . . .

In the present case the purpose of the grantor is clearly manifested and the trust in favor of Charles Wittmeier clearly created. The trust is fully and finally declared in the instrument creating it. With a competent grantee of the deed, no further act was necessary to give it effect. Massey v. Huntington, 118 Ill. 80, 7 N.E. 269. Viewing the trust as we think it should be properly held here, we do not discuss the issue of the consideration of the trust. The grantor intended the deed to establish a trust in favor of Wittmeier. Although the deed did not, in fact, transfer title from her, we think it sufficient to impress the trust upon the property in the hands of the grantor and of the heirs to whom it descended. We are of the opinion that the incapacity of the church to take the property does not defeat the purpose of the grantor, and that the heirs take the property impressed with a trust in favor of Wittmeier. The fact that the grantor had two purposes in mind, one of which must fail, is no reason why the other should fail, when it is expressed with sufficient definiteness and can be legally carried out.

It is suggested it would be possible to take the view that Josephine Wittmeier, while making her purpose clear, did not make it effective, because of the incompetent grantee, and that therefore the property descends to her heirs, free from all obligations sought to be impressed upon it in favor of Charles Wittmeier, as in Meyer v. Holle, 83 Tex. 623, 19 S.W. 154; but such a conclusion, in our judgment, by weight of authority, is not required, and would unreasonably and unnecessarily defeat the purpose of the grantor. . . .

Reversed and remanded.

HEBREW UNIVERSITY ASSOCIATION v. NYE
148 Conn. 223, 169 A.2d 641 (1961)

[Plaintiff, a university in Israel, obtained a judgment declaring it the rightful owner of the Library of Abraham Yahuda, a distinguished Hebrew scholar who died in 1951. The collection belonged to his widow, Ethel, until the time of her death in 1955, unless her actions before then transferred ownership to plaintiff. The executors of her will are defendants in this action, but the real controversy is between plaintiff and other charities to which Ethel left the bulk of her estate. In 1953 Ethel went to Israel; at a luncheon attended by university officials and the president of Israel, she described the library and announced its gift to plaintiff. The next day she approved and signed a newspaper release announcing the gift. Thereafter she stated orally and in letters to various persons that she "had given" the library to plaintiff; on that ground, she refused offers to purchase the collection; and she began the task of cataloging the material and arranging for its crating and shipment to Israel. These activities continued until about the time of her death, but without completion or shipment. The trial court found that Ethel had made a declaration of trust by "indicating and making public 'her intention to create such a trust.'"]

KING, A.J. . . .

We construe [the court's] language [to be] a determination that . . . Ethel orally constituted herself a trustee of the library for future delivery to the plaintiff. The difficulty with the trust theory . . . is that . . . Ethel [n]ever regarded herself as trustee of any trust whatsoever, or as having assumed any enforceable duties with respect to the property. The facts . . . indicate that Ethel intended to make, and perhaps attempted to make, not a mere promise to give, but an executed, present, legal gift inter vivos of the library to the plaintiff without any delivery whatsoever.

. . . A gift which is imperfect for lack of a delivery will not be turned into a declaration of trust for no better reason than that it is imperfect for lack of a delivery. Courts do not supply conveyances where there are none. . . .

It is true that one can orally constitute himself a trustee of personal property for the benefit of another and thereby create a trust enforceable in equity, even though without consideration and without delivery. 1 Scott, [Trusts] §28; §32.2, p. 251. But he must in effect constitute himself a trustee. There must be an express trust, even though oral. . . . There are no subordinate facts in the finding to indicate that Ethel ever intended to, or did, impose upon herself any enforceable duties of a trust nature with respect to this library. The most that could be said is that the subordinate facts in the finding might perhaps have supported a conclusion that at the luncheon she had the requisite donative intent so that, had she subsequently made a delivery of the property while that intent persisted, there would have been a valid, legal gift inter vivos. . . .

The judgment, however, is not based on the theory of a legal gift inter vivos but on that of a declaration of trust. Since the subordinate facts give no support for a judgment on that basis, it cannot stand. . . .

[N]ew trial ordered.

HEBREW UNIVERSITY ASSOCIATION v. NYE
26 Conn. Supp. 342, 223 A.2d 397 (1966)

[On remand, in addition to the facts stated in the case above, the trial court found that the decedent gave plaintiff a memorandum listing most of the contents of the "Yahuda Library" at the time of the luncheon announcement, that the Hebrew University began the project of fund-raising and erecting a library with a Yahuda Room indicated on the plan, thus removing that room from possible subscription by and designation for other contributors, thereby depriving the university "of a possible source of substantial revenue." In this proceeding plaintiff asserted three theories: (1) a gift inter vivos based on constructive or symbolic delivery; (2) constructive trust based on plaintiff's action in reliance on a promise to make a gift; and (3) constructive trust arising out of an ineffective conveyance of an intended gift made by one who died believing an effective gift had been made.]

PARSKEY, J. . . .

[1. Constructive Delivery]

A gift inter vivos is complete when there is an intention to give, accompanied by a delivery of the thing given and an acceptance by the donee. . . . It is not necessary that there should be a manual delivery of the thing given; nor is there any particular form or mode in which the transfer must be made or by which the intention of the donor must be expressed. . . . While the change of possession may be either actual or constructive, it must be such as is consistent with the nature of the property and the situation of the parties. . . . For a constructive delivery, the donor must do that which, under the circumstances, will in reason be equivalent to an actual delivery. It must be as nearly perfect and complete as the nature of the property and the circumstances will permit. Hebrew University Assn. v. Nye, 148 Conn. 223, 232, 169 A.2d 641. The gift may be perfected when the donor places in the hands of the donee the means of obtaining possession of the contemplated gift, accompanied with acts and declarations clearly showing an intention to give and to divest himself of all dominion over the property. . . . It is not necessary that the method adopted be the only possible one. It is sufficient if manual delivery is impractical or inconvenient. Constructive delivery has been found to exist in a variety of factual situations: delivery of keys to a safe deposit box; pointing out places where money is hidden; informal memorandum.

Examining the present case in the light of the foregoing, the court finds that the delivery of the memorandum coupled with the decedent's acts and declarations, which clearly show an intention to give and to divest herself of any ownership of the library, was sufficient to complete the gift. If the itemized memorandum which the decedent transmitted had been incorporated in a formal document, no one would question the validity of the gift. But formalism is not an end in itself. "Whatever the value of the notion of forms, the only use of the forms is to present their contents." Holmes in Justice Oliver Wendell Holmes — His Book Notices and Uncollected Letters and Papers, p. 167 (Shriver Ed.). This is not to suggest that forms and formalities do not serve a useful and sometimes an essential purpose. But where the purpose of formalities is being served, an excessive regard for formalism should not be allowed to defeat the ends of justice. The circumstances under which this gift was made — a public announcement at a luncheon attended by a head of state, accompanied by a document which identified in itemized form what was being given — are a sufficient substitute for a formal instrument purporting to pass title.

[2. Constructive Trust — Action in Reliance]

If it be assumed that there was an insufficient constructive delivery to consummate the gift, the question arises whether the facts justify the imposition of a constructive trust. It is undisputed that the decedent intended to give the Yahuda Library to the Hebrew University. Her purpose in so doing was to establish a "centre for Biblical and Semitic research and a meeting place for scholars" as a memorial to her illustrious husband, Professor Abraham Shalom Yahuda. She had reason to expect that the plaintiff would act in reliance on the eventual delivery of the library. In fact it did so act. It removed from the fund-raising market a room which was set aside to house the Yahuda collection.

> A promise which the promisor should reasonably expect to induce action or forebearance of a definite and substantial character on the part of the promisee and which does induce such action or forebearance is binding if injustice can be avoided only by enforcement of the promise.

Restatement, 1 Contracts §90. . . . The conditions justifying the application of §90 of the Restatement of the Law of Contracts are present.

[3. Constructive Trust — Ineffective Conveyance] . . .

Although it is true that even in the case of a charity an imperfect gift will not be turned into a declaration of trust for no better reason than that it is imperfect; . . . there is ample reason on the facts of this case for equity to impose a constructive trust. It is abundantly clear from the evidence that Ethel Yahuda wanted to house her husband's collection of rare books and manuscripts in a single repository so that they might be easily accessible to scholars. Yet if this collection remains part of the estate the trustees, who are directed under the second clause of will to sell, call in and convert into money such parts of the trust as shall not consist of money, may have no alternative but to sell these books and documents piecemeal, in which event the library may be scattered over universities and colleges throughout the world. The net effect would be to frustrate the foundation which Ethel Yahuda established in the fifth clause of her will, for of what value would be a foundation in Israel, one of the purposes of such foundation being to complete the publication of the work of decedent's husband, if the source material was scattered? Rules of law must, in the last analysis, serve the ends of justice or they are worthless. For a court of equity to permit the decedent's wishes to be doubly frustrated for no better reason than that the rules so provide makes no sense whatsoever. "[T]he plastic remedies of the chancery are moulded to the needs of justice." Foreman v. Foreman, 251 N.Y. 237, 242, 167 N.E. 428, 429. Who is helped by completing the gift to the plaintiff? The plaintiff, obviously; scholars, of course; the Ethel Yahuda foundation, to be sure. Who is hurt? No one. According to the will, after the specific bequests the remainder of the estate is to be converted into money and this money is to be used to establish Ethel Yahuda's foundation. The Yahuda Library, however, is essential if the foundation is to serve the purpose for which it is founded. By the housing of the library at the Hebrew University, the decedent's wishes will be carried out in full.

The court recognizes, in arriving at this result, that it is abrogating in some respects the requirement of delivery in a case involving an intended gift inter vivos. Obviously, it would be neither desirable nor wise to abrogate the requirement of delivery in any and all cases of intended inter-vivos gifts, for to do so, even under the guise of enforcing equitable rights, might open the door to fraudulent claims. But neither does it mean that the present delivery requirement must remain inviolate. . . .

Accordingly, judgment [for] plaintiff. . . .

See Love, Imperfect Gifts as Declarations of Trust: An Unapologetic Anomaly, 67 Ky. L.J. 309 (1979).

2. Formalities: Requirement of a Writing

Assuming a valid transfer of the intended trust property has been made, or that a declaration of trust is involved, does it matter that the existence and terms of the trust agreement are not evidenced by a writing? The statutory setting in which this question may arise will vary from state to state. Consideration must be given to rules such as the parol evidence rule, and in most states the question will require a consideration of a statute of frauds provision relating to trusts of land.

RESTATEMENT (SECOND) OF TRUSTS

§38. The Parol Evidence Rule.

(1) If the owner of property transfers it inter vivos to another person by a written instrument in which it is declared that the transferee is to take the property for his own benefit, extrinsic evidence, in the absence of fraud, duress, mistake or other ground for reformation or rescission,

is not admissible to show that he was intended to hold the property in trust.

(2) If the owner of property transfers it inter vivos to another person by a written instrument in which it is declared that the transferee is to hold the property upon a particular trust, extrinsic evidence, in absence of fraud, duress, mistake or other ground for reformation or rescission, is not admissible to show that he was intended to hold the property upon a different trust or to take it beneficially.

(3) If the owner of property transfers it inter vivos to another person by a written instrument in which it is not declared that the transferee is to take the property for his own benefit or that he is to hold it in trust, extrinsic evidence may be admitted to show that he was intended to hold the property in trust either for the transferor or for a third party.

(4) If the owner of property by a written instrument declares that he holds the property upon a particular trust, extrinsic evidence, in the absence of fraud, duress, mistake or other ground for reformation or rescission, is not admissible to show that he intended to hold the property upon a different trust or to hold it free of trust.

The above section of the Restatement is particularly significant in cases where there is no statutory requirement of a writing for the creation of trusts or where (as in most states) the statute of frauds is inapplicable because the subject matter is not an interest in land. In parol evidence cases, despite the absence of grounds for reformation or rescission in equity, extrinsic evidence may be admitted (1) in the process of interpreting ambiguous language in the instrument, and (2), by the majority view, for the purpose of proving a trust where the deed or bill of sale transferring legal title is silent as to the possible existence of a trust. This latter rule, adopted in §38(3) of the Restatement, is rationalized on the basis that proof of a trust purpose does not vary but merely supplements the writing. To establish a trust by parol in such a case the proof is generally required to satisfy some such standard as that of "clear and convincing evidence." Some cases have at least purported to distinguish between oral trusts for the grantor and those for third persons where the instrument is silent, and to exclude extrinsic evidence only in the former.

In holding that the existence of an oral partnership agreement need not be established by clear and convincing evidence, the court in Weiner v. Fleischman, 54 Cal. 3d 476, 489, 286 Cal. Rptr. 40, 47-48, 816 P.2d 892, 899-900 (1991), distinguished "other areas of the law where courts have traditionally required clear and convincing evidence." The court observed: (1) "Oral agreements to make wills are disfavored because such claims arise after the testator . . . is deceased . . . "; (2) "Allegations that deeds absolute . . . are subject to a trust . . . have also been historically disfavored because society and the courts have a reluctance to tamper with duly executed instruments and documents of legal title"; and (3) "Finally, the higher burden of proof required to prove oral trusts of personal property is derived from the special care that courts have historically shown in recognizing the creation of trusts . . . because of special concerns that the terms of the trusts specify the information needed for courts to deal with the trust, such as the identification of the trust property and purpose, the beneficiaries and trustees, and any special administrative provisions."

STATUTE OF FRAUDS
29 Car. II. c. 3 (1677)

VII. . . . [A]ll declarations or creations of trusts or confidences of any lands, tenements or hereditaments, shall be manifested and proved by some writing, signed by the party who is by law enabled to declare such trust, or by his last will in writing, or else they shall be utterly void and of none effect.

VIII. [Exempts resulting and constructive trusts. See pages 305-306, supra.]

IX. And be it further enacted, that all grants and assignments, of any trust or confidence shall likewise be in writing, signed by the party granting or assigning the same, or by such last will or devise, or else shall likewise be wholly void and of none effect.

A statute of frauds becomes involved whenever the statute's requirement of a writing is expressly made applicable to trusts of interests in land. It also becomes a factor, even in the absence of such an express reference to trusts, whenever the general writing requirement applicable to contracts and conveyances concerning interests in land has been held to apply to trusts of interests in land. Interests in land generally include leaseholds but not debts secured by a mortgage. A few statutes require a writing to establish trusts of personalty.

Except in cases to which these various statutes apply, oral trusts are enforceable, assuming the parol evidence rule does not preclude proof of them. The following basic rules of the Restatement assume the applicability of a statute of frauds.

RESTATEMENT (SECOND) OF TRUSTS

§42. . . . Where the owner of an interest in land transfers it inter vivos to another person in trust, a memorandum properly evidencing the trust is sufficient to satisfy the requirements of the Statute of Frauds if it is signed

      (a) by the transferor prior to or at the time of the transfer; or

      (b) by the transferee

        (i) prior to or at the time of the transfer; or

        (ii) subsequent to the transfer to him but before he has transferred the interest to a third person.

§43. . . . Where an oral trust of an interest in land is created inter vivos, the trustee can properly perform the trust if he has not transferred the interest, although he cannot be compelled to do so.

§46. . . . A memorandum properly signed is sufficient to satisfy the requirements of the Statute of Frauds if, but only if, it sets forth with reasonable definiteness the trust property, the beneficiaries and the purposes of the trust.

§50. . . . Although a trust of an interest in land is orally declared and no memorandum is signed, the trust is enforceable if, with the consent of the trustee, the beneficiary as such enters into possession of the land or makes valuable improvements thereon or irrevocably changes his position in reliance upon the trust.

§51. . . . Although a trust of an interest in land is orally declared and no memorandum is signed, no one except the trustee or persons succeeding to his interest can take advantage of the unenforceability of the trust.

The statute of frauds may be satisfied by one or several writings, whether or not intended as a memorandum of a trust. The loss or destruction of a memorandum does not preclude proof of a trust of land by oral evidence which is otherwise admissible under the law of evidence. See IA W. Fratcher, Scott on Trusts §§47-49 (4th ed. 1987).

PROBLEM

11-C.   Several months before his recent death, A conveyed the Blackacre Apartments (real property valued at about $200,000) to his brother B, a real estate broker. The deed was in the form of a standard warranty deed, reciting merely that it was "for a valuable consideration" and making no reference to the existence or nonexistence of a trust. A's daughter, D, has come to consult you about this conveyance. D states that B had orally agreed to serve as trustee for A and then on A's death to distribute the trust estate to D. D further reveals that, in D's presence before the conveyance, A had told B that he did not wish to be bothered with investment management because he wished to be free to travel, now that his wife had died and he was alone; furthermore, at his age (68), A thought that following the stock market would be too burdensome and he could not continue to supervise the apartments. *D* recalls that *A* and *B* had talked generally about the possibility of the apartments being sold and the proceeds being invested in stocks and mortgages or deeds of trust, since *B* was often able to find good investment opportunities of these types. Then *A* persuaded *B* to act as a trustee, not just as his agent, and *B* agreed. *B* had not made any payments to *A* and now claims the apartments as his own, refusing to transfer the property to *D*. *A* left no will and very little other property. He is survived by *D* and by *X* and *Y*, *A*'s two sons, both of whom are successful businessmen.

(a) As you study the three cases and related notes in the next two subsections, consider what additional information you need to determine, what facts you might seek to establish, and in general how you might go about preparing a case for *D* under a typical statute patterned after the English statute of frauds.

(b) If the fairly representative case of Gregory v. Bowlsby, infra, were the latest decision by the highest court of your state, and if you were *B*'s lawyer, how would you argue the *law* in support of your case? How would the cases for *D* and *B* differ under the statute of frauds in your state? Where there is no applicable statute of frauds?

(c) If you were appointed to a bar association committee for the purpose of considering statutory amendments or new legislation to deal with the constantly troublesome problems of this type, what would you propose?

a.   Oral Trust for the Settlor

GREGORY v. BOWLSBY
115 Iowa 327, 88 N.W. 822 (1902)

[Plaintiffs' petition, which the court recognized "must be treated as presenting the facts," stated: that plaintiffs' father, defendant Benjamin Bowlsby, requested them to deed him their interest in land left by their deceased mother, in order that he might use the land to better advantage; that he orally promised to hold the land, not to sell or dispose of it, and to allow it to descend to the plaintiffs at his death; that plaintiffs executed deeds to defendant reciting a consideration of $1; that by reason of relations existing between them and their father, they relied on his statements without legal advice; that neither the defendant nor his attorney, who was present at the time, advised them that the promises could not be enforced; that defendant paid no consideration for the conveyance, which was induced by his representations; that the defendant made the promises solely to defraud the plaintiffs and without intention to perform; and that he gratuitously conveyed a one-third interest in the land to the co-defendant, his second wife, who knew of the defendant's agreement. The petition asks that the deeds be canceled, that plaintiffs be adjudged owners of interests in the land, and that an accounting be had of rents and profits. Demurrer was sustained on the ground that the alleged agreement was within the statute of frauds.]

DEEMER, J. . . .

That plaintiffs, in the first instance, are seeking to establish an express trust is too clear for argument; and it is equally clear that such a trust cannot rest in parol. . . . As the deed was absolute on its face, and recited the payment of a valuable consideration, plaintiffs will not be permitted to establish a trust by showing that there was in fact no consideration but the parol agreement to hold the title in trust.

As an express trust cannot be shown by parol, and as there was no resulting trust, we have one question left, and that is, was there such a fraud perpetrated by defendant Benjamin Bowlsby as entitles plaintiffs to the relief asked? That relief is not a reformation of the contract, but its cancellation; not a judgment at law as for fraud, but a decree quieting title, and for an accounting. If there is any cause of action stated, it is for the declaration and establishment of a constructive trust, growing out of the alleged fraud of the defendants. While some facts are recited for the purpose of showing fiduciary relations between the parties, we apprehend they are insufficient for that purpose. A father bears no such confidential or fiduciary relations to his adult children as to bring transactions between them relating to the lands of either under suspicion. He may deal with them as with strangers, and no presumption of fraud or undue influence obtains. It is charged, however, that, with intent to cheat and defraud, defendant made the representations charged, fully intending at the time he made them not to carry them out, but to obtain the title to the land, and thus defraud the grantors. Does this make such a case of fraud as that a court will declare a constructive trust in the land in favor of the grantors? This instrument was in the exact form agreed upon by the parties, and there was no promise to execute defeasances or other instruments to witness the trust. The sole claim is that defendant made the promises and agreements with intent to cheat and defraud the plaintiffs. Mere denial that there was a parol agreement as claimed will not constitute a fraud. If it did, the statute would be useless. Nor will a refusal to perform the contract be sufficient to create a constructive trust. But the statute was not enacted as a means for perpetrating a fraud; and, if fraud in the original transaction is clearly shown, the grant[ee] will be held to be a trustee ex maleficio. If, then, there was a fraudulent intent in procuring the deed without intention to hold the land as agreed, and pursuant to that intent the grantee disposed of the property, or otherwise repudiated his agreement, equity will take from the wrongdoer the fruit of his deceit by declaring a constructive trust. Mere breach of or denial of the oral agreement does not, as we have said, constitute a fraud. . . . [A]s said by Mr. Pomeroy, in his work on Equity Jurisprudence (section 1055): "There must be an element of positive fraud accompanying the promise, and by means of which the acquisition of the legal title is wrongfully consummated." Breach of the agreement may, of course, be considered, but it is not alone sufficient. There must be also some clear and explicit evidence of fraud or imposition at the time of the making of the conveyance to constitute the purchaser a trustee ex maleficio. The instant case, however, does not present the question of the quantity of proof required, for, as has been stated, it was decided upon a demurrer to the petition, which pleads fraud in the inception of the transaction, and specifically alleges that the deed was made through defendant's agency, and upon his promise and representations, with the specific intent to cheat and defraud. Our observations regarding the character of the evidence required will perhaps prevent misapprehension of the role in the future. The authorities are not harmonious on the questions discussed, although the points of difference seem to relate more to the quantum of proof in addition to the mere breach of promise than to the rule itself. . . .

We think the petition on its face recites facts showing a constructive trust, and that the demurrer should have been overruled. Reversed.

Section 182 of the Restatement of Restitution provides:

> Where the owner of an interest in land transfers it inter vivos to another upon an oral trust in favor of the transferor or upon an oral agreement to reconvey the land to the transferor, and the trust or agreement is unenforceable because of the Statute of Frauds, and the transferee refuses to perform the trust or agreement, he holds the interest upon a constructive trust for the transferor, if
>
>   (a) the transfer was procured by fraud, misrepresentation, duress, undue influence or mistake of such a character that the transferor is entitled to restitution, or
>
>   (b) the transferee at the time of the transfer was in a confidential relation to the transferor, or
>
>   (c) the transfer was made as security for an indebtedness of the transferor.
>
> Caveat: The Institute takes no position on the question whether the transferee holds upon a constructive trust for the transferor an interest in land transferred to him inter vivos, where he orally agreed with the transferor to hold it in trust for the transferor or to reconvey it to the transferor, except under the circumstances stated in this Section.

It is stated in IA W. Fratcher, Scott on Trusts §44 (4th ed. 1987): "By the weight of authority in the United States, however, the transferee of land upon an oral trust or contract [for the settlor] is allowed to retain the land." A considerable number of the cases cited for this proposition, however, actually involved a failure to prove the existence of the alleged oral agreement adequately rather than a holding that the plaintiff's evidence of an agreement was inadmissible or that his pleadings failed to state a claim upon which relief could be granted.

Stewart v. Hooks, 372 Pa. 542, 546, 94 A.2d 756, 758 (1953), discussing the confidential relationship exception, states:

> We likewise find little merit in plaintiff's argument that a confidential relationship is here established [by the testimony of a witness] . . . that plaintiff "said he had confidence in her [the grantee] and he knew everything would be done as he wanted it." . . . Confidence of this character is obviously present in every case where title is transferred upon an oral promise to reconvey. The Statute of Frauds would wholly fail to render unenforceable such an oral promise if it could be circumvented merely by having the transferor say to the transferee in the presence of a third party: "I have confidence that you will reconvey this property when I ask you to do so."

See also the concurring opinion of Allen, J., in Horsley v. Hrenchir, 146 Kan. 767, 771-772, 73 P.2d 1010, 1012-1013 (1937), which states:

> [I]f it is shown there was a confidential relationship between the parties . . . the court will compel restitution by raising a constructive trust. The same is true if the transfer was secured by fraud, duress or mistake. If it is possible to show the oral agreement in such cases, no valid reason has been given why the statute of frauds should forbid showing the oral trust to prevent unjust enrichment. . . .
>
> By a long line of cases it seems settled in this state that the transferee can keep the property. One reason given is that deeds would no longer be valuable as muniments of title. . . . The reason given seems unsubstantial, for it would prevent enforcing restitution when a transfer of land was procured by fraud, misrepresentation, mistake, duress, undue influence, or where the transfer was made as a security transaction. But in any view of the question it must be conceded that the rule followed in this case is too firmly established to be departed from at this late day.

An aside on precedent and the role of courts. Consider whether the attitude reflected in the concluding sentence of the quotation immediately above represents a workable view of the judicial function or a satisfactory approach to precedent in this particular type of case. What reasons are there *in general* for adhering to precedent? Which of these reasons would prevent a court in the type of case under consideration here from reconsidering the rule it has laid down in prior decisions? Note that this is a different question from the ultimate question of which of several possible rules is preferable on the merits. Consider what reasons there might be — in general, and then in this type of case — for not reaching the issue of the substantive merits of the possible rules.

The opinion that follows is representative of what is referred to in Restatement (Second) of Trusts §44, comment *a*, as "a growing body of authority."

ORELLA v. JOHNSON
38 Cal. 2d 693, 242 P.2d 5 (1952)

[Appeal from a judgment for defendants entered after the granting of a motion for nonsuit. In 1933 plaintiff borrowed $1,000 from the defendant, May (his stepdaughter), to pay off a mortgage on his home, known as the Harder Road place. In 1938 he and his wife conveyed the land to May, who sold it for $3,900 in 1941 and retained $1,400 in payment of the debt and interest thereon. $1,800 of the remaining $2,500 was used to purchase a new home, the Winton Road place, for plaintiff, with title again taken in May's name. In 1943 this property was sold for $4,500, of which $2,300 was used to buy land in Santa Cruz, also in May's name. After his wife's death, plaintiff asked May to convey the land to him, and she refused. Plaintiff then brought suit to impress a constructive trust on the Santa Cruz property and to obtain an accounting of amounts realized by May on the previous sales, alleging that the 1938 conveyance was made on the understanding that May would reconvey the land on request. The trial court excluded evidence offered to prove a conversation between plaintiff and his wife in which his wife presented him with "a proposition May wants me to put to you" and as a result of which the deed was executed.]

TRAYNOR, J. . . .

If a grantor conveys property to another in reliance on the oral promise of the latter to hold the property in trust for the grantor or a third person and the grantee subsequently repudiates the trust, it is settled that a constructive trust may be enforced against the grantee if the conveyance was induced by fraud or if there was a confidential relationship between the parties. Such trusts are enforced under the provisions of section 2224 of the Civil Code that "One who gains a thing by fraud . . . is . . . an involuntary trustee of the thing gained, for the benefit of the person who would otherwise have had it." It is either the actual fraud that induced the conveyance, or the constructive fraud arising from the confidential relationship coupled with the breach of the oral promise, that brings the provisions of the section into play. Since under this section the trust is in favor of the person who, but for the fraud, "would otherwise have had" the property, the effect of its application when the grantee refuses to perform his oral promise, is to enforce the trust in favor of the intended beneficiary.

Whether or not there is a confidential relationship or whether or not the original transfer was induced by fraud, the fact remains that the grantee will be unjustly enriched, if he is allowed to repudiate his promise and retain the property. Accordingly, the view has been forcefully advocated that although the grantee cannot be compelled to perform his promise in view of the statute of frauds, unjust enrichment should be prevented by compelling him to make specific restitution to the grantor. See, I Scott on Trusts §44, p. 248, and authorities cited. This view is sup-

ported by the rule that a purchaser under an invalid oral contract to buy
land may recover the amount he has paid if the seller refuses to perform
the contract, see Moresco v. Foppiano, 7 Cal. 2d 242, 247, 60 P.2d 430;
Rest., Restitution, §108(d), and the rule that a person who renders services under an invalid oral contract to devise property may secure quantum meruit for the value of those services. Zellner v. Wassman, 184 Cal.
80, 88, 193 P. 84. Although there are cases where recovery has been
denied despite an apparent unjust enrichment, in none of them was the
question raised or considered of the availability of the remedy of specific
restitution as distinct from the remedy of a constructive trust based on
the abuse of a confidential relationship. In cases where the question has
been considered, however, the right to relief has been recognized.
Accordingly, it is unnecessary to decide whether there was a confidential
relationship in this case. The nonsuit must be reversed if there is evidence, either that plaintiff conveyed his property in reliance on an oral
promise to reconvey it to him, or that the conveyance was induced by
fraud. . . .
   The judgment is reversed.

b.   Oral Trusts for Persons Other Than the Grantor

   The preceding cases dealt with transfers by *A* to *B* on oral trust for *A*.
How are the results affected by the fact that the deed is from *A* to *B* on
oral trust for *C*? Can *B* retain the property? If not, should a constructive
trust be imposed for *C*, the intended beneficiary? Or would it be appropriate to impose a constructive trust for the transferor, *A*?

JONES v. GACHOT
217 Ark. 462, 230 S.W.2d 937 (1950)

McFADDIN, J.
   This is a suit seeking to impress a trust on real property.
   In 1932 Mrs. Felice Field executed a regular warranty deed to L. C.
Gachot and J. F. Gachot (her nephews), conveying certain lands in
Pulaski County. There was nothing in the deed to indicate, or even suggest, that the grantees received the title in any way except as the owners
thereof. Under an agreement with J. F. Gachot, L. C. Gachot went into
possession of the property here involved and so remained until his death
in 1948. Then, in 1949, this suit was filed alleging (and evidence was
offered to that effect) that when Mrs. Felice Field made the deed to
L. C. Gachot and J. F. Gachot in 1932, the said grantees agreed with the
grantor to hold the property as trustees for themselves and their brothers and sisters. Such agreement is the trust that is sought to be impressed

on the property against the widow and heirs of L. C. Gachot. The Chancery Court rejected the evidence as to the alleged trust agreement and dismissed the complaint for want of equity; and this appeal ensued.

At the outset, appellants concede that an *express trust* cannot be established by oral evidence. But appellants contend that the trust here sought to be imposed is not an express trust but a *constructive trust* and they cite, inter alia, Section 45 of the Restatement of the Law of Trusts:

> Where the owner of an interest in land transfers it inter vivos to another in trust for a third person, but no memorandum properly evidencing the intention to create a trust is signed, and the transferee refuses to perform the trust, the transferee holds the interest upon a constructive trust for the third person, if, but only if,
>
> (a) — the transferee by fraud, duress or undue influence prevented the transferor from creating an enforceable interest in the third person, or
>
> (b) — the transferee at the time of the transfer was in a confidential relation to the transferor, or
>
> (c) — the transfer was made by the transferor in contemplation of death.

It is conceded that sub-paragraph (a) does not apply to this case; but it is earnestly insisted that a trust should be decreed in the case at bar under either sub-paragraph (b) or sub-paragraph (c).

In the briefs no Arkansas case is cited as going to show that such sub-paragraphs (b) and (c) are recognized by holdings in the State. But even if the rules stated in sub-paragraphs (b) and (c) prevail in Arkansas (which it is unnecessary to decide), nevertheless the proof in the case at bar is entirely insufficient to justify the application of either of these sub-paragraphs. As to sub-paragraph (b), there was no more of a "confidential relation" existing between the grantor, Mrs. Field, and the grantee, L. C. Gachot, than exists between any other aunt and nephew; there was a kinship, but not a confidential relationship; he did not importune her to make the deed; they were not living in the same home; she consulted an attorney who prepared the deed for her. As to sub-paragraph (c), there was no more "contemplation of death" on the part of Mrs. Field, the grantor, when she made the deed in question than there is such contemplation by any person of advanced years: she was both physically and mentally active at the time she had the attorney prepare the deed; she was not in extremis; she lived fourteen months after its delivery.

A study of the evidence in the case at bar reflects that this suit — filed after the death of L. C. Gachot — is an effort to establish an express trust by oral evidence, and is within the interdiction of Sec. 38-106, Ark. Stats. 1947. . . .

Leflar, J.

I concur in the conclusion that the evidence in this case was insufficient to establish a constructive trust in appellants' favor. But I wish to make it clear that, our statute prohibiting express oral trusts in lands,

Ark. Stats. §38-106, does not in any wise inhibit the establishment of constructive trusts. The next following section in the statute of frauds, §38-107, provides:

> Where any conveyance shall be made of any lands or tenements, by which a trust or confidence may arise or result by implication of law, such trust or confidence shall not be affected by anything contained in this act.

The great weight of American authority recognizes the validity of constructive trusts under the circumstances set out in the Restatement of Trusts, §45, as quoted in the majority opinion. Unless constructive trusts are enforced in those circumstances the statute of frauds will be made an instrument for achieving fraud, by vesting in nominal grantees the title to lands for which they have paid nothing and to which in equity and good conscience they are not entitled. Under §38-107 it is clear that this was never the intent of the statute of frauds.

Whether the constructive trust in such circumstances should run in favor of the ones for whom the oral trust was declared, as the Restatement suggests, thus effectuating it as though it were an express trust, or should run in favor of the grantor or his successors, on the theory that the parties should be restored as nearly as possible to the position they were in prior to the making of the deed, is another matter. Certainly, the latter disposition of the property would be more nearly in keeping with the law of constructive trusts generally. See 3 Bogert, The Law of Trusts, p. 215; 1 Scott, The Law of Trusts, p. 269. This form of relief, however, was not sought in the present case.

In Person v. Pagnotta, 75 Or. 2d 362, 541 P.2d 483 (1975), the grantor, elderly and seriously ill, executed and delivered a deed to a close friend, expressly reserving a life estate. The transfer was based on the grantee's oral promise to transfer the land to the grantee's daughter at the grantor's death, which appeared imminent. Later the grantor's conservator sued to recover the land on the theory of a resulting trust based on the failure of the intended trust under the statute of frauds. Recovery was denied because a valid constructive trust of the remainder was created for the grantee's daughter, with the grantee as constructive trustee.

Instead of being absolute on its face, a deed may recite simply that a transfer is "in trust" or that the transferee takes "as trustee," without stating the terms of the trust. If clear evidence is available that by oral agreement the land was to be held in trust for X, can the trust be enforced? The limited number of cases in point hold that it cannot. Because it is clear from the deed itself that the transferee takes title in trust, and because the intended trust fails if the transferee refuses to perform the agreement, the transferee holds the property on a resulting trust for the transferor. There is no need to allow a constructive trust to avoid an unjust enrichment. On the other hand, if the grantee under such a deed chooses, an enforceable written trust agreement can apparently be executed or the agreed oral trust can be carried out. Just as in cases where the deed is absolute on its face, the intended trust will fail only if the grantee, or the grantee's successor in interest, asserts the defense of the statute of frauds.

3. Special Problems of Revocable Trusts

During life one may execute and deliver a deed of certain property to another, or declare oneself trustee of certain property, and even though the existence and terms of a trust are so specified as to comply fully with the requirements of the statute of frauds, it is still possible that the trust will be deemed illusory and thus "testamentary" in character and then be held invalid for failure to comply with the statutory formalities prescribed for wills. At this point we are concerned with determining what circumstances may lead to such a result. In particular we are concerned with determining what trust provisions might be a source of danger in this regard, and you should consider carefully what steps might be taken to eliminate this hazard. Compare the cases in Chapter 8, section C, particularly Noble v. Tipton, 219 Ill. 182, 76 N.E. 151 (1905).

William Nicholls established a living trust in which he reserved for life the right to receive $230 a month and also such amounts as the trustee "may deem necessary for his benefit." The remainder was to pass to such persons as Nicholls might appoint or, in default of appointment, to his next of kin under Massachusetts law. He also reserved the power to alter, amend, or revoke the trust. Nicholls's business adviser, one Neville, was given power to control the trustee's investments. Following Nicholls's death, the lower court instructed the trustee to distribute the remainder in accordance with the provisions of the trust, rather than to certain legatees whose bequests under Nicholls's will could not be paid due to insufficiency of other assets. The legatees contended that Nicholls retained full dominion over the property, that the provisions of the instrument were testamentary in nature and created a mere agency, and consequently that the intended disposition of the remainder failed for noncompliance with the formal requirements of the wills act. In rejecting these contentions and affirming the decree below, the court, in National Shawmut Bank v. Joy, 315 Mass. 457, 474-476, 53 N.E.2d 113, 124-125 (1944), stated that the power to appoint and the power to revoke, in addition to an interest for life, did not render the remainder disposition incomplete or testamentary. The court added:

> The same is true, a fortiori, of a reservation of the lesser powers to alter or amend the trust, or to withdraw principal from it, either with or without

the consent of the trustee. Obviously an exercise of the power to revoke would enable the settlor to establish a new trust changed as he might desire. There is no reason why he may not reserve the right to take a short cut by altering or amending the original trust instrument. . . .

But the legatees contend that by reserving power to alter, amend or revoke the trust the settlor made it possible for him as a practical matter to dominate Neville, and that the power to control the investments was in effect reserved to Nicholls himself. We assume without deciding that this contention is true. It does not follow that the gift over to the statutory next of kin is therefore testamentary and void. We need not decide whether the trust would have been invalid had the trustees been reduced to passive impotence, or something near it. A reservation by a settlor of the power to control investments does not impair the validity of a trust.

PROBLEM

11-D.   Nine years ago S entered into a trust agreement with the T Trust Company under which he delivered to the trust company securities then worth $80,000 and certain life insurance policies in the face amount of $100,000 on his life. The beneficiary designated in each policy was the T Trust Company. S expressly reserved the power to change the beneficiaries of the policies and to amend or revoke the trust. The agreement provided that the trust company, as trustee, acknowledged receipt of the securities and the policies and that it agreed to accumulate the income from the securities and on the death of S to collect the proceeds and hold all of the properties in trust to be paid in equal shares — that is, one-fifth to W, his wife of 25 years, and one-fifth to each of his four children as they severally attained age 21 — if, but only if, W took under his will. In the event that W renounced his will, the properties were to be paid in equal shares to his four children.

S died last month. The value of the securities in the inter vivos trust is now $170,000. His will, which has just been filed for probate, disposes of his net probate estate, consisting of $100,000 in securities and $50,000 in realty, in five equal shares to his wife and his four children. T Trust Company is executor and is directed to hold the shares of minor children in trust until they reach their majority. Only two of the children are minors, one age 15 and the other age 17.

(a) Under the law of your state, what approach would you expect W to take in claiming a maximum share in these assets and how would you support her claims? How would your answers be affected if the Uniform Probate Code applies?

(b) As attorney for the children, how would you attempt to resist W's claims?

(c) Outline the opinion you would give to support the decision you think would be appropriate in this case. Would your conclusion differ if the trust had been created nine days rather than nine years before S's death?

(d) How would you advise a client in *S*'s position during his lifetime?

(e) Is this an area in which applicable policies could be given greater effect by statute? If so, what provisions would you suggest? Consider the Uniform Probate Code.

INVESTORS STOCK FUND, INC. v. ROBERTS
179 F. Supp. 185 (D. Mont. 1959), *affd.,*
286 F.2d 647 (9th Cir. 1961)

[Interpleader action filed by Investors Stock Fund, Inc. against Franklin H. Roberts, as "beneficiary" (actually, remainder beneficiary) under a declaration of trust executed by George W. Roberts, and against Loretto Lohman Roberts, as widow and sole heir of George W. Roberts, seeking a determination of the rights and conflicting claims of the defendants in certain stock. Loretto Roberts and Franklin Roberts each moved for summary judgment.]

MURRAY, C.J. . . .

Two questions are presented by the motions for summary judgment: . . .

Is the Decree of Distribution in the Estate of George W. Roberts, Deceased, Conclusive as to the Ownership of the Stock? Loretto Lohman Roberts' first contention is that, regardless of the validity or invalidity of the declaration of trust made by George W. Roberts, the ownership of the stock in question was conclusively determined by the decree in the George W. Roberts' estate distributing said stock to her as the widow and sole heir at law of George W. Roberts, deceased, and that . . . the decree of distribution of the probate court is res judicata in this action.

. . . [R]egardless of the sufficiency or insufficiency of the notice to Franklin H. Roberts, and regardless of whether or not the probate court was aware at the time it made the decree of distribution of the fact that the stock certificate was issued in the name of George W. Roberts, as trustee for Franklin H. Roberts, it is clear under Montana law, as well as the law generally, that the probate court in the Roberts estate was without jurisdiction to try the title to the stock in question as between Franklin H. Roberts, on the one hand, and either the Estate of George W. Roberts, deceased, or Loretto Lohman Roberts, as the widow and sole heir of George W. Roberts, deceased, on the other. . . .

Is the "Declaration of Trust-Revocable" Executed by George W. Roberts in His Lifetime Valid as a Trust? The [next] contention of plaintiff is that the instrument is ineffective as . . . a trust . . . because it was merely an attempt on the part of George W. Roberts to make a testamentary disposition of the stock to Franklin H. Roberts without complying with the Montana statutes on wills. . . .

The contention . . . is based on two premises: first, it is claimed that by virtue of the declaration of trust George W. Roberts parted with none of the rights or incidents of ownership of the stock, and in reality retained complete ownership, both legal and equitable, and all of the rights and incidents of such ownership; and, second, that by virtue of the declaration of trust Franklin H. Roberts, the alleged beneficiary, acquired no interest of any kind in the stock.

This being a diversity case, it is governed by Montana law. However, the problems presented here have never been passed upon by the Montana Supreme Court, so recourse must be had to the law of trusts generally as announced by text writers and courts of other jurisdictions in an attempt to determine how the Montana Supreme Court would view the matter. . . .

. . . While it is true that there can be no trust when the full legal and equitable ownership vests in a single person, it is also true that a person may occupy two capacities with regard to a trust. Thus, the settlor of a trust may make himself trustee thereof (Restatement of Trusts, Sec. 100), or the settlor may likewise be a beneficiary of the trust (Restatement of Trusts, Sec. 114). . . .

By the declaration of trust George W. Roberts declared that he held said stock in trust for Franklin H. Roberts. That a valid trust may be created in this manner is clear (Restatement of Trusts, Secs. 17 and 28; 54 Am. Jr. "Trusts," Sec. 61, p. 69). In declaring the trust, George W. Roberts reserved to himself *in his capacity as settlor or trustor* the following rights with respect to the trust property.

1. The right to receive during his lifetime all cash dividends.
2. The right at any time to change the beneficiary of the trust, or to revoke the trust by written notice to Investors Stock Fund, Inc., in such form as that Company prescribed, and regain the entire ownership of the property, and
3. Upon the sale or redemption of the stock by the trustee, the right to retain the proceeds of such sale or redemption.

Likewise the trust was to terminate upon the death of the beneficiary.

Under the declaration of trust, George W. Roberts, *in his capacity as trustee,* had the right to vote, sell, redeem, exchange, or otherwise deal in or with the stock, but in the event of sale or redemption, the trust was to terminate as to the stock sold or redeemed, and the proceeds of the stock sold or redeemed were to become the property of George W. Roberts as settlor.

By this distribution of the rights incidental to ownership of the stock in question between George W. Roberts, in his capacity as settlor, and George W. Roberts, in his capacity as trustee, George W. Roberts as settlor effectively relinquished some of the incidents of complete ownership of the stock. While he was free to sell or redeem the stock and apply the proceeds to his own use under the trust, his right to vote, exchange or deal with the stock in any manner otherwise than by sale or redemption was subject to the obligation which the law imposes on trustees. . . . As an absolute owner of the stock, George W. Roberts would be free to exchange the $5,000 worth of stock for a $10 hat, if he chose, but as trustee he would not be free to make such an exchange without first revoking the trust. And if George W. Roberts died after having committed any violation of his duties as trustee without revoking the trust, the beneficiary could hold his estate liable for any loss resulting to the trust fund as a result of such violations. . . .

On the other hand, immediately upon the execution of the declaration of trust, Franklin H. Roberts became vested with an equitable interest in the stock. This interest consisted essentially in a right to the performance of the trust, that is the right to have the trustee perform the duties imposed upon him by law, and eventually to succeed to complete ownership of the stock. That this interest was not to vest in enjoyment until the future, and was contingent in character, does not make it any less a vested interest. . . .

Much of the attack of the plaintiff upon the validity of the trust is necessarily based upon the erroneous proposition that the reserved power of revocation invalidates the trust. It seems clear to the Court that were the power of revocation not contained in the declaration of trust, there would be no question of its validity. Yet the right to reserve the power to revoke and still establish a valid trust is so well established in the law of trusts, that it cannot be questioned. Such right is indeed recognized by statute in Montana. Section 86-602, R.C.M. 1947, provides:

> A trust cannot be revoked by the trustor after its acceptance, actual or presumed, by the trustee and beneficiaries, except by the consent of all the beneficiaries, *unless the declaration of trust reserves a power of revocation to the trustor,* and in that case the power must be strictly pursued.

Likewise, the reservation of the right to revoke by George W. Roberts, coupled with the reservation of the cash dividends, and the reservation of the right to the proceeds of any of the stock sold or redeemed do not render the trust testamentary in character. . . .

In Cleveland Trust Co. v. White, 134 Ohio St. 1, 15 N.E.2d 627, 118 A.L.R. 475 at page[s] 478 and 479, the Court said:

> By the weight of authority, a trust, otherwise effective, is not rendered nugatory because the settlor reserves to himself the following rights and powers: (1) The use of the property and the income therefrom for life; (2) the supervision and direction of investments and reinvestments; (3) the amendment or modification of the trust agreement; (4) the revocation of the trust in whole or in part; (5) the consumption of the principal.

Finally, it is elementary that the creation of a trust is primarily dependent upon the intention of the settlor, and his manifestation of such intention. . . . By declaring that he held the stock in question for his brother, Franklin H. Roberts, George W. Roberts clearly manifested his intention to create a trust, and there is nothing elsewhere in the declaration of trust or in the record of this case to refute that manifestation of his intention. And . . . there is nothing in the law which requires the Court to thwart that intention by holding the trust invalid.

The Court is fortified in this opinion by the fact that "Declarations of Trust-Revocable," identical with the one involved here, were considered by the Supreme Courts of the States of Illinois and North Carolina, in the face of attacks similar to those made here, and were held to be valid, in the cases of Farkas v. Williams, 5 Ill. 2d 417, 125 N.E.2d 600, and Ridge v. Bright, 244 N.C. 345, 93 S.E.2d 607. Not only were the instruments in those cases identical word for word with the instrument here involved, but the subject of the trust was stock of the same company as in this case. . . .

The Court is therefore of the opinion that the "Declaration of Trust-Revocable," executed by George W. Roberts, created a valid inter vivos trust, and upon the death of George W. Roberts the 375.094 shares of Investors Stock Fund, Inc., represented by Certificate No. 1738, became the absolute property of the beneficiary, Franklin H. Roberts. . . .

––––––––––

Although it is now generally accepted without question that revocable inter vivos trusts can serve as will substitutes without compliance with the wills act, litigation continues in abundance. The question of "illusory" or "testamentary" character therefore remains a significant one to be understood and handled by lawyers in both planning and litigation contexts. The question is no doubt confused by the unfortunate tendency of courts (as in *Roberts,* above) to use the term "vested" when they mean to refer to interests that are legally recognized as presently existing property rights, which do not depend on whether they are, for example, vested or contingent, and which in any event begs the very question at issue. Most importantly, it is evident today in nearly all states that the question before the court is not whether revocable trusts *can* be used as will substitutes but generally whether in a given situation the transferor really intended a trust or something less — whether the transferor's actions and intentions were such that the law should take the alleged trust disposition seriously. Nearly all "trusts" that have "failed" in recent cases have been the result of informal and casual, if not sloppy, handling (sometimes by lawyers) leaving the transferor's understanding of the transaction or true intentions in the matter in substantial doubt. In some of these instances, as in the preceding case, the alleged settlor and trustee were the same person, although this situation does not readily lend itself to an "agency" explanation either. Usually, however, in reported cases finding no trust, the clouded role of "trustee" or "agent" is played by a family member or other trusted individual, with whom either oral or written communications are understandably ambiguous. Yet an occasional case is still encountered in which a formal arrangement, even one with a corporate fiduciary, falls on the wrong side of the vague line between trust and agency. The portion of the Ohio opinion reproduced below serves as a warning and suggests some of the danger signals, even though this portion of the opinion may only be dictum because of the result of another but omitted issue in the case.

OSBORN v. OSBORN
10 Ohio Misc. 171, 226 N.E.2d 814 (1966)

CORRIGAN, J. . . .

[T]he mere designation of "trustee" does not elevate a custodian or an agent to that status. In that event, the death of the so-called settlor or donor revokes the agency and the property of the decedent passes either under a will or pursuant to the intestate laws. The question for determination then is whether you are dealing with a trust or merely an agency.

[The Henry C. Osborn Trust, established in 1920 with the Cleveland Trust Company as trustee, also referred to as] the No. 1 Trust, must be viewed in the light of the facts and surrounding circumstances. In the instant case the mere retention of the income rights in the No. 1 Trust by Mr. Osborn together with the right to amend or revoke did not equal such control or dominion which would vitiate the trust. In serving its proper function an inter vivos trust provides management during the settlor's life, expeditiously disposes of the property at his death, limits costs of administration and widespread publicity on the probate of a will. During his lifetime he can observe how the trustee manages the trust, participate to some degree in the management, modify or even revoke the trust entirely. If the law is to recognize these rights of the settlor and sanction inter vivos trusts, the courts are charged with the responsibility of determining whether or not the trust is, in fact, a true trust.

After hearing all the testimony on this issue and reviewing the scores upon scores of exhibits received into the evidence, the court concludes that the Henry C. Osborn Trust fails to meet the requirements of a true trust, "both in the manner of administration by the bank and in the pervasive dominion and control which Mr. Osborn continually exercised, solely for his own personal advantage." Without attempting to list all the instances of domination and practically exclusive control of the bulk of the corpus of the trust, we will refer to some of the facts supporting this conclusion. As was suggested by counsel for plaintiff it served more as a combination bank account and safety deposit box for his benefit. Not only were all of his securities included, but an insurance policy issued by the Cleveland Automobile Club to its members and qualifying shares in various private clubs. His Cleveland home was carried as an asset of the trust, but he paid no rent and when it was of no more use to him as a home he took it back and used it to cut his income tax by a charitable deduction. Trust assets were used as collateral on personal loans and to pay his personal expenses, although he dutifully completed the revocation forms from a supply he kept available. A loan arrangement worked out with the bank provided him with a device to raise cash without incurring substantial tax liability and to defer sales until after his death when no capital gains tax would be payable, with the interest in the interim used as a tax deduction.

Although the trust agreement called for nothing more than obtaining "whenever practicable" his approval of the trustee's investment determinations, he made the decisions and continually rejected the trustee's demands for trust diversification. According to a former vice-president who handled the matters for the trust and Mr. Osborn, he could not think of an instance in which the bank ever changed a decision or refused a request by Mr. Osborn, after discussing the matter with him. Further all the indicia of ownership of the stocks which were issued in his name were sent to him, not the trustee. With one exception, Mr. Osborn's income and personal property tax returns show this income as received directly by him rather than through the trust. . . .

Several exhibits revealed:

> While cash additions and withdrawals were often large in amount (in the years 1956 through 1960, the cash revocations alone total over $580,000), they include amounts as low as $12.19 (addition) and $10.94 (withdrawal). The number and scope of these "additions" and "revocations" transactions reveal a use of the account not unlike the use one would make of an ordinary commercial bank account or a custodianship.

Without further enlarging this memorandum with additional details, we believe the evidence reflects that the arrangement between the bank and Mr. Osborn was so completely dominated by him that although it was referred to as a trust it remained an agency account. While conceding that [a contrary] argument might be advanced [on the basis of certain facts], the court looking at the total picture believes that such a working arrangement was a custodial account and in the nature of a testamentary disposition and certainly did not meet the true concept of a trust.

With the increasing popularity of the revocable living or inter vivos trust in modern estate planning, it should be made clear that the phraseology used in the trust instrument is meaningless, if the so-called settlor or donor actually remains in virtual control and the so-called trustee for fear of losing the business acquiesces in his every act and wish. Where the trustee continually yields and makes adjustments in an attempt to keep a semblance of a true trust, a mere agency or custodianship is bound to result.

By way of summary, then, under the current law of Ohio, a person can observe the operation of one's estate plan and provide for the consolidation of the entire estate in a trust program, but the trust must meet the test of a true trust in order to maintain its non-testamentary character. The trust instrument executed by Henry C. Osborn in 1920 and modified over the years meets the test as to form [if] there had been full compliance with the terms and spirit of the No. 1 Trust. . . . However, due to the complete dominance of Henry C. Osborn and the meek acquiescence of the bank the trust in question was not a trust in fact. . . .

4.   Savings Bank Trusts

PROBLEM

11-E.   Five years ago, *X,* a single person, deposited $25,000 in a savings account opened in her own name "in trust for *Y.*" Shortly thereafter she wrote to *Y,* stating at one point: "Incidentally, several days ago I put $25,000 in trust for you." A year later *X* withdrew $8,000 from the account, and six months ago she executed a will bequeathing $10,000 to *A,* $10,000 to *B,* and the residue of her estate to *C.* At the time of her death last month *X*'s assets consisted solely of marketable securities worth $12,000, a personal checking account containing about $600, and her interest, if any, in the savings account mentioned above (the balance of which was then slightly over $19,000, including interest). What are the rights of *A, B, C,* and *Y* in these assets? What other facts would you seek to determine?

It is not uncommon for a person to deposit funds in a bank or savings and loan association in the depositor's own name as trustee for another without specifying the real intent or the terms of a trust. Thus *A* may deposit money in a savings account in the name of "*A* in trust for *B*." What are the consequences of this act? Is a trust created? If so, is the trust revocable or irrevocable, and what are its other terms? We are dealing with what has come to be known as a tentative or *Totten* trust.

In the leading case of Matter of Totten, 179 N.Y. 112, 120, 125-126, 71 N.E. 748, 750, 752 (1904), Judge Vann's opinion states:

> [W]hen it became common practice for persons to make deposits in that form, in order to evade restrictions upon the amount one could deposit in his own name and for other reasons, the courts . . . sought to avoid

unjust results by adapting the law to the customs of the people. A brief review of the cases will show how the subject has gradually developed so as to accord with the methods of the multitude of persons who make deposits in these banks. . . .

It is necessary for us to settle the conflict [in opinions from different appellate divisions] by laying down such a rule as will best promote the interests of all the people in the state. . . . A deposit by one person of his own money, in his own name as trustee for another, standing alone, does not establish an irrevocable trust during the lifetime of the depositor. It is a tentative trust merely, revocable at will, until the depositor dies or completes the gift in his lifetime by some unequivocal act or declaration, such as delivery of the pass book or notice to the beneficiary. In case the depositor dies before the beneficiary without revocation, or some decisive act or declaration of disaffirmance, the presumption arises that an absolute trust was created as to the balance on hand at the death of the depositor.

Evidence is admissible to show the actual intent of the depositor, and if his intention is discovered it will be given effect. "The evidence bearing upon the intent of the depositor, aside from the deposit itself, may be divided into three classes, namely: (a) Express statements of intent; (b) acts or omissions of the depositor with respect to the deposit or the supposed beneficiary, aside from express statements; (c) the circumstances of the depositor." G. Bogert, Trusts §20 (3d ed. 1952).

From the form of the deposit alone any of several inferences might be drawn. Some cases infer no intent to create a trust. Some others infer that an irrevocable trust is created. By the weight of authority the inference is that stated in Matter of Totten, supra. See also Uniform Probate Code §§6-201 to 6-216.

In Abbale v. Lopez, 511 So. 2d 340 (Fla. App. 1987), *H* deposited his funds in a bank account in the names of *H* and *W* (his wife) "in trust for *B*." When *H* died, the court concluded that this deposit had created a *Totten* trust with cotrustees, that the trust continued with *W* as sole trustee, but that she had no power to revoke. Does this seem like an appropriate interpretation? Contrast Hillyer v. Hillyer, 499 N.E.2d 569 (Ill. App. 1986). Should the result be different (and, if so, how) if both *H* and *W* had contributed to the account, such as if the deposited funds had been their community property or partly the property of each?

RESTATEMENT (SECOND) OF TRUSTS

§58. . . . *Comment*: . . .

c. *Revocation of tentative trust.* A tentative trust of a savings deposit can be revoked by the depositor at any time during his lifetime, by a manifestation of his intention to revoke the trust. No particular formalities are necessary to manifest such an intention. If he withdraws any part of the deposit during his lifetime, the withdrawal operates as a revocation of the trust to the extent of such withdrawal, and the beneficiary will be entitled only to the amount remaining on deposit at the death of the depositor. . . .

A tentative trust of a savings deposit can be revoked by the depositor by his will. It is so revoked where by will he makes a disposition of the deposit in favor of anyone other than the beneficiary. . . .

d. *Creditors of depositor.* Although creditors of the settlor cannot reach the trust property merely because he has reserved a power of revocation (see §330, Comment o), creditors of a person who makes a savings deposit upon a tentative trust can reach his interest, since he has such extensive powers over the deposit as to justify treating him as in substance the unrestricted owner of the deposit. . . .

In re ESTATE OF KRYCUN
24 N.Y.2d 710, 249 N.E.2d 753 (1969)

SCILEPPI, J. . . .

In the case at bar, the testatrix had six separate bank accounts, four of which were in the *Totten* Trust form and two in her name alone. The language in paragraph SEVENTH of the will relied upon by the respondents states: "I give and bequeath any and all funds on deposit to my credit, in any bank or trust company or similar financial institution." The majority of the Appellate Division held that this language, in itself, was "clear and absolute to show the intention of the testatrix to revoke any prior trust bank accounts and to have such proceeds become part of the assets of the estate." We do not agree.

If the money on deposit in the four trust accounts comprised all or most of the assets of the estate or if the trust accounts were the only bank accounts in the decedent's name, that would be a strong indication that the testatrix intended to revoke the *Totten* Trusts. Such, however, was not the case. The money on deposit in the trust accounts only comprised a little more than one third of the total estate, and as indicated earlier the testatrix had two bank accounts in her name alone. We conclude, therefore, that the language in paragraph SEVENTH, in itself, under the facts of this case, is insufficient to overcome the presumption of non-revocation. In such a case it is necessary to scrutinize the surrounding circumstances and the will as a whole, very carefully, in determining the true intention of the testatrix. It is our opinion that the posting of interest to the trust accounts up to the date of death [and] the language in paragraph THIRTEENTH of the will which contemplated "property passing outside [the] Will" . . . manifest an intention on the part of the testatrix not to revoke. . . .

See also Litsey v. First Federal Savings and Loan Assn., 243 So. 2d 239 (Fla. App. 1971). The abatement of legacies where funds do not permit payment in full is considered in Chapter 20.

5.   Life Insurance Trusts

The use of life insurance trusts (typically a form of revocable inter vivos trust) is an important and common feature of estate planning. Where trusts are to be employed for any of the reasons already considered with regard to estates generally (see Chapter 9, section C), there are a variety of reasons for using insurance trusts for any life insurance owned by the client rather than simply having the proceeds made payable to the estate for inclusion in a testamentary trust. Among the major reasons are (1) avoidance of the costs and delays that would result from insurance proceeds being administered as part of the insured's estate; (2) the fact that such trusts are inter vivos trusts rather than testamentary trusts where retained jurisdiction in the probate court is provided for the latter by statute or practice and where the particular circumstances render such retained jurisdiction undesirable; and (3) avoidance of unnecessary state inheritance taxation under fairly common state rules taxing insurance proceeds payable to the estate of the insured but exempting proceeds payable to named beneficiaries. Inasmuch as the various insurance options also avoid probate and qualify for the typical inheritance tax exemption, what advantages do you see in an insurance trust over the selection of an annuity or interest option under the policy?

Life insurance trusts are generally created in either of two ways. Frequently, the owner of the insurance policy will designate the trustee as the beneficiary under the policy, normally designating that payee as trustee but occasionally without mention of the fiduciary capacity in the policy; the settlor and trustee will also execute a trust agreement. Under this method the trustee is usually given custody of the policy for convenience. The second method is to assign the insurance policies to the trustee pursuant to a trust agreement. Under each method the trust may be either funded or unfunded. The funded insurance trust involves also a transfer of other property to the trustee, with the income from the property used by the trustee to pay the premiums on the policies. Insurance trusts are often made wholly revocable, with the insured (or other owner of the policy) reserving all rights under the policies; this is common even where the policies are assigned to the trustee. Thus, the settlor of such a revocable trust would have the right to change the beneficiary designation or to surrender or borrow against the policies.

PROBLEM

11-F.   Your client, *H,* who has $100,000 worth of insurance and very little else, wishes to make his insurance payable to *W,* his wife, if she survives him; but if *W* does not survive him, *H* wants the proceeds to be payable to his sister, *S,* to hold in trust for *H*'s minor children. What steps would you take to bring about the desired result, and what beneficiary designations would be written into the policies? Does this arrangement pose any special problems regarding the validity of the trust as a nontestamentary disposition? If so, can you recommend any step that might be taken at the planning stage to protect against such a challenge? On what theory or theories might you argue to sustain such a trust if a challenge materializes?

GURNETT v. MUTUAL LIFE INSURANCE CO.
356 Ill. 612, 191 N.E. 250 (1934)

[Knowlton Ames and the Central Trust Company entered into a trust agreement in 1930. The agreement stated that Ames deposited with the trust company insurance policies (acquired between 1906 and 1927) insuring his life for a total of $1 million and making it beneficiary of all the policies. The agreement further provided that Ames would continue to pay the premiums and that he retained all rights under the policies, including the right to change the beneficiary, to borrow against the policies, and to surrender any policy for its cash value. He also reserved powers to revoke and amend the trust and twice exercised the latter power. During Ames's lifetime the trustee's only duty was to return the policies to Ames on his demand; on his death the trustee was to collect and administer the proceeds as provided in the trust instrument. Following Ames's death in 1931, complainants, creditors of his estate, brought suit against the insurance companies, the trustee, the executors of Ames's will, and his heirs at law. They sought to have the trust agreement declared void and to have the trustee ordered to hold the proceeds of the life insurance policies under a resulting trust in favor of Ames's estate. Complainants alleged, inter alia, that the rest of Ames's estate was insufficient to pay the claims of creditors, that Ames had not assigned the policies to the trustee but had treated them as his sole property, including borrowing on several of them, even after the date of the agreement, that there was no actual corpus of the trust and no transfer of property during Ames's lifetime, and that the intended trust fails with the proceeds rightfully belonging to the executors via resulting trust. Fraud was not alleged. The chancellor found a valid trust and entered a decree dismissing complainants' bill.]

DE YOUNG, J. . . . .

A life insurance policy is property and may constitute the subject-matter of a trust. . . . The designated beneficiary of the policy may, by the provisions of collateral trust agreement, be named as the trustee. . . . When the beneficiary promises the insured to pay either the whole or a portion of the proceeds of the policy to a third person, the proceeds will be impressed with a trust to the extent of the promise made. . . .

The date of the death of the insured merely fixed the time when the obligation of the insurers to pay and the right of the beneficiary to receive the proceeds of the policies became enforceable. . . . The trust agreement and the change of beneficiaries, however, became effective during the lifetime of the settlor. The continuing right to receive the proceeds of an insurance policy is not impaired by the unexercised right or privilege of the insured to designate another beneficiary. The designation of a beneficiary in a policy of life insurance creates an inchoate gift of the proceeds of the policy, which, if not revoked by the insured in his lifetime, vests in the beneficiary at the time of the former's death. A policy of life insurance is not deemed an asset of the estate of the insured unless it is made payable to him, his executors or administrators. The mere fact that the insured may change the beneficiary does not make the policy or its proceeds a part of his estate. Neither the policies nor their proceeds constituted a part of the estate of Knowlton L. Ames, deceased. Since his death, the trust agreement is merely evidence of the trustee's contract under which it must collect the policies and hold the proceeds for the purposes of the trust. . . .

. . . [I]n the case of Hirsh v. Auer, 146 N.Y. 13, 40 N.E. 397, 398, [the court stated:]

> The fact that the trust dealt with a contingent interest of the insured in the certificate of insurance is of no moment. That interest became vested at the death of the insured, and, the beneficiary having collected the insurance money, the trust, under the agreement creating and acknowledging it, attached to the fund. A trust of this character is not to be distinguished from assignments of contingent interests, which courts of equity recognize as valid.

The reservation of the power to revoke an entire trust does not invalidate the agreement presently creating it or render it testamentary. The plaintiffs in error concede the validity of the provision reserving power to the settlor to terminate the trust agreement in whole or in part. Naming new beneficiaries in one or more of the policies would have produced precisely the same effect as the termination of the trust with respect to such policies. The power to designate another beneficiary in an insurance policy is a privilege personal to the insured. The powers and privileges reserved do not affect the obligations of the insurers to pay the proceeds of the policies to the trustee upon the death of the insured. . . .

The judgment of the Appellate Court is affirmed. . . .

The above case is illustrative of the consistent response of courts to the assertion that insurance trusts are testamentary. See also Gordon v.

Portland Trust Bank, 201 Or. 648, 653-655, 271 P.2d 653, 655 (1954),
2 U.C.L.A. L. Rev. 151:

> The older rule which gave a vested interest to the beneficiary does not,
> of course, square with the modern notions of life policies. . . . But the
> courts are by no means in accord on the issue. Many hold that the bene-
> ficiary takes a vested interest subject to divestment upon change of ben-
> eficiary in accordance with the provisions of the policy. . . . Where this
> view obtains, there is no problem concerning the testamentary aspect of
> the transaction, for the vested right of the beneficiary is without doubt a
> proper subject for a trust. . . .
>
> Under the general view that the beneficiary has no more than an expec-
> tancy, it is more difficult to find the necessary res for a present trust.
> Rather, the transaction appears to be a contract . . . to create a trust at the
> insured's death. The courts, however, have not felt constrained to arrive
> at this conclusion, and the cases are legion which have upheld the usual
> form of unfunded insurance trust even where the court had previously
> announced that the beneficiary has no more than a mere expectancy. In
> some of the earlier cases, the rationale appeared to be that, since a life
> insurance policy payable to an ordinary third-party beneficiary is not tes-
> tamentary, then neither is one wherein the third-party beneficiary is also
> trustee, for in both cases the legal title to the proceeds is in the beneficiary
> according to the doctrine of the third party beneficiary as it has developed
> in the law of contracts. In the insurance trust device, the trustee-benefi-
> ciary takes a divided interest in the property, but this is specifically a trust
> problem and has no bearing on the testamentary character of the
> device. . . . We observe, therefore, that both under the old view, where the
> beneficiary is considered the owner, and under the new view where he has
> only an expectancy, the result is the same, for even in the new view, the
> third-party beneficiary has a present right to fulfillment of the insurer's
> promise to pay. There is no inconsistency in this position.

PROBLEM

11-G. John died nine days after changing the beneficiary of his
$50,000 life insurance policy from his wife to the Peoples Bank "to be
held in Trust," but without specifying the trust terms in the beneficiary
designation. Six days before his death, he executed a will bequeathing
his estate, without mention of the insurance, to Peoples Bank in trust for
his wife for life, remainder to their children. An apparent suicide note
in the decedent's handwriting stated that Peoples Bank "will have control of all the property and insurance money for the family." Peoples
Bank, as executor and trustee, petitioned for instructions with respect
to the insurance proceeds, which it had collected as beneficiary under
the policy. Claims against the decedent's estate exceeded $51,000; the
estate was worth less than $1,000 without the insurance proceeds, the
bulk of the family assets being jointly held land that passed to decedent's
widow by right of survivorship. From an order that the insurance pro-

ceeds were to be held by the bank in an inter vivos trust under the terms
set out in the will, one of the estate creditors appealed. What arguments
would you expect by the various parties? What result would you anticipate? Why? See Pavy v. Peoples Bank & Trust Co., 195 N.E.2d 862 (Ind.
App. 1964).

Even in those decisions in which, because of some defect in the
intended trust arrangement or some peculiar facts of the case, an
intended insurance trust has been found to be illusory or otherwise held
invalid, the opinions have usually recognized the general validity of
insurance trusts. See, e.g., Bickers v. Shenandoah Valley National Bank,
197 Va. 145, 88 S.E.2d 889 (1955), noted in 54 Mich. L. Rev. 880, 31
N.Y.U. L. Rev. 967, 42 Va. L. Rev. 256.

Where the beneficiary under an insurance policy has orally agreed to
hold the proceeds for a particular purpose or on a particular trust, the
trust is generally enforceable. Shaull v. United States, 161 F.2d 891
(D.C. Cir. 1947) (oral promise by brother to hold for children of
insured); Fahrney v. Wilson, 180 Cal. App. 2d 694, 4 Cal. Rptr. 670
(1960) (oral promise by widow to pay insured's debts); Cooney v. Montana, 347 Mass. 29, 196 N.E.2d 202 (1964). In Ballard v. Lance, 6 N.C.
App. 24, 169 S.E.2d 199 (1969), an oral trust of flight insurance was
sustained although the insured's intention and instructions were conveyed to someone other than the trustee to whom the policies were made
payable. Under a few statutes of frauds, however, these oral agreements
or directions may be difficult to sustain. See, e.g., Desnoyers v. Metropolitan Life Insurance Co., 108 R.I. 100, 272 A.2d 683 (1971) (intended
trust of insurance failed because trusts of personalty must be in writing);
but see Blanco v. Valez, 295 N.Y. 224, 66 N.E.2d 171 (1946) (enforcing
oral promise).

With these various insurance trusts, compare the situation in which
the insured wishes the proceeds to be held in trust by a testamentary
trustee. Frost v. Frost, 202 Mass. 100, 88 N.E. 446 (1909), involved a
purported *assignment* of life insurance policies to "the trustees to be
named in my will." The intended trust failed for want of a completed
transfer, no delivery of the policies having been made to the "trustees"
who remained unascertained during the insured's lifetime. Do you see
why this trust was not upheld on the theories of the *Gurnett* and *Gordon*
cases, supra?

Statutes permitting designation of testamentary trustees as beneficiaries of life insurance policies have been enacted in a growing number
of states. The principal provision of one of these statutes is set out below.
Would this statute have changed the result of the *Frost* case? See generally discussion in Schlesinger, Paying Insurance to Testamentary Trustees, 104 Tr. & Est. 1095 (1965), and compare discussion of "pour-over
trusts" infra this chapter.

CALIFORNIA PROBATE CODE

§6321. *Trustees; Designation as Beneficiary, Payee, or Owner.* A contract or plan [defined to include an insurance, annuity, or endowment contract or an employee's or self-employed person's pension, retirement, profit-sharing, or similar plan] may designate as a primary or contingent beneficiary, payee, or owner a trustee named or to be named in the will of the person entitled to designate the beneficiary, payee or owner. The designation shall be made in accordance with the provisions of the contract or plan or, in the absence of such provisions, in a manner approved by the insurer if an insurance, annuity, or endowment contract is involved, and by the trustee, custodian, or person or entity administering the contract or plan, if any. The designation may be made before or after the execution of the designator's will and is not required to comply with the formalities for execution of a will.

Insurance trusts pose a peculiar conceptual problem. Does the trust come into existence when the trust agreement and beneficiary designation are executed, or does it arise on the death of the insured by operation of two contracts? See the quotation from Gordon v. Portland Trust Bank, supra. Does it matter whether the policies are assigned or whether the trustee is merely designated as beneficiary of the policies? The effective date of the trust can be a crucial issue in cases involving the rule against perpetuities. Properly analyzed, however, this latter question does not arise where the insurance trust remains wholly revocable until the insured's death because the period of the rule against perpetuities does not begin to run until the trust becomes irrevocable. Cook v. Horn, 214 Ga. 289, 104 S.E.2d 461 (1958).

C. Will Substitutes and Policies Restricting Testation

We have seen that, for the most part, even thin inter vivos trusts that are used as will substitutes survive quite well against the charge that they circumvent the *formal* requirements imposed on testation. We now turn to cases in which trusts that have the character of will substitutes are employed to circumvent — or at least may have the effect of circumventing — what might be called *substantive* policies governing testamentary disposition. As earlier observed, the history of the trust's development reveals its frequent use to avoid undesired consequences of legal ownership. One of the trust's particular contributions has been avoiding outmoded rules and technical restrictions in advance of legal reform; equity does not necessarily follow the law.

Modern tax law reveals the efforts that are being made to prevent the use of trusts to circumvent tax policy. Express provisions of the federal estate tax law now treat property as belonging to the settlor when it has been placed in a trust that has the nature of a will substitute. (See Chapter 8, section E, supra.) For example, sections 2036 and 2038 of the Internal Revenue Code of 1954 require inclusion in a decedent's taxable estate of certain property that had been transferred with retention of various rights, benefits, or powers. On the other hand, statutes restricting bequests and devises to charity are generally held not to invalidate trusts for charitable purposes, despite the settlor's retention of a life interest and a power of revocation. IA W. Fratcher, Scott on Trusts §57.5 (4th ed. 1987). This is consistent with the generally accepted policy of narrowly construing such statutes.

Another area of problems involves the use of living trusts to circumvent statutes intended to prevent disinheritance of a surviving spouse. The American cases have historically taken the position that "if it is provided by statute that the wife of a testator shall be entitled to a certain portion of his estate of which she cannot be deprived by will, a married man can nevertheless transfer his property inter vivos in trust and his widow will not be entitled on his death to a share of the property so transferred, even though he reserves a life estate and power to revoke or modify the trust." 1 Restatement (Second) of Trusts §57, cmt. c. This statement is predicated on the basic rule that, in the absence of contrary statute, a person may defeat a spouse's forced share by giving away property during life. The statement does not apply, of course, when even an outright gift of the property would not defeat the spouse's right, such as in the case of land subject to dower.

A small but increasing number of cases have reached results contrary to the traditional position reflected in the Restatement (Second) of Trusts. The diversity of the views adopted by various courts and the uncertainty created by some of the opinions can be sources of considerable difficulty. See generally W. MacDonald, Fraud on the Widow's Share 67 et seq. (1960).

NEWMAN v. DORE
275 N.Y. 371, 9 N.E.2d 966 (1937)

Lehman, J.

The Decedent Estate Law . . . does not limit or affect disposition of property inter vivos. In terms and in intent it applies only to decedents' estates. Property which did not belong to a decedent at his death and which does not become part of his estate does not come within its scope. . . .

[B]y section 18 of the revised Decedent Estate Law . . . "a personal right of election is given to the surviving spouse to take his or her share of the estate as in intestacy, subject to the limitations, conditions and exceptions contained in this section." These limitations and exceptions include a case where "the testator has devised or bequeathed in trust an amount equal to or greater than the intestate share, with income thereof payable to the surviving spouse for life. . . . "

Ferdinand Straus died on July 1, 1934, leaving a last will and testament dated May 5, 1934, which contained a provision for a trust for his wife for her life of one-third of the decedent's property both real and personal. In such case the statute did not give the wife a right of election to take her share of the estate as in intestacy. She receives the income for life from a trust fund of the amount of the intestate share, . . . [which] includes no property which does not form part of the estate at the decedent's death. The testator on June 28, 1934, three days before his death, executed trust agreements by which, in form at least, he transferred to trustees all his real and personal property. If the agreements effectively divested the settlor of title to his property then the decedent left no estate and the widow takes nothing. The widow has challenged the validity of the transfer to the trustees. The beneficiary named in the trust agreement has brought this action to compel the trustees to carry out its terms. The trial court has found that the "trust agreements were made, executed and delivered by said Ferdinand Straus for the purpose of evading and circumventing the laws of the State of New York, and particularly sections 18 and 83 of the Decedent Estate Law." Undoubtedly the settlor's purpose . . . could not [be accomplished] by testamentary disposition of his property. The problem in this case is whether he has accomplished that result by creating a trust during his lifetime.

The validity of the attempted transfer depends upon whether "the laws of the State of New York and particularly sections 18 and 83 of the Decedent Estate Law" prohibit or permit such transfer. . . . [A] "purpose of evading and circumventing" the law [cannot] carry any legal consequences. . . . "The fact that it desired to evade the law, as it is called, is immaterial, because the very meaning of a line in the law is that you intentionally may go as close to it as you can if you do not pass it." Superior Oil Co. v. State of Mississippi, 280 U.S. 390, 395. . . .

Under the trust agreements executed a few days before the death of the settlor, he reserved the enjoyment of the entire income as long as he should live, and a right to revoke the trust at his will, and in general the powers granted to the trustees were in terms made "subject to the settlor's control during his life," and could be exercised "in such manner only as the settlor shall from time to time direct in writing." Thus, by the trust agreement which transferred to the trustees the settlor's entire property, the settlor reserved substantially the same rights to enjoy and control the disposition of the property as he previously had possessed, and the inference is inescapable that the trust agreements were executed by the settlor, as the court has found, "with the intention and for the purpose of diminishing his estate and thereby to reduce in amount the share" of his wife in his estate upon his death and as a "contrivance to deprive . . . his widow of any rights in and to his property upon his death." They had no other purpose and substantially they had no other effect. Does the statute intend that such a transfer shall be available as a means of defeating the contingent expectant estate of a spouse?

In a few states where a wife has a similar contingent expectant interest or estate in the property of her husband, it has been held that her rights may not be defeated by any transfer made during life with intent to deprive the wife of property, which under the law would otherwise pass to her. In those states it is the intent to defeat the wife's contingent rights which creates the invalidity and it seems that an absolute transfer of all his property by a married man during his life, if made with other purpose and intent than to cut off an unloved wife, is valid even though its effect is to deprive the wife of any share in the property of her husband at his death. . . .

Motive or intent is an unsatisfactory test of the validity of a transfer of property. In most jurisdictions it has been rejected, sometimes for the reason that it would cast doubt upon the validity of all transfers made by a married man, outside of the regular course of business; sometimes because it is difficult to find a satisfactory logical foundation for it. Intent may, at times, be relevant in determining whether an act is fraudulent, but there can be no fraud where no right of any person is invaded. "The great weight of authority is that the intent to defeat a claim which otherwise a wife might have is not enough to defeat the deed." Leonard v. Leonard, 181 Mass. 458, 462. . . . Since the law gives the wife only an expectant interest in the property of her husband which becomes part of his estate, and since the law does not restrict transfers of property by the husband during his life, it would seem that the only sound test of the validity of a challenged transfer is whether it is real or illusory. That is the test applied in Leonard v. Leonard, supra. The test has been formulated in different ways, but in most jurisdictions the test applied is essentially the test of whether the husband has in good faith divested himself of ownership of his property or has made an illusory transfer. . . . In Pennsylvania the courts have sustained the validity of the trusts even where a husband reserved to himself the income for life, power of revocation, and a considerable measure of control. In other jurisdictions transfers in trust have been upheld regardless of their purpose where a husband retained a right to enjoy the income during his life. . . . In some of these cases the settlor retained, also, a power of revocation. In no jurisdiction has a transfer in trust been upheld where the conveyance is intended only to cover up the fact that the husband is retaining full control of the property though in form he has parted with it. Though a person may use means lawfully available to him to keep outside of the scope of a statute, a false appearance of legality, however attained, will not avail him. Reality, not appearance, should determine legal rights.

In this case the decedent, as we have said, retained not only the income for life and power to revoke the trust, but also the right to control the trustees. We need not now determine whether such a trust is, for any purpose, a valid present trust. It has been said that, "where the settlor transfers property in trust and reserves not only . . . a power to revoke and modify the trust but also such power to control the trustee as to the details of the administration of the trust that the trustee is the agent of the settlor, the disposition so far as it is intended to take effect after his death is testamentary. . . . " American Law Institute, Restatement of the Law of Trusts, §57, subd. 2. We do not now consider whether the rule so stated is in accord with the law of this state or whether in this case the reserved power of control is so great that the trustee is in fact "the agent of the settlor." We assume, without deciding, that except for the provisions of section 18 of the Decedent Estate Law the trust would be valid. Perhaps "from the technical point of view such a conveyance does not quite take back all that it gives, but practically it does." That is enough to render it an unlawful invasion of the expectant interest of the wife. Leonard v. Leonard, supra; Brownell v. Briggs, 173 Mass. 529, 54 N.E. 251.

Judged by the substance, not by the form, the testator's conveyance is illusory, intended only as a mask for the effective retention by the settlor of the property which in form he had conveyed. We do not attempt now to formulate any general test of how far a settlor must divest himself of his interest in the trust property to render the conveyance more than illusory. Question of whether reservation of the income or of a power of revocation, or both, might even without reservation of the power of control be sufficient to show that the transfer was not intended in good faith to divest the settlor of his property must await decision until such question arises. In this case it is clear that the settlor never intended to divest himself of his property. He was unwilling to do so even when death was near.

The judgment should be affirmed, with costs. . . .

In Matter of Halpern, 303 N.Y. 33, 100 N.E.2d 120 (1951), the executrix, the testator's widow and the sole beneficiary of his will, sought to have included in his otherwise insignificant estate certain savings accounts (tentative trusts) created by the testator in his name as trustee for a grandchild. In modifying the surrogate's decision that the trusts were illusory, the Appellate Division held that the tentative trusts failed only to the extent required to satisfy the widow's statutory share computed as though the accounts were included in the estate. The executrix appealed but the grandchild did not. The Court of Appeals, however, stated:

> We hold that respondent's legal position is correct, and that these *Totten* trusts were, on this record, valid, effective and not illusory. It is, perhaps, regrettable that any husband resorts to such transfers to keep his money from his wife. But *Totten* trusts, if real and not merely colorable or pretended, are valid transfers with legally fixed effects. . . .
>
> The Appellate Division, reasoning . . . from its conclusion that these trusts were illusory because destructive of section 18 benefits, decided that only so much thereof should be set aside as was required to put the widow in the section 18 position. . . . We see no power in the courts to divide up such a *Totten* trust and call part of it illusory and the other part good. The only test is that quoted above, from Newman v. Dore, . . . and the results of its applications would necessarily be either total validity or total invalidity, as to any one transfer.

303 N.Y. at 37-40, 100 N.E.2d at 122-123.

A review of the New York experience and legislation expanding the spouse's protection can be found in Amend, The Surviving Spouse and the Estates, Powers and Trust Law, 33 Brooklyn L. Rev. 530 (1967).

SULLIVAN v. BURKIN
390 Mass. 864, 460 N.E.2d 572 (1984)

[Mary Sullivan elected against the will of her husband, Ernest, and sought unsuccessfully in the probate court to have included in his estate for that purpose the assets of a revocable inter vivos trust of which he was settlor, sole trustee, and income beneficiary with a right to principal on demand. The Sullivans had been separated for many years before the husband's death.]

WILKINS, J. . . .

[T]he wife's claim was simply that the inter vivos trust was an invalid testamentary disposition. . . . If [that were so] the trust assets would be a part of the husband's probate estate [and] we would not have to consider any special consequences of the wife's election. . . .

We conclude, however, that the trust was not testamentary in character and that the husband effectively created a valid inter vivos trust. . . . We [further] conclude that, in this case, we should adhere to the principles expressed in Kerwin v. Donaghy, [59 N.E.2d 299 (1945)], that deny the surviving spouse any claim against the assets of a valid inter vivos trust created by the deceased spouse, even where the deceased spouse alone retained substantial rights and powers under the trust instruments. For the future, however, as to any inter vivos trust created or amended after the date of this opinion, we announce that the estate of a decedent, for the purposes of G.L. c. 191, §15, shall include the value of assets held in an inter vivos trust created by the deceased spouse as to which the deceased spouse alone retained the power during his or her life to direct the disposition of those trust assets for his or her benefit, as, for example, by the exercise of a power of appointment or by revocation of the trust. Such a power would be a general power of appointment for Federal estate tax purposes (I.R.C. §2041(b)(1) [1983]) and a "general power" as defined in the Restatement (Second) of Property §11.4(1) (Tent. Draft No. 5, 1982).

We consider first whether the inter vivos trust was invalid because it was testamentary. . . . We believe that the law of the Commonwealth is correctly represented by the statement in Restatement (Second) of Trusts §57, comment *h* (1959), that a trust is

> not testamentary and invalid for failure to comply with the requirements of the Statute of Wills merely because the settlor-trustee reserves a beneficial life interest and power to revoke and modify the trust. The fact that as trustee he controls the administration of the trust does not invalidate it.

We come then to the question whether, even if the trust was not testamentary on general principles, the widow has special interests which should be recognized.

. . . In considering this issue at the May, 1982, annual meeting of the American Law Institute the members divided almost evenly on whether a settlor's surviving spouse should have rights, apart from specific statutory rights, with respect to the assets of an inter vivos trust over which the settlor retained a general power of appointment. See Proceedings of the American Law Institute, May, 1982, pp. 59-117; Restatement (Second) of Property — Donative Transfers, Supplement to Tent. Draft No. 5 at 28 (1982).[1] . . .

In this Commonwealth a husband has an absolute right to dispose of any or all of his personal property in his lifetime, without the knowledge or consent of his wife, with the result that it will not form part of his

---

1. The reporter, Professor A. James Casner, recommended the following statement:

> §13.7 *Spousal Rights in Appointive Assets on Death of Donee.* The spouse of the donee of a power of appointment is entitled to treat appointive assets as owned assets of the donee on the donee's death, only to the extent provided by statute.

Restatement (Second) of Property — Donative Transfers, Tent. Draft No. 5 at pp. 108-109 (1982). This statement is consistent with the principles expressed in Kerwin v. Donaghy, supra. By a vote of 63 to 60, the members rejected the substitution of the following statement under §13.7, recommended by an adviser to the project, Justice Rava S. Dreben of the Massachusetts Appeals Court:

> Appointive assets are treated as owned assets of a deceased donee in determining the rights of a surviving spouse in the owned assets of the donee if, and only if, the deceased spouse was both the donor and donee of a general power that was exercisable by the donee alone, unless the controlling statute provides otherwise.

Restatement (Second) of Property — Donative Transfers, Supplement to Tent. Draft No. 5 at pp. 6 and 28 (1982).

estate for her to share under the statute of distributions (G.L. [Ter. Ed.] c. 190, §§1, 2), under his will, or by virtue of a waiver of his will. That is true even though his sole purpose was to disinherit her. In the *Kerwin* case, we applied the rule to deny a surviving spouse the right to reach assets the deceased spouse had placed in an inter vivos trust of which the settlor's daughter by a previous marriage was trustee and over whose assets he had a general power of appointment. The rule of Kerwin v. Donaghy has been adhered to in this Commonwealth for almost forty years and was adumbrated even earlier. The bar has been entitled reasonably to rely on that rule in advising clients. In the area of property law, the retroactive invalidation of an established principle is to be undertaken with great caution. . . . We conclude that, whether or not Ernest G. Sullivan established the inter vivos trust in order to defeat his wife's right to take her statutory share in the assets placed in the trust and even though he had a general power of appointment over the trust assets, Mary A. Sullivan obtained no right to share in the assets of that trust when she made her election under G.L. c. 191, §15.

We announce for the future that, as to any inter vivos trust created or amended after the date of this opinion, we shall no longer follow the rule announced in Kerwin v. Donaghy. There have been significant changes since 1945 in public policy considerations bearing on the right of one spouse to treat his or her property as he or she wishes during marriage. The interests of one spouse in the property of the other have been substantially increased upon the dissolution of a marriage by divorce. We believe that, when a marriage is terminated by the death of one spouse, the rights of the surviving spouse should not be so restricted as they are by the rule in Kerwin v. Donaghy. It is neither equitable nor logical to extend to a divorced spouse greater rights in the assets of an inter vivos trust created and controlled by the other spouse than are extended to a spouse who remains married until the death of his or her spouse.

The rule we now favor would treat as part of "the estate of the deceased" for the purposes of G.L. c. 191, §15, assets of an inter vivos trust created during the marriage by the deceased spouse over which he or she alone had a general power of appointment, exercisable by deed or by will. This objective test would involve no consideration of the motive or intention of the spouse in creating the trust. We would not need to engage in a determination of "whether the [spouse] has in good faith divested himself [or herself] of ownership of his [or her] property or has made an illusory transfer" (Newman v. Dore, 275 N.Y. 371, 379, 9 N.E.2d 966 [1937]) or with the factual question whether the spouse "intended to surrender complete dominion over the property" (Staples v. King, 433 A.2d 407, 411 [Me. 1981]). Nor would we have to participate in the rather unsatisfactory process of determining whether the inter vivos trust was, on some standard, "colorable," "fraudulent," or "illusory."

What we have announced as a rule for the future hardly resolves all the problems that may arise. There may be a different rule if some or all of the trust assets were conveyed to such a trust by a third person. Cf. Theodore v. Theodore, 356 Mass. 297, 249 N.E.2d 3 (1969). We have not, of course, dealt with a case in which the power of appointment is held jointly with another person. If the surviving spouse assented to the creation of the inter vivos trust, perhaps the rule we announce would not apply. We have not discussed which assets should be used to satisfy a surviving spouse's claim. We have not discussed the question whether a surviving spouse's interest in the intestate estate of a deceased spouse should reflect the value of assets held in an inter vivos trust created by the intestate spouse over which he or she had a general power of appointment. That situation and the one before us, however, do not seem readily distinguishable. See Schnakenberg v. Schnakenberg, 262 A.D. 234, 236-237, 28 N.Y.S.2d 841 (N.Y. 1941). A general power of appointment over assets in a trust created by a third person is said to present a different situation. Restatement (Second) of Property — Donative Transfers, Supplement to Tent. Draft No. 5, reporter's note to §13.7 at 29 (1982). Nor have we dealt with other assets not passing by will, such as a trust created before the marriage or insurance policies over which a deceased spouse had control. Id. at 30, 38.

The question of the rights of a surviving spouse in the estate of a deceased spouse, using the word "estate" in its broad sense, is one that can best be handled by legislation. See Uniform Probate Code, §§2-201, 2-202, 8 U.L.A. 74-75 (1983). See also Uniform Marital Property Act, §18 (Natl. Conference of Commrs. on Uniform State Laws, July, 1983), which adopts the concept of community property as to "marital property." But, until it is, the answers to these problems will "be determined in the usual way through the decisional process." Tucker v. Badoian, 376 Mass. 907, 918-919, 384 N.E.2d 1195 (1978) (Kaplan, J., concurring).

We affirm the judgment of the Probate Court dismissing the plaintiff's complaint.

So ordered.

See also Moore v. Jones, 44 N.C. App. 578, 261 S.E.2d 289 (1980), holding a revocable trust "ineffective" to impair the surviving spouse's statutory rights. Except to that extent, the court upheld the trust and directed that it otherwise be carried out, as far as practicable, in accordance with its terms. The court expressly declined to find the trust illusory or to base its decision on fraud or intention to impair the spouse's rights; in the court's view, the record would not support such an interpretation.

For a decision relying on the "illusory trust" basis for recognizing the spouse's right in "*Totten* trust" property, see Johnson v. LaGrange State Bank, 73 Ill. 2d 342, 383 N.E.2d 185 (1978).

An interesting approach to the allocation of the legislative and judicial responsibilities in this matter is reflected in In re Jeruzal's Estate, 269 Minn. 183, 194-196, 130 N.W.2d 473, 481-482 (1964), noted in Note, 34 U. Cin. L. Rev. 179 (1965), in which it is stated:

> [I]t appears that in Minnesota a motive to deprive one's spouse of the statutory inheritance by inter vivos transfer generally is irrelevant, the only test being whether the transaction is real. This principle, if extended to *Totten* trusts, would lead to the adoption of the New York rule enunciated in the *Halpern* case. . . . We are not satisfied that [a] rule should be adopted [under which] the trust is either good against the spouse or void altogether. We would prefer the Restatement [(Second) of Trusts §58, comment *e*] rule, by which the beneficiaries receive what the decedent intended them to have except so far as [*Totten*] trust funds are necessary to satisfy statutory interests of the spouse after the general assets of the estate have been exhausted. However, in view of the widespread use of *Totten* trusts in the area of testamentary disposition we do not feel free to adopt the Restatement rule without first giving the legislature an opportunity to provide for it by statute as was done in Pennsylvania. . . .
>
> However, this court will feel free to follow the Restatement rule hereafter if the legislature declines to act on this matter. The *Totten* trust itself is a judicial creation, [and it] is therefore our duty to subject this judicially-created doctrine to such limitations as are necessary to prevent the defeat of substantive statutory policies. . . . The statutory policy against allowing the widow to be left destitute should not be subordinated to the policy of giving broad effect to saving account trusts, however desirable the latter may be. We cannot overlook the danger that lies in the general use of *Totten* trusts as they may affect the surviving spouse. Actually, a depositor accomplishes nothing by a *Totten* trust which he could not accomplish by will. Only the procedure, not the substance, is changed. . . . We feel that the Restatement rule . . . provides a satisfactory balance of the two policies here involved. . . .
>
> This conclusion does not limit the effect of any of our earlier decisions on the extent to which marital rights may be defeated by the use of trusts. *Totten* trusts are a special case not necessarily subject to rules governing trusts generally.

Legislative solutions to this conflict are gradually emerging. In a number of states statutes have been enacted specifically to protect the forced share of a surviving spouse against revocable trusts and certain other will substitutes. Pennsylvania enacted one of the earliest of these, and after the *Jeruzal* case Minnesota enacted legislation patterned after Pennsylvania's. (Subsequently, with the adoption of versions of the Uniform Probate Code in these states, both statutes have been revised or replaced.) Since the New York decisions, supra, N.Y. Estates, Powers &

Trusts Law §5-1.1(b) was enacted. It excludes life insurance and employee benefits, based on the experience of Pennsylvania, which had initially included life insurance but which eight years later dropped it (and still continues to exclude insurance and "broad-based" employee benefit plans) from the coverage of the legislation. Pa. Stat. Ann. tit. 20, §2203(b). A similar approach, also excluding insurance, annuities, and pensions, is now found in California Probate Code §§101, 102, protecting a surviving spouse's forced right to half of a decedent's foreign-acquired marital ("quasi-community") property from gratuitous transfers in which the decedent retained income, control, or right of survivorship. Federal law, however, mandates provision (unless waived) for surviving spouses of participants in pension plans governed by the Employee Retirement Income Security Act (ERISA), 29 U.S.C.A. §§1001 et seq. (1974), as amended by the Retirement Equity Act, 98 Stat. 1426 (1984). Compare the comprehensive provisions of the "augmented estate" in Uniform Probate Code §§2-201 to 2-207, set out in Chapter 3, supra.

PROBLEM

11-H. Your client, W, resides in state X, which has enacted legislation providing: "A conveyance of assets by a person who retains a power of revocation over the principal thereof shall, for purposes of the forced share election of his or her surviving spouse, be treated as a testamentary disposition." H, her husband, died six weeks ago. His probate estate consists of property, mostly land in state X, valued at $200,000. H's will has been admitted to probate and provides for the property to be divided equally between W and H's only child, D, a daughter by a previous marriage.

About a year before his death H established an inter vivos trust in state Y, with the T Trust Company of that state as trustee, although H then resided in state X. Under this trust H reserved the income for life and a power of revocation, providing for the principal to go on H's death to D, who lives in state Z. This trust consists of securities valued at $250,000.

W wants to establish whatever rights she may have in H's estate and in the trust estate. How would you proceed to obtain as much of the property as you think possible? What type of evidence would you seek to present, and how would you argue the case in W's behalf? What other factual and legal information do you need to know? Your research reveals that the Restatement rule, noted supra page 396, represents the law of the state Y and was recently quoted in an opinion of the Y Supreme Court. Consider the case that follows. Would the result differ if State X is a state of the United States but States Y and Z are foreign countries? Consider The Hague Convention excerpts, infra.

NATIONAL SHAWMUT BANK v. CUMMING
325 Mass. 457, 91 N.E.2d 337 (1950)

WILKINS, J.

The plaintiff bank is the surviving trustee under a declaration of trust, dated August 25, 1944, in which the bank and the settlor, William Gray Cumming, of Barre, Vermont, were named as trustees. The settlor died on August 19, 1947. The defendants are the settlor's widow, Cora Mann Cumming, and the mother, brother, and three sisters of the settlor, and constitute all the surviving life beneficiaries under the trust instrument. This bill in equity seeks (1) the removal of a cloud upon the plaintiff's title as trustee to the trust property, as well as upon the beneficial interests of the defendants, the said cloud consisting of a claim asserted by the widow that the trust is invalid; and (2) a binding declaration of the rights of the parties under the trust instrument. G.L. (Ter. Ed.) c. 231A, inserted by St. 1945, c. 582, §1. The answers of the defendants other than the widow admit the allegations of the bill and join in the prayers for relief. The widow's answer sets up that the trust was created in bad faith with intent to defraud her of rights under Vermont law after waiver of the will, and that the validity of the trust is to be determined by the laws of the State of Vermont. The widow (hereinafter called the defendant) appealed from a final decree adjudging that the trust is valid, and that she has no claim to the trust property except as a beneficiary under the trust instrument. The judge filed "Findings, ruling and order for decree." The evidence is reported.

We summarize certain facts found by the judge or by ourselves.

The trust agreement provided that the income, and such amounts of the principal as the settlor might direct in writing, should be paid to him for life; and that after his death the income should be paid equally to his widow, his mother, two brothers (one of whom predeceased him), and three sisters, the principal, if necessary, to be used to insure the receipt of $150 monthly by each beneficiary. Upon the death of the settlor and the last survivor of the life beneficiaries, the trust was to terminate and distribution be made to the nieces and nephews of the settlor then living and to the living issue of each deceased niece or nephew by right of representation. The settlor reserved the power to amend, to revoke in whole or in part, and to withdraw principal. The last paragraph reads, "This instrument shall be construed and the provisions thereof interpreted under and in accordance with the laws of the Commonwealth of Massachusetts." Extensive powers of management were reserved to the trustees, but by an amendment of September 26, 1945, the settlor "delegated" his powers as cotrustee to the plaintiff.

The settlor died domiciled in Vermont at the age of fifty-seven. On January 5, 1925, when in Florida, he married the defendant. It was his first marriage. She was "several years" his senior and a widow with three children. The settlor, who until then had lived with his mother, was an eldest son who had assumed the obligation of the head of the family. He took these obligations very seriously, and strong family ties continued throughout his life. . . .

The settlor and the defendant "had not gotten along well," and the "rupture became more pronounced in December, 1944. . . ."

The judge stated:

> I find that the settlor meticulously and designedly arranged his holdings and his business affairs so that his mother, wife, brothers and sisters would share the income, or principal, if necessary, equally after his death. That he knew that but for this arrangement his widow would have been entitled under the laws of Vermont to $4,000 and one half of his estate. But I do not find that in doing what he did . . . he was actuated by bad faith, or that he sought to accomplish something which he under all the circumstances considered to be unjust or unfair to his wife. I do not find that he set up the trust, with the fraudulent intent of preventing his wife from obtaining her distributive share of his property. I find and rule that the trust is valid. I find that the settlor intended that the trust be administered in Boston by the National Shawmut Bank as trustee. . . .

If the settlor had been domiciled in this Commonwealth and had transferred here personal property here to a trustee here for administration here, the transfer would have been valid even if his sole purpose had been to deprive his wife of any portion of it. Kerwin v. Donaghy, 317 Mass. 559, 571, 59 N.E.2d 299. The Vermont law we understand to be otherwise and to invalidate a transfer made there by one domiciled there of personal property there, if made with an actual, as distinguished from an implied, fraudulent intent to disinherit his spouse. In re O'Rourke's Estate, 106 Vt. 327, 331, 175 A. 4.

The plaintiff contends that the validity of the trust is to be determined by the law of this Commonwealth, and, in the alternative, that should the question be determined by Vermont law, the trust would still be valid on the judge's findings. The defendant, on the other hand, contends that the "trust is not valid under either Vermont or Massachusetts law." This argument is founded upon alleged illegality according to the law of Vermont and an assertion that our courts must look to the law of the State of domicil, which determines the right of succession to the settlor's personal property here. Reliance is placed upon . . . Phelan v. Conron, 323 Mass. 247, 253, 81 N.E.2d 525. See G.L. (Ter. Ed.) c. 199, §1.2; Restatement: Conflict of Laws, §301, comment *b*. . . .

One answer to the defendant's contention is that, wholly apart from what may be the law of Vermont, it was not shown that the trust was created to defraud the wife of statutory rights in Vermont. The judge was not plainly wrong in not making such a finding. There was no evidence which compelled it. The findings which he did make, including the finding that the settlor knew that but for the trust arrangement his wife would be entitled to $4,000 and one half of his estate, meaning, of course, at its then valuation, are not tantamount to findings that the trust was created, or added to, with intent to defraud her, nor are the findings inconsistent with one another.

Another independent and insuperable difficulty is that before death the settlor had effectively disposed of the trust property, which had its situs in this Commonwealth and was not subject here to any equity in favor of a wife or to any similar limitation upon his power of disposition. He had expressed an intent in the trust instrument that it should be construed and interpreted according to the laws of this Commonwealth.

The elements entering into the decision as to the law of which State determines the validity of the trust are, on the one hand in Vermont, the settlor's domicil, and, on the other hand in Massachusetts, the presence of the property or its evidences, the completion of the trust agreement by final execution by the trustee, the domicil and the place of business of the trustee, and the settlor's intent that the trust should be administered by the trustee here. The general tendency of authorities elsewhere is away from the adoption of the law of the settlor's domicil where the property, the domicil and place of business of the trustee, and the place of administration intended by the settlor are in another State. The situation is unchanged by the fact that the one seeking to set aside the transaction is the widow of the settlor. We are of the opinion that the question of validity is to be determined by the law of this Commonwealth. There was no error under our law in adjudging the trust to be valid when created, or in omitting to adjudge it to be invalid at the time of the additions to principal made in 1945.

We are not sure whether any contention is made that the trust instrument is illusory on its face apart from alleged fraud toward the widow. The trust is not illusory. . . .

Decree affirmed.

THE HAGUE CONVENTION ON THE LAW APPLICABLE TO TRUSTS AND ON THEIR RECOGNITION
(1985)

Article 1

This Convention specifies the law applicable to trusts and governs their recognition.

Article 6

A trust shall be governed by the law chosen by the settlor. The choice must be express or be implied in the terms of the instrument creating or the writing evidencing the trust, interpreted, if necessary, in the light of the circumstances of the case.

Where the law chosen under the previous paragraph does not provide for trusts or the category of trust involved, the choice shall not be effective and the law specified in Article 7 shall apply.

Article 7

Where no applicable law has been chosen, a trust shall be governed by the law with which it is most closely connected.

In ascertaining the law with which a trust is most closely connected reference shall be made in particular to —

a) the place of administration of the trust designated by the settlor;

b) the situs of the assets of the trust;

c) the place of residence or business of the trustee;

d) the objects of the trust and the places where they are to be fulfilled.

Article 15

The Convention does not prevent the application of provisions of the law designated by the conflicts rules of the forum, in so far as those provisions cannot be derogated from by voluntary act, relating in particular to the following matters —

a) the protection of minors and incapable parties;

b) the personal and proprietary effects of marriage;

c) succession rights, testate and intestate, especially the indefeasible shares of spouses and relatives;

d) the transfer of title to property and security interests in property;

e) the protection of creditors in matters of insolvency;

f) the protection, in other respects, of third parties acting in good faith.

If recognition of a trust is prevented by application of the preceding paragraph, the court shall try to give effect to the objects of the trust by other means.

THE HAGUE CONVENTION ON THE LAW APPLICABLE TO SUCCESSION TO THE ESTATES OF DECEASED PERSONS
(1988)

Article 1

(1) This Convention determines the law applicable to succession to the estates of deceased persons.

410

11. Creation of Trusts

(2) The Convention does not apply to —

    a) the form of dispositions of property upon death;

    b) capacity to dispose of property upon death;

    c) issues pertaining to matrimonial property;

    d) property rights, interests or assets created or transferred otherwise than by succession, such as in joint ownership with right of survival, pension plans, insurance contracts, or arrangements of a similar nature.

Article 3

(1) Succession is governed by the law of the State in which the deceased at the time of his death was habitually resident, if he was then a national of that State.

(2) Succession is also governed by the law of the State in which the deceased at the time of his death was habitually resident if he had been resident there for a period of no less than five years immediately preceding his death. However, in exceptional circumstances, if at the time of his death he was manifestly more closely connected with the State of which he was then a national, the law of that State applies.

(3) In other cases succession is governed by the law of the State of which at the time of his death the deceased was a national, unless at that time the deceased was more closely connected with another State, in which case the law of the latter State applies.

Article 5

(1) A person may designate the law of a particular State to govern the succession to the whole of his estate. The designation will be effective only if at the time of the designation or of his death such person was a national of that State or had his habitual residence there.

(2) This designation shall be expressed in a statement made in accordance with the formal requirements for dispositions of property upon death. The existence and material validity of the act of designation are governed by the law designated. If under that law the designation is invalid, the law governing the succession is determined under Article 3.

(3) The revocation of such a designation by its maker shall comply with the rules as to form applicable to the revocation of dispositions of property upon death.

(4) For the purposes of this Article, a designation of the applicable law, in the absence of an express contrary provision by the deceased, is to be construed as governing succession to the whole of the estate of the deceased whether he died intestate or wholly or partially testate.

Article 6

A person may designate the law of one or more States to govern the succession to particular assets in his estate. However, any such designation is without prejudice to the application of the mandatory rules of the law applicable according to Article 3 or Article 5, paragraph 1.

Article 7

(1) Subject to Article 6, the applicable law under Articles 3 and 5, paragraph 1, governs the whole of the estate of the deceased wherever the assets are located.

(2) This law governs —

    a) the determination of the heirs, devisees and legatees, the respective shares of those persons and the obligations imposed upon them by the deceased, as well as other succession rights arising by reason of death including provision by a court or other authority out of the estate of the deceased in favour of persons close to the deceased;

    b) disinheritance and disqualification by conduct;

    c) any obligation to restore or account for gifts, advancements or legacies when determining the shares of heirs, devisees or legatees;

    d) the disposable part of the estate, indefeasible interests and other restrictions on dispositions of property upon death;

    e) the material validity of testamentary dispositions.

(3) Paragraph 2 does not preclude the application in a Contracting State of the law applicable under this Convention to other matters which are considered by that State to be governed by the law of succession.

D. *Pour-over Trusts*

UNIFORM PROBATE CODE

§2-511. *Testamentary Additions to Trusts.*

(a) A will may validly devise property to the trustee of a trust established or to be established (i) during the testator's lifetime by the testator, by the testator and some other person, or by some other person, including a funded or unfunded life insurance trust, although the settlor has reserved any or all rights of ownership of the insurance contracts, or (ii) at the testator's death by the testator's devise to the trustee, if the trust is identified in the testator's will and its terms are set forth in a written instrument, other than a will, executed before, concurrently with, or after the execution of the testator's will or in another individual's will if that other individual has predeceased the testator, regardless of the existence, size, or character of the corpus of the trust. The devise is not invalid because the trust is amendable or revocable, or because the trust was amended after the execution of the will or the testator's death.

(b) Unless the testator's will provides otherwise, property devised to a trust described in subsection (a) is not held under a testamentary trust of the testator, but it becomes a part of the trust to which it is devised, and must be administered and disposed of in accordance with the provisions of the governing instrument setting forth the terms of the trust, including any amendments thereto made before or after the testator's death.

(c) Unless the testator's will provides otherwise, a revocation or termination of the trust before the testator's death causes the devise to lapse.

PROBLEM

11-I. *A* entered into an unfunded life insurance trust agreement on January 20, 1972, designating *T* Trust Company as beneficiary under several policies insuring *A*'s life for a total of $50,000. The trust agreement reserved to *A* the power to amend or revoke the trust. Shortly thereafter *A* executed his will leaving the residue of his estate, amounting to about $100,000, "to the *T* Trust Company as trustee of that life insurance trust executed on January 20, 1972, of which I am the settlor, this property to be added to and administered as a part of said trust as it exists at the date of my death." Subsequent to the execution of this will, *A* amended the trust agreement. Although both the original trust agreement and the amendment were in writing, neither was executed with testamentary formalities. According to the original terms of the agreement, on *A*'s death the trustee was to invest the trust estate and to pay the income in equal shares to *A*'s son *S* and daughter *D,* and on the death of each, the child's issue were to receive outright the share of corpus from which the child had been receiving the income. The amendment removed *S* and his issue as beneficiaries, providing instead that the entire trust estate should be held for *D* for life, remainder to her issue. *A* has just died, survived by *S* and *D* and several children of each.

(a) What rights might *S* assert and how might his case be argued? What arguments can be made by the lawyer for *D* and her children, seeking to uphold the intended disposition of *A*'s estate and the insurance proceeds? Cf. State ex rel. Citizens National Bank v. Superior Court, 236 Ind. 135, 138 N.E.2d 900 (1956). Under what theory, if any, do *S*'s issue have a claim to some interest in the estate of *A*? Consider the cases and notes that follow. How would the case be affected if it arose under the law of your state? Under the Uniform Probate Code?

(b) In the absence of legislation authorizing testamentary additions to trusts, how would you have planned the will and trust for a client who wished to create a revocable and amendable trust and, at death, to provide for unified administration of the assets of the trust and those passing by will? What reasons might there be for "pouring over," other than the objective of unified administration?

In Atwood v. Rhode Island Hospital Trust Co., 275 Fed. 513 (1st Cir. 1921), the settlor created an amendable inter vivos trust and later executed a will providing for the residue of his estate to go to the "Rhode Island Hospital Trust Co., to be held, managed and disposed of as a part of the principal of the estate and property held by it in [the inter vivos trust] in the same manner as though the [residue] had been deposited by me as a part of said trust estate." He thereafter twice amended the remainder provisions of the trust. In invalidating this attempted pour-over, the court stated that the

> plan disclosed in the will and the inter vivos trust together is obnoxious to the statute of wills. . . . "A testator cannot by his will prospectively create for himself a power to dispose of his property by an instrument not duly executed as a will or codicil." . . .
>
> Manifestly, then, the real disposition of this residuary estate is made, not by the will, but by the shifting provisions in the trust instrument. No amount of discussion could make plainer the absolute destruction by such plans of the safeguarding provisions in the statute of wills. . . .
>
> It seems equally clear to us that this case does not fall within the rule which permits a testator to determine to some degree the objects of his testamentary bounty by his own subsequent conduct, as, for instance, in the cases of gifts to servants in the employ of a testator at his decease, or to surviving partners, or to the persons or institutions caring for the testator in his last sickness. . . . There is a great practical as well as legal difference between such relationships — arising "in the ordinary course of his affairs or in the management of his property" — and a relationship which arises solely out of the bounty-giving volition of the testator.

See also President & Directors of Manhattan Co. v. Janowitz, 260 App. Div. 174, 179, 21 N.Y.S.2d 232, 236-237 (1940):

> Here, while the original trust indenture and the first two supplemental indentures were in existence at the time the will was executed, the third supplemental indenture did not become effectual until after the will was executed, and the fourth supplemental indenture did not come into existence until approximately two months after the will was executed. . . . [T]he settlor reserved the right to alter and revoke the trust indenture and in fact modified it both prior and subsequent to the execution of his will. Therefore, the disposition . . . was not made by the will "but by the shifting provisions in the trust instrument." [Citing *Atwood.*] To permit the incorporation of the trust indenture, as amended, would allow the testator to alter his will by an instrument not published and attested as required by the statute of wills. The statute may not be so circumvented. Moreover, if the property is to pass under the original and three supplemental indentures, as the court below has decreed, then the purpose and intention of

the testator is frustrated because he intended that his property should be disposed of as provided in the original and four supplemental indentures. As stated by Professor Scott: " . . . [I]t would seem that the testamentary disposition should fail altogether, since the doctrine permits incorporation only of an instrument existing at the time of the execution of the will, and it would defeat the purpose of the testator to have the property pass according to the original terms of the inter vivos instrument."

Nor may article "Third" be upheld on the ground that the trust indenture and its amendments were facts of independent significance. . . . The reservation of the power to amend the trust indenture and its repeated exercise eliminated all independent significance that might be attached to the trust indenture.

Compare Clark v. Citizens National Bank, 38 N.J. Super. 69, 118 A.2d 108 (1955). On March 1, 1952, Clark, ill and confined to his home, executed two instruments, a will and an amendable inter vivos trust agreement. The will bequeathed the residue of Clark's estate to a named bank "subject to the terms and provisions of a certain agreement of trust entered into between the said Citizens National Bank and myself, and bearing even date herewith, including such amendments to and modifications of the same, if any, as may hereafter and during my life be made." There was no evidence showing the order of Clark's signing of the two instruments, but the court treated the trust as having been signed first since "it is to be presumed that the prescribed order has been followed." It was established, however, that the trust property had not been delivered to the bank or the trust accepted by the bank until Monday, March 3, 1952. After the will was admitted to probate, the attempted pour-over was challenged. The court held the residuary bequest invalid because (1) "one of the essential elements [of incorporation by reference] is lacking, i.e., the existence of a valid trust on the date of the execution of the will" and (2) "the trust instrument has no independent significance." In what respect is the court's statement about incorporation by reference fallacious? Would it have mattered if the trust had not been amendable?

Contrast Koeninger v. Toledo Trust Co., 49 Ohio App. 490, 197 N.E. 419 (1934), in which a preexisting inter vivos trust was amended subsequent to the execution of the will; the amendment was effective to modify the disposition of the original trust estate, but held under the doctrine of incorporation by reference the testamentary assets were to be held in trust according to the terms of the trust as they existed at the time the will was executed, unaffected by the subsequent amendment.

Today, the vast majority of states have pour-over legislation akin to Uniform Probate Code §2-511, supra, but the judicially recognized issues and concepts are still important to understand for marginal cases and analogous problem areas.

CANAL NATIONAL BANK v. CHAPMAN
157 Me. 309, 171 A.2d 919 (1961)

WILLIAMSON, C.J.

On report. This is an action by the Canal National Bank of Portland, executor under the will of Marion P. Harmon for construction of a "pour over" provision in the will. The issue is whether the property under paragraph Sixth of the will passes into an inter vivos trust as amended subsequent to the execution of the will, or passes into an inter vivos trust as it existed when the will was executed or passes by intestacy.

The facts are not in dispute. The testatrix, who is also the settlor of the trust, executed her will on September 24, 1948, and died on January 31, 1960. Paragraph Sixth of the will reads:

> *Sixth:* I hereby give, bequeath and devise all and any other rights and credits, cash on hand, monies in banks or on deposit, any notes, obligations and securities of any and all kinds to the Canal National Bank of Portland as well as any shares in any loan and building associations, the same to be added to and made a part of the Trust Fund created by me under a Trust Agreement with said Bank dated August 24, 1934, as well as any Supplemental Agreement or amendments thereof, in which Agreement provisions are made for additions to said fund.

The trust agreement of August 24, 1934 between the settlor and the plaintiff bank as trustee was a revocable and amendable inter vivos or living trust. At the time of the execution of the will the trust had been amended in 1942 and again on the day of the execution of the will in 1948.

On September 23, 1955, the trust was again amended with changes in the ultimate disposition of the trust property after the death of the settlor. The amendment was signed and sealed by the settlor and the trustee before one witness. In short, the amendment was not made with the formalities required for the execution of a will under the Statute of Wills (e.g., "subscribed in his presence by 3 credible attesting witnesses" — R.S. c. 169, §1).

It is unquestioned that the property held in the trust has been of substantial value since its inception in 1934, and likewise that property of substantial value passes under paragraph Sixth of the will. Indeed, in argument, without objection, it was indicated that at the death of the testatrix the trust amounted roughly to $120,000 and the estate to $93,000.

> The cardinal rule to be applied in the construction of a will is that the intention of the testator when clearly expressed in the will must be given effect, provided it be consistent with legal rules. . . . The intention of the testator is that which existed at the time of the execution of the will.

First Portland Natl. Bank v. Kaler-Vaill et al., 155 Me. 50, 57, 58, 151, A.2d 708, 712.

The testatrix beyond doubt intended under paragraph Sixth to add property to the trust as it existed at her death. We can think of no sound reason why the testatrix would have intended in 1948 that property should be added to the trust as it then existed, and not to the trust as it might later be amended. One trust and only one trust was intended, and this was the trust created by her in 1934 and continuing after her decease.

The doctrine of incorporation by reference is not applicable under the circumstances. First: The 1955 amendment to the trust was not in existence in 1948 when the will was executed. By definition, therefore, it could not have been incorporated by reference in the will. First Portland Natl. Bank v. Kaler-Vaill et al., supra; In re Sleeper (Littlefield), 129 Me. 194, 151 A. 150, 171 A.L.R. 518. Second: The testatrix intended, as we have discussed above, to add property not to the trust existing by virtue of the 1934 agreement as amended when the will was executed, but to the trust existing on her death in 1960. Lastly, the testatrix intended to create not a testamentary trust, but to add property to an existing continuing non-testamentary trust, revocable and amendable in her lifetime.

Our decision is reached through the operation of the doctrine of the facts of independent significance. Here we have in the inter vivos trust as amended after the execution of the will such a fact. The 1934 trust as amended in 1955 is itself of unquestioned validity. The case arises as we have seen not with reference to the validity of the trust, but with reference to the validity of the provision of the will for "pouring over" assets from the estate to the trust.

The trust from 1934 until the death of the testatrix at no time was a mere shell without the body of a trust. The trust with substantial assets has had since 1934 and continues to have an active independent life of its own. We are not concerned here, for example, with a trust with nominal or no assets in the settlor's lifetime which in substance is created by will. There is not the slightest suggestion that the trust will wither away unless nourished by the gift under paragraph Sixth. On the separate entity of the inter vivos trust see Swetland v. Swetland, 102 N.J. Eq. 294, 140 A. 279; In re York's Estate, 95 N.H. 435, 65 A.2d 282, 8 A.L.R.2d 611; Matter of Rausch's Will (In re Locke), 258 N.Y. 327, 179 N.E. 755, 80 A.L.R. 98, which, however, do not involve amendments after the will.

There are situations not uncommon in the settlement of estates which bear a strong analogy to the case before us. In Lear v. Manser, 114 Me. 342, 96 A. 240, we held valid a gift in trust "to such person or persons, or to such institution as shall care for me in my last sickness." The identification of the beneficiary was considered sufficiently certain and capable of proof.

The "receptacle cases" so-called, are also in point. In Merrill v. Winchester, 120 Me. 203, at page 216, 113 A. 261, at page 267, the following provision was sustained:

> To said Clossen C. Hanson I give in trust for himself and wife and children as may suit the needs and wishes of each, the libraries in my house in rooms below and above and all books, magazines, papers, etc. and all articles of personal property in said house not herein otherwise disposed of; and also all personal property of every kind in my stable and buildings, not heretofore mentioned.

In Gaff v. Cornwallis, 219 Mass. 226, 106 N.E. 860, the Court upheld the gift of the contents of a drawer. The opportunity, for example, of adding or removing books from libraries or contents from a drawer after the execution of a will is obvious.

In each of the cases noted there is a fact of independent significance, that is to say, a fact of significance apart from its effect upon the disposition of property under the will. The "pour over," the future identification, the "receptacle" are alike in this respect.

The "pour over" problem has not been decided specifically by our Court. . . .

In Second Bank-State Street Trust Co. v. Pinion, Mass., 170 N.E.2d 350, decided in 1960, a "pour over" from an estate to an amendable, revocable inter vivos trust amended after the execution of the will was upheld. The court said, at page 352:

> We agree with modern legal thought that a subsequent amendment is effective because of the applicability of the established equitable doctrine that subsequent acts of independent significance do not require attestation under the statute of wills. . . .

We find no solid ground for refusing to give effect to the intention of the testatrix. The trust is adequately identified in the will. The provisions of the trust for amendment were duly carried out. The amendments and indeed the trust as amended are facts of independent significance. The "pour over" under paragraph Sixth from estate to trust as it existed at the death of the testatrix is valid and the executor should make distribution to itself as trustee thereunder.

The entry will be remanded for judgment in accordance with this opinion. Cost and reasonable counsel fees to be determined by the single justice to be paid from the estate.

Note on "court" and "noncourt" trusts — retained jurisdiction in the probate court. In some states, statutes provide that testamentary trusts (then called *court trusts*) are subject to continuing jurisdiction in the court of probate, whereas in most of these same states trusts that are created inter vivos are not. The latter then remain subject to the traditional jurisdiction of equity courts. A few of these probate statutes apply to inter vivos trusts as well, or provide that living trusts become subject to continuing jurisdiction of the probate court once the court's jurisdiction is invoked by one of the parties. The retained jurisdiction is likely to entail required periodic accountings in court and judicial supervision and control. These are often considered to be burdensome and costly, especially for nonprofessional trustees. The often unreleasable attachment to the court of probate may prove to be a particular nuisance when administration of the trust in another state is desirable, and court-trust status often precludes the appointment of a foreign (that is, out-of-state) corporate fiduciary as trustee. By contrast, *noncourt trusts* are subject to no continuing jurisdiction of court, but justiciable matters are generally brought to a convenient court of equity that has a basis for jurisdiction. Court trusts are sometimes favored by settlors and their lawyers because they offer trustees and beneficiaries broader and more expeditious access to court, whereas noncourt trusts are often preferred for their greater administrative flexibility, simplicity, and freedom. The preference in any given case will depend on such things as the nature of the property to be administered and the expected location of the beneficiaries. Pour-overs may be resorted to as a means of attempting to manipulate the court or noncourt character of trusts and thus court jurisdiction where arbitrary distinctions are drawn between testamentary and living trusts. Sometimes the inverse of the pour-overs in the above cases is used, the objective being to add the assets of an inter vivos trust (sometimes an insurance trust) to a testamentary trust after the latter has been established. Article 7 of the Uniform Probate Code seeks to eliminate these distinctions between trusts created by will and those created inter vivos, providing for interstate mobility and offering ready access to a single court for all trusts without the disadvantages of continuing jurisdiction.

PROBLEM

11-J. *A* created a revocable living trust on June 10, 1985, with *T* Trust Company as trustee. In 1986 *A* executed a will leaving the residue of his estate "to *T* Trust Company, as trustee of the trust created by me on June 10, 1985, to be held and administered in accordance with the provisions of said trust." In 1990 *A* revoked the living trust but made no changes in his will. *A* has just died. What is the effect of the residuary bequest? How would you argue the case for *A*'s next of kin? For the beneficiaries designated in the original trust instrument? What facts would be relevant for purposes of guiding your investigation? See Fifty-Third Union Trust Co. v. Wilensky, 79 Ohio App. 73, 70 N.E.2d 920 (1946);

but cf. Bank of Delaware v. Bank of Delaware, 39 Del. Ch. 187, 161 A.2d 430 (1960).

If *A*'s will had provided that if his wife, *W*, should predecease him the residue of his estate was to pass "to the trustee under the will of my wife, executed on this date, upon the terms therein provided," what is the result if at *A*'s death *W* had changed her will and predeceased him? See Marshall v. Northern Trust Co., 22 Ill. 2d 391, 176 N.E.2d 807 (1961); cf. In re Brandenburg's Will, 13 Wis. 2d 217, 108 N.W.2d 374 (1961).

With the above cases and problems, compare the situation in which *A*'s will provides that certain property shall be disposed of as *B* directs by her will. *A* has given *B* a *power of appointment*, and if after *A*'s death *B* makes a will appointing to *C*, the power is validly exercised. If *B* had executed her will before *A*'s death but survived *A*, it is also generally held that the power was validly exercised, unless this is found to be contrary to the intent of *A* or of *B*. Restatement (Second) of Property §17.6. If *B* had predeceased *A*, however, she could not have exercised the power because it had not yet come into existence. The power is not created by *A*'s will until *A*, the donor of the power, dies. Consequently the power of appointment lapses. Can the disposition to persons in *B*'s will still be given effect if it is found that *A* so intended? See Restatement (Second) of Property §18.4.

E. Some Further Questions

PHILLIPS, TOWARD A TRUST SETTLEMENT OPTION
24 Chartered Life Underwriters J. 38-43 (1970)

. . . Historically, [a major source of investment activity] for life insurance companies has been death proceeds left with the company. The lack of flexibility both in investment policy and in payment provisions available through life insurance settlement options has caused insureds and their beneficiaries to take their money elsewhere. . . .

One prime reason for the shift from settlement options to trusts is the ability of trustees to invest in equities as well as fixed dollars. A hedge against inflation and a potentially higher rate of return have been offered by the trusts. . . . Life insurance companies have been creating competitive vehicles for equity investment. The variable annuity plans and mutual funds offered by life insurance companies have had excellent investment returns. . . .

Estate planners recommend trusts more often for their flexibility in payment provisions than for their investment return or as a hedge against inflation. Trusts permit the use of discretionary powers, while life settlement options are much more restricted. Life insurers permit invasion of proceeds only in specific dollar or percentage amounts by the beneficiaries, or in full. Withdrawal privileges subject proceeds to estate tax in the estate of the beneficiary. Trustees, on the other hand, may [if authorized by the trust terms] invade proceeds at their discretion, sprinkle income among beneficiaries according to the needs of the beneficiaries and even accumulate income. These discretionary powers are extremely valuable. No insured can predict during his lifetime the needs of his beneficiaries after his death. . . .

Life insurance companies have, I submit, two choices: (1) They can continue to abdicate payout and investment of death proceeds to banks and trust companies or (2) they can create a new vehicle to compete in this area. The thesis of this article is that a new settlement option, perhaps called a "Trust Settlement Option," should be developed by life insurance companies.

Insurers would have to become trust companies or seek special enabling legislation. But why not? . . . A number of dormant charters already exist. Many United States life insurers had trust powers from their inception. . . .

I believe that charters would be available for one compelling reason — it would be good for the insuring public. Let me suggest the advantages:

(1) "Trust Settlement Options" would be less costly to the buyer. Now the public must pay the cost of transferring funds out of one investment medium, the insurance company, into another financial institution. Reinvestment commissions, trustees' opening and closing fees could be saved.

(2) More trusts would be created. Life insurance agents are trained to get action. They are able to inform and convince the owners of life insurance policies to adopt trusts where appropriate. How many wills, trusts and buy-sell agreements exist solely because a conscientious life insurance agent persuaded a client to act in his own interest?

(3) Geographic problems of trust companies would be overcome. Banks and trust companies do not cross state lines. Life insurers, on the other hand, have offices all over the country. Regional trust administration offices could be created. . . .

The insurance companies are uniquely equipped to do a better job [than is currently being done in the field]. Insurance companies have investment and service departments without peer. These departments, which are highly computerized, can provide trust settlements profitably at low cost to beneficiaries. Most important, insurers have highly trained agents in the field, able to explain the advantages of trusts to the public and to get action. . . .

In the long run, many observers believe that life insurance companies will have complete trust powers and will also be providing full banking services. Conversely, banks and trust companies will be competing in the insurance arena. This competition should provide better services and products for the insuring public.

How do you react to this proposal, especially insofar as it might involve simplified creation of trusts in several more or less standardized forms through insurance settlement options? Compare this with the use of "canned" trusts in the form of custodianships via Gifts to Minors legislation. See Chapter 8. The Uniform Custodial Trust Act (1987) provides for the creation of a complete, revocable, discretionary trust by a simple designation or registration in statutory form. The Act has been enacted in Hawaii, Idaho, Minnesota, Missouri, Rhode Island, and Virginia. The Prefatory Note to this Act states:

> This Uniform Act provides for the creation of a statutory custodial trust for adults to be governed by the provisions of the Act whenever property is delivered to another "as custodial trustee under the (Enacting state) Uniform Custodial Trust Act." . . . The Custodial Trust Act is designed to provide a statutory standby inter vivos trust for individuals who typically are not very affluent or sophisticated, and possibly represented by attorneys engaged in general rather than specialized estate practice. The most frequent use of this trust would be in response to the commonly occurring need of elderly individuals to provide for the future management of assets in the event of incapacity. The statute will also be available for accomplishing distribution of funds by judgment debtors and others to incapacitated persons for whom a conservator has not been appointed. Since this Act allows any person, competent to transfer property, to create custodial trusts for the benefit of themselves or others, with the beneficial interest in custodial trust property in the beneficiary and not in the custodial trustee, its potential for use is extensive. . . .
>
> This Act follows the approach taken by the Uniform Transfers to Minors Act and allows any kind of property, real or personal, tangible or intangible, to be made the subject of a transfer to a custodial trustee for the benefit of a beneficiary. However, the most typical transaction envisioned would involve a person who would transfer intangible property, such as securities or bank accounts, to a custodial trustee but with retention by the transferor of direction over the property. Later, this direction could be relinquished, or it could be lost upon incapacity. The objective of the statute is to provide a simple trust that is uncomplicated in its creation, administration, and termination. . . . A simple transfer document, examples of which are set forth in the Act, and a receipt from the custodian, also in the Act, would provide for identification of beneficiaries or distributees upon death of the beneficiary. Protection is extended to third parties dealing with the custodian. . . .

See G. W. Beyer, Simplification of Intervivos Trust Instruments, 32 S. Tex. L. Rev. 203 (1991). Also compare the widespread use of statutory trusts in England since 1925 in certain intestate situations and for family provision. See Chapters 2 and 3. Consider the possible pros and cons of attempting to develop more general legislation offering several alternative forms of statutory trusts that could be easily invoked, if one wished to do so instead of having one's own trust tailor-made, by a simple reference in a will or other instrument of transfer to the desired statutory trust option. See generally Halbach, Probate and Estate Planning: Reducing Need and Cost Through Change in the Law (Ch. 11), in Death, Taxes and Family Property 169-174 (American Assembly 1977); G. W. Beyer, Statutory Will Methodologies, 94 Dick. L. Rev. 231 (1990).

In the last few years legislation has been enacted establishing statutory forms for complete wills, first in California (one simple and one with trust for minor children), and then in a number of other states. Another legislative effort is the Uniform Statutory Will Act (1984). The Prefatory Note to this act states:

> The Uniform Statutory Will Act is a proposed statute to provide a scheme of testamentary disposition of broad utility. This Act contemplates that a testator will *adopt* the statutory *will through incorporation by reference* in a "simple will." This Act does not provide a battery of optional schemes or provisions, but it does permit modifications and additions to be made by the will which adopts the statutory-wills scheme generally or for some portion of the testator's estate. The statutory will may be the entire will of a testator and thus apply to all of the testator's testamentary estate, or it is adaptable to apply to a portion of the testator's estate as part of a will which includes other devises. . . .
>
> If the testator's intent is that the statutory will is to dispose of the entire testamentary estate, the plan can be adopted by the simplest kind of will. [This permits a] testator to achieve the desired testamentary scheme not only simply and at a lower cost, but the statutory will also probably reduces the risk of error and mistake.
>
> In effect, the statutory will is an optional alternative to intestacy. . . . Since the statutory will is an expression of testator's intent (as contrasted with intestacy statutes based on the absence of any expression of decedent's intent), this Uniform Statutory Will Act adopts some provisions based on the probable intent of the testator, which provisions will not be consistent with provisions applicable in intestacy in the enacting state. . . .

As you reflect on this chapter's major problem areas involving (1) oral promises and the statute of frauds, (2) the possible testamentary character of revocable inter vivos trusts, and (3) the validity of pour-over transactions, consider how the handling of these problems by the courts does or does not reflect the considerations and policies discussed in the excerpts from the Gulliver and Tillson article in the introduction to Chapter 4 and the Mechem article in Chapter 8.

12

The Nature of the Beneficiaries' Interests

This chapter deals with the rights of a beneficiary to enforce the interest the settlor intended to confer, as the court determines the settlor's intent from the terms of the trust interpreted in light of the relevant circumstances. This chapter also concerns certain of the characteristics of various beneficial interests, including transferability and susceptibility to the claims of a beneficiary's creditors.

A. Enforceability of Beneficial Interests

1. General Principles

A beneficiary can compel the trustee to carry out the terms of the trust and to administer the trust in accordance with fiduciary standards. Problems of administration and management of trust property are taken up in subsequent chapters. At this point we are concerned with the trustee's duties and the beneficiaries' rights as they relate to the dispositive provisions of the trust. Certain closely related matters, such as the determination of what receipts and disbursements are allocable to principal and income, are also deferred.

Arising from the recognition that a beneficiary's rights can be enforced not only against the trustee but can also be asserted against third parties is the conceptual question, What is the true nature of a beneficial interest under a trust? Is the beneficiary an equitable owner of the trust property, or does the cestui que trust have something more akin to a personal claim against the trustee? One leading scholar expressed the "considered judgment . . . that the traditional and historically sound view (namely, that the beneficiary of a trust has only a chose in action plus collateral and supplementary protections against interferences by third persons) is still pragmatically the preferable modern rule." 4 R. Powell, Real Property §515 (1967). But see Restatement (Second) of

Trusts §130. Chemical Bank New York Trust Co. v. Steamship West-
hampton, 358 F.2d 574, 584 (4th Cir. 1965), states:

> Scholars have long debated whether the beneficiary of a trust has a prop-
> erty interest in the trust res or merely a personal right against the trustee.
> The courts have had less trouble with this question. The Supreme Court
> has held that beneficiaries of a trust have an interest in the property to
> which the trustee holds legal title.

SCOTT, THE IMPORTANCE OF THE TRUST
39 U. Colo. L. Rev. 177-179 (1967)

The great historian of the English law, Professor Maitland, has said:
"The idea of a trust is so familiar to us all that we never wonder at it. And
yet surely we ought to wonder." He went on to say that the greatest and
most distinctive achievement performed by Englishmen in the field of
jurisprudence is the development from century to century of the trust
idea.

Foreign scholars, trained in the civil law, have difficulty in grasping the
trust idea. The German historian Gierke said to Maitland, "I can't
understand your trust." Many books have been written by scholars in
Germany and in France, in Italy and in Holland, in Central and South
America, undertaking to explain the Anglo-American trust. They find
great difficulty in trying to insert it into their jurisprudential systems.
Should it be classified under Obligations or under Property? As the Ger-
mans would put it, is the trust to be put under the head of *Obligationen-
recht* or under *Sachenrecht*?

The truth is that the chancellors in England who invented the trust
were practical men rather than jurists. They did not bother with problems of juristic classification.

It all started with transfers of land made to the use of the transferor
or of a third person. Such transfers began not long after the Norman
Conquest and had become common before the fifteenth century. At first
no legal problems were involved since the beneficiaries of the use had
no legal remedies. They had to trust to the honor of the transferee. But
early in the fifteenth century the chancellors began to enforce the claim
of the beneficiary against the transferee. They held that he should be
compelled in equity to do what conscience required him to do. They
punished him for contempt if he refused to carry out the purposes for
which the property was given to him. There was no remedy in the courts
of law but there was now a remedy in equity.

At first it was unnecessary for the chancellors to consider whether they
were merely enforcing a personal obligation of the transferee or
whether they were protecting a property interest of the beneficiary. But
they were soon compelled to deal with the question whether the bene-

ficiary had something more than merely a personal claim against the transferee.

In the first place, the question arose whether on the death intestate of a beneficiary of a use or trust of land his interest should be treated as a chose in action which would pass to his next of kin, or as an interest in land which would descend to his heir. The chancellors held that equity should follow the law, and that the beneficiary's interest should descend on his death to the person who would be entitled to a corresponding legal interest. At that time most of the land in England was held subject to uses, and to hold that the use should pass to the next of kin would upset the whole policy of primogeniture. The use was accordingly treated at least for this purpose as an interest in land rather than merely as a claim against the holder of the legal title. Moreover it was held that the beneficiary's interest was transferable by him, although at that time choses in action were not transferable.

In the second place, the question arose whether the beneficiary was entitled to relief against subsequent transferees of the property. After some hesitation the chancellors held that the beneficiary had a remedy against subsequent transferees who took with notice of the beneficiary's claim, against the heir or devisee of the transferee, against donees of the property and against creditors of the transferee. Thus they recognized that the beneficiary had something more than merely a personal claim against the original transferee. They treated his interest as an interest in the property. They refused, however, to give the beneficiary relief against a purchaser for value and without notice, thus making the interest of the beneficiary more vulnerable than that of a legal owner of property.

In the third place, they held that if the transferee exchanged the property for other property, the beneficiary was entitled to follow the res and compel the transferee to surrender the other property, since it was the product of property of the beneficiary.

All this seems to make it clear that the chancellors had come to recognize that the beneficiary had a property interest and not merely a claim against the trustee. . . .

Today it is generally agreed in England as well as in the United States that the beneficiaries of a trust have a proprietary interest in the subject matter of the trust and not merely a personal claim against the trustee. Although the trustee has the legal title, the beneficiaries are the equitable owners. The chancellors created a new kind of property interest. . . .

In the common situation in which a beneficiary is entitled to the income from the trust estate, or from a portion thereof, the trustee can be compelled to make the income payments at reasonable intervals where payment dates are not fixed by the terms of the trust. The trustee is liable for interest on amounts unreasonably withheld. If there is an overpayment or payment to the wrong person, the trustee is liable to the proper beneficiary, even though the trustee acted in good faith. Misinterpretation of the trust instrument and mistakes of law or fact, even though reasonable, are generally no defense. In order to be protected in the event of doubt, a trustee should apply to the proper court for instructions. If granted, such instructions will normally protect the trustee from liability. Where reasonable doubt exists as to who is entitled to a distribution, a delay is justifiable, and the trustee is not personally liable for interest on amounts reasonably withheld.

A trustee may generally withhold income reasonably required as a reserve for those anticipated expenses that, although extraordinary, would be chargeable to income. This is treated merely as an aspect of determining the proper net income of a period. On the other hand, where a beneficiary is entitled to the income, a trustee may not retain any of the net income merely because it is not needed by the beneficiary; nor can the trustee distribute principal that is ultimately to be paid to another because the income is inadequate for the needs of the income beneficiary, assuming no provision authorizing such payments.

2. Discretionary Distributions

Much of the essential character of the trust relationship and of the rights of beneficiaries is revealed by the issues posed by trusts in which some of the beneficial interests are subject to the discretion of the trustee. It has become common, particularly in recent years, for the trustee to be given the power to decide certain matters relating to the benefits to be received by the beneficiaries. Most well-drawn trusts include a provision for invasion of principal for the needs of the income beneficiary, who is often the primary object of the settlor's bounty. Sometimes a life beneficiary is not given the right to income but is entitled only to such payments as are required for a certain purpose, typically support. Trusts occasionally provide that the income, or part of the income, is to be distributed among a group of beneficiaries in amounts to be decided by the trustee. Modern tax law often encourages the use of discretionary powers to determine the distributive rights of beneficiaries. As the rights of beneficiaries and the problems of their enforcement are studied, consider the significance of these problems in the interviewing of clients and in the planning and drafting of trust provisions. See generally Halbach, Problems of Discretion in Discretionary Trusts, 61 Colum. L. Rev. 1425 (1961).

See Judge Learned Hand's widely quoted dictum in Stix v. Commissioner of Internal Revenue, 152 F.2d 562, 563 (2d Cir. 1945):

[N]o language however strong, will entirely remove any power held in trust from the reach of a court of equity. After allowance has been made for every possible factor which could rationally enter into the trustee's decision, if it appears that he has utterly disregarded the interests of the beneficiary, the Court will intervene. Indeed, were that not true, the power would not be held in trust at all; the language would be no more than a precatory admonition.

PROBLEM

12-A.   You have been asked to review the draft of a will by which *H*, if survived by his wife, *W*, wishes to create a trust for *W*'s life with remainder on her death to certain of *H*'s collateral relatives, there being no issue. The draft presently provides in relevant part:

a. The Trustee shall pay the net income annually to my wife.

b. In addition to such income, the Trustee may pay to my wife such amount of the principal of the trust as the Trustee in its absolute discretion deems appropriate.

What problems do you see in paragraph *b*? If those problems become issues in litigation, how would you expect them to be handled by a court? In particular, what types of changes would you suggest be made in this provision for invasion of principal before the will is executed? Consider the materials that follow and what additional information you need to know about *H*'s purposes and the circumstances of *H* and *W* in order to make specific changes of the types you would suggest.

ROWE v. ROWE
219 Or. 599, 347 P.2d 968 (1959)

[Suit for declaratory judgment to construe the provisions of two similar testamentary trusts under which plaintiff is the surviving life beneficiary and the trustee and remainderman are defendants. The trusts, created by the wills of Enoch and Nellie Peterson (who died in a common disaster), were for the primary benefit of Mrs. Peterson's parents. Mrs. Peterson's cousin, as trustee, had power to distribute income and principal to the two beneficiaries "entirely according to his own judgment and discretion." In five years or so since the trust was created its income approximated $7,500, of which a total of $600 had been paid out to the plaintiff and his now deceased wife.]

O'CONNELL, J. . . .

The provision in question was effective to create a discretionary trust. Such a trust may be created even though there is no *specific* standard to guide the trustee in exercising his authority. Stated differently, a settlor may create a valid trust which vests in the trustee the discretion to pay or apply only so much of the income or principal as the trustee sees fit. 2 Scott on Trusts (2d ed.) §§128.3 and 155; 3 Bogert, Trusts and Trustees, §560. The standard in such a case is not a specific one, such as the beneficiaries' need, but is, rather, a general standard of reasonableness in exercising the discretion granted to him. The standard is stated in 2 Scott on Trusts, §128.3, p. 936 as follows:

> . . . If the settlor manifested an intention that the discretion of the trustee should be uncontrolled, the court will not interfere unless he acts dishonestly or from an improper motive.

The court will not interfere if the trustee acts within "the bounds of a reasonable judgment." 2 Scott on Trusts, §187, p. 1375. What these bounds are will vary with the terms and purposes of the trust and the circumstances of each case. Although there are some cases which seem to express a contrary view, there would appear to be no reason why a settlor could not, if he wished, vest in the trustee the authority to dispose of, or withhold, the income of a trust upon the basis of the trustee's own judgment unrelated to any standard. There is no policy precluding a person from vesting in another the uncontrolled authority to dispose of the property of the donor of the power. This is evident from the fact that the law has long recognized that a general power of appointment may be conferred upon a donee permitting him to dispose of the property to whomsoever he pleases and for reasons which are left entirely to his own choice. . . .

There is an abundance of authority recognizing the proposition that the trustee may be given a discretion so broad that he may refuse to make a disposition of the trust property for reasons which he is pleased to withhold. The rule is stated in 2 Scott on Trusts, §187.2, p. 1388, as follows: "By the terms of the trust the requirement of reasonableness in the exercise of a discretionary power by the trustee may be dispensed with." . . .

> . . . In such a case the exercise by the trustee of his discretion will not be interfered with by the court, even though he acts beyond the bounds of a reasonable judgment, if he acts in good faith and does not act capriciously. . . .
>
> Even though there is no standard by which it can be judged whether the trustee is acting reasonably or not, or though by the terms of the trust he is not required to act reasonably, the court will interfere where he acts dishonestly or in bad faith, or where he acts from an improper motive. . . .

We must decide, however, whether the language of the provision, read in light of the circumstances existing at the time of the creation of the trust, conferred upon the trustee a more restricted power.

When the specific purpose or purposes of the settlor can be ascertained the trustee's choice of action, if it is to constitute a reasonable judgment, must be within the limits set by the settlor's purpose. The difficulty in many if not in most of these cases is finding the purpose of the settlor with sufficient definiteness to be helpful in marking out the limits beyond which the trustee should not be permitted to go in dealing with the trust property. The settlor's specific design in framing a discretionary trust is normally unexpressed or vaguely outlined. In looking outside of the terms of the trust itself the court is permitted to consider the circumstances attendant upon the creation of the trust in attempting to determine the scope of the trustee's power, but frequently these circumstances are not particularly illuminating.

The instant case presents an example of this difficulty of finding the settlor's purpose in the creation of a particular trust. We receive no aid to construction from the language directing the trustee "to pay to and for the use and benefit" of the life beneficiaries. This language is . . . not equivalent to the words "for the maintenance and support." Huffman v. Chasteen, 1948, 307 Ky. 1, 209 S.W.2d 705. . . .

The beneficiaries were the natural objects of Nellie's bounty; but not of Enoch Peterson's bounty. As the will recites, the life tenants were at an advanced age in life, one being 74 and the other 75 years of age. At the time of the death of the settlors the life beneficiaries owned property the total value of which was not made clear by the testimony, but it was at least $24,000. There was no other evidence of the circumstances existing at the time of the making of the wills from which we might derive the trust purpose.

The trustee indicated in his testimony that he understood that he had the duty to pay income to the life beneficiaries in case of "need." He stated that he was guided in the exercise of his judgment by what was stated in the will and by what Enoch Peterson, one of the settlors, told him. Statements made by a testator at the time of the execution of his will generally are not admissible for the purpose of showing his intention with respect to the disposition of his property. There is an exception where the evidence is necessary to aid in interpreting an equivocation. Since the scope of the trustee's power under the trust before us was not clear his declaration of purpose in vesting discretion in the trustee may have been admissible to resolve the uncertainty. However, it is not necessary for us to pass upon this question. . . . [B]oth plaintiff and defendants have proceeded upon the assumption that trustee's power is limited to a determination of the needs of the life beneficiaries; it is assumed that the only question is whether the trustee properly interpreted the meaning of "needs" by limiting payments to such small amounts and to the few instances mentioned. The trustee understood that he was to pay over income to the beneficiaries only if they were in need in the sense that they lacked the essential things in life or were substantially inconvenienced by the lack of money. . . . The trustee explains that he made such limited payments because the life beneficiaries were getting along fairly well with the income they were receiving from other sources.

Plaintiff testified that he had "about eight or ten thousand" dollars in cash; a pension of $100 a month; social security of $87.90; a little income from property and investments. Plaintiff owned his own home free of encumbrances; he also owned a television set, an automobile (which was later destroyed, however), a Wurlitzer organ, and other items of furniture and equipment. With respect to house furnishings plaintiff testified that he and his present wife had "everything we need."

There is no question of the trustee's good faith in making his decision to limit the payments as he did. The only question presented is the reasonableness of his judgment. It is quite possible that we would have been more liberal in our treatment of the life beneficiaries had the power to decide been vested in us. But we have no right to substitute our judgment for that of the trustee. 3 Bogert, Trusts and Trustees §560; 2 Scott on Trusts §187. We are permitted to control the trustee only if we can say that no reasonable person vested with the power which was conferred upon the trustee in this case could have exercised that power in the manner in which it was exercised. We cannot say that the trustee's conduct in the instant case was unreasonable in this sense. . . .

It should be noted that the trust in question was created not only for the life beneficiaries but for the remaindermen as well. In vesting a broad discretion in the trustee it is possible that the settlors intended that the trustee should consider the needs of the remaindermen as well as the needs of the life beneficiaries. There is nothing in the record to show the needs of the remaindermen. . . . Irrespective of whether this was a consideration, we are without authority to interfere with the trustee's function under the circumstances of this case. . . .

What is the significance of a provision granting a trustee "absolute" or "sole and uncontrolled discretion"? Restatement (Second) of Trusts §187, comment j (1959), widely quoted by courts, states that words like these are not taken literally but "are ordinarily construed as merely dispensing with the standard of reasonableness," so that courts will not intervene where the trustee has merely "acted beyond the bounds of reasonable judgment" so long as the trustee acts "in a state of mind . . . contemplated by the settlor." Can you suggest why an extended discretion of this type might be granted? Can you think of drafting alternatives for accomplishing the objectives you suggest? Is the language in the above case ("entirely according to his own judgment and discretion") the equivalent of "absolute" or "sole and uncontrolled" discretion? Also, consider the difficulties that standardless discretionary powers like the one in the *Rowe* case present to the trustee and ultimately to a court. And consider what dangers this type of discretion poses in the hands of fiduciaries and, on review, even in the hands of judges. Compare K. Davis, Discretionary Justice: A Preliminary Inquiry v (1969):

If all decisions involving justice to individual parties were lined up on a scale, with those governed by precise rules at the extreme left, those involving unfettered discretion at the extreme right, and those based on various mixtures of rules, principles, standards, and discretion in the middle, where on the scale might be the most serious and the most frequent injustice? I believe that officers and judges do reasonably well at the rules end of the scale, because rules make for evenhandedness, because creation of rules usually is relatively unemotional, and because decision-makers seldom err in the direction of excessive rigidity when individualization is needed. And probably injustice is almost as infrequent toward the middle of the scale, where principles or other guides keep discretion limited or controlled. I think the greatest and most frequent injustice occurs at the discretion end of the scale, where rules and principles provide little or no guidance, where emotions of deciding officers may affect what they do, where political or other favoritism may influence decision, and where the imperfections of human nature are often reflected in the choices made.

See also Davis, Judicial Review of Fiduciary Decisionmaking — Some Theoretical Perspectives, 80 Nw. U.L. Rev. 1 (1985), especially at 40-49.

The issue before the court in the case that follows is today, as the Surrogate noted it was at the time of the decision, one of the most frequently litigated questions in the trust law. Yet it continues to be much neglected in drafting.

In re GATEHOUSE'S WILL
149 Misc. 648, 267 N.Y. Supp. 808 (Surr. Ct. 1933)

WINGATE, S.

The present proceeding raises again the frequently litigated question of testamentary interpretation, as to whether, on a gift for support and maintenance, the private resources of the beneficiary shall be taken into consideration in determining the amount properly payable to him for this purpose from the funds of the estate. An examination of reported cases on the subject indicates that this question is one of growing interest, since it has been raised almost as many times in the last decade as during the entire preceding period of New York legal history.

In the case at bar, the testator, by the "fourteenth" item of his will, gave the residue of his estate to his executors and trustees with directions:

> To pay the entire income therefrom to my wife, Kathryn H. Gatehouse, for and during her natural life, and should the income prove insufficient to maintain my wife in her accustomed style of living, then I direct my Trustees in their discretion to apply from the principal so much as may be necessary to maintain my wife in her accustomed style of living. I further direct my Trustees to pay from the principal all necessary expenses

incurred for hospital or medical attention or other extraordinary expenses that may be necessary for the care and comfort of my wife. In the event of any unforeseen or unexpected emergency that will require additional funds for the necessary care of my wife, I authorize and direct my Trustees, or either of them, in their discretion, to make such payment as to them or either of them may seem best. It is my intention to amply provide for the care and comfort of my wife and the discretion given to my Trustees is to be used by them in a broad sense, and I hereby expressly relieve them or either of them from the necessity of accounting to any person except my wife for the exercise of their discretion. . . .

At the time of the executorial accounting in 1929, a question having arisen in respect to the annual sum necessary to maintain the beneficiary in her accustomed style of living, the matter was fully litigated, and such sum was fixed at $3,600 a year, which, in view of the income of the trust at that time, involved an annual invasion of principal to the extent of $740.

It has now been made to appear that the widow was remarried, with consequent obligation upon her present husband to support and maintain her, and it is contended that by reason of this fact, further payments for this purpose from the estate of her first husband are improper.

This position is contested by the cestui que trust for two reasons: First, on the ground that the terms of the will absolutely entitle her to support; and, secondly, that her second husband has fallen on evil days and is unable to maintain her. If her first contention were to be overruled, an issue of fact would be presented for trial on the second; but if the first position is sound, the second is immaterial.

Under ordinary circumstances, as has been pointed out on innumerable occasions, particular precedents are substantially valueless in testamentary interpretation. In the present instance, however, the paucity of possible variations in testamentary language in this regard arouses interest in previous adjudications respecting the subject. Of the . . . most frequently cited decisions of New York courts bearing on the question, seventeen have determined that the private sources of support of the beneficiary have no bearing upon his rights in a testamentary gift for that purpose, [while six] have reached contrary results. . . .

Holden v. Strong, 116 N.Y. 471, 22 N.E. 960, 961 . . . is, perhaps, the leading precedent in this state on the general subject. The testator there gave the residue of his estate in trust for his son, vesting the trustee with "full power and authority to use so much of the said trust fund, either interest or principal" as shall, in the "judgment and discretion" of said trustee "be necessary for the proper care, comfort and maintenance" of his son. In determining that the beneficiary was entitled to receive his entire support from the fund irrespective of his other means or sources of income, the court said at page 475 of 116 N.Y., 22 N.E. 960, 961:

> We do not understand that in order to receive the benefit of the provisions of the will it is necessary for him to remain idle and refrain from all per-

sonal exertion, neither does the fact that he is frugal and saving and has accumulated a fund which he has deposited in the bank deprive him of the right to the support provided for him.

An analysis of the foregoing precedents demonstrates that in all except two of their number the courts have carefully analyzed the donative language to determine precisely what was given by the will. . . .

As has many times been indicated, the purpose in the mind of the testator in the making of a gift is wholly immaterial so long as such purpose does not modify the terms of the gift itself, and the latter remains absolute and unqualified. A gift of "support and maintenance," if absolute, is therefore merely a gift of a sum of money, the amount of which is ascertainable by a calculation of the component effect of extraneous circumstances and contributing factors, and differs neither in nature nor in kind from an ordinary gift of income; the sole diversity arising from the difference of the factors which unite in determining the particular number of dollars which the donee thereof is entitled to receive.

It follows, therefore, that when an absolute gift is made of the sum which is compounded from the elements going into the computation of "support and maintenance," it assumes the nature of any other absolute gift and is not subject to defeat by an extraneous condition. No one would have the temerity to assert that because a legatee of a gold watch already possessed such an article, or because a 'ife tenant, who was given the income of a $100,000 trust, had income of his own, the testamentary gift to the legatee would be defeated for this reason. The same considerations apply to an absolute gift of "support and maintenance," and the fact that the intended recipient may be able to supply his needs in this regard from other sources is wholly immaterial in any evaluation of his rights to the testamentary gift of the sum which would ordinarily be required for this purpose. . . .

In [four of the cases reviewed courts determined that] the income was given absolutely to the life tenant, but power to invade principal was expressly made subject to conditions; that in Matter of Briggs' Will [223 N.Y. 677, 119 N.E. 1032] was that such use be "necessary and proper"; in Matter of Niles' Will [122 Misc. 17, 202 N.Y. Supp. 475], "if necessary for his support and maintenance"; in Matter of Johnson's Will [123 Misc. 834, 207 N.Y. Supp. 66], in case he "needs it for care, support and maintenance"; and in Matter of Hogeboom's Will [219 App. Div. 131, 219 N.Y. Supp. 436], "he shall need it for support and maintenance." In all of these cases, an affirmative demonstration respecting the state of the financial affairs of the possible recipient was made an express condition precedent to any right to receive more than the income. . . .

Applying these principles to the case at bar, the testamentary direction made an absolute gift of all income to the wife. It also directed an invasion of principal to the extent necessary to maintain the wife "should the *income* prove insufficient" for that purpose, not as in Matter of Hogeboom's Will, and similar cases, if *she* needed it. Here is therefore an absolute gift of maintenance to the wife which is charged on the entire estate. She is entitled to receive it irrespective of her outside resources in like manner to the supposed donee of the watch who already possessed one. . . .

One of the respondents who may be entitled to receive a part of the remainder, if there is any, upon the death of the life tenant, has suggested that the allowance to the widow of $3,600 per year may be too high, in view of a change of living costs since the prior determination of this matter. This, if seriously asserted, obviously presents a question of fact for decision, the issue in respect to which the court would remit to a referee for hearing and report. Since the presumption of a continuance of conditions so recently determined carries with it a strong inference that the sum awarded is presently reasonable, the court would be inclined to grant an application to compel the nonresident remainderman to furnish security for costs in the event that she elects to litigate the question.

Proceed accordingly.

See also Martin v. Simmons First National Bank, 467 S.W.2d 165 (Ark. 1971), finding that the trustee was not to consider the life beneficiary's independent resources. Concerning the manner in which such issues are to be resolved, the court stated:

> Examination of the will can only lead to the conclusion that appellant was intended to be the primary object of Mrs. Nichol's bounty. . . . This preference standing alone, however, is not of sufficient significance to control the construction of the clause. . . .
>
> Whenever there is uncertainty as to the intention of a testator which cannot be clearly ascertained when the words of his will are considered in their ordinary sense, the court must read the language employed by the testator in the light of the circumstances existing when the will was written and, in order to put itself in the place of the testator as nearly as possible, may consider all surrounding facts and circumstances known to him, including the condition, nature and extent of the testator's property, his relations with his family and other beneficiaries named, the motives which may reasonably be supposed to influence him, the subject matter of the gift, the financial condition of the beneficiary and other such matters. . . .

Restatement (Second) of Trusts §128, comment e, states: "It is a question of interpretation whether the beneficiary is entitled to support out of the trust fund even though he has other resources. The inference is that he is so entitled." Accord, Godfrey v. Chandley, 811 P.2d 1248 (Kan. 1991). Contra, Guaranty Trust Co. v. New York City Cancer Commission, 145 Conn. 542, 144 A.2d 535 (1958) (trustee must consider all other means of support). Under the facts and language involved in Sibson v. First National Bank, 64 N.J. Super. 225, 165 A.2d 800 (App. Div. 1960), it was held that the trustee was to consider the beneficiary's outside income but was not to require her to consume the principal of her independent estate.

Boston Safe Deposit & Trust Co. v. Boynton, 443 N.E.2d 1344 (Mass. App. 1983), involved a petition brought by a trustee to be instructed whether, in exercising its discretionary power to invade principal, the beneficiary's independent resources were to be considered. The declaration of trust provided that the settlor's widow was to receive the net income quarterly "and in addition if such net income should be insufficient to provide for her comfortable maintenance, support and medical care, the trustee in its sole discretion may from time to time use such part of the principal as it deems necessary therefore." The court noted that whether "Mrs. Boynton's separate resources are to be considered . . . is a 'question of interpretation' of the intent" of the settlor and that the Massachusetts Supreme Judicial Court has stated "that where such terms as 'when in need' or 'if necessary' are used, other resources of the life beneficiary are to be considered." The court further noted that "the circumstances of the parties at the time the instrument was drawn shed light on the meaning of the clause." The trust was executed in connection with an antenuptial agreement that

> set forth the parties' intent to retain the right to leave their property to their respective children and to waive their rights in the other's estate. We do not think it consistent with that intent to ignore the outside resources of Mrs. Boynton in determining when principal is "necessary" for her support, or to permit Mrs. Boynton, when in need of income for herself, voluntarily to dispose of productive assets so as to deplete her husband's estate and the shares of his children in order to increase the amounts to be received by her own.

The court did not consider whether real estate given by Mrs. Boynton to her children was "impressed with a trust for her benefit" but decided "only that the trustee is required, under the terms of the trust, to consider Mrs. Boynton's other resources, including the resources distributed to her children, in determining whether and to what extent she is entitled to receive payments from the principal of the trust."

Should it matter whether the trustee's power is expressed in terms of "absolute discretion"? See First National Bank v. Howard, 149 Tex. 130, 136, 229 S.W.2d 781, 785 (1950) (such discretion does not apply to the question of whether to consider other resources). But see Offutt v. Offutt, 204 Md. 101, 102 A.2d 554 (1945).

What benefits are included in a provision for the welfare or the support of a beneficiary? It is generally implied that "support" is to be in the manner to which the beneficiary was accustomed at the time the trust was created. Does this include the support and education of the beneficiary's family? See Robison v. Elston Bank & Trust Co., 113 Ind. App. 633, 654, 48 N.E.2d 181, 189 (1943):

> The needs of a married man include . . . the needs of his family living with him and entitled to his support. It would not be consistent with his welfare for his family to be in want, and it is hardly probable that the testator intended to provide for his needs and let his wife and children go without.

Does the support of a minor beneficiary include the support of that minor's parent or guardian in the event of need? Where the testator desires to create a trust for minor grandchildren if a child should predecease, provision for the possible needs of a widowed daughter-in-law or son-in-law ought not to be omitted by inadvertence. The nature and extent of the benefits intended for the various distributees should be given careful consideration in the drafting of discretionary trusts. The discretionary power conferred on the trustee to determine the amount and purpose of distributions is likely to be the most significant provision of such a trust, particularly in a trust for minor children or grandchildren.

When discretionary interests are conferred on each of multiple beneficiaries under a single trust, are inequalities in distributions during the trust period to be taken into account in fixing the shares of the beneficiaries or their descendants on termination? See Hartford National Bank v. Turner, 21 Conn. Supp. 437, 156 A.2d 800 (Super. Ct. 1959) (disregarding prior inequalities). See also New England Merchants National Bank v. Morin, 449 N.E.2d 682 (Mass. App. 1983).

B.   Transfer of a Beneficiary's Interest

1.   In General

a.   Voluntary Assignment

As a general principle, and subject to exceptions we will study later in this chapter, the beneficiary's equitable interest in trust property can be transferred if and to the extent the beneficiary has capacity to transfer other property. Thus it can be sold or mortgaged; a gift can be made of it, absolutely or subject to another trust; if the interest is not so limited as to terminate on the beneficiary's death, it can be devised or bequeathed, and if this is not done, it will pass by intestacy. In a few jurisdictions special problems are presented by the fact that a beneficiary's interest is a contingent future interest, but these problems are the result of future interest rules that relate to the alienability of certain legal as well as equitable interests and are not peculiar to trusts.

The transfer of a beneficiary's interest need not be in writing except as required by statute. In most states the statute of frauds requires, or is interpreted as requiring, a writing for the assignment of a beneficiary's interest in a trust of land. In a few states a writing is not required although the trust property is land, while in a few other states a writing is required for a transfer of a beneficial interest in any trust, including trusts of personality.

When a beneficiary's interest is assigned to another, the assignee acquires only the interest that the beneficiary owned. If A assigns to B her right to income for life, B's right to the income ceases on A's death; if B predeceases A, the right to income for A's life continues and passes by B's will or to B's next of kin. Where X is entitled to receive the trust principal on A's death if X is then living, a valid assignment of X's interest to Y will entitle Y or his legatees, devisees, or heirs to the principal on A's death if and only if X is then alive.

If the trustee has notice of the transfer of a beneficiary's interest, the trustee is liable to the transferee if payments are thereafter made to the original beneficiary. In the absence of notice of the transfer, however, a trustee is not liable for continued payments to the transferor.

When the interest of a beneficiary is assigned first to A and subsequently to B, which of the assignees prevails? A number of states have adopted the rule that A prevails over B even though B was the first to give notice of the assignment to the trustee. In other words, priority in the time of the assignment is controlling in these states. This view is reflected in 1 Restatement (Second) of Trusts §163. A number of states, however, have followed the leading English decision of Dearle v. Hall, 3 Russ. 1, 48 (1828), which concludes:

> [T]he Plaintiffs . . . , having neglected to give the trustees notice of their assignments, . . . could not come into this Court to avail themselves of the priority of their assignments in point of time, in order to defeat the right of a person who had acted as Hall had acted [having corresponded with one of the trustees], and who, if the prior assignment were to prevail against him, would necessarily sustain a great loss. . . .
>
> [I]t does not appear that the precise question has ever been determined. . . . But the case is not new in principle. . . . [O]n the assignment of a bond debt, the bond should be delivered, and notice given to the debtor; and . . . with respect to simple contract-debts, for which no securities are holden, such as book-debts for instance, notice of the assignment should be given to the debtor in order to take away from the debtor the right of making payment to the assignor, and to take away from the assignor the power and disposition over the thing assigned. In cases like the present, the act of giving the trustee notice, is, in a certain degree, taking possession of the fund. . . .

b.   Rights of Creditors of a Beneficiary

Subject to exceptions taken up in the succeeding portions of this chapter, the interest of a trust beneficiary may generally be reached by the beneficiary's creditors in satisfaction of a judgment. The procedure by

438   **12. The Nature of the Beneficiaries' Interests**

which creditors subject a beneficiary's interest to their claims varies from state to state, often requiring that other available assets be exhausted before the creditor may resort to equitable process (such as creditor's bill) to reach the debtor's equitable interests.

Except in the rare case in which a debtor is the sole beneficiary of a trust and can presently demand conveyance of the trust property, a creditor cannot reach the trust property itself. It is the beneficial interest of the debtor that is subjected to the claim. The basic remedy of the creditor is to have the beneficial interest sold and the proceeds of the sale applied to satisfy the claim. The buyer acquires the rights that the debtor owned as beneficiary, whether it be the right to receive periodic income payments or the right to share in the principal on termination. The element of sacrifice involved in a forced sale of such rights is likely to work a hardship on the beneficiary. Consequently courts of equity generally refuse to order sale of an income interest, instead directing that the trustee pay the creditor the income to which the beneficiary is entitled, if it can be expected that this remedy will satisfy the debt within a reasonable time. If this milder remedy is inadequate or if the debtor's interest is a future interest, the court will normally direct a sale of the interest. The beneficiary can avoid this result if the needed funds can be raised by mortgaging the interest.

In numerous jurisdictions, certain future interests (particularly if subject to a condition precedent) are immune to creditors' claims, either because of their general inalienability under outmoded local property law or, more frequently today, because of the sacrifice involved in their forced sale. For present purposes (deferring questions of restraints on alienation), it is sufficient to note that the mere fact that the future interest is equitable rather than legal generally does not affect the rights of creditors.

c. Disclaimer by a Beneficiary

The principles governing renunciation of a beneficiary's interest in a trust are fundamentally the same as those governing nonacceptance of gifts and disclaimer of rights under a will. At this point certain aspects of renunciation are considered, including examination of cases and doctrine relating to the rights of beneficiaries of decedents' estates, rather than attempting to restrict our study to situations in which trusts are involved.

Although acceptance of a bequest or devise is generally implied, a person need not accept and retain benefits conferred by will or by the laws of descent and distribution. Whether a beneficiary can, by renouncing or disposing of the interest, avoid the usual consequences of property ownership, however, is not a simple matter.

UNIFORM PROBATE CODE

§2-801. *Disclaimer of Property Interests.*

(a) [Right to Disclaim Interest in Property.] A person, or the representative of a person, to whom an interest in or with respect to property or an interest therein devolves by whatever means may disclaim it in whole or in part by delivering or filing a written disclaimer under this section. The right to disclaim exists notwithstanding (i) any limitation on the interest of the disclaimant in the nature of a spendthrift provision or similar restriction or (ii) any restriction or limitation on the right to disclaim contained in the governing instrument. For purposes of this subsection, the "representative of a person" includes a personal representative of a decedent, a conservator of a disabled person, a guardian of a minor or incapacitated person, and an agent acting on behalf of the person within the authority of a power of attorney.

(b) [Time of Disclaimer.] The following rules govern the time when a disclaimer must be filed or delivered:

(1) If the property or interest has devolved to the disclaimant under a testamentary instrument or by the laws of intestacy, the disclaimer must be filed, if of a present interest, not later than [nine] months after the death of the deceased owner or deceased donee of a power of appointment and, if of a future interest, not later than [nine] months after the event determining that the taker of the property or interest is finally ascertained and his [or her] interest is indefeasibly vested. The disclaimer must be filed in the [probate] court of the county in which proceedings for the administration of the estate of the deceased owner or deceased donee of the power have been commenced. A copy of the disclaimer must be delivered in person or mailed by registered or certified mail, return receipt requested, to any personal representative or other fiduciary of the decedent or donee of the power.

(2) If a property or interest has devolved to the disclaimant under a nontestamentary instrument or contract, the disclaimer must be delivered or filed, if of a present interest, not later than [nine] months after the effective date of the nontestamentary instrument or contract and, if of a future interest, not later than [nine] months after the event determining that the taker of the property or interest is finally ascertained and his [or her] interest is indefeasibly vested. If the person entitled to disclaim does not know of the existence of the interest, the disclaimer must be delivered or filed not later than [nine] months after the person learns of the existence of the interest. The effective date of a revocable instrument or contract is the date on which the maker no longer has power to revoke it or to transfer to himself [or herself] or another the entire legal and equitable ownership of the interest. The

disclaimer or a copy thereof must be delivered in person or mailed by registered or certified mail, return receipt requested, to the person who has legal title to or possession of the interest disclaimed.

(3) A surviving joint tenant [or tenant by the entireties] may disclaim as a separate interest any property or interest therein devolving to him [or her] by right of survivorship. A surviving joint tenant [or tenant by the entireties] may disclaim the entire interest in any property or interest therein that is the subject of a joint tenancy [or tenancy by the entireties] devolving to him [or her], if the joint tenancy [or tenancy by the entireties] was created by act of a deceased joint tenant [or tenant by the entireties], the survivor did not join in creating the joint tenancy [or tenancy by the entireties], and has not accepted a benefit under it.

(4) If real property or an interest therein is disclaimed, a copy of the disclaimer may be recorded in the office of the [Recorder of Deeds] of the county in which the property or interest disclaimed is located.

(c) [Form of Disclaimer.] The disclaimer must (i) describe the property or interest disclaimed, (ii) declare the disclaimer and extent thereof, and (iii) be signed by the disclaimant.

(d) [Effect of Disclaimer.] The effects of a disclaimer are:

(1) If property or an interest therein devolves to a disclaimant under a testamentary instrument, under a power of appointment exercised by a testamentary instrument, or under the laws of intestacy, and the decedent has not provided for another disposition of that interest, should it be disclaimed, or of disclaimed, or failed interests in general, the disclaimed interest devolves as if the disclaimant had predeceased the decedent, but if by law or under the testamentary instrument the descendants of the disclaimant would take the disclaimant's share by representation were the disclaimant to predecease the decedent, then the disclaimed interest passes by representation to the descendants of the disclaimant who survive the decedent. A future interest that takes effect in possession or enjoyment after the termination of the estate or interest disclaimed takes effect as if the disclaimant had predeceased the decedent. A disclaimer relates back for all purposes to the date of death of the decedent.

(2) If property or an interest therein devolves to a disclaimant under a nontestamentary instrument or contract and the instrument or contract does not provide for another disposition of that interest, should it be disclaimed, or of disclaimed or failed interests in general, the disclaimed interest devolves as if the disclaimant has predeceased the effective date of the instrument or contract, but if by law or under the nontestamentary instrument or contract the descendants of the disclaimant would take the disclaimant's share by representation were the disclaimant to predecease the effective date of the instru-

ment, then the disclaimed interest passes by representation to the descendants of the disclaimant who survive the effective date of the instrument. A disclaimer relates back for all purposes to that date. A future interest that takes effect in possession or enjoyment at or after the termination of the disclaimed interest takes effect as if the disclaimant had died before the effective date of the instrument or contract that transferred the disclaimed interest.

(3) The disclaimer or the written waiver of the right to disclaim is binding upon the disclaimant or person waiving and all persons claiming through or under either of them.

(e) [Waiver and Bar.] The right to disclaim property or an interest therein is barred by (i) an assignment, conveyance, encumbrance, pledge, or transfer of the property or interest, or a contract therefor, (ii) a written waiver of the right to disclaim, (iii) an acceptance of the property or interest or a benefit under it or (iv) a sale of the property or interest under judicial sale made before the disclaimer is made.

(f) [Remedy Not Exclusive.] This section does not abridge the right of a person to waive, release, disclaim, or renounce property or an interest therein under any other statute.

(g) [Application.] An interest in property that exists on the effective date of this section as to which, if a present interest, the time for filing a disclaimer under this section has not expired or, if a future interest, the interest has not become indefeasibly vested or the taker finally ascertained, may be disclaimed within [nine] months after the effective date of this section.

PROBLEM

12-B. *A*'s will left the residue of her estate to *T* in trust for her son, *S*, for life, remainder per stirpes to the issue of *S* who survive him. Specifically the trust provisions for *S* were the right to receive all of the trust income during his lifetime plus an unrestricted power to demand onefourth of the trust principal after attaining age 25 and one-third of the remaining principal after attaining age 35. At the date of *A*'s death *S* was 38 years of age. Two months later, following lengthy discussions with his lawyer, *S* filed a statement with the probate court declaring his acceptance of his right to the trust income for life but purporting to renounce "any and all other rights I may have under the will of my mother, and in particular disclaiming all powers to withdraw any portions of the trust estate whether now or hereafter exercisable by me."

C, a creditor of *S*, has come to you for advice. *C* reports that, as a result of business reverses and heavy borrowing, *S* has been insolvent for some time and owes $25,000 to *C*.

Preliminary research reveals several possibly relevant code provisions in your state. One is a section that exempts from creditor's claims "any right of a trust beneficiary to receive the income of a trust created by another person." The second is a section that provides that creditors may reach, among other listed items, any property over which the debtor has at the time "a power of appointment to the extent such power is presently exercisable for his own benefit," the annotation indicating that this "section reverses the usual American rule that such powers, unless exercised, cannot be reached by creditors except under the Federal Bankruptcy Act." The third is a series of sections adopting the Uniform Fraudulent Conveyances Act, section 4 of which provides: "Every conveyance . . . by a person who is or will thereby be rendered insolvent is fraudulent as to creditors without regard to his actual intent if the conveyance is made . . . without a fair consideration." Section 9 of the Act allows one in *C*'s position to set aside a fraudulent conveyance to the extent necessary to satisfy a claim.

How would you advise *C*? What other information would you wish to determine? Consider the cases that follow and any other material in this chapter that appears pertinent. Would Uniform Probate Code §2-801 supra resolve the problems you identify?

The opinion in First City National Bank v. Toombs, 431 S.W.2d 404 (Tex. Civ. App. 1968), states:[1]

The right of a devisee or legatee under a will to decline a devise or bequest in toto is generally recognized. . . . A beneficiary may disclaim or renounce his rights under a will, even where the gift is beneficial, provided he has not already accepted it, and provided that the rights of third persons are not involved; and the motives which prompt a renunciation are immaterial in the absence of fraud or collusion. . . . However, there is a division of authorities with regard to partial renunciations under a will. Some jurisdictions do not recognize the right of partial renunciation. Other jurisdictions permit a partial renunciation in a proper case. . . . There are some Texas cases which contain inferential language to the effect that one who accepts a benefit under a will must adopt the whole contents of the will. These Texas decisions . . . involve situations where the donee is put to an election and are not factually similar to the case involved here. . . .

In those jurisdictions which permit a partial renunciation, a controlling determination is whether the gifts are separate and independent gifts, or one single aggregate gift. Where two or more separate and independent gifts are made by a will to a beneficiary he is, as a general rule, entitled to accept one or more and disclaim others, unless a contrary intention on the

---

1. One is led to suspect that this is friendly litigation, possibly to establish tax consequences by carrying the case through the appellate stage in a manner unfortunately invited by the highly unsatisfactory opinions in Commissioner v. Bosch, 387 U.S. 456 (1967), dealing with the question of when state court decisions are "binding" on the Internal Revenue Service as a determination of the property rights of taxpayers.

part of the testator appears from other provisions of the will. . . . Some courts appear to place great emphasis on the principle that a donee cannot disclaim the burdensome gift and accept the beneficial one. Perhaps the leading case upholding renunciation in part and acceptance in part is Brown v. Routzahn, 63 F.2d 914 (C.C.A. 6th 1933), *certiorari denied,* 290 U.S. 641, 54 S. Ct. 60, 78 L. Ed. 557, where the Court said:

> Where a testator makes two separate and distinct gifts one beneficial and the other burdensome, the donee may undoubtedly accept the beneficial gift and reject the other, but, where there is a single gift, including burdensome and beneficial properties as an aggregate, then unless a contrary intention appears from the will, the donee cannot disclaim the burdensome gift and accept the beneficial one. . . .

It is our opinion that the judgment of the trial court [upholding the partial renunciation] was correct for the following reasons: (1) The two gifts, one a cash bequest . . . and the other an income interest for life in a trust are separate, distinct and independent gifts. (2) Both gifts were beneficial . . . and neither involved burdensome features. (3) The renunciation of the . . . interest for life . . . does not result in loss or hardship to any other devisees or legatees in such will. (4) There is nothing in the decedent's will which intimates that the decedent conditioned the acceptance of one gift upon the full acceptance of both gifts.

A concurring opinion would not restrict "the right of partial renunciation to cases where there are 'separate' and 'distinct' gifts, as distinguished from a 'single aggregate gift,'" noting:

> The right of partial renunciation should exist in all cases except where the testator indicates an intent that the beneficiary shall take all or none, or in cases where the exercise of the right would impose a burden on other recipients of the testator's estate. The distinction between "separate" and "distinct" gifts, on the one hand, a "single aggregate gift," on the other, besides having all the earmarks of being slippery, can be productive of nothing other than judicial opinions replete with "nice" differentiations placing misdirected emphasis on the literary style of the draftsman rather than on the practical effect of the attempted renunciation.

HARDENBERGH v. COMMISSIONER OF INTERNAL REVENUE

198 F.2d 63 (8th Cir.), *cert. denied,* 344 U.S. 836 (1952)

[George Hardenbergh, of St. Paul, Minnesota, died intestate. His sole heirs at law were his widow, Ianthe, a daughter, Gabrielle, and a son by a former marriage, George. According to the Minnesota laws of intestate succession each of the heirs was entitled to one-third of the net estate of about $250,000. Because his wife and daughter were independently wealthy, the decedent had his lawyer prepare a will leaving his estate to his son but died before executing the will. Decedent's widow and daughter filed a document in the estate proceedings, renouncing their respective interests in the estate in order to carry out the intent of the decedent. Accordingly, the Probate Court entered a final decree providing for distribution of the estate to the son, George.]

RIDDICK, C.J. . . .

The Commissioner determined that Ianthe and Gabrielle had each made a gift to George of one-third of the net estate, and the Tax Court sustained his action, 17 T.C. 166. These petitions for review challenge the Tax Court's decision on the ground that the Minnesota Probate Court by its order of final distribution of decedent's estate made the only effective transfer thereof to George Hardenbergh. . . .

Section 1000 of the Internal Revenue Code, 26 U.S.C.A. §1000, imposes a tax upon the transfer of property by gift whether the property is real or personal, tangible or intangible and whether the gift is direct or indirect. Section 86.2 of Treasury Regulations 108 provides that all transactions whereby property or rights or interests in property "are gratuitously passed or conferred upon another, regardless of the means or device employed, constitute gifts subject to tax." The words "property," "transfer," "gift," and "indirect," as used in the section of the Revenue Code are to be read in the broadest and most comprehensive sense. . . .

We think the decision of the Tax Court is right. The general rule as to intestate succession is that the title to the property of an intestate passes by force of the rules of law . . . and that those so entitled by law have no power to prevent the vesting of title in themselves. The rule is otherwise as to legatees or devisees under a will. Brown v. Routzahn, 6 Cir., 63 F.2d 914, since the beneficiary under a will may accept or reject a testamentary gift. The controlling fact here is that title to an interest in decedent's estate vested in taxpayers by operation of law which neither had the power to prevent.

It is true, as taxpayers contend, that the Minnesota Probate Court acquired jurisdiction of decedent's estate; that the administration of the estate was a proceeding in rem; that during the administration the Probate Court held possession and control of all the estate property and had jurisdiction to determine "Who is entitled to share therein, the proportions in which they take, and to assign to each his share"; and that the final decree of distribution is for the distributees the conclusive evidence of their rights. . . .

But it is also true, as shown by the . . . cases relied on by taxpayers, that the exercise of a probate court's jurisdiction is circumscribed by the Minnesota Statute of Intestate Succession. All that these cases hold of importance on the question here is that the probate court having jurisdiction of the property of the estate in administration to determine the identity of the parties entitled to take the estate has jurisdiction to make a wrong decision. Its decision, erroneous in law or fact, is final and binding upon the world, except upon direct attack by appellate review. That is to say, that if in the present case the Probate Court, without the intervention of the taxpayers, had vested the decedent's estate in George, its decree, though contrary to the Minnesota Statute, would be binding on taxpayers until vacated on appeal. The probate decree acquired the effect claimed for it as a transfer of decedent's property to George Hardenbergh because and only because of the consent or acquiescence of the taxpayers. It could not have survived a direct attack.

That the probate decree derived its vitality from the consent of the taxpayers closely appears from the language of the taxpayer's renunciation and the final decree of distribution. The source of the rights acquired by George Hardenbergh was not the decree of the Probate Court, but the affirmative acts of taxpayers in relinquishing the shares of the estate which Minnesota law vested in them. . . .

The decision of the Tax Court is affirmed.

Stoehr v. Miller, 296 Fed. 414, 425 (2d Cir. 1923), states:

In the case of a trust the creator of the trust cannot compel a third person to be the trustee against his consent, but his acceptance of the office is necessary to constitute him trustee and to vest the title in him. It is equally true that property cannot be forced upon a cestui que trust against his will, and a valid trust does not exist if the cestui que trust when informed of it clearly and unequivocally rejects or renounces its benefits. . . . If the cestui que trust when he learns of the trust accepts it his acceptance relates back to the date of the declaration. If he repudiates it when he learns of it his repudiation relates back in the same manner and the title must be regarded as having been in the settlor all of the time.

The record in this case discloses that the cestuis que trustent under the declaration herein involved renounced their rights in them when they learned of their existence. . . . This court is not concerned with the motive which may have induced the renunciation. . . . [Even] if their renunciation had been made in order to defeat the seizure which the Alien Property Custodian had made it would be quite immaterial.

Coomes v. Finnegan, 233 Iowa 448, 451, 7 N.W.2d 729, 730 (1943), distinguished testate situations from the intestate situation before the court as follows:

A testamentary trust, bequest or devise may, prior to any act of acceptance, be renounced by the beneficiary . . . and such renunciation when made will revert back to the death of the testator, and will displace the lien of any personal judgment against the beneficiary existing at that time or of any levy upon the property made subsequent thereto. Such a renunciation will prevent the testamentary disposition from having any effect to pass any title or interest, and since it relates back to the death of the testator, or the taking effect of the gift, there is nothing to which a lien or levy may attach. Renunciation is not an assignment.

For a rare modern case finding a *legatee's* renunciation to constitute a fraudulent conveyance, see Estate of Reed, 566 P.2d 587 (Wyo. 1977). Contrast Tompkins State Bank v. Niles, 127 Ill. 2d 209, 537 N.E.2d 274 (1989), finding no fraudulent conveyance under a modern disclaimer statute.

For federal gift and estate tax purposes, the significance of the conceptual distinctions based on state law and much of the variation in application of the federal taxes from state to state have been largely removed by the enactment in 1976 of Internal Revenue Code §2518. That section prescribes limitations of both timing and substance that must be complied with if a disclaimer is to be "qualified" so as not to constitute a "transfer" for tax purposes. The details of federal law vary from those of most state disclaimer statutes (see, e.g., Uniform Probate Code §2-801, supra), and counseling and drafting must take account of both bodies of law. Tax objectives of disclaimers, or their favorable incidental tax treatment even when not tax motivated, require compliance with the mandates of both state and federal doctrine.

2. Restraints on Alienation: Spendthrift Trusts

PROBLEM

12-C.   *A* conveyed Blackacre to *B* in fee simple absolute and the deed contained a sentence which stated: "Provided, however, that *B* shall not convey the same nor shall it be subject to his creditors until ten years from the date hereof." Can *B* sell or mortgage and give good title in five years? Can *B*'s creditors successfully attach the property? Could *A* have better accomplished his apparent objectives had he been fully advised? Would your response to the last question differ if the creditors were *B*'s wife and child seeking support?

BROADWAY BANK v. ADAMS
133 Mass. 170, 43 Am. Dec. 504 (1882)

MORTON, C.J.

The object of this bill in equity is to reach and apply in payment of the plaintiff's debt due from the defendant Adams the income of a trust fund created for his benefit by the will of his brother. The eleventh article of the will is as follows:

> I give the sum of $75,000 to my said executors and the survivors or survivor of them, in trust to invest the same in such manner as to them may

seem prudent, and to pay the net income thereof, semi-annually, to my said brother Charles W. Adams, during his natural life, such payments to be made to him personally when convenient, otherwise, upon his order or receipt in writing; in either case free from the interference or control of his creditors, my intention being that the use of said income shall not be anticipated by assignment. . . .

There is no room for doubt as to the intention of the testator. It is clear, that if the trustee was to pay the income to the plaintiff under an order of the court, it would be in direct violation of the intention of the testator and of the provisions of his will. The court will not compel the trustee thus to do what the will forbids him to do, unless the provisions and intention of the testator are unlawful. . . .

It is true that the rule of the common law is, that a man cannot attach to a grant or transfer of property, otherwise absolute, the condition that it shall not be alienated; such condition being repugnant to the nature of the estate granted. Co. Litt. 223 a; Blackstone Bank v. Davis, 21 Pick. 42.

Lord Coke gives as the reason of the rule, that "it is absurd and repugnant to reason that he, that hath no possibility to have the land revert to him, should restrain his feoffee in fee simple of his power to alien," and that this is "against the height and puritie of a fee simple." By such a condition, the grantor undertakes to deprive the property in the hands of the grantee of one of its legal incidents and attributes, namely, its alienability, which is deemed to be against the public policy. But the reasons of the rule do not apply in the case of a transfer of property in trust. By the creation of a trust like one before us, the trust property passes to the trustee with all its incidents and attributes unimpaired. He takes the whole legal title to the property, with the power of alienation; the cestui que trust takes the whole legal title to the accrued income at the moment it is paid over to him. Neither the principal nor the income is at any time inalienable. . . .

[F]rom the time of Lord Eldon the rule has prevailed in the English Court of Chancery . . . that when the income of a trust estate is given to any person . . . for life, the equitable estate for life is alienable by, and liable in equity to the debts of, the cestui que trust, and that this quality is so inseparable from the estate that no provision, however express, which does not operate as a cesser or limitation of the estate itself, can protect it from his debts.

The English rule has been adopted in several of the courts of this country.

Other courts have rejected it, and have held that the founder of a trust may secure the benefit of it to the object of his bounty, by providing that the income shall not be alienable by anticipation, nor subject to be taken for his debts.

The precise point involved in the case at bar has not been adjudicated in this Commonwealth. . . . The founder of this trust was the absolute owner of his property. He had the entire right to dispose of it, either by an absolute gift to his brother, or by a gift with such restrictions or limitations, not repugnant to law, as he saw fit to impose. His clear intention, as shown in his will, was not to give his brother an absolute right to the income which might hereafter accrue upon the trust fund, with the power of alienating it in advance, but only the right to receive semi-annually the income of the fund, which upon its payment to him, and not before, was to become his absolute property. His intentions ought to be carried out, unless they were against public policy. There is nothing in the nature or tenure of the estate given to the cestui que trust which should prevent this. The power of alienating in advance is not a necessary attribute or incident of such an estate or interest, so that the restraint of such alienation would introduce repugnant or inconsistent elements.

We are not able to see that it would violate any principles of sound public policy to permit a testator to give to the object of his bounty such a qualified interest in the income of a trust fund, and thus provide against the improvidence or misfortune of the beneficiary. The only ground upon which it can be held to be against public policy is, that it defrauds the creditors of the beneficiary.

It is argued that investing a man with apparent wealth tends to mislead creditors, and to induce them to give him credit. The answer is, that creditors have no right to rely upon property thus held, and to give him credit upon the basis of an estate, which by the instrument creating it is declared to be inalienable by him, and not liable for his debts. By the exercise of proper diligence they can ascertain the nature and extent of his estate, especially in this Commonwealth, where all wills and most deeds are spread upon the public records. There is the same danger of their being misled by false appearances, and induced to give credit to the equitable life tenant when the will or deed of trust provides for a cesser or limitation over, in case of an attempted alienation, or of bankruptcy or attachment, and the argument would lead to the conclusion that the English rule is equally in violation of public policy. . . . Under our system, creditors may reach all the property of the debtor not exempted by law, but they cannot enlarge the gift of the founder of a trust, and take more than he has given.

The rule of public policy which subjects a debtor's property to the payment of his debts does not subject the property of a donor to the debts of his beneficiary, and does not give the creditor a right to complain, that in the exercise of his absolute right of disposition, the donor has not seen fit to give the property to the creditor, [but] has left it out of his reach.

Whether a man can settle his own property in trust for his own benefit, so as to exempt the income from alienation by him or attachment in advance by his creditors, is a different question, which we are not called upon to consider in this case. But we are of opinion that any other person, having the entire right to dispose of his property, may settle it in trust in favor of a beneficiary, and may provide that it shall not be alienated by him by anticipation, and shall not be subject to be seized by his creditors in advance of its payment to him.

It follows that under the provisions of the will which we are considering, the income of the trust fund created for the benefit of the defendant Adams cannot be reached by attachment, either at law or in equity, before it is paid to him.

Bill dismissed.

G. BOGERT, TRUSTS
(6th ed. 1987)

§40. *Spendthrift Clauses.* A spendthrift trust is one in which, either because of a direction of the settlor or because of a statute, the beneficiary is unable to transfer his right to future payments of income or principal and his creditors are unable to subject the beneficiary's interest to the payment of their claims. Such a trust does not involve any restraint on alienability or creditors' rights with respect to property after it is received by the beneficiary from the trustee, but rather is merely a restraint with regard to his rights to future payments under the trust.

An attempted transfer of his right to future income by the beneficiary of a spendthrift trust does not give the assignee a right to compel the trustee to pay income to him, but if the assignment has not been repudiated by the beneficiary, the trustee may treat it as an order to pay to the assignee and the trustee will be protected in making payments to the assignee until the order is revoked, unless the instrument directed payment into the hands of the beneficiary alone.

Spendthrift clauses are void, as creating an unlawful restraint on alienation and as against public policy, in England and a few American states. In the majority of the American states such clauses are valid, either to an unlimited extent or subject to some statutory restrictions. Where the spendthrift clause is declared invalid, the remainder of the trust is enforced.

SCOTT v. BANK ONE TRUST CO.
62 Ohio St. 3d 39, 577 N.E.2d 1077 (1991)

PER CURIAM.

. . . Since we may constitutionally answer certified questions, we shall now consider the . . . certified question. The federal court has asked us whether spendthrift trusts are enforceable under Ohio law. . . .

. . . Most states enforce such trusts, at least to some degree. . . . How-

ever, in Sherrow v. Brookover (1963), 174 Ohio St. 310, 189 N.E.2d 90,
. . . we held that, absent legislative authorization, a restraint on the involuntary transfer of the beneficiary's continuing and enforceable rights in
the trust property is invalid.

In a technical sense, it is arguable that the trust provision at issue here
is not a true spendthrift provision. It does not expressly restrain the
alienability of McCombe's interest in the trust property. [Another provision of the trust, however, while for some reason "not at issue here,"
was (and was so described by the present court) a "classic spendthrift
provision" of the type considered by Sherrow, supra.] Instead, it provides
that Bank One shall distribute the trust property outright to McCombe
unless he is, inter alia, insolvent ("the insolvency clause"), has filed a petition in bankruptcy ("the bankruptcy clause"), or would not personally
enjoy the property ("the nonenjoyment clause"). When any of these
things occurs, the trust becomes a discretionary trust. Only when all the
conditions cease to exist will McCombe again be entitled, under the
terms of the trust, to outright distribution of the trust property.

However, Brewer [the settlor] intended this provision to accomplish
the same goal as a spendthrift trust. The federal district court found that
Brewer "wanted to leave her estate to John McCombe, but did not want
to have her estate end up in the hands of John McCombe's creditors."
While the trust provision in issue does not forbid the alienation of
McCombe's interest in the trust property, it does in effect prevent such
alienation.

. . . [T]he nonenjoyment clause precludes Bank One from distributing
trust property outright unless McCombe will personally enjoy it. Therefore, if McCombe's [right to future distributions] is transferred to the
bankruptcy trustee, . . . McCombe would continue to be the beneficiary
of a discretionary trust, the property of which his creditors cannot
reach. . . . Thus the nonenjoyment clause makes McCombe's future
interest [sic] in the trust property worthless to anyone but McCombe.

Under such circumstances, it is unlikely that creditors would trouble
to attach the future interest. . . . Even if they did, McCombe would simply receive distributions at the discretion of a trustee selected by his
mother.

Enforcement of the Brewer trust as written would neatly circumvent
Sherrow and allow McCombe to enjoy the property free of his creditors'
claims. A rule so easily avoided would be no rule at all. We therefore
agree with the federal court's characterization of the Brewer trust as a
spendthrift trust. We must either apply Sherrow or overrule it. So we turn
to the question raised by Amici: Should Sherrow be overruled?

. . . In evaluating Sherrow's viability, we recognize that "the principle
of stare decisis is necessary to an orderly and predictable system of law."
. . . However, we are also mindful "that our adherence to former decisions [must] not be arbitrary, but founded on their continuing reason
and logic." . . .

Amici raised several arguments in favor of overruling *Sherrow* and allowing spendthrift trusts. Most persuasively, they argue that a property owner should have the right to dispose of her property as she chooses. This is why most courts . . . have enforced spendthrift trusts. . . .

On the other hand, an owner's rights over her property are not absolute. We endorsed that notion in *Sherrow;* we do not shrink from it today. As Dean Griswold rightly says [see excerpt infra this chapter]: "The validity of spendthrift trusts is a matter of policy, not logic." . . .

However, as a matter of policy, it is desirable for property owners to have, within reasonable bounds, the freedom to do as they choose with their own property. This freedom is not absolute . . . [but] is a policy consideration to be balanced against other policy considerations. In a society that values freedom as greatly as ours, this consideration is far from trivial.

The most important argument against spendthrift trusts is that they are unfair to the beneficiary's creditors because they allow the beneficiary to enjoy the trust property without paying his debts. . . .

As a matter of logic, *Sherrow*'s reasoning [on this point] begs the question. Of course, we agree that McCombe's creditors may collect from any property he has, including whatever interest he has in the trust property. But McCombe *has* no greater interest in the trust property than the trust agreement gives him. And McCombe's interest in the trust property is contingent on his personal enjoyment of it. If his interest in the trust property passes to his creditors, he will not personally enjoy it; if he will not personally enjoy it, then he has no interest in it to transfer to his creditors.

More important *Sherrow*'s reasoning fails as a matter of policy. Suppose that Brewer had said to McCombe: "I will give you this property when you are out of debt, but not before." No one would suggest that McCombe's creditors . . . could take the property from Brewer. . . . McCombe's creditors are no worse off than they would be if the Brewer trust is enforced. The results are identical: McCombe enjoys Brewer's property and the creditors get no share of it. . . . [E]nforcing a spendthrift trust provision "takes nothing from the prior or subsequent creditors as the beneficiary loses nothing to which they previously had the right to look for payment." . . .

Some have suggested that spendthrift trusts, like other restraints on alienation, are economically inefficient. . . . However, the overwhelming majority of states recognize such trusts, and we know of no evidence that spendthrift trusts have harmed those states' economies. . . .

We certainly cannot dispute the general proposition that "an individual [property] owner" may claim only such exemptions as the Revised Code allows him. But we think the *Sherrow* court drew the wrong conclusion from that proposition . . . [begging] the question of what the "individual [property] owner" *actually owns* as the beneficiary of his spendthrift trust. The beneficiary owns no greater interest in the trust property than the settlor has given him. In the case of a spendthrift trust, the settlor has not given the beneficiary an alienable interest. . . .

. . . It is true that a judgment debtor's equitable interests are liable to execution . . . [but the statute so providing] speaks only of those interests "which . . . [the judgment debtor] *has*. . . . " (Emphasis added [by the court].) And the beneficiary of a spendthrift has no interest that can be executed upon, because the trustor did not give him such an interest. The General Assembly undoubtedly could have outlawed spendthrift trusts, but it has not . . . [so] we must, as the *Sherrow* court did, make our best effort to balance the competing policies favoring and disfavoring spendthrift trusts.

We are no longer satisfied with the balance struck 28 years ago. The policy reasons against spendthrift trusts, which seemed so strong then, now look weak. The *Sherrow* court too easily dismissed the countervailing policy that the law should allow the property owner, within reason, to dispose of her property as she chooses. We can no longer sustain the *Sherrow* doctrine.

Accordingly we overrule *Sherrow* and hold that spendthrift trusts will be enforced in Ohio. Our answer to the second certified question, therefore, is that the spendthrift contained in the Brewer Trust is enforceable under Ohio law. . . .

No particular language is required to create a spendthrift trust. If the terms of the trust manifest such an intention, the trust will be deemed a spendthrift trust.

There remains considerable doubt whether a spendthrift provision can validly apply to future rights in the principal of a trust, even where such provisions are valid as to income interests. The trend of modern decisions is to uphold spendthrift restraints on equitable future interests in corpus, assuming the intent (which is often narrowly construed) is made clear and also that the statute of uses does not execute the interest converting it to a legal future interest. An extension of the spendthrift trust doctrine to remainders is criticized in Niles, Matter of Vought's Will: A Tighter Grip by the Dead Hand, 45 N.Y.U.L. Rev. 421 (1970).

PROBLEMS

12-D.   *S* created an inter vivos trust with $100,000 in securities to pay *B* income for life, remainder to *B*'s children, *X*, *Y*, and *Z*. At the same time *S* executed a will leaving her residuary estate to this trust by a pour-over clause. *S* executed a later will leaving the residue to *X*, *Y*, and *Z*, and died soon thereafter. *B* filed a contest against *S*'s second will. On compromise settlement *X*, *Y*, and *Z* each received $25,000 in cash, and the

$50,000 balance of the residue went into the trust. A few years ago *B* retired and transferred a $50,000 piece of realty to this same trust.

Four months ago *B* was involved in a boat collision while uninsured. Judgment for $100,000 was obtained against *B*, who owns outright about $50,000 in assets. What are the judgment creditor's chances against the trust? Why? What effect would a spendthrift clause have in *S*'s trust?

12-E.   *X* devised an apartment house to her son, *S*, $50,000 to her daughter, *D*, and the residue of her substantial estate to *T* as trustee to pay the income in equal shares to *S* and *D* for life, remainder on the survivor's death to *X*'s then living issue. A trust provision stated: "The interests of the beneficiaries hereunder shall not be alienable nor subject to anticipation by assignment or claims of creditors." Both *S* and *D* were single and childless when *X* died. *S* accepted the trust income interest but filed a timely renunciation under state law, properly disclaiming the devise of the apartment building.

Fifteen years after *X*'s death, *S* became involved in litigation concerning a partnership liability, and a judgment for $100,000 was obtained against him. The judgment creditor has retained you to initiate a garnishment proceeding to reach *S*'s interest in the trust to satisfy the judgment. What arguments can you reasonably make on behalf of the creditor? What result would you anticipate? Why?

RESTATEMENT (SECOND) OF TRUSTS

§157. *Particular Classes of Claimants.*   Although a trust is a spendthrift trust . . . , the interest of the beneficiary can be reached in satisfaction of an enforceable claim against the beneficiary,

> (a) by the wife or child of the beneficiary for support, or by the wife for alimony;
>
> (b) for the necessary services rendered to the beneficiary or necessary supplies furnished to him;
>
> (c) for services rendered and materials furnished which preserve or benefit the interest of the beneficiary;
>
> (d) by the United States or a State to satisfy a claim against the beneficiary.

A substantial number of cases have refused to recognize exception *(a)*, relating to support and alimony, and in many states the law is unclear or changing. Recent legislation on this matter in various states, the policy influence of uniform acts, and the details of spendthrift trust legislation in a particular state must be carefully considered.

In re MATT
105 Ill. 2d 330, 473 N.E.2d 1320 (1985)

[Garnishment action against petitioner's former husband to enforce a $7,000 child-support judgment. Respondent is entitled to receive $3,600 per year as life beneficiary of a testamentary trust established by his mother, and the garnishee bank responded to the petition by filing a "no funds" answer based on a spendthrift provision in the trust instrument, which included language expressly referring to "claims for alimony or support of any spouse of such beneficiary." Because of this reference to spousal support with no reference to child support, the circuit court concluded that respondent's mother had no intent to protect the trust from his child-support obligations, but the appellate court reversed on the ground that the applicable *statute* prohibits the garnishment of trust income.]

SIMON, J. . . .

[T]he issue involves a construction of section 2-1403 of the Code of Civil Procedure (Ill. Rev. Stat. 1983, ch. 110, par. 2-1403) and section 4.1 of the Non-Support of Spouse and Children Act (Non-Support Act) (Ill. Rev. Stat. 1983, ch. 40, par. 1107.1), the relationship between these sections, the public policy established by the General Assembly when it enacted the latter section, and our decision in a recent case involving a closely analogous issue. Because we dispose of the case on these grounds, we need not determine, as the circuit court did, whether the spendthrift clause itself excludes claims for child-support arrearages. . . .

The [first] statute provides: "No court shall order the satisfaction of a judgment out of any property held in trust for the judgment debtor if such trust has, in good faith, been created by, or the fund so held in trust has proceeded from, a person other than the judgment debtor." (Ill. Rev. Stat. 1983, ch. 110, par. 2-1403.) The respondent contends that because this trust was created in good faith by . . . a person other than the judgment debtor, the circuit court's order that the trust income be subject to a claim for the respondent's child-support arrearages was improper.

However, section 4.1 of the Non-Support Act (Ill. Rev. Stat. 1983, ch. 40, par. 1107.1) now provides for the withholding of "income," "regardless of source," for the purpose of securing collection of unpaid support obligations. . . .

Significantly, the same section of the statute provides: "Any other State or local laws which limit or exempt income or the amount or percentage of income that can be withheld shall not apply." (Ill. Rev. Stat. 1983, ch. 40, par. 1107.1(A)(4)(e).) We read this provision to indicate the General Assembly's intention that section 4.1 prevail over all laws to the contrary, including section 2-1403 of the Code of Civil Procedure.

Section 2-1403 must therefore be construed as allowing the garnishment of trust income in situations in which garnishment is authorized by another statute, as it is by section 4.1.

In enacting section 4.1, together with corresponding provisions in the Illinois Marriage and Dissolution of Marriage Act (Ill. Rev. Stat. 1983, ch. 40, par. 706.1), the Revised Uniform Reciprocal Enforcement of Support Act (Ill. Rev. Stat. 1983, ch. 40, par. 1201 et seq.), and the Illinois Public Aid Code (Ill. Rev. Stat. 1983, ch. 23, par. 1-1 et seq.), the General Assembly established that it is the public policy of Illinois to ensure that support judgments are enforced by all available means. However, the accommodation that the General Assembly devised between that policy and the long-standing policy of protecting spendthrift trusts from invasion does not entail a serious infringement of the latter policy. Only the income and not the principal of such a trust is subject to garnishment, and then only when the obligor is delinquent in support payments. (Ill. Rev. Stat. 1983, ch. 40, par. 1107.1(B)(1).) Moreover, the obligor has a number of procedures available to avoid garnishment. Thus, it is only in circumstances in which the obligor cannot be located, as here, or takes no steps to avoid garnishment that the income from a spendthrift trust would become subject to withholding. . . .

Reversed and remanded.

Without aid of legislation, Council v. Owens, 770 S.W.2d 193 (Ark. App. 1989), concluded that public policy requires that spendthrift restraints not be given the effect of barring claims for arrearages in child support and alimony and held that the beneficiary's former spouse could reach trust income in the hands of a trustee who had no discretion to withhold the income from the beneficiary.

It is well settled that the person who creates a trust is not protected from creditors by a spendthrift provision relating to *retained* interests. Thus, if a settlor retains a right to the income for life in an irrevocable trust containing a spendthrift clause, even assuming the transfer to the trustee was not a fraudulent conveyance, the income right can be subjected to the claims of the settlor's creditors just as if there were no spendthrift clause. See Johnson v. Commercial Bank, 284 Or. 675, 588 P.2d 1094 (1978). (The question of the rights of creditors under a revocable trust is considered in the next chapter.)

When is a person the settlor of a trust? When *A* pays the consideration for *B*'s transfer to *C* in trust for *A* for life, remainder to *A*'s children, it is clear that *A* is to be treated as the settlor. Some cases are more difficult, and authority is insufficient to state a general conclusion. For example, is the mere election by a widow to take under her husband's will, instead of asserting her forced share, sufficient to constitute her a "purchaser" of her interest in the trust, so she would be deemed the settlor? Cf. Bal-

aban v. Willett, 305 Ill. App. 388, 27 N.E.2d 612 (1940). If a devisee who
is also income beneficiary of a residuary trust renounces his devise so
that the land falls into the residue, would a spendthrift restraint in the
trust be effective to protect his income interest?

Legislation. Statutes in some states have dealt with the problems of voluntary and involuntary alienation of a beneficiary's interest. They vary
widely in their approaches.

Based on legislation dating back to 1830, N.Y. Est. Powers & Trusts
Law §7-1.5 provides:

> The right of a beneficiary of an express trust to receive the income from
> property and apply it to the use of or pay it to any person may not be trans-
> ferred by assignment or otherwise, unless a power to transfer such right,
> or any part thereof, is conferred upon such beneficiary by the instrument
> creating or declaring the trust.

(Recent amendments, patently motivated by income tax considerations,
then follow providing limited exceptions permitting certain gratuitous,
intrafamily assignments.) According to N.Y. Est. Powers & Trusts Law
§7-3.4 (having the same early origin), in the absence of a valid direction
for accumulation, the income of the above described trusts "in excess of
the sum necessary for the education and support of the beneficiary is
subject to the claims of his creditors in the same manner as other property which cannot be reached by execution." Unfortunately for the creditor, "support" under the New York statute (and others similar to it) has
been construed to require application of a "station-in-life" or "accus-
tomed-standard-of-living" test. This protection for the beneficiary has
been partially impaired in New York, however, by various provisions of
the Civil Practice Law and Rules.

In several other states, as in New York (but in some without the exceptions), the interests of trust beneficiaries are made automatically unas-
signable, even without an express spendthrift provision. A second group
of statutes merely provides that a trust beneficiary *may* be restrained by
the terms of the trust instrument from voluntarily disposing of a beneficial interest, occasionally limiting this authorization to interests for life
or for a term of years; this type of provision is likely to be accompanied
by a section dealing with the rights of creditors under such trusts —
often with limitations along the lines of N.Y. Est. Powers & Trusts Law
§7-3.4, supra. In a third but numerically declining group of states there
are statutes dealing only with the rights of creditors, as in the *Matt* case,
supra. These states permit the beneficiary to assign his interest voluntarily unless the terms of the trust contain a valid spendthrift restriction.
The statute's automatic restraint applies only to involuntary alienation.

If *A* creates a trust to pay the income to *B* for life, remainder to *B*'s
issue, and the terms of the trust state merely that *B*'s creditors cannot
reach his interest in the trust, can *C*, a creditor of *B*, reach that interest

if *B* is insolvent? Would *C*'s position be improved if *C* could force *B* into bankruptcy? See Eaton v. Boston Safe Deposit & Trust Co., 240 U.S. 427 (1916), and especially see the excerpt below from the recently revised Federal Bankruptcy Act. Would *C*'s position be affected if the trust instrument contained no express restraint on alienation but applicable state law made *B*'s interest assignable voluntarily but not reachable by creditors? (The Bankruptcy Act §522(b) allows the debtor to elect to exempt, inter alia, "any property that is exempt under . . . [domiciliary] State or local law.") Cf. Young v. Handwork, 179 F.2d 70 (7th Cir. 1949), *cert. denied,* 339 U.S. 949 (1950).

BANKRUPTCY ACT
11 U.S.C. §541(c) (1978)

(c)(1) Except as provided in paragraph (2) of this subsection, an interest of the debtor in property becomes property of the [bankruptcy] estate under subsection (a)(1), (a)(2), or (a)(5) of this section notwithstanding any provision —

(A) that restricts or conditions transfer of such interest by the debtor; or

(B) that is conditioned on the insolvency or financial condition of the debtor, on the commencement of a case under this title, or on the appointment of or the taking possession by a trustee in a case under this title or a custodian, and that effects or gives an option to effect a forfeiture, modification, or termination of the debtor's interest in property.

(2) A restriction on the transfer of a beneficial interest of the debtor in a trust that is enforceable under applicable nonbankruptcy law is enforceable in a case under this title.

It has become a widespread practice to insert spendthrift provisions routinely in wills and trust agreements. Is this a good practice? Consider when it might be disadvantageous to include such a clause.

PROBLEM

12-F.   *H,* a wealthy client who has just become a widower, has come to you for advice. His late wife's will bequeaths to him a portion of her estate of well over $1 million to take advantage of the marital deduction under the federal estate tax. The residue of her estate is left in trust to pay *H* the income for life, remainder to her issue, with provision for invasion of principal for certain needs of *H* and the issue. The trust includes a spendthrift provision. Because *H* is also the life beneficiary of a large trust (also containing a spendthrift clause) under his father's will, he is certain he will not need the income from his wife's residuary trust and realizes that his income tax position will be most unfavorable for the rest of his life. How would you advise him in an effort to relieve his tax burdens?

———————————

Restraints on alienation of *legal* interests in property, even life estates, are generally invalid. Forfeiture restraints, however, have met with limited acceptance, particularly in relation to legal life estates. See generally 6 American Law of Property §§26.13-26.54 (J. Casner ed. 1952). For purposes of evaluating spendthrift trusts as a matter of policy, consider the extent to which there are material differences relevant to restraints on alienation between legal interests and the equitable interests of trust beneficiaries. To what extent, on the other hand, are the policy considerations substantially similar in the two cases? What other policy considerations ought to enter into legislative or judicial judgments as to whether and to what extent spendthrift trusts are to be permitted?

E. GRISWOLD, SPENDTHRIFT TRUSTS
(2d ed. 1947)

§32. *Gray's Futile Attack on Spendthrift Trusts*

The most careful and thoughtful text on the subject was of course John C. Gray's Restraints on the Alienation of Property which first appeared in 1883. Gray attacked the doctrine of spendthrift trusts, thoroughly and with not a little vehemence. The arguments which he set forth have never been completely answered, but, as so frequently happens with such arguments, they have had little influence in shaping the law. Gray's text was frequently cited and quoted by the courts, but rarely followed. A second edition of the work appeared in 1895. During the twelve year interval a very considerable number of cases had been decided. Almost without exception, however, they had upheld the validity of spendthrift trusts.

In the preface of the second edition of his book, Gray wrote what has become the classic statement of the opposition to spendthrift trusts. For reasons which seem hard to understand now, he found these to be an earmark of socialism. He argued that the judges who had aided in the introduction of spendthrift trusts must

> have been influenced, unconsciously it may well be, by those ideas which
> the experience of the last few years has shown to have been fermenting in
> the minds of the community; by that spirit, in short, of paternalism, which
> is the fundamental essence alike of spendthrift trusts and of socialism.

At this day, it seems easy to see that this argument went too far. We can readily agree with the observation of a recent writer

> That socialism should rise through a device designed to protect the fortunes of Pennsylvania manufacturers and Massachusetts shipping and textile overlords from the depredations of their extravagant, and none too competent, progeny now seems a curious idea indeed.

[Manning, The Development of Restraints on Alienation Since Gray, 48 Harv. L. Rev. 373, 404 (1935).] . . .

§552. *The Basis of Spendthrift Trusts as Developed in the Decisions*

The origin of spendthrift trusts has been traced in the earlier sections of this book (see §§25-33). Although the factors which lead to such results are not always expressed in written opinions, the reasoning advanced by the Court in Nichols v. Eaton [91 U.S. 716 (1875)] may be examined as typical of that adopted and followed in other cases. Apart from the authorities cited, all of which seem to have been distinguishable, the decision there was based on what was apparently regarded as a logically necessary conclusion. A person who owns property, it was said, may give it as he pleases, and may therefore "attach to that gift the incident of continued use, of uninterrupted benefit of the gift, during the life of the donee." A similar basis was expressed for the decision in Broadway Natl. Bank v. Adams. There, too, the court proceeded on grounds based on supposed logic. It held that the power of alienation was not "a necessary attribute or incident" of a beneficiary's interest. On this basis, it concluded that the founder of a trust "has the entire jus disponendi, which imports that he may give it absolutely, or may impose any restrictions or fetters not repugnant to the nature of the estate which he gives."

This reasoning had been foreshadowed in the earlier Pennsylvania cases. In Ashhurst v. Given [5 W. & S. 323, 330 (Pa. 1843)], the court spoke in sweeping terms:

> Whoever has the right to give, has the right to dispose of the same as he pleases. Cujus est dare ejus est disponere, is the maxim which governs in such case.

The same line of argument has been relied on in many of the later cases. Typical of these is Morgan's Estate [223 Pa. 228, 230, 72 Atl. 498, 499 (1909)], where the court again quoted "cujus est dare ejus est disponere," and said:

> It is always to be remembered that consideration for the beneficiary does not even in the remotest way enter into the policy of the law; it has regard solely to the rights of the donor. Spendthrift trusts can have no

other justification than is to be found in considerations affecting the donor alone.

There is in all this a deference to the dead hand which is perhaps typical of the nineteenth century's attitude toward property. Closer examination, however, makes it clear that the conclusion so generally adopted is certainly not a logically necessary one, regardless of whatever other merit it may have. The difficulty is that the major premise — that the owner of property may dispose of it as he desires — is patently fallacious. . . .

[Section 553 summarizes a few limitations on the disposition of property: dower, forced heirship, and restrictions on charitable bequests; prohibitions against trusts that have indefinite beneficiaries or illegal purposes or that unreasonably restrain marriage or encourage divorce or neglect of duties; rules relating to perpetuities; and, most closely analogous, rules prohibiting restraints on alienation of legal interests.]

§554.   The Validity of Spendthrift Trusts Is a Matter of Policy, Not of Logic

It is apparent from the summary statement in the previous section that the bundle of rights known as ownership of property does not embrace an unqualified power of disposition in any way desired. There is no syllogistic basis for the spendthrift trust. If such trusts are valid it is not because the owner of property may dispose of it as he sees fit, but because the particular restriction in question is not contrary to public policy. The question therefore involves an examination of public policy. Such an examination has rarely, if ever, been attempted by the courts. It is obviously a matter difficult to approach and one about which dogmatic conclusions cannot be reached. It is well, however, to recognize its fundamental place in the question of the validity of spendthrift trusts.

§555.   The Question of Policy

The fundamental question, then, is whether spendthrift trusts should be sustained. This question, like many others in law, presents intangible elements in many fields, including, among others, ethics, economics, and psychology. In the past this question has generally been disposed of by assertion. And, indeed, it is difficult to dispose of it otherwise.

Spendthrift trusts have been attacked on the ground that the assurance of a guaranteed income destroys the initiative and the self-reliance of the beneficiary. Thus, it has been asserted that the commercial decline of New England has been caused in part by the spendthrift trust [Gerish, Commercial Structure of New England (1929) 65, 66]:

> Those with the initiative, foresight, and purpose to undertake new enterprises have been hampered in many instances by the "spendthrift

trust." . . . The "spendthrift trust" has tended to develop a class of what has been termed "four percenters." . . .

Absenteeism in industry, the lack of an aggressive community spirit, and the "spendthrift trust," coupled with an education that has weaned away from commerce and industry the natural recruits from among the descendants of former leaders, may have tended to stifle the development of leadership so necessary to a vitalized and dynamic social order.

But assertions like this will not withstand more critical examination. Spendthrift trusts are not confined to [New England]. . . . The reason for the decline in New England, if it exists, must be found elsewhere. Moreover, the argument in question, so far as it has validity, is directed against all trusts, not against spendthrift trusts alone. It is the trust, not the spendthrift provision, that tends to take property out of commerce.

The effect of spendthrift trusts on the commerce of the nation obviously does not lend itself to statistical analysis. Speculation is scarcely worthwhile when the answer depends upon so many unknown variables. Certainly assertion is not warranted. Similarly, it does not seem possible to dogmatize as to the effect of spendthrift trusts upon the character of the beneficiaries themselves. The percentage of failures among those who do not inherit fixed incomes is perhaps as large as among those who do. We have no figures and they would be extremely difficult to obtain, especially since so much of judgment is bound up in determining the question of an individual's success or failure.

An argument which is perhaps less difficult to evaluate is found in the unfairness of spendthrift trusts to creditors. It will not do to say that creditors should not extend credit to apparently opulent spendthrift beneficiaries because the restraints on their interests are a matter of public record which could be looked up. The argument is obviously not applicable to tort creditors. Moreover, many trusts, including nearly all of those created inter vivos, are not a matter of record. And finally, the argument is most unrealistic in holding creditors responsible for not doing what no one really expects a creditor to do. The fact remains that a decision allowing the beneficiary of a trust to refuse to pay bills for lodging and clothes though her trust income amounts to more than $171,000 a year [Congress Hotel Co. v. Martin, 312 Ill. 318, 143 N.E. 838, (1924)] must be shocking even to the most hardened conscience. And the same is true of the early New York case which so aroused Mr. Gray's wrath, where the beneficiary was allowed a larger exemption from the claims of his creditors because of his "high social standing," because "his associations are chiefly with men of leisure," and because he "is connected with a number of clubs."

There would seem, too, to be little reason why a matter of so great importance not only to the beneficiary but also to the public generally should be left to the control of individuals. Property in the hands of its owner is normally subject to his debts. The spendthrift trust allows the owner in transferring it to another to create an exemption from this general liability, an exemption which the settlor himself did not have. Exemptions of this sort should be regulated by the state, not by the wishes of individual testators. They should be open to all, not limited to a favored few. The language of a decision [Swan v. Gunderson, 51 S.D. 588, 590-591, 215 N.W. 884, 885 (1927)] rejecting an attempt to restrain the alienation of a legal interest is in point here. After referring to the statutes relating to exemptions and executions, the court concluded: "It is elementary that no testator or other nonsovereign donor by a condition or restriction in a devise or gift of the absolute legal title to real property, can take such property out from under the operation of these statutes and pro tanto repeal them." There seems obviously to be no *reason* why this conclusion is not equally applicable to private attempts to restrain the alienation of *equitable* interests.

A similar argument has been well stated in Brahmey v. Rollins [87 N.H. 290, 17 A. 186 (1935)], where the New Hampshire Supreme Court rejected the doctrine of spendthrift trusts after a thorough consideration of the question. In reaching this conclusion, the court said, "If the statute law permits creditors to reach the rights of the beneficiary, the settlor may not provide that they shall not." And again, "If he may bar seizure, why may he not as well bar taxability?"

POWELL, THE RULE AGAINST PERPETUITIES AND SPENDTHRIFT TRUSTS IN NEW YORK: COMMENTS AND SUGGESTIONS
71 Colum. L. Rev. 688, 704-706 (1971)

What New York needs is a thoroughgoing reconsideration of the whole topic of spendthrift trusts. . . . It would not be wise to prohibit *all* spendthrift trusts. There are times when a possessor of substantial wealth has, close to his heart, a relative who lacks the business experience to protect himself from the ever-present vultures. A modest sum, so set up as to protect such a person from dissipating his substance and unreachable by his creditors generally, constitutes no threat to social welfare. The trouble arises when the amount entrusted becomes large and the immunities of the beneficiaries cease to be reasonable. . . .

In the Law Revision Commissions Report for 1938 . . . the following language appears:

The Commission has concluded:

(a) That the allowance of spendthrift trusts within limits, is in harmony with public opinion but that under the present system larger sums may be made inalienable than is desirable.

(b) That the creation of spendthrift trusts should not be required by statute but should depend upon the settlor's intention. . . .

(d) That spendthrift trusts should be controlled and regulated as to size and duration by direct provision.

On this basis the Commission recommended statutory changes [but the] proposed legislation was not enacted. Austin Scott in all three editions of his great treatise has urged a ceiling on such trusts. Perhaps additional provisions could be usefully borrowed from the regulatory statutes of this type now operative in six of these United States, namely, Alabama, Louisiana, New Jersey, North Carolina, Oklahoma and Virginia.

I respectfully urge a prompt reconsideration of the social wisdom of the New York law on spendthrift trusts, and that this reconsideration concern itself with:

(1) the abandonment of the present rule that every trust of the most commonly created type must be spendthrift in character whether the settlor wishes it or does not; and the confining of permissible spendthrift trusts to those set up pursuant to the express manifestation by settlor that such is his desire;

(2) the rounding out of the rule now stated in EPTL section 7-1.5(d) so as not only to authorize the beneficiary of a spendthrift trust to transfer his income to or for the benefit of his dependents, but also expressly to authorize such persons to reach the trust income for maintenance and support;

(3) the confining of the doctrine of spendthrift trusts exclusively to income, thus reversing the recent decision in the *Vought* case;

(4) the allowance of the creation of a spendthrift trust only for the benefit of a relation by blood or marriage of the settlor;

(5) (and this is the most important of my suggestions) the establishment of a ceiling, stated either in terms of corpus (maybe $200,000, as is now the rule in Virginia) or of income (maybe $10,000, as is now the rule in Louisiana) upon the amount which any one person can put into a spendthrift trust for another. This would need careful safeguarding against multiple trusts of this character for the same beneficiary. . . .

Any such program would render unnecessary the present station-in-life statute and the present income executions (formerly called garnishments). They could be repealed with few mourners.

3. Discretionary, Protective, and Related Trusts

PROBLEM

12-G. *A* left his estate to *T* in trust "to pay such amounts of income or principal, or both, to *B* as *T* may, in her absolute discretion, deem appropriate for *B*'s support, welfare and happiness," remainder to *B*'s issue. *B* is now insolvent. His major creditor, *C*, asks your advice concerning the availability of the trust assets, or any of *B*'s rights therein, to satisfy *C*'s claim. How would you advise *C*? Consider the materials that follow.

TODD'S EXECUTORS v. TODD
260 Ky. 611, 86 S.W.2d 168 (1935)

[Paulina Todd died in 1933. Her will left a portion of her estate to her executor in trust

> to use the income or principal in the support, maintenance and comfort of Romulus Todd during his life, and is to have an absolute discretion as to what part of either he shall use for said purpose or pay to said Romulus, and this discretion is not to be controlled by any other person and in no event is any portion of the principal or interest to be applied to any debt of said Romulus, and . . . this trust is to cease and the principal is to go to the remaindermen [Romulus's children], if the Court should adjudge that any part could be subjected to the claims of any creditor.

Iva Todd, who had divorced Romulus in 1923, asked for an attachment against the trust fund to satisfy her personal judgment against Romulus for unpaid alimony and child support. The three minor children of Iva and Romulus filed an intervening petition alleging that the interest of Romulus was subject to Iva's claim and that they were thus entitled to the principal of the trust estate.]

REES, J. . . .

[I]t was adjudged that Iva Todd was entitled to have her judgment for $3,420 paid out of the trust fund. The executors and Romulus Todd have appealed.

The question squarely presented is whether the provision of Paulina E. Todd's will creating a trust estate for the benefit of her son, Romulus Todd, is void and unenforceable as in violation of section 2355 of the Kentucky Statutes, which reads:

> Estates of every kind held or possessed in trust, shall be subject to the debts and charges of the persons to whose use, or for whose benefit, they shall be respectively held or possessed, as they would be subject if those persons owned the like interest in the property held or possessed as they own or shall own in the use or trust thereof.

This depends upon whether or not the will creates a beneficial interest that can be enforced by the cestui que trust. Where the trustee is authorized in his discretion to withhold all payments, the cestui has no absolute right which he can enforce or which can be reached by creditors. In Cecil's Trustees v. Robertson & Brother, 105 S.W. 926, 927, 32 Ky. Law Rep. 357, it was said:

> The rule is that, when the trustee has the discretion to withhold from the beneficiary all interest in the trust fund, then the fund may not be sub-

jected to the debts of the beneficiary, but that, if the beneficiary may in equity compel the trustee to pay her a certain part of the estate or income, the creditors may do the same.

Where a testator provides in his will that property actually devised shall not be subject to the debts of the devisee, such provision is void, and where the income from certain property is devised to one for life, with the provision that if any court should ever hold it subject to the devisee's debts his interest therein should cease and the title should vest at once in the remaindermen, such provision is valid. . . .

The provision in the will of Paulina E. Todd falls in neither of these classifications. There is no misconstruing the intent of the testatrix in the instant case. The language of the will is direct and unambiguous. It was the manifest intent of the testatrix that the legal title and the absolute control of the property should pass to the trustees, and that they should be vested with absolute discretion in the matter of payments to the cestui out of the principal and income. No interest vested in the cestui. He has no rights which he can enforce. The property is given to the trustees to be applied in their discretion, uncontrolled by any other person, to the use of Romulus Todd, and no interest goes to him until the trustees have exercised this discretion. Section 2355 of the Statutes has no application where the cestui is without any interest in the trust estate which he can enforce. Davidson's Executors v. Kemper, 79 Ky. 5; Hackett's Trustee v. Hackett, 146 Ky. 408, 142 S.W. 673.

In Louisville Tobacco Warehouse Co. v. Thompson, 172 Ky. 350, 189 S.W. 245, 247, the provision of the will there under consideration was very similar to the provision of Paulina E. Todd's will heretofore quoted, and it was held that no interest was created which could be subjected to the debts of the beneficiary. After reviewing a number of cases, the court said:

> From the brief review we have given these cases, it becomes apparent that the rule is that, where the beneficiary whose interest is sought to be subjected is given an enforceable interest in the property devised, that interest may be subject to his debts. Such an interest is given when a specific sum is directed to be paid to him, and the payment of which sum he can legally enforce. It is likewise given when the language creating the interest is sufficient to give him an estate in the property devised, but when neither of these is given, and the sum which he is to receive is discretionary with the trustee, no interest is created which may be subjected to the payment of his debts.

Our conclusion is that the will under consideration gives to Romulus Todd no interest in his mother's estate which can be subjected to the payment of his debts. . . .

The judgment is reversed, with directions to enter a judgment in conformity with this opinion.

RESTATEMENT (SECOND) OF TRUSTS

§155. *Discretionary Trusts.*

(1) Except as stated in §156 [where the settlor is a beneficiary], if by the terms of a trust it is provided that the trustee shall pay to or apply for a beneficiary only so much of the income and principal or either as the trustee in his uncontrolled discretion shall see fit to pay or apply, a transferee or creditor of the beneficiary cannot compel the trustee to pay any part of the income or principal.

(2) Unless a valid restraint on alienation has been imposed in accordance with the rules stated in §§152 and 153, if the trustee pays to or applies for the beneficiary any part of the income or principal with knowledge of the transfer or after he has been served with process in a proceeding by a creditor to reach it, he is liable to such transferee or creditor.

§154. *Trusts for Support.*   Except as stated in §§156 and 157, if by the terms of a trust it is provided that the trustee shall pay or apply only so much of the income and principal or either as is necessary for the education or support of the beneficiary, the beneficiary cannot transfer his interest and his creditors cannot reach it.

G. BOGERT, TRUSTS
(6th ed. 1987)

§43. *Blended Trusts.*   If a trust is for the benefit of described persons as a group and no member of the group is intended to have a right to any individual benefits separate and apart from the others, then no member has an alienable interest or one which his creditors can reach.

§44. *Protective Trusts.*   The phrase "protective trust" has been used in England to describe a trust of an ordinary type which, on attempted alienation of his interest by the cestui or attempted attachment by his creditors, becomes a discretionary trust to apply the income for the benefit of any one or more or all of the group consisting of the original beneficiary and his spouse and issue, or if he has no spouse or issue, for the original beneficiary and his prospective next of kin. . . .

––––––––––––

Bogert's third edition (1952) pointed out that in England "the protective trust takes the place of the outlawed spendthrift trust," and stated that a protective trust "can be created in the United States but the validity of spendthrift or other similar trusts renders it of little use." Can you think of reasons for using protective trust provisions even where spendthrift trusts are valid?

MATTHEWS v. MATTHEWS
450 N.E.2d 278 (Ohio App. 1982)

[Action against the beneficiary of a trust to recover alimony and child support. The trustee was directed to pay to or for defendant Matthews such part of the income "as the trustee in his sole discretion shall deem necessary for his reasonable support, maintenance and health" and also to pay or apply principal for these purposes as the trustee "shall deem necessary and proper under the circumstances." The trial court found that there was nothing in the trust instrument indicating an intent by the settlor to provide for defendant's children and that no "vested interest existed because the trust was fully discretionary."]

MOYER, J. . . .

[D]efendant's ex-wife . . . attempted to reach defendant's interest in the trust to satisfy her judgment against defendant [but] Martin v. Martin, [54 Ohio St. 2d 101, 374 N.E.2d 1384 (1978)], clearly holds that a former spouse may not attach the interest of a beneficiary of a discretionary trust. Defendants rely on *Martin* also for their argument that defendant Matthews' child may not attach [his] interest. . . .

The trial court erred in concluding that the trust was fully discretionary. The first branch of the syllabus in *Martin* reads as follows:

> A trust conferring upon the trustees power to distribute income and principal in their "absolute discretion," but which provides standards by which that discretion is to be exercised with reference to needs of the trust beneficiary for education, care, comfort or support, is neither a purely discretionary trust nor a strict support trust, and the trustees of such trust may be required to exercise their discretion to distribute income and principal for those needs. . . .

The trust before us, as the trust in *Martin*, is neither a purely discretionary trust, nor a strict support trust. It follows that, at least to the extent of his needs, defendant Matthews has an interest in . . . the income of the trust.

The next question is whether plaintiffs may claim an interest in the beneficiary's income interest in the trust. We find no decision of the Supreme Court that disposes of the issue. A review of the cases from other jurisdictions . . . causes us to conclude that there is no unanimous view of the law. [One view] is that the child may, in the absence of an express exclusion in the trust instrument, recover from the trust. The reasoning upon which this position is based is that beneficiary should not be allowed to enjoy his interest while neglecting to support his children. We believe this to be the better rule.

The trial court held that there was no indication that the settlor intended to provide for defendant Matthews' children. However, the trust document states that the trustee shall pay what he deems necessary for the beneficiary's "reasonable support, maintenance and health." Support of one's children is mandated by R.C. 3103.03. "Reasonable support" includes payment of all the beneficiary's normal, expected and legal responsibilities. It would have been unreasonable, had defendant Matthews lived with his child, for the trustee to have refused to pay defendant Matthews sufficient funds from the trust to support both himself and his child. We have been given no reason why "reasonable support" should have a different application simply because defendant lived apart from his daughter. . . . The final question is, from what fund the judgment should be satisfied. Plaintiffs claim that [the will] authorizes payment from the corpus of the trust . . . when the income from the trust is insufficient to provide for the beneficiary's needs. . . .

Assuming no significant change in the trust income, the judgment for child support could reasonably be expected to be paid from the trust income within 3 to 5 years. It would, therefore, be imprudent to order the trustee to invade the principal to satisfy said judgment. This amount constitutes over one-tenth of the entire principal, and the payment of such an amount might jeopardize the trust itself. Therefore, we hold that the trustee did not abuse its discretion by refusing to invade the corpus of the trust to pay the judgment. . . .

Judgment reversed and cause remanded.

MOYER, J. [reaffirming the reversal on reconsideration]. . . .

The general rule is that the income from a trust which is neither a purely discretionary nor a strict support trust and which contains no express exclusion therefrom of the beneficiary's children, may be attached for the purpose of paying for the support of the beneficiary's children. . . .

DEPARTMENT OF MENTAL HEALTH v. PHILLIPS
114 Ill. 2d 85, 500 N.E.2d 29 (1986)

WARD, J. . . .

[This court has] found it "proper and fitting" that a patient, his estate or relatives should reimburse the State as they are able, or to [the extent required by statute], thereby lessening the burden on the public. . . . This court has held that the income yielded by trust assets is part of a recipient's estate against which the Department may bring a claim . . . , and later rejected the contention that only the income and not the principal is subject to service charges. . . . [Courts in this state and] in other jurisdictions have held that a spendthrift trust established for the benefit of an incompetent is subject to reimbursement proceedings brought under statute by public agencies. . . . We are aware that there are decisions to the contrary. . . .

Here [the trust instrument] authorizes the trustee to expend as much of the trust assets "as the trustee deems necessary or advisable for the beneficiary's education (including a college or professional education), maintenance, medical care, support, general welfare and comfortable living." It is not clear from this provision whether the settlor intended to establish a fund to provide services for Steven supplemental to the care provided by the State, or whether her intent was simply to provide for Steven's support regardless of whether or not Steven is in a public institution. The circumstances surrounding the execution of the trust instrument, however, support the conclusion that the settlor's intent was to provide that which the Department was unwilling or unable to furnish.

Sue Phillips executed the trust instruments shortly after Steven reached his 18th birthday. . . . Thus it is clear that at the time the trust instrument was executed, [she] was under no legal obligation . . . to reimburse the Department for services. . . . It is also significant that the trust assets would be exhausted if the Department were to prevail in its claim against the trust.

. . . [O]ur construction of the trust preserves the settlor's intent to create a fund for Steven's education, maintenance, medical care, support, general welfare and comfortable living beyond that which the State is willing or able to provide. . . .

MATTER OF ROBERTS
61 N.Y.2d 782, 461 N.E.2d 300 (1984)

MEMORANDUM [Opinion of the Court]. . . .

In 1957, the grantor created a trust providing in part that the income be applied, as the trustees saw fit, for the support and maintenance of her daughter, and permitting the trustees "in their absolute discretion" to apply all or part of the corpus for the daughter's support and maintenance. After the grantor's death, the daughter was hospitalized at Kings County Hospital for a considerable period at public expense. Appellant [City Health and Hospital Corporation] obtained a judgment against the daughter of $111,000 for the unpaid charges and seeks to satisfy this judgment from the trust principal, now valued at approximately $45,000.

Special Term declined to order the trustees to expend the trust funds in partial satisfaction of appellant's judgment. It found, both from the terms of the trust indenture and from the surrounding circumstances, that the grantor did not intend to exhaust the trust principal to provide for her daughter's hospitalization; knowing of her daughter's disability, the grantor nonetheless made no amendment of the pertinent trust provisions, which gave the trustees discretion to determine what funds would be used for her welfare and provided for remaindermen. . . . The Appellate Division unanimously affirmed, and the affirmed findings have support in the record. The trustees did not abuse their discretion as a matter of law by refusing to pay over the trust corpus to appellant.

See extensive and thoughtful discussion in Frolik, Discretionary Trusts for a Disabled Beneficiary: A Solution or a Trap for the Unwary?, 46 U. Pitt. L. Rev. 335 (1985), discussing the social and personal utility of discretionary trusts but pointing out the danger that the existence of such a trust may disqualify a disabled beneficiary from state or federal assistance. See also Silber, The Effect of a Trust on the Eligibility or Liability of the Trust Beneficiary for Public Assistance, 26 Real Prop., Prob. & Trust J. 133 (1992), with appendix (id. at 168-212) reviewing the law in twenty-nine of the states.

Moloshok v. Blum, 109 Misc. 2d 660, 441 N.Y.S.2d 331 (Sup. Ct. 1981), involved a proceeding to annul and reverse the determination of the New York State Department of Social Services (respondent Blum) and to direct respondent to make certain payments for nursing care services without reduction for payments that petitioner could receive under a trust. "Respondent Blum contends that the petitioner may not be considered a person who requires public assistance until she has made a bona fide effort to seek an invasion of the corpus of the trust," but, the court concludes, "[a]ssets denied to petitioner within the authorized discretion of the trustees cannot be considered assets available to her" for these purposes. The opinion states:

> The testamentary trust gives absolute discretion to the trustees and further states that they "shall not be held accountable to any court or to any person for the exercise or non-exercise of this completely discretionary power." Since the creator of the trust was the owner of the funds, their disposition must comply with his wishes. His direction that the discretion of the trustees be absolute cannot be invaded by the court nor by anyone else. The trustees' conduct in [retaining principal] cannot be held to be either illegal, arbitrary or capricious. Implicit in their designation is a fiduciary obligation to preserve the corpus for the remaindermen. . . .
>
> Furthermore, the discretion of the Court is limited under [special legislation enabling New York courts to authorize invasion of trust principal] by the phrase "unless otherwise provided in the disposing instrument." The disposing instrument herein does otherwise provide and specifically precludes an interference by the court with the complete discretionary power given to the trustee.

Compare the increasingly common practice of establishing discretionary trusts in personal injury judgments or settlements, discussed in Berkness, Abusive Discretion: Discretionary and Supplemental Trusts Created in Settlement of Personal Injury Claims, 67 Wash. L. Rev. 437 (1992), arguing for creditor access on policy grounds and because such trusts are "self-settled."

Creditors of settlor-beneficiary. Greenwich Trust Co. v. Tyson, 129 Conn. 211, 222-225, 27 A.2d 166, 172-174 (1942), states:

> The trust before us is not a spendthrift trust but, by reason of the discretion reposed in the trustee as to the use of the income, it is a "discretionary" trust. If in such a trust the settlor is the sole person entitled to the income, that income can be reached by his creditors. Griswold, Spendthrift Trusts 481; Restatement, Trusts, §156(2). A provision in the trust instrument that the trustee might in his discretion withhold the income from the settlor and accumulate it would not in itself place the income beyond the reach of his creditors. . . . We are brought, then, to the question of the effect of the provision that the trustee in his "absolute discretion" might expend any part of the income for the support and maintenance of the wife of the settlor or the support, education and maintenance of a named son and of other children who might be born to him. . . .
>
> The outstanding factor in the situation is that, under a trust where the trustee has absolute discretion to pay the income or expend it for the settlor's benefit, the trustee could, even though he had a like discretion to expend it for others, still pay it all to the settlor. Such a trust opens the way to the evasion by the settlor of his just debts, although he may still have the full enjoyment of the income from his property. To subject it to the claims of the settlor's creditors does not deprive others to whom the trustee might pay the income of anything to which they are entitled of right; they could not compel the trustee to use any of the income for them. The public policy which subjects to the demands of a settlor's creditors the income of a trust which the trustee in his discretion may pay to the settlor applies no less to a case where the trustee might in his discretion pay or use the income for others. The trial court was correct in holding that the plaintiff was entitled to reach the income if necessary to satisfy its judgment, but was in error in holding that its rights were limited to so much only of that income as the trustee in his discretion deemed not to be required for the support, maintenance or education of the settlor's wife and children.
>
> The fact that the provisions of the trust agreement are ineffective to protect the income of the trust from the claims of Tyson's creditors does not invalidate the trust as a whole or in itself destroy the remainder interests created.

13

Modification and Termination of Trusts

In the typical case a trust is terminated according to its terms when its purpose has been fulfilled in due course. After the creation of a trust but before the time fixed for its regular termination, questions sometimes arise regarding possible modification or premature termination of the trust. This chapter deals with certain of the problems presented by such questions and also with express powers to modify or to terminate.

A. *Power of the Settlor to Modify or Revoke*

Can the settlor, once an inter vivos trust has been created, terminate the trust, take away the rights given the beneficiaries, and recover the trust property? Essentially this depends on whether the trust is revocable. In a properly drawn trust agreement or declaration the question would be answered expressly. Sometimes, however, the question is not adequately covered by the terms of the trust — that is, either the provisions of the trust instrument or some other admissible evidence of the settlor's intent. In certain informal trusts a power of revocation may be implied, as in the case of tentative or *Totten* trusts. Occasionally it is asserted that the settlor intended to reserve a power to revoke the trust but omitted it by mistake.

In most states the settled rule is that, in the absence of grounds for reformation or rescission, a trust created or declared by a written instrument is irrevocable unless a power of revocation is expressly reserved or may be implied from language contained in the instrument. Restatement (Second) of Trusts §330. In a few states there are statutory provisions reversing this standard common law rule. For example, California Probate Code §15400 provides that "[u]nless expressly made irrevocable by the trust instrument, the trust is revocable by the settlor."

A trust may be reformed or rescinded on the same grounds as a transfer free of trust. Yet problems in the reformation of trusts, particularly on the ground of unilateral mistake, are made somewhat distinctive by the donative character of the typical trust, and the problems are shaped by the circumstances of a trust's planning and preparation. "The creation of a trust being substantially a unilateral transaction, the mistake of the settlor, not shared by the trustee or beneficiary, is sufficient to avoid the transfer if it induces a conveyance whose consequences the settlor does not understand or intend." Nossaman and Wyatt, Trust Administration and Taxation §21.12 (rev. 2d ed. 1969).

Coolidge v. Loring, 235 Mass. 220, 223-224, 126 N.E. 276, 277 (1920), states:

> [T]he mistaken "belief" of the settlors as set forth in the agreed facts affords no ground for relief. Misconception of the legal effect of the language in the instrument is not a "mistake of law" against which our courts afford a remedy. The parties are bound by the legal effect of what has really been agreed on, and cannot have the declaration set aside on the ground that they did not fully understand the legal effect of the language used, and that certain legal consequences which were not anticipated by the settlors flowed from its execution. . . . The language is entirely consistent with a view that the subject of . . . termination in the lifetime of the settlors did not occur to the parties at the time of the declaration of trust. . . . It is settled that an instrument will not be reformed on the ground of mistake, except upon "full, clear and decisive proof" of the mistake.

In Atkinson v. Atkinson, 157 Md. 648, 651-652, 147 A. 662, 663 (1929), involving a trust of all of the settlor's property, the court stated:

> The record convinces us that the grantor did not intend to relinquish control of his estate to that extent. His physical and mental debility . . . was sufficient to account for his apparent failure to comprehend clearly the real effect of the deed of trust and the true intent of his attorney's explanations. There was no consideration for the deed, and, as it appears not to be in accord with the grantor's actual purpose and understanding, we shall affirm the decree.

In a number of cases a settlor or donor has been allowed to rescind a trust or gift on the grounds of mistake as to the tax consequences of the transfer. See IV W. Fratcher, Scott on Trusts §333.4 (4th ed. 1989). For an example of reformation to salvage a deceased settlor's tax objectives (qualification for estate tax marital deduction), see Berman v. Sandler, 399 N.E.2d 17 (1980).

The power to revoke is generally held to include the power to amend. See Heifetz v. Bank of America, 147 Cal. App. 2d 776, 305 P.2d 979 (1957); Annot., 62 A.L.R. 1043 (1957). Is there any reason for not implying the power to amend from a power to revoke? On the other hand, it has been held that the reservation of a power to modify a trust during the settlor's lifetime does not allow modification by will. Magoon v. Cleveland Trust Co., 101 Ohio App. 194, 134 N.E.2d 879 (1956). Is there any justification for this?

There is divergence of views on the question of whether creditors of the settlor, under otherwise appropriate circumstances, can avail themselves of the settlor's power to revoke a trust. Can the creditors reach this power and exercise it, terminating the trust and even restoring the interests of other beneficiaries to the settlor to the extent needed to satisfy his debts? (Compare the claim of the settlor's spouse, supra Chapter 11 at page 396.) The right of creditors in bankruptcy is clear. Section 541 of the Federal Bankruptcy Act (11 U.S.C. §541) excludes from the bankruptcy estate only those powers that are exercisable "solely for the benefit of [persons or entities] other than the debtor." Bankruptcy, however, is available only during the debtor's lifetime. Under state law, absent a statute comparable to the bankruptcy provision, case law generally supports the anomalous combination of rules set out in the Restatement (Second) of Trusts. Comment *c* of §156 states that if the settlor reserves "not only a life interest but also a general power to appoint the remainder by deed or by will or by deed alone or by will alone, his creditors can reach the principal of the trust as well as the income." But §330, comment *o*, states:

> Unless it is otherwise provided by statute a power of revocation reserved by the settlor cannot be reached by his creditors. . . . [T]hey cannot compel him to revoke the trust for their benefit.

Does this combination of rules make sense? Is there any conceivable reason why creditors should fare better when the settlor retains the right to receive corpus only in the trustee's discretion (Restatement (Second) of Trusts §156, comment *e*, recognizing that the rights of creditors are measured by the maximum amount the settlor might receive) than when the trust property can be taken by revocation at the whim of the settlor?

Should states adopt the position that revocable trust assets are subject to the claims of the settlor's creditors? If so, should these assets also be reachable by creditors after the settlor's death?

STATE STREET BANK & TRUST CO. v. REISER
389 N.E.2d 768 (Mass. App. 1979)

KASS, J.

State Street Bank and Trust Company (the bank) seeks to reach the assets of an inter vivos trust in order to pay a debt to the bank owed by the estate of the settlor of the trust. . . .

Wilfred A. Dunnebier created an inter vivos trust on September 30, 1971, with power to amend or revoke the trust and the right during his lifetime to direct the disposition of principal and income. He conveyed to the trust the capital stock of five closely held corporations. Immediately following execution of this trust, Dunnebier executed a will under which he left his residuary estate to the trust he had established.

About thirteen months later Dunnebier applied to the bank for a
$75,000 working capital loan. A bank officer met with Dunnebier, exam-
ined a financial statement furnished by him and visited several single
family home subdivisions which Dunnebier, or corporations he controlled, had built or were in the process of building. During their conversations, Dunnebier told the bank officer that he had controlling
interests in the corporations which owned the most significant assets
appearing on the financial statement. On the basis of what he saw of
Dunnebier's work, recommendations from another bank, Dunnebier's
borrowing history with the bank, and the general cut of Dunnebier's jib,
the bank officer decided to make an unsecured loan to Dunnebier for
the $75,000 he had asked for. To evidence this loan, Dunnebier, on
November 1, 1972, signed a personal demand note to the order of the
bank. The probate judge found that Dunnebier did not intend to
defraud the bank or misrepresent his financial position by failing to call
attention to the fact that he had placed the stock of his corporations in
the trust.

Approximately four months after he borrowed this money Dunnebier
died in an accident. His estate has insufficient assets to pay the entire
indebtedness due to the bank.

Under Article Fourteen of his inter vivos trust, Dunnebier's trustees
" . . . may in their sole discretion pay from the principal and income of
this Trust Estate any and all debts and expenses of administration of the
Settlor's estate." The bank urges that, since the inter vivos trust was part
of an estate plan in which the simultaneously executed will was an integrated document, the instruction in Dunnebier's will that his executor
pay his debts should be read into the trust instrument. This must have
been Dunnebier's intent, goes the argument. . . . [W]e find the trust
agreement manifests no such intent by Dunnebier. Article Fourteen
speaks of the sole discretion of the trustees. Subparagraphs *A* and *B* of
Article Five, by contrast, direct the trustees unconditionally to pay two
$15,000 legacies provided for in Dunnebier's will if his estate has insuf-
ficient funds to do so. It is apparent that when Dunnebier wanted his
trustees unqualifiedly to discharge his estate's obligations, he knew how
to direct them. As to those matters which Dunnebier, as settlor, left to
the sole discretion of his trustees, we are not free to substitute our judgment for theirs. . . .

During the lifetime of the settlor, to be sure, the bank would have had
access to the assets of the trust. When a person creates for his own benefit a trust for support or a discretionary trust, his creditors can reach
the maximum amount which the trustee, under the terms of the trust,
could pay to him or apply for his benefit. Ware v. Gulda, 331 Mass. 68,
70, 117 N.E.2d 137 (1954). . . . Under the terms of Dunnebier's trust,
all the income and principal were at his disposal while he lived.

We then face the question whether Dunnebier's death broke the vital chain. His powers to amend or revoke the trust, or to direct payments from it, obviously died with him, and the remainder interests of the beneficiaries of the trust became vested. . . .

Traditionally the courts of this Commonwealth have always given full effect to inter vivos trusts, notwithstanding retention of powers to amend and revoke during life, even though this resulted in disinheritance of a spouse or children and nullified the policy which allows a spouse to waive the will and claim a statutory share, G.L. c. 191, §15. It might then be argued that a creditor ought to stand in no better position where, as here, the trust device was not employed in fraud of creditors.

There has developed, however, another thread of decisions which takes cognizance of, and gives effect to, the power which a person exercises in life over property. When a person has a general power of appointment, exercisable by will or by deed, and exercises that power, any property so appointed is, in equity, considered part of his assets and becomes available to his creditors in preference to the claims of his voluntary appointees or legatees. These decisions rest on the theory that as to property which a person could appoint to himself or his executors, the property could have been devoted to the payment of debts and, therefore, creditors have an equitable right to reach that property. It taxes the imagination to invent reasons why the same analysis and policy should not apply to trust property over which the settlor retains dominion at least as great as a power of appointment. . . .

Frequently, as Dunnebier did in the instant case, the settlor retains all the substantial incidents of ownership because access to the trust property is necessary or desirable as a matter of sound financial planning. Psychologically, the settlor thinks of the trust property as "his," as Dunnebier did when he took the bank's officer to visit the real estate owned by the corporation whose stock he had put in trust. See Fiduciary Trust Co. v. First Natl. Bank, 344 Mass. 1, 9, 181 N.E.2d 6 (1962). In other circumstances, persons place property in trust in order to obtain expert management of their assets, while retaining the power to invade principal and to amend and revoke the trust. It is excessive obeisance to the form in which property is held to prevent creditors from reaching property placed in trust under such terms. . . .

The Internal Revenue Code institutionalizes the concepts that a settlor of a trust who retains administrative powers, power to revoke or power to control beneficial enjoyment "owns" that trust property and provides that it shall be included in the settlor's personal estate. I.R.C. §§2038 and 2041.

We hold, therefore, that where a person places property in trust and reserves the right to amend and revoke, or to direct disposition of principal and income, the settlor's creditors may, following the death of the settlor, reach in satisfaction of the settlor's debts to them, to the extent not satisfied by the settlor's estate, those assets owned by the trust over which the settlor had such control at the time of his death as would have enabled the settlor to use the trust assets for his own benefit. Assets which pour over into such a trust as a consequence of the settlor's death or after the settlor's death, over which the settlor did not have control during his life, are not subject to the reach of creditors since, as to those assets, the equitable principles do not apply which place assets subject to creditors' disposal.

The judgment is reversed. . . .

See also Johnson v. Commercial Bank, 284 Or. 675, 679, 588 P.2d 1096, 1100 (1978):

> Defendants argue, correctly, that "creditors can reach the trust only to the extent of the settlor's interest." . . . But this principle argued by defendants is not on point. Defendants cite a case where the settlor gave himself a life estate with remainder to specified persons and did not retain the power to revoke. We agree that creditors could not reach the remainder interests under such facts because such conveyances give the remaindermen present vested interests in the property that cannot be defeated by any act of the settlor. Such remainder interests are present gifts that are no more subject to the claims of creditors than are any other gifts. See A. Scott, The Law of Trusts §156 at 1192 (3d ed. 1967); E. Griswold, Spendthrift Trusts §544 (2d ed. 1947). In the case at bar, Elmer did not divest himself of the remainder interests; they were subject to complete defeasance at any time during his life if he chose to exercise his right to revoke.

B. *Termination by the Trustee*

The trustee has power to terminate or modify a trust only to the extent expressly or impliedly granted by the terms of the trust. Such a power is to be exercised in accordance with fiduciary standards and the intent of the settlor as manifested in the terms of the trust. The general principles encountered in the preceding chapter relating to trustees' discretionary powers over distributions are applicable to discretionary powers to terminate. See Watling v. Watling, 27 F.2d 193 (6th Cir. 1928).

Where the trustee is not expressly given a power to terminate the trust but is given discretion to invade principal, the latter power would presumably permit termination by distribution of all of the principal if reasonably required to carry out the settlor's purpose. See Boyden v. Stevens, 285 Mass. 176, 188 N.E. 741 (1943). But the trustee may not exercise a discretionary power of invasion to terminate a trust for reasons beyond the intended purpose of the power. See Kemp v. Paterson, 6 N.Y.2d 40, 159 N.E.2d 661 (1959), in which three dissenting judges thought that the purpose of saving taxes fell within the expressed standard relating to the beneficiary's "best interest."

C. Termination and Modification by the Beneficiaries

PROBLEMS

13-A.   S left the residue of his estate to T in trust "to pay the income to my wife, W, for life, remainder to such of my children as survive her." No spendthrift provision was included in the trust. W, age 65, and S's only children, A and B, ages 40 and 35, jointly petition the court to terminate the trust and to convey the trust assets to them. What result?

Would the inclusion of a spendthrift clause alter the result? What if this spendthrift trust had been created inter vivos and S were still alive and gave his consent to the requested termination? (Careful!)

13-B.   Suppose in the spendthrift trust situation in Problem 13-A, W, A, and B request T to convey the trust assets to them in termination of the trust. T does so and they receipt for it. Later, W files suit to require T to reestablish the trust and to pay her the income until her death. What result?

Assume further while suit is pending, T pays W, A, and B $100 each for a release of all liability in settlement of the suit. What would be the effect of this transaction?

In the landmark case of Claflin v. Claflin, 149 Mass. 19, 20 N.E. 454 (1889), the settlor created a testamentary trust to pay his son $10,000 at age 21, $10,000 at age 25, and the balance of the principal at age 30. Following his twenty-first birthday the son sought to compel the trustees to pay the entire trust fund over to him. The court conceded that the son was the sole beneficiary and that all equitable interests in the property were indefeasibly vested in him; it also concluded that the trust was not a dry or passive trust and that all purposes of the trust had not been accomplished. The question then was whether, under such circumstances, the sole beneficiary could compel termination. The court stated, 149 Mass. at 23-24, 20 N.E. at 456:

> In the case at bar nothing has happened which the testator did not anticipate, and for which he has not made provision. It is plainly his will that neither the income nor any part of the principal should now be paid to the plaintiff. It is true that the plaintiff's interest is alienable by him, and can be taken by his creditors to pay his debts, but it does not follow that, because the testator has not imposed all possible restrictions, the restrictions which he has imposed should not be carried into effect.
>
> The decision in Broadway National Bank v. Adams, 133 Mass. 170, rests upon the doctrine that a testator has a right to dispose of his own property with such restrictions and limitations, not repugnant to law, as he sees fit, and that his intentions ought to be carried out, unless they contravene

some positive rule of law, or are against public policy. The rule contended for by the plaintiff in that case was founded upon the same considerations as that contended for by the plaintiff in this, and the grounds on which this court declined to follow the English rule in that case are applicable to this, and for the reasons there given we are unable to see that the directions of the testator to the trustees to pay the money to the plaintiff when he reaches the age of 25 and 30 years, and not before, are against public policy, or are so far inconsistent with the rights of property given to the plaintiff, that they should not be carried into effect. It cannot be said that these restrictions upon the plaintiff's possession and control of the property are altogether useless, for there is not the same danger that he will spend the property while it is in the hands of the trustees as there would be if it were in his own. . . . The existing situation is one which the testator manifestly had in mind, and made provision for. The strict execution of the trust has not become impossible; the restriction upon the plaintiff's possession and control is, we think, one that the testator had a right to make; other provisions for the plaintiff are contained in the will, apparently sufficient for his support; and we see no good reason why the intention of the testator should not be carried out.

Where, after the creation of a trust, one beneficiary or a third person acquires all of the beneficial interests, whether by assignment or by testate or intestate succession, premature termination is frequently appropriate. Thus, the *Claflin* opinion quoted and distinguished the earlier case of Sears v. Choate, 146 Mass. 395, 15 N.E. 786 (1888), as follows:

> In Sears v. Choate it is said:
>
> Where property is given to certain persons for their benefit, and in such a manner that no other person has or can have any interest in it, they are in effect the absolute owners of it; and it is reasonable and just that they should have the control and disposal of it, unless some good cause appears to the contrary.
>
> In that case the plaintiff was the absolute owner of the whole property, subject to an annuity of $10,000 payable to himself. The whole of the principal of the trust fund, and all the income not expressly made payable [via the annuity] to the plaintiff had become vested in him . . . by way of resulting trust, as property undisposed of by the will. Apparently the testator had not contemplated such a result, and had made no provision for it, and the court saw no reason why the trust should not be terminated and the property conveyed to the plaintiff.

149 Mass. at 22-23, 20 N.E. at 455-456.

A few American courts have followed the English rule under which the beneficiaries, if all consent and are sui juris, can modify or compel termination even though the purposes of the trust have not been accomplished. In most of the states, however, some version of the so-called *Claflin* doctrine prevails. The doctrine, as it is interpreted and applied in many states, is summarized by the American Law Institute, Restatement (Second) of Trusts, as follows:

> §337.   *Consent of Beneficiaries.*
>
> (1) Except as stated in Subsection (2), if all of the beneficiaries of a trust consent and none of them is under an incapacity, they can compel the termination of the trust.
>
> (2) If the continuance of the trust is necessary to carry out a material purpose of the trust, the beneficiaries cannot compel its termination.

The doctrine is discussed in Speth v. Speth, 8 N.J. Super. 587, 592, 598, 74 A.2d 344, 347, 350 (1950), as follows:

> The American cases recognize primarily the privilege of the donor to qualify his gift as he pleases within legal limits. . . . The English courts concentrate their predominant attention upon the situation of the beneficiary who being substantially the owner of the trust estate should be permitted in their judgment to deal with it as he wished. . . .
>
> This retrospective exposition of the subject may well be concluded in the words of Chief Justice Vanderbilt . . . :
>
>> The English authorities are of no force here because of our fundamentally divergent view of the power of the settlor and the beneficiaries of a trust over the trust res. In England the beneficiaries of the trust may by united action terminate, notwithstanding the fact that to do so may nullify the intention of the settlor. In this State it is the intention of the settlor of the trust that governs and not the desires of the beneficiaries.

Consent of settlor. Where the settlor of an inter vivos trust is alive and joins with all of the beneficiaries in seeking termination or modification, even under the *Claflin* doctrine the trust will be terminated or modified as requested without regard to the original purposes of the settlor.

> There would seem to be no good reason for holding that the courts owe it to the settlor to carry out his intention once expressed, if neither he nor anyone else any longer desires to have it carried out. . . . It is true that in the United States the beneficiaries alone cannot terminate the trust if its purposes have not been accomplished. It is true that where some of the beneficiaries do not consent, the others, even with the consent of the settlor, cannot terminate the trust. But where the settlor and all of the beneficiaries are of full capacity and consent, there seems to be no good reason why they should not have power to make such disposition of the trust property, as they choose.

A. Scott, Trusts §338 (Abridgment 1960). Similarly, §339 of the Restatement (Second) of Trusts provides: "If the settlor is the sole beneficiary of a trust and is not under an incapacity, he can compel the termination of the trust, although the purposes of the trust have not been accomplished."

In particular applications of the *Claflin* doctrine the problems generally center about one or both of two issues:

1. Do the parties to the agreement or petition hold all of the potential beneficial interests?
2. Is there a "material purpose" of the trust that would be defeated by its premature termination or by the proposed modification?

Consent of all beneficiaries. When modification or premature termination of a trust is sought by the beneficiaries, the court must initially determine who are the beneficiaries of the trust and whether each has capacity to give consent, for under the traditional general rule guardians ad litem or others cannot give this consent. (Contrast, however, Hatch v. Riggs National Bank, infra, as to representation by a guardian ad litem.) Determining all of the beneficiaries is not always an easy matter. Even when the meaning of the dispositive provisions of a trust instrument is clear, however, it will not be possible to obtain the consent of all beneficiaries in the typical modern trust. The presence of unborn, unascertained, or incompetent beneficiaries, even those holding contingent interests, will preclude obtaining the consent of all beneficiaries as required.

In re LEWIS' ESTATE
231 Pa. 60, 79 A. 921 (1911)

[Petition to compel termination of a testamentary trust. The trust provided for investment of the property and payment of the income to the settlor's widow for life and, in effect, for corpus thereafter to be distributed to the settlor's then-living descendants, per stirpes. Petitioners are the widow and the only living child of the settlor, his other two children having died without issue prior to the time of the petition. The trial court denied the petition.]

PER CURIAM.

The widow of the testator, for whose benefit he created the trust which she and their sole surviving child wish to have terminated, is still alive. Who will be the ultimate distributees of the fund under the will of her husband cannot be determined until her death, and the court below could not have made a decree determining the trust without the consent of all parties in interest. Such parties were not before it, for some who may ultimately participate in the fund may not yet be in existence.

Decree affirmed at appellants' costs.

For purposes of giving consent to termination or modification of a trust, should the donee of a power of appointment be treated as holding the interests that are subject to the power? Certainly the donee who holds only a special power of appointment is not so treated, but the donee who holds a *presently exercisable* general power *is* so treated. Do you see why? But what of the holder of a general power exercisable only by will? Assume that *A* is the life beneficiary of a trust and also holds a general testamentary power to appoint the trust property at death, remainder in default of appointment to *B*. If no substantial purpose of the settlor will be impaired by doing so, can the trust be terminated by *A* as a sole beneficiary? Cf. Restatement (Second) of Property §§16.1, 16.2.

LEVY v. CROCKER-CITIZENS NATIONAL BANK
14 Cal. App. 2d 102, 94 Cal. Rptr. 1 (1971)

[The attorney for plaintiff's mother prepared the trust instruments here in question, and plaintiff executed them in 1956 shortly after his twenty-first birthday.]

GUSTAFSON, J. . . .

Plaintiff is the trustor and the beneficiary of the net income for his life. Upon his death, the corpus is to be distributed pursuant to his exercise of a testamentary general power of appointment, or, in default of such appointment, to his then surviving lawful issue per stirpes or, if he has no surviving issue, to the then surviving lawful issue of his mother.

Plaintiff's testimony concerning his intent and the circumstances existing at the time of his execution of the trust instruments was objected to by the trustee (the only defendant) on the ground that the trust instruments were clear and unambiguous thus precluding extrinsic evidence of the meaning of the words used. . . . [N]o matter how clear and unambiguous language may appear to the reader, extrinsic evidence is admissible for the purpose of ascertaining what was meant by the person using the words in question. The extrinsic evidence, however, may not show that what was meant by the words used was something to which, under all of the circumstances, the words are not reasonably susceptible. . . . Plaintiff's testimony would have been relevant in an action to rescind the trust instruments on the ground of mistake or undue influence. . . . But here the action was not to rescind the trust instruments on the ground of mistake or undue influence, but rather an action by the trustor, assuming the validity of the trust instruments, to terminate the trusts. Plaintiff's testimony that he did not know what was in the documents he signed is not evidence that he intended by the words used therein not to make a gift to anyone.

It is conceded that if a trustor is the sole beneficiary of a trust, he may revoke it even though by its terms the trust is irrevocable. (Rest. 2d Trusts §339.) If there are other beneficiaries, however, consent of all beneficiaries is generally necessary to revoke the trust. (Rest. 2d Trusts §340.) Putting aside for the moment the existence of a testamentary power of appointment in the trustor, [plaintiff argues that the surviving] issue of the trustor, whose existence and identity will not be known until the trustor dies, are [not] beneficiaries. . . . The only answer to plaintiff's argument is that the authorities binding on us compel a contrary result. . . .

We now consider the effect of the trustor's general power to appoint by will. If a trustor receives a general power to appoint by deed or will, by appointing to himself by deed he becomes the sole beneficiary and obviously can terminate the trust. Plaintiff argues, again quite persuasively, that he has a will, that in all likelihood he will not die intestate and that there is therefore little likelihood that anyone will take in default of exercise of the power of appointment. The existence of the power, plaintiff argues, manifests an intent not to make a gift to those who would take in default of the exercise of the power of appointment.

But again the authorities compel us to reject plaintiff's argument. . . . While it is true that in neither [of the leading California cases] did the court explain why the existence of the power did not alter the result which would have been reached had there been no power of appointment, we are nevertheless bound by the decisions in those cases. (See also Rest. 2d Trusts §127, Com. b.)

The judgment is affirmed.

HATCH v. RIGGS NATIONAL BANK
361 F.2d 559 (D.C. Cir. 1966)

[Appellant seeks modification of a trust she created in 1923, reserving the income (with a spendthrift restraint) for life and a general power to appoint corpus by will; the unappointed remainder on her death is to go to her next of kin. The instrument expressly declared the trust irrevocable.]

LEVENTHAL, C.J. . . .

Appellant does not claim that the declaration of trust itself authorizes her to revoke or modify the trust. In effect she invokes the doctrine of worthier title, which teaches that a grant of trust corpus to the heirs of the settlor creates a reversion in the settlor rather than a remainder in his heirs. She claims that since she is the sole beneficiary of the trust under this doctrine, and is also the settlor, she may revoke or modify under accepted principles of trust law.

The District Court, while sympathizing with appellant's desire to obtain an additional stipend of $5000 a year, out of corpus, "to accommodate recently incurred expenses, and to live more nearly in accordance with her refined but yet modest tastes," felt that denial of the requested relief was required by this court's decision in Liberty National Bank v. Hicks, 173 F.2d 631 (1948). Summary judgment was granted for appellees. We affirm. . . .

The abbreviated discussion in *Hicks* may be taken as an implied rejection of [the] doctrine of worthier title. . . . This appeal squarely raises the question, and we deem it appropriate that we rely not on the aura of *Hicks,* but on an express consideration of the applicability of the doctrine of worthier title.

The doctrine of worthier title had its origins in the feudal system which to a large extent molded the English common law which we inherited. In its common law form, the doctrine provided that a conveyance of land by a grantor with a limitation over to his own heirs resulted in a reversion in the grantor rather than creating a remainder interest in the heirs. It was a rule of law distinct from, though motivated largely by the same policies as, the Rule in Shelly's Case. Apparently the feudal overlord was entitled to certain valuable incidents when property held by one of his feoffees passed by "descent" to an heir rather than by "purchase" to a transferee. The doctrine of worthier title — whereby descent is deemed "worthier" than purchase — remained ensconced in English law, notwithstanding the passing of the feudal system, until abrogated by statute in 1833.

The doctrine has survived in many American jurisdictions, with respect to inter vivos conveyance of both land and personalty, as a common law "rule of construction" rather than a "rule of law." In Doctor v. Hughes, 225 N.Y. 305, 122 N.E. 221 (1919), Judge Cardozo's landmark opinion reviewed the common-law history of the doctrine and concluded that its modern relevance was a rule of construction, a rebuttable presumption that the grantor's likely intent, in referring to his own heirs, was to reserve a reversion in his estate rather than create a remainder interest in the heirs. Evidence might be introduced to show that the grantor really meant what he said when he spoke of creating a remainder in his heirs. . . .

The views of the critics of the doctrine, which we find persuasive against its adoption, and borne out by the experience of the New York courts in the series of cases which have followed Doctor v. Hughes, supra, may be summarized as follows. The common-law reasons for the doctrine are as obsolete as those behind the Rule in Shelley's Case. Retention of the doctrine as a rule of construction is pernicious in several respects.

First, it is questionable whether it accords with the intent of the average settlor. It is perhaps tempting to say that the settlor intended to create no beneficial interest in his heirs when he said "to myself for life, remainder to my heirs" when the question is revocation of the trust, or whether creditors of the settlor's heirs should be able to reach their interest. But the same result is far from appealing if the settlor-life beneficiary dies without revoking the trust and leaves a will which makes no provision for his heirs-at-law (whom he supposed to be taken care of by the trust). In short, while the dominant intent of most such trusts may well be to benefit the life tenant during his life, a subsidiary but nevertheless significant purpose of many such trusts may be to satisfy a natural desire to benefit one's heirs or next of kin. In the normal case an adult has a pretty good idea who his heirs will be at death, and probably means exactly what he says when he states in the trust instrument, "remainder to my heirs."

It is said that the cases in which such is the grantor's intent can be discerned by an examination into his intent; the presumption that a gift over to one's heirs creates a reversion can thereby be rebutted in appropriate cases. . . . After three decades of observing the New York courts administer the rule of construction announced in Doctor v. Hughes, supra, Professor Powell [Cases on Future Interests 88 n.14 (3d ed. 1961)] observed that

> there were literally scores of cases, many of which reached the Appellate Division, and no case involving a substantial sum could be fairly regarded as closed until its language and circumstances had been passed upon by the Court of Appeals. . . . This state of uncertainty was the product of changing an inflexible rule of law into a rule of construction.

An excellent example of this confusion is the effect to be given the fact that, as in the case at bar, the settlor has reserved the power to defeat the heirs' interest by appointing the taker of the remainder by will. One might think that the reservation of a power of appointment was an index intent which buttressed the presumption of a reversion by demonstrating that the settlor did not wish to create firm interests or expectations among his heirs, but intended to retain control over the property. Most courts, including the New York Court of Appeals in its most recent pronouncement on the subject, have disagreed, albeit over the voice of dissent. They have reasoned that the retention of the testamentary power of appointment confirms the intent to create a remainder in the heirs, since the settlor would not have retained the power had he not thought he was creating a remainder interest in the heirs.

We see no reason to plunge the District of Columbia into the ranks of those jurisdictions bogged in the morass of exploring, under the modern doctrine of worthier title, "the almost ephemeral qualities which go to prove the necessary intent." The alleged benefit of effectuating intent must be balanced against the resulting volume of litigation and the diversity and difficulty of decision. We are not persuaded that the policy of upholding the intention of creators of trusts is best effectuated by such a rule of construction with its accompanying uncertainty.

The rule we adopt, which treats the settlor's heirs like any other remaindermen, although possibly defeating the intention of some settlors, is overall, we think, an intent-effectuating rule. It contributes to certainty of written expression and conceptual integrity in the law of trusts. It allows heirs to take as remaindermen when so named, and promises less litigation, greater predictability, and easier drafting. These considerations are no small element of justice.

We hold, then, that the doctrine of worthier title is no part of the law of trusts in the District of Columbia, either as a rule of law or as a rule of construction. Any act or words of the settlor of a trust which would validly create a remainder interest in a named third party may create a valid remainder interest in the settlor's heirs. It follows that the District Court was correct in granting summary judgment for appellees in this case since appellant's action is based on the theory that she was the sole beneficiary and hence could revoke the "irrevocable" trust she had created. . . .

Appellant's invocation of worthier title was premised in part on the injustice alleged to result in many cases from holding such a trust irrevocable. The irrevocability was supposed to be riveted into the trust by the impossibility of obtaining consent to revocation from all the beneficiaries, since some of them are still unborn. Appellant's argument reflects a misunderstanding of the consequence of the judgment of the District Court.

It is hornbook law that any trust, no matter how "irrevocable" by its terms, may be revoked with the consent of the settlor and all beneficiaries.

The beneficiaries of the trust created by appellant are herself, as life tenant, and her heirs, as remaindermen. Her heirs, if determined as of the present time, are her two sisters. There is no assurance that they will in fact be the heirs who take the remainder under the trust; appellant might survive one or both. Yet their consent is necessary, we think, to revocation, since they are at least the persons who would be beneficiaries if the settlor died today.

In addition, it is necessary to protect the interests of those additional persons, both living and unborn, who may, depending on circumstances, be members of the class of heirs at the time the corpus is distributed. We think that upon an adequate showing, by the party petitioning to revoke or modify the trust, that those who are, so to speak, the heirs as of the present time consent to the modification, and that there is a reasonable possibility that the modification that has been proposed adequately protects the interest of those other persons who might be heirs at the time the corpus is to be distributed, that the District Court may appoint a guardian ad litem to represent the interests of those additional persons.

Although the question has not been previously discussed by this court we think basic principles of trust law are in accord with appointment of a guardian ad litem to represent interests of unborn or unascertained beneficiaries for purposes of consent to modification or revocation of a trust. This use of a guardian ad litem is not uncommon in other jurisdictions. In a number of states authority for [the appointment of guardians ad litem] is provided by statute. These statutes reflect a broad sentiment of the approaches that are consistent with the Anglo-American system of law and adopted to promote the objective of justice. Where it is at least debatable whether rulings must await express legislative authorization, this court must take into account the fact that the legislature for the District of Columbia is primarily concerned with awesome questions of national policy, and we should be more ready to accept our obligation as a court to refine and adapt the corpus of law without waiting for a legislative go-ahead. Here we are certainly in a field where it is not inappropriate for courts to act without statutory foundation. . . . "Courts of justice as an incident of their jurisdiction have inherent power to appoint guardians ad litem." [Quoting Mabry v. Scott, 51 Cal. App. 2d 245, 258, 124 P.2d 659, 665 (1942), set out hereafter in Chapter 15, section C.] The efficacy of a guardian ad litem appointed to protect the interest of unborn persons is no different whether he be appointed pursuant to statute or the court's inherent power. Given such protection, the equitable doctrine of representation embraces the flexibility, born of convenience and necessity, to act upon the interests of unborn contingent remaindermen to the same effect as if they had been sui juris and parties.

The use of guardians ad litem to represent interests of unborn and/or otherwise unascertainable beneficiaries of a trust seems to us wholly appropriate. Though the persons whose interests the guardian ad litem represents would be unascertainable as individuals, they are identifiable as a class and their interest, as such, recognizable.

The settlor seeking to revoke or modify the trust may supplement his appeal to equity with a quid pro quo offered to the heirs for their consent. In many cases it may well be consistent with or even in furtherance of the interest of the heirs to grant such consent. The case at bar provides a good example. Here the interest of all heirs is contingent, since appellant can defeat their remainder by exercising her testamentary power of appointment. If the modification agreed upon not only increased the annual income of the life tenant but also transferred assets in trust for the benefit of the heirs, without any power of alteration in the settlor, the heirs' remainder interest would be secure, and accordingly more valuable than it is now. The pattern of such a modification is clearly available where the remaindermen of a trust are specific named persons, and, we think, should also be available where the remaindermen are recognizable as a class even though the members of the class are not now individually ascertainable.

Appellant, proceeding on a different theory, has not taken steps to obtain the consent of heirs. We think it important to make clear that, in rejecting the doctrine of worthier title, we do not mean to put settlors and life tenants of trusts in which the remaindermen are the settlor's heirs at an unwarranted disadvantage with respect to legitimate efforts to modify trust arrangements concluded largely for their own benefit. Our affirmance of the judgment for appellees is without prejudice to a future submission by appellant on such a basis.

Affirmed.

The settlor-life beneficiary seized the court's invitation to modify this trust with consent of the living remaindermen and of a guardian ad litem acting for other possible remaindermen. The modification agreement was approved in Hatch v. Riggs National Bank, 284 F. Supp. 396 (D.D.C. 1968), which does not discuss the contents or merits of the modification agreement but is concerned solely with the issue of the court's inherent authority to appoint a guardian ad litem, this question having been raised again by the trustee out of concern that the opinion of the court of appeals on this point was purely dictum.

Judge Leventhal's opinion, first rejecting the doctrine of worthier title and then dealing with the dilemma arising from a desire to leave open to settlors the possibility of amendment in these appealing types of cases, actually skirts a significant issue, and a particularly important one for our purposes. The opinion asserts that basic principles of trust law support the use of guardians ad litem for the purpose of consenting to proposed modifications of trusts, yet the court's discussion then deals only with the more general issue of a court's power, without legislative authority, to appoint guardians ad litem for any purpose. One need not question the wisdom or propriety of finding such an inherent judicial power (although authorities are divided) in order to note that such a determination does not reach the most novel aspect of the opinion — that of then allowing a guardian ad litem to give *consent* to an *agreement* authorizing modification by action of the beneficiaries. It is a traditional function for guardians ad litem to represent and defend beneficiaries in *litigation* (such as where the rights of unborn beneficiaries are being litigated or, in the more immediate context, where the court is exercising its own power, independent of consent, to modify a trust, as discussed infra), and as an adjunct of this probably also to compromise litigation in order to protect the represented interests. This, however, is different from allowing the guardian ad litem to enter into a transaction — that is, to consent to a contract that involves, in effect, a transfer — which then newly *creates* a basis for altering the beneficiaries' interests. This latter, without any real discussion of the point in the opinion, eliminates the traditional requirement, recognized even where the use of guardians ad litem is well established, that all beneficiaries must be sui juris and must consent to modification or termination of the trust.

These comments are not at all intended to suggest that the thrust of Judge Leventhal's innovative and potentially influential opinion is undesirable. In fact, it may be a very good judicially designed solution to the dilemma presented by the competing objectives of properly construing "heirs" provisions and yet of preserving flexibility of amendment for settlors in this type of case. Certainly the widespread abolition of worthier title by legislation speaks for itself, and the all too rare, clear-cut undertaking by a court to clean up the common law is both admirable and refreshing. A major concern of legislatures in considering abolition of worthier title has been the consent problem and the effect the recognition of an interest in unascertainable heirs would have on the ability of the settlor and other living persons to terminate or modify inter vivos trusts. Here too, though on a far lesser scale, some legislatures have acted. In order to facilitate revocation and amendment of living trusts by the beneficiaries, several statutes have provided, in some form, essentially that for those particular purposes the actions of the settlor and the other persons beneficially interested can bind interests created in a presently undeterminable class described as the settlor's heirs (or equivalent) or, under one statute, described solely by relationship to a consenting person. See N.Y. Est. Powers & Trusts Law §7-1.9 (originating as a response to the messy aftermath of Doctor v. Hughes, discussed supra in the *Hatch* case) and Wis. Stat. Ann. §701.13 (1969). See also California Probate Code §15405, which provides:

> For the purposes of [modification of trusts], the consent of a beneficiary who lacks legal capacity, including a minor, or who is an unascertained or unborn person may be given in proceedings before the court by a guardian ad litem, if it would be appropriate to do so. In determining whether to give consent, the guardian ad litem may rely on general family benefit accruing to living members of the beneficiary's family as a basis for approving a modification or termination of the trust.

All of the foregoing is to be contrasted with the limited powers of courts under special circumstances to modify trusts without the consent of the beneficiaries, to be discussed in section D of this chapter. Nevertheless, the approach of the *Hatch* case should be kept in mind, particularly as section D2 is studied, for it may be applicable to that type of situation in the District of Columbia and may be suggestive of an approach different from the traditional approach in other jurisdictions. For another recent case that is apparently unique but is significantly analogous to *Hatch,* see Estate of Lange, 75 N.J. 464, 383 A.2d 1130 (1978), set out infra at section D1 of Chapter 17; that case involves estoppel, or waiver of trust beneficiaries' rights, by vicarious consent obtained through the doctrine of virtual representation, also a concept normally confined to the necessities of representation in court.

Material purpose. What constitutes a "material purpose" of a trust for purposes of the second requirement that no significant objective of the settlor be defeated by a revocation or modification by the beneficiaries? How readily should such a purpose be inferred? See Rust v. Rust, 176 F.2d 66, 67 (D.C. Cir. 1949):

> To say that the beneficiaries cannot compel termination of a trust if its continuance is necessary to carry out a *material purpose* of the settlor is not to say they cannot do so if continuance is necessary to carry out his *intent* regarding duration of the trust. Such a proposition would go farther than our law in preferring the dead over the living. . . . The "purpose" with which the rule is concerned is not the settlor's intent but the aim, object or motive underlying his intent.

When the settlor creates a trust to protect one or more of the beneficiaries from their own improvidence, the beneficiaries cannot compel termination of the trust where the *Claflin* doctrine prevails. It is often difficult, however, to ascertain whether such a purpose exists.

It is accepted that even the unanimous consent of the beneficiaries cannot compel termination of a spendthrift trust. This is sometimes explained on the ground that termination would be a prohibited alienation or exchange of a beneficiary's trust interest. It is also explained on the ground that the spendthrift provision demonstrates that protection from the beneficiary's own improvidence was a material purpose of the settlor. The routine inclusion of spendthrift clauses by many lawyers removes the possibility of total or partial termination by the beneficiaries in a great number of trusts. For example, a life income beneficiary might like (often for tax reasons) to assign part or all of the income interest to the remainder beneficiaries (often the life beneficiary's children), but this assignment and the desired termination of some or all of the trust will be frustrated by the spendthrift restraint.

BENNETT v. TOWER GROVE BANK & TRUST CO.
434 S.W.2d 560 (Mo. 1968)

WELBORN, C.

Action to terminate a testamentary trust for the reason that the life beneficiary transferred her interest in the trust to the remaindermen. The court below refused to decree termination and the remaindermen and life tenant appeal.

[Under the will in question the respondent bank, as trustee, was to pay a share of the trust income to testator's widow and a share to his daughter, Lois Bennett, and on the death of either both shares to the survivor; on the death of the survivor, the remainder was to go free of trust to three named nephews. The trust provided for no invasion of principal, no discretion over income payments, and no spendthrift restraints. The widow elected her statutory share against the will.]

Respondents do not question two preliminary propositions advanced by appellants: First, that the renunciation by the widow resulted in an acceleration of the trust and Lois Bennett became the sole life tenant. Second, that the remainder interests of the three nephews are vested interests. Conceding these propositions, the respondents assert that termination of the trust would thwart the intention of the testator, whose wishes must prevail without regard for the desires of the beneficiaries. The appellants, on the other hand, contend that, in the circumstances of this case, the only purpose of the trust was preservation of the corpus for the benefit of the remaindermen, and, therefore, when they acquired the outstanding life estate, the trust had no further purpose and should be terminated. . . .

Appellants acknowledge that [Peugnet v. Berthold, 183 Mo. 61, 81 S.W. 874 (1904),] is the only [Missouri] case in which the trust in question was terminated. They contend, however, that the three subsequent cases recognize the rule laid down by *Peugnet,* and that the cases represent exceptions to the *Peugnet* rule, not a repudiation of it. Respondents, on the other hand, contend that the *Peugnet* rule has been repudiated and that the three subsequent cases lay down the applicable rule which prevents termination of the trust in this case. . . .

Appellants would distinguish [the first case] Evans [v. Rankin, 329 Mo. 411, 44 S.W.2d 644 (1931),] because the trustee there had absolute discretion as to payment of any part of the income and corpus to the life tenant. Hamilton [v. Robinson, 236 Mo. App. 289, 151 S.W.2d 504 (1941),] is distinguished by reason of the express provision for continuation of the trust until the beneficiary reached the age of 28 years. Thomson [v. Union National Bank, 291 S.W.2d 178 (Mo. 1956), the most recent case,] would be distinguished on the grounds that it involved a trust for support of the widow during her life.

The Restatement of Trusts, Second, adopts the rule that, if all of the beneficiaries of a trust consent and none is under an incapacity, they can compel termination of a trust, unless its continuance is necessary to carry out a material purpose of the trust. 2 Rest. of Trusts, Second §337, p. 158. Comment *f* to this section is as follows (Id., pp. 159-160):

> f. Successive beneficiaries — Purposes accomplished. The mere fact that the settlor has created a trust for successive beneficiaries does not of itself indicate that it was a material purpose of the trust to deprive the beneficiaries of the management of the trust property for the period of the trust. If a trust is created for successive beneficiaries, in the absence of circumstances indicating a further purpose, the inference is that the only purpose of the trust is to give the beneficial interest in the trust property to one beneficiary for a designated period and to preserve the principal for the other beneficiary, and if each of the beneficiaries is under no incapacity, and both of them consent to the termination of the trust, they can compel the termination of the trust. . . .

The Restatement recognizes that continuation is essential to carry out the material purpose of a trust when the enjoyment of the interest of the sole beneficiary is postponed (Id., Comment *j*, p. 163), the situation in *Hamilton,* trusts for support of a beneficiary (Id., Comment *m*, p. 165), the situation in *Evans,* and discretionary trusts (Id., Comment *n*, p. 165).

The respondents argue that the primary purpose of the trust here must have been to care for the testator's wife and daughter, not to preserve the corpus for his nephews. However, [absent] other circumstances to show the intention of the testator, we are of the opinion that the mere creation of the trust for successive beneficiaries did not indicate a purpose other than preservation of the corpus for the remaindermen and, therefore, the trust may be terminated by the action here taken. See IV Scott on Trusts, 3rd ed. §337.1, p. 2664.

Although it may not be possible to reconcile the language in all of our cases with the rules laid down by the Restatement, the actual results of such cases are consistent with such rules. As above noted, *Evans* and *Hamilton* clearly fit into situations recognized by the Restatement when continuation is necessary to effectuate an essential purpose of the trust. The *Thomson* case does not so clearly fit within such situations. However, the close restrictions upon investment which the testator there laid down evidenced a strong desire on the part of the testator to preserve the corpus of the estate during his widow's lifetime. Evidence of such intention is not to be found in this case. In our opinion, the rules laid down by the Restatement adequately protect the scheme of the testator in those cases where there is a genuine necessity for continuation of the trust, but the situation of continuing a trust for the benefit of the trustee is avoided.

The decree below is reversed. . . .

The *Hamilton* case mentioned in the above opinion involved a trust designed from the outset for a single beneficiary whose right to principal was postponed beyond age 21, as in the *Claflin* case, which additionally involved staggered principal payments. A later case (also with principal distributions staggered beyond age 21), however, departed from the normal refusal to terminate prematurely trusts established for longer than the minority of a sole beneficiary. Ambrose v. First National Bank, 482 P.2d 828 (Nev. 1971). This result, from which two of the five judges dissented, may best be explained as reflecting an attitude falling somewhere between the usual American rule and England's rule allowing termination by unanimous consent regardless of the settlor's purposes. The concluding paragraph of Justice Thompson's opinion states:

> We are not persuaded that the doctrine of the leading American case of Claflin v. Claflin should rule the trust before us. . . . No reason is

expressed in the trust instrument for delaying the daughter's enjoyment beyond the settlor's death. No provision is made therein for the daughter's support between the ages of 21 and 28. Should the daughter die during that period of time she would be denied enjoyment of the corpus. All these factors together with a strong public policy against restraining one's use and disposition of property in which no other person has an interest leads us to conclude that termination should be decreed and the beneficiary spared the expense incident to the continued administration of the trust.

482 P.2d at 831.

It should be observed that up to this point we have been dealing with the question of whether the beneficiaries can *compel* the trustee to convey the trust property to them. Assume now that we are dealing with a trust in which all of the beneficiaries seek but cannot compel termination due to an unaccomplished purpose of the trust. What if the trustee in such a case *does* convey the trust property either to a sole beneficiary or in accordance with an agreement entered into by all of the beneficiaries? If the funds are thereafter dissipated, can the trustee be held liable by a beneficiary, assuming the latter was under no incapacity when the consent was given? The cases quite consistently hold that the trustee cannot be held liable for so terminating a trust. The beneficiary is precluded by consent from recovering from the trustee for breach of trust.

Should the consenting beneficiary of a spendthrift trust be treated differently? Section 342, comment *f*, of the Restatement (Second) of Trusts has adopted the position that the beneficiary is estopped and cannot hold the trustee liable for terminating the trust. Because the few cases in point are divided, the comment adds:

> In a State which rejects the rule here stated . . . if the trustee is compelled . . . to make restitution to the trust, he can recover the amount from the property of the beneficiary other than his interest under the trust.

D. Judicial Power to Modify or Terminate

1. Equitable Deviation from Administrative Provisions of the Instrument

RESTATEMENT (SECOND) OF TRUSTS

§167. *Change of Circumstances.*

(1) The court will direct or permit the trustee to deviate from a term of the trust if owing to circumstances not known to the settlor and not anticipated by him compliance would defeat or substantially impair the

accomplishment of the purposes of the trust; and in such case, if necessary to carry out the purposes of the trust, the court may direct or permit the trustee to do acts which are not authorized or are forbidden by the terms of the trust.

(2) Under the circumstances stated in Subsection (1), the trustee can properly deviate from the terms of the trust without first obtaining the permission of the court if there is an emergency, or if the trustee reasonably believes that there is an emergency, and before deviating he has no opportunity to apply to the court for permission to deviate.

(3) Under the circumstances stated in Subsection (1), the trustee is subject to liability for failure to apply to the court for permission to deviate from the terms of the trust, if he knew or should have known of the existence of those circumstances.

MATTER OF PULITZER

139 Misc. 575, 249 N.Y.S. 87 (Surr. Ct. 1931), *affd. mem.*, 237
A.D. 808, 260 N.Y.S. 975 (1932)

FOLEY, S.

This is a proceeding for . . . instruction and determination of the court as to the propriety, price, manner, and time of sale of a substantial portion of the assets of the Press Publishing Company, the stock of which constitutes a material part of the assets of the trust here involved. . . . A serious and imperative emergency is claimed to exist, whereby, if such a sale is not made, a valuable asset of the trust estate may be in great part or wholly lost to the trust, the life tenants, and remaindermen. . . .

Joseph Pulitzer died in the year 1911. He left a will and four codicils which were admitted to probate by this court on November 29, 1911. The provisions directly pertinent to the issues here are contained in the first codicil, which is dated March 23, 1909. By its terms he gave the shares of the capital stock of the Press Publishing Company, which were owned by him, and his shares of the Pulitzer Publishing Company, of St. Louis, in trust for the life of each of the two youngest of his sons, Joseph Pulitzer, Jr., and Herbert Pulitzer. . . .

To distinguish it from the residuary trust, the particular trust here has been called the "Newspaper Trust." Its trustees are the testator's three sons, Ralph Pulitzer, Herbert Pulitzer, and Joseph Pulitzer, Jr. The Pulitzer Publishing Company publishes the St. Louis Post Dispatch. The Press Publishing Company publishes the New York World, the Sunday World, and the Evening World. The trustees of the so-called "Newspaper Trust" hold within the trust a very large majority of shares of the Press Publishing Company. The remaining shares are owned by the trustees individually. The paragraph particularly sought to be construed here, which deals with the powers of the trustees and the limitations thereon, is contained in article seventh of the codicil of March 23, 1909, and reads as follows:

> I further authorize and empower my Executors and Trustees to whom I have hereinbefore bequeathed my stock in the Pulitzer Publishing Company of St. Louis, at any time, and from time to time, to sell and dispose of said stock, or any part thereof, at public or private sale, at such prices and on such terms as they may think best, and to hold the proceeds of any stock sold in trust for the beneficiaries for whom such shares were held in lieu thereof, and upon the same trusts. This power of sale is not to be construed as in any respect mandatory, but purely discretionary. This power of sale, however, is limited to the said stock of the Pulitzer Publishing Company of St. Louis, and shall not be taken to authorize or empower the sale or disposition under any circumstances whatever, by the Trustees of any stock of the Press Publishing Company, publisher of "The World" newspaper. I particularly enjoin upon my sons and my descendents the duty of preserving, perfecting and perpetuating "The World" newspaper (to the maintenance and upbuilding of which I have sacrificed my health and strength) in the same spirit which I have striven to create and conduct it as a public institution, from motives higher than mere gain, it having been my desire that it should be at all times conducted in a spirit of independence and with a view to inculcating high standards and public spirit among the people and their official representatives, and it is my earnest wish that said newspaper shall hereafter be conducted upon the same principles.

There are fifteen remaindermen in existence. One of them is an adult; the other fourteen are infants. Because of a possible adversity of interest they are represented here by two separate special guardians. The adult life tenants and remaindermen join in requesting the relief sought by the trustees.

Counsel for the trustees contend that the express denial of a power of sale contained in the paragraph was modified and cut down, as a matter of testamentary intent, by Mr. Pulitzer in subsequent language. . . .

But I prefer to place my determination here upon broader grounds and upon the power of a court of equity, in emergencies, to protect the beneficiaries of a trust from serious loss, or a total destruction of a substantial asset of the corpus. The law, in the case of necessity, reads into the will an implied power of sale. . . .

The same rule applies to emergencies in trusts not only where there is an absence of power of sale in a will, but also where there is a prohibition against sale. It has been satisfactorily established by the evidence before me that the continuance of the publication of the newspapers, which are the principal assets of the Press Publishing Company, will in all probability lead to a serious impairment or the destruction of a large part of the trust estate. The dominant purpose of Mr. Pulitzer must have been the maintenance of a fair income for his children and the ultimate reception of the unimpaired corpus by the remaindermen. Permanence of the trust and ultimate enjoyment by his grandchildren were intended. A man of his sagacity and business ability could not have intended that from mere vanity, the publication of the newspapers, with which his name and efforts had been associated, should be persisted in until the entire trust asset was destroyed or wrecked by bankruptcy or dissolution. His expectation was that his New York newspapers would flourish. Despite his optimism, he must have contemplated that they might become entirely unprofitable and their disposal would be required to avert a complete loss of the trust asset. The power of a court of equity, with its jurisdiction over trusts, to save the beneficiaries in such a situation has been repeatedly sustained in New York and other jurisdictions. . . .

The trustees here find themselves in a crisis where there is no selfhelp available to them. A judicial declaration is necessary, not only as to their general authority, but as to the effect of the words of Mr. Pulitzer contained in his will. The widest equity powers exist in the Surrogate's Court of this state by the grant of legislative authority contained in section 40 of the Surrogate's Court Act. Matter of Raymond v. Davis' Estate, 248 N.Y. 67, 71, 161 N.E. 421.

I accordingly hold, in this phase of the decision, that the terms of the will and codicils do not prohibit the trustees from disposing of any assets of the Press Publishing Company, that the trustees have general power and authority to act in the conveyance of the assets proposed to be sold, and that this court, in the exercise of its equitable jurisdiction, should authorize them by an appropriate direction in the decree to exercise such general authority. . . .

PAPIERNIK v. PAPIERNIK
45 Ohio St. 3d 337, 544 N.E.2d 664 (1989)

[The settlor established an inter vivos trust with a bank serving as trustee and with the settlor's wife, Elizabeth (now the life beneficiary), and R.B. Cohen (settlor's accountant) serving in the position of "trust advisors." Without the advisors' approval, the trustee could not sell, lease, exchange, or reinvest assets of the trust; and the advisors had joint authority to remove any trustee and appoint a successor, with each having the power and duty to appoint a successor if the other ceased to act. The trust advisors had no other responsibilities and could not require the trustee to sell or make specific investments. Certain remainder beneficiaries brought the present action seeking modification of the trust and injunctive relief against the trust advisors because of alleged abuses by the advisors. The Court of Common Pleas entered judgment removing the trust advisors and modifying the trust agreement by deleting the trust advisor positions.]

Evans, J. . . .

Deviation from the administrative provisions of a trust will be permitted by a court of equity, if owing to circumstances not known to the grantor and not anticipated by him, compliance would defeat or substantially impair the accomplishment of the purposes of the trust. . . . Furthermore, the doctrine of deviation is to be applied with caution and only to the extent necessary to accomplish the purpose of the grantor. In this case, deviation by eliminating the position of trust advisor could serve to defeat the intent of the grantor . . . [and] goes well beyond that which is necessary to correct the circumstances which threaten the purpose of the trust. We therefore hold that it was error to delete the trust advisor provisions from the trust.

Finally, we consider the issue of the removal of both Elizabeth and Cohen from the position of trust advisor.

The record in this case clearly establishes that Elizabeth completely misunderstood the office of trust advisor and acted irrationally, irresponsibly and unsuitably in relation to the trust. . . . Instead of confining herself to the given duties, Elizabeth inserted herself into the management of the trust . . . to the extent that the continued existence of the trust [was] threatened. . . .

Elizabeth had a duty to limit her activities . . . to those duties assigned to a trust advisor.

The [remainder beneficiaries] argue that the role of trust advisor is akin to that of a fiduciary, but we believe it is unnecessary to make this determination to decide this case. The conduct of Elizabeth was unsuitable whether or not she was a fiduciary by virtue of her position of trust advisor. . . .

It is apparent that the trial court properly exercised its equity jurisdiction in removing Elizabeth as a trust advisor.

However, there is nothing in the record which justifies the removal of Cohen from office. . . .

We remand this cause to the trial court with instructions to restore the trust provisions which create the position of trust advisor and to restore Cohen to his position of trust advisor with an appropriate period of time to permit Cohen to fill the vacancy created by the removal of Elizabeth as trust advisor.

Judgment affirmed in part, reversed in part and cause remanded.

PROBLEM

13-C. Assume that the opinion that immediately follows is an opinion just handed down by an intermediate appellate court in your state. The lawyer for whom you work has now been retained to handle the petitioners' appeal of that decision to the state's highest court. Following the *Stanton* opinion are a Minnesota case and a note about a Delaware case;

these two recent decisions are among the most favorable authorities available to you. In order to begin preparations, study the subject opinion and the case and note case following it. Then consider and prepare to discuss the following questions:

Do you see why the desired modification could not be effectuated by *consent of all beneficiaries* under principles studied in the previous section? How might you nevertheless argue for modification based on consent?

According to the *Stanton* opinion, precisely what appears to be lacking in your case to permit *deviation under judicial power* according to the usual rule as stated in §167 of the Restatement, supra? How might the matters of inflation and trust purposes be handled in your brief and arguments so that the court can fit your case within the Restatement rule, assuming you can persuade the judges to want to decide your way but find them unwilling to depart from that widely accepted formulation of the applicable law?

Are there good reasons for adopting a less restrictive rule for deviation from trust investment provisions than the rule of the Restatement? If the court is so inclined, it will wish to spell out a principled course for lower courts to follow in future cases. In what terms might we suggest that such a rule be framed?

STANTON v. WELLS FARGO BANK & UNION TRUST CO.
150 Cal. App. 2d 763, 310 P.2d 1010 (1957)

[Petition by the life beneficiaries of a trust, created by will in 1931, to authorize the trustee to make investments pursuant to the statutory "prudent man rule" of the California Civil Code and to deviate from the terms of the trust, which specifically limit the trustee to investments

in bonds of the United States government, in bonds of the States of the United States, and municipalities thereof, and in such other bonds . . . as shall be rated "AA" by Moody's Investor's service,

and then provide an alternative if Moody's service ceases to exist. Under the trust the income was payable to certain beneficiaries for life, and these beneficiaries held general testamentary powers to appoint the remainders following their respective life interests, and in default of appointment the remainder in each share was to pass to the descendants of the life beneficiary. From the decree of the superior court authorizing deviation, one of the trustees has appealed.]

PETERS, P.J. . . .

The main contention of respondent . . . is that if the trustees are compelled to adhere to the terms of the trust the settlor's intent and his main trust purpose would be frustrated. It is argued that all of the interested beneficiaries, including the living remaindermen, have consented to the deviation, and all will benefit by the proposed modification. Respondent refers specifically to the evidence showing a marked decline in the purchasing power of the dollar, and to the return on bonds as compared to the return on stocks. It is urged that since the settlor drafted this trust the following unanticipated events have occurred: The depression of the thirties; World War II and the cold war; the current defense program; the increase in income taxes; and the government controls on capital. In order to keep the record straight, it is obvious that respondent erroneously refers to the depression as an unanticipated event. The trust was drafted in the middle of the depression and undoubtedly the depression was one of the reasons that motivated the trustor to insert the provision in question.

The power to permit deviation from the terms of private trusts is analogous to the cy-pres doctrine applicable to charitable trusts. . . . A few generalizations can be made. Normally, of course, the trust instrument constitutes the measure of the trustee's powers. . . . Except in unusual or emergency situations the courts will limit the trustees to the powers conferred. But the courts will not permit the main purpose of a trust to fail by compelling slavish adherence to the administrative limitations of the trust instrument. Where the main purpose of the trust is threatened the courts will and should grant permission to deviate from restrictive administrative provisions. But the court should not permit a deviation simply because the beneficiaries request it where the main purpose of the trust is not threatened and no emergency exists or is threatened. It must be remembered that it is the theory of this rule that, by the exercise of this power, the court is not defeating the trust, but in fact is furthering it. The equity court is simply doing what the testator, presumably, would have done had he anticipated the changed conditions. In other words, the specific intent of the testator is disregarded in order to enforce his general intent.

In the instant case all persons interested in the trust except one trustee, and unlikely unborn contingent remaindermen request that the modification be made. This is a factor to be considered. Also, the requested modification concerns only the method of administration of the trust and does not affect any rights of the beneficiaries between themselves. This, too, is important. It should also be mentioned that the objecting trustee concedes that the existing restriction is ill advised. No doubt economic changes have occurred since 1931.

On the other hand, the considered conclusions of the settlor regarding what should constitute appropriate investments cannot be lightly disregarded. He had managed to preserve a large fortune during a terrible depression. He had seen stock investments wiped out overnight. He knew that in the past there had been recurring periods of inflation and deflation. He, the man who had accumulated this fortune, whose property it was, wanted to protect his niece and her children from such vicissitudes, and to provide them with an adequate income. He decided that this could best be done by limiting the trustee's reinvestment powers to the purchase of certain types of bonds. While the equity court has power in an emergency to disregard these directions, the express and considered wishes and desires of the settlor should not be cavalierly disregarded. In the instant case the judgment of the settlor, to date, has not proved devastatingly erroneous. . . . The distributable annual income was $88,890.66 in 1938, and by 1954 this had increased to $109,942.84. There is no evidence that any beneficiary is in want or that the distributable income is not sufficient to supply the reasonable needs of all beneficiaries. No emergency exists. The existing inflationary cycle has continued for some years. The government has adopted many economic measures to try to control and stop this inflationary trend. Some economists predict an era of deflation and others warn us of a depression. These matters are mentioned to indicate that, while the settlor might not have been omniscient, neither are the beneficiaries nor the courts, omniscient. No one can forecast, with any certainty, future events. Certainly, it is true that misguided restrictions imposed by a settlor should not be permitted to defeat his fundamental trust purpose, but it is equally true that the court should not try to guess what economic conditions may be in a few years by permitting deviations when no real emergency exists or is threatened. . . .

It is not the function of courts to remake the provisions of trust instruments. Generally, it is the duty of courts to enforce the provisions of the trust instrument. A court should not presume to remake a trust instrument even though the court believes that it could do a better job. The court's power to permit a deviation exists so that the settlor's main trust purpose will not fail, and to take care of grave emergencies. That is not this case. The trial court should not have permitted the deviation. . . .

The judgment appealed from is reversed.

BRAY and WOOD, J.J., concur.

In re TRUSTEESHIP UNDER AGREEMENT
WITH MAYO
259 Minn. 91, 105 N.W.2d 900 (1960)

[In 1917 and 1919 Dr. Charles H. Mayo created two trusts that remained revocable until his death in 1939. The trustees were authorized under both instruments to invest "in real estate mortgages, municipal bonds or any other form of income bearing property (but not real estate nor corporate stock)." This is an appeal by a number of the beneficiaries from the district court's denial of a petition to authorize deviation from the investment restrictions to permit investment in corporate stock. One trust containing assets worth approximately $1 million will last for at least another twenty-one years, while the other, with assets of about $186,000, will probably terminate somewhat sooner.]

DELL, C.J. . . .

In support of the petition, evidence was submitted that an inflationary period, which could not have been foreseen, had commenced shortly after the donor's death in 1939; that it had reduced the real value of the trust assets by more than 50 percent; that a further inflationary period of a permanent "creeping inflation," which the donor could not have foreseen, must be expected; . . . [and] that the provisions of the trust prohibiting investments in real estate and corporate stocks had caused such shrinkage. . . . Appellants state that even in the short period between March 1959 and November 1959 the Consumer Price Index of the Bureau of Labor Statistics has increased from 123.7 to 125.6, representing an increase of almost 2 percent in 8 months.

Petitioner urges that the donor's ultimate and dominant intention was to preserve the value of the trust corpus and that this will be circumvented unless the court authorizes the trustees to deviate from the investment provisions of the trusts and invest part of the funds in corporate stocks; that it is common practice of trustees of large trusts which have no restrictive investment provisions (including the First National Bank of Minneapolis, one of the trustees in both trusts here) to invest substantial proportions of trust assets in corporate stocks to protect such trusts against inflation, and . . . that if no deviation is permitted and the next 20 years parallel the last 20 years the ultimate beneficiaries of these trusts will be presented with assets having less than one-fourth of the value which they had at the time of the donor's death.

In opposition to the petition, the trustees refer to the donor's clear intention, as expressed in the trust instruments, that no part of the trust funds should be invested in real estate or corporate stocks, and urge that, since no emergency or change of circumstances which could not have been foreseen or experienced by the donor during his lifetime has been shown, no deviation from the donor's clearly expressed intention would be justified. They urge that the rule is well established that where prospective changes of conditions are substantially known to or anticipated by the settlor of a trust the courts will not grant a deviation from its provisions. They point out that the donor here had survived some 20 years after the creation of the trusts during a period in which there had been both a great inflation and a severe depression; that after creating such trusts he had observed the inflation of the post-World-War-I period, the stock market fever of the pre-1929 era, the market crash of 1929, and the subsequent depression and lowering of bond interest rates during the late 1930's; that despite these economic changes he had never altered the investment restrictions in these trusts; and that he was always aware of his right to amend the trust instruments. . . . Petitioner offered expert testimony favoring deviation and respondents' expert testimony was to the contrary. The lower court found in favor of respondents and these appeals followed.

1. The principles governing construction of trust instruments are well settled. One of the court's highest duties is to give effect to the donor's dominant intention as gathered from the instrument as a whole. Neither the court, a beneficiary, nor the legislature is competent to violate such intention. When the language of the instrument is clear, the intention of the donor must be ascertained therefrom. In determining such intention the court is not at liberty to disregard plain terms employed in the trust instrument.

2. With respect to trust provisions restricting investments in which a trustee may invest trust funds, the courts are especially concerned in giving full effect to the donor's intention. . . .

3. . . . The general principles governing deviation to which this court has adhered whenever the question has been presented are set forth in Restatement, Trusts (2 ed.) §167, comment *c*:

> Where by the terms of the trust the scope of investment which would otherwise be proper is restricted, the court will permit the trustee to deviate from the restriction, if, but only if, the accomplishment of the purposes of the trust would otherwise be defeated or substantially impaired. Thus the court will permit the investment if owing to changes since the creation of the trust, such as the fall in interest rates, the danger of inflation, and other circumstances, the accomplishment of the purposes of the trust would otherwise be defeated or substantially impaired. Where by the terms of the trust the trustee is not permitted to invest in shares of stock, the court will not permit such an investment merely because it would be advantageous to the beneficiaries to make it.

In applying the foregoing rule the courts have adopted certain rules for guidance. It is only in exceptional circumstances described as cases of emergency, urgency, or necessity that deviation from the intention of the donor, as evidenced by the trust instrument, has been authorized. In most of the cases where deviation was authorized, the fact that the donor could not have foreseen the changed circumstances played an important part. Even under such circumstances deviation will not be authorized unless it is reasonably certain that the purposes of the trust would otherwise be defeated or impaired in carrying out the donor's dominant intention.

4. In our opinion the evidence here, together with economic and financial conditions which may properly be judicially noticed, compels us to hold that unless deviation is ordered the dominant intention of the donor to prevent a loss of the principal of the two trusts will be frustrated. When the trusts were created and for many years prior thereto, the dollar, based upon the gold standard, remained at a substantially fixed value. [I]t was not until after the death of the donor that inflation

commenced to make itself really known and felt. Since then it has gradually increased. . . . While the experts called by the respective parties disagreed as to when inflation, which they felt was then dormant, would start again and at what percentage it would proceed, there was no disagreement between them that further inflation "in the foreseeable future" could be expected. [F]rom the date of trial to November 1959 there was an increase of almost 2 percent in the cost of living index.

At the time these trusts were created it was common practice for businessmen, in protecting their families through the creation of trusts, to authorize investments to be made by their trustees only in high-grade bonds or first mortgages on good real estate. Many of the states then had statutes preventing trustees from investing in corporate stocks or real estate. Since that time many of the states, including Minnesota, have enacted statutes permitting trustees to invest in corporate stocks and real estate. In recent years most trust companies have encouraged donors, when naming the companies as trustees, to permit investment in common stocks as well as bonds and mortgages. And these trustees maintain competent and efficient employees, well acquainted with the various aspects of corporations having listed stocks, so as to enable them to make reasonably safe and proper corporate-stock purchases.

Throughout the trial considerable reference was made to the 1929 stockmarket crash as a reason why deviation should not be granted. There are many reasons, however, why the market action of that period is not a controlling factor today. [Omitted is the court's discussion of earlier practices, conditions, and abuses in business and in the stock market, plus various developments, curative measures, and regulations believed to make stock investments safer than previously.] Since 1932, because of heavy Federal expenditures, the national debt has grown . . . to approximately $290,000,000,000 at the present time. Inflation has been steadily increasing. None of this was foreseeable by an ordinarily prudent investor at the time these trusts were created, nor at the time of the donor's death in 1939, since these inflationary practices did not become noticeably fixed and established until after his death.

It appears without substantial dispute that if deviation is not permitted the accomplishment of the purposes of the trusts will be substantially impaired because of changed conditions due to inflation since the trusts were created; that unless deviation is allowed the assets of the trusts, within the next 20 years, will, in all likelihood, be worth less than one-fourth of the value they had at the time of the donor's death. To avoid this we conclude that in equity the trustees should have the right and be authorized to deviate from the restrictive provisions of the trusts by permitting them, when and as they deem it advisable, to invest a reasonable amount of the trust assets in corporate stocks of good, sound investment issues. Through an investment in bonds and mortgages of the type designed by the donor, plus corporate stocks of good, sound investment issues, in our opinion, the trusts will, so far as possible, be fortified against inflation, recession, depression, or decline in prices. Corporate trustees of the kind here are regularly managing trusts consisting of corporate stocks, bonds, and mortgages, on a successful basis. There appears to be no sound reason why they cannot do the same thing here.

Reversed and remanded for further proceedings in conformity with this opinion.

In Bank of Delaware v. Clark, 249 A.2d 442 (Del. Ch. 1968), the trustee, adult beneficiaries, and guardian ad litem all agreed that deviation from a provision restricting investments to mortgages on local land was "in the interest of the trust estate and the beneficiaries." Although Delaware courts have statutory power to authorize deviation, cases indicate that they are to do so "with extreme caution, and only when clearly required for the benefit of all interested and for the preservation of the corpus of the trust fund." The court found there had been a change of economic conditions and a sharp decline in the purchasing power of corpus since the creation of the trust. It also concluded that the settlor could not have anticipated these changes and that if he had "it is fair to say" he would not have restricted investments as he did. In authorizing deviation, the court said there was no need to consider cases from other states because it was satisfied that Delaware cases had adopted a different rule involving a "so-called substitution of judgment approach."

FRATCHER, FIDUCIARY ADMINISTRATION IN ENGLAND
40 N.Y.U. L. Rev. 12, 35-36 (1965)

If there is reasonable doubt as to the construction or legal effect of the terms of a trust [in the United States and in England], the trustee may apply to the court for instructions, and they will protect him, and the persons dealing with him, against the beneficiaries. In the absence of statute, courts of equity have inherent power to authorize deviation from the terms of a trust if, because of circumstances not known to the settlor when the trust was created and not anticipated by him, failure to do so would defeat or substantially impair the accomplishment of the purposes of the trust. . . . This narrow doctrine . . . is of no assistance in the common case in which the circumstances are known or anticipated, but the draftsman of the trust is unaware of the necessity of inserting express powers to do acts required for prudent administration. Moreover, even if circumstances which the settlor did not anticipate occur, the doctrine is operative only when action is necessary to prevent defeat or substantial impairment of the trust purposes; it is not sufficient that it would make administration of the trust more efficient or economical or would be advantageous to the beneficiaries, as by increasing the trust income.

The English statutes greatly enhance the powers of the court to authorize deviations from the terms of trusts. The court may authorize any transaction affecting or concerning settled land, or any part thereof, which in the opinion of the court would be for the benefit of the settled land, or any part thereof, or [for the benefit of] the persons interested under the settlement, if it is one which could validly have been effected by an absolute owner. [Settled Land Act of 1925, 15 & 16 Geo. 5, c. 18 §64, as amended.] The court may empower a trustee of any other type of trust to make any investment or engage in any transaction not otherwise authorized by the terms of the trust or by law, which is in the opinion of the court expedient. [Trustee Act of 1925, 15 & 16 Geo. 5, c. 19 §57, as amended.] . . .

COLONIAL TRUST CO. v. BROWN
105 Conn. 261, 135 A. 555 (1926)

[Suit to construe a will establishing a trust that originally consisted of two parcels of land, referred to as the Exchange Place and the Homestead. The will restricted the height of buildings on the properties to three stories and limited all leases to periods of one year. The trustee was to pay certain long-term annuities and then to distribute the remainder "among the heirs of the blood" of the testator's father, per stirpes.]

MALTBIE, J. . . .

The Exchange Place property . . . is located in the heart of the financial and retail business district of Waterbury. . . . There is, and for a long time has been, upon it a group of several old buildings. They are costly to maintain, expenditures for this purpose during the last seven years absorbing more than fifty per cent of the gross rentals. . . . Tenants of the most desirable class cannot be secured for the property, and could not be, even if the properties were improved, unless leases for more than one year could be given. This reacts upon rental values and the character of the business done in the neighborhood and retards the normal development of the property in use and value. . . .

The Homestead property . . . cannot be improved, so long as the height of buildings upon it is restricted to three stories, or, if improved, cannot be rented so long as leases upon it are restricted to one year, so as to secure the best income return from it, and the effect of these restrictions is likely to be more serious in the future. . . .

The effect which would be caused by the restrictions as to height of buildings and length of leases to be given, inserted in the will, was apparent when the testator executed it and thereafter until his death was known to him. . . . [A]lthough the annuities provided in the will have been paid, there has been an accumulation of excess income. . . .

We are asked to advise whether the provision in the fourth article, restricting leases of the property to one year and forbidding any promises of longer leases, and that in the eleventh article, directing that no new buildings placed upon the Exchange Place property and the Homestead shall exceed three stories in height, are binding upon the trustee. In Holmes v. Connecticut Trust & Safe Deposit Co., 92 Conn. 507, 514, 103 Atl. 640, . . . we said:

> As a general rule, a testator has the right to impose such conditions as he pleases upon a beneficiary as conditions precedent to the vesting of an estate in him, or to the enjoyment of a trust estate by him as cestui que trust. He may not, however, impose one that is uncertain, unlawful or opposed to public policy.

So it may be said of the directions and restrictions which a testator may impose upon the management of property which he places in a trust, that they are obligatory upon the trustee unless they are uncertain, unlawful or opposed to public policy. Lewin on Trusts (12th Ed.) 90. In the instant case, the length of time during which the testator directed that the property should remain in the trust and the complete uncertainty as to the individuals to whom it would ultimately go, preclude any thought of an intent on his part to forbid the encumbering of the property by long leases or the burdening of it with large buildings, lest the beneficiaries be embarrassed in the development of it along such lines as they might themselves prefer. The only other purpose which can reasonably be attributed to him is to compel the trustee to follow his own peculiar ideas as to the proper and advantageous way to manage such properties. That the restrictions are opposed to the interests of the beneficiaries of the trust, that they are imprudent and unwise is made clear by the statement of agreed facts, but that is not all, for their effect is not confined to the beneficiaries. The Exchange Place property is located at a corner of the public square in the very center of the city of Waterbury, in the heart of the financial and retail business district, is as valuable as any land in the city, and is most favorably adapted for a large building containing stores and offices, and the Homestead is located in a region of changing character, so that its most valuable use cannot now be determined. . . . The effect of such conditions cannot but react disadvantageously upon neighboring properties, and to continue them, as the testator intended, for perhaps seventy-five years or even more, would carry a serious threat against the proper growth and development of the parts of the city in which the lands in question are situated. The restrictions militate too strongly against the interests of the beneficiaries and the public welfare to be sustained, particularly when it is remembered that they are designed to benefit no one, and are harmful to all persons interested, and we hold them invalid as against public policy. . . .

2. Deviation from Distributive Provisions

In re VAN DEUSEN'S ESTATE
30 Cal. 2d 285, 182 P.2d 565 (1947)

[The testatrix died in 1944, bequeathing her residuary estate in trust to pay the net income equally to her two daughters, Gladys and Hazel, for their joint lives and then all of the income to the survivor for life. On the death of the survivor the trust was to terminate, with the principal to go to the testatrix's descendents by right of representation. In 1945 the life beneficiaries petitioned the probate court to instruct the trustee to pay each of them $200 a month from income and, if necessary, from corpus. The petition alleged that the provision for the daughters was to provide enough income for their needs, that on the basis of a contemplated trust income of $400 a month when the will was executed the testatrix intended each daughter to receive at least $200 a month, that since the creation of the trust one daughter has come to require special medical care, and that the other daughter must rely on trust income for the necessities of life. The court granted the petition after determining that the trust income was now less than $250 a month and finding that the petitioners were the primary objects of the trust, that they were intended to receive $200 each month, and that the primary purpose of the trust could not be accomplished by strict adherence to its terms. From this order the trustee, who appeared at the hearing in opposition to the petition, has appealed.]

TRAYNOR, J. . . .

[T]he order appealed from is erroneous on its merits. The theory of the order, and the only basis for granting it after the decree of distribution, was to allow a modification or deviation from the trust to carry out the purpose of the testatrix in view of changed conditions. A court of equity may modify a trust on a proper showing of changed conditions occurring after the creation of a trust if the rights of all the beneficiaries may be protected. If it is assumed that a probate court has the same power under section 1120, the order appealed from is nevertheless erroneous, since it provides for an invasion of the corpus of the trust contrary to the express provisions of the decree of distribution without any attempt to protect the interests of the residuary beneficiaries in that corpus.

The only interest given respondents in either the will or the decree of distribution is the net income from the corpus. The grandchildren of the testatrix, children of the respondents, are entitled to distribution of the corpus on the death of the surviving respondent. To allow an invasion of the corpus without the consent of the residuary beneficiaries contrary to the provisions of the trust instrument is to take property from one without his consent and give it to another. (See 3 (pt. 1) Bogert, Trusts and Trustees, 504.) As stated in the Restatement of Trusts (168, comment *d*):

> The court will not permit or direct the application of the principal to the support or education of one beneficiary where by the terms of the trust income only is to be so applied, if the result would be to deprive another beneficiary of property to which he is or may become entitled by the terms of the trust, whether the interest of such other beneficiary is vested or contingent, or unless such other beneficiary consents to such application.

(See also, Hughes v. Federal Trust Co., 119 N.J. Eq. 502, 504 [183 Atl. 299]; Scott on Trusts, §168.)

In Whittingham v. California Trust Co., 214 Cal. 128, 134 [4 P.2d 142], the claimant, a beneficiary of a testamentary trust, was the only person interested in the estate. It was held that a court of equity could modify the trust to allow distribution of part of the corpus to the beneficiary on a proper showing of the beneficiary's need therefor and of changed circumstances occurring since the execution of the will. In the present case, the respondent life beneficiaries are not the only persons interested in the trust, and the rights of the residuary beneficiaries must be protected. The respondents contend, however, that the probate court did not have to protect the interests of the residuary beneficiaries, and that the trustees had no right to attempt to do so, since the living residuary beneficiaries were all served with notice of the filing of the petition and two of them, who appeared through counsel, stated that they had no objection to increasing the payments to $150. This can hardly be considered consent by all the residuary beneficiaries to an invasion of the corpus of the trust to provide each of the life beneficiaries with at least $200 a month. . . .

Sympathy for the needs of the respondents does not empower the court to deprive the residuary beneficiaries of their interests in the corpus of the trust without their consent, nor does it enable the court to construe the nontestamentary declarations of the testatrix into an expression of her plan or purpose in providing for the trust some eleven years previous thereto. If the courts could increase the payments under testamentary trusts without the consent of all the beneficiaries merely because the income therefrom is not what it was at the time the will was executed and because at one time or another the testator expressed the desire to provide adequately for the beneficiaries, there would be no stability to any testamentary trust in this state.

The order is reversed.

See also Staley v. Ligon, 239 Md. 61, 210 A.2d 384, 388-389 (1965):

> Inasmuch as the testator clearly gave the widow . . . the net income of the estate and gave no right to corpus, express or implied, to anyone other

than the grandchildren, the.court was without power to order corpus to be given to the widow, for to do so would be to give one cestui part of a fund which the testator gave to another, without the consent of that other. This the decisions and the text writers say cannot be done. Hughes v. Federal Trust Co., 119 N.J. Eq. 502, 183 A. 299. . . . To the argument that the testatrix would want the life tenant to have this relief, the New Jersey Court said it had no doubt this might be true "but the fact remains that she gave [her daughter] only a life interest. I cannot rewrite the will." See also In re Cosgrave's Will, 225 Minn. 443, 31 N.W.2d 20, in which there is a full discussion of the reasons why corpus may not be invaded for the benefit of one who has only a life interest. In the Anno. "Invasion of Trust Principal," 1 A.L.R.2d 1328, 1333-1334, the editor summarizes the authorities thus:

> [In] most jurisdictions the power of a court of equity to authorize an invasion or deviation from the terms of a trust in unforeseen circumstances not contemplated by the trustor is rightly exercised only in matters of administration — such as the sale, mortgage, or pledge of trust property, the making of investments, the hastening of enjoyment, or the early termination of the trust contrary to the instrument — and is not in any case to be extended to an extinction or reduction of the interest of any of the beneficiaries.

It is surprising how often a fiduciary power to invade principal is apparently omitted by oversight or thoughtlessness in the drafting of trusts. Although a statement of Policies for the Acceptance of Trust Business by the Trust Division of the American Bankers Association indicates a reluctance to accept powers requiring the trustee to pass on the character and judgment of beneficiaries, the inclusion of powers to pay principal to meet the *needs* of beneficiaries is an important factor in making a trust instrument acceptable to corporate fiduciaries. See Sanders, An Examiner's Views on Estate Planning, 99 Tr. & Est. 485 (1960). Even when the income beneficiary is in grave need of additional funds, the *Van Deusen* and *Staley* cases are representative of the standard refusal of courts to authorize invasion of principal, absent one of the rare statutes to the contrary, if to do so would impair the interest of any nonconsenting beneficiary or potential beneficiary. See, e.g., Matter of Rotermund, 61 Misc. 2d 324, 305 N.Y.S.2d 413 (1969), where the life beneficiary's testamentary general power of appointment did not change this result. A virtually unique case openly reaching the opposite result is Petition of Wolcott, 95 N.H. 23, 56 A.2d 641 (1948), under most appealing circumstances and with the encouragement of those of the remaindermen who were adults, authorizing the trustee to do what the settlor "presumably would have authorized had he foreseen the emergency." Also compare the approach of Hatch v. Riggs National Bank in section C, supra. Occasionally courts "discover" an implied power to invade corpus, as in Longwith v. Riggs, 123 Ill. 258, 14 N.E. 840 (1887); and as noted in *Van*

Deusen, supra, invasion is also permitted by deviation where the beneficiary is indefeasibly entitled to the principal later so that only an acceleration at no possible cost to others is involved.

In Probasco v. Clark, 58 Md. App. 683, 474 A.2d 221 (1984), the testator left his estate in trust to pay his son $300 per month for life with the principal to go to a church on the son's death. The estate was over $250,000 and produced substantially more than $300 per month. The church and trustee petitioned the court to terminate the trust after purchasing a $300 per month annuity for the son. Although the trial court granted the petition, the appellate court reversed and refused to terminate because the court could not rewrite the trust to permit the acceleration of the remainder over the objections of the son. Is this an appropriate application of Maryland's Staley v. Ligon, supra, and of the *Van Deusen* principles?

As we have already seen, in England statutes broaden considerably the power of courts to expand the administrative powers of trustees, and the Trustee Act of 1925, 15 Geo. 5, c. 19 §32, authorizes trustees in their discretion to advance limited amounts of capital to persons holding absolute or *contingent* future rights to it, as long (the courts have held) as the instrument does not manifest a contrary intention of the settlor. Nevertheless in Chapman v. Chapman, [1954] A.C. 429 (H.L.), the House of Lords held that courts could not modify trusts in a way that would alter the interests of minor or unborn beneficiaries except in the limited ways set out in the Trustee Act. In response, Parliament enacted new legislation four years later.

The English Variation of Trusts Act of 1958, 6 & 7 Eliz. 2, c. 53, empowers courts to give assent on behalf of unborn, unascertained, infant and otherwise disabled beneficiaries to "any arrangement . . . varying or revoking . . . trusts, or enlarging the powers of trustees" provided the court is satisfied that "the carrying out thereof would be for the benefit of" the person on whose behalf the consent is given. The act does not, but for very limited exceptions, permit courts to alter the interests of nonconsenting beneficiaries who are sui juris.

The Pennsylvania Estates Act of 1947 (Pa. Stat. Ann. tit. 20, §301.2) provides that a court "in its discretion may terminate [a] trust in whole or in part, or make an allowance from principal" (not to exceed $25,000 in total) to any one or more of "the conveyor, his spouse, issue [and] parents," provided that the person or persons benefited are income beneficiaries and that the court "is satisfied that the original purpose of the conveyor cannot be carried out or is impractical of fulfillment and that termination, partial termination, or allowance more nearly approximates the intention of the conveyor, and notice is given to all parties in interest."

In 1965 the New York legislature enacted what is now N.Y. Est.

Powers & Trusts Law §7-1.6, authorizing limited principal invasion for income beneficiaries who also have some interest in the principal of a trust created before June 1966. More important, however, as to trusts created thereafter, where the terms fail to authorize invasion of principal but do not manifest an intention to preclude it, the statute empowers a court in its discretion, after notice and hearing, to make an allowance from principal for the benefit of any income beneficiary who is in need of additional funds for support or education if the court finds that the allowance will further the settlor's intention. Neither an interest in principal nor the consent of affected beneficiaries is required. Consider California Probate Code §15409(a), which provides:

> On petition by a trustee or beneficiary, the court may modify the administrative or dispositive provisions of the trust or terminate the trust if, owing to circumstances not known to the settlor and not anticipated by the settlor, the continuation of the trust under its terms would defeat or substantially impair the accomplishment of the purposes of the trust. In this case, if necessary to carry out the purposes of the trust, the court may order the trustee to do acts that are not authorized or are forbidden by the trust instrument.

A thorough and thoughtful analysis of this area is found in a student note, the proposals and some of the conclusions of which are excerpted below.

HYDE, VARIATION OF PRIVATE TRUSTS IN RESPONSE TO UNFORESEEN NEEDS OF BENEFICIARIES: PROPOSALS FOR REFORM
47 B.U.L. Rev. 567, 600, 608 (1967)

A statute responsive to the preceding discussions would authorize a court to permit invasion of corpus for a needy income beneficiary (1) without any requirement of consent, and (2) when the beneficiary is a parent, issue or spouse of the donor or (3) where there is evidence of a general intent to provide for the needs of the beneficiary. . . .

The following model statute is drafted as a suggested approach to the problems of intent and consent, taking into special consideration the nature of the donor's relation to the beneficiary. It is, in one sense, an attempt to place the ingrained notion of a right to free disposition of property in some equitable balance with the manifest needs of beneficiaries. It also explicitly rejects the idea that a donor says absolutely all that he intends, that what he intends is always wholly expressed in the provisions of the trust instrument, and that a court has a "sacred" duty to distribute property under trust by rigid adherence to explicit terms.

1. A court having jurisdiction of a trust shall authorize an allowance

of principal for any person who is an income beneficiary whose support or education is not sufficiently provided for by said trust or otherwise

(a) when an intent so to provide can be gathered from the terms of said trust or from circumstances surrounding the creation of said trust,

(b) when notice is given to all parties in interest or to their duly appointed representatives,

(c) without regard to (i) the inability or refusal of any party in interest to consent or (ii) the date of execution of the trust.

2. It shall be presumed that the donor of a trust intended to provide support and education for any beneficiary of said trust who is the parent, issue or spouse of said donor, and this presumption is rebuttable only

(a) by evidence of a contrary intent in a trust heretofore executed,

(b) by an express statement of a contrary intent in a trust hereafter executed.

14

Charitable Trusts

Charitable trusts are accorded a number of special privileges by the law. On the other hand, to qualify for these privileges charitable trusts are in some respects subject to restrictions not applicable to other trusts. Thus, certain aspects of charitable trusts are taken up separately at this point. You have already encountered in Chapter 3 the subject of limitations on testamentary gifts to or for charity. Other restrictions and privileges that are more or less peculiar to charitable trusts are taken up in this chapter.

A. History of Charitable Trusts

The English Statute of Charitable Uses, 43 Eliz. c. 4 (1601), included a list of charitable purposes and provided a method of enforcing charitable trusts. Historical research now makes it clear, however, that charitable trusts for like purposes were enforced at common law in England long before the enactment of this statute. Where gifts to charitable "corporations" (which included religious associations and individuals) were restricted, transfers to individuals to the use of charities offered a means of circumventing the restrictions. For example, uses (then apparently honorary rather than enforceable) were employed to avoid mortmain statutes, prohibiting ownership of land by religious corporations, until the statutes were amended to prevent this circumvention.

When the enforcement procedures of the Statute of Charitable Uses were subsequently repealed, the attorney general undertook the primary burden of enforcing charitable trusts. The attorney general had apparently assumed responsibility for enforcing charitable trusts in a few cases prior to the statute.

In the United States the common law of charitable trusts in most states followed the English law, including enforcement by the attorney general. In several states, however, statutes specifying purposes for which trusts could be created did not include charitable purposes; and in a number of states legislation declared that only certain English statutes remained in force, either not mentioning the Statute of Charitable Uses or excluding it among others. How did such legislation affect charitable trusts? Both illustrative and influential were two United States Supreme Court cases. In Trustees of Philadelphia Baptist Association v. Hart's Executor, 17 U.S. (4 Wheat.) 1 (1819), the opinion by Chief Justice Marshall concluded that charitable trusts were not enforceable under the common law in England but depended on the Statute of Charitable Uses, which was not a part of the law of the state (Virginia) involved in the case. Twenty-five years later, in Vidal v. Girard's Executors, 43 U.S. (2 How.) 127 (1844), it was decided that charitable trusts were not dependent on the Statute of Charitable Uses. The opinion of Justice Story points out that authoritative historic publications since 1819 establish the fact that charitable trusts were enforced in Chancery before the statute. Today, by statute if not by common law, charitable trusts are valid and enforceable in all the states.

B. General Nature of Charitable Trusts

Note, in the materials that follow, not only the issues about what constitutes a charitable purpose but also the advantages that follow from a finding that a particular purpose is charitable.

Restatement (Second) of Trusts §368 states that charitable purposes include

> (a) the relief of poverty; (b) the advancement of education; (c) the advancement of religion; (d) the promotion of health; (e) governmental or municipal purposes; (f) other purposes the accomplishment of which is beneficial to the community.

In re FRESHOUR'S ESTATE
185 Kan. 345, 345 P.2d 689 (1959)

[The testator's heirs challenged the clause of his will leaving a share of his residuary estate in trust "for the benefit of the Parish of St. Joseph's Catholic Church" and "for the benefit of the members of the First Methodist Church," both of Hays, Kansas. This is an appeal from the decision of the district court holding that the trusts were private trusts for the benefit of the individual members of the two churches and that they were therefore invalid for indefiniteness of beneficiaries and for violation of the rule against perpetuities.]

SCHROEDER, J. . . .

A trust may be valid as a trust for the advancement of religion although in the terms of the trust it is not stated in specific terms that the purpose is religious. Thus, the fact that a legatee or devisee is a religious organization or a person holding a religious office *may indicate* that it is to be applied for religious purposes, although by the terms of the trust its application is not specifically so limited. Restatement of Law, Trusts, §371c, p. 1150. . . .

A charity is broadly defined as a gift for general public use. In the legal sense a charity may be more fully defined as a gift to be applied consistently with existing laws for the benefit of an indefinite number of persons, *either by bringing their minds or hearts under the influence of education or religion,* by relieving their bodies from disease, suffering or constraint, by assisting them to establish themselves in life, or by erecting or maintaining public buildings, or works or otherwise lessening the burdens of government.

It is essential to a valid charitable gift that it be for a purpose recognized in law as charitable. To constitute a charitable use or purpose, it must be a public as distinguished from a private one. It must be for the public use or benefit, and it must be for the benefit of an indefinite number of persons. However, this does not prevent the donor from selecting some particular class of the public and limiting his benefaction to that class, provided the class is composed of an indefinite number of persons rather than certain designated and named individuals.

The most important differences between private trusts and charitable trusts relate to the validity of the trust. There cannot be a private trust unless there is a beneficiary who is definitely ascertained at the time of the creation of the trust or definitely ascertainable within the rule against perpetuities (See, Restatement of Law, Trusts, §112, p. 288). On the other hand, a charitable trust can be created although there is no definite or definitely ascertainable beneficiary designated (See, Restatement of Law, Trusts, §364, p. 1136), and a charitable trust is not invalid although by the terms of the trust it is to continue for an indefinite or unlimited period (See, Restatement of Law, Trusts, §365, p. 1136). . . . As long as the property given in trust vests in the trustee immediately or within the period prescribed by the rule [against perpetuities], trusts for charitable uses are not obnoxious to the rule although they may continue forever and beneficial interests may arise under them at a remote time.

The law must find in the trust, if it is to achieve the status of being "charitable," some social advantages which more than offset the detriments which arise out of the special privileges accorded to that trust. 2A Bogert, The Law of Trusts and Trustees, §361, p. 3. While the human beings who are to obtain advantages from charitable trusts may be referred to as beneficiaries, the real beneficiary is the public and the human beings involved are merely the instrumentalities from whom the benefits flow. Whether a gift is or may be operative for the public benefit is a question to be answered by the court. . . .

In our opinion, the testator's use of the words "parish" and "members" in association with the organizations named in the will was intended to refer to the respective ecclesiastical societies, and we are confident he intended the word "members" to have the same connotation as the word "parish." . . . The words "parish" and "members" were simply used by the testator to limit the trustees in the use of the trust property to the respective congregations, rather than to permit the trustees to use it for the benefit of other localities. It was his intention to confine the trustees in activities of the two religious organizations to the area which they served.

It remains to inquire whether the respective bequests and devises are void because the testator designated no uses to which the property should be applied. . . . [A] gift to a church or a church society by name, without declaration or restriction as to the use to be made of the subject matter of the gift, must be deemed to be a gift for the promotion of the purposes for which the church was organized. Courts look with favor upon trusts for charitable purposes and construe language creating such trusts most favorable to their validity. . . .

The judgment of the trial court is reversed.

HIGHT v. UNITED STATES
256 F.2d 795 (2d Cir. 1958)

MOORE, C.J. . . .

The testatrix by will left all her residuary estate to "such charitable, benevolent, religious or educational institutions as my executors hereinafter named may determine." Despite the fact that all institutions which received legacies are conceded to be "so created and constituted that a legacy to any one of them is deductible under Federal law in determining the net estate subject to the Federal estate tax" (Stip. of Facts, par. 15), the Commissioner disallowed all such legacy deductions "upon the theory that the plaintiffs had power to appoint said remainder and residue exclusively to benevolent institutions that were not also charitable" (Id. par. 22).

The question to be determined is whether the word "benevolent" included with the words "charitable," "religious" or "educational" is sufficient to deprive this estate of the tax benefits bestowed by Congress upon public-minded citizens who desire to devote their estates to public purposes.

The word "benevolent" has no fixed meaning which is self-defining. Webster's New International Dictionary (1934 Ed.) defines it in part as "disposed to give to good objects; kind; charitable" thus giving it a place within the category of "charitable." . . .

Restatement of Trusts, section 398, comment *d*, singles out the phrase "charitable or benevolent" as an example of the application of the principle of ejusdem generis to uphold a charitable trust:

> Where by the terms of the trust a word is used which standing alone would be broader than charity, it may in view of the other terms of the

trust be interpreted as limited to charity. Thus, where a testator devises or bequeaths property to be applied to "charitable or benevolent" purposes, the word "benevolent" may be interpreted as a synonym for "charitable," and not as including purposes which are not charitable, even though the word "benevolent" standing alone might be interpreted as including purposes which are not charitable. . . .

[Omitted is the court's review of evidence showing that the testatrix gave generously during her lifetime to institutions whose tax-exempt status she had verified in advance and that she had prepared for the guidance of her executor a list of suggested charities all of which were tax exempt.]

From these facts there can be no doubt that Mrs. Cochran during her lifetime gave ample proof of the type of institution which she selected for her benefactions. Her wishes were conveyed to her executors both orally and in writing. The executors understood these wishes and explicitly carried them out. . . .

[In an action for declaratory judgment brought by the executors of this will, the Supreme Court of Errors of Connecticut, in Cochran v. McLaughlin, 128 Conn. 638, 24 A.2d 836] specifically upheld the validity of the disposition of residuary estate, thereby indicating that the term "benevolent" was a sufficiently definite direction to her executors. The district court in the instant case distinguished the federal decisions allowing deductions where the devises were to "benevolent institutions" on the ground that the Connecticut court had precisely delineated the term "benevolent" so as to encompass "institutions whose principal function is to provide pleasure and cheer to their members." However, had the Connecticut court reached such a conclusion, it would have had no alternative but to find the trust incapable of being enforced, and would have been compelled to strike out the disposition of the entire residuary estate as void for uncertainty and indefiniteness. . . .

The judgment below is reversed and the case is remanded to the District Court for recomputation of the tax and entry of judgment in conformity with this opinion. . . .

Contrast Morice v. Bishop of Durham, 10 Ves. 521 (Ch. 1805), discussed supra Chapter 10, section D, holding "benevolence and liberality" noncharitable. In Hegeman's Executor v. Roome, 70 N.J. Eq. 562, 62 A. 392 (1905), a trust for "such religious, benevolent, or charitable objects as my husband may select" was held not valid as a charitable trust. The trend of judicial attitudes in this country, however, is better illustrated by a later New Jersey decision.

In Wilson v. Flowers, 58 N.J. 250, 277 A.2d 199 (1971), the issue was whether the testator intended *philanthropic* to be limited to charitable or to have its broader dictionary meaning. The next of kin urged (1) that the court adhere to its cases following the English rule that terms such as *benevolent* and *philanthropic* are broader than charitable, and (2) that even if such terms have come generally to mean charitable for these purposes, this testator's usage indicated a broader intention inasmuch as he gave the property to "such philanthropic causes as my trustee may select, *special consideration,* however, to be given to charitable, educational and scientific fields" (emphasis added). The court considered at length the admissibility of extrinsic evidence in such cases and approved the flexible use of a broad range of evidence showing the particular testator's intention. It then concluded:

> While "philanthropic" may be technically broader than "charitable," we think it has come to mean the same thing in modern usage. However, even if it has not, it is ambiguous enough to be construed as such. . . . And if there were any doubt, well established rules of construction would lead us to lean in favor of a construction which upheld the gift as charitable.

58 N.J. at 263-264, 277 A.2d at 206-207.

Dispositions in trust simply for "such charitable purposes as my trustee may select" and bequests to "such charitable institutions as my executor may select" are valid. E.g., Boyd v. First National Bank, 145 Tex. 206, 196 S.W.2d 497; Annot., 168 A.L.R. 1326 (1946); Rabinowitz v. Wollman, 174 Md. 6, 197 A. 566 (1939). See also Newick v. Mason, 581 A.2d 1270 (Me. 1990). So are bequests and intended trusts for "charity" or for some class of charity without naming a trustee, for trusts do not fail for want of trustees, which courts can appoint. See In re Jordan's Estate, 329 Pa. 427, 197 A. 150 (1938) ("to charity"); In re Vanderhoofen's Estate, 18 Cal. App. 3d 940, 96 Cal. Rptr. 260 (1971) ("to some Protestant school . . . of engineering").

In contrast to the broad purposes considered above, the purposes of a trust may be so restricted as to be challenged on the ground that the limited purpose is not charitable. If such a trust is too indefinite as to its beneficiaries or duration to be upheld as a private trust, it must fail if not found to be charitable. When is a specific purpose not charitable? "A trust is not a charitable trust if the persons who are to benefit are not a sufficiently large or indefinite class so that the community is interested in the enforcement of the trust." Restatement (Second) of Trusts §375. Thus, a trust for the care of unspecified stray animals is charitable, but the notorious trusts for the care of specific pets are not. (The latter, however, may be permitted as *honorary trusts,* as noted in Chapter 10, section D.) A trust for Masses for the soul of a particular person is now considered to be charitable; this is because the religious purpose is not limited to particular souls, according to Restatement §371, comment *g.* A trust to establish a museum to exhibit objects that the particular testator regarded as works of art but that have no artistic value will not be enforced. Restatement §374, comment *m*. When troublesome cases arise, how is it decided whether the required interest or benefit to the community is present? This is for the court, not the donor, to decide. But how is this to be done if we are to avoid personalized decision-making, which merely substitutes the values and attitudes of the individual judge or panel of judges on a given court at a given time for those of the donor, especially in particularly controversial areas?[1]

Certain types of trusts tend to pose difficult questions regarding what is of benefit to the community. A trust to disseminate beliefs that are judged to be so irrational or inconsequential as to be of no community interest is not valid. The mere fact that views are unpopular or have but a few adherents, however, is not sufficient to deprive a trust of the educational or religious purpose to which the special privileges of a charitable trust attach. Where is the line drawn in such cases? On which side does spiritualism fall? See 4 A. Scott, Trusts §370 (3d ed. 1967). And what of a trust the income of which is to be used as the trustee deems appropriate to further a specific radical or reactionary political philosophy? What of partisan political purposes, or advocacy of a particular change in the law (as distinct from general support of the work of a law revision commission)?

In Jackson v. Phillips, 96 Mass. (14 Allen) 539 (1867), a trust to "create a public sentiment that will put an end to negro slavery" was upheld, along with a trust "for the benefit of fugitive slaves who may escape from the slave-holding states." The very same case, however, held invalid another bequest to create a trust to promote women's suffrage because the purpose was "to change the laws." A later Massachusetts case also invalidated a trust to promote "women's rights," interpreted as meaning

---

1. With the Restatement references above on Masses and personal museums, compare two modern English cases that are illustrative of problems concerning the meaning of public benefit and how that benefit may be determined. In invalidating a gift for the "purposes of the Roman Catholic community known as the Carmelite Priory," Lord Simonds's opinion in Gilmore v. Coats [1949] A.C. 426, 444-446, states:

> It is said . . . that religious purposes are charitable, but that can only be true [of activities] tending directly or indirectly towards the instruction or edification of the public. . . . [A court does not] accept as proved whatever a particular church believes [for] the court can act only on proof. A gift to one or two or a hundred cloistered nuns in the belief that their prayers will benefit the world at large does not from that belief derive validity any more than does the belief of any other donor for any other purpose.

In the other case the quality of a testator's collection of his own and others' paintings, plus some antique furnishings, led one expert witness to express "surprise that so voracious a collector should not by hazard have picked up even one meritorious object," and Davies, L.J., to observe that in such cases the court must

> receive expert evidence on the question whether the display [is] for the advancement of education or otherwise of benefit to the public. For without such evidence the court would be unable to decide the question.

Re Pinion, [1965] 1 Ch. 98, 197 (C.A.).

the right to vote and hold office, while upholding two other trusts in the same will to promote "the cause of temperance" and the "best interests of sewing girls in Boston." Bowditch v. Attorney General, 241 Mass. 168, 134 N.E. 796 (1922).

RESTATEMENT (SECOND) OF TRUSTS

§374. . . . A trust for the promotion of purposes which are of a character sufficiently beneficial to the community to justify permitting property to be devoted forever to their accomplishment is charitable.

Comment: . . .

j. *Change in existing law.* A trust may be charitable although the accomplishment of the purpose for which the trust is created involves a change in the existing law. If the purpose of the trust is to bring about changes in the law by illegal means, such as by revolution, bribery, illegal lobbying or bringing improper pressure to bear upon members of the legislature, the purpose is illegal. See §377. The mere fact, however, that the purpose is to bring about a change in the law, whether indirectly through the education of the electors so as to bring about a public sentiment in favor of the change, or through proper influences brought to bear upon the legislators, does not prevent that purpose from being legal and charitable. . . .

k. *Political purposes.* A trust to promote the success of a particular political party is not charitable. Thus, a trust of a large sum of money to use the income forever in the discretion of the chairman of a party committee to assist the party in the election of members of the party or otherwise to promote the interests of the party is not a charitable trust. There is no social interest in the community in the underwriting of one or another of the political parties. If, however, the promotion of a particular cause is charitable, the mere fact that one or another of the political parties advocates the cause, does not make the promotion of the cause non-charitable. Thus, a trust . . . to promote an economic doctrine, such as the desirability of free trade or of protective tariffs, is charitable although the political parties take different stands on these questions.

PROBLEM

14-A.   George Bernard Shaw left the residue of his estate to trustees to use the income for twenty-one years to support the study of the advantages of a phonetic alphabet consisting of forty letters (one for every sound and having but one sound per letter), to finance publication and free distribution to libraries of his play *Androcles and the Lion* in this alphabet, and to fund a campaign to promote the adoption of the proposed alphabet. How would you argue to uphold this intended trust in the United States? How would you argue against it?[2]

FRATCHER, BEQUESTS FOR PURPOSES
56 Iowa L. Rev. 773, 773-783, 800-802 (1971)

Your client is an elderly widower. His only relatives are wealthy, greedy nephews whom he does not wish to benefit. He insists upon keeping control of his substantial fortune while he lives. He wishes it devoted after his death, for so long as the law permits, to the support of three projects in which he is interested:

1. promotion of the game of royal or court tennis, which flourished in the days of Henry VIII but is now in danger of extinction;
2. promotion of legislation to facilitate the docking of entails and to prohibit the docking of horse tails;
3. erection and operation of non-profit apartment house specially designed for the comfortable accommodation of elderly persons of modest means.

None of these purposes is against public policy. Your client deems all of them to be beneficial to the public. In each case, however, the individuals who will benefit from the project constitute an indefinite class, whose identity is not ascertainable. Your problem is to determine what legal devices exist for the effectuation of your client's wishes and which of these will best accomplish his purposes. This article will explore the various devices in order to ascertain those which will properly serve your client's posthumous . . . purposes, whether or not they are charitable.

A. Charitable Trusts

Your first thought is the charitable trust. . . . If usable for these purposes, [it] would be an ideal device for carrying out your client's wishes. Any person or corporation with general capacity to execute trusts may serve as trustee. The attorney general may sue to compel proper performance. The persons to benefit need not be a definite group or class and their interests need not vest within the period of the Rule Against Perpetuities. There is no limit on the duration of the trust. If changing cir-

_____

2. A major asset of Shaw's estate eventually turned out to be the royalties from the musical *My Fair Lady,* based on his *Pygmalion,* in which a professor of phonetics was portrayed. As pointed out in an omitted portion of the Fratcher article excerpted here, Shaw's project was invalidated as noncharitable and not within the limited purposes for which honorary trusts are allowed. In re Shaw, [1957] 1 All F.R. 745 (Ch.), but the other charitable residuary beneficiaries, whose rights accelerated, have allowed these purposes to be pursued.

cumstances make effectuation of the purposes impossible or illegal, or if they can be accomplished without using the entire fund, a court of equity, acting under the cy pres doctrine, may authorize the trustee to apply funds to other purposes as near as possible to those in which your client is interested. . . .

By 1940 all of the states had adopted, with some minor deviations, the English law of charitable trusts. There is still danger with many of these statutes that the courts will revert, in a particular case, to older decisions hostile to charitable trusts. If your client's purposes are charitable, however, the risk of this hostility is bearable. Hence, the chief problem connected with use of the charitable trust device is determining whether your client's purposes are charitable.

Trusts for the promotion of education or health, or both, among the public or a substantial segment of it are charitable, even if not limited to the poor. A trust to promote chess tournaments has been upheld as an educational charity in England, but trusts to promote athletic sports, such as tennis or baseball, have not been deemed charitable unless connected with the program of an established school or a program of military training. No doubt a trust to finance court tennis as part of the rehabilitation or physical therapy program of a hospital would be deemed charitable as promoting public health. Your client's first purpose, the promotion of court tennis without reference to the programs of a school, a hospital, or a military training establishment, is not, however, charitable according to the reported cases.

It could be argued that your client's second purpose, the promotion of legislation to facilitate the docking of entails and to prohibit the docking of horse tails, is charitable as designed to promote public education, improve the economy, and relieve the suffering of animals. The English decisions, however, are to the effect that a trust to promote change in existing law is never charitable. Some American decisions follow the English view. Others will enforce bequests as charitable when they are for purposes that include the promotion of change in existing law. Federal tax legislation has recently become increasingly hostile to the treatment of the promotion of legislation as a charitable purpose. Although qualification as a charity under the Internal Revenue Code is not necessarily required for treatment as a charity in determining validity under state law, the effect of the federal attitude may well be to incline the courts toward returning to the English rule. Perhaps your client's second purpose is charitable, but you should proceed cautiously.

The Preamble to the Statute of Charitable Uses of 1601, often used by the courts as a guide in formulating a list of permissible charitable purposes, lists first as a charitable purpose, "Relief of aged, impotent and poor people." . . . Nevertheless, a growing number of decisions in this country deny charitable status to such homes. The decisions involve exemption from property taxation and so are not necessarily conclusive on the question of the validity of a trust for this purpose, [but] a decision that a purpose is not charitable for tax purposes tends to influence decision on the question of validity.

It would seem, then, that none of your client's three purposes is certain to be held to be charitable. If an attempt to create a charitable trust by the residuary clauses of a will fails, the property is held on resulting trust for the heirs or next of kin of the testator. As your client's heirs and next of kin are his wealthy, greedy nephews, who are almost certain to attack his testamentary dispositions if they stand to benefit, no attempt should be made to create trusts for these purposes by the residuary clause. If any attempt is made it should be by specific or general legacies to trustees and the residue should be devised and bequeathed to someone less likely to attack the trusts. . . . Although homes for elderly human beings are no longer charitable in several states, homes for [indefinite] elderly cats are clearly charitable. If the residue is devised and bequeathed to a friend who hates cats, upon trust to establish a home for elderly cats, neither the trustee nor the attorney general is likely to attack prior dispositions made by the will.

B. Honorary Trusts

In view of the uncertainty as to whether your client's purposes are charitable, your second thought is to create testamentary trusts in such a manner that, if their purposes are held to be non-charitable, they will be [permitted] as honorary trusts. This will involve restricting their duration to the period of the Rule Against Perpetuities. It will also involve the risk that the trusts will not be carried out if the named trustee dies or fails to perform the duties sought to be imposed on him. If the purposes are not charitable and no definitely ascertainable persons or class of persons are to benefit, neither the attorney general nor anyone else will have standing to sue to compel performance of the trusts. As in the case of an ineffective attempt to create a charitable trust, the property will be held on resulting trust for the heirs or next of kin if the disposition is by the residuary clause; otherwise for the residuary devisees or legatees.

In England honorary trusts limited in duration to the period of the Rule Against Perpetuities have been upheld. The trustee has been permitted to apply the property to the designated purpose, if he chose to do so, for [certain narrowly limited purposes]. In this country honorary trusts, similarly limited in duration, have been upheld to the same limited extent for: (1) manumission of slaves; (2) erection of sepulchral monuments; (3) care of graves; and (4) care of a definite group of animals; and (5) saying of masses. The Restatement of Trusts takes the position that an honorary trust is not a true trust but a power which may be conferred on a "trustee" for any purpose not in conflict with public policy. The English courts have rejected the Restatement view in cases holding [various] bequests to trustees to apply funds during the period of the Rule Against Perpetuities . . . wholly void in the sense that . . . willing trustees would not be permitted to carry out the testator's wishes by way of honorary trust. . . . The English cases suggest that the honorary trust is an unjustifiable anomaly which will be permitted in the future only for care of graves and pet animals. Consequently, there is danger that an honorary trust for any of your client's purposes may fail if the recent trend in British law is applied. . . .

[The author then reviewed other possibilities: nonimperative powers of appointment; outright bequests to trusted friends who share the client's interests; bequests subject to forfeiture on the legatees' failure to devote stipulated amounts of their own funds to the purposes; contracts; servitudes; equitable charges; bequests for the benefit of unincorporated associations devoted to the purposes the client has in mind; corporate foundations to be formed for the purposes; and the bequests to existing nonprofit corporations.]

Anglo-American law provides no risk-free device for devoting property to non-charitable purposes for extended periods. Perhaps it should not. As Thomas Jefferson was wont to urge, wealth should be controlled by the living, not the dead. On the other hand, it ought to be possible for a testator with ample means to ensure the continuation, for at least a few years after his death, of an undertaking in which he is interested. An elderly person who is engaged in research or writing a book knows that he may die before his project is completed. His lawyer should be able to assure him that, if he does, the project will not collapse. . . .

The trust device failed [in England] to ensure the execution of Mr. Shaw's purpose and it might fail to accomplish your client's purposes of promoting court tennis, legislation, and housing for the elderly. Of the other devices which have been discussed, the last, bequests to existing non-profit corporations, is probably the most dependable for effectuating your client's wishes during at least a reasonable period after his death. The affirmative legal easement device and the equitable charge device could be combined with it without serious risk that, if they failed, there would be a resulting trust for the wealthy, greedy nephews.

PROBLEM

14-B. The will of Jack Robbins left property to named trustees, the income

> to be used for the support, education, and welfare of such minor Negro child or children as they may select whose father or mother or both have been convicted of a crime of a political nature. Wishing to preserve the right of dissent and being aware of the changing nature of attempts to restrict free expression and to circumscribe activity in unorthodox causes,

I authorize my Trustees to decide what Negro child or children shall receive benefits under this trust.

What recognized charitable purpose is involved? Is this trust valid? In re Robbins' Estate, 57 Cal. 2d 718, 371 P.2d 573 (1962). Consider the material below.

A. SCOTT, TRUSTS
Vol. 4 (3d ed. 1967)

§377. *Illegal purposes.*   A trust cannot be created for a purpose which is illegal. The purpose is illegal if the trust property is to be used for an object which is in violation of the criminal law, or if the trust tends to induce the commission of crime, or if the accomplishment of the purpose is otherwise against public policy. Questions of public policy are not fixed and unchanging, but vary from time to time and from place to place. A trust fails for illegality if the accomplishment of the purposes of the trust is regarded as against public policy in the community in which the trust is created and at the time when it is created. Where a policy is articulated in a statute making certain conduct a criminal offense, then, of course, a trust is illegal if its performance involves such criminal conduct, or if it tends to encourage such conduct. . . .

A trust is illegal, even if it does not involve the performance of an illegal act by the trustees, if the natural result of the performance of the trust would be to induce the commission of crime. Thus a bequest to purchase the release of persons committed to prison for nonpayment of fines under the game laws was held illegal.

The trust that came before the United States Supreme Court in 1844 in Vidal v. Girard's Executors, mentioned in section A supra, returned to the Court in 1957. In 1776 a one-eyed sea captain named Stephen Girard began a shipping business in Philadelphia and died in 1831, a lonely man but one of the country's wealthiest tycoons. Most of his estate was bequeathed in trust to the mayor, aldermen, and citizens of Philadelphia to establish a "college" (an elementary and secondary school) for "poor male white orphan children." In Girard Will Case, 386 Pa. 548, 127 A. 287 (1956), the Pennsylvania Supreme Court upheld the trust, which was then administered by a statutory body created to accept and execute charitable trusts for the City of Philadelphia. The decision was reversed in Pennsylvania v. Board of Directors of City Trusts, 353 U.S. 230 (1957), on the ground that the refusal of admission to applicants because of their race by a state agency, though acting as a trustee, was discrimination forbidden by the fourteenth amendment. On remand the orphans' court removed the board and appointed thirteen private citizens as trustees. The Pennsylvania Supreme Court upheld the substitution of trustees and affirmed the decree of the orphans' court providing for execution of the trust according to its terms. In re Girard College Trusteeship, 391 Pa. 434, 138 A.2d 844, *appeal dismissed, cert. denied sub nom.* Pennsylvania v. Board of Directors of City Trusts, 357 U.S. 570 (1958). After the Supreme Court decided Evans v. Newton, infra, Pennsylvania v. Brown, 392 F.2d 120 (3d Cir.), *cert. denied,* 391 U.S. 921 (1968), concluded that, in light of the "fairly comparable" facts and trusteeship histories of the college and of the park in Evans v. Newton, the latter decision "governs the issue before us" and required that applicants to Girard College be admitted without regard to race.

EVANS v. NEWTON
382 U.S. 296 (1966)

DOUGLAS, J., delivered the opinion of the Court.

In 1911 United States Senator Augustus O. Bacon executed a will that devised to the Mayor and Council of the City of Macon, Georgia, a tract of land which, after the death of the Senator's wife and daughters, was to be used as "a park and pleasure ground" for white people only, the Senator stating in the will that while he had only the kindest feeling for the Negroes he was of the opinion that "in their social relations the two races (white and negro) should be forever separate." The will provided that the park should be under the control of a Board of Managers of seven persons, all of whom were to be white. The city kept the park segregated for some years but in time let Negroes use it, taking the position that the park was a public facility which it could not constitutionally manage and maintain on a segregated basis.

Thereupon, individual members of the Board of Managers of the park brought this suit in a state court against the City of Macon and the trustees of certain residuary beneficiaries of Senator Bacon's estate, asking that the city be removed as trustee and the court appoint new trustees, to whom title to the park would be transferred. The city answered, alleging it could not legally enforce racial segregation in the park. The other defendants admitted the allegation and requested that the city be removed as trustee.

Several Negro citizens of Macon intervened, alleging that the racial limitation was contrary to the laws and public policy of the United States, and asking that the court refuse to appoint private trustees. Thereafter the city resigned as trustee and amended its answer accordingly. Moreover, other heirs of Senator Bacon intervened and they and the defendants other than the city asked for reversion of the trust property to the Bacon estate in the event that the prayer of the petition were denied.

The Georgia court accepted the resignation of the city as trustee and appointed three individuals as new trustees, finding it unnecessary to pass on the other claims of the heirs. On appeal by the Negro intervenors, the Supreme Court of Georgia affirmed, holding that Senator Bacon had the right to give and bequeath his property to a limited class, that charitable trusts are subject to supervision of a court of equity, and that the power to appoint new trustees so that the purpose of the trust would not fail was clear. 220 Ga. 280, 138 S.E.2d 573. The case is here on a writ of certiorari. 380 U.S. 971.

There are two complementary principles to be reconciled in this case. One is the right of the individual to pick his own associates so as to express his preferences and dislikes, and to fashion his private life by joining such clubs and groups as he chooses. The other is the constitutional ban in the Equal Protection Clause of the Fourteenth Amendment against state-sponsored racial inequality, which of course bars a city from acting as trustee under a private will that serves the racial segregation cause. Pennsylvania v. Board of Trusts, 353 U.S. 230. A private golf club, however, restricted to either Negro or white membership is one expression of freedom of association. But a municipal golf course that serves only one race is state activity indicating a preference on a matter as to which the State must be neutral. . . . [W]hen private individuals or groups are endowed by the State with powers or functions governmental in nature, they become agencies or instrumentalities of the State and subject to its constitutional limitations.

Yet generalizations do not decide concrete cases. [T]he fact that government has engaged in a particular activity does not necessarily mean that an individual entrepreneur or manager of the same kind of undertaking suffers the same constitutional inhibitions. While a State may not segregate public schools so as to exclude one or more religious groups, those sects may maintain their own parochial educational systems. Pierce v. Society of Sisters, 268 U.S. 510.

If a testator wanted to leave a school or center for the use of one race only and in no way implicated the State in the supervision, control or management of that facility, we assume arguendo that no constitutional difficulty would be encountered.[3]

This park, however, is in a different posture. For years it was an integral part of the City of Macon's activities. From the pleadings we assume it was swept, manicured, watered, patrolled, and maintained by the city as a public facility for whites only, as well as granted tax exemption under Ga. Code Ann. §92-201. The momentum it acquired as a public facility is certainly not dissipated ipso facto by the appointment of "private"

3. It is argued that this park was a product of Georgia's [statutory] policy to allow charitable trusts of public facilities to be segregated. . . . We do not, however, reach the question whether the state facilitated, through its legislative action, the establishment of segregated parks.

trustees. So far as this record shows, there has been no change in municipal maintenance and concern over this facility. Whether these public characteristics will in time be dissipated is wholly conjectural. If the municipality remains entwined in the management or control of the park, it remains subject to the restraints of the Fourteenth Amendment. . . . We only hold that where the traditions of municipal control had become firmly established, we cannot take judicial notice that the mere substitution of trustees instantly transferred this park from the public to the private sector.

'This conclusion is buttressed by the nature of the service rendered the community by a park. The service rendered even by a private park of this character is municipal in nature. It is open to every white person, there being no selective element other than race. Golf clubs, social centers, luncheon clubs, schools such as Tuskegee was at least in origin, and other like organizations in the private sector are often racially oriented. A park, on the other hand, is more like a fire department or police department that traditionally serves the community. . . . [A]nd state courts that aid private parties to perform that public function on a segregated basis implicate the State in conduct proscribed by the Fourteenth Amendment. . . .

Under the circumstances of this case, we cannot but conclude that the public character of this park requires that it be treated as a public institution subject to the command of the Fourteenth Amendment, regardless of who now has title under state law. . . .

Reversed.

WHITE, J. . . .

That the Fourteenth Amendment prohibits operation of the park on a segregated basis so long as the city is trustee is of course not disputed. . . . Whether the successor trustees may themselves operate the park on a segregated basis is the question. The majority holds that they may not, I agree, but for different reasons. . . .

[T]he record does not show continued involvement of the city in the operation of the park — the record is silent on this point. . . . That the city's own interest might lead it to extricate itself at once from operation of the park does not, of course, necessarily mean that it has done so [but what] the majority has done . . . is simply a disguised form of conjecture and, I submit, is an insufficient basis for decision of this case.

I would nevertheless hold that the racial condition in the trust may not be given effect by the new trustees because, in my view, it is incurably tainted by discriminatory state legislation validating such a condition under state law. The state legislation to which I refer is §69-504 and §69-505 of the Georgia Code, which were adopted in 1905, just six years before Senator Bacon's will was executed. . . .

As this legislation does not compel a trust settlor to condition his grant upon use only by a racially designated class, the State cannot be said to have directly coerced private discrimination. Nevertheless, if the validity of the racial condition in Senator Bacon's trust would have been in doubt but for the 1905 statute and if the statute removed such doubt only for racial restrictions, leaving the validity of non-racial restrictions still in question, the absence of coercive language in the legislation would not prevent application of the Fourteenth Amendment. For such a statute would depart from a policy of strict neutrality in matters of private discrimination by enlisting the State's assistance only in aid of racial discrimination and would so involve the State in the private choice as to convert the infected private discrimination into state action subject to the Fourteenth Amendment. . . .

Apart from §69-504 and §69-505, the Georgia statute governing the determination of permissible objects of charitable trusts is §108-203. This statute "almost copies the statute of 43d Elizabeth," Newson v. Starke, 46 Ga. 88, 92 (1872), and has the effect of fully adopting in Georgia the common law of charities. Jones v. Habersham, 107 U.S. 174, 180. We may therefore expect general charitable trust principles to be as fully applicable in Georgia as elsewhere in the several States. Under such principles, there is grave doubt concerning whether a charitable trust for a park could be limited to the use of less than the whole public. . . . Professor Scott states this principle as follows:

> As we have seen, a trust to promote the happiness or well-being of members of the community is charitable, although it is not a trust to relieve poverty, advance education, promote religion or protect health. In such a case, however, *the trust must be for the benefit of the members of the community generally* and not merely for the benefit of a class of persons.

IV Scott on Trusts §375.2, at 2715 (2d ed. 1956). (Emphasis added.) . . .

On the whole, therefore, I conclude that prior to the 1905 legislation it would have been extremely doubtful whether §108-203 authorized a trust for park purposes when a portion of the public was to be excluded from the park. . . .

BLACK, J., dissenting. . . .

[T]he narrow question of whether a city could resign such a trusteeship and whether a state court could appoint successor trustees depended entirely on state law. . . . [S]ince the Georgia courts decided no federal constitutional question, I agree with my Brother Harlan that the writ of certiorari should have been dismissed as improvidently granted. . . .

HARLAN, J., whom STEWART, J., joins, dissenting. . . .

In my view the writ should be dismissed as improvidently granted. . . . To infer from the Georgia Supreme Court's opinion, as the majority here does, a further holding that the new trustees are entitled to operate Baconsfield on a racially restricted basis, is to stretch for a constitutional issue. . . .

On the merits, which I reach only because the Court has done so, I do not think that the Fourteenth Amendment permits this Court in effect to frustrate the terms of Senator Bacon's will, now that the City of Macon is no longer connected, so far as the record shows, with the administration of Baconsfield. If the majority is in doubt that such is the case, it should remand for findings on that issue and not reverse. . . .

Quite evidently uneasy with its first ground of decision, the majority advances another which ultimately emerges as the real holding. This ground derives from what is asserted to be the "public character" of Baconsfield. . . .

More serious than the absence of any firm doctrinal support for this theory of state action are its potentialities for the future. [Despite similarities of parks and schools in terms of "public functions" involved,] the majority assumes that its decision leaves unaffected the traditional view that the Fourteenth Amendment does not compel private schools to adapt their admission policies to its requirements, but that such matters are left to the States acting within constitutional bounds. I find it difficult, however, to avoid the conclusion that this decision opens the door to reversal of these basic constitutional concepts, and, at least in logic, jeopardizes the existence of denominationally restricted schools while making of every college entrance rejection letter a potential Fourteenth Amendment question.

While this process of analogy might be spun out to reach privately owned orphanages, libraries, garbage collection companies, detective agencies, and a host of other functions commonly regarded as nongovernmental though paralleling fields of governmental activity, the example of schools is, I think, sufficient to indicate the pervasive potentialities of this "public function" theory of state action. . . .

Following the above decision, a Georgia trial court ruled that Senator Bacon's trust was not enforceable according to its terms and that the trust property reverted to his heirs, rejecting the arguments of certain Macon citizens and the Georgia Attorney General that the trust should continue and that the doctrine of cy pres, infra, should be applied to modify the trust terms by striking the racial restrictions. The court found the doctrine inapplicable because the park's segregated character was so essential a part of the testator's plan as to preclude finding the general charitable intent required to vary the terms of the trust instead of allowing the property to revert to the heirs. Evans v. Abney, 396 U.S. 435 (1969) (Justices Douglas and Brennan dissenting), affirmed the decision of the Georgia Supreme Court (224 Ga. 826, 165 S.E.2d 160 (1968)) affirming the trial court's ruling. Justice Black, writing for the Court, stated:

> We do not understand petitioners to be contending here that the Georgia judges were motivated either consciously or unconsciously by a desire

to discriminate against Negroes. . . . What remains of petitioners' argument is the idea that the Georgia courts had a constitutional obligation in this case to resolve any doubt about the testator's intent in favor of preserving the trust. Thus stated, we see no merit in the argument. The only choice the Georgia courts either had or exercised in this regard was their judicial judgment in construing Bacon's will to determine his intent, and the Constitution imposes no requirement upon the Georgia courts to approach Bacon's will any differently than they would approach any will creating any charitable trust of any kind. Surely the Fourteenth Amendment is not violated where, as here, a state court operating in its judicial capacity applies its normal principles of construction to determine the testator's true intent in establishing a charitable trust and then reaches a conclusion with regard to that intent which, because of the operation of neutral and nondiscriminatory state trust laws, effectively denies everyone, whites as well as Negroes, the benefits of the trust.

396 U.S. at 447.

The opinion had earlier noted (id. at 445) that the case was distinguishable from Shelley v. Kraemer, 334 U.S. 1 (1948), in that here "the effect of the Georgia decision eliminated all discrimination against Negroes in the park by eliminating the park itself."

In comparable cases facing the choice between having trust property revert or eliminating racially discriminatory restrictions by cy pres, cases have usually found the requisite general charitable intent to reform the trust. E.g., Howard Savings Institution v. Trustees of Amherst College, 61 N.J. Super. 119, 160 A.2d 177 (1960). But not always. See La Fond v. City of Detroit, 357 Mich. 362, 98 N.W.2d 530 (1959). The racial restriction in a trust for the support and education of "poor white citizens of Kent County" was held invalid and cy pres was applied to delete the word *white* in In re Will of Potter, 275 A.2d 574 (Del. Ch. 1970), where again the finding of state action was based on peculiar facts of the case rather than deciding that charitable trusts inherently involve state action because of special functions and privileges or that state *trust* law requires that, in order to be charitable, trusts must not involve invidious racial discrimination.

In Ebitz v. Pioneer National Bank, 372 Mass. 207, 361 N.E.2d 225 (1977), a trust (with a bank trustee) to provide law scholarships to worthy "young men" was construed in a generic sense to include women, partly on the basis that "declared policy of the Commonwealth . . . regarding equal treatment of the sexes" should lead the court to resolve any ambiguity in that fashion rather than raise a question of the trust's validity.

MATTER OF ESTATE OF WILSON
59 N.Y.2d 461, 452 N.E.2d 1228 (1983)

[Companion cases involving testamentary trusts for college scholarships: the Wilson trust income to aid five "young men" who have graduated from a designated high school with certain academic achievements, to be certified by the superintendent of schools for that school district; and the Johnson trust income to be used for "bright and deserving young men" who have graduated from another high school, who meet certain need requirements, and who are selected by the principal and board of education of that school. Following complaints lodged with the Civil Rights Office of the U.S. Department of Education in each case, and certain investigations, negotiations, and agreements, both cases ended up in court. The Surrogate's Court in *Wilson* held that the school superintendent's cooperation with the trustee, a bank, violated neither federal statute or regulation nor the equal protection clause of the fourteenth amendment. The Appellate Division (Third Department), however, found administration of the trust according to its literal terms impossible because of the superintendent's agreement not to certify the students and exercised its cy pres power to reform the trust by striking the clause in the will providing for the school superintendent's certification, permitting candidates to apply directly to the trustee. In *Johnson,* the school district having agreed not to serve as trustee, the Surrogate replaced the school district with a private trustee. The Appellate Division (Second Department) held that a court's reformation by substitution of trustees would constitute state action and a violation of the fourteenth amendment's equal protection requirement; accordingly the Appellate Division exercised its cy pres power to reform the trust by eliminating the gender restriction.]

CooK, C.J. . . .

These appeals present the question whether the equal protection clause of the Fourteenth Amendment is violated when a court permits the administration of private charitable trusts according to the testator's intent to finance the education of male students and not female students. When a court applies trust law that neither encourages, nor affirmatively promotes, nor compels private discrimination but allows parties to engage in private selection in the devise or bequest of their property, that choice will not be attributable to the State and subjected to the Fourteenth Amendment's strictures. . . .

There can be no question that the trusts, established for the promotion of education, are for a charitable purpose within the meaning of the law. Charitable trusts are encouraged and favored by the law. . . . [U]nlike other trusts, a charitable trust will not necessarily fail when the settlor's specific charitable purpose or direction can no longer be accomplished. . . .

The court, of course, cannot invoke its cy pres power without first determining that the testator's specific charitable purpose is no longer capable of being performed by the trust. In establishing these trusts, the testators expressly and unequivocally intended that they provide for the education expenses of male students. It cannot be said that the accomplishment of the testator's specific expression of charitable intent is "impossible or impracticable." So long as the subject high schools graduate boys with the requisite qualifications, the testator's specific charitable intent can be fulfilled.

Nor are the trusts' particular limitation of beneficiaries by gender invalid and incapable of being accomplished as violative of public policy. It is true that the eradication in this State of gender-based discrimination is an important public policy. Indeed, the Legislature has barred gender-based discrimination in education, employment, housing, credit, and many other areas. . . . The restrictions in these trusts run contrary to this policy favoring equal opportunity and treatment of men and women. A provision in a charitable trust, however, that is central to the testator's or settlor's charitable purpose, and is not illegal, should not be invalidated on public grounds unless that provision, if given effect, would substantially mitigate the general charitable effect of the gift (see 4 Scott, Trusts [3d ed.], section 399.4).

Proscribing the enforcement of gender restrictions in private charitable trusts would operate with equal force towards trusts whose benefits are bestowed exclusively on women. "Reduction of the disparity in economic condition between men and women caused by the long history of discrimination against women has been recognized as . . . an important governmental objective" (Califano v. Webster, 430 U.S. 313, 317 . . .). There can be little doubt that important efforts in effecting this type of social change can be and are performed through private philanthropy. And, the private funding of programs for the advancement of women is substantial and growing. Indeed, one compilation of financial assistance offered primarily or exclusively to women lists 854 sources of fundings. Current thinking in private philanthropic institutions advocates that funding offered by such institutions and the opportunities within the institutions themselves be directly responsive to the needs of particular groups. It is evident, therefore, that the focusing of private philanthropy on certain classes within society may be consistent with public policy. Consequently, that the restrictions in the trust before this court may run contrary to public efforts promoting equality of opportunity for women does not justify imposing a per se rule that gender restrictions in private charitable trusts violate public policy.

Finally, this is not an instance in which the restriction of the trusts serves to frustrate a paramount charitable purpose. In Howard Sav. Inst. v. Peep, 34 N.J. 494, 170 A.2d 39, . . . [d]ue to the religious restrictions, the college declined to accept the bequest as contrary to its charter. The court found that the college was the principal beneficiary of the trust, so that removing the religious restriction and thereby allowing the college to accept the gift would permit administration of the trust in a manner most closely effectuating the testator's intent.

In contrast, the trusts subject to these appeals were not intended to directly benefit the school districts. Although the testators sought the school districts' participation, this was incidental to their primary intent of financing the college education of boys who attended the schools. Consequently, severance of the school districts' role in the trusts' administration will not frustrate any part of the testators' charitable purposes. Inasmuch as the specific charitable intent of the testators is not inherently "impossible or impracticable" of being achieved by the trusts, there is no occasion to exercise cy pres power.

Although not inherently so, these trusts are currently incapable of being administered as originally intended because of the school districts' unwillingness to cooperate. These impediments, however, may be remedied by an exercise of a court's general equitable power over all trusts to permit a deviation from the administrative terms of a trust and to appoint a successor trustee.

A testamentary trust will not fail for want of a trustee and, in the event a trustee is unwilling or unable to act, a court may replace the trustee with another. Accordingly, the proper means of continuing the Johnson Trust would be to replace the school district with someone able and willing to administer the trust according to its terms.

When an impasse is reached in the administration of a trust due to an incidental requirement of its terms, a court may effect, or permit the trustee to effect, a deviation from the trust's literal terms. This power differs from a court's cy pres power in that "[t]hrough exercise of its deviation power the court alters or amends administrative provisions in the trust instrument but does not alter the purpose of the charitable trust or change its dispositive provisions." The Wilson Trust provision that the school district certify a list of students is an incidental part of the trust's administrative requirements, which no longer can be satisfied in light of this district's refusal to cooperate. The same result intended by the testator may be accomplished by permitting the students to apply directly to the trustee. Therefore, a deviation from the Wilson Trust's administrative terms by eliminating the certification requirement would be the appropriate method of continuing the trust administration. . . .

It is argued before this court that the judicial facilitation of the continued administration of gender-restrictive charitable trusts violates the equal protection clause of the Fourteenth Amendment (see U.S. Const., 14th Amdt., section 1). The strictures of the equal protection clause are invoked when the State engages in invidious discrimination. Indeed, the State itself cannot, consistent with the Fourteenth Amendment, award scholarships that are gender restrictive.

The Fourteenth Amendment, however, "erects no shield against merely private conduct, however discriminatory or wrongful." (Shelley v. Kraemer, 334 U.S. 1, 13; . . . Evans v. Abaney, 396 U.S. 435, 445 . . .). Private discrimination may violate equal protection of the law when accompanied by State participation in, facilitation of, and, in some cases, acquiescence in the discrimination. Although there is no conclusive test to determine when state involvement in private discrimination will violate the Fourteenth Amendment, the general standard that has evolved is whether "the conduct allegedly causing the deprivation of a federal right [is] fairly attributable to the state." . . .

The Supreme Court has identified various situations in which the State may be deemed responsible for discriminatory conduct with private origins. . . .

"The court has never held, of course, that discrimination by an otherwise private entity would be violative of the Equal Protection Clause if the private entity receives any sort of benefit at all from the State, or if it is subject to state regulation in any degree whatever." Rather, "the State must have 'significantly involved itself with invidious discriminations' . . . in order for the discriminatory actions to fall within the ambit of the constitutional prohibition."

The state generally may not be held responsible for private discrimination solely on the basis that it permits the discrimination to occur. Nor is the state under an affirmative obligation to prevent purely private discrimination. Therefore, when the state regulates private dealings it may be responsible for private discrimination occurring in the regulated field only when enforcement of its regulation has the effect of compelling the private discrimination.

In Shelley v. Kraemer (supra), for example, the Supreme Court held that the equal protection clause was violated by judicial enforcement of a private covenant that prohibited the sale of affected properties "to people of Negro or Mongolian Race." When one of the properties was sold to a black family, the other property owners sought to enforce the covenant in State court and the family was ordered to move from the property. The Supreme Court noted

> that the restrictive agreement standing alone cannot be regarded as violative of any rights guaranteed to petitioners by the Fourteenth Amendment. So long as the purposes of those agreements are effectuated by voluntary adherence to their terms, it would appear clear that there has been no action by the State and the provisions of the Amendment have not been violated

(334 U.S. at p. 13). The court held, however, that it did not have before it cases

> in which the States have merely abstained from action leaving private individuals free to impose such discriminations as they see fit. Rather, these are cases in which the states have made available to such individuals the full coercive power of the government to deny petitioners on the grounds of race or color the enjoyment of property rights

(id., at p. 19). It was not the neutral regulation of contracts permitting parties to enter discriminatory agreements that caused the discrimination to be attributable to the State. Instead it was that the State court's exercise of its judicial power directly effected a discriminatory act. . . .

More recently, the Supreme Court considered whether a State's regulation of private clubs licensed to serve liquor caused a club's restrictive membership policy to be attributable to the State (see Moose Lodge No. 107 v. Irvis, 407 U.S. 163, 92 S. Ct. 1965, 32 L. Ed. 2d 627). The court held that although the State extensively regulated these private clubs, it was not responsible for the private discrimination simply because the regulation permitted the discrimination to occur. . . .

A court's application of its equitable power to permit the continued administration of the trust involved in these appeals falls outside the ambit of the Fourteenth Amendment. Although the field of trusts is regulated by the State, the Legislature's failure to forbid private discriminatory trusts does not cause such trusts, when they arise, to be attributable to the State. It naturally follows that, when a court applies this trust law and determines that it permits the continued existence of private discriminatory trusts, the Fourteenth Amendment is not implicated.

In the present appeals, the coercive power of the State has never been enlisted to enforce private discrimination. . . . The court's power compelled no discrimination. That discrimination has been sealed in the private execution of the wills. Recourse to the courts was had here only for the purpose of facilitating the administration of the trust, not for enforcement of their discriminatory dispositive provisions.

This is not to say that a court's exercise of its power over trusts can never invoke the scrutiny of the Fourteenth Amendment. This court holds only that a trust's discriminatory terms are not fairly attributable to the State when a court applies trust principles that permit private discrimination but do not encourage, affirmatively promote, or compel it.

The testators' intention to involve the State in the administration of these trusts does not alter this result, notwithstanding that the effect of the court's action respecting the trusts was to eliminate this involvement. The court's power to replace a trustee who is unwilling to act as in *Johnson* or to permit a deviation from an incidental administrative term in the trust as in *Wilson* is a part of the law permitting this private conduct and extends to all trusts regardless of their purposes. It compels no discrimination. Moreover, the minimal State participation in the trust's administration prior to the time that they reached the courts for the constructions under review did not cause the trusts to take on an indelible public character.

In sum, the Fourteenth Amendment does not require the State to exercise the full extent of its power to eradicate private discrimination. It is only when the State itself discriminates, compels another to discriminate, or allows another to assume one of its functions and discriminate that such discrimination will implicate the Amendment.

Accordingly, in Matter of Wilson, the order of the Appellate Division should be affirmed. . . . In Matter of Johnson, the order of the Appellate Division should be reversed . . . and the decree of the Surrogate's Court . . . reinstated.

JASEN, JONES, WACHTLER, and SIMONS, J.J., concur with COOKE, C.J.

MEYER, J. (concurring in Matter of Wilson and dissenting in Matter of Johnson). . . .

In [the latter] the trustee is the Board of Education, a public body. The establishment of a public trust for a discriminatory purpose is constitutionally improper. . . . For the State to legitimize that impropriety by replacement of the trustee is unconstitutional State action. The only permissible corrective action is, as the Appellate Division held, excision of the discriminatory limitation.

Contrast the decision to use the cy pres power, infra, to remove gender restrictions rather than to replace state agencies with private trustees in In re Certain Scholarship Funds, 133 N.H. 227, 575 A.2d 1325 (1990), 90 A.L.R.4th 811.

C. Cy Pres

Among the peculiar advantages of the charitable trust is its potential indefinite existence. In considering the *Freshour* case at the outset of this chapter, you may have wondered what would happen to the trusts if the designated churches eventually ceased to exist. What *would* happen? You have, of course, just encountered a form of this problem immediately above.

PROBLEM

14-C. *A* died in 1965, leaving her residuary estate to the trustees of Blackstone University in trust "to use the income, or as much of the income or principal as the Trustees deem appropriate, for the sole purpose of acquiring books, periodicals, and other research materials devoted to the subject of Law and Anthropology for the library of the College of Law of Blackstone University." At the present time, mainly as a result of this trust, the Blackstone Law Library possesses a singularly outstanding collection on law and anthropology, but the income of the trust is no longer being expended. As the collection has developed, annual expenditures have declined, and the fund has begun to accumulate in increased amounts each year. The librarian and the appropriate university and law school committees agree that further duplication is unnecessary and that normal current acquisitions will require only a portion of the income. No one associated with the law library doubts that much better use can be made of much of the trust income. As counsel for the Trustees of the University, how would you advise on this matter and how might you proceed? What factual inquiries would you make? What possibilities and what obstacles do you see?

JACKSON v. PHILLIPS[4]
96 Mass. (14 Allen) 539 (1867)

[Bill for instructions as to the validity and effect of certain provisions of the will of Francis Jackson. The fourth article of the will named a board of trustees and bequeathed $10,000 to them in trust to be used

> for the preparation and circulation of books, newspapers, and delivery of speeches, lectures, and such other means, as, in their judgment, will create a public sentiment that will put an end to negro slavery in this country. . . . My desire is that they [the board of trustees] may become a permanent organization; and I hope and trust that they will receive the services and sympathy, the donations and bequests, of the friends of the slave.

The fifth article of the will bequeathed $2,000 to the same board of trustees in trust "for the benefit of fugitive slaves who may escape from the slave-holding states of this infamous Union from time to time." These dispositions were upheld as valid charitable trusts, but while the case was under advisement the thirteenth amendment was adopted.]

GRAY, J. . . .

By the thirteenth amendment of the Constitution of the United States, adopted since the earlier arguments of this case, it is declared that

> neither slavery nor involuntary servitude, except as a punishment for crime whereof the party shall have been duly convicted, shall exist within the United States or any place subject to their jurisdiction.

The effect of this amendment upon the charitable bequests of Francis Jackson is the remaining question to be determined; and this requires a consideration of the nature and proper limits of the doctrine of cy pres.

It is contended for the heirs at law, that the power of the English chancellor, when a charitable trust cannot be administered according to its terms, to execute it so as to carry out the donor's intention as nearly as possible — cy pres — is derived from the royal prerogative or the St. of 43 Eliz., and is not an exercise of judicial authority; that, whether this power is prerogative or judicial, it cannot, or, if it can, should not, be exercised by this court; and that the doctrine of cy pres, even as admin-

---

4. Portions of this early influential case, which have been mentioned in section B, supra, are omitted here.

istered in the English chancery, would not sustain these charitable bequests since slavery has been abolished.

Much confusion of ideas has arisen from the use of the term cy pres in the books to describe two distinct powers by the English chancellor in charity cases, the one under the sign manual of the crown, the other under the general jurisdiction in equity. . . .

The principal, if not the only, cases in which the disposition of a charity is held to be in the crown by sign manual, are of two classes: the first, of bequests to particular uses charitable in their nature, but illegal, as for a form of religion not tolerated by law; and the second, of gifts of property to charity generally, without any trust interposed, and in which either no appointment is provided for, or the power of appointment is delegated to persons who die without exercising it. . . .

[The first] is clearly a prerogative and not a judicial power, and could not be exercised by this court. . . .

The jurisdiction of the court of chancery to superintend the administration and decree the performance of gifts to trustees for charitable uses of a kind stated in the gift stands upon different grounds; and is part of its equity jurisdiction over trusts, which is shown by abundant evidence to have existed before the passage of the Statute of Charitable Uses. . . .

A charity, being a trust in the support and execution of which the whole public is concerned, and which is therefore allowed by the law to be perpetual, deserves and often requires the exercise of a larger discretion by the court of chancery than a mere private trust; for without a large discretionary power, in carrying out the general intent of the donor, to vary the details of administration, and even the mode of application, many charities would fail by change of circumstances and the happening of contingencies which no human foresight could provide against; and the probabilities of such failure would increase with the lapse of time and the remoteness of the heirs from the original donor who had in a clear and lawful manner manifested his will to divert his estate from his heirs for the benefit of public charities.

It is accordingly well settled by decisions of the highest authority, that when a gift is made to trustees for a charitable purpose, the general nature of which is pointed out, and which is lawful and valid at the time of the death of the testator, and no intention is expressed to limit it to a particular institution or mode of application, and afterwards, either by change of circumstances the scheme of the testator becomes impracticable, or by change of law becomes illegal, the fund, having once vested in the charity, does not go to the heirs at law as a resulting trust, but is to be applied by the court of chancery, in the exercise of its jurisdiction in equity, as near the testator's particular directions as possible, to carry out his general charitable intent. . . .

The intention of the testator is the guide, or, in the phrase of Lord

Coke, the lodestone, of the court; and therefore, whenever a charitable gift can be administered according to his express directions, this court, like the court of chancery in England, is not at liberty to modify it upon considerations of policy or convenience. But there are several cases, where the charitable trust could not be executed as directed in the will, in which the testator's scheme has been varied by this court in such a way and to such an extent as could not be done in the case of a private trust. Thus bequests to a particular bible society by name, whether a corporation established by law or a voluntary association, which had ceased to exist before the death of the testator, have been sustained, and applied to the distribution of bibles through a trustee appointed by the court for the purpose. . . .

In all the cases cited at the argument, in which a charitable bequest, which might have been lawfully carried out under the circumstances existing at the death of the testator, has been held, upon a change of circumstances, to result to the heirs at law or residuary legatees, the gift was distinctly limited to particular persons or establishments. . . .

The charitable bequests of Francis Jackson cannot, in the opinion of the court, be regarded as so restricted in their objects, or so limited in point of time, as to have been terminated and destroyed by the abolition of slavery in the United States. They are to a board of trustees for whose continuance careful provision is made in the will, and which the testator expresses a wish may become a permanent organization and may receive the services and sympathy, the donations and bequests, of the friends of the slave. Their duration is not in terms limited, like that of the trust sought to be established in the sixth article of the will, by the accomplishment of the end specified. They take effect from the time of the testator's death, and might then have been lawfully applied in exact conformity with his expressed intentions. The retaining of the funds in the custody of the court while this case has been under advisement cannot affect the question. The gifts being lawful and charitable, and having once vested, the subsequent change of circumstances before the funds have been actually paid over is of no more weight than if they had been paid to the trustees and been administered by them for a century before slavery was extinguished.

Neither the immediate purpose of the testator — the moral education of the people; nor his ultimate object — to better the condition of the African race in this country; has been fully accomplished by the abolition of slavery. . . .

Slavery may be abolished; but to strengthen and confirm the sentiment which opposed it will continue to be useful and desirable so long as selfishness, cruelty, and the lust of dominion, and indifference to the rights of the weak, the poor and the ignorant, have a place in the hearts of men. Looking at the trust established by the fourth article of this will as one for the moral education of the people only, the case is within the principle of those, already cited, in which charities for the relief of leprosy and the plague were held not to end with the disappearance of those diseases. . . .

The mode in which the funds bequeathed by the fourth and fifth articles of the will may be best applied to carry out in a lawful manner the charitable intents and purposes of the testator as nearly as possible must be settled by a scheme to be framed by a master and confirmed by the court before the funds are paid over to the trustees. In doing this, the court does not take the charity out of the hands of the trustees, but only declares the law which must be their guide in its administration. Shelford on Mortmain, 651-654, Boyle on Charities, 214-218. The case is therefore to be referred to a master, with liberty to the attorney general and the trustees to submit schemes for his approval; and all further directions are reserved until the coming in of his report.

FREME v. MAHER
480 A.2d 783 (Me. 1984)

[The will in question, executed two years before decedent's death, left her entire estate to "Ricker Classical Institute and Ricker College . . . to be . . . held by it in trust . . . , the net income only to be used for such general purposes of said Institution as the Board of Trustees of said Institution may determine." Several months after decedent's death in 1978, Ricker College was adjudicated bankrupt in a Chapter 11 proceeding initiated in 1974. Ricker's physical plant was subsequently closed. On the executor's petition for directions, the superior court ordered the matter to be heard by a referee. The college trustees urged that they be permitted to hold the bequest in trust for college scholarships for Maine students. The referee found a general charitable intent and recommended that the cy pres power be exercised to allocate the estate in equal shares to Bates, Bowdoin, and Colby Colleges. The superior court agreed with the recommendation except that it scheduled a hearing to determine the propriety of selecting those three colleges; but it refused to enlarge the scope of the hearing to include consideration of the Ricker proposal, noting that the decedent intended to support "a functional school."]

ROBERTS, J. . . .

In In re Estate of Thompson, 414 A.2d 881, 886 (Me. 1980), we listed three prerequisites for the application of the cy pres doctrine. First, the gift must create a valid charitable trust. Second, the specific purpose of the trust must be impossible or impracticable to carry out. Third, the settlor must have had a general charitable intent. On appeal, the trustees of Ricker contend that resort to cy pres was unnecessary because the second prerequisite was not met. . . .

In addressing the second prerequisite to the application of cy pres, therefore, we focus on two issues. Does Ricker College, as it exists in its present form, qualify as the beneficiary? If it does, can it still carry out the general charitable purpose for which the trust was intended? Cy pres is often applied when a testamentary charitable trust has been established in favor of a corporation or institution that ceases to exist by the time of the testator's death. . . . We note that Ricker was a functioning institution at the time of Mrs. Knox's death, and that a bequest speaks as of the time of the testatrix's death. See Pushor v. Hilton, 123 Me. 225, 227, 122 A. 673, 673 (1923). Moreover, while Ricker College is bankrupt, no longer maintains a physical campus, and has no faculty or students, its corporate existence continues. The trustees retain the power to receive, to hold, and to disburse assets. As discussed at oral argument, there is no evidence that Ricker's corporate existence will in any way change or be dissolved in the future. In addition, the Knox will does not suggest a clear attachment to Ricker, the college, as opposed to Ricker, the corporation. See State v. Rand, 366 A.2d 183, 196 (Me. 1976). Instead, the bequest was made "unto Ricker Classical Institute and Ricker College, a corporation organized and existing under the laws of the State of Maine and maintaining an educational institution at Houlton. . . . " The Ricker corporation possesses the legal capability of accepting the Knox bequest. We conclude, therefore, that the trust does not fail, and the doctrine of cy pres need not be applied, based upon any want of a qualified, existing beneficiary.

Nevertheless, at oral argument the counsel for Bates, Bowdoin and Colby Colleges argued that Ricker's continuing corporate existence was not necessarily determinative. Instead, they contend, the issue is whether Ricker, in its present form, is capable of carrying out the purpose of the bequest. We agree with that posture of the issue. We emphasize that the Knox will sought to establish a trust fund at Ricker the income from which would be used for "such general purposes of said Institution as the Board of Trustees of said Institution may determine." The language of the will is determinative.

We note that the testamentary language refers to the "general purposes of said Institution," having referred earlier to "Ricker Classical Institute and Ricker College, a *corporation* organized and existing under the laws of the State of Maine and maintaining an educational institution at Houlton. . . . " (emphasis added). The referee interpreted the will's language to mean "general (college) purposes." He assumed, therefore, that "the demise of Ricker College as a functional education institution . . . made it impossible to make the trust operative in its precise terms." We disagree. We consider instead the relevant general purposes of Ricker to be among those enunciated by the Legislature at various times through Ricker's history: "to promote the cause of education," P. & S.L. 1847, ch. 10; . . . and to furnish "the opportunity for a college education at modest cost to great numbers of deserving youths of Aroostook County." P. & S.L. 1955, ch. 42.

The trustees' proposal to use the trust income to provide scholarships to Aroostook area students is fully consistent with these general purposes. The referee erred in concluding that the trustees could not, without a functioning college, carry out the testatrix's intent. . . . A resort to cy pres would tend to defeat, rather than further, the general charitable intent expressed in the Knox will, . . . and application of the doctrine under the circumstances of this case was therefore error as a matter of law. . . .

Remanded to the Superior Court for further proceedings consistent with the opinion herein.

RESTATEMENT (SECOND) OF TRUSTS

§399. . . . If property is given in trust to be applied to a particular charitable purpose, and it is or becomes impossible or impracticable or illegal to carry out the particular purpose, and if the settlor manifested a more general intention to devote the property to charitable purposes, the trust will not fail but the court will direct the application of the property to some charitable purpose which falls within the general charitable intention of the settlor.

§400. . . . If property is given upon trust to be applied to a particular charitable purpose, and the purpose is fully accomplished without exhausting the trust property, and if the settlor manifested a more general intention to devote the whole of the trust property to charitable purposes, there will not be a resulting trust of the surplus, but the court will direct the application of the surplus to some charitable purpose which falls within the general charitable intention of the settlor.

According to generally accepted principles, cy pres may be exercised even though it is possible to carry out the particular trust specified by the settlor if the court finds that it would be "impracticable" to do so, in the sense that the settlor's intention would not be fulfilled by adhering to his specified purpose. As long as the purpose specified by the settlor is both legal and practicable, however, that purpose must be carried out even though the court recognizes that another purpose would be more useful. The line, of course, can be a difficult one to draw. Statutes in several states seemingly provide a more liberal standard for the exercise of cy pres. E.g., Minn. Stat. Ann. §501.12(3) (1977) ("impracticable, inexpedient, or impossible").

If a particular charitable purpose fails or the funds for its accomplishment are excessive, a provision in the trust instrument for disposition of the property or the surplus will be controlling. Typically no such provision is made because the situation was not contemplated by the settlor. Consequently it is frequently difficult to determine whether a resulting trust arises for the settlor, or for the settlor's next of kin or residuary legatees, or whether the doctrine of cy pres is applicable. It is generally said that this depends on whether the settlor had a "general charitable purpose." The mere fact that the terms of the trust provide for application of the funds to a particular charitable purpose and no other, or that the funds are given upon condition that they be applied to a specified purpose, is not controlling.

In re Scott's Will, 8 N.Y.2d 419, 171 N.E.2d 326 (1960), involved a remainder "to St. Thomas' Church in the City of New York, for the purpose of erecting and maintaining . . . buildings for the care of persons suffering from tuberculosis to be called the Scott Memorial Home." At the termination of the life estates the testamentary trustee petitioned for a determination of the effect of this provision. The parties to the proceeding, including the attorney general, agreed that modern methods of treating tuberculosis no longer require special hospitals and that at current costs the funds were inadequate to erect and maintain an appropriate building. The Surrogate, later affirmed by the Appellate Division, had directed a modification of the terms of the disposition to provide a Scott Memorial Fund to be used "for the care of persons suffering from respiratory and thoracic diseases." The church appealed on the ground that the funds should be applied to the purposes of the church. The court of appeals decided that the testator's intention is a matter of law where it is to be determined from the terms of the will and undisputed surrounding circumstances and that it could review the Surrogate's exercise of cy pres. The court of appeals found the Surrogate's exercise improper but declined to substitute its judgment for that of the court below, remanding for the Surrogate to exercise the power with appropriate respect for all three of the basic purposes of the testator: a memorial building in his name, to be erected by St. Thomas's Church, for the aid of tuberculosis patients. Three judges dissented on the ground that the discretion inherent in the exercise of cy pres had not been abused by the lower court.

BURR v. BROOKS
75 Ill. App. 3d 80, 393 N.E.2d 1091 (1979)

GREEN, J. . . .

The dispute arises because the will provides [both for a primary charitable trust and] for an alternate charitable trust, and literal compliance with either the primary or alternate charitable trust is not possible or practical.

The City [which is interested in the primary trust purpose] seeks to avoid [arguing] a cy pres theory by asserting that its proposals should have been accepted under the doctrine of "equitable deviation." As with cy pres this doctrine is applicable when literal compliance with the terms of the trust endowment is impractical, illegal or impossible. This power is distinguishable from cy pres in that the former is applicable to all trusts and can be applied where the settlor manifests a specific as well as a general charitable intent. (15 Am. Jur. 2d Charities §§157 and 164 (1976).) The two doctrines are further distinguished by the statement in comment (a) to Restatement (Second) of Trusts §381 (1959) that equitable deviation concerns the administration of the trust while cy pres permits the application of the trust proceeds to purposes other than those provided for in the trust instrument.

A general rule has developed that the cy pres doctrine cannot be applied where the settlor provides for an alternate use of the trust corpus if the primary purpose fails or is refused, but it is clear that "equitable deviation" is permissible even though such an alternate use has been stated. . . .

The proposals of the City here are more . . . than merely a matter of administration as described in the comment to §381 of the Restatement. . . .

Accordingly, we are required to consider the general rule that a cy pres application of charitable trust funds may not be made if there is an alternate charitable gift. . . . [I]n all cases cited by the parties, the alternate trust was capable of being performed literally. Under those circumstances, the general rule makes sense. . . . [But] logic requires a different interpretation of the rule when a trust instrument (1) provides for a primary and alternate charitable gift *neither* of which can be carried out, and (2) also indicates a strong desire that the charitable interest of the document be followed. . . .

[Accordingly, the requested cy pres modification of the primary trust purpose is granted.]

D. Supervision of Charitable Trusts

Although only the beneficiaries have the right to enforce a private trust, the indefiniteness of the beneficiaries of a typical charitable trust poses special problems. Suit to enforce a charitable trust is brought by or in the name of the attorney general, or, in a few states, by some local official such as the county attorney. This power of the attorney general exists even in the absence of a statute so providing.

The attorney general must typically be made a party to any action brought by another person or organization to enforce, construe, modify, or determine the validity of a charitable trust.

One who is entitled to a specific benefit, other than the general benefit of members of the community, may maintain a suit for enforcement of a charitable trust. A trustee may also enforce the trust against a cotrustee and may bring suit for instructions or to have the terms of the trust construed. A person who has no special interest in the performance of the trust — and this category includes the settlor or his representatives, according to the majority of decisions — cannot maintain a suit to enforce a charitable trust. Such a person can only hope to induce action by the attorney general.

Unfortunately, busy attorneys general and their staffs do not always satisfactorily discharge their general obligations concerning charitable trusts, nor do they always respond to legitimate pleas for action on the part of interested citizens. This presents practical difficulties of supervision of and performance by trustees and foundation boards. Nor have common law (and post-1950 federal tax law) restrictions on "unreasonable" accumulations proved adequate either in substantive content or enforcement. All of this has aggravated and reinforced other concerns of tax policy makers, among others, over the special privileges accorded charitable giving. It is already clear that much of the current concern has not been removed, even for tax purposes, by the Tax Reform Act of 1969. See discussion in section E, infra.

In the way just mentioned and others, the procedures for enforcing and supervising charitable trusts are often uncertain or inadequate. In a number of states patchwork or comprehensive legislation is being enacted to clarify procedures and improve enforcement of charitable trusts and corporations. For example, versions of the Uniform Supervision of Trustees for Charitable Purposes Act have recently been enacted in a number of states, with several of the larger states (California in 1959 and Illinois in 1961) leading the way. Cal. Govt. Code §§12580-12595; Ill. Rev. Stat. ch. 14, §§51-64. See also Mich. Comp. Laws Ann. §14.251; Or. Rev. Stat. §128.610. In order to give some indication of the general nature and content of these modern statutes, a brief description of New York's recent overhaul of charitable trust supervision legislation is provided in the excerpt below. Also, in recent years legislation has been enacted in some states to facilitate compliance with the requirements of Internal Revenue Code §508(e) added by the Tax Reform Act of 1969. (In general, these latter statutes provide for distribution of income annually and set out prohibitions against self-dealing, excess business holdings, and the making of certain investments and expenditures.)

At this point it is worthwhile at least to note the potentially serious risks facing clients (and lawyers, for that matter) who serve, often almost casually, as trustees or as members of boards of trustees or directors for charitable trusts, associations, foundations, and like institutions. Charitable entities — especially the smaller ones — are frequently operated, with the best of intentions, in an informal and excessively lax manner, with inadequate accounting procedures and inadequate attention to legal requirements and sound business practices. The absence of reliable public or private monitoring often makes it easy for part-time, civic-minded volunteers to participate unwittingly in breaches of trust. Essentially, the rules of fiduciary conduct and liability to be studied hereafter, primarily in the context of decedents' estates and private trusts, apply to uncompensated charitable trustees, whose outlook and behavior patterns often reflect little or no awareness of their obligations and risks.

GLASSER, TRUSTS, PERPETUITIES,
ACCUMULATIONS AND POWERS UNDER THE
ESTATES, POWERS AND TRUSTS LAW
33 Brooklyn L. Rev. 551, 562-563 (1967)

[N]ew legislation, which confers upon the attorney general broad supervisory powers over charities, has been incorporated into the EPTL as section 8-1.4. In broad outline, the new statute requires the attorney general to maintain a register of trustees containing such information as he deems appropriate. For the purpose of establishing and maintaining that register, the attorney general may conduct such investigations and examine such documents as he deems necessary. Every trustee is required to file with the attorney general the instrument from which he derives his title, powers and duties. The attorney general must be notified of any action or proceeding in which the disposition for charitable purposes may be affected. Trustees are required to file periodic written reports (for which filing fees are to be paid) disclosing the assets held and how they are administered. The failure of a trustee to register or file reports may justify his removal from office. The register, instruments and reports which are filed shall be available for public inspection, subject to stated exceptions. The attorney general may investigate the administration of such trusts and is given the power of subpoena and the power to administer oaths to facilitate any investigation he may make. He may also institute proceedings to secure compliance with the new law and to secure the proper administration of the trust.

A. SCOTT, TRUSTS, ABRIDGEMENT
(1960)

§348.1. *Charitable Corporations.* . . . Certainly many of the principles applicable to charitable trusts are applicable to charitable corporations. In both cases the Attorney General can maintain a suit to prevent a diversion of the property to other purposes than those for which it was given; and in both cases the doctrine of cy pres is applicable. . . .

It is not infrequently stated in the cases that a charitable corporation does not hold upon a charitable trust property conveyed or bequeathed to it. In fully as many cases, however, it is stated that a charitable corporation holds its property in trust. It is sometimes said that a charitable corporation holds property in trust if the property is to be used only for a particular charitable purpose or if only the income is to be used.

A charitable corporation certainly does not hold its property beneficially in the same sense in which an individual or noncharitable corporation can hold it beneficially, since in the case of a charitable corporation the Attorney General can maintain a suit to prevent a diversion of the property from the purposes for which it was given. Where property is conveyed to a charitable corporation, a provision restricting the use of the property to a particular purpose, or a provision that only the income of the property shall be used, is binding and enforceable at the suit of the Attorney General.

Where property is left by will to a charitable corporation, whether it may be used for the general purposes of the corporation or whether the devise or bequest is subject to restrictions as to its use, and the property is conveyed by the executor to the corporation, the corporation is not thereafter bound to account as if it were a testamentary trustee. The situation is quite different from that which arises where property is left by will to individual trustees, or to a trust company, charged with a duty to make the property productive and to pay the income to a charitable corporation.

E.   *Observations on the Role and Regulation of Foundations and Other Charities*

STONE, FEDERAL TAX SUPPORT OF CHARITIES AND OTHER EXEMPT ORGANIZATIONS: THE NEED FOR A NATIONAL POLICY
20 U. So. Cal. 1968 Tax Inst. 27-34

Few matters of federal income taxation have been the subject of such extensive discussion in the last two decades as the treatment of charities and other exempt organizations and the closely related problems of deductions for charitable contributions. The debate has included congressional hearings, Treasury Department studies and reports, extensive statistical compilations and analyses, scores of articles, symposia and books, and significant legislation and court decisions. . . . In England,

Canada and other countries, similar debate, proposals and some changes in public policy have also occurred. . . .

The steady growth of indirect government [tax] support to charities, . . . now about $5 billion annually at the federal level alone (enough to provide an across-the-board 10% reduction of all individual income taxes at 1965 levels), has undoubtedly led to increasing concern about whether all of such revenue loss is justifiable. This concern is buttressed by an increasing emphasis upon the need for analyzing the costs and benefits of alternative government expenditure programs. . . . The pressure of high tax rates since World War II has led to what many consider abuses of the tax benefits which in turn have adverse side effects on tax administration, tax morality and tax equity. The magnitude and nature of the tax benefits also give rise to concern over some competition by the tax-exempt sector with private enterprise, possible improper allocation of resources in our society and long-run erosion of the tax base. The increasing anxiety over church-state issues has also become a reason for questioning the more than 50% portion of the $5 billion that is attributable to the tax benefits granted churches and their donors. . . .

Few basic issues have been resolved or put to rest. A simple, but hopefully provocative, explanation is the absence of any real national policy in this area. . . . Perhaps our ad hoc approach has resulted in the correct national policy. Perhaps we can, in an area fraught with as many intangibles and sensitive issues, expect nothing more than a series of compromises and patch-quilt policy. But unless we make a comprehensive overall assessment we shall not know and shall not put the questions to rest.

[In the remainder of the article, the author, who served as the Tax Legislative Counsel of the Treasury Department during preparation of the 1965 report infra, which led to the 1969 act, discusses the principal issues and sets out an outline for a long-range policy study.]

ROSS, LET'S NOT FENCE IN THE FOUNDATIONS
Fortune 148, 166-172 (June 1969)

One of the great virtues of foundations is the broad charter now permitted them in law. Their freedom is essential to their leavening role in society. They must be free to pioneer, to aid projects that lack majority support, indeed to aid unpopular causes. Without such freedom there would be little point in maintaining private philanthropy. . . .

The foundations' increasing involvement in the domestic arena underscores a simple fact that was less apparent in the past: to be effective a foundation must make choices, take sides, support causes. In such matters as population control, civil rights, and school decentralization, a foundation takes sides by merely funding a project. To be above the battle is to be irrelevant; to be relevant is to risk controversy. . . .

This plea for freedom embraces only the program area of foundations. But when it comes to the financial operations of foundations, there is a compelling case for tighter government regulations. In this area many abuses have occurred, particularly on the part of small foundations. The more blatant abuses can be reached by present law. . . .

In general, however, the Internal Revenue Code has been too permissive. It does not deal, for example, with the conflict between public and private interest that arises when a foundation is used to preserve control of a corporation. . . . When a foundation is used in this way, its public obligations do not necessarily get slighted. [Example omitted.] Philanthropy does get shortchanged, however, when the corporate stock that a foundation holds for control purposes produces meager income. . . .

The Treasury advocates abolishing all self-dealing. It also recommends that mandatory civil penalties be imposed on foundation personnel who violate any of the proposed new rules, and that the federal courts be given the authority to ensure that foundation assets are used for charitable purposes. Among other things, the courts could fine or remove trustees, rescind transactions, and divest assets. Up to now, the states alone have had this power, and only a dozen states have enforcement programs.

U.S. TREASURY DEPARTMENT, REPORT ON PRIVATE FOUNDATIONS
1, 5 (1965)

Since the Federal tax laws encourage and, in substantial measure, finance private charity, it is proper — indeed, it is imperative — for Congress and the Treasury Department periodically to reexamine the character of these laws and their impact upon the persons to which they apply to insure that they do, in fact, promote the values associated with philanthropy and that they do not afford scope for abuse or unwarranted private advantage. . . .

Private philanthropy plays a special and vital role in our society. Beyond providing for areas into which government cannot or should not advance (such as religion), private philanthropic organizations can be uniquely qualified to initiate thought and action, experiment with new and untried ventures, dissent from prevailing attitudes, and act quickly and flexibly.

Private foundations have an important part in this work. Available even to those of relatively restricted means, they enable individuals or small groups to establish new charitable endeavors and to express their own bents, concerns, and experience. In doing so, they enrich the pluralism of our social order. Equally important, because their funds are frequently free of commitment to specific operating programs, they can shift the focus of their interest and their financial support from one charitable area to another. They can, hence, constitute a powerful instrument for evolution, growth, and improvement in the shape and direction of charity.

Three broad criticisms have been directed at private foundations. It has been contended that the interposition of the foundation between the donor and active charitable pursuits entails undue delay in the transmission of the benefits which society should derive from charitable contributions; that foundations are becoming a disproportionately large segment of our national economy; and that foundations represent dangerous concentrations of economic and social power. Upon the basis of these contentions, some persons have argued that a time limit should be imposed on the lives of all foundations. Analysis of these criticisms, however, demonstrates that the first appears to be susceptible of solution by a measure of specific design and limited scope, the second lacks factual basis, and the third is, for the present, being amply met by foundations themselves. As a consequence, the Treasury Department has concluded that prompt and effective action to end the specific abuses extant among foundations is preferable to a general limitation upon foundation lives.

[Preceding the proposals, a description of major specific problems lists self-dealing; delay in benefiting charity, including accumulation of income and low-yield, growth investments; foundation involvement in business, family control, and unrelated transactions; and need for broadened management.]

CALKINS, THE ROLE OF THE PHILANTHROPIC FOUNDATION
11 Found. News 1-13 (1970)[5]

The philanthropic foundation during this century has been an important innovative force in the life of this country and throughout much of the free world. I propose to review its role in a rapidly changing society. It began with the efforts of a few wealthy men, who sought to leave their fortunes in competent hands to be administered for the public good. It has become a vastly expanded and diversified enterprise with resources undreamed of even a generation ago.

Meanwhile, the growing role of government has altered the setting in

5. Paper delivered in mid-1969, before the Tax Reform Act of 1969 was enacted.

which the private foundations operate. . . . My purpose is to clarify the role of foundations in American life and to reappraise that role in light of the new environment and threatened restraints by public authorities.

[The early history of philanthropy began] as an "expression of family sympathy" beyond the family, to members of the tribe and community. . . . The practice of charity toward the poor and suffering was early embraced by the Hebrews and others in tithing, and by the Greeks and Romans, who expanded the concept of charity from merciful giving to include the enrichment of life of those in the community. . . .

With the rise of Christianity, charity was encouraged as a duty. . . . In England [controversies between the church and political authorities] became long and bloody under the Norman kings after 1066. There in the 12th century one-third to one-half of the public wealth of the country was under ecclesiastical control. . . . The confiscation of church properties by Henry VIII and Edward VI finally broke the influence of the church. The Statute of Charitable Uses approved in 1601, in the reign of Elizabeth, became a landmark in the secular control of charitable funds. . . .

To these shores the English settlers brought religiously inspired moral convictions of their charitable duties and the doctrines of the Christian stewardship of wealth. . . . Not until after the Civil War did the independent foundation in its modern form arise. . . . By 1967, according to the latest Foundation Directory, there were about 18,000 active foundations, of which 6,803 [held] assets of almost $20 billion. . . . The proportion of Gross National Product going to benevolences has persisted over the years at about 2 percent. . . .

The foundations which have had the greatest impact on American life are the large general and special purpose foundations which make over 60 percent of the grants. . . . Their object is not charity, or the alleviation of distress by palliatives, but the correction of evils through discovery, knowledge, and innovations, through which important correctives may be achieved. They are not operated to maintain existing institutions, or to finance what others will finance, but to pioneer. . . . Thus their search is ceaseless for those who with financial help may achieve objectives of wide import and impact. . . .

While the evidence is too fragmentary to be conclusive, [the growth of foundations] appears not exceptional as compared to the growth of GNP or the growth of individual incomes and wealth. Though tax exemption has doubtless promoted charitable and philanthropic contributions, as the law intended, the results have not been exceptional, save perhaps in the number of foundations established — mainly small family foundations.

Among the most notable changes confronting foundations during the past three decades have been those created by government. The most important has been the expansion of federal support for education, research, and the arts, often for activities formerly pioneered by private foundations. The second has been rising taxes, which make tax exemption appear more and more as a special privilege rather than as a national policy to encourage private philanthropy in the public interest. The third is the growing surveillance of foundation activities by the Congress and the Internal Revenue Service. . . .

Even the $200-300 million budget of the Ford Foundation is dwarfed by the large and expanding effort of the federal government. This federal aid is not so much a competitor of foundation philanthropy as a welcome supplement to it. . . . The National Science Foundation, with a budget of nearly $500 million, and the National Foundation for the Arts and Humanities, which still receives only token support, operate most nearly like private foundations, and yet they lack the flexibility, promptness, and innovative freedom of the major private foundations. They leave untouched large areas for private philanthropic effort. The diverse federal programs permit, and indeed impose, an obligation on the private foundations to abandon traditional programs and to look for new opportunities. The safe, easy, and non-controversial support of medical research, health and welfare activities, fellowships, and the major universities is no longer sufficiently discriminating to be pioneering. But highly informed, perceptive, and strategic efforts in these and new areas will assure a continuing role for the foundations that seek the opportunities ahead rather than the safe ruts suggested by past experience.

The early foundations were established before the income tax of 1913 and the estate tax of 1916. [Charity and philanthropy] have been so much a part of the American philosophy that their encouragement through tax exemption has until recently been rarely an issue. . . . But under current tax rates, and more especially with the disclosure that numbers of persons with high incomes pay little or no federal taxes because of loopholes and charitable contributions, there has arisen a Congressional and public clamor to "make them pay." This, combined with the disclosure of abuses by a few foundations, could prompt hasty, restrictive legislation without proper consideration of its consequences. Although there have been abuses that should be outlawed, the means to the end are varied and deserving of more detailed analysis than has yet been made, or made public. . . .

The third environmental change instigated by government has been the closer surveillance of foundations by the Internal Revenue Service and the Congress. Three investigations of foundations have been conducted by Congressional committees since 1952. . . . The common motivation leading to the recent Congressional inquiries has been a suspected abuse of the power and independence of at least some foundations.

The first [two inquiries] sought to determine whether foundations were using their resources for purposes other than those for which they were established, and especially whether they were using them "for Un-American and subversive activities or for purposes not in the interest or tradition of the United States" . . . or "for political purposes, propaganda, or attempts to influence legislation." . . .

The Patman Committee. The third inquiry was begun by Representative Wright Patman in 1961 as chairman of the House Select Committee on Small Business. This has been essentially a one-man inquiry. . . . The investigations have been conducted by "staff" and are submitted as "reports" by the Chairman to the Committee. . . . [C]areless or politically motivated staff work has all but discredited many of the Chairman's findings. However, the sensational charges have made large headlines for avid readers.

Notwithstanding the defects in these reports, it must be said that Chairman Patman has contributed towards the improvement of reporting rules and practices, and he has called attention to the abuses of several foundations which deserve to be corrected. But his suggested remedies have often been drastic. . . . Some of the proposals if adopted would severely discourage the establishment of new foundations, and a limited life of 25 years would in a generation remove all currently existing foundations. One may argue that to disburse their capital assets to other nonprofit organizations, such as universities, research institutions, welfare organizations, and churches, would enrich the programs foundations now support. But it would at the same time dry up the central springs of innovative influence. Operating organizations quickly commit operating revenues to on-going programs, and usually look outside for innovative support and challenge funds for new ventures. The destruction of the present foundation system would accordingly be a major blow to innovation in our society.

Treasury Report. Prompted by Patman's complaints against the Internal Revenue Service for lax surveillance of foundations, the Treasury undertook its own study and issued its own report in 1965. The Treasury Report on Private Foundations is moderate in its proposed reforms. It suggests a prohibition of business dealings between a donor and his foundation; a limit on a foundation's ownership of voting stock to 20 percent in any one corporation; restrictions on the tax deductibility of gifts to a foundation when the donor retains control of the property; and limiting after 25 years the membership of the donor and relatives on the governing body of the foundation. These and other proposals would curb the major abuses that have been discovered and would prevent the use of foundations for control over business. . . .

In the Congressional haste . . . there is danger that the role of foundations in advancing the public good may be overlooked. It is well, therefore, to remind ourselves of some of the many achievements foundations have helped to bring about. . . .

I may summarize foundation accomplishments . . . in these words:

foundations have pioneered and assisted pioneers, scientists, scholars, and innovators; they have helped to create and strengthen colleges, universities, research laboratories, research institutions, scientific and scholarly organizations, welfare and religious institutions; they have often anticipated social and international problems and mobilized knowledge for dealing with them. In doing these things, they have freed large parts of the world from the curse of diseases, such as malaria and yellow fever; have advanced the art of medical care and the treatment of illness; have provided knowledge for the control of population and the expansion of food supplies; have aided the development of emerging nations; have encouraged educational opportunities for minority groups, and the establishment of area and language studies to afford a better understanding of other cultures. They have demonstrated the value of liberal support for basic research and encouraged large public support; have contributed importantly to our growing knowledge of physical and living nature, and of social organization; have made possible the development of new scientific instruments for studying the atom, the cell, the star, and the nature of life itself; have contributed toward a better understanding of social behavior and informed social policy; have helped to clarify the goal of humanistic scholarship, aided the arts, and broadened the cultural interests and enjoyments of millions of people. They have also supported the development of thousands of scientists, scholars, creative writers, artists, and professional personnel, as well as leaders for business, government, and education. They have encouraged informed approaches to domestic problems, promoted international understanding, and assisted in the search for peace. They have contributed to the international community of scholarship and learning, and built bridges of communication and mutual respect.

They have admittedly made some mistakes and encountered some failures along with their many successes. Some ventures have failed, some opportunities have been overlooked, some have not been supported long enough for fruition. Some have aroused public criticism with or without warrant. But the extent of these miscalculations, by any fair appraisal, is small to insignificant compared with the thousands upon thousands of grants that have been made successfully for the good of society. . . . Even if [the $20 billion of foundations'] tax-exempt resources had been taxable, only a modest fraction would have gone into public coffers as tax revenues. No refined analysis of social costs and social benefits is required to reach the conclusion that the national policy of granting tax exemption to foundations has paid off handsomely.

One of the greatest virtues of the American foundation system is that it reinforces and contributes to our pluralistic society. . . . To curb the creation of new foundations and to impose life terms on all would in time place innovation and innovators largely at the mercy of governmental financing. That the welfare of this country and mankind would be better served in this way I leave to your judgment. My own view is that it would not.

GOHEEN, LET'S REMOVE FOUNDATIONS FROM SECOND-CLASS PHILANTHROPIC CITIZENSHIP
L.A. Times, July 24, 1973

. . . During the late 1960's, the public — through its elected representatives in the Congress — took a hard look at American foundations, and it found that too often they were wanting. In some cases, the privilege of tax exemption had been perverted into advantageous business arrangements, friends and relatives had benefited at the public's expense, and assets had been hoarded with subminimal returns to charity. Some indiscreet intrusions into the political process further clouded the reputation of foundations generally.

The upshot was the Tax Reform Act of 1969, which gave the private foundations a heavy working over and closed off the kinds of abuse and misfeasance that existed. No responsible person can quarrel with the main thrust of this legislation or deny that it is working in salutary ways to insure that foundations will be held accountable for the philanthropic mandate vested in them both by the fact of their tax exemption and their claims to be charitably intended.

Yet, if the public's hard look at foundations in 1969 has had these positive results, it also was in certain ways more punitive than remedial. A number of provisions of the act treat foundations like "least-favored charities" and portend a progressive weakening of their collective capability to respond to the sorts of educational, cultural and social service needs that now press so insistently upon them.

Most notable of these punitive provisions are the following:

- The extraordinary tax placed on the net investment income of foundations.
- The special restrictions on gifts of appreciated securities to foundations.
- The lower limit of deductibility on gifts to foundations.
- A high level of required annual pay-out (which does not become fully effective until 1975).

The sure consequence of these combined "disincentives" is a gradual diminishment in the capacity of foundations to sustain the support which the country's various educational, medical, cultural and other charitable services have drawn from them.

It is, I submit, time to look again at the significance and the potential of our grant-making foundations.

The human needs with which they are concerned — and whose insistent pressures today flood their phones, their mail and their offices — are not likely to diminish in the near future.

Assistance for needy students, improved health care, the alleviation of poverty and hunger at home and abroad, environmental protection, scientific discovery, the search for better intercultural communication and understanding — these and other traditional objectives of private philanthropy will be pressing problems for years to come, if not forever.

In years past, foundations have compiled a telling record of useful contributions in all these areas. Are we to believe that at least comparable contributions will not be needed from them in the future? Can government do it all? — indeed, should it?

The people say "No." A survey by the Gallup organization shows that 70% of the public thinks that foundations and government should work to solve the same problems, and nearly 75% thinks present tax incentives to charitable giving should be maintained — or increased.

The task of regulating foundations to foreclose abuses and misfeasance was well accomplished in the 1969 act. The reform beyond that reform — the one now needed — would embody a positive view toward the humanitarian character and the creative potential of organized philanthropy. It would encourage, not discourage, those who would commit their personal wealth to achieving benefits for others, and it will do so with respect to estates and lifetime giving alike. . . .

Also, see generally American Assembly: The Future of Foundations (F. Heimann ed. 1973).

15

Introduction to Fiduciary Administration

During the administration of a decedent's estate or trust, the drafting skill of the estate planner is put to its most stringent test, for this is the period in which most of the provisions must be put into effect. In the case of a will, this is when the validity of the instrument is determined, and then its directions must be carried out while coping with administrative requirements. In the case of a trust, over the period of administration the trustee will encounter a number of specific problems, some inherently troublesome and others arising out of changed circumstances that can be anticipated only in a general way.

Even though the general purposes of estate and trust administration differ, there are so many common aspects of the fiduciary relationships that treating them together is desirable for purposes of comparison and contrast. As you begin now to study these matters you should review, quickly at least, that portion of Chapter 1, sections E3 and E4, that tells the story of an estate and trust administration. This should help place the portions of the course ahead into context; section E3 should be particularly helpful as background for your necessarily piecemeal study of the administration of decedent's estates.

A. *Function and Necessity of Administration*

In the estate of any decedent, intestate as well as testate, it is necessary to go through a liquidation process, that is, winding up the property and business affairs of the deceased. This process, whether formal or informal, is essentially one of collecting and conserving the assets of the deceased, paying from the assets all debts and charges thereon, and making the distribution that is proper. More specifically, formal estate administration involves publicizing the fact of the decedent's death; discovering and collecting assets; determining and paying the taxes, debts, and funeral expenses of the decedent, and the administration expenses of the estate; determining and making distribution to persons entitled to receive the property under the decedent's will or by operation of law; and, throughout this process, managing estate assets.

Many problems similar to those of decedent's estates arise in administering trust estates, but the basic purpose differs. Rather than being a liquidating process, the general purpose of trust administration is securing efficient management of assets to provide continuing benefit to the family. In a testamentary trust, administration of the trust begins with distribution to the trustee, generally after the full cycle of estate administration has been completed.

Because of the differences of function, the possible liability of a fiduciary who is named to serve both as executor and as trustee may depend on whether certain acts were performed in the former or the latter capacity. For example, if the fiduciary, without negligence, invests funds of the estate and a loss is incurred, liability may depend on whether there was authority to invest at all at the time. The capacity in which the fiduciary acted may be decisive, since a trustee's function is to make the estate productive by investment while an executor generally has no inherent power to invest. Assuming the power to invest is not expressly conferred on an executor by will or by statute, the fiduciary must prove (1) that the investment was made in the capacity of trustee, which normally must be preceded by some overt act such as the settling of accounts as executor in the probate court, or (2) that the power to invest is implied from the dual capacity or from other facts, such as that the estate will remain open for a considerable period of time. For an interesting case involving questions of these types, see Estate of Beach, 15 Cal. 3d 623, 542 P.2d 994 (1975).

Model Probate Code §133, which influenced the legislation in many states during the 1950s and 1960s, authorized the personal representative to make investments of the kind permitted to trustees, subject to "his primary duty to preserve the estate for prompt distribution." See also Uniform Probate Code §§3-711 and 3-715(5).

AN OUTLINE OF TYPICAL STEPS IN THE
SETTLEMENT OF ESTATES

Preliminary Steps

Meet with family.

Review funeral arrangements and obtain proof of death.

Obtain and review will or ascertain fact of intestacy.

Ascertain and safeguard assets, notify banks, review books and records, and inquire into insurance and business interests.

Meet with others than family members who are interested in the estate, confer with persons familiar with decedent's legal and financial affairs (such as the attorney who drew the will), and locate witnesses to will.

Open Estate Administration

Probate will, if any, and obtain letters testamentary or of administration.

Issue Notice to Creditors.

Collect and Inventory Estate Assets

Obtain transfer of bank accounts, store or protect personal effects and furnishings, and obtain custody of securities.

Collect income, debts, and any insurance payable to estate.

Ascertain out-of-state assets (and the possible need for ancillary administration) and interests in trusts or other estates.

Inspect real estate (check mortgages, taxes) and look into leases and business ventures (collection of rents, arrange management, supervision, and representation in these activities).

Determine asset values, and obtain appraisals.

Prepare and file inventory of estate assets (note distinctions between assets to be accounted for and nonprobate assets or will substitutes for tax returns).

Claims and Taxes

Receive, analyze, and allow or disallow claims, to be paid in order of priority.

Obtain information about and file tax returns (decedent's final and estate's fiduciary income tax returns, federal and state death tax returns, and, if applicable, final year's or even overdue gift tax returns); pay taxes in a timely manner; obtain releases or waivers; and handle audits and possible assessments or tax controversies.

Management of Estate Assets

Determine liquidity requirements (debts, family allowance, administration expenses, taxes, and legacies).

Analyze, safeguard, and manage investments, including securities (sale or retention in light of authority and responsibilities under will or local law and market necessities/opportunities), real estate (sale or supervision), and business interests (liquidation, sale or retention, and supervision in light of fiduciary authority and duties).

Fund cash needs through sales or otherwise (including possible borrowing from or sales to recipients of insurance proceeds, especially life insurance trusts).

Accounting and Distribution

Determine rights and needs of beneficiaries.

Prepare and submit accountings (receipts, disbursements, principal/ income allocations), interim and final, in or out of court, as appropriate.

Determine the need or desirability, and the nature and timing, of allowance payments and possible preliminary distributions (including their tax effects and whether they should be in cash or in kind) with respect to bequests and devises, including residuary and trust interests; make distributions during administration accordingly.

Plan and make final distributions; obtain receipts and releases.

In section C of Chapter 9 we considered some of the important reasons for having property administered under a trust. The materials that follow are concerned with some of the quite different reasons for having a decedent's estate formally administered.

Creditors. The law relating to the administration of decedent's estates has always reflected a strong policy to protect creditors of the decedent who have usually contributed, indirectly at least, to the assets of the estate. Although this policy that a decedent should be just before being generous gives creditors priority over gratuitous distributees, it does conflict with those policies calling for protection of the family and for prompt, secure distribution of assets to those next entitled. The resolution of these policy conflicts are reflected in nonclaim statutes, as well as in those (see Chapter 3, supra) providing homestead rights and family allowances.

UNIFORM PROBATE CODE

§3-801. *[Notice to Creditors.]*

(a) Unless notice has already been given under this section, a personal representative upon appointment [may] [shall] publish a notice to creditors once a week for three successive weeks in a newspaper of general circulation in the [county] announcing the appointment and the personal representative's address and notifying creditors of the estate to present their claims within four months after the date of the first publication of the notice or be forever barred.

(b) A personal representative may give written notice by mail or other delivery to a creditor, notifying the creditor to present his [or her] claim within four months after the published notice, if given as provided in subsection (a), or within 60 days after the mailing or other delivery of the notice, whichever is later, or be forever barred. Written notice must be the notice described in subsection (a) above or a similar notice.

(c) The personal representative is not liable to a creditor or to a successor of the decedent for giving or failing to give notice under this section.

§3-802. *[Statutes of Limitations.]*

(a) Unless an estate is insolvent, the personal representative, with the consent of all successors whose interests would be affected, may waive any defense of limitations available to the estate. If the defense is not waived, no claim barred by a statute of limitations at the time of the decedent's death may be allowed or paid.

(b) The running of a statute of limitations measured from an event other than death or the giving of notice to creditors is suspended for four months after the decedent's death, but resumes thereafter as to claims not barred by other sections.

(c) For purposes of a statute of limitations, the presentation of a claim pursuant to Section 3-804 is equivalent to commencement of a proceeding on the claim.

§3-803. *[Limitations on Presentation of Claims.]*

(a) All claims against a decedent's estate which arose before the death of the decedent, including claims of the state and any subdivision thereof, whether due or to become due, absolute or contingent, liquidated or unliquidated, founded on contract, tort, or other legal basis, if not barred earlier by another statute of limitations or non-claim statute, are barred against the estate, the personal representative, and the heirs and devisees of the decedent, unless presented within the earlier of the following:

(1) one year after the decedent's death; or

(2) the time provided by Section 3-801(b) for creditors who are given actual notice, and within the time provided in 3-801(a) for all creditors barred by publication.

(b) A claim described in subsection (a) which is barred by the non-claim statute of the decedent's domicile before the giving of notice to creditors in this State is barred in this State.

(c) All claims against a decedent's estate which arise at or after the death of the decedent, including claims of the state and any subdivision thereof, whether due or to become due, absolute or contingent, liquidated or unliquidated, founded on contract, tort, or other legal basis, are barred against the estate, the personal representative, and the heirs and devisees of the decedent, unless presented as follows:

(1) a claim based on a contract with the personal representative, within four months after performance by the personal representative is due; or

(2) any other claim, within the later of four months after it arises, or the time specified in subsection (a)(1).

(d) Nothing in this section affects or prevents:

(1) any proceeding to enforce any mortgage, pledge, or other lien upon property of the estate;

(2) to the limits of the insurance protection only, any proceeding to establish liability of the decedent or the personal representative for which he is protected by liability insurance; or

(3) collection of compensation for services rendered and reimbursement for expenses advanced by the personal representative or by the attorney or accountant for the personal representative of the estate.

Many nonclaim statutes do not apply, as the above does, to claims of the state and its subdivisions or to claims arising at or after death. Subsequent sections spell out the methods of presenting (including by commencing an action within the claim period), allowing, paying, and compromising claims. Section 3-810 provides that unmatured, contingent, and unliquidated claims may be paid at their present (discounted) or other agreed value, or that provision for future payment may be made by retention of funds in trust or by the distributees' limited liability secured by lien or bond.

Section 3-805 specifies priorities among claimants of insolvent estates, giving the usual preferences to the expenses of administration, followed in order by funeral expenses, debts, and taxes preferred under federal law, last illness expenses, and then debts and taxes preferred under state laws.

Many statutes contain provisions allowing claimants who receive no notice "by reason of being out of the state" to present claims after the claim period but "before a decree distribution is entered." Some offer other special and limited exceptions to the bar of the statute. See application of a statute exempting claims covered by liability insurance in Collier v. Connolley, 400 A.2d 1107 (Md. 1979), and application of a fairly broad statute allowing late filing without culpable neglect (while protecting recipients of prior distributions) in Hastoupis v. Gargas, 398 N.E.2d 745 (Mass. App. 1980).

Do due process requirements concerning the necessity and quality of notice apply to nonclaim statutes? See materials beginning with *Mullane* case infra.

PROBLEM

15-A. *H* and his wife, *W*, executed mutual wills pursuant to a contract not to revoke. Under the wills and the agreement the property of the first of them to die was to pass to the survivor, and the survivor was to leave an estate as follows: one half was to go to *H*'s child, *C*, by a former marriage; the other one-half was to be divided between *S* and *D*, *W*'s two children by a prior marriage. *H* died leaving his estate to *W* as agreed. *H*'s net estate of $110,000 consisted of $50,000 cash in banks and a $60,000 parcel of real estate. On *W*'s later death eleven months ago her entire estate was left to *S* and *D* by the terms of a subsequent will. *W*'s estate is now about to be distributed. Inventoried in *W*'s net estate of $200,000 are the parcel of land she received from *H* and $10,000 in one of the bank accounts *H* had at death. Also in *W*'s estate were $70,000 in securities, a $20,000 piece of real estate, $10,000 worth of chattels, and $20,000 on deposit in another bank. *C* has not filed a claim in *W*'s estate and the statutory nonclaim period has expired. Can *C* now enforce his claim to half of the estate? How would you advise him to proceed and how would you argue his case? What arguments do you anticipate would be made in behalf of *S* and *D*? Compare O'Connor v. Immele, 77 N.D. 346, 43 N.W.2d 649 (1950), with Abrams v. Schlar, 27 Ill. App. 2d 237, 169 N.E.2d 583 (1960).

Vanderpool v. Vanderpool, 48 Mont. 448, 453-455, 138 P. 772, 774 (1914), states:

> [T]he trial court proceeded upon the theory that if plaintiff was led into error in filing her claim, by the attorney for the estate, the estate itself is estopped to deny that the claim was presented as required by law. . . . The executor or administrator is in effect a trustee of the funds of the estate for the benefit of the creditors and heirs, and cannot waive any substantial right which materially affects their interest, and, for the same reason, cannot be estopped by his own conduct. He cannot, by failure to plead the statute of nonclaim . . . , preclude the heirs or other creditors of the estate from setting it up upon settlement of his accounts, and he renders himself personally liable for devastavit in case of payment of such a claim. While an equitable estoppel might be invoked as against an executor or administrator so far as his individual interest in the estate is concerned, it cannot operate to the prejudice of the heirs or other creditors. Even his misleading statements, his assurances or his conduct which induces a creditor to omit compliance with the statute, will not operate to estop him from contesting the claim upon the ground of noncompliance. The reason for these rules ought to be manifest at once, and with reference to them there is substantial unanimity of opinion among the authorities. . . .
>
> If [the claimant] has any cause of action which she can now assert, it must be one against Mr. Burleigh and not against this estate.

Thompson v. Owen, 249 Mass. 229, 144 N.E. 216 (1914), involved an action on a note that matured after the decedent's death. The executor gave notice of his appointment by posting and by publication in the local newspaper. After the executor's final accounting, the plaintiffs made application to the probate court to have the accounting reopened and to have assets retained to pay their claim, which had not been presented within the statutory period. Plaintiffs alleged that they had no knowledge of the debtor's death. The court stated:

> This . . . is not a claim which "could not legally be presented to the Probate Court." Presentation of such claims at "any time before the estate is fully administered" is specifically provided for. . . . [A]s they neglected to do so, it follows that they cannot maintain a bill against the heirs, next of kin, devisees or legatees of the testator. Before the estate was fully administered they could have been given the relief afforded by §10 of the same chapter, if justice and equity so required. . . .
>
> It is strenuously urged by the plaintiffs that they are entitled to maintain the bill because they did not learn of the death of the decedent or of the appointment of the executor until after the estate had been fully administered; but there is no allegation that such want of information was due to any fraud or deception practised upon them. There is nothing in the statutes under which the bill is brought which gives the plaintiffs a remedy because of their failure seasonably to learn of the death of the decedent, or because they did not seasonably know of the taking out of administration.

249 Mass. at 233-234, 144 N.E. at 217-218.

Compare Estate of Pfaff, 41 Wis. 2d 159, 163 N.W.2d 140 (1968), that an often routine will direction to pay "my just debts" required payment of just debts whether or not they were otherwise legally enforceable.

PROBLEM

15-B.   A friend and regular client of mine has just telephoned my secretary and has made an appointment to see me late this afternoon. Her mother, a widow, recently died. My client and her brother are the only children, and they are to receive everything under the will, which has not been probated. They would like to avoid probate proceedings and have worked out how they will divide the property, essentially equally as their mother's will provides.

My secretary's note says that my client stated: "Probate was a pointless nuisance, and a waste, when Dad died a few years ago." She also said that the estate was surely more than adequate to cover all her mother's debts and concluded:

> Even though I suppose I'll be told it's always possible we could be wrong, we have discussed the matter and will gladly take that risk. There's no one who might possibly question our right to the estate, and anyway we're pre-

pared to run any risks of that sort as well. So, I'd like to know if there are any really good reasons for going through administration again.

We will no doubt be able to take care of tax returns without formal probate. Under these circumstances, are there any reasons why I should advise my client to go through formal proceedings? If so, what are they? In order to reach an informed judgment, what more will I need to know about the estate or other matters, and why? Consider the cases and notes in the rest of this section.

HEINZ v. VAWTER

221 Iowa 714, 266 N.W. 486 (1936)

[Millie Vawter died intestate and without issue in 1930, survived only by her husband, H. M. Vawter, and her father, Edward Heinz. No administration was had on her estate of about $11,300. Her husband took possession of her entire estate, paid all of her known debts and burial expenses aggregating about $1,900, and paid her father $2,000, for which Heinz signed a receipt "in full settlement of my distributive share as heir at law." Vawter retained the residue in satisfaction of his statutory rights. About four years later Heinz petitioned and was appointed to serve as administrator of his daughter's estate and brought suit against H. M. Vawter for the sum of $11,300 that it might be administered on. He alleges no fraud or overreaching.]

ANDERSON, J. . . .

[I]n the face of the facts as disclosed by the record in this case, there was no good reason for the appointment of an administrator. Under the statute the husband was entitled to $7,500.00 of the estate of his deceased wife. . . . [In paying his wife's debts and] making the payment to the father of $2,000 the husband used $114.57 of his own share of the estate, and the record further shows that some of the property of the deceased wife was turned over to the sisters of the deceased, to wit, a diamond ring and a fur coat; and a shotgun was turned over to the father, Edward Heinz; and that the father knew of the distribution, was present when it was made, and agreed and acquiesced therein. It appears conclusively by the record that at the time the father petitioned for his appointment as administrator of the estate of his daughter there was nothing to administer. All debts and expenses had been paid, and the entire estate disbursed and distributed. There was no expense whatever incident to the settlement of the estate by the husband. The father, having acknowledged the receipt in full of his distributive share in the estate, had no further interests therein. . . .

Where there are no debts and the property of an estate is such that it can be divided and the persons entitled thereto agree upon a division thereof, there is nothing either in law or reason to prevent them from settling and distributing the estate without the appointment of an administrator. . . .

Affirmed.

BROBST v. BROBST

190 Mich. 63, 155 N.W. 734 (1916)

[Action on a promissory note executed by the defendant payable to Almanda Adams, who died intestate in 1913. Plaintiff is a daughter of Mrs. Adams, whose other heirs assigned their interests in the note to the plaintiff. No administration was had of Mrs. Adams's estate. Uncontradicted testimony was given that there were no debts or claims against Mrs. Adams's estate, and judgment was given for the plaintiff. Exception by the defendant is on the ground that the plaintiff has not shown such title to the note as to authorize recovery by her on it.]

PERSON, J. . . .

It is unquestionably the law, as stated in Foote v. Foote, 61 Mich. 181, 28 N.W. 90, that:

. . . When there are no creditors, the heirs or legatees may collect, if they can, the estate together, and make such distribution among themselves as they may agree to and carry into effect, without the intervention of any administrator; and the law favors such arrangements. . . .

And where there is no fraud or mistake, such an arrangement, particularly when carried into effect, will be binding upon the heirs and distributees; and, in the absence of creditors, they will be estopped from disturbing it by asking for the appointment of an administrator. Needham v. Gillett, 39 Mich. 574. The heirs themselves being bound by such settlement, and no creditors existing, there is no one with authority to question the distribution they may make; they are the equitable owners of the estate, and, in the absence of administration, there is no one to assert the legal title against them. It will be observed, however, that while this rule recognizes the right of the heirs and distributees to divide among themselves such property of the estate as may be in their possession, and such as they may be able to get into their possession, it does not recognize any authority upon their part, they not having the legal title, to enforce the payments of debts owing to the estate and unpaid.

Notwithstanding the right of heirs and distributees to make such arrangements among themselves, "It is well settled in this State that, on the decease of an intestate, the title (legal title) to his personal effects remains in abeyance until the appointment of an administrator, and then vests in him, in trust, in his official capacity, as of the time of the intestate's death, and he is entitled to the possession of such assets, and to manage the property for the purposes of his trust." Parks v. Norris, 101 Mich. 71, 59 N.W. 428. And, except under special circumstances, such administrator, or other personal representative, as holder of the legal title, is alone authorized to bring an action for the recovery of a debt due to the estate. . . .

If the heirs and distributees of an estate were entitled to receive and enforce payments of debts due the estate whenever it was believed that there were no creditors, then every debtor would be under the necessity of determining, at his peril, whether there were such creditors or not. And for a stranger to the estate to reach such a conclusion would ordinarily be no safe or assured matter. There might be debts depending upon a contingency that had not happened, or incurred in a fiduciary relation not falling within the bar of the statute of limitations. As was said in Powell v. Palmer, 45 Mo. App. 236:

> From the nature of the case, the proposition that there are no debts provable against the estate of a deceased person is therefore a negative proposition, which is not susceptible of absolute proof. No evidence which could be offered in support of such a proposition could go further than to reach a strong degree of probability. . . .

The judgment will be reversed, and a new trial granted.

In reversing the lower court's refusal to appoint an administrator on petition of a debtor who wished to pay his debt to the estate and receive discharge of the mortgage on his land, In re Collins' Estate, 102 Wash. 697, 698-700, 173 P. 1016, 1017 (1918), states:

> This court has held that a claim against an estate is not barred by lapse of time where no notice to creditors has been published as required by law. . . .
> So it is plain that there may be debts, and if there are . . . such debts are not now barred, because no administrator has been appointed and no notice to creditors has been published. . . . When the appellant pays the note he is entitled to have the mortgage satisfied by one authorized to do so, in order that he may not again be liable to pay the note or any part thereof. . . . We are satisfied, therefore, that there is necessity for the appointment of an administrator of this estate, in order that . . . appellant's mortgage, when paid, may be legally satisfied.

In Matter of Estates of Thompson, 226 Kan. 437, 601 P.2d 1105 (1979), the parties did not find the will in question, but an executed copy was in the files of the decedent's lawyer. The heirs and the sole legatee under the will entered an agreement settling the rights to the estate. Later the will was found, and the legatee petitioned for probate and for a decree setting aside the settlement agreement on the basis of mutual mistake. In enforcing the agreement and reversing the lower court, the

Kansas Supreme Court (at 442, 601 P.2d at 1109) stated that "the parties clearly intended to resolve all disputes," and added:

> . . . They knew that a will had been written and executed. They were uncertain whether it had been revoked, destroyed, lost or merely mislaid. . . . Appellee undoubtedly believed that an original will would not be found or he would not have agreed to the settlement. He was mistaken in his belief as to this uncertainty but relief will not be granted for a mistake in prophecy, opinion or in belief relative to an uncertain event. . . .
>
> [W]e have frequently stated that family settlement agreements are favorites of the law and, when fairly made, are to be given liberal interpretation and should not be disturbed by those who entered into them or by those claiming under or through them. . . . In the instant case there is no claim of fraud, misrepresentation, concealment or other inequitable conduct. . . .

PROBLEM

15-C.   *T* died eighteen years ago survived by *D* as sole heir. No will was found, and *D* went into possession of land owned by *T* at her death. Eleven years after *T*'s death, *D* conveyed the land to *E* by warranty deed, and two years later it was transferred by warranty deed to *P*. The following year a will was found and probated under which *T* devised the land to *D* for life with remainder in fee to *D*'s children, *A* and *B*. Thereafter *P* filed a bill to quiet title in him as an innocent purchaser free of any claims of *A* and *B* and praying that their claims be removed as clouds on his title. What are the arguments in behalf of *P*? What are the arguments for *A* and *B*? What result would you anticipate in absence of statute? Under the laws of your state? (Consider the cases that follow.)

Is there anything *P* might have done at the time of purchase to protect himself? Do the statutes of your state adequately meet the problems raised under these and similar circumstances? If not, what statutory provisions would you suggest to remedy the matter? See Uniform Probate Code §3-108 (limiting the time within which a will may be probated) and cf. §3-910 (protecting purchasers from distributees holding deeds from personal representatives). Consider Uniform Probate Code §3-312 (succession without administration).

MURPHREE v. GRIFFIS
215 Ala. 98, 109 So. 746 (1926)

[Action of ejectment, commenced in 1923. D. M. Murphree died in 1910 owning the land in question, which he devised to his widow. He left no children and was survived by his wife and by the plaintiffs, who are his heirs at law. In 1910 Murphree's widow conveyed the land to the defendant. The widow died in 1922. The will by which Murphree devised the land was not probated until 1925, when it was duly admitted to probate after notice to the heirs.]

MILLER, J. . . .

It is true, . . . "An instrument, testamentary in character, cannot be recognized as valid in any form until it has been admitted to probate." [But this is] not consistent with . . . Whorton v. Moragne, 62 Ala. 201, 207, in which this court said:

> At the common law, the authority and duty of an administrator extended only to personal assets. Lands descended immediately on the death of the ancestor to the heir, who was invested with the title and all its incidents. The title of an executor, if there was no devise of the lands to him, and no power over them conferred by the will of the testator, was also confined to the personal assets. Lands devised passed immediately on the death of the testator to the devisee. . . .

To prove [the widow's] title, it was necessary that the will should be probated; and, when duly probated, either before or after her death, it was evidence of her title, which was vested in her at the time of the testator's death, by this instrument. The title to his land of this devisee vested in her at the death of the testator; and not at the time of the probate of the will. The title cannot be kept in abeyance. The will and its probate are the proof of her title; and when probated it relates back to the death of the testator, so as to make valid whatever she had previously done with the land, which under the will, after probate, she could have lawfully done. . . .

[T]he title to the land sued for is in the defendant. . . .

Affirmed.

Where there is no statute limiting the time for probating a will, if a prior will has been admitted to probate and another will is thereafter discovered, what is the effect of a statute providing that a will that has been probated cannot be attacked or contested after a specified period of time, which has now expired? The cases are divided, but the prevalent view is that the probate of a second will is permissible as it is not a "contest" of the previously admitted will. Thus, it is reasoned, probate establishes the valid execution of the will but not that it was the *last* will of the testator. E.g., In re Bentley's Will, 175 Va. 456, 9 S.E.2d 308 (1940); 2 J. Woerner, The American Law of Administration §§217, 227 (3d ed. 1923). When a probate of a subsequent will revokes the order admitting a prior will to probate, bona fide purchasers from the devisees under the earlier will are generally protected if the time has expired within which the prior order could have been contested. See T. Atkinson, Wills §96 (2d ed. 1953).

SEIDEL v. SNIDER

241 Iowa 1227, 44 N.W.2d 687 (1950)

MANTZ, J.

Plaintiff's husband died intestate April 19, 1949, owning an [undivided] interest in common — not in joint tenancy in the premises involved here. The contract sought to be enforced is dated September 17, 1949, five months later. By it plaintiff, as vendor, agreed to furnish defendant, the purchaser, an abstract showing merchantable title of record. She later tendered one which showed various affidavits designed to serve in lieu of administration proceedings on her husband's estate, in order to show heirs, freedom from debts and the homestead character of the premises from date of their acquisition, November 17, 1944.

The one question presented is the sufficiency of such showing on the abstract to comply with the requirement of the contract as to "merchantable title," whether, within the five year period allowed for administration, affidavits are competent to make of record for title purposes facts that are normally and properly shown by administration proceedings. . . .

Affidavits are not eligible to record except as provided by statute, Fagan v. Hook [134 Iowa 381, 388], 105 N.W. 155, 158. . . .

There is of course no law to compel resort to administration by the heirs and surviving spouse of an intestate decedent. The title to his property passes whether administered upon or not. Reichard v. Chicago, B & Q.R. Co., 231 Iowa 563, 578, 1 N.W.2d 721. The surviving spouse and heirs may agree among themselves to its distribution. Heinz v. Vawter, 221 Iowa 714, 716, 266 N.W. 486. But we are speaking here of the manner of making that devolution of title a matter of record so it may be properly reflected by an abstract.

Under the language of Code section 558.8 affidavits are recordable only to *explain* defects in the chain of title. To hold that affidavits are competent to be filed *in lieu* of administration proceedings during the time in which such proceedings can be instituted would make the statute a device to create defects rather than to explain them, to encourage omission of administration, thereby making defects to be "explained." That surely is not its purpose. Rather it is designed as a practical remedy for defects due to failure to follow orderly procedure when such procedure was available.

Our conclusion is somewhat based on judicial knowledge of the practice of lawyers to whom is usually entrusted the duty of examining abstracts and of advising clients as to the merchantability of title shown by them. That is perhaps the best index to the mental processes of purchasers of real estate as reasonably prudent men. Fortunately, at this point we have concrete justification for taking such judicial notice. The Title Standards Committee of our State Bar Association has adopted standards that would limit the use of affidavits in lieu of administration proceedings (in the case of decedents dying within the state) to cases where the affidavit shows:

> (1) that the decedent died intestate at least five years prior [because there is a five-year limit on the commencement of original administration in Iowa]; (2) (applicable only to nonresident decedents); (3) that the estate of said decedent had not been administered upon; (4) that all debts and claims, including the expense of last sickness and burial, have been paid; (5) that the decedent was survived by the persons named in the affidavit, specifying their relationship to said decedent; and (6) such statements of the assets of decedent's estate, . . . and such statement of estate liabilities as to enable the title examiner to determine what further showing, if any, to require as to inheritance and estate taxes.

Iowa Land Title Examination Standards (1950), pages 47, 48 (problem 9.18). . . .

From all the foregoing it follows that plaintiff did not tender an abstract showing merchantable title of record and the decision of the trial court is accordingly reversed.

Reversed.

Although it is important to understand the purpose and necessity of putting a particular estate through administration under our existing law, awakened concern over the delivery and cost of legal services demands that we also ask what needs of society our present probate system serves. Can these requirements of our legal system be met by a fundamentally revised probate system, simplified and less costly to both society and the interested individuals? Indeed, can these functions be fulfilled, at least for normal estate situations, by a system that requires *no* fiduciary intervention and estate administration as we know it?

In addition to summary procedures for the handling of very small estates in nearly all jurisdictions, some states now offer noteworthy opportunities for succession without administration. A limited opportunity of this type (applicable initially to community property and now to any property that passes outright to the surviving spouse) is authorized by California Probate Code §13650. The state of Washington has for many years had a statute allowing spouses to enter into an agreement with respect to the disposition of all or any part of their community property at death. Wash. Rev. Code §26.16.12. "The statute does not limit the parties to survivorship dispositions, nor in any other fashion (except for preserving the rights of creditors), and despite the lack of a definitive decision, the writer believes that any conceivable disposition not otherwise proscribed could be made, even cutting off the survivor entirely or vesting only a life interest in the survivor with remainders over, etc." Cross, The Community Property Law in Washington, 15 La.

L. Rev. 640, 645 (1955). One study found that more married persons disposed of their property at death in this fashion than by any other method. Price, The Transmission of Property at Death in a Community Property Jurisdiction, 50 Wash. L. Rev. 277, 299 (1975). There is apparently no reason why such laws and practices need be confined to community property or to transfers between spouses. See additional, more recent Washington legislation discussed in Note, Property: Probate Law and Procedure — No More Probate? (Wash. Rev. Code §11.02.090 (1974)), 51 Wash. L. Rev. 451 (1976). Can agreements analogous to Washington's community property agreements be used for similar probate avoidance purposes under Uniform Probate Code §6-101, without relying on the more traditional forms of will substitutes encountered in Chapters 8 and 11, supra?

The Uniform Probate Code was amended in 1982 to provide a procedure (not yet widely adopted in UPC states) for succession without administration; and the Uniform Succession Without Administration Act, a freestanding act for states not adopting the UPC, was promulgated in 1983.

UNIFORM PROBATE CODE

SUCCESSION WITHOUT ADMINISTRATION. *Prefatory Note.* This amendment to the Uniform Probate Code is an alternative to other methods of administering a decedent's estate. The Uniform Probate Code otherwise provides procedures for informal administration, formal administration and supervised administration. This amendment adds another alternative to the system of flexible administration provided by the Uniform Probate Code and permits the heirs of an intestate or residuary devisees of a testator to accept the estate assets without administration by assuming responsibility for discharging those obligations that normally would be discharged by the personal representative.

The concept of succession without administration is drawn from the civil law and is a variation of the method which is followed largely on the Continent in Europe, in Louisiana and in Quebec.

This proposed amendment contains cross-references to the procedures in the Uniform Probate Code and particularly implements the policies and concepts reflected in Sections 1-102, 3-101 [devolution of estate at death; restrictions] and 3-109 [successors' rights if no administration]. . . .

§3-312. *Universal Succession; In General.* The heirs of an intestate or the residuary devisees under a will, excluding minors and incapacitated, protected or unascertained persons, may become universal successors to the decedent's estate by assuming personal liability for (1) taxes, (2) debts of the decedent, (3) claims against the decedent or the estate, and (4) distributions due other heirs, devisees, and persons entitled to property of the decedent as provided in Sections 3-313 through 3-322.

§3-316. *Universal Succession; Universal Successors' Powers.*   Upon the Registrar's issuance of a statement of universal succession: (1) Universal successors have full power of ownership to deal with the assets of the estate subject to the limitations and liabilities in this [Act]. The universal successors shall proceed expeditiously to settle and distribute the estate without adjudication but if necessary may invoke the jurisdiction of the court to resolve questions concerning the estate.

(2) Universal successors have the same powers as distributees from a personal representative under Section 3-908 and 3-909 and third persons with whom they deal are protected as provided in Section 3-910.

(3) For purposes of collecting assets in another state whose law does not provide for universal succession, universal successors have the same standing and power as personal representatives or distributees in this State.

§3-317.   *Universal Succession; Universal Successors' Liability*
            to Creditors, Other Heirs, Devisees and Persons
            Entitled to Decedent's Property; Liability of Other
            Persons Entitled to Property.

(a) In the proportions and subject to the limits expressed in Section 3-321, universal successors assume all liabilities of the decedent that were not discharged by reason of death and liability for all taxes, claims against the decedent or the estate, and charges properly incurred after death for the preservation of the estate, to the extent those items, if duly presented, would be valid claims against the decedent's estate.

(b) In the proportions and subject to the limits expressed in Section 3-321, universal successors are personally liable to other heirs, devisees, and persons entitled to property of the decedent for the assets or amounts that would be due those heirs, were the estate administered, but no allowance having priority over devisees may be claimed for attorney's fees or charges for preservation of the estate in excess of reasonable amounts properly incurred.

(c) Universal successors are entitled to their interests in the estate as heirs or devisees subject to priority and abatement pursuant to Section 3-902 and to agreement pursuant to Section 3-912.

§3-321. *Universal Succession; Liability of Universal Successors for Claims, Expenses, Intestate Shares and Devises.*   The liability of universal successors is subject to any defenses that would have been available to the decedent. Other than liability arising from fraud, conversion, or other wrongful conduct of a universal successor, the personal liability of each universal successor to any creditor, claimant, other heir, devisee, or person entitled to decedent's property may not exceed the proportion of the claim that the universal successor's share bears to the share of all heirs and residuary devisees.

§3-322. *Universal Succession; Remedies of Creditors, Other Heirs, Devisees or Persons Entitled to Decedent's Property.* In addition to remedies otherwise provided by law, any creditor, heir, devisee or person entitled to decedent's property qualified under Section 3-605, may demand bond of universal successors. If the demand for bond precedes the granting of an application for universal succession, it must be treated as an objection under Section 3-314(c) unless it is withdrawn, the claim satisfied, or the applicants post bond in an amount sufficient to protect the demandant. If the demand for bond follows the granting of an application for universal succession, the universal successors, within 10 days after notice of the demand, upon satisfying the claim or posting bond sufficient to protect the demandant, may disqualify the demandant from seeking administration of the estate.

SCOLES, SUCCESSION WITHOUT
ADMINISTRATION: PAST AND FUTURE
48 Mo. L. Rev. 371-374, 386-387 (1983)

One of the most persistent problems in private law has concerned the process by which private assets pass from their owner on the owner's death to those who, by law, are next entitled to enjoy them. In primitive societies organized around the family, many assets probably were viewed as belonging to the family. However, since social and governmental organizations have become more complex and individual ownership of real and personal property has developed, the law has experienced a continual state of evolution. As commercial activity and demands of the public fisc increased, the law became concerned about assuring that creditors, who had indirectly contributed to the decedent's accumulation of wealth, were paid and that a fair share of the costs of government, which permitted and protected the accumulation, were recovered before the assets were distributed to the new owners. Although many of the concepts found in modern laws of succession can be traced to early Roman law, most European countries developed different methods of accommodating the interests of the various parties involved in succession from those developed in England and the United States. Most of the civil law countries, like France and Germany, have utilized the concept of universal succession by which the heirs receive the title to the decedent's assets directly on death and also become obligated to pay any liabilities of the decedent. The heirs, who were viewed as succeeding to the decedent's person and standing in the decedent's shoes, received the benefit of his assets and the burden of his obligations. Third parties, who would have looked to the decedent, looked to the heirs after the decedent's death. In brief, the heirs owned the assets and, upon acceptance of the inheritance, owed the decedent's debts as their own. Consequently, the heirs reduced the decedent's assets to possession, paid the decedent's debts and creditors, paid any taxes due, and also paid the legacies in any will of the decedent. On the other hand, English law interposed a personal representative, the administrator or executor, as an independent responsible person to collect the assets, discharge debts and claims before making distribution of the net balance to the heirs or distributees who were to be the next beneficial owners. Nearly all of the states of the United States adopted and further developed the English system of probate and administration. However, Louisiana, with its background of the French civil law, followed the civil law pattern, as did Quebec and nearly all the Latin American countries.

The objectives of both the civil law and the common law approaches are the same: to collect the decedent's assets with dispatch, to satisfy any obligations to creditors, government, or others incident to the termination of the decedent's life, and to complete the transmission of his property to those beneficially entitled with the minimum expense of time and money. In both systems, the process is one of liquidation so the new owners can enjoy the assets free and clear without interruption from the claimants of the past. As both systems developed, modifications were made to accommodate the interests of different parties. In the civil law, the heir could avoid liability to the decedent's creditors in excess of the value of the estate by renouncing, by accepting only to the extent of the value of the assets, i.e., with benefit of inventory, or by instituting a process similar to bankruptcy to separate the assets of the decedent from those of the heir and, in that way, protect the heir's own assets. Under the civil law in most countries, a person could be appointed to intercede as an administrator in an insolvent estate and often this would be the heir himself. In the United States and England, procedures were frequently developed by which formal administration could be shortened or avoided and the decedent's assets distributed or passed directly into the possession and enjoyment of the heirs or devisees. Because land was often not available for creditors except in extreme cases, the law of most states of the United States provided for direct devolution of title and possession of land to the heirs or devisees without administration. As the western United States developed, with some civil law antecedents and a quite general lack of concern for judicial formalities reinforced by great distances from the courthouse, many experiments emerged providing for informal means of satisfying the functions of formal administration. Homestead and exemption laws permitted continued possession and enjoyment of assets with only modest affidavit procedures. Community property was often set off to the surviving spouse with little in the way of formalities. Texas and Washington provided for the independent executor who essentially accounted only to the family, and nearly all states provided for summary administration of small estates. As a consequence, the approaches of the civil law's universal succession and the common law's administration of decedent's estates were frequently different in name only and were often functionally quite similar.

This Article will attempt to demonstrate these common developments as an introduction to the consideration in the United States of a statutory form of succession without administration somewhat similar to civil law universal succession, which, it is submitted, is the result of the normal evolution in American efforts to transmit assets from generation to generation with maximum economy of time and value. . . .

It is generally recognized that the underlying purpose of administering a decedent's estate is to collect the assets, pay those who have claims against the decedent and the assets, and transmit possession with unencumbered title to the next owner as quickly and as inexpensively as possible. The foregoing brief review of experience in the United States with procedures dispensing with some or all of the usual steps in administration demonstrates that the policy concerns really are not with the size of the estate or the nature of its assets, but with the protection usually afforded to the parties by formal administration. If the functional protection of those concerned can reasonably be obtained by less expensive alternatives to administration, those alternatives should be employed.

The functions to which attention should be addressed begin with the collection process. Someone needs to be identified as an appropriate party to initiate the process of collecting the decedent's assets. This is the personal representative in formal administration, but under the statutes and in the cases allowing administration to be avoided, the successors, i.e., heirs and devisees, can and have nearly everywhere been permitted to do this. The size of the estate or the nature of its assets does not affect this problem of identity. Second, in considering collection, the persons from whom the assets or obligations are to be collected need to be protected from the risk of double liability. An efficient transfer system requires the ability to rely on the receipt of the transferee to foreclose further liability. We see that the facility of payment statutes have successfully provided this protection, even though administration does not occur. Again, it appears that the value of the assets involved does not control the protection of the debtor in making payment or transfer to the successors.

The next function with which we need be concerned is the protection and payment of the decedent's creditors, tax authorities, and others who have prior claim to the assets. If these creditors and claimants are given essentially the same protection by an alternative procedure that they receive by administration, the alternative seems viable. The experience both under statutes in which size limitations on small estates exceed the allowable exemptions and statutes providing for avoiding administration in any estate demonstrate that we can rely upon the successors to pay the debts and taxes, as individuals normally do, under the latent threat of enforcement action from the claimant. If a claimant can trace assets and assert the claim against those assets, the claimant's position is no different than when a family member is a personal representative under obligation to pay debts. Similarly, tax collection relies on the reporting process and that does not depend on the character of the person making the report. If these obligations are imposed on the successors, the lack of formality would not alter the obligations. Furthermore, if it results in lower costs, more assets may be available to the claimants.

Finally, there is a need to identify the distributees who are the new owners of the free and clear assets. We have seen that this is perhaps the easiest task in an informal process since people simply have more knowledge about their close relatives than other information in decedents' estates. And if any unknown or unidentified potential successors are given reasonable opportunity to come forward and prove their identity, the function of administration in that regard is satisfied. Further, to the extent that successors are identified at the outset and given the function of collecting the assets and clearing the assets from claims, costs of transfer are avoided. The economies of owners managing their own assets are thereby achieved.

These considerations seem to identify the requirements of an efficient alternative to formal administration. It is submitted that these requirements are met by the approach of the recent amendment to the Uniform Probate Code providing for succession without administration. In the belief that succession without administration is a normal and timely development of the probate and administration law in all states, enactment of an adaptation of the Uniform Probate Code amendment seems appropriate in states that have not yet enacted the Uniform Probate Code.

W. FRATCHER, PROBATE CAN BE QUICK AND CHEAP: TRUSTS AND ESTATES IN ENGLAND[1]
i, 48, 52, 55, 102-104 (1966)

When an Englishman dies, leaving an estate worth $14,000, his widow can, within three weeks after his death, secure ownership of the estate by making a single half-hour visit to a District Probate Registry near her

---

1. This study, in almost identical form, can be found in Fratcher, Fiduciary Administration in England, 40 N.Y.U. L. Rev. 12 (1965).

home, signing three printed forms, and paying a fourteen-dollar fee, without ever going near a court. When an American man dies, leaving an estate worth $14,000 his widow is unlikely to be able to secure ownership of his estate in less than a year and then only by attending, personally or through a lawyer, numerous hearings in a probate court and paying fees and other expenses amounting, probably, to a hundred times the expense of the English widow. . . .

An American lawyer is likely to wonder whether [in uncontested applications, conveniently processed through registries and subject for a time to subsequent challenge] the fact that most grants of probate and administration are made without notice to anyone and without any real proof of the execution of wills tends to work injustice. The English officials who operate the system think that it does not. In this connection it may be noted that there are more safeguards than are provided in either England or the United States for the recording or registration of *inter vivos* conveyances. . . .

In the great bulk of English estates there are no judicial proceedings after the grant of probate or administration. The personal representative simply collects the assets, pays claims and expenses of administration, distributes the residue to the persons entitled [to it] and secures discharges from the distributees. This is what is known as "independent administration" in Texas and [Washington]. [Also, several states have now adopted Uniform Probate Code article 3 (see infra), which is the heart of the Code.] . . .

A personal representative who distributes the estate without paying debts is personally liable to creditors, even though he had no notice of their claims. He may protect himself against such liability, however, by publishing notice in newspapers of his intended distribution, requiring any person interested to send in particulars of his claim within a time stipulated in the notice, not less than two months. At the expiration of the time fixed by the notice the personal representative may effect the intended distribution without liability to any person of whose claim he had no notice prior to distribution. This does not bar a claimant from proceeding against the property so distributed in the hands of a distributee or anyone else who is not a [bona fide] purchaser. . . .

Modern English legislation has revolutionized the position and powers of trustees by conferring upon them broad statutory powers of investment, disposition and management. . . . It accords executors and administrators the same title, status and powers over [estate] property. . . .

[T]he fiduciary [can] exercise all his powers without authorization, supervision or approval of any court or tribunal. An interested person [can, however], for good reason, secure a court supervised administration of the estate. . . .

Most American states compel [personal representatives] to secure

court authorization for the exercise of some or all of their powers. . . .
Court supervision is bound to involve considerable expense and delay.
In light of the English experience and our own experience with trust
administration, might not . . . independent administration of the estates
of decedents . . . be given serious consideration?

V. EMMERICH, ESTATE PRACTICE IN THE
UNITED STATES AND EUROPE
7-8, 17-18, 38-41 (1950)

Roman law developed the conception of universal succession. Like in
many ancient cultures, the heir was regarded as continuing the personality of the deceased. This concept was expressed by the legal theory that
the estate of the deceased passed on automatically to his heirs, property
and possession, rights and obligations. No special administration was
necessary. The heir adopted the obligations of the deceased as his own.
Several heirs shared in the estate like other co-owners of property. If the
deceased had property in different countries, one uniform law, the personal law of the deceased, was applied to all his property. . . .

The Anglo-American system offers a unified procedure under careful
and detailed supervision of the government. The solutions enjoy the
authority and definiteness of court decisions. The proceeding also takes
care of the tax interests of the government. It necessitates the interference of various persons and institutions besides the heirs, generally the
employment of a lawyer, and appointment of an executor or administrator, the supervision by the court. The influence of the real parties in
interest, the heirs and legatees, is restricted, the position of the executor
or administrator rather independent. In consequence of all that, the
transfer and distribution of an estate is generally a lengthy affair lasting
for a year or more, sometimes even considerably longer. The interested
parties have to be satisfied with the exclusion from their inherited property for a long time, and are burdened with heavy expenses for the complicated work to be performed by experienced and trustworthy experts.

In countries of French, Western-European and Germanic laws the
heirs take the estate over without formalities, very often without the
interference of any executor or administrator, or employment of a lawyer. Then they take all the necessary steps themselves. There is practically no administration. Debts and legacies are paid informally. No
formal accounting is necessary. No court is approached.

If the heir is only one individual, he becomes the owner and possessor
of the estate without any formality. If several persons become the heirs,
the whole work to be done takes often only a few days. . . .

The contrast between Anglo-American and continental European conceptions of estate law becomes most apparent in the subjects of administration and distribution. Here, all fundamental ideas are different.

In Anglo-American law, an estate generally requires administration. Every administration is based upon a grant of the court. . . . The executor or administrator is independent of the heirs or relatives. . . . He is party to procedures concerning assets and debts. He pays the debts during administration. He distributes the estate among the beneficiaries. He accounts to the court. All or nearly all of these rules are part of the adjective law laid down in statutes and rules on court procedure.

In continental European law, the separate administration of an estate is necessary only in special cases, like insufficiency of the estate to pay the debts, or where the heirs are unknown. No grant of the court is required or provided for except in the special cases just mentioned. . . .

In [most] Western-European countries, wills are not filed in or probated by the court. The notaries who assist in the execution of a will retain it. In case no notary was employed, the heirs keep it. The heirs themselves decide upon the validity and construction of the will, and disagreements can be brought to . . . court like in any other cases. The notaries are usually of great help to the heirs and practice has clothed their certificates with great authority. The acts lack however the power of decisions with final force and can be attacked collaterally.

According to German law, a will of a German national must be filed in court after the death. The court informs relatives and beneficiaries. Probate is not necessary but is granted upon application. Similar rulings are also given in cases of intestacy. Such decisions cannot be attacked collaterally. Even if a later will is discovered and filed, application to the court for revision of the former decision is necessary. . . .

In Western-European law the ipso iure transfer of the estate makes the heirs the owners of the assets and debtors of the obligations. Execution and administration do not change these consequences. If no executor has been appointed, the heirs themselves perform the acts of administration or distribution without any supervision. If an executor or administrator has been appointed, his work is restricted to the functions entrusted to him. The heirs are entitled to take over the estate immediately, notwithstanding the appointment of an executor, in so far as he does not need the assets for the performance of his duties, and even the whole estate if they insure this performance.

On the other hand, the personal liability of the heirs for the debts of the deceased can be a heavy burden. The law then provides special institutions by which the heirs can restrict their liability to the assets of the estate, by special declarations and registrations, inventories, and proper administration and accounting.

B. Opening Administration

Before the administration of a decedent's estate can begin, there are certain preliminary matters that must be cared for by someone. The matter of making the funeral arrangements is usually handled by the family. The person making the arrangements should be aware that the court may not allow more than a reasonable amount in funeral expenses as a claim against the estate, and the balance, if any, may be the personal obligation of the one making the arrangements. Some states also give a priority for the payment of a fixed maximum amount for funeral expenses, and any balance must be presented as a general claim after administration expenses are paid. Although family members rarely object to any excessive expenses, creditors may object in the event the assets are insufficient for their claims.

Another of the matters that should be handled promptly after the death of a person is to suspend transactions in the name of the deceased, and sometimes to notify banks and brokerages to stop payment on checks outstanding. The powers of agents are terminated by the death of the principal, and in order to avoid the problem of transactions that may be completed after the death of the principal, prompt notification to persons who may have powers of attorney or other agencies may prevent costly litigation. If a check is a gift, the payee may not collect after the donor's death; however, if a check has been given in payment for goods or services, then the payee can come as a creditor and be paid the amount due.

Promptly after the death of the deceased there should be an investigation to discover any life insurance on the deceased so a claim for the proceeds can be filed. Life insurance has as one of its principal functions the provision of funds that will financially carry the family over the period of estate administration. Life insurance proceeds are usually payable promptly so the family can be in funds during this period in which the need is great.

One of the unpleasant but nevertheless important jobs at the outset of administering a decedent's estate is the process of going through the private papers of the deceased. The first reason for doing so is of course to find a will if any exists. It is important that this be done promptly because subsequent proceedings depend on whether a will is found. There is the practical problem of making certain the latest will has been found and protecting against the possibility of someone destroying or hiding it. Should the will be in the custody of some person, it is necessary to obtain the will and file it with the court. If the custodian should refuse to file it with the court, summary proceedings are available by which the filing may be obtained. The problem of going through the private papers can be a considerable task. Most persons accumulate a vast amount of relevant and irrelevant papers during their lifetime. These must be searched and classified in order to determine whether any have significance. It is often better to destroy nothing even though the papers seem to be insignificant. In several instances circulars or old envelopes with odd notations on them have become important. It also avoids the possibility of any assertion that a will or other important paper was destroyed during the process of destroying what appeared to be waste paper. One of the places to be searched in this process is any safety-deposit box of the deceased. A court order may be necessary to open the box. It is often required by statute and advisable to have a public official, such as a representative of the taxing authority, as well as a bank representative present at the time the box is opened and searched in order to avoid any question of concealment of assets at a later date. An inventory should be taken of contents at the time of the initial opening and witnessed by those present.

Finally it is necessary to determine the appropriate court in which to file the petition for administration or for probate of the will if one is found. Once the court is chosen, it is necessary to proceed with probate and to petition for the appointment of the personal representative. Determining the place of administration or the court that has jurisdiction in administrative matters is not always easy. The concepts of in rem jurisdiction and in personam jurisdiction are particularly confused in decedent's estates. The in rem concept still prevails generally to determine where administration must be taken out; that is, administration is required or excused by the law of the place where the assets are located. But even so, the principal or domiciliary administration is taken out in the state and county of the domicile of the deceased. Administration in other states is ancillary. Traditionally under the in rem concept the service of process by publication has been thought to be adequate, but in recent years there has been increased recognition of the personal service requirement under both state and federal law.

In administration of trust estates the matter of jurisdiction is usually less complex. An inter vivos trust usually will not come to a court's attention until a party seeks judicial relief of some kind. Ordinarily jurisdiction of such matters is taken by a court of equity at the place where the trust is administered, which in most instances is where the trustee lives or does business. On the other hand, statutes in some states subject testamentary trusts to the probate court's jurisdiction by reason of statute, and then administration of a testamentary trust is in the state where principal administration of the decedent's estate occurred. See generally the note on court and noncourt trusts near the end of section D of Chapter 11. Also compare the approach of Uniform Probate Code, Article 7 (especially §§7-107, 7-103, and 7-203) discussed in that note.

UNIFORM PROBATE CODE

§3-201. *Venue for Estate Proceedings; Location of Property.*

(a) Venue for the first informal or formal testacy or appointment proceedings after a decedent's death is:

(1) in the [county] where the decedent had his domicile at the time of his death; or

(2) if the decedent was not domiciled in this state, in any [county] where property of the decedent was located at the time of his death. . . .

C. Estate and Trust Proceedings

PROBLEM

15-D. *D*, a retired executive, recently died and his son, *S*, comes to you for legal advice. *D*'s usual residence and most of his continuing business activities were in the state where you practice. He died while vacationing in a sunbelt state where he and his wife, *W*, owned a condominium as joint tenants; in recent years *D* and *W* had spent increasing amounts of their time at the condo. *D* was survived by *W*, *S*, and *G*, the child of a deceased daughter. *G* lives in another state halfway across the country. *D* left a will naming *S* as executor and dividing his property equally among *W*, *S*, and *G*. *W* now expects to live in the sunbelt condo and would like to sell the residence in this state. *H* owned a number of valuable paintings, some kept at the condo and others in the residence. At the time of his death he had deposits in the savings banks in this state and in the sunbelt state and had automobiles registered in both states. He had major shareholdings in a Delaware corporation and also in a company incorporated in this state; in addition, he was a partner in a business operated in this state, with local land, buildings, and equipment in the partnership name. There are two life insurance policies on *D*'s life, one payable to *W* and the other payable to his estate. Where would you open administration, and what procedures would you plan to follow? Do you see reason for any particular procedural concerns?

UNIFORM PROBATE CODE

Article 3. *General Comment.* The provisions of this Article describe the Flexible System of Administration of Decedents' Estates. Designed [for] both testate and intestate estates and to provide [interested persons] as little or as much by way of procedural safeguards as may be suitable under varying circumstances, this system is the heart of the Uniform Probate Code. . . .

(1) Post-mortem probate must occur to make a will effective, and appointment of a personal representative by a public official . . . is required in order to create the duties and powers attending the office of personal representative. Neither are compelled, however, but are left to be obtained by persons having an interest in the consequence of probate or appointment. . . .

(2) Two methods of securing probate of wills which include a nonadjudicative determination (informal probate) on the one hand, and a judicial determination after notice to all interested persons (formal probate) on the other, are provided.

(3) Two methods of securing appointment of a personal representative [informal and formal] are provided. . . .

(5) Probate of a will by informal or formal proceedings or an adjudication of intestacy may occur without any attendant requirement of appointment of a personal representative.

(6) One judicial, in rem, proceeding encompassing formal probate of any wills (or a determination after notice that the decedent left no will), appointment of a personal representative and complete settlement of an estate under continuing supervision of the Court (supervised administration) is provided for testators and persons interested in a decedent's estate, whether testate or not, who desire to use it.

(7) Unless supervised administration is sought [interested persons] may use an "in and out" relationship to the Court so that any question . . . may be resolved . . . by adjudication after notice without necessarily subjecting the estate to the necessity of judicial orders in regard to other or further questions. . . .

(8) The [testate or intestate] status of a decedent [may] be resolved by adjudication after notice in proceedings commenced within three years of death. If not so resolved, any will probated informally becomes final, and if there is no such probate the status of the decedent as intestate is finally determined, by a statute of limitations which bars probate and appointment unless requested within three years after death.

(9) Personal representatives appointed informally, or after notice, and whether supervised or not, have statutory powers enabling them to collect, protect, sell, distribute and otherwise handle all steps in administration without further order of the Court, except that supervised personal representatives may be subjected to special restrictions on powers as endorsed on their letters.

[(10) and (11) mention protections for purchasers and personal representatives to make nonadjudicated settlements safe and feasible.]

(12) Statutes of limitation bar creditors of the decedent who fail to present claims within four months after legal advertising of administra-

tion, and unsecured claims not barred by non-claim statutes are barred after three years from the decedent's death.

Overall, the system [is based on] the premise that the Court's role in regard to probate and administration . . . is wholly passive until some interested person invokes its power to secure resolution of a matter. The state, through the Court, should provide remedies which are suitable and efficient to protect any and all rights regarding succession, but should refrain from intruding into family affairs unless relief is requested, and limit its relief to that sought.

The cases that follow involve certain procedural aspects of estate and trust administration proceedings and of related litigation that is likely to arise during the administration of a trust. These cases are concerned primarily with problems of jurisdiction and notice and with the representation and protection of the interest of minors, incompetents, and unascertained or unborn persons.

RILEY v. NEW YORK TRUST CO.
315 U.S. 343 (1941)

[Coca-Cola International Corporation, incorporated in Delaware, filed a bill of interpleader in a Delaware court against the Georgia executors (Riley and Spalding) of the will of Julia Hungerford and against the New York Administrator c.t.a. (New York Trust Co.) of the same decedent. Each claimed the right to receive transfer of the Coca-Cola stock now standing in the decedent's name. The outstanding certificates are now in the hands of the Georgia executors. The parties agreed that Delaware was the situs of the stock. The petitioners (Georgia executors) asserted that original domiciliary probate was obtained in Georgia, with the husband and all beneficiaries and heirs at law of the testatrix as actual parties by personal service; the respondent (administrator c.t.a.) was not a party. The Georgia record of probate included a finding that the testatrix was domiciled in Georgia. Petitioners offered to pay all Delaware taxes and charges on the stock and requested issuance of new certificates to them on the basis that the Georgia domicile had been conclusively established against "all persons," relying on the full faith and credit clause (art. IV, §1) of the federal Constitution. Respondent admitted that all parties entitled to oppose probate in Georgia were actually before the Georgia court but denied that the testatrix was domiciled in Georgia or that the Georgia judgment was binding on the respondent trust company; it averred that New York was the domicile of the testatrix at death, that there were New York creditors, and that New York had claims for estate and inheritance taxes. As domiciliary administrator c.t.a., respondent prayed issuance to it of the certificates for the stock in controversy. The Supreme Court of Delaware, reversing the trial court's finding of fact, determined that New York was the testatrix's domicile and denied that the full faith and credit clause required issuance of the certificates to the Georgia executors. Certiorari was granted to review the alleged error in denying full faith and credit to the Georgia judgment.]

REED, J., delivered the opinion of the Court. . . .

The constitutional effect of the Georgia decree on a claim in his own name in another state by a party to the Georgia proceedings is not here involved. The question we are to decide is whether this Georgia judgment on domicile conclusively establishes the right of the Georgia executors to demand delivery to them of personal assets of their testatrix which another state is willing to surrender to the domiciliary personal representative; when another representative, appointed by a third state, asserts a similar domiciliary right. For the purpose of this review, the conclusion of Delaware that the testatrix was in fact domiciled in New York is accepted. The answer to the question lies in the extent to which Article IV, §1, of the Constitution, . . . nevertheless controls Delaware's action.

This clause of the Constitution brings to our Union a useful means for ending litigation. Matters once decided between adverse parties in any state or territory are at rest. Were it not for this full faith and credit provision, so far as the Constitution controls the matter, adversaries could wage again their legal battles whenever they met in other jurisdictions. Each state could control its own courts but could not project the effect of its decisions beyond its own boundaries. Cf. Pennoyer v. Neff, 95 U.S. 714, 722. That clause compels that controversies be stilled, so that, where a state court has jurisdiction of the parties and subject matter, its judgment controls in other states to the same extent as it does in the state where rendered. . . . By the Constitutional provision for full faith and credit, the local doctrines of res judicata, speaking generally, become a part of national jurisprudence, and therefore federal questions cognizable here. . . .

The full faith and credit clause allows Delaware, in disposing of local assets, to determine the question of domicile anew for any interested party who is not bound by participation in the Georgia proceeding. . . . But, while allowing Delaware to determine domicile for itself where any interested party is not bound by the Georgia proceedings, the full faith and credit clause . . . [does] require that Delaware shall give Georgia judgments such faith and credit "as they have by law or usage" in Georgia. . . .

We find nothing . . . , however, which would lead to the conclusion that, in Georgia, the New York administrator c.t.a., was in privity, so far as the . . . estate is concerned, with any parties before the Georgia court. . . . Hence, if the Georgia judgment is to bind the New York administrator, it can be considered to do so only in rem.

By §113-602, Georgia Code of 1933, set up by petitioner as a basis for his contention as to the finality of the Georgia judgment in Delaware it is provided that the Court of Ordinary is given exclusive jurisdiction over the probate of wills and that "such probate is conclusive upon all parties notified, and all the legatees under the will who are represented in the executor." All the parties entitled to be heard in opposition to the probate, including Mr. Hungerford, were actually before the Court of Ordinary. It may be assumed that the judgment of probate and domicile is a judgment in rem and therefore, as "an act of the sovereign power," "its effects cannot be disputed" within the jurisdiction. But this does not bar litigation anew by a stranger, of facts upon which the decree in rem is based. Hence it cannot be said, we think, that because respondent would have no standing in Georgia to contest the probate of a will . . . thereafter respondent could not file a claim in Delaware, dependent upon domiciliary representation of testatrix, for assets in the latter state. While the Georgia judgment is to have the same faith and credit in Delaware as it does in Georgia that requirement does not give the Georgia judgment extra-territorial effect upon assets in other states. So far as the assets in Georgia are concerned, the Georgia judgment of probate is in rem; so far as it affects personalty beyond the state, it is in personam and can bind only parties thereto to their privies. . . . Phrased somewhat differently, if the effect of a probate decree in Georgia in personam was to bar a stranger to the decree from later asserting his rights, such a holding would deny procedural due process.

It seems quite obvious that the administrator c.t.a. appears in Delaware as an agency of the State of New York, and not as the alter ego of the beneficiaries of the Hungerford estate. In its answer to the petitioners' statement of claim, it established its status by alleging that . . . creditors residing in New York and the State of New York were interested in the estate, that its appointment as temporary administrator had been sought by the New York Tax Commissioners "to protect the claim of the State of New York to inheritance and succession taxes," [asserted] on the theory that the domicile was New York. . . .

Georgia and New York might each assert its right to administer the estates of its domiciliaries to protect its sovereign interests, and Delaware was free to decide for itself which claimant is entitled to receive the portion of Mrs. Hungerford's personalty within Delaware's borders.

Affirmed.

STONE, C.J.

I concur upon the single ground that the New York administrator was not bound by the Georgia judgment. He was not a party to the Georgia proceedings, nor was he represented by any of those who were parties. As administrator appointed under the New York statutes, he was charged with the duty of administering the estate of the decedent and paying inheritance taxes upon it. His interest so far as he owes duties to the state is therefore adverse to that of the husband and the next of kin, who alone were parties to the Georgia proceeding. To have bound him by representation of those so adverse in interest would have been a denial of due process. . . . A judgment so obtained is not entitled to full faith and credit with respect to those not parties. . . . Any other conclusion would foreclose New York from litigating its right to collect taxes lawfully due by simple expedient of a probate by the next of kin of the will of the decedent as the domiciled resident of another state, without notice to any representative of New York or opportunity to be heard.

It is unnecessary to consider the other questions discussed by the opinion.

FRANKFURTER and JACKSON, J.J., concur in this opinion.

Hanson v. Denckla, 357 U.S. 235 (1958), involved a controversy over the right to $400,000 of the corpus of a trust of securities established in Delaware. In 1935, while domiciled in Pennsylvania, the settlor established the trust in question with a Delaware trustee. She reserved the income to herself for life and a variety of powers, including powers of revocation, amendment, and appointment. In 1944 the settlor became domiciled in Florida. In 1949 she executed an inter vivos instrument appointing $400,000 of the corpus at her death to trusts previously established with another Delaware trustee and the balance to her executrix. The settlor died domiciled in Florida in 1952. The residuary legatee under her will sought a declaratory judgment in Florida, where the will was probated, holding the trust and inter vivos appointment of the remainder invalid as being testamentary in nature. The trustee and some of the beneficiaries were not served in Florida; the executrix and several of the beneficiaries were personally served in Florida. While the Florida case was pending, a suit was started in Delaware to determine the disposition of the assets under the trust. The Florida court held the trust and the appointment void, while the Delaware court held both the trust and the appointment valid. Delaware refused to give effect to the Florida decree on the basis that it had been rendered without jurisdiction. Certiorari was granted by the United States Supreme Court in both cases. The Supreme Court affirmed the Delaware decree, holding it valid, and reversed the Florida decree, holding that it was void. In holding that Florida had no jurisdiction either in rem or in personam, the majority opinion, written by Chief Justice Warren, stated:

> *In rem jurisdiction.* . . . The . . . assets that form the subject matter of this action were located in Delaware and not in Florida. . . .
> The Florida court held that the presence of the subject property was not

essential to its jurisdiction. Authority over the probate and construction
of its domiciliary's will, under which the assets might pass, was thought
sufficient to confer the requisite jurisdiction. But jurisdiction cannot be
predicated upon the contingent role of this Florida will. Whatever the efficacy of a so-called "in rem" jurisdiction over assets admittedly passing
under a local will, a State acquires no in rem jurisdiction to adjudicate the
validity of inter vivos disposition simply because its decision might augment an estate passing under a will probated in its courts. If such a basis
of jurisdiction were sustained, probate courts would enjoy nationwide service of process to adjudicate interests in property with which neither the
State nor the decedent could claim any affiliation. The settlor-decedent's
Florida domicile is equally unavailing as a basis for jurisdiction over the
trust assets. For the purpose of jurisdiction in rem the maxim that personalty has its situs at the domicile of its owner is a fiction of limited utility. . . . The fact that the owner is or was domiciled within the forum State
is not a sufficient affiliation with the property upon which to base jurisdiction in rem. . . .

In personam jurisdiction. Appellees' stronger argument is for in personam jurisdiction over the Delaware trustee. They urge that the circumstances of this case amount to sufficient affiliation with the State of Florida
to empower its courts to exercise personal jurisdiction over this nonresident defendant. Principal reliance is placed upon McGee v. International
Life Ins. Co., 355 U.S. 220 [and] International Shoe Co. v. State of Washington, 326 U.S. 310. But it is a mistake to assume that [these cases herald]
the eventual demise of all restrictions on the personal jurisdiction of state
courts. . . . However minimal the burden of defending in a foreign tribunal, a defendant may not be called upon to do so unless he has had the
"minimal contacts" with the State that are a prerequisite to its exercise of
power over him. . . .

We fail to find such contacts in the circumstances of this case. The
defendant trust company has no office in Florida, and transacts no business there. None of the trust assets has ever been held or administered in
Florida, and the record discloses no solicitation of business in that State
either in person or by mail. . . .

The cause of action in this case is not one that arises out of an act done
or transaction consummated in the forum State. In that respect, it differs
from McGee v. International Life Ins. Co. . . . In contrast, this action
involves the validity of an agreement that was . . . executed in Delaware by
a trust company incorporated in that State and a settlor domiciled in
Pennsylvania. The first relationship Florida had to the agreement was
years later when the settlor became domiciled there, and the trustee remitted the trust income to her in that State. From Florida Mrs. Donner carried on several bits of trust administration that may be compared to the
mailing of premiums in *McGee*. But the record discloses no instance in
which the *trustee* performed any acts in Florida that bear the same relationship to the agreement as the solicitation in *McGee*. . . . This case is also
different from *McGee* in that there the State had enacted special legislation
. . . to exercise what *McGee* called its "manifest interest" in providing
effective redress for citizens who had been injured by nonresidents

engaged in an activity that the State treats as exceptional and subjects to special regulation. . . .

The execution in Florida of the powers of appointment under which the beneficiaries and appointees claim does not give Florida a substantial connection with the contact on which this suit is based. It is the validity of the trust agreement, not the appointment, that is at issue here. . . . [W]e think it an insubstantial connection with the trust agreement for purposes of determining the question of personal jurisdiction over a nonresident defendant. The unilateral activity of those who claim some relationship with a nonresident defendant cannot satisfy the requirements of contact with the forum state. The application of that rule will vary with the quality and nature of the defendant's activity, but it is essential in each case that there be some act by which the defendant purposely avails itself of the privilege of conducting activities within the forum state, thus invoking the benefits and protections of its laws. International Shoe Co. v. State of Washington, 326 U.S. 310, 319. The settlor's execution in Florida of her power of appointment cannot remedy the absence of such an act in this case.

It is urged that because the settlor and most of the appointees and beneficiaries were domiciled in Florida the courts of that State should be able to exercise personal jurisdiction over the nonresident trustees. This is a non sequitur. With personal jurisdiction over the executor, legatees, and appointees, there is nothing in federal law to prevent Florida from adjudicating concerning the respective rights and liabilities of those parties. But Florida has not chosen to do so. As we understand its law, the trustee is an indispensable party over whom the court must acquire jurisdiction before it is empowered to enter judgment in a proceeding affecting the validity of a trust. It does not acquire that jurisdiction by being the "center of gravity" of the controversy, or the most convenient location for litigation. The issue is personal jurisdiction, not choice of law. It is resolved in this case by considering the acts of the trustee. As we have indicated, they are insufficient to sustain the jurisdiction. . . .

As we have noted earlier, the Florida Supreme Court has repeatedly held that a trustee is an indispensable party without whom a Florida court has no power to adjudicate controversies affecting the validity of a trust. For that reason the Florida judgment must be reversed not only as to the nonresident trustee but also as to appellants, over whom the Florida court admittedly had jurisdiction.

357 U.S. at 246-255. Justices Black and Douglas dissented.

L. SIMES, FUTURE INTERESTS
(2d ed. 1966)

§49. In some situations the person to whom a future interest in property is limited is not a necessary party to a proceeding involving the title to the property, but may be represented by some other person. A trustee may sometimes represent the beneficiaries of a trust, and a guardian ad litem may sometimes represent his ward. There is also a doctrine of representation based upon the fact that the representing person has an interest in the property which will be affected by the judgment or decree in the same way as the interest of the represented person or in a similar way. This kind of representation is commonly limited to cases where an unborn or unascertained person is represented.

MABRY v. SCOTT
51 Cal. App. 2d 245, 124 P.2d 659 (Dist. Ct. App.), *cert. denied,*
317 U.S. 670 (1942)

[In 1931 the defendant trust company executed an irrevocable declaration of trust acknowledging receipt of $1,350,000 to be held in trust. The living beneficiaries were the settlor, W. J. Garland, and his then wife Alzoa, and their four minor children. The trust was to terminate on the death of the last survivor of these six beneficiaries, and the corpus was to go to Mr. and Mrs. Garland's then living issue, and in default of issue to the living spouses of the four children, if any, and otherwise to the settlor's heirs. The trust, which bore the same date as a property settlement agreement between Mr. and Mrs. Garland, provided for payment of income essentially as follows: (1) $15,000 annually to Mrs. Garland; (2) any remaining income to the settlor; and (3) on various contingencies and on the death of Mr. and Mrs. Garland, part or all of the income was distributable to the four children. About four months after the creation of the trust, Alzoa Garland secured a divorce from the settlor. Thereafter she married M. L. Scott, and the settlor also remarried and had a minor child of that marriage. In 1936 the settlor brought suit to set aside the trust, alleging fraud and undue influence. The allegations were denied by all defendants, including the trustee and all beneficiaries appearing in person or by guardians ad litem. The plaintiff and his former wife, Alzoa, agreed on a compromise of the litigation: each of them was to receive $60,000 cash from principal, and 75 percent of the income was to be paid equally to them or their successors until termination of the trust, with 25 percent of the income to be divided among the children. With the exception of the trustee, all parties (including contingent remaindermen) personally or by guardians ad litem joined in a petition to the court to authorize and approve the proposed compromise. On the hearing of the petition the guardians ad litem recommended approval of the compromise, and the court entered judgment accordingly, ordering the agreed modification. The trustee argued below and on appeal that judgment deprived unborn remaindermen of property without due process of law in that their interests are impaired by the $120,000 reduction of corpus and the elimination of certain contingent rights to income.]

DRAPEAU, J. PRO TEM. . . .

When the litigation is between them, all beneficiaries of a trust are indispensable parties; without their presence the trial court has no jurisdiction to proceed.

The latest expression of the rule is by Mr. Chief Justice Gibson in the case of First National, etc., Bank v. Superior Court, 19 Cal. 2d 409, 417, 121 P.2d 729, 733:

> The law is settled in this state that, where one of several beneficiaries seeks to fix his share in a trust fund and where judgment in his favor would inevitably determine the amount available for others similarly situated, such other beneficiaries are indispensable parties. A judgment rendered in their absence and purporting to determine their rights is in excess of the court's jurisdiction.

But this rule of indispensable parties has one manifest exception. It is founded on the paramount duty of every court to see that justice be done. It takes effect when there are remaindermen not in being and when it is apparent that it is essential, in the interests of justice, to adjudicate rights of living persons.

This exception has been stated, approved, and applied by our courts in numerous cases in which future estates of unborn or unknown contingent remaindermen in real property and the relationship of such estates to rights of living persons have been under consideration. One of the best statements of it is to be found in section 182, chapter 12, Restatement of the Law, Property, Future Interests:

> Prerequisites for binding effect as against interest limited in favor of an unborn person. A judicial proceeding has binding effect as against the future interest limited in favor of a person who was unborn at the time of the commencement of such proceeding when the requirements stated in some one of the clauses of this section are satisfied, but not otherwise: (a) Such person was duly represented in such proceeding in accordance with one of the rules stated in sections 183 [involving virtual representation] and 186 [involving representation by a trustee]; (b) Such person was duly represented by a guardian ad litem appointed to protect the interests limited in favor of unborn persons. . . .

The reason behind the exception is a simple one of human relationships, implicit in the principle that human laws, and all other temporal things, are for the living; not for the dead or for those not yet in being, if to hold otherwise would result in injustice to living persons. Because parties are not in being, and therefore cannot be brought before the tribunal, is not sufficient reason for a court to stand by, helpless and impotent, when rights of living persons, in ordinary common sense ought to be adjudicated.

Were the unborn contingent remaindermen represented in the litigation? . . .

The trial court was correct in its determination that there was virtual representation of the unborn contingent remaindermen by the living children of Mr. and Mrs. Garland. There were no living members of this class of unborn contingent remaindermen. . . .

[In County of Los Angeles v. Winans, 13 Cal. App. 234, 244, 109 P. 640, 645 (1910)] it is said: "The interests of representative and represented must, however, be so identical that the motive and inducement to protect and preserve may be assumed to be the same in each." That case held that there was hostility of interest which precluded representation because a parent life tenant and a child remainderman had acted adversely to the interests of other child remaindermen who might later be born.

Appellant contends that by the compromise in the present case the living children secured a better participation in income than in the trust as originally drawn. Indeed a close reading of the trust agreement supports a theory of the appellant that the living children were to receive no income from the original trust until the death of their mother, or upon the nomination of their father, and that it is necessary to read the property settlement agreement into the trust to give any income to the children. But, assuming that by the compromise the living children received income not provided by the original trust, we are unable to agree with either minor premise or conclusion of appellant's suggested syllogism: that this caused them to profit at the expense of their unborn issue: and that there was thereby created hostility of interest as between the living children and their unborn issue which prevented virtual representation by the living children of the unborn contingent remaindermen.

The principal argument in support of this proposition is that . . . the living children consented to these changes in the trust agreement so that they might get the better participation in income provided by the compromise, and thereby deprived the contingent remaindermen of $120,000 which otherwise would eventually have gone to them, and of contingent income. To thus hold would involve conclusions of collusion and conspiracy which the facts of this case will not sustain. The decisive fact still remains that the remaindermen had no interest in the income: the living children had no interest in the corpus, except in the contingencies above stated. These contingencies are too remote to require a decision that the incentive on the part of the living children to protect and preserve the rights of their issue was destroyed. And computations are in the briefs which indicate that should any of these contingencies come to pass, neither income nor corpus will be depleted to the disadvantage of the remaindermen. Therefore, there was no adverse interest as between the living children and their issue which prevented the living children from representing the unborn contingent remaindermen. Under the doctrine of virtual representation the contingent remaindermen were represented and the court had jurisdiction over them and their interests in the trust. . . .

Under the pleadings, when the issues were joined in fraud, undue influence, failure of consideration, and mistake, the court had jurisdiction to hear and determine the controverted facts. If an affirmative finding could have been made as to any such facts, supported by competent testimony, the court had power to terminate the trust. Therefore it had the right and it was its duty to adjudicate this case, unless the action of all of the parties except the trustee in presenting the petition to approve the compromise, divested the court of jurisdiction. Obviously, there is here involved all of the aspects of the case, and the terms and conditions of the compromise.

In this connection there has been presented a most persuasive argument. It is that courts should always have in mind the rights of remaindermen not in being; that by affirming the judgment in this case, there may be sanctioned a method whereby trusts may be destroyed at will by combinations of living beneficiaries; that this may be done by pleadings framing issues giving jurisdiction to courts of equity to modify trusts, and then by securing judgments based on compromises giving to living beneficiaries property of unborn remaindermen.

The answer to this argument is equally persuasive. It is that courts may be safely entrusted with the protection of rights of unborn remaindermen. And it is in cases of this sort, in which there is jurisdiction in equity of the controversy, that such rights are protected by the courts themselves. In the present case we can confidently assume that this duty was performed by the trial court.

In actions for rescission, when a jurisdiction of equity attaches, it is the duty of equity to adjust all the differences arising from the cause of action presented and to leave nothing for further litigation. To aid it in the exercise of its jurisdiction to hear and determine this matter, the court appointed a guardian ad litem to represent and protect the interests of the contingent remaindermen. Courts of justice as an incident of their jurisdictions have inherent power to appoint guardians ad litem. . . .

There has been considerable argument in the briefs, and citation of authority, as to whether the trustee in this case represented the interests of the unborn contingent remaindermen. In view of there being virtual representation and equitable jurisdiction, it is not necessary to go into this question to any particular extent. There is strong authority for the statement that if it were necessary in order that justice might be done to living parties, the interests of contingent remaindermen in this trust estate could be represented by the trustee. . . .

The . . . judgment is affirmed.

MATTER OF WILL OF SANDERS
123 Misc. 2d 424, 474 N.Y.S. 2d 215 (Surr. 1984)

RADIGAN, Surrogate.

In this executor's account proceeding the court is required to pass on the question of virtual representation (SCPA 315). Article TWENTIETH of the will provides for the establishment of a sprinkling trust of the entire residuary estate with income in the trustee's discretion payable to testatrix's son, Robert, and any of his issue, with principal invasion [on limited terms] for the benefit of the son [and] any child or grandchild of the son. . . . The trust is to terminate on the death of the son and his two children, Ian and Zara (grandchild) with the principal and all accrued and accumulated income to be paid to the issue of the decedent's son living at the termination of the trust per stirpes.

Both Ian and Zara have children of their own (great grandchildren). It is these three great grandchildren upon whom service of process is sought to be disposed of on the ground that they are virtually represented by their parents, the decedent's grandchildren. Petitioner's argument is based upon the theory that the grandchildren and the great grandchildren have the requisite "same interests" under the virtual representation statute in this executor's accounting; that is, the maximization of the trust principal and therefore their interests are not in conflict. . . .

The interests of the grandchildren and the infant great grandchildren, both of whom are presently interested in income and principal as beneficiaries of the sprinkling trust, are identical as to those [sprinkling] interests. . . . In addition, . . . the three infant great grandchildren are the remaindermen as far as this application is concerned, subject to the trustee's limited power to invade principal.

The court must be ever mindful of its obligation to expedite the administration of estates and avoid unnecessary expenses including that of fees to be paid to guardians ad litem where possible. At the same time, the court, mindful of our litigious society, seeks to secure decrees from attack and not permit them to lie in waiting for an adult representee or for an incapacitated person to reach majority and with his disability unshackled to move to vacate same on the basis that they were not adequately represented. The court has an obligation to seek to insure finality of its decrees and to avoid a possible later attack based on lack of jurisdiction. Accordingly, a court must carefully evaluate the petitioner's request to use virtual representation, especially where any doubt may exist in the court's mind as to the adequacy of the representation. . . .

The Third Report 1984 P. 284 of the Temporary State Commission on Estates (The Bennett Commission) indicates that a present income interest is not the same and is in fact antagonistic to a future remainder interest. . . . [H]ere in an accounting proceeding . . . the income and principal interest can be adverse, especially under the terms of the will herein where the grandchildren may prefer to focus on their income interest [while] in the long term the great grandchildren would have more of an interest in the preservation of the corpus. The grandchildren and great grandchildren both have a potential to receive income and limited principal but the great-grandchildren are the only ultimate takers of the remainder and may therefore be benefited by a portfolio that consists of assets which have a growth potential rather than favoring a high yield potential which may be more beneficial to their parents. . . .

[N]ecessarily an accounting by an executor with a trust involved must include allocations of receipts and expenses between principal and interest which may create conflicts. Here the trust indeed was funded and there may be diversity of interests between the income beneficiaries and the remaindermen concerning the funding of the trust. While both income and principal interests ostensibly have the identical interest of maximizing the trust, they may have a diversity of interest as to the specific assets to be distributed to the trust in addition to potential diversity concerning allocation of receipts and expenditures.

The court must be concerned with whether or not the representees are being actively represented and not [merely] with whether or not they could be represented. . . . The court is not satisfied that the great grandchildren will be adequately represented [by the grandchildren] under the statute.

Accordingly, the court directs citation be served on the great grandchildren.

A statutory provision for virtual representation in appropriate cases and appointment of guardians ad litem can be found in §1-403 of the Uniform Probate Code. Paragraph 3 of that section and §1-401 prescribe methods for giving notice efficiently and in accordance with due process requirements.

MULLANE v. CENTRAL HANOVER BANK & TRUST CO.
339 U.S. 306 (1950)

JACKSON, J., delivered the opinion of the Court.

This controversy questions the constitutional sufficiency of notice to beneficiaries on judicial settlement of accounts by the trustee of a common trust fund. . . . The New York Court of Appeals considered and overruled objections that the statutory notice contravenes requirements of the Fourteenth Amendment and that by allowance of the account beneficiaries were deprived of property without due process of law. . . .

Common trust fund legislation is addressed to a problem appropriate for state action. . . . In order that donors and testators of moderately sized trusts may not be denied the service of corporate fiduciaries, the District of Columbia and some thirty states other than New York have permitted pooling small trust estates into one fund for investment administration. The income, capital gains, losses and expenses of the collective trust are shared by the constituent trusts in proportion to their contribution. By this plan, diversification of risk and economy of management can be extended to those whose capital standing alone would not obtain such advantage.

Statutory authorization for the establishment of such common trust funds is provided in the New York Banking Law. . . . Under this act a trust company may, with approval of the State Banking Board, establish a common fund and, within prescribed limits, invest therein the assets of an unlimited number of estates, trusts or other funds of which it is trustee. Each participating trust shares ratably in the common fund, but exclusive management and control is in the trust company as trustee, and neither a fiduciary nor any beneficiary of a participating trust is deemed to have ownership in any particular asset or investment of this common fund. The trust company must keep fund assets separate from its own, and in its fiduciary capacity may not deal with itself or any affiliate. Provisions are made for accountings twelve to fifteen months after the establishment of a fund and triennially thereafter. The decree in each such judicial settlement of accounts is made binding and conclusive as to any matter set forth in the account upon everyone having any interest in the common fund or in any participating estate, trust or fund.

In January, 1946, Central Hanover Bank and Trust Company established a common trust fund in accordance with these provisions, and in March, 1947, it petitioned the Surrogate's Court for settlement of its first account as common trustee. During the accounting period a total of 113 trusts, approximately half inter vivos and half testamentary, participated in the common trust fund, the gross capital of which was nearly three million dollars. The record does not show the number or residence of the beneficiaries, but they were many and it is clear that some of them were not residents of the State of New York.

The only notice given beneficiaries of this specific application was by publication in a local newspaper in strict compliance with the minimum requirements of N.Y. Banking Law §100-c(12). . . . Thus the only notice required, and the only one given, was by newspaper publication [four times] setting forth merely the name and address of the trust company, the name and the date of establishment of the common trust fund, and a list of all participating estates, trusts or funds.

At the time the first investment in the common fund was made on behalf of each participating estate, however, the trust company, pursuant to the requirements of §100-c(9), had notified by mail each person of full age and sound mind whose name and address was then known to it and who was "entitled to share in the income therefrom . . . [or] . . . who would be entitled to share in the principal if the event upon which such estate, trust or fund will become distributable should have occurred at the time of sending such notice." Included in the notice was a copy of those provisions of the Act relating to the sending of the notice itself and to the judicial settlement of common trust fund accounts.

Upon the filing of the petition for the settlement of accounts, appellant was, by order of the court pursuant to §100-c(12), appointed special guardian and attorney for all persons known or unknown not otherwise appearing who had or might thereafter have any interest in the income of the common trust fund; and appellee Vaughan was appointed to represent those similarly interested in the principal. There were no other appearances on behalf of any one interested in either interest or principal.

Appellant appeared specially, objecting that notice and the statutory provisions for notice to beneficiaries were inadequate to afford due process under the Fourteenth Amendment, and therefore that the court was without jurisdiction to render a final and binding decree. Appellant's objections were entertained and overruled. . . .

The effect of this decree, as held below, is to settle "all questions respecting the management of the common fund." We understand that every right which beneficiaries would otherwise have against the trust company, either as trustee of the common fund or as trustee of any individual trust, for improper management of the common trust fund during the period covered by the accounting is sealed and wholly terminated by the decree.

We are met at the outset with a challenge to the power of the State — the right of its courts to adjudicate at all as against those beneficiaries who reside without the State of New York. It is contended that the proceeding is one in personam in that the decree affects neither title to nor possession of any res, but adjudges only personal rights of the beneficiaries to surcharge their trustee for negligence or breach of trust. Accordingly, it is said, under the strict doctrine of Pennoyer v. Neff, 95 U.S. 714, the Surrogate is without jurisdiction as to nonresidents upon whom personal service of process was not made.

Distinctions between actions in rem and those in personam are ancient and originally expressed in procedural terms what seems really to have been a distinction in the substantive law of property under a system quite unlike our own. The legal recognition and rise in economic importance of incorporeal or intangible forms of property have upset the ancient simplicity of property law and the clarity of its distinctions, while new forms of proceedings have confused the old procedural classification. American courts have sometimes classed certain actions as in rem because personal service of process was not required, and at other times, have held personal service of process not required because the action was in rem.

Judicial proceedings to settle fiduciary accounts have been sometimes termed in rem, or more indefinitely quasi in rem, or more vaguely still, "in the nature of a proceeding in rem." It is not readily apparent how the courts of New York did or would classify the present proceeding, which has some characteristics and is wanting in some features of proceedings both in rem and personam. But in any event we think that the requirements of the Fourteenth Amendment to the Federal Constitution do not depend upon a classification for which the standards are so elusive and confused generally and which, being primarily for state courts to define, may and do vary from state to state. . . . It is sufficient to observe that, whatever the technical definition of its chosen procedure, the interest of each state in providing means to close trusts that exist by the grace of its laws and are administered under the supervision of its courts is so insistent and rooted in custom as to establish beyond doubt the right of its courts to determine the interests of all claimants, resident or nonresident, provided its procedure accords full opportunity to appear and be heard.

Quite different from the question of a state's power to discharge trustees is that of the opportunity it must give beneficiaries to contest. Many controversies have raged about the cryptic and abstract words of the Due Process Clause but there can be no doubt that at a minimum they require that deprivation of life, liberty or property by adjudication be preceded by notice and opportunity for hearing appropriate to the nature of the case.

In two ways this proceeding does or may deprive beneficiaries of property. It may cut off their rights to have the trustee answer for negligent or illegal impairments of their interests. Also, their interests are presumably subject to diminution in the proceeding by allowance of fees and expenses to one who, in their names but without their knowledge, may conduct a fruitless or uncompensatory contest. Certainly the proceeding is one in which they may be deprived of property rights and hence notice and hearing must measure up to the standards of due process.

Personal service of written notice within the jurisdiction is the classic form of notice always adequate in any type of proceeding. But the vital interest of the state in bringing any issues as to its fiduciaries to a final settlement can be served only if interest or claims of individuals who are outside of the State can somehow be determined. A construction of the Due Process Clause which would place impossible or impractical obstacles in the way could not be justified.

Against this interest of the State we must balance the individual interest sought to be protected by the Fourteenth Amendment. This is defined by our holding that "The fundamental requisite of due process of law is the opportunity to be heard." Grannis v. Ordean, 234 U.S. 385. This right to be heard has little reality or worth unless one is informed that the matter is pending and can choose for himself whether to appear or default, acquiesce or contest.

The Court has not committed itself to any formula achieving a balance between these interests in a particular proceeding or determining when constructive notice may be utilized or what test it must meet. Personal service has not in all circumstances been regarded as indispensable to the process due to residents, and it has more often been held unnecessary as to nonresidents. We disturb none of the established rules on these subjects. No decision constitutes a controlling or even a very illuminating precedent for the case before us. But a few general principles stand out in the books.

An elementary and fundamental requirement of due process in any proceeding which is to be accorded finality is notice reasonably calculated, under all the circumstances, to apprise interested parties of the pendency of the action and afford them an opportunity to present their objections. . . . The notice must be of such nature as reasonably to convey the required information, . . . and it must afford a reasonable time for those interested to make their appearance. . . . But if with due regard for the practicalities and peculiarities of the case these conditions are reasonably met the constitutional requirements are satisfied. "The criterion is not the possibility of conceivable injury, but the just and reasonable character of the requirements, having reference to the subject with which the statute deals." American Land Co. v. Zeiss, 219 U.S. 47, 67, and see Blinn v. Nelson, 222 U.S. 1, 7.

But when notice is a person's due, process which is a mere gesture is not due process. The means employed must be such as one desirous of actually informing the absentee might reasonably adopt to accomplish it. The reasonableness and hence the constitutional validity of any chosen method may be defended on the ground that it was in itself reasonably certain to inform those affected, . . . or, where conditions preclude reasonable certainty of actual receipt of notice, that the form chosen is not substantially less likely to bring home notice than other of the feasible and customary substitutes.

It would be idle to pretend that publication alone as prescribed here, is a reliable means of acquainting interested parties of the fact that their rights are before the courts. It is not an accident that the greater number of cases reaching this Court on the question of adequacy of notice have been concerned with actions founded on process constructively served through local newspapers. Chance alone brings to the attention of even a local resident an advertisement in small type inserted in the back pages of a newspaper, and if he makes his home outside of the area of the newspaper's normal circulation the odds that the information will never reach him are large indeed. The chance of actual notice is further reduced when as here the notice required does not even name those whose attention it is supposed to attract, and does not inform acquaintances who might call it to attention. In weighing its sufficiency on the basis of equivalence with actual notice we are unable to regard this as more than a feint.

Nor is publication here reinforced by steps likely to attract the parties' attention to the proceeding. It is true that publication traditionally has been acceptable as notification supplemental to other action which in itself may reasonably be expected to convey a warning. . . .

In the case before us there is, of course, no abandonment. On the other hand these beneficiaries do have a resident fiduciary as caretaker of their interest in this property. But it is their caretaker who in the accounting becomes their adversary. . . . Not even the special guardian is required or apparently expected to communicate with his ward and client, and of course, if such a duty were merely transferred from the trustee to the guardian, economy would not be served and more likely the cost would be increased.

This Court has not hesitated to approve of resort to publication as a customary substitute in another class of cases where it is not reasonably possible or practicable to give more adequate warning. Thus it has been recognized that in the case of persons missing or unknown employment of an indirect and even a probably futile means of notification is all that the situation permits and creates no constitutional bar to a final decree foreclosing their rights.

Those beneficiaries represented by appellant, whose interests or whereabouts could not with due diligence be ascertained come clearly within this category. As to them the statutory notice is sufficient. However great the odds that publication will never reach the eyes of such unknown parties, it is not in the typical case much more likely to fail than any of the choices open to legislators endeavoring to prescribe the best notice practicable.

Nor do we consider it unreasonable for the state to dispense with more certain notice to those beneficiaries whose interests are either conjectural or future or, although they could be discovered upon investigation, do not, in due course of business come to knowledge of the common trustee. Whatever searches might be required in another situation under ordinary standards of diligence, in view of the character of the proceedings and the nature of the interests here involved we think them unnecessary. We recognize the practical difficulties and costs that would be attendant on frequent investigations into the status of great numbers of beneficiaries, many of whose interests in the common fund are so remote as to be ephemeral; and we have no doubt that such impracticable and extended searches are not required in the name of due process. The expense of keeping informed from day to day of substitutions among even current income beneficiaries and presumptive remaindermen, to say nothing of the far greater number of contingent beneficiaries, would impose a severe burden on the plan, and would likely dissipate its advantages. These are practical matters in which we should be reluctant to disturb the judgment of the state authorities.

Accordingly we overrule appellant's constitutional objections to published notice insofar as they are urged on behalf of any beneficiaries whose interests or addresses are unknown to the trustee.

As to known present beneficiaries of known place of residence, however, notice by publication stands on a different footing. Exceptions in the name of necessity do not sweep away the rule that within the limits of practicability notice must be such as is reasonably calculated to reach interested parties. Where the names and post office addresses of those affected by a proceeding are at hand, the reasons disappear for resort to means less likely than the mails to apprise them of its pendency.

The trustee has on its books the names and addresses of the income beneficiaries represented by appellant, and we find no tenable ground for dispensing with a serious effort to inform them personally of the accounting, at least by ordinary mail to the record addresses. . . . Certainly sending them a copy of the statute months and perhaps years in advance does not answer this purpose. The trustee periodically remits their income to them, and we think that they might reasonably expect that with or apart from their remittances word might come to them personally that steps were being taken affecting their interests.

We need not weigh contentions that a requirement of personal service of citation on even the large number of known resident or nonresident beneficiaries would, by reasons of delay if not expense, seriously interfere with the proper administration of the fund. . . . This type of trust presupposes a large number of small interests. The individual interest does not stand alone but is identical with that of a class. The rights of each in the integrity of the fund and the fidelity of the trustee are shared by many other beneficiaries. Therefore notice reasonably certain to reach most of those interested in objecting is likely to safeguard the interests of all since any objections sustained would inure to the benefit of all. We think that under such circumstances reasonable risks that notice might not actually reach every beneficiary are justifiable. . . .

The statutory notice to known beneficiaries is inadequate not because in fact it fails to reach everyone, but because under the circumstances it is not reasonably calculated to reach those who could easily be informed by other means at hand. However it may have been in former times, the mails today are recognized as an efficient and inexpensive means of communication. . . .

We hold the notice of judicial settlement of accounts required by the New York Banking Law §100-c(12) is incompatible with the requirements of the Fourteenth Amendment as a basis for adjudication depriving known persons whose whereabouts are also known of substantial property rights. Accordingly the judgment is reversed and the cause remanded for further proceedings not inconsistent with this opinion.

Reversed.

TULSA PROFESSIONAL COLLECTION SERVICES v. POPE
485 U.S. 478 (1988)

Justice O'CONNOR delivered the opinion of the Court.

This case involves a provision of Oklahoma's probate laws requiring claims "arising upon a contract" generally to be presented to the executor or executrix of the estate within 2 months of the publication of a notice advising creditors of the commencement of probate proceedings. Okla. Stat., Tit. 58, §333 (1981). The question presented is whether this provision of notice solely by publication satisfies the Due Process Clause.

I

Oklahoma's probate code requires creditors to file claims against an estate within a specified time period, and generally bars untimely claims. Ibid. Such "nonclaim statutes" are almost universally included in state probate codes. See Uniform Probate Code §3-801, 8 U.L.A. 351 (1983); Falender, Notice to Creditors in Estate Proceedings: What Process is Due?, 63 N.C.L. Rev. 659, 667-668 (1985). Giving creditors a limited time in which to file claims against the estate serves the State's interest in facilitating the administration and expeditious closing of estates. See, e.g., State ex rel. Central State Griffin Memorial Hospital v. Reed, 493 P.2d 815, 818 (Okla. 1972). Nonclaim statutes come in two basic forms. Some provide a relatively short time period, generally 2 to 6 months, that begins to run after the commencement of probate proceedings. Others call for a longer period, generally 1 to 5 years, that runs from the decedent's death. See Falender, supra, at 664-672. Most States include both types of nonclaim statutes in their probate codes, typically providing that if probate proceedings are not commenced and the shorter period therefore never is triggered, then claims nonetheless may be barred by the longer period. See, e.g., Ark. Code Ann. §28-50-101(a), (d) (1987) (3 months if probate proceedings commenced; 5 years if not); Idaho Code §15-3-803(a)(1), (2) (1979) (4 months; 3 years); Mo. Rev. Stat. §473.360(1), (3) (1986) (6 months; 3 years). Most States also provide that creditors are to be notified of the requirement to file claims imposed by the nonclaim statutes solely by publication. See Uniform Probate Code §3-801, 8 U.L.A. 351 (1983); Falender, supra, at 660, n.7 (collecting statutes). Indeed, in most jurisdictions it is the publication of notice that triggers the nonclaim statute. The Uniform Probate Code, for example, provides that creditors have 4 months from publication in which to file claims. Uniform Probate Code §3-801, 8 U.L.A. 351 (1983). See also, e.g., Ariz. Rev. Stat. Ann. §14-3801 (1975); Fla. Stat. §733.701 (1987); Utah Code Ann. §75-3-801 (1978).

The specific nonclaim statute at issue in this case, Okla. Stat., Tit. 58, §333 (1981), provides for only a short time period and is best considered in the context of Oklahoma probate proceedings as a whole. . . .

Immediately after appointment, the executor or executrix is required to "give notice to the creditors of the deceased." §331. Proof of compliance with this requirement must be filed with the court. §332. This notice is to advise creditors that they must present their claims to the executor or executrix within 2 months of the date of the first publication. As for the method of notice, the statute requires only publication: "[S]uch notice must be published in some newspaper in [the] county once each week for two (2) consecutive weeks." §331. A creditor's failure to file a claim within the 2-month period generally bars it forever. §333. The nonclaim statute does provide certain exceptions, however. If the creditor is out of State, then a claim "may be presented at any time before a decree of distribution is entered." §333. Mortgages and debts not yet due are also excepted from the 2-month time limit.

This shorter type of nonclaim statute is the only one included in Oklahoma's probate code. Delays in commencement of probate proceedings are dealt with not through some independent, longer period running from the decedent's death, see, e.g., Ark. Code Ann. §28-50-101(d) (1987), but by shortening the notice period once proceedings have started. Section 331 provides that if the decedent has been dead for more than 5 years, then creditors have only 1 month after notice is published in which to file their claims. A similar 1-month period applies if the decedent was intestate. §331.

II

H. Everett Pope, Jr. was admitted to St. John Medical Center, a hospital in Tulsa, Oklahoma, in November 1978. On April 2, 1979, while still at the hospital, he died testate. His wife, appellee JoAnne Pope, initiated probate proceedings in the District Court of Tulsa County in accordance with the statutory scheme outlined above. The court entered an order setting a hearing. Record 8. After the hearing the court entered an order admitting the will to probate and, following the designation in the will, id., at 2, named appellee as the executrix of the estate. Id., at 12. Letters testamentary were issued, id., at 13, and the court ordered appellee to fulfill her statutory obligation by directing that she "immediately give notice to creditors." Id., at 14. Appellee published notice in the Tulsa

Daily Legal News for 2 consecutive weeks beginning July 17, 1979. The notice advised creditors that they must file any claim they had against the estate within 2 months of the first publication of the notice. Id., at 16.

Appellant Tulsa Professional Collection Services, Inc., is a subsidiary of St. John Medical Center and the assignee of a claim for expenses connected with the decedent's long stay at that hospital. Neither appellant, nor its parent company, filed a claim with appellee within the 2-month time period following publication of notice. In October 1983, however, appellant filed an Application for Order Compelling Payment of Expenses of Last Illness. Id., at 28. In making this application, appellant relied on Okla. Stat., Tit. 58, §594 (1981), which indicates that an executrix "must pay . . . the expenses of the last sickness." Appellant argued that this specific statutory command made compliance with the 2-month deadline for filing claims unnecessary. The District Court of Tulsa County rejected this contention, ruling that even claims pursuant to §594 fell within the general requirements of the nonclaim statute. Accordingly, the court denied appellant's application. App. 3.

The District Court's reading of §594's relationship to the nonclaim statute was affirmed by the Oklahoma Court of Appeals. App. 7. Appellant then sought rehearing, arguing for the first time that the nonclaim statute's notice provisions violated due process. In a supplemental opinion on rehearing the Court of Appeals rejected the due process claim on the merits. Id., at 15.

Appellant next sought review in the Supreme Court of Oklahoma. That court granted certiorari and, after review of both the §594 and due process issues, affirmed the Court of Appeals' judgment. . . . We noted probable jurisdiction, 484 U.S. 813, 108 S. Ct. 62, 98 L. Ed. 2d 26 (1987), and now reverse and remand.

III

Mullane v. Central Hanover Bank & Trust Co., 339 U.S. 306, at 314, 70 S. Ct. 652, at 657 (1950), established that state action affecting property must generally be accompanied by notification of that action: "An elementary and fundamental requirement of due process in any proceeding which is to be accorded finality is notice reasonably calculated, under all the circumstances, to apprise interested parties of the pendency of the action and afford them an opportunity to present their objections." In the years since *Mullane* the Court has adhered to these principles, balancing the "interest of the State" and "the individual interest sought to be protected by the Fourteenth Amendment." Ibid. The focus is on the reasonableness of the balance, and, as *Mullane* itself made clear, whether a particular method of notice is reasonable depends on the particular circumstances. . . .

Applying these principles to the case at hand . . . [a]ppellant's interest is an unsecured claim, a cause of action against the estate for an unpaid bill. Little doubt remains that such an intangible interest is property protected by the Fourteenth Amendment. . . .

The Fourteenth Amendment protects this interest, however, only from a deprivation by state action. Private use of state sanctioned private remedies or procedures does not rise to the level of state action. . . . Nor is the State's involvement in the mere running of a general statute of limitation generally sufficient to implicate due process. See Texaco, Inc. v. Short, 454 U.S. 516, 102 S. Ct. 781, 70 L. Ed. 2d 738 (1982). . . . But when private parties make use of state procedures with the overt, significant assistance of state officials, state action may be found. . . . The question here is whether the State's involvement with the nonclaim statute is substantial enough to implicate the Due Process Clause.

Appellee argues that it is not, contending that Oklahoma's nonclaim statute is a self-executing statute of limitations. Relying on this characterization, appellee then points to *Short,* supra. Appellee's reading of *Short* is correct — due process does not require that potential plaintiffs be given notice of the impending expiration of a period of limitations — but in our view, appellee's premise is not. Oklahoma's nonclaim statute is not a self-executing statute of limitations.

It is true that nonclaim statutes generally possess some attributes of statutes of limitations. They provide a specific time period within which particular types of claims must be filed and they bar claims presented after expiration of that deadline. Many of the state court decisions upholding nonclaim statutes against due process challenges have relied upon these features and concluded that they are properly viewed as statutes of limitations. . . .

As we noted in *Short,* however, it is the "self-executing feature" of a statute of limitations that makes *Mullane* . . . inapposite. . . . The State's interest in a self-executing statute of limitations is in providing repose for potential defendants and in avoiding stale claims. The State has no role to play beyond enactment of the limitations period. . . .

Here, in contrast, there is significant state action. The probate court is intimately involved throughout, and without that involvement the time bar is never activated. The nonclaim statute becomes operative only after probate proceedings have been commenced in state court. The court must appoint the executor or executrix before notice, which triggers the time bar, can be given. Only after this court appointment is made does the statute provide for any notice; §331 directs the executor or executrix to publish notice "immediately" after appointment. . . . It is only after all of these actions take place that the time period begins to run, and in every one of these actions, the court is intimately involved. This involvement is so pervasive and substantial that it must be considered state action subject to the restrictions of the Fourteenth Amendment.

Where the legal proceedings themselves trigger the time bar, even if those proceedings do not necessarily resolve the claim on its merits, the time bar lacks the self-executing feature that *Short* indicated was necessary to remove any due process problem. Rather, in such circumstances, due process is directly implicated and actual notice generally is required. . . . Our conclusion that the Oklahoma nonclaim statute is not a self-executing statute of limitations makes it unnecessary to consider appellant's argument that a 2-month period is somehow unconstitutionally short. See Tr. of Oral Arg. 22 (advocating constitutional requirement that the States provide at least 1 year). We also have no occasion to consider the proper characterization of nonclaim statutes that run from the date of death, and which generally provide for longer time periods, ranging from 1 to 5 years. . . .

Nor can there be any doubt that the nonclaim statute may "adversely affect" a protected property interest. In appellant's case, such an adverse effect is all too clear. The entire purpose and effect of the nonclaim statute is to regulate the timeliness of such claims and to forever bar untimely claims, and by virtue of the statute, the probate proceedings themselves have completely extinguished appellant's claim.

In assessing the propriety of actual notice in this context consideration should be given to the practicalities of the situation and the effect that requiring actual notice may have on important state interests. . . . Creditors, who have a strong interest in maintaining the integrity of their relationship with their debtors, are particularly unlikely to benefit from publication notice. As a class, creditors may not be aware of a debtor's death or of the institution of probate proceedings. Moreover, the executor or executrix will often be, as is the case here, a party with a beneficial interest in the estate. This could diminish an executor's or executrix's inclination to call attention to the potential expiration of a creditor's claim. There is thus a substantial practical need for actual notice in this setting.

At the same time, the State undeniably has a legitimate interest in the expeditious resolution of probate proceedings. Death transforms the decedent's legal relationships and a State could reasonably conclude that swift settlement of estates is so important that it calls for very short time deadlines for filing claims. As noted, the almost uniform practice is to establish such short deadlines, and to provide only publication notice. . . . Providing actual notice to known or reasonably ascertainable creditors, however, is not inconsistent with the goals reflected in nonclaim statutes. Actual notice need not be inefficient or burdensome. We have repeatedly recognized that mail service is an inexpensive and efficient mechanism that is reasonably calculated to provide actual notice. . . . In addition, *Mullane* . . . disavowed any intent to require "impracticable and extended searches . . . in the name of due process." . . . [A]ll that the executor or executrix need do is make "reasonably diligent efforts" . . . to uncover the identities of creditors. For creditors who are not "reasonably ascertainable," publication notice can suffice. Nor is everyone who may conceivably have a claim properly considered a creditor entitled to actual notice. Here, as in *Mullane*, it is reasonable to dispense with actual notice to those with mere "conjectural" claims. . . .

On balance then, a requirement of actual notice to known or reasonably ascertainable creditors is not so cumbersome as to unduly hinder the dispatch with which probate proceedings are conducted. Notice by mail is already routinely provided at several points in the probate process. In Oklahoma, for example, §26 requires that "heirs, legatees, and devisees" be mailed notice of the initial hearing on the will. Accord Uniform Probate Code §3-403, 8 U.L.A. 274 (1983). Indeed, a few States already provide for actual notice in connection with short nonclaim statutes. See, e.g., Calif. Prob. Code Ann. §§9050, 9100 (Supp. 1988); Nev. Rev. Stat. §§147.010, 155.010, 155.020 (1987); W. Va. Code §§44-2-2, 44-2-4 (1982). We do not believe that requiring adherence to such a standard will be so burdensome or impracticable as to warrant reliance on publication notice alone.

In analogous situations we have rejected similar arguments that a pressing need to proceed expeditiously justifies less than actual notice. . . . Probate proceedings are not so different in kind that a different result is required here.

Whether appellant's identity as a creditor was known or reasonably ascertainable by appellee cannot be answered on this record. Neither the Oklahoma Supreme Court nor the Court of Appeals nor the District Court considered the question. Appellee of course was aware that her husband endured a long stay at St. John Medical Center, but it is not clear that this awareness translates into a knowledge of appellant's claim. We therefore must remand the case for further proceedings to determine whether "reasonably diligent efforts" . . . would have identified appellant and uncovered its claim. If appellant's identity was known or "reasonably ascertainable," then termination of appellant's claim without actual notice violated due process.

IV

We hold that Oklahoma's nonclaim statute is not a self-executing statute of limitations. Rather, the statute operates in connection with Oklahoma's probate proceedings to "adversely affect" appellant's property interest. Thus, if appellant's identity as a creditor was known or "reasonably ascertainable," then the Due Process Clause requires that appellant be given "[n]otice by mail or other means as certain to ensure actual notice." . . . Accordingly, the judgment of the Oklahoma Supreme Court is reversed and the case is remanded for further proceedings not inconsistent with this opinion.

It is so ordered.

Justice BLACKMUN concurs in the result.

Chief Justice REHNQUIST, dissenting.

In Texaco, Inc. v. Short, 454 U.S. 516, 102 S. Ct. 781, 70 L. Ed. 2d 738 (1982), the Court upheld . . . an Indiana statute providing that severed mineral interests which had not been used for a period of 20 years lapsed and reverted . . . unless the mineral owner filed a statement of claim. . . .

Obviously there is a great difference between the 20-year time limit in the Indiana statute and the 2-month time limit in the Oklahoma statute, but the Court does not rest the constitutional distinction between the cases on this fact. Instead, the constitutional distinction is premised on the absence in *Texaco, Inc.,* of the "significant state action" present in this case. . . .

The "intimate involvement" of the Probate Court in the present case was entirely of an administrative nature. . . .

. . . Virtually meaningless state involvement, or lack of it, rather than the effect of the statute in question on the rights of the party whose claim is cut off, is held dispositive.

. . . [T]here is no reason to conclude that the perfunctory administrative involvement of the Oklahoma probate court triggers a greater level of due process protection. . . .

Uniform Probate Code §§3-801 et seq., supra pages 561–563, contain amendments made in response to the *Pope* case. Are they adequate, and are they valid? See Reutlinger, State Action, Due Process and the New Non-Claim Statutes: Can No Notice Be Good Notice When Bad Notice Is Not?, 24 Real Prop., Prob. & Tr. J. 433 (1990). Other concerns were earlier expressed about probate notice statutes (following a case that presaged *Pope*) in Wade, Notice and Due Process in Probate, 10 Probate Notes 356 (1985):

> Initially it seems clear that the typical state law provisions regarding notice to creditors . . . are constitutionally inadequate as to "known creditors." It is less clear, however, as to what is meant by "known creditors." In *Mennonite* [Board of Missions v. Adams, 462 U.S. 791 (1983),] the interest of the mortgage holder may not have been actually known to the taxing authority [but] the interest was of record and was reasonably ascertainable. Similarly, the personal representative may reasonably be required to examine the decedent's records for the existence of creditors. Does the constitution impose a duty to inquire further?

The article goes on to note that most statutes prescribing notice of hearings for probate of wills fail

> to provide for notice to persons whose interests would often be most seriously affected, that is the successors under the decedent's "next to the

last" will or other prior wills. Such prior wills may, in fact, be logged with the court or their existence may be known to the petitioner for probate. The rationale of *Mullane* would seem to require a notice at least to those apparent successors under the prior wills in order to give the court jurisdiction to enter a fully binding order of probate.

In re ESTATE OF THOMPSON

484 N.W.2d 258 (Minn. App. 1992)

LANSING, J.

Anchor Realty challenges (1) the trial court's determination that [personal representative] Doris Thompson conducted a reasonably diligent search for creditors . . . and (2) the court's refusal to allow a late claim against the estate. . . .

The Due Process Clause of the United States Constitution requires the personal representative of an estate to provide actual notice of probate proceedings to known or reasonably ascertainable creditors. Tulsa Professional Collection Servs., Inc. v. Pope, 485 U.S. 478, 489-90, 108 S. Ct. 1340, 1347, 99 L. Ed. 2d 565 (1988). Consistent with that requirement, the Minnesota probate statute [enacted in 1990] provides that within three months of publication of notice of probate proceedings, the personal representative must serve notice upon all known and identified creditors. Minn. Stat. §524.3-801(b)(2). Further, the personal representative may determine, in the personal representative's discretion, that it is or is not advisable to conduct a reasonably diligent search for creditors of the decedent who are either not known or not identified. If the personal representative determines that a reasonably diligent search is advisable, the personal representative shall conduct the search. Minn. Stat. §524.3-801(b)(1). Any creditors discovered in the search must then be served with notice. Minn. Stat. §524.3-801(c).

Due process does not require "impracticable and extended searches." *Pope*, 485 U.S. at 490. . . . Rather, the personal representative must make "reasonably diligent efforts." Id. (quoting Mennonite Bd. of Missions v. Adams, 462 U.S. 791, 798 n.4, 103 S. Ct. 2706, 2711 n.4, 77 L. Ed. 2d 180 (1983)). No Minnesota case law has defined the scope of a "reasonably diligent search" for creditors. See generally Thomas L. Waterbury, Notice to Decedents' Creditors, 73 Minn. L. Rev. 763 (1989).

If a reasonably diligent search for ascertainable creditors is interpreted to require an extensive search, the timely and efficient administration of estates will be impaired, while few additional creditors will be discovered. Id. at 782. A statute giving the personal representative discretion on whether to search suggests a corresponding duty to avoid an abuse of that discretion. Id. Thus, the personal representative must act with good faith and from proper motives, and within the bounds of reasonable judgment. Id. at 782-83 n.97. . . .

Doris Thompson retrieved her husband's records from his secretary and his attorney. She reviewed the records of stores currently owned by herself and her husband, talked to his business associates, the board of directors of his company, and the partners and shareholders in his current business transactions. She paid off or served the required notice on all creditors she knew about or discovered. Nowhere in her search did Thompson encounter information about the [claim in question].

Anchor contends that Thompson's search was not reasonably diligent because she did not speak with all the employees of the stores owned by her husband or with all former business associates, and because the law firm that represented the Thompsons examined only files kept under Robert Thompson's name and not files kept under the names of businesses in which Thompson was involved. Information about the [claim] was contained in the files of Midwest 10, Inc. and DARB Investors, but in a branch office of the firm.

Robert Thompson was involved in numerous business transactions over the course of many years. To require his personal representative to determine the status of every past business transaction and contact all past associates approaches the "extended search" that *Tulsa* rejects. Doris Thompson pursued all current, potentially productive sources of information known to her. She exercised her discretion and acted in good faith.

The trial court applied the statutory language to essentially undisputed facts, therefore, its conclusion was one of law and does not bind this court. . . . We agree with the trial court, however, that Doris Thompson's search was reasonably diligent.

A court may allow a claim to be filed against an estate after expiration of the statutory filing time if the creditor can show good cause. Minn. Stat. §524.3-803(c)(4)(ii). The trial court has broad discretion to determine whether good cause exists, and its finding will not be disturbed unless clearly erroneous. . . .

. . . This court has identified hardship, misunderstanding, and diligent but mistaken procedures as reasons for granting a petition to file a late claim. . . .

The trial court denied Anchor's petition to file a late claim because although Anchor did not delay filing a claim once it discovered Robert Thompson was deceased, it had done little to protect itself up to that time. . . .

Doris Thompson conducted a reasonably diligent search for creditors under the statute. The trial court did not abuse its discretion in refusing to allow the late claim.

Affirmed.

D. Ancillary Administration

Nearly all estates are administered at the domicile of the decedent, and this is known as the *principal* or *domiciliary administration.* But for various reasons, administration elsewhere may also be required. This nondomiciliary administration is called *ancillary administration.* The in rem jurisdictional concepts applicable in many instances in estate matters in the United States, together with the strong policy of protecting the decedent's creditors, have led to the general requirement that the assets of an estate be administered in each state in which they are found at the decedent's death. State death tax obligations often require a similar result. Thus, for example, in absence of statutory modification of this view by the situs, administration proceedings must be had in each state in which the deceased owned property at death. Because this requirement is not limited to land, it is important to distinguish the question of where administration must be had from the question of what state's law governs rights of succession to various assets. Although situs law has traditionally governed nearly all issues concerning succession to immovables, under an increasing number of modern statutes various issues may be controlled by domiciliary law, such as UPC §2-201 and California Probate Code §120 relating to the rights of surviving spouses, or by other law, such as the place of execution under UPC §2-506. Normally the law of the decedent's domicile will determine who are the successors to movables even though they are administered where located. Determining the location of tangible movable property (that is, chattels) is not difficult, but intangibles raise many questions. Nonnegotiable debts and causes of action are generally subject to administration wherever suit may be brought to collect them. Negotiable paper and documents of title, to the extent interests represented thereby have been chattelized in the paper, are generally subject to administration where the paper is found. Corporate shares may also be embodied in the share certificates under the law of the place of incorporation of the issuing company. (This is now so in all states as to negotiable securities.) If all assets owned by the decedent are not thus "located" at the domicile, additional ancillary proceedings may be necessary. See generally Scoles and Hay, Conflict of Laws ch. 22 (2d ed. 1992).

Because traditional doctrine treats the administration in different states as separate, the acts of one personal representative may not be binding on another. As a result, many problems arise concerning the effect of suits by and against different personal representatives. Unusual applications of the doctrine of res judicata are to be expected and call for exceedingly close analysis of the interests of the parties and the statutes of the states involved.

Creditors may file their claims in any jurisdiction where administration is open and usually may force administration where assets can be found. Once paid, however, the creditor's claim is discharged everywhere. As a notable exception to the separate administration concepts, an insolvent estate is generally administered as a unit by paying a creditor's dividend based on the ratio of all claims wherever filed to all assets wherever located. Illustrative of the ease with which traditional concepts requiring separate administrations can be overcome, even without statute, the insolvent estate cases point the way for much-needed reform in the handling of multistate estates by our judicial system.

After ancillary administration is completed, local creditors and tax collectors being satisfied, the movable property remaining normally may be and usually is sent to the principal (that is, domiciliary) personal representative for distribution with the other assets there. This is, however, within the discretion of the ancillary court, and in some circumstances distribution may be made directly in the ancillary proceedings to those persons entitled thereto by the law of the domicile. These and other exceptions or limitations on transfer to the domiciliary representative may result from provisions in the will or statute. E.g., Cal. Prob. Code §§12540, 1132; Ill. Prob. Act §7-6 (1988). Title to land is determined locally in ancillary administration and possession granted by that court according to the situs law.

In most instances initial administration should be opened in the state of the decedent's domicile to take advantage of the opportunities for avoiding multiple administrations. This rule of thumb may not, however, apply in many situations, and careful inter vivos and postmortem planning is necessary to avoid the costly and complex problems of multistate administration. These estate administration problems should be anticipated by the parties and their attorneys on such occasions as the incorporation of a business, the making of investments, and extending business operations into other states. Of course, the use of will substitutes should also be considered. Such matters are particularly important when a property owner retires or has an estate plan reviewed. These matters are explored in Scoles and Rheinstein, Conflict Avoidance in Succession Planning, II Law 4 Contemp. Probs. 499, 520 (1956).

Some states have noted the additional expense and trouble caused by needless ancillary administration and have provided statutory exceptions or modifications of the requirements of separate administrations. Provisions permitting summary probate of a foreign will (such as Wis. Stat. Ann. §868.01 (1971)) and provisions permitting a domiciliary personal representative to collect assets within the state without local appointment (such as Fla. Stat. §734.101 (1975)) are among the most significant. Such provisions often permit avoidance of ancillary administration by careful planning and prompt action.

The Uniform Probate Code offers a simplified, rational approach to multistate administration. Article 4 provides a comprehensive set of provisions to minimize the needs for as well as complexities of ancillary administration. In part this is done by expanding the recognition and authority of domiciliary representatives in nondomiciliary states that adopt the Code. Key provisions include §§4-201, 4-301, 4-302, and 4-401 of Article 4, plus §§2-506, 3-203(g), 3-602, 3-703, 3-815, and 3-816.

16

Probate and Contest of Wills

In a testate estate, probate of the will is a prelude to administration in most instances. *Probate* is here used in its restrictive sense to mean the judicial proof of the will. Two general types of probate are in common usage in the United States. The first is probate in an informal ex parte proceeding, often referred to as *probate in common form,* in which no notice need be given at the initiation of the proceedings. This is a development from the early form of probate commonly used in England. Ex parte probate has the advantage of speed and economy, but because of lack of notice the decree admitting the will is subject to attack by one aggrieved. On the other hand, formal probate with notice to all interested parties — that is, *probate in solemn form* — is slow, allowing parties an opportunity to appear, and expensive, with costs of notice and a formal hearing, but is generally conclusive if not successfully appealed or contested within a limited time allowed by statute. In the ex parte scheme of probate, a contest of the will is usually conducted on a petition to revoke the probate of the will brought within a specified period after its admission to probate or on a caveat to the will. The filing of a caveat to a will normally brings up the question of its validity for trial after notice to interested parties prior to its admission to probate and thus converts the ex parte proceeding to probate in solemn form.

Both of these concepts of probate are employed in varying forms in the United States. Under each, the general theory is that probate is a proceeding in rem to establish the will and to administer certain assets. This reliance on a single proceeding to establish or disestablish the will as against all parties reduces litigation expense and permits maximum reliance on a single decree. However, characterizing the proceeding as in rem does not remove the procedural safeguards calculated to assure potential litigants a reasonable opportunity to be heard. Notice that is reasonably calculated under the circumstances to bring knowledge of the litigation to interested parties is required in all cases without regard to the classification employed. Recall Mullane v. Central Hanover Trust Co., 339 U.S. 306 (1950), and Tulsa Professional Collection Services v. Pope, 485 U.S. 478 (1988), Chapter 15 supra. Perhaps it is preferable not to classify the proceedings rigidly as in rem or in personam but rather to consider the needs that are to be served and the results achieved by any classification. In order to satisfy due process requirements, the tendency of modern legislation is to increase the requirements of notice in proceedings for the establishment of wills; for example, it may be provided that the period beyond which ex parte probate may not be attacked must be commenced by the giving of notice after probate or that notice must be given before the hearing on admission to probate, after which a period is allowed within which the probate may be set aside. You should consider whether the procedures prescribed by your local statute are adequate in light of the notice requirements under the *Mullane* doctrine.

Certain limitations on the rights of probate and contest and some of the grounds for successful contests are treated in this chapter. In addition to the technicalities of execution, which have been considered previously, the grounds of contest usually consist of the failure on the part of the testator to meet the requirements of testamentary capacity and its voluntary exercise.

The entire probate procedure is one that might well be subjected to considerable reform, and the student should constantly consider whether the procedures here explored could not be improved to accomplish economies of time and effort. See generally American Assembly: Death, Taxes and Family Property, chs. 9-11 (E. Halbach ed. 1977).

A. *Proving the Will*

In the typical case, probate of a will is a simple matter. At the hearing on probate the sole question before the court is whether the propounded instrument is the authentic will of the decedent; the validity and meaning of its provisions are not in issue. Some duty of producing the will is generally imposed on any person having custody of it, and a person nominated to serve as executor or some other person interested in the will normally petitions for its probate. (In the absence of a will someone interested in the estate will usually petition for the issuance of letters of administration.) Local statutes prescribe in some detail the contents of the petition, the procedure for giving notice, and the time and method of hearing the petition.

Assuming no contest, the proponent of the will is generally required to offer evidence of jurisdictional facts, compliance with notice requirements, due execution, and often testamentary capacity. The nature of evidence required to prove these matters varies, but typically the requirements are slight when the will is uncontested. The modern trend is to reduce the burdens of proving wills in uncontested proceedings. Many states permit reliance on affidavits. For example, the Uniform Probate Code §3-303 requires only the affidavit of the proponent in an informal probate proceeding. It is further provided in §3-405 and §3-

406 that proof by the affidavits of one or more of the attesting witnesses
to due execution is adequate in a formal proceeding. The self-proved
will, UPC §2-504, requires only the affidavit of the testator and the
attesting witnesses for prima facie proof of due execution even in contested cases. UPC §3-406.

PROBLEM

16-A.   The proponents seek to probate a homemade will executed
several years ago. It was signed by three witnesses. One witness has since
died, one does not recall the execution, and the third, an illiterate,
signed the will by mark. The former county health nurse was also present
at the execution of the will but did not attest it. She is an intelligent,
mature woman who was well acquainted with the testator and remem-
bers the circumstances of the valid execution at the testator's home. As
attorney for the proponents, in what order would you call the witnesses
and how would you examine each? What would you do if all witnesses
had predeceased the testator? If the will had been executed in your
office, what would you have done to avoid the difficulties present in this
problem?

Gillis v. Gillis, 96 Ga. 1, 15-17, 23 S.E. 107, 111-112 (1895), states:

. . . The fact to be established is the proper execution of the will. If that is
proved by competent testimony, it is sufficient, no matter from what quarter the testimony comes, provided the attesting witnesses are among those
who bear testimony, or their absence is explained. . . . The law does not
allow proof of the valid execution and attestation of a will to be defeated
at the time of probate by the failure of the memory on the part of any of
the subscribing witnesses. . . .

The main reason of the rule for calling all witnesses in a proceeding for
probate in solemn form is to give the other party an opportunity of cross-
examining them; and while the law requires a will to be attested by three
witnesses, it does not necessarily mean that all three must concur in their
testimony to prove it on probate. To do this would make the validity of the
will depend upon the memory and good faith of the witnesses, and not
upon that reasonable proof the law demands in other cases.

In re THURMAN'S ESTATE
13 Utah 2d 156, 369 P.2d 925 (1962)

CROCKETT, J. . . .

The will bore an adequate attestation clause which recited full compliance with the requirements of our statute. . . .

Appellant asserts that notwithstanding those *written* recitals, the actual *testimony* adduced at the hearing left the proof of proper execution deficient in certain particulars: that it did not show affirmatively that [the testator] had declared the document was his will; nor that he requested the witnesses to act as such.

It has been held, and we think correctly, that under such circumstances the fact that the witness does not recall or relate [that] the full detail of the statutory formalities were complied with will not defeat the will. Where there is an attestation clause reciting observance of the statutory requirements for the execution of a will, and the genuineness of the signatures is proved, a presumption arises that the recitals contained therein are true and that the will was duly executed. This is justified because it is reasonable to assume that persons acting in regard to something this important will do so seriously and deliberately; and that they therefore know the contents of what they signed. The presumption of due execution is of such strength that it will support a finding to that effect; and it can be overcome only by clear and convincing evidence to the contrary. There being no such evidence here, the finding that the will was valid is sustained. . . .

See also In re Estate of Koss, 84 Ill. App. 2d 59, 70, 228 N.E.2d 510, 515-516 (1967):

It is settled law that execution of an instrument may be sufficiently proved where one attesting witness testified positively to the requisites of execution and the other witness does not recollect or denies compliance with the statutory requisites. . . .

Where an attestation clause is in due form and the will bears the genuine signatures of the testatrix and of the witnesses this is prima facie evidence of the due execution of the will, which cannot usually be overcome by the testimony of a witness that there was no compliance with all of the statutory requisites. The testimony of a subscribing witness which seeks to impeach a will is to be viewed with suspicion and received with caution.

Proof of lost or destroyed wills. In In re Murray's Estate, 404 Pa. 120, 129, 171 A.2d 171, 175-176 (1961), the court stated:

Certain proof is essential to establish a destroyed or suppressed will: (1) that testatrix duly and properly executed the original will; (2) that the contents of the executed will were substantially as appears on the copy of the will presented for probate; (3) that, when testatrix died, the will remained undestroyed or unrevoked by her. . . . The difficulty arises in proving the status of the will when decedent died. In determining such status, we must bear in mind that where a testatrix retains the custody and possession of her will and, after her death, the will cannot be found, the presumption arises, in the absence of proof to the contrary, that the will was revoked or destroyed by the testatrix. To overcome that presumption, the evidence must be positive, clear and satisfactory.

In re Estate of Gardner, 69 Wash. 2d 229, 236-237, 417 P.2d 948, 952-953 (1966), stated:

> The contents of [a lost] will need be clearly and distinctly proven [under our statute] by two witnesses who are not required to be the attesting witnesses to the will. The two witnesses . . . must be able to testify to the provisions of the will from [their] own knowledge, and not from the declarations of another. . . . Auritt's Estate, 175 Wash. 303, 27 P.2d 913 (1933):
>
>> [I]n establishing the terms and provisions of a will, it is not necessary that the witnesses testify to its exact language but only to the substantive provisions. The cases in this and other jurisdictions have used various terms as to the quantum of evidence needed to establish the provisions of the will [such as] "clear and satisfactory," [and] "to a reasonable certainty." . . .

But the court then further observed that "the rule seems to be well settled that where one deliberately destroys or purposely induces another to destroy a written instrument of any kind, and the contents of such instrument subsequently become a matter of judicial inquiry between the spoliator and an innocent party, the latter will not be required to make strict proof of the contents."

Often the probate of lost and destroyed wills is governed by statute. The possible conflict between such statutes and rules governing the revocation of wills is treated in Chapter 6, section A, supra.

B.   Limitations on the Rights of Probate and Contest

Aside from statutes that may limit the time within which a will must be offered for probate (such as Uniform Probate Code §3-108) or within which a will must be contested, the law, the provisions of a will, or the acts of interested parties may limit or deter rights to petition for probate of a will or to contest it.

1.   Parties: The Requirement of Interest

In an effort to reduce litigation in the area of will contests, courts and legislatures have required the parties to the suit to show an "interest" in its outcome in order to have standing to sue. Although this standing requirement typically exists with reference to petitions for probate, the requirement is more often significant and more strictly interpreted in will contests. For example, one nominated as an executor may petition for probate but often is not allowed to contest a subsequent will. Also, a creditor of the decedent may petition for the opening of testate or intestate administration although denied any right to contest a will. As far as the right to contest is concerned, courts generally require the showing of a direct pecuniary interest in the denial or setting aside of probate, whatever language may be used in the statute relating to contests. Thus, where the interests of a person are the same whether probate is granted or denied, that person has no right to contest. Is there any reason why the law should permit contest of a will by the decedent's creditors, as such, or by a pretermitted heir, who will take an intestate share by statute regardless of the will's validity?

Consider whether, if a person entitled to contest a particular will died without having contested it, the right to contest should survive and pass to the personal representative. What facts might influence your decision in a particular case, or is a fixed rule one way or the other appropriate? Compare the question of whether the right of a surviving spouse to renounce the will and receive a statutory share can be exercised by the personal representative in the event the spouse dies before making an election. See Chapter 3, section B, supra.

PROBLEMS

16-B.   *D* was a citizen of the United States domiciled in Maryland but spent much of his life abroad, mostly in Spain. He died recently in London.

Two years before his death, *D* executed a will in Spain in Spanish, leaving his substantial asset holdings in Spain to *R*, a stepchild (the child of his third wife, who predeceased him) and leaving all assets located elsewhere to his brother *B*, who lives in the United States. The next month *D* traveled to Maryland and, while there, executed a similar will in English also leaving the Spanish assets to *R* and all other property to *B*. Several months ago, back in Spain, *D* executed another will in Spanish, purporting to revoke "prior wills" and to devise all the Spanish assets to *B* but making no reference to assets in the United States.

In addition to *B* and *R*, *D* is survived by two children of his second marriage, which had been annulled in Spain prior to his third marriage. He had no children by his first marriage, which had ended in divorce in Maryland. The Maryland will has been admitted to probate in Maryland, and *B* was appointed executor. *D*'s two children now move to probate the third (that is, the last Spanish-language) will in the same Maryland court. *B* objects on the grounds that the children lack standing because they are not legatees of the proposed will or any other will and are disinherited by the previously admitted Maryland will.

How would you support the children's petition for probate of the latest will? How would you expect the executor to resist it? What result would you expect? Why? See Lowenthal v. Rome, 57 Md. App. 728, 471 A.2d 1102 (1984).

16-C.   *H*, who died a number of years ago, created a testamentary trust for *W*, his wife by his second marriage, for life, remainder "to such persons or corporations as *W* may appoint by her last will and testament," and in default of appointment to *X*, a child of *H*'s first marriage. Recently *W* died leaving an instrument purporting to be her last will and to dispose of her property, including that over which she held a power of appointment, to *Z*. *X* is to take nothing under *W*'s will, but he believes he can prove that *W* lacked testamentary capacity when she executed her will. *X* is in no way related to *W*. *X* has come to you for advice. How would you advise *X* to proceed? How would you argue the case for *Z* on the question of interest? See Hogarth-Swann v. Weed, 274 Mass. 125, 174 N.E. 314 (1931).

Assuming it is decided that *X* has no interest permitting him to oppose probate of *W*'s will, is there any hope for *X*'s case? How would you proceed? How is *X*'s case affected by the "in rem character" of a probate decree and its "immunity from collateral attack"?

In re O'Brien's Estate, 13 Wash. 2d 581, 584-588, 126 P.2d 47, 49-52 (1947), states that

> there has been sharp disagreement as to whether or not an executor under a prior will or a previously appointed administrator is eligible [to contest a will]. . . .
>
> [Numerous cases have] held that an executor under an earlier will cannot caveat, or contest, a later will. . . .
>
> [However], . . . a trustee named in the earlier will could prosecute a contest. The basic reason for making the distinction seems to be that a testamentary trustee has a more substantial interest than an executor under an earlier will; that the trustee is clothed with title, and . . . "In fact a trustee is a legatee." . . . Some courts have gone so far as to hold that the administrator of an estate, who has been appointed and has qualified and assumed the duties of his office, cannot contest. . . .
>
> In In re Browning's Will (1937), 274 N.Y. 508, 10 N.E.2d 522, the New York court of Appeals held that an executor named in a will was entitled to contest a second codicil. . . . However, . . . in that case, the governing New York statute *expressly* authorized an executor to wage a will contest. . . .
>
> To contest a will, one must have a direct, pecuniary interest therein. An executor under a prior will has no interest other than the prospect of receiving compensation for his services, and that interest is not a direct, pecuniary one. . . . [I]n this state, the proposition that the executor receives only the value of his services is not merely a theory. It is a clearly defined statutory rule. . . .

It is our conclusion that . . . both the weight of authority and the better reasoning favor the rule that a will contest cannot be initiated by an executor named in a prior will.

Nearly all authorities agree that the interest of general creditors of an heir or beneficiary under a prior will is not sufficient to permit them to contest a will. However, there is disagreement as to the right of a creditor whose judgment would give rise to a lien on the interest of an heir or a devisee under a prior will. See Lee v. Keech, 151 Md. 34, 133 A. 853 (1926), noted in 36 Yale L.J. 150 (1926).

In re LENT
142 N.J. Eq. 21, 59 A.2d 7 (1948)

[An instrument purporting to be Ella Lent's will, executed in 1946, was admitted to probate. It bequeathed two-thirds of her estate to charitable institutions and one-third to the respondent. In 1927 testatrix had executed a will leaving her entire estate to charity. Appellants, testatrix's next of kin, sought to contest the 1946 will and then to appeal from the adverse findings of the Orphans' Court. The Prerogative Court reasoned that if the 1946 will failed, the 1927 will would be effective and thus that appellants would have no standing to attack the 1946 will unless the 1927 will were also attacked. When no proof of the invalidity of the 1927 will was offered on the appointed day, the Prerogative Court dismissed the appeal. This is an appeal from that dismissal.]

DONGES, J. . . .

It seems clear that in a case of this kind, involving the validity of a will, the next of kin, those who would take an interest in the event of intestacy, do have a standing to attack any and all wills of a decedent. They may have a valid ground of attack upon the 1927 will, but they are in no position to attack that instrument unless and until it is offered for probate. With a decree of the Orphans' Court sustaining the 1946 will in effect, the 1927 instrument will most certainly not be offered for probate. The 1927 will could not have been attacked in this proceeding, as has been suggested, because, besides not having been offered for probate, the parties in interest, the beneficiaries and the executor, are not in court and could not be bound by a decree against their interests in a proceeding to which they were not parties. Therefore, it would seem that the only course which the appellants could pursue was to make their attack upon the will offered and if successful then make a further attack upon the earlier will when it was offered, as it would have to be.

The rule applied by the court below if carried to an extreme case would certainly work an injustice. Suppose, for instance, an insane man made a series of wills cutting off his family and benefitting strangers, even unscrupulous fortune seekers, could it be that upon the last of these wills being offered for probate, the man's immediate family, perhaps his minor children, would have no standing to attack it because of the existence of earlier wills under which they were not beneficiaries? No such rule of law applied and appellants were entitled to file a caveat and to appeal from the adverse decree. . . .

The decree is reversed and the case remanded in order that the Prerogative Court may pass on the merits of the appeal.

See also on the effect of an unprobated prior will on an heir's right of contest In re Powers' Estate, 362 Mich. 222, 106 N.W.2d 833 (1961), 15 Vand. L. Rev. 308 (1962).

2.   Anticontest Clauses

> If any devisee, legatee, or beneficiary under this will shall contest it or any of its parts or provisions, any share or interest given to that person shall be revoked and augment proportionately the share of such of the beneficiaries hereunder as shall not have joined or participated in said contest.

Sample form from G. Stephenson, Drafting Wills and Trust Agreements: Dispositive Provisions §17.12 (1955).

BARRY v. AMERICAN SECURITY & TRUST CO.
77 App. D.C. 351, 135 F.2d 470 (1943)

[The will in question provided for forfeiture and a gift over of the interest of any person contesting its provisions. Appellant Samuel Barry and others filed an unsuccessful caveat to the will on the grounds of mental incapacity, fraud, and undue influence. The court held that their interests under the will were forfeited by this contest.]

PARKER, C.J. . . .

[V]erdict was directed for the propounders. So far as the record before us shows, there was not a scintilla of evidence to justify the allegations of the caveat. . . . Under these circumstances, the court below was unquestionably correct in holding that the interest of Barry under the will was forfeited by his filing of the caveat. Under the law applicable in the District of Columbia, the forfeiture provision contained in the will was valid and the filing of the caveat worked the forfeiture of the interest of the devisee filing it, irrespective of the question of good faith or probable cause for the litigation. Smithsonian Institution v. Meech, 169 U.S. 398. But even if good faith and probable cause could avoid the forfeiture, there is no evidence in the record before us upon which the court could base a finding of probable cause. . . . Even if probable cause were held to exist with respect to undue influence, this would not justify a contest based on a number of other grounds for which no cause whatever existed.

The validity of provisions for forfeiture in case of contest has been denied in bequests of personalty in the absence of a gift-over. This exception, even if valid, has no application here, as the devise is of an interest in realty and there is a gift-over to the residuary legatee in case of breach of condition. In some jurisdictions, it is held that a contest in good faith and upon probable cause will not work a forfeiture under such a provision. What we regard as the weight of authority, however, is to the contrary. A contest on the ground of forgery or subsequent revocation, neither of which is here involved, would seem to stand on different footing from the ordinary contest based on defective execution, mental incapacity or undue influence.

In the District of Columbia, the law is settled in accordance with the weight of authority, we think, by Smithsonian Institution v. Meech, supra, [in which] the Supreme Court stated the philosophy underlying the rule as follows [169 U.S. 398]:

> Experience has shown that often, after the death of a testator, unexpected difficulties arise; technical rules of law are found to have been trespassed upon; contests are commenced wherein not infrequently are brought to light matters of private life that ought never to be made public, and in respect to which the voice of the testator cannot be heard either in explanation or denial; and, as a result, the manifest intention of the testator is thwarted. It is not strange, in view of this, that testators have desired to secure compliance with their dispositions of property, and have sought to incorporate provisions which should operate most powerfully to accomplish that result. And, when a testator declares in his will that his several bequests are made upon the condition that the legatees acquiesce in the provisions of his will, the courts wisely hold that no legatee shall without compliance with that condition, receive his bounty, or be put in a position to use it in the effort to thwart his expressed purposes.

We feel ourselves bound by this decision of the Supreme Court; but, even in its absence, we would follow the rule that it lays down as being supported by the weight of authority and as embodying the sounder reasoning. The view that the wishes of the testator should be disregarded with respect to the disposition of his property in the interest of greater freedom of litigation does not impress us as resting on a sound or logical basis. Studies which have been made show that only a very small percentage of will contests made on the grounds of defective execution, mental incapacity or undue influence are successful; and the public interest in freeing such contests from the restraining influence of conditions like that here involved seems of little importance compared with enforcing the will of the testator that those who share in his bounty shall not have been guilty of besmirching his reputation or parading the family skeletons after his death. But, as stated above, even if the rule avoiding forfeiture where contest is based on probable cause were recognized here, it would not avail appellant, since there was no probable cause shown for the contest.

For the reasons stated, the judgment appealed from will be affirmed. Affirmed.

MILLER, A.J. (concurring in part, dissenting in part).

I concur in the result and in the conclusion that no probable cause was shown for the contest. I join also in believing that the public interest will be better served if, in cases which involve no more of merit than is revealed by the present record, those who share the bounty of the testator should be strongly deterred from "besmirching his reputation or parading the family skeletons after his death." However, I doubt the wisdom of closing the door completely to contests calculated to reveal the use of fraud, coercion and undue influence in procuring the execution of wills. It seems to me that public policy may be well served by keeping the door a little open for some extreme situations, as where one person or a group of heirs conspire to shut out another; or, perhaps, to prevent the probate of an earlier will containing a bequest for charitable purposes. The object of an in terrorem clause may be to protect the family reputation, but it may be to silence a legatee who, otherwise, would be a material witness.

Where a legatee or devisee is fully competent, armed with adequate legal counsel, and financially able to hazard a contest, public policy may be satisfied by the assumption that fraud or undue influence will be challenged. Under such circumstances a successful contest may break the will and cause a distribution different from the one therein directed. But, while the rule as declared by the majority opinion would, perhaps, be consistent with public policy in such a case, it will not much affect the type of case which it is supposed to affect, or restrain the person whom it purports to restrain, namely, the litigious troublemaker. He will be most apt to take his chances on a successful contest. The person who *will be* discouraged and restrained is just the person whose right to litigate, the public policy should be most concerned to protect: poor, timid people; children, widows, incompetents. It is against the interests of such persons that the schemer, the confidence-man and the ruthless rascal are most apt to operate. If fraud, coercion and undue influence — rarely as they now may be used in procuring the execution of wills — can be covered up and made secure by the insertion of a forfeiture condition into a will, then, far from establishing a beneficent rule of public policy, we may, instead, be putting another weapon into the hands of the racketeer.

Text and other legal writers, generally, favor treating the forefeiture clause as invalid where probable cause for contest exists. The history of the contrary rule and the artificial distinctions which were written into it, do not much commend it for present day uses. On the other hand, the rule of probable cause seems a safe one to apply. Probable cause is a term of well-established meaning. An honest, upright person would not act upon a lesser showing of improper conduct. A lawyer would hesitate to advise a legatee to act on less, in the face of such a rule. In the present case, as we have seen, it would not have availed the appellant. . . .

Cf. American Bar Association, Model Rules of Professional Conduct, Rules 1.2, 4.1

ESTATE OF LARSEN
161 Cal. App. 3d 564, 207 Cal. Rptr. 526 (1984)

STONE, Presiding Justice.

William Edwin Larsen appeals from a judgment forfeiting his interest in his mother's estate because he violated the in terrorem clause in her will. We affirm the judgment.

By will dated July 28, 1973, Mother Larsen specifically bequeathed one parcel of real property to her son Edwin and two parcels of real property to her daughter Alberta. The residue of her estate was to be divided equally between the siblings.

The will contains two provisions which are pertinent here: "Any apparent inequality in value of the properties in favor of my daughter [Alberta] is intended to equalize the gifts my children shall have received from me, in that my son has received substantial amounts from me during my lifetime," and "If any beneficiary under this Will in any manner, directly or indirectly, contests or attacks this Will or any of its provisions, any share or interest in my estate given to that contesting beneficiary under this Will is revoked and shall be disposed of in the same manner provided herein as if that contesting beneficiary had predeceased me without issue."

When his mother died in 1978 Edwin presented a creditor's claim to her estate seeking $41,786 for services to his mother during her lifetime and for travel expenses incurred by him in rendering those services. The creditor's claim expressly states: "All of the foregoing services were rendered in accordance with an oral agreement between claimant and decedent by which she agreed to devise certain property [plus half the rest of her estate] in exchange therefor and which was breached by decedent."

Alberta, the executrix, denied the claim. On January 24, 1979, Edwin filed a "Complaint for Services Rendered." . . .

Edwin informs us that "this case presents a single, straightforward issue of law: Is a beneficiary's suit on a creditor's claim for services to a decedent a 'contest' of or 'attack' upon the decedent's will, compelling forfeiture of the claimant's gifts under the will?" We disagree. "We recognize that while no-contest clauses 'are to be given effect according to the intent of the testator, yet it is also the rule . . . that such a provision — being by way of forfeiture and condition subsequent — is to be strictly construed and not extended beyond what was plainly the testator's intent.' . . . By the same token, however, we must not rewrite the testatrix's will in such a way as to immunize legal proceedings plainly intended to frustrate her unequivocally expressed intent from the reach of the no-contest clause." (Estate of Kazian (1976) 59 Cal. App. 3d 797, 802, 130 Cal. Rptr. 908.)

"Whether there has been a contest within the meaning of the language used in a no-contest clause is to be determined according to the circumstances in each case." . . . "The answer cannot be sought in a vacuum, but must be gleaned from a consideration of the purpose that the testatrix sought to attain by the provisions of her will." (Estate of Kazian, supra, 59 Cal. App. 3d at p. 802, 130 Cal. Rptr. 908.)

There may be instances where a beneficiary of a will who is also a legitimate creditor of the estate could file a creditor's claim without violating an in terrorem clause. However, the facts in this case support the implied finding that Edwin was using his creditor's claim to disguise his attack upon the will. . . .

Except for the parcels of real property and the small residue, the balance of her property passed to the children outside of probate by way of joint tenancy bank accounts. Thus, in order to satisfy Edwin's $41,786 creditor's claim, one of the parcels of real property would have to be sold. That would plainly frustrate Mother Larsen's testatmentary intent. . . .

The in terrorem clause here prevents a beneficiary from "contesting or attacking" the provisions of the will "directly or indirectly." That clause is sufficiently broad to include what the probate court found to be Edwin's "indirect attack." . . .

Edwin himself fatally describes the nature of his suit for services rendered: "The claim is premised upon the fact that the will does not leave appellant the property he claims was promised him, and therefore that he did not receive the consideration for his services." This argument admits that, if the will had read the way Edwin had expected it to read, as opposed to the manner in which Mother Larsen intended that it read, there would have been no creditor's claim and no lawsuit. That is the definition of a "contest of" or "attack upon" a will.

We are mindful that equity abhors a forfeiture, and that forfeiture provisions should be strictly construed. . . . [But] loss of an inheritance due to the violation of an in terrorem clause is not a "forfeiture" in the strict sense of that term. An heir's "right" to take under a will is not absolute. Mother Larsen was entitled to dispose of her assets in whatever manner she chose. (Estate of Fritschi (1963) 60 Cal. 2d 367, 373, 33 Cal.

Rptr. 264, 384 P.2d 656.) She chose to make her legacies subject to the condition that an heir not attack her intended testamentary disposition. Edwin did not abide by the condition.

The judgment is affirmed.

Just prior to the decision in the above case, Estate of Black, 160 Cal. App. 3d 582, 206 Cal. Rptr. 663 (1984), had decided "that petitioner, a beneficiary under the will and alleged unmarried partner of decedent, may seek a determination of claimed property right arising during the couple's lengthy relationship [a so-called *Marvin* petition] without forfeiting, by operation of the will's no-contest clause, the specific gift of their residence." In re Estate of Wojtalewicz, 93 Ill. App. 3d 1061 (1981), refused to enforce a clause calling for forfeiture of the rights of a beneficiary who initiates a "proceeding to challenge or deny any of the provisions" of the will, concluding that enforcement would be contrary to public policy when the beneficiary opposed appointment of an executor who had failed for nearly a year to offer the will for probate. See also Estate of Watson, 177 Cal. App. 3d 569, 223 Cal. Rptr. 14 (1986), finding no violation of a no-contest clause in testator's daughter filing a claim against the estate of testator's spouse and an action for constructive trust against the heirs of that spouse, alleging (unsuccessfully) that testator's residuary bequest to the spouse was based on the latter's oral agreement to bequeath that property at her death to the claimant daughter. Under a narrow but reasonable construction of her recently deceased father's will, this claim was not a contest of the will or an attempt "to impair or invalidate any of its provisions."

If a contest of a will in its entirety is successful, of course, the no-contest provision will fail along with the will. Furthermore, it is generally said by courts that no-contest clauses are to be narrowly construed for purposes of determining what conduct constitutes a contest under the provision. On each of these points, however, note the facts of Smithsonian Institution v. Meech, 169 U.S. 398 (1898), discussed in the *Barry* case, supra. In *Smithsonian* the will read, in relevant part: "These bequests are all made upon the condition that the legatees acquiesce in this will." Does this language explain the application of the forfeiture provision to a mere dispute (won by the legatee) over the ownership of property? Is that case, then, more like those involving the problems of election discussed in Chapter 3? On the question of what constitutes a "contest," note that the form quoted from Stephenson, supra, refers not only to contesting the will but also to contesting "any of its parts or provisions." Is this desirable?

How far should a court allow no-contest clauses to be extended? Commerce Trust Co. v. Weed, 318 S.W.2d 289 (Mo. 1958), required forfeiture of the interests of the *issue* of the testator's son because of a contest

by the *son,* under a provision that a contest should forfeit the interest of
the issue as well as that of the son, whose own interest was slight. The
court also rejected the probable cause exception.

The quotation from the *Smithsonian* case recited in the *Barry* case
supra emphasizes, in support of provisions against contest, that "the
voice of the testator cannot be heard either in explanation or denial."
Should this not be a consideration in will contests generally? In studying
the latter portions of this chapter, consider whether this is or should be
a persuasive factor in the receipt of parol evidence. Also, is it a factor in
the willingness of courts to find that evidence is sufficient to submit a
case to a jury on possible questions of fact, particularly in the mental
derangement cases? On the other hand, in questions of the validity of
no-contest clauses, is it not equally true that the testator is unable to
speak out against forgery, fraud, or undue influence? And is not a fore-
sighted perpetrator of undue influence likely to include such a clause for
protection and as a threat against those who would challenge the will?

Estoppel and claims or contests. Matter of Estate of Joffe, 493 N.E.2d 70,
72 (Ill. App. 1986), states:

> Under that doctrine [equitable election], one . . . accepts or rejects the
> instrument in its entirety, and cannot pick and choose those clauses one
> finds most advantageous. . . . [O]nce a beneficiary under a will has
> accepted a benefit granted by the will, he is estopped from asserting any
> claim contrary to the [terms or] validity of the will.
>
> The doctrine of election, however, is not absolute and is subject to
> exception. . . . [O]ne may take under a will and still be free to challenge
> any provisions which are contrary to law or public policy. Additionally,
> acceptance of a bequest under a will must have been made with full knowl-
> edge of the facts and circumstances surrounding the execution of the will,
> and acceptance of the benefit must not have been procured by fraud or
> mistake . . . or such acceptance will not function to preclude a beneficiary
> from challenging the will. . . . [Under] a "possible third exception" to the
> doctrine of election, not yet recognized in Illinois, the timely tender or
> repayment of the benefits received under a will, where the estate is not
> prejudiced by the temporary acceptance, may allow the beneficiary to
> challenge the validity of the will.

3.   Settlement Agreements

After the testator has died, the beneficiaries are able to transfer their
interests in the estate and to contract with regard to those interests. Such
actions are not viewed as defeating a testator's intent but as the beneficiary's exercise of property rights the testator has bestowed. Thus,
threatened or pending controversy over the probate of a will is likely to
be avoided by a settlement providing for probate of the will and for certain changes in the distribution of the estate. In such a case the problem

is essentially a simple one of contract. The parties to such a contract would be bound, while others who are not parties would not be. (Difficulties may arise, however, as to the methods of enforcement if such a contract is dishonored.) On the other hand, certain modes of settlement may be undertaken that would interfere with the rights of others if special provision is not made to assure those rights. For example, either to prevent contest or for some other reason, the parties may agree not to probate the will in question but to administer the estate as if it were intestate, in which case provision must be made for the testamentary beneficiaries to look to the heirs for the satisfaction of their agreed rights.

PROBLEM

16-D. The testator's will left his entire estate, valued at about $200,000, in trust to pay the income to *A* for life, with remainder to *B.* The heirs at law of the testator commenced an action to set aside the will. *A, B,* and the heirs subsequently entered into a compromise agreement providing for distribution of 40 percent of the estate to *A,* 30 percent to *B,* and 30 percent among the testator's heirs. All of the heirs and trust beneficiaries were sui juris and joined in the agreement, but the executor and trustee have opposed it. The latter argued that the court should refuse to approve the settlement on the grounds that the trust cannot be terminated on the consent of *A* and *B* because, under the usual American rule (the *Claflin* doctrine, discussed in Chapter 13), a material purpose of the settlor would thereby be defeated. See Adams v. Link, 145 Conn. 634, 145 A.2d 753 (1958). See also the note that follows. But see IV W. Fratcher, Scott on Trusts §337.6 (4th ed. 1989).

(a) How should the case be decided? Why?

(b) Assume that the court rejects the settlement agreement but that *A* and your client, *B,* still wish to compromise the issues in litigation, and the heirs are still willing to accept 30 percent of the estate in settlement. Can you suggest any solution? Would the presence of a spendthrift clause in the trust provisions of the will affect your proposed solution? Consider the possible utility of disclaimers.

In In re Estate of Swanson, 239 Iowa 294, 31 N.Y.2d 385 (1948), probate of a will, under which the proponents were nominated as executors, was opposed by the decedent's widow and heirs on the basis of an agreement among themselves providing for settlement of the estate entirely as if it were intestate. In sustaining the position of the heirs, the court stated:

> [I]t is generally held that the beneficiaries under a will may agree to disregard the instrument and have the estate distributed as intestate or in any other manner they see proper. . . .

It is sometimes said family settlements are favored by courts. In upholding such settlements, courts have reasoned that beneficiaries under a will may, immediately after the distribution, divide the property as they see fit and there is no reason why they may not make such division before they receive the property. Also the beneficiaries are not compelled to accept provisions of the will. . . .

There are two exceptions to, or limitations upon, the rule permitting family settlements: (1) Beneficiaries under a will cannot defeat a trust. (2) Such an agreement may not deprive one not a party thereto of his interest in the estate or prejudice the rights of non-consenting creditors.

Neither of these exceptions is applicable here. The will creates no trust. . . . [O]ne who, like these proponents, has been nominated executor in a will but not appointed by the court cannot be called a trustee. . . . The nomination in the will may be disregarded by the court if the best interests of this estate so require.

Unlike an heir, legatee or creditor of decedent, proponents had no interest in the estate of which they were deprived by the settlement agreement. That they would be compensated as executors, if appointed by the court, gave them no such interest. Such compensation would be only in return for services rendered.

Id. at 301-303, 31 N.W.2d at 390.

In Altemeier v. Harris, 403 Ill. 345, 351, 86 N.E.2d 229, 236 (1949), the court stated:

The appellants rely entirely upon the application of the family-settlement doctrine, which has been before this court on several occasions. . . .

Undoubtedly, the members of a family are not privileged to alter the terms and provisions of a will merely for the convenience of the family or for the sole purpose of securing greater individual financial advantages than those specified in the will and intended by the testator. However, the rule is well established that courts of equity favor the settlement of disputes among members of a family by agreement rather than by resort to law. Where there is a reasonable or substantial basis for the belief or assurance that prolonged and expensive litigation will result over the proceeds or distribution of an estate, that the estate will be materially depleted and that the family relationship will be torn asunder, the parties interested therein are warranted in preventing such bona fide family controversy by a settlement agreement. . . .

It is observed that in every one of the cases just cited, wherein the family-settlement doctrine is announced, no trust existed, and no contingent beneficiaries were interested, and no spendthrift provisions changed or set aside. . . .

Settled rules apply to the administration of trusts, and, where all of the persons are of age and sui juris and no principle of law is violated, the trust may generally be terminated if all of the cestuis que trustent consent. It has likewise been held by this court that where the trust makes provision for distribution to contingent beneficiaries, or upon uncertain contingencies, a trust may not be terminated even by the unanimous consent of all the beneficiaries, or the prospective beneficiaries, before the time fixed by the terms of the trust. . . . Likewise, the rule is clear that a spendthrift trust may not be destroyed or terminated by the unanimous consent of the beneficiaries. . . .

In view of the foregoing, we are of the opinion that the object and purpose of a trust created by a will cannot be varied or terminated unless the purpose of the trust is accomplished, nor can such a trust be terminated by unanimous consent where it contains spendthrift provisions or where contingent interests cannot be definitely ascertained. All three of these conditions exist in the instant case.

A very few courts have refused to permit agreements among all beneficiaries to suppress probate of a will. They generally do so out of respect for the testator's wishes and particularly because of the fact that all possible interests (such as those of the creditors or devisees) cannot be accounted for with complete certainty. Can these objections be answered?

Under appropriate circumstances, other courts uphold settlements providing for the avoidance of the probate of a will. When trusts or successive legal estates have been provided for in the will, should it be required that such a settlement also satisfy all of the requirements for premature termination of a trust or for transfer of complete title to the property in which a legal life estate and remainder have been created? Can contingent future interests be extinguished by agreement not joined in by unborn or unknown remainder beneficiaries in the face of a will contest? If not, how can a settlement be arranged where the will creates interests in unborn persons? In a few states, statutes facilitate agreements of this sort, and the Uniform Probate Code suggests possible statutory solutions. In addition to the two following sections, see UPC §2-801, Chapter 12 supra, dealing with renunciation. On the problems posed by statutes dealing with these matters, see Schnebly, Extinguishment of Contingent Future Interests by Decree and Without Compensation, 44 Harv. L. Rev. 378 (1930).

UNIFORM PROBATE CODE

§3-912. *Private Agreements Among Successors to Decedent Binding on Personal Representative.* Subject to the rights of creditors and taxing authorities, competent successors may agree among themselves to alter the interests, shares, or amounts to which they are entitled under the will of the decedent, or under the laws of intestacy, in any way that they provide in a written contract executed by all who are affected by its provisions. The personal representative shall abide by the terms of the agreement subject to his obligation to administer the estate for the benefit of creditors, to pay all taxes and costs of administration, and to carry out the responsibilities of his office for the benefit of any successors of the decedent who are not parties. Personal representatives of decedents' estates are not required to see to the performance of trusts if the trustee thereof is another person who is willing to accept the trust. Accordingly, trustees of a testamentary trust are successors for the purposes of this section. Nothing herein relieves trustees of any duties owed to beneficiaries of trusts.

§3-1101. *Effect of Approval of Agreements Involving Trusts, Inalienable Interests, or Interests of Third Persons.*   A compromise of any controversy as to admission to probate of any instrument offered for formal probate as the will of a decedent, the construction, validity, or effect of any probated will, the rights or interests in the estate of the decedent, of any successor, or the administration of the estate, if approved in a formal proceeding in the Court for that purpose, is binding on all the parties thereto including those unborn, unascertained or who could not be located. An approved compromise is binding even though it may affect a trust or an inalienable interest. A compromise does not impair the rights of creditors or of taxing authorities who are not parties to it.

C.   Grounds of Contest

There are various grounds for contesting wills, and it is common that a contestant will assert several of these grounds in opposing probate or in seeking to set aside a will. The formal requirements of the due execution have already been studied and are not taken up again at this point, although it is obvious that improper execution is a possible ground of contest. Usually the proponent of the will bears the risk of nonpersuasion in proving its due execution. This burden, however, may readily be carried by aid of various presumptions, such as that arising from recitations in an attestation clause, or by inferences or even presumptions based on the appearance of the instrument once the required signatures have been identified. After a will has been admitted to probate, the contestant in a subsequent contest typically has at least the burden of going forward with the evidence in order to raise a question of fact on the matter of due execution.

Many statutes provide a right of jury trial as to at least some issues in will contests. As the materials involving grounds of contest are studied, consider the problems of proof, the way in which a party's burden is carried, and the quantum of evidence required to permit submission of a case on a question of fact. Consider whether there seems to be a different "feeling" for what constitutes a question of fact for a jury and for what is proper as a matter of appellate review in will contest cases as against the civil cases you have sampled in other courses, and whether there is a particular need for caution in submitting will contests to a jury. Under some statutes provision for jury trials in will contest cases is severely limited.

1.   Testamentary Capacity

The age requirements for execution of wills have rarely been the cause of litigation, although under a few statutes the age requirement is unclear as a result of vague references to full or lawful age. Litigation concerning testamentary capacity generally centers on mental capacity. Basically, mental incapacity is of two types: (1) mental deficiency and (2) mental derangement.

Traditionally the risk of nonpersuasion is on the proponent with regard to testamentary capacity. However, the burden of going forward with the evidence is often cast on the contestants as a result of a presumption of capacity arising from a mere showing of due execution. On the other hand, it is often held or at least stated that the burden of proof is on the contestant, particularly once the will has been admitted to probate, and statutes sometimes describe the contestants as the plaintiff in an action to set aside probate. Judicial references to the "burden of proof" may only refer to the burden of going forward with the evidence, however, and the true risk of nonpersuasion may remain with the proponent in many such cases. As you study the cases in this section consider the relationship between burdens of proof and procedure in will contest cases. An examination of many cases would suggest that the traditional relationships are sometimes overlooked or disregarded by probate courts and in appeals from probate decrees.

MATTER OF ESTATE OF KUMSTAR
105 App. Div. 2d 747, 481 N.Y.S.2d 646 (1984)

Supreme Court, Appellate Division, Second Department. Nov. 13, 1984. . . . In a contested probate proceeding, the proponent of the purported will of the deceased Rose B. Kumstar, dated Sept. 1, 1982 appeals from a decree of the Surrogate's Court, Orange County (Green, J.), dated Jan. 5, 1984, which, after a jury trial, inter alia, denied probate to the purported will. Decree affirmed, with costs payable by appellant personally. The evidence on the record was sufficient to raise a jury question as to the issues of incompetence and undue influence, and there is no reason to disturb the jury's findings. We have considered appellant's other arguments and find them to be without merit. . . .

MATTER OF ESTATE OF KUMSTAR
66 N.Y.2d 691, 487 N.E.2d 271 (1985)

MEMORANDUM.

The order of the Appellate Division [affirming denial of probate] should be reversed and the matter remitted to Surrogate's Court for entry of a decree granting the petition for probate.

It is the indisputable rule in a will contest that

> the proponent has the burden of proving that the testator possessed testamentary capacity and that the court must look to the following factors: (1) whether she understood the nature and consequences of executing a will; (2) whether she knew the nature and extent of the property she was disposing of; and (3) whether she knew those who would be considered the natural objects of her bounty and her relations with them. . . .

When there is conflicting evidence or the possibility of drawing conflicting inferences from undisputed evidence, the issue of capacity is one for the jury. . . .

Here, there was insufficient evidence adduced at trial to warrant submitting that issue to the jury. The subscribing witnesses and those who were close to decedent when the will was drafted each testified that decedent was alert and capable of understanding the nature of her actions. Decedent's treating physician testified that it was his opinion, based on a reasonable degree of medical certainty, that decedent was competent when she signed the will. By contrast a physician called by the objectant who reviewed decedent's medical records was unable to state with a degree of medical certainty that decedent was incompetent at the time in question. That the will contained a bequest to a "brother," long since deceased, "in Cuba, Cattaraugus County, New York" does not raise a question of decedent's competence in light of her attorney's testimony that, without knowing of the brother's death, he had assumed that the person referred to was decedent's brother. . . . Also without significance are the bequests establishing trust funds in relatively small amounts and the omission of a specific devise of certain land to a historical site contrary to a wish mentioned on several occasions by decedent. . . .

It was likewise error to submit the question of undue influence to the jury. That the willdrafter stood to benefit by being named trustee of the estate and that he possessed an "opinionated and domineering personality," as indicated by his propensity to write "letters to the editor," is of no import. . . .

On review . . . , order reversed, with costs payable out of the estate to all parties appearing separately and filing separate briefs. . . .

Mental deficiency. In general the test to be applied in the mental deficiency cases is well settled and agreed on by courts in this country. Of course, the real problems in these cases are those of fact and proof. The test of competence to make a will may be differently worded by different courts, but in substance the rule is generally accepted to be that a person is of sound mind for testamentary purposes if the person is able to understand "(1) The nature and extent of his property, (2) The persons who are the natural objects of his bounty, and (3) The disposition which he is making of his property," and if he is "capable of (4) Appreciating those elements in relation to each other, and (5) Forming an orderly desire as to the disposition of his property." T. Atkinson, Wills §51 (2d ed. 1953).[1] "One may have testamentary capacity though he is under guardianship or lacks the ability to make a contract or transact business." Ibid.[2] As emphasized in a recent decision, a testator need only "have capacity to know the nature and extent of his bounty" and other matters mentioned above, "as distinguished from [a] requirement that he have actual knowledge thereof." In re Estate of Jenks, 291 Minn. 138, 141, 189 N.W.2d 695, 697 (1971). Essentially similar principles apparently apply to the validity of inter vivos gifts, the donative creation of joint tenancies, transfers in trust, and the like. See, e.g., Estate of Payton, 398 N.E.2d 977 (Ind. App. 1979); see also Re Beaney, [1978] 2 All Eng. Rep. 595.

Mental derangement. The cases involving mental derangement or insane delusions cannot so easily be summarized. Note, however, that irrational beliefs *that do not affect the will* do not render the will invalid on the ground of insane delusion. Nevertheless, in such a situation the holding of beliefs that are clearly contrary to fact and reason may be some *evidence* of mental *deficiency*. The effect and definition of insane delusion, as widely recited in judicial opinions, are succinctly stated in In re

---

1. Compare Estate of Basich, 398 N.E.2d 1182 (Ill. App. 1980): "To have testamentary capacity, the testator must possess sufficient mental capacity to know the natural objects of his bounty, comprehend the kind and character of his property, understand the nature and effect of his act, and make disposition of his property according to some plan formed in his mind."

Occasionally statutes impinge on doctrine in this area, as in Georgia Code §13-106, providing that a will may disregard the testator's family and leave the entire estate to strangers but that in such a case "the will should be closely scrutinized and, upon the slightest evidence of aberration of intellect . . . probate should be refused." (This language may be of greater relevance in derangement cases, infra.) For purposes of this statute a common law spouse is not a stranger to the family. See Yuzamas v. Yuzamas, 241 Ga. 577, 247 S.E.2d 73 (1978).

2. See In re Estate of Teel, 14 Ariz. App. 371, 483 P.2d 603 (1971), where testator was found to be "mentally retarded," possessing a mental "age level of ten to twelve years," but where there was also a trial court finding that he "was aware of those who had some claim to benefit from his property"; "comprehended generally the kind and nature of his property"; "understood the nature and effect of his testamentary act"; and "could make a disposition of his property according to a plan formed in his mind." On that basis, the testator possessed testamentary capacity even though he was declared incompetent and had a guardian appointed not long after the will was executed, the court noting that even having a guardian when a will is executed does not necessarily preclude a testator from having the required capacity.

Nigro's Estate, 243 Cal. App. 2d 152, 160, 52 Cal. Rptr. 128, 133 (1966), as follows:

> [T]he possession of an insane delusion which leads a testator to dispose of his property otherwise than he would have done had he not possessed such insane delusion is sufficient to invalidate a will. [A]n insane delusion is "the conception of a disordered mind which imagines facts to exist of which there is no evidence and the belief in which is adhered to against all evidence and argument to the contrary, and which cannot be accounted for on any reasonable hypothesis. One cannot be said to act under an insane delusion if his condition of mind results from a belief or inference, however irrational and unfounded, drawn from facts which are shown to exist."

Is this distinction between "facts" and "beliefs" really a workable one? Try to utilize it in the *Honigman* case, infra.

In Pendarvis v. Gibb, 328 Ill. 282, 159 N.E. 353 (1927), the testator bequeathed $1,000 to a cemetery association, $500 to each of two churches, $3,000 to the family physician, $500 to each of twelve persons "as slight recognition of kindness shown to me," $100 to his only surviving brother, William, and $250 to each of two nieces. The residue was left in equal shares to such of the children of the testator's deceased brothers and sisters as might be living at his death. One Milligan was nominated as executor. The testator's brother William and several nieces contested the will; the jury found in their favor, and the will was set aside. On appeal, the Illinois Supreme Court reversed, holding the verdict based on unsoundness of mind to be "contrary to the manifest weight of evidence." As the facts appeared, the testator was a bachelor who lived alone on his farm and who had little contact with people, except for irregular visits by relatives and occasional visits by neighbors to help him or to play cards and drink whiskey. Some of these neighbors were remembered in the will by $500 bequests. The testator's home and person were typified by filth and odor. Many witnesses testified he was sound of mind, while several testified he was not. The testator's own physician testified that testator was not of sound mind at a particular time that was more than eighteen months after execution of the will. Two doctors, who examined the testator just before a hearing on the appointment of a conservator shortly after the will was executed, testified that the testator was not of sound mind, but that he could name his brothers and sisters and some of his nieces and nephews and that he knew the size of his farm and had a general understanding of its condition. Substantial testimony evidenced that at the time the will was executed the testator believed that there were people in the trees around his house, that they were a threat to his property, that there were also cattle in the trees, and that the people were butchering them and hanging the beef in the trees.

The testator recognized his need for a conservator and testified at the proceedings that his eyesight was bad, that there were things in the trees, and that he did not know whether they were people but that it looked like they were butchering out there.

The court stated at 291-295, 159 N.E.2d 357-358:

> [A] testator does not have to be absolutely of sound mind and memory in every respect. . . . It is not every insane delusion that will avoid a will. In order to avoid a will the insane delusion must affect the testamentary disposition of the property. . . . Even if the testator has an insane delusion on certain subjects, still if he has mental capacity to know his property, the objects of his bounty and to make a disposition of his property according to a plan formed by him, the will cannot be set aside on the ground of mental incapacity. . . .
>
> Apart from the evidence concerning this delusion [about the people in the trees] there is very little evidence on which a charge of unsoundness of mind could be sustained. Even if it be conceded that the testator had an insane delusion in the respect claimed, the evidence does not show that it in any way affected or entered into the execution of the will. The burden of proof was on appellees not only to overcome by the preponderance of the evidence the prima facie case made by appellants based upon the testimony of the subscribing witnesses to the will, but . . . to prove . . . that the testator was mentally incapable of making a will at the time it was executed. . . .
>
> The preponderance of the evidence shows that the testator knew who were the objects of his bounty. He knew he had one brother living and two sisters who were dead, leaving children. He named . . . some of his nieces and nephews to Drs. Marshall and Babcock. He specifically named two of them in his will and none of them were omitted. The will stated that they were the children of his deceased brothers and sisters, who were named in the will. It is possible that he could not call each of these eleven nieces and nephews by name. One reason for this might have been that five of them were nonresidents, the children of his sister Eliza Fort.
>
> The preponderance of the evidence also shows that the testator knew the kind and character of his bounty to be bestowed. He knew the amount of land he owned and that he had some personal property. . . . [T]he testator made disposition of his property according to a plan of his own. . . . The fact that he gave only $100 to the brother is in keeping with the facts. The brother was two years older than the testator. He had as much property as the testator. He had never been married and had no children. The heirs of each of the brothers were identical. The will, when considered as a whole, shows a rational and reasonable disposition of the estate under the facts in evidence.

Is there any doubt that a different result would be required by the *Pendarvis* case if the testator had also left $25,000 to Jones, a contractor, for the purpose of removing all the trees from the area of his home in order to protect his neighbors from the people residing in the trees (assuming, at least for purposes of discussion, that there were no people in the trees)? In that event, to what extent would the court hold the will invalid? With this variation of the facts in *Pendarvis* compare the same court's earlier treatment of bequests to promote spiritualism. In Owen v. Crumbaugh, 228 Ill. 380, 81 N.E. 1044 (1907), the testator, Crumbaugh, appeared to be a believer in spiritualism and purported to have frequent communications from residents of the spirit world, including mostly acquaintances long deceased and his spirit guide, Bright Eyes, his son who had died in infancy but who had grown to manhood in the spirit world. In order to bring the benefits of spiritualism to his home town, the testator left most of his estate in trust to build a spiritualist church and public library. After hearing twenty-four lay witnesses and eight physicians for the contestants and fifty-five lay witnesses and twelve physicians for the proponents, the jury found against the will. At the conclusion of a thirty-page opinion reversing the lower court's decree setting aside probate, it was stated (228 Ill. at 413, 81 N.E. at 1055-1056):

> Proponents requested the court to direct a verdict in their favor, which was refused. If there was evidence requiring the court to submit the case to the jury the refusal of the request was not error. If, upon the whole case, there was evidence fairly tending to support contestants' bill the motion was properly denied. After giving this case the careful examination which its importance requires, we are firmly convinced that there is no evidence here even raising a suspicion in our minds that the testator was not entirely sane and as competent to make a will or transact any other kind of business as the average business man. We have examined the evidence with great care, and when it is all summarized and reduced to its final results it only proves that Crumbaugh was a believer in spiritualism; that he thought that he was doing a philanthropic work for his friends . . . , and however much one may differ from him as to the advisability of such a devise, that has nothing to do with the legal status of the will. If the testator had the capacity to make the will he had the capacity to select the beneficiaries. . . .
>
> The court erred in refusing to direct a verdict for proponents, for which the decree must be reversed, which is accordingly done and the cause remanded to the circuit court, for further proceedings not inconsistent with the views herein expressed.

In considering the appropriate functions of the trial judge, the jury, and the appellate court in will contest cases, the rest of the litigation involving Mr. Crumbaugh's will, along with the above quoted opinion, affords considerable food for thought.

On remand in the *Crumbaugh* litigation, the circuit court dismissed the contestants' bill for want of equity without the cause being again submitted to a jury on the theory that the supreme court had determined the cause on its merits in favor of the proponents. From this, the contestants successfully appealed, and the supreme court again reversed and remanded in Crumbaugh v. Owen, 232 Ill. 191, 196, 83 N.E. 803, 805 (1908), stating:

> When this case is again re-docketed in the circuit court it will be for trial by jury precisely as in the first instance. If it is again submitted to a jury and the proof is not substantially different from that offered upon the first trial, the chancellor should, upon proper motion made either at the close of the evidence for the contestants or at the close of all the evidence, direct a verdict for the proponents. If the evidence should be substantially different and such motion should be made, the chancellor, in disposing of it, should be governed by the ordinary rules applicable in such case.

On the second remand, the case was again submitted to the jury, which found for the contestants, and a decree was entered accordingly. Proponents appealed again, and again the court reversed but this time without remand, in Crumbaugh v. Owen, 238 Ill. 497, 87 N.E. 312 (1909). The court concluded its opinion by stating:

> This case has been submitted to two juries, and all the evidence which either of the parties to this litigation has been able to discover and bring forward, or can reasonably be expected to discover and bring forward upon another trial is found in the record now before us. We are therefore satisfied that nothing will be gained by protracting this litigation and by submitting this case to another jury, as it is evident if a jury should again return a verdict against the validity of the will that the court would be bound to set the verdict aside. We therefore think it to the interest of all the parties that this case should not be remanded for a new trial.
> The decree of the circuit court will therefore be reversed but the cause will not be remanded, the result of which will be to leave the judgment of the county court of McLean county admitting the will of James T. Crumbaugh, deceased, to probate, in full force and effect.

238 Ill. at 509, 87 N.E. at 316. (About one-third of this estate was consumed by costs of litigation. Champaign-Urbana Courier, May 21, 1966, at 19.)

In re HONIGMAN'S WILL
8 N.Y.2d 244, 168 N.E.2d 676 (1960)

Dye, J.
Frank Honigman died May 4, 1956, survived by his wife, Florence. By a purported last will and testament, executed April 3, 1956, just one

month before his death, he gave $5,000 to each of three named grand-nieces, and cut off his wife, with a life use of her minimum statutory share, plus $2,500, with direction to pay the principal upon her death to his surviving brothers and sisters and to the descendants of any pre-deceased brother or sister, per stirpes. The remaining one half of his estate was bequeathed in equal shares to his surviving brothers and sisters and to the descendants of any predeceased brother or sister, per stirpes, some of whom resided in Germany.

When the will was offered for probate in Surrogate's Court, Queens County, the widow Florence filed objections. A trial was had on framed issues, only one of which survived for determination by the jury, namely: "At the time of the execution of the paper offered for probate was the said Frank Honigman of sound and disposing mind and memory?" The jury answered in the negative, and the Surrogate then made a decree denying probate to the will.

Upon an appeal to the Appellate Division, Second Department, the Surrogate's decree was reversed upon the law and the facts, and probate was directed. Inconsistent findings of fact were reversed and new findings substituted.

We read this record as containing more than enough competent proof to warrant submitting to the jury the issue of decedent's testamentary capacity. By the same token the proof amply supports the jury findings, implicit in the verdict, that the testator, at the time he made his will, was suffering from an unwarranted and insane delusion that his wife was unfaithful to him, which condition affected the disposition made in the will. The record is replete with testimony, supplied by a large number of disinterested persons, that for quite some time before his death the testator had publicly and repeatedly told friends and strangers alike that he believed his wife was unfaithful, often using obscene and abusive language. Such manifestations of suspicion were quite unaccountable, coming as they did after nearly 40 years of a childless yet, to all outward appearances, a congenial and harmonious marriage, which had begun in 1916. During the intervening time they had worked together in the successful management, operation and ownership of various restaurants, bars and grills and, by their joint efforts of thrift and industry, had accumulated the substantial fortune now at stake.

The decedent and his wife retired from business in 1945 because of decedent's failing health. In the few years that followed he underwent a number of operations, including a prostatectomy in 1951, and an operation for cancer of the large bowel in 1954, when decedent was approximately 70 years of age.

From about this time, he began volubly to express his belief that Mrs. Honigman was unfaithful to him. This suspicion became an obsession with him, although all of the witnesses agreed that the deceased was normal and rational in other respects. Seemingly aware of his mental state, he once mentioned that he was "sick in the head" ("Mich krank gelassen in den Kopf"), and that "I know there is something wrong with me" in response to a light reference to his mental condition. In December, 1955 he went to Europe, a trip Mrs. Honigman learned of in a letter sent from Idlewild Airport after he had departed, and while there he visited a doctor. Upon his return he went to a psychiatrist who Mr. Honigman said "could not help" him. Finally, he went to a chiropractor with whom he was extremely satisfied.

On March 21, 1956, shortly after his return from Europe, Mr. Honigman instructed his attorney to prepare the will in question. He never again joined Mrs. Honigman in the marital home.

To offset and contradict this showing of irrational obsession the proponents adduced proof which, it is said, furnished a reasonable basis for decedent's belief, and which, when taken with other factors, made his testamentary disposition understandable. Briefly, this proof related to four incidents. One concerned an anniversary card sent by Mr. Krauss, a mutual acquaintance and friend of many years, bearing a printed message of congratulation in sweetly sentimental phraseology. Because it was addressed to the wife alone and not received on the anniversary date, Mr. Honigman viewed it as confirmatory of his suspicion. Then there was the reference to a letter which it is claimed contained prejudicial matter — but just what it was is not before us, because the letter was not produced in evidence and its contents were not established. There was also proof to show that whenever the house telephone rang Mrs. Honigman would answer it. From this Mr. Honigman drew added support for his suspicion that she was having an affair with Mr. Krauss. Mr. Honigman became so upset about it that for the last two years of their marriage he positively forbade her to answer the telephone. Another allegedly significant happening was an occasion when Mrs. Honigman asked the decedent as he was leaving the house what time she might expect him to return. This aroused his suspicion. He secreted himself at a vantage point in a nearby park and watched his home. He saw Mr. Krauss enter and, later, when he confronted his wife with knowledge of this incident, she allegedly asked him for a divorce. This incident was taken entirely from a statement made by Mr. Honigman to one of the witnesses. Mrs. Honigman flatly denied all of it. Their verdict shows that the jury evidently believed the objectant. Under the circumstances, we cannot say that this was wrong. The jury had the right to disregard the proponents' proof, or to go so far as to hold that such trivia afforded even additional grounds for decedent's irrational and unwarranted belief. The issue we must bear in mind is not whether Mrs. Honigman was unfaithful, but whether Mr. Honigman had any reasonable basis for believing that she was.

In a very early case we defined the applicable test as follows:

> If a person persistently believes supposed facts, which have no real existence except in his perverted imagination, and against all evidence and probability, and conducts himself, however logically, upon the assumption of their existence, he is, so far as they are concerned, under a morbid delusion; and delusion in that sense is insanity. Such a person is essentially mad or insane on those subjects, though on other subjects he may reason, act and speak like a sensible man.

(American Seamen's Friend Soc. v. Hopper, 33 N.Y. 619, 624-625.)

It is true that the burden of proving testamentary incapacity is a difficult one to carry (Dobie v. Armstrong, 160 N.Y. 584, 55 N.E. 302), but when an objectant has gone forward, as Mrs. Honigman surely has, with evidence reflecting the operation of the testator's mind, it is the proponents' duty to provide a basis for the alleged delusion. We cannot conclude that as a matter of law they have performed this duty successfully. When, in the light of all the circumstances surrounding a long and happy marriage such as this, the husband publicly and repeatedly expresses suspicions of his wife's unfaithfulness; of misbehaving herself in a most unseemly fashion, by hiding male callers in the cellar of her own home, in various closets, and under the bed; of hauling men from the street up to her second-story bedroom by use of bed sheets; of making contacts over the household telephone; and of passing a clandestine note through the fence on her brother's property — and when he claims to have heard noises which he believed to be men running about his home, but which he had not investigated, and which he could not verify — the courts should have no hesitation in placing the issue of sanity in the jury's hands. To hold to the contrary would be to take from the jury its traditional function of passing on the facts. . . .

The proponents argue that, even if decedent was indeed laboring under a delusion, the existence of other reasons for the disposition he chose is enough to support the validity of the instrument as a will. The other reasons are, first, the size of Mrs. Honigman's independent fortune, and second, the financial need of his residuary legatees. These reasons, as well as his belief in his wife's infidelity, decedent expressed to his own attorney. We dispelled a similar contention in American Seamen's Friend Soc. v. Hopper, supra, 33 N.Y. at page 625, where we held that a will was bad when its "dispository provisions were or *might have been* caused or affected by the delusion" (emphasis supplied). . . .

The order appealed from should be reversed and a new trial granted, with costs to abide the event.

FULD, J. (dissenting).

I am willing to assume that the proof demonstrates that the testator's belief that his wife was unfaithful was completely groundless and unjust. However, that is not enough; it does not follow from this fact that the testator suffered from such a delusion as to stamp him mentally defective or as lacking in capacity to make a will. . . . "To sustain the allegation," this court wrote [in Clapp v. Fullerton,] 34 N.Y. 190, 197,

> it is not sufficient to show that his suspicion in this respect was not well founded. It is quite apparent, from the evidence, that his distrust of the fidelity of his wife was really groundless and unjust; but it does not follow that his doubts evince a condition of lunacy. The right of a testator to dispose of his estate, depends neither on the justice of his prejudices nor the soundness of his reasoning. . . .

In short, the evidence adduced utterly failed to prove that the testator was suffering from an insane delusion or lacked testamentary capacity. The Appellate Division was eminently correct in concluding that there was no issue of fact for the jury's consideration and in directing the entry of a decree admitting the will to probate. Its order should be affirmed.

DESMOND, C.J., and FROESSEL and BURKE, J.J., concur with DYE, J.; FULD, J., dissents in an opinion in which VAN VOORHIS and FOSTER, J.J., concur.

Should there be some way by which these issues and those that follow could be determined while the testator is still alive? See Alexander, The Conservatorship Model: A Modification, 77 Mich. L. Rev. 86 (1978); Alexander and Pearson, Alternative Models of Ante-Mortem Probate and Due Process Limitations on Succession, 78 Mich. L. Rev. 89 (1979); Fellows, The Case Against Living Probate, 78 Mich. L. Rev. 1066 (1980); Cavers, Ante-Mortem Probate, 1 U. Chi. L. Rev. 440 (1934); Fink, Ante-Mortem Probate Revisited, 37 Ohio L.J. 264 (1976); Langbein, Living Probate: The Conservatorship Model, 77 Mich. L. Rev. 63 (1978); Beyer and Leopold, Ante-Mortem Probate, 43 Ark. L. Rev. 131 (1990). See also Ark. Stat. Ann. §§28-40-201 et seq. (1987); Ohio Rev. Code §§2107.081 et seq. (1981); N.D. Cent. Code §30.1-08.1-01 (Supp. 1977). Much support for legislation of this type comes from charities. Why? Is there a need for such legislation? Does determination of potential contest issues during life offer an option a testator would freely choose? Is such a procedure fair and humane to family members who have serious doubts about a living person's will, and is a genuine and hence just determination of the issues likely? In light of increasing interest in this subject, questions like these should be given thoughtful consideration not only with respect to the question of desirability but also with respect to matters of form and content.

The case that follows is representative of important issues and illustrative of evolving principles in an important area of estate planning, especially for dying individuals who are under disability. Counterpart issues arise under modernized conservatorship legislation, durable power of attorney statutes, and evolving common law principles.

MATTER OF JONES
379 Mass. 826, 401 N.E.2d 351 (1980)

ABRAMS, J. . . .

This case is before us on the reservation and report by a Probate Court judge of certain questions of law arising from a petition by a conservator for approval of an estate plan for his ward under G.L. c. 201 §38.[3] . . .

The proposed estate plan principally consists of the creation of two inter vivos trusts: one, a revocable trust, providing for distributions to or for the ward during her lifetime from income or principal as necessary or advisable for her health and comfortable support, with reminders to certain charitable organizations; the other, an irrevocable charitable remainder trust which provides for an annual payment to or for the ward, during her lifetime, of an amount equal to nine percent of the fair market value of the trust assets, determined annually, with remainders to certain charitable organizations.

As we read the judge's reservation and report, three basic questions are presented: (1) whether the creation of revocable and irrevocable trusts specifying the ultimate distribution of trust assets to other than the estate of the ward is the same as making a will; (2) whether G.L. c. 201, §38, as amended through St. 1976, c. 515, §§25-26, authorizes making a will; and (3) whether the proposed estate plan could be

---

3. General Laws c. 201, §38, as amended through St. 1976, c. 515 §§25-26, reads as follows: . . .

> The probate court, upon the petition of a conservator or guardian, other than the guardian of a minor, and after such notice to all other persons interested as it directs, may authorize such conservator or guardian to take such action, or to apply such funds as are not required for the ward's own maintenance and support, in such fashion as the court shall approve as being in keeping with the ward's wishes so far as they can be ascertained and as designed to minimize insofar as possible current or prospective state or federal income, estate and inheritance taxes, and to provide for gifts to such charities, relatives and friends as would be likely recipients of donations from the ward.

> Such action or application of funds may include but shall not be limited to the making of gifts, to the conveyance or release of the ward's contingent and expectant interests in property including marital property rights and any right of survivorship incident to joint tenancy or tenancy by the entirety, to the exercise or release of his powers as donee of a power of appointment, the making of contracts, the creation of revocable or irrevocable trusts of property of the ward's estate which may extend beyond his disability or life, the exercise of options of the ward to purchase securities or other property, the exercise of his rights to elect options and to change beneficiaries under insurance and annuity policies, and the surrendering of policies for their cash value, the exercise of his right to an elective share in the estate of his deceased spouse, and the renunciation or disclaimer of any interest acquired by testate or intestate succession or by inter-vivos transfer. . . .

> Gifts may be for the benefit of prospective legatees, devisees or heirs apparent of the ward or may be made to individuals or charities in which the ward is believed to have an interest. The conservator or guardian shall . . . not, however, be required to include as a beneficiary any person whom he has reason to believe would be excluded by the ward.

approved in a proceeding in which the Commonwealth's representation may have been neutralized by a conflict of interest, and in which the ward's next of kin were represented by a guardian ad litem for unborn and unascertained heirs. Although not reported by the judge, the parties have also asked whether an estate plan which is found to be in accordance "with the ward's wishes so far as they can be ascertained, although speculative" complies with the requirements of G.L. c. 201, §38.

We hold that the proposed estate plan is not a testamentary disposition and is authorized by the statute. Furthermore, we find no infirmities arising from representation of the next of kin by the guardian ad litem or of the Commonwealth by the Attorney General. Finally, we uphold the judge's finding that the estate plan complied with the statutory criteria. . . .

Wanda W. Jones is [90 years old,] mentally incompetent and unlikely to recover sufficient mental capacity to execute a will. [In about 1959,] the conservator became the ward's attorney [and] he alleges that to the best of his knowledge, the ward has no husband, issue or other kindred. On her death, [it appears] her estate would pass by escheat to the commonwealth. The conservator believes his ward never made a will.

In 1968, the conservator drafted a will for the ward under which virtually all her estate would pass to various charities, but she never executed the will. Although the ward refused to sign the will, she never repudiated the dispositive provisions. The ward claimed that she had consulted with unidentified advisors who told her that the will was not properly drafted. There was no evidence as to the ward's competency at the time she refused to sign the will. Although the will was presented to the ward for signature only once, the conservator reminded her of it on several occasions, the last being either in 1974 or 1975. The conservator also testified that the ward made small annual gifts, shown in her tax returns, to the charities named in the draft will; however, no individual charitable gift exceeded seventy-five dollars.

Prior to the hearing on the petition, the judge ordered that notice be given to the Attorney General of the Commonwealth and to the Department of Mental Health, and both filed acknowledgments of notice. The Attorney General's acknowledgment stated that the Attorney General assented to the allowance of the petition. Pursuant to the court order, a notice of the proceedings was also published in a major Boston newspaper once a week for three successive weeks. The judge found that the conservator made no special effort to investigate the possible existence of kindred, but simply relied on his long-standing acquaintance with the ward and her deceased husband, the ward's statements to the conservator and others that she had no relatives, and the failure of any party claiming a relationship to have responded to the newspaper publication of notice in the conservatorship proceedings. In addition, the conservator made inquiries of the ward's brother-in-law, and others who knew her well. All reported that they did not know of any person claiming a relationship to the ward. However, no professional heir search was undertaken.

The court below appointed a guardian ad litem for the ward. The guardian ad litem's report opposed the allowance of the petition in so far as the petition proposed that ninety percent of the ward's property be transferred to the irrevocable trust and only ten percent to the revocable trust. The guardian ad litem for the ward recommended that fifty percent of the ward's assets should be transferred to the revocable trust in order to assure the availability of sufficient funds; including principal, for the ward's needs. With that modification, the guardian ad litem for the ward recommended approval of the estate plan. . . .

The court also appointed a guardian ad litem to represent the interests of the unascertained heirs. He filed a report opposing the allowance of the petition on the ground that heirs who might with reasonable diligence be discovered at the time of the ward's death would be deprived of any rights they might have under the laws governing the estates of deceased persons.

The [probate] judge made the following findings. First, the proposed estate plan, modified as recommended by the guardian ad litem of the ward, includes adequate provision for the ward's own maintenance and support. Second, the estate plan is in keeping with the ward's wishes, so far as they can be ascertained, although speculative, and provides gifts to such charities, relatives and friends as would be likely recipients of donations from the ward. Third, the estate plan is designed to minimize in so far as possible current and prospective State and Federal income, estate and gift taxes.

The judge indicated that the plan might be substantially similar to making a will, and therefore not authorized by the statute, G.L. c. 201, §38. We do not think the proposed estate plan is objectionable for that reason.

In Strange v. Powers, 358 Mass. 126, 260 N.E.2d 704 (1970), we held that the prior version of §38 did not empower the court to approve the making of a will because that would involve "an unduly broad construction of the term 'estate plan.'" Id. at 133, 260 N.E.2d at 710. We think that the amendment to §38 still does not permit a conservator to execute a will on behalf of his ward. The 1976 amendment to §38 was largely drawn from §5-408(3)[4] of the Uniform Probate Code, which specifically prohibits the conservator from making a will. . . .

4. The Uniform Probate Code, §5-408(3) (Uniform Laws Annotated, Master ed. 1972), reads:

> After hearing and upon determining that a basis for an appointment or other protective order exists with respect to a person for reasons other than minority, the Court has, for the benefit of the person and members of his household, all the powers over his estate and affairs which he could exercise if present and not under disability, except the power to make a will. These powers include, but are not lim-

Moreover, our case law does not support the view that the creation of an inter vivos trust is "the making of a will." . . .

The fact that a certain disposition of property, here the creation of revocable and irrevocable trusts with charitable remainders, is virtually a substitute for a will is unobjectionable.

> If an owner of property can find a means of disposing of [the property] inter vivos that will render a will unnecessary for the accomplishment of his practical purposes, he has a right to employ it. The fact that the motive of a transfer is to obtain the practical advantages of a will without making one is immaterial.

National Shawmut Bank v. Joy, 315 Mass. at 471, 53 N.E.2d at 122.

The amendment to §38 grants the ward through a conservator most of the powers that the ward would have if the ward were of full capacity. "[T]he purpose is to carry out the ward's wishes so far as they can be ascertained, and not solely for tax minimization. . . ." Young, Probate Reform, 18 Boston B.J. No. 3, 7, 19 (1974). . . . There is no reason not to allow the ward to use inter vivos trusts in estate planning. Given the legislative policy to carry out "the ward's wishes so far as they can be ascertained," the arguments of the guardian ad litem for unborn and unascertained heirs to the effect that authorization of the estate plan in question will undermine the well-established laws of this Commonwealth governing devolution and descent of property are not persuasive. . . .

The guardian ad litem for persons unborn and unascertained complains that the notice by publication ordered by the court is constitutionally inadequate. We disagree.

Due process permits notice by publication, for "[t]hose beneficiaries . . . whose interests or whereabouts could not with due diligence be ascertained." Mullane v. Central Hanover Bank & Trust Co., 339 U.S. 306, 317 (1950). Notice by publication is prohibited "with respect to a person whose name and address are known or very easily ascertainable." Schroeder v. City of N.Y., 371 U.S. 208, 212-213 (1962). Our cases hold that due process "does not demand the impossible. It is impossible to mail a copy of a citation to a person unborn, and as a practical matter it is impossible to mail one to a person whose identity cannot with reasonable diligence be ascertained." Young v. Tudor, 323 Mass. 508, 514, 83 N.E.2d 1, 5 (1948). . . .

---

ited to power to make gifts, to convey or release his contingent and expectant interests in property including marital property rights and any right of survivorship incident to joint tenancy or tenancy by the entirety, to exercise or release his powers as trustee, personal representative, custodian for minors, conservator, or donee of power of appointment, to enter into contracts, to create revocable or irrevocable trusts of property of the estate which may extend beyond his disability or life, to exercise options of the disabled person to purchase securities or other property, to exercise his rights to elect options and change beneficiaries under insurance and annuity policies and to surrender the policies for their cash value, to exercise his right to an elective share in the estate of his deceased spouse and to renounce any interest by testate or intestate succession or by inter vivos transfer.

The record is clear that the conservator had no actual knowledge of the existence of any heirs, and furthermore, that he possessed no information which, if pursued, might have led to the discovery of kindred. Compare McCabe v. Rourke, 301 Mass. 180, 16 N.E.2d 659 (1938) and Cleaveland v. Draper, 194 Mass. 118, 80 N.E. 227 (1907), with Tucker v. Bowen, 354 Mass. 27, 234 N.E.2d 896 (1968), and Welch v. Flory, 294 Mass. 138, 200 N.E. 900 (1936).

The question then is whether the conservator is required to retain the services of a professional genealogist in this case. We think not. . . .

Finally, it is by no means clear that the heirs' participation in the proceedings would affect the outcome. General Laws, c. 201, §38, authorizes the conservator to exclude "as a beneficiary any person whom he has reason to believe would be excluded by the ward." Thus, the interest of any person whose existence was unknown to the ward or whose existence she denied in conversations with family and friends is very attenuated. There is no evidence that the ward ever intended to benefit her next of kin.

Under similar provisions of North Carolina law, the North Carolina Supreme Court said persons who had a contingent or potential financial interest in the death of the incompetent are limited "to present[ing] to the court facts which will assist the court in determining whether the action proposed by the trustee is detrimental to the estate of the incompetent or whether the incompetent, if then competent, would probably not act as the trustee proposes to act." In re Kenan, 262 N.C. 627, 638 (1964). In the case at bar, the judge had appointed a guardian ad litem for persons unborn and unascertained, who very ably represented their interests. As a result, it is hard to imagine what further arguments could be presented on their behalf. . . .

The remaining question briefed by the parties is whether an estate plan which is found to accord "with the ward's wishes, so far as they can be ascertained, although speculative" complies with the requirements of G.L. c. 201, §38. . . . In a petition under §38, the conservator is not required to prove that a proposed estate plan conforms with absolute certainty to the ward's wishes. The court is merely required to "approve [the estate plan] as being in keeping with the ward's wishes so far as they can be ascertained," and "as designed to minimize insofar as possible current or prospective state or federal income, estate and inheritance taxes." G.L. c. 201, §38. The plan may "provide for gifts to such charities, relatives and friends as would be likely recipients of donations from the ward . . . [i.e., those] individuals or charities in which the ward is believed to have an interest." Id.

The guardian ad litem for unascertained heirs argues that the estate plan sought to be established is substantially based on the terms of a will the ward refused to sign. While this is true, the evidence indicated that the will was drafted according to her instructions, instructions which were never changed. The ward continued to make modest annual gifts to the same charitable institutions named in the will. Where the record is not clear as to the ward's wishes, §38 creates a presumption that the ward would favor a reduction in estate taxes and a distribution of her estate to achieve that goal. "[T]here is [no] evidence of any settled intention of the incompetent, formed while sane, to the contrary." Estate of Christiansen, 248 Cal. App. 2d 398, 423, 56 Cal. Rptr. 505, 521 (1967). Compare In re Turner, 6 Misc. 2d 153, 305 N.Y.S.2d 387 (Sup. Ct. 1969) (gifts to three minor children denied where incompetent's will postponed distribution of any portion of his estate until his children reached twenty-five); In re Myles, 57 Misc. 2d 101, 291 N.Y.S.2d 71 (Sup. Ct. 1968) (gifts to son and daughter denied pending testimony as to the survival clause in incompetent's will). Although the evidence offered as to the ward's wishes is not conclusive, we cannot say that the Probate Court judge is plainly wrong in finding that the estate plan is "in keeping with the ward's wishes." See G.L. c. 201, §38. . . .

Since specific questions were reserved and reported, we remand the case to the Probate Court for consideration of the proposed estate plan in light of this opinion.

See Uniform Probate Code §§5-407, 5-408; Cal. Prob. Code §2580; 20 Pa. Con. Stat. §5536(b) (1989). Consider also the durable power of attorney designed to assist persons to utilize non-court procedures for the management of their affairs in the event of later incompetency. The UPC sections that follow are illustrative.

UNIFORM PROBATE CODE

§5-501. *[Definition.]* A durable power of attorney is a power of attorney by which a principal designates another his attorney in fact in writing and the writing contains the words "This power of attorney shall not be affected by subsequent disability or incapacity of the principal, or lapse of time," or "This power of attorney shall become effective upon the disability or incapacity of the principal," or similar words showing the intent of the principal that the authority conferred shall be exercisable notwithstanding the principal's subsequent disability or incapacity, and, unless it states a time of termination, notwithstanding the lapse of time since the execution of the instrument.

§5-502. *[Durable Power of Attorney Not Affected by Lapse of Time, Disability or Incapacity.]* All acts done by an attorney in fact pursuant to a durable power of attorney during any period of disability or incapacity of the principal have the same effect and inure to the benefit of and bind the principal and his successors in interest as if the principal were competent and not disabled. Unless the instrument states a time of termination, the power is exercisable notwithstanding the lapse of time since the execution of the instrument.

2.   Undue Influence

The effect of undue influence is to invalidate the portion of the will procured thereby. Unaffected portions of the will may be allowed to stand as written. "It has been stated in numerous cases that undue influence, such as will invalidate a will, must be something which destroys the free agency of the testator, at the time when the instrument is made, and which, in effect, substitutes the will of another for that of the testator." Toombs v. Matthesen, 206 Okla. 139, 142, 241 P.2d 937, 940 (1952). Thus, it is generally said, an influence is not undue if it merely involves persuasion, pleas calculated to arouse the testator's sympathy, or the courting of favor, even with the intent to obtain benefits under a will. What actions then may constitute undue influence? Certainly the answer varies depending on the circumstances, particularly susceptibility of the testator as it appears from mental, emotional, and physical conditions at the time; but the answer is also likely to vary with the court's concept of undue influence. With the dictum of *Toombs*, supra, compare in particular the *Reddaway* opinion in the ensuing pages, and compare that opinion with the one that follows it.

It is self-evident that the actual facts of alleged acts of undue influence will rarely be known or provable by direct evidence. Undue influence must almost inevitably be shown by circumstantial evidence. The burden of proof, which generally rests on the contestant in the issue of undue influence, may be carried by a showing of facts from which an inference of undue influence may be drawn or that create a presumption of such influence, shifting to the proponent the burden of going forward with the evidence. A few courts have taken the position that undue influence must be proven by clear and convincing evidence, but usually the preponderance-of-the-evidence requirement of ordinary civil litigation is held applicable.

Most cases of undue influence are proven, or sought to be proven, in one of two primary ways, as indicated by the fairly representative dicta set out below. But again the court's formulation and handling of doctrine can make a considerable difference in the outcome of a given contest.

(1) In Will of Leisch, 221 Wis. 641, 648, 650, 267 N.W. 268, 271, 272 (1936), a showing of four elements is generally said to give rise to a permissible inference of undue influence:

> The proof of undue influence generally rests in circumstantial evidence. . . . The four elements necessary to be proved in order to establish

undue influence are as follows: (1) a person unquestionably . . . [suscep-
tible] to undue influence; (2) opportunity to exercise such influence and
[to] effect the wrongful purpose; (3) a disposition to influence unduly for
the purpose of procuring an improper favor; and (4) a result clearly
appearing to be the effect of the supposed influence. . . . "[Y]et the clear
establishment of three of these essential elements may with slight additional evidence as to the fourth compel the inference of its existence. This
is particularly true where the will is not what may be termed a natural one,
such as relationship usually dictates."

(2) Compare In re Hopper, 9 N.J. 280, 282, 88 A.2d 193 (1952):

[I]f a will benefits one who stood in a confidential relationship to the testator and there are additional circumstances of a suspicious character, a
presumption of undue influence is raised and the burden of proof is
shifted to the proponent. A confidential relationship arises where trust is
reposed by reason of the testator's weakness or dependence or where the
parties occupied relations in which reliance is naturally inspired or in fact
exists, as the relation between client and attorney.

See also In re Ausseresses' Estate, 178 Cal. App. 487, 488, 3 Cal. Rptr.
124, 125 (1960): "It is now settled that " . . . when the contestant has
shown that the proponent of a will sustains a confidential relationship
toward the testator, and actively participates in procuring the execution
of the will, and unduly benefits thereby, the burden then shifts to the
proponent to prove that the will was not induced by his undue influence." And see Estate of Osborn, 470 N.E.2d 1114, 1117, 1118 (Ill.
App. 1984):

The necessary fiduciary relationship exists where there is a special confidence reposed in one who, by reason of such confidence, must act in
good faith and with due regard to the interests of the person reposing such
confidence. This relationship "may exist as a matter of law between attorney-client, guardian-ward, trustee-beneficiary, and the like, or it may be
the result of a more informal relationship — moral, social, domestic or
even personal in its origin." . . . While the plaintiff . . . asserts that a confidential relationship arose because of the Diocese's role as religious and
spiritual adviser to the decedent, we are aware of no authority . . . that
such a relationship is fiduciary as a matter of law. The further allegations
. . . fail to indicate that the decedent reposed any "special confidence" in
the Diocese or, indeed, that the relationship between the decedent and
her religious advisors was any different than that between other elderly
persons and their religious or spiritual advisers.
    Even if we were to assume the existence of a fiduciary relationship . . .
[a] presumption of undue influence arises, not from the mere fact of a
fiduciary relationship, but from the fiduciary's participation in procuring
execution of the will, as undue influence that will invalidate a will must be
directly connected with its execution and operate at the time it was made.

In re REDDAWAY'S ESTATE
214 Or. 410, 329 P.2d 886 (1958)

[William Reddaway executed a will in 1931; the original was destroyed and purportedly revoked in 1957, but a copy was admitted to probate following his death in 1957 on a finding that the revocation had been procured by undue influence. The primary beneficiary of the will is Walter, the testator's son by his second marriage; the contestants are the son and daughter of the testator's first marriage, Dallas and Dorlis. Walter had worked for nearly twenty years for his father, until several months before the latter's death. A series of paralytic strokes in 1956 left William almost helpless; at the suggestion of Dallas, Golda Ritzau (Dallas's mother-in-law) was then employed as a practical nurse to care for William and lived in his home until his death. During this period, according to Walter's testimony, his father's previously warm attitude toward him changed dramatically, but no evidence was introduced to explain the change. Shortly before William's death, and all apparently at William's direction, Dallas obtained the will from William's lawyer, read it to William, and then burned it in the presence of William, Golda, and Dallas's wife, Zena. Other evidence indicated that Golda seldom allowed anyone to be alone with William and that she and Dallas were involved in various ways in his financial affairs during his last months. A later will in favor of Golda, Dallas, and Dorlis was drafted but never executed.]

O'CONNELL, J. . . .

Although much of the testimony is conflicting, as is usual in cases of this type, we are of the opinion that the proponent has carried his burden of proof. . . .

[I]n the usual case in which undue influence is relied upon as a basis of attack, the object of the suit is to set aside the will. In the instant case the object of the suit is to sustain the will, it being asserted that undue influence was exerted upon the testator so as to cause him to destroy his will. However, the underlying principle is the same. Briefly stated, that principle is that the law will not permit improper influences to control the disposition of a person's property. We speak of this in the law as "undue influence." The term, like so many other legal terms, cannot be specifically defined. . . . [E]very will is the product of some kind of influence. It is the task of the courts to determine whether the influence in the particular case is "undue." . . .

Rather than approach the problem from the standpoint of the testator's freedom of will, it would be more profitable to focus the emphasis on the nature of the influencer's conduct in persuading the testator to act as he does. The question is, has the influencer by his conduct gained an unfair advantage by devices which reasonable men regard as improper? The idea is expressed in Morris v. Morris, 1942, 192 Miss. 518, 6 So. 2d 311, 312, where the court says that undue influence

> denotes "something wrong, according to the standard of morals which the law enforces in the relations of men, and therefore something legally wrong, something, in fact, illegal. . . . The nature of the influence can be judged only by its result. It is the end accomplished which colors the influence exerted, and entitles us to speak of it as wrongful, fraudulent, or undue, on the one hand, or as proper or justifiable on the other hand. . . . We are to understand the word 'undue' as describing not the nature or the origin of the influence existing, nor as measuring its extent, but as qualifying the purpose with which it is exercised or the result which it accomplishes. . . . "

It is not expected that all courts would hold to the same moral standard in appraising the influencer's conduct, and further, the consequences of upholding the influenced gift are important. It would be expected that there would be less concern with the influencer's motive in a contest between him and the state claiming by escheat than there would be in a contest between him and the donor's deserving spouse.

Definitions of undue influence couched in terms of the testator's freedom of will are subject to criticism in that they invite us to think in terms of coercion and duress, when the emphasis should be on the unfairness of the advantage which is reaped as the result of wrongful conduct. "Undue influence does not negative consent by the donor. Equity acts because there is want of conscience on the part of the donee, not want of consent on the part of the donor." 3 Modern L. Rev. 97, 100 (1939). Said in another way, undue influence has a closer kinship to fraud than to duress. It has been characterized as "a species of fraud."

We shall now consider the application of the law more specifically as it relates to the facts recited above. We first consider the burden of proof. The burden of proving that the will was destroyed free from influence was on the contestants. This court has held that where a confidential relation exists between a testator and the beneficiary, slight evidence is sufficient to establish undue influence. In re Estate of Rosenberg, 196 Or. 219, 256 P.2d 858, 248 P.2d 340. The rule is more specifically stated in In re Southman's Estate, 1946, 178 Or. 462, 482, 168 P.2d 572, 581, as follows: "The existence of a confidential relationship . . . when taken in connection with other suspicious circumstances may justify a suspicion of undue influence so as to require the beneficiary to go forward with the proof and present evidence sufficient to overcome the adverse inference. . . . " It will be noted that the burden does not exist unless there are circumstances in addition to the confidential relation. As was said in Roblin v. Shantz, 1957, 210 Or. 371, 378, 311 P.2d 459, 462, "We must be shown suspicious circumstances." Suspicious circumstances are abundant in the case at bar. We also find that there was a confidential relation between William and his son Dallas, and between William and Golda. . . . The record shows that during the crucial period immediately preceding and during the burning of the will, William was guided by the judgment and advice of Dallas with respect to a variety of matters, some of which have been recited above. The inference is strong that Golda participated in these activities. See In re Estate of Rosenberg, supra.

It has been held that a confidential relation may exist between patient and nurse. . . .

We shall now consider the factors of importance in determining whether undue influence was exercised upon the testator in the present case.

Procurement. One of the circumstances frequently relied upon in the cases as indicating improper influence is the participation of the beneficiary in the preparation of the will, or in its destruction, if it is urged, as here, that the destruction of the will did not revoke it. . . .

In the instant case the participation of Dallas, Golda and Zena in the burning of the 1931 will . . . is described above. Their activity manifested a concern over the disposition of William's estate which might well have been prompted by a selfish motive in view of the fact that the changes which were to be made in the new will would have increased [Dallas's] interests in William's estate. This motive may have caused them to improperly persuade William. The contestants had the burden of producing evidence that such persuasion was not used. They did not carry that burden.

Independent Advice. As stated by Mr. Justice McAllister in Toomey v. Moore, Or. 1958, 325 P.2d 805, 810:

> This court has uniformly held that it is the duty of a beneficiary who participates in the preparation of a will and who occupies a confidential or fiduciary relationship to the testator to see that the testator receives independent and disinterested advice. . . .

. . . It may be noted, however, that on the occasion of [each of two visits] of William's attorney . . . Golda was present. Although there was the opportunity for independent advice under these circumstances it is quite possible that it would not have been heeded. . . .

Secrecy and Haste. Among the circumstances justifying an inference of undue influence is the "secrecy and haste attendant upon the making of the will." In the present case most of the events relating to the destruction of the old will and the making of the new one could be testified to only by Golda, Zena and Dallas. Walter was never informed of his father's plans. There was also testimony that Golda discouraged others from coming to the Reddaway home, and that when visitors came to see William she exercised a watchful eye during that time. Viewed together with the other facts in this case, we regard these as suspicious circumstances.

Change in Decedent's Attitude Toward Others. The unexplained change in the donor's attitude toward those for whom he had previously expressed affection is evidence of improper influence. . . . It is probable that Golda played a part in effecting this change of attitude.

Change in the Testator's Plan of Disposing of His Property. . . . The "variance" between the testator's first will and a later will has been regarded as a "suspicious circumstance" justifying an inference of undue influence in [prior cases]. . . .

Soon after Golda was employed at the Reddaway home William decided to reduce Walter's share in the estate. . . . Yet there was no evidence of estrangement between William and Walter as a result of Walter's conduct in his relation to his father.

Unnatural or Unjust Gift. A person may make a legally effective disposition of his estate which reasonable men would regard as unfair. He may favor his mistress over his wife, or he may disinherit a deserving son, and the law will not concern itself with his moral duty. In re Estate of Riggs, 1926, 120 Or. 38, 241 P. 70, 250 P. 753. But if he does make an unfair or unnatural disposition it is a circumstance to be weighed in determining whether improper influence had been used. . . .

Where there is a confidential relation between the donor and donee and the [revocation] results in shunting the property away from those who had a reasonable expectation of being the recipients of the donor's bounty, the law places the burden on the donee to produce evidence that improper influence was not used. . . .

Donor's Susceptibility to Influence. The physical and mental condition of the donor is regarded as a factor of importance in determining whether a disposition of property was the result of undue influence. . . . And in the present case the contestants argue that since William Reddaway was a man of strong will as evidenced by various acts referred to by contestants, his mind was not overpowered by the influence exerted by others and therefore the influence was not "undue." As we understand undue influence, we need not find that the donor's mind is captured by another. The mental and physical weakness of the donor is merely a circumstance in determining whether the persuasion was improper and an unfair advantage resulted. It is apparent from the evidence in this case that William Reddaway's mental and physical condition made him an easy mark for one who might wish to influence him. We do not think that it is necessary to recite this evidence.

Although there is other evidence in the record which is relevant to the issue of improper influence, the combination of circumstances recited above is sufficient to sustain the proponent's claim that undue influence was exercised upon the testator in causing him to destroy his will. As this court has pointed out previously, cases of this type ordinarily must rest upon circumstantial evidence. We can only view the evidence from the bare record without the opportunity of watching the witnesses as they testify. The trial judge had this opportunity. He concluded that undue influence was exercised. We agree with him. The decree is affirmed.

In re ESTATE OF KAMESAR
81 Wis. 2d 151, 259 N.W.2d 733 (1977)

[Samuel Kamesar died in 1974 at age 84, survived by his two daughters, Jeanette Feldman and Bernice Lee, his son Armon Kamesar, and his second wife, Doris, to whom he was married in March of 1971. The will in question was executed in June of 1971. It incorporated the terms of a prenuptial agreement with Doris, bequeathed $5,000 to a grandchild, and left the rest of his estate to Bernice, explaining that his omission of Armon and Jeanette was because he had made special provisions for them during life. The latest of his prior wills contained bequests to all of his grandchildren and would have left his residuary estate equally to his three children. The 1971 will was propounded by Bernice and contested by Armon and Jeanette, alleging it was the result of undue influence by Bernice. The trial court found in favor of Bernice and admitted the will to probate.

Samuel lived nearly all of his adult life in Milwaukee; Armon lived there until 1971 and managed his father's financial affairs until Armon moved to California that year. Jeanette also lives in California. Both did, in fact, receive substantial funds from their father during his lifetime. Bernice had lived abroad until 1968, when she returned to Milwaukee; after Armon's departure she managed her father's financial affairs and held a power of attorney executed by him in March 1971. There is no record of gifts to Bernice or her children, but after June 1971 she and her children received $3,000 apiece each year. Friends and relatives testified that Samuel had been forgetful and confused in 1971, but all except Armon testified that he was of sound mind when he married Doris. Armon doubted his father's mental capacity at the time but had never said so because he approved of the marriage and antenuptial agreement. A physician testified that Samuel had been in ill health for a number of years and that he lacked the ability to make a decision when he became hospitalized in 1973.]

DAY, J. . . .

While the record shows that there was much ill feeling between Bernice and her brother and sister, it seems clear that Samuel Kamesar had equal affection for all of them.

All of the wills were drawn by the deceased's lifetime friend and attorney, Mr. George Laikin. Mr. Laikin testified that on March 18, 1971, when Samuel Kamesar and Doris Kamesar executed the prenuptial agreement, Mr. Laikin recommended that Mr. Kamesar amend his will to incorporate the terms of the agreement. Mr. Kamesar told him that "other changes" should be made in the will also and that he would advise him of those changes later. Mr. Laikin testified that Mr. Kamesar did not personally contact him but communicated the changes to be made in the will by telephone through Bernice Lee. Mr. Laikin stated that Mr. Kamesar customarily communicated with him in that manner, first through Armon and later through Bernice.

When the June will was ready to sign, Bernice Lee made an appointment with Mr. Laikin and drove Samuel and Doris Kamesar to his office. Doris Kamesar and Bernice Lee were present when the will was executed. Mr. Laikin and Bernice Lee both testified that Mr. Laikin reviewed the specific terms of the will. Bernice Lee testified Mr. Laikin asked her to go through the terms again with her father and she read it to him. She testified Mr. Laikin told her father that the will would make some people unhappy but her father replied that one has to take a chance in life. Doris Kamesar testified that Mr. Laikin did not review the will but merely gave it to Samuel Kamesar to read and asked him if he understood it. She and Mr. Laikin testified Samuel Kamesar did ask to have the will changed to provide that his wife could remain in the apartment for one year after his death instead of six months.

Mr. Laikin testified that Samuel Kamesar said the will was what they had talked about and said, "let's proceed to sign the will." Mr. Laikin also testified he questioned Samuel Kamesar whether he knew this will left all to Bernice and he said he did. Mr. Laikin believed Samuel Kamesar was competent at the time and not under any undue influence.

Doris testified that some months after the will was signed, when she reminded Samuel Kamesar that he had cut his two children out of the will, he could not remember doing so. . . .

There are two avenues by which an objector to a will on the theory of undue influence may challenge its admission.

One is by proving the elements that this court has said show undue influence. Those are: (1) susceptibility to undue influence, (2) opportunity to influence, (3) disposition to influence, and (4) coveted result. The burden is on the objector to prove by clear, satisfactory and convincing evidence that the will was the result of undue influence. However, when three of the four elements have been established by the required quantum of proof, only slight evidence of the fourth is required.

The second method of challenge is to prove the existence of (1) a confidential relationship between the testator and the favored beneficiary and (2) suspicious circumstances surrounding the making of the will.

1. Four Elements Test

A. SUSCEPTIBILITY TO UNDUE INFLUENCE

The objectors must establish by clear, satisfactory and convincing evidence that the testator in this case was susceptible to the influence of Bernice Lee. Factors to be considered are age, personality, physical and mental health and ability to handle business affairs. This court has stated that the infirmities of old age, such as forgetfulness, do not incapacitate one from making a valid will . . . [but] evidence of impaired mental powers on the part of a testator is itself a circumstance which gives rise to a reasonable inference that the testator is susceptible to undue influence. . . .

The objectors argue that the fact that Samuel Kamesar entrusted the management of his business affairs to Bernice, coupled with his impaired mental powers, made him susceptible to her influence. But the evidence is conflicting. The testator did suffer from arteriosclerosis, and there was testimony that in June of 1971 he was forgetful and confused. But several witnesses testified he was of sound mind three months before when he was married, and his wife testified he never forgot what he owned or who his children were. Mr. Laikin, the attorney, who was present when all the wills were executed and had known the testator for most of his own life, testified that the deceased was of sound mind and not under any undue influence when the will in question was executed. At that conference the testator made one request for a change with regard to his wife's occupancy of the apartment in the event of his death. This request shows his awareness of the will's provisions. The trial court's conclusion that the objectors did not establish susceptibility is not against the great weight and clear preponderance of the evidence.

B. OPPORTUNITY TO INFLUENCE

The trial court found and the proponents agree that Bernice Lee had ample opportunity to exert undue influence on the decedent. This conclusion is not against the great weight of the evidence.

C. DISPOSITION TO INFLUENCE

Disposition to unduly influence means more than a desire to obtain a share of the estate. It implies a willingness to do something wrong or unfair.

The evidence in this case shows that Bernice Lee had taken over the decedent's business affairs completely, but as the trial court pointed out, she had merely taken up where her brother had left off when he moved from Milwaukee. Bernice Lee testified that in December 1973, she did consult another attorney other than Mr. Laikin and procured a declaration of intent signed by her father to give her and her children $9,000 in tax free gifts every year. This document was executed twenty-one days before Samuel Kamesar died, at a time when his attending physician testified that he was incapable of making any kind of decision. But this was remote in time from the date of execution of the will in question here. . . .

The evidence here is quite clear that Armon Kamesar and Jeanette Feldman received substantial gifts from their parents during the parents' lives and that Bernice Lee had not. Even if she had tried to influence her father to make his will more favorable to her than to her brother and sister who had already benefitted from Samuel Kamesar's generosity, such influence would not necessarily be undue. . . .

D.   COVETED RESULT

This element goes to the naturalness or expectedness of the bequest. The fact that the testator has excluded a natural object of his bounty is a "red flag of warning." But that fact alone does not render the disposition unnatural where a record shows reasons as to why a testator would leave out those who may be the natural beneficiaries of his bounty.

In the case at bar, the will expressly states that Armon Kamesar and Jeanette Feldman are excluded because the testator believed he had adequately provided for them during his lifetime. Mr. Laikin testified that it was he who suggested that this language be used in drafting the will. . . .

While conflicting inferences may be drawn from the evidence presented and even though the June 1971 will manifests a drastic change in attitude from that manifested just three months before when Armon Kamesar had been the close confidant of his father, the trial court's finding in favor of the proponent on this issue is not against the great weight and clear preponderance of the evidence.

We conclude, therefore, that on the basis of the four classic elements the trial court must be sustained.

II.   *Was the Trial Court's Refusal to Raise a Presumption of Undue Influence Contrary to the Great Weight and Clear Preponderance of the Evidence?*

Undue influence may also be proved by the existence of (1) a confidential relationship between the testator and the favored beneficiary, and (2) suspicious circumstances surrounding the making of the will. When the objector proves the existence of both elements by the required quantum of evidence, a presumption of undue influence is raised, which must be rebutted by the proponent. The trial court held that the record did not substantiate a finding of either element.

(1) CONFIDENTIAL RELATIONSHIP

This court has described the confidential relationship that is sufficient to raise a presumption of undue influence as follows:

> The basis for the undue influence presumption lies in the ease in which a confidant can dictate the contents and control or influence the drafting of such a will either as the draftsman or in procuring the drafting. . . . If one is not the actual draftsman or the procurer of the drafting, the relationship must be such that the testator depends upon the advice of the confidant in relation to the subject matter of the will. . . .

Estate of Steffke, 48 Wis. 2d at 51, quoted in Estate of Velk, 53 Wis. 2d 500, 507, 192 N.W.2d 844 (1972).

The objectors argue that Bernice Lee's role in the execution of the June 1971 will made her the procurer of the drafting and execution of the will. To "procure" is "to initiate," "to instigate," or "to cause a thing to be done." Black's Law Dictionary 1373 (1968). However, the record shows that it was Mr. Laikin who recommended that Samuel Kamesar change his will to reflect the provisions of the pre-nuptial agreement. Samuel Kamesar himself stated that he intended to make "other changes" as well. Bernice Lee's role in communicating these changes to Mr. Laikin and in arranging for the execution of the will was a role customarily played by one of Samuel Kamesar's children.

The record is clear, however, that Bernice Lee did manage all of her father's business and personal affairs, and this court has held that where a child has also served as a testator's financial advisor that a confidential relationship can be found to exist. . . .

Bernice Lee testified that she took over the role that had previously been played by her brother and it appears to us that the reasonable inference to be drawn from the evidence is that Samuel Kamesar did rely on Bernice Lee in relation to the subject matter of the will. We conclude, therefore, the finding of the trial court, that there was no confidential relationship between Bernice Lee and her father is against the great weight and clear preponderance of the evidence.

(2) SUSPICIOUS CIRCUMSTANCES

The suspect circumstances requirement is satisfied by proof of facts "such as the activity of the beneficiary in procuring the drafting and execution of the will, or a sudden and unexplained change in the attitude of the testator, or some other persuasive circumstance." "The basic question to be determined from the evidence is always whether 'the free agency of the testator has been destroyed.'" . . .

[A]lthough Bernice Lee called the attorney, Mr. Laikin, made the appointment to see him to have the will signed, drove Samuel Kamesar to the lawyer's office and communicated to the attorney the terms of the will which made her the sole beneficiary, these were all routine practices for this particular testator. The evidence showed that at the time of execution, Samuel Kamesar was aware of the terms of his will. The will was also drafted by his long-time personal friend and attorney who testified there was nothing irregular in the drafting or in the execution. The will itself contained the explanation that Samuel Kamesar believed that he had adequately provided for his son and his other daughter during their lifetime, and the fact was that they had received substantial gifts and that Bernice Lee had not received such gifts. The will was not made in haste but over a period of three months. There was no reluctance shown in signing the will and while the testator was forgetful, he was functioning on his own, outside of a nursing home when the will was executed. It was also established that Armon Kamesar had been informed by Doris Kamesar of the new will before his father died and all parties were aware of the testator's failing health. The . . . court's conclusion that no suspicious circumstances were proven . . . is not against the great weight and clear preponderance of the evidence. . . .

By the Court, Judgment affirmed.

COMMENT, WILLS, UNDUE INFLUENCE
50 Mich. L. Rev. 748, 759-760 (1952)

. . . Can it be said that an examination of the cases shows results consistent with the definition that undue influence is the destruction of the free agency of the testator so that he has lost his ability to weigh motivations and reach an independent decision? While the ultimate fact required by the courts may be in keeping with such a definition, it must be recognized that it is most difficult to prove that the free agency has been destroyed. As a result, the courts have been forced to accept a lower standard. It is clear that testators, especially when enfeebled, ought to be protected from certain "activity" on the part of others. Yet the courts are aware that many a disappointed heir attempts to break a will on any pretext handy even though no real grounds of undue influence exist; and the courts have observed that no jury should be permitted to rewrite a will merely because it disagrees with the propriety of the disposition made by the testator. These latter facts are borne out by the observations that in the great majority of cases appellate courts have either reversed jury findings of undue influence or have affirmed the trial judge in taking the case from the jury. It is submitted that on the whole the courts have succeeded in steering a course so as to accomplish both aims. But just what "activity" the testator is to be protected from can only be "felt" by reading of many cases. When a testator becomes old and mentally enfeebled, he is apt to be affected by the influences of others much more than in his younger days. While such a testator may not be a mere rubber stamp for the will of others, the courts have refused to permit such influences on the ground that society's interest is better served by allowing him to be free of importunities. This is not removing the testator's right to dispose of his property as he chooses, but is making sure that he is not imposed upon when his better judgment may be absent. By the same token, the courts have felt that a person, who is in such a position that his influence might be held unduly in esteem by the testator, ought to refrain from participation in the procurement of the will; and where there is a flavoring of other suspicious factors, the chances that the testator was unsocially influenced are so great that the will should be set aside, even though free agency in the philosophical sense probably was not destroyed.

In re ESTATE OF REILAND
292 Minn. 460, 194 N.W.2d 289 (1972)

PER CURIAM.

This is a will contest in which one of the decedent's stepchildren seeks to prove . . . that the will was the product of undue influence exerted by an attorney-scrivener whose father was a beneficiary. . . .

[This raises the] question [of] the effect of an attorney's drafting a will in which he or his family have a beneficial interest. We have unequivocally condemned this practice in In re Estate of Keeley, 167 Minn. 120, 208 N.W. 535 (1926), and more recently, in In re Estate of Peterson, 283 Minn. 446, 168 N.W.2d 502 (1969). In the *Keeley* case, we adopted the following rule (167 Minn. 124, 208 N.W. 537): "[W]hen a beneficiary of a substantial portion of the estate sustains a fiduciary or confidential relation with the testator and acts as the scrivener in drawing the will or controls its drafting, such facts alone will make a prima facie case and will sustain a finding of undue influence." We went on to brand the preparation of a will by the beneficiary as unethical and said that professional honor dictates that under such circumstances the will be prepared by someone other than the beneficiary. In the *Peterson* case, we extended the rule to apply where the attorney-scrivener's children are beneficiaries. . . .

In the case at hand, the . . . father was not only a personal friend of decedent's, but had acted as his counsel. The trial court pointed out that the testator was an alert, strong-minded person who had taken the initiative to have the scrivener prepare the will. Recognizing that an inference of undue influence arises under these circumstances, the [trial] court held that there was other evidence sufficient to overcome that inference. We are of the opinion that the record fully supports the court's finding and affirm.

In re ESTATE OF PEDRICK
505 Pa. 530, 482 A.2d 215 (1984)[5]

HUTCHINSON, J. . . .

The sole question before us is the effect of appellee's conduct as attorney-scrivener-beneficiary on his right to use Orphans' Court process to secure a benefit under the will [resulting] from conduct which, while not illegal, is not only far below those standards acceptable in the legal profession, but additionally plainly frustrates full equitable inquiry into the substantive issues presented. On the undisputed facts of this case, we hold that appellee, proponent of the September 27, 1979 will, came into equity with unclean hands. Thus, the Orphans' Court erred in granting him affirmative relief. Therefore, we reverse.

The testator, Joseph C. Pedrick, unmarried and childless, . . . made at least four wills in his lifetime. The first two were prepared in 1959 and 1972 by his long time personal attorney, appellee's father. In them he left his modest estate to that attorney. In the course of time the father was joined in his legal practice by his sons, this appellee and Edmund, appellee's brother. Still later, in 1975, death came to the father, but his two sons continued the family law firm. In August of 1977 testator came one day to the law firm his dead friend had founded. That he did so is undisputed. Whether he and appellee quarreled is unclear. However, about one month later he sought the services of Thomas Mettee, Esquire. Mr. Mettee prepared a third will in which Mr. Pedrick left his entire estate to a boy he had raised, John Gregory, the appellant here.

On September 27, 1979, Mr. Pedrick, old and sick, lay in St. Mary's Hospital. . . . [H]e asked a nursing sister to call the Butler law firm to see to his will. The nurse, Sister Catherine Joseph, called appellee to come to the hospital. In response to that call appellee went to the hospital although he found it most inconvenient. There, on that day, in that condition, while alone with the son and namesake of his dead friend and attorney, testator signed his fourth will leaving his still modest estate to the scrivener and the scrivener's brother. No witness, disinterested or otherwise, attested that will. That will was not re-executed or republished in the presence of any witness whatsoever when appellee returned alone two days later to have testator name appellee himself beneficiary on testator's federal pension.

The Register had a hearing and denied appellee's will probate. Appellee then sought the aid of the Orphans' Court Division, a court in which equitable principles apply. [Pennsylvania law permits an unwitnessed will to be established in an equity proceeding.] That court noted appel-

---

5. See more recent ABA recommendations on professional responsibility in Chapter 8, section G. — EDS.

lee's "unfortunate and inexcusable" conduct, but nevertheless opened its halls to aid him because it could not find undue influence under our governing case law. However, it did ignore the maxim that he who asks the sovereign, in its conscience, to support him, must put out hands undirtied in the matter where he seeks the sovereign's aid.

The Code of Professional Conduct to which members of appellee's profession were held at the time he did this "unconscionable" act does not have the force of substantive law. . . . Thus, appellee's failure to live up to that Code, standing alone, would not invalidate this will. Here, however, we have not only a clear departure from ethical standards, but other conduct which plainly frustrates a determination based on untainted disinterested evidence as to whether this testator freely willed his worldly goods to appellee and appellee's brother. Appellee's failure to secure any witness to what transpired between him and the testator, despite the second opportunity created when he came back two days later to effect a beneficiary change in his own favor, effectively insulated the will he prepared to his own benefit from any acceptable inquiry into the very issue before the court, undue influence. A court applying equitable principles is not open to such a supplicant. . . .

Appellee admitted that he was familiar with Ethical Consideration 5-5 of the Code of Professional Responsibility which provides:

> A lawyer should not suggest to his client that a gift be made to himself or for his benefit. If a lawyer accepts a gift from his client, he is peculiarly susceptible to the charge that he unduly influenced or over-reached the client. *If a client voluntarily offers to make a gift to his lawyer, the lawyer may accept the gift, but before doing so, he should urge that his client secure disinterested advice from an independent, competent person who is cognizant of all the circumstances. Other than in exceptional circumstances, a lawyer should insist that an instrument in which his client desires to name him beneficially be prepared by another lawyer selected by the client.*[6]

Emphasis added. However, he stated that he did not have someone else draft the will because "the call I received from Sister Catherine placed emphasis on the fact that he wanted to see me that night." . . . [T]hat explanation fails in the face of appellee's own testimony that he returned to the hospital on September 29 to obtain Mr. Pedrick's signature on a change of beneficiary form naming appellee himself beneficiary. . . . He excused his failure to have someone else draft a will before that second visit by his belief that the will was valid and because "it was a busy time

---

6. The proposed Model [Rules] of Professional [Conduct] more explicitly [prescribe] the conduct barred by Ethical Consideration 5-5 of the present Code. We note it without implying our position on it. Rule 1.8(c) of the proposed [Rules] states:

> A lawyer shall not prepare an instrument giving the lawyer or a person related to the lawyer as parent, child, sibling or spouse any substantial gift from a client including a testamentary gift, except where the client is related to the donee.

at the office and time was of an absolute premium." There was no evidence that he made any effort to have the will benefitting him and his brother re-executed and republished in the presence of disinterested subscribing witnesses.

Mr. Pedrick died six months after he executed this fourth will. . . .

The Orphans' Court considered only the issues of testamentary capacity and undue influence. . . .

Here, however, an attorney whose conduct the record shows was "unfortunate and inexcusable" comes into a court applying equitable principles to secure a benefit from the very conduct which the accepted standards of the profession preclude. Such conduct may constitute "unclean hands" which bars relief in equity. . . .

We base our holding not on Mr. Butler's violation of an Ethical Consideration of the Code of Professional Responsibility; rather, we find that Mr. Butler's conduct in this matter, when viewed on the whole record, shocks the conscience of this Court.

Reversed and remanded to the Orphans' Court for proceedings consistent with this opinion. . . .

MAGEE v. STATE BAR OF CALIFORNIA
58 Cal. 2d 423, 24 Cal. Rptr. 839, 374 P.2d 807 (1962)

PER CURIAM.

Petitioner challenges a finding by the Board of Bar Governors that he abused the confidence placed in him by an aged [81 years old] client, Mary Rohde, in drawing a will naming him the residuary beneficiary of her estate and in accepting a substantial cash gift from her. The Board recommended that he be suspended from the practice of law for two years.

The Board's finding followed two hearings by a local administrative committee. The committee twice concluded that petitioner obtained the testamentary gift and the inter vivos gift by undue influence, emphasizing that he had "gained an advantage over his client" and that he presented "no substantial evidence . . . to show that these transactions were fair and just." . . .

Petitioner was admitted to practice in 1930. He met Mrs. Rohde, who was a friend of his mother, at a meeting in 1941 of the Auxiliary of Miles Camp, Spanish American War Veterans. Between 1941 and 1949 petitioner had only brief conversations with Mrs. Rohde several times a year at functions of the veterans' organization. After the death of her husband in 1949, Mrs. Rohde consulted petitioner for assistance in applying for a government pension. He did not see Mrs. Rohde again until October 16, 1951, when the will was drawn. . . .

Petitioner's testimony is the only direct evidence of what occurred during the 10 to 15 minutes he was alone with Mrs. Rohde in his office. He stated that they had a few moments of pleasant conversation and that she then told him how she wished to dispose of her estate. He took notes of her wishes, including her wish to make him the residuary legatee. He asked her why she wished to give him the residue, and she stated that she had no relatives, that he and his mother had been good to her, and that she was fond of him. . . .

A relative of Mrs. Rohde's deceased husband contested the will [see Cal. Prob. Code §6402(e)] and a jury determined that petitioner had exercised undue influence over her and that she was mentally incompetent. The trial judge held that the evidence of incompetence was insufficient to support the verdict, but sustained the verdict of undue influence, apparently in reliance on the presumption that arises from the attorney-client relationship. The decision was affirmed by the District Court of Appeal. (Estate of Rohde, 158 Cal. App. 2d 19, 323 P.2d 490.)

An attorney who by undue influence obtains a gift from a client inter vivos or in a will is guilty of an act involving moral turpitude. In determining whether the evidence is sufficient to sustain the finding that petitioner exercised undue influence, however, we are not bound by the decision in the action setting aside Mrs. Rohde's will on this ground.

The highest good faith an attorney owes his client requires the attorney to rebut the inference of undue influence that arises when he receives a gift from the client under circumstances that reasonably suggest such influence. Although the circumstances of the instant case gave rise to a presumption of undue influence, petitioner rebutted the presumption and raised reasonable doubts that he committed this offense. Of utmost significance is the testimony of Mr. Devlin [another attorney who witnessed the will] that he read the will to Mrs. Rohde paragraph by paragraph, questioned her about her intention, and explained to her the nature of the residuary gift. She stated that this was exactly what she wished to do, and she seemed to resent all the questioning. By this procedure, intended by Mr. Devlin to be a "taking over" of the will, Mrs. Rohde was in fact given much of the protection she would have received had petitioner sent her to another attorney when she first declared her intention to make him a beneficiary. There was no evidence that Mrs. Rohde was not fully competent on the morning in question. Indeed, all the evidence indicated that she appeared alert and in complete command of herself. The fact that she did not again make a will during the year preceding her death is some evidence that she was content with the will petitioner drew for her. Moreover, it seems unlikely that in the 10 to 15 minutes he was alone with Mrs. Rohde (a woman described variously as "tough," "firm," and "definite in . . . [her] ideas") petitioner could have persuaded her to discard a previous testamentary plan and make him the principal beneficiary of her estate.

If petitioner's version of the making of the will is accepted, the gift of cash was a normal and understandable act on Mrs. Rohde's part. We conclude, therefore, that the Board did not prove by "convincing proof and to a reasonable certainty" that petitioner obtained either the testamentary or inter vivos gift by undue influence. . . .

An attorney's duty of fidelity to his client involves far more than refraining from exercising undue influence. . . . In civil cases, "there are no transactions respecting which courts . . . are more jealous and particular, than dealings between attorneys and their clients, especially where there is great intellectual inequality, and comparative inexperience on the part of the latter." (Mills v. Mills, 26 Conn. 213, 219.) . . .

There is no rule that attorneys should never draw wills in which they receive gifts. There is nothing improper in an attorney's drawing wills for his family or for relatives, provided the gift to him is reasonable under the circumstances. Similarly, there is nothing improper in drawing wills for close friends or for clients if the gift to the attorney is a modest one. . . . As the instant case suggests, however, attorneys take a grave risk in drawing wills in which they receive more than a modest gift that is in keeping with the nature of the relationship they have with the client. Petitioner took this risk, unwisely, and one consequence was that he lost the substantial gift in Mrs. Rohde's will when it was contested. Even though an attorney may be acting only to carry out the wishes of his client in drawing a will containing a gift to himself, he should send the client to another lawyer when the circumstances would support an inference of wrongdoing. In the instant case, petitioner should have taken the initiative in having Mrs. Rohde consult another lawyer. Since, however, the purpose of such consultation was adequately served by Mr. Devlin, although on his own initiative, and since there is no convincing proof of petitioner's wrongdoing, we have concluded that his conduct does not call for discipline or reprimand.

The proceeding is dismissed.

WHITMAN AND HOOPES, THE CONFIDENTIAL RELATIONSHIP IN WILL CONTESTS
122 Tr. & Est. 53, 54 (1985)

The existence of a confidential relationship between a testator and beneficiary of a will can be an important factor in a will contest. Indeed, these rules often decide will contests. While it has been suggested that we ultimately develop better legal rules by considering each state as a separate experimental laboratory, the confusion created by widely varying state rules also has been noted. The authors believe it is time to unify and standardize the rules of confidential relationship applied in will contests.

In many jurisdictions, courts now hold that if a substantial beneficiary is found to stand in a confidential relationship with a testator, and that beneficiary actively participated in the preparation or execution of the will, a rebuttable presumption of undue influence arises. But some jurisdictions additionally require that the benefits received be "undue" or "unnatural," or permit other "suspicious circumstances" to substitute for active participation. While the presumption of undue influence applies, in one form or another, in nearly every jurisdiction, the definition of what constitutes a confidential relationship clearly lacks uniformity.

Confusion also exists as to the effect of the finding of the existence of the presumption. Generally, if the proponent offers no evidence in rebuttal, the contestant is entitled to a directed verdict. If rebuttal evidence is presented, the presumption disappears from the case, leaving the burden of persuasion on the contestant. In a few jurisdictions, however, the presumption creates a prima facie case, permanently shifting the burden of persuasion to the proponents. . . .

While it is clear that a confidential relationship exists as a matter of law between a testator and his doctor, lawyer, clergyman or close business associate, when other categories of relationships are involved, each state's law must be consulted; for state law varies widely.

For example, consider the question of whether there is a confidential relationship between husband and wife. In some states, "[i]t is generally held that there is no such thing as a confidential relation between husband and wife in the law governing will contests." Yet other jurisdictions follow the rule that the issue of whether a confidential relationship exists between husband and wife is a question of fact.

The law's treatment of consanguinity is similarly erratic. In one jurisdiction, consanguinity is "an important and material fact in considering the question of whether in fact a confidential relationship exists. . . . " Yet elsewhere, consanguinity is considered irrelevant.

When a rule of law does not govern the question of whether a particular relationship is confidential for purposes of will contests, then an issue of fact exists. A typical judicial statement of the standard to be used is that a confidential relationship exists "whenever trust and confidence is reposed by one person in the integrity and fidelity of another." In this area there is uniformity. The difficulty arises in determining whether one of the various rules of law applies to render a particular relationship either confidential, or not, as a matter of law.

Active Participation

There is also a lack of uniformity in the requirement of a showing of active participation in the preparation or execution of the will on the part of the person alleged to have unduly influenced the testator by means of a confidential relationship.

In some states, a showing of active participation is necessary in addition to the existence of a confidential relationship between a beneficiary and a testator. In other states, *additional* suspicious circumstances, such as a substantial gift or a weakness of mind of the testator, *must* be shown. And in still other jurisdictions, weakness of mind or other suspicious circumstances may serve as *substitutes* for active participation, in that *either* active participation *or* other suspicious circumstances may be shown.

Compounding the confusion, there are differing views as to what constitutes active participation. There appear to be two schools of thought. According to one, there is no active participation unless there is personal participation in the actual drafting or execution of the will. According to the other, active participation may be found to exist where there is only conduct by a beneficiary prior to the drafting or execution of the will.

It has been held, moreover, that a presumption of undue influence does not arise where a beneficiary participated in the preparation of the will at the request of the testator.

Unnatural Disposition

Another trap for unwary practitioners in the area of confidential relationship is the rule that, to raise a presumption of undue influence, it must be shown that the person alleged to have unduly influenced the testator received unnatural or undue benefits under the will. This is the law in some states, in others it is not, and, no doubt, in still others no one can be sure what the law is. . . .

The diversity of rules in the area of confidential relationship in will contests suggests a need for uniformity more than a need for any particular set of uniform rules.

The root issue is whether the presumption of undue influence is favored or disfavored. On the side of the presumption is a need to protect testators and the expectant objects of their bounty from the machinations of those who would thwart the free will of testators. Also on the side of the presumption is the fact that undue influence is difficult to prove affirmatively. The only evidence is usually circumstantial, and it is easy for wrongdoers to cover their tracks.

Other considerations, however, militate against too much enthusiasm for the presumption of undue influence. In particular, there is the policy, deeply rooted both in the common law and in Anglo-American notions of individual liberty, of freedom of testation. There is every reason to believe that when the issue of confidential relationship is one of fact, jurors will often allow their own feelings as to how the testator should have disposed of his property to influence their conclusion on the confidential relationship issue. Justice Tobringer of California has stated that "[i]t does appear, from the cases appealed, that the jury finds for the contestant in over 75 percent of the cases submitted to it. But the fact that juries exhibit consistent unconcern for the wishes of testators should come as no surprise. Indeed, the tendency of juries in this respect is so pronounced that it has been said to be a proper subject of judicial notice."

Another view sometimes appearing in the judicial decisions, which is used to justify restriction of the presumption of undue influence, is that influence arising from a husband and wife relationship is always proper, and should therefore never result in a presumption of undue influence. One court has stated that "a wife ought to have great influence over her husband, and it is one of the necessary results of proper marriage relations, and that it would be monstrous to deny to a woman who is generally an important agent in building up domestic prosperity, the right to express her wishes concerning its disposal."

This view, however, is far from universal. It could be argued that, in an age in which second marriages are common, there is an increased danger that children of first marriages will be unfairly disinherited by a susceptible parent. . . .

Whatever the rules that might ultimately be adopted, an organized move towards creating a nationally uniform set of rules seems clearly called for.

What form might you suggest the rules urged by Whitman and Hoopes should take? Is such legislation appropriate?

3.   Fraud and Mistake

Closely related to other grounds of contest are fraud and some types of mistake. Certain forms of mistake (mainly in description and inducement) are treated as problems in the use of extrinsic evidence in Chapter 5, section E, supra.

Although difficult factual problems arise in proving fraud, there is generally little trouble in defining it. "[F]alse representations . . . constitute fraud if it can be shown that they were designed to and did deceive the testator into making a will different in its terms from that which he would have made had he not been misled." In re Newhall's Estate, 190 Cal. 709, 718, 214 P. 231, 235; Annot., 28 A.L.R. 778 (1923). The fraud may be either in the execution of a will or in its inducement, and in either form it is similarly treated.

The *remedy* for fraud poses a more difficult legal problem, especially in deciding whether and in what manner a disposition was, or — more realistically — should be deemed to have been, affected by deceit practiced upon a testator. Also, when is it sufficient merely to deny probate to the will or a portion of it? What other remedies are available? In what circumstances, and then how, must it be shown what the testator would have done but for the fraud? Cf. Pope v. Garrett, supra page 306.

In re CARSON'S ESTATE
184 Cal. 437, 194 P. 5 (1920)

[Alpha Carson's will left a number of bequests to relatives and her residuary estate to "my husband J. Gamble Carson." Within the statutory period following probate, her heirs petitioned to have probate revoked primarily on the ground of fraud, and contestants appeal the denial of their petition. The facts indicate that the testatrix and Carson had gone through a marriage ceremony a year before her death and that she made her will and died believing that he was her husband, which he was not because he was already married to and not divorced from another woman who was still living. It was alleged that Carson knew he was not free to marry but represented that he was.]

OLNEY, J. . . .

Was the evidence for the contestants, both what they introduced and what they sought to introduce, sufficient to justify revocation of the probate of the will? . . .

So far as the other beneficiaries are concerned . . . the will is perfectly valid. . . . [O]nly the portions of the will in favor of Carson should be revoked in case the contestants should succeed. . . . If it were not possible to separate the portions affected by the fraud from those unaffected, it may be that the whole will would have to fail, but that question is not present here. . . .

The gross fraud upon the testatrix is, of course, apparent. According to the evidence, she was seduced by a marital adventurer into a marriage with him which was no marriage in the eyes of the law. . . . There can be no question also that if the bequest to Carson were the direct fruit of such fraud, it is void.

The only question in the case, assuming the contestants' evidence to be true, as we must, is, Was the bequest in fact the fruit of the fraud? This is a question of fact which it was for the jury to determine; and, unless it can be said that the jury could have reasonably reached but one conclusion concerning it, and that was that the bequest to Carson was not the direct fruit of his fraud, the evidence was sufficient to prevent a nonsuit.

Now a case can be imagined where, nothing more appearing, as in this case, than that the testatrix had been deceived into a void marriage and had never been undeceived, it might fairly be said that a conclusion that such deceit had affected a bequest to the supposed husband would not be warranted. If, for example, the parties had lived happily together for 20 years, it would be difficult to say that the wife's bequest to her supposed husband was founded on her supposed legal relation with him, and not primarily on their long and intimate association. It might well be that if undeceived at the end of that time her feeling would be, not one of resentment at the fraud upon her, but of thankfulness that she had been deceived into so many years of happiness. But, on the other hand, a case can easily be imagined where the reverse would be true. If in this case the will had been made immediately after marriage, and the testatrix had then died within a few days, the conclusion would be well-nigh irresistible, in the absence of some peculiar circumstance, that the will was founded on the supposed legal relation into which the testatrix had been deceived into believing she was entering. Between these two extreme cases come those wherein it cannot be said that either one conclusion or the other is wholly unreasonable, and in those cases the determination of the fact is for the jury. Of that sort is the present.

We are not unmindful of the fact that the contestants offered no evidence other than that the testatrix had been tricked into the marriage; that in particular they did not offer any direct evidence that the inducing reason in her mind for her bequest to Carson was her belief that he was her legal husband, and that the bequest would not have been made except for that belief. But such direct evidence is not necessary, and not improbably could not possibly be had. It is not an unreasonable inference, from the fact that she has been so recently married when the will was made, that she left the bulk of her estate to Carson because she believed he was her lawful husband, and would not have so left it if she had believed otherwise. Such inference, of course, was subject to being strengthened or weakened by evidence of other circumstances throwing light upon the matter, such as the views of the testatrix upon the sanctity of marriage, her harmonious or other relations with Carson, and the strength of her affection for him. But in the absence of such circumstances the inference mentioned is yet not an unreasonable one from the facts that appear. Our conclusion therefore is that the order of nonsuit should not have been made. . . .

Judgment reversed.

Was the fraudulent marriage in the *Carson* case "designed to . . . deceive the testator into making a will"? (See quotation from *Newhall's Estate* at the start of this subsection.) Should a case such as this be an exception to that requirement? On the question of whether, if the truth were known to the testatrix before her death, she would have made a different disposition, should a jury be allowed to draw its own inferences from the circumstances?

MARKELL v. SIDNEY B. PFEIFER FOUNDATION
402 N.E.2d 76 (Mass. App. 1980)

[This action was brought by Minnie Hey three days before her death (and was continued by her executor) principally to set aside an irrevocable trust on the ground of fraud, mistake, or undue influence. The sole remainder beneficiary under the trust is the defendant foundation; the beneficiaries of Minnie Hey's will are certain of her friends and their families. She had been predeceased by her nephew Sidney Pfeifer, who was a lawyer, close friend, and an original cotrustee of the trust in question. The trial judge found that Minnie Hey signed the trust documents in question without understanding that their effect was to relinquish her capacity freely to control and dispose of the trust assets, and set aside the trust for mistake.]

ARMSTRONG, J. . . .

We start from the proposition, "settled in this Commonwealth, 'that a voluntary trust completely established, with no power of revocation reserved, cannot be revoked or set aside at the will of the person by whom and with whose property it was set on foot . . . without proof of mental unsoundness, mistake, fraud or undue influence.'" . . . Here, we have no allegation of mental unsoundness on the part of Minnie Hey at the time she executed the [trust,] and the judge's finding fell short of showing fraud or deceit on the part of Sidney Pfeifer. Rather, the plaintiff argues that the judge's ruling that the trust was voidable was properly grounded on the law of mistake.

The validity of that view turns on whether a mistake sufficient to warrant rescission of the trusts may be found in the misconception by Minnie Hey . . . as to the revocability of the trust. In some circumstances a trust executed with the mistaken impression that it is revocable is subject to being declared void on complaint of the settlor. And while there is long-settled precedent for declaring rescission of an instrument where the mistake was mutually held by the parties to it, it is now settled that in the case of a trust, where the settlor receives no consideration for its creation, a unilateral mistake on the part of the settlor is ordinarily sufficient to warrant rescission. See Berman v. Sandler, 399 N.E.2d 17 (Mass. 1980). That principle is relevant, for there is no suggestion in the record that Sidney Pfeifer, a lawyer of long experience, was at all unclear as to the revocability of the trusts in question.

But our chief concern here is whether Minnie Hey's misconception was a "mistake" of the type that would warrant reformation or rescission of the trusts. A party "asserting [mistake] must present evidence of an actual mistake and cannot prevail on a showing of mere inadvertence on the part of the [settlor]. . . . Misconception of the legal effect of the language used in [an] instrument is not a 'mistake of law' against which our courts afford a remedy. The parties are bound by the legal effect of what has really been agreed on, and cannot have the declaration set aside on the ground that they did not fully understand the legal effect of the language used, and that certain legal consequences which were not anticipated by the settlors flowed from its execution." The judge's findings, and the evidence on which they were based, did not show that "there was [a] mistake, in the sense that [the settlor] thought that the [declaration of trust] contained any other or different provision than in fact it contained, and no accident in the sense that anything was omitted which was intended to be put in. . . . " Taylor v. Buttrick, 165 Mass. 547, 550, 43 N.E. 507, 508 (1896). . . . One who knowingly signs a writing that is obviously a legal document without bothering to ascertain the contents of the writing is ordinarily bound by its terms, in the same manner as if he had been fully aware of those terms, unless it can be proved that he was induced to sign it by fraud or undue influence. That he does not know the terms that he is agreeing to is not a mistake, but a conscious choice and a known risk. Such a document is not ordinarily subject to rescission.

There is an exception to the foregoing principles, however, where a person is induced to sign a legal document by one standing in a fiduciary relation to that person and where the fiduciary has an interest in the document's execution. In such a case, the document can generally be avoided by its signer on a showing merely that the fiduciary failed to make him aware of the legal significance of the signing of the document, provided that the rights of innocent third persons have not intervened. . . . The rule is based on the principle that the fiduciary owes complete and undivided loyalty to the person towards whom he stands in such a relation and should not permit any other consideration to influence his actions or advice. Thus, it has been said that an attorney

> who bargains with his client in a matter of advantage to himself must show, if the transaction is afterwards called in question, that it was in all respects fairly and equitably conducted; that he fully and faithfully discharged all his duties to his client, not only by refraining from any misrepresentation or concealment of any material fact, but by active diligence to see that his client was fully informed of the nature and effect of the transaction proposed and of his own rights and interests in the subject matter involved, and by seeing to it that his client either has independent advice in the matter or else receives from the attorney such advice as the latter would have been expected to give had the transaction been one between his client and a stranger.

Hill v. Hall, 191 Mass. 253, 262 77 N.E. 831, 835 (1906); Israel v. Sommer, 292 Mass. 113, 122, 197 N.E. 442 (1935); Goldman v. Kane, 3 Mass. App. 336, 341, 329 N.E.2d 770 (1975). Similar principles govern analogous dealings in other fiduciary contexts, as, for example, in dealings between a trustee and a beneficiary of the trust. Brown v. Cowell, 116 Mass. 461, 465 (1875). It is manifest that Sidney Pfeifer's dealings with Minnie Hey in relation to the creation of the trust cannot stand if they are to be measured by the standard applicable to the conduct of a fiduciary; for Sidney Pfeifer and the foundation that was to perpetuate his name were interested parties to the execution of the trust and, by the judge's findings, Sidney Pfeifer failed to make that fact, as well as the extent of her alienation of the trust assets, known to Minnie Hey.

The plaintiff argues that the relationship of Sidney Pfeifer to Minnie Hey was fiduciary as matter of law, because as regards the execution of the trust he acted in fact as her attorney. It is true that the relationship between attorney and client, like those between trustee and beneficiary, director and corporation, guardian and ward, is fiduciary as matter of law, Smith v. Smith, 222 Mass. 102, 106, 109 N.E. 830 (1915); and that if an attorney or a member of his family is personally advantaged by a transaction with his client, the transaction is presumptively improper and voidable; the burden is on the attorney to prove that the transaction was fully understood by the client, that he attempted to have the client obtain independent advice, and that, if the client declined to receive independent advice, the attorney gave him forthrightly disinterested advice as to any aspect of the transaction which was arguably against the client's best interests. But it is not invariably true that, when an attorney performs a legal service for another, a strict attorney-client relationship exists. Not infrequently an attorney will draft a will or do estate planning work for a relative or close friend and associate; and in such a case, if the attorney or a member of his immediate family is named as a beneficiary, a court called upon to examine the transaction, although it may suggest that the better practice would be for an independent attorney to do such work and although it may state that such a transaction "should be viewed with great circumspection," will not apply to such a transaction the presumption of impropriety which is applied when dealing with one whose fiduciary status is uncomplicated by ties of blood, marriage, or close friendship. The reason for the distinction is that in the case of an exclusively fiduciary relationship, it can reasonably be presumed that that relationship influenced the transaction, and the policy of the law is to favor the fiduciary's duty of loyalty and to discourage business or donative transactions which inure to the personal benefit of the fiduciary. But where there is also a relationship of family or friendship, gifts or other acts of generosity are natural and to be expected; in such a setting the reason for the presumption of impropriety dissolves. . . . There is here no presumption of impropriety, whether that result is rationalized by saying that the relation was not strictly that of attorney and client or by recognizing that an attorney-client relationship is not fiduciary as matter of law when there is an overriding relationship of family or friendship.

But that is as far as the cases relied upon by the foundation will take it. Apart from the strictly fiduciary relationships (trustee-beneficiary, executor-legatee, attorney-client, guardian-ward, etc.), the law recognized the existence of fiduciary responsibilities arising out of other relationships of trust and confidence and provides a remedy against one who abuses the confidence reposed in him by another, turning it to his own advantage. Such a relationship does not arise merely by reason of family ties. Whether a relationship of trust and confidence exists is a question of fact and may be found on evidence indicating that one person is in fact dependent on another's judgment in business affairs or property matters. . . .

The case at bar is governed by the principles stated. Minnie Hey had the utmost trust and confidence in Sidney Pfeifer and relied on his judgment and integrity in committing to him the management of her securities. Taking advantage of her confidence, he prepared or caused to be prepared the 1960 trust document and obtained her signature to it knowing that she had not read it and had no understanding of its far-reaching legal effects. We can assume that he intended it for her benefit as a protective trust; but he owed her a duty as a fiduciary personally interested in the execution of the document to disclose fully all adverse legal effects of the document or to cause her to obtain independent legal advice before execution. He did neither, permitting her to sign the document without knowing that she was thereby relinquishing control of the principal irrevocably. . . .

It follows that the judgment was correct. . . .

17

The Fiduciary Office

This chapter is concerned with the fiduciary and with the essential nature of the office. The material in this chapter includes an examination of the basic standards and duties by which the conduct of a trustee or personal representative is judged. It also covers the rights and liabilities that accompany the fiduciary office.

A. Qualification, Selection, Appointment, and Removal of Fiduciaries

UNIFORM PROBATE CODE

§3-203. *Priority Among Persons Seeking Appointment as Personal Representative.*

(a) Whether the proceedings are formal or informal, persons who are not disqualified have priority for appointment in the following order:
(1) the person with priority as determined by a probated will including a person nominated by a power conferred in a will;
(2) the surviving spouse of the decedent who is a devisee [which term includes legatee in the UPC] of the decedent;
(3) other devisees of the decedent;
(4) the surviving spouse of the decedent;
(5) other heirs of the decedent;
(6) 45 days after the death of the decedent, any creditor. . . .
(c) A person entitled to letters under (2) through (5) of (a) above, and a person aged [18] and over who would be entitled to letters but for his age, may nominate a qualified person to act as personal representative. . . . When two or more persons share a priority, those of them who do not renounce must concur in nominating another to act for them, or in applying for appointment. . . .
(g) A personal representative appointed by a court of the decedent's domicile has priority over all other persons except where the decedent's will nominates different persons to be personal representative in this state and in the state of domicile. The domiciliary personal representa-

tive may nominate another, who shall have the same priority as the domiciliary personal representative. . . .

PROBLEM

17-A.   The decedent died leaving as sole survivors and equal beneficiaries of his will his wife, *W,* and two adult children, *D* who lives in another state and *S* who lives in this state. The will named *D* as executor and provided that "my executor shall receive as compensation $6,000 per year." Consider the following matters under Uniform Probate Code §3-203 and the law of your state.

(a) *D* petitions for letters. May she be appointed?

(b) *D* declines and seeks to have a local bank appointed. What result?

(c) *D* declines and *W* seeks to have a local bank appointed. May *W* do this? What could *W* do to obtain assistance in business matters with which she is unfamiliar if she were appointed?

(d) *D* and *W* decline, but *W* nominates a local bank. *S* has no business experience but objects strenuously to the appointment of the bank because of a strong dislike for, and a prior disagreement with, the president of the bank.

(e) If *D, W,* or the bank is appointed, what compensation may each expect?

All states have statutes specifying persons entitled to appointment as personal representatives. (In such a statutory scheme, preference for males over females violates the right of equal protection. Reed v. Reed, 404 U.S. 71 (1971).) In a testate situation, the decedent's nominee is preferred, but in intestate situations or where a will does not nominate an executor, priorities for the selection of a personal representative are generally based on interest in the estate and relationship to the decedent. Some jurisdictions require that personal representatives be residents, while other statutes contain no such requirement; some others permit nonresident personal representatives subject to restrictions or distinguish between executors and administrators, imposing a residency requirement only for the latter.

In Estate of Svacina, 239 Wis. 436, 1 N.W.2d 780 (1942), it was argued that because the person nominated as executrix was indebted to the estate her appointment should be denied on the ground that her personal interests were antagonistic to those of the estate. In reversing the lower court's refusal to issue letters testamentary to the person named in the will, the court pointed out that the decedent's nominee *must* be confirmed unless precluded by mental incompetency or other legal disability, and that such a disqualification does not exist by reason of an indebtedness that was known to the testatrix at the time she made her will. The court noted that it "has ever been the policy of the law of this state that every citizen making a will has the right to select according to his own judgment the person or persons whom he would have execute it" and that "the court might well follow the maxim 'Whom the testator will trust so will the law.'" Cf. In re Estate of Moss, 183 Neb. 71, 157 N.W.2d 883 (1968).

In general, any natural person capable of taking title to property may take title to like property as a trustee. If a trustee has the capacity to take and to hold title but lacks the legal or practical capacity to *administer* the trust, the trustee may be removed in an appropriate proceeding and replaced by another trustee. For example, infants and insane persons can administer trust property only to the extent they can manage their own and therefore would normally not be suitable trustees because of their legal disabilities. Nonresident individuals who have capacity to administer their own property are generally eligible to act as trustees of testamentary as well as inter vivos trusts, although special requirements may be imposed on them, and a court may refuse to confirm an appointment under a will or may remove a nonresident from office if unavailability is likely to impede the administration or enforcement of the trust.

An unincorporated association may be a trustee only where it is recognized as a legal entity for purposes of taking and holding property for its own benefit. The defective appointment of an unincorporated association to act as trustee does not cause the trust to fail, however, since another trustee will be appointed. This assumes, of course, that the transfer on which the creation of the trust would depend has not been defective because of the association's inability to take the property. See Wittmeier v. Heiligenstein, 308 Ill. 434, 139 N.E. 871 (1923), supra Chapter 11. Much the same principles apply to partnerships as trustees, but if the transfer is deemed to be to the *partners* they can act as trustees. This solution does not pose the same practical difficulties as would be posed by treating the purported appointment of an unincorporated association as an appointment of the persons who comprise its shifting membership.

A corporation may be a trustee, although its capacity to administer a trust is dependent on the corporate objectives and the powers conferred on it by law. Thus, in all states, corporations locally chartered to conduct a trust business, typically banks and trust companies, may be appointed to act as trustee, subject to whatever limitations and requirements are imposed by applicable state law. The field includes state banks and trust companies and national banks, which have the same privileges in the state in which they are located as a bank or trust company chartered there. Both legal and practical problems may arise when a foreign corporation is designated to serve as trustee. State law frequently excludes foreign corporations from carrying on trust business in the state or imposes severe burdens on foreign corporations seeking appointment. Many statutes permit a foreign corporation to act as trustee only if it qualifies to do business in the state; others will admit a foreign corporation to engage in trust activities if reciprocal privileges are extended by the company's state of incorporation. It is important for a lawyer to be aware of the problems posed by these statutes, particularly with regard to testamentary trusts for estates that will require estate administration in several jurisdictions. A settlor's desire to use a foreign corporation as trustee of an inter vivos trust is not likely to present problems of these types unless real property is involved.

In recent years the constitutionality of state discrimination against nonresident individuals and foreign corporations has come into question in connection with both personal representative and trustee positions. See recent cases arising in Florida: Fain v. Hall, 463 F. Supp. 661 (1979); BT Investment Managers v. Lewis, 461 F. Supp. 1187 (1978). A flexible system for the selection and substitution of trustees is provided in Article 7 of the Uniform Probate Code, including provisions for registration of trusts and for taking account of the mobility and multistate character of modern estates.

It is apparent from the above that the selection of a trustee involves the initial legal question of capacity to hold and administer trust property in the relevant state or states. The settlor should also be led to consider the practical problems of administration presented whenever the settlor owns land in a state other than where the intended trustee resides. The practicalities of trust administration and of the trustee's problems may require the creation of several trusts or the appointment of multiple trustees. Furthermore, the selection of trustees requires a consideration of the alleged advantages and disadvantages of corporate trustees, professional individual trustees, and interested or disinterested relatives. Where a relative is a possible candidate for the office of trustee, consideration should be given to any special knowledge that person may have of the settlor's property or business affairs and also to the possibility of such a person serving gratuitously.

One solution might be to appoint cotrustees, one a trust company and the other an individual, but the potential practical operating difficulties of this ready solution should be carefully considered. Is it appropriate to place on a family member, particularly a person of little business experience, the burdens and responsibilities of general trusteeship merely to provide a "family voice" in distributive or managerial decisions? Is an advisory role more appropriate? Can the same objectives be accomplished by a special power of appointment? If cotrusteeship is decided on, should the authority of each fiduciary be specified, or should one of them be given limited duties? Should the usual unanimity of decision required of cotrustees be changed or broad delegation permitted? Questions of this type should be kept in mind as the administration of trusts is studied.

What accounts for the significant growth of the corporate trustee's role in modern trust activities? What factors enter into the choice between corporate and individual trustees? In McAvinchey, Worthy of Its Hire, 96 Tr. & Est. 976 (1957), a probate court judge mentions the corporate fiduciary's reliability, the reduced or eliminated bonding costs, specialization within the trust department, and impartiality. Lowndes, Corporate Trustees in the United States, 1958 J. Bus. L. 332, attributed the popularity of corporate trustees (1) to "the increasing complexity of trust administration owing to the complicated tax forms and reports which make a trustee's duties well nigh intolerable for an individual who is not equipped with the clerical facilities and experience to cope with them" and (2) to the trend today in which wealth "typically takes the form of stocks and securities of national and international enterprises . . . [requiring] the familiarity with national and international markets supposedly possessed by the large trust company." Porter, Professional Opinion of Trust Departments, 95 Tr. & Est. 439 (1956), reporting the results of a survey, indicated a 93 percent yes response to the question: "Is the permanence of a trust department, as opposed to an individual, an important factor in your recommendations?" Although evaluations of trust companies certainly vary widely from place to place, from time to time, and from person to person within a given location, it might be worth noting that Porter, supra, also reported certain common criticisms, including cold and indifferent attitude toward beneficiaries; conservatism in invasion of principal for beneficiaries' needs; shrinking from business decisions, particularly in going enterprises; the competence of a trust department too often depends on its size; and excessive fees, especially in small trusts. On this latter point, however, note that fee-setting practices vary; for example, in some parts of the country it has become the custom of trust companies, for various reasons, not to charge higher percentages on smaller than on medium-sized trusts, once a modest minimum fee is reached.

The court that is responsible for the supervision of a trust has the power to remove a trustee. Often that court will be a court of equity, but in any given state the supervisory power over trusts, particularly testamentary trusts, may be conferred by statute on some other court, such as the probate court.

Trust provisions should normally nominate alternate and successor trustees and deal with the question whether, when co-trustees are nominated, one may be appointed or may continue to act alone in the event of the other's failure or inability to serve. Wills and trust instruments often provide procedures for appointing alternate or successor fiduciaries if the transferor does not wish to make additional nominations or if the list of nominees is exhausted. These procedures frequently authorize beneficiaries or prior fiduciaries to make nominations. In such cases, the attitude of In re Trust of Selsor, 13 Ohio App. 3d 164, 468 N.E.2d 745 (1983), is fairly typical. Finding the lower court's failure to follow the recommendation of a surviving trustee arbitrary, contrary to the terms of the trust, and an abuse of discretion, the opinion states:

> Where a will provides for the selection process of a successor trustee, the "intention of the testator as it affects the power of the Court to name a successor trustee is controlling." . . . Since the surviving testamentary trustee [was] given the authority to nominate the successor of a deceased trustee, full effect is to be given to the intent of the testator as expressed in the will. . . . "Under such circumstances it [is] the duty of the Probate Court to follow the recommendations of such person [surviving trustee] as to who should be a cotrustee unless the person chosen as a cotrustee was incompetent to administer the trust or such appointment would be detrimental to the trust."

Id. at 167, 468 N.E.2d at 748.

In the absence of special statutory provisions, the matter of a trustee's removal is left to the sound discretion of the court in an appropriate proceeding. This discretion is, of course, reviewable for abuse.

PROBLEM

17-B. *H* died six years ago. His will bequeathed to his son, *S,* $115,000 worth of stock representing *H*'s entire interest in a family corporation owned by *H* and *S*. The residue of *H*'s estate was valued at $260,000 and was left to *S* in trust to pay the income to *W, H*'s wife, for her life, remainder on *W*'s death to *D, H*'s only daughter. Under the terms of the trust *S,* as trustee, was authorized to distribute principal to *W* "in such amounts as may be deemed appropriate in the absolute discretion of the trustee."

Several months ago *D,* who had never married, died leaving her entire estate to her brother, *S.* The only property of any consequence owned by *D* was her vested remainder in the above described trust created by her father's will.

Since the establishment of the trust on distribution of *H*'s estate about a year after his death, *W* has received principal in amounts of between $4,000 and $11,000 each year. She is concerned that *S* will no longer be as generous with her and wishes to have *S* removed as trustee because the trust property consists of securities requiring no special managerial skills peculiar to *S.* How would you argue for *S*'s removal? How would you argue for his retention as trustee? Compare In re Borthwick's Estate, 102 N.H. 344, 156 A.2d 759 (1959) (the fact that the survivor of two cotrustees was a life beneficiary was to be taken into consideration in deciding whether to appoint a successor to replace the deceased cotrustee).

Also consider: Was *S* a wise choice as trustee? If *S* had been an intended remainder beneficiary at the time *H*'s will was drawn, how would you have advised *H* on the selection of the trustee? Why?

In re ESTATE OF BEICHNER
432 Pa. 150, 247 A.2d 779 (1968)

JONES, J.

This appeal challenges the propriety of a decree of the Orphans' Court of Beaver County removing an executrix of an estate and revoking letters testamentary granted to her. . . .

A testamentary executor or trustee is one whose choice was made by the person whose estate was to be administered and managed and represents an expression of trust and confidence in the person or persons so selected; an administrator appointed by the Register of Wills represents not the choice of the decedent nor are the person or persons appointed those in whom, necessarily, the decedent placed trust and confidence.

That an Orphans' Court possesses the power to remove an executor is clear beyond question. . . . [S]uch removal lies largely within the discretion of such courts, [but] an abuse of such discretion renders its exercise subject to appellate review. . . .

The removal of a personal representative chosen by the testator is a drastic action which should be undertaken only when the estate within the control of such personal representative is endangered. To justify the removal of a testamentary personal representative the proof of the cause for such removal must be clear. . . .

The only cause assigned for Mrs. Groom's removal by the court below was that animosity existed between Mrs. Groom and her stepmother, Mrs. Beichner, such cause being shown only by an admission in the pleadings. Such animosity may have arisen, as it too often and unfortunately does, because Mrs. Beichner was the second wife and Mrs. Groom a daughter of the first wife or it might have arisen through the fault of Mrs. Beichner or Mrs. Groom; nothing of record indicates *why* the animosity existed. Moreover, there is not a scintilla of evidence on this record that indicates that, assuming this animosity to exist, the estate is being mismanaged or wasted or that such animosity has jeopardized the estate or the interest therein of Mrs. Beichner. Animosity per se, absent any showing of any adverse effect on the estate or the rights of any beneficiary by reason of such animosity, does not constitute a ground for removal of an executor in whom the testator placed trust and confidence. . . .

We recognize that Mrs. Groom . . . had failed to file an inventory or a statement of debts and deductions or pay the transfer inheritance tax, failures which Mrs. Groom attempted to account for in her answer to the removal petition. Such failures could have been promptly rectified by action on the part of Mrs. Beichner's counsel had the executrices been cited to file an inventory, etc. For some unexplained reason such remedies were not resorted to.

On this record, absent a showing of any impact on the handling and
management of this estate arising from any ill-feeling existing between
Mrs. Groom and her stepmother or that Mrs. Beichner's interest in this
estate has been jeopardized by such animosity, the court below should
not have removed Mrs. Groom.

Decree reversed. Costs on Mrs. Beichner.

McDONALD v. O'DONNELL
56 App. D.C. 31, 8 F.2d 792 (1925)

[Appeal from a decree removing the appellant, McDonald, as sole
trustee under the will of Michael O'Donnell, who died in 1910. The
terms of the trust provided, among other things, for payments to the
testator's widow of $25 monthly and such additional sums as the trustee
deems necessary "for her needs, condition, and station in life."]

MARTIN, C.J. . . .

In November, 1920, the widow, Mary O'Donnell, filed a bill of complaint in the court below against said trustee, wherein, as amended, she
charged that he had for a long time past continuously refused to pay her
sufficient funds from said estate to maintain her in her station of life,
although sufficient funds were available, thereby humiliating and embar-
rassing her, and imposing great hardship upon her; also that he had
maintained an attitude of harshness, antagonism, and hostility towards
her ever since about two years after the testator's death; and for these
reasons she prayed that the defendant should be removed as trustee and
a successor be appointed. . . . The court below granted the prayer of the
bill, removed the appellant as trustee, and appointed a successor. . . .

It is unnecessary for us to discuss in detail the evidence contained in
the record. We find nothing in it which reflects upon the integrity of the
trustee, nor do we find grounds there for any condemnation of the discretion with which he has managed the trust in his dealings with third
parties. But we are convinced from the record that the relations between
the trustee and the testator's widow have become irreconcilably hostile,
to such an extent and with such results as to defeat the true purpose
which the testator had in mind when he created the trust.

It is clear, from a reading of the testator's will, that his wife and his
adopted daughter were the principal objects of his bounty. The entire
income of the trust estate, as well as a part of its principal, were made
subject to their reasonable needs. The latter is now deceased, and the
former is a woman of advanced years. Her claim upon the estate is in
part founded upon a property consideration, since she accepted it in lieu
of her legal dower in the estate. The duties of the trustee toward her,
under the terms of the will and codicil, are intimate and personal. The
trustee is required to pay her such sums from the estate as may seem to

him to be necessary, proper, and suitable for her needs, condition, and station of life. The relations existing for a long time between them make the proper performance of such duties almost impossible under the circumstances.

It is true that the testator selected the appellant as trustee, but it should be remembered that the selection was made more than 15 years ago, and the relations of the parties have changed since that time. Where the trustee occupies antagonistic relations to the trust property, because of his personal interest therein, or where inharmonious or unfriendly relations exist between the trustees, or between them and the cestui que trust, there may be sufficient reason for removal. . . .

A trustee, who is beneficiary's son, may be removed, on application of beneficiary, because a state of mutual hostility has arisen between them since the creation of the trust, attributable in part to the fault of the trustee, and which would naturally pervert the feelings and judgment of the trustee, who is given full power to determine what allowance the beneficiary shall have, limited only by the duty of exercising a fair and reasonable discretion, although there is no distinct proof of misconduct in consequence of such hostility. . . .

It may be conceded that where a trustee is charged with an active trust, which gives him some discretionary power over the rights of the cestui que trust, and which brings him into constant personal intercourse with the latter, the mere existence of strong mutual ill feeling between the parties will, under some circumstances, justify a change by the court. . . .

We may say, moreover, that the decision of the trial court upon such a complaint should not be disturbed, except upon clear and convincing grounds.

The decree of the lower court is affirmed, with costs.

RESTATEMENT (SECOND) OF TRUSTS

§107. *Removal of a Trustee.* . . .

b. *Grounds for removal.* The following are, among others, grounds for removal of a trustee: lack of capacity to administer the trust . . . ; the commission of a serious breach of trust; refusal to give a bond, if bond is required; refusal to account; the commission of a crime, particularly one involving dishonesty; unfitness, whether due to old age, habitual drunkenness, want of ability or other cause; permanent or long-continued absence from the State; the showing of favoritism to one or more beneficiaries; unreasonable or corrupt failure to co-operate with his cotrustees.

c. *Friction.* Mere friction between the trustees and the beneficiary is not a sufficient ground for removing the trustee unless such friction interferes with proper administration of the trust.

    d. *Insolvency.* If the trustee becomes bankrupt or insolvent, the court may remove him but will not necessarily do so. . . .

    Even assuming a beneficiary who is named to act as trustee would be suitable to a court, practical considerations may make it preferable not to appoint a person who, as trustee, would be subject to conflicting interests. The possible personal and administrative problems of such arrangements should not be overlooked. This is not at all to suggest that beneficiaries or other interested persons should not be named as trustee in an appropriate case. In fact, it is quite common today for such persons to act, frequently as one of two or more cotrustees. In trusts that are prompted by tax considerations, the use of a family member as trustee or cotrustee involves special tax problems and requires that the family trustee's powers be carefully limited to avoid certain income and estate tax hazards. In small trusts it is often necessary to appoint an interested person who will serve gratuitously as trustee; and when some of the shares of, or assets used in connection with, a closely held business are placed in trust it is sometimes considered desirable to have the surviving co-owner of the business serve as trustee, despite the obvious possibility of divided loyalties. This does suggest, however, that careful planning and drafting are required in such cases and particularly that special administrative provisions will almost certainly be necessary. Interested trustees not only pose practical problems in the administration of the trust but also significant, concealed problems affecting income and estate taxation. The tax dangers are particularly acute in the case of irrevocable inter vivos trusts that are intended to relieve the settlor of the income and estate tax consequences of owning the property.

    Of mainly academic interest is the rule that a trust will be extinguished by merger in the event the sole trustee is or becomes the sole beneficiary. The rule is generally recognized to be that no merger results if a sole trustee is one of several beneficiaries, if a sole beneficiary is one of several cotrustees, or even if all of several beneficiaries are also the only trustees. See generally IA W. Fratcher, Scott on Trusts §§99-99.5 (4th ed. 1987).

    It is sometimes provided in the terms of the trust that the trustee may be removed by one or more beneficiaries or by some other person. Unless the power is subject to limitation, such as removal "for good and sufficient cause," it may validly be exercised without justification as long as it is not found that the exercise will jeopardize the interests and rights of the beneficiaries. In the absence of a provision authorizing removal by the beneficiaries, they possess no such power over the trustee, except under circumstances in which all beneficiaries could terminate the trust.

RESTATEMENT (SECOND) OF TRUSTS

§102. *Disclaimer by Trustee.*

(1) If a trustee has not accepted the trust either by words or by conduct, he can disclaim.

(2) If a trustee has accepted the trust, whether the acceptance is indicated by words or by conduct, he cannot thereafter disclaim.

(3) In the case of a trust created by a transfer inter vivos if a trustee has disclaimed he cannot thereafter accept; in the case of a testamentary trust a trustee who has disclaimed can thereafter accept, but only with permission of the court.

(4) A trustee cannot accept a trust in part and disclaim in part.

§106. *Resignation of Trustee.* A trustee who has accepted the trust cannot resign except

(a) with the permission of a proper court; or

(b) in accordance with the terms of the trust; or

(c) with the consent of all of the beneficiaries, if they have capacity to give such consent. . . .

Comment on Clause (a):

c. *Permission of court.* It is within the discretion of the court whether to allow a trustee to resign. Ordinarily a trustee will be allowed to resign if such resignation will not be unduly detrimental to the administration of the trust, particularly if it would be unduly burdensome to the trustee to compel him to continue to act as trustee. . . .

B.   *Rights to Compensation and Indemnification*

PROBLEM

17-C. *T* died several years after she had retired from business activities. At her death, her estate consisted primarily of securities, all of which were listed and marketable on the national exchanges. The only parcel of real property, a condominium, was held in joint tenancy with a child. The administration of the estate proceeded smoothly and the executor, County Bank and Trust Co., has just filed with the court its final accounts and petition for approval and discharge. The bank included a request to the court for allowance of its executor fees and submitted in support of the allowance its printed schedule of charges, which are based on a percentage of the gross value of the estate.

You represent the residuary legatee who is surprised and irritated at the size of the fee. What advice would you give?

Unless personal representatives and trustees accept appointment to serve gratuitously, they are entitled to compensation for their services. In many states the fee is left to the discretion of the court pursuant to a flexible standard. For example, see Uniform Probate Code §3-719, infra. Under these "reasonable compensation" standards, local courts have sometimes developed an informal schedule of fees as a guide. In some states a standard schedule of fees is set by statute. The 1991 California statutory schedule, infra, is illustrative of compensation for personal representatives. Consider the policies reflected in the parallel provisions of §§10810-10814 for attorneys.

UNIFORM PROBATE CODE

§3-719. *Compensation of Personal Representative.* A personal representative is entitled to reasonable compensation for his services. If a will provides for compensation of the personal representative and there is no contract with the decedent regarding compensation, he may renounce the provision before qualifying and be entitled to reasonable compensation.[1] A personal representative also may renounce his right to all or any part of the compensation. . . .

CALIFORNIA PROBATE CODE

§10800. *[Compensation of Personal Representative] Based on Value of Estate.*

(a) Subject to the provisions of this part, for ordinary services the personal representative shall receive compensation based on the value of the estate accounted for by the personal representative, as follows:

(1) Four percent on the first fifteen thousand dollars ($15,000).

(2) Three percent on the next eighty-five thousand dollars ($85,000).

(3) Two percent on the next nine hundred thousand dollars ($900,000).

---

1. In the absence of legislation, the usual view (applicable at least in the absence of unanticipated circumstances) is stated in Bailey v. Crosby, 226 Mass. 492, 494, 116 N.E 238, 239 (1917): "The executor was not bound to accept the trust, but having done so he is entitled to receive only the compensation named in the will, whether that sum be more or less than a reasonable sum."

(4) One percent on the next nine million dollars ($9,000,000).

(5) One-half of one percent on the next fifteen million dollars ($15,000,000).

(6) For all above twenty-five million dollars ($25,000,000), a reasonable amount to be determined by the court.

(b) For the purposes of this section, the value of the estate accounted for by the personal representative is the total amount of the appraisal value of property in the inventory, plus gains over the appraisal value on sales, plus receipts, less losses from the appraisal value on sales, without reference to encumbrances or other obligations on estate property.

§10801. *Additional Compensation; Employment of Tax Experts.*

(a) Subject to the provisions of this part, in addition to the compensation provided by Section 10800, the court may allow additional compensation for extraordinary services by the personal representative in an amount the court determines is just and reasonable.

(b) The personal representative may also employ or retain tax counsel, tax auditors, accountants, or other tax experts for the performance of any action which such persons, respectively, may lawfully perform in the computation, reporting, or making of tax returns, or in negotiations or litigation which may be necessary for the final determination and payment of taxes, and pay from the funds of the estate for such services.

§10802. *Compensation Provided by Will; Petition for Relief from Provision; Notice.*

(a) Except as otherwise provided in this section, if the decedent's will makes provision for the compensation of the personal representative, the compensation provided by the will shall be the full and only compensation for the services of the personal representative.

(b) The personal representative may petition the court to be relieved from a provision of the will that provides for the compensation of the personal representative.

(c) Notice of the hearing on the petition shall be given. . . .

(d) If the court determines that it is to the advantage of the estate and in the best interest of the persons interested in the estate, the court may make an order authorizing compensation for the personal representative in an amount greater than provided in the will.

§10803. *Agreement Between Personal Representative and Heir or Devisee.*
An agreement between the personal representative and an heir or devisee for higher compensation than that provided by this part is void.

§10804. *Personal Representative Who Is an Attorney.* Unless expressly authorized by the decedent's will, a personal representative who is an attorney may receive the personal representative's compensation but not compensation for services as the estate attorney.

§10805. *Two or More Personal Representatives.* If there are two or more personal representatives, the personal representative's compensation shall be apportioned among the personal representatives by the court according to the services actually rendered by each personal representative or as agreed to by the personal representatives.

§10810.   *Compensation [of Estate Attorney] for Conducting Ordinary Proceedings.*

(a) Subject to the provisions of this part, for ordinary services the attorney for the personal representative shall receive compensation based on the value of the estate accounted for by the personal representative, as follows:

(1) Four percent on the first fifteen thousand dollars ($15,000).

(2) Three percent on the next eighty-five thousand dollars ($85,000).

(3) Two percent on the next nine hundred thousand dollars ($900,000).

(4) One percent on the next nine million dollars ($9,000,000).

(5) One-half of 1 percent on the next fifteen million dollars ($15,000,000).

(6) For all above twenty-five million dollars ($25,000,000), a reasonable amount to be determined by the court.

(b) For the purposes of this section, the value of the estate accounted for by the personal representative is the total amount of the appraisal value of property in the inventory, plus gains over the appraisal value on sales, plus receipts, less losses from the appraisal value on sales, without reference to encumbrances or other obligations on estate property.

§10811.   *Extraordinary Services; Additional Compensation.*

(a) Subject to the provisions of this part, in addition to the compensation provided by Section 10810, the court may allow additional compensation for extraordinary services by the attorney for the personal representative in an amount the court determines is just and reasonable.

(b) Extraordinary services by the attorney for which the court may allow compensation include services by a paralegal performing the extraordinary services under the direction and supervision of an attorney. The petition for compensation shall set forth the hours spent and services performed by the paralegal.

§10812. *Compensation Provided by Will; Petition for Relief.*

(a) Except as otherwise provided in this section, if the decedent's will makes provision for the compensation of the attorney for the personal representative, the compensation provided by the will shall be the full and only compensation for the services of the attorney for the personal representative.

(b) The personal representative or the attorney for the personal representative may petition the court to be relieved from a provision of the will that provides for the compensation of the attorney for the personal representative.

(c) Notice of the hearing on the petition shall be given as provided. . . .

(5) If the court determines that it is to the advantage of the estate and in the best interest of the persons interested in the estate, the court may make an order authorizing compensation of the attorney for the personal representative in an amount greater than provided in the will.

§10813. *Agreements for Higher Compensation.* An agreement between the personal representative and the attorney for higher compensation for the attorney than that provided by this part is void.

§10814. *Apportionment of Compensation.* If there are two or more attorneys for the personal representative, the attorney's compensation shall be apportioned among the attorneys by the court according to the services actually rendered by each attorney or as agreed to by the attorneys.

ESTATE OF EFFRON
117 Cal. App. 3d 920, 173 Cal. Rptr. 93, *appeal dismissed,*
454 U.S. 1070 (1981)

WIENER, A.J. . . .

[Appellants] challenged on theoretical and practical grounds both customary probate practices fostered by corporate fiduciaries and statutory attorney's fees. On a theoretical level, they claim as a matter of law statutory attorney's fees violate the antitrust laws and their application denies due process of law to those affected. As a practical matter, they question the ethical and legal propriety of what they allege to be the customary practice involving reciprocal back scratching between corporate fiduciaries and lawyers in which the lawyer drafting the will is always retained as counsel for the executor. In describing this scenario where the corporation's only purpose is to perpetuate corporate trust and probate business, they claim a conflict of interest is created causing a breach of the executor's duty, reflected here by the Bank's failure to negotiate a lesser fee for its lawyer than that allowed by statute and its failure to discharge counsel when Beneficiaries believed it was in their best interest to do so.

As we will explain, we conclude the system of statutory fees is valid, falling within the state action exemption to the Sherman antitrust Act enunciated in Parker v. Brown (1943) 317 U.S. 341. We also decide the Bank did not breach its fiduciary responsibilities. We affirm the order. . . .

The Sherman Act of 1890, enacted to prevent undue restraints upon trade having a significant effect on competition, provides simply, "Every contract, combination in the form of trust or otherwise, or conspiracy, in restraint of trade or commerce among the several States . . . is . . . illegal." (15 U.S.C. §1.) Lawyers can no longer take solace in the naive belief that, as members of a learned profession, they are exempt from the Act. "In the modern world it cannot be denied that the activities of lawyers play an important part in commercial intercourse, and that anticompetitive activities by lawyers may exert a restraint on commerce." (Goldfarb v. Virginia State Bar (1975) 421 U.S. 773, 788.) . . .

Within this framework, the applicability of the Sherman Act turns on our determination of whether statutory probate fees fall within the state action exemption of Parker v. Brown, supra.

> These decisions establish two standards for antitrust immunity. . . . First, the challenged restraint must be "one clearly articulated and affirmatively expressed as state policy"; second, the policy must be "actively supervised" by the State itself. [Citation.]

(Cal. Retail Liquor Dealers Assn. v. Midcal Alum., . . . 445 U.S. 97, 105 (1980).)

> It is clear that no exemption applies if the anticompetitive act is performed by a private association and is not compelled by the state (Goldfarb) or if the state merely approves anticompetitive conduct initiated by a private agency and the program does not effectuate any statewide policy (Cantor v. Detroit Edison Co., 428 U.S. 5 (1976).)

(Rice v. Alcoholic Bev., etc., Appeals Bd., . . . 21 Cal. 3d 431 at p. 444, 146 Cal. Rptr. 585, 579 P.2d 476 (1978).) . . .

The Legislature, after expending enormous energy on attorney's fees in probate proceedings, pointedly examining and reexamining the issue in various contexts, has determined the present statutory system of compensating lawyers is both cost effective and fair. Presumably, the public's interest is served where those bereaved are insulated from negotiating over a lawyer's fee during the traumatic post-death period.

Efficiency and economy are present in the use of judicial time which would otherwise be spent verifying fees and trying cases over questions of time, need, and reasonableness of the hourly rate charged. Theoretically, the present system also works in favor of smaller estates, for percentage fees are a financial incentive to lawyers to develop expertise and efficiency in the handling of those estates on a profitable basis, at lower fees than would otherwise be charged, thereby promoting greater access to competent legal services in such matters.

Our State Supreme Court also periodically reviews questions pertaining to the setting of attorneys' fees when it considers and approves State Bar Rules of Professional Conduct. Present rule 2-107 contains the factors which are to be considered in determining the reasonableness of a fee. The rules do not contain any prohibition against a lawyer charging a statutory fee nor do they suggest any ethical impropriety when he does so.

We do not wish to minimize the soundness of many of Beneficiaries' arguments criticizing the present system. One appellate court from another state, in describing legislative changes in probate, has referred to "the public outcry over antiquated and expensive probate laws" criticizing the percentage fee system as unnecessary and expensive. It commended the legislature for passing a law which authorizes payment to the attorney for the personal representative on a basis of numerous factors, only one of which is the monetary value of the estate. (See Matter of Estate of Painter (1977) 39 Colo. App. 506, 567 P.2d 820, 822.)

The caldron of public dissatisfaction over probate fees, which many view as having been forged through an amalgam of lawyer self-interest and lawyer mistrust, continually bubbles. A recent article in the Washington Post bemoaning a $1,908 hourly fee in a probate matter said, in part,

> Percentage fees . . . for settling estates . . . are generally a rip-off. Some lawyers, to be sure, can't stomach them; but most . . . think they are just dandy. There is little chance that this Legislature [Maryland], or any other, will do anything about this situation this year. But sooner or later lawyers are going to have to accept, or have imposed on them, the revolutionary idea that how much they charge a client should be related to how much work they do.

(Quoted in Los Angeles Daily Journal (Mar. 27, 1981) §1, p. 4.)

The fact that others, including legislatures from other states, have different views on the best system for compensating lawyers in probate matters does not mean this court may encroach upon the legislative prerogative where it has been lawfully exercised. We may not substitute our view for a legislative decision which legislators have made after the weighing of the relevant policy considerations. . . .

We also reject Beneficiaries' claim [that] the Bank's adherence to the statutory procedure and consequent failure to negotiate attorney's fee is private, anticompetitive conduct not mandated by the statute and thus constitutes a violation of the antitrust laws. This factual record, establishing what this Bank's practice is in hiring counsel for executors, is insufficient to establish a form of conspiracy falling within the purview of the Sherman Act. . . .

Beneficiaries say the Bank must be removed as executor because it breached its fiduciary duty when it did not fire the Rose firm upon their request. They claim the proper rule of law is that an executor, upon unanimous demand of an estate's beneficiaries, must discharge the attorneys for the executor, with or without cause, unless the executor will be subjected to some economic liability to third parties arising out of its duties as executor as a result of the discharge. . . .

An executor . . . is charged with the statutory duties of collecting, preserving and protecting the assets of the estate until distribution, subject to the continuing control of the probate court. . . . In the performance of those duties, the executor has the right to retain counsel whose fees for ordinary services, determined by statute, are treated as an expense of administration entitled to priority in payment of the decedent's debts. . . .

Beneficiaries argue the Bank's judgment over terminating the Rose firm was colored by its concern not to jeopardize its favorable trust business relationship with that firm. There is no doubt that economic self-interest is a factor which motivates a corporate fiduciary to retain the same lawyer who drafts the will. Nevertheless, where the testator's selection of the executor is free and voluntary, his wish may not be annulled except on a clear showing the best interests of the estate require it. (Estate of Sherman (1936) 5 Cal. 2d 730, 744, 56 P.2d 230.) The executor has the right to choose independent counsel to perform the necessary legal services on behalf of the estate. Presumably, the lawyer with familiarity of the decedent's property is a reasonable choice. Where lawyers' fees are governed by statute and require court approval, the element of the executor's self-interest standing alone does not create an absolute bar to retaining the same lawyer who drafted the will.

The order is affirmed.

ESTATE OF DAVIS
509 A.2d 1175 (Me. 1986)

WATHEN, J.

On a petition to review fees filed by personal representative Stuart E. Hayes, the Somerset County Probate Court approved a fee of $44,700 for services as personal representative of the estate of Linea A. Davis. Benjamin D. Harrington, Sr., and James B. Harrington, Jr., residual beneficiaries under the will of Linea Davis, appeal the Probate Court's order, challenging the reasonableness of the fee, which Hayes admitted was based on a fixed percentage of the decedent's estate, under the Maine Probate Code. We conclude that the court erred in its determination of reasonableness, and accordingly, we vacate the Probate Court's order.

Hayes, an attorney, testified that he calculated his fee on a percentage basis. From decedent's gross estate, valued at $1,388,000, he deducted a total of $590,400 attributable to real and personal property situated in Florida, leasehold property located in Maine, and lifetime transfers made by the decedent. He then charged five percent of the remaining $797,600 value of the estate and five percent of $96,000 in income earned by the estate, for a total fee of $44,700.

Hayes testified that the handling of the Davis estate required performance of numerous tasks. The will listed many charities as beneficiaries but did not provide addresses for the various charitable legatees. Name changes increased the difficulty of locating some of the charities. In addition, payment to one individual beneficiary was impossible because she was incompetent and, as best Hayes could ascertain, did not have a representative to handle her affairs. The federal estate tax return had to be prepared under some time pressure due to delay in resolving a dispute between beneficiaries regarding the valuation of certain property. Hayes also testified that he encountered difficulty in obtaining information from various institutional trustees regarding four trusts created by decedent during her lifetime.

With regard to certain leasehold property held by the estate, Hayes testified that he had to negotiate the transfer of the leases to the beneficiaries and also described becoming embroiled in a dispute between beneficiaries as to whether the personal representative should undertake repairs on the leased property. Hayes was also responsible for overseeing the maintenance and subsequent sale of Florida real estate. Finally, Hayes testified that he timed certain distributions to minimize the beneficiaries' ultimate tax liability.

The record reveals that Hayes was familiar with the decedent's estate. He had acted as personal representative of the estate of decedent's husband in 1978. Thereafter, he prepared decedent's will in which he was named personal representative. Later, the decedent granted him a power of attorney to handle her financial affairs. . . .

The Probate Court made the following factual findings: Attorney Hayes is an experienced, able, and reputable practitioner of probate law. Personal representatives in the locality customarily charge five percent of the taxable estate for their services. Hayes and his staff spent approximately 250 hours working on the estate. The estate required considerable skill on the part of the personal representative and was handled in an efficient and competent manner. Finally, the court found that under the circumstances of this case, the fee charged constituted reasonable compensation for Hayes' services as personal representative.

The Harringtons argue that the Probate Court's decision must be vacated because the personal representative based his fee on a percentage of the estate, a practice the Legislature has sought to eliminate. We agree that with the enactment of the Maine Probate Code in 1981, the Legislature intended to abolish the prevailing practice in determining compensation for personal representatives as a percentage of the estate and to substitute a system based on reasonable compensation.

Prior to 1981, personal representatives were authorized by statute to charge up to five percent of the personal assets of an estate for their services. . . .

> One important, and highly undesirable, aspect of the . . . present Maine system is the tying of compensation to various percentages of the estate's value. It is precisely this kind of approach that has led to criticism of probate expense and has given rise to anti-trust problems when used as a general and pervasive standard for attorneys' fees throughout the bar. . . . Compensation should be based on the amount and value of the work done, under a variety of relevant circumstances.

Maine Probate Law Commission, Report of the Commission's Study and Recommendations Concerning Maine Probate Law 305 (October 1978). The Maine Probate Code, enacted in 1981, implemented the commission's recommendation regarding fees for personal representatives. Section 3-719 states that a personal representative "is entitled to reasonable compensation for his services." 18-A M.R.S.A. §3-719 (1981). Section 3-721 sets forth the following criteria for determining the reasonableness of a fee:

(1) The time and labor required, the novelty and difficulty of the questions involved, and the skill requisite to perform the service properly;
(2) The likelihood, if apparent to the personal representative, that the acceptance of the particular employment will preclude the person employed from other employment;
(3) The fee customarily charged in the locality for similar services;
(4) The amount involved and the results obtained;
(5) The time limitations imposed by the personal representative or by the circumstances;
(6) The experience, reputation and ability of the person performing the services.

18-A M.R.S.A. §3-721(b) (1981).[2]

The current provisions of the Probate Code, along with the legislative history surrounding their enactment, demonstrate that the Legislature intended to abolish the determination of fees for personal representa-

---

2. 18-A M.R.S.A. §3-719 is identical to sections 3-719 of the Uniform Probate Code. The formulation of the factors designated in 18-A M.R.S.A. §3-721(b) for determining the reasonableness of a fee, is not contained in the uniform act. Other states, however, have adopted similiar additions to the Uniform Probate Code. See, e.g., Colo. Rev. Stats. §15-12-721 (1974); Fla. Stat. Ann. §733.617 (West Supp. 1986).

tives on a percentage basis and to mandate that in all cases, such fees be governed by a standard of reasonable compensation. The clear expression of legislative intent is not dispositive of the present case, however, because the order of the Probate Court recites consideration of most[3] of the factors set forth in section 3-721 and ultimately finds the fee assessed to be reasonable. The determination of a reasonable fee is reviewed only for abuse of discretion, and the court's factual findings are final unless demonstrated to be clearly erroneous. . . .

Nevertheless, the court abused its discretion in concluding that a fee of $44,700 constitutes reasonable compensation for the services provided in this case.

Section 3-721 places complexity of the services required and the time and skill necessary to perform those services first among the factors to be considered in arriving at a reasonable fee. Courts in other jurisdictions with similar statutory provisions have emphasized that the reasonableness of a fee depends on the services actually performed rather than on the size of the estate. In re Estate of Painter, 39 Colo. App. 506, 508, 567 P.2d 820, 822 (1977); In re Estate of Kottrasch, 63 Ill. App. 3d 370, 374-75, 20 Ill. Dec. 349, 352, 380 N.E.2d 26, 29 (1978).

Although the estate in this case cannot be described as simple, the personal representative himself testified that it involved no difficult negotiations or litigation and presented no novel legal questions. In cases such as this, when the services required are routine rather than extraordinary, the amount of time expended should be the predominant factor. In re Estate of Painter, 39 Colo. App. at 508-09, 567 P.2d at 822-23.

The Probate Court found that Hayes and his staff devoted 250 hours to handling the estate. Utilizing this figure, over half of which consists of secretarial and bookkeeping time, the fee amounts to an hourly rate of $180. If only the hours put in by attorney Hayes are considered, the hourly rate exceeds $400. It is evident that in finding such extraordinary hourly compensation to constitute a reasonable fee, the Probate Court relied heavily on the local custom of charging a five percent fee for estate work. Given that sections 3-719 and 3-721 embody a legislative intent to abolish the percentage fee system, any continuing practice of charging percentage fees should carry little or no weight in evaluating the reasonableness of a fee under the new statutory scheme. The Probate Court's reliance on the local custom of percentage charges was improper.

Because we conclude that the Probate Court abused its discretion, we vacate the order and remand for further proceedings. . . .

---

3. The Probate Court made no findings regarding the extent to which work on the estate precluded Hayes from accepting other employment, §3-721(b)(2), or as to time constraints involved in handling the estate, §3-721(b)(5). In his petition to review fees, Hayes admitted that work on this estate did not preclude his accepting other employment. The only evidence in the record as to time constraints was noted above with regard to filing of the federal estate tax return.

AMERICAN BAR ASSOCIATION, STATEMENT OF PRINCIPLES REGARDING PROBATE PRACTICES AND EXPENSES[4]
(1975)

2. Where, as is the usual case, the testator has made no prior arrangements for compensation, then (a) the commissions of the personal representative and the fee of the attorney for services in settlement of a decedent's estate should bear a reasonable relationship to the value of the services rendered by each and the responsibility assumed by each . . . ; and (b) the following factors, in particular, should be given significant weight in determining reasonable fees for the attorney and for the personal representative for their respective services in the settlement of the estate: (A) The extent of the responsibilities assumed and the results obtained. (B) The time and labor required, the novelty and difficulty of the questions involved, and the skill requisite to perform the services properly. (C) The sufficiency of assets properly available to pay for the services.

3. Rigid adherence to statutory or recommended commission or fee schedules, even when not illegal,[5] is a frequent source of unfairness to beneficiaries of estates, to personal representatives or the attorney, as the case may be. Where such a schedule is consulted, it should (a) be considered to have been projected upon the assumption of the full and timely performance of the normal services involved in the proceeding and the full assumption of the responsibilities attached thereto, and (b) not be regarded automatically as either a maximum or a minimum, but only as a possible or suggested starting point to be considered in determining reasonable compensation, which, depending upon the circumstances, could be more or less than the amount (or amounts) indicated by the schedule.

4. Even if he is the sole personal representative an attorney may serve both as a personal representative of a decedent's estate and as counsel to the personal representative and may receive reasonable compensation for his aggregate services and responsibilities. . . .

6. When an attorney or personal representative, either by choice or by lack of experience, has certain of his normal duties performed by others, his compensation should, generally, be lower than otherwise to reflect the fact that certain services and responsibilities were not performed and assumed. . . .

7. When a personal representative or any attorney is required to ren-

4. Developed by the Section of Real Property, Probate and Trust Law and approved by the House of Delegates of the American Bar Association in 1975.

5. On antitrust prohibitions affecting bar association fee schedules, see Goldfarb v. Virginia State Bar, 421 U.S. 773 (1975).

der services with regard to nonprobate property, he should be reasonably compensated for such services and a determination should be made with respect to the amount to be charged and the property against which the charge should be made. . . .

A trustee is also entitled to compensation. The right to a commission is generally expressed in terms of "reasonable compensation," either by statute or judicial decision. Again, some statutes provide a fee schedule. In the absence of a statutory schedule local practice often tends to become more or less standardized.

When compensation has been fixed by the terms of the trust, that provision normally controls. An unanticipated change of circumstances or the rendering of extraordinary services may lead the court to authorize a different compensation. Sometimes when a trust company is appointed, the settlor will provide in the instrument for normal compensation in accordance with the trustee's standard fee schedule as it exists from time to time. With the advent of devices facilitating the investment of small estates, such as the development of the common trust funds described in the *Mullane* case, supra page 597, some trust companies use a flat rate rather than a sliding scale for all trusts of moderate size. For example, the rate may be in the neighborhood of six-tenths of 1 percent of principal annually for a trust of securities, and nine-tenths of 1 percent for real estate managed in trust. In addition, trustees sometimes receive extra compensation as a receiving fee when property is initially transferred to the trustee and as a termination fee when principal is distributed or the trust terminated. Uniform Probate Code §7-205 provides for judicial review of a trustee's compensation. Compare §3-721 dealing with review of personal representatives' compensation.

A. LORING, A TRUSTEE'S HANDBOOK
(6th ed. J. Farr 1962)

§65. *Indemnity.* . . .   The right of exoneration permits the trustee to pay directly from the estate all of the expenses which he properly incurs as owner, including taxes, repairs, insurance and other legitimate expenses of management, traveling expenses, the cost of justifible litigation, and expenses of consulting counsel when there is reasonable cause.

This right of exoneration is coupled with a right of reimbursement for sums paid from the trustee's own pocket for expenses properly incurred.

The existence and extent of each of the foregoing rights is strictly dependent upon the propriety of the expense in question; if the expense has been incurred without authority, the trustee is without recourse. . . . If the trustee has made an excessive payment for the services of an agent, or paid for work he should have performed, or has made an unauthorized payment, he is left without the right of indemnity. . . .

The trustee is not entitled to indemnity from the beneficiary as distinguished from the trust estate, unless the beneficiary has expressly agreed to indemnify him. . . .

Where unauthorized expenses have been incurred in good faith, it has generally been held that the trustee is entitled to indemnification to the extent the trust estate has actually been benefited. There is some authority for the contrary result, however. Even though the estate is benefited, the trustee is not entitled to be reimbursed for an expense incurred in bad faith.

MATTER OF ESTATE OF GREATSINGER
67 N.Y.2d 177, 492 N.E.2d 751 (1986)

MEYER, J. . . .

The order of the Appellate Division affirming the Surrogate's order fixing counsel fees [is] reversed, with costs, and the application of the unsuccessful contestants [in a will construction proceeding] for an award of counsel fees out of the estate should be denied. . . .

The Appellate Division [position was that] "the instant proceeding has served to resolve a justifiable doubt as to the testator's intent caused by the language used in the will." . . . Chauncey's heirs . . . argued that Edna's remaindermen, having been unsuccessful, were not entitled to allowance of attorney's fees. . . .

SCPA 2301(4) . . . provides that, "[e]xcept where special provision is otherwise made by law, costs or an allowance may be [granted] any party personally or out of the assets of the estate or out of the share or interest of any person or from both in such proportion as directed by the court as justice requires." The phrase "as justice requires" . . . vests in the court a "discretion which is not to be exercised arbitrarily, and which is subject to review in the Court of Appeals, but only as to whether or not it has been abused and not on its merits." . . .

The factors to be considered in making an award of counsel fees in a will construction proceeding are spelled out by the case law. Prior to the amendment in 1928 of Surrogate's Ct. Act §278, the predecessor of SCPA 2302(6), there was no authority to award fees to a party in a construction proceeding other than an executor or trustee, except in cases in which the estate had been enhanced by a surcharge against the executor or trustee. The theory being that the attorneys for individual beneficiaries acted to protect the individual interests of the beneficiaries. . . .

Doubt as to the testator's intent is a proper basis for the bringing of a construction proceeding and for the allowance of counsel fees to the successful petitioner's attorneys payable from the general estate. . . .

[From] the above cases . . . can be distilled factors to be considered in determining whether a fee award should be made and from what source . . . , no one of which is by itself determinative: whether there was a justifiable doubt necessitating construction; who instituted the proceeding; whether the party seeking a fee award acted solely in his own interest or in the common interest of himself and the estate; whether he was successful; whether there was a benefit from the attorneys to the entire estate or only to the share of the party seeking the award; what the effect of payment of the award will be upon the estate's share of the successful party. . . . [T]he only factor justifying award of counsel fees at all was that "the instant proceeding has served to resolve a justifiable doubt as to the testator's intent caused by the language used in the will." . . .

In sum, it was an abuse of discretion as a matter of law to allow attorney's fees of Edna's remaindermen payable from the corpus . . . without taking into consideration that Edna's remaindermen . . . acted in their own rather than any other interest common with the trustee, and were unsuccessful, and the substantial detriment . . . to Chauncey's heirs that would result from the fees paid from the trust corpus rather than by those remaindermen personally.

For the foregoing reasons, the order . . . should be reversed, with costs and the application of Edna's remaindermen for an award of counsel fees out of the estate should be denied.

Compare Becht v. Miller, 279 Mich. 629, 636-641, 273 N.W. 294, 297-299 (1937):

> It has been held that the attorney must look to the one who employed him for his compensation even though others were incidentally benefited by his services and accepted such benefits. On the other hand . . . there exists the generally recognized equitable principle that where one, among others interested in a particular fund, employs an attorney by whose service the fund is enhanced, preserved or protected, the others entitled to claim in the fund, and so benefited, shall share the expenses of such services. . . .
>
> [T]he case at bar presents the question of the allowance from an estate as administrative expenses of fees and expenses incurred not by the executor or administrator but by a residuary legatee. . . . [A]s a general proposition it may be stated that before such an item may be charged against the estate it must be shown that the services rendered were beneficial to the estate as a whole rather than to an individual or group of individuals

interested therein. A doctrine which permits a decedent's estate to be so charged, should, however, in our opinion, be applied with caution and its operation limited to those cases in which the services performed have not only been distinctly beneficial to the estate, but became necessary either by reason of laches, negligence or fraud of the legal representative of the estate. . . .

We, therefore, are of the opinion that it was not error to charge the estate with payment of the reasonable value of the services of [the attorney].

Was the fee of $7500 allowed him excessive? In ascertaining the reasonable value of legal services, the court should consider the time spent, the amount involved, the character of the services rendered, the skill and experience called for in the performance of the work, and the results obtained. . . . He contends that a total of some 1400 hours in addition to 26 days in court were devoted by him to the matters involved. There were no complicated legal questions involved in this case. The facts seem to have been quite readily ascertainable, and from our experience we cannot understand how an attorney could devote nearly 10 months' work upon the issues that were there involved. . . . We are, therefore, constrained to hold that there was an abuse of discretion on the part of the trial court in making an allowance of $7,500 for attorney's fees . . . and are of the opinion that [the services] were reasonably worth $2,000.

C. General Fiduciary Duties and Standards

The functions of the fiduciary, and the standards and duties to which a fiduciary is held, reflect the nature of the interests that the fiduciary and beneficiary have in the property subjected to the relationship. The beneficiary has the beneficial interests and the fiduciary the management and administration of the property. Consequently we find that the fiduciary's functions are such as to enable and require the property to be managed for the exclusive benefit of those having the beneficial interest in it. The fiduciary owes the highest obligation to the beneficiaries to protect the property and to manage it solely in their interest, without regard to the fiduciary's own interests. As we consider the duties, powers, and liabilities of fiduciaries at different stages in these materials, it should be borne in mind that we are discussing different aspects of the fiduciary relationship.

There is some variation in the specific powers and liabilities of trustees as contrasted with those of personal representatives and with those of guardians, but usually these differences are but variations on the general theme of the fiduciary relationship. The law governing trustees is largely decisional, growing out of the practice of the early chancery courts. That governing personal representatives is largely statutory, though often also reflective of early chancery and common law practice. However, both common law and statutory techniques for the development of doctrine are important in these areas, as no statute is without some gap and no common law doctrine without some legislative embroidery.

Even though the various aspects of the fiduciary's functions are treated in greater detail later, it is worthwhile to consider them in general terms at the outset. The trustee has the duty to administer the property in the trust for the beneficiaries, and the personal representative has the duty to administer the property in the estate first for the benefit of the creditors of the estate and second for the distributees. Both fiduciaries are obligated to observe the utmost loyalty to those with whom they are in a fiduciary relationship and to refrain from all manner of self-dealing whereby there may even be so much as temptation to place the interests of the beneficiaries second to the fiduciary's own. As we shall see, the law has hedged the relationship with many safeguards to prevent any division of loyalties. Because the fiduciary is the one charged with the responsibility of making decisions in the administration of the estate, there is a duty not to delegate this responsibility to others. The fiduciary is required to keep records and to render accounts to those interested in the estate in order to provide adequate information regarding the administration of the estate or trust. Appropriate to the obligation to preserve the property is the duty to keep the trust property separated from assets of the fiduciary and others in order that confusion of title may be avoided. We have already seen that the functions of a trustee require that the property be kept productive, while an executor or administrator, who is primarily involved in a liquidation process, ordinarily has no such affirmative duty. Should administration of a decedent's estate be unduly extended, however, the personal representative may very well be obligated to make the property productive in order to avoid unnecessary loss to the beneficiaries. In carrying out the many duties of administration, a fiduciary is required to use reasonable care and skill and to treat all of the beneficiaries impartially.

The details of an administrator's functions are governed by statute. Most of the powers, duties, and liabilities of executors and trustees are, for the most part at least, subject to the control of the testator or the settlor. The extent to which the usual procedures or obligations may be modified by appropriate directions in the will or trust instrument will be explored as the particular problems are treated.

1. Prudence: The Standards of Care, Skill, and Caution

UNIFORM PROBATE CODE

§7-302. *Trustee's Standard of Care and Performance.* Except as otherwise provided by the terms of the trust, the trustee shall observe the stan-

dards in dealing with the trust assets that would be observed by a prudent
man dealing with the property of another, and if the trustee has special
skills or is named trustee on the basis of representations of special skills
or expertise, he is under a duty to use those skills.

A fiduciary is required to exercise reasonable care and skill to act prudently in the performance of the functions of the office. The standard of
care and skill is expressed in various ways. In later chapters we will see the
possible effect of various formulations of the standard and its application
in different aspects of estate and trust administration. Modern cases often
quote the language of Professor Scott and the Restatement, which provide that a trustee is to exercise "such care and skill as a man of ordinary
prudence would exercise in dealing with his own property." 1 Restatement (Second) of Trusts §174; IIA Fratcher, Scott on Trusts §174 (4th
ed. 1987). The element of prudence — the caution implicit in this standard — is frequently emphasized by stating that the test is not how one
would act with regard to one's *own* property but how a prudent trustee
would act in administering the property of *others* or how a trustee would
act in *conserving* the property.

In re Mild's Estate, 25 N.J. 467, 136 A.2d 875 (1957), involved the surcharge of an administratrix for delegation of duties and failure to supervise the activities of her attorney. To the assertion that the administratrix
was not capable of adhering to the usual standard of care and skill, the
court responded:

> This standard does not admit of variation to take into account the dif-
> fering degrees of education or intellect possessed by a fiduciary. The stan-
> dard of the "ordinary prudent person" is of necessity an ideal one and is
> not tailored to the imperfections of any particular person. Mr. Justice
> Holmes aptly stated the rule as follows:
>
> > The standards of the law are standards of general application. The
> > law takes no account of the infinite varieties of temperament, intel-
> > lect and education which make the internal character of an act so
> > different in different men. . . .
>
> Holmes, The Common Law, p. 108 (1881).
> Mrs. Dorn's conduct must be measured by the standard of the mythical
> ordinary prudent administratrix, notwithstanding her natural limitations.

25 N.J. at 480-481, 136 A.2d at 882.

On the other hand, a fiduciary possessing greater than ordinary skill
and more than ordinary facilities is under a duty to exercise the skill and
to utilize the facilities at hand. Thus, in Liberty Title & Trust Co. v. Plews,
142 N.J. Eq. 493, 509, 60 A.2d 630, 642 (1948), it is stated:

> In the present case, the corporate trustee held itself out as an expert in
> the handling of estates and trust accounts. It also held itself out as having
> particular departments for investments and statistical information, and

especial skill in this respect. It had so advertised for a number of years. . . .
It therefore represented itself as being possessed of greater knowledge
and skill than the average man and, " . . . if the trustee possesses greater
skill than a man of ordinary prudence, he is under a duty to exercise such
skill as he has." . . . The manner in which investments were handled must
be viewed and assayed in the light of such superior skill and ability.

2. Duty of Loyalty

HALLGRING, THE UNIFORM TRUSTEES' POWERS ACT AND THE BASIC PRINCIPLES OF FIDUCIARY RESPONSIBILITY
41 Wash. L. Rev. 801, 808-811 (1966)

The trustee may justify a self-dealing transaction only by showing (1)
that the beneficiaries consented, (2) that their consent was given after
full disclosure of all facts material to the transaction, and of the beneficiary's legal rights in the light of those facts, and (3) that the transaction
was fair and reasonable. The "uncompromising rigidity"[6] of the rule
requiring undivided loyalty is not an arid formalism. The courts have
consistently held that this inflexibility is essential to its effective
operation.

In refusing to make ready exceptions to the rule, the courts have recognized three principal considerations. I will discuss these briefly, in the
belief that the reasons which gave rise to the present state of the law go
far to commend its retention.

First, the courts have acknowledged that it is difficult, if not impossible
for a person to act impartially in a matter in which he has an interest.
Lord Loughborough said, in Whichcote v. Lawrence:[7] "Where a trustee
has a prospect of advantage to himself, it is a great temptation to him to
be negligent." A similar statement may be found in Thorp v. McCullum.[8]
"Between two conflicting interests, it is easy to foresee, and all experience has shown, whose interests will be neglected and sacrificed." . . .

6. I shall not be the first to depart from tradition by failing to quote Judge Cardozo's
classic, if florid, statement of the principle of fiduciary loyalty in Meinhard v. Salmon, 249
N.Y. 458, 464, N.E. 545, 546 (1928):

Many forms of conduct permissible in a workaday world for those acting at arm's
length, are forbidden to those bound by fiduciary ties. A trustee is held to something stricter than the morals of the market place. Not honesty alone, but the punc-
tilio of an honor the most sensitive, is then the standard of behavior. As to this there
has developed a tradition that is unbending and inveterate. Uncompromising rigidity has been the attitude of courts of equity when petitioned to undermine the rule
of undivided loyalty by the "disintegrating erosion" of particular exceptions. Only
thus has the level of conduct for fiduciaries been kept at a level higher than that
trodden by the crowd. It will not be consciously lowered by this court.

7. 3 Ves. Jr. 740, 750, 752 (1978).
8. 6 Ill. 614 (1844).

Just as no one may be a judge in his own cause, so a trustee can not be expected to utilize his best, most objective and disinterested judgment in situations where that judgment may run counter to his own interest. This observation, as earlier suggested, seems to be something of a constant in human affairs. It is not confined to the law of trusts, but has its analogies in the law of agency and of public officers.

It should be noted that the stricture against conflicting interest does not rest upon an imputation of dishonesty. That the most conscientious and judicious of men cannot be unmoved by the obtrusion of his own interest has long been recognized. It should, if anything, be more obvious in our own time in view of our increasing understanding of the importance of subconscious factors in human motivation. However upright the trustee, if the intrusion of personal advantage does not tip the scales of judgment against the interest of his beneficiary (perhaps without his conscious recognition), it will, by causing him to "lean over backwards" or in some still more subtle way, distort his objectivity. In any case, the beneficiary is deprived of that disinterested and impartial judgment to which he is entitled. The man of intelligent and refined sensitivity will be the first to recognize this, and to give wide berth to situations in which his freedom of judgment will be encumbered by a prospect of personal advantage.

Secondly, the courts have realized that fiduciary relationships lend themselves to exploitation. This is especially true in the case of the trust, in which the fiduciary aspect is peculiarly "intense." The trustee, by reason of his more-or-less complete control and day-to-day management of the trust property, often for long periods, has a large advantage over the beneficiary with respect to any matter in which their interests conflict. Normally, the trustee's position gives him superior knowledge of all the facts and circumstances relating to the trust property and its administration. Furthermore, the main purpose of his appointment is often to relieve the beneficiary of the cares of management, and to confer upon him the benefit of the trustee's superior skill and judgment. For these reasons, the success of the trust relationship will depend on the ability of the beneficiary to trust the trustee. The morals of the market place will not suffice. If the beneficiary must deal with the trustee at arm's length, look behind his representations, and supervise his conduct, the utility of the trust is greatly impaired. The only way to insure that the beneficiary can sleep at night in free and easy reliance on the loyalty of the trustee is to remove all serious temptations to disloyalty.

Finally, the courts have made much of the fact that disloyal conduct is hard to detect. Lord Loughborough, quoting Lord Hardwicke, said, in Whichcote v. Lawrence:[9]

> Where a trustee has a prospect of advantage to himself, it is a great temptation to him to be negligent; acting in a manner, that does not quite fix

9. 3 Ves. Jr. 740, 750, 752 (1798).

an imputation on him. His conduct may be so covered, that it may be difficult to fix direct fraud upon him. . . .

The reasons why disloyalty will often go undetected are plain enough. The trustee, by reason of his day-to-day management of the trust estate, generally commands better information concerning its affairs than the beneficiary. Even a court, inquiring into his administration at a later date, cannot expect to match the trustee's knowledge. Furthermore, many decisions of a trustee are matters of refined judgment and discretion. On such subjects as the value of trust property, the wisdom of the retention or reinvestment of assets, and the needs of the beneficiaries, judgments are rarely clear-cut. A wide variety of determinations can generally be supported by plausible argument, and rationalizations made after the fact will generally be unassailable. As to these decisions of the trustee, undivided loyalty can be guaranteed only by removing all factors which might give rise to a contrary motivation. This, of course, will not insure that the trustee's judgments are infallible or even that they are the best of which he is capable; but it will insure that they are not influenced by motives adverse to the interest of the beneficiary.

See Matter of Rothko, 43 N.Y.2d 305, 372 N.E.2d 291, 401 N.Y.S.2d 449 (1977), and also Surrogate Midonick's opinion at 84 Misc. 2d 830, 379 N.Y.S.2d 923 (1975); Wellman, Punitive Surcharges Against Disloyal Fiduciaries — Is *Rothko* Right?, 77 Mich. L. Rev. 95 (1979).

PROBLEMS

17-D. The testator left his residuary estate to three of his children in trust in equal shares for the exclusive benefit of the testator's five children. The trust included a parcel of valuable industrial real estate that was subject to a mortgage. Four years after the testator's death, the lessee of the property became insolvent and defaulted on the rent. After evicting the tenant, the trustees were unable to obtain another tenant because of a temporary business recession in the community. The five children discussed the matter and decided to try to negotiate an extension of the mortgage to avoid selling other assets of the trust. The trustees were unable to secure an extension and the mortgagee threatened foreclosure. Thereafter S, the spouse of one of the trustees, purchased the mortgage from the mortgagee for $100 more than any offer received by the mortgagee and granted an extension of six months, which was acknowledged by the three trustees. One of the other children was overseas at the time and was the only child who had no knowledge of the purchase and extension of the mortgage by S. At the end of the six months, the amount due on the mortgage remained unpaid. S foreclosed the mortgage and bought in the property at the public foreclosure sale. Five months later S sold the property to an industrial concern for a profit of $105,000.

The children, with the exception of S's spouse, sue to impress this $105,000 with the trust. How would you proceed if you represented the different parties involved? What result should the court reach?

How could the parties have protected themselves if they had secured counsel at the outset? Would the problem of protecting the transaction be complicated if the trust had provided for remainders to the testator's grandchildren and the issue of deceased grandchildren?

17-E.   D died leaving a large estate including real estate, securities, notes receivable, some limited partnership interests, and some valuable works of art. Her will directed payment of several pecuniary legacies, sale of certain assets, and distribution of the residue of her estate to her son T as trustee for certain family members and their descendants.

The estate has been in administration for about three years and First Bank, as executor, is preparing for final distribution, accounting, and discharge. T has retained you to advise him on the executor's accounting. The executor had regularly deposited estate cash receipts with its commercial banking department in a no-interest checking account entitled "First Bank as Executor of the Estate of D." It had drawn on this account for estate purposes, such as payment of debts and expenses, but maintained a minimum balance of $10,000 entitling it to free checking privileges. On the first of each month, First Bank transferred any amounts in the checking account over $10,000 to a 4 percent passbook savings account in its commercial department, using the same account title. When the balance in the passbook account exceeded $60,000, the executor invested $50,000 in six-month certificates of deposit in its commercial department, again designated by the same title. These CDs paid about 6 percent interest at maturity, after which the funds were reinvested in similar certificates. All accounts and certificates of deposit were insured by the Federal Deposit Insurance Corporation.

During the time the estate was in administration, the prime rate of interest at which the bank loaned to its best customers fluctuated between 8 percent and 9 percent. The bank also made other loans in its regular business at rates up to 14 percent.

The applicable state law includes Uniform Probate Code §3-715(5) authorizing a personal representative, "if funds are not needed to meet debts and expenses currently payable and are not immediately distributable," to "deposit or invest liquid assets of the estate, including moneys received from the sale of other assets, in federally insured interest-bearing accounts, readily marketable secured loan arrangements or other prudent investments which would be reasonable for use by trustees generally," and a Banking and Trust Code section entitled "Deposits by Corporate Fiduciaries" stating:

Principal and income received and held by corporate fiduciaries awaiting investment or distribution may be invested temporarily in deposit
accounts or other investment vehicles of such corporation, provided that
it shall first set aside in its trust department obligations of the United
States or securities wholly guaranteed, both as to principal and interest,
by the United States having an aggregate market value, at all times, of at
least 100% of the amount of such trust funds, unless such trust funds are
insured by the Federal Deposit Insurance Corporation.

What advice would you give *T* in this situation? Why?

TRACY v. CENTRAL TRUST CO.
327 Pa. 77, 192 A. 869 (1937)

SCHAFFER, J.

In this proceeding in equity two of the three trustees of the Estate of
David E. Tracy seek to compel the third one, Central Trust Company, to
take back mortgages which it sold to the trust estate and properties
obtained by foreclosure of some of them and to substitute therefor the
money it received for them. The court below refused to grant the relief
prayed for and dismissed the bill. From the decree so ordering we have
this appeal by plaintiffs.

There is no dispute that defendant, having in its banking department
and owning in its own right certain mortgages, sold them to the trust
estate of David E. Tracy, of which it was one of the trustees and received
from all of the trustees funds of the estate in payment therefor. The
amount of the mortgages was $204,380.

The decedent under his will created a trust, the income from which is
payable to his wife Gertrude H. Tracy for life and the principal in the
main to named charities. The court below found as a fact, and there is
no dispute of the finding, that plaintiffs participated in the purchases of
the mortgages and knew that the trust company owned them. There is
no question of bad faith on the part of defendant.

Appellants state the controlling question to be: Whether it is a breach
of trust for a corporate trustee to sell to a trust estate, of which it is a
cotrustee, mortgages originally taken and held by it for its own corporate
purposes. While there are minor questions suggested and debated, an
answer to the main one disposes of the controversy. It has long been an
outstanding principle of the law of trusts that a trustee violates his duty
to the trust estate if he sells to himself as trustee property which he individually owns. This principle has been crystallized in the Restatement,
Trusts, sec. 170, comment *h,* (p. 435) thus: "The trustee violates his duty
to the beneficiary if he sells to himself as trustee his individual property."
We have always held to this principle: Painter v. Henderson, 7 Pa. 48;
Everhart v. Searle, 71 Pa. 256. That the trustee acted in good faith makes

no difference: Restatement, Trusts, Sec. 170, comment *h*. The doctrine applies, though the purchaser be one of several trustees: 26 R.C.L. 1327. And, covering the exact factual situation before us, in comment *i* of Sec. 170, (p. 436) of the Restatement, Trusts, it is stated: "A corporate trustee violates its duty to the beneficiary if it purchases property for the trust from one of its departments, as where it purchases for the trust securities owned by it in its securities or banking department." This rule is incorporated in our statutory law. "A bank and trust company shall not, directly or indirectly, purchase with funds held by it as fiduciary, or exchange for any real or personal property held by it as fiduciary, any asset of its commercial department": Act May 15, 1933, P.L. 624, Art. XI, Sec. 1111, 7 PS Secs. 819-1111.

The remedy for such a breach of trust is clear.

> If the trustee in breach of trust sells his individual property to himself as trustee and the price paid by him as trustee was more than the value of the property at the time of sale, the beneficiary can compel him to repay the difference; or, at his option, the beneficiary can set aside the purchase and compel the trustee to repay the amount of the purchase price with interest thereon, in which case the trustee will be entitled to receive from the trust estate the property and any income thereon actually received by the trust estate.

Restatement, Trusts, Sec. 206, comment *c* (p. 560).

A subordinate question arises out of the fact that plaintiffs, two of the trustees, participated in the purchases of the mortgages. This does not prevent relief.

> If there are several trustees, each trustee is under a duty to the beneficiary to participate in the administration of the trust and to use reasonable care to prevent a cotrustee from committing a breach of trust or to compel a cotrustee to redress a breach of trust.

Restatement, Trusts, Sec. 184.

> If there are several trustees, one or more of them can maintain a suit against another to compel him to perform his duties under the trust, or to enjoin him from committing a breach of trust, or to compel him to redress a breach of trust committed by him. A trustee is not precluded from maintaining such a suit by the fact that he himself participated in the breach of trust, since the suit is on behalf of the beneficiary.

Id., Sec. 200, comment *d* (p. 529). See also Abbott v. Reeves, Buck & Co., 49 Pa. 494.

Bill reinstated, with direction to enter a decree in accordance with this opinion. Costs to be paid by defendant.

In re ESTATE OF SWIECICKI
460 N.E.2d 91 (Ill. App. 1984)

HARRISON, P.J. . . .

During its tenure as guardian, the Bank invested [the minor ward's] money in two six-month certificates of deposit in itself. . . . During the times [the] money was not invested in these certificates, it was placed in a passbook savings account at the Bank. . . . By making commercial loans at an interest rate higher than that which it paid on its own certificates of deposit and savings accounts, the Bank made a profit on the estate's funds during its term as guardian. . . . The sole question presented by this appeal is whether [the Bank] must account to the estate for that profit. . . .

[W]e are compelled to conclude that the estate is entitled to the profit which the Bank made through the use of the estate's money. . . . [I]n the instant case, the Bank's financial motives and fiduciary responsibilities were incompatible. As "buyer" of [the ward's] money for its own use, the Bank had an interest in acquiring the money at the lowest possible rate, in order to insure the profitability of that acquisition. As "seller" of that same money for the purpose of earning interest income for the estate, the Bank as guardian was faced with the conflicting responsibility of considering only the interests of the estate in determining how to invest the estate funds. While it is not claimed and there is no evidence to suggest that the bank acted with anything less than good faith in carrying out its responsibilities as guardian, this fact does not preclude application of the rule prohibiting the trustee from dealing with the trust property on its own account. " . . . [T]he only safe rule is one which absolutely forbids a trustee to occupy two positions inconsistent with each other." Joliet Trust and Savings Bank v. Ingalls (1934) 276 Ill. App. 445, 451. In making the determination which we reach here, we are cognizant of the fact that courts in other jurisdictions have found no conflict of interest on facts similar to those presented in this case. These cases essentially treat the institutional trustee as two separate entities, one which acts as trustee and the other which acts as custodian of the estate. From this premise it is reasoned that the trustee is not actually buying trust property on its own account, or that money made by the institution through its handling of the trust fund constitutes a reasonable profit for the institution in its capacity as custodian, provided that the trust is paid at least the prevailing rate of interest on the fund. We find these cases unpersuasive, because we reject the premise underlying them. There is nothing to suggest that, in reality, the Bank here is anything other than one business entity, controlled by one board of directors and owned by a single set of stockholders. That the acquisition of money at a low rate and subsequent loaning of money at a higher rate inures to the benefit of the Bank as a whole is a fact undoubtedly within the understanding of both the trust and the commercial departments of the Bank. . . .

Nothing in the statute permitting a guardian to invest in obligations guaranteed by the United States indicates a legislative attempt to override the common law duty owed by the guardian, and we will not infer the existence of such an intention. . . .

Section 21-1.03 of the Probate Act . . . expressly permits the representative of a decedent's estate to invest in savings accounts or certificates of deposit in a state or national bank "even though the bank of deposit is the representative of the estate." [Section 21-2.06] of the [same] Act allowing the representative of a ward's estate to make similar investments, however, contains no provision permitting the representative to invest in itself. . . . [W]e will not presume in this case that the legislature intended to significantly alter the common law fiduciary rules pertaining to guardians without saying so. Nor do we believe that Section 3 of the Trust Companies Act . . . , discussed in the dissenting opinion, affects the result here. The funds in question were not "awaiting investment or distribution" as contemplated by Section 3. . . .

Reversed and remanded. . . .

JONES, J., dissenting. . . .

The majority's holding . . . is, I believe, contrary to legislative intent regarding a bank's investment of funds held in trust. Notwithstanding the general common law rule that a trustee shall not make any advantage to itself of a trust fund, the legislature of this state has specifically authorized the deposit of trust funds by a corporate trustee in its own banking department under certain conditions. Such a deposit of funds "awaiting investment or distribution" is proper . . . provided the deposit is protected by securities set aside for that purpose or is guaranteed by the Federal Deposit Insurance Corporation. . . .

In considering whether, under the general common law rule regarding a trustee's duty of complete loyalty to its cestui que trust, a bank may deposit funds in its own banking department, courts of other jurisdictions have reached different conclusions. Courts dealing with this question have noted the inherent conflict of interest that arises from a bank lending trust money to itself individually. Thus, it has been said, a corporate trustee may be tempted to leave large amounts of trust monies on deposit for an unnecessarily long time due to the convenience and profit derived from the use of such funds and may be tempted to make and continue such deposits despite knowledge by the bank's officers that the bank is in a precarious financial position.

The potential for self-dealing resulting from the temptation to consider the commercial activities of a bank in administrating its trusts (see 2 Scott, Trusts §170.23(A), at 100 (Supp. 1983)) has led in some instances to a flat prohibition against a corporate trustee depositing trust funds in its own account. Indeed, the American Law Institute, after much deliberation, adopted the position in its Restatement of Trusts that a bank or trust company that makes a general deposit of trust funds in its own banking department thereby commits a breach of trust, unless it is authorized to do so by the terms of the trust. This rule was continued in the Restatement (Second) of Trusts §170, comment *m* (1959). It is, however, common practice for banks and trust companies to deposit trust funds in their own institutions, and, despite the view of some courts that such transactions involve disloyalty, this practice is sanctioned by the weight of authority at common law. Bogert, Trusts and Trustees §598, at 488-89 (2d. ed. rev. 1980). . . .

A federal statute (12 U.S.C. §92a(d) (Supp. 1983)) makes similar provision [to that of the Illinois Trust Companies Act] for national banks operating in the state. See Comptroller of the Currency Regulation 9.10, 12 CFR §9.10 (1983). These statutes . . . provide an exception to the general rule prohibiting a trustee from dealing with trust property on its own account.

This exception can be justified on policy grounds as allowing "efficient temporary investment of funds held in a trust by a bank pending their ultimate disposition, while providing maximum security for those funds." (Humane Society of Austin v. Austin National Bank, 531 S.W.2d 574, 579.) The convenience for a corporate trustee of making such deposits in itself rather than in another institution is evident. . . . "Under the . . . statutory rule there is great security for the trust deposits, first through the insurance provided by the FDIC, and secondly, through the fund which is set apart in the trust department of the bank as security for all trust deposits." Bogert on Trusts and Trustees, §598, at 495 (2d. ed. rev. 1980).

While it may be objected that, despite these considerations of convenience and security, there remains the potential for self-dealing inherent in a bank's use of trust funds deposited in its own accounts, the statutes here referred to reflect a legislative recognition of the distinctive character of corporate trustees. . . . Such trust companies operate in a regulated environment under the supervision of banking authorities and are required to be examined, separately from an affiliated banking department, regarding their investment of funds and their actions generally. . . . In any event, the legislature of this state . . . has made a policy decision that the benefits to be afforded outweigh the potential for self-dealing inherent in such transactions. For this reason, the omission, referred to by the majority, of expressed statutory language permitting the representative of a ward's estate to invest in its own accounts must be disregarded as merely legislative oversight rather than as an expression of legislative intent.

Although the statutes here noted authorize the use of trust funds in the conduct of the trustee bank's business, these statutes do not relieve the bank of its fiduciary duty as trustee. . . . The deposit of trust funds in itself by a corporate trustee, then, must be consonant with principles of good faith and reasonableness in order to come within the cloak of immunity afforded by the statutes authorizing such deposits. . . .

In the absence of a basis for holding the bank liable for profits from the use of the minor's funds, the bank's payment of interest at the market rate leads to the same result as if the bank had taken the funds to any other institution and deposited them in similar accounts. Thus, the bank's actions here were proper, and the decision of the trial court approving the bank's final report and account should be affirmed.

MATTER OF ESTATE OF ALLISON
488 N.E.2d 1035 (Ill. App. 1986)

[Hazel Allison died in 1982, survived by five children. Her will nominates her son John as executor, and she left her residuary estate to three of her other children. The residue included the farm in question, which was apparently to be sold and the proceeds divided among the residuary distributees. Prior to her death, Hazel had executed a 50/50 crop share lease with Allison Farming Co., of which John was sole owner. The lease was terminable on certain notice by either party, and absent notice the year-to-year tenancy would automatically extend into the next year. On Hazel's death, John petitioned for and received letters testamentary, assuming, the court noted, "the awkward position of both landlord and tenant," but the will granted the executor "full power to engage in farming operations . . . to lease on shares . . . and to perform any other acts necessary or desirable in [his] discretion to operate such farm properties." The next spring (1983) the Department of Agriculture instituted the Payment in Kind (PIK) program allowing farmers to draw a certain amount of surplus commodities in exchange for their not planting those commodities; small cash diversion payments were also part of the program. As executor, John enrolled in the program and, pursuant to the crop share agreement, divided the receipts (grain and cash) between the estate and Allison Farming Co. The receipts by the estate were reported in his first and second accounts, but neither mentioned Allison Farming's receipts from the PIK program. The residuary legatees would now have John account to the estate for all receipts from the PIK program. John's responses were: at the date of his mother's death the tenancy under the lease had continued automatically into 1983, so that "there were no dealings, therefore no self-dealing"; the will purportedly created and sanctioned his conflict of interest by allowing the executor to carry on farming operations; and there is no allegation that his decision to enroll in PIK was either in bad faith or contrary to the best interests of the estate. The trial court construed the lease and will together and concluded that it was Hazel's intention to allow such a conflict to exist.]

HEIPLE, P.J. . . . .

The net effect of [prior cases] is to call John's actions as executor and de facto tenant into serious question. The first questionable act was the acceptance of the office of executor. He knew that the lease would automatically extend into the 1983 farming year when he became executor. At this point, he should have either refused the position or assigned the lease, [although] assignment might have disqualified the farms from the PIK program. . . . Turning to the decision to opt into the PIK program, it is undisputed that the decision was sound and that the estate was not harmed thereby. It is also the case that the profit realized by John from the set-aside would have occurred even if someone else had made the decision to participate. However, these circumstances are not entirely relevant. The profits earned by a fiduciary as the result of self-interested transactions belong to the beneficiaries. . . . Had John either petitioned the court for permission to enroll the farms in PIK or resigned and allowed a substitute executor to serve, then he could have received the tenant's share of the PIK bounty without adverse consequences. However, because he allowed himself to remain in a position to profit from a self-interested transaction, the profit must be accounted for and returned to the estate.

The argument that John raised before the trial court concerning the intent of the testatrix to create such a conflict is misplaced. While there is an exception to the general principles of fiduciary responsibility where the instruments creating the relationships sanction a conflict of interest, the exception does not govern here. . . .

Paragraph Six of the will makes it abundantly clear that John was to sell the farm as soon as reasonably possible and divide the proceeds among the residuary legatees. As such, the only conflict sanctioned by Hazel was a brief, limited period of John in the dual role of landlord and farm tenant. Unfortunately, the PIK program entered into the equation. It is impossible for Hazel to have foreseen the redistribution of profits and expenses occasioned by PIK when she executed her will. Thus, the windfall profit that John earned as a result of his decision as executor to enroll the farms in PIK constituted a self-interested transaction the kind of which Hazel did not sanction.

We reiterate that the decision to participate in PIK was a sound exercise of discretion and in the best interests of the estate. Moreover, John would have been entitled to this profit if a different executor had made the decision to participate. He also could have petitioned the court for instructions or sought prior approval from the legatees. However, because John used his fiduciary office to profit from a self-interested transaction with estate property, he must account to the estate.

John argues that he did not deal with himself because the lease was between the estate and his solely-owned corporation. We can not agree. The prohibition against self-dealing by a fiduciary cannot be avoided by use of the corporate persona. . . .

John further contends that the propriety of the PIK transactions was adjudicated as a result of the approval of the First Current Account and Report. Thus, objections to the second report are subject to the defenses of res judicata and collateral estoppel. The only transaction reported on the first accounting was the . . . payment to the estate. Nothing was mentioned regarding Allison Farming Company. . . . The record suggests that the trial court did not decide in approving the first account that the payments to the tenant were proper.

Accordingly, the order overruling the legatee's objection . . . is reversed and remanded for further proceedings consistent with this opinion. . . .

See also Amalgamated Clothing & Textile Workers, etc. v. Murdock, 861 F.2d 1406 (9th Cir. 1988). In Matter of Scarborough Properties Corp., 25 N.Y.2d 553, 558, 255 N.E.2d 761, 763-764 (1969), Chief Justice Fuld stated:

> The rule has long been established that a trustee "should not be allowed to become a purchaser of the trust property, because of the danger in such a case that the interests of the beneficiary might be prejudiced." However, there is little danger of such prejudice if the transaction is subjected to prior judicial scrutiny and given court approval. Accordingly, the rule against self-dealing has not been applied, and does not apply, to interdict the purchase of trust property by a trustee where the court, after conducting a full adversary hearing at which all interested parties are represented, approves and authorizes the sale.

Compare Estate of Halas, 568 N.E.2d 170, 178 (Ill. App. 1991) (citations omitted):

> The creator of the trust can waive the rule of undivided loyalty by expressly conferring upon the trustee the power to act in a dual capacity, or he can waive the rule by implication where he knowingly places the trustee in a position which might conflict with the interests of the beneficiaries.
>
> . . . Where a conflict of interest is approved or created by the testator, the fiduciary will not be held liable for his conduct unless the fiduciary has acted dishonestly or in bad faith, or has abused his discretion. Further, where the will approves the conflict of interest, the burden of proof remains on the party challenging the fiduciary's conduct as there is no presumption against the fiduciary despite the divided loyalty.

UNIFORM PROBATE CODE

§1-108. *Acts by Holder of General Power.*   For the purpose of granting consent or approval with regard to the acts or accounts of a personal representative or trustee, including relief from liability or penalty for failure to post bond, to register a trust, or to perform other duties, and for purposes of consenting to modification or termination of a trust or to deviation from its terms, the sole holder or all co-holders of a presently exercisable general power of appointment, including one in the form of a power of amendment or revocation, are deemed to act for beneficiaries to the extent their interests (as objects, takers in default, or otherwise) are subject to the power.

CITY BANK FARMERS TRUST CO. v. CANNON
291 N.Y. 125, 51 N.E.2d 674 (1943)

[Appeal from Appellate Division order affirming a judgment settling plaintiff's accounts as trustees. The Appellate Division made findings of fact as follows:

1. Although the interest of the trustee, City Bank Farmers Trust Company, in its own stock, evidenced by the certificates of stock of The National City Bank of New York received by the trustee upon said Bank and Trust Company becoming affiliated, was such as to place the trustee in a position of divided loyalty as a matter of law, there was no divided loyalty in fact.

2. Mary E. Cannon, the settlor and life beneficiary, had knowledge of the facts which placed City Bank Farmers Trust Company as trustee in a position of divided loyalty as a matter of law, and of her right to remedy the situation by revoking the trust or amending it so as to substitute another trustee, or requiring the trustee to sell the shares of stock of The National City Bank of New York, the ownership of which gave to the trustee a beneficial interest in shares of its own stock, but she consented to the City Bank Farmers Trust Company continuing to occupy the said position giving rise to divided loyalty as a matter of law.

The conclusions of law read:

1. The interest of the trustee, City Bank Farmers Trust Company, in its own stock . . . was such as to place the trustee in a position of divided loyalty, which would have constituted a breach of trust if the settlor had not consented to said Trust Company continuing to occupy such position.

2. The settlor had the power to revoke the trust or to amend it so as to remove the trustee or to require the trustee to sell the stock of The National City Bank of New York. Since the settlor had knowledge of the facts which, as a matter of law, placed the trustee in a position of divided loyalty, and of her right to remedy the situation, and she consented to the City Bank Farmers Trust Company continuing to occupy such position, said trustee was not guilty of a breach of trust in continuing as trustee and in continuing to hold such stock.

The appeal is from every part of the judgment that directly or by implication determines that the corporate trustee should not be surcharged for loss in the value of bank stock while the trustee was in a position of divided loyalty.]

THACHER, J.

The action was brought by City Bank Farmers Trust Company and two individuals, as trustees, under a deed of trust for the judicial approval and settlement of their accounts. The only questions presented on this appeal were raised by the guardian ad litem of the infant defendants interested in the trust who sought to surcharge the corporate trustee for loss on investments in National City Bank stock incurred after the Bank's affiliation with the trustee. None of the other defendants has objected to the accounts. . . .

The trustee was expressly authorized to retain securities "so long as it may seem proper" and also to sell the same from time to time in its discretion and to invest and reinvest the proceeds thereof and any other cash at any time in its hand as trustee in such securities as to it may seem wise without being limited to investments legally authorized for trust investments.

Included in the securities delivered to the trustee under the deed of trust were 300 shares of National City Bank stock of the par value of $100. During the years 1926, 1927 and 1928 the donor requested the trustee to increase this holding of National City Bank stock through the exercise of subscription rights and to this end made additions of cash and securities to the trust to be used in partial payment for the additional shares. The result of these transactions was that prior to the affiliation of the National City Bank with the trustee there were held in the trust 3,000 shares of the Bank stock having a par value of twenty dollars a share. There is no suggestion that these investments were improper when made. . . . It is, however, contended that by the affiliation of the Bank and the Trust Company the latter as trustee became the beneficial owner of its own stock, was thus placed in a position of divided loyalty and should be surcharged for retaining the Bank shares which were inseparable from beneficial ownership of its own shares. The affiliation was accomplished by increasing the capital stock of the Bank and exchanging the new shares for all of the shares of the Trust Company on a basis of five Bank shares for one Trust Company share. The Trust Company shares were placed in trust for all the shareholders of the Bank each of whom acquired a pro rata beneficial interest in all the shares of the Trust Company. . . . After affiliation the two companies had several common officers and directors. Earnings distributed as dividends by the trustee were paid to the shareholders of the Bank. . . . The trustee with the donor's approval and active participation turned in the old certificates of stock of National City Bank held in the trust and received for them new certificates exactly like the old ones except for an additional endorsement showing that ownership of the stock carried with it a proportionate beneficial interest in the stock of the trustee. Thus the trustee acquired as an asset of the trust a substantial beneficial interest in its own stock which could only be sold by selling its shares in the National City Bank with which it was so closely affiliated. The fact is established that Mrs. Cannon not only approved the investment but insisted that the shares be retained by the trustee and as long as she lived was opposed to a sale of these shares. In this opposition she was supported by the honest judgment of the trustee. Nor is there any doubt that the donor was fully cognizant of her full powers of revocation and modification.

The standard of loyalty in trust relations does not permit a trustee to create or to occupy a position in which he has interests to serve other than the interest of the trust estate. Undivided loyalty is the supreme test, unlimited and unconfined by the bounds of classified transactions. . . . Undivided loyalty did not exist after affiliation of the trustee and the Bank because of the ownership by the trust of the shares of the Bank. The officers of the trustee responsible for the administration of the trust were under a duty with unremitting loyalty to serve both the interest of the Trust Company and the interest of the trust estate. These were conflicting interests insofar as the trust investment in the National City Bank shares required a decision whether to hold or to sell the shares in a falling market. The sale of this large number of shares might have seriously affected the interests of the Trust Company by depressing the value of these shares in a rapidly deteriorating market. Consequently the trustee had conflicting interests to serve in deciding to sell or not to sell. We do not for a moment suggest that the trustee did not act in the utmost good faith. Both courts below so found. But that is not enough for when the trustee has a selfish interest which may be served, the law does not stop to inquire whether the trustee's action or failure to act has been unfairly influenced. It stops the inquiry when the relation is disclosed and sets aside the transaction or refuses to enforce it, and in a proper case, surcharges the trustee as for an unauthorized investment. It is only by rigid adherence to these principles that all temptation can be removed from one acting as a fiduciary to serve his own interest when in conflict with the obligations of his trust. The rule is designed to obliterate all divided loyalties which may creep into a fiduciary relationship and utterly to destroy their effect by making voidable any transactions in which they appear.

In continuing to act as trustee and retaining the shares, the respondent Trust Company violated the rule of undivided loyalty and is accountable for the loss on the shares unless the donor by approving the investment and its retention has estopped the guardian ad litem and the infant remaindermen he represents from objecting to the investment. A similar problem was presented in Central Hanover Bank & Trust Co. v. Russell (290 N.Y. 593 [1943]). There we held that a settlor of a trust, who retained a testamentary power of appointment over the remainder limited upon life estates of the settlor and of her sister, by joining with her sister in approving investments of funds of the trust in the stock of the corporate trustee precluded the appointees named in her will from objecting to the investments thus approved. In the *Russell* case, the power retained was a power to appoint by will. Here we are concerned with powers to change and to revoke the trust.

A settlor who reserves absolute power of modification and revocation possesses all the powers of ownership and for many purposes is treated as the absolute owner of the property held in trust. . . .

Since the settlor reserved the right to exercise all the powers of ownership insofar as the trust was concerned, we hold that her action in approving the exchange of National City Bank shares for shares carrying a beneficial interest in the shares of the corporate trustee and in opposing any sale of the new shares was an effective estoppel not only against her own objections but also against an objection by the recipients of her bounty to the acts of the trustee which she approved. . . .

The judgment should be affirmed, without costs.

Compare with the above case the situation in which a testator names a bank as executor and trustee under his will and the estate includes a block of the shares of the named bank. Although it is probably the duty of the bank to dispose of its own stock, this may cause problems. In a relatively small community the available market for such shares may be limited to — or at least significantly impaired by the absence of — persons who are already substantial shareholders, officers, and directors of the bank. What problems does this situation pose? Particularly consider the responsibility of the lawyer who draws a will for a person in the circumstances of such a testator.

BERLE, OUR PROBLEM OF FINANCIAL POWER?
Washington Post, Aug. 11, 1968

Who controls American finance and industry — and how? The evidence now points to two groups: the managements of several hundred big American corporations and, increasingly, the trust departments of the large commercial banks that vote stock they hold in trust for others.

Until recently, the power of these banks was suspected but unproved. A huge gap in our knowledge of American economic power has now been filled by an excellent staff report to the Domestic Finance Subcommittee of the House Committee on Banking and Currency. . . .

The salient facts are these. Some 500 corporations make 60 percent of all the sales in the United States. . . . These corporations are "owned" by 24 million or more shareholders. So numerous and so scattered a group obviously cannot "control" anything. . . . Somebody has to make nominations, mobilize stockholders' votes and tell them what to do. Until recently, the corporate management did this.

Then came the . . . development, almost entirely since World War II [of] big employee pension trusts. . . .

The trust departments of big banks do a great deal more, however, than manage pension and employee benefit funds. They also are executors and trustees for an enormous number of individual holdings.

The trust department of the commercial banks hold altogether $253 billion of trust assets — of which $72 billion are employee benefit funds, another $126 billion are the total of private trusts and a further $54 billion are held in agency accounts. This quarter-trillion dollars of assets are held by less than 400 banks — the 10 largest banks alone hold about 37 percent of the total. Prudently, the trust companies have invested an increasing proportion of this huge aggregate in common stocks.

The Patman committee staff estimates that by 1970, institutions will hold more than one-third of all the stocks listed on the New York Stock Exchange and there is no reason to suppose that their holdings will not increase.

Now add another factor. Banks not only run trust departments; through their loan powers, they are also creators as well as lenders of money. They supply credit to American corporations which are, perhaps, the largest users of it. As lenders, they have considerable influence. When to this is added their ability to vote large blocks of the stock held in their trust departments, their power-position becomes formidable.

Who controls the banks? Here a curious situation emerges. According to the report, six percent of these trust companies hold (in trust, of course) stock of their own banks — many of them more than 10 percent. In seven big banks, their trust departments hold more than 30 percent of the bank stock itself — a clearly controlling minority where the stock is widely distributed. Each trust department also has trust investments in substantial blocks of stock in other, often competing, trust companies.

The possibilities of self-dealing and self-service are enormous, to put it mildly. But it is one thing to say that the possibility is there and another to conclude that the whole system is dangerous or rotten and should be changed. The companion fact is that the system in our time has not worked badly.

Individuals have regularly confided their assets to trust companies and these concerns have made their money not by manipulating corporate controls but by collecting their fees as trustees. Opportunity has existed and undoubtedly does exist for huge manipulation, but so far as appears, it has not been used.

[Professor Berle then stated that he had no ready-made solution to the vacuum created by scattered ownership, noting that the real problem is to devise an effective method of control as an alternative to the present situation. His concluding observations included a suggestion that self-perpetuating machinery for control be outlawed and specifically that no trust department be allowed to vote the stock of its own bank.]

STAFF STUDY, SENATE SUBCOMMITTEE ON
REPORTS, ACCOUNTING, AND MANAGEMENT,
COMMITTEE ON GOVERNMENTAL AFFAIRS,
VOTING RIGHTS IN MAJOR CORPORATIONS
59th Cong., 1st Sess. 1-4 (1978)

Voting rights to stock in large U.S. corporations are concentrated among relatively few bank trust departments (led by Morgan Guaranty Trust Co. of New York), insurance companies, mutual funds and their related investment advisory companies. . . .

Institutional investors' management powers frequently include voting authority — which is usually exercised — and investment discretion, which is the power to buy and sell stock. . . . Institutional votes decide a wide range of social, economic, environmental and ethical issues which are considered at stockholder meetings.

These large investors' power to influence corporate policy through authority to vote, buy and sell large blocks of stock is often augmented by two other powerful levers of control, interlocking directorates and debt holdings. . . .

No further studies nor hearings are necessary . . . to suggest that Federal regulatory agencies inform themselves, the Congress and the public, on a regular basis, regarding who has an actual or potential position of control or influence within the corporations they are supposed to regulate. This should include identification of influential institutional investors about whom public information is scant, such as some of the investment advisory complexes. . . . The regulatory agencies need to be motivated by their own leadership and by the standing committees of Congress to which they report. The Administration should use its considerable powers to expedite accurate and adequate reports, dealing with ownership and control. They are needed now for consideration of a broad range of public issues, including economic and tax policy, divestiture, foreign ownership restriction, Federal chartering of corporations, antitrust enforcement, securities regulation, rights of stockholders, encouragement of small businesses, conflicts of interest and ethics.

The hands on the levers of control of giant private corporations must be visible to the public, for its own protection. The time has come, this study suggests, for institutional investors to be required to pass through voting rights to other people's stock to the beneficial owners, or to withhold votes if pass-through is not practical. . . .

See also P. Harbrecht, Pension Funds and Economic Power (1959); D. Kotz, Bank Control of Large Corporations in the United States (1978); Twentieth Century Fund, Abuse on Wall Street (Schotland ed. 1980).

Legislation that is relevant — or at least potentially relevant — to a trustee's voting of its own stock frequently takes one of two forms. The Ohio litigation reported in the two opinions that follow is affected by both of these types of statutes and ultimately becomes concerned with the common law on the question, with differing viewpoints on the latter being reflected in the two opinions.

One form of legislation is patterned after a federal statute providing that a national bank that holds its own stock as a sole trustee may not vote those shares in the election of its directors unless it is directed to do so by a beneficiary or settlor who is authorized to so direct by the terms of the trust, and where the bank is a cotrustee its shares may be voted by the *other* trustee or trustees. 48 Stat. 186 (1933), as amended by 80 Stat. 242 (1966), 12 U.S.C. §61. Comparable legislation now exists in some states. See Cal. Corp. Code §703; N.Y. Banking Law §6012. See also Ohio Rev. Code §1109.10(c), enacted after the start of the litigation below.

The other form of legislation, more general but arguably applicable, is illustrated by Ohio Rev. Code §1701.47(c), originally enacted prior to the litigation below. In relevant part, it provides: "No corporation shall directly or indirectly vote any shares issued by it." A similar prohibition was held inapplicable to shares held by a bank *in trust.* Graves v. Security Trust Co., 369 S.W.2d 114 (Ky. 1963).

CLEVELAND TRUST CO. v. EATON
11 Ohio Misc. 151, 229 N.E.2d 850 (Ct. App. 1967)

CORRIGAN, J.

Stated in its simplest form the issue facing this court is: May the present management of the Cleveland Trust Company at the stockholders meeting for the election of directors vote directly or through its nominee the shares of Cleveland Trust stock held by it in a fiduciary capacity? . . .

While there are some Ohio cases . . . dealing with this general problem, no court in this state has been called to rule upon the direct question of whether the prohibition of Section 1701.47(C), Revised Code [text, supra], against an Ohio corporation voting stock issued by it applies to a bank and trust corporation. . . . [We conclude] that the plaintiffs herein, the Cleveland Trust Company, are not entitled to vote Cleveland Trust stock held by the bank in a fiduciary capacity. . . .

The law is clear that self-dealing or breach of good faith on the part of a trustee can not be excused on the ground that the instrument creating the trust and making him trustee has given him broad authority and unlimited discretion in the administration of the trust . . . unless express authorization is contained in the instrument creating the trust or in a provision of law. . . . [Furthermore, it] is elementary that to bind a beneficiary in a breach of trust, by acquiescence, it must be made to appear not only that he was aware of all the material facts, but that he was also advised of his legal rights and failed thereafter to register objection. . . .

CLEVELAND TRUST CO. v. EATON
21 Ohio St. 2d 129, 256 N.E.2d 198 (1970)

[In 1968, after the above decision, Ohio Rev. Code §1109.10(c) and other sections applicable to trust companies were enacted; at the outset of this opinion the Supreme Court of Ohio determined that the present case was governed by pre-1968 law without §1701.47(c) — that is, by the common law.]

TAFT, C.J. . . .

[When a corporation owns its own shares, the] voting rights have been regarded in effect as corporate property [and might accordingly be allocated] to each stockholder in proportion to the amount of his ownership interest in the corporation. Because of the impracticability of doing this and because the same effect can be obtained by suppressing the exercise of voting rights with respect to such stock, the common law developed a rule preventing a corporation from exercising, in the election of directors, voting rights on those of its shares owned by it. . . .

[T]he reason for not allowing a bank to vote its own shares for directors does not exist where those shares are held by it as trustee for others. . . . If shares so held by the bank in trust cannot be voted, voting rights belonging to those beneficiaries are in effect given without consideration to the remaining shareholders.

We conclude therefore that any common-law rule, against a corporation in an election for its directors voting shares of stock owned by the corporation, does not apply to such corporations so voting its own shares held by it as a trustee for others. . . .

In our opinion, the mere fact that a corporate trustee might acquire some advantage from voting [those shares] does not require the conclusion that a trust should be deprived of the protection that the trustee can and should give to the trust by voting such shares so as to benefit the trust.

We recognize that, in voting shares held by it in trust, a bank may commit a breach of trust. . . . [W]here it does commit such a breach of trust it can be held accountable to the trust. . . .

Judgment reversed.

[Concurring and dissenting opinions omitted.]

PROBLEM

17-F. Your client owns half of the stock of an incorporated department store. The other half of the stock is owned by your client's brother. The building in which the store operates under a long-term lease is owned by the client and her brother as tenants in common. Your client's interests in the department store and the building are valued at about $250,000 and $300,000 respectively. The rest of the client's estate is comprised of listed securities. The client's situation calls for the use of a trust, and she would like to have the securities administered by the *T* Trust Company and to have her brother administer the business interest and the store building. The brother knows the business well, and your client has complete confidence in him; as a matter of fact, the client feels a great loyalty to her brother and would not want the management of his own interests to be hampered by the independent decisions of a trust company, particularly by sale to a person who would not be a satisfactory "partner" to the brother. Although it is likely that on the death of either sibling the building and stock of both may be sold, the properties will be difficult to sell without sacrifice, and continuation of the business for a number of years for profit or for an advantageous sale is likely to be necessary or at least desirable. What problems do you see in your client's wishes? What solutions would you recommend, and what drafting details would you want covered in the will?

Some states tacitly encourage lawyers to name themselves as fiduciaries in instruments they draw by permitting an attorney who acts as a fiduciary to receive additional compensation for performing legal services. For example, Wash. Rev. Code §11.48.210 (1990) provides that "[a]dditional compensation may be allowed for his services as attorney and for other services not required of a personal representative." See also N.C. Gen. Stat. §28A-23.4 (1989). Cf. Cal. Prob. Code §10805. But cf. State v. Gulbankian, 54 Wis. 2d 599, 196 N.W.2d 730 (1972). Characterization of legal services as extraordinary services was criticized in the leading case of Estate of Parker, 200 Cal. 132, 139, 251 P. 907, 910 (1926), in which the court stated:

> It clearly is the duty of every executor, when engaging counsel to render professional services for the estate, to employ the best legal talent available for the stipulated compensation. But he would place himself in a position where there would be a clash between his own personal interest and his duty to employ the ablest counsel obtainable for the agreed compensation if, being himself a lawyer, he should undertake to perform that service himself with the intention of charging the estate therefor, or if, being a member of a law firm and sharing in the profits to be made, he should employ his firm to render the necessary professional services. Again, it is the duty of every executor to oppose any charge which the attorney or attorneys employed by him might make against the estate for extraordi-

nary legal services, if there be no substantial ground for the claim that the services were indeed extraordinary. But his personal interest would conflict with this duty, if the services were rendered by his own law firm and he is to share in the earnings. These examples will suffice to show how an executor might be tempted to look with too friendly an eye upon improper claims for legal services if we were to relax the salutary rule . . . merely because our Code provides that an executor may be allowed extra compensation for extraordinary service. . . . [10]

See also In re Estate of Schuldt, 428 N.W.2d 251 (S.D. 1988); C. Wolfram, Modern Legal Ethics §8.12.4 (1986).

AMERICAN BAR ASSOCIATION, CODE OF PROFESSIONAL RESPONSIBILITY

Canon 5. *A Lawyer Should Exercise Independent Professional Judgment on Behalf of a Client*

EC 5-6 A lawyer should not consciously influence a client to name him as executor, trustee, or lawyer in an instrument. In those cases where a client wishes to name his lawyer as such, care should be taken by the lawyer to avoid even the appearance of impropriety.

In re ESTATE OF DEARDOFF
10 Ohio St. 2d 108, 461 N.E.2d 1292 (1984)

[The testator directed his executrix to employ either of two named attorneys to represent his estate and that, if she failed to do so, she "shall be replaced" and the court shall appoint "a suitable person" who will do so. The named executrix declined to serve, and testator's alternative nominee sought to employ counsel of her choice. On this basis the designated attorneys objected to her appointment, but the probate court appointed her and the court of appeals affirmed.]

---

10. Cf. Williams v. Barton, [1927] 2 Ch. 9, 12 (Ch. D.), where the court stated with regard to the actions of a cotrustee who was a member of a firm of stockbrokers employed by the trust to value securities:

> From this it seems to me evident that the case falls within the mischief which is sought to be prevented by the rule [prohibiting a fiduciary from making a profit from opportunities arising out of his trusteeship]. The case is clearly one where his duty as trustee and his interest in an increased remuneration are in direct conflict. As a trustee it is his duty to give the estate the benefit of his unfettered advice in choosing the stockbrokers to act for the estate; as the recipient of half of the fees [received by his own firm] on work introduced by him his obvious interest is to choose or recommend [that firm] for the job.

As to whether the prohibition against profits arising from the trusteeship is different from or purely derivative from the prohibition against conflicts of interest, see McLean. The Theoretical Basis of the Trustee's Duty of Loyalty, 7 Alberta L. Rev. 218 (1970), which also provides a thorough review of Canadian authorities on the duty of loyalty.

HOLMES, J. . . .

It cannot be questioned that an executor has the right to employ counsel to assist in the performance of various duties in the administration of an estate. The employment of counsel, however, is not mandatory as the executor may perform all such duties.

R.C. 2109.03 provides that upon court appointment, the fiduciary has discretion to select counsel who will represent him during the administration of the estate. Under this statutory scheme, it is important to note that the attorney represents the fiduciary, not the estate. In light of this fact, we believe that although he may well accede to the wishes of the testator, the fiduciary must have unfettered discretion to select an attorney, as said fiduciary may incur personal liability for the attorney's unlawful conduct concerning matters of the estate.

In addition, the attorney-client relationship is quite personal and usually involves confidential matters. The relationship demands complete faith and trust between the parties. Such a relationship thrust upon the client against his will would be ill-conceived and not conducive to an atmosphere of reciprocal confidence. This, in turn, would interfere with the administration of the estate.

We further note that today's decision is in line with the majority of jurisdictions which have addressed this issue. . . . Therefore, we hold that a provision of a will which designates an attorney to represent the executor in the administration of the estate may not be considered as a condition precedent to the appointment of the executor, but is merely precatory and not binding upon the fiduciary or the probate court. . . .

Judgment affirmed.

The trustee is not prohibited from dealing individually with a beneficiary as an individual, but in doing so must act with the utmost fairness. In such dealings the presumption is that any advantage obtained by the trustee was fraudulent. The burden is on the trustee to prove that no advantage was taken of the fiduciary relationship and that the beneficiary was fully informed of all relevant matters. If this burden is not sustained, the beneficiary has the choice of affirming or avoiding the transaction.

3. Duty Not to Delegate

PROBLEM

17-G. *T* left the residue of his estate to his daughter *X*, as trustee, to pay the income equally to his daughters *X*, *Y*, and *Z* for their lives and thereafter to distribute the principal equally among his surviving issue.

X often took extensive trips in this country and abroad. Before one such trip to Europe, X entered into an "Agency Account Agreement" with the Fidelity Trust Company, which provided:

> The Fidelity Trust Company hereby acknowledges receipt of the assets listed in the attached inventory. The Trust Company hereby is appointed and becomes the agent and attorney-in-fact of X, trustee, and agrees to invest and reinvest the funds so received as authorized by said trustee under the terms of the will of T deceased. The Trust Company further agrees to collect the rents, dividends, interest, and other income and after deducting proper charges including three percent of such income as agency fee to distribute the same in accordance with the will of T.

The trust company acted under this agreement for a period of eleven years. For the first three years, the trust company secured prior approval for all transactions concerning the estate. After that X arranged to have the trust company make a semiannual report to her, which she would approve and return to them. During the last three years X lived in France and did not return the semiannual reports but accumulated them. After her return to this city and after a conference with Fidelity Trust Company, X signed a statement ratifying and approving all reports for the intervening period.

The securities in the trust have depreciated in value although they are all shares in which the trustee was authorized to invest. Y and Z and several of the grandchildren seek to surcharge X and the Fidelity Trust Company for the loss in the value of the securities. As attorney for the complainants, on what do you base your claim of surcharge? If you represented the defendants, what position would you take? What result would you anticipate?

Meck v. Behrens, 141 Wash. 676, 678-688, 252 P. 91, 94-96 (1927), states:

> It is undoubtedly the rule that, while a trustee may delegate to someone else a purely ministerial duty, he may not delegate to another his discretionary powers. 39 Cyc., at page 304, states:
>
> > It is a general rule that a trustee in whom there is vested discretionary powers involving personal confidence cannot delegate his powers and shift his responsibility to other persons. . . .
>
> The authorities seem to be practically harmonious in holding that when a trustee unlawfully delegates and surrenders his discretionary powers to someone else, with reference to the control and management of the trust property, he becomes a guarantor and is responsible for any loss that may have resulted, whether or not such loss can be shown to be the result of the delegation of power; the theory being that it is against public policy for one to delegate powers which have been entrusted to him alone, and

that the trustee who has placed the trust property in the hands of others will not, after the property has been lost, be heard to say that the delegation of power was not responsible for the loss and that, if he had performed his duties as the law required, the loss would also have occurred. . . .

We are fully conscious of the fact that we have not measured the amount of cross-appellant's rightful claim against appellants with any sort of mathematical accuracy. Indeed, it is impossible to do so from the much involved record before us. . . . Appellants are in no position to complain of want of exactness in measuring their liability.

Contrast G. Bogert, Trusts §92 (6th ed. 1987), which states that a trustee may delegate the exercise of a power

> where a reasonably prudent owner of property of the same type as the trust property who was acting for objectives similar to those of the trust would employ assistance. In the case of such highly important transactions as would be managed personally by a property owner following customary business practices, the trustee must personally make the decisions and perform the acts involved.

See also McClure v. Middletown Trust Co., 95 Conn. 148, 153, 154, 110 A. 838, 840, 841 (1920):

> While the trustee may not delegate his duties and powers to others, it is obvious that he must act frequently through agents or attorneys. This is not a delegation of his powers, for the trustee remains responsible for the reasonable diligence of his agent or attorney. He must select his agents with reasonable care and he must supervise their acts with the same care. Whether, in a given case, the trustee will be justified in entrusting the specific asset of the administration of the trust to an agent, must depend upon whether such act would be the act of the reasonably prudent trustee in a similar situation. The necessities of the trust may require the services of an agent, on account of the complexity or extent of the business or the special expert knowledge required. . . .
>
> There is no question of the diligence of the defendant in selecting [the particular] attorney to entrust this matter to. But reasonable diligence on the part of the trustee required it to know generally what the attorney was doing in the carrying out of its business. It could not commit the cause to the attorney and relieve itself of all further supervision. In a general way it should know what steps the attorney was taking, and it should use due care to have him fulfill his employment.

Concerning delegation or division of duties between cotrustees, see In re Mueller's Trust, 28 Wis. 2d 26, 46-47, 135 N.W.2d 854, 865-866 (1965), stating:

> According to the Restatement, a co-trustee is liable to beneficiaries for a breach of trust committed by another co-trustee if he:
>
> (b) improperly delegates the administration of the trust to his co-trustee; or . . . (d) by his failure to exercise reasonable care in the

administration of the trust has enabled his co-trustee to commit breach of trust.

. . . In the present case there is no evidence that the respondent . . . expressly authorized appellant to handle the trust affairs. It appears that any fault on the part of the appellant was passive rather than active. There is no good reason why subsection (b) should not apply when one trustee impliedly consents to letting the other do the administering, or why (d) would not apply in a situation where the breach results from mere omission. Professor Scott says:

> Where there are several trustees, each of them is under a duty to participate in the administration of the trust and to use reasonable care to prevent the co-trustee from committing a breach of trust. . . .

Respondent . . . was content to let appellant alone handle the trust affairs from the date of its inception. The record shows that she made no inquiries of him regarding trust affairs subsequent to the time the Worthington stock was acquired in 1954. Having assumed the position of trustee, she was bound to perform the duties required of her, and cannot escape liability merely because she relied entirely on the co-trustee to actually run the show. Any other result would drive co-trustees into the weeds for safety's sake.

Having established that respondent . . . was at fault, the question of whether appellant is entitled to indemnity or contribution from her is reached.

The general rule is that when two trustees are liable for a breach of trust, each is entitled to contribution from the other except that "if one of them is substantially more at fault than the other, he is not entitled to contribution from the other but the other is entitled to indemnity from him. . . ." [Restatement (Second) of Trusts §258(1)(a).] The Restatement lists four factors to be considered in determining whether one trustee is substantially more at fault than the other:

> (1) whether he fraudulently induced the other to join in the breach of trust; (2) whether he intentionally committed a breach of trust and the other was at most guilty of negligence; (3) whether because of his greater experience he controlled the conduct of the other, as in the case where he was an attorney and the other was a person without business experience who was accustomed to rely upon his judgment; (4) whether he alone committed the breach of trust and the other is liable only because of an improper delegation, or failure to exercise reasonable care to prevent him from committing a breach of trust, or neglect to take proper steps to compel him to redress the breach of trust.

[S]ince her consent was required before any trust assets could be sold, Jean Mueller knew that the Worthington stock was the sole asset of the trust, and knew that no sales of Worthington were being made to diversify the trust. As a trustee she was bound, as much as appellant, to diversify the trust assets unless it was imprudent not to do so.

One trustee is not more at fault so as not to be entitled to contribution merely because he was more negligent or active than the other. The mere fact that the other trustee did not actively participate in the breach does not necessarily put him in the position of being substantially less at fault.

We conclude, therefore, that Harold Mueller was not "substantially more at fault" than Jean Mueller. It follows that, although each is surcharged for the entire amount of the charge as to the two testamentary trusts where they were co-trustees, if the appellant pays the entire amount he is entitled to a contribution from Jean Mueller of half that amount. If she pays the entire amount then she is entitled to contribution from appellant of half the amount. In other words, they should share equally in these particular surcharges.

Restatement (Third) of Trusts (Prudent Investor Rule, 1992) adopts a more affirmative view of delegation. It states in §171 that trustees have "a duty personally to perform the responsibilities of the trusteeship except as a prudent person might delegate those responsibilities to others" and adds that in "deciding whether, to whom and in what manner to delegate fiduciary authority in the administration of a trust, and thereafter in supervising agents, the trustee is under a duty to the beneficiaries to exercise fiduciary discretion and to act as a prudent person would act in similar circumstances." Comment *a* to that section states:

> Decisions of trustees concerning delegation are matters of fiduciary judgment and discretion. Therefore these decisions may not be controlled by a court except to prevent abuse of that discretionary authority. . . .
>
> A trustee's authority in the matter of delegation may be abused by imprudent failure to delegate as well as by making an imprudent decision to delegate. Abuse of discretion may also be found in failure to exercise prudence in the degree or manner of delegation. Prudence thus requires the exercise of care, skill, and caution in the selection of agents and in negotiating and establishing the terms of the delegation. Significant terms of delegation include those involving the compensation of the agent, the duration and conditions of the delegation, and arrangements for monitoring or supervising the activities of agents. . . .

4. Duty to Identify and Segregate Trust Property

MILLER v. PENDER
93 N.H. 1, 34 A.2d 663 (1943)

Bill in Equity, for an accounting by the defendant trustee. The bill alleged that after the decease of the father John Pender, a trust agreement was executed April 2, 1928, whereby the defendant George E. Pender was to hold in trust the sum of $13,500 of the estate of the father for the benefit of a brother of the trustee, John L. Pender, during his life, and to pay over the principal on the decease of the life tenant to his issue if any. John L. Pender died December 13, 1940. This action is brought by the children of John L. Pender and by the executrices of his estate.

Trial by the Court (Lorimer, J.) who found the facts and entered a decree in favor of the plaintiffs against the defendant trustee, and dismissed the bill as to the defendant surety company. The plaintiffs have transferred no exception to the dismissal of the bill in favor of the surety. The defendant trustee excepted to the ruling of the Court that he was liable for the sum of $7,666.44 and certain interest thereon, which sum was the depreciation in value of the amount invested in trust securities by December 13, 1940. These securities had no designation on them that they belonged to a trust. The plaintiffs excepted to various findings and rulings. The facts and the exceptions will be stated more in detail in the opinion.

JOHNSON, J. . . .

Clearly the defendant had authority to invest in securities that were not legal under our statutes, but in view of the fact that the trial Court adopted the standard of the care and skill of a man of ordinary prudence in dealing with his own property rather than that of a prudent man whose duty it is to conserve the property, this exception is sustained and there should be a new trial, since it is being held that the trustee is not liable for the sum of $7,666.44 as decreed by the trial Court. If it should be found that the defendant was guilty of a breach of trust in investing according to this stricter standard, then the plaintiffs are entitled to recover for the losses suffered thereby. The damages for this breach of the trust duty would be the losses from securities that the trustee was not authorized to invest in to the extent that said losses were due to the lack of prudence as stated above and not due to general economic conditions without such lack of prudence in conserving the trust estate. . . .

The plaintiffs excepted to interest being limited to 3½%. . . . In Knowlton v. Bradley, 17 N.H. 458, the Court charged the trustee with interest at the rate of 5% per annum. This case was decided at the December term, 1845. The legal rate of interest then was 6%. R.S., c. 190 s.2. Because of the present lower rates of interest, the amount of 3½% allowed by the Court is equitable.

The securities invested in by the trustee were taken in his own name without any marks on them to show that they belonged to the trust estate. The plaintiffs excepted to the finding that the trustee did this in good faith and that his purpose was to make the securities more readily exchangeable. As stated above, the finding of good faith was properly made by the Court. Whether the reason for the trustee's action was as stated by the Court or was simply neglect, the important point to decide is to what extent, if any, the trustee should be held liable.

Further facts found are as follows: that the trustee kept the original trust certificates apart from his own in a safe in his house; that he made notations of income and remittances on separate slips of paper from which with duplicate deposit slips it was possible for the accountant to trace the income and remittances of the trust fund; that the accountant was able to trace and learn the condition of the trust affairs and the administration of the trust.

It is the duty of a trustee to earmark assets of the trust as trust property. Certificates of stock should be issued in the name of the trustee as trustee.

Failure to do this, however, is not so contrary to public policy that it cannot be authorized by the trust instrument. . . .

A trustee guilty of a breach of trust in failing to have the securities properly tagged is liable for any loss occasioned by such breach. So if personal creditors of the trustee attach the trust securities, written in the name of the trustee personally and cause loss to the estate, the trustee is liable in damages.

In the present case, however, it has been found that the depreciation amounting to $7,666.44 was not due to the breach of trust in taking the securities in the name of George E. Pender individually, but was caused by general economic conditions. The securities would have had the same value and would have sustained the same losses if they had been properly earmarked.

According to Professor Scott the authorities have held that a trustee is liable for any loss that is only simultaneous with a breach of the duty to earmark and not at all caused by it.

> By the weight of authority it is held that the trustee is liable for any loss resulting from a fall in value of the shares, even though the loss did not result from the fact that the shares were taken in the name of the trustee individually. The courts seem to have felt that the practice is so dangerous that the trustee should be held liable for any loss which results from the purchase of the shares, even though he acted in good faith in making the purchase and in taking the title to the shares in his own name.

2 Scott, Trusts, s.205.1. See also s.179.3 of the same work, and cases cited.

The purpose of the rule has been stated to be the prevention of any false claim on the part of the trustee or his estate as to the ownership of the securities of the trust or of the trustee. 3 Bogert, Trusts and Trustees, s.596. This reasoning of course applies only to the prevention of losses that cannot be known. Losses that are known can be dealt with according to the ordinary principles of causation. Losses due to commingling of trust property, whether intentional or not, or due to conversion can be properly compensated for by the usual rules of causation and damages. The reasoning involved in the above stated purpose of the rule would seem to have little application where it is found that a trustee has been acting in good faith in the trust management. There should be little likelihood of such a trustee making false claims as to the title or property between himself and the trust estate.

A similar rule with regard to earmarking deposits has been said to be a harsh one. 2 Scott, Trusts, s.205.1.

The rule requires the loss to be borne by the trustee as a penalty for the technical breach of the trust duty to earmark, since the loss is not caused by the breach but merely takes place during the time of the breach.

There is a tendency in the more recent cases involving investments in mortgages to adopt a more liberal view and to hold the trustee liable only for such loss as results from the failure to earmark and not for losses due to general economic conditions. 2 Scott, Trusts, s.179.3; 3 Bogert, Trusts and Trustees, s.596, Cumulative Pocket Part. . . .

Under the above circumstances a trustee should not be held liable according to Restatement, Trusts, s.179, comment *d.*

> If the trustee takes title to the trust property in his individual name in good faith, and no loss results from his so doing, he is not liable for breach of trust. Thus, if the trustee of a mortgage accepts a conveyance of the property from the mortgagor, and in order to prevent a merger takes the conveyance in his individual name, acting in good faith and crediting the trust estate in his accounts with all receipts from the property, and the only objection to the transaction is that he took title in his own name, he is not liable merely because the property depreciates in value. The breach of trust in such a case is merely a technical breach of trust, and no loss has resulted therefrom. If, however, he took title in his own name in bad faith, intending to misappropriate the property, he is liable for the full amount of the mortgage and interest thereon. Even if he acted in good faith, if a loss resulted from the fact that he took title in his own name, as for example if his personal creditors were thereby enabled to reach the property free of trust, he would be liable for the loss.

Potter v. Bank, 105 F.2d 437, supports this view. Certain stock certificates were transferred to a copartnership consisting of employees of the defendant bank acting as its agent. The purpose was to facilitate the investment of the trust fund. Book entries showed the true ownership although the stock certificates were not earmarked as belonging to a trust. There was no bad faith and the loss suffered was caused by economic conditions and not by the failure to earmark. The Court held that the breach of trust was technical only and that the defendant bank was not liable for the loss.

> Where the failure to earmark is bona fide, the good faith of the trustee diminishes the probability that he will be guilty of the subsequent wrongful conduct that must occur before the risk can develop into a loss. Therefore, if the trustee is able to show clearly that he has acted in good faith and that he has not manipulated the accounts of the trust to the prejudice of the beneficiary, there seems to be little justification for charging him for any loss which is not in fact caused by the failure to earmark.

50 Harv. L. Rev. 317, 321. Again on page 322, "The innocent trustee, however, whose failure to earmark has not caused a loss to the trust estate, should not be thus penalized."

The practice of failing to earmark the securities of a trust has been said to be dangerous because of wrongful claims on the part of the trustee or his estate that cannot be known. A penalty may be needed to stop a dangerous practice, but the penalty should be in proportion to the culpability of the offense. It should not consist of a loss in no wise caused by the offense but one that merely occurs during the time of the offense. The State of New York has made it a misdemeanor for a testamentary trustee to engage in this practice. This is an appropriate way of curbing a dangerous practice. It is inequitable for a Court of Equity to substantially penalize a trustee acting in good faith for a neglect of duty that in no way caused the loss complained of when the administration of the trust estate can be accounted for in all essential details.

The rule of penalizing the trustee by making him an insurer against losses not caused by his conduct is inequitable and illogical. It imposes the penalty when the trust estate has suffered misfortune and there are losses but not when there are no losses. Yet there is danger of false claims on the part of the trustee as to title when there are no losses in the trust estate.

The defendant is not liable for the said sum of $7,666.44 because of the reason given, namely, failure to designate the securities as trust property.

The trial Justice properly decreed that the defendant should pay the expense of the accountant. This was made necessary by the inadequacy of the trustee's accounts.

New trial.

All concurred.

Cf. Gump v. Wells Fargo Bank, 192 Cal. App. 3d 222, 237 Cal. Rptr. 311 (1987); Stokes v. Henson, 217 Cal. App. 3d 187, 265 Cal. Rptr. 836 (1990); Daniels and Martin, Myth and Reality in Punitive Damages, 75 Minn. L. Rev. 1 (1990); Schwartz and Magarian, Challenging the Constitutionality of Punitive Damages, 28 Am. Bus. L.J. 499 (1990).

AMERICAN BAR ASSOCIATION, MODEL RULES OF PROFESSIONAL CONDUCT

Rule 1.15 *Safekeeping Property.*

(a) A lawyer shall hold property of clients or third persons that is in a lawyer's possession in connection with a representation separate from the lawyer's own property. Funds shall be kept in a separate account maintained in the state where the lawyer's office is situated, or elsewhere with the consent of the client or third person. Other property shall be identified as such and appropriately safeguarded. Complete records of such account funds and other property shall be kept by the lawyer and shall be preserved for a period of [five years] after termination of the representation.

(b) Upon receiving funds or other property in which a client or third person has an interest, a lawyer shall promptly notify the client or third person. Except as stated in this rule or otherwise permitted by law or by agreement with the client, a lawyer shall promptly deliver to the client or third person any funds or other property that the client or third person is entitled to receive and, upon request by the client or third person, shall promptly render a full accounting regarding such property.

(c) When in the course of representation a lawyer is in possession of property in which both the lawyer and another person claim interests, the property shall be kept separate by the lawyer until there is an accounting and severance of their interest. If a dispute arises concerning their respective interests, the portion in dispute shall be kept separate by the lawyer until the dispute is resolved.

Comment:

[1] A lawyer should hold property of others with the care required of a professional fiduciary. Securities should be kept in a safe deposit box, except when some other form of safekeeping is warranted by special circumstances. All property which is the property of clients or third persons should be kept separate from the lawyer's business and personal property and, if monies, in one or more trust accounts. Separate trust accounts may be warranted when administering estate monies or acting in similar fiduciary capacities. . . .

Wills and trust instruments sometimes provide for a relaxation of the requirements of keeping separate and earmarking the property of a trust or decedent's estate. In fact it is common practice to authorize trustees to hold trust property in the name of another as nominee. It may also be provided that the funds of various trusts may be commingled or that estate or trust property may be commingled with the fiduciary's own. Such provisions are generally given effect by courts so that commingling or failure to earmark will not constitute a breach of trust. The purpose of such provisions may include the economy of managing commingled funds and the simplicity of acquiring and transferring title to trust property.

Most of the states have now enacted legislation to simplify the transfer of securities by fiduciaries, generally in the form of the Uniform Act for Simplification of Fiduciary Security Transfers or provisions of the Uniform Stock Transfer Act or Uniform Commercial Code. Supportive rules have been adopted by the New York, American, and regional stock exchanges and by the National Association of Securities Dealers (over-the-counter market), so that securities registered in the names of "domestic individual" trustees, personal representatives, and guardians (or conservators) are effectively delivered when accompanied by a properly executed and guaranteed assignment or power.

In most of the states some legislation exists relating to the use of nominees, especially by banks and trust companies. For example, Uniform Probate Code §3-715(14) authorizes the personal representative to "hold a security in the name of a nominee or in other form without disclosure of the interest of the estate but the personal representative is liable for any act of the nominee in connection with the security so held."

5. Duty to Take Control of Assets and to Render Accounts

Every fiduciary has an obligation to take control of the assets of the estate he is to administer and to keep a record of those assets and of his administration of them. In the inter vivos trust, the schedule of assets transferred to the trustee represents the starting point of the accounting procedure. On the other hand, the assets constituting a decedent's estate are likely to be uncertain and the subject of conflicting claims of ownership. The accounting procedure is initiated by the filing of an inventory by the personal representative of property he considers to be assets of the decedent's estate. Nearly all states require the inventory to be filed promptly after the appointment of the personal representative. In all states it includes personalty, and in most real property is also required to be inventoried whether or not it is subject to administration in the hands of the personal representative.

REPORT OF FIDUCIARY ACCOUNTING STANDARDS COMMITTEE[11]
(1980)

"Fiduciary Accounting" does not have one commonly understood meaning. In a broad sense, it can mean the entire process whereby a fiduciary — normally a personal representative, trustee or guardian — com-

11. A joint project (Robert Whitman, Reporter) of the American Bar Association, the American Bankers Association, the American College of Probate Counsel, the American Institute of Certified Public Accountants, the National Center for State Courts, the National College of Probate Judges, and the Uniform Probate Code Project.

municates information on an on-going basis regarding his administration of a fund and periodically justifies his administration to the
parties in interest and, perhaps, to a court. In another sense, it may be
the process whereby a fiduciary — here more often a trustee — periodically keeps parties in interest currently informed of transactions and
investment policies being followed.

In a narrower sense, to which this report is directed, a fiduciary
accounting may refer to the statement prepared by a fiduciary at the
close of his administration of a fund (or at some appropriate intermediate stage) to reflect transactions that have occurred and to be presented to the parties in interest as part of a process whereby the fiduciary
seeks discharge from liability for the events disclosed. . . .

The fundamental objective of an account should be to provide essential and useful information in a meaningful form to the parties interested
in the accounting process. It is also important that the account should
be sufficiently simple to enable its preparation without unreasonable
expense to the fund, or undue distraction from the on-going administration of the estate. Finally, although the parties should understand the
nature of the accounting process and the need to protect their interests,
the relationship of trust and confidence existing between the fiduciary
and the beneficiaries is itself important and the account should not be
presented in an adversary format that will unnecessarily impair this
relationship.

Maximum clarity, full disclosure and complete description and explanation of all events to be disclosed appear to be standards that all would
accept. But, in combination, they may present many difficulties. For
example, clarity may be obscured by the detail that is required for a disclosure that omits nothing. Full explanation of all investment decisions
might produce a massive document that few beneficiaries would read.
On balance, a set of flexible principles keyed to the standard of good
faith supports the utmost protection of the parties and permits accounting standards to change and mature as circumstances require.

Fiduciary accounts rarely will be identical. In addition to the predictable variables of the size and composition of the assets, the period covered and the position of those interested, the significance of particular
issues in a controversy may be illuminated by special accounting treatment of some portion of a fund. This suggests that a fiduciary should
have enough flexibility to state an account in the manner best adapted
to the particular circumstances and discourages any effort to prescribe
a totally rigid format. Accordingly, the following principles are suggested as general standards for fiduciary accounting. . . .

I. Accounts should be stated in a manner that is understandable by
persons who are not familiar with practices and terminology
peculiar to the administration of estates and trusts. . . .

II. A fiduciary account shall begin with a concise summary of its purpose and content. . . .

III. A fiduciary account shall contain sufficient information to put the interested parties on notice as to all significant transactions affecting administration during the accounting period.

Commentary: The presentation of the information in an account shall allow an interested party to follow the progress of the fiduciary's administration of assets during the accounting period without reference to an inventory or earlier accounting that is not included in the current account.

An account is not complete if it does not itemize assets on hand at the beginning of the accounting period.

Illustrations:

3.1 The first account for a decedent's estate or a trust should detail the items received by the fiduciary and for which he is responsible. It should not simply refer to the total amount of an inventory filed elsewhere or assets described in a schedule attached to a deed of trust.

3.2 In later accounts for an estate or trust, the opening balance should not simply refer to the total value of principal on hand as shown in detail in the prior account, but should list each item separately. . . .

IV. A fiduciary account shall include both carrying values — representing the value of assets at acquisition by the fiduciary — and current values at the beginning and end of the accounting period. . . .

V. Gains and losses incurred during the accounting period shall be shown separately in the same schedule. . . .

VI. The account shall show significant transactions that do not affect the amount for which the fiduciary is accountable. . . .

UNIFORM PROBATE CODE

§3-706. *Duty of Personal Representative; Inventory and Appraisement.* Within 3 months after his appointment, a personal representative, who is not a special administrator or a successor to another representative who has previously discharged this duty, shall prepare and file or mail an inventory of property owned by the decedent at the time of his death, listing it with reasonable detail, and indicating as to each listed item, its fair market value as of the date of the decedent's death, and the type and amount of any encumbrance that may exist with reference to any item.

The personal representative shall send a copy of the inventory to interested persons who request it. He may also file the original of the inventory with the court.

[§3-707 authorizes employment of appraisers.]

[§3-708 requires a supplementary inventory for revised valuations and after discovered property.]

§3-709. *Duty of Personal Representative; Possession of Estate.*   Except as otherwise provided by a decedent's will, every personal representative has a right to, and shall take possession or control of, the decedent's property, except that any real property or tangible personal property may be left with or surrendered to the person presumptively entitled thereto unless or until, in the judgment of the personal representative, possession of the property by him will be necessary for purposes of administration. The request by a personal representative for delivery of any property possessed by an heir or devisee is conclusive evidence, in any action against the heir or devisee for possession thereof, that the possession of the property by the personal representative is necessary for purposes of administration. The personal representative shall pay taxes on, and take all steps reasonably necessary for the management, protection and preservation of, the estate in his possession. He may maintain an action to recover possession of property or to determine the title thereto.

The trend of modern legislation is to provide for immediate vesting of *title* to personal as well as real property in beneficiaries; but most of these statutes provide that the beneficiaries' rights are subject to the personal representative's *right of possession* over some or all of the estate. In the absence of statute, the courts of most of the states continue to adhere to traditional concepts under which title to and possession of personal property pass to the personal representative of a decedent, whereas both title and right of possession in real property pass directly to devisees or heirs on the decedent's death.

Trustees, like personal representatives, have a duty to keep and render accounts and to furnish the beneficiaries information at reasonable times. This duty is commonly regulated by statute and local practice. Periodic accounting to the courts may be required, especially in the case of testamentary trusts. In the absence of statute, the power to compel an accounting is an inherent aspect of the general jurisdiction of courts of equity over trusts. See also Uniform Probate Code §7-303.

WOOD v. HONEYMAN
178 Or. 484, 169 P.2d 131 (1946)

[Appeal from decree finding that defendant, Honeyman, failed to account, removing him from the office of trustee, entering judgment against him for conversion of trust assets, and denying him compensation for his services as trustee. The trust instrument purported to relieve the trustee of all obligation to account.]

ROSSMAN, J. . . .

We believe that the principal contention which the appellants wish to submit under these two assignments of error is that the defendant was under no duty to account.

It must be apparent that when one becomes a trustee and thus undertakes to administer an estate for the benefit of another, he must maintain records of his transactions so complete and accurate that he can show by them his faithfulness to his trust. It is not enough for him to know that he is honestly performing his duty. Since, generally, the burden of proof rests upon him to prove his fidelity, he must be able to sustain his position by honest records. Bogert on Trusts and Trustees, §962, says: . . .

> The principal penalty usually stated to apply to a trustee who fails to keep proper records of his trust is that "all presumptions are against him" on his accounting, or that "all doubts on the accounting are resolved against him." He has the burden of showing on the accounting how much principal and income he has received and from whom, how much disbursed and to whom, and what is on hand at the time.

It must be obvious that since a trustee administers the estate, not for his own benefit, but for that of the beneficiary, he must render his records available for the inspection of the beneficiary and supply the latter with information pertinent to the trust. The requests must, of course, be made at reasonable times. The reasonableness of the rule just stated becomes more apparent when we bear in mind the fact that the records, documents and account books which a trustee procures so that he can perform his duty do not belong to him personally, but are parts of the trust estate. The rule which authorizes the beneficiary to inspect the trust records is essential in order that the beneficiary may be assured that he is obtaining the income or other advantages which the settlor intended. . . .

The trust instrument . . . , however, contains the clause which says:

> The said trustee is hereby relieved from all obligations to account to the beneficiaries of this trust, or to any one, for any of the trust funds or income therefrom; the provisions above that receipts by the mother or custodian of said children shall fully acquit said trustee, and that having made payments to said mother or custodian, he shall not be further bound to see to the application of said trust funds or income, being merely for the guidance and protection of the trustee, and not obligatory on him, and he is hereby relieved from any duty of accounting whatsoever. . . .

Colonel Wood [the settlor] and those who signed the writing did not make a gift to the defendant of the $15,000 fund by signing that paper. The document refers to the defendant many times as trustee and repeatedly used the word "trust." Although the legal title to the fund was in the defendant, the beneficial interest was not in him but in the three beneficiaries. Clearly, he was not made a gift of the money, and it was his duty to administer the trust in harmony with the trust instrument. The latter conferred upon the defendant wide discretion concerning the investment of the fund; the use of principal as well as of income; the amount to be distributed to each beneficiary; the periods, whether quarterly or semi-annually, when distributions should be made; and the time when the final distribution should take place. Yet, notwithstanding those facts, the fund was not his, but was entrusted to him in a capacity — a trust relationship — which is a favorite of our law. The law attaches such great social value to trusts of the kind now before us that virtually every duty owed by a trustee is enforcible by a decree of the chancellor. In the present instance, whether expressly set forth in the trust instrument or not, the defendant was required to distribute nothing to any one except to the three beneficiaries, to refrain from self-dealing, and to give to the beneficiaries, before the expiration of the trust, the entire amount of the principal and income, less lawful expenses. The settlors of the trust expected him to perform those duties, and the only way by which obedience could be enforced was by suit in equity. For a violation of any of those duties, a court of equity could remove the defendant from his office, deny him compensation for his services or enter judgment against him for any sum misspent. But remedies of that kind normally are not feasible unless an accounting has first been had. . . .

If a fiduciary can be rendered free from the duty of informing the beneficiary concerning matters of which he is entitled to know, and if he can also be made immune from liability resulting from his breach of the trust, equity has been rendered impotent. The present instance would be a humiliating example of the helplessness into which courts could be cast if a provision, placed in a trust instrument through a settlor's mistaken confidence in a trustee, could relieve the latter of a duty to account. Such a provision would be virtually a license to the trustee to convert the fund to his own use and thereby terminate the trust. When we mentioned mistaken confidence, we had in mind the words of the Wood Trust instrument: "I think Dave Honeyman would be an ideal trustee." It was that mistaken impression which caused Colonel Wood to write the provision which the defendant now seeks to employ as an impenetrable shield.

Bogert on Trusts and Trustees, §972, says:

> A settlor who attempts to create a trust without court accountability in the trustee is contradicting himself. A trust necessarily means rights in the cestui, enforcible, in equity. If the trustee cannot be called to account, the cestui cannot force the trustee to any particular line of conduct with regard to the trust property or sue for breach of trust. The trustee may do as he likes with the property, and the cestui is without remedy. If the court

finds that the settlor really intended a trust, it would seem that accountability in chancery or other court must inevitably follow as an incident. Without an account the cestui must be in the dark as to whether there has been a breach of trust and so is prevented as a practical matter from holding the trustee liable for a breach. . . .

We come now to an expression of our own views. We are completely satisfied that no trust instrument can relieve a trustee from his duty to account in a court of equity. We are, however, prepared to adopt the point of view of the Restatement that a trust instrument may lawfully relieve a trustee from the necessity of keeping formal accounts. When such a provision is found in a trust instrument, a beneficiary can not expect to receive reports concerning the trust estate. But even when such a provision is made a part of the trust instrument, the trustee will, nevertheless, be required in a suit for an accounting to show that he faithfully performed his duty and will be liable to whatever remedies may be appropriate if he was unfaithful to his trust. Such being our views, it follows that, so far as the Educational Trust is concerned, the defendant was not required to maintain formal records and supply information to the beneficiaries concerning the condition of the corpus of the trust. The provision under consideration did not, however, relieve him from the accounting which the circuit court exacted of him. . . .

Decree afirmed.

Informal accountings. The trustee's duty to render accountings may be satisfied by privately settling his accounts with the beneficiaries. A beneficiary who participates in such a settlement may be estopped or subject to a defense of laches if questions later arise concerning the trustee's administration for the period covered. Often corporate trustees follow a practice of obtaining an instrument from the beneficiaries approving an informal accounting and discharging the trustee for the acts reported. In Matter of James, 173 Misc. 1042, 1045, 19 N.Y.S.2d 532, 535 (1940), the beneficiary had executed an instrument of this type after consultation with a lawyer, and the court said of such settlements:

> The law encourages the making of agreements for the release of fiduciaries and for the approval of their informal accounts principally because they avoid expense and delay. Except where fraud or imposition is shown, such agreements and releases are approved. . . . [The beneficiary] "may not be heard to say that the accounting trustee owed him . . . an affirmative duty to detail an open state of facts as to which he was content to waive inquiry."

The terms of trusts sometimes go further and provide that the trustee is to submit an accounting to a particular person, such as an adult beneficiary, and that approval of the account by that person discharges the trustee as to all beneficiaries. There is some doubt that such a provision is effective, but the American Law Institute takes the position that it is effective as long as the approval is given in good faith and the accounting makes proper disclosure of the trustee's acts. Restatement (Second) of Trusts §172, comment *d*. For further discussion of this matter and related problems, see Westfall, Nonjudicial Settlement of Trustees' Accounts, 71 Harv. L. Rev. 40 (1957).

A trustee may also voluntarily render account in court. By periodic judicial settlements the trustee may wish to obtain a discharge from further liability for previous acts of administration and to receive compensation for those acts. In some states the practice of courts of equity may limit voluntary settlements in court to final accountings, in the absence of an actual controversy between trustee and beneficiary.

In re ENGER'S WILL
225 Minn. 229, 30 N.W.2d 694 (1948)

[Trustees appeal from a court order that had vacated prior orders as far as necessary to enable the beneficiaries to litigate claims against the trustees for alleged self-dealing. The court stated that the primary question raised was whether the prior order allowing the trustees' account was res judicata.]

PETERSON, J. . . .

An order made in proceedings under §501.35 allowing the annual account of a trustee has the legal effect of a final judgment. The statute, so far as here material, provides that a trustee may file and petition the court for the settlement and allowance of any account, whereupon the court shall set the matter for hearing and give notice thereof as therein provided; and that "[u]pon such hearing the court shall make such order as it deems appropriate, which order shall be final and conclusive as to all matters thereby determined and binding in rem upon the trust estate and upon the interests of all beneficiaries, . . . except that appeal to the supreme court may be taken from such order within 30 days from the entry thereof. . . . " The statute denominates an order allowing an account thereunder an "order," and, because that is true, we are bound by that characterization. But the statute also provides that the legal effect of such an order is that it is *final and conclusive* as to all matters thereby determined, the meaning of which we think is that the determinative effect of such order shall be the same as a final judgment. . . .

In a trustee's accounting, the "matters" involved include the transactions set forth in the trustee's account and the petition for the allowance thereof and the objections thereto, if any. The pleadings consist of the account and the petition on the one side and of the objections thereto on the other. . . . The issues are framed by the account and the petition and the objections thereto as the pleadings in an accounting proceeding. . . . Here, since there were no objections to the annual accounts, the matters determined by the orders allowing the annual accounts were those put in issue by the accounts and the petitions for the allowance thereof filed by the trustees. The proceedings having been by default, the court had jurisdiction to determine only the questions thus raised. . . .

Self-dealing by a trustee is not a matter involved in an accounting proceeding by a trustee where the account and the petition for the allowance thereof do not apprise the beneficiaries of the fact. It is the trustee's duty to disclose to the beneficiary fully, frankly, and without reservation all facts pertaining to the trust. In re Trusteeship under Will of Rosenfeldt, 185 Minn. 425, 430, 241 N.W. 573, 575. In the cited case, our decision related to the trustee's duty of disclosure in extra-judicial transactions. The duty of disclosure does not end at the commencement of a legal proceeding, but continues to be just as obligatory therein as it was prior thereto. That being true, the duty rests on the trustee in accounting proceedings to make the fullest measure of disclosure. . . .

Because a beneficiary may rely upon the disclosures in the trustee's account and the petition for its allowance, a proceeding for the allowance of the account does not impose upon the beneficiary as an ordinary adversary the burden of making his own inquiry to ascertain the truth of the trustee's disclosures. The beneficiary may accept them as true. In this respect the rule is different from what it is in ordinary litigation, where the parties are not only adversary, but where there is no fiduciary relationship. . . .

Here, there is not one word in any of the petitions and accounts or in the proceedings for the allowance of the annual accounts apprising the beneficiaries of any self-dealing on the part of the trustees. On the contrary, all information with respect to the matter was concealed. Hence no issue was tendered by the trustees in any of the prior proceedings concerning any self-dealing. The self-dealing was not, therefore, a matter determined by any of the orders relied on as having that effect.

From what has been said it must be apparent that the orders allowing the trustees' annual accounts are not res judicata as to self-dealing by the trustees. Section 501.35, as the controlling statute, determines the extent to which such orders are res judicata. . . . The statute in express terms provides that such orders shall be final and conclusive as to all matters thereby determined. The effect of this provision is that if the matter was determined by the order the order is res judicata, and if the matter was not so determined the order is not res judicata. This is the rule independent of statute. . . . It has been held that where an investment is listed in the account, but the facts showing its illegality are not, the order is not res judicata as to the question of the illegality of the investment, because the mere listing of it fails to apprise the beneficiaries of the fact of illegality. . . .

Since the orders allowing the annual accounts of the trustees are not res judicata of the question whether the trustees are liable for self-dealing, it can make no possible difference whether they were vacated to permit litigation of the question. . . .

Affirmed so far as orders relate to orders allowing trustees' annual accounts and appeal dismissed as to other parts of the order.

D. Liability of Fiduciaries

1. Liability to Beneficiaries

In other parts of this chapter we have encountered the matter of a fiduciary's personal liability for failure to comply with the duties and standards appropriate to the office. The subject continues to arise in various contexts throughout these materials. This section deals simply with fundamentals of the fiduciary's potential liability to the beneficiaries.

A cause of action against a fiduciary may be brought by a beneficiary, and in the case of a decedent's estate also by a creditor of the estate; or it may be brought by a successor or cofiduciary. Typically, questions of liability arise on accounting or in actions to surcharge or remove a trustee or personal representative. In the usual case where the fiduciary has given bond with sureties for the performance of duties, recovery may be against the surety, a matter that depends on the construction of the bond and the cause of the fiduciary's liability. The judgment against a fiduciary usually is not a preferred claim but has the same status as general claims of the fiduciary's personal creditors, except where the beneficiary is granted a lien on certain property of the trustee or is able to trace particular trust property into the hands of the trustee.

The measure of a fiduciary's liability may best be understood in the context of the various cases involving such liability, but as a general principle it has been stated that the "measure of damages is usually the difference between the values of the capital and income of the trust as they would have been if the trust had been performed and as they existed as a result of the wrongful conduct of the trustee." G. Bogert, Trusts §157 (6th ed. 1987). It is stated in Restatement (Second) of Trusts §205 that when a trustee commits a breach of trust the amount he is chargeable with may be measured in terms of "any loss or depreciation in value of the trust estate resulting from the breach," or "any profit made by him through the breach of trust," or "any profit which would have accrued to the trust estate if there had been no breach."

The materials below are concerned with the basic principles governing the occasions of a fiduciary's liability and the measure of it.

CREED v. McALEER
275 Mass. 353, 175 N.E. 761 (1931)

PIERCE, J. . . .

C. James Connelly died on July 10, 1914. By his will, after payment of minor bequests, he left the rest of his estate in trust, the income to be paid to his wife, Agnes G. Connelly, during her lifetime, and the remainder over on her death. The widow died on August 22, 1929. On September 14, 1929, some of the remaindermen filed a petition in the Probate Court for partial distribution in kind of stocks of the trust estate. Not all of the remaindermen agreed to the distribution of the securities in kind; the petition was dismissed on December 19, 1929, and the stocks were ordered to be sold within a reasonable time.

The sale price of most of the stock exceeded their appraised value when they were turned over to the trustees by the executors under the will. At times, however, during the term of the trust many of the stocks could have been sold at higher prices. The appellants seek to charge the trustees for the difference between the price of the stocks at their peak and the price at which they were sold. A trustee, to invest, is required to conduct himself faithfully and to exercise a sound discretion, observing how men of prudence, discretion and intelligence manage their own affairs. . . . The trustee is chargeable, therefore, with failure to sell such stocks at the peak price only if such failure was an abuse of "the sound discretion and good judgment of a prudent man dealing with his own permanent investments." Boston Safe Deposit & Trust Co. v. Wall, 254 Mass. 464, 467. The delay in selling the stocks after the death of the life tenant was not unreasonable. As a reasonable man, the trustee could await the outcome of the petition for partial distribution in kind. He could not be held to forecast the sudden drop in stock prices in October and November, 1929. He is not chargeable with the difference between the market price of the stock at the life tenant's death and the price of such stock at the time of the actual sale. . . .

In the absence of specific direction in the creation of a trust, an investment in property of a wasting nature in order to increase the income is not consistent with the duty of a trustee. The same rule obtains in regard to property which comes to trustees from the testator not specifically bequeathed as obtains in respect to new investments, and when so received it should not be allowed to continue but should be converted promptly into safe investments. . . .

The Probate Court charges the trustee with the "loss . . . sustained by the trustee" by reason of the retention of the stocks beyond a reasonable time after he received them. This charge in legal contemplation compensates the remaindermen for the failure of the trustee to convert. . . . For all practical purposes such shares as were held by the trustee were worth what they were quoted in the market. The holder of these stocks was under no obligation to retain them until the mines were exhausted and he could at any time escape from the possibility of diminished value by reason of wastage by selling the stocks in the market. . . .

There was a slight gain in the sale of the group copper mining stocks over the inventory value. There was a substantial gain over inventory values in the sale of all stocks. The trustee contends that "the total gains should be taken into consideration in considering whether or not the trustee should be held for any losses." . . . As above stated, with citation of authorities, a trustee must exercise reasonable skill and prudence and sound discretion in making or retaining each investment and is chargeable with any loss by failing to do so. The gain in each investment belongs to the trust estate and in no way can a trustee reap a personal profit from it. . . . A trustee cannot offset a loss for which he is liable by a gain belonging not to him but to his cestui. . . . The failure to [offset gain from the sale of the *same* stock on which losses were surcharged, however, was] an apparent oversight, and [that offset] should be allowed. . . .

Decree accordingly.

FALL v. MILLER
462 N.E.2d 1059 (Ind. App. 1984)

[The decedent bequeathed certain corporate stock to Fall. During administration, although there was no necessity to sell the stock, the executrix petitioned the court (without Fall's knowledge or consent) to sell the stock, erroneously alleging that it was necessary to do so to pay debts and expenses of the estate. The petition was granted, and the executrix sold the stock. About eight months later her attorney acknowledged the mistake in a letter to Fall and promised to compensate him or replace the stock. Thereafter, without further disclosure, the executrix reacquired on the market equal shares of the same stock for $8,804.60 less than the earlier sale price. In her final account she proposed to distribute the specific shares to Fall and to retain the profit in the residue, which was to be divided among herself and others. From an adverse ruling on his objections to that proposal, Fall appeals; the executrix argues that Fall is entitled to and did receive his distribution in kind, fully satisfying her fiduciary duty to him.]

NEAL, P.J. . . .

[I]t is conceded that the Executrix had no right to sell the stock and it was a breach of her duty to do so. A personal representative is regarded as a trustee appointed by law for the benefit of and protection of creditors and distributees. . . .

There is a thread which runs through the law governing fiduciary relationships which forbids a person standing in a fiduciary capacity to another from profiting by dealing in the property of his beneficiary, and any profit realized must be disgorged in favor of that beneficiary. . . . In Ross v. Thompson, (1957) 128 Ind. App. 89, 146 N.E.2d 259, the court . . . said:

> . . . [W]hen the legal identity of a chattel is destroyed, or cannot be specifically traced into another thing, [a court of law] is unable to give relief except by action for damages. . . . But courts of equity, having greater powers, endeavor to afford a more complete remedy. . . . The equity rule is that trust property may be followed by the beneficiary so long as its identity can be ascertained [and] equity imposes a constructive trust upon the new forms or species into which it is converted, so long as it can be traced or followed and its identity ascertained. . . . The trust property rightfully belongs to the cestuis que trust and a change in its form does not change its ownership. . . . As between the cestuis que trust and the trustee and all parties claiming under the trustee, except purchasers for value and without notice, all the property belonging to the trust, however much it may have been changed in its form or in its nature or character, and *all the fruits of such property,* whether in its original or altered state, continue to be subject to and affected by the trust. (Emphasis added by court.)

Ind. Code 30-4-3-11(b), applicable to trusts, provides that if the trustee commits a breach of trust he is liable to the beneficiary: "(2) *for any profit* made by the trustee through the breach." (Emphasis by court.)

A legatee may either charge the personal representative with the value of the converted property, or elect to claim and pursue the property for which it has been exchanged. . . .

The Executrix held Fall's stock in a fiduciary capacity, and wrongly sold it, even if by mistake. Neither she nor anyone claiming through her should be permitted to retain the profits or fruits of the transaction. Fall, as equitable owner of the stock, subject only [if needed] to abatement for payment of debts, is entitled to his stock and all profits made by the Executrix in wrongfully dealing in it. One rationale for the rule is that the property which generated the profit belonged to Fall, and in equity and good conscience the property should belong to him. A more persuasive rationale is that if a fiduciary is not allowed to retain any gain or profit from wrongful, speculative or self-dealing transactions in his beneficiary's property and at the same time can be held liable for any loss incurred, an effective deterrent to such activity exists. Any other rule would encourage residuary legatees in control of the estate to speculate in estate assets. Policy forbids such conduct. . . .

Judgment reversed.

When a fiduciary undertakes an act that is forbidden or not authorized, it is no defense that the action was taken in good faith and with
reasonable care and skill. Thus, as must be apparent from earlier cases
in this chapter, the trust is breached any time there is a violation of a duty
imposed by law or by the terms of the trust, regardless of compliance
with general standards of care and skill. The trustee must know or ascertain and then must obey the valid terms of the trust and the applicable
rules of law. Although in most respects a fiduciary is not a guarantor of
the success of actions undertaken in the course of estate or trust administration, under principles of strict liability, traditional doctrine (with
some modern cases contra) does not excuse a fiduciary for reasonable,
honest mistakes concerning the nature and extent of the fiduciary's powers and duties, nor for payment of trust funds to one who is not the
proper beneficiary.

If there is reasonable doubt as to the powers and duties of a trustee,
for example, or as to the proper interpretation of administrative or distributive provisions of the instrument, it is generally recognized that
application may be made to the appropriate court for instructions at the
expense of the trust estate. A court will ordinarily refuse to instruct a
trustee when reasonable doubt does not exist or where the question is
one of business judgment or one that is within the discretion of the
trustee. The readiness of courts to provide instructions varies with local
practice, and sometimes within a given jurisdiction courts of equity are
stricter than are courts that supervise testamentary trusts. See Wile,
Judicial Assistance in the Administration of Trusts, 14 Stan. L. Rev. 231
(1962). The trustee will be protected if an act is pursuant to court
instructions obtained in good faith and on full disclosure, assuming the
beneficiaries were parties to the proceeding.

A trustee may also obtain protection through consent of the beneficiaries. A beneficiary who participates in a breach of trust cannot complain of it. Where powers or duties are uncertain or where contemplated
actions are likely to exceed proper authority, a trustee may seek to obtain
the approval of the beneficiaries. As a practical matter it is rarely possible
to obtain consent of all beneficiaries, but those who are sui juris and give
their informed consent to a particular act are estopped to object. This
assumes that the trustee has concealed no material facts and has acted
in a manner consistent with the fiduciary relationship to the beneficiary
in obtaining the consent. Beneficiaries who do not or cannot give their
consent are not bound by the act of those who do consent, in the absence
of special circumstances such as where the consent of the settlor of a
revocable trust binds all beneficiaries, as in City Bank v. Cannon, page
719 supra. The case that follows, however, involves an innovative use of
vicarious consent: is it a desirable reversal of conventional doctrine to
be considered by other courts or by legislatures? Compare Hatch v.
Riggs National Bank, page 483 supra, the note at page 488 supra, and
Mabry v. Scott, supra page 592.

In re ESTATE OF LANGE
75 N.J. 464, 383 A.2d 1130 (1978)

PASHMAN, J.

The issue presented by this appeal is the propriety of surcharging executrices for acts beyond the scope of their powers under the will. . . . The County Court, Probate Division, held, and the Appellate Division agreed, that any [consent of interested parties] was ineffective to exonerate the executrices from liability. . . . [U]nder the circumstances of this case, we reverse the judgment of the courts below. . . .

[Philip Lange bequeathed his residuary estate in trust for his widow for life, remainder on her death to his three children (all adults), if living, or "to their surviving issue, per stirpes." Mrs. Lange (the widow) and Catherine Lennox (a daughter) were coexecutrices and cotrustees.]

In early 1969, the attorney for the estate advised the executrices that approximately $60,000 would be needed to pay the estimated federal estate tax liability. Since liquid assets sufficient to meet this obligation were apparently not available, the attorney recommended that certain of the residuary assets of the estate be liquidated in order to obtain the necessary funds. It was then determined that 1500 of the estate's 4500 shares of stock in the Colonial National Bank (hereinafter Colonial) should be sold and the proceeds applied to the payment of the estate tax. Five hundred shares of the Colonial stock were sold in March 1969 at a price considered to be very unfavorable by Mrs. Lange, who thereupon determined to refrain from selling any more of the stock until market conditions improved. The proceeds of the shares sold were used for partial payment of the estate taxes. No attempt was made to liquidate other residuary assets, although estate taxes were still owing. Later that month, apparently at the suggestion of Elizabeth Dixon, the executrices negotiated a loan from the Delaware Valley National Bank (hereinafter Delaware Valley) on behalf of the estate for the balance of the tax indebtedness. Mrs. Lennox agreed to the loan transaction on the understanding that it was to be only a temporary measure and would be repaid as soon as possible by the sale of small increments of the Colonial stock. This loan was secured by the pledge of a substantial amount of the estate's shares of Colonial stock as collateral. The attorney for the estate had given his opinion that the executrices would be acting within their powers under the will in procuring this loan. In addition, the lending bank agreed to the loan only after it had examined the will and satisfied itself that the executrices were authorized to so obligate the estate. Neither George Lange nor Elizabeth Dixon, the other [children], made any objection or otherwise questioned the propriety of the loan transaction. The monies obtained from the loan were used to pay the balance of the estate tax due. Interest on the loan was paid out of income from the residuary assets of the estate, including the pledged Colonial stock.

In late summer of 1971 the attorney for the estate recommended to

Mrs. Lennox that a portion of the estate's Colonial stock sufficient to pay off the loan be sold. In March 1972 Mrs. Lennox's husband became the attorney for the estate and made a similar recommendation to the executrices, with which Mrs. Lennox agreed. However, Mrs. Lange, her coexecutrix and the income beneficiary under the trust, refused to consent to liquidation of any of the estate's Colonial stock. Her resistance resulted from the opposition to the proposal by George Lange and Elizabeth Dixon [who] believed that the stock continued to be undervalued and that any such sale would still yield an unfavorable price for the shares. When the attorney formally requested the consent of those two beneficiaries to the retention of the shares as estate assets, both indicated their opposition to any sale of the Colonial stock. Mrs. Lange thereafter remained adamant in her refusal to consent to any liquidation of the Colonial stock. In August 1972 the three children, by agreement, received their specific bequests in kind by way of shares of the estate's Colonial stock and executed the appropriate refunding bonds and releases. All subsequent efforts by Mrs. Lennox and her husband, as attorney for the estate, to persuade Mrs. Lange, Elizabeth Dixon and George Lange to liquidate the remaining Colonial stock held by the estate and to pay off the Delaware Valley loan proved unsuccessful. In May 1973 an informal accounting rendered by the executrices to all interested parties [George Lange's two sons had succeeded to his remainder interest as his surviving issue upon his death in 1973] revealed the outstanding Delaware Valley loan, the pledge of the Colonial stock and the monthly interest payments on the loan. None of the beneficiaries objected to the continuation of the loan or the estate's retention of the pledged and non-pledged Colonial stock. As late as May 1974 Mrs. Lange, through her counsel, reiterated her continuing refusal to liquidate any of the Colonial stock for the purpose of satisfying the loan even though the value of the stock had steadily declined since her husband's death. None of the residuary remaindermen, other than Catherine Lennox, ever objected to the continuance of the Delaware Valley loan or the retention of the Colonial stock during the decline in its market value.

As a result of other unrelated disputes among the parties in interest, in September 1974 Mrs. Lennox filed a complaint with the account annexed in the Probate Division of the Camden County Court. She sought, inter alia, to have her final and formal accounting approved and distribution of the residuary assets to the testamentary trustees ordered. She also sought an order directing the executrices to liquidate sufficient estate assets to retire the Delaware Valley loan, the outstanding amount of which was some $33,000 at that time. Mrs. Lennox's formal accounting revealed the outstanding status of the loan and the retention of both the pledged and nonpledged Colonial stock as estate assets. Mrs. Lange filed exceptions to this accounting, in which she had not joined as a co-accountant, in October 1974. None of her exceptions was addressed to the Delaware Valley loan transaction. Neither Elizabeth Dixon nor the two sons of George Lange filed any exceptions to the formal accounting.

Prior to filing her exceptions, Mrs. Lange had filed a complaint in the Probate Division seeking to have Delaware Valley restrained from liquidating any of the pledged Colonial stock for purposes of reducing the principal balance on the loan. It also sought to have Catherine Lennox ordered to take the necessary steps to have another estate asset (a certificate of deposit) liquidated and the proceeds applied to the principal on the Delaware Valley loan. Mrs. Lange alleged that the intervention of the court was required because her co-executrix refused to make any estate assets available to reduce the Delaware Valley loan.

Temporary restraints against the bank and an order to show cause against Catherine Lennox were issued by the probate judge. On the October 4, 1974 return date, the probate judge, prompted by Mrs. Lange's action for injunctive relief against her co-executrix, sua sponte raised the issue of the executrices' authority to have negotiated the Delaware Valley loan and temporarily restrained the executrices from paying any interest on the loan until he ruled on that issue. In her subsequently filed answer to Mrs. Lennox's original complaint, Mrs. Lange requested that retirement of the Delaware Valley loan be held in abeyance until the court determined the propriety of the loan. She also asked that the court surcharge the executrices if the loan was found to be illegal. In late November 1974 the probate judge ordered that the pledged Colonial stock be sold and the proceeds applied to pay the Delaware Valley loan in full, with any excess monies resulting from the sale to be paid into the estate. However, by that time the value of the Colonial stock had so dwindled that the liquidation of the collateral was insufficient to satisfy the outstanding balance on the loan.

At the several hearings on the legality of the loan and other disputed matters, Mrs. Lange advanced the contention that she and her coexecutrix daughter had acted improperly and in excess of their powers under the will in negotiating the Delaware Valley loan. As the life tenant with the right to the entire income from the corpus and with the power to invade, when necessary, the principal of the testamentary trust, Mrs. Lange would suffer no real harm from any surcharge imposed on her. Mrs. Lennox's position, however, was substantially more vulnerable and she vigorously contested the alleged impropriety of the loan.

In February 1975 the probate judge held, inter alia, that the executrices' negotiation of the Delaware Valley loan for the purpose of meeting the tax liability of the estate was an ultra vires act, notwithstanding the fact that no interested party had indicated any objection to the estate's obtaining the loan and no party other than Catherine Lennox had ever objected to the continuance of the loan. The basis for this ruling was the judge's finding that the procurement of a loan to pay a tax obligation contravened specific instructions in the will as to how taxes were to be paid. Consequently, he concluded that it was not the testator's intention that his wife and daughter, as executrices, have the power to obtain a loan to pay the taxes imposed on the estate. The judgment specifically surcharged the executrices jointly and severally in the amount of $26,819.19, which the probate judge found to be the loss sustained by the estate as a result of the procurement of the Delaware Valley loan. This amount was calculated as the decrease in the value of the number of Colonial shares whose liquidation would have been necessary to satisfy the balance of the tax indebtedness in March 1969, the approximate date of the Delaware Valley loan, from that date to the November 1974 date when the collateral was sold at the court's direction. Appropriate adjustments were made for the value of dividends and fractional shares received from the Colonial shares. With respect to Catherine Lennox's contention that even if ultra vires the loan transaction was consented to originally and ratified thereafter by all interested beneficiaries, the probate judge held that any such conduct by the adult beneficiaries in this case was ineffective to bind their living minor children and any unborn issue who might be the actual takers in remainder under the trust upon the death of Mrs. Lange. . . .

[T]he Appellate Division . . . affirmed the probate judge's holding that the Delaware Valley loan was improper. . . . Without reaching the probate judge's ruling that the negotiation of the Delaware Valley loan by the executrices exceeded their authority under the will, a holding whose correctness for present purposes will be assumed, we disagree with his conclusion that validation by all interested beneficiaries of an otherwise ultra vires act by a fiduciary cannot preclude the imposition of a surcharge for that breach of duty.

The principle that a fiduciary may be relieved from liability for the consequences of an otherwise surchargeable transaction as a result of legally sufficient validation thereof by all parties in interest is firmly rooted in the law. The rationale underlying this principle is that such validation results in a preclusion of the right of the interested parties to subsequently object to the propriety of the transaction. An eminent commentator has stated this general rule in a more comprehensive fashion: "If a beneficiary, legatee or next of kin of age and under no disability had knowledge of acts constituting a breach of trust which are about to be or have been committed by the fiduciary and consents to or acquiesces in them voluntarily, knowing his legal rights, he will be barred from objecting to the breach of trust." 6 N.J. Practice (Clapp, Wills and Administration), §1124 at 741 (3d ed. 1962). Such validation does not have the effect of enlarging the powers of the fiduciary; it merely operates to prevent the parties in interest from holding the fiduciary accountable for the consequences of the validated conduct. See Scott on Trusts §216. . . .

Before such validation will be held effective to exonerate a fiduciary, the showing must meet exacting standards. A party in interest will not be precluded from challenging a fiduciary's acts or held to have validated his misdeeds in the absence of full knowledge of all the relevant facts and full appreciation of what was being done. . . .

[I]n the instant case, we conclude that the interested parties possessed an awareness of the facts and circumstances, including the legal consequences, of the Delaware Valley loan sufficient for an effective validation of that assumedly ultra vires transaction. . . .

[W]e find ample evidence of consensual conduct with respect to the negotiation and continuation of the Delaware Valley loan in the totality of circumstances in this case. Elizabeth Dixon originally suggested the idea of procuring a loan (instead of liquidating additional Colonial stock to pay the estate taxes) to her mother and sister and later resisted all suggestions to liquidate estate assets to retire the Delaware Valley loan. George Lange acquiesced in the original loan and pledge of Colonial stock and also opposed the various recommendations that the loan be paid through liquidation of the estate assets. Both Elizabeth Dixon and George Lange (as well as Catherine Lennox) signed "boiler plate" releases purporting to relieve the executrices of any liability with respect to their interests in the estate upon receiving their specific bequests. Neither Elizabeth Dixon nor George Lange's surviving issue, the successors to his remainder interest in the residuary trust, objected to the loan transaction at the time of the informal accounting or filed any exceptions with respect thereto in the formal accounting proceeding below. Both accountings fully disclosed the continued existence of the Delaware Valley loan and the pledge of the Colonial stock to secure it. . . . Catherine Lennox, in her dual capacity as coexecutrix and beneficiary in remainder, was also involved in obtaining the loan, although her original consent to its procurement was limited and her later informal objections to its continuation were persistent. However, she never took formal action to expedite its repayment until filing her complaint in September 1974. . . .

Accordingly, the adult beneficiaries, including the two sons of George Lange, would a fortiori have been precluded from seeking to hold the executrices liable for their ultra vires act.

Our finding of validation by the adult remaindermen is dispositive of this case only if the resulting preclusion is binding on their minor children and unborn issue, who also are potential takers in remainder under the residuary trust upon the death of the income beneficiary, Mrs. Lange. The probate judge perceived no authority for holding these potential beneficiaries to be so bound and thus viewed any validation by their predecessors in interest as posing no obstacle to a surcharge of the executrices.

The terms of the testamentary trust established by Philip Lange created a present one-third interest on the part of each of his three children in the trust remainder. Thus, at the time of the trust's creation, the presumptive takers in remainder were Catherine Lennox, Elizabeth Dixon and George Lange. If any of the children predeceased his mother, the life tenant, his respective issue would succeed to his remainder interest per stirpes. This in fact occurred in the case of George Lange, whose two sons acquired the status of presumptive takers of his one-third share of the trust remainder upon his death. The identities of the persons who would be the actual takers in remainder are, of course, unascertainable until the death of the life tenant. Thus, the interests of the original beneficiaries in remainder were contingent on their surviving their mother. The interests of their issue were more remote — for any of them to be the actual takers, they not only must be "in being" at the time of the death of the life tenant, but also must have been predeceased by the ancestor to whose remainder interest they would succeed. When the proceedings below were commenced in September 1974, it appears that the beneficiaries who were the presumptive takers in remainder at that time, Catherine Lennox, Elizabeth Dixon and the two sons of George Lange, were the only potential beneficiaries who were sui juris. The remaining members of the three classes of potential beneficiaries included the minor children and any unborn issue of each who might be the actual takers of the respective shares at the time the trust principal is distributed.

We believe that the proper approach to resolution of this issue entails application of the principles of virtual representation by a presumptive taker presently embodied in R. 4:26-3(a). Where the identities of the actual takers of a future interest are unascertainable or otherwise difficult to determine with certainty, joinder of the presumptive takers of that interest as of the time of the commencement of the action will, in appropriate circumstances, be sufficient to enable any judgment entered therein to be binding upon all persons, whether in being or not, in the class of potential takers of that interest. While the members of that class may not be individually ascertainable at the time of the action, they are identifiable as a class and their interests as such cognizable. The presumptive takers are persons who would be the actual takers of the future interest if the contingency occurred at the time of the commencement of the proceeding affecting the property in which the future interest exists. They are permitted to represent the entire class of potential takers, but only in the absence of any demonstrable conflict of interest or other hostility between the presumptive takers and the other members of the class sought to be represented. The assumption underlying the doctrine of virtual representation is the existence of a relationship between the presumptive takers and the class of potential takers sufficiently close to guarantee an identity of interest between the representatives and the class and thus to assure that the representation will be adequate. See Mabry v. Scott, 51 Cal. App. 2d 245, 124 P.2d 659, 663-

664 (Dist. Ct. App. 1942), *cert. den. sub nom.*, Title Ins. & Trust Co. v. Mabry, 317 U.S. 670 (1942); 5 N.J. Practice (Clapp, Wills and Administration), §295 and n.31 at 136 (1977 Supp.). See also Restatement, Property, §§180-185 (1936). Utilization of virtual representation enables the court to act upon the interests of unascertainable contingent remaindermen to the same effect as if they all had been sui juris and parties to the action without any infringement of their right to due process. See Mullane v. Central Hanover Bank & Trust Co., 339 U.S. 306, 317-318 (1950).

Thus, if Catherine Lennox, Elizabeth Dixon and the sons of George Lange could have qualified as the respective virtual representatives of the three classes of potential takers of the trust remainder, their validation of the Delaware Valley loan transaction should have the same preclusive effect on the right of any members of the class to have the executrices surcharged as it does with respect to the right of those presumptive takers who were joined as parties.[12] Each class is comprised of the potential takers of the respective one-third interests in the remainder of the residuary trust originally held by the three children of Philip Lange and includes all potential successors to those interests. The representatives of the three classes are the persons who, as of September 1974, stood in the relation of ancestral predecessors-in-interest to the other members of the respective classes. We are satisfied that in such circumstances there is a sufficient nexus between the representatives and the members of each class of potential takers in remainder to justify a conclusion that the class members are bound by the representatives' validation of the loan transaction. We perceive no hostility between the interests of the presumptive takers and the interests of the other members of the respective classes such as would render virtual representation inequitable and disqualify the presumptive takers from binding those who may be the ultimate remaindermen. Accordingly, we hold that the members of the three classes of potential takers of the respective shares of the trust remainder were bound by their predecessors-in-interest's validation of the loan transaction and their right to have the executrices surcharged therefor was consequently precluded as well. . . .

For reversal and remandment. . . .

---

12. Although R. 4:26-3(a) itself is not precisely applicable to the proceedings in this case since we are not concerned with the binding effect of a judgment in an action affecting a future interest, we nevertheless feel that the principles of virtual representation can serve as useful guidelines in determining whether the conduct of a predecessor in interest may in any way disentitle his successor to assert a right whose vindication he would otherwise be able to seek. Our court rule does not purport to specify the only set of circumstances in which virtual representation by a presumptive taker may be given effect. Resort to the doctrine in other appropriate contexts, such as that of the instant case, where it is "essential, in the interests of justice, to adjudicate rights of living persons," Mabry v. Scott, supra, 124 P.2d at 663, is to be encouraged. [Court's footnote.]

As a general rule a fiduciary is not liable to the beneficiaries for the wrongful or negligent act of another if the fiduciary is not also personally at fault. Thus, an individual trustee is not liable to the beneficiaries for the acts of an agent in the absence of an improper delegation of authority, unless the trustee participated or acquiesced in the agent's wrongful act or neglected to compel the agent to make good a loss for which the agent was liable, or unless the trustee failed to use reasonable care in the selection, supervision, and retention of the agent. A corporate trustee, which necessarily acts through its employees, is generally liable for their negligence as the negligent act of the company itself.

One of several fiduciaries is normally not liable for the acts of a cofiduciary unless there has in some way been a failure in the former's own duties. Each cofiduciary, however, must participate in the administration of a decedent's estate or trust, assuming at least that such participation is not excluded by the terms of the governing instrument. Thus, a trustee is under a duty "to use reasonable care to prevent a cotrustee from committing a breach of trust or to compel a cotrustee to redress a breach of trust." Restatement (Second) of Trusts §184. A fiduciary must not delegate duties to a cofiduciary, at least in the absence of compelling circumstances that require it in the interest of proper administration. A cofiduciary who violates these duties is liable. When cofiduciaries are both liable, their liability is joint and several; and when neglect renders one liable for the wrongful act of the other, either may be required to make good the entire loss. In such a case the greater fault of one may create a right of indemnity in the other.

Normally a fiduciary is not liable for the acts of a predecessor in office. On the other hand, a fiduciary will generally be held liable for failing to compel redress of a breach of trust by the predecessor, and even for negligent failure to detect the predecessor's breach of trust. Therefore, in order to be safe, a trustee must require an accounting of the predecessor and inquire into the condition of the trust estate. In the absence of a valid provision excusing such inquiry, this admonition would apply whether the successor fiduciary is assuming the administration from another trustee or receiving distribution from an executor or administrator.

Exculpatory clauses. It is common to find wills and trust agreements that purport to restrict or even eliminate the liability of a fiduciary. The extent to which a trustee or personal representative generally may be relieved by the terms of the instrument of normal liability for breach of duty is reflected in Fleener v. Omaha National Co., 131 Neb. 253, 257, 267 N.W. 462, 464-465 (1936):

> Appellants contend that, as the trust deed was drawn by the trustee, it ought to be construed against it. This would be true if the provisions of the trust deed were so worded as to require a construction, but where the language used is definite and unambiguous, its usual and ordinary mean-

ing should be adopted by the court. We conclude therefore that the exculpatory provisions of the trust deed may be invoked by the trustee to relieve it of all liability except for gross negligence and wilful default. The proper rule is stated by a highly regarded authority as follows:

> (1) Except as stated in subsections (2) and (3), the trustee, by provisions in the terms of the trust, can be relieved of liability for breach of trust.
>
> (2) A provision in the trust instrument is not effective to relieve the trustee of liability for breach of trust committed in bad faith or intentionally or with reckless indifference to the interest of the beneficiary, or of liability for any profit which the trustee has derived from a breach of trust.
>
> (3) To the extent to which a provision relieving the trustee of liability for breaches of trust is inserted in the trust instrument as the result of an abuse by the trustee of a fiduciary or confidential relationship to the settlor, such provision is ineffective.

Restatement, Trusts §222.

In Browning v. Fidelity Trust Co. (C.C.A.) 250 F. 321, 324, the court said:

> The plaintiff admits that as a general proposition parties creating a trust can, by their agreement, limit the liability which is imposed by one and accepted by the other, Tuttle v. Gilmore, 36 N.J. Eq. 617, but maintains, very properly, that the law, dictated by considerations of public policy, determines a point beyond which the parties cannot agree to relieve a trustee from liability for breach of a trust duty. For instance, a trustee cannot contract for immunity from liability for acts of gross negligence or for acts done in bad faith. Such contracts are invalid because repugnant to law.

Contrast Committee Report, Current Investment Questions and the Prudent Person Rule, 13 Real Prop., Prob. & Tr. J. 650, 669 (1978):

With respect to any employee benefit plan subject to ERISA, section 410(a) provides as follows:

> Except as provided in sections 405(b)(1) and 405(d), any provision in an agreement or instrument which purports to relieve a fiduciary from responsibility or liability for any responsibility, obligation, or duty under this part shall be void as against public policy.

The first exception referred to permits the allocation of fiduciary duties among co-trustees, in which case a trustee to whom a given duty has not been allocated is not liable for a loss due to a breach on the part of the trustee to whom that duty has been allocated. The second exception provides that a trustee is not liable for the acts or omissions of a qualified investment manager who has been properly appointed to manage plan assets, unless the trustee knowingly participates in or knowingly conceals an act or omission of the investment manager which it knows constitutes a breach.

Section 410(b), however, does permit a fiduciary to purchase personal fiduciary liability insurance at his own expense, or at the plan's expense if the insurance policy permits recourse by the insurer against the fiduciary in the event of a breach by the fiduciary. To permit a plan to purchase such insurance with plan assets without a recourse provision would constitute a prohibited relief from personal liability for the fiduciary.

Statutes of limitations and laches. "It is the settled rule that as between a trustee and cestui que trust the statute of limitations does not commence to run so long as the trust continues." Meck v. Behrens, 141 Wash. 676, 681, 252 P. 91, 93 (1927). Compare Developments in the Law — Statutes of Limitations, 63 Harv. L. Rev. 1177, 1214-1215 (1950):

> [Actions for breach of fiduciary duty] have been accorded . . . special treatment under statutes of limitations . . . because . . . the plaintiff will not ordinarily learn of the wrong for some time after the defendant's defalcation. This consideration is especially appropriate to the express formal trust, a relationship used frequently for the preservation and management of property for the young, infirm, or inexperienced, who are unlikely to have sufficient business acumen to determine when a breach has occurred. . . . Thus, the statute does not begin to run during the existence of the relationship unless the beneficiary knows, or reasonably should know, of the facts constituting the breach of duty.

The frequent judicial assertion that statutes of limitations have no application to express trusts has been said to mean merely that the statute does not begin to run until the beneficiary had actual or constructive notice of the trustee's breach or repudiation of the trust. G. Bogert, Trusts §170 (6th ed. 1987). The more common view, however, is that statutes of limitations of most states are not applicable to equitable claims but that the barring of a beneficiary's cause of action against a trustee is a matter of laches, for which the length of time necessarily depends upon the circumstances. Restatement (Second) of Trusts §219, comments *a, b.* "The arbitrary operation of the statutes of limitations is very different from the operation of the equitable doctrine of laches, which is a very flexible doctrine." III W. Fratcher, Scott on Trusts §219 (4th ed. 1988).

2. A Fiduciary's Liability to Third Parties

PROBLEM

17-H. *E,* as executor of an estate valued at $350,000, has continued the hardware store business that the testator had operated as a sole proprietorship. The business assets are worth $190,000, constituting slightly more than half the estate. An employee, driving the store truck to make a delivery, ran over a pedestrian. The pedestrian has filed suit for $400,000. What are the potential liabilities under the materials that follow? Under the law of your state? Under the UPC?

Would the problems differ if a cornice stone fell from a building held in trust and injured a pedestrian on the sidewalk? If the building had been specifically devised to X?

The general concept of the fiduciary relationship is that the fiduciary is the owner of the property as far as third persons are concerned. In absence of statute, the fiduciary is personally liable on contracts relating to the property and its management and is the only person who can make contracts involving the administration of the trust or estate. Similarly, the fiduciary is subjected to personal liability for tax assessments and for torts arising out of the administration. The position of a trustee or personal representative must be distinguished from that of an agent, who has a principal to respond for his acts. Because of the harshness of the common law rule, the Uniform Probate Code provides for personal liability in contract only if the fiduciary fails to reveal the representative capacity to the third party and in tort only if the fiduciary is personally at fault. Uniform Probate Code §§3-808, 5-428, 7-306. These provisions attempt to make an estate or trust a corporate-like entity as far as third parties are concerned. As we have already seen, even at common law if the administration is proper, the fiduciary will be reimbursed from the estate for expenses.

The normal contract liability of a fiduciary at common law can be eliminated or limited by the terms of the contract. In attempting to so limit liability, the fiduciary should be certain that the intended limitation is clearly expressed. See Torrey Pines Bank v. Hoffman, 231 Cal. 3d 308, 282 Cal. Rptr. 354 (1991) (trustee's contract prior to effective date of Cal. Prob. Code §18000, which adopted UPC principles). Absent legislation similar to the UPC, for example, it is quite generally accepted that the mere addition of the word *trustee* or *executor* to one's signature is not sufficient; nor is a provision of the trust instrument effective to preclude a trustee's personal liability, at least in the absence of knowledge by the third party or contractual reference to the instrument. An innocent third party does not lose recourse against the fiduciary where the contract limiting the latter's liability was improper so as not to bind the trust estate.

Under traditional rules an action in tort or on a contract is brought and judgment is entered against the fiduciary in his individual capacity. Thus, to satisfy a judgment against a trustee, the creditor may look to the trustee's own assets. The trust assets may be reached only in equity through subrogation, and then the right of the creditor is dependent on the trustee's right of indemnification. See generally on these matters Cook v. Holland, 575 S.W.2d 468 (Ky. App. 1978). Rules relating to the personal liability of fiduciaries and the procedures to be followed by creditors have been modified by statute or judicial decision in some of the states.

In Kirchner v. Muller, 280 N.Y. 23, 28-29, 19 N.E.2d 665, 667-668 (1937), the court stated:

> The general rule as contended for by appellant is that for their torts trustees or executors are liable in their individual, and not in their representative, capacity. Judgments obtained against executors or trustees are collectible out of their private property, and not out of the trust or estate assets. Although the question appears to have arisen infrequently, the trustee or executor has been held entitled to reimbursement from the estate where he was free from willful misconduct in the tort which occurred during his administration of the estate. A few States have gone so far as to hold that where a trustee or executor would be entitled to reimbursement, the injured third party may sue him in his representative capacity, on the ground that thereby circuity of action may be avoided. No New York authorities are found supporting this procedure. Such a procedure would involve a trial in the same action of both the tort liability and whether the nature of the tort was such as to entitle the trustees or executors to reimbursement, out of the estate, which might entail an undesirable clash of interests between the trustee in his individual capacity and in his representative capacity. In Matter of Raybould ([1900] 1 Ch. 199) it was held that where a judgment was recovered by a third party against a trustee for a tort committed in the administration of the trust, the third party, where his judgment against the trustee proves uncollectible, may then proceed directly against the trust estate. Whether such procedure would be sanctioned in this State need not now be decided.

Compare Smith v. Rizzuto, 133 Neb. 655, 659-660, 276 N.W. 406, 408-409 (1937), in which it is stated:

> It is the general rule that a "trustee is subject to personal liability to third persons for torts committed in the course of the administration of the trust to the same extent that he would be liable if he held the property free of trust." . . . We therefore conclude that the petition states a cause of action against the defendant.
>
> The question immediately arises as to the nature of the liability and the right of the defendant to be indemnified from the trust estate. While "the trustee is personally liable to third persons for torts committed by him in the course of the administration of the trust, if the liability was incurred in the proper administration of the trust and the trustee was not personally at fault in incurring the liability, he is entitled to indemnity out of the trust estate." Restatement, Trusts, sec. 247, comment a. As to whether a trustee is personally liable for the amount of a judgment in excess of the amount that the trust estate is able to pay raises another question. We are constrained to the view that, if the liability arises from the mere fact that the fee title to the trust property is in the trustee, the liability of the trustee to third persons is limited to the extent to which the trust estate is sufficient to indemnify him where he is without fault and where he is not responsible for the insufficiency of the estate to make indemnity. See Restatement, Trusts, sec. 265.

The reference to the Restatement, in support of the last sentence quoted above, is to a section dealing with items such as property taxes and assessments.

JOHNSTON v. LONG
30 Cal. 2d 54, 181 P.2d 645 (1947)

TRAYNOR, J.

Defendant appeals from a judgment entered in favor of plaintiff for damages for personal injuries sustained by the latter when an overhead door fell on him as he was entering a garage of the C. A. Gray automobile agency in San Diego. The garage was owned and operated by C. A. Gray during his lifetime. At the time of the accident it was operated as part of his estate according to the terms of his will and pursuant to section 572 of the Probate Code by Ralph C. Long and A. J. Verheyen as executors. . . .

Eight months after the accident occurred, the assets of the estate were distributed to J. O. Miller, as trustee, the estate was closed and the executors were discharged. Four months later plaintiff brought this action [against] Long and Verheyen, both as individuals and as executors of the estate of C. A. Gray. . . . Demurrers filed by defendant Long were overruled. A. J. Verheyen, the coexecutor, died before the trial, and the action was dismissed as to him. . . .

The jury returned a verdict for $87,575 "against defendant Ralph C. Long, an individual acting as executor of the estate of C. A. Gray, deceased." . . . Defendant Long appeals. . . .

A basic issue in this case is whether an executor is personally liable for torts committed by employees of a business operated by him pursuant to section 572 of the Probate Code. An executor has always been liable for any torts committed by him in the administration of the estate. Before the 1929 amendment to section 1581 of the Code of Civil Procedure (now Prob. Code, §572), if an executor elected to carry on decedent's business without authorization in the will . . . he did so at his own risk and his liability for anything that occurred in the course of conducting the business was a personal one, with no right of reimbursement from the estate. . . .

Section 572 of the Probate Code provides:

> After notice to all persons interested in an estate, given in such manner as may be directed by the court or judge thereof, the court may authorize the executor or administrator to continue the operation of the decedent's business to such an extent and subject to such restrictions as may seem to the court to be for the best interest of the estate and those interested therein.

Defendant contends that since an executor authorized under this section to operate a decedent's business no longer does so at his own risk, he is not liable for torts committed in the course of business operations when he is free from fault, and that to construe the section otherwise would impose too heavy a burden on executors who must operate businesses. This contention overlooks not only the fact that the executor is not required to operate the business, but must petition the court for permission to do so, but the fact that the rule as to the personal liability of an executor for torts committed during the course of his administration is not confined to cases in which the executor carries on operations that are outside the scope of his authority. Personal liability for torts committed during operations that are otherwise within the proper scope of the executor's authority is not a new burden. There is nothing in section 572 to indicate that any change in the rule as to personal liability was intended. The principal effect of the 1929 amendment was to provide an authorization, should the will fail to provide one, for the executor to carry on the decedent's business.

Defendant also contends that the rule of respondeat superior cannot be applied against an administrator or executor who gains no personal advantage from the operation of a decedent's business. . . .

Under the doctrine of respondeat superior, except where the rule may have been changed by statute, torts committed by employees of a trustee in the course of administration of the trust estate subject the trustee to personal liability. Most cases have recognized that the same rules determine the personal liability of an executor for torts committed in the course of administration.

The rule of personal liability of a trustee or executor for the torts of his agents in the course of administration is now generally qualified by giving the executor or trustee a right to reimbursement against the assets of the estate when he is personally without fault. The Restatement also provides that when the claim against the trustee is uncollectible because his personal assets are insufficient, the plaintiff may reach the trust assets to the extent that the trustee would have had a right of reimbursement. (Rest., Trusts §268; see, also, Scott on Trusts §268; Stone, A Theory of Liability of Trust Estates for the Contracts and Torts of the Trustee, 22 Colum. L. Rev. 527.) A few cases have gone further and allowed the trustee to be sued in his representative capacity in order to avoid circuity of action. None of these authorities, however, holds that the trustee is absolved from personal liability . . . and it is clear that any right of action that the plaintiff has against the estate is purely a derivative one. . . .

It has been contended, however, that the doctrine of respondeat superior should apply directly against the executor in his representative capacity and not subject him to personal liability when he is without fault. Although this precise question has never previously been decided by the California courts, there are good reasons for not departing from the general rule. To hold the estate rather than the executor primarily liable for the torts of the agents of the estate, it would be necessary to apply the rules governing the liabilities of a corporate officer and to abandon those governing a trustee, which have heretofore been held applicable to executors. It is clear that an officer of a corporation is not liable under the doctrine of respondeat superior for the torts of corporate employees except where the officer is at fault. The liability falls upon the corporation. Unlike a corporation, however, an estate is not a legal or corporate entity . . . and cannot be a principal. Nor can the executor properly be regarded as the agent of the heirs or distributees, for his authority is derived from the will, and the control that is exercised over him is the control exercised by the probate court. . . . His position is more nearly that of a trustee or of the decedent himself than that of an agent. The employees are thus regarded as his employees and his liability for their actions should be that of any employer. . . .

Moreover, even if it be assumed possible by some procedure to hold the estate directly liable for the torts of employees without any right against the executor personally, where the executor is not personally at fault, there are practical objections to such a procedure. Under the existing system of administration such a procedure would not afford the heirs adequate protection. The only method available for reaching the assets of the estate is an action against the executor in his representative capacity. If the plaintiff could recover directly from the estate in an action against the executor in his representative capacity, the heirs would have no assurance that the question of the personal fault of the executor would be properly tried. It would not be to the interest of either the plaintiff, who would be attempting to recover out of the assets of the estate, or the defendant, whose interest as an individual and as an executor would be in conflict (see Kirchner v. Muller, 280 N.Y. 23, 28 [19 N.E.2d 665]), to show personal fault on the part of the executor. Under the general rule that the executor is personally liable for the torts committed by him or his agents in the course of administration, the plaintiff may recover a judgment against the executor personally and the question of the executor's fault is determined in the probate court, where the interest of the heirs may properly be protected. (See Atkinson on Wills 611.)

It is contended that this application of the respondeat superior doctrine may have harsh results if the executor is not able to recover against the estate and his own property is subject to execution under the judgment. Ordinarily, if the executor is without fault he is protected by his right of reimbursement out of the assets of the estate. Moreover, this application of the doctrine of respondeat superior is no harsher than its usual application to a principal who may gain no profit from the actions of his agent . . . and there is no estate from which he can get reimbursement. The principal justification for the application of the doctrine of respondeat superior in any case is the fact that the employer may spread the risk through insurance and carry the cost thereof as part of his costs of doing business. . . . Under the broad power granted to the probate court under section 572 of the Probate Code, the court may require, as a condition to the right to continue decedent's business, the executor to insure against any tort liability arising out of the conduct of the business, with the premiums for such insurance payable out of the assets of the estate as a proper expense of the business.

In the present case, even if there were either a direct or derivative right against the executor in his representative capacity, defendant Long could not be held liable in that capacity, for he was no longer an executor and there was no estate for him to represent at the time of the suit. The purpose of such a suit is to reach the assets of the estate under the executor's control. Where the executor has been discharged and the estate distributed, the executor is therefore no longer subject to suit in his representative capacity. . . . There would be no purpose in such a suit, for the executor has no assets of the estate under his control.

Similarly, after an executor has been removed, his connection with the estate is severed and a judgment against him does not bind the estate. . . .

In this case, therefore, the plaintiff could proceed directly against the assets of the estate only by suing the distributee. This action was originally instituted against the distributee as well as against the executors, but a demurrer was sustained without leave to amend, and a judgment, which has now become final, was entered in favor of the distributee. Since the distributee is not a party to this appeal, it cannot be decided in this case whether the executor has a right of indemnity against the distributee or to the extent of the assets distributed. (See Rest., Trusts §§249(2) and 279 for the Restatement rules as to the trustee's right of indemnity after distribution and the derivative rights of a tort plaintiff.) The suggestion that a plaintiff should have only a direct right against the distributee after an estate has been closed and the assets distributed is completely unsupported by authority. Moreover, such a rule would impose a considerable burden on the plaintiff in a case in which the assets are widely distributed among many legatees, who may all be residents of other jurisdictions and have no property within this state. There are not, therefore, sufficient reasons for deviating from the general rule of personal liability of the executor for the torts of himself and his agents in the course of administration, and it is clear that in closing the estate an executor does not thereby cut off his personal liability for such torts. . . .

[D]efendant Long, as an executor of the estate authorized to run the business, was liable for the negligence of the employees of the estate in regard to the condition of the door. . . .

The judgment is affirmed.

SCHAUER, J.

I dissent. In liberal construction of section 572 of the Probate Code I would hold that in such a case as this the executor should be liable exclusively in his representative capacity. . . . His actions in the premises are purely in the capacity of executor. The employee whose fault causes the injury to another is not the employee of the executor personally. He is the employee of the executor only in the latter's representative status. The doctrine of respondeat superior, then, should pass the burden on to the real employer, to the executor in his representative capacity but not against him otherwise.

It is asserted that the law which holds that an officer of a corporation is not liable under the doctrine of respondeat superior for the torts of corporate employees except where the officer is at fault, cannot be applied to executors; that the corporate employee's liability can be related directly to the corporation because the latter is an entity and can be sued, but that the estate of a decedent is not an entity and cannot be sued. I do not find this proposition persuasive. If the estate of a decedent is enough of an entity to carry on a business, to contract and pay debts, and realize profits and losses, it should be enough of an entity to be sued. . . . If it is to be recognized that the liability is ultimately and in justice that of the estate, then that liability should be imposed directly on the estate rather than through the round-about method espoused in the opinion. The opinion says, in effect, that the nonnegligent executor is personally liable in legalistic form but not in actual substance because he may ultimately recover from the estate. Such method must inevitably tend to multiply litigation and often may result in leaving a nonnegligent executor with the actuality as well as the form of personal liability.

Section 572 (Prob. Code) in its present substance is before us for initial construction in this case. We should not, on this open question, evolve a construction which seems so certain to produce multiplicity of suits, delays in final settlement of estates, and, at least occasionally, admittedly unjust actual responsibility, all stemming from the unrealistic concept that authorization to an executor to conduct a business in his official capacity does not carry with it authorization to sue or be sued *in the same capacity* in respect to torts committed in doing the very thing authorized. . . .

E. Third Party Liability for Breach of Duty by a Fiduciary

In this portion of the present chapter we are concerned with the extent to which obligations of the fiduciary affect persons who are not themselves parties to the fiduciary relationship. The other side of this problem is the question of when a beneficiary's interests may be impaired by the dealings of the trustee or personal representative with outsiders. We have previously considered the fiduciary's liability to third persons, as well as to the beneficiaries. We now turn to those situations in which a third person, allegedly at least, has interfered with the fiduciary relationship or has dealt with a fiduciary who has exceeded its powers or otherwise violated its duties.

It has been said that a trustee "is in many respects like a buffer between the beneficiaries and the outer world." IV W. Fratcher, Scott on Trusts §279A (4th ed. 1989). In this buffer role the fiduciary is entitled to bring actions against outsiders when required by the interests of the estate. In fact there normally is an obligation to do so. Thus, the burden of enforcing contract and tort claims against third parties falls on the fiduciary. For example, in seeking redress for a tortious interference with trust property, a trustee can sue the wrongdoer without joinder of the beneficiaries. Although in equity, and under modern codes at law, joinder of beneficiaries is permissible, this is not necessary unless a complete determination cannot be had without their being made parties. (This limitation is best illustrated by litigation involving controversies among beneficiaries or between beneficiaries and the trustee.) The beneficiary cannot ordinarily maintain an action against a third party. Exceptions are generally recognized (1) where the beneficiary had a possessory right that was interfered with and (2) where the trustee neglects or declines to act. In the latter case the interests of a beneficiary may be protected by bringing suit in equity against the trustee, joining the third party as codefendant; when required by jurisdictional considerations, beneficiaries have been allowed to bring suit directly against the third party alone. The foregoing generalizations assume situations in which the third person has acted independently of the fiduciary.

In the class of cases of particular concern in this section, the procedural aspects may be quite different from the cases referred to in the preceding paragraph. Here we deal with cases in which the alleged liability of the third party stems from a violation of duty by the fiduciary. In a sense, and quite realistically in certain situations, the "buffer" between the beneficiaries and the outside world has been lost. If the third party in the example in the preceding paragraph had been a participant with the trustee in a breach of trust, the beneficiary would be entitled to bring suit against the outside wrongdoer directly. Here the interference is with the fiduciary relationship. The better view is that an action could also be brought against the third person by the trustee, but a difference of opinion exists on this point, particularly where the trustees had acted in bad faith rather than by inadvertence. Where a cotrustee or a successor trustee is available to seek redress, the right of a beneficiary to bring suit is doubtful.

PROBLEM

17-I.   *X* opened a *fiduciary* bank account in a proper form reading, "The Estate of *A*, by *X* as executor." He subsequently drew checks on that account payable to himself and also to the same bank for deposit to his *personal* account. Thereafter, *X* withdrew funds from his personal account, including withdrawals by checks payable to the bank to discharge his personal liabilities, even after the balance of his personal account had been reduced to a level below the total of deposits transferred from the fiduciary account. When *X* is unable to repay his misappropriations from the estate's account, is the bank liable, and if so for what?

In Bischoff v. Yorkville Bank, 218 N.Y. 106, 111, 112 N.E. 759, 760 (1916), the court, although acknowledging the existence of decisions to the contrary, observed that a bank that is aware that trust funds have been deposited in the fiduciary's individual account "has the right to presume that the fiduciary will apply the funds to their proper purposes under the trust." But the court went on to state:

> Inasmuch as the defendant [bank] knew that the credits to [the fiduciary's personal account were by checks drawn on a fiduciary account,] were of a fiduciary character and were equitably owned by the executor, it had not the right to participate in a diversion of them from the estate or the proper purposes under the will. Its participation in a diversion . . . with actual notice or knowledge . . . [made the bank a] party to it. . . . A bank does not become privy to a misappropriation by merely paying or honoring the checks of a depositor drawn upon his individual account in which there are, in the knowledge of the bank, credits created by deposits of trust funds. The law does not require the bank, under such facts, to assume the hazard of correctly reading in each check the purpose of the drawer or, being ignorant of the purpose, to dishonor the check. The presumption is, and . . . remains until annulled by adequate notice or knowledge, that the depositor would preserve or lawfully apply the trust funds. [But] notice may come from circumstances which reasonably support the sole inference that a misappropriation is intended, as well as directly.
>
> In the present case [as soon as] the defendant knew that [the executor] had appropriated . . . funds for his private benefit [the] presumption that he would not thus violate his duty . . . then ceased to exist. . . . Having such knowledge, [the bank] was under the duty to make reasonable inquiry and endeavor to prevent a diversion. . . . It did nothing of that sort, and . . . [thereafter] became privy to the misapplication.

Where a trustee transfers trust property in breach of trust to a purchaser who takes in good faith and without notice, the transferee takes free of the trust and is not liable to the beneficiaries. This is because the interest of the beneficiary is equitable. The result is not dependent upon principles of estoppel, although decisions are occasionally worded in this fashion. Today, of course, the result is facilitated by recording acts in the case of real property when the trust is not of record and by special legislation dealing with negotiable instruments and corporate stock, but the basic rule exists independently of statute as well. By the better view it applies to nonnegotiable choses in action as well as to chattels held in trust. See 4 A. Corbin, Contracts §900 (1951).

The rule that a bona fide purchaser cuts off outstanding equities of which the purchaser has no notice is well settled. It is to be distinguished from the rule of common law, often carried to harsh extremes, that the legal owner prevails over a bona fide purchaser from a wrongdoer in the absence of grounds for estoppel, assuming that the subject matter is not of a negotiable character. The doctrine that a bona fide purchaser takes free of *equitable* interests is understandable only by recognizing that each of the claimants has roughly equal claim on the conscience of the court and that in such cases courts have traditionally refused to disturb the status quo. As a result the party having the legal title prevails. Thus, when the prior right was merely an equitable one, the innocent purchaser of the legal title prevailed. The equitable claimant is left with only his claim against the wrongdoer and can no longer obtain the property itself. See generally Brown, Personal Property §70 (2d ed. 1955); IV W. Fratcher, Scott on Trusts §284 (4th ed. 1989). The typical trust case is a ready demonstration that this result does not depend on estoppel, for rarely would grounds for estoppel exist with respect to the beneficiary — especially minors and unborn beneficiaries.

Because these results depend on the passage of legal title, the rule does not apply in favor of a bona fide purchaser who has paid consideration but has not yet received the legal title. IV W. Fratcher, Scott on Trusts §310 (4th ed. 1989). This limitation on the success of the bona fide purchaser does not apply where there are grounds for estoppel or where the purchaser can claim the protection of a recording act.

The result of the rules stated above is that the main area of difficulty is in determining whether a particular purchaser from a trustee satisfies the requirements of a bona fide purchaser. Certain aspects of this issue are peculiar to situations involving dealings with fiduciaries who hold legal title. Beyond the initial question of whether the purchaser had notice of the *existence* of a trust, for example, there is the further issue of whether, assuming such notice, there was notice of the *breach* of trust.

PROBLEM

17-J.   Your client, *C*, has entered into a contract to purchase Blackacre from *T*. A search of the record reveals that *T* holds title to Blackacre in the name of "*T* as trustee." At this point, how would you advise *C* to proceed, assuming that she wishes to go through with her purchase?

If *C* had completed this transaction before consulting you and the beneficiaries later sought to set aside the deed to her from *T,* who was not authorized to sell Blackacre, what would *C*'s rights be? Would she be charged with whatever knowledge a reasonable inquiry would have disclosed? What would constitute a reasonable inquiry?

Suppose that you are still advising *C* and that she has not yet accepted *T*'s deed or paid the purchase price, and suppose that on examination you find the trust instrument entirely silent on the question of whether *T* has power to sell Blackacre. How would you advise *C* to proceed now? For purposes of this and other questions in this problem, consider the materials that follow and also consider, as you subsequently begin your study of Chapter 18, whether the trustee has an implied power to sell Blackacre.

FIRST NATIONAL BANK v. NATIONAL BROADWAY BANK
156 N.Y. 459, 51 N.E. 398 (1898)

[Action to compel National Broadway Bank to transfer certain shares of its stock to the plaintiff, which had made a loan to Philo Hotchkiss by discounting the note of Hotchkiss & Co. The securities in question, standing in Hotchkiss's name as trustee, were pledged as part of the collateral for this note. Hotchkiss was at the time serving as trustee under a trust created by W. H. Imlay for his daughter Georgiana (Hotchkiss's wife) and her issue. At the time of the loan the plaintiff also received a writing signed by Georgiana Hotchkiss authorizing her husband to borrow on "the stock standing in his name as trustee for my benefit, and owned by me." When Hotchkiss defaulted on the note, the plaintiff purchased the shares at a public auction held pursuant to the terms of the note. When the defendant bank refused to transfer the stock on its books and to issue a new certificate to the plaintiff, this action was instituted, the lower courts holding that the successor trustee to Hotchkiss was entitled to the stock and accrued dividends thereon because the plaintiff had constructive notice that the shares were the subject of a trust and that the pledge was contrary to its terms.]

GRAY, J. . . .

I do not understand the appellant as disputing the general rule, which imposes upon a party dealing with a trustee, in respect of the trust estate in his hands, the duty of inquiry as to the character of the trust, and a consequent responsibility for the property received, if it turns out that a reasonable inquiry would have disclosed that the property had been transferred in violation of the duty or power of the trustee. Nor does the appellant appear to dispute that the presence of the word "trustee" upon the stock certificate was, of itself, notice of the character of the property, and sufficient to put the plaintiff upon inquiry as to Hotchkiss' authority to pledge it. The argument is that [appellant's] . . . duty of inquiry was performed in a way that an ordinarily prudent and careful man would pursue in his own affairs. . . . [E]vidence is lacking to show what inquiry was made, or what the . . . information [might have] disclosed, at the time. The court therefore is more or less remitted to the presumptions which arise from the known facts of the transaction, and which it is bound to entertain in view of the settled rule of law. Any person who receives property knowing that it is the subject of a trust, and that it has been transferred in violation of the duty or power of the trustee, takes it subject to the right, not only of the cestui que trust, but also of the trustee, to reclaim possession of the property. Knowledge of the trustee's violation of the trust conditions will be chargeable to the person dealing with him, if the facts were such as, in reason, to put him upon inquiry, and to require him to make some investigation, as the result of which the true title and authority of the trustee might have been disclosed. He will then be regarded as having constructive notice of the terms of the trust, whence the trustee derives his power to act. . . . In Story, Eq. Jur. §400, it is laid down that "a purchaser is . . . supposed to have knowledge of the instrument under which the party with whom he contracts as executor, or trustee, or appointee derives his power"; and quite lately this court has affirmed that doctrine. Such an inquiry was called for in this case as was reasonably possible to the plaintiff, in order to discover what was the character of the trust impressed upon the property, and if there was a right in the trustee to use it by way of pledge for a loan or an advance of moneys for the benefit of Hotchkiss & Co. The proof shows that the Broadway Bank, whose stock was offered to be pledged, had transferred the title thereto to Hotchkiss as trustee, upon the requirements of an order of the Connecticut court, which appointed him as trustee in succession to a prior trustee. This order referred to "the matter of the Imlay trust, dated January 17, 1857," . . . [which] would, presumably, have disclosed further facts about the trust. . . . Its examination would have shown that the only power which the trustee had to deal with the trust securities was to sell the same, and invest the proceeds thereof in other good bank stocks "in his own name as trustee." It would have shown that Georgiana's interest in them was only that of a life beneficiary. . . .

I see nothing unreasonable in holding the plaintiff to such a rule of diligence as would require the examination of the trust instrument before it undertook to loan moneys upon trust property in behalf or for the benefit of any person. The burden was upon it to prove what inquiry was made, and failing that proof, the presumption should obtain that it was made up to the instrument of trust itself, an inspection of which would show that the trustee could not pledge the trust securities. . . . Doubtless, the circumstances of each case must determine whether the person has acted prudently and cautiously. Whether he was constructively notified in the transaction with the trustee, may depend upon how far those circumstances pointed out the path of inquiry.

On the face of this stock, the plaintiff's attention was called to the fact that it was dealing with a trustee, and inquiry of the Broadway Bank would have produced the order appointing Hotchkiss trustee "in the matter of the Imlay trust, dated January 17, 1857." It then became chargeable with the knowledge of such facts about the trustee's duty and power as would have been revealed by such an inquiry as a prudent regard for the rights of others, if not for its own interest, would, naturally, dictate. That a knowledge of the limitations of the trustee's power of disposition would have, or should have, deterred the plaintiff from advancing moneys to a business concern upon a pledge of the stock, is not to be doubted. That such knowledge was obtainable, if not through the trustee himself, then through other available means, is also clear. . . .

But I do not think we should affirm the judgment below in so far as it denies the plaintiff's claim upon the life interest of Georgiana Hotchkiss in the dividends accumulated and to be declared upon the stock. . . . I think she is estopped by her acts from setting up any claim to the income upon the stock received, and which may be hereafter, during her life, received, by way of dividends, by the trustee. If this were not so, then the court would be aiding her in the perpetration of a fraud upon the plaintiff. . . . The conclusion I reach, therefore, is that this judgment should be modified so that it shall adjudge that the dividends upon the stock in question, accumulated and to be declared, shall be paid to the plaintiff during the lifetime of Georgiana I. Hotchkiss. . . .

In re ESTATE OF DILLON
441 Pa. 206, 272 A.2d 161 (1971)

Roberts, J.

This case involves the question of the disposition of certain funds deposited in a savings account in the Pittsburgh National Bank by a testamentary trustee, who later pledged the savings account as collateral for his personal obligation to the Bank. The Bank asserts that a Totten trust was created between it and the depositor-trustee and that it did not know the funds were assets of a testamentary trust. The beneficiary claims the funds under the trust instrument. The Bank refused to turn over the funds to the beneficiary, holding them as a set-off for the trustee's personal obligation. In a well considered opinion the orphans' court ordered the Bank to release the money, and the Bank has appealed. We affirm. . . .

The Bank asserts it had no knowledge that the funds in the savings account were testamentary trust assets. However, the orphans' court found that the record clearly established that the Tax Department of the Bank knew in 1963 that J. Pierre Vogel was a testamentary trustee . . . and the ledgers of the Bank Real Estate Department indicate that that department had knowledge as early as 1961. [The borrowing and the pledge in question occurred in 1964.] The orphan's court was clearly correct in its determination. . . .

The Bank further contends that a tentative or "Totten" trust was created. However, it is settled, as noted by the orphans' court that a tentative trust is created only when one person deposits his *own* money, in his own name as trustee for another in a savings bank. See, e.g., Brose Estate, 416 Pa. 386, 206 A.2d 301 (1965). The orphans' court was entirely correct when it stated:

> . . . Since this was not a tentative trust it would fall into the same category with other trusts. The form of the account would give notice that the account was trust property and any person dealing with the trustee with reference to it was bound to inquire into the nature of the trust and the powers of the trustee. If the bank had made inquiry of [the beneficiary] it would have learned that J. Pierre Vogel did not own the funds in the now disputed savings account and that he had no right to pledge the funds in this account for his individual debt.

Accordingly, the decree . . . is affirmed. . . .

See also Kurowski v. Burch, 8 Ill. App. 3d 716, 719-720, 290 N.E.2d 401, 404-405 (1972):

> [A]lthough it be assumed that the purchasers knew they were dealing with trustees and receiving a conveyance of trust property, there is absent from the second amended complaint any allegation that the purchasers knew or should have known that they were dealing with trustees who were committing a breach of trust in making the conveyance of the property in question. In order to declare the purchasers trustees and impress a trust upon the property it must appear that they either knew or should have known that the trustees with whom they were dealing were committing a breach of trust in conveying the property to them. The purchasers would have notice that a breach of trust was taking place if they had actual knowledge of the breach or if they possessed knowledge of facts that would lead a reasonably intelligent and diligent person to make further inquiry as to whether the trustees were committing a breach of trust. . . . [A] trustee is presumed to act rightfully, and in the absence of facts putting purchasers on inquiry they are not bound to presume wrongful conduct on his part.

ADLER v. MANOR HEALTHCARE CORP.
7 Cal. App. 4th 1110, 9 Cal. Rptr. 2d 732 (1992)

CHIN, Associate Justice. . . .

Rossmoor is a privately owned and operated retirement community. . . . Appellants allege that they are shareholders in the Golden Rain Foundation . . . and beneficiaries under a trust Golden Rain administers. As trustee, Golden Rain holds titles to and maintains all commonly owned property for the benefit of Rossmoor residents and its shareholders.

In September 1987, UDC . . . , the Rossmoor developer, agreed to sell Manor [Healthcare Corp.] an unimproved parcel of land (Lot 4) in Rossmoor. Because Rossmoor property surrounded Lot 4, Manor [also] needed an easement of access. . . .

In October 1987, . . . First American [Title and Guaranty Co.] prepared and recorded a grant deed that conveyed an access easement from Golden Rain to UDC. A grant deed conveying Lot 4 from UDC to Manor incorporates the easement. In a letter to First American with supporting documents, Golden Rain confirmed its authority to transfer the easement. On November 16, 1987, escrow closed, and First American recorded UDC's grant deed of Lot 4 and the access easement to Manor. Appellant sued Golden Rain, UDC, Manor, and First American, alleging that Golden Rain's transfer of the easement to UDC violated the trust. . . . The complaint alleged that First American, as title insurer, escrow holder, and agent for Manor, had either actual, constructive, or inquiry notice . . . that Golden Rain exceeded its powers as trustee [and that this knowledge] was also imputed to Manor. . . .

This case turns on the applicability of [Prob. C. §18100], which states: "with respect to a third person dealing with a trustee or assisting a trustee in the conduct of a transaction, if the third person acts in good faith and for a valuable consideration and without actual knowledge that the trustee is exceeding the trustee's powers or improperly exercising them: (a) The third person is not bound to inquire whether the trustee has power to act or is properly exercising a power and may assume without inquiry the existence of a trust power and its proper exercise. (b) The third person is fully protected in dealing with or assisting the trustee just as if the trustee has and is properly exercising the power the trustee purports to exercise."

Section 18100 replaces former Civil Code section 2243, which the courts consistently interpreted as creating a duty of inquiry making constructive notice as binding on third-party purchasers as actual notice. . . . The new statute is drawn from section 7 of the Uniform Trustees' Powers Act of 1964. (See Cal. Law Review Com. comment, 54A West's Ann. Prob. Code (1991 ed.) foll. §18100, p. 241.)

In recommending replacement of former Civil Code section 2243 with section 18100, the Law Revision Commission expressly intended to give greater protection to the rights of a third-party purchaser of trust property. The commission's report states: "The proposed law protects a third person who acts in good faith and for a valuable consideration unless the third person has *actual knowledge* that the trustee is improperly exercising powers under the trust. *Constructive knowledge or inquiry notice of the trustee's powers is not sufficient to deprive a good faith transferee of protection.* This rule is generally consistent with changes that have been made in the law concerning negotiable instruments, securities, and bank accounts. The proposed law also continues the existing provisions that protect third persons who rely on documents relating to real property recorded with the county recorder." . . .

Thus, section 18100 was specifically adopted to change the prior law, which placed third-party purchasers of trust property on constructive or inquiry notice of possible breaches of trust. The new law gives such purchasers protected bonafide status except where they have *actual knowledge* of a breach. . . .

In this case, the Golden Rain trust agreement was recorded in the official records of Contra Costa County in April 1964. . . . On the other hand, under the clear and express provisions of section 18100 third parties dealing with Golden Rain in good faith and without *actual knowledge* that it was (allegedly) exceeding or improperly exercising its trust powers were not bound to inquire into those powers, and could assume without inquiry that Golden Rain had authority to act as it did.

. . . In our opinion, the record in this case supports the trial court's conclusion [no evidence to the contrary having been offered] that Manor had no actual knowledge of any of Golden Rain's alleged breaches of its trust agreement. Therefore, Manor was not bound to inquire further into the extent or exercise of Golden Rain's powers and could rely absolutely on Golden Rain's express representation of its authority to enter into the transaction at issue. . . .

UNIFORM COMMERCIAL CODE

§3-304. *Notice to Purchaser.* . . .

(2) The purchaser has notice of a claim against the instrument when he has knowledge that a fiduciary has negotiated the instrument in payment of or as security for his own debt or in any transaction for his own benefit or otherwise in breach of duty. . . .

(4) Knowledge of the following facts does not give the purchaser notice of a defense or claim: . . . (e) that a person negotiating the instrument is or was a fiduciary. . . .

§8-304. *Notice to Purchaser of Adverse Claims.* . . .

(2) The fact that the purchaser (including a broker for the seller or buyer) has notice that the security is held for a third person or is registered in the name of or endorsed by a fiduciary does not create a duty of inquiry into the rightfulness of the transfer or constitute notice of adverse claims. If, however, the purchaser (excluding an intermediary bank) has knowledge that the proceeds are being used or that the transaction is for the individual benefit of the fiduciary or otherwise in breach of duty, the purchaser is charged with notice of adverse claims.

§8-403. *Limited Duty of Inquiry.*

(1) An issuer to whom a security is presented for registration is under a duty to inquire into adverse claims if: (a) a written notification of an adverse claim is received at a time and in a manner which affords the issuer a reasonable opportunity to act on it prior to the issuance of a new, re-issued or re-registered security and the notification identifies the claimant, the registered owner and the issue of which the security is a part and provides an address or communications directed to the claimant; or (b) the issuer is charged with notice of an adverse claim from a controlling instrument which it has elected to require under subsection (4) of Section 8-402.

(2) [Omitted is the paragraph specifying how the issuer may discharge a duty of inquiry.]

(3) Unless an issuer is charged with notice of an adverse claim from a controlling instrument which it has elected to require under subsection (4) of Section 8-402 or receives notification of an adverse claim under subsection (1) of this section, where a security presented for registration is endorsed by the appropriate person or persons the issuer is under no duty to inquire into adverse claims. [Omitted is the remaining portion of the paragraph, the provisions of which are comparable to the terms of the acts set out immediately below.]

UNIFORM SIMPLIFICATION OF FIDUCIARY SECURITY TRANSFERS ACT

§2. *Registration in the Name of a Fiduciary.* A corporation or transfer agent registering a security in the name of a person who is a fiduciary or who is described as a fiduciary is not bound to inquire into the existence, extent, or correct description of the fiduciary relationship. . . .

§3. *Assignment by a Fiduciary.* Except as otherwise provided in this act, a corporation or transfer agent making a transfer of a security pursuant to an assignment by a fiduciary: (a) may assume without inquiry that the assignment, even though to the fiduciary himself or to his nominee, is within his authority and capacity and is not in breach of his fiduciary duties; (b) may assume without inquiry that the fiduciary has complied with any controlling instrument and with the law of the jurisdiction governing the fiduciary relationship, including any law requiring the fiduciary to obtain court approval of the transfer; and (c) is not charged with notice of and is not bound to obtain or examine any court record or any recorded or unrecorded document relating to the fiduciary relationship or the assignment, even though the record or document is in its possession.

UNIFORM PROBATE CODE

§3-714. *Persons Dealing with Personal Representative; Protection.* A person who in good faith either assists a personal representative or deals with him for value is protected as if the personal representative properly exercised his power. The fact that a person knowingly deals with a personal representative does not alone require the person to inquire into the existence of a power or the propriety of its exercise. . . . A person is not bound to see to the proper application of estate assets paid or delivered to a personal representative. . . . The protection here expressed is not by substitution for that provided by comparable provisions of the laws relating to commercial transactions and the laws simplifying transfers of securities by fiduciaries.

18

Management Functions

In order that the administration of a decedent's estate or trust can be carried out, the fiduciary must have the power to act. The powers of a fiduciary may be expressed or implied. The practice today is to extend the powers of fiduciaries by broad grants of powers in the controlling document or by statutory presumptions in favor of certain powers. A power that is not granted by the instrument or by statute may be implied so that the purposes of the administration may be carried out.

In this chapter we consider first whether certain powers need be expressed or may be implied. Then we explore the significant function of investment and problems associated with the fiduciary's investment power. Throughout, the student should consider how particular matters might be dealt with in the planning and drafting of wills and trust instruments.

A. Powers of Fiduciaries

1. General Managerial Powers

RESTATEMENT (SECOND) OF TRUSTS

§186. *Extent of Trustee's Powers.*[1] Except as stated in §§165-168 [dealing with impossibility, illegality, and change of circumstances], the trustee can properly exercise such powers and only such powers as

(a) are conferred upon him in specific words by the terms of the trust, or

(b) are necessary or appropriate to carry out the purposes of the trust and are not forbidden by the terms of the trust.

---

1. The case law of some states may be less liberal in finding implied powers and in construing express powers than is suggested by the Restatement section above and the comments thereto. See generally Fratcher, Trustees' Powers Legislation, 37 N.Y.U. L. Rev. 627 (1962).

SMITH v. MOONEY
5 N.J. Misc. 1087, 139 A. 513 (1927)

BACKES, V.C.

The surviving executor and trustee under the last will and testament of Mary Ann Smith, deceased, entered into a written contract with the defendant to sell him a piece of land belonging to the estate. The bill is filed to compel the defendant to perform his contract, and he is willing to do so, but contends that the complainant cannot give him a marketable title, asserting that the executor has not the power to sell. That depends upon the true construction of the will. The testatrix, after some specific bequests and devises, . . . devised and bequeathed all the rest, residue and remainder of her property to her executors upon trust . . . the income . . . to be paid to the children and one Catherine Burke in equal shares. . . . Upon the death of all the children the will directs that the principal of the estate, the accumulations of income, if any, be divided among the issue of the testatrix's six sons and Catherine Burke. . . .

The testatrix died possessed of considerable personal property and many houses and vacant lots of land in and about Newark, and if distribution of the estate were made at this time some of the pro rata shares would be as low as a one-seventy-second of the whole.

There are, it is true, no words expressly authorizing the sale of the real estate, but full effect could not be given to the testatrix's direction to *divide* the estate — the real and personal property as a unit — at the time fixed by her for its *distribution* unless there was a conversion of the realty. The testatrix obviously contemplated that the division should be in money-shares, and to that end that the real estate should be sold. The power of sale in the trustee is clearly implied. . . .

The complainant can unquestionably convey a marketable title and a decree that the contract be enforced will be advised.

In the case of personal property, particularly securities held as an investment, a trustee normally has an implied power of sale. This is true even though the property in question is proper as a trust investment. Courts have traditionally been less willing, however, to imply a power to sell land where a sale is not necessitated by the purposes of the trust, although the modern tendency is to do away with the assumption that land is to be retained. The inference of the existence or nonexistence of a power of sale may be strengthened or weakened by the circumstances. For example, any of the following may be relevant in determining whether a trustee has a power of sale: the propriety of particular property as a trust investment; whether the property is productive or unproductive; whether the instrument suggests that the property is to be distributed in specie to the remaindermen; the uses to which the property may be devoted in the interests of the life beneficiary; and the general purposes of the trust. See generally III W. Fratcher, Scott on Trusts §190.3 (4th ed. 1988).

The power of a personal representative to sell property of a decedent's estate, as well as the manner of its exercise, is frequently determined by statute. Often, approval by a court is required. The powers and procedures may be different as between real and personal property, although the trend is to abolish this distinction in administration of estates.

In general, the contrasting functions of trustees and personal representatives suggest significant differences with regard to the powers likely to be implied in these two instances of fiduciary administration. Nevertheless, the tendency is to set out a broad statutory set of powers for executors and administrators and to confer on them powers comparable to those typically granted to trustees. For example, §3-715 of the Uniform Probate Code is patterned after the Uniform Trustees' Powers Act.

In re STRASS' TRUST ESTATE
11 Wis. 2d 410, 105 N.W.2d 553 (1960)

[On petition of the testamentary trustee, an order was entered authorizing him to sell certain land (appraised at $15,000) at private sale. Several months thereafter, he accepted an offer of $16,000 for the property subject to the approval of the court. Then the trustee petitioned the court setting forth the agreement, reporting a subsequent offer of $17,000, and asking the court to vacate his acceptance of the prior agreement of sale, although reciting that $16,000 was not an unfair price. The county court declined to confirm the sale and proceeded to auction the property from the bench. The person who had made the second offer eventually bid $18,300, and the court ordered the trustee to accept this bid and confirmed the sale.]

BROWN, J. . . .

[T]he rule which controls the case above [is] as follows:

. . . that an offer or agreement to advance a bid upon a resale which is made before the sale is confirmed, not accompanied by a showing of mistake, misapprehension or inadvertence, is insufficient to sustain an order setting aside the sale. . . .

The contract . . . was expressly subject to the approval of the court. . . . We fail to recognize that there is, or should be, a different treatment accorded a court confirmation required by statute and one required by contract. A case very like the present one in its essential facts is Evans v. Hunnold, 1946, 393 Ill. 195, 65 N.E.2d 373, 376, stating:

. . . In this case the only reason appellee seeks disapproval of the sale is because more money was offered. The fact that events subsequent to a sale in good faith result in trust estate being deprived of a substantial sum of money, does not outweigh the injustice which a denial of confirmation would work upon appellant.

There is a public policy in having stability of contracts which are made with trustees in good faith and for adequate consideration. Unless there is stability prospective purchasers cannot be expected to make good offers if their offers can be set aside after they have been accepted in favor of later ones.

In the transaction [before the court] there is no claim that there was any mistake, misapprehension or inadvertence, no suspicion of fraud, and the trustee acknowledged that $16,000 was not disproportionate to the value of the property. . . . The facts are insufficient to sustain an order setting aside the sale [or refusing] to confirm it.

Order reversed. . . .

HALLOWS, J. (dissenting).

The reasons [for the rule quoted in the majority opinion] apply only to public judicial sales where all persons interested have an equal chance to bid on the property in competition with other interested bidders. The finality of such sales as to price insures some stability to such sales and the highest bid being made. Such reasoning does not apply to private sales by fiduciaries authorized by the court. In such sales the trustee is at a disadvantage because of a lack of prospective purchasers. . . . This is especially true when a private sale by a fiduciary is ordered by a court expressly subject to its approval. In such cases the court should have the power to disapprove the sale because of the inadequacy of price whether such price exceeds the appraised value or not, if at that time a better offer of purchase exists. . . .

ALLARD v. PACIFIC NATIONAL BANK
99 Wash. 2d 394, 663 P.2d 104 (1983)

DOLLIVER, J.

Plaintiffs Freeman Allard and Evelyn Orkney are [life]beneficiaries of trusts established by their parents, J. T. and Georgiana Stone. Defendant Pacific National Bank (Pacific Bank) is the trustee of the Stone trusts. Plaintiffs appeal a King County Superior Court decision dismissing their action against Pacific Bank for breach of its fiduciary duties as trustee of the Stone trusts. . . .

We conclude, however, that Pacific Bank breached its fiduciary duties regarding management of the Stone trusts. We also find the Superior Court incorrectly awarded attorney fees and costs to Pacific Bank. . . .

In 1978 the sole asset of the Stone trusts was a fee interest in a quarter block located on the northwest corner of Third Avenue and Columbia Street in downtown Seattle. The trust provisions of the wills gave Pacific

Bank "full power to . . . manage, improve, sell, lease, mortgage, pledge, encumber, and exchange the whole or any part of the assets of [the] trust estate" and required Pacific Bank to "exercise the judgment and care under the circumstances then prevailing, which prudent men exercise in the management of their own affairs, not in regard to speculation but in regard to the permanent disposition of their funds, considering the probable income as well as the probable safety of their capital."

The Third and Columbia property was subject to a 99-year lease, entered into by the Stones in 1952 with Seattle-First National Bank (Seafirst Bank). The lease contained no rental escalation provision and the rental rate was to remain the same for the entire 99-year term of the lease. The right of first refusal to purchase the lessor's interest in the property was given to the lessee. . . .

In June 1977 Seafirst Bank assigned its leasehold interest in the Third and Columbia property to the City Credit Union of Seattle (Credit Union). Eight months later, on February 14, 1978, Credit Union offered to purchase the property from Pacific Bank for $139,900. On April 25, 1978, Pacific Bank informed Credit Union it was interested in selling the property, but demanded at least $200,000. In early June 1978, Credit Union offered $200,000 for the Third and Columbia property. Pacific Bank accepted Credit Union's offer, and deeded the property to Credit Union on August 17, 1978. On September 26, 1978, Pacific Bank informed Freeman Allard and Evelyn Orkney of the sale to Credit Union.

On May 1, 1979, plaintiffs commenced the present action against Pacific Bank for breach of its fiduciary duties. . . .

At the culmination of the trial, the court entered judgment dismissing plaintiffs' action against Pacific Bank. It determined Pacific Bank acted in good faith and in conformance with its duties under the Stone trust instruments. The court concluded Pacific Bank neither had a duty to inform the trust beneficiaries prior to sale of the Third and Columbia property nor a duty to obtain an independent appraisal of the property or to place the property on the open market. Finally, the trial court awarded Pacific Bank $51,507.07 attorney fees and costs from the income and principal of the Stone trusts. From this judgment plaintiffs bring appeal. . . .

The beneficiaries of the Stone trusts essentially allege Pacific Bank improperly depleted the trust assets by selling the Third and Columbia property for less than its fair market value. The trial court properly determined plaintiffs' action against Pacific Bank was equitable in nature. The denial of plaintiffs' demand for a jury trial was proper. None of the beneficiaries have a present right to receive distribution of the trust corpus. Their only remedy for depletion of the trust corpus is restoration of the value of the corpus by the trustee, often referred to as a "surcharge" on the trustee. . . .

II

We now consider the crux of the case before us. Defendant contends it had full authority under the trust instrument to exercise its own judgment and impartial discretion in deciding how to invest the trust assets and a duty to use reasonable care and skill to make the trust property productive. . . . It further contends the sale of the property was conducted in good faith and with honest judgment. . . . Plaintiffs assert this discretion was limited by its fiduciary duties and that defendant in its management of the trusts breached its fiduciary duty.

Plaintiffs' argument regarding Pacific Bank's alleged breach of its fiduciary duties is twofold. First, Pacific Bank had a duty to inform them of the sale of the Third and Columbia property. Second, Pacific Bank breached its fiduciary duties by failing either to obtain an independent appraisal of the Third and Columbia property or to place the property on the open market prior to selling it to Seattle Credit Union. We agree with plaintiffs' position in both instances and hold defendant breached its fiduciary duty in its management of the trusts.

A

Initially, plaintiffs and amicus curiae the Attorney General of the State of Washington contend Pacific Bank should be held to a higher standard of care than the ordinary, prudent investor standard provided in RCW 30.24.020. Plaintiffs and amicus curiae argue the ordinary, prudent investor standard is inappropriate where the trustee represents that it has greater skill than that of a nonprofessional trustee. They fail to mention, however, the terms of the Stone trust agreements which specifically adopt the prudent investor standard of care provided in RCW 30.24.020. . . .

Significantly, the statute recognizes the standard of care required of a trustee is "subject to any express provisions or limitations contained in any particular trust instrument." . . . Although in some future case we may be called upon to determine if a corporate professional trustee should be held to a higher standard, because of the language in the trust instruments, this issue need not be decided here. Cf. Restatement (Second) of Trusts §227, comment *d* (1959).

B

The Stone trusts gave Pacific Bank "full power to . . . manage, improve, sell, lease, mortgage, pledge, encumber, and exchange the whole or any part of the assets of [the] trust estate." Under such an agreement, the trustee is not required to secure the consent of trust beneficiaries before selling trust assets. The trustee owes to the beneficiaries, however, the highest degree of good faith, care, loyalty, and integrity.

Pacific Bank claims it was obligated to sell the property to Credit Union since Credit Union, as assignee of the lease agreement with Sea-first Bank, had a right of first refusal to purchase the property. Since it did not need to obtain the consent of the beneficiaries before selling trust assets, Pacific Bank argues it also was not required to inform the beneficiaries of the sale. We disagree. The beneficiaries could have offered to purchase the property at a higher price than the offer by Credit Union, thereby forcing Credit Union to pay a higher price to exercise its right of first refusal as assignee of the lease agreement. Furthermore, letters from the beneficiaries to Pacific Bank indicated their desire to retain the Third and Columbia property. While the beneficiaries could not have prevented Pacific Bank from selling the property, they presumably could have outbid Credit Union for the property. This opportunity should have been afforded to them.

On a previous occasion, we ruled the trustee's fiduciary duty includes the responsibility to inform the beneficiaries fully of all facts which would aid them in protecting their interests. . . .

The duty to provide information is often performed by corporate trustees by rendering periodic statements to the beneficiaries, usually in the form of copies of the ledger sheets concerning the trust. G. Bogert, Trusts §141 (5th ed. 1973). For example, such condensed explanations of recent transactions may be mailed to the beneficiaries annually, semi-annually, or quarterly. G. Bogert, Trusts, supra. Ordinarily, periodic statements are sufficient to satisfy a trustee's duty to beneficiaries of transactions affecting the trust property. The trust provisions here, for example, provide the trustee "shall furnish on or before February 15 of each year to each person described in Section 1 of Article IV who is then a beneficiary . . . a statement showing how the respective trust assets are invested and all transactions relating thereto for the proceeding calendar year."

The trustee must inform beneficiaries, however, of all material facts in connection with a nonroutine transaction which significantly affects the trust estate and the interests of the beneficiaries prior to the transaction taking place. The duty to inform is particularly required in this case where the only asset of the trusts was the property on the corner of Third and Columbia. Under the circumstances found in this case failure to inform was an egregious breach of fiduciary duty and defies the course of conduct any reasonable person would take, much less a prudent investor.

C

We also conclude Pacific Bank breached its fiduciary duties regarding management of the Stone trusts by failing to obtain the best possible price for the Third and Columbia property. Pacific Bank made no attempt to obtain a more favorable price for the property from Credit Union by, for example, negotiating to cancel the restrictive provisions in the lease originally negotiated with Seafirst Bank. Cf. Hatcher v. United States Natl. Bank, 56 Or. App. 643, 643 P.2d 359 (1982) (trustee had not fulfilled its fiduciary duties by merely examining offer to purchase and altering the terms slightly). The bank neither offered the property for sale on the open market, nor did it obtain an independent, outside appraisal of the Third and Columbia property to determine its fair market value.

Washington courts have not yet considered the nature of a trustee's duty of care regarding the sale of trust assets. Other courts, however, generally require that a trustee when selling trust assets try to obtain the maximum price for the asset. The Oregon Court of Appeals required a trustee to determine the fair market value of trust property prior to selling the property by obtaining an appraisal or by "testing the market" to determine what a willing buyer would pay. Hatcher v. United States Natl. Bank, 56 Or. App. at 652, 643 P.2d 359. Some courts specifically require trustees to obtain an independent appraisal of the property. See, e.g., Belcher v. Birmingham Trust Natl. Bank, 348 F. Supp. 61 (N.D. Ala. 1968); Webb & Knapp, Inc. v. Hanover Bank, 214 Md. 230, 133 A.2d 450 (1957). Other courts merely require that a trustee determine fair market value by placing the property on the open market. See, e.g., . . . State v. Hartman, 54 Wis. 2d 47, 194 N.W.2d 653 (1972).

We agree with the Oregon Court of Appeals in *Hatcher* that a trustee may determine the best possible price for trust property either by obtaining an independent appraisal of the property or by "testing the market" to determine what a willing buyer would pay. The record discloses none of these actions were taken by the defendant. By its failure to obtain the best possible price for the Third and Columbia property, defendant breached its fiduciary duty as the prudent manager of the trusts. . . .

III

Finally, we consider whether the trial court improperly awarded attorney fees to Pacific Bank. A trial court may allow and properly charge attorney fees to a trust estate for litigation that is necessary to the administration of the trust. The award of attorney fees against the trust estate is vested in the discretion of the trial court. A trial court's discretion to award attorney fees, however, is not absolute. The court must determine the litigation is indispensable to the proper administration of the trust; the issues presented are neither immaterial nor trifling; the conduct of the parties or counsel is not vexatious or litigious; and that there has been no unnecessary delay or expense. Furthermore, the trial court must consider the result of the litigation. G. Bogert, Trusts and Trustees §871 (2d rev. ed. 1982).

The court's underlying consideration must be whether the litigation and the participation of the party seeking attorney fees caused a benefit to the trust. A trustee who unsuccessfully defends against charges of breach of fiduciary duties obviously has not caused a benefit to the trust. Therefore, a trial court abuses its discretion when it awards attorney fees to a trustee for litigation caused by the trustee's misconduct.

Here the trial court awarded attorney fees to Pacific Bank based on its decision Pacific Bank properly exercised its discretion in the management of the Stone trusts. Since we rule here that regardless of the discretion of the trustee it breached its fiduciary duties, the award of attorney fees was based on untenable grounds. We hold this was an abuse of discretion. . . . A trustee may be awarded attorney fees and costs for litigation alleging breach of the trust agreement only if the trustee successfully defends against the action. . . .

We also hold that since defendant breached its fiduciary duty plaintiffs should be granted their request to recover all attorney fees expended at both the trial and on appeal on behalf of the plaintiffs and all minor beneficiaries and unknown beneficiaries. . . . Where litigation is necessitated by the inexcusable conduct of the trustee, . . . the trustee individually must pay those expenses. . . .

The case is remanded for a determination of the damages caused to plaintiffs by defendant's breach of its fiduciary duties as trustee of the Stone trusts and a determination of the amount of attorney fees to be awarded plaintiffs from the trustee individually.

ALLARD v. FIRST INTERSTATE BANK OF WASHINGTON
112 Wash. 2d 145, 768 P.2d 998 (1989)

CALLOW, C.J.

First Interstate Bank (Bank) challenges the trial court's award of attorneys' fees to plaintiffs. . . .

On remand [following the 1983 *Allard* decision, supra], the trial court awarded approximately $2.5 million in damages to the plaintiffs. The court also awarded approximately $1 million in attorneys' fees. . . .

Both the Bank and the Court of Appeals have framed the issues in terms of the propriety of the trial court's reliance on the contingent fee agreement and the award of hourly fees in addition to those awarded under the agreement. However, the issue should be framed as to whether the trial court's award of attorneys' fees, as a whole, was reasonable. . . .

In this case, the trial court considered three primary factors in determining the amount of attorneys' fees to be awarded: 1) RPC 1.5(a); 2) the contingent fee agreement between plaintiffs and their attorney; and 3) the court's belief that the plaintiffs should be made whole. . . .

The trial court acted reasonably when it considered the factors set forth in RPC 1.5(a) in determining the amount of attorneys' fees to be awarded. These factors include:

(1) The time and labor required, the novelty and difficulty of the questions involved, and the skill requisite to perform the legal service properly;
(2) The likelihood, if apparent to the client, that the acceptance of the particular employment will preclude other employment by the lawyer;
(3) The fee customarily charged in the locality for similar legal services;
(4) The amount involved and the results obtained;
(5) The time limitations imposed by the client or by the circumstances;
(6) The nature and length of the professional relationship with the client;
(7) The experience, reputation, and ability of the lawyer or lawyers performing the services; and
(8) Whether the fee is fixed or contingent.

. . . Furthermore, the trial court also acted reasonably when it considered the contingent fee agreement between plaintiffs and their attorney in making its award. . . .

. . . [It] did not apply the contingent fee agreement mechanically to determine the amount of attorneys' fees to be awarded to the plaintiffs. The court also considered the factors set forth in RPC 1.5(a) and its intent to make the plaintiffs whole. Because the court considered several factors in making its award, we cannot say that its award of $596,646 according to the contingent fee agreement constituted an abuse of discretion. . . .

The Bank also contends that the trial court abused its discretion by awarding $80,000 in hourly fees for the services of Mr. Wiggins in addition to the $596,646 awarded under the contingent fee agreement. The Bank asserts that had Mr. Luvera chosen to associate someone from the Mullavey firm, the fees awarded to that attorney would have been covered by the contingent fee agreement. Instead, by going outside the firm, the Bank has been required to pay the entire 25 percent contingent fee plus an additional $80,000 to Mr. Wiggins.

The contingent fee agreement provided that outside counsel might be required, and that such counsel would be paid on an hourly basis in addition to payment of the contingent fee. . . .

. . . [T]here was evidence that Mr. Wiggins' role was limited to research, briefing, and motions practice during much of the litigation, and his role expanded only when the Bank noted last-minute depositions of the plaintiffs' experts and made last-minute disclosures of its own

expert witnesses. The plaintiffs should not have to bear the burden of
the Bank's late-hour tactics, especially in light of the purpose of making
plaintiffs whole. . . .

Finally, Mr. Wiggins and the guardian ad litem have requested [and
received] attorneys' fees for services rendered during this appeal. . . .

. . . We conclude that [the fees awarded in this litigation] are not
unreasonable and did not constitute an abuse of discretion. We uphold
the award of attorneys' fees. . . .

DORE, J. (dissenting).

. . . On remand, the trial court based its award of attorney fees on an
attorney fee agreement that permits counsel to collect both a contingent
fee and an hourly fee for the same result. I believe such a fee agreement
is unreasonable and contrary to public policy. Attorney fees based upon
such an agreement amount to an unjustifiable penalty. I would disallow
Wiggins' fees in the amount of $80,000. . . .

PROBLEM

18-A. T is the trustee of an estate consisting of about $190,000
worth of securities and one parcel of land. The will expressly empowers
T, among other things, "to sell the land or to retain it as an investment."
Having carefully weighed the alternatives available to her, T believes she
should accept an offer she has received from B, who wishes to buy the
land for a price of $150,000. One-third of this price is to be paid in cash,
and the remaining $100,000 is to be in the form of a note, bearing an
appropriate rate of interest, payable in installments over a fifteen-year
period and secured by a first mortgage on the land. T wishes to know
whether she can accept this offer. How would you advise her?

DURKIN v. CONNELLY
84 N.J. Eq. 66, 92 A. 906 (Ch. 1915)

[By the testator's will, the executrix was given "full power and authority to sell and convey . . . real estate . . . and to invest the proceeds . . . at
her discretion." The executrix contracted to sell land of the estate for
$45,000, to be paid $5,000 in cash, $16,000 by proceeds of a bank loan
secured by a first mortgage, and $24,000 by note secured by a second
mortgage to the executrix. The executrix refused to perform, alleging
lack of power, and the purchaser filed a bill for specific performance.]

LEAMING, V.C.

It is obvious that this court cannot by its decree require the specific
performance of a contract of sale which has been made by a trustee if by
the terms of the trust the trustee had no power to do what he contracted
to do; in such circumstances a trustee will not be compelled to commit

a breach of his trust. Repetto v. Baylor, 61 N.J. Eq. 501, 506. In Repetto v. Baylor, supra, it is also held that a mere power to sell does not include any power to arrange terms of postponed payment of price, or to accept a mortgage or anything else than money in satisfaction of it. If the principles defined in Repetto v. Baylor are here followed, it is clear that no relief can be afforded complainant in this case, for, by the terms of the contract here sought to be enforced, a postponed payment of more than one-half of the purchase price is provided for and a second mortgage on the premises conveyed is contemplated to secure such postponed payment.

With the power of sale here involved there is added the power "to invest the proceeds," but this added power cannot be made the basis of a decree herein, for, if the acceptance of a second mortgage on the property sold to secure the payment of a part of the purchase price is regarded as an investment of a part of the proceeds of sale, such investment is proposed to be secured in a manner not authorized by our Orphans Court Act (3 Comp. Stat. p. 3864 §137); the trustee cannot be properly required by decree of this court to make such an investment.

It is urged in behalf of complainant that Repetto v. Baylor, supra, is not in harmony with the earlier case of Woodruff v. Lounsberry, 40 N.J. Eq. 545. In that case a will authorized and directed executors to sell and convey real estate and to invest the proceeds thereof upon first bond and mortgage on property worth double the amount or in stocks or bonds of the United States or the State of New Jersey, and pay the income to testator's widow. The executors sold certain real estate at a good price and accepted in payment forty percent cash and purchase-money mortgages — first liens — to secure the sixty percent deferred payments. Losses having been sustained on these mortgages, the question before the court was whether the executors should be compelled to make good these losses. It will be observed that the mortgages accepted by the executors were in amount the percentage of value of the mortgaged premises authorized by the Orphans Court Act. In determining that the executors should not be charged the losses, the learned ordinary said:

> Although the executors were, by the will, directed to invest the proceeds of the sale of the property upon first bond and mortgage of property worth twice the amount invested, or in stocks or bonds of the United States, or of this state, it would not be just to hold them bound by that provision in taking mortgages for part of the purchase-money of the property. Those mortgages were not taken as an investment of proceeds of sales, but to secure the payment of part of the price at which the property was sold. They were themselves proceeds of sales. In taking the mortgages for which the accountant asks allowance, the executors appear to have acted in good faith and for the best interest of the estate. They, therefore, ought not to be charged with them.

It is, therefore, insisted in behalf of complainant that Woodruff v. Lounsberry recognizes a power to sell as including a power to postpone payments of the purchase price for a period subsequent to the sale, and also determines that the acceptance of a purchase-money mortgage for a part of the purchase price is not to be regarded as an exercise of the power of investment. I am unable to adopt that view. In Woodruff v. Lounsberry the primary inquiry was whether under the special circumstances of that case the executor should be compelled to bear the loss which had arisen from shrinkage of the value of the tracts of land on which he had taken purchase-money mortgages. The learned chancellor points out with clearness and emphasis that the sales had been made at good prices and that the purchase-money mortgages taken were in amount but sixty percent of the values of the land covered by them, and that the executors had acted in good faith and for the best interest of the estate; he accordingly held that although the will limited mortgage investments to fifty percent of the value of the land, it would not be just to hold the executors in the circumstances stated. In Williams on Executors, §1530, it is laid down as a general rule adopted by the courts in suits to establish liability of executors for breach of trust duties, that while care must be taken to guard against an abuse of their trust, yet, in order not to deter persons from undertaking these offices, the court is extremely liberal in making every possible allowance, and cautious not to hold executors and administrators liable upon slight grounds. In Perrine v. Vreeland, 33 N.J. Eq. 102, affd., 33 N.J. Eq. 596, an executor, acting in good faith and under advice of counsel, retained a fund after it was payable to one who was entitled to it by the will, and in good faith invested the fund, after the time when it should have been by him paid over, in a mortgage on property then worth more than three times the amount of the loan, but which property so depreciated in value that the executor was compelled to buy it in upon foreclosure. In a suit to charge the executor with the loss, it was held that, notwithstanding his breach of trust duties, he should not be charged, but should be allowed to turn over the land in lieu of the fund. It may well be, as suggested in Woodruff v. Lounsberry, that in a suit in which the primary issue is whether an executor shall be made personally liable for losses sustained a purchase-money mortgage should not be regarded as so clearly an unauthorized investment as to justify an imposition of personal liability based on a breach of trust duties, and in like circumstances a postponement of payment of purchase price under a mere power of sale may not be deemed adequate to impose personal liability for loss. But in a suit for specific performance of a contract of sale made by an executor the primary inquiry is whether the contract is one which the executor had power to make and which a court of equity should compel him to specifically perform; before that form of relief should be administered both these inquiries must be clearly answered in the affirmative.

As already stated, in Repetto v. Baylor, supra, this court is committed to the view that a mere power of sale does not include any power to arrange terms of postponed payments of price, or to accept a mortgage or anything else than money in satisfaction of it. If the added power to invest proceeds of sale justifies the arrangement of postponed payments secured by a purchase-money mortgage, it is necessarily because the purchase-money mortgage is in the nature of an investment.

The second mortgage, in which the funds of this estate are proposed to be in effect invested, is $24,000 in amount, and is to be second to lien to a mortgage of $16,000. The total proposed purchase price is $45,000. This makes the combined encumbrances $40,000, or eight-ninths of the entire purchase price. The testimony at the hearing disclosed that $16,000 was the largest amount that could be procured as a loan on first mortgage security. This court is therefore asked to compel this executrix, in effect, to invest $24,000 of trust money in a second mortgage (subject to a prior lien of $16,000) on a property on which $16,000 was the utmost amount that any moneyed concern was willing to invest on first mortgage security. It is clear that no court would advise such an investment of trust funds, and the cestuis que trust, whose interest in the transaction are paramount, are not made parties to the bill. In such circumstances, specific performance should not be decreed even though the contract of the trustee be deemed within his powers; complainant should be left to his remedy at law. In 1 Lewin, Trusts 423, it is said:

> If trustees, or those who act by their authority, fail in reasonable diligence in inviting competition, or in the management of the sale (as if they contract under circumstances of haste or improvidence, or contrive to advance the interests of one party at the expense of another) they will be personally responsible for the loss to the suffering party; and the court, however correct the conduct of the purchaser, will refuse at his instance to compel the specific enforcement of the agreement.

In the cases cited in the footnote to the text above quoted will be found numerous cases in which courts of equity have refused this form of relief against a trustee out of considerations alone involving the best interests of the cestuis que trust.

I am obliged to advise a decree denying the relief sought by the bill.

RUSSELL v. RUSSELL
109 Conn. 187, 145 A. 648 (1929)

MALTBIE, J.

The first question we propose to consider concerns the authority of the trustees to cause extensive and permanent improvements upon the premises in their charge. The plaintiffs in their brief quote from the note to 2 Perry on Trusts & Trustees (6th Ed.) §477, a statement to the effect that American decisions show a strong tendency to modify the rule which forbids permanent and extensive improvements unless clearly authorized in the will or unless the expenditures are necessary to save the trust property from destruction or irreparable loss. This statement hardly seems borne out by the authorities. In England the matter is now largely governed by statute, but where it is not, it still seems true that the trustees will not be authorized to make such improvements. It should be borne in mind that the question is usually not so much one of authority in the trustees to make such improvements as of their authority to use the capital of the estate for such a purpose, and, so understood, the cases cited in the note in Perry to support its text are seen to be rather exceptions to than illustrations of a general rule; for in Stevens v. Melcher, 152 N.Y. 551, 567, 46 N.E. 965, authority in the trustees to invest the principal of the fund in real estate was found in the will; in Massachusetts, as pointed out in Warren v. Pazolt, 203 Mass. 328, 348, 89 N.E. 381, the general rule is that trustees have authority to invest the funds in their possession in real estate; and in both cases the making of permanent improvements was regarded as tantamount to an investment in lands. The fact that investment in real estate is not among those authorized for trustees by our statute, would seem to preclude the adoption of the Massachusetts rule in this State, and ordinarily to limit the right of trustees to use the principal of a trust fund for permanent improvements to situations where authority to do so can be found in the instrument creating the trust or in the powers of trustees to make investments under the law. General Statutes §4903, as amended by Public Acts of 1925, Chap. 171.

If we turn to the will before us we find, on the one hand, that the testator has expressly stated, in the eighth paragraph of his will, his intent that none of the premises should be sold during the trust, and as the trust is to terminate when the youngest child reaches the age of twenty-one, which cannot be later than 1937, this restriction is valid. Colonial Trust Co. v. Brown, 105 Conn. 261, 279, 135 A. 555. On the other hand, in seeking any intent the testator had as to changes and improvements in the premises during the trust, the provisions of the fourth paragraph of the codicil require scrutiny. He there directs that "any and all monies and income belonging to my estate and remaining in the hands of my executors and trustees after the payment of all legacies, bequests, unsecured indebtedness, and expenses of settling my estate," is to be used to pay off his mortgage indebtedness, and if any remains after the mortgages are paid, he directs its investment as trust funds are allowed to be invested by law. . . . His direction contained in the fourth paragraph of the codicil as to money or income in the hands not only of his executors . . . but also of the trustees, . . . indicates pretty clearly that he meant to include also in the expression "monies and income belonging to my estate" such income as should be received during the period of the trust. . . .

Such being the intent of the testator as expressed in the codicil, it would follow that he must have contemplated that the properties should be retained during the trust in virtually the condition in which they were at his death, ordinary repairs excepted; for, had he contemplated substantial improvements in the premises, any excess income would have been the fund to which he would have first pointed to defray the necessary expenses. Certainly he would hardly have directed the use of the money to discharge the mortgages upon the properties existing at his death when it must have been obvious that only by its use, or by creating additional mortgage indebtedness, could such improvements be made. Nor is there anything remarkable in attributing such an intent to him. The will was executed in 1923, and the codicil in 1925. The trust would not last longer than the time when his youngest son became twenty-one, that is, 1937, a period of twelve years. Except for the fire, the premises when the codicil was executed must have been in practically the same situation as now. It would not be strange if he did not wish his trustees, his brother and son, the latter still a young man, to embark upon extensive building operations, but preferred to have the premises remain substantially as they were until the end of the trust, which at most would be some twelve years after the codicil was executed. There is nothing in the facts stipulated which makes unreasonable or contrary to public policy the purpose of the testator that no permanent or extensive improvements should be made on the premises and consequently no reason why it might not be given effect.

There being, then, no authority given to the trustees in the will to make extensive permanent improvements on the premises but rather the contrary, their right to do so must arise, if at all, out of the situation created by the fire upon the premises at 73 to 81 Bank Street, and cannot extend beyond those premises. In the administration of a trust, circumstances sometimes bring about a situation where adherence to the directions given by its creator for its management or the application of the ordinary rules of law, would defeat the very purpose which the trust is meant to accomplish. . . .

It appears from the facts stipulated that, while in the last year before the fire the building on the premises in question brought in a net income of $2,610.35, the rentals now reasonably to be anticipated from it will not be sufficient to pay the necessary charges upon the property, that the upper floors are now untenantable and are boarded up, so that the whole building presents an unsightly appearance; and that it is a liability which it would cost $5,000 to remove. . . . The trustees have not asked us to approve any particular plan for the improvement of the property, and properly so. It would hardly be possible to arrive at a satisfactory solution upon a stipulation of facts which leaves out so many elements which ought to be considered, and upon an ex parte argument. The trial court is in a far better position to advise the trustees upon the basis of the evidence produced before it, as to any particular plan of development, having as it does the right to require further disclosure of facts if it is not satisfied by the evidence produced and, in view of the fact that the interests of minors are involved, being under the duty to satisfy itself in this way, if it be in doubt. . . .

As any plan of improvement will in all probability necessitate the raising of funds from the capital of the trust, it becomes necessary to consider what authority, if any, the trustees can secure to encumber the property of the estate with a mortgage. We have a statute which authorizes the Court of Probate, upon application of a trustee under a will and upon notice given to all parties in interest and hearing had, to order the sale or mortgage of any real estate held by trustees whenever in the opinion of the court it will best promote the interests of the beneficiaries under the trust, provided such sale or mortgage is not prohibited by the will, and the statute proceeds that the court may make any orders necessary to protect the rights of all parties in interest and to carry the sale or mortgage into effect. . . . It follows that if the plaintiffs secure the approval by the Superior Court of a plan for the improvement of the premises injured by the fire which will save the estate from loss and that plan involves mortgaging them to secure the necessary funds, the plaintiffs may apply to the Court of Probate for, and under the statute the court may grant them, authority to make such a mortgage. There is no reason in law why it should not be placed upon properties held by the trustees other than that one affected by the fire, but in all such cases regard must be had for the fact that very likely the best interests of the estate will be served if, when the time for distribution comes, different pieces of property may be dealt with as separate units, and upon the facts stipulated in this case, the mortgage must be confined to the premises to be improved, numbers 73 to 81 Bank Street.

The remaining questions concern the power of the trustees to execute leases of the property. No power to lease is expressly given them in the will or codicil, but they are directed to hold, manage and care for the property given them by the testator, to collect the income therefrom and to expend it for the purposes we have before stated; and, in view of the nature of the property and of these obligations, a power to make leases is necessarily implied. The real question upon which the trustees desire advice is as to the length of time such leases may be made to run. In general, trustees having a power to lease must exercise that power reasonably, having regard to the rights of the beneficiaries and those ultimately entitled to the property, the nature of the property, the uses to which it may advantageously be put and the usual and customary methods of dealing with such property in the locality where it is situated; and this rule applies to the duration of leases they may properly make. A trustee may unquestionably be expressly authorized, by the instrument creating the trust, to execute leases which will or may run beyond the duration of the trust, the legal effect of such authority being to couple to his estate at law a power, and to limit the estate of those entitled at the end of the trust to the extent of any leases so validly executed under it. Authority to execute leases which may run beyond the term of the trust may also be impliedly given, as, for instance, where the power to execute them is necessary to accomplish the purposes of the trust. In the case of a trust whose duration is uncertain because made for the life of some person or, as in the one before us, until the youngest of testator's children reaches a certain age, to deny the right to make any lease which might run beyond the end of the trust period would in many instances destroy the rentability of the property. On the other hand, the right of those entitled to the property at the termination of the trust to receive it free of incumbrance or charge is one not lightly to be disregarded and is an important consideration in determining the duration of leases which a trustee may be regarded as having authority to execute. Leases by trustees which will not run beyond the termination of the trust, or if its termination is indefinite in time, beyond its probable duration, are ordinarily within their implied powers, and leases extending beyond those limits may be, if it appears that they are reasonably necessary for the accomplishment of the purposes of the trust or the preservation of the trust property. Unless the necessity to make leases of the latter class is clear, trustees should seek the advice of the Superior Court as to the period they may be made to run. These principles, we believe, may be deduced from the leading authorities dealing with this question.

The sole statement in the stipulation bearing upon this matter is that it is not and will not be possible, even if the buildings upon the premises are improved, to secure the most desirable and stable class of tenants for them unless leases for long terms are made. The words "long terms" are most indefinite and would afford no basis for any present advice to the trustees as to the length of time as to which they may execute leases. Moreover, it is to be noted that the stipulation does not state that it will not be possible to fulfill all the purposes of the trust by granting leases which will not run beyond its probable termination. When the trust ends, in 1937, if not before, it seems probable that all persons interested will be of full age and in that case such arrangements may be made for the management of the property as will best meet the wishes of all. That time is so near at hand that the present making of leases for any very long period would seem questionable. If, however, the trustees deem it reasonably necessary for the proper performance of their duties to grant leases in excess of the probable duration of the trust, they may seek the advice of the court, not, as they suggest in one of their questions, the Court of Probate, but our court of general chancery powers, the Superior Court. . . .

Purdy v. Bank of America, 2 Cal. 2d 298, 304, 40 P.2d 481, 484 (1935), states:

the authority to borrow money is regarded in law as one of the most dangerous powers which may be conferred upon an agent, and the courts are slow to find that such a power may be implied. The wisdom of that policy may not be gainsaid, but it is not conclusive in the present case, and is not indicative that the power may not be held to be implied where the facts establish the necessity and the trustee has acted in good faith.

2. Power to Continue Decedent's Business

PROBLEM

18-B. The testator, who died recently, left a simple will that devised one-half of his property to his wife and one-half to his eight-year-old child. His wife is named executrix. The testator operated an explosives delivery and storage service as a sole proprietorship. The storage igloos are located in a small secluded valley on land that he had owned. Four expert and trusted employees drive the trucks and handle the dynamite and other explosives. This is a highly profitable business but with an obviously high risk of loss and liability. The surviving spouse, who has run the business office, comes to you for advice. She would like to keep the business operating through administration and indefinitely thereafter, but she is concerned about insurance costs, the risks involved, and her child's interests. What problems do you foresee, and what advice would you give regarding possible solutions and why?

Consider how her situation would be affected by Uniform Probate Code §3-715, which empowers a personal representative to:

> (24) continue any unincorporated business or venture in which the decedent was engaged at the time of his death (i) in the same business form for a period of not more than 4 months from the date of appointment of a general personal representative if continuation is a reasonable means of preserving the value of the business including good will, (ii) in the same business form for any additional period of time that may be approved by order of the Court in a formal proceeding to which the persons interested in the estate are parties; or (iii) throughout the period of administration if the business is incorporated by the personal representative and if none of the probable distributees of the business who are competent adults object to its incorporation and retention in the estate.
>
> (25) incorporate any business or venture in which the decedent was engaged at the time of his death.

SPIVAK v. BRONSTEIN
367 Pa. 70, 79 A.2d 205 (1951)

[Jacob Spivak died intestate in 1943, survived by his widow and a minor son. At the time of his death the decedent was the partner of Jules

Bronstein in a restaurant business. The partnership agreement contained no provision governing continuation or dissolution in case of death. Decedent's widow, Anne Spivak, was appointed administratrix of the estate. Without approval of the Orphan's Court, she executed a new partnership agreement with the defendant on her own behalf, as administratrix, and "as guardian of the minor heir," although she had not been appointed the guardian of her son. The new partnership agreement provided that Bronstein should retain all profits after making stated weekly payments to Mrs. Spivak. The new partnership continued until 1946, when it was terminated by Mrs. Spivak's sale, "individually and as Administratrix" of the estate, of "her" half of the business to Bronstein. Later in 1946 Mrs. Spivak, as administratrix, filed a bill in equity against Bronstein for an accounting and other relief, reciting, inter alia, that the estate's share of the profits greatly exceeded the sums paid to plaintiff under the agreement. The chancellor found against the plaintiff on her allegations of fraud and mismanagement; he also found that under the agreement she was not entitled individually to an accounting, but that the rights of the minor son, for whom she purported to act as guardian, were not affected by her acts and that she was without authority as administratrix "to invest the minor's share of his father's estate in a partnership." Defendant has appealed the decree ordering an accounting to the plaintiff for the one-fourth interest in the partnership belonging to the son and for the profits derived therefrom.]

LANDNER, J. . . .

The agreement was with a fiduciary whose limitations to enter into such a contract defendant was bound to know. Personal representatives may not carry on the business of a decedent unless authorized by a will or by the court, and when they do so, directly or in the guise of a new partnership, the gain, if any, belongs to the estate and the loss, if any falls on them. . . . Defendant should have known that without approval of the court, the contract he entered into with the plaintiff afforded him no protection against anyone beneficially interested in the estate whether as creditor of the estate or as heir who had not consented to it. So also he was bound to know that the minor son of his deceased partner (whose share he admitted to be ¼ of the whole) could act only through his lawfully appointed guardian. . . .

Having participated therefore in the unlawful act of the administratrix in hazarding the assets of her decedent in the business, the defendant cannot now plead innocence of liability to account for the full earnings to which the share of the minor is entitled. We hold, therefore, the learned chancellor was entirely correct in so ruling, and he is amply sustained in principle by the authorities he cites. . . . The situation here is one for the application of the rule as it appears in the Restatement of the Law of Trusts, Sec. 288, viz., "If the trustee in breach of trust transfers trust property to a person who takes with notice of the breach of trust, the transferee does not hold the property free of the trust, although he paid value for the transfer." The unauthorized conduct of a business by a personal representative has been recognized to be a breach of trust whether it be a continuance of decedent's sole business or one in which he had been a partner. . . .

[The surviving partner's] duty was to account as trustee to the personal representative of his deceased partner for the value of the deceased's interest and until that was done and settlement made, the personal representative had the option to claim either the profits attributable to the decedent's interest or legal interest. Here she relieved him of that obligation by entering into the new partnership agreement so far as she was able, that is individually, but she could not relieve him as to those she represented in a fiduciary capacity without approval of the Orphan's Court. . . .

As heir, Mrs. Spivak was, of course, bound by her agreement and the court below so found, but in her representative capacity of fiduciary representing possible creditors of the estate and as guardian (which she was not), she was utterly without authority to risk the assets of the estate and certainly not the share of the minor in what was virtually a continuation of the business. . . .

T. ATKINSON, WILLS
(2d ed. 1953)

§121. A representative who continues the decedent's business without authority incurs personal obligation to those with whom he deals and is liable for all losses and must account to the estate for all profits.

Authority to operate the business of the deceased may exist temporarily to preserve the assets of the estate or to realize thereon, and also by reason of:

    (1) Express provision of testator's will, or

    (2) Consent of the interested parties, or

    (3) Order of the court (at least if the statute so provides).

The personal representative who is so authorized to conduct the business has the same liabilities as the unauthorized representative, except that he is not obliged to bear the losses incurred in good faith.

In re ESTATE OF MULLER
24 N.Y.2d 336, 248 N.E.2d 164, 300 N.Y.S.2d 341 (1969)

JASEN, J. . . .

One of the issues raised by the objectant bears on the right of an executor to use assets of the general estate to pay corporate obligations where the testator specifically conferred the executor with the power to continue decedent's businesses.

The intention of a testator to confer upon an executor power to use general assets of the estate to continue various businesses of the testator "must be found in the direct, explicit and unequivocal language of the will, or else it will not be deemed to have been conferred."

Although the will did authorize the executor to continue the various businesses of the testator "if in his discretion it [was] for the best interest of [the] estate," such authorization merely grants to the executor the power to conduct the various businesses with the funds already invested in them at the time of the testator's death, and to subject only these funds, and not the general assets of the estate, to the hazards of the businesses.

Moreover, a clause in the will giving the executor authority to sell, invest and reinvest the general assets of the estate will not be taken as authority to invest additional money in the decedent's businesses. . . . While there may be a valid purpose in continuing a business to preserve its value as a going concern, rather than to sell it piecemeal, assets of the general estate may not be used for this purpose unless the will specifically so provides. Such was not the case here. . . .

WILLIS v. SHARP
113 N.Y. 586, 21 N.E. 705 (1889)

[Fida Sharp's will directed the carrying on of some legitimate business and empowered her executors and trustees "to sell or make such other disposition" of her properties as "the safe conduct of such business shall seem to require." Plaintiffs sold goods on credit to the executor for use in the business. When the price was not paid, plaintiffs brought suit alleging that the executor individually was unable to pay the amounts claimed but that the estate property was sufficient to do so. Judgment against the executor is appealed.]

ANDREWS, J. . . .

In every case where a trade is carried on by an executor under authority of the will, questions may arise as to the respective rights of existing and subsequent creditors, that is creditors of the testator and creditors of the trade whose debts were contracted in the business carried on by the executor. The creditors of the testator, under our statute and the general rule of law for the administration of assets of a decedent, are entitled to have the assets collected in and applied upon their debts, a reasonable time being allowed for the ascertainment of the debts and the conversion of the assets. It would seem that direction of the testator that his business should be continued would not be allowed to interfere with this right of existing creditors, or put to hazard the property of the testator applicable to the payment of their debts. . . .

The provision in the will of Mrs. Sharp, empowering her executors to "sell or make such other disposition of my real and personal estate as the safe conduct of such business shall seem to require," indicates we think, unmistakably, an intention on her part to subject her general assets to the debts of the business and to authorize the executor to contract debts therein binding her general estate. The executor could, unquestionably, have withdrawn from the assets money to purchase the goods, and a purchase on credit was, we think, a pledge of the general assets for their payment. . . .

Judgment affirmed.

DURAND, RETENTION OF DECEDENT'S BUSINESS
95 Tr. & Est. 907 (1962)

The retention of business interests as normal investment components of the businessman's estate is a most significant development in the changing concepts of trust investment of our generation. . . . Attorneys who plan their client's estates and fiduciaries who handle them now find and will continue to find that the treatment of business interests must be dealt with with increasing frequency. . . .

Decedent's business may, of course, be of such a kind that it may be made liquid before or shortly after death. Partnerships, in the absence of a provision in the articles of partnership, dissolve upon the death of a partner and must in ordinary circumstances be liquidated. The practice of the professions, whether individually or in partnership form, necessarily terminates upon the death of the doctor, lawyer or engineer. As businesses mature, the owner sometimes establishes a market for the business by participating employees and others in the enterprise. Unlisted stocks, in relatively closely held corporations, can often be sold even in large blocks when, over a period of years, a market has been established by a few transactions involving a small number of shares. The closely held corporation is often merged into a larger one, the stock of which may be marketable and liquidity achieved in this manner. . . . The buy-sell agreement is effectively employed in certain instances to liquidate the estate's interest in decedent's business.

Yet in many cases, a businessman cannot, no matter how much planning he does, provide for the liquidation of his business. Business, once set in motion, cannot be stopped upon the owner's death. The obligations of the business to its customers and to its employees and their families may effectively prevent the consummation of any plan for the liquidation of decedent's interest in the business and may impose upon the decedent and his estate the burden of providing increased capital, incurring increased obligations to meet the demands of the business and assuring continuity of employment to employees who, like the decedent, may have spent their lives in the development of the business. In other cases, the businessman fails to evolve an adequate plan to liquidate his interest during life.

Finally, some businesses are of a kind that should be retained and managed for the benefit of decedent's family. It may be desirable to retain a relatively secure enterprise, producing a high rate of return, provided competent and cooperative management is available, as a normal component of the trust, either indefinitely or until a child attains business age and competence and is able to succeed to the management of the business. . . .

An executor, unless specifically authorized by statute or by decedent's will to retain and operate decedent's business, is under a duty to liquidate the business within a reasonable time and distribute the proceeds. An executor is said to continue the business at his own risk. He is accountable to the beneficiaries for all profits, but is individually liable for all losses.

These sweeping statements apply to unincorporated, and not incorporated businesses. . . .

The fiduciary's authority to continue to hold the stock of a closely held corporation is derived from the following principal sources:

First: Many states have enacted statutes which authorize trustees in the exercise of their discretion to retain investments made by decedent in securities. Such statutes are usually broad enough to authorize trustees to retain the stock of a closely held corporation. In prudent man states, trustees in the exercise of reasonable discretion may retain stock in a closely held corporation in the absence of statute.

Second: Decedent may, by his will, grant to trustees power to retain the stock of such closely held corporation, and may undertake to give to the trustees instructions to guide them in the discharge of their duties. The authority to retain may be granted to one of the trustees, frequently the individual trustee, as distinguished from the corporate trustee.

Third: A court, having general equitable jurisdiction, will in some states advise and instruct trustees as to their duties in the retention of investments made by decedents. Trustees, as officers of the court, may in such cases submit their problems to the court by applying for advice and instructions at frequent intervals and thereby eliminate or reduce the hazard of personal liability. If the interests of the family will be served, the court in the exercise of such jurisdiction, may go to extreme lengths to protect the trustee in the continuance of decedent's incorporated business by giving advice and instructions. The power of the court to advise the continuance of an unincorporated business, in the absence of statute, remains obscure. . . .

HILLYARD v. LEONARD
391 S.W.2d 211 (Mo. 1965)

PRITCHARD, C. . . .

Defendants say that the phrase "to deal with said property and every part thereof in all other ways and for such other considerations as it would be lawful for any person owning the same to deal with same" gives them full power to incorporate the trust and distribute to beneficiaries the capital stock of the corporation. . . . There is no applicable statute governing the powers of trustees in the situation which we have here, and the trustees did not apply to a court of equity for any determination of their powers prior to incorporation and purported distribution. . . .

[T]here is one controlling precedent in this state: Garesche et al. v. Levering Inv. Co. et al., 146 Mo. 436, 48 S.W. 653, cited and relied upon by plaintiffs. In that case, a will gave the trustees power to manage the estate, and to sell the property or in any other way to dispose of it, and to reinvest it, during the life of the testator's wife, and directed a distribution among remaindermen at her death. Pending the administration the Levering Investment Company was formed, and its board of directors purchased from the trustees practically all of the property (mostly realty) in the estate, for which 3,000 shares were issued to the trustees. . . .

The trustees contended the transaction of incorporation was to prevent and avoid the expense of partition of the property, and to preserve the estate intact, and prevent a sacrifice of the property at a public partition sale; and that it was done in good faith, under advice of counsel (as here). The court said, loc. cit., 48 S.W. 656,

> Yet the case is not dependent upon any of these considerations. It is a question of the power of the executors and trustees under the terms of the Levering will — of whether the power to sell and reinvest gives the authority to the executors and trustees to incorporate the estate. If there is no such power conferred by the will, the bona fides of the executors and trustees, and the benefits accrued to the trust property, cannot justify the proceeding. The will itself nowhere gives any intimation of any such idea in the mind of the testator. . . .
>
> When Levering directed that upon the death of his wife the property remaining, "real, personal, and mixed," should be distributed among the devisees share and share alike, he cannot fairly be said to have intended that the Leverings should become minority stockholders in a corporation that was to hold the property he left for 50 years, and that those devisees

were only to have the benefit of his devise whenever the majority of the stockholders chose to declare dividends, nor that the management of the interests bequeathed to the Leverings should be . . . exercised by a majority vote of the stock, and executively attended to by the officers. . . . The executors and trustees were clothed with power over the property only until termination of the life estate. Then the trust ceased. They were not authorized to prolong their tenure of office.

There are striking similarities between the case now before the court and the *Garesche* case. . . . We hold that they were not authorized to incorporate the trust and make a final stock distribution in lieu of trust assets over the objection of these plaintiffs. The interest of these plaintiffs was converted into minority stock, the dividends upon which were controlled by adverse majority interests in the Leonard Land Company. Such interests were tied up for the duration of the corporation. At the death of Mrs. Leonard, these plaintiffs were deprived of their right to immediate liquidation of their interests in the trust, and were at the mercy of the majority stockholders with respect to such liquidation and income from dividends in this close family corporation. . . .

3.   Powers of Successor Fiduciaries

TATMAN v. COOK'S ADMINISTRATRIX
302 Ky. 529, 195 S.W.2d 72 (1946)

DAWSON, J. . . .

The only question presented on this appeal is whether the power of sale conferred by the will is personal to the executors named therein, or whether such power passed to the administratrix with the will annexed. . . .

In the Restatement of the Law of Trusts, Vol. 1, Section 196, in treating the question under consideration, subsections b., d., and f. state the rule as follows:

> b. Powers which are essential to the trust or powers which relate to the effective administration of the trust can ordinarily be exercised by successor trustees. Thus, a power of sale can ordinarily be exercised by successor trustees.
>
> d. Where the exercise of a power is not discretionary, the inference is that the settlor intended that it might be exercised by successor trustees. There is ordinarily the same inference where the trustee is given discretion and there is a standard by which the reasonableness of the exercise of the discretion can be judged. If the exercise of a power is within the discretion of the trustee and there is no such standard the inference is not as strong, but ordinarily the power may be exercised by successor trustees, unless it

appears from the terms of the trust that the confidence placed in the original trustee should be personal to him.

f. The relation between the settlor and the original trustee may be such as to show an intention to place confidence in him personally and only in him. It is less difficult to draw an inference that the settlor intended powers to be exercised by successor trustees where the original trustee was a person not related to or closely connected with the settlor, especially where the original trustee was a corporate trustee, than it is where the trustee was a near relative or close friend of the settlor. . . .

Taking the will as a whole, it is apparent that the testator had one purpose uppermost in his mind, and that was that his executors convert his estate, including his realty, into cash and have the proceeds invested for the benefit of his sister and niece. . . . Applying the rule set out in the Restatement of the Law we are impelled to hold that the testator's intention was to confer the power of sale upon the executors by virtue of that office. It follows that the power passes to the administratrix with the will annexed. . . .

B.   *The Investment Function*

It has already been noticed that the functions of the personal representative and the trustee are likely to be quite different, particularly as affects the matter of power and duty to invest.

Most of our attention in this section of this chapter is focused on situations, such as the typical trust situation, in which it is assumed that the fiduciary has an obligation to make the property productive. We might begin, however, with a brief look at the situation of a decedent's estate and the limitations traditionally placed on the personal representative. "Ordinarily it is not the function of an executor or administrator, as such, to invest the money even in land mortgages or government bonds, though this is authorized by statute in some jurisdictions and under certain circumstances would be proper even in absence of such legislation." T. Atkinson, Wills §124 (2d ed. 1953).

In Jones v. O'Brien, 58 S.D. 213, 235 N.W. 654 (1931), the question was whether the administrator, and thus the surety on his bond, was absolutely liable for losses sustained in connection with estate funds placed on deposit in a bank that subsequently failed. There was no allegation of negligence or bad faith but only that the placing of funds on a time deposit at interest constituted an improper investment. The court's opinion (at 218-227, 235 N.W. at 656-660) stated:

> The general rule is universally held to be that an executor or administrator may deposit money in a bank temporarily as a trust account. . . . [T]here is some question as to the protection of the executor or administrator

where a deposit is not payable on demand or where the executor or administrator parts with his right of exclusive dominion over the deposit. . . .

. . . The word "investment" has been variously defined in the cases with some considerable attention to the circumstances of the inquiry in each particular case. It has been held that any deposit in a bank which bears interest is an "investment," whether the deposit is for a fixed period or not. On the other hand, it has been held that the deposit of money in a bank at interest temporarily pending closing of administration, under statutes similar to our own, is not an "investment" in any such sense as contemplated by the statute. . . .

[T]here was a very considerable tendency among the earlier cases to treat every time deposit as a loan upon time. . . . With the growth of deposit banking . . . the courts have tended more and more to consider certificates of deposit as evidence of deposit rather than a loan. . . .

. . . We do not wish to establish any general rule to the effect that an executor or administrator is authorized to part with control of trust funds in his hands for any fixed period of time, either to a bank or to anyone else. . . . In the instant case, however, we think the defendant administrator was justified, by reason of such general custom and practice [in the community of treating time deposits as demand deposits despite the terms of the certificate], in believing that the money would be paid him at any time upon demand (without interest if demanded prior to six months).

UNIFORM PROBATE CODE

§3-715. [*Transactions Authorized for Personal Representatives; Exceptions.*]   Except as restricted or otherwise provided by the will or by an order . . . , a personal representative, acting reasonably for the benefit of the interested persons, may properly:

(1) retain assets owned by the decedent pending distribution or liquidation including those in which the representative is personally interested or which are otherwise improper for trust investment; . . .

(5) if funds are not needed to meet debts and expenses currently payable and are not immediately distributable, deposit or invest liquid assets of the estate, including moneys received from the sale of other assets, in federally insured interest-bearing accounts, readily marketable secured loan arrangements or other prudent investments which would be reasonable for use by trustees generally. . . .

DICKINSON, APPELLANT
152 Mass. 184, 25 N.E. 99 (1890)

FIELD, C.J.

The general principles which should govern a trustee in making investments, when the creator of the trust has given no specific directions concerning investments, have been repeatedly declared by this court. . . .

The rule in general terms is, that a trustee must in the investment of the trust fund act with good faith and sound discretion, and must, as laid down in Harvard College v. Amory, [26 Mass. (9 Pick.) 446,] at page 461, "observe how men of prudence, discretion, and intelligence manage their own affairs, not in regard to speculation, but in regard to the permanent disposition of their funds, considering the probable income, as well as the probable safety of the capital to be invested."

It is said in the opinion in Brown v. French, [125 Mass. 410]: "If a more strict and precise rule should be deemed expedient, it must be enacted by the Legislature. It cannot be introduced by judicial decision without working great hardship and injustice." It is also said, "The question of the lawfulness and the fitness of the investment is to be judged as of the time when it was made, and not by subsequent facts which could not then have been anticipated." A trustee in this Commonwealth undoubtedly finds it difficult to make satisfactory investments of trust property. The amount of funds seeking investment is very large; the demand for securities which are as safe as is possible in the affairs of this world is great; and the amount of such securities is small, when compared with the amount of money to be invested. Trusts frequently provide for the payment of income to certain persons during their lives, as well as for the ultimate transfer of the corpus of the trust property to persons ascertained, or to be ascertained, at the termination of the trust; and a trustee must, so far as is reasonably practicable, hold the balance even between the claims of the life tenants and those of the remaindermen. The life tenants desire a large income from the trust property, but they are only entitled to such an income as it can earn when invested in such securities as a prudent man investing his own money, and having regard to the permanent disposition of the fund, would consider safe. A prudent man possessed of considerable wealth, in investing a small part of his property, may wisely enough take risks which a trustee would not be justified in taking. A trustee, whose duty is to keep the trust fund safely invested in productive property, ought not to hazard the safety of the property under any temptation to make extraordinary profits. Our cases, however, show that trustees in this Commonwealth are permitted to invest portions of trust funds in dividend paying stocks and interest bearing bonds of private business corporations, when the corporations have acquired, by reason of the amount of their property, and the prudent management of their affairs, such a reputation that cautious and intelligent persons commonly invest their own money in such stocks and bonds as permanent investments.

The experience of recent years has, perhaps, taught the whole community that there is a greater uncertainty in the permanent value of railroad properties in the unsettled or newly settled parts of this country than was anticipated nine years ago. Without, however, taking into consideration facts which are now commonly known, and confining ourselves strictly to the evidence in the case, and the considerations which ought to have been present to the mind of the appellant, when in May and August, 1881, he made the investment in the stock of the Union Pacific Railroad Company, we think it appears that he acted in entire good faith, and after careful inquiry of many persons as to the value of the stock and the propriety of the investments. We cannot say that it is shown to our satisfaction that the trustee so far failed to exercise a sound discretion that the investments should be held to be wholly unauthorized. Still, it must have been manifest to any well informed person in the year 1881, that the Union Pacific Railroad ran through a new and comparatively unsettled country; that it had been constructed at great expense, as represented by its stock and bonds, and was heavily indebted; that its continued prosperity depended upon many circumstances which could not be predicted; and that it would be taking a considerable risk to invest any part of a trust fund in the stock of such a road.

. . . On May 9, 1881, the trustee bought thirty shares of the stock of the Union Pacific Railroad Company at $119 per share. . . . This is an investment of between one fourth and one fifth of the whole trust fund in this stock, and is certainly a large investment relatively to the whole amount of the trust fund to be made in the stock of any one corporation. After this, on August 16, 1881, he purchased twenty shares more at $123 per share. . . . The last investment, we think, cannot be sustained as made in the exercise of a sound discretion. While we recognize the hardship of compelling a trustee to make good out of his own property a loss occasioned by an investment of trust property which he has made in good faith, and upon the advice of persons whom he thinks to be qualified to give advice, we cannot on the evidence hold that the trustee was justified in investing in such stock as this so large a proportional part of the property.

It appears by the report of the single justice before whom the case was tried, that "the time has now come for a final distribution of said trust fund." It does not appear that, when the first account was allowed, there was any adjudication of the questions now before us, and they are not therefore res judicata, and no assent to these investments is shown on the part of the persons now entitled to the trust property. The result is, that this last investment is disallowed, and that the trustee must be charged with the amount of it, to wit: $2,475, and with simple interest thereon from August 16, 1881, and must be credited with any dividends therefrom which he has received and paid over, with simple interest on each, from the time each dividend was received.

The decree of the Probate Court must be modified in accordance with this opinion.

Decree accordingly.

ST. LOUIS UNION TRUST CO. v. TOBERMAN
235 Mo. App. 559, 140 S.W.2d 68 (1940)

[This is a suit by a trust company seeking instructions with respect to the character of investments it may be permitted to make as trustee under a will. The court below decreed, inter alia, that the plaintiff was authorized to invest "in corporate preferred and common stocks, provided, however, that it shall exercise reasonable care" in selecting the stocks.]

BENNICK, C. . . .

. . . A trustee . . . may take only such risks as an ordinarily prudent man would take in the investment of the funds of others, bearing in mind that it is the preservation of the estate, and not an accumulation to it, which is the chief object and purpose of his trusteeship. . . .

In many jurisdictions the question of the nature of the investments that a trustee may make of trust funds in his possession has come to be explicitly regulated by statute, but such is not the case in our own jurisdiction, save as respects the inhibition placed upon the right of any trust company to invest trust funds held by it in its own capital stock. . . .

Neither is there any decision in our own state which purports to arbitrarily classify, define, or limit the character of investments that a trustee may or may not make for his estate. . . .

Apart from the requirement of statutes which have been enacted in many of the states, and in the absence of any specific authority conferred by the instrument creating the trust, there would seem to exist two rules having to do with the general investment powers of trustees, the one, the New York, or more strict, rule, which holds that a trustee may not invest trust funds in common or preferred stocks, and permits investment only in government securities and first mortgages on real estate; and the other, the Massachusetts, or more liberal, rule, which permits the reasonable investment of trust funds in corporate stocks, where the corporations have acquired, by reason of the amount of their property and the prudent management of their affairs, such a reputation for safety and stability that cautious and prudent persons commonly invest their own money in such stocks as permanent investments. . . .

As we view the situation, not only do reason and experience establish the soundness of the above statement of the law, but indeed a proper conception of judicial power and authority would hardly warrant a court in holding otherwise. By this we mean that a court, within the limits of its prerogatives, deals with the question of due prudence and good faith when it is called upon to determine whether, in a particular case, a trustee has faithfully and properly discharged his trust in the matter of the investment of the funds committed to his care, and it therefore has no function to perform with respect to arbitrarily classifying and defining the character of investments which he may make for his estate, unless it can say, from the evidence before it, that a particular type of security or investment is improper as a matter of law. On the contrary, if there is to be an arbitrary classification of the character of investments that a trustee may be permitted to make for his estate, the making of such classification would seem to be purely a legislative, and not a judicial, function. . . .

With the true judicial function thus kept in mind, we know of no reason why a court . . . should attempt to say, as a matter of law, that corporate stocks, as such, can never be a proper form of investment for money held in trust. We appreciate that many years ago there may have been sound reason for a holding to the contrary. The corporations were in their infancy, and at that time a contemplated investment in such new and unproved enterprises necessarily involved a contemplated investment of a more or less speculative nature. Now, however, there are many corporations in the land with years of good management and demonstrated stability and earning capacity behind them, in the stocks of which the most prudent and cautious persons are accustomed to invest their savings with a primary view to the safety and permanency of their investments. . . .

With the so-called prudent man rule of the above cases, contrast the version of what is often called the "New York rule" expressed in Taylor's Estate, 277 Pa. 518, 121 Atl. 310 (1923): "Pennsylvania has long stood with the majority of jurisdictions favoring the view that, in the absence of express authority, a fiduciary has no power to invest . . . in the stock or bonds of private corporations." Early in the development of American trust law and continuing well into the twentieth century, this highly restrictive approach to the investment authority of fiduciaries was reaffirmed or adopted by legislation in many of the states. These "legal list" statutes, prescribing with varying degrees of specificity the types and characteristics of permissible investments, still apply in a few jurisdictions to some or all trustees or to other fiduciaries.

Is it proper for trustees, in their investment policies, to take into account the effects of inflation on purchasing power and the prospect that market values and dividend levels of equity securities are likely to increase during extended periods of inflation, even though risk tends to be higher and income yield lower for these securities than for high-grade debt securities? See Bulk, Prudence Will Be Prosecuted, 39 Tr. Bull. 4 (1960). Consider the language of the traditional "prudent man rule" as stated by the Massachusetts court (supra) or as often codified in statutes instructing trustees to consider "the probable income as well as the probable safety of their capital."[2]

As you read the case that follows (and subsequent material in this chapter will be relevant as well), consider whether the trustees' investment policy adequately took account of the interests of the remainder beneficiaries and whether the trustees appropriately balanced their duties to all of the various beneficiaries. Is the court's concept of the duty to diversify and of the risks to be guarded against through diversification an adequate one in an age of long-run inflationary trends? Also consider whether, even if a trustee is not *required* to invest with one eye on the cost-of-living index, a fiduciary duty is or may be violated if the trustee adjusts — and admits to adjusting — investment policy to expectations regarding inflation.

COMMERCIAL TRUST CO. v. BARNARD
27 N.J. 332, 142 A.2d 865 (1958)

[In 1920 Isaac Guggenheim created a trust of 6 percent corporate bonds having a face value of $1,267,000. The net income was to be divided equally among the settlor's three daughters, the remainder of the share of each to her issue. A bank and an individual were cotrustees. Certain of the settlor's brothers were given power to veto investments, and all investments were made with their approval until they relinquished their veto power in 1937. From the time the original bonds were redeemed for $1,393,700 in 1927 until the present intermediate accounting (1955), the corpus was invested in tax-exempt government bonds pursuant to the policy developed under the advice of the Guggenheim brothers while possessed of their veto power. Exceptions were filed by the three daughters, by the adult remaindermen, and by the guardians ad litem of unborn and infant remaindermen. The trial court disallowed the exceptions, refused to surcharge the trustees for their low-return investments, and approved the account as stated. Exceptants have appealed.

The evidence showed descending yields on the trust estate: an annual average of 4.27 percent in 1927, 2.34 percent in 1944, 2.17 percent in 1945, and 1.51 percent in 1955. Exceptants maintained that a change

---

2. In recent years questions have begun to arise (such as in meetings of boards of trustees), and occasionally even to surface in court, over the possibility of taking account of noneconomic (especially social or political) criteria in making investment decisions with respect to charitable, employee benefit, and even family trusts. See, e.g., Withers v. Teachers Retirement Sys., 447 F. Supp. 1248 (S.D.N.Y. 1978) (upholding purchase of $2.5 billion of speculative city bonds to help stave off city's possible bankruptcy); Restatement (Third) of Trusts §227 (1992), comment *c* and Reporter's Notes thereto.

of investment policy should have been considered, but was not, in 1945 when the yield went below 2¼ percent; they also introduced evidence to support their allegation that other trusts appropriate for comparison were averaging yields of 4¼ percent or better and sought surcharge for the difference. The trustees introduced evidence that during the period from 1945 through 1954 the tax brackets reached by one daughter averaged over 83 percent and the second daughter averaged over 68 percent. In comparing net disposable incomes after taxes for these two daughters, the trustees' policy produced decidedly better results than would have been produced by fully taxable yields at any reasonably likely trust rates.]

BURLING, J. . . .

Helen G. Ward [the third daughter] had an average tax rate of 64.8 percent of the years 1950 through 1954. . . . For the years 1945 through 1949 she had the status of a non-resident alien and was therefore only subject to a 15 percent federal income tax rate. This fact has no appreciable bearing on the duty of the trustees since they were required to deal with the corpus as a whole for the benefit of all three life income beneficiaries as well as the remaindermen. They could not be expected or required to change their investment policy because of the temporary tax status of one of the income beneficiaries. . . .

Exceptants' primary contention is that the trustees have failed to exercise any judgment with regard to the propriety of investing in higher-yield securities. They allege an adamant refusal over the years to even consider investments other than tax-exempts.

It is the duty of a trustee, imbued by the settlor with discretionary powers, to exercise active judgment and not to remain inert. The standard is set forth in 2 Scott on Trusts, §187.3, 995-996 (1939) as follows:

> Where by the terms of the trust a discretionary power is conferred upon the trustee and the exercise of the power is left to his judgment, the court will interpose if the trustee fails to use his judgment. This is true even though what is done by the trustee or what he fails to do would have been proper if he had used his judgment. . . .

The facts in the present case would not sustain a finding that the trustees have failed to exercise judgment with respect to investments, but rather support the conclusion that they have been alert to the relative advantages to be derived from the investment policy pursued.

Exceptants contend that by investing solely in governmental securities the trustees have breached their duty to diversify investments. Exceptants have misconceived the import of the doctrine that the trustees have a duty to diversify investments.

The Restatement [Second] of Trusts, §228, comment (a) provides: "The trustee is under a duty to the beneficiary to exercise prudence in diversifying the investments so as to *minimize the risk of large losses,* and therefore he should not invest a disproportionately large part of the trust estate in a particular security or type of security."

The italicized phrase is the reason for the rule, i.e., avoidance of large losses resulting from the deflation in value of a particular security. It is difficult to perceive how the trustees could have better protected the trust assets from the hazards of the market than by investing in governmental securities.

In Scott on Trusts, supra, §227.3 p. 1203, it is stated:

> The primary purpose of a trustee should be to preserve the trust estate, while receiving a reasonable amount of income, rather than to take risks for the purpose of increasing the principal or income. In other words, a trustee must be not merely careful and skillful but also cautious.

The law requires that a trustee exercise that degree of care, prudence, circumspection and foresight that an ordinary prudent person would employ in like matters of his own.

We conclude that the trustees have fully acquitted the duties imposed upon them by pursuing the investment policy that they have, bearing in mind the high income status of the beneficiaries. . . .

The investments of trustees are judged primarily on two bases: (1) whether the investment is of a type in which the trustee can properly invest; and (2) whether the particular investment chosen from the permissible types is proper. The latter depends on the care, skill, and caution exercised by the trustee, whose actions may be defended by showing compliance with these standards as long as the type of investment is permissible under the first test, which has to do with the outer limits of the trustee's discretion. The first test is often controlled by statutory provision or by the terms of the particular trust, which may serve to enlarge or restrict the range of investments permissible under applicable common law rule or statute. Compliance with the general fiduciary duty to exercise care, skill, and caution is not a defense when the investment is of a type not permitted to the trustee.

Even in the absence of a statutory rule or restriction in the governing instrument, courts have often developed from the general standard of prudence, particularly the duty of caution, subsidiary rules regarding investments that are and are not permissible. This is true even in jurisdictions that have adopted the more flexible doctrine rooted in the early Massachusetts cases and now recognized in judicial opinions or adopted by legislation in nearly all of the various states. In such situations it was recognized several decades ago that "what was decided in one case as a question of fact tends to be treated as a precedent establishing a rule of law." 3 A. Scott, Trusts §227 (2d ed. 1956). Rules of thumb have thus tended to forbid investment in bonds and stocks of "new and untried" enterprises, a prohibition that has applied as well to the securities of small, closely held businesses under ordinary circumstances. Such rules, of course, preclude all "speculative" investments or courses of action. At the more conservative end of the spectrum, however, traditional doctrine allows trustees to invest in the bonds of federal, state, and municipal governments, and normally also in high-grade corporate bonds and in first mortgages or deeds of trust secured by land of sufficient value to offer a comfortable margin of safety, always assuming that care, skill, and caution are exercised. In between are significant areas of authorized investment that now generally include the preferred and common shares of stable, well established, and financially sound corporations.

Trust investment law under the Third Restatement. The "general standard of prudent investment" in §227 of the Restatement (Third) of Trusts (the "prudent investor rule") instructs a trustee to "invest and manage the funds of the trust as a prudent investor would, in light of the purposes, terms, distribution requirements and other circumstances of the trust." The blackletter of the section goes on to explain that this standard "requires the exercise of reasonable care, skill and caution, and is to be applied to investments not in isolation but in the context of the trust portfolio and as a part of an overall investment strategy." That strategy must ordinarily provide for reasonable diversification of trust investments and should incorporate "risk and return objectives reasonably suitable to the trust." The rule further directs the trustee, in making and implementing investment decisions, to "conform to fundamental fiduciary duties of loyalty and impartiality" and to "incur only costs that are reasonable in amount and appropriate to the investment responsibilities of the trusteeship." In addition, the trustee is to "act with prudence in deciding whether and how to delegate authority and in the selection and supervision of agents."

The manner in which these investment duties, and the trustee's authority and responsibilities, may be affected by the terms of a trust or applicable statute is discussed in §228. The duty with respect to "inception assets" is then dealt with in §229. That section calls for the trustee, "within a reasonable time after the creation of the trust, to review the contents of the trust estate and to make and implement decisions concerning the retention and disposition of original investments in order to conform to the requirements of §§227 and 228."[3]

---

3. Both §228 and §229 struggle to offer guidance to fiduciaries and courts in the difficult matters of interpretation presented by increasingly common but unfortunately casual authorizations or grants of discretion with respect to the acquisition or retention of particular trust investments. The struggle particularly involves a conflict between (a) the objective of giving respect and meaning to the terms of a trust or statute and (b) concerns over the possible nonexercise of judgment or disregard of basic prudence by trustees who are sometimes willing to rely on permissive provisions as a source of exculpation or as justification for simply giving no attention to "authorized" portions of their portfolios.

The evolution of the traditional "prudent man rule" over the years resulted in considerable rigidity and arbitrariness, despite the generality and flexibility of the language in which that rule was originally expressed in the classic dictum of Harvard College v. Amory, quoted in *Dickinson, Appellant,* supra. As we have seen, decisions dealing with essentially factual issues tended later to become crystallized into rather specific subsidiary rules prescribing the permissible types or required characteristics of trust investments. These rules in turn were usually based on some perceived but unarticulated degree of risk that was abstractly viewed as excessive not only for a particular trustee but for trustees in general. Typically, inadequate or no concern was shown for the portfolio context or role of a challenged investment, or for the particular trust's purposes or risk tolerance. In short, the tendency to judge and classify investments in isolation generally resulted in broad categories of assets (such as venture capital) or courses of action (e.g., borrowing, in many contexts) being labeled "speculative" or imprudent per se, and thus impermissible, usually without regard to the degree of care and skill exercised by the trustee.

Knowledge, experience, and practice in the modern investment world have demonstrated that arbitrary restrictions on trust investments are generally unwarranted and likely to be counterproductive, not to mention their potential for inhibiting the judgment of skilled trustees and even for causing unjustified fiduciary liability. The need for change in trust investment law has been well documented in scholarly research and in legal and financial literature in recent years. The need is also evidenced by recent legislative trends at both federal and state levels, even if rather selectively, and by the judgments and behavior of expert fund managers. Particularly concerned are fiduciaries whose circumstances would otherwise invite, or at least permit, management strategies that would include some relatively high risk-and-return investment programs (involving, for example, venture capital or real estate), or some abstractly high-risk courses of action of types that are now widely employed by fund managers for the purpose of reducing the risk level of a portfolio as a whole (e.g., certain uses of options and futures).

The American Law Institute's prudent investor project was undertaken with a clear recognition that trust investment law should reflect and accommodate current concepts and knowledge within the financial community. It had become evident that trust investment law must be general and flexible enough both (a) to adapt to changes that have occurred and will continue to occur in the financial world and in our economic knowledge and (b) to take account of the differing needs and circumstances of the broad variety of trusts, trustees, and settlor purposes to which that body of law will inevitably apply. These objectives required that revised Restatment doctrine draw only on consistent themes of legitimate financial theories and express only those principles upon which general agreement exists. Thus, the objectives called for a prudent investor rule the mandates of which would not exceed what was needed in order to articulate standards by which the conduct of trustees may be guided and judged, while also protecting settlor objectives and the interests of trust beneficiaries.

With these various goals in mind, the modernized prudent investor rule begins with the fundamental proposition that no investments or courses of action are imprudent per se. In addition, given the broad variety in the goals and composition of different trust estates, the rule also recognizes that it would be inappropriate for the law to attempt to prescribe some universal standard of acceptable risk or even of risk characteristics for permissible investments and techniques. Each investment or course of action is thus to be judged by its role in the trust portfolio and in relation to the objectives and circumstances of the particular trust in question. The rule of §227 and its commentary then go on to prescribe a few relatively flexible principles of prudence for the guidance of trustees, their counsel, and the courts.

First, sound diversification is fundamental to risk management and is therefore ordinarily required of trustees as a means of moderating the dangers inherent in investing and, most notably, as a means of minimizing "uncompensated" risk. Thus, a trustee has the duty to diversify investments unless, under the circumstances, the objectives of both prudent risk management and impartiality (primarily as between income and remainder beneficiaries) can be satisfied without doing so, or unless special considerations make it prudent not to diversify in a particular trust situation.

Second, risk and expected return are so directly related that a trustee has a duty to consider, and to make conscious decisions concerning, the level of risk appropriate to the purposes, distribution requirements, and other circumstances of the trust being administered. Although carrying "uncompensated" (i.e., diversifiable) risk is viewed negatively, the same cannot so simply be stated concerning risks that are rewarded by expectation of increased return.[4] This so-called "compensated" (or "market" or "systematic") risk is unavoidable in investing, and fiduciary decisions are therefore concerned with the appropriate degree of that risk. As an integral part of investment strategy, these decisions call for the trustee to make reasonable judgments about a suitable level of risk and reward for the trust. These decisions are thus to be made and reviewed with due regard for portfolio context and objectives and in light of such factors as the particular trust's return requirements and risk tolerance.

---

4. The commentary and Reporter's Notes to §227 contain, in addition to suggested readings for a lawyer audience, rather lengthy explanations of the nature and types of risk, as well as discussion of efficient market theories and other financial background and concepts that are important to a proper understanding of modern trust investment principles. See also Macey, An Introduction to Modern Financial Theory (ACTEC, 1991).

Third, trustees and the rules that govern their investment activities must be sensitive to the competition between the needs of the present and the future, and also to the different meanings impartiality might have depending on the nature, purposes, and circumstances of different trusts. This sensitivity is especially important in light of modern experience with inflation and taxation and with the differing impact these factors may have on different beneficiary interests. Conflicting objectives in these matters are especially but not exclusively evident between income and principal beneficiaries. In particular, the prudent investor rule recognizes that traditional concern for protection of principal should include reasonable consideration of an objective of preserving purchasing power and real, after-tax values. It also recognizes that life beneficiaries' concerns over trust-accounting income are not the same (or even necessarily present) in all trusts, and in any event that productivity requirements focus on the portfolio as a whole, rather than on each investment. The rule further recognizes that family financial and tax circumstances and settlor objectives will sometimes justify a deliberate effort to achieve real growth in the value of the trust estate. Accordingly, the new Restatement seeks to increase, or at least clarify, both the flexibility of the duty of impartiality and the breadth of the concerns it addresses.

Fourth, prudence may require or at least benefit from expert assistance in investment matters. Accordingly, the prudent investor rule views delegation by trustees much more positively than has traditional doctrine accompanying the "prudent man" standard. In very different ways, delegation is likely to advance the management activities of trustees ranging from skilled professional fiduciaries (who may seek, for example, to pursue challenging investment strategies) to family members or friends selected as trustees for quite valid reasons other than financial expertise.

Finally, trustees should avoid incurring unwarranted expenses in fulfilling their investment responsibilities. Cost-conscious administration should take account of market efficiency concepts and the importance of comparing the additional research and transaction costs of active management strategies with realistically appraised prospects for increased return from such strategies. It should also take account of increased legal acceptance of delegation and pooled investing by trustees, as well as the availability and continuing emergence not only of investment products with significantly varied characteristics but also of virtually identical products being offered at significantly different costs.

Related portions of the initial volume of the Restatement (Third) of Trusts give particular attention to several issues of trustee liability. The traditional rule limiting a trustee's ability to offset gains against losses from multiple breaches of trust, for example, has attracted considerable criticism in recent discussions of modernizing trust investment law.

Much of the criticism stems from a mistaken belief that the general rule against netting prevents reliance on modern portfolio theory. This belief fails to recognize that a breach of trust depends on fiduciary conduct rather than on investment performance, so that the anti-netting rule is not involved in determining *whether* there has been a breach of trust but only in determining the measure of damages when breaches do occur. Nevertheless, the commentary to revised §213 attempts to be more careful than its predecessors in identifying when breaches should be treated as "separate and distinct" so as to preclude offset.

In addition, as a part of the prudent investor rule's effort to be more careful about the distinction between "total return" and income "yield," the new Restatement generally measures a trustee's liability for improper investment conduct by reference to total return. It thus allows, in most situations, for example, recovery for the trustee's failure to produce gains that would reasonably have been expected from an appropriate investment program. In part, this seeks to assure that trustees who have ignored important aspects of their fiduciary obligations by employing inadequate investment strategies will not be insulated from liability merely because their portfolios escaped loss of dollar value during periods of significantly rising markets. Restatement (Third) §§205 and 208-211 recognize that earlier concern over the "speculative" character of such damages is alleviated today by the availability of relevant data and the suitability of current investment principles to serve as guides in identifying reasonably appropriate "benchmark portfolios" for this purpose.

The principles and underlying portfolio concepts of Restatement (Third) of Trusts §§227-229 are reflected in Illinois Ann. Stat. ch. 17, ¶1675, §5 (1992), which provides:

§5. *Investments.* (a) Prudent Investor Rule. A trustee administering a trust has a duty to invest and manage the trust assets as follows:

(1) The trustee has a duty to invest and manage trust assets as a prudent investor would considering the purposes, terms, distribution requirements, and other circumstances of the trust. This standard requires the exercise of reasonable care, skill, and caution and is to be applied to investments not in isolation, but in the context of the trust portfolio as a whole and as a part of an overall investment strategy that should incorporate risk and return objectives reasonably suitable to the trust.

(2) No specific investment or course of action is, taken alone, prudent or imprudent. The trustee may invest in every kind of property and type of investment, subject to this Section. The trustee's investment decisions and actions are to be judged in terms of the trustee's reasonable business judgment regarding the anticipated effect on the trust portfolio as a whole under the facts and circumstances prevailing at the time of the decision or action. The prudent investor rule is a test of conduct and not of resulting performance.

(3) The trustee has a duty to diversify the investments of the trust unless, under the circumstances, the trustee reasonably believes it is in the interests of the beneficiaries and furthers the purposes of the trust not to diversify.

(4) The trustee has a duty, within a reasonable time after the acceptance of the trusteeship, to review trust assets and to make and implement decisions concerning the retention and disposition of original pre-existing investments in order to conform to the provisions of this Section. The trustee's decision to retain or dispose of an asset may properly be influenced by the asset's special relationship or value to the purposes of the trust or to some or all of the beneficiaries, consistent with the trustee's duty of impartiality.

(5) The trustee has a duty to pursue an investment strategy that considers both the reasonable production of income and safety of capital, consistent with the trustee's duty of impartiality and the purposes of the trust. Whether investments are underproductive or overproductive of income shall be judged by the portfolio as a whole and not as to any particular asset.

(6) The circumstances that the trustee may consider in making investment decisions include, without limitation, the general economic conditions, the possible effect of inflation, the expected tax consequences of investment decisions or strategies, the role each investment or course of action plays within the overall portfolio, the expected total return (including both income yield and appreciation of capital), and the duty to incur only reasonable and appropriate costs. The trustee may but need not consider related trusts and the assets of beneficiaries when making investment decisions.

(b) The provisions of this Section may be expanded, restricted, eliminated, or otherwise altered by express provisions of the trust instrument. The trustee is not liable to a beneficiary for the trustee's reasonable and good faith reliance on those express provisions.

(c) Nothing in this Section abrogates or restricts the power of an appropriate court in proper cases (i) to direct or permit the trustee to deviate from the terms of the trust instrument or (ii) to direct or permit the trustee to take, or to restrain the trustee from taking, any action regarding the making or retention of investments.

(d) The following terms or comparable language in the investment powers and related provisions of a trust instrument, unless otherwise limited or modified by that instrument, shall be construed as authorizing any investment or strategy permitted under this Section: "investments permissible by law for investment of trust funds," "legal investments," "authorized investments," "using the judgment and care under the circumstances then prevailing that men of prudence, discretion, and intelligence exercise in the management of their own affairs, not in regard to the speculation but in regard to the permanent disposition of their funds, considering the probable income as well as the probable safety of their capital," "prudent man rule," and "prudent person rule."

(e) On and after the effective date of this amendatory Act of 1991, this Section applies to all existing and future trusts, but only as to actions or inactions occurring after that effective date.

DENNIS v. RHODE ISLAND HOSPITAL TRUST
NATIONAL BANK
744 F.2d 893 (1st Cir. 1984)

BREYER, Circuit Judge.

The plaintiffs are the great-grandchildren of Alice M. Sullivan and beneficiaries of a trust created under her will. They claimed in the district court that the Bank trustee had breached various fiduciary obligations owed them as beneficiaries of that trust. The trust came into existence in 1920. It will cease to exist in 1991 (twenty-one years after the 1970 death of Alice Sullivan's last surviving child). The trust distributes all its income for the benefit of Alice Sullivan's living issue; the principal is to go to her issue surviving in 1991. Evidently, since the death of their mother, the two plaintiffs are the sole surviving issue, entitled to the trust's income until 1991, and then, as remaindermen, entitled to the principal.

The controversy arises out of the trustee's handling of the most important trust assets, undivided interests in three multistory commercial buildings in downtown Providence. The buildings (the Jones, Wheaton-Anthony, and Alice Buildings) were all constructed before the beginning of the century, in an area where the value of the property has declined markedly over the last thirty years. During the period that the trust held these interests the buildings were leased to a number of different tenants, including corporations which subsequently subleased the premises. Income distribution from the trust to the life tenants has averaged over $34,000 annually.

At the time of the creation of the trust in 1920, its interests in the three buildings were worth more than $300,000. The trustee was authorized by the will to sell real estate. When the trustee finally sold the buildings in 1945, 1970, and 1979, respectively, it did so at or near the lowest-point of their value; the trust received a total of only $185,000 for its interests in them. These losses, in plaintiffs' view, reflect a serious mishandling of assets over the years.

The district court, 571 F. Supp. 623, while rejecting many of plaintiffs' arguments, nonetheless found that the trustee had failed to act impartially, as between the trust's income beneficiaries and the remaindermen; it had favored the former over the latter, and, in doing so, it had reduced the value of the trust assets. To avoid improper favoritism, the trustee should have sold the real estate interests, at least by 1950, and reinvested the proceeds elsewhere. By 1950 the trustee must have, or should have, known that the buildings' value to the remaindermen would be small; the character of downtown commercial Providence was beginning to change; retention of the buildings would work to the disadvantage of the remaindermen. The court ordered a surcharge of $365,000, apparently designed to restore the real value of the trust's principal to its 1950 level.

On appeal, plaintiffs and defendants attack different aspects of the district court's judgment. We have reviewed the record in light of their arguments. We will not overturn a district court's factual determination unless it is "clearly erroneous," Fed. R. Civ. P. 52(a). And, in a diversity case such as this one, involving a technical subject matter primarily of state concern, we are "reluctant to interfere with a reasonable construction of state law made by a district judge, sitting in the state, who is familiar with that state's law and practices." Application of these principles leads us, with one minor exception, to affirm the district court's judgment. . . .

The trustee first argues that the district court's conclusions rest on "hindsight." It points out that Rhode Island law requires a trustee to be "prudent and vigilant and exercise sound judgment," Rhode Island Hospital Trust Co. v. Copeland, 39 R.I. 193, 98 A. 273, 279 (1916), but "[n]either prophecy nor prescience is expected." Stark v. United States Trust Co. of New York, 445 F. Supp. 670, 678 (S.D.N.Y. 1978). It adds that a trustee can indulge a preference for keeping the trust's "inception assets," those placed in trust by the settlor and commended to the trustee for retention. See Peckham v. Newton, 15 R.I. 321, 4 A. 758, 760 (1886); Rhode Island Hospital Trust Co. v. Copeland, supra. How then, the trustee asks, can the court have found that it should have sold these property interests in 1950?

The trustee's claim might be persuasive had the district court found that it had acted *imprudently* in 1950, in retaining the buildings. If that were the case, one might note that every 1950 sale involved both a pessimistic seller and an optimistic buyer; and one might ask how the court could expect the trustee to have known then (in 1950) whose prediction would turn out to be correct. The trustee's argument is less plausible, however, where, as here, the district court basically found that in 1950 the trustee had acted not imprudently, but *unfairly,* between income beneficiaries and remaindermen.

Suppose, for example, that a trustee of farmland over a number of years overplants the land, thereby increasing short run income, but ruining the soil and making the farm worthless in the long run. The trustee's duty to take corrective action would arise from the fact that he knows (or plainly ought to know) that his present course of action will injure the remaindermen; settled law requires him to act impartially, "with due regard" for the "respective interests" of both the life tenant and the remainderman. Restatement (Second) of Trusts §232 (1959). See also A. Scott, The Law of Trusts §183 (1967); G. G. Bogert & G. T. Bogert, The Law of Trusts and Trustees §612 (1980). The district court here found that a sale in 1950 would have represented one way (perhaps the only practical way) to correct this type of favoritism. . . .

To be more specific, in the court's view the problem arose out of the trustee's failure to keep up the buildings, to renovate them, to modernize them, or to take other reasonably obvious steps that might have given the remaindermen property roughly capable of continuing to produce a reasonable income. This failure allowed the trustee to make larger income payments during the life of the trust; but the size of those payments reflected the trustee's acquiescence in the gradual deterioration of the property. In a sense, the payments ate away the trust's capital.

The trustee correctly points out that it did take certain steps to keep up the buildings; and events beyond its control made it difficult to do more. In the 1920's, the trustee, with court approval, entered into very longterm leases on the Alice and Wheaton-Anthony buildings. The lessees and the subtenants were supposed to keep the buildings in good repair; some improvements were made. Moreover, the depression made it difficult during the 1930's to find tenants who would pay a high rent and keep up the buildings. After World War II the neighborhood enjoyed a brief renaissance; but, then, with the 1950's flight to the suburbs, it simply deteriorated.

Even if we accept these trustee claims, however, the record provides adequate support for the district court's conclusions. There is considerable evidence indicating that, at least by 1950, the trustee should have been aware of the way in which the buildings' high rents, the upkeep problem, the changing neighborhood, the buildings' age, the failure to modernize, all together were consuming the buildings' value. There is evidence that the trustee did not come to grips with the problem. Indeed, the trustee did not appraise the properties periodically, and it did not keep proper records. It made no formal or informal accounting in 55 years. There is no indication in the record that the trust's officers focused upon the problem or consulted real estate experts about it or made any further rehabilitation efforts. Rather, there is evidence that the trustee did little more than routinely agree to the requests of the trust's income beneficiaries that it manage the trust corpus to produce the largest possible income. The New Jersey courts have pointed out that an impartial trustee must "view the overall picture as it is presented from all the facts, and not close its eyes to any relevant facts which might result in excessive burden to the one class in preference to the other." Pennsylvania Co. v. Gillmore, 137 N.J. Eq. 51, 43 A.2d 667, 672 (1945). The record supports a conclusion of failure to satisfy that duty.

The district court also found that the trustee had at least one practical solution available. It might have sold the property in 1950 and reinvested the proceeds in other assets of roughly equivalent total value that did not create a "partiality" problem. The Restatement of Trusts foresees such a solution, for it says that "the trustee is under a duty to the beneficiary who is ultimately entitled to the principal not to . . . retain property which is certain or likely to depreciate in value, although the property yields a large income, unless he makes adequate provision for amortizing the depreciation." Restatement (Second) of Trusts §232, comment b. Rhode Island case law also allows the court considerable discretion, in cases of fiduciary breach, to fashion a remedy, including a remedy based on a hypothetical, earlier sale. In, for example, Industrial Trust Co. v. Parks, 190 A. at 42, the court apportioned payments between income and principal "in the same way as they would have been apportioned if [certain] rights had been sold by the trustees immediately after the death of the testator" for a specified hypothetical value, to which the court added hypothetical interest. In the absence of a showing that such a sale and reinvestment would have been impractical or that some equivalent or better curative steps might have been taken, the district court's use of a 1950 sale as a remedial measure of what the trustee ought to have done is within the scope of its lawful powers.

In reaching this conclusion, we have taken account of the trustee's argument that the buildings' values were especially high in 1950 (though not as high as in the late 1920's). As the trustee argues, this fact would make 1950 an unreasonable remedial choice, other things being equal. But the record indicates that other things were not equal. For one thing, the district court chose 1950, not because of then-existing property values, but because that date marks a reasonable outer bound of the time the trustee could plead ignorance of the serious fairness problem. And, this conclusion, as we have noted, has adequate record support. For another thing, the district court could properly understand plaintiffs' expert witness as stating that the suburban flight that led to mid-1950's downtown decline began before 1950; its causes (increased household income; more cars; more mobility) were apparent before 1950. Thus, the court might reasonably have felt that a brief (1948-52) downtown "renaissance" should not have appeared (to the expert eye) to have been permanent or longlasting; it did not relieve the trustee of its obligation to do something about the fairness problem, nor did it make simple "building retention" a plausible cure. Finally, another expert testified that the trustee should have asked for power to sell the property "sometime between 1947 and 1952" when institutional investors generally began to diversify portfolios. For these reasons, reading the record, as we must, simply to see if it contains adequate support for the district court's conclusion as to remedy (as to which its powers are broad), we find that its choice of 1950 as a remedial base year is lawful.

Contrary to the trustee's contention, the case law it cites does not give it an absolute right under Rhode Island law to keep the trust's "inception assets" in disregard of the likely effect of retention on classes of trust beneficiaries. Cf. Peckham v. Newton, supra (original holdings should be retained but only so long as there is no doubt as to their safety); Rhode Island Hospital Trust Co. v. Copeland, supra (court not sufficiently informed on safety of holding to order sale or retention). The district court's conclusion that the trustee should have sold the assets if necessary to prevent the trust corpus from being consumed by the income beneficiaries is reasonable and therefore lawful. . . .

The judgment of the district court [on a matter of damages that is omitted here] is modified and as modified affirmed.

PROBLEM

18-C.   *D*'s will left her entire estate in trust to pay the income to her husband for life, remainder at his death to their issue. The trustee is "directed to invest only in bonds of the United States or bonds of any of the top 100 largest corporations whose shares are listed on the New York Stock Exchange." The executor administered *D*'s estate promptly and distributed to the trustee, *T*: $100,000 in cash; $20,000 worth of stock in Neighbors, Inc., a small, local corporation; $50,000 in bonds of Acme Corporation, which was the seventy-fifth-largest corporation listed on the New York Stock Exchange; and $280,000 in United States bonds.

The week after receiving the assets from the executor, *T* invested $50,000 in the common stock of Best Corporation and $40,000 in bonds of Western Co., which were numbers nine and sixty, respectively, on the New York Stock Exchange list of the largest corporations. The remaining cash was placed in an interest-bearing account at a competitive rate in a savings and loan institution. A year later *T* has made no further changes in the investments and asks you to review the trust portfolio and advise him.

T reports that a few months after *D*'s death Neighbors, Inc. paid its regular semi-annual cash dividend and that several stockholders then offered to buy the trust's stock for $25,000. Later, however, Neighbors' board of directors announced that it was passing the next semi-annual dividend because of a severe loss of sales. *T* has just received an offer to buy the trust's shares for $10,000.

T also shows you a copy of a letter from a broker reporting that Acme has lost its imaginative chief executive officer and that its natural resource holdings had been greatly overvalued, and advising *T* to sell before a further drop occurs in the market for Acme bonds.

The trust's holding in Best has now risen in value to $60,000.

The bonds of Western have held steady, but *T*'s broker reports that Western was just denied an important line of credit, and slipping sales have raised the possibility that Western is overextended and considering a financial restructuring.

What advice would you give *T* under the law of your state? Under a statute such as that set out below? Under the Illinois statute, supra?

> In acquiring, investing, reinvesting, exchanging, retaining, selling and managing property for the benefit of another, a fiduciary shall exercise the judgment and care under the circumstances then prevailing, which persons of prudence, discretion and intelligence exercise in the management of their own affairs, not in regard to speculation but in regard to the permanent disposition of their funds, considering the probable income as

well as the probable safety of their capital. Within the limitations of the foregoing standard, a fiduciary is authorized to acquire and retain every kind of property, real, personal or mixed, and every kind of investment, specifically including, but not by way of limitation, bonds, debentures, and other corporate or government obligations, preferred or common stocks, interests in common trust funds, securities of any open-end or closed-end management type investment company, or investment trust, and contracts of life insurance, which persons of prudence, discretion and intelligence acquire or retain for their own account.

In Miller v. Pender, 93 N.H. 1, 2-4, 34 A.2d 663, 665-666 (1943), the court stated:

> The defendant trustee . . . under the instrument setting up the trust fund had the power "To invest the same in such securities as said trustee shall deem proper (even though the same shall not be classified as trust investments under the laws of New Hampshire). . . . " The [trial] Court found and ruled as follows:
>
>> The trustee had a broad discretion under the provisions of the trust agreement in making and changing investments and he acted within his authority as trustee. In these matters he exercised his best judgment and the care and skill which a man of ordinary prudence would exercise in dealing with his own property.
>
> To this the plaintiffs excepted. The test applied is too liberal. In making investments for a trust, the proper standard to follow is the care and skill of a prudent man in conserving the property — not that of a man of ordinary prudence. . . . "[He] must use the caution of one who had primarily in view the preservation of the estate entrusted to him, a caution which may be greater than that of a prudent man who is dealing with his own property." 2 Scott, Trusts, §174. . . .
> It is true that the powers of a trustee in making investments can be determined by the terms of the trust instrument. However, provisions enlarging the powers to invest are strictly construed.
>
>> More frequently the terms of the trust instead of restricting the trustee enlarge his powers in making investments. It is in each case a question of interpretation whether or not the terms of the trust enlarge the scope of permissible investments and if so to what extent. This depends upon how broad the scope of proper trust investments is in the particular state in the absence of a provision in the trust instrument and upon the breadth of the language used in the instrument. Where by statute or by judicial decision the scope of the trust investments is narrow, an authorization to the trustee to make investments "in his discretion" is ordinarily interpreted to enlarge his powers so that he can properly make such investments as a prudent man would make. In states in which in the absence of a provision of the trust instrument the trustee can properly make such

investments as a prudent man would make a provision authorizing him to make investments "in his discretion" ordinarily does not extend his powers. A provision in the terms of the trust authorizing the trustee to exercise his discretion in making investments is not interpreted as permitting him to make investments which a prudent man would not make.

2 Scott, Trusts §227.14. . . .

Clearly the defendant had authority to invest in securities that were not legal under our statutes, but in view of the fact that the trial Court adopted the standard of care and skill of a man of ordinary prudence in dealing with his own property rather than that of a prudent man whose duty is to conserve the property, this exception is sustained and there should be a new trial.

TAYLOR'S ESTATE
277 Pa. 518, 121 Atl. 310 (1923)

[William Taylor died in 1899, leaving part of his residuary estate to the Fidelity Trust Company in trust to pay the income to his daughter for her life, remainder to her children who survive her.]

Moschzisker, C.J. . . .

The present account was filed, at the instance of the daughter and her son, to determine whether the will authorized either the retaining or acquiring of certain classes of securities in which the funds of the estate were invested.

The auditing judge decided that the will did not authorize the purchase or undue retention of nonlegal securities, and surcharged sums aggregating $9,087.60 for losses . . . [on] bonds . . . , which originally had come to accountant as trustee from itself as executor, [plus] $43,018.75 representing the price of sundry nonlegal securities originally purchased and still held by the trustee. . . .

Perry on Trusts, 6th ed., sec. 465, correctly states:

There is said to be a distinction between an original investment improperly made by trustees, and an investment made by the testator himself and simply continued by a trustee, but it is a distinction that cannot be safely acted upon (as controlling). . . . It is true, a testator during his life may deal with his property according to his pleasure, and investments made by him are some evidence he had confidence in that class of investments; but, in the absence of directions in the will, it is more reasonable to suppose that a testator intended that his trustees should act according to law. Consequently, in states where the investments which trustees may make are pointed out by law, the fact that the testator has invested his property in certain stocks, or loaned it on personal security, will not authorize trustees to continue such investments beyond a reasonable time for conversion and investment in regular securities.

In Pennsylvania we have a number of cases where this court refused to surcharge executors with losses sustained through holding, for several years after a testator's death, dividend-paying corporate stocks purchased by their decedent . . . but each of these decisions stands on its own facts rather than on any controlling principle . . . ; and the rule in respect to holding nonlegal securities owned by a decedent, which governs executors and other personal representatives with their presumably short-duration trusts, should for obvious reasons, be more liberal than that governing trustees fixed with the duty of managing an estate during a long period of years.

. . . The general rule, — in jurisdictions which, like Pennsylvania, limit the investment of trust funds, — is that ordinarily a fiduciary has no right to retain, beyond a reasonable period, investments made by the decedent in unauthorized securities, unless specially empowered so to do; that when a trustee continues to possess such nonlegal investments after a time when he could properly dispose of them, and a loss occurs, he may be held liable for a failure of due care, unless he shows that his retention of the securities in question represents, not a mere lack of attention, but the honest exercise of judgment based on actual consideration of existing conditions; in other words, he is expected to be ordinarily watchful and to exercise normally good judgment. . . .

FIRST ALABAMA BANK v. SPRAGINS
515 So. 2d 962 (Ala. 1987)

ADAMS, J.

The Spragins family, as beneficiaries, brought suit against First Alabama Bank of Huntsville (hereinafter "First Alabama" or "the Bank"), trustee of a trust created by the last will and testament of Marion Beirne Spragins, Sr., for breach of fiduciary duty and mismanagement of the trust fund. . . . The jury returned a verdict in favor of the Spraginses for $533,000.00 in compensatory damages and $1,500,000.00 in punitive damages. . . . First Alabama Bank of Huntsville v. Spragins, 475 So. 2d 512 (Ala. 1985). The Bank was then permitted to withdraw as trustee.

We reversed and remanded the case to the trial court with instructions, having determined that the case should not have been tried to a jury . . . and that no reasonable inferences existed to support a finding of bad faith or willful mismanagement which would justify an award of punitive damages.

On re-trial before Judge Watson, the parties agreed to submit the case on the record previously established; no further evidence was presented. The court elected to treat the prior jury verdict as advisory. Judge Watson ruled in favor of the Spraginses and ordered the Bank to pay $685,560.00 in compensatory damages and $79,224.00 in interest. We affirm the judgment of the circuit court.

The issues presented on appeal are whether the trial court erred in awarding damages; whether the trial court's reliance on the plaintiffs' method of calculating damages was erroneous; and whether the court erred in awarding the Spraginses pre-judgment interest.

The facts reveal that Marion Beirne Spragins, Sr., was formerly the president and later chairman of the board of trustees of the defendant (appellant) Bank. . . . After settlement of his estate, the net value of the trust was $556,881.73, at least 70% of which consisted of stock in First Alabama's own holding company.

. . . [T]he Bank does not argue that the trial court's application of the "prudent person" rule to the Bank's alleged breach of fiduciary duty was erroneous under Alabama law. Instead, the Bank contends that the general rule is modified by the terms of the trust. That agreement [grants the trustee power]:

> . . . To sell, exchange, transfer, convey, either before or after option granted, all or any part of said Trust Estate and any trust created herein, upon such terms and conditions as it sees fit to invest and reinvest such Trust Estate and any trust created herein and the proceeds of sale or disposal of any portion thereof, in such loans, stocks, common or preferred, bonds, insurance contracts, or other securities, mortgages, common trust funds, or other property, real or personal, whether so-called "legal" investments of trust funds, or not, as to it may seem suitable, and to change investments and to make new investments from time to time as it may seem necessary or desirable, regardless of any lack of diversification, risk, or nonproductivity.

The Bank argues that the trial court's award of damages was based on First Alabama's failure to diversify the trust holdings, when in fact, the power not to diversify was granted to the Bank by the trust agreement. The alleged "loss" suffered by the trust, the Bank argues, is illusory because the trust principal increased and "substantial income" was earned throughout the Bank's tenure as trustee. First Alabama contends that the court erroneously based its finding that the trust suffered a compensable loss on the Spraginses' calculations of what the trust might have earned had the trust portfolio been more diversified. The Bank argues that no loss was suffered, and, therefore, that the law will not recognize any loss to the trust.

We noted in our earlier consideration of this case, 475 So. 2d at 516, that although a trustee's duties and obligations are governed largely by the trust agreement, that agreement cannot be employed to vitiate "the duty imposed by the 'prudent person' standard." The circuit court found that the trust agreement provided:

> (3) POWERS OF TRUSTEE. . . . However, none of these powers shall be exercisable if to exercise the power would defeat my intention regarding my trust estate. . . .
>
> . . .

(d) To hold any property or securities originally received by it as a part of said trust estate or any trust estate created herein *so long as it shall consider the retention thereof for the best interest of said trust estate* . . . [emphasis added].

The Spraginses argue that a loss was incurred by the trust and that the trial court properly found that damages were due. The Bank's concentration of the trust property in its own stock, First Alabama Bancshares, was a violation of its duty of loyalty to the trust beneficiaries and constituted self-dealing, the Spraginses contend. The Spraginses claim, and the trial court found, that the Bank's failure to diversify the trust portfolio was "at least, insensitivity" by the trustee to the duty of loyalty it owed the trust beneficiaries. We agree. As we stated in the earlier appeal of this case:

> The trustee is under a duty to the beneficiary in administering the trust to exercise such care and skill as a man of ordinary prudence would exercise in dealing with his own property; and if the trustee has or procures his appointment as trustee by representing that he has greater skill than that of a man of ordinary prudence, he is under a duty to exercise such skill.

475 So. 2d at 516, quoting Restatement (Second) of Trusts, §174 (1959). We agree with the circuit court that the donor did not intend to vest in the trustee Bank a power to diversify so little as to prejudice the interests of the beneficiaries.

From the evidence presented to the circuit court, the advisory jury, and later, Judge Watson, found that the Bank failed to provide a reasoned plan of investment calculated to accomplish the testator's purpose. That purpose was to provide for present and future generations of the testator's family. Testimony by the Bank's senior trust officer revealed that eight years after the Bank had assumed administration of the trust, i.e., by 1982, the needs of the testator's grandchildren had still not been determined by the trustee, a basic step which should have preceded formulation of a prudent plan for management of the trust property. The Bank argued, nevertheless, that it had adopted an investment strategy of "moderate income and moderate growth," in its management of the trust. Again, from the facts presented, the circuit court had more than ample evidence from which to conclude that the plan of investment which the Bank claims to have adopted to manage the Spragins trust was "designed to provide a justification for the failure of the trustee Bank to more fully diversify the trust holdings by selling all or substantially all of the First Alabama Bancshares stock." At a time when the trustee Bank's own investment advisory service was recommending that investment in bank stock be limited to five percent of a trust's portfolio, approximately seventy-five percent of the Spragins trust assets were invested in First Alabama Bancshares. We hold that the circuit court was not in error in concluding that the trustee Bank's management of the Spragins trust was, at least, imprudent, and demonstrated the insensitivity of the trustee Bank in the performance of its duty of loyalty to the trust's beneficiaries.

The appellant argues, however, that liability is irrelevant; that even if the Bank is guilty of a breach of trust, no damages should have been awarded because the Trust suffered no loss. Again, we disagree.

The net value of the Trust was $556,881.73 when the testator's estate was settled. The court found that the trust property, 70 to 75% of which was composed of First Alabama Bancshares during the Bank's tenure as trustee, fluctuated in value from a low of approximately $200,000.00 in 1975 to $776,168.00 by 1983. By contrast, the Spraginses offered the testimony of James C. King, a recognized expert in the field of trust management, to show what active, prudent management might have achieved. The Bank disputes King's conclusion, attributing his estimation of loss suffered by the trust to hindsight and speculation. We conclude that the circuit court was not in error in finding that the trust suffered a compensable loss and, further, that the method employed by Mr. King was not mere speculation and hindsight.

As the circuit court observed, speculation is not a sufficient basis for an award of damages in Alabama. See Mall, Inc. v. Robbins, 412 So. 2d 1197 (Ala. 1982), Preston v. Alabama Power Company, 401 So. 2d 107 (Ala. 1981); Taylor v. Shoemaker, 34 Ala. App. 168, 38 So. 2d 895 (1948), *cert. denied*, 251 Ala. 601, 38 So. 2d 900 (1949).

The Spraginses argue that the court correctly determined the amount of the loss by weighing the actual value of the trust principal against what the value would have been had it been prudently managed. The increase in principal cited by the Bank is largely attributable to inflation, the Spraginses contend, and is far less than the increase which would have been realized if the Bank had acted on the investment advice it gave its other customers regarding limiting investment in bank stocks. . . .

Mr. King's approach, the court said, was one of fiscally sound, conservative, active management of the trust estate. His alternative to the Bank's investment in First Alabama Bancshares was to concentrate the assets in the Standard and Poor's 500 index and in fixed income treasury bills. Although the Bank argues strenuously that Mr. King's approach was speculative and mere hindsight, the trial court had substantial evidence upon which to base its conclusion that King's approach was a responsible investment alternative to the Bank's management method. Indeed, the Bank's investment approach appears to have been based upon the assumption that, at all times during its tenure as trustee, First Alabama Bancshares represented the best possible investment of the trust property. More than sufficient evidence supports the circuit court's finding that the Bank's continued investment of 70 to 75% of the trust assets in bank stock was not in the best interest of the beneficiaries. . . .

Affirmed. . . .

TORBERT, Chief Judge (dissenting).

The conclusion that damages are properly awardable in this case is wrong. The central issues presented are whether the failure of the trustee to sell the stock of the trustee bank was a breach of trust and, if it was a breach, whether any compensable injury ensued. . . . [The trial judge erred in concluding that there was a breach when] the trust instrument authorized the very conduct at issue . . . [and in] then conclud[ing] that, even though the supposed breach resulted in no actual loss, the trustee is liable for *lost profits*. . . .

. . . [N]o one really argues that investing in some shares of the bank stock was imprudent. . . . The specific issue is whether the bank was imprudent in failing to diversify the portfolio, which consisted primarily of bank stock [which the instrument authorized the bank to retain "regardless of any lack of diversification"]. . . .

We have been very restrictive with regard to allowing recovery for lost profits, primarily because such awards would often be based on very questionable evidence. The Restatement appears to take a similar view, by limiting recovery for lost profits for breach of trusts in the absence of a breach of loyalty to situations where the trustee had a duty to purchase a specific piece of property. Restatement (Second) of Trusts §205(c) and comment (c) and §211. . . . Lost profits are easily ascertained with respect to failure to purchase a specific item, such as shares of XYZ Corporation. . . .

. . . [Furthermore,] Mr. King starts with the premise that all bank stock would be sold and reinvested. However, Mr. King agreed that the bank stock was a good investment in general, and his objection was solely that the trust res was too heavily concentrated in that stock. "[T]he trustee is liable only for such loss as results from the investment of the excess beyond the amount which it would have been proper so to invest." Restatement (Second) of Trusts §228 comment 1. Therefore, Mr. King began from the wrong starting point.

UNION COMMERCE BANK v. KUSSE
251 N.E.2d 884 (Ohio Prob. Ct. 1969)

[The executor's petition for instructions asks whether a will provision precluding the executor and trustee from selling securities received from the probate estate relieves them from possible liability for holding the securities.]

ANDREWS, CHIEF REFEREE (opinion approved by MERRICK, P.J.). . . .

The answer to that question is definitely "no." Even though a fiduciary is without power of sale, he is still not relieved from his duty to manage the estate with due care and prudence. If the circumstances are such that it becomes imprudent to retain a certain security or other item of property, the fiduciary must apply to the court for permission to sell it. And in an emergency or what the fiduciary reasonably believes to be an emergency, if he has no opportunity to apply to the court, he may sell the security without first obtaining the court's permission, although his action is subject to the court's later approval. 1 Restatement, Trusts 2d, sec. 167(2) and Comment *e* [dealing with deviation from trust terms based on changed circumstances (see Chapter 13, section D1)]. . . .

Questions relating to the retention of investments coming to a fiduciary at the beginning of his service start with the common law rule that where the fiduciary receives securities which are not proper trust investments (often called "nonlegals"), it is his duty to dispose of them within a reasonable time.

Statutes or provisions in wills or trust instruments authorizing the fiduciary to retain any property coming to him relieve the fiduciary of this common law duty. But they do not relieve him of his duty to exercise due care and prudence with reference to the retention or disposal of such property. . . .

Mr. Kusse's will also grants to his executor and trustee the power to invest in any property without regard to statutory or judicial restrictions. Consequently, no investments made by either fiduciary can be classed as nonlegals, and the same is true of the property originally coming to the fiduciary. 3 Scott, Trusts (3d ed.) sec. 230.1, p. 1870.

But even the unlimited investment authority given in Mr. Kusse's will does not relieve the fiduciary from the obligation of due care and prudence. . . .

When the fiduciary is a corporate executor and trustee, with greater skill and facilities for handling trust estates than those possessed by the "ordinary prudent man," such fiduciary is held to a higher degree of care, consonant with its greater skill and facilities. . . .

BOSTON SAFE DEPOSIT & TRUST CO. v. BOONE
489 N.E.2d 209 (Mass. App. 1986)

[The will of W. T. Pearson, who died in 1968, established a marital deduction trust giving his widow income for life and a general power to appoint the remainder by her will, with a gift in default of appointment to Brown University. Pearson's attorney, who had died by the time this action was brought, and Boston Safe were cotrustees. When Mrs. Pearson died in 1972, a codicil to her will provided for various appointments of the trust remainder with any balance to go to her estate. Brown University contested the appointments, causing the distribution of the trust to be delayed for a period during which a severe decline and a partial recovery in the stock market reduced the estate assets by about

$100,000, so that no balance was available for Mrs. Pearson's executors.]

KAPLAN, J. . . .

Boston Safe recognized, as a general proposition, that upon the falling in of a trust (as upon the death of a life tenant like Mrs. Pearson), a trustee should consider itself — in the words of one of its trust officers — a "stake holder" with some obligation to "back off to a conservative position." The law is in agreement. Usually the "stake holder" will discharge its duty by liquidating and distributing with reasonable promptness. There is, however, no iron or absolute duty to do so, and prudence may indeed suggest (or even demand) that liquidation be deferred. . . . Where distribution will necessarily be long deferred, common sense tells us that a trustee can properly consider keeping the corpus of the trust reasonably productive meanwhile. . . . One can well imagine a claim of surcharge if a trustee in these circumstances liquidates precipitately, say upon an obviously depressed market. . . .

Neither the record or common experience suggests that the trustee could fairly be held for failing to predict the movement of stock prices after April, 1974, and in this period it faced the problem of what to do in a declining market. . . . When the slump comes, it often appears too late to sell; even then it may not be unreasonable to expect, and count upon an upturn. In consideration of the vagaries of the market, our courts have not been harsh about charging trustees for investment judgments which, on reflection after the event, appear to have been mistaken, although an extreme case could warrant surcharge. . . .

Mr. Pearson's will provided: "No one of them [executors and trustees] shall be liable for any act or omission except for his or its own willful default or bad faith." In light of the discussion above, we are not required to deal with the effect of this "exculpatory" clause. However, we note our agreement with the judge that the trustee's behavior cannot in any view be properly characterized as having involved "willful default" or "bad faith." The judge's evident view that the clause was effective according to its terms and not against public policy, is supported by past decisions.

The executors [of Mrs. Pearson's estate] attempt on this appeal for the first time to argue the point that one who drafts a will in which he is named as a fiduciary should not include an exculpatory clause that might apply to himself, without first advising the testator specifically of the effect of this provision. . . . Without attempting to delineate the scope of the rule which the executors seek to invoke, . . . we say that any claimed delict of the cotrustee should have been brought forward by the executors at an early stage. We may pass by the question whether or in what circumstances an infraction by one trustee might deprive a fellow trustee of the protection of an exculpatory clause.

The judgments dismissing the executors' objections to the accounting and allowing the accounts are affirmed.

PROBLEM

18-D. The testator bequeathed his residuary estate, valued at about $3 million, to the Towne Trust Company. The trust company has administered the estate for many years. The terms of the trust authorized investment "in government securities and such other mortgage loans, stocks or securities as the trustee deems in the best interest of my estate."

At a time when 70 percent of the trust assets were invested in common and preferred stocks, the trustee purchased $80,000 worth of stock in Continental Shares, Inc., an investment company organized five years earlier. By the charter of Continental Shares, its management had authority to buy and sell holdings without consulting its stockholders and regularly exercised this authority. The holdings of Continental Shares, at the time of the trustee's purchase, consisted of stock in established companies in the iron, steel, public utilities, rubber, paint, and petroleum industries. At the time of the purchase, the trust portfolio contained no shares of these industries.

Subsequent to the purchase, a business recession occurred and a substantial loss was sustained in the value of the trust's investment in Continental Shares. A beneficiary objected to this item on the trustee's accounting and sought to have the trustees surcharged for the amount of the loss. The trial court ruled in favor of the trustee on the propriety of the investment. A memorandum accompanying the court's ruling (see In re Rees' Estate, 53 Ohio L. Abs. 385, 85 N.E.2d 563 (1949)) reads as follows:

> Because of the lack of judicial authority on the subject in this state, the Court has had to look elsewhere and has been benefited by a recent article written by Mayo Shattuck, former President of the Massachusetts Bar Association and author of the Massachusetts Annotations to the Restatement of Trusts, in 25 Boston University Law Review (1945) at pages 12 and 13, where he states:
>
> > When we are speaking of acquiring shares of an investment trust are we describing an *abandonment* of the duties of a trust in any real sense or are we describing a *discharge* of those duties by participation in a reputable management enterprise, the evidence of which participation consists of a readily marketable certificate? Is the trust management in any real or practical sense abandoned? To me it seems that exactly the opposite has taken place. Nor am I alone in this view. Men of prudence, intelligence and discretion are every day acquiring the shares of well seasoned management type investment companies and investment trusts as desirable securities. . . .
> >
> > Now, if it is the intention of modern trust law to place the trustee as nearly as possible in the position of the man of prudence, intelligence and discretion who is making permanent disposition of his own capital, why should not the trustee be extended the same privilege which is everyday being exercised by the prudent man who is

his model? My answer is that the trustee ought to have that privilege; that there is no sound reason for denying it to him and that the law must therefore be expected to advance in this direction.

This court believes that the arguments of Mr. Shattuck are well founded. Therefore the exceptions to the account are overruled.

How would you argue in behalf of the beneficiary on an appeal of this decision? What arguments would be made in behalf of the trustee? How do you evaluate your chance of success for purposes of deciding whether to advise an appeal? See generally G. Bogert, Trusts and Trustees §679 (2d ed. 1960).

Assume that the Banking and Financial Code of your state, comparable to provisions in almost all of the states, contains the following provision:

> Any trust company may establish and administer common trust funds composed of property permitted by law for the investment of trust funds, for the purpose of furnishing investments to itself as fiduciary, and may invest funds held by it as fiduciary in interests in such common trust funds, if not prohibited by the instrument, decree, or order creating such fiduciary relationship.

(The *Mullane* case, Chapter 15, section C, supra, involved and describes the nature of a common trust fund.) You have also determined that the larger trust companies in the state utilize common trust funds extensively, but that the Towne Trust Company had never found it worthwhile to do so. Your research also produces the *Springfield Safe Deposit & Trust Co.* case, which follows, as the nearest case in point decided by the highest court of your state.

SPRINGFIELD SAFE DEPOSIT & TRUST CO. v. FIRST UNITARIAN SOCIETY
293 Mass. 480, 200 N.E. 541 (1936)

[Petition for allowance of accounts by the trustee of a fund of $6,000 under the will of Sarah Spaulding. The disputed items relate to an investment of $2,000 in a "participating interest" in a note and mortgage and to the losses resulting therefrom. The objection is essentially that this constituted an unauthorized form of investment.]

Rugg, C.J. . . .

The facts relating to the original investment now assailed were these in substance: In 1925 the trust department of the petitioner, from uninvested funds held by it in various trusts, lent $65,000 to William M. Young, a man of substantial means and owner of a considerable amount of real estate, on his note payable on demand after three years with interest at five and a half percent per annum, payable quarterly, and secured by a first mortgage in usual form on real estate in the business section of Springfield. . . . The officers of the petitioner appraised the land at $100,000 and the buildings at $20,000. The executive committee of the petitioner, consisting of its president and five directors, all men of extensive experience in real estate matters, approved the loan as a conservative mortgage and a proper investment for the trust estates contributing thereto. The note and mortgage ran to the petitioner without designation as trustee. This method was for the convenience of the various trust estates interested therein and to enable the petitioner as trustee to hold, administer and deal with the note and mortgage for the best interests of the trusts. This method was in accordance with uniform practice of other similar institutions and was the only practicable way to manage such an investment. The money advanced on this note and mortgage was derived exclusively from various trust funds in the control of the trust department of the petitioner; no portion of it belonged to the commercial department of the petitioner. When the loan was made and the necessary funds contributed by the various trust estates from uninvested capital in the several trust estates, proper entries were promptly and duly made upon the books of the trust department of the petitioner showing the sums respectively advanced from each contributing trust estate, the proportion of each contribution to the amount of the note and mortgage, and the face amount of the participating beneficial interest therein received by each contributing trust estate, which participating beneficial interests were evidenced and represented by "Certificates of Interest in Real Estate Mortgage," so called, identical in form, which were on the same date duly executed by the petitioner and placed in the portfolio of each contributing trust estate. These certificates showed that the particular trust estate had a participating interest in the mortgage with a face value equal to the amount contributed by it. . . . In 1932, during the depression, it became necessary to foreclose this mortgage. The property was sold at a loss. A new note and first mortgage were taken by the petitioner covering the same property and a new participating interest certificate issued to represent the share of the Spaulding trust on the same plan as before. This was known as the Okum mortgage. The loss thus suffered by the Spaulding trust was in no respect due to the method of holding the Young mortgage or caused by the fact that it was a participating mortgage. The same loss would have occurred if the mortgage had been held entirely by one trust estate. It is stated in the agreed facts:

> Investment of trust funds held by corporate fiduciaries in participating interests in mortgages, similar to those held in this trust, have been made since 1892 and continuously thereafter. . . .

Conditions which have led to this form of investment are narrated at some length in the record but need not be here recited. This device was adopted and has grown in favor because of the difficulty which corporate fiduciaries have experienced in obtaining first mortgages upon real estate in the Commonwealth in amounts small enough to be held in smaller trusts and to provide the diversification desired in larger trusts. The plain inference from the facts stated is that this form of investment for trust funds has been regarded as safe and conservative by the men charged with the responsibility of managing large and small trusts by trust companies. . . .

The precise question is whether as a matter of law such investments are permissible. That question has not arisen hitherto in this Commonwealth. Investment of trust funds in securities of this nature has been upheld in other jurisdictions. The general principle is found in Am. Law Inst. Restatement: Trusts, in §227, comment *j*, in these words:

The mere fact that trust funds are combined with funds not held in trust or with funds of other trusts in making investments does not necessarily make the investments improper, provided that the investments are in other respects proper. Thus, an investment of trust funds in a participating interest in one or more first mortgages on land, or in a group of securities which are all proper trust investments, may be a proper trust investment. Such investments are not proper if they are not such as a prudent man would make of his own property having primarily in view the preservation of the estate and the amount and regularity of the income to be derived. . . .

It was said in Matter of Union Trust Co. 219 N.Y. 514, 519:

The advantages that are frequently to be secured by combining trust funds to make a large and more satisfactory investment than can be made of the funds of one trust without combination are of sufficient importance and value to the several trust funds to overcome any disadvantage that may arise from the fact that the several owners of the investment may thereafter differ in the matter of handling the same. Trust funds have been from time to time combined for investment with satisfactory results and the practice is generally recognized as proper for a trustee. . . .

Individual trustees ought to be scrupulously careful not to make investments of trust funds in their own names but always to indicate that they are made in a trust capacity. They are held to strict liability for violation of this duty. But the books of account of the petitioner, the stringent provisions of statute as to the separation of trust investments, and the constant public supervision of its affairs show that no harm has come to the beneficiaries. . . .

It is the duty also of trustees holding two or more distinct trust funds to keep them separate and ordinarily not to invest them together. . . . That principle has not been violated in the case at bar in its essential features. The mortgage was a single investment, but it was divided forthwith by the issuance of the certificates of interest to the several trusts, which became at once a matter of record in its trust department and subject to periodical inspection and examination by the bank commissioner. Objection based on the possibility of transfer of certificates from one trust to another by the trustee, if in good faith, and otherwise not open to just criticism, is without merit. . . .

In the case at bar there is no contention that the petitioner did not exercise good faith and act for a proper purpose. The loss that has resulted to the beneficiaries is not due to conduct of the petitioner or the kind of investment made, but to adverse general financial conditions. In such circumstances there is no liability for breach of trust. . . .

The contention is made by the beneficiaries that the Young mortgage was not a proper investment in point of security when originally made in 1925. The circumstances attendant upon making that investment have already been stated. The amount of the loan seems large in view of what happened since it was made. The propriety of an investment must be determined with reference to facts and conditions existing at the time it was made and not in the light of subsequent and unforeseen events. The depreciation in the value of the real estate resulting from the depression and the consequent loss on the mortgage occurring after it was taken have no direct bearing on the soundness of the original investment. No hard and fast rule can be formulated to determine with exactness the amount of a loan on real estate permissible for trust funds. . . . The fair and conservative market value of productive real estate as basis for a loan in its last analysis is a matter of opinion. No opinion evidence is set out in the record, except the appraisal of the trust officers and the executive committee of the petitioner. No evidence challenges the soundness of their judgment. The case on this point appears to be close, but we do not think that the loan can be pronounced excessive.

Decree may be entered allowing each account. Ordered accordingly.

One of the most important efforts to codify rules covering trustee investment duties is the Employee Retirement Income Security Act of 1974 (29 U.S.C.A. §§1001 et seq.). ERISA §404 (29 U.S.C. §1104(a)(1)(B) and (C)) requires trustees of employee benefit trusts "to discharge [their] duties with the 'care, skill, prudence, and diligence under the circumstances then prevailing that a prudent man acting in a like capacity would use in the conduct of an enterprise of a like character and with like aims,' and by diversifying the investments so as to minimize the risk of 'large losses,' unless under the circumstances it is clearly prudent not to do so." Fleming, Prudent Investment Standards: The Varying Standards of Prudence, 12 Real Prop., Prob. & Tr. J. 243, 247 (1977), continues:

> Many lawyers have been perplexed by this provision of ERISA. But if one takes the time to make the comparison, it will be found that much of

the language is lifted almost verbatim from sections 227 and 228 of the Restatement of Trusts (Second), and from section 7-302 of the Uniform Probate Code, including the reference to "large losses." The word "diligence" has been added to "care, skill and prudence" but it, too, appears in the Restatement's commentary and adds only an element of attentiveness to what is already implicit in the term "care." The reference to an "enterprise of like character and with like aims" means much the same as "dealing with the property of another" found in the Uniform Probate Code and in Scott on Trusts.

In spite of ERISA's rhetoric, it is reasonable to expect that the courts will interpret its provisions in accordance with the standards of prudence applicable under state law to trusts generally. What is now in ERISA is the extension of fiduciary accountability to others besides trustees and the outlawing of [exculpatory] clauses frequently found in express trusts and the listing of prohibited transactions.

But compare Committee Report, Fiduciary Responsibility and The Employee Retirement Income Security Act of 1974, 12 Real Prop., Prob. & Tr. J. 285, 286 (1977):

Although the ERISA prudent man rule has its genesis in the common law prudent man rule, it differs in several material respects from that familiar rule. Congress expressly stated its intent to impose principles of fiduciary conduct "adopted from existing trust law, but with modifications appropriate for employee benefit plans." Indeed, Congress expected that the "courts will interpret the prudent man rule and other fiduciary standards bearing in mind the special nature and purposes of employee benefit plans. . . . " To predict the responsibilities which will be imposed on fiduciaries under ERISA will therefore require an understanding of the basic principles of fiduciary responsibility under existing state law, coupled with an estimate of those modifications which are appropriate in the administration of employee benefit plans under ERISA.

And see Committee Report, Current Investment Questions and the Prudent Person Rule, 13 Real Prop., Prob. & Tr. J. 650, 661-662 (1978):

Finally, it should be noted that the Department of Labor has indicated approval of investment by ERISA fiduciaries in small businesses. In a speech delivered in Chicago in August, 1977, Ian D. Lanoff, Administrator of the Pension and Welfare Benefit Programs of the Labor Department addressed the concerns of fiduciaries who are uncertain of their authority to invest in new small companies. Mr. Lanoff indicated that as far as the Department of Labor is concerned, investment in small companies is permissible based on modern portfolio management methods. [Securities Week, Sept. 12, 1977.]

Once the whole portfolio is accepted as the proper focus for legal analysis, it is easy to see that pension investments in small companies are not prohibited. . . . The prudence of any investment by a pension fund can be determined in its relation to the overall structure of the pension portfolio and the functions and funding requirements of the pension plan. These are the factors to examine in determining the prudence of an investment in a small company.

Finally, Mr. Lanoff supports the position that amending ERISA to permit investment in small companies is not necessary. . . .

> The empirical data does not support the factual allegations that ERISA has caused a concentration of pension investments in "blue-chip" companies. A legal analysis of section 404 does not lead to the conclusion that ERISA prohibits pension investments in small companies. In fact, when viewed against the whole portfolio, an investment in a small company may be perfectly appropriate and proper.

Mr. Lanoff's views are restated in his April 21, 1978 announcement of Proposed Regulation section 2500.404a-1, Investment Duties. The proposed regulation itself rather innocuously defines the factors to be considered in investments as including diversification, volatility, liquidity, projected return, and projected economic conditions. Mr. Lanoff states that this "makes it clear" that the riskiness of a specific investment does not make it per se prudent or imprudent.

> Thus, although securities issued by a small or new company may be a riskier investment than securities issued by a "blue-chip" company, the investment in such a company may be entirely proper under the Act's "prudence" rule.

How Mr. Lanoff finds this clear in the proposed regulation may not be altogether clear to others.

Mr. Lanoff may give comfort to ERISA fiduciaries, and his statements may help protect fiduciaries from surcharge under ERISA for investing in new small companies. For the rest of fiduciaries under the present state of the law, either they will need very specific language in the governing instrument, or they will be entering that rather unsatisfactory game where any profit realized on the investment will belong to the trust, but any loss will come out of their own pocket.

LANGBEIN AND POSNER, THE REVOLUTION IN TRUST INVESTMENT LAW
62 A.B.A.J. 887 (1976)

There are growing indications that the investment practices of fiduciaries are undergoing fundamental change. Although the new developments have occurred in institutional investing circles, ordinary private trustees who lag behind may soon be risking surcharge. A principal sphere of legal counseling is therefore affected.

A large and still growing body of empirical evidence demonstrates that conventional investment practices have produced consistently disappointing results. Not only have institutional portfolios as a group underperformed the broad stock market averages like the Standard and Poor's 500, but there appear to have been no significant exceptions among individual funds. Despite their heavy research and trading expenditures, professional fund managers have been unable to "beat the market." As this evidence has mounted, economic science has produced a convincing explanation of why their efforts have been doomed to futility — the so-called theory of efficient markets. Recent articles in the business press — the Wall Street Journal, Forbes, and elsewhere — have popularized the theory.

In response to these advances in our understanding of investment, a new investment strategy has been devised and is being ever more widely adopted. Portfolios that track the performance of the market as a whole ("market funds" or "index funds") have been constructed successfully and at astonishingly low cost. The legal analysis developed to sustain the prudence of this new investment strategy will inevitably bring into question and litigation whether the courts should continue to sanction the outmoded investment practices of the past. The trustee's duty to diversify investments is taking on a new scope and meaning, while the former duty of care respecting the selection of individual securities is being significantly de-emphasized.

This article is only an introduction to the important legal questions the market-fund phenomenon raises for trustees. Readers who want greater detail are referred to our article, "Market Funds and Trust-Investment Law" [(parts 1 and 2) 1976 Am. B. Foundation Research J. 1, and 1977 Am. B. Foundation Research J. 1].

Mutual Funds May Underperform

Between 1962 and 1972 several studies of the postwar investment performance of the American mutual fund industry were undertaken, beginning with the Wharton School investigation commissioned by the Securities and Exchange Commission. The results of the studies were stunning. Mutual funds as a group had not outperformed the market as a whole, despite the *expertise* of their managers. Profs. James H. Lorie and Mary T. Hamilton summarized the studies in their 1973 book, The Stock Market: Theories and Evidence: "The funds did not show superior judgment either in picking stocks or anticipating general market movements." No individual fund consistently outperformed the market. Some did better than others, but none outperformed the market with a consistency greater than the law of averages would predict. Indeed, when brokerage costs and management fees were taken into account, the average mutual fund underperformed the market.

Although academic investigators have concentrated on mutual funds because the reporting and disclosure requirements of the Investment Company Act of 1940 have produced a superior, uniform, and easily

accessible data base, there is every indication that the investment record
of other large institutional investors, such as bank trust departments,
insurance companies, foundations, universities, and pension funds, is no
better. According to the Wall Street Journal of November 13, 1975, 77
percent of a large sample of pension fund managers "performed worse
than the S&P 500 over the 10 years ended Dec. 31, 1974. In the five
years ended that date, 90% of the funds failed to beat the market."

Theory of Efficient Markets Formulated

Why have the financial experts and analysts been unable to turn their
research skills to the advantage of their clients' portfolios? The answer,
it seems clear, is that the experts have cancelled out each other. To see
why this should be, we start with some truisms.

First, the price of a security represents the present value of its future
earnings. Second, for every buyer there must be a seller — someone who
has formed an opposite judgment about the value of the security at its
current price. If there were universal consensus that a particular stock
was a bargain at its current price, no one who owned it would be willing
to sell at that price. The price would have to rise to induce sellers to sell.
Hence, we can say that presumptively any stock is correctly priced at its
current trading level.

The only way to outperform the market — that is, consistently to identify undervalued or overvalued securities in advance of other investors
— is to predict future earnings with superior speed and accuracy. But
how are prophetic powers to be developed? Political, economic, and
social changes at home and abroad profoundly affect security prices, but
these phenomena are notoriously difficult to foresee; new information
about individual companies is disseminated rapidly as a result of modern
communications systems; and the securities laws have all but choked off
inside information as a source of advantage in trading.

Stock analysts are thus largely limited to interpreting information in
the public domain and available to other analysts, so that to outperform
the market an analyst has to be better at making interpretations than his
competitors. But as Professor Lorie and Hamilton conclude: "The
ardent quest for undervalued or overvalued securities by 11,000 trained
security analysts has made it extremely unlikely that more than very small
and transient margins of superiority can be achieved by any of these
analysts."

The theory of efficient markets posits that everything that is known or
knowable about the price of a security is *already fully reflected in its price.*
To be sure, there are some bargains — some securities that in retrospect
will turn out to have been incorrectly priced. But they are so few that the
cost of attempting to identify them, together with the cost of being
wrong much of the time, outweighs any gain.

And make no mistake about it: picking and trading stocks are very costly activities. Analysts have to be paid, housed, and supplied with data, equipment, and supporting personnel. The brokerage fees incident to trading constitute a significant drain on performance. The large blocks of shares characteristic of institutional trading often suffer unfavorable market spreads. The expense of researching individual securities in the hunt of bargains induces investment managers to hold a smaller number of stocks than they otherwise hold, and this underdiversification should also be reckoned as a costly feature of conventional portfolio management.

Market Funds Develop

In recognition of the expense and futility of attempting to outperform the market, a new investment strategy for fiduciaries and other investors has been developed: the "market" or "index" fund. A market fund creates and holds essentially unchanged a portfolio of securities designed to approximate some broad index of capital-asset performance, such as Standard and Poor's 500, the entire New York Stock Exchange, or conceivably an even broader cross-section of investment opportunities.

Within the past year or so, market funds have grown phenomenally. . . .

Market funds have three salient characteristics:

First, the fund manager does not research the prospects of individual securities. He assumes that securities are correctly priced and saves his fund the expense of conducting research to locate bargains. Instead he buys each individual stock in the portfolio in proportion to its value relative to that of all other stocks in the market. For example, since I.B.M. constitutes about 6 percent of the total value of all listed New York Stock Exchange stocks, and A.T. and T. about 5 percent, the market portfolio will keep 6 percent of its assets in I.B.M. and 5 percent in A.T. and T. The smaller the company, as measured by its (value-weighted) common stock, the smaller its representation in the market portfolio. The smallest company in the S. and P. 500 on this basis is Sonesta Corporation, which would have a weight of one thousandth of 1 percent in the market portfolio.

Second, as a corollary to its mode of stock selection, a market fund follows a "buy-and-hold" investment strategy that reduces trading costs to an absolute minimum. Trading is conducted only when cash inflows or redemptions require alteration in the net size of the fund or when substantial changes in the market price of a security require its inclusion in or exclusion from the portfolio in order to maintain the portfolio's fidelity to the market as a whole.

Third, market funds maximize diversification, a benefit worth pausing to explain.

The Advantages of Built-in Diversification

The principle of diversification is captured at the intuitive level in the maxim that you should not put all your eggs in one basket. Modern capital market theory has developed an understanding of diversification that, if less quaint, is rather more compelling. It asserts a distinction between the diversifiable and nondiversifiable risks incident to a particular stock.

For example, in an industry that does not have industry-wide collective bargaining the risk of a strike against one firm can be offset (diversified away) by buying stocks in the same industry, because a strike against a single firm, while it will hurt that firm, will lead to a corresponding increase in the sales of the other firms. A risk may affect all the firms in an industry yet still be diversifiable away. The 1973 Arab oil embargo damaged the fortunes of all automobile makers, motel chains, and makers of recreational vehicles but benefited domestic oil producers, the coal industry, and oil exploration service companies. Owning shares in the last three groups of stocks would have enabled an investor to offset, in part anyway, the losses he would have incurred on his holdings in the first three groups.

On the other hand, much of the risk of stock ownership obviously cannot be diversified away simply by broadening one's stock holdings. Many of the factors that will depress the value of one stock simultaneously will depress the value of most (sometimes all) other stocks: a rise in short-term interest rates, a threat of war, a president's assassination, a general economic downturn, a change in tax law adverse to corporations or to corporate shareholders, to mention a few. This is why the day-to-day and even year-to-year fluctuations of the stock market as a whole are so steep, notwithstanding that the market as a whole represents a broadly diversified portfolio of equity securities.

The capital market investigators have shown that the degree of risk that cannot be diversified away (the so-called systematic risk) is compensated risk, in the sense that the greater the degree of nondiversifiable risk to a stock, the higher the average return. Conversely, they have shown that diversifiable risk is uncompensated risk. No one pays the investor a premium because his portfolio is underdiversified. Although an investment policy that achieves optimal diversification cannot eliminate nondiversifiable risk, it can eliminate the uncompensated diversifiable risk, which represents a deadweight loss for the investor who dislikes risk when it does not produce a higher return.

There is a serious misconception about what degree of diversification is optimal. The point has been made that if one carefully selects about thirty stocks, the portfolio will be as much as 90 to 95 percent correlated with the movements of the market. But a 90 or even 95 percent correlation by no means eliminates all or even 90 to 95 percent of the diversifiable risk. In any given year the expected return of this thirty-stock portfolio would not be the same as the expected return of the market as a whole; rather, the expected return of the portfolio would be a fairly broad range on either side of the expected return. If the market as a whole rose in value (including dividends and appreciation) by 10 percent in one year, . . . the thirty-stock portfolio [might] rise by as little as 5.5 [or as much as 14.5] percent. It is only when the portfolio reaches about two hundred stocks that the range within which its return can be expected to fall is reduced to 1 percent on either side of the market's expected return.

Conventionally managed portfolios have been chronically underdiversified, in large part because of the expense of doing fundamental research on such a vast number of stocks. The market funds have been able to achieve optimal diversification because they do no research. They have rid themselves of this uncompensated risk. (For detail, see James H. Lorie, "Diversification: Old and New," in the winter, 1975, issue of the Journal of Portfolio Management.)

Seeing the Portfolio as an Entity

The two great discoveries of postwar investment experience — the futility of bargain-hunting for undervalued or overvalued securities and the central importance of optimally diversifying investments — have brought about a reorientation in thinking about the investment process that has major significance for the future shape of trust investment law.

It is now being recognized that a trustee's investment decision involves two conceptually distinct steps. One is evaluating specific assets that might be included in the trust. The other is combining specific assets to form the trust's portfolio, i.e., the package of assets constituting the corpus of the trust. The law of trusts traditionally placed greater emphasis on the first step and much less on the design of the portfolio. Yet from the beneficiary's standpoint what counts is the performance of the portfolio rather than the performance of its individual components.

If the value of the portfolio rises from $500,000 to $600,000, what does it matter to the beneficiary whether this increase resulted from a uniform 20 percent increase in the value of all of the assets in the portfolio or from larger gains in the few of the assets partially offset by losses in others? Conversely, if the portfolio has declined in value, it is of small comfort to the beneficiary to know that one of the components did spectacularly well rather than that all declined. From the beneficiary's standpoint, the portfolio is the relevant security.

Prudent Investor Rule and Market Funds

Virtually all of the money now flowing into market funds is trust money. Most market fund investors are pension funds, and they must satisfy the prudent investor standard of the Employee Retirement Income Security

Act as well as the common law standard. Obviously, the substantial institutions that are placing trust money in market-matching vehicles have
been counseled that the new investment strategy satisfies the legal
standard.

It is true that trust investment law as reflected in case reports in many
jurisdictions mirrors the old-fashioned investment strategy of individual
stock-picking and consequent underdiversification. But this is only
because most of the case law interpreting the trustee's duty of prudence
dates from the 1930s or earlier. In applying the prudent investor standard, the courts of that day were guided by the investment practices then
current in the investment community. Modern courts have not yet been
presented with an occasion to apply modern principles of portfolio
construction.

The trustee's duty to diversify, although recognized in a few cases and
. . . in Section 228 of the Restatement of Trusts, Second, has been
largely dormant because in the past the idea of risk spreading was an
intuitive notion unaided by scientific understanding of the advantages
and requisites for optimal diversification. Likewise, in reviewing the
trustee's discharge of his duty of prudence in selecting investments,
courts followed then current investment practice and disregarded the
portfolio as a whole: because trustees had invested on a stock-by-stock
basis, the courts reviewed their investment results on that basis. So long
as the universal custom of the investment community was to hunt for
individual bargains, the courts asked only whether the trustee had conducted the hunt with due care.

The market funds of the 1970s have been constructed on the premise
that the courts will apply the prudent investor standard differently to
them. The trustee who recognizes the import of the new learning and
who intentionally avoids individual stock picking in favor of a market-
matching vehicle expects to be judged on how effectively his portfolio
matches the market. His case is overwhelming. Whereas the vast majority
of pension funds have underperformed the market, the existing market
funds are tracking the market within a variance of 1 percent. And these
superior results are being achieved at greatly reduced management and
trading costs, yielding savings that are passed through to the beneficiaries of the fund.

Objections to Market Funds

How can the use of market funds be reconciled with the law of trust
administration?

The trustee who pursues the market-matching strategy all but inevitably will acquire some stocks that if individually selected would be characterized as speculative and hence as imprudent for trust investment.
The stocks of imperiled companies will not bulk large in a market port-

folio, because it weights each stock by the aggregate market value of the outstanding shares of the company. Since market value is the greater of (1) the capitalization of future earnings and (2) liquidation value (which is normally small), stocks of companies having poor earnings prospects already will have been bid down, and a further drop in their prices will have little impact on the fund. An attempt to exclude those stocks, if rigorously pursued, would impair the diversification of the fund and burden it with research costs — the very evils that the market fund was created to avoid.

There is in truth no reason for believing that the stocks of troubled companies are characteristically overvalued. The time to sell stock in a company headed for trouble is before the market discovers the trouble and discounts the price of the stock accordingly. But to beat the market to the punch is precisely what the investor cannot be expected to do with any consistency. In a market fund the portfolio is the relevant security, and there is no reason to examine the performance of its separate components.

In discussion of market funds the point is often made that if all investors adopted the passive "buy-the-market-and-hold" strategy, the market would cease to be efficient. There would be enormous gains to be made from stock picking because no one would be gathering or interpreting the information necessary to value stocks correctly in terms of their anticipated earnings. Although this point is correct, it has no practical significance. Even if all trustees adopted the passive strategy, there would still be many other investors, they would continue to search out undervalued stocks to buy and overvalued stocks to sell, and their activities would make it unnecessary and unprofitable for trustees to do any picking.

It is sometimes asked whether market funds are appropriate vehicles for specialized investment objectives. A trust fund set up to accumulate for a long period before making distributions will be seeking growth of its corpus, whereas a trust that is making heavy current distributions must have a portfolio selected to maximize income. Since the market fund is a suit that comes in only one basic size, is it unfit for these cases? The question is a legitimate one, but the example chosen to illustrate it — maximizing capital appreciation by selecting only "growth" stocks — a poor one. Growth is not an objective concept, as most of the owners of self-styled "growth" mutual funds have discovered to their rue. So-called growth stocks can underperform the market in spectacular fashion — Polaroid is one notorious recent example. Since the prospects for growth in the earnings of every company already will have been capitalized into the price of its shares, picking growth stocks is just another version of stock picking. It is a strategy that entails severe underdiversification as well as the other costs of conventional stock picking.

It is nonetheless true that a pure market fund will not suit the needs of every trust beneficiary, but adaptation of the concept to the specific needs of the beneficiary will be possible ordinarily without compromising the basic principle itself. For example, the principle of indexing equity investments does not prevent the fund from buying whatever proportion of nonequities, such as government and corporate fixed-income securities, it needs to increase its current income yields. The resulting portfolio will be less risky than the equity market as a whole, although by the same token it will not appreciate as rapidly in a rising market. Similarly, the specific tax status of the beneficiary may require some departure from the pure market fund idea. But this is a detail (although an important one) that can be handled within the broad framework of the market fund approach.

Implications for Conventionally Managed Funds

Trustees who invest in market funds will not be engulfed in lawsuits challenging the prudence of their investment, although a test case or two is perhaps inevitable. The advantages of market funds are so overwhelming and so palpable that their legal validation cannot be in serious doubt.

The real impact of market funds on trust investment law will be felt in the opposite arena — that of conventionally managed funds. Beneficiaries of conventionally managed funds will begin to complain of their trustees' failure to achieve results comparable to the market funds. Trustees who ignore the new learning and who underperform the market will be hard pressed to justify their adherence to an investment strategy of demonstrated riskiness, costliness, and futility.

The biggest impact of the market fund on trust investment law will be a greatly augmented conception of the duty to diversify. The same body of economic research that has demonstrated the hopelessness of stock picking also has shown what significant and virtually costless returns are achievable from optimal diversification. Portfolios of fifty growth stocks or a handful of bonds are now indefensible for a trustee. If a trust fund is too small to diversify adequately at reasonable cost, the law will move toward the recognition and enforcement of a trustee's duty to pool small trust funds to the extent necessary to achieve sufficient diversification.

On the question of trust investment law in the above article, compare the *Spitzer* case, infra, and see Committee Report, Current Investment Questions and the Prudent Person Rule, 13 Real Prop., Prob. & Tr. J. 650, 654-657 (1978):

> To the extent that estimates are available as to the relative value of portfolios declared to be "indexed," a figure in the neighborhood of 1 percent of institutional portfolios appears to be realistic. . . .

For those trust portfolios which must be judged by the "Prudent Person Rule," whether in one of its common law or statutory permutations, how does indexing meet the standard of prudence?

One challenge to indexing is improper delegation of duty. A trustee who invests in an index fund has, it may be presumed, taken two steps. First, he has examined the index fund concept and concluded that the concept has validity and that a prudent person would invest in such funds. Second, he has selected a particular fund. . . . It is unrealistic to assume that a trustee investing in an index fund will investigate the individual securities held by the fund. . . . The mix of stocks in each index is changed from time to time . . . imposing a further independent decision on the trustee's investment. . . . The counter argument would take a unitary approach to the index fund investment. That is, the fund as a whole is the investment. A change in its parts is no more the creature of an improper delegation than is corporate management's decision to sell off a division of a corporation whose stock is held by a trust.

A second challenge to index fund investing is the general prohibition against offsetting gains and losses. . . . Here again, the counter argument is bottomed on the unitary concept, with the speculative stock included in the index no more significant than the new division in the diversified corporation.

A third question is the general wisdom of index funds. There is evidence that index funds have in recent years outperformed individually managed portfolios. If such is the case presumably a prudent trustee should give serious consideration to the concept in the performance of his duties within the prudent person rule. Knowledgeable fiduciaries and investors have established and invested in index funds, and [fiduciaries are] "to observe how men of prudence, discretion and intelligence manage their own affairs. . . . " Also, an index fund certainly enables a trustee to diversify to a degree beyond that which could be achieved by most trustees without an unwarranted increase in administrative costs. Counter arguments against the wisdom of index funds include the widespread hostility in the investment community against index funds, and the relative novelty of the concept with the attendant lack of seasoning. . . .

[T]he trustee investing in index funds without specific authority to do so in the instrument is running a risk, pending further seasoning by time or further development of judicial precedent.

The Report, id. at 662-663, then considers "modern portfolio theory"·

[Securities] which might be quite risky when taken alone may, according to the theory, decrease total portfolio risk and, accordingly, be a more "prudent" purchase than a security which appears less risky by itself. Proponents chafe at the alleged restrictions of the Prudent Person Rule, which, say they, insists that each investment within a portfolio be "analyzed in a vacuum."

The uncertainty risk of the portfolio is the aggregate of the uncertainty risk of the securities which compose it. This aggregation of risks is not an arithmetic total but recognizes that securities which

strongly covary add more to portfolio risk than securities which do
not. . . . [T]he addition of a speculative security may actually reduce
the risk of the portfolio as a whole. Thus, because the economic
approach to risk views the risk of particular securities in terms of the
risk they contribute to the whole portfolio, it is more appropriate
than the legal concept.

[Note, Regulation of Risky Investments, 83 Harv. L. Rev. 603 (1970).]
And so mathematical techniques are developed which allegedly quantify
the concepts of speculation, volatility, covariance, investment productivity, and diversification. Those few doubting Thomases who remain are
heard to remark that math can be a substitute for thought, and that quantification can give a dangerous and misleading aura of certainty. . . .
    . . . [I]s not the fiduciary embracing this concept rushing into greater
danger? If his performance does not measure up to the averages, or that
of his competitors, is not the contention available that he was prima facie
negligent? Is not the fiduciary better protected by a rule of conduct,
rather than a test of performance?
    In any event, modern portfolio theory and its methodology have not yet
been endorsed by the courts, although the Department of Labor offers a
ringing endorsement for ERISA purposes. Ian Lanoff's announcement
April 21, 1978 of proposed regulation section 2550.401a-1 states that the
Act goes beyond what he alleges to be the common law doctrine of judging
prudence of an investment alone, without regard to its role in the total
investment portfolio.
    Perhaps the *Spitzer* case comes closest to addressing the portfolio issue,
and its consideration is balanced. The Court of Appeals decision held that
if a trust portfolio shows an overall increase in value, this does not prevent
the trustee from being held responsible for imprudence or negligence
with respect to a particular investment. . . . Nor, however, is the security
to be reviewed in a "watertight compartment" or "in a vacuum." On the
contrary, individual investment decisions are properly affected by considerations of the portfolio as a whole, as, e.g., diversification and sound tax
planning. But the focus, nevertheless, is on the individual security as such,
with factors relating to the entire portfolio to be weighed only along with
others in reviewing particular investment decisions. And that appears to
be the extent of present legal recognition of the relation of the portfolio
to the particular investment.

MATTER OF BANK OF NEW YORK
("THE *SPITZER* CASE")
35 N.Y.2d 512, 323 N.E.2d 700 (1974)

[The bank as trustee of its own common trust fund submitted an
accounting for a four-year period (as prescribed by N.Y. Banking Law
§100-c) ending September 30, 1968. The guardian ad litem (as "attorney for principal") challenged four investments; after examination of

witnesses, summary judgment on the four objections was granted, two by the Surrogate and the other two by modification in the Appellate Division.]

JONES, J. . . .

We now affirm the [dismissal] of all objections raised by the guardian [ad litem]. . . .

The guardian had completed the examination desired by him both of the trustee's records and its personnel. . . . There is no factual dispute between the parties as to what the trustee and its representatives did or omitted to do. The difference between them relates only to the legal conclusion to be drawn from conceded facts — the one contends that the trustee did not meet the duty imposed on it by law; the other, that such duty was discharged. . . .

[W]e do not agree with what appears to have been in part the basis on which the majority at the Appellate Division reached its conclusion. The fact that this portfolio showed substantial overall increase in total value during the accounting period does not insulate the trustee from responsibility for imprudence with respect to individual investments for which it would otherwise be surcharged (cf. King v. Talbot, 40 N.Y. 76, 90-91; 3 Scott, Trusts [3d ed.], §213.1, pp. 1712-1713). To hold to the contrary would in effect be to assure fiduciary immunity in an advancing market such as marked the history of the accounting period here involved. The record of any individual investment is not to be viewed exclusively, of course, as though it were in its own water-tight compartment, since to some extent individual investment decisions may properly be affected by considerations of the performance of the fund as an entity, as in the instance, for example, of individual security decisions based in part on considerations of diversification of the fund or of capital transactions to achieve sound tax planning for the fund as a whole. The focus of inquiry, however, is nonetheless on the individual security as such and factors relating to the entire portfolio are to be weighed only along with others in reviewing the prudence of the particular investment decisions. . . .

The record discloses that with respect to each investment the trustee acted in good faith and cannot be said to have failed to exercise " 'such diligence and such prudence in the care and management [of the fund], as in general, prudent men of discretion and intelligence in such matters, employ in their own like affairs.' " . . . It was not shown in any instance that the losses to the trust fund resulted from imprudence or negligence. There was evidence of attention and consideration with reference to each decision made. Obviously it is not sufficient that hindsight might suggest that another course would have been more beneficial: nor does a mere error of investment judgment mandate a surcharge. Our courts do not demand investment infallibility, nor hold a trustee to prescience in investment decisions. . . .

Whether a trustee is to be surcharged in these instances, as in other cases, must necessarily depend on a balanced and perceptive analysis of its consideration and action in the light of the history of each individual investment, viewed at the time of its action or its omission to act. In our opinion no sufficiently useful purpose would be served by a detailed description of the analysis by which we reach the conclusion that there is no basis for surcharge with respect to any of the four investments here called into question. . . .

Decree affirmed. . . .

ESTATE OF KNIPP
489 Pa. 500, 414 A.2d 1007 (1980)

FLAHERTY, J. . . .

[T]he Orphans' Court . . . denied a claim for surcharge . . . against the appellee corporate executor, Central Penn National Bank, for alleged mismanagement of estate investments. . . .

On November 9, 1972, letters testamentary were issued to appellee as executor of decedent's estate. His will created a testamentary trust, the beneficiaries of which included the appellants, and designated appellee to serve as trustee. The estate property included 4314 shares of Sears Roebuck & Co. common stock valued at the commencement of the estate's administration at approximately $470,000, a figure which represented 71% of the estate's total asset value and 97% of the value of all stocks in the estate. Only 400 of the Sears shares were sold by the executor during the first year of administration, the sales being made primarily to cover costs of administration rather than for reinvestment purposes. The will gave appellee, as executor and trustee, an absolute discretionary power either to retain or sell such property. Appellants' surcharge claim was brought because of a very substantial drop in the market price of Sears stock during the period of its being held in trust.

Appellants' first contention is that the attention, supervision, and group judgment given the investment account by the appellee did not measure up to that required of an expert corporate fiduciary under the rule of Killey Trust, 457 Pa. 474, 477-478, 326 A.2d 372, 375 (1974), where we stated:

> [T]he corporate trustee held itself out as an expert in the handling of estate and trust accounts. It represented itself as being possessed of greater knowledge and skill than the average man. It was therefore under a duty to exercise a skill greater than that of an ordinary man and the manner in which investments were handled must accordingly be evaluated in light of such superior skill.

After a thorough review of the record, we find, at least minimally, sufficient evidence to support the conclusion of the court below that the appellee exercised the degree of care, skill, and judgment required of a fiduciary. The testimony included an expert opinion from an investment advisor that appellee's investment practices conformed to generally followed corporate trust standards of skill and prudence. In addition, testimony was presented that appellee utilized respected outside sources of information and advice and closely followed trust account activity by frequent reviews, analyses, and group judgments. The evidence establishes that Sears stock was, during the period in question, reasonably believed to be a sound, national, broadbased stock worthy of investment by a fiduciary.

As it turned out, however, performance of the Sears stock was poor: the price per share dropped from $117 at the time of testator's death to approximately $88 by February of 1974 and continued to decline thereafter. Hindsight, however, is not the test of liability for surcharge. . . .

On the other hand, we are not prepared to say that authorization to retain assets gives an executor or trustee an absolute and unbridled discretion to sit idly by while those assets depreciate in value. Rather, when challenged, every such administration should be carefully scrutinized to determine whether an expert corporate fiduciary has performed according to the higher standards required of it.

In addition to the heretofore discussed assertion of a lack of attention to the estate account, appellants contend that the trustee's failure to substantially diversify the stock holdings within three months of commencement of administration constituted unskillful and imprudent trust asset management. Where, as in the present case, a testator vests a fiduciary with discretion to retain assets, the fiduciary is not thereby excused from the duty of making the retention decision prudently. . . . It is not, however, per se imprudent for an executor, vested with absolute discretion to hold property, to refrain from immediately diversifying a large block of stock received at the commencement of administration. In Saeger's Estates, 340 Pa. 73, 76-77, 16 A.2d 19, 21-22 (1940), where a surcharge was sought solely on the ground that the trustee had not diversified holdings, we said:

> Nor does it appear that in any case thus far brought before this Court has a trustee been surcharged solely for the reason now urged. In the absence of controlling precedent and particularly in the absence of such requirement in the statutory law relating to the investment of trust funds, we conclude that . . . there is no authority in the law of this State for the doctrine, contended for by appellants, that trust investments, otherwise legal and entirely proper under all the recognized standards, are necessarily improvident per se for any claimed lack of proper diversification.

Although many financial authorities advocate diversity of investment as a desirable course for trust management, a judicial decision declaring non-diversification to be presumptively imprudent would arbitrarily foreclose executors and trustees from opportunities to retain beneficial holdings. The preferable approach, therefore, is to determine on a case by case basis whether the particular investment approach meets the standard in Killey Trust, supra. Here we cannot say that the record does not adequately support the determination of the court below that retention of the Sears stock, without diversification, was not imprudent.

Decree affirmed. Each party to pay own costs.

Nix, J., dissenting. . . .

While it is true that the corporate fiduciary does not act as guarantor of the investment's success, I do not agree with the majority's conclusion that appellee in the instant appeal "has performed according to the higher standards required of it." The drop in price per share of the Sears & Roebuck & Co. stock which comprised a large portion of the trust corpus, did not occur suddenly, but rather took place over an extended period of time. From November, 1972 to February, 1974, the price dropped from $117 to $88 per share. Yet, in the face of the steadily increasing losses, the appellee retained the stock continuing to hope for its market recovery. These circumstances should have forced the conclusion that some diversification was required to attempt to offset the possible loss.

CHURCH AND SNITZER, DIVERSIFICATION, RISK AND MODERN PORTFOLIO THEORY
124 Tr. & Est. 32 (Oct. 1985)

The investment industry has undergone dramatic changes in recent years reflecting in part its efforts to convert ever-increasing amounts of information into knowledge. And while investors have always been concerned with diversification and risk, only recently have they had the tools to adequately quantify them.

Traditionally, professional investors, including bank trust departments, have relied on analysts to research companies and industries and provide reports for review by their organizations' investment committees. Portfolio managers, in turn, translated these recommendations into action for their assigned accounts. Though the methodology varied, the process remained essentially subjective.

Conventional wisdom held that diversification served to reduce risk, but that notion could not be proved quantitatively. Moreover, efforts at diversification were prone to error. Many professionals in the early '70s, for example, invested in an array of growth stocks spread over several industries only to see them drop as a group when high-multiple stocks fell out of favor. Thus, diversification by industry was inadequate. Risk itself was not well qualified and was usually defined by qualitative standards much as a treasury bond is considered to be less risky than a BAA bond.

In 1952, Prof. Harry Markowitz, in a pioneering effort to quantify these factors, conceived Modern Portfolio Theory. This theory held that all investors are risk-averse and will seek the highest rate of return at a particular level of risk. Prof. Markowitz also concluded that since most investors used basically the same precepts and quickly factored all published information into their investment decisions, markets tended to be efficient.

Prof. Markowitz recognized, however, that by creating a sufficiently large portfolio, non-market risk could be largely eliminated. . . . As computers became available and professional managers [were recognized as] underperforming popular market averages, Modern Portfolio Theory gained in popularity. By the mid '70s passive or index funds became fashionable. These funds, however, raised an important question — should the holdings of an indexed portfolio be confirmed by independent research?

By the late '70s the notion of efficient markets had become less credible. A consensus developed that large, well-researched and efficiently priced companies were appropriate for passive core holdings, but that opportunities for superior investment results lie in the inefficient market, i.e., small companies that are not fully researched.

Concurrently, the concept of covariance emerged. This is a measurement of how a security moves in relation to other securities and to the market. Covariance has become an accepted portfolio management tool. Simply, different types of stocks tend to move in opposite directions; this phenomenon can be quantified by itself, as well as in terms of its effect on a particular portfolio.

Covariance, then, represents a further evolution and refinement of Modern Portfolio Theory. . . .

Today's version of Modern Portfolio Theory is characterized by analysis of greater amounts of data — some unconventional such as earnings and price momentum, volatility and others — while reducing decision time. Moreover, it reflects the need to increase productivity through use of computer data bases and screens to identify specific issues for constructing portfolios with optimal characteristics.

In March of this year, the Chase Lincoln First of Rochester, New York obtained approval from the New York State banking authorities to use stock index options and market futures in common trust funds.

The investment world is changing rapidly and professional trustees may not be able to cling to past procedures and strategies to protect themselves from surcharge.

The basics of this approach are probably here to stay, particularly quantification of risk and portfolio characteristics vis-à-vis client investment objectives. The new methods are less subjective and more precise, thereby substantially enhancing the odds for successful investment performance.

By way of example, in the Estate of Knipp [supra] the Supreme Court of Pennsylvania held that a bank would not be surcharged for losses sustained by failure to diversify stock holdings of an estate within the first 90 days of account administration. . . .

Modern Portfolio Theory teaches that the financial principle underpinning the duty to diversify, is the need to modulate the effect of unanticipated events on the performance of a portfolio and to reduce risk.

One generally accepted measurement of portfolio risk is the standard deviation of return, a statistical method measuring the extent to which the actual return of a portfolio differs from its average return. For example, if a portfolio over time returned 10 percent on average, but could have returned from -20 percent to $+40$ percent, in any one time segment, its standard deviation is said to be 30 percent. Such a portfolio would seem volatile, and therefore more risky, than one with an average return of 10 percent and a standard deviation of 10 percent.

Now let us examine the *Knipp* portfolio vs. Standard & Poors over a 12 year period (Jan. 1961 to Dec. 1972) as shown in Table 1.

Therefore, on a total return basis with dividends and capital gains reinvested, a dollar in January 1961 of Sears stock became $4.52 by 1972. On the same basis, a dollar of the S&P 500 became $2.75. Sears was 60 percent riskier than the S&P 500. The risk, in retrospect, was worth it (.45 is better than .36). (However, it certainly was not worth the risk from Jan. 1, 1973 to Jan. 1, 1983 when the S&P 500 outperformed Sears by a margin of three to one even though Sears was 85 percent riskier than the market in *that* period.) The odds of securing such risk-adjusted results are between 5 and 50 percent.

The court did not address the issue now quantified by professional money managers: How much risk was the bank taking and was it appropriate for its beneficiaries?

Table 1

Sears & Roebuck & Co.	*Results*
Average Annual Return	13.4% (income and capital)
Standard Deviation	20.2
Risk-Free Return (T bills)	4.4
Risk Premium (13.4% − 4.4%)	9.0
Risk-Adjusted Return	
(9.0% ÷ 20.2%)	.45% reward per risk unit

S&P 500	*Results*
Average Annual Return	8.8% (income and capital)
Standard Deviation	12.5
Risk-Free Return (T-bills)	4.4
Risk Premium (8.8% − 4.4%)	4.4
Risk-Adjusted Return	
(4.4% ÷ 12.15%)	.36% reward per risk unit

It is not often that a fiduciary for widows and children takes 60 percent greater risk than market, a risk comparable to the most aggressive portfolio managers. A trustee who does not know the past and current risk of a portfolio is ignorant of what modern financial ideas can teach of an important element of fiduciary duty.

As for the legal implications, because it is now possible to define with reasonable mathematical precision the past risk of individual securities and portfolios, a criteria of investment competence should be that a trustee *know* such risk.

In addition, it would be imprudent for a fiduciary to assume "much" more than market risk no matter what the expected return. The duty to diversify should become more of an immediate imperative than was permitted in *Knipp*. And, finally, it should be gross negligence, subject to surcharge, for a fiduciary to assume the risk of *Knipp* (i.e., 60 percent more risk than market), a risk level higher than the most aggressive portfolios. The courts will undoubtedly catch up with available technology. Trustees cannot afford to be complacent.

The excerpt below is in one sense most directly related to principal/income accounting questions, and thus may usefully serve here as an introduction to the next chapter. It may be more significantly related, however, to an understanding of investment principles and decisions in an inflationary economy, including issues about possible applications of portfolio theory and at least about portfolio balance.

YOUNG, RUSSELL, ET AL., CURRENT INVESTMENT QUESTIONS AND THE PRUDENT PERSON RULE
13 Real Prop., Prob & Tr. J. 650, 664-668 (1978)

Based on our current inflation trends and projections for the future, is the purchase of long-term bonds with high interest rates prudent, considering what is apt to be left for the remaindermen after the passage of time? It has been suggested that some of this "interest" is an inflation factor which should be added to principal.

Such an adjustment to the income of a life income beneficiary is at present unsupported by the law. Does the law need changing, or should trust documents direct the trustee to undertake such an allocation? . . .

Interest rates (yields) on long-term bonds are a function of a "real" interest rate and the degree of "risk" incurred by the lender or investor. . . . The "risk" component represents the premium demanded and obtained to compensate for the risk assumed, [and inflation is] incorporated into the rate, or yield, structure . . . as a risk [causing] devaluation in the purchasing power of money. . . .

Conceptually, this interest rate now consists of two components, "a real rate of interest . . . and an inflation premium." Indeed, "inflation has almost always coincided with rising interest rates, and interest rates have rarely risen without inflation."

A possible way to avoid this might be to allocate some portion of the nominal interest rate return to principal. This allocation would spread the inflation "premium" (as a portion of the nominal interest rate) and therefore the inflation risk, to both the income beneficiary and to the remainderman.

The problem, of course, is that it is not precisely known how much of the nominal interest rate is attributable to inflation factors . . . because many factors may be involved in the setting of an interest rate. . . .

Since such an adjustment is currently unsupported by the law, when a large portion of any trust portfolio would be bonds, a trustor or his attorney might wish to develop a formula provision for the trust making an allocation of interest to the remainders. . . .

There is substantial support for the idea that some increment of interest does reflect an inflation factor and also some support for allocating to principal some interest for the purpose of protecting the purchasing power of a remainder. The balancing of interests between income beneficiaries and remaindermen has always been an important concern of fiduciaries. While it may be tempting to create as many guidelines as possible to aid in this process, the practical problem of measurement probably vitiates any substantial interest in making such an allocation and an amendment to our principal and income laws to accomplish this purpose seems remote.

19

Matters of Accounting and Successive Enjoyment

Some of the more technical and troublesome problems in fiduciary administration are considered in this chapter. Here we take up the day-to-day detail of allocating receipts and expenditures to the appropriate accounts, particularly as between principal and income. Most trusts and estates have purposes for which income is to be used or beneficiaries to whom income must be paid. At the same time usually there will be purposes and beneficial interests to which principal is allocable. At the time of each receipt or disbursement the fiduciary is forced to decide whether it is to be charged or credited to income or to principal, or whether it is to be apportioned between these accounts. Charged with the duty of impartiality, the fiduciary is subject to surcharge for improper allocation on any of these many transactions.

In the course of administering a trust or decedent's estate, a fiduciary will also find it necessary to make certain choices that will affect the various beneficial interests differently. Thus, the problem arises: How does the fiduciary's duty of impartiality to successive or multiple beneficiaries affect administrative decisions, and, if a decision benefits one beneficiary to the detriment of another, is any adjustment required or permitted?

Each item of a fiduciary's account is reviewable by the beneficiaries and, if objected to, must be supported as to its accuracy and propriety. This means not only that the allocation to the proper account or beneficiary must be correct but also that the validity and amount of the entry must be sustained. Thus, the fiduciary must show that each expenditure has been made for a proper purpose and in a reasonable amount and has been charged to the appropriate account. Only after this burden has been sustained will the fiduciary's accounts be approved.

In the case that follows, note the two types of problems it introduces. First, there is the question of a fiduciary's possible duty to insure, arising out of the obligation to protect and benefit potentially diverse interests. This type of problem quite often reflects itself in the investment function, where it affects the selection of properties to be held by the fiduciary. Second, there is the question of how the costs of fulfilling a fiduciary duty are to be borne by the various interests. This is one side of the general principal and income problem, which is a fundamental burden of fiduciary life.

WILLIS v. HENDRY
127 Conn. 653, 20 A.2d 375 (1940)

MALTBIE, C.J. . . .

We are asked whether it is the duty of the trustees to insure the premises given to them in the fourth article against loss by fire, and if so, whether the premium should be apportioned between the widow and the remaindermen. It is the duty of the trustees to exercise that care and prudence which an ordinarily prudent person would who was entrusted with the management of like property for another. . . . It is today a general custom among prudent business men to insure buildings in their charge against loss by fire; and ordinarily it is the duty of trustees holding property for remaindermen to see that such provision is made. . . . We are not informed of any facts in this case which would make inapplicable this rule. The premises are not to become a part of the residuary trust in the will until the widow dies, and, so long as she occupies them, the trustees are without any income from the property with which to pay such charges. The apparent intent of the testator was that the widow should bear all ordinary charges incident to the maintenance of the property so long as she lives on it, and the word "upkeep" is to be so construed. . . . In the absence of any facts taking the case out of the general rule, we advise that it is primarily the duty of the widow to insure the buildings; but if she fails to do so, the trustees should insure them and charge the premiums against her. Should the term of any policy run beyond the life of the widow, the portion of the premium representing the period thereafter would be a charge upon the trustees and the widow's estate would be entitled to reimbursement to that extent. . . .

A. Principal and Income

In the area of principal and income matters there have been many legislative attempts to spell out the rights of the various parties. These statutes on the whole have been helpful, but, as is seen below, many problems remain and new ones have arisen either in spite of or because of the statutory provisions. The administration of a decedent's estate has its principal and income problems and also the related problems of interest and increase. Thus, the interests of residuary beneficiaries are often at odds with those of the recipients of specific or general bequests and devises. Particular attention is required, however, to trust problems, and recent legislative efforts in this area are especially noteworthy.

1. Introductory Information

a. Increase and Related Problems of Decedents' Estates

For purposes of the present subject and certain other matters it becomes necessary to classify bequests and devises. Classification is considered further in Chapter 20, but at this point a brief introduction to the classes of bequests and devises is necessary.

A *specific* bequest or devise is a gift of a particular thing or parcel of land, such as a devise of Blackacre or a bequest of "my twenty-five shares of Acme Corporation stock." A *general* bequest is one payable out of the general assets of the estate, typified by a legacy of a stated sum of money. A bequest of "twenty-five shares of Acme Corporation stock" would also be general, provided the testator intended the executor to purchase the shares out of the general funds of the estate. The term *residuary bequest* is more or less self-explanatory and, along with the term *demonstrative bequest,* is taken up subsequently as further examination of the classes of gifts becomes appropriate.

A specific bequest or devise normally carries with it any increments that are not separable from the property itself. The legatee or devisee is also entitled to the income from specifically bequeathed or devised property after the death of the testator. Because the legatee or devisee is not entitled to income received by the testator during life, it becomes necessary to know what receipts by the testator constitute *income* from, rather than the *principal* of, the property involved.

There are also problems of when income is deemed to arise because the specific legatee gets only the income after the death of the testator. Certain general rules have been developed for application in the absence of provision in the will or in a statute to the contrary. For example, interest, as distinguished from other forms of income, is "earned from day to day" for purposes of apportioning receipts between income and principal at the beginning of a trust or at the termination of a right to trust income. At common law, in absence of statute, a devisee was entitled to rent becoming due after the testator's death, even though it might cover a period preceding the death, but did not receive that payable — even though in advance — during the testator's lifetime. Statutes now generally apportion rents received after the testator's death. Dividends declared to stockholders of record during the testator's lifetime, though paid to the executor or administrator, are held not to pass to the legatee of the stock specifically bequeathed.

Unless the contrary is provided by will, general legacies are usually held to bear interest at the legal rate beginning a year after the death of the testator, or, under some statutory rules, as of some other date. At common law and by statute, exceptions are typically recognized for legacies in payment of debts, in lieu of dower, for support of a minor child, and for the creation of testamentary trusts under which the income is payable to a designated beneficiary. In these exceptional cases interest usually commences at death.

Because income received by the personal representative and not allocable to specific bequests and devises enlarges the residue, and because interest charges are borne by the residuary estate, residuary gifts do not bear interest.

The income beneficiary of a trust is ordinarily entitled to the earnings of the trust property commencing with the testator's death. Generally speaking, specific and general gifts in trust cause no difficulty because the earnings accruing to the trustee under the above rules are simply allocated to the income beneficiary. On the other hand, if the trust is residuary, as is typically the case in modern wills, the determination of income and principal for the period of estate administration is likely to become more complex. As we shall see subsequently, there is disagreement among the cases regarding the rights of the income beneficiary and the remaindermen.

b. Trust Principal and Income Legislation

The original Uniform Principal and Income Act (1931) (9-B Uniform Laws Annotated 569) is still in effect in some states. Most of the statutes contain significant changes from the provisions of the recommended uniform act.[1] A revised uniform act was approved in 1962 and has now been adopted in a substantial number of states. The uniform act purports to be comprehensive and affords a useful frame of reference for our study. The Revised Uniform Principal and Income Act (1962) is printed below. As particular matters are taken up in this chapter, you should refer back to the relevant provisions of the act.

REVISED UNIFORM PRINCIPAL AND
INCOME ACT
(1962)

Section 1. *Definitions.* As used in this Act:

(1) "income beneficiary" means the person to whom income is presently payable or for whom it is accumulated for distribution as income;

---

1. The changes contained in one of these statutes are discussed at length in Bogert, The Illinois Principal and Income Act, 9 U. Chi. L. Rev. 30 (1941).

An extensive discussion of the pros and cons and implications of the Revised Act, infra, can be found in Gamble, The Revised Principal and Income Act (Mich. Inst. Continuing Legal Educ. 1966).

(2) "inventory value" means the cost of property purchased by the trustee and the market value of other property at the time it became subject to the trust, but in the case of a testamentary trust the trustee may use any value finally determined for the purposes of an estate or inheritance tax;

(3) "remainderman" means the person entitled to principal, including income which has been accumulated and added to principal;

(4) "trustee" means an original trustee and any successor or added trustee.

Section 2. *Duty of Trustee as to Receipts and Expenditures.*

(a) A trust shall be administered with due regard to the respective interests of income beneficiaries and remaindermen. A trust is so administered with respect to the allocation of receipts and expenditures if a receipt is credited or an expenditure is charged to income or principal or partly to each —

(1) in accordance with the terms of the trust instrument, notwithstanding contrary provisions of this Act;

(2) in the absence of any contrary terms of the trust instrument, in accordance with the provisions of this Act; or

(3) if neither of the preceding rules of administration is applicable, in accordance with what is reasonable and equitable in view of the interests of those entitled to income as well as of those entitled to principal, and in view of the manner in which men of ordinary prudence, discretion and judgment would act in the management of their own affairs.

(b) If the trust instrument gives the trustee discretion in crediting a receipt or charging an expenditure to income or principal or partly to each, no inference of imprudence or partiality arises from the fact that the trustee has made an allocation contrary to a provision of this Act.

Section 3. *Income; Principal; Charges.*

(a) Income is the return in money or property derived from the use of principal, including return received as

(1) rent of real or personal property, including sums received for cancellation or renewal of a lease;

(2) interest on money lent, including sums received as consideration for the privilege of prepayment of principal except as provided in section 7 on bond premium and bond discount;

(3) income earned during administration of a decedent's estate as provided in section 5;

(4) corporate distributions as provided in section 6;

(5) accrued increment on bonds or other obligations issued at discount as provided in section 7;

(6) receipts from business and farming operations as provided in section 8;

(7) receipts from disposition of natural resources as provided in sections 9 and 10;

(8) receipts from other principal subject to depletion as provided in section 11;

(9) receipts from disposition of underproductive property as provided in section 12.

(b) Principal is the property which has been set aside by the owner or the person legally empowered so that it is held in trust eventually to be delivered to a remainderman while the return or use of the principal is in the meantime taken or received by or held for accumulation for an income beneficiary. Principal includes

(1) consideration received by the trustee on the sale or other transfer of principal or on repayment of a loan or as a refund or replacement or change in the form of principal;

(2) proceeds of property taken on eminent domain proceedings;

(3) proceeds of insurance upon property forming part of the principal except proceeds of insurance upon a separate interest of an income beneficiary;

(4) stock dividends, receipts on liquidation of a corporation, and other corporate distributions as provided in section 6;

(5) receipts from the disposition of corporate securities as provided in section 7;

(6) royalties and other receipts from disposition of natural resources as provided in sections 9 and 10;

(7) receipts from other principal subject to depletion as provided in section 11;

(8) any profit resulting from any change in the form of principal except as provided in section 12 on underproductive property;

(9) receipts from disposition of underproductive property as provided in section 12;

(10) any allowances for depreciation established under sections 8 and 13(a)(2).

(c) After determining income and principal in accordance with the terms of the trust instrument or of this act, the trustee shall charge to income or principal expenses and other charges as provided in section 13.

Section 4.   *When Right to Income Arises; Apportionment of Income.*

(a) An income beneficiary is entitled to income from the date specified in the trust instrument, or, if none is specified, from the date an asset becomes subject to the trust. In the case of an asset becoming subject to a trust by reason of a will, it becomes subject to the trust as of the date of the death of the testator even though there is an intervening period of administration of the testator's estate.

(b) In the administration of a decedent's estate or an asset becoming subject to a trust by reason of a will

(1) receipts due but not paid at the date of death of the testator are principal;

(2) receipts in the form of periodic payments (other than corporate distributions to stockholders), including rent, interest, or annuities, not due at the date of the death of the testator shall be treated as accruing from day to day. That portion of the receipt accruing before the date of death is principal, and the balance is income.

(c) In all other cases, any receipt from an income producing asset is income even though the receipt was earned or accrued in whole or in part before the date when the asset became subject to the trust.

(d) On termination of an income interest, the income beneficiary whose interest is terminated, or his estate, is entitled to

(1) income undistributed on the date of termination;

(2) income due but not paid to the trustee on the date of termination;

(3) income in the form of periodic payments (other than corporate distributions to stockholders), including rent, interest, or annuities, not due on the date of termination, accrued from day to day.

(e) Corporate distributions to stockholders shall be treated as due on the day fixed by the corporation for determination of stockholders of record entitled to distribution or, if no date is fixed, on the date of declaration of the distribution by the corporation.

Section 5. *Income Earned During Administration of a Decedent's Estate.*

(a) Unless the will otherwise provides and subject to subsection (b), all expenses incurred in connection with the settlement of a decedent's estate, including debts, funeral expenses, estate taxes, interest and penalties concerning taxes, family allowances, fees of attorney and personal representatives, and court costs shall be charged against the principal of the estate.

(b) Unless the will otherwise provides, income from the assets of a decedent's estate after the death of the testator and before distribution, including income from property used to discharge liabilities, shall be determined in accordance with the rules applicable to a trustee under this Act and distributed as follows:

(1) to specific legatees and devisees, the income from the property bequeathed or devised to them respectively, less taxes, ordinary repairs, and other expenses of management and operation of the

property, and an appropriate portion of interest accrued since the death of the testator and of taxes imposed on income (excluding taxes on capital gains) which accrue during the period of administration;

(2) to all other legatees and devisees, except legatees of pecuniary bequests not in trust, the balance of the income, less the balance of taxes, ordinary repairs, and other expenses of management and operation of all property from which the estate is entitled to income, interest accrued since the death of the testator, and taxes imposed on income (excluding taxes on capital gains) which accrue during the period of administration, in proportion to their respective interests in the undistributed assets of the estate computed at times of distribution on the basis of inventory value.

(c) Income received by a trustee under subsection (b) shall be treated as income of the trust.

Section 6. *Corporate Distributions.*

(a) Corporate distributions of shares of the distributing corporation, including distributions in the form of a stock split or stock dividend, are principal. A right to subscribe to shares or other securities issued by the distributing corporation accruing to stockholders on account of their stock ownership and the proceeds of any sale of the right are principal.

(b) Except to the extent that the corporation indicates that some part of a corporate distribution is a settlement of preferred or guaranteed dividends accrued since the trustee became a stockholder or is in lieu of an ordinary cash dividend, a corporate distribution is principal if the distribution is pursuant to

(1) a call of shares;

(2) a merger, consolidation, reorganization, or other plan by which assets of the corporation are acquired by another corporation; or

(3) a total or partial liquidation of the corporation, including any distribution which the corporation indicates is a distribution in total or partial liquidation or any distribution of assets, other than cash, pursuant to a court decree of final administrative order by a government agency ordering distribution of the particular assets.

(c) Distributions made from ordinary income by a regulated investment company or by a trust qualifying and electing to be taxed under federal law as a real estate investment trust are income. All other distributions made by the company or trust, including distributions from capital gains, depreciation, or depletion, whether in the form of cash or an option to take new stock or cash or an option to purchase shares are principal.

(d) Except as provided in subsections (a), (b), and (c), all corporate distributions are income, including cash dividends, distributions of or rights to subscribe to shares or securities or obligations of corporations other than the distributing corporation, and the proceeds of the rights or property distributions. Except as provided in subsections (b) and (c), if the distributing corporation gives a stockholder an option to receive a distribution either in cash or in its own shares, the distribution chosen is income.

(e) The trustee may rely upon any statement of the distributing corporation as to any fact relevant under any provision of this Act concerning the source or character of dividends or distributions of corporate assets.

Section 7. *Bond Premium and Discount.*

(a) Bonds or other obligations for the payment of money are principal at their inventory value, except as provided in subsection (b) for discount bonds. No provision shall be made for amortization of bond premiums or for accumulation for discount. The proceeds of sale, redemption, or other disposition of the bonds are principal.

(b) The increment in value of a bond or other obligation for the payment of money payable at a future time in accordance with a fixed schedule of appreciation in excess of the price at which it was issued is distributable as income. The increment in value is distributable to the beneficiary who was the income beneficiary at the time of increment from the first principal cash available or, if none is available, when realized by sale, redemption, or other disposition. Whenever unrealized increment is distributed as income but out of principal, the principal shall be reimbursed for the increment when realized.

Section 8. *Business and Farming Operations.*

(a) If a trustee uses any part of the principal in the continuance of a business of which the settlor was a sole proprietor or a partner, the net profits of the business, computed in accordance with generally accepted accounting principles for a comparable business, are income. If a loss results in any fiscal or calendar year, the loss falls on principal and shall not be carried into any other fiscal or calendar year for purposes of calculating net income.

(b) Generally accepted accounting principles shall be used to determine income from an agricultural or farming operation, including the raising of animals or the operation of a nursery.

Section 9. *Disposition of Natural Resources.*

(a) If any part of the principal consists of a right to receive royalties, overriding or limited royalties, working interests, production payments, net profit interests, or other interests in minerals or other natural resources in, on or under land, the receipts from taking the natural resources from the land shall be allocated as follows:

(1) If received as rent on a lease or extension payments on a lease, the receipts are income.

(2) If received from a production payment, the receipts are income to the extent of any factor for interest or its equivalent provided in the governing instrument. There shall be allocated to principal the fraction of the balance of the receipts which the unrecovered cost of the production payment bears to the balance owed on the production payment, exclusive of any factor for interest or its equivalent. The receipts not allocated to principal are income.

(3) If received as a royalty, overriding or limited royalty, or bonus, or from a working, net profit, or any other interest in minerals or other natural resources, receipts not provided for in the preceding paragraphs of this section shall be apportioned on a yearly basis in accordance with this paragraph whether or not any natural resource was being taken from the land at the time the trust was established. Twenty-seven and one-half percent of the gross receipts (but not to exceed 50% of the net receipts remaining after payment of all expenses, direct and indirect, computed without allowance for depletion) shall be added to principal as an allowance for depletion. The balance of the gross receipts, after payment therefrom of all expenses, direct and indirect, is income.

(b) If a trustee, on the effective date of this Act, held an item of depletable property of a type specified in this section, he shall allocate receipts from the property in the manner used before the effective date of this Act, but as to all depletable property acquired after the effective date of this Act by an existing or new trust, the method of allocation provided herein shall be used.

(c) This section does not apply to timber, water, soil, sod, dirt, turf, or mosses.

Section 10.   *Timber.*   If any part of the principal consists of land from which merchantable timber may be removed, the receipts from taking the timber from the land shall be allocated in accordance with section 2(a)(3).

Section 11.   *Other Property Subject to Depletion.*   Except as provided in sections 9 and 10, if the principal consists of property subject to depletion, including leaseholds, patents, copyrights, royalty rights, and rights to receive payments on a contract for deferred compensation, receipts from the property, not in excess of 5% per year of its inventory value, are income, and the balance is principal.

altics, even though the income beneficiary also has rights in the principal.

(d) Regularly recurring charges payable from income shall be apportioned to the same extent and in the same manner that income is apportioned under section 4.

Section 14. *Application of Act.* Except as specifically provided in the trust instrument or the will or in this Act, this Act shall apply to any receipt or expense received or incurred after the effective date of this Act by any trust or decedent's estate whether established before or after the effective date of this Act and whether the asset involved was acquired by the trustee before or after the effective date of this Act.

Section 15. *Uniformity of Interpretation.* This Act shall be so construed as to effectuate its general purpose to make uniform the law of those states which enact it.

Section 16. *Short Title.* This Act may be cited as the Revised Uniform Principal and Income Act.

Section 17. *Severability.* If any provision of this Act or the application thereof to any person or circumstance is held invalid, the invalidity does not affect other provisions or applications of the Act which can be given effect without the invalid provision or application and to this end the provisions of this Act are severable.

2. Allocation and Apportionment of Receipts

Stock dividends and splits. No satisfactory answers have yet been found for the recurring questions involving basically whether a corporation's distributions of its own shares should be treated as income or as principal for various purposes. The questions typically arise in one of two forms.

(1) Should shares received by a trustee as a stock *dividend* be retained in corpus, or should they be allocated to income for distribution to the income beneficiaries? Although legislation has tended to quiet most of the litigation in this area, trustees and drafters continue to find any solution unsatisfactory. Therefore, both legislative and private-planning interest in this problem remains widespread. Stock splits have tended not to be very troublesome for trustees, with allocation to principal being generally accepted.

(2) Does a bequest of corporate stock carry with it additional shares that are attributable to those bequeathed and that are received by the

testator via stock dividends or splits occurring after the execution of the will but before the testator's death? Or are the additional shares a form of "income" to the testator during life and thus general assets of the estate belonging to the residuary beneficiaries? Here the greatest difficulty has been with *splits,* on which litigation is voluminous. Some seems to be invited by judicial reliance on distinctions that appear, to many at least, to be irrelevant to the issue and subject to manipulation. Furthermore, modern sophistication about the nature of stock *dividends* and their general tax treatment may be undermining the traditional probate law treatment of the dividend shares as income of the testator (and hence as general assets enlarging his residuary assets) for this purpose. Obviously, there are drafting lessons to be learned from these difficulties; legislative solutions have been slow to appear.

PROBLEM

19-A. *T* executed a will reading, in relevant part, as follows: "I bequeath 800 shares of *X* Co. stock to my Sister, *S.* The residue of my estate I give to the children of my deceased Brother, *B.*" Ten years later, *T* executed a valid codicil, simply stating, "I hereby bequeath $1,000 to my nurse, *N.*"

At the time the original will was executed *T*'s portfolio of listed securities included 1,000 shares of *X* Company common stock. Seven years thereafter, *X* Company distributed to its common stockholders one additional share of common stock for each two shares previously held, thereby increasing *T*'s holdings to 1,500 shares, which are now in the estate. Your investigation reveals that *X* Company designated this distribution a dividend and transferred to capital stock and capital surplus an amount of its retained earnings equal to the fair market value of the newly issued shares. *X* Company's retained earnings had grown considerably over the preceding ten-year period because of high earnings and relatively low cash dividends.

T died a year ago, and it is now time for *T*'s estate to be distributed. Instructions are sought regarding the rights of *S* and the two children of *B.* To what is *S* entitled? How would you argue her case? How would you argue the case for *B*'s children?

Consider what additional facts, if any, you would want determined. Consider, along with the preceding materials in this section, the notes and the cases that follow. Cf. Knight v. Bardwell, 32 Ill. 2d 172, 205 N.E.2d 249 (1965); Loeb's Will, 206 So. 2d 615 (Miss. 1968).

The first four cases discussed below were all decided at about the same time by different courts. Each involved a *stock split* and the question of whether the increased number of shares passed to the legatee of a stated number of shares in a named corporation.

In Igoe v. Darby, 343 Mass. 145, 177 N.E.2d 676 (1961), the testatrix owned seventy-six shares of certain common stock ($100 par value) and gave twenty-five shares to *A,* twenty-five to *B,* and twenty-six to *C.* A three-for-one split (reducing par to $33.33) occurred prior to the death of the testatrix. The Supreme Judicial Court of Massachusetts stated:

> Usually a gift of stock (such as "*X* shares of *Y* stock") is general; but . . . the testator's intent must prevail if it can be ascertained. . . . Doubtless the tendency of courts to favor general, rather than specific legacies, is chiefly to avoid the harshness of ademption [under which a specific bequest is extinguished if the thing bequeathed is not a part of the estate at the testator's death; see Chapter 20]. . . .
>
> But ademption is not involved here and the reason for preferring to treat a bequest of stock in a named corporation as a general legacy does not exist. At all events, the rule of preference in such a case is merely one of construction and must yield in a case where the intent of the testator to make a specific legacy can be, as we think it can be here, ascertained from the entire will. . . . It will be noted that the number of shares bequeathed corresponds exactly with the number of shares (76) owned by the testatrix at the time of the execution of the will. This may not be very significant in the case of round numbers, but it is of considerable significance in the case, as here, of an odd amount. . . . Following the stock split the interest of the testatrix in American remained precisely the same; the change was one of form rather than substance. In receiving all of the shares the legatees are getting no more than they would have received had there been no split. It would be manifestly unjust to hold that they were not entitled to the additional shares resulting from the split.

343 Mass. at 147-148, 177 N.E.2d at 677-678.

In Shriners Hospital v. Emrie, 347 S.W.2d 303 (Mo. 1961), a bequest of 200 shares of stock, without possessory words, was held specific even though the testatrix owned many more shares in the named corporation at the date the will was executed. In holding that the legatee was to receive 1,000 shares when the stock was split five for one before the testatrix died, the court said that in the case of a specific bequest "a will speaks as of the time of execution and . . . is not ambulatory as to the meaning of . . . such a bequest."

On the other hand, in Matter of Brown's Will, 26 Misc. 2d 1011, 1017-1018, 209 N.Y.S.2d 465, 472 (Surr. Ct. 1961), additional shares acquired through a stock split were held not to pass to the legatees because a bequest of stock "available for purchase on the open market is a general legacy where the testator does not specify any particular share of stock . . . despite the fact that the testator may own on the date of the execution of his Will an equal or larger amount of shares than the legacy."

In re Helfman's Estate, 193 Cal. App. 2d 704, 14 Cal. Rptr. 482 (1961), in giving the legatee the enlarged number of shares resulting from a stock split, the court did not consider it important whether a bequest of X shares of Y stock was general or specific because in either case the issue was a matter of the testator's intent when the will was executed.

More recently, the case of Egavian v. Egavian, 102 R.I. 740, 232 A.2d 789 (1967), a case of first impression, reviewed the decisions of other states and adopted a rather forceful position on this problem. The court began by observing that many courts have struggled to permit the new shares resulting from a split to pass to the legatee as a part of the shares originally bequeathed, and that the unmanageable distinction between general and specific bequests invited manipulation to that end. The opinion then referred to sophisticated recent cases that recognize that a stock split "in no way alters the testator's total interest or rights in the corporation" but merely divides the "outstanding shares of a corporation into a greater number of units without disturbing the stockholder's original proportional participating interest." It quotes from one case to the effect that in today's world it seems "logical to assume that, in absence of language to the contrary, a testator, in making a gift of a given number of shares of stock in a corporation, intends that the legatee be entitled to the future profits of the corporation in the same fractional share as the testator received at the time of the will," and from another that a court should not so construe a will "as to deprive a beneficiary of a value which the testatrix intended to be given." The court concluded:

> To rely [on] a formalistic and almost arbitrary analysis as to how this gift should be classified is clearly lacking in common sense and reason. It would give undue credence to pure fiction to hold that a testator's true intent as to whether a legatee should receive the increased number of shares due to a stock split could be determined from the degree of specificity with which the bequest was drafted when the contingency which has subsequently occurred was one the testator had little reason to anticipate at the time he drew his will and was one over which he had little control.
>
> It is our firm belief that the rule first expressed by the Pennsylvania supreme court . . . and subsequently adopted in four other jurisdictions, which removed the distinction between specific, general or demonstrative legacies as a necessary incident when considering the effects of a stock split, is far sounder, and more just than the others which require an initial classification. In Allen v. National Bank, 19 Ill. App. 2d 149, 160, 153 N.E.2d 260, 265, an Illinois court said ". . . that in the absence of an intention to the contrary, a legatee of shares of stock is entitled to additional shares issued as a result of a stock split occurring after execution of the will." Whereas it has in the past been generally held that a legatee receives the surplus shares of stock split only if the testator is deemed to have specifically bequeathed the stock in question, today we embrace the rule as announced in Allen, supra, and hold that it is presumed that the prime

intent of the testator is that the legatee is to benefit from any increased shares coming by way of a stock split provided no contrary intent is evident in the will.

See also In re Estate of Marks, 435 Pa. 155, 159, 255 A.2d 512, 515 (1969): "Other jurisdictions . . . have not been unanimous in their views; however, the more recent case law would award the fruits of a stock split to the legatees to whom stock gifts were provided in the will."

After reviewing the *Helfman*, *Egavian*, and *Marks* cases, among others, and its own earlier dicta in *Igoe* about splits producing a change of form and not substance, the Massachusetts Court has abandoned its prior distinction between general and special bequests in order to reflect both corporate realities and probable testamentary intent, holding that presumptively the additional shares resulting from a stock split go to the legatee regardless of the elusive, litigation-breeding distinction previously employed in that state. Bostwick v. Hurstel, 364 Mass. 282, 304 N.E.2d 186 (1973). Compare Estate of Holmes, 821 P.2d 300 (Colo. App. 1991), where bequests of "my" 180 X Company shares and of "my" 124 Y Company shares passed, respectively 360 and 248 shares, the additional shares in each case having been acquired by splits during testator's lifetime, the court concluding that the "conflict" between "my" and the numbers of shares should be resolved by holding that the testator had intended to bequeath all of her shares in the X and Y companies.

Unlike the rule governing stock splits (at least as it is applied to specific bequests), the usual holding has been that the recipient of either a general or a specific bequest of stock is not entitled to receive *stock dividends* distributed between execution of the will and the testator's death. See, e.g., In re Doonan's Estate, 110 N.H. 157, 262 A.2d 281 (1970) (involving stock dividends and also stock splits and, as to the latter, adding New Hampshire to the group of states that reject distinctions between "general" and "specific" bequests for the purpose, although not laying down a generalized rule as to the result as did the *Egavian* case, supra). This is said to be because the legatee is not entitled to the "income" from the stock during that period. T. Atkinson, Wills §135 (2d ed. 1953).

A few courts, however, have disagreed with this general rule for stock dividends. See Succession of Quintero, 209 La. 279, 24 So. 2d 589 (1945), finding the same form/substance argument used by *Bostwick* and similar stock split cases, supra, equally appropriate to the stock dividend cases. The majority of the Louisiana court held that shares received as stock dividends between the date of the will and the date of death belonged to the person to whom the original shares were bequeathed, the additional shares being, in changed form, a part of the originally bequeathed shares rather than general increments in the estate resulting from "income" of the decedent during life.

See also Uniform Probate Code §2-605, which treats stock dividends and splits alike without regard to whether the devise is specific or general, including the share distribution in the devise.

AMERICAN INSTITUTE OF CERTIFIED PUBLIC ACCOUNTANTS COMMITTEE ON ACCOUNTING PROCEDURE, ACCOUNTING RESEARCH BULLETIN
No. 43, ch. 7(B) (1953)

Stock Dividends

10. As has been previously stated, a stock dividend does not, in fact give rise to any change whatsoever in either the corporation's assets or its respective shareholders' proportionate interests therein. However, it cannot fail to be recognized that, merely as a consequence of the expressed purpose of the transaction and its characterization as a *dividend* in related notices to shareholders and the public at large, many recipients of stock dividends look upon them as distribution of corporate earnings and usually in an amount equivalent to the fair value of the additional shares received. Furthermore, it is to be presumed that such views of recipients are materially strengthened in those instances, which are by far the most numerous, where the issuances are so small in comparison with the shares previously outstanding that they do not have any apparent effect upon the share market price and, consequently, the market value of the shares previously held remains substantially unchanged. The committee therefore believes that where these circumstances exist the corporation should . . . account for the transaction by transferring from earned surplus to the category of permanent capital . . . an amount equal to the fair value of the additional shares issued. . . .

11. Where the number of additional shares issued . . . is so great that it has, or may reasonably be expected to have, the effect of materially reducing the share market value, the committee believes that the implications and possible constructions discussed in the previous paragraph are not likely to exist and that the transaction clearly partakes of the nature of a stock split-up. . . .

13. Obviously, the point at which the relative size of the additional shares issued becomes large enough to materially influence the unit market price of the stock will vary with individual companies and under differing market conditions and, hence, no single percentage can be laid down as a standard for determining when capitalization of earned surplus in excess of legal requirements is called for and when it is not. However, . . . it would appear that there would be a few instances involving

the issuance of additional shares of less than, say, 20% or 25% of the number previously outstanding where the effect would not be such as to call for the procedure referred to in paragraph 10.

New York E.P.T.L. §11-2.1(e)(2) provides:

A distribution by a corporation or association made to a trustee in the shares of the distributing corporation or association held in such trust, whether in the form of a stock split or a stock divided, at the rate of six percent or less of the shares of such corporation or association upon which the distribution is made, is income. Any such distribution at a greater rate is principal.

See also 20 Pa. Purdon's Stat. §8105 (1984).

MATTER OF FOSDICK'S TRUST
4 N.Y.2d 646, 152 N.E.2d 228 (1958)

[The settlor created two inter vivos trusts of General Electric stock for the benefit of each of two nieces and then two grandnieces, with the reversions on the beneficiaries' deaths to the settlor or his estate. A special provision of the trusts, however, directs "any and all stock dividends which [the trustee] may from time to time receive on any stocks held by it hereunder" to be distributed to the settlor or, if he is dead, to his executor. A number of years after the settlor's death the stock distributions in question were received by the trusts.]

BURKE, J. . . . .

The effect of [the corporate action was] summarized by the lower court [as follows]: (1) all the old stock was cancelled; (2) 36,057,409.2 shares of $5 par value stock (aggregate par $180,287,046) were issued for the old capital of $180,287,046; (3) 50,480,372.88 shares of $5 par value stock were issued and were backed by a capitalization of earned surplus in the amount of $252,401,864.40 which amount was equivalent to the aggregate par value of the said shares. Mathematically, $\frac{7}{12}$ths of the new shares represented new capital, transferred, as pointed out, from earned surplus.

A proxy statement and notice of election sent before the adoption of the resolution suggested that the new stock distribution would serve a two-fold purpose, viz.: it would most likely reduce the market value of the individual shares thus rendering them more saleable and it would, by means of the low par value, result in a savings on the Federal transfer tax.

The lower court held that $\frac{7}{12}$ths of the new stock which was attributed to the transfer from reinvested earnings to capital account constituted a stock dividend within the meaning of the trust deed and was distributable, therefore, to the [settlor's executor] as required by the instrument. He reached this conclusion by application of the definition of the term "stock dividends" as it appears in our decisional law. The Appellate Division unanimously affirmed his determination.

Appellants beneficiaries assert that the substance and intent of the distribution was not to distribute earnings, but rather was merely to split up the shares and apportion the additional capital and that, therefore, it did not constitute a stock dividend. They point out that distributions of stock, like the one under discussion, which substantially increase the number of shares outstanding, ordinarily reduce both the market value of and income upon the original shares so that in a case like the present one if the additional shares are permitted to leave the trust principals it will bring about a considerable reduction in the amount of annual income distributable to the beneficiaries. This result, it is concluded, could not have been intended by the settlor. . . .

In our view the courts below were correct. The term "stock dividends" has been frequently the subject of litigation and has acquired a fixed judicial meaning which clearly includes the corporate action in question. Since before the execution of the subject deed in 1918 it has been held and understood that a stock dividend consists of a distribution of stock by a corporation to its shareholders evidencing and accompanied by the transfer of accumulated surplus to the corporation's capital account. . . . The term "dividend" signifies a distribution of profits or earnings to the shareholders. In its most obvious form it consists of a distribution of cash. It may also be in shares of the corporation. When in this form it is accomplished by segregating that part of the earnings it represents. The segregation is accomplished by capitalization. Therein lies the distinction, as found in the cases, between a mere stock split and a stock dividend. The stock dividend evidences that "the company's accumulated profits have been capitalized, instead of distributed to the stockholders or retained as surplus available for distribution in money or in kind should opportunity offer" (Eisner v. Macomber, 252 U.S. 189, 211). A stock split, on the other hand, results from the simple increase in the number of shares without altering surplus or segregating earnings. . . .

It is the almost exceptionless holding of the later cases on this subject that the distribution of additional stock to shareholders in conjunction with the capitalization of earned surplus constitutes a stock dividend. It is established with equal clarity that in apportioning the amount of newly issued shares attributable to the new capital no reference is had to market value — that proportion of the shares whose par or stated value is represented by the new capital constitutes the stock dividend. . . .

PROBLEM

19-B.   *S* died on January 2, leaving his residuary estate in trust to pay *W* the income for her life, with remainder to *R.* Included in the assets are *X* Company and *Y* Company shares, on which an ordinary cash dividend and a 5 percent stock dividend, respectively, are received after *S*'s death. Both the cash and stock dividends were declared by corporate resolutions adopted one month before *S*'s death, payable to stockholders of record on February 1 following. Also in the estate are several interest-bearing corporate bonds paying interest in semiannual installments as of June 30 and December 31, but the checks for the December installment were received on February 3. How should each of these receipts be allocated under the Revised Uniform Principal and Income Act? Absent legislation, how should the stock dividend be allocated?

Suppose that three years later on December 28 *W* dies, and the same corporations again declare cash and stock dividends on December 1, payable to stockholders of record on February 1. Assume further that these are the only dividends by these companies since the testator's death. The corporate bonds are still held by the trustee and are still paying interest as noted above. What allocation do you suggest?

APPEAL OF NEW BRITAIN BANK & TRUST CO.
39 Conn. Supp. 157, 472 A.2d 1305 (1983)

[The testator left his residuary estate to appellant bank, as trustee, to pay the net income to or for his widow during her lifetime, plus principal as needed for her support, with the remainder at her death to go to eight charities. Certain income had accrued but had not been received at the date of the widow's death. The bank's final account, proposing to distribute this income to the remainder beneficiaries, was disapproved by the probate court, which directed that it be distributed to the widow's estate. This accrued income (about $20,000) consisted of (1) cash dividends declared and of record prior to the widow's death and (2) income from certain bonds and common funds since the last scheduled payment date prior to the widow's death.]

DOYLE, J. . . .

The basic issue before the court is whether the estate of the life tenant is entitled to income accrued but not actually received by its trustees at the time of the death of the life tenant.

The general rule, in the absence of a contrary intent expressed in the testamentary trust, is that income which accrues prior to the death of the life tenant passes to the estate of the life tenant. Gorham v. Gorham, 99

Conn. 187, 193-94, 121 A. 349 (1923); 1 Restatement of Trusts (Second), §235A(a). If the right to income has accrued during the tenancy of an income beneficiary but has not been received, and the income is received after the beneficiary's death, it should be paid to the representative of the deceased beneficiary. . . .

The bank claims that paragraph sixteen expressly directs the trustee to pay over the income of the trust only "during the term of her [the life tenant's] natural life" and only for her support and maintenance. Therefore, they conclude that upon the death of the life tenant the duty to pay over the income to the life tenant ceases and the accrued income is to be added to the principal and paid over to the remaindermen. The phrase in paragraph sixteen, however, "to pay over the net income to or for the maintenance and support of my wife . . . during the term of her natural life," in fact requires the bank to pay over *all* net income either to the decedent's widow *or* for her maintenance and support. It does not mean that the net income must be used *only* for her maintenance and support. The use of the word "or" compels payment of "the net income" to her directly, or, in the alternative, for her maintenance and support by payment to a third party. The phrase should not be construed to prohibit payment of accrued income to her estate.

It is inconceivable that the testator had intended his wife to be without income for her maintenance and support for *any* period of her life. He knew that obligations occur in one period and may be payable in a later period. If his wife should die at any time within the period between payments, he knew that obligations of her contracting would be liable to be outstanding, but that income earned upon the trust and in the hands of the bank for the purpose of providing for her maintenance and support would, if applied to the payment of the outstanding accounts, probably liquidate them. This testator surely did not contemplate or desire that any portion of the income from this trust for the maintenance of his widow, which income had accrued prior to her death, would not be available to pay for her debts, but would instead pass to the eight remaindermen.

Paragraph sixteen of the will reads as follows: "Upon the decease of my said wife, I direct my said trustee to divide the balance of said rest, residue and remainder, *together with any accumulations thereof,* equally between [eight charitable remaindermen]." (Emphasis added.) The bank urges that the testator's use of the word "accumulations" in the gift over to the remaindermen expresses an intention to include accrued income therein. The word "accumulations" by itself, however, has no technical or fixed legal meaning. Commercial Trust Co. of New Jersey v. Spiegelberg, 117 N.J. Eq. 171, 174, 175 A. 164 (1934); 90 C.J.S., Trusts §354, pp. 638-39 n.88. Nowhere in the will does the testator herein define what he means by "any accumulations." He does not state that "accumulations" are "income accumulations," [for] accumulations can also include funds of principal because of failure of other dispositions [or] . . . denote principal assets of whatever nature which became a part of the remainder assets after the establishment of the paragraph sixteen trust, whether by lapse of bequests or devises, the acquisition of after-discovered assets, or otherwise.

Since his widow was clearly the primary object of the testator's bounty, this testamentary objective should not be destroyed without a clear and unmistakable direction to that effect. No such direction or intent can be found in his will. An overall examination of the will discloses no clear testamentary intent to include accrued income within the word "accumulations" as used in paragraph sixteen.

Connecticut adopted the Uniform Principal and Income Act in 1939, which enactment is now codified in General Statutes §§45-110 through 45-119. Such legislation applies to the present trust and to all trusts, no matter when created. These statutes do not change the applicable common law as set forth above, but they reinforce it. . . .

DAVIDSON'S ESTATE
287 Pa. 354, 135 A. 130 (1926)

FRAZER, J.

These two appeals raise the same questions and will be disposed of in one opinion.

John H. Davidson died in 1909, leaving a will in which he devised his residuary estate in trust to invest, with provision that "the dividends, rents, and interest arising from my said residuary estate, after paying the necessary expenses and taxes, shall every three months be divided into nine equal shares," four of which shares were devised to his wife, Mary E. Davidson, and four to his son, Clayton T. Davidson, with right of survivorship between them. Mary E. Davidson died in 1921. Included as part of the estate of John H. Davidson was a promissory note for $60,000, on which no interest had been paid from January, 1914, to December, 1923, at which latter date, as a result of legal proceedings, the whole of the principal and interest, amounting in all to $99,061.71, was collected.

The portion of the interest which accumulated before the death of Mary E. Davidson amounted to $24,677.04. Four-ninths of this amount, or $10,967.57, less proper expenses was claimed by the administrator of Mrs. Davidson's Estate, and also by Clayton T. Davidson by reason of the gift over to him after the death of his mother, his contention being that while the interest accrued previous to his mother's death, it was not actually paid until after her death, and, accordingly, never became part of her estate. The question thus arising is whether the failure to collect the accrued income before the death of Mrs. Davidson prevented it from vesting in her under the terms of her husband's will.

The gift of the income is clearly a vested interest. It was a gift of the income "arising" from the trust fund, not of only such part of the income as might have been actually received or collected before her death. It was payable "while she lives and remains my widow" and the mere fact that the will directed the executors to render a statement to each of the devisees every three months did not affect the interest given, but merely established a convenient time for the rendering of an account or statement and to avoid the inconvenience of possible demands made at more frequent or at irregular periods. This case is an appropriate illustration of the injustice which would arise from the application of the opposite rule. The income had not been collected for approximately seven years previous to the widow's death, and, in the meantime, had been permitted to accrue. The failure to collect was not due to the default of the trustees, but to the insolvency or bankruptcy of one of the makers of the note. This circumstance should not prevent the life tenant from receiving the benefit of her share of the income if it is, in fact, finally collected in full, especially where there is a clearly vested remainder. The general rule is that interest on money is apportionable because presumed to accrue from day to day, regardless of whether payable quarterly, semiannually or at other fixed periods: Wertz's App., 65 Pa. 306, 309; Wilson's App., 108 Pa. 344, 346. We are of opinion the court below reached a proper conclusion in holding the interest was apportionable up to the death of the life tenant.

In affirming the conclusion of the court below we take this opportunity to approve the method adopted by that court in apportioning the amount paid for counsel fees in collecting the principal and interest of the note between the life tenant and remaindermen in proportion to the total amount of principal and interest collected. While the income and not the principal is generally liable for the expense of administering the fund (Crawford's Est., 256 Pa. 504), yet this rule has an exception where unusual or extraordinary expenses are necessarily incurred, and although the will in this case expressly directs that the dividends should be paid "after deducting necessary expenses and taxes," it must be presumed that this had reference only to the usual expenses of administration and will not be construed as extending to a case like the present, where expensive legal proceedings were necessary not only to collect the interest but also to preserve the corpus of the estate from actual loss. The court below, consequently, properly divided the counsel fees and expenses pro rata between the life tenants and remaindermen.

The decree of the court below is affirmed.

UNITED STATES TRUST CO. v. COWIN
121 Neb. 427, 237 N.W. 284 (1931)

GOOD, J.

Plaintiff, as trustee, brings this action, seeking direction and guidance as to the proper disposition of a stock dividend, declared upon corporate stock constituting a part of the trust estate. . . .

The question is new in this jurisdiction. It has been a fruitful source of litigation in other courts. Their holdings are not harmonious. The courts of last resort in this country which have passed upon the question have taken three distinctly divergent views. They are generally referred to as the Massachusetts rule, the Kentucky rule, and the Pennsylvania rule.

Briefly speaking, the Massachusetts rule is that [stock dividends are] not income but a part of the corpus of the trust. The Kentucky rule is that a stock dividend, declared during the existence of the trust, is income and belongs to the life tenant or settlor, regardless of whether the stock dividend was declared from earnings accumulated before or after the creation of the trust, or partly before and partly thereafter. The Pennsylvania rule, under such circumstances, apportions the stock dividend, holding that so much of the stock dividend as represents earnings of the corporation prior to the creation of the trust is a part of the corpus of the trust, and that such part of the stock dividend as represents earnings, made subsequent to the creation of the trust, is income and belongs to the settlor or life tenant.

Plausible arguments have been adduced in support of each of these rules. Practically all of the courts, regardless of which rule obtains, hold that the intention of the settlor, if sufficiently specific and violative of no statute or rule of public policy, shall guide the courts in the determination of the question. . . . In the instant case the settlor has not evinced by the language used any specific direction with regard to a stock dividend. . . .

It may be observed that the Kentucky rule has not been generally accepted and followed by other jurisdictions.

The Pennsylvania rule appears to have been first specifically announced in Earp's Appeal, 28 Pa. St. 368, decided in 1857. That rule has been followed in a number of jurisdictions, but has been severely criticized, and we think the more recent trend of authority is in favor of the Massachusetts rule. The Ohio supreme court, in the case of Lamb v. Lehmann, 110 Ohio St. 59, after reviewing the reasons supporting the various rules, announced its adherence to the Massachusetts rule. Commenting upon this decision in 34 Yale Law Journal, 195, it is said (p. 196):

The apportionment rule (meaning the Pennsylvania rule) is unfortunately blessed with an implication of fairness. . . . The first cases figured the value of the corpus from the market value of the shares on the day of testator's death. It was soon seen that this measure of value was inadequate, and the test in later Pennsylvania cases seems to be "actual value." In New York we find the courts making findings of "intrinsic value" from the books, records, and reports of the corporation. In a very recent case the court made its findings on the basis of a report of capital and earnings furnished by the executor. Through all of the decisions one is conscious of faulty methods of valuation. To ascertain the value of the corpus the courts must order an independent and complete inventory of assets as of the time of the testator's death. In cases where the courts must find value of the assets of one of our modern industrial giants, the cost is so great as to render the rule of apportionment impracticable.

In the comment it is further said:

The decisions, therefore, have been based upon an approximation of "value." They represent, not apportionment, but a more or less arbitrary allotment of stock dividends a part to the life tenant, and at times a part to the remainderman. . . .

Out of sympathy for the life tenant the apportionment rule might be condoned were it not for certain other legal consequences which seem to have been entirely overlooked. Valuable legal relations attach to the ownership of stock, and those legal relations have a value which is a part of the value of the corpus. . . .

The fairness of the apportionment rule is only theoretical and illusory. Its application is dangerously variable, and it is really unfair to the remainderman. The supreme court of Ohio has chosen wisely in its adoption of the Massachusetts rule. The advantage of simplicity is obvious.

It seems to us that the inherent fallacy of the Pennsylvania rule is that it regards the corpus of the trust as of its value at the time the trust was created, while the fact is, where the trust property consists of corporate stock, the stock, itself, is the corpus, and it may rise or fall in value. Still, the corporate stock is the corpus or principal. If corporate stock, held in trust, greatly increases in value for a time, and a stock dividend is declared and goes to the life tenant, and thereafter the stock falls in value until it is worth much less than when the trust was created, by what process can the value of the corpus be maintained? We know of no means by which it can be maintained. If real estate is conveyed in trust the corpus is the realty. It may rise or fall in value as the market goes up or down; so corporate stock, placed in trust, remains the corpus or principal of the trust; its value may rise or fall with the market; but because its value rises with the market it should not be reduced by declaring a stock dividend and thereby dividing the corpus.

One of the best expositions of the Massachusetts rule may be found in Gibbons v. Mahon, 136 U.S. 549, wherein it is said (p. 557):

[T]he intention of the testator, so far as manifested by him, must of course control; but when he has given no special direction upon the question as to what shall be considered principal and what income, he must be presumed to have had in view the lawful power of the corporation over the use and apportionment of its earnings, and to have intended that the determination of that question should depend upon the regular action of the corporation with regard to all its shares.

Therefore, when a distribution of earnings is made by a corporation among its stockholders, the question whether such distribution is an apportionment of additional stock representing capital, or a division of profits and income, depends upon the substance and intent of the action of the corporation, as manifested by its vote or resolution; and ordinarily a dividend declared in stock is to be deemed capital, and a dividend in money is to be deemed income, of each share.

A stock dividend really takes nothing from the property of the corporation, and adds nothing to the interests of the shareholders. Its property is not diminished, and their interests are not increased. After such a dividend, as before, the corporation has the title in all the corporate property; the aggregate interests therein of all the shareholders are represented by the whole number of shares; and the proportional interest of each shareholder remains the same. The only change is in the evidence which represents that interest, the new shares and the original shares together representing the same proportional interest that the original shares represented before the issue of new ones. . . .

In the case of Hayes v. St. Louis Union Trust Co., 317 Mo. 1028, decided in 1927, there is a full and thorough review of all the cases. In that case it is held:

If . . . the corporate stock so held in trust increases in value through the accumulation of corporate earnings after the beginning of the trust, and if no dividends are declared, the whole increase belongs to the corpus, even upon a sale of the stock. . . .

The earnings and profits of a corporation remain the property of the corporation until severed from corporate assets and distributed as dividends. . . .

A stock dividend is in no true sense a dividend. A dividend implies a division, a severance from the corporate assets to the amount of the dividend, and a distribution thereof among the stockholders. A stock dividend is the increasing of the fixed capital of the corporation; it takes nothing from the corporation; it gives nothing to the shareholder; the title to all corporate property remains in the corporation as before, and the proportional interest of the stockholder continues the same. . . .

In our view, the Massachusetts rule is the more logical and based on the better reason. We therefore adopt that rule, and hold that where corporate stock is placed in trust, reserving the income therefrom to the settlor, a stock dividend, declared during the existence of the trust, is not income, but is a part of the corpus of the trust and goes to the beneficiary of the trust.

It follows that the judgment of the district court is right, and it is therefore affirmed.

In Bowles v. Stilley's Executor, 267 S.W.2d 707 (Ky. App. 1954), the court reviewed the "three divergent views" and concluded:

> Notwithstanding our previous adherence to the Kentucky rule, this Court, as presently constituted, is convinced that it is unsound. It fosters inequities, and usually ignores the intention of the testator where the life estate is created by will. . . .
>
> At one time the trend of the courts in the various jurisdictions seemed to be away from the Massachusetts rule. In fact, this trend continued until about 1930. However, during the last fifteen or twenty years the pendulum has swung in the opposite direction. The courts of last resort of several jurisdictions in which the question of distribution of extraordinary dividends was squarely presented for the first time have decided with no little emphasis, in favor of the Massachusetts rule, commending it for its directness, simplicity, and ease of application. In addition to those states which have made it the rule by judicial interpretation, several states have adopted it by legislative enactment through the passage of the Uniform Principal and Income Act.
>
> The basic argument in favor of the Massachusetts rule is the fact that a stock dividend is not in any true sense a dividend at all, since it involves no division or severance from the corporate assets of the subject of the dividend. A stock dividend does not distribute property but simply dilutes the shares as they existed before. There is no more reason in principle and justice for giving the life beneficiary any part of the new shares represented by the stock dividends . . . than there is in the case of accumulation of earnings by the corporation during the life interest without the declaration of any dividends at all. . . .
>
> [This view] is also consistent with the position taken by the Supreme Court in holding that stock dividends representing surplus profits transferred to capital account are not income within the meaning of the Federal Income Tax Law.

267 S.W.2d at 708-709.

Is there any statutory solution that might be considered, other than one representing one of the three views already discussed? Is the uniform act fair to the income beneficiary? Assuming a desirable statutory solution is enacted, is it to be applied prospectively only or retroactively? Consider the problems that may arise in either approach. See In re Dunham's Estate, 433 Pa. 273, 249 A.2d 531 (1969); South Carolina National Bank v. Arrington, 165 S.E.2d 77 (S.C. 1968). If a trustee held a substantial block of stock of a company that pursued a regular policy of retaining its earnings and declaring periodic stock dividends in lieu of cash dividends, could the trustee retain the stock without fear of surcharge? Is this danger a good thing for trusts generally, especially where the beneficiaries are or may be in high income tax brackets? How might the draftsman for the settlor provide an adequate solution without becoming involved in excessive detail?

TAIT v. PECK
346 Mass. 521, 194 N.E.2d 707 (1963)

CUTTER, J.

Letitia M. Tait (the widow) seeks a declaratory decree with respect to an inter vivos trust (the trust) executed in 1935 by her late husband (the settlor). She asks the court to determine whether a certain distribution of capital gains to the trust, made by Broad Street Investing Corporation (Broad Street) in December, 1961 is to be treated as principal or income of the trust. The widow, life beneficiary of the trust, asserts that the capital gains distribution is income. The individual remaindermen and the trustees assert that it is a return of capital and hence should be added to principal. . . .

In 1961, . . . Broad Street paid to the trustees of the trust two cash dividends from income and in addition, in December, 1961, Broad Street delivered to the trustees 1,463 additional shares of Broad Street as "distributions of gain," as distinguished from "dividend from income," on the shares then held by the trustees. The trustees paid to the widow the 1961 dividends from income paid to them by Broad Street in 1961 (less expenses and taxes) "but refused and still refuse to transfer" to the widow the 1,463 shares of Broad Street (less any expense or taxes thereto allocable). The trustees, in support of their position, state that under Int. Rev. Code of 1954 §852, the trustees must pay a Federal capital gains tax on these shares of Broad Street so received as "distributions of gain." . . .

In its statements to the public, Broad Street says that its investments have two goals — (1) favorable current income, and (2) long term growth in both income and capital value. Dividends payable out of net income are paid quarterly, whereas distributions of gain realized on the sale of investments are paid at the end of each year. . . . The 1,463 shares were paid to the trustees in December, 1961, at their request. At their option, they could have received the equivalent of these shares in cash.

1. No party contends that the inter vivos trust shows what the settlor's intent was with respect to capital gains dividends. . . .

2. The usual Massachusetts rule for the allocation of dividends was stated in Minot v. Paine, 99 Mass. 101, 108:

> A trustee needs some plain principle to guide him; and the cestuis que trust ought not to be subjected to the expense of going behind the action

of the directors, and investigating the concerns of the corporation, especially if it is out of our jurisdiction. A simple rule is, to regard cash dividends, however large, as income, and stock dividends, however made, as capital.

. . . This simple rule, in practice, has come to be based . . . upon the substance . . . of the transaction as carried out by the entity declaring the dividend. Dividends in cash in substance paid out of capital or in liquidation have been treated as belonging to principal. The substance of a transaction has been examined to determine whether it was equivalent to a stock dividend. Where the trustee, as shareholder, is given the option to receive a dividend in stock or in cash, the later cases, in effect, treat the dividend as a cash dividend and as income. We look at the substance of the capital gain distribution made by Broad Street in December, 1961, against the background of these authorities. No prior Massachusetts case has presented the question whether such a distribution, received by a trustee, is to be treated as capital or income. . . .

Some commentators have felt that dividends from net capital gains from the sales of securities held in a mutual fund's portfolio are income from the ordinary conduct of the fund's business, that the portfolio holdings are bought and sold like inventory or other corporate property of a business corporation, and that distribution from such gains, at least where there is opportunity to receive the distribution in cash, should be treated as income. Weight is given by these commentators to the circumstances that investors in investment companies rely on both income and capital gains as a part of the expected yield. It is suggested by at least one author (Professor Bogert) that to invest in mutual funds would be a breach of trust, about which the life beneficiary could complain, unless the investment produced a normal trust investment yield. The contrary view is that the sale of a security in an investment company portfolio involves the sale of a capital item, so that, if the gain is distributed the capital is necessarily reduced. In some years such a company may experience net losses. It is argued that if capital gain distributions of other years have been paid to the income beneficiary, the trust principal will inevitably suffer in years of losses, which must be expected even in an era generally inflationary, so that, in effect, the investment company shares may become a wasting investment. It is also urged that a trustee's investment in an investment company is in substance nothing more than a fractional ownership in a diversified portfolio of securities, as to which the trustee should account as if he held the portfolio securities directly. The special character of regulated investment companies and their specialized tax treatment under the Internal Revenue Code also have some tendency to give capital gains distributions the aspect of principal.

If the dividends and distributions of a regulated investment company should be regarded as inherently the same as those of an ordinary industrial company, then the rule of Smith v. Cotting, 231 Mass. 42, 48-49, 120 N.E. 177, should be applied to Broad Street's 1961 capital gain distribution, which the trustees, at their option, could have received either in cash or in shares. It seems to us, however, that, when a fiduciary invests in investment company shares, he is entering into an arrangement more closely like participation in a common trust fund (see G.L. c. 203A) than like an investment in the shares of an industrial company. His purpose generally will be to obtain for his trust beneficiaries (usually of a small trust) the same type of a spread of investment risk which the trustee of a common trust fund can obtain for its participating trusts, or which the trustee of a large trust fund can obtain by a well conceived program of diversified direct investment. . . .

The method of determining the purchase and sales prices of investment company shares, in relation to the net asset value of shares, is consistent with the concept that the trustee is obtaining diversification by an indirect participation in the investment company's portfolio. It is apparent that if a fiduciary were to redeem his shares at a profit just before a capital gain distribution, he would necessarily allocate any gain to principal. No practical reason requires treating the capital gain distribution, when made, in any different way, or prevents retaining it as a part of the principal of the trust.

One major virtue of our Massachusetts rule for allocation between principal and income has been its simplicity as a rule of convenience. To treat capital gains distributions of registered investment companies as principal will not impair the simplicity of our rule, for no inquiry need be made as to the source of the distribution. The source must be announced [§19 of the Investment Company Act of 1940, 15 U.S.C. §80a-19 (1958)], as it was in respect of Broad Street's capital gain distribution in December, 1961.

Since no binding precedent controls our decision, we are guided by the substance of the situation. We adopt the rule that distributions by a regulated investment company, from capital gains (whether made in the form of cash or shares or an option to take or purchase new shares), are to be allocated to principal. This is essentially the view adopted by the Commissioners on Uniform State Laws in 1962 after full deliberation. The Commissioners' action can be taken as reflecting a considered current view of what is in the public interest. In effect, we think that the regulated company, from the standpoint of a trustee investing in its shares, is merely a conduit of its realized gains to the trust fund and that, in the hands of the trustee, the gains should retain their character as principal. . . .

3. Overproductive and Underproductive Property

When a fiduciary has an investment function, serious problems are posed by the retention or acquisition of property that either (1) produces periodic returns that are abnormally *high* and that cause an impairment of principal values or (2) provides abnormally *low* receipts of income or none at all. There are, in such cases, questions of apportionment between principal and income of periodic receipts or of proceeds on the eventual sale of the property. There are also allied questions relating to the propriety of the investment and to the possible duty of the fiduciary to dispose of the investment in order to fulfill the duty of impartiality. Several of the more common situations of this character are considered hereafter.

a.   Bond Premium and Discount

It may be observed that the element of premium or discount in the price paid for a bond represents a means by which the rate of return fixed on the bond is adjusted to the return demanded by investors. Thus, a premium is an increased price attributable to the fact that the stated interest rate exceeds the rate of return appropriate in the relevant market for obligations involving similar risk and maturity date. A discount is a reduction of the amount invested reflecting an inadequate rate of interest and a demand for some payment on maturity in excess of the acquisition price. In general, then, in order to avoid negotiations over interest and the use of complicated fractions in the rate at issuance, and to deal with interest problems on subsequent transactions, uncomplicated interest rates are used with the purchase price serving as an adjustment to market conditions. Discounts and premiums therefore are factors in the true return on a fiduciary's investments. What obligations does this suggest may be imposed on a fiduciary in investing in bonds? Consider especially the effect of Revised Uniform Principal and Income Act §7(a). Also compare the discussion of inflation and interest at the end of Chapter 18, supra.

RESTATEMENT (SECOND) OF TRUSTS

§239. . . .

Comment *f. Bonds purchased at a premium.* The trustee can properly purchase bonds which are otherwise proper trust investments, although the purchase price is greater than the face value of the bonds and accrued interest. Since, however, if the bonds are held until maturity only the face value of the bonds will be paid, they are to a certain extent wasting investments. The trustee need not, therefore, pay the whole of the interest received upon the bonds to the beneficiary entitled to the income, but can properly retain so much of the income as is necessary to amortize on the maturity of the bonds the amount of the premiums paid by him. Whether the trustee is under a duty to the beneficiaries in remainder to amortize the premiums depends upon the application of the general rule imposing upon him a duty to deal impartially with the beneficiaries. See §183. It would be a violation of his duty of impartiality to invest a considerable portion of the trust estate in bonds purchased at a premium, particularly where the premiums are large. If, however, he happens to purchase a few bonds at a small premium, particularly if he also purchases other bonds at a discount, he does not necessarily violate his duty of impartiality by failing to make provision for amortization.

Any method of amortization which the trustee may adopt is proper, if the result would be on the maturity of the bonds to accumulate the amount of the premiums. Even though he sells the bonds before their maturity at a price greater than the purchase price paid by him, the amount retained by him to amortize the premiums remains principal.

Where the trust estate at the time of the creation of the trust includes bonds selling at a premium, the trustee cannot properly make provision for amortization, unless the settlor manifested a different intention. In such a case the inference is that the settlor intended that the beneficiaries entitled to the income should receive the whole income without deduction for amortization.

The rule requiring or permitting a trustee to amortize bonds acquired at a premium has been done away with by statute in a number of States. It has been done away with by the Uniform Principal and Income Act, §6 (see Comment *i*), and it has been done away with by statute in a number of States which have not adopted the Act.

§240. . . .

Comment *h*. *Bonds acquired at a discount.* If the trustee purchases bonds at a discount, that is at less than the amount which will be due thereon at their maturity, and which are otherwise proper trust investments, the trustee cannot properly prior to the maturity or sale or other realization of the bonds pay to the beneficiary who is entitled to income an additional sum out of the principal of the estate, even though if the bonds are held to maturity and are then paid there will be an appreciation of the principal of the estate. Prior to such realization, it is not certain that the appreciation will actually be received. If, however, the trustee has purchased some bonds at a premium and others at a discount, in determining whether he should make provisions for amortizing the premiums he can properly take into consideration the fact that he has purchased other bonds at a discount, even though the amounts of the premiums and discounts are not exactly the same. See §239, Comment *f*.

Even if the bonds purchased by the trustee at a discount are held until they mature and are then paid, the trustee is not under a duty to the beneficiary entitled to income to pay him any part of the appreciation realized on the bonds.

The trustee, however, cannot properly invest a considerable part of the trust estate in bonds purchased at a discount for the sake of increasing the principal of the trust estate, thereby diminishing the amount of income payable to the beneficiary entitled to income substantially below the usual rate of return on trust investments, since the trustee is under a duty to deal impartially with the beneficiaries. See §183.

Where the trust estate at the time of the creation of the trust includes bonds selling at a discount, the trustee cannot properly pay to the beneficiary who is entitled to income anything more than the interest paid on the bonds, unless the settlor manifested a different intention. In such case the inference is that the settlor intended that the beneficiary entitled to the income should receive only the interest paid on the bonds.

The rule here stated is not applicable to non-interest-bearing securities sold on a discount basis. See §233, Comment *d*. [See §7(b) of Revised Uniform Principal and Income Act, supra.]

b.   Unproductive Assets

PROBLEM

19-C.   The trust estate in question, as originally constituted, included a note in the principal amount of $100,000, bearing annual interest at 6 percent. No interest payments have been received for a five-year period, at the end of which the debtor, following insolvency proceedings, paid $60,000 in discharge of this obligation. The trustee was unable to dispose of this note or to realize on it earlier, despite diligent efforts since the time of default. He now asks you to advise whether the $60,000 he has received belongs to principal or whether some of this amount is allocable to income. What answer would you give under the Revised Uniform Principal and Income Act? What result in absence of statute?

In re PAGE'S ESTATE
199 Cal. App. 2d 550, 18 Cal. Rptr. 886 (1962)

Fox, P.J.

This litigation arose by way of a petition for distribution to the remaindermen of the assets of a testamentary trust upon the death of the income beneficiary. The pleadings constitute an accounting, report and petition filed by the trustees (who are also the remaindermen) and objections thereto filed by the widow and executrix of the estate of the income beneficiary.

Lottie Page died testate in 1938, leaving four children as her sole heirs. In August of 1940 the estate was distributed pursuant to a Decree of Distribution which was based on Lottie's holographic will. Pursuant to the Decree each of the three children, Lottie Ray, Mary Simonsen and Albert Johnson, were given an undivided one-fourth interest in the entire estate. The remaining undivided one-fourth interest was distributed to the same three children as trustees, with the income attributable to that interest to be paid to John Johnson for his life. On John's death the trust estate was to be distributed to the trustees as remaindermen.

The estate, insofar as is here pertinent, consisted in part of completely unproductive desert land, together with some income properties. The income properties and some of the desert properties were never sold. A number of the desert properties were sold in 1957 and 1958 [during the life estate]. None of the desert properties ever became productive of income. All of the properties appreciated substantially in value. By her objections to the accounting, John Johnson's executrix, whom we shall call "contestant," seeks two things: A portion of the appreciated value of the properties in the estate as "delayed income"; and a surcharge upon the trustees for an alleged breach of trust in not making productive the portion of the estate which produced no income and in not making more productive the remaining portion.

By its judgment the trial court awarded contestant a portion of the appreciated value of the desert properties (both those which were sold and those retained), held that she was not entitled to any of the appreciated value of the income properties, and refused to surcharge the trustees. Both sides, being unsatisfied with the judgment, have appealed.

At this point it would seem appropriate to set forth in its entirety Civil Code §730.13 of the Principal and Income Law, originally enacted in 1941, on which the judgment is based. [See similar provision in Revised Uniform Principal and Income Act §12, supra.]

It will be noticed that 1 percent is the stated test of productivity for the purpose of apportionment. The trial court found that the desert properties which were sold were unproductive and that the trustees were under a duty to sell them within a year, and "imprudently neglected [to sell them] within a reasonable time." The same was found as to the unsold desert properties, and delayed income was computed, the record reveals, according to the formula in Section 730.13(2). Concerning the income properties in question, it was found "That the net income from the trust's interest in inventory items #1 and #3 did not at any time fall below one percent per annum of the appraised value of said interest." This finding is not challenged and it of course takes the income properties out of the operation of Section 730.13. In its conclusions of law the trial court sets forth certain amounts as "delayed income apportionable to John Johnson" from the desert properties. Concerning the income properties, the trial court concluded "That inasmuch as the net income from inventory items #1 and #3 did not at any time fall below one percent per annum, the trustees are deemed to have acted as prudent men in the management of the trust's interest in said inventory items."

Contestant challenges the judgment in two ways. She claims that certain allegations of fraud on the part of the trustees were improperly stricken, and that if she were allowed to prove these allegations she would be entitled to a surcharge equal to all the appreciated value of the estate. She further contends that although the one percent figure is the dividing line between productive and unproductive property for purposes of Section 730.13, the fact that one percent was earned on the income properties does not mean that as a matter of law the trustees met their trust responsibility to the income beneficiary with respect to those properties. The trustees' appeal is based on claims that the evidence is insufficient to establish a duty or the amount of the judgment; that the trial court erred in failing to find on the question of estoppel and various other matters; and that there were certain evidentiary errors.

The contention of the trustees that is dispositive of this appeal is that Section 730.13 does not apply to this trust. The Decree of Distribution establishing the trust became effective in August of 1940. Section 730.02 of the Principal and Income Law reads in part:

> This chapter [of which §730.13 is a part] shall apply to all transactions by which principal shall be established which become legally effective on or after September 13, 1941. It shall also apply to all revocable trusts existing on and prior to that date and to all other trusts to the extent to which they may be at that time or any later time amendable by the settlor in respect to matters covered by this chapter. . . .

This section was apparently included to protect the constitutionality of the law. (See Annot. 69 A.L.R.2d 1137.) It clearly does not embrace the instant trust within its terms.

This is not to say that the principle of apportionment does not exist in this State independent of statute. Estate of Bothwell, 65 Cal. App. 2d 598, 151 P.2d 298, 868, was the first appellate decision in California to consider the question. It adopted the Restatement rule. Section 241 of the Restatement of Trusts reads:

> (1) Unless it is otherwise provided by the terms of the trust, if property held in trust to pay the income to a beneficiary for a designated period and thereafter to pay the principal to another beneficiary is property which the trustee is under a duty to sell, and which produces no income or an income substantially less than the current rate of return on trust investments, or which is wasting property or produces an income substantially more than the current rate of return on trust investments, and the trustee does not immediately sell the property, the trustee should make an apportionment of the proceeds of the sale when made, as stated in Subsection (2).
>
> (2) The net proceeds received from the sale of the property are apportioned by ascertaining the sum which with simple interest thereon at the

current rate of return on trust investments from the day when the duty to sell arose to the day of the sale would equal the net proceeds; and the sum so ascertained is to be treated as principal, and the residue of the net proceeds as income.

(3) The net proceeds are determined by adding to the net sale price the net income received or deducting therefrom the net loss incurred in carrying the property prior to the sale.

It will be noted that there are several important differences between Section 730.13 and the Restatement rule. The "one percent" rule of Section 730.13 becomes "no income or income substantially less than the current rate of return on trust investments" in the Restatement. Section 730.13 uses 5 percent in calculating the amount to be apportioned to income, whereas the Restatement uses "the current rate of return on trust investments." There are many other differences which should receive judicial comment only when interpretation is necessary in the resolution of a case. It is sufficient here to say that the differences are such as to alter substantially the complexion of the litigation. It is impossible to ascertain what the trial court would have done had it applied Estate of Bothwell, supra, and Section 241 of the Restatement instead of Section 730.13. . . .

Since the other matters giving rise to alleged error are less than likely to occur on a new trial, it would not be appropriate to discuss them here.

Because of the unusual circumstances of this case, each side will bear its own costs on appeal.

The judgment is reversed.

For other cases involving problems of "unproductive" property, see Bowen v. Safe Deposit & Trust Co., 188 Md. 490, 53 A.2d 413 (1947) (involving proceeds from the sale of rights to new securities received pursuant to the reorganization of a corporation whose bonds were in default and on which no interest was paid during the period of the trust); Matter of Rowland, 273 N.Y. 100, 6 N.E.2d 393 (1937) (involving proceeds of sale of real estate on which the rental activities had produced a large net loss); In re Nirdlinger's Estate, 327 Pa. 171, 193 A. 30 (1937) (involving proceeds of foreclosing a mortgage that had been in default and on which less than the principal amount of the mortgage was realized).

c. Depreciable and Wasting Assets

PROBLEM

19-D.   When *H* died three years ago, he left a life insurance policy payable to his widow, *W.* On the advice of an insurance agent, *W* elected an option under which she would receive annual payments of $8,000 for the rest of her life but providing that even in the event of death within ten years the payments were to continue until ten such annual payments were made. Because of her failing health at the time of election, *W* believed this "term certain" option was preferable to the straight life annuity under which the annual payments to her would have been larger.

Recently, *W* died. Her will, executed before *H*'s death, left her entire estate to *T* Trust Company to pay the income to *M*, the widowed mother of *H*, and then to distribute the corpus on *M*'s death to *B* and *S*, who were *W*'s brother and sister. Among the assets of *W*'s estate was the right to receive the seven remaining annual payments under the insurance settlement option previously mentioned. The other assets paid over to the trust estate consisted of about $160,000 worth of securities.

T consults you and informs you that *B* and *S* insist that *M* is not entitled to receive the $8,000 payment to be received by *T* from the insurance company each year, while *M* insists that she is. How would you advise *T*? What possibilities are open? Should a court give instructions to *T*, and if so what should the instructions be? Cf. Matter of Pennock, 285 N.Y. 475, 35 N.E.2d 177 (1941) (deceased life insurance agent's right to percentage of renewal premiums). Assume that the cases below were decided in your state. What would be the result under the Revised Uniform Principal and Income Act?

In Union County Trust Co. v. Gray, 110 N.J. Eq. 270, 159 A. 625 (1932), the testamentary trust contained almost 50,000 shares of the Gray Processes Corporation, the assets of which consisted primarily of a patented process invented by the testator. The corporation also received about $110,000 of insurance proceeds on the testator's death in April 1931, increasing the company's "surplus" to $275,000. Thereafter in June 1931 the corporation declared a "regular" dividend of $50,000 and an "extra" dividend of $50,000, each being payable in January 1932, first out of earnings since July 1, 1931, and if insufficient then out of prior earnings. The question of whether these dividends were income or principal or were to be apportioned was presented to the court, which stated:

> A neat answer, that [one] . . . dividend is extraordinary and the other is not, would be of no assistance, for solution of the meritorious question is not to be found in nomenclature. The tags "regular" and "extra" are presently of no significance. . . .
>
> The regular and extra dividends of June 11th, 1931, are apportionable. . . . So much of the dividends as represents life insurance, obviously was capital; the earnings for the six months preceding the dividend, $3,769.30 are apportionable to corpus and income. . . .
>
> The income from license fees and royalties will end with the life of the patent, and, meanwhile, paying it out in dividends to the life tenants may

result in disappointing the remaindermen. . . . [F]or the protection of the remaindermen, the value of the certificates is to be ascertained as of the testator's death and the life tenants paid interest on the sum, as in Helme v. Strater, 52 N.J. Eq. 591, where the principle was laid down and applied by Chancellor McGill:

> Where a testator bequeaths the residue of his property without specific description, or, in other words, indicating an intention that it shall be enjoyed in specie, first to a tenant for life and then to a remainderman, and thus manifests that the same fund shall be successively enjoyed by both, the necessary inference and established rule in equity is that it must be invested as a permanent fund so that the successive takers shall enjoy it in an equally productive capacity. But where it consists in whole or in part of property which is in its nature perishable, which for some reason cannot be converted into money or cannot be so converted without great sacrifice of both principal and interest, the tenant for life will not be entitled to the annual product which the property thus perishing is actually making, but to interest from the testator's death on the value thereof estimated as of that time.

> . . . The rule of the court (says Lewin) under which perishable property is converted does not proceed upon the assumption that the testator in fact intended his property to be sold, but is founded upon the circumstance that the testator intended the perishable property to be enjoyed by different persons in succession, which is accomplished by means of a sale. . . . Lewin, Trusts 300. Here . . . the power given to the trustees to "invest and reinvest" the estate implies that it should be converted. There is no indication of intention to vary the relative rights of the legatees, or, that the rule of conversion should not obtain. Constructive conversion will be ordered. . . .

> There will be a reference to a master to determine the value of the certificates, and lawful interest will be allowed if the annual income equals the rate.

> It is the fact that only about ten per cent of the oil industry is presently using the patented process, and that the rest of the field is open to exploitation which may greatly swell the annual profits. The possibility requires that the valuation be periodically adjusted to increased annual profits.

110 N.J. Eq. at 274-279, 159 A. at 628-630.

CHAPIN v. COLLARD
29 Wash. 2d 788, 189 P.2d 642 (1948)

[Action by trustees for declaratory judgment. Included among the assets originally received by the trustees from the settlor's estate were two apartment houses, two commercial buildings, and several other buildings. The trustees requested authority to deduct reasonable depreciation on these buildings from gross income before arriving at distributable net income. The trial court decreed that depreciation was not authorized by the will or by law and directed that amounts previously withheld be paid over to the income beneficiary and that no such deductions be made in the future.]

ROBINSON, J. . . .

In Laflin v. Commissioner of Internal Revenue, 69 F.2d 460, the law is tersely stated:

> It is a rule of general application that the beneficiary of a trust entitled thereunder to receive the income from such property may not be required to suffer a deduction from such income for the creation of a sinking fund to provide for depreciation and obsolescence, unless, indeed, the trust instrument or the law of the state makes provision therefor.

Appellants concede this to be the general rule, but urge that the language of the whole will . . . manifests an intention on the part of the testator that a reserve for depreciation be established.

This is no more than wishful thinking. The trustees were directed, "after payment of the necessary expenses of this trust," to pay to the named beneficiaries "the entire net income from said trust." There is nothing in the will to evidence any intention that a reserve for depreciation be deducted from that income, and no ambiguity that warrants the admission of extrinsic evidence of such an intention. . . .

Appellants then invite us to say that the rule referred to is outmoded, and to declare that modern business conditions and practice justify the establishment of a rule of law in this state that trustees of a trust including rental property may deduct a depreciation reserve from rental income which would otherwise be distributed to a life tenant. . . .

In re Roth's Estate, 52 A.2d (N.J.) 811, [in denying a request for depreciation charges the court] said:

> Such a course is in harmony with modern accounting practice, but generally, as between life tenant and remainderman, the latter must bear any loss due to depreciation and obsolescence. . . . A tenant for life is bound to repair only to the extent of preventing permissive or actual waste. . . . But he is under no obligation in respect to the loss of economic value of a building which normally occurs.

We find no substantial authority, either "old" or "modern," supporting the position of the appellants, and both the number and the reasoning of the cases which adhere to the rule as stated in the *Laflin* case, supra, impel us to decline the invitation to establish a different rule in this state.

The courts diligently protect the right of the life tenant to enjoy the full benefits intended for him or her, because, as Mr. Justice Swayze said, in McCracken v. Gulick, 92 N.J. Eq. 214, 112 A. 317:

> Clearly when he [the testator] has created a trust fund and directed that the income be paid a beneficiary for life, he intends to secure that income

to the life tenant; that is the very object of the fund . . . the testator can hardly mean to starve the life tenant for the benefit of remaindermen, whom he often has never seen.

That statement is particularly appropriate in this case, where the trust terminates on the death of the life tenant. . . .

Note that, in following the traditional view rather than modern accounting practice, the above court was considering depreciation on assets initially received by the trustee. Should the result be different as to properties acquired, buildings erected, or improvements made by the trustee? See section A4, infra. An important California decision established the rule providing for depreciation on the *trustee's* investments and then reasoned back to modify the traditional rule on property received from the settlor over which the trustee had power of sale. (After this decision, the California legislature made it a matter of the trustee's "absolute discretion" whether to provide "a reasonable allowance for depreciation under generally accepted accounting principles.") This case, Estate of Kelly, 63 Cal. 2d 679, 685-690, 408 P.2d 353, 357-359 (1965), states:

> Ordinary repairs are those incidental repairs that do not materially add to the value of the property or appreciably prolong its life, but keep it in efficient operating condition. They are customarily treated as charges against income by accountants and accepted as such for both federal and state tax purposes. . . . The renovation of the store building constituted a capital improvement. The work was undertaken, not to maintain a state of repair existing when the property was received by the trustees, but to off-set obsolescence brought about by changes in merchandising techniques. It materially increased the value of the property. . . . The installation of new fixtures was also a capital improvement. Although replacement of fixtures, component parts of a structure, or of mechanical apparatus may be ordinary repairs when done to maintain operating efficiency, that was not the purpose of the expenditures here. The purpose was to provide the lessee with essentially a new store, adapted for modern merchandising techniques. The trial court therefore erred in treating the expenditures for fixtures as ordinary repairs. . . .
>
> The improvement generates additional income for the life beneficiary, but if it depreciates in value with the passage of time, it will not benefit the remaindermen unless the trust terminates before the end of the useful life of the improvement. To require the remaindermen to pay the entire cost of a trust activity undertaken for the benefit of all the beneficiaries would contravene both the intent of the testator and the express provisions of the Principal and Income Law that ordinary expenses of trust management be met by income. . . .
>
> Allocation of the amounts withheld from income to a depreciation

reserve account will provide a fund to meet the expense of making the improvements and of needed upkeep [by replacement of fixtures].

> It avoids the necessity of speculating upon the probable duration of the trust and deducting immediately a gross sum from the income for the whole period. It results in an equalization of the income from year to year instead of the deduction of a large amount all in one year. If the life beneficiary lives as long as the probable duration of the improvements, he will ultimately have paid for the improvements, which is just, because in that case the remainderman ordinarily will have no advantage from the improvements. If the life beneficiary dies within a short time after the improvements are made, he pays for no more than the actual enjoyment he has had, and the remainderman who profits in that case pays the balance of the cost.

(3 Scott, Trusts (2d ed.) §233, p. 1760.) . . .

Depreciation of commercial or rental realty that formed part of the original trust corpus is also a proper trust expense unless the testator has expressed a contrary intent. Rules to the effect that the remainderman must bear the burden of shrinkage of trust capital due to depreciation were the outgrowth of concepts developed during the last century to govern the relation between legal life tenants and remaindermen. Such rules are not adequate to assure either profitable or equitable administration of a contemporary trust. . . . [A trustee can invest in realty] only if the interests of both the income beneficiary . . . and the remainderman . . . are protected. When a trustee who has the power to sell realty held in the trust and to invest the proceeds therefrom elects instead to retain the property, the duty to preserve corpus remains. . . . [H]e must adopt a method of accounting that will prevent the impairment of the principal unless the testator has clearly indicated a contrary intent. . . . An awareness that sound trust management requires that business properties be managed by trustees in such a way that they are not permitted to deteriorate at the expense of the remainderman is reflected in the decision of the Commissioners on Uniform State Laws to provide for a depreciation reserve account in the Uniform Revised Principal and Income Act (1962). . . .

When realty other than that to be occupied by the beneficiary is retained in a trust, the trustee must administer it as a business, allocating expenses in accordance with accepted accounting procedures if he is to fulfill his obligation to income beneficiary and remainderman and fulfill the normal intentions of the testator. . . . Property used in a trade or business continued by trustees is depreciable. As commercial or rental realty retained by trustees cannot be meaningfully distinguished from property used in a trade or business, it should be treated in a similar manner. . . .

. . . [T]he trustees should establish a depreciation schedule under which the improvements to the store building, including fixtures, will be depreciated on a straight line basis over their anticipated useful life. . . . Additionally, the value of the store building itself, before the modernization, is subject to depreciation. . . .

4. Expenses

PROBLEM

19-E.   X is executor and trustee under the will in question. The entire estate was left to X as trustee, and probate administration is now ready to be closed. One of the main assets of the estate is an apartment building the trustee is authorized to retain. It is appraised at $500,000. Two matters have been brought to your attention as attorney for X. The first is that the taxes on the apartment building had not been paid for several years preceding the testator's death and were paid from the rental receipts during estate administration. The second is that the municipality in which the building is located recently built a new sewage disposal plant. An ordinance was adopted increasing real estate taxes for a period of five years by raising the tax base from 60 percent to 75 percent of appraised values. It is anticipated that the increased revenue will enable the city to pay for the sewage plant in five years after which the tax base is to return to 60 percent. How should X account for the taxes he has paid and expects to pay in the future, as between income and principal?

MATTER OF CRONISE
167 Misc. 310, 6 N.Y.S.2d 392 (Surr. Ct. 1937)

FEELY, S.

In this final judicial settlement of the account of the executor, several matters are to be determined, mainly, the apportionment of the estate or death taxes laid both by the Federal government and by the State of New York; and next the allocation of certain disbursements of the executor as between the life beneficiary and the residuary legatees.

Testatrix was domiciled in Rochester, N.Y., where she made her last will on April 2, 1933, and died on the eighteenth of the next August. After the will had been probated in this court, it was re-probated in Stockton, Cal., where testatrix also had both real and personal property. Her last will was that her debts and funeral expenses be paid; and also $5,000 be given to Mills College for a scholarship. By the third paragraph she gave to her sister, Mrs. Eliza F.H. Middlecoff, now by marriage, Mrs. Emery, of Stockton, Cal., "all real estate owned by me situate in the State of California"; and by the next paragraph to the same sister there was given "as her absolute property all my personal effects such as jewelry, clothing, household furniture and all other articles of domestic and personal use." These personal effects lay in Rochester, N.Y. The general residue of her estate was given to Security Trust Company, in trust, "(a) to collect and receive the rent, issues, income and profits thereof, and after paying therefrom all lawful dues and expenses in respect thereof, to pay the net income thereof to my said sister, Eliza F.H. Middlecoff, in monthly payments as long as she shall live; and (b) on the death of my said sister, the corpus, with any unpaid net income to" two named nephews, who are the children of the life beneficiary, and are residents of the State of California.

1. There is nothing else in the will that bears on the matter of allocation or apportionment.

The general rule, as shown by Surrogate Wingate in Matter of Shepard, 136 Misc. 218, is to charge principal only with such expenses as tend to enhance the value of the principal of the trust while income must bear all ordinary expenses connected with the continuance of the property in substantially its existing state; and this is especially so where the will gives only the "net" income. See, also, Matter of Lichtenstein, Rochester Daily Record of July 11, 1932.

In other words, Mr. H. W. Jessup summarizes the rule by saying that expenditures to protect the integrity of the corpus, to avert wastage, etc., are charged to principal; but those made to assure productivity, or for ordinary administration costs are charged to income.

In Matter of Brewster (148 Misc. 390, 392), from which the foregoing summary of the rules is copied, the same distinction is also expressed by referring to one class as items made to assure productivity, but to the other class as items of a structural or defensive character.

The facts bearing on the allocation of outlays, other than for death or estate taxes, are undisputed. The homestead is a large, spacious house, on a large city lot, in a somewhat central section of this city and in a neighborhood that has changed from a fine residential section to one of a boarding house and professional office class; and at death of testatrix was not the kind of a house that could be let to an ordinary family. This real property is valued at $15,000. Despite the executor's efforts, the house was neither sold nor leased, except that the life tenant was in occupancy of it from November 1, 1933, till December twentieth following; and thereafter it stood idle until October, 1935, when it was let at a rental that hardly meets the carrying charges. The expenses of fitting up the property for this tenant is one of the items in question.

In the meantime, the executor paid a caretaker to watch the property and keep the yard and walks in condition; and in the house there were living for a time, for the purpose of caring for the house and its contents, a maid and a sister-in-law of the testatrix, for whom food, etc., was supplied by the executor until the arrival here of the life beneficiary. These outlays kept the property in good condition, and protected it from the dangers to which vacant houses are nowadays exposed, especially when filled, as this house was, with furniture, etc., of the appraised value of $5,612 (New York tax deposition), which had been specifically bequeathed to the life beneficiary as the latter's absolute property. This movable property the executor could as well have put into a public storage warehouse at the charge of the specific legatee. On the basis of the value of the lot and house alone at about $15,000, and this specific legacy at $5,612, one-fourth of these caretaking charges, with insurance premiums on personalty, should be borne by the specific legatee, and the remaining three-fourths should be apportioned between the life beneficiary and the residuary legatees in such ratio as the value of the life estate bears to that of the residuary, because to that extent a common benefit was derived therefrom by both parties in interest. A like apportionment should be made of the expense of caretaking (other than fire insurance) from the time the life beneficiary moved out, taking the personal property with her, until the present tenant was found in October, 1935. The city and county taxes that became liens before the death of testatrix for ordinary purposes other than for local improvements, must be borne wholly by the residuary legatees, but those that became liens after the death of testatrix fall entirely to the charge of the life beneficiary under the provision of the will giving her only "net" income.

On September 14, 1933, a plumbing bill of six dollars was incurred, which was paid December 13, 1933. This appears to have been an ordinary repair. The fact that it was the culmination of wear that probably was given it mainly in the lifetime of the testatrix does not lessen the obligation of the life beneficiary, now that the latter has accepted benefits under the will, from bearing the whole of this charge, as she is deemed to have accepted the condition of the property as it was on the date of the death of the testatrix. No authority for apportionment of any such repair charge has come to the attention of this court.

Most of the other outlay in question arose out of the fitting up of the large outmoded family residence so that it could be used as a boarding house. In this adaptation, the making of a new bathroom was required in addition to the existing two; and $22 was laid out on a partition, $10 on resetting a door, and $100.63 for decoration after these changes. The plumber's bill for the fixtures installed in this new bathroom, with ventilation, amounts to $233. As the only call in this neighborhood is for a lay-out suitable either for boarding house purposes or for the offices of medical or dental doctors, this adaptation was necessary rather than optional, and was designed to "assure productivity," and at the same time it consisted of a permanent addition to the structure of the house; and the cost should be apportioned.

The same is true of the bill of thirty-five dollars spent to run a new pipe line from the heater to the old front bathroom on the second floor, which never before had been heated, except by the seepage from adjoining rooms. Likewise, the seven dollars and five cents spent for new door bells; and the forty-eight dollars and sixty-six cents spent for new wire screens for windows that never had been so equipped before; and the thirty dollars spent for firebelt and rope to comply with the ordinance in respect of the apartment on the third floor. All of these should be apportioned between the life beneficiary and the residuary legatees in such ratio as the value of the life estate bears to that of the residuary interests. (Matter of Laytin, 2 Con. Surr. 106. See, also, Peerless Candy Co. v. Kessler, 123 Misc. 735; Matter of Whitney, 75 id. 610; Peck v. Sherwood, 56 N.Y. 615.)

Then there is a group of replacement of outworn items, like the ninety-one dollars spent to replace a worn-out water heater with a new one. The residuaries were not required either to repair or to replace it (Stevens v. Melcher, 80 Hun. 514, 524); but the life beneficiary would find her income impaired without one, in the peculiar circumstances of this case. Similarly, the removal of the old coal range, and the replacing of it with a used one, at a cost of fourteen dollars and sixty-three cents; and also the replacement of an old ice box with a used electric refrigerator at a cost of $139.50; and likewise in the heating system, an old oil burner, that had been fitted to the furnace had worn to uselessness, and was replaced with a used burner, and the furnace reset, at a cost of $150; these replacements were substantial, and were all put in to stay as long as they should last; although the manner in which some were connected or fastened was not in itself enough to indicate the permanency of the intention with which they were installed. All these replacements, in the circumstances, should be apportioned between the life beneficiary and the residuaries, as aforesaid.

Then there is a group of ordinary repairs, such as the leak in the water pipe, repaired at a cost of fifteen dollars; the repairs to the trap under the tile floor in the old bathroom, at a cost of fifty-nine dollars and seven cents; also the two dollars and forty-seven cents paid to relieve stoppage in the laundry trays; the synchronizing of the thermostat, and repair of leaks, at a cost of six dollars and twenty-four cents; the twenty-five dollars paid for painting the living room; and the twenty-three dollars and thirty cents paid for repairs to the oil burner; and the replacement of the fallen ceiling with plasterboard at a cost of seventeen dollars and twenty-five cents, probably necessitated by the leaks mentioned above — all these fall entirely to the charge of the life beneficiary. To this class should be added the ten dollars paid to clear the garage of the two useless and worthless old safes.

2. The executor's expense in probating this will in California inured to the benefit of the legatee to whom testatrix had devised specifically "all real estate owned by me situate in the State of California"; and it also benefited the residuary trust inasmuch as there was considerable personal property, also situate in that State, which will go into this trust. May the expense be allocated or apportioned for that reason? An executor, by accepting the nomination as such, becomes obliged to execute the last will; and to that end a decree of probate is practically indispensable. The will is thus formally established in several respects — as one integral act, and also conclusively as to all parties in interest, and as to

all the property of the testatrix wheresoever situate — at least, such is the policy of New York as to regularly foreign-made wills that are in writing and subscribed by testator. Re-probate is usually not required in New York, although it is practiced in some other jurisdictions. The integral character of the act of probate — whatever be its procedural incidents in other jurisdictions — whether by record there of an exemplified copy, or by a decree re-probating the original instrument — appears to have caused it to be ever regarded here as a fundamental administrative expense, properly chargeable to corpus on account of its general structural nature. While the executor was not obliged, in an amply solvent estate like this, to take possession of the sometime property of the testatrix situate in other jurisdictions that had been specifically devised or bequeathed by her, nor to make actual physical delivery thereof to its specific legatee (Matter of Columbia Trust Co., 186 App. Div. 377), still the executor was obliged to execute the last will whereby the property had been given, and also to establish title thereto in the ordinary manner as an inseparable part of the integral will he undertook to execute. To ask the legatee of specified property, other than the residue, to pay the expense of formally establishing the wish that the legatee should have it before others were served — as is usually the intention of testators — is not in line with that intention, nor justified by any authority known to this court. This applies not only to the specified land but also to the rest of the California property, to wit, the personalty there, which will go into the residuary trust for the respective benefit of the life beneficiary and of the residuaries solely by virtue of the indivisible act of probating and establishing the wish that it should ultimately benefit them, among others also remembered in the last will. It is not the practice, and to a large extent impracticable to apportion or allocate any such fundamental expense among all the various interests created or benefited by the will, including tax gatherers, lawyers and funeral directors. None of the expense of the California probate, nor that of obtaining possession of the movable property situate there should be apportioned, but should all be borne by the corpus of the estate as a general administrative expense.

3. Some of the ordinary taxes of the California real estate had become liens on January 1, 1933, three months before the date of her will and eight months before the death of the testatrix. While she may not have been liable therefor personally, still they had become liens on her landed interests in her lifetime, and for that reason fall wholly to the charge of the estate at large, to wit, the residue; and without any right of apportionment, because they antedate the inception of the estate and the erection of the trust therein. (See Matter of Babcock, 115 N.Y. 450.) These liens fall in the statutory class of "taxes assessed on property of the deceased previous to his death," which are to be paid as debts in the order or priority defined in subdivision 2 of section 212 of the Surrogate's Court Act.

Mrs. Emery, having paid $7,659.96 of taxes on the California land which had been assessed in the lifetime of the testatrix, is now entitled to credit therefor.

4. As to apportionment of death or estate taxes, . . . New York in 1930 enacted [legislation] for the apportionment of Federal and State estate taxes, and authorized therein the executor either to deduct the apportioned share from the distribution, or to recover it from the person benefited. . . .

The objectant, Mrs. Emery, being subject to the New York law of apportionment, is thereby made liable to an action to recover the portion of the Federal estate tax allotted to her in respect either of her specific legacy, or of her right to income from the residuary trust. To facilitate a prompt settlement of this estate, and to avoid the delay and expense of pursuing that administrative cause of action in some other jurisdiction, this court under its broadened equity powers will decree that enough of her income may be impounded to fully satisfy this obligation now and be applied thereto, unless sooner met otherwise.

5. The outlays made to preserve the lien of certain mortgages subject now to the Alberta Moratorium Act, as set out in Schedule H, should be temporarily charged to principal, until that matter can be finally adjusted.

On notice to counsel, or on voluntary appearance, submit for signature and enter a decree in accord with this decision.

The problem of the estate tax burden and apportionment in the above case is considered further in a subsequent section. One particular aspect of the apportionment problem in the *Cronise* case should be noted, however. As a practical matter the New York apportionment rule was enforced against the devisee of the California land through her interest in the residuary trust, which was under the control of the New York court. If this devisee had received no interest under the will other than the land in California, how might the matter of the tax burden have been handled? Could the testator have required apportionment?

The allocation and apportionment of expenses of a trust estate are detailed in §13 of the Revised Principal and Income Act, supra; and compare id. §5.

5. Fiduciary Fees and Related Matters

ESTATE OF LOPEZ
79 Cal. App. 2d 399, 179 P.2d 621 (1947)

GOODELL, J. . . .

The respondent trustee filed in the superior court its first account and report in each of two trusts created by the will of Robert F. Lopez. . . .

In the orders settling the accounts the court allowed compensation to the trustee and its attorneys for their services during said first year of administration and charged one-half thereof against the corpus and one-half against the income, of the respective trusts. From those orders this appeal was taken. . . .

The appellant [contends "that] the trustee may not impair the principal of the trust estate by paying therefrom compensation for itself and its attorneys but must pay such out of the income." . . . The testamentary provision creating each trust provides:

> 2. The said trustee shall collect and receive any . . . income, issues and profits . . . and shall dispose of all such cash revenue from said trust fund:
>
> (a) By first paying . . . taxes and the reasonable expenses of this trust which shall include the reasonable compensation of said Trustee for its service as Trustee hereunder, and the reasonable compensation of any attorney employed by said Trustee in the administration of said trust fund; and
>
> (b) By paying . . . the surplus to [the life beneficiary] for her support and maintenance during her life.

Appellant contends that the provisions of paragraph (a) that the net income shall be arrived at after the deduction, inter alia, of the trustees and attorney's compensation from the gross income so circumscribes the court's action that it cannot make any charge whatever against corpus. She also invokes section 2 of the Principal and Income Act . . . which provides that:

> This act shall govern the ascertainment of income and principal, . . . except that . . . the person establishing the principal may himself direct the manner of ascertainment of income and principal and the apportionment of receipts and expenses or grant discretion to the trustee or other person to do so, and such provision and direction, where not otherwise contrary to law, shall control notwithstanding this act.

The year covered by these two accounts, it must be remembered, was the first year of the administration of both trusts. The duties of the trustee and its attorneys during that first year embraced the acceptance of the trust property which, in turn, involved putting both trusts into operation, the determination of questions of corpus and income in organizing the trust funds, the settling of tax problems consequent upon the new administration, setting up the necessary accountancy machinery, and in the case of the Leonardini trust, the purchase of a home in Stockton for the use and occupancy of Mrs. Leonardini, the life beneficiary. None of these can be classified as ordinary, routine, recurring, or year-round duties any more than the tasks connected with the distribution or winding up of a trust can be.

Section 12 of the act provides that the trustee's compensation upon or for acceptance or distribution of principal shall be paid out of principal, [but as] we view this case it is not necessary for us to decide whether or not the court's action was taken under the Principal and Income Act.

In Estate of Kruce, 10 Cal. App. 2d 426, 51 P.2d 1174, the testamentary provision was not substantially different from that in paragraph 2(a) of the Lopez will quoted above. . . . The court said, page 430:

> We do . . . not think the provisions of the will depart from this rule. *The direction of the will would seem to apply to the current compensation and expenses of the trustees and not to anything of an extraordinary nature.* The services for which the allowances were made consisted of closing the trust and distributing the property remaining therein after the death of the life tenant. They were performed necessarily for the benefit of the remaindermen and were unrelated to the management of the trust for the benefit of the life estate. *They were not such ordinary and current expenses as would have to be deducted from the income periodically in order that the net income might be computed and paid to the life tenant each month as directed by the will.*

(Emphasis added.)

The language just quoted is particularly applicable to this case and we think is controlling. . . .

The orders settling the two accounts and approving the trustees' reports are affirmed.

Cf. Creed v. McAleer, 275 Mass. 353, 358-359, 175 N.E. 761, 763 (1931).

6. Income During Transitional Periods

PROBLEM

19-F.   The decedent died leaving a gross estate of $550,000 and a will bequeathing:

1. My 1,000 shares of stock in W.G. Corporation to *G*.
2. $20,000 to *A*.
3. $100,000 to *X* Trust Co. to pay the income to *B* for life, remainder to *C*.
4. $100,000 to *Y* Trust Co. to pay the income to *D* for life, remainder to *D*'s surviving children or their issue by representation.
5. Residue to *T* Trust Co. to pay the income to *E* for life, remainder to *F*.

(1) At the end of one year, the executor delivered 1,000 shares of W.G. Corporation stock (worth $25,000) to *G* and paid $100,000 to *X* Trust Co. in trust for *B* and *C*. (2) At the end of eighteen months, the executor

paid $20,000 to *A* and $100,000 to *Y* Trust Co. to fund the *D* family trust. (3) Then at the end of twenty-four months, the executor paid $150,000 in debts, costs of administration and taxes, and is now ready to distribute the residue to *T* Trust Co.

The estate earned income of:

(a) $6,000 in the first year after the decedent's death, including a $500 cash dividend on the W.G. stock;
(b) $13,000 during the period from twelve to eighteen months after the decedent's death; and
(c) $10,000 during the period eighteen to twenty-four months after decedent's death.

How are these items of income to be accounted for in a state that has adopted §5 of the Revised Uniform Principal and Income Act? In your state? Are interest payments due to any of the beneficiaries?

TILGHMAN v. FRAZER
199 Md. 620, 87 A.2d 812 (1950)

MARKELL, J. . . .

The basic question now before us is whether, as between life tenant and remainderman, in the absence of indication of a contrary intent by the testator, income received, during the period of administration, from that part of the testator's assets which eventually was sold and used to pay debts, administration expenses and legacies, goes to the life tenant as income, or, together with the assets so sold and used, is part of the corpus. This question was decided by this court, by holding that such income goes to corpus, fifty-eight years ago. Wethered v. Safe Deposit and Trust Co., (1894) 79 Md. 153, 28 A. 812. . . .

The *Wethered* case was followed in [York v. Maryland Trust Co., 150 Md. 354, 133 A. 128 (1926)], in which the court said,

> We do not find in the testator's will any expression of intention that the debts should be paid from income, but we do think there is an indication that the wife was only to receive the income from the residue of the estate, after the payment of the debts, and under these circumstances it is clear that the rules laid down in the *Wethered* case and the other authorities heretofore cited should apply, and these rules are: (1) that the debts and expenses are payable from the corpus and not from the income; and, (2) that where a life tenant is entitled to the income, such income, in the absence of a contary intention expressed in the will, is confined to that received from the residue, and does not ordinarily include the income derived from that part of the principal used to pay debts, expenses and specific legacies. It accordingly follows that in this case the . . . items

should have been charged against the corpus of the estate, but it also follows that, since there was no contrary intention expressed in the will, the life tenant was not entitled to receive the dividends derived from the securities sold to pay the testator's debts. . . .

Long since the *Wethered* case . . . a conflict in the authorities has developed. In the greater number of jurisdictions the law is in accord with the Maryland law, but a few jurisdictions have adopted a so-called "Massachusetts rule," which is at variance with the "general," or Maryland, or former New York, or "English" rule. In [Proctor v. American Security and Trust Co., 98 F.2d 599, 601-606] the court, by Judge Vinson, said,

> It is fair to say that there are two irreconcilable rules which have grown up in this country in respect to the point involved. There is the general rule, supported by the decided weight of authority in this country, and, likewise, the English cases, that the earnings upon testator's property, derived during the course of administration, used to pay costs of administration, debts and legacies, if not disposed of by the express terms of the will, are added to the residuary trust as part of its corpus. Then there is the so-called Massachusetts rule, which crystallized in 1929 (Old Colony Trust Co. v. Smith, 266 Mass. 500, 165 N.E. 657), which holds that the earnings upon testator's property used to pay costs of administration, debts and legacies derived during the course of administration, if not disposed of by the express terms of the will, are distributable to the life beneficiaries as income. The general rule finds support in the courts of New York, Maryland, Connecticut, Kentucky, New Hampshire, Delaware, New Jersey and the English cases. The Massachusetts rule is followed in the courts of Rhode Island and North Carolina.

In New York the former rule was changed by statute. Laws of 1931, c. 706, Personal Property Law, sec. 17-b, McK. Consol. Laws, c. 41. In Maryland the Act of 1949, ch. 672, Code, Art. 93, sec. 372, apparently modeled after the New York statute, is applicable only to testators who die after the passage of the act. Appellant says the Act of 1949 substitutes the Massachusetts rule for the *Wethered* case. As to the construction or operation of the Act of 1949 we express no opinion.

The merit of the Massachusetts rule is simplicity, i.e., it can be applied, without the use of arithmetical — or algebraical — formulas in more or less complicated computations. The defects of the rule are that it (1) is unsound in principle in distributing, as income of the residue, income from property that never was part of the residue, and (2) consequently is unsound in practice in giving the life tenant more income from the initial year or years than for subsequent years. When administration of an estate is promptly completed the defects of the rule are often mitigated by the circumstance that the difference between the results of the two rules is small. In the instant case the results of the defects of the rule are magnified by the inordinate delay in administering the estate.

This court has not had occasion to express in a formula the principle established and applied in the *Wethered* and *York* cases. In the instant case the auditor followed the formula stated in Section 234, comment *g*, of the Restatement of Trusts:

> g. *Income on property used in paying legacies, debts and expenses.* To the extent to which the income received by the executor during the period of administration is derived from property which is subsequently used in paying legacies and discharging debts and expenses of administration, and has not been applied to the payment of interest on such legacies, debts and expenses, the trustee is entitled to receive the same, but it should be added to principal and not paid to the beneficiary entitled to income. A proper method of determining the extent to which legacies, debts and expenses of administration should be paid out of principal is by ascertaining the amount which with interest thereon at the rate of return received by the executor upon the whole estate from the death of the testator to the dates of payment would equal the amounts paid. This amount is charged to principal and the balance of the amount paid is charged to income.
>
> *Illustrations:* 3. A bequeaths $30,000 to B and all the residue of his property to C in trust to pay the income to D for life and on D's death to pay the principal to E. The value of A's estate at his death is $100,000. During the year after his death the income received by his executor is $5,000. At the expiration of the year the executor pays the legacy of $30,000 to B and pays $10,000 in discharging A's debts and the expenses of administration. Of the $40,000 so paid, $38,095.23 (the sum which with interest at five percent for one year would equal $40,000) is charged to principal, and $1,904.77 is charged to income. D is entitled to receive as income for the first year after A's death $3,095.23; the remainder of the estate amounting to $61,904.77 is principal of the trust estate. . . .

The auditor followed the correct method. . . .

Order affirmed and cause remanded, costs to be paid by appellant individually.

The American Law Institute adopted the Massachusetts rule in Restatement (Second) of Trusts §234, comment *g*. See also Revised Uniform Principal and Income Act §5, supra.

UNIFORM PROBATE CODE

§3-904. *Interest on General Pecuniary Devise.* General pecuniary devises bear interest at the legal rate beginning one year after the first appointment of a personal representative until payment, unless a contrary intent is indicated by the will.

Comment. Unlike the common law, this section provides that a general pecuniary devisee's right to interest begins one year from the time when administration was commenced, rather than one year from death. The rule provided here is similar to the common law rule in that the right to interest for delayed payment does not depend on whether the estate in fact realized income during the period of delay. The section is consistent with Section 5(b) of the Revised Uniform Principal and Income Act which allocates realized net income of an estate between various categories of successors.

In drawing wills, lawyers often find it desirable to include special provisions covering questions of the types raised above. For example, it is not uncommon for drafters to make special provision to prevent the "doubling up" of payments to a surviving spouse that results from the recurring situation in which the spouse is entitled to (1) an allowance from the decedent's estate for support during the period of estate administration and (2) the income of the residuary trust created by the decedent's will. Compare In re King's Estate, 367 Mich. 503, 116 N.W.2d 897 (1962), where the widow was to receive a stated amount monthly from the trust under her husband's will and was also awarded a monthly allowance for the statutory period of one year during probate. Although recognizing that the testator could provide for a different result, the court held that the widow was entitled to both payments for the period of her allowance. Even though an annuity or a right to trust income generally runs from the date of the testator's death, actual payment to the beneficiary is usually not made until the estate is distributed by the executor to the trustee. Typically, however, courts of probate can authorize preliminary distributions before completion of administration under appropriate circumstances.

7. Trustee's Discretionary Power of Allocation

DUMAINE v. DUMAINE
301 Mass. 214, 16 N.E.2d 625 (1938)

. . . The sole question for determination is the power of the trustee under the following clause of the trust indenture:

> The trustee under this instrument shall have full power and discretion to determine whether any money or other property received by him is principal or income without being answerable to any person for the manner in which he shall exercise that discretion.

Frederic C. Dumaine, Jr., the plaintiff trustee, and Frederic C. Dumaine, Sr., a defendant, are the life tenants under the trust indenture, and the trustees of "Dumaines," defendants, are the remaindermen. By the terms of the trust instrument certain property was conveyed to the plaintiff in trust "[t]o hold, manage, invest and reinvest the same with all the powers hereinafter set forth, and, after paying the expenses of administering the trust in this instrument set forth," to pay the net income as therein directed. The trustee is not required to give any bond, and

> [n]o trustee under this instrument shall ever be held responsible for any act or omission of any other person nor for any loss or depreciation of any of the trust property unless such loss or depreciation shall have been directly caused by his own dishonesty or gross negligence. . . . He shall not be responsible for any loss which may occur if he shall have in his absolute and uncontrolled discretion mortgaged, pledged or otherwise encumbered any of the property of this trust fund for the benefit of "Dumaines."

Absolute and uncontrolled discretion is given the trustee as to the purchase and retention of securities. . . .

Our inquiry will be limited to the question raised by the amendment to the bill, that is, whether the trustee may, in his discretion, distribute to himself, as life tenant, as income, the profit derived by the sale of certain shares of stock in 1938, over and above their cost. The general rule is that, in case of a trust, gains resulting from the purchase and sale of securities are accretions belonging to the principal of the trust fund, rather than income. . . .

The defendant trustees do not appear to argue that a settlor has no power to confer a discretion upon his trustees to determine what is income and what is principal, but do contend that, under the trust instrument in question, the trustee has no power to determine, contrary to established rules of law in this Commonwealth, what money or other property received by him as trustee is principal or income. This court has uniformly held that trustees in whom a discretion is vested are under an obligation to exercise a "sound judgment and a reasonable and prudent discretion," Davis, appellant, 183 Mass. 499, 502; that kind of "power and discretion which inheres in a fiduciary relation and not that illimitable potentiality which an unrestrained individual possesses respecting his own property," Corkery v. Dorsey, 223 Mass. 97, 101; a "soundness of judgment which follows from a due appreciation of trust responsibility," Boyden v. Stevens, 285 Mass. 176, 179, unless the settlor has expressed an intention that the power of discretion conferred is such that "the court will not interfere except upon clear proof that the trustees are abusing their authority and acting in perversion of the trust." . . .

On the other hand "full power and discretion" to determine whether any money or other property received by the trustee is principal or income, in the light of attendant circumstances and the language of the trust instrument as a whole, would have little significance if construed to mean a discretion so to determine only in cases where there is no settled law to guide. By the terms of the trust instrument he is to have that power and discretion "without being answerable to any person for the manner in which he shall exercise that discretion."

The court may properly have in mind that, when a settlor reposes a discretion in a trustee, he does so because he desires the honest judgment of the trustee, perhaps even to the exclusion of that of the court. In reposing a discretion he must be held to have known that human judgment is not infallible. It is not for the court to read into a trust instrument provisions which do not expressly appear or which do not arise by implication from the plain meaning of the words used, and the court will not substitute its discretion for that of the trustee except when necessary to prevent an abuse of discretion. It has been said that doubtless a trust might be created which by its terms would make his judgment, however unwise it might be, the final test.

The power, if uncontrollable, to determine whether any money or other property received by the trustee is principal or income, coupled with the power to pay over to the present life tenant so much of the net income as in his absolute and uncontrolled discretion he shall determine, would give the trustee power to destroy the trust. The settlor has no such intention. In deciding the question which is before us, we think that the scope of our inquiry properly embraces the needs of the life tenants, the continuance of the trust until its manifest purposes are accomplished, and the protection and well-being of the "Dumaines," of which latter trust the plaintiff is not only a trustee but also a beneficiary. We do not think the clause in issue confers an absolute and uncontrolled discretion. Nor do we think that it limits the trustee to the determination of the matter involved in cases where there is a question of doubt or no rule of law to guide him. We have nothing before us to show the amount of the trust fund. The trust known as "Dumaines" was created on July 31, 1920, twelve years prior to the trust involved. It made immediate provisions for the children of Frederic C. Dumaine, with ultimate provisions for a substantial educational charity. The power is reserved, in the trust before us, in Frederic C. Dumaine, to make additions to the trust property, and to appoint other trustees instead of or in addition to the one named in the instrument. The trust known as "Dumaines" stands out as an important consideration in the mind of the settlor of the trust before us. Clearly he contemplated no destruction of his trust by any discretionary act of the trustee. But he did intend to give the trustee a power to determine what was principal and income, although he refrained from conferring that power as an absolute and uncontrolled discretion, and we regard this as significant, in the light shed upon the inquiry by a consideration of all factors. The discretion conferred is not an empty one. It confers an important responsibility to make a determination which, if honestly exercised, calls for no revision by the court. Am. Law Inst. Restatement: Trusts, §§187, 233. . . .

Upon consideration of the entire matter, we are of the opinion that the trustee under the clause in question has full power and discretion, after serious and responsible consideration, short of arbitrary or dishonest conduct or bad faith or fraud, when he has to determine whether any money or other property received by him is principal or income; and that upon this record there is nothing disclosed to prevent him from distributing to himself, in his personal capacity, the profit derived during the year 1938 as the result of selling certain shares of stock, a part of the trust property, at a price "over and above cost." . . .

Ordered accordingly.

In Sherman v. Sherman, 5 Ohio St. 2d 27, 213 N.E.2d 360 (1966), the question before the court was whether, for purposes of a clause giving trustees "discretion" to allocate "all receipts" between principal and income, certain stock dividends (clearly otherwise allocable to principal under Ohio law) were "receipts" to which the trustees' power would apply. A four-judge majority held the power did apply, but three judges dissented on the ground that "stock splits and stock dividends are not *receipts* which may be allocated to income by a trustee unless the trust instrument specifically confers [that authority] by unequivocal and express language."

In the widely discussed case of State Street Trust Co. v. United States, 263 F.2d 635 (1st Cir. 1959),[2] the question was whether the powers retained by the settlor as cotrustee were such as to render the property of an irrevocable trust includible in his gross estate for federal estate tax purposes. This question in turn depended on whether the powers amounted to "the right . . . to designate the person who shall possess or enjoy the property or the income therefrom." (See Internal Revenue Code §§2036, 2038.) The court held that the settlor, as cotrustee, possessed such a right because of the express power

> to exchange property for other property; . . . to retain and invest and reinvest in securities or properties of a kind . . . ordinarily . . . not considered suitable for a trust investment, including, but without restriction, investments that yield a high rate of income or no income at all and wasting investments, intending hereby to authorize . . . investments [which] might not otherwise be proper; . . . to determine what shall be charged or credited to income and what to principal notwithstanding any determination by the courts and specifically, but without limitation, to make such deter-

---

2. This case was ostensibly overruled on the basis of changed Massachusetts trust doctrine in Old Colony Trust Co. v. United States, 423 F.2d 601 (1st Cir. 1970).

mination in regard to stock and cash dividends . . . and to decide whether
or not to make deductions from income for depreciation, amortization or
waste and in what amount; . . . all such acts and decisions made by the
Trustees in good faith shall be conclusive.

263 F.2d at 638. The majority opinion stated:

It is true that it is not at all unusual to clothe trustees with power to
invest trust assets in securities other than so-called "legals." And it is also
true that it is far from uncommon to provide that trustees shall have the
power in their discretion to allocate accretions to the property they hold
in trust to principal or to income, at least when there is no settled rule of
law to apply and proper allocation is open to honest doubt. Certainly in
the exercise of one or both of these powers trustees can to some extent
affect the interests of the various beneficiaries. Indeed, even in a trust
wherein investment is limited to "legals," a trustee can effect some shifting
of benefits between life beneficiaries and remaindermen by his choice of
investment with respect to rate of income return or growth potential.
[And here] the trustees' discretionary power to allocate trust assets to corpus or income is not limited to situations where the law is unsettled and
there is honest doubt whether a given accretion or receipt should be classified as capital or income. . . . Furthermore, the trustees may make
deductions from income for depreciation, amortization or waste in whatever amounts they see fit. . . .
    We may . . . assume that a Massachusetts court of equity at the behest
of a beneficiary would intervene not only in the event of a wilful act or
default by the trustees, but would also intervene in the event the trustees
should act in utter disregard of the rights of a beneficiary. . . . But short
of utter disregard of the rights of a life tenant or a remainderman . . . a
Massachusetts court would have no external standard with which to measure the trustees' conduct. The area of the trustees' discretion, although
not untrammelled, is about as broad as language can make it and the law
permits, and within that area the trustees can act in the administration and
management of their trusts to confer or withhold very substantial benefits
as between the life tenants and remaindermen.

263 F.2d at 638-639.

Chief Judge Magruder, dissenting, argued:

The investment powers, although obviously designed to permit a more
imaginative program of investment than trustees usually may pursue, were
not uncontrolled. . . .
    The accounting power given to the trustees is obviously corollary to this
investment power and necessary to the successful maintenance of this balance; I believe it must be limited to this purpose and restricted to the best
interests of the trust as a whole.

263 F.2d at 641-642.

8. Special Problems Posed by Business Interests Administered in Trust

HOLMES v. HROBON
93 Ohio App. 1, 103 N.E.2d 845 (1950)

[Action for declaratory judgment instituted in 1946 by H. B. Holmes, as trustee under the will of C. M. Thomas, seeking construction of the will and instructions concerning the administration of the trust. Thomas died testate in 1938 leaving the residue of his estate to Holmes, his attorney for many years, in trust to pay his widow, Mae Thomas,

> all the income after the payment of operating expenses and taxes and other charges from my business at The Atlas Linen Laundry [an unincorporated business], or any other income that I may have after the payment of the other monthly legacies which I herebefore have set out.

A codicil authorized continuation of any business of the testator and added the "wish that the said trustee shall continue my linen and laundry business as long as the same may be profitable." The trust was to terminate on the widow's death, and the property was then to be distributed to the testator's "legal heirs." The trust property consisted of the assets of the Atlas business (net worth about $75,000) and certain unrelated real estate.

During the period until August 1946 the widow, who has remarried and is now Mae Thomas Hrobon, received from the trustee an average of nearly $33,000 annually, or a total in excess of $260,000. In September 1946 she demanded additional sums primarily as income of the Atlas business from prior periods. Her demands included amounts of income expended for the purchase of five competing businesses ($104,000) and for the purchase of machinery and equipment, designated in the subsequent report of a referee as "replacements" ($140,000) and "additions" ($62,000). Other facts appear in the opinion of the Court of Appeals printed below; certain issues have been omitted.]

WISEMAN, J. . . .

The referee held that income payable to the life tenant should be arrived at by computing the gross income from the operation of the Atlas Plant and other income producing properties of the decedent; and deducting therefrom all operating costs recognized . . . for [federal] income tax purposes; [and] that in the operating costs of the Atlas Plant there should be included maintenance, *expansion necessary to keep pace with the increase or progress and continued operation of the business of the plant,* the cost of the management of the trust, including the trustee's compensation, court costs, fees of counsel necessarily incurred in the administration of the trust, *and the interpretation of the will, also expenses occasioned by litigation and other charges incurred under the supervision and control of the court.* . . . We disagree with the referee with respect to that part of the finding which is [italicized]. . . .

The words in the will, the meaning of which is in dispute, are "other charges." The life tenant contends that the rule of ejusdem generis applies, restricting the meaning of the term to items of expense similar to operating expenses and taxes. We do not believe that the testator intended to give these words such a restricted meaning.

The trustee and remaindermen contend that the words "other charges" should be given a broad meaning because of the broad powers conferred on the trustee [to continue the business]. The trustee and the remaindermen contend, and the referee finds, that the powers thus conferred authorized the trustee to conduct the laundry business in the same manner as if it were his own enterprise [including discretion whether] any of the income from the business should be used for expansion purposes, such as purchasing competing businesses, purchasing additional land and additional machinery for such expanded business, in order that the laundry business "may be profitable." In other words, the trustee interpreted the will, and the referee agreed, that it was the intention of the testator that the trustee could do anything necessary to operate successfully. Record, p. 917. We do not agree. The testator had in mind that the trustee may not be able to operate the business profitably and so provided for the sale of the business.

We recognize that in operating a business, such as a laundry business, it would be advisable to confer wide discretionary power on the trustee in determining whether a certain given expense, such as money expended for the purchase of competing businesses and for additional land and machinery for the operation of the expanded business, would be for the best interest of the trust. However, unless the provisions of the will expressly provide that the trustee shall have such wide discretionary power to take income, which would otherwise be distributed to the life tenant, and to use it for such purpose, the trustee has no authority to make such expenditures. Authority to operate does not confer power on trustee to allocate the costs of replacements and additions to the detriment of the life tenant and benefit of the remaindermen. . . . We find no provision in the will which would permit a construction that it was the intention of the testator that the trustee in the operation of the laundry business could deprive the life tenant of a portion of her income to expand the business, thereby increasing the corpus at her expense. . . .

We now apply the principle herein announced to several controversial matters in which the trustee expended from the income substantial sums of money in the conduct of the laundry business.

A. *Cost of Linens — Float*

The referee found that "float" is a term used to denote linens and garments in use; that is, in the hands of customers, in trucks, and at the Atlas Plant being laundered. The life of these linens and garments, according to the evidence, is considerably less than one year. The referee properly found from the evidence that "float" is expensed as soon as it is put into use, and appears as an "operating expense" on the statement of income. The referee also found that the testator in the operation of the laundry business and in his income tax returns followed the policy of expensing float as of the date it went into use, and that the trustee, upon assuming charge of the trust, followed the same policy. . . .

The increase in the value of material in stock, and also the material in use, known as float, was largely due to the persistent effort on the part of the trustee to expand the business and particularly in the purchase of like competing businesses. . . . [T]he purchase of competing businesses, which will be treated later under an additional heading, resulted in the expansion of the business and necessitated the purchase of additional machinery, additional trucks, additional supplies, and resulted in a tremendous increase [$14,000 to almost $100,000] in the amount and value of float. . . . All of the cost of float was paid from income.

It is the contention of the trustee and the legatees that the life tenant was the direct beneficiary of this expansion of the business and this manner of operation for the reason that her income increased correspondingly each succeeding year. The life tenant contends that since the material in stock and float has been tremendously increased in value a credit should be given the life tenant at this time for the increased inventory value of the material on hand and for float over and above the inventory value for such material and float at the beginning of the trust. If these were done the effect would be to permit the life tenant to receive the income from the use of float in the business and, also, a credit for the estimated value of float at the end of the accounting period. We cannot accept this view of the matter, since it is the fact that linens, etc., are totally consumed and depreciated within a few months after being taken out of stock and put into use, and that it is the accepted practice to expense linens, etc., as soon as such material is taken from stock and put into use.

The life tenant has received and now claims the income derived from the use of float in the business. In order to keep the business operating on a high level of income, the trustee must annually expend large sums for material which goes into stock. The purchase of such material is properly charged to income. The increased cost of material going into stock in turn produces an increase in net income distributable to the life tenant.

We are in accord with the contention of the life tenant to the extent that the trustee should not be permitted to gradually build up the inventory of such material during the conduct of the trust and charge it to income and at the termination of the trust regard such material in inventory and float as corpus. In respect to float we fail to find any injustice resulting to the life tenant during the continuation of the trust. It is upon the termination of the trust that an adjustment must be made, otherwise the remaindermen would be unjustly enriched at the expense of the life tenant. Then, too, in the event of the sale of the business material in inventory and in float would be a substantial item in determining the value of the business. It would be at that juncture in the relationship of the parties that an adjustment would be required. . . .

B. Expansion — Businesses Purchased

The referee found from the record that from January 18, 1940 to and including the 19th day of May, 1945, the trustee purchased five similar competing businesses. The total costs of purchase of the several businesses were paid out of the gross income of the trust. The trustee contends that since the will placed no limitation upon the trustee respecting the purchase of new businesses that, therefore, the trustee may do so. This Court holds to the proposition that the trustee has not the power to purchase new businesses unless the will expressly confers the power on him to do so. "Full power and authority to conduct and carry on the laundry business," and "to do all things necessary or proper in the usual course of said business," which was the power conferred on the trustee in the will, does not authorize him to purchase new businesses. To do "all things necessary" means to do all things necessary as trustee and not as sole proprietor. . . . A private individual may use income to expand at will; a trustee may not unless authority is clearly given.

But it is claimed that the life tenant consented to the purchase of other businesses by the trustee. The record does not show that the trustee discussed with the life tenant the purchase of the first three businesses. . . . However, it does appear that an application was filed in the Probate Court by the trustee to purchase The 5¢ Towel and Supply business and The Bowden Towel and Supply Company. The Court in an ex parte order granted the application. The life tenant had no notice and such order would not be binding on her. . . .

This situation presents two questions: First, the power and authority of the trustee under the will to make the purchases. On this issue we conclude that the trustee exceeded his powers in the purchase of these businesses. Second, the trustee, having made the purchases, against whom should the cost be charged? . . . The physical assets received through these purchases fall into the category of additional equipment and machinery purchased by the trustee. The physical assets received by the trustee, such as trucks, machinery, etc., should be charged to corpus in the same manner as any other additional equipment and machinery, and depreciated over a period of years in the same manner; the life tenant to be charged annually for depreciation during the life of such assets. The difference between the value of the physical assets and the purchase price is the amount paid for good will and becomes a part of and should be charged to corpus. This method of accounting is discussed more fully under the next sub-heading.

C. Replacements — Additions to Laundry Building

It is conceded that repairs to machinery, equipment and buildings are properly charged to income.

The referee found from the record that between May 1, 1938 and August 31, 1946, new property assets, such as machinery and equipment, were purchased during this period at a total cost of $201,883.33, of which amount $140,091.20 was for replacements and $61,792.13 was for additions. The purchase price of these various property assets was deducted from the net income as "other charges" in the year purchased, so that the distributable income to the life tenant was reduced over this period by reason of the cost of these property assets. The referee further found that in each year the amount of depreciation on the items so purchased was credited to net income in determining the distributable income to the life tenant [thereby relieving distributable income of depreciation charges on the replacements and additions]; that during this period these credits amounted to $39,823.18 for replacements and $18,163.25 for additions, or a total of $57,986.43. The difference between the latter figure and $201,883.33, the total cost of such assets so purchased up to the year of 1946, will be credited back to net income of life tenant in succeeding years so that by 1955 the total depreciation credits will equal the amount of the cost of the assets.

The trustee and the legatees contend . . . that in the event of the death of the life tenant at a time prior to the receiving by the life tenant of all of such depreciation credits there will be due her estate the balance of such depreciation credits. . . . This method of operation of the trust, and this system of accounting of charges and credits forces the life tenant to finance the operation of the business out of her income from year to year, and because of the increase of the business and the expansion of the business by the trustee from year to year, the life tenant is required to forego each succeeding year a larger share of her income; so that at no time during the operation of the trust would she receive the total amount of income due her for any current year. As a result there would be from year to year an increasing total amount of depreciation credits

due her. It is contended by the remaindermen that at her death her
estate could make claim against the trust for the total amount of such
depreciation credits due her.

The life tenant is not interested in depreciation credits. The life tenant
is entitled to receive each calendar year the net income from the Atlas
business after deducting operating expenses, taxes and other charges as
defined by this Court. If some of the assets which are considered to be
corpus are replaced the cost [should be] charged to the corpus and a
depreciation charge should be made against the income of the life tenant
for each year during the life of such replacement. The same is true with
respect to additions which depreciate through use and produce income.
In Restatement of the Law, Trusts, Vol. I, Section 233, Note 1, page
688, the author states:

> . . . [T]he result is that if the trust does not terminate before the end of
> the probable life of the improvements, the whole cost of the improve-
> ments will be paid out of income. This is fair because the beneficiary enti-
> tled to the income gets the full benefit of the improvements and the
> remainderman gets no benefit. On the other hand, if the trust terminates
> prior to the end of the probable life of the improvements, the payments
> from income will cease on the termination of the trust. This is fair because
> the beneficiary entitled to the income has not received the full benefit
> from the improvements but the remainderman receives a part of the ben-
> efit. . . .

However, the trustee now contends that he will experience financial
difficulty if he is required to operate the trust as directed by this Court.
The trustee contends that since he has no working capital, and the net
income is distributed to the life tenant, he is required of necessity to
charge the cost of replacements and additions to income and give the
life tenant a depreciation credit each year during the useful life of the
article. As we have heretofore stated, we have rejected this method on
the ground that it forces the life tenant to finance the operation of the
trust out of income, and therefore deprives the life tenant of a substantial portion of her income each accounting period. In our judgment this
method is neither fair nor just to the life tenant, and, is contrary to fundamental principles of trust law.

We do not believe the trustee will experience serious difficulty in operating the trust as directed by this Court. We have found that the trustee
has no power to purchase additions except machinery and equipment
required to take care of the normal increase of trade. Had the trustee,
in the conduct of the trust thus far, confined his purchases of replacements and additions to take care of the normal increase of trade, it is our
opinion he would have been able to conduct the trust by making bank
loans and mortgaging trust property. As a matter of fact the record
shows that the trustee did make repeated bank loans and applied to the

Probate Court for authority to mortgage the trust res. This is the accepted procedure to be followed by the trustee where there is no working capital. However, it is the duty of the trustee to find working capital. There are assets in the trust, exclusive of the laundry business, which may be liquidated and the proceeds placed in a working capital account or a reserve account. . . . See Scott on Trusts, Section 233.3 in the 1951 supplement, page 116, which reads as follows:

> Where a trust is created for successive beneficiaries, the trustee cannot properly set up a reserve out of income for future improvements. . . .

The finding of the referee is sustained in part and overruled in part. . . .

[Dissenting opinion omitted.]

HOLMES v. HROBON
158 Ohio St. 508, 110 N.E.2d 574 (1953)

[The opinion that follows involves the next reported step of the litigation in the above case. Parts of the opinion of the Supreme Court of Ohio are omitted; these deal with issues omitted in the printed portions of the preceding opinion.]

MIDDLETON, J. . . .

Giving full consideration to the desire of the testator that the Atlas business be continued, the history of its past operation, the fact that it had always been operated and expanded out of earnings, the complete lack of capital with which the trustee could operate, the amount of the profits realized from the business during the latter years of operation by the testator and the impossibility of operation by the trustee without using a portion of the income as capital, we conclude that it was the intention of the testator to and he did authorize the use by the trustee of income in the operation and expansion of Atlas, even though such use reduced the amount of profits currently available for payment to the widow. The right of the trustee to so use income would exist only so long as the business was operated profitably and the widow received a reasonable amount of the income. That the widow has not suffered hardship is evidenced by payment to her of $263,299.72 up to August 31, 1946. Although the record does not contain evidence of the amounts paid to the widow since 1946, photostatic copies of checks in her favor included in the briefs indicate payment of $100,000 to her during the first ten months of 1952.

The right of the trustee to use income in operation extends to all phases of operation which sound business judgment would approve, but such right of the trustee to use a portion of the income does not authorize accounting such as will result in currently increasing the corpus of the trust estate or confiscation of income payable to the life tenant.

This court does not undertake to direct the detailed manner in which the trustee's accounts should be kept. It is hoped, however, that such general principles may be herein stated as will enable accountants to rewrite or amend the trustee's books of accounts so that they will satisfy all legal requirements. . . .

The first item of capital is the value of the corpus of the trust. The "corpus" of the trust as here used is that portion of the total assets of the estate remaining after deduction of all debts of the testator as they existed at the time of his death, all taxes, the widow's year's allowance, the amount exempt from administration and the entire cost of the administration. Upon determination of that amount it should be shown in the books of account and it will represent the amount as to which the remaindermen were entitled to the protection of law at the inception of the trust. The corpus of the trust is an amount of money representing the net assets of the estate as above stated. It does not consist of specific property. When so set up on the books of account, the amount of money representing the corpus of the trust will not be reduced as a result of the operation of the business. On the other hand, the use of income by the trustee in the operation, maintenance or expansion of the business must not be permitted to result in currently increasing the value of the corpus of the trust.

Expenditures by the trust out of income may, and in all probability will, result in increasing the total net assets used in operation of the business. This may be considered as increasing the capital. Since, as we have stated, such increase does not currently change the value of the corpus of the trust, that increase in the capital belongs to the widow and she is entitled to receive it upon sale of the business or termination of the trust. The books of account must be so kept that annual statements will reflect the total net assets of the trust and reflect both the unchanging value of the corpus and the additional capital resulting from expenditure of income. It would seem obvious that at a given time the latter element of capital, to wit, the amount thereof resulting from investment of income, will be the difference between the total net assets and the original and unchanged value of the corpus.

The court is mindful of the fact that upon sale of the business or termination of the trust there may be an item of intangible value, goodwill or going value, not represented by physical assets or cash in the hands of the trustee, the disposition of which may call for the court's determination at that time. No such issue is now before this court and this decision is not to be considered as dispositive of any such questions or issues except to the limited extent herein stated. . . .

The words "other charges," which appear in item V of the will have been given much consideration by the lower courts and have been discussed in briefs at great length. Is their meaning to be limited to items similar to operating expenses and taxes under the rule of ejusdem generis or should they be given a broader interpretation in harmony with the broad powers given to the trustee? We adopt the latter interpretation.

Referring to specific transactions affected by that interpretation, we hold that the trustee had the right and authority to use income as needed with which to purchase five competing businesses. We do not, however, approve the accounting now in the records of the trustee with respect to those purchases. . . . The trustee included the items of equipment in appropriate accounts but charged the entire balance covering "float" (linen in service) and intangibles to operating expense in the years of the respective purchases. Such accounting does not protect the interests of the life tenant. . . . [T]he amount of the purchase price remaining after deduction of cost of equipment and value of linen in service — in other words, the amount representing intangible ["goodwill"] value — should be included in the capital assets but should be amortized and written out of the capital account over a period of years. . . . Income of the widow would thus be used to purchase those items of goodwill but, the investment having been made in the exercise of sound business judgment, it is to be assumed that the income of the widow during the succeeding years would be increased by reason of such expenditure of income. . . .

Upon sale of the business or termination of the trust, the unamortized portions of the cost of goodwill of the five businesses purchased [may] still be present in the statement of capital assets and the widow would be entitled to receive such unamortized amounts, provided, however, that such payment to her may not effect any reduction in the stated value of the "corpus."

Since the life of linen in service is shown to be less than one year, the trustee's practice of charging the linen to expense when put into service is approved. For like reasons we approve of charging the value of "float," purchased with the five businesses, to expense in the year of purchase. . . .

The judgment of the Court of Appeals is affirmed in part and reversed in part, and the cause is remanded for accounting consistent herewith.

For a thorough and informative examination of the above litigation and related problems, see Krasnowiecki, Existing Rules of Trust Administration: A Stranglehold on the Trustee-Controlled Business Enterprise, 110 U. Pa. L. Rev. 506 (Part I, The Unincorporated Business), 816 (Part II, The Incorporated Business) (1962).

How might the drafter attempt to deal with such problems of operating an unincorporated business in trust, such as setting up reserves for depreciation, depletion, replacement, or expansion? Does statutory or testamentary authorization "to continue the decedent's business" mean the trustee can do anything an owner could do? Does the customary business practice reflected in the income tax law, federal or state, impliedly authorize a trustee to establish depreciation reserves in order to obtain a tax benefit for the trust or some beneficiaries? Compare Uniform Trustees Powers Act §3(b), (c)(3), (21); Revised Uniform Principal and Income Act §§8, 13. Would these problems be any different if the business interest bequeathed to the trustee had been in the form of the capital stock of an incorporated business? How would these matters be affected if the corporate shares involved represented a controlling interest in the business but not all of the outstanding stock? Can the trustee who receives an unincorporated business interest hope to solve these problems by incorporation? Compare Uniform Trustees Powers Act §3(c)(3). If the law of the state does not authorize the trustee to incorporate a business, could the matter be resolved by the executor of the decedent's estate before distribution to the trustee? Compare Uniform Probate Code §3-715(24), (25); cf. supra Chapter 18, section A2. Be prepared to discuss these questions, particularly in the context of an inflationary economy.

It would appear that the attorney has three opportunities to suggest solutions to these problems of handling business interests in the decedent's estate or trust: (1) lifetime and testamentary estate planning during the owner's life; (2) postmortem estate planning during the administration of the decedent's estate; and (3) postmortem planning during the administration of the trust. The opportunities and available alternatives decrease sharply with the passage of time in each instance. Does this failure of the attorney to see the problems and take corrective steps at the earliest opportunity constitute malpractice or only excusable incompetence?

B. Burden of Death Taxes

A significant problem that arises in all substantial estates is that of allocating or apportioning the burden of estate and inheritance taxes. The nature of an inheritance tax, often levied by states, is such that the burden is borne by each distributee on whose interest an inheritance tax is levied, assuming no express provision for its payment from another source. The federal estate tax, to the extent it is based on probate assets and nonprobate assets for which no contrary provision is made in the Internal Revenue Code, is payable by the personal representative and generally from the residuary estate unless state legislation or will provision prescribes a different result. Most states, however, either by statute or by judicial decision, now provide for apportionment of the estate tax among the various recipients of the taxable estate on a basis of the tax attributable to their respective shares. See Scoles, Estate Tax Apportionment in the Multi-State Estate, 5 Miami Inst. Est. Plan. 7-1 (1971). Nonprobate assets often contribute to the total tax imposed upon an estate. The Internal Revenue Code (§§2206 and 2207) directs that certain of these assets (insurance proceeds and appointive assets) are to bear the tax attributable to them, while other taxable nonprobate assets remain a source of uncertainty and diverse results in the absence of well-tailored estate plans.

In the case of Riggs v. Del Drago, 317 U.S. 95 (1942), the United States Supreme Court was presented with the question of whether certain cash bequests, aggregating $500,000, were to bear a proportionate part of the tax as directed by the apportionment statute of New York, the only state whose laws were an issue, or whether the state legislation was "repugnant to the federal estate tax law" and thus "in violation of the supremacy and the uniformity clauses of the Constitution." The New York Court of Appeals had, under the latter view, held the statute unconstitutional, causing the entire burden of the tax to fall on the residuary estate. In reversing, the United States Supreme Court stated:

> Section 826(b) [of the Internal Revenue Code] does not command that the tax is a nontransferable charge on the *residuary* estate. . . . [R]esort must then be had to state law to determine whether personalty or realty, or general, demonstrative or special legacies abate first, . . . leaving to state law the determination of where the final impact [of the tax] shall be.
>
> Respondents also rely on §826(b), authorizing the executor to collect the proportionate share of the tax from the beneficiary of life insurance includable in the gross estate [and] authorizing similar action against a person receiving property subject to a power which is taxable under §811(f), as forbidding further apportionment by force of state law against other distributees. But these sections deal with property which does not pass through the executor's hands and the Congressional direction with regard to such property is wholly compatible with the intent to leave the determination of the burden of the estate tax to state law as to properties actually handled as part of the estate by the executor.

317 U.S. at 101-102.

In recommending the New York Apportionment Statute, the Decedent Estate Commission had stated (Combined Reports of the Decedent Estate Commission (1930), reprint edition, page 338):

> The principal objection to an estate tax has been that where the decedent dies leaving a will, and makes no provision therein to the contrary, the entire burden of the tax must be borne by the residuary legatee or legatees. Experience has demonstrated that in most estates the residuary legatees are the widow, children, or nearer and more dependent relatives. This has been one of the objections to the Federal Estate Tax Law in New York. The burden of the tax has been imposed upon the residuary legatees not only as to the property passing under the will, but also upon transfers

whether by gift or inter vivos trust, or other form of transfer taking effect at death. These transfers are included both in the Federal Estate Tax Law and under the proposed New York State Estate Tax Law as subject to taxation. Thus the residuary legatees have been compelled to pay the entire estate tax. . . .

The foregoing proposed section [is intended to provide] statutory authority for an equitable apportionment of the estate taxes — both Federal and State — as against all transfers of property included in the gross estate. . . . Of course, if the will directs the method or source of the payment of the estate taxes no apportionment can be made in violation of its terms; thus the testator, in his discretion, may provide for the method and source of the payment of the tax. . . .

A provision has been inserted in the proposed section governing the method of apportionment of the taxes where there are life estates either primary or contingent, and either legal or equitable. In such cases it is intended that the taxes on the transfer to all the beneficiaries, either life tenants or other temporary beneficiaries and remaindermen, whether vested or contingent, shall be paid out of the property or principal of the fund. No separate valuation of the life or other temporary interest is to be made, but the transfer is to be treated as if it were a single legacy of the property or fund.

UNIFORM PROBATE CODE

§3-916.   *Apportionment of Estate Taxes.* . . .

(b) Except as provided in subsection (i) and, unless the will otherwise provides, the tax shall be apportioned among all persons interested in the estate. The apportionment is to be made in the proportion that the value of the interest of each person interested in the estate bears to the total value of the interests of all persons interested in the estate. The values used in determining the tax are to be used for that purpose. If the decedent's will directs a method of apportionment of tax different from the method described in this Code, the method described in the will controls.

(c)(1) The Court in which venue lies for the administration of the estate of a decedent, on petition for the purpose may determine the apportionment of the tax.

(2) If the Court finds that it is inequitable to apportion interest and penalties in the manner provided in subsection (b), because of special circumstances, it may direct apportionment thereof in the manner it finds equitable.

(3) If the Court finds that the assessment of penalties and interest assessed in relation to the tax is due to delay caused by the negligence of the fiduciary, the Court may charge him with the amount of the assessed penalties and interest.

(4) In any action to recover from any person interested in the

estate the amount of the tax apportioned to the person in accordance with this Code the determination of the Court in respect thereto shall be prima facie correct.

(d)(1) The personal representative or other person in possession of the property of the decedent required to pay the tax may withhold from any property distributable to any person interested in the estate, upon its distribution to him, the amount of tax attributable to his interest. If the property in possession of the personal representative or other person required to pay the tax and distributable to any person interested in the estate is insufficient to satisfy the proportionate amount of the tax determined to be due from the person, the personal representative or other person required to pay the tax may recover the deficiency from the person interested in the estate. If the property is not in the possession of the personal representative or the other person required to pay the tax, the personal representative or the other person required to pay the tax may recover from any person interested in the estate the amount of the tax apportioned to the person in accordance with this Act.

(2) If property held by the personal representative is distributed prior to final apportionment of the tax, the distributee shall provide a bond or other security for the apportionment liability in the form and amount prescribed by the personal representative.

(e)(1) In making an apportionment, allowances shall be made for any exemptions granted, any classification made of persons interested in the estate and for any deductions and credits allowed by the law imposing the tax.

(2) Any exemption or deduction allowed by reason of the relationship of any person to the decedent or by reason of the purposes of the gift inures to the benefit of the person bearing such relationship or receiving the gift; but if an interest is subject to a prior present interest which is not allowable as a deduction, the tax apportionable against the present interest shall be paid from principal.

(3) Any deduction for property previously taxed and any credit for gift taxes or death taxes of a foreign country paid by the decedent or his estate inures to the proportionate benefit of all persons liable to apportionment.

(4) Any credit for inheritance, succession or estate taxes or taxes in the nature thereof applicable to property or interests includable in the estate, inures to the benefit of the persons or interests chargeable with the payment thereof to the extent proportionately that the credit reduces the tax.

(5) To the extent that property passing to or in trust for a surviving spouse or any charitable, public or similar purpose is not an allowable deduction for purposes of the tax solely by reason of an inheritance tax or other death tax imposed upon and deductible from the property, the property is not included in the computation provided for in subsection (b) hereof, and to that extent no apportion-

ment is made against the property. The sentence immediately preceding does not apply to any case if the result would be to deprive the estate of a deduction otherwise allowable under Section 2053(d) of the Internal Revenue Code of 1954, as amended, of the United States, relating to deduction for state death taxes on transfers for public, charitable, or religious uses.

(f) No interest in income and no estate for years or for life or other temporary interest in any property or fund is subject to apportionment as between the temporary interest and the remainder. The tax on the temporary interest and the tax, if any, on the remainder is chargeable against the corpus of the property or funds subject to the temporary interest and remainder.

(g) Neither the personal representative nor other person required to pay the tax is under any duty to institute any action to recover from any person interested in the estate the amount of the tax apportioned to the person until the expiration of the 3 months next following final determination of the tax. A personal representative or other person required to pay the tax who institutes the action within a reasonable time after the 3 months' period is not subject to any liability or surcharge because any portion of the tax apportioned to any person interested in the estate was collectible at a time following the death of the decedent but thereafter became uncollectible. If the personal representative or other person required to pay the tax cannot collect from any person interested in the estate the amount of the tax apportioned to the person, the amount not recoverable shall be equitably apportioned among the other persons interested in the estate who are subject to apportionment.

(h) A personal representative acting in another state or a person required to pay the tax domiciled in another state may institute an action in the courts of this state and may recover a proportionate amount of the federal estate tax, of an estate tax payable to another state or of a death duty due by a decedent's estate to another state, from a person interested in the estate who is either domiciled in this state or who owns property in this state subject to attachment or execution. For the purposes of the action the determination of apportionment by the Court having jurisdiction of the administration of the decedent's estate in the other state is prima facie correct.

(i) If the liabilities of persons interested in the estate as prescribed by this act differ from those which result under the Federal Estate tax law, the liabilities imposed by the federal law will control and the balance of this Section shall apply as if the resulting liabilities had been prescribed herein.

PROBLEM

19-G.   *E*, the executor of *T*'s will, has come to consult you regarding certain aspects of his accounting for estate tax payments, and regarding the consequences of a decision made by him in the determination of the estate tax.

Under T's pre-1981 will, Blackacre was devised to A and $100,000 was bequeathed to B. T also made a bequest to his wife, W, "in an amount equal to one-half of my adjusted gross estate as finally valued for federal estate tax purposes." The residue was left in trust to accumulate any income not needed for W's support, taking into account her other resources, and on W's death to be distributed to C. The only nonprobate property included in T's gross estate was half of the value of Whiteacre, a valuable ranch that was held in joint tenancy by T and his brother, D. T's will provided that all taxes on his estate were to be apportioned in accordance with the apportionment act of his state, which is identical to the Uniform Probate Code §3-916, supra. Both Blackacre and White-acre are situated in other states, and under the decisional law of these states the burden of all estate taxes falls on the residuary estate, in accordance with the earlier common law rule.

E also informs you that, in order to minimize estate taxes, he elected the alternate valuation date for purposes of the federal estate tax. (Under §2032 of the Internal Revenue Code the executor is allowed under certain circumstances to choose either of two dates, the date of death or the date six months later, for purposes of determining the value of the gross estate.) By choosing the later date E was able to reduce the value of the estate by an amount that effected a substantial estate tax saving. In doing so, however, the "adjusted gross estate" was reduced, and W's marital deduction bequest was impaired by $40,000, in contrast to what she would have received had the earlier date been elected.

(a) E wishes to know how the estate tax is to be borne as among A, B, C, D, and W. He also wishes to know what he is to do with respect to W's complaint that his decision cost her $40,000 and particularly whether he may have some liability for this decision. How would you advise E? Consider, in addition to the statute above, the rest of the material in this chapter.

(b) If you had been advising T in the planning of his estate, how could you have better handled the problems created by the present situation?

JOHNSON v. HALL
283 Md. 644, 392 A.2d 1103 (1978)

Digges, Judge.

Confronting us in this case is the task of finding a final resting place for the federal estate tax obligation which was assessed on the worldly goods owned at the time of her death by Catherine W. Johnson, M.D., of Fort Foote, Prince George's County, Maryland. The orphans' Court of that county concluded that the federal estate tax should be apportioned among the beneficiaries named in Dr. Johnson's last will and testament; however, the Court of Special Appeals reversed and placed the entire burden of this tax upon the residuary legatee. Hall v. Johnson, 38 Md. App. 589, 382 A.2d 332 (1978). We granted certiorari and now reverse the judgment rendered by the Court of Special Appeals.

Upon her death in 1973, Dr. Johnson left a gross estate slightly in excess of one-half million dollars which, by her will, she divided among her close relatives and friends. After making a number of specific bequests, she left the residue of her estate in trust for the benefit of her son, Carman, who had a history of recurring mental illness. Among these specific bequests were gifts of stock to Dr. W. Luther Hall and Dr. James M. Bacos, the respondents here, both of whom, the will indicates, had attended Dr. Johnson as her personal physicians. The will was admitted to probate in December 1973 with another son of the testatrix, Jule Abner Johnson, who is the petitioner here, being named as personal representative. In January of 1977, preparatory to making a final accounting and distribution, the personal representative sought the approval of the orphans' Court to apportion the federal estate taxes on a pro rata basis among all the beneficiaries. The two physicians opposed apportionment on the ground that the will directed payment of these taxes from the residuary estate. It is the resolution of this dispute to which we now turn our attention.

We begin by noting that, except in instances when life insurance proceeds pass directly to the beneficiary and in cases when property subject to a general power of appointment is devised, the burden of paying federal estate taxes, because of the absence of any federal statute regulating the subject, is determined by reference to state law. Riggs v. Del Drago, 317 U.S. 95, 97-98, 101-02 (1942); see I.R.C. §§2206-07. Historically, estate taxes were viewed, like any other transfer tax or administrative expense, as being part of the cost of administration and, absent an expression of intent in the will to the contrary, payable from the residuary portion of the estate. Scoles & Stephens, The Proposed Uniform Estate Tax Apportionment Act, 43 Minn. L. Rev. 907, 915 (1959). The inequity which frequently resulted from the application of this "common law" rule, especially when the residue was left to sustain a widow or minor children, spurred many state legislatures to revise that rule through statutory enactment. Id. These statutes, the first of which was adopted in New York in 1930, usually provide that, in the absence of an expression of intent in the will to the contrary, federal and state estate taxes are to be apportioned among the beneficiaries in proportion to the value of the gifts they receive.[3] Id. Maryland adopted its first apportion-

---

3. One commentator who recently surveyed the law of the 50 states and the District of Columbia found that, when the will is silent as to the testator's intent, 29 jurisdictions apportion all estate taxes, 8 apply apportionment only to nonprobate assets, and 14 still follow the common law rule and place the burden of estate taxes upon the residue. Minan, The Allocation of Estate Taxes by Judicial Rule: A Case for Reform, 38 Ohio St. L.J. 539, 540 nn.7-9 (1977).

ment statute by the enactment of chapter 546 of the 1937 Laws of Maryland. This early law was substantially revised by chapter 156 of the 1947 Laws, which, in turn, was replaced in 1965 with a new enactment that largely tracks the 1964 revision of the Uniform Estate Tax Apportionment Act. This statute is now codified as Md. Code (1974), §11-109 of the Estates and Trusts Article and in pertinent part provides:

> (b) *Persons among whom tax to be apportioned.* — The [federal and Maryland estate taxes] shall be apportioned among all persons interested in the estate. The apportionment shall be made in the proportion that the value of the interest of each person interested in the estate bears to the total value of the interests of all persons interested in the estate. . . .
>
> (k) *Applicability.* — Except as otherwise provided in the will, or other controlling instrument, the provisions of this section shall apply to the apportionment of, and contribution to, the federal and Maryland estate taxes.

It is evident from a reading of subsection (k) of the act that the application of the rule of apportionment set out in subsection (b) is mandatory, unless the will evinces an expression of intent to the contrary. This enactment, therefore, is in harmony with the firmly established rule that, unless prohibited by statute or public policy, the intent of the testator as ascertained from the four corners of the will controls the disposition of a decedent's estate. . . . Most, if not all courts, including the Court of Special Appeals in its opinion below, have recognized, however, that under tax apportionment statutes an intention not to apportion must be plainly stated in the will or other controlling instrument before the legislative scheme can be ignored. See Hall v. Johnson, 38 Md. App. 589, 596 & n.7, 382 A.2d 332, 336 & n.7; Annot., 71 A.L.R.3d 247, 315 & n.81 (1976) (citing cases). . . . Put another way, "[i]n a tax allocation problem the text of the will is to be scanned only to see if there is a clear direction *not* to apportion; and if such *explicit* direction is not found, *construction of text ceases because the statute states the rule.*" In re Mills Estate, 189 Misc. 136, 64 N.Y.S.2d 105, 110 (1946) (emphasis in original), *affd.,* 272 App. Div. 229, 70 N.Y.S.2d 746 (1947), *affd.,* 297 N.Y. 1012, 80 N.E.2d 535 (1948). . . .

In seeking to show that the contents of Dr. Johnson's will demonstrate a clear intent to avoid the rule of apportionment set out in section 11-109, respondents, who bear the burden of proof . . . have focused almost exclusively on the initial item of the will.

> FIRST: I direct that all lawful debts I owe at the time of my death, including funeral and administration expenses and the expense of my last illness (but not including debts secured by mortgages on real property, except matured obligations as they fall due), and *all estate and inheritance taxes, be paid as soon after my death as can lawfully and conveniently be done.*

[(Emphasis supplied.)] While we have no doubt that words similar to those used in this first clause are contained in many wills which have been probated in this State, including wills which have been before this Court on other occasions for other reasons, we have not been presented previously with the question of whether such language constitutes a direction that the residuary portion of the estate provide the funds to pay estate taxes. Faced as we are with scant precedent from our previous cases, we explore the decisions of our sister states to see whether they have confronted this same constructional problem. In doing so, we find numerous states have adopted statutes similar to ours and a number of their courts have been presented with the contention that language almost identical to that contained in the first clause of the Johnson will expresses an intent not to apportion. Of those, a vast majority have held that a direction against apportionment is signified by such language.

Typical of the analysis utilized primarily by these authorities is the opinion of the Supreme Court of Virginia in Baylor v. National Bank of Commerce of Norfolk, 194 Va. 1, 72 S.E.2d 282 (1952). There . . . the court opined:

> The testator made no distinction between debts, funeral expenses and State inheritance and Federal transfer taxes. It is clear from the language used that he intended all of the items to be treated alike and to be paid in the same manner and from the same fund[, the residue].

[72 S.E.2d at 284.] Using this same analysis when dealing with similar testamentary provisions, a number of other courts have reached the same result as did the Supreme Court of Virginia. . . .

Although we recognize that this very substantial authority merits our serious consideration before rejecting it, we nonetheless conclude that the decisions constituting the majority are not soundly reasoned and we decline to follow them; instead, we prefer to join the ranks of a small minority of courts which have reached the opposite but, in our view, the correct result. . . . Accepting the premise, as all courts on both sides of this controversy do, that a statute directing apportionment will only be ignored if the testator clearly and unambiguously indicates that to be his intention, we fail to see how the first clause, whether read in isolation or examined in the context of the entire will, in any way expresses Dr. Johnson's desire that all the beneficiaries should not share proportionately the bite of the federal estate tax. . . .

No magic or mystical word or phrase is required to shift the burden of estate taxes from the legatees and devisees to the residue; however, for us to recognize that the testatrix's ritualistic, "boiler plate" reference to the payment of debts, expenses, and taxes in the first clause of her will states an intent not to apportion would require that we be clairvoyant. In short, we detect no direction by the decedent in the first paragraph of her will not to apportion taxes as section 11-109 provides. . . .

MURPHY, Chief Judge, dissenting. . . . Because I think that Articles FIRST and TENTH [giving executors discretion to pay expenses from either real or personal property], when read together, sufficiently express Dr. Johnson's intention to direct against apportionment under Maryland Code (1974), §11-109(k) of the Estates and Trusts Article, I respectfully dissent. . . .

McLaughlin v. Green, 136 Conn. 138, 69 A.2d 289 (1949), illustrates another issue that continues to trouble courts and to arise from imprecise drafting. Under an apportionment statute, does a will clause directing payment "from my residuary estate of all estate, inheritance and other death taxes imposed on my estate" (or "all succession, transfer and inheritance taxes," as in *McLaughlin*) include taxes payable with respect to joint tenancy property, life insurance proceeds, and other nonprobate assets (inter vivos trust properties in *McLaughlin*)? Or is this direction insufficiently clear to overcome the statute's allocation of a portion of the tax burden to the recipients of all nonprobate assets that contribute to (that is, are not deductible or excludable in determining) the estate's overall tax liability? Like many such cases, *McLaughlin* concluded that the language of the clause in question applied only to the testamentary estate and failed to show the requisite intention to overcome the statutory apportionment. Compare Yoakley v. Raese, 448 So. 2d 632 (Fla. App. 1984), where both statute and will provision were clear enough in placing the primary burden for all death taxes on the residuary estate, with respect to probate and nonprobate assets alike, but the residue proved inadequate to pay the taxes — in what should not have been a surprise to the lawyer who handled the planning for that estate.

In Isaacson v. Boston Safe Deposit & Trust Co., 325 Mass. 469, 91 N.E.2d 334 (1950), an executor sought declaratory relief against the trustee of a trust created by the testator while he resided in Massachusetts. The testator died in Maine, where he was domiciled at death. The plaintiff was both executor of the will in Maine and ancillary executor in Massachusetts. The value of the inter vivos trust was included in the testator's taxable estate. The only estate "asset" in Massachusetts was the alleged claim against the trust estate for its alleged share of the federal estate tax in accordance with the apportionment statute of the state of Maine. The Maine statute provides for the tax to "be equitably apportioned and prorated among the persons interested in the estate" in proportion to the values of their respective interests. The statute defines "persons interested in the estate" to include persons entitled to property under inter vivos trusts that are included in the gross estate for federal estate tax purposes. (The Massachusetts Apportionment Statute was not applicable, and therefore the Massachusetts law would impose no tax burden upon the trust in question.) The opinion states:

> The trust upon which it is now sought to fasten a liability by virtue of a
> statute of Maine was created by the decedent while he was a resident of

Massachusetts. The original trustee was a national bank located in this Commonwealth, and the present trustee is a corporation of this Commonwealth. The trust indenture was acknowledged in this Commonwealth. By fair inference from the facts agreed it appears that the indenture was delivered in this Commonwealth, and that the trust property was then and has since remained here. It is apparent that the trust owes its validity to the law of this Commonwealth. All rights of the beneficiaries of the trust are derived from our law. The trust is from every point of view a Massachusetts trust. The laws of Maine never had anything to do with it. The trustee has done nothing by which it has submitted itself to the jurisdiction of Maine. The persons who succeeded to Smith's interest in the trust upon his decease did so not through the laws of Maine but according to the terms of the trust as previously established under Massachusetts law. The fact that Smith was a resident of Maine when he died is of no consequence. His interest in the trust ceased upon his death. The trust fund did not become part of his estate in Maine or anywhere else. The only possible connection between this trust and the State of Maine which we are able to discover is that the Federal government in imposing an estate tax has seen fit to aggregate the probate estate in Maine and the trust fund in Massachusetts into a single "gross estate." We cannot see how this circumstance gives power to either State to impose the statutory fiat liabilities upon the fiduciary or the property under the exclusive jurisdiction of the other State. The Federal government could have provided for apportionment of the tax, and did so in certain particulars not reaching the question in this case. U.S.C. (1946 ed.) Title 26, §826(b), (c), (d). But for the most part apportionment was left to the States. Riggs v. Del Drago, 317 U.S. 95. Of course the failure of the Congress to provide for complete apportionment gives no extraterritorial effect to State statutes. It seems to us that to apply the Maine statute in this case would be to give to that statute extraterritorial effect contrary to first principles. There is nothing to the contrary in New York Trust Co. v. Brewster, 241 Mass. 155. In that case the defendants, while residents of New York, acquired an interest in the estate of a New York decedent, which interest carried with it a liability under a statute of New York. It was held that the existing liability followed the defendants and the property into this Commonwealth. The case is clearly distinguishable.

325 Mass. at 472-473, 91 N.E.2d at 336.

If a revocable inter vivos trust established by the decedent directs the payment of all death taxes on both probate and nonprobate assets from the trust estate and if the decedent's will also directs payment of all taxes from the residue of the probate estate, how are these contradictory directions to be resolved? Should the will prevail if executed later than the trust? See Estate of Cord, 462 N.Y.S.2d 622, 449 N.E.2d 402 (App. Div. 1983). In First National Bank v. Shawmut Bank, 389 N.E.2d 1002 (Mass. 1979), the later will did "not qualify as an amendment to the trust" (amendment of which required the trustee's signature), and the Supreme Judicial Court reversed the trial court's exclusion (based on the will's "clarity") of extrinsic evidence intended primarily to show the size of the nontrust estate at the time the will was executed. The opinion states:

> If these conflicting provisions appeared in a single document, such as a will, we would admit extrinsic evidence to assist in resolving the ambiguity. . . . [W]hen a slip-up has obviously occurred in the estate planning process, evidence of the circumstances known to a testator-settlor may be particularly instructive in achieving the ultimate goal of recognizing and carrying out the testator-settlor's intention. Here, if the allegations of the Florida executor concerning the tax obligations of [the] estate are proved, the view espoused by the trustees would result in total failure of all testamentary gifts, including the gift of income to [testatrix'] friend, who is not an income beneficiary of the trust. There may be no logic in a result which would fully achieve an expressed testamentary purpose of paying all taxes from the residue while in the process destroying the only gifts expressed in the will.

389 N.E.2d at 1006. The court also observed:

> We need not decide at this time whether the suggestion of the *Isaacson* and *Warfield* [Warfield v. Merchants National Bank, 337 Mass. 14, 147 N.E.2d 809 (1958)] opinions on choice of law would be accepted today. Refusal to apply the law of the decedent's domicil has been criticized. See Scoles, Apportionment of Federal Estate Taxes and Conflict of Laws, 55 Colum. L. Rev. 261 (1955). In several jurisdictions the law of the decedent's domicil has been applied. . . . The application of the law of the decedent's domicil, if followed universally, would tend to ensure uniformity of treatment among nonprobate assets included in the decedent's gross estate.

389 N.E.2d at 1007.

DOETSCH v. DOETSCH
312 F.2d 323 (7th Cir. 1963)

[Diversity action by Caroline Doetsch against defendants as remaindermen under inter vivos trust created by plaintiff's husband, now deceased. The value of the trust corpus, which was distributed to defendants prior to this action, had been included in the gross estate of plaintiff's husband for federal estate tax purposes, as property transferred by the decedent with a retained life estate. As executrix and sole beneficiary of her husband's will, plaintiff had been held liable for the full amount of the estate tax and brought this action to recover from defendants a portion of the tax attributable to the inclusion of the trust corpus in the estate. Neither the husband's will nor the trust agreement provided where the ultimate burden of the estate tax should fall or what law should govern this question. The district court entered judgment against defendants for a portion of the tax, and defendants have appealed.]

HASTINGS, C.J. . . .

We conclude, since neither of the apportionment sections in the [Internal Revenue Code, dealing with insurance proceeds and appointive assets] is applicable here, that under the *Del Drago* Case [Riggs v. Del Drago, 317 U.S. 95] applicable state law is determinative of the issue involved in the instant case.

The district court found that John A. Doetsch was domiciled in Arizona at the time of his death, and such finding is not clearly erroneous. Rule 52(a), Federal Rules of Civil Procedure, 28 U.S.C.A. Decedent's will was duly admitted to probate in Arizona, and plaintiff, decedent's widow, is a citizen of that state. The trust involved, however, must be considered an Illinois trust. It appears from the trust agreement that the corpus of the trust was an interest in a partnership doing business in Illinois, the trustee was a resident of Illinois and the settlor, John A. Doetsch, was a resident of Illinois when he established the trust.

Under the doctrine of Erie R. Co. v. Tompkins, 304 U.S. 64 (1938), we are obliged to apply the law of Illinois, including its conflict of laws rules. . . .

The question which we must initially determine is whether Illinois would apply its own law, as the state of the situs of the trust, or that of Arizona, as the state of decedent's domicile, in deciding the ultimate question of whether the federal estate taxes should be apportioned against defendants, the remainder beneficiaries.

The parties have not cited any Illinois case in which this question has been raised, and we have found none. Furthermore, it appears that this precise question has been decided in only five jurisdictions. The Supreme Judicial Court of Massachusetts had held that the question of apportionment is governed by the law of the situs and refused to refer the question to the law of decedent's domicile. Isaacson v. Boston Safe Deposit & Trust Co., 325 Mass. 469, 91 N.E.2d 334, 16 A.L.R.2d 1277 (1950). . . .

In First National Bank of Miami v. First Trust Co. of St. Paul, 242 Minn. 226, 64 N.W.2d 524 (1954), the Supreme Court of Minnesota adopted the reasoning of the *Isaacson* case and held accordingly. In Knowles v. National Bank of Detroit, 345 Mich. 671, 76 N.W.2d 813 (1956), the court refused to follow a decree of a Florida court, a court of the state of decedent's domicile, ordering apportionment with respect to Michigan trust assets. The court stated:

"[T]he order of the Florida court, based on a proration statute in that State, does not control decision here, absent such a statute in this State." Id. at 816. The decision is not so clear as *Isaacson* and *First National Bank of Miami* because the court relied on what it discerned to be the testatrix's intent in refusing apportionment.

The courts of New York and New Jersey, however, have adopted a rule which refers the question of apportionment of estate taxes to the law of decedent's domicile. In re Gato's Estate, 276 App. Div. 651, 97 N.Y.S.2d

171 (1950), *affd.*, 301 N.Y. 653, 93 N.E.2d 924; Central Hanover Bank & Trust Co. v. Peabody, 190 Misc. 66, 68 N.Y.S.2d 256 (1947); Trust Co. of Morris County v. Nichols, 62 N.J. Super. 495, 163 A.2d 205 (1960). In each of the two New York cases, the application of the domiciliary law led to apportionment of the taxes, but New York follows the same conflicts rule where the domiciliary laws fail to require apportionment. In re Peabody's Estate, 115 N.Y.S.2d 337 (Sup. Ct. 1952).

In our opinion the better rule, and the one which the courts of Illinois would follow, is that adopted in New York and New Jersey. When questions of apportionment of estate taxes arise in courts of a state of the situs of a trust whose assets are includible in decedent's gross estate for tax purposes, the law of the situs refers to the law of decedent's domicile to resolve the questions.

This rule brings about the desirable result of uniform treatment of all those who benefit from the property included in decedent's gross estate for tax purposes, for regardless of the situs of the property there is a single point of reference — decedent's domicile.[4]

The decedent's domicile is a traditional point of reference in the solution of many problems involving decedent's estates. Problems concerning movables transferred upon death which involve questions such as intestate distribution and validity of a will are traditionally referred to the domiciliary law. In addition, a non-domiciliary forum state whose local law governs control of land titles may look to the domiciliary law to aid in interpreting the testator's intent. The problems of apportionment are closely akin to these problems of decedent's estate, for they are all concerned with the extent to which various persons are to share in the decedent's wealth. The domicile provides an easy and convenient point of reference for the solution of these problems.

Finally, referring to the law of decedent's domicile results in observing that state's policy with respect to protecting the widow and family. The extent of a decedent's inter vivos transfers brought into the gross estate could be such that the entire probate estate would be used up in payment of federal estate taxes.[5] Recognizing this possibility a state may have adopted a policy of apportionment. Thus, some assets are left for the

---

4. The inconsistency which could result under the rule adopted by Massachusetts, Minnesota, and Michigan may be demonstrated. A decedent has died domiciled in state *A*. Before his death, he has established trusts in states *B* and *C* the value of which have been included in his gross estate. Local law in state *B*, the situs of one of the trusts, requires apportionment while local law in the state *C*, the situs of the other trust, does not so require. Neither states *B* nor *C* look to the law of decedent's domicile but apply their local law in determining the question of apportionment. Those who benefit under the trust in state *B* must contribute to the estate tax burden, but those who benefit under the trust in state *C* do not. This anomalous situation is undesirable and is avoided when each situs state refers to the law of decedent's domicile to resolve the question.

5. See In re Gato's Estate, 276 App. Div. 651, 97 N.Y.S.2d 171 (1950), *affd.*, 301 N.Y. 653, 93 N.E.2d 924, where the net estate distributable by the administrator amounted to $180,924 while the total estate tax, because of inter vivos transfers brought into the gross estate, amounted to $190,532.

estate beneficiaries as well as the trust beneficiaries. Protection of the widow and family is a matter in which the domiciliary state has a dominant interest, and without reference by the situs state to the state of decedent's domicile, this policy can not be fulfilled.[6]

Having decided to look to the law of the state of decedent's domicile, Arizona, we find there is neither a statute commanding or precluding apportionment nor a judicial pronouncement on the subject.

The parties in the instant case have devoted much effort to cataloguing the cases pro and con from various jurisdictions on the issue of apportionment. We do not feel compelled to do so. In our opinion, Arizona would adopt the rule of apportionment.

In passing on this question, the Supreme Court of New Mexico stated in In re Gallagher's Will, 57 N.M. 112, 255 P.2d 317, 37 A.L.R.2d 149 (1953):

> We have not tallied the jurisdictions on each side, but although the earlier rule may still represent the majority opinion of jurisdictions passing upon the question, we feel no compunction to adhere inelastically to a rule which in the view of this court is not productive of substantial justice. Certainly the vitality of our legal system derives in large part from the function of our courts in applying its *root* concepts, among them that of equal treatment, to ever new and diversified problems. . . . Therefore, the rule is nonprobate assets includible in the gross taxable estate shall bear their proportionate share of the burden of the federal estate tax. . . .

Id. at 328.

We feel this statement adequately expresses our reasons for holding that Arizona would apportion the tax burden under the circumstances of the instant case. . . .

Defendants contend the amount of plaintiff's marital deduction should not have been excluded from the formula used in determining defendants' share of the tax. The amount of the marital deduction, however, did not contribute to the tax burden, and was properly excluded by the district court in arriving at its apportionment formula. Seymour National Bank v. Heideman, 178 N.E.2d 771 (Ind. App. 1961).

For the foregoing reasons, the judgment of the district court is affirmed.

Affirmed.

C. The Principle of Impartiality

The fiduciary's duty of loyalty to the beneficiaries imposes more than an obligation to avoid conflicts of interest and personal profit arising from

---

6. For a thorough treatment of the conflict of laws problems involved in cases such as the case at bar see Scoles, Apportionment of Federal Estate Taxes and Conflict of Laws, 55 Colum. L. Rev. 261 (1955).

his fiduciary activities. Those are problems an alert and scrupulous fiduciary will normally avoid. More pervasive, and usually unavoidable, are the almost inevitable problems of conflicts among the various beneficial interests that the fiduciary (especially a trustee) must represent and to which are owed duties of care and loyalty. Consequently the purely fiduciary obligations are in conflict, giving rise to what is often called a *duty of impartiality*. We have previously encountered various manifestations of this duty, most noticeably in connection with the investment function and then throughout this chapter in relation to principal-income accounting, for which this duty is in a sense the basic, underlying principle.

The problem of impartiality is particularly acute today in the context of tax burdens and the related decisions of personal representatives and trustees. Examples are the alternate valuation date election under the federal estate tax and the situations in the cases below. As these opinions are studied, consider the effect of the fiduciary's duty of impartiality on (1) the actual decisions to be made in tax matters arising in the course of administering a decedent's estate or trust and on (2) the allocation or apportionment of the benefits and detriments flowing from these decisions. This array of tax-related issues is both significant and interesting in its own right, as well as revealing for purposes of other fiduciary situations, because these problems — recognized or not — confront the fiduciary as everyday matters although yet remaining doctrinally on the frontiers of the law. See generally Dobris, Equitable Adjustments in Postmortem Tax Planning: An Unremitting Diet of *Warms*,[7] 65 Iowa L. Rev. 103 (1979); Moore, Conflicting Interests in Postmortem Planning, 1975 U. Miami Est. Plan. Inst. §§1900 et seq. The cases that follow fairly represent the still modest number of decisions so far available.

In re DWIGHT'S TRUST
204 Misc. 204, 128 N.Y.S.2d 23 (Sup. Ct. 1952)

DICKSTEIN, J.

Upon this application to settle the accounts of a trustee, the guardian ad litem has interposed an objection which presents one of the facets of a recurring problem in trust administration today. Due to increased income tax rates, trustees are being met with demands by life beneficiaries, who are in high income tax brackets, to invest in tax exempt securities. In most cases such securities sell at a premium, with the result that upon maturity there is a loss in principal, even though the securities are redeemed at par. Such loss is visited upon the remaindermen of the trusts. It is unnecessary in the instant case to decide the broad questions of the liability of trustees under such circumstances, for here it is undis-

---

7. Reference is to Estate of Warms, 140 N.Y.S.2d 169 (Surr. Ct. 1955).

puted that the trustee, when informed of the high tax bracket in which the life beneficiary found herself, deliberately sold United States Savings Bonds, which it held as principal in the trust, at a loss to the estate, so that it could invest the proceeds in tax free securities. The redemption of the United States Bonds resulted in a loss of $3,290.70. I hold that the objection of the guardian to such loss is well taken and that the action of the trustee constituted an unwarranted subordination of the interests of the remaindermen to that of the life beneficiary. There was no power in the trustee to redeem the bonds at a loss for the sole purpose of effecting a higher net income for the life beneficiary. The trustee will, therefore, be surcharged the amount of the loss so sustained. The motion to settle the accounts is otherwise granted.

ESTATE OF BIXBY
140 Cal. App. 2d 326, 295 P.2d 68 (1956)

Fox, J. . . . .

The executor or administrator . . . represents all the beneficiaries of the estate and must not favor one over another.

Estates are treated for tax purposes as separate entities, the tax on whose income is payable by the executor or administrator. The tax applies to the entire taxable income of the estate.

Bearing these principles in mind, we turn now to a consideration of who must bear the thrust of income taxes paid by the executor upon income accruing to the estate while in the course of administration. In the instant case, we are concerned with the dividends amounting to $76,000 which the executor received upon the 19,000 shares of stock of which Mrs. Bixby was the outright legatee. As legatee of this stock, title thereto vested in her eo instante as of the date of the testator's death, at which time there also originated her right to receive the income (dividends) produced by this stock subsequent to the testator's death. Had the legatee received this income when her right thereto accrued, it is undisputed that the payment of an income tax on these funds would have been the legatee's obligation. However, distribution not having as yet been made and the estate being a taxable entity, the executor was required to pay an income tax on this and other income received by him during the course of administration. Since such taxes are the subject of and measured by the income, it seems only fair that they should be paid therefrom and not from the principal of the residue of the estate. . . .

We pass now to the problem presented by the trustees' appeal, viz.: What is the effect on the rights of the beneficiaries of the executor's utilization of expenses of administration as federal income rather than federal estate tax deductions? In order to strip the problem of its esoteric trappings and place it in its proper perspective, a few prefatory observations are in order by way of clarification of the treatment of deductions in connection with the fiduciary returns which an executor is required to file under the provisions of the Internal Revenue Code, 26 U.S.C.A.

The taxable income of an estate, with certain exceptions not here germane, is computed in the same manner as that of an individual. The tax imposed upon the taxable income of an estate must be paid by the executor. The period of administration or settlement of the estate is, of course, the period actually required by the executor to perform his normal administration functions. During this period administration expenses accrue, and these expenses, in the case at bar, have been paid from the principal of the residue of the estate. The propriety of using that fund as the source of payments is not challenged. Taxwise, administration expenses of estates may be treated as a deduction under the income tax return or under the estate tax return. However, to obviate double deductibility, administration expenses are allowable as a deduction only once, and the executor is afforded an election as to whether he will apply the deduction against the estate tax or against the income tax. (§162(e), Internal Revenue Code, 26 U.S.C.A., reenacted as §642(g) of the Internal Revenue Code of 1954.) This gives the executor an opportunity of determining under which return it would prove more advantageous taxwise to claim the administrative expense deduction, and places him in a position to minimize the aggregate of taxes paid by the estate. Confronted with this elective treatment of deductions, the discreet executor will, of course, study the applicable estate tax and estate income rates and if he finds that there is a wide disparity between them, it would be judicious to avail himself of the deduction in the place where the optimum advantage will accrue to the estate, that is, by diminishing the aggregate amount of taxes payable to the federal government.

In the case at bar, the executor discharged his responsibility wisely under the circumstances by electing to utilize the administration expenses as an income tax deduction, although such expenses were borne by the principal of the residuary estate. In so doing, having reported an income of some $160,000, he paid a tax of $18,728.16. Had he not utilized this deduction on the estate income tax return, the tax would have been $120,378.11. He thus effected a tax saving of $101,649.95, resulting in a very substantial benefit to the legatees and beneficiaries entitled to the income. While this is a most obviously desirable result, its correlative effect on those entitled to corpus is unfortunate. For had the administrative expenses been used as a deduction in the federal estate tax return, the succession taxes payable from decedent's estate would have been reduced by $58,932.44. To that extent the remainder beneficiaries of the residuary trusts have been penalized to effect the income tax saving previously described.

It is at once manifest that the election to effect a tax saving afforded the executor under the Revenue Code does not justify the severe disruption and disarrangement of what would otherwise constitute the beneficial interests of the legatees and remaindermen under the will. Recognizing this inequity, the court below charged Mrs. Bixby's income account with the sum of $8,713.40, this sum being the part of the $18,728.16 in federal and state income taxes paid by the executor which is allocable to the dividends on the stock bequeathed to her. This, however, does not go far enough in adjusting the rights of the parties and in repairing the detriment occasioned to the corpus of the estate by giving only the income beneficiaries the benefit of the deduction for administration expenses. The total income tax saving, as we have seen was $101,649.95. The consequent impairment of corpus was $58,932.44, the amount by which the estate tax was increased by being deprived of the deduction of administration expenses. The impact of this loss to corpus is borne by the remaindermen. In such a situation, the equitable solution is to reallocate enough of the tax saving to the principal account to make whole the detriment suffered by corpus. (Estate of Warms, 140 N.Y.S.2d 169.) The virtue of this approach is that while a significant benefit in the form of tax saving still accrues to Mrs. Bixby, and the income beneficiaries, it is not exacted in the form of an unjust enrichment at the expense of the residuary beneficiaries. . . .

Such a rule commends itself to the conscience of the court as one under which no one is injured by an unjust encroachment on his inheritance. Apart from its simplicity of application, we adopt this rule because it places the burden of the income tax on the income legatee, where it properly belongs, and obviates any dislocation of the testator's bounty by shifting the burden of an income tax to a residuary legatee. While the executor's election as to the use of deductions under the present circumstances still enables the income beneficiaries to receive an actual cash benefit in the form of tax savings, by the process of reallocating an appropriate portion of such savings to principal, no part of any beneficiary's inheritance is diminished so that another may reap a profit at his expense. It is within the province of the probate court to bring to its aid the full equitable powers with which as a superior court it is invested to insure that income beneficiaries do not profit at the expense of the remaindermen. . . .

WILL OF PROSS
90 Misc. 2d 895, 396 N.Y.S.2d 309 (Surr. 1977)

EVANS V. BREWSTER, Surrogate.

One of the co-trustees of the residuary trust for the benefit of decedent's wife has petitioned the court for advice and directions with respect to the allocation between principal and income, of certain taxes paid by the trustees attributable to capital gains realized by the trust. Decedent's wife, the income beneficiary and co-trustee, urges that the tax be charged to the principal of the trust. The remaindermen of the trust have been made parties but failed to appear in the proceeding.

Decedent owned a fractional interest in property known as 1855 Broadway, New York City which was valued for estate tax purposes at $10,326.93. This property was subsequently transferred to the trustees of the residuary trust. On October 1, 1964, the trustees in order to facilitate the management of this property, entered into a limited partnership agreement with the other owners of the aforesaid property for the purpose of carrying on the business of owning and operating the real property. Depreciation on the property was deducted annually in the partnership tax returns and for five (5) years preceding 1975, the depreciation deduction resulted in the partnership showing a net loss. In fact the trust's share of the loss was in excess of the amount of dividend and income received from the other investments held by the trust. As a consequence, the trust reported no "distributable net income" for the five (5) calendar years preceding 1975 and the income beneficiary of the trust has been able to report no income from the trust despite having received the dividend interest income earned by the trust investments other than this property.

The partnership real property was subject to a mortgage in excess of $1,650,000.00. After having an operating loss for several years, the partnership defaulted in making the required payments under the bond and mortgage as a result of which the mortgagee foreclosed its lien on July 1, 1976. Under the tax law, a foreclosure is treated as a regular sale of the property and any resulting gain or loss must be reported. The depreciation deductions which had been taken on the real property (and which gave rise to the losses reported for income tax purposes) served to reduce the basis of the partnership property to such an extent that the adjusted basis was less than the mortgage debt which was cancelled on the foreclosure. Thus, for tax purposes, the foreclosure resulted in a long-term capital gain for which the trust is charged $13,479.77 for its share of federal income taxes and $7,960.32 for state income taxes.

While in theory and for accounting purposes, depreciation allowed on property is placed in a capital account for replacement of the depreciated property, frequently, as in the present case, no sums are set aside in a capital replacement account. The capital gain earned on the property because of the depreciation deductions was also a bookkeeping or accounting profit and the questions posed by the petitioner are (1) whether a capital gain was in fact received by the trust where nothing was received and the entire benefit has inured to the income beneficiary and (2) whether the income taxes payable on this illusive capital gain should be borne by the capital or principal of the trust or by the person benefitted.

EPTL §11-2.1(a)(1) provides as follows:

> (a) Duty of trustee as to receipts and expenditures.
> (1) A trust shall be administered with due regard to the respective interests of income beneficiaries and remaindermen. A trust is so administered with respect to the allocation of receipts and expenditures if a receipt is credited or an expense is charged to income or to principal or partly to each (A) in accordance with the terms of the trust instrument, notwithstanding any contrary provisions in this section; (B) in the absence of any contrary terms of the trust instrument, in accordance with the provisions of this section; or (C) if neither of the preceding rules of administration is applicable, in accordance with what is reasonable and equitable in view of the interests of those entitled to income as well as those entitled to principal and in view of the manner in which men of ordinary prudence, discretion and judgment would act in the management of their own affairs.

Insofar as subdivision (A), supra, is concerned, it reaffirms the basic rule that the intention of the testator is controlling with respect to the provisions of the trust. In the will before the court, there is nothing therein contained that reveals any intention expressed or implied with respect to the allocation to be made of a charge for taxes of any kind.

Subdivision (B), supra, refers to the provisions set forth in this section with respect to the allocation charges. EPTL §11-2.1(l)(4) provides that the "following charge shall be made against principal: . . . ; (C) any tax levied upon profits, gain or other receipts allocated to principal notwithstanding denomination of the tax as an income tax by the taxing authority." It would thus appear that since depreciation of capital was responsible for a capital gain, a literal application would require the capital gains tax should be charged to principal. It appears to the court, however, that the words "any tax levied upon profits, gain or other receipts allocated to principal" must have reference to such cases where in fact a profit, gain or receipt was realized. In the usual case, capital gains are a return or an addition to trust corpus and principal of the trust should bear the tax attributable thereto. If the trustees set aside the amount deducted for depreciation to preserve principal in fulfillment of their duty, the reserve would be wholly applicable to principal and the source of the capital gain. However, in this case, there was no reserve. The capital gain is nothing more than a paper entry which has come about by reason of the depreciation deduction having reduced the base of the property below the amount realized upon the foreclosure. There was no addition to, appreciation of or replacement for the trust principal. As applied here it is more closely akin to property which has been depleted and which under the statute [EPTL §11-2.1(d)(5)] would require a tax allocation in accordance with what is reasonable and equitable. To the extent that the income beneficiary received the benefits of the deduction for depreciation without any concomitant benefit to trust principal, equity requires that the charge for the capital gains tax be placed on the person receiving the capital gain.

In Matter of Holloway, 68 Misc. 2d 361, 327 N.Y.S.2d 865, the court was similarly faced with a question of allocation of taxes by reason of a distribution of principal to four residuary trusts where those distributions were "deemed" income by the taxing authorities. In its first consideration of the case (reported 67 Misc. 2d 132, 323 N.Y.S.2d 534) the court charged the entire tax to principal under a literal interpretation of §11-2.1(*l*)(4)(C). However, upon reargument, the court recognized that the tax, in fact, was attributable to a receipt by a trust of income for accounting purposes and directed that the adjustment of taxes be made from income to principal stating "The court believes that a realistic view of this problem requires a determination based upon the purely equitable principle that the burden of income taxes should be charged to the account into which the taxed item goes (Matter of Mankowski, Sur., 110 N.Y.S.2d 677, 681; Matter of Bixby, [140 Cal. App. 2d 326] p. 335, 295 P.2d 68, 73; Ann. 108 A.L.R. 1138)." Matter of Holloway, 68 Misc. 2d 361, 365, 327 N.Y.S.2d 865, 869.

Since it would appear that §11-2.1(a)(1), subdivision (A) or (B) is not applicable, subdivision (C) requires a reasonable and equitable adjustment. Accordingly, the court directs that the income beneficiary be charged with the capital gains tax to the extent that the capital gain is attributable to the utilization of the depreciation deduction which augmented the income received by her. In accordance with EPTL §11-2.1(*l*)(3) the trustee may by means of reserves or other reasonable means charge the payment of tax by the income beneficiary over a reasonable period of time and withhold from distribution sufficient sums to regularize distributions.

20

Constructional Problems in Estate Distribution

An enormous amount of litigation occurs each year to determine the meaning of particular wills and trusts. Most of this litigation centers on the meaning of dispositive provisions, although the preceding chapters reveal the significance of interpretation and construction in the administration of trusts and decedents' estates. A natural starting point in studying the construction of dispositive provisions is to examine the problems created by such basic provisions as outright bequests and devises in simple wills. These matters are taken up in this chapter. The present discussion omits problems peculiar to trusts and other arrangements involving future interests and fiduciary and appointive powers, some of which are treated elsewhere in these materials. The often complicated constructional problems posed by future interest provisions of trusts and successive legal estates are, for the most part, dealt with in courses on future interests.

Subsequent to the execution of a will but prior to the date of distribution of an estate, many events may occur affecting the operation of the will and the rights of the beneficiaries. There may, of course, be births and deaths among the beneficiaries or within described classes after the will is executed. Some problems arising from births and deaths are taken up in section B of this chapter. There may also be changes in the assets of the estate, or there may be transactions between the testator and the legatees and devisees affecting estate assets or the beneficiaries' interests therein. These occurrences frequently create problems in the distribution of the estate and are the subject of section A of this chapter.

PROBLEM

20-A.   The testator left a will providing:

1.   "I leave the spinet piano to *A*."
2.   "I bequeath $5,000 to *B*."
3.   "I bequeath $10,000 to *C*."
4.   "I bequeath $50,000 to the children of *D*."

5. "The residue of my estate to *E, F,* and *G* in equal shares, i.e., ⅓ to *E,* ⅓ to *F,* and ⅓ to *G.*"

As you proceed through this chapter, consider the effect of the following facts under the Uniform Probate Code; under the law of your state:

(a) The testator sold the piano after the will was executed; the piano was destroyed in a residential fire several years ago after the will was executed; the piano was destroyed by fire one month before the testator's death.

(b) *B* received a check for $3,500 from the testator during his lifetime with a note "This is in lieu of a bequest in my will."

(c) *C* died shortly before the testator, survived by a daughter.

(d) *D* had four children, one of whom died before the will was executed, and one of whom died shortly before the testator; both children of *D* left issue.

(e) The net estate was $100,000. How would the problems differ if the net estate were $50,000?

A. *Distributive Problems*

As noted in Chapter 19 and as will become more apparent as this section is studied, the traditional solution to certain distributive problems often requires bequests and devises to be classified. In deciding a particular question, a court may first find it necessary to determine whether a testamentary gift is specific, general, demonstrative, or residuary. Also, purely for convenience, it is useful to have accepted terminology by which reference can readily be made to common types of testamentary gifts.

Specific bequests and devises. A specific bequest or devise is a gift of some particular thing or parcel of land. A devise of "the house and land at 185 4th Street" is specific. "My 100 shares of *X* Corporation stock" and "the grandfather clock in the living room" are examples of specific bequests.

General bequests. A general bequest is one that is payable out of the general estate rather than one requiring distribution of or payment from particular assets. The typical general bequest is a pecuniary legacy, such as "$1,000 to *A*." Occasionally a general bequest will be made in terms other than an amount of money. "One hundred shares of *X* Corporation stock" would be general if the testator is found to have intended his executor to use the general funds of the estate or, if necessary, to sell other assets in order to buy 100 shares of *X* stock for distribution to the legatee. Although it was once held that all devises of land were specific, it is now generally agreed that devises may be residuary or general under the same circumstances as bequests.

Demonstrative bequests. A demonstrative bequest is a gift, typically of an amount of money, payable primarily from a particular source and then from the general assets of the estate if that source fails or is inadequate. A legacy of "$1,000 to A, payable out of my account in B Bank, and if this is insufficient then out of my other property," is demonstrative.

Residuary disposition. A residuary disposition is a gift of whatever remains of the estate after the payment of all obligations and after all other bequests and devises have been satisfied. Thus it is a gift of "the residue of the estate."

How would you classify the following bequests and devises?

1. "I give all of my living-room furniture to A."
2. "I give A any money X owes to me at my death."
3. "I give A $1,000 worth of my X Corporation stock."
4. "I give A $1,000 out of my account at X Bank."
5. "I give A all of my personal property."
6. "I give the rest of my land to A."
7. "I give A 100 shares of X Corporation stock."

(Does it matter if the testator owned no X Corporation stock at his death? What if he owned 200 X Corporation shares when he executed the will? Or 200 when he died? What if he owned 100 when he died? Or 100 when he executed the will?)

1. Ademption

PROBLEM

20-B.   *T*'s will bequeathed $50,000 to A, devised Blackacre to B and Greenacre to C, and left the residue of her estate to D. After executing the will, *T* was declared incapacitated and a conservator was appointed. Thereafter, Blackacre was taken by eminent domain by the state highway commission, and the condemnation award of $200,000 was paid to the conservator and deposited in a savings account. By the time of *T*'s death five years later, the funds in this account were reduced to $25,000, the rest having been properly expended by the conservator for the support of *T*, whose incapacity continued until her death. The other assets of *T*'s estate consisted of Greenacre, listed securities worth $100,000, and $10,000 in a checking account. How is the estate to be distributed, assuming the jurisdiction in question has no legislation in point? What result in your state? What result under Uniform Probate Code §2-606 (infra) and §3-902 (infra, section A3)? Explain.

Ademption, sometimes referred to as *ademption by extinction,* occurs when the particular property bequeathed or devised is not a part of the testator's estate at the time of death, and the gift thereby fails. The doctrine of ademption applies only to specific bequests and devises. Thus, it is often necessary for this purpose to decide whether a particular testamentary gift is general or specific.

Today, in the absence of statute, the doctrine is often applied without regard to the testator's intention at the time the property is removed from the estate. The earlier New York cases offered illustrations of this view. For example, in Matter of Ireland, 257 N.Y. 155, 177 N.E. 405 (1931), the testator became incompetent after executing his will, and when the specifically bequeathed shares were sold and used for the testator's support by the committee of his person and estate, the bequest was held to fail. The opinion stated (at 158-160, 177 N.E. at 406):

> The Appellate Division was of the opinion that the intention of the testator was the governing factor in the case, and that, as he had become incompetent to change or modify his will, his committee had no power to dispose of his property or, in this instance, the preferred shares, so as to work an ademption of the legacy. The rule as it existed at common law, and still exists, admits of no such exception. . . .
>
> Out of the moneys received from the sale of the preferred shares by the committee there was left a balance over and above expenditures for the incompetent of $1,848.40, which was turned over to the executor as part of the estate. To give this to Lena M. Whitmore in place of the preferred shares might seem equitable, but it is not in accordance with the directions or will of the testator. He gave her the preferred shares of stock, not the proceeds thereof, and according to all the decisions, when the specific thing given ceases to exist the legacy falls; it cannot be made up out of property in the estate. . . .
>
> The wisdom of adhering to this rule is apparent when we reflect that [the testator], when he made his will, probably never contemplated physical and mental incapacity and the appointment of a committee to handle his affairs. An intention to hold the shares of the preferred stock for the benefit of a stranger, while spending the remainder of his estate which would naturally go to his children, for doctors, nurses and maintenance, can hardly be imagined. At least a court should not say that a man in his right mind would not under such contemplation have changed his will.

An earlier New York case, Ametrano v. Downs, 170 N.Y. 388, 63 N.E. 340 (1902), had held a devise of land to be adeemed by its sale under condemnation proceedings, stating (at 391-392, 63 N.E. at 341):

> Had the deceased voluntarily alienated her property . . . the devisee would have no claim to the proceeds of the sale. . . . We see no such difference between a voluntary and an involuntary sale of the devised land as justifies a distinction in principle in the application of the rule.

More recently, in In re Wright's Will, 7 N.Y.2d 365, 165 N.E.2d 561 (1960), the question was whether a specific bequest of all furs and jewelry was adeemed as to a diamond ring that was missing at the time of the death of the testatrix even though the value of the ring had been paid to the estate by an insurance company. In holding the gift adeemed, the court observed (at 366, 165 N.E.2d at 562):

> Although, in the early days of our law, ademption was based on the intention of the testator, today in New York, as well as in many other jurisdictions, intention has nothing to do with the matter; the bequest fails and the legatee takes nothing if the article specifically bequeathed has been given away, lost or destroyed during the testator's lifetime.

A number of jurisdictions, however, have rejected the view that the intent to adeem is irrelevant. "[A]demption requires some act of the testator indicative of an intention to revoke. . . . The trial court should have . . . conducted a hearing as to whether the decedent disposed of the stock with intent to revoke plaintiff's bequest." Hobin v. O'Donnell, 451 N.W.2d 30, 32 (Ill. App. 1983). A shift in attitude is reflected in Newbury v. McCammant, 182 N.W.2d 147, 149 (Iowa 1970):

> Historically the courts of this country, and England, in early times followed the dictates of Justinian, holding testator's intention crucial to operation of the doctrine. . . . There then came a period during which judicial tribunals encountered troublesome problems or witnessed opportunities for abuse in application of the pure intention theory. Seeking a practical solution, they held ademption occurred, regardless of testator's intention, if property specifically bequeathed was not found in the estate on death. . . .
> We followed this strict identity theory in [one] case. . . . But this application of the doctrine was often harsh and frequently at odds with testator's intention. . . .
> More recently we have therefore taken the position, at least sotto voce, that the Justinian concept of intention is involved in application of the ademption principle, coupled with reliance on identity of the thing bequeathed or devised. . . .
> This appears to be entirely proper for it has long been held the primary consideration in will construction is intent of the testator.

And White v. White, 105 N.J. Super. 184, 186, 251 A.2d 470, 472-473 (1969), responding to defendant's reliance on *Wright's Will,* supra, states:

> There is some support for the proposition that such was the law in this state at one time. Since that time, however, it has become clear that probable intent of the testator is the determining factor. . . . "The rule that the nonexistence of the subject of a legacy evidences its ademption is but a rule of evidence, rebuttable by other evidence indicating that ademption was not intended." . . .

Cases having to do with the execution of a contract for the sale of premises specifically devised are not applicable for the obvious reason that in such cases the testator has evidenced his intention for a testamentary change. Here the partial destruction of the house did not occur through any voluntary act of the decedent. . . .

Where a testator has specifically devised real property upon which a house stands, which house is destroyed or damaged by fire before death and the testator dies without regaining capacity to indicate a contrary intention, the proceeds of fire insurance on the house replace the house and pass under the devise.

Even where intent to adeem *is* said to be essential to an ademption by extinction, courts often require that the legatee, in order to take other property, find an identifiable replacement or trace proceeds to a fund that remains in the estate, thus not allowing resort to the general assets of the estate. This limitation itself may apply to some types of potential ademption situations but not to others. Thus, e.g., in In re Mason's Estate, 62 Cal. 2d 213, 215, 397 P.2d 1005, 1007-1008 (1965), it is stated:

Although a specific testamentary gift is adeemed regardless of the testator's intention when the specific property has been disposed of *by the testator* and cannot be traced to other property in the estate, or when the *testator* has placed the proceeds of such property in a fund bequeathed to another, it does not follow that there is an ademption when the specific property has been sold and the proceeds spent *by a guardian* during an incompetency from which the testator does not recover. . . .

. . . [The legislature] has set forth rules to govern the abatement of testamentary gifts when the assets of the estate are insufficient to satisfy them in full. We believe that those rules provide a better alternative than the rule of pro tanto ademption and that they therefore constitute an appropriate model for this court to adopt.

Even where intent is *not* an element in ademption, some exceptions are likely to be recognized. For example, it has been held that the rule of ademption does not apply to a bequest of an automobile "where the decedent dies and the object of the specific legacy is simultaneously destroyed with his death," the legatee being entitled to the insurance proceeds received by the estate. In re Buda's Will, 21 Misc. 2d 931, 197 N.Y.S.2d 824 (1960). What would the legatee's rights be if the automobile had not been insured? Other courts have also refused to follow the rule of the *Ireland* case, supra, where the testator's guardian disposes of specifically bequeathed or devised property. E.g., Lewis v. Hill, 287 Ill. 542, 56 N.E.2d 619 (1944); Walsh v. Gillespie, 338 Mass. 278, 154 N.E.2d 906 (1959). See also Diaz v. Duncan, 406 N.E.2d 991 (Ind. App. 1980) (result of no ademption based on statute). Legislation on this matter is frequent.

UNIFORM PROBATE CODE

§2-606. *Nonademption of Specific Devises; Unpaid Proceeds of Sale, Condemnation, or Insurance; Sale by Conservator or Agent.*

(a) A specific devisee has a right to the specifically devised property in the testator's estate at death and:

(1) any balance of the purchase price, together with any security agreement, owing from a purchaser to the testator at death by reason of sale of the property;

(2) any amount of a condemnation award for the taking of the property unpaid at death;

(3) any proceeds unpaid at death on fire or casualty insurance on or other recovery for injury to the property;

(4) property owned by the testator at death and acquired as a result of foreclosure, or obtained in lieu of foreclosure, of the security interest for a specifically devised obligation;

(5) real or tangible personal property owned by the testator at death which the testator acquired as a replacement for specifically devised real or tangible personal property; and

(6) unless the facts and circumstances indicate that ademption of the devise was intended by the testator or ademption of the devise is consistent with the testator's manifested plan of distribution, the value of the specifically devised property to the extent the specifically devised property is not in the testator's estate at death and its value or its replacement is not covered by paragraphs (1) through (5).

(b) If specifically devised property is sold or mortgaged by a conservator or by an agent acting within the authority of a durable power of attorney for an incapacitated principal, or if a condemnation award, insurance proceeds, or recovery for injury to the property are paid to a conservator or to an agent acting within the authority of a durable power of attorney for an incapacitated principal, the specific devisee has the right to a general pecuniary devise equal to the net sale price, the amount of the unpaid loan, the condemnation award, the insurance proceeds, or the recovery.

(c) The right of a specific devisee under subsection (b) is reduced by any right the devisee has under subsection (a).

(d) For the purposes of the references in subsection (b) to a conservator, subsection (b) does not apply if after the sale, mortgage, condemnation, casualty, or recovery, it was adjudicated that the testator's incapacity ceased and the testator survived the adjudication by one year.

(e) For the purposes of the references in subsection (b) to an agent acting within the authority of a durable power of attorney for an incapacitated principal, (i) "incapacitated principal" means a principal who is an incapacitated person, (ii) no adjudication of incapacity before death is necessary, and (iii) the acts of an agent within the authority of a durable power of attorney are presumed to be for an incapacitated principal.

Assuming that under applicable law a specific gift cannot be saved from ademption on the basis of the testator's intent when the property was removed from this estate, several other possibilities remain. One of these possibilities is to salvage the gift through construction. Courts have often tended to classify a questionable bequest as general rather than specific when confronted with a question of ademption. If such a classification is not permitted by the language of the bequest, the court may construe the specific bequest to refer to certain property which is found in the estate at death. As an example of this latter, a bequest of "the automobile I now own" could, despite the usual tendency to relate the word "now" in a will to the time of execution, be held to refer to the automobile owned at the time of death to avoid ademption by a sale of the original and a later acquisition of a new automobile. See In re Cooper's Estate, 107 Cal. App. 2d 592, 237 P.2d 699 (1951) (avoiding issue of intent at the time of sale).

A second possibility, even where intent at the time of disposal is not relevant, is through application of the accepted principle that a mere change of form does not work an ademption. Of course, the problem then is to decide what changes constitute mere changes of form. Consider the materials that follow.

PROBLEM

20-C.   *T*'s will, executed five years ago, reads: "I bequeath to *A* my checking accounts in *X* Bank and in *Y* Bank. I give *B* any interest I may have in the estate of my deceased sister, *S*. The residue of my estate I bequeath and devise to *C*." After executing this will:

(a) *T* closed out both of the above-mentioned bank accounts two years ago and with the same funds opened a checking account (with a deposit of $5,000) in *Z* Bank and a savings account (with a $10,000 deposit) in the *S-L* Savings & Loan Association. Cf. In re Estate of Hall, 60 N.J. Super. 597, 160 A.2d 49 (1960); Baybank Harvard Trust Co. v. Grant, 23 Mass. App. 653, 504 N.E.2d 1072 (1987).

(b) Also two years ago, *T* received a preliminary distribution of $6,000 in cash and two months later a final distribution of $5,346 cash, together representing his full rights in the estate of *S*; *T* endorsed each check over to *Z* Bank, on each occasion purchasing a certificate of deposit in the amount of $5,000 and having the excess ($1,000 and $346 respectively) deposited in his checking account in that bank. See In re Estate of Brown, 252 N.E.2d 142 (Ind. App. 1969).

T died a year ago. Who is entitled to the two $5,000 certificates of deposit and the *Z* and *S-L* accounts, then containing $6,500 and $10,450, respectively? Does it matter whether an intent test is applied in the state in which the questions arise? Consider UPC §2-606 (supra). Are there additional facts you need to determine?

FIRST NATIONAL BANK v. PERKINS INSTITUTE
275 Mass. 498, 176 N.E. 532 (1931)

CARROLL, J.

This is a petition for instructions by the executor of the will of Amelia G. Dyer who died July 4, 1928. In the sixteenth clause of her will the testatrix gave to her nephew, John Baker, hereinafter referred to as the legatee, "all of my stock in the Standard Oil Company of New York and the Standard Oil Company of New Jersey." Instructions are sought as to the disposition of $7,000 in principal amount of the debentures of the Standard Oil Company of New Jersey, which the legatee contends passed to him under this clause of the will, and the other respondents contend belong to them under the residuary clause.

It was agreed that at the time of the execution of the will the testatrix owned one hundred ten shares of the seven percent preferred stock of the Standard Oil Company of New Jersey; that this stock was callable at $115 a share and accrued dividend and was called for payment by vote of the directors on November 15, 1926. To meet this call debentures totalling $120,000,000 were to be issued; these debentures were sold to bankers in New York. The bankers agreed to give the holders of the stock a preferential right to subscribe for these debentures. The testatrix sent to the bankers her one hundred ten shares of stock, subscribing for a sufficient number of debentures to absorb the stock. The issue of the debentures was oversubscribed; accordingly, there was allowed to Mrs. Dyer seven of these debentures in payment for sixty-two shares of stock. The remainder of her stock was redeemed by the New Jersey company. At the time of her death Mrs. Dyer owned the $7,000 of debentures.

There was no stock of the Standard Oil Company of New Jersey in the estate of the testatrix when she died. Her stock in that company had been taken up by the payment in cash from the New Jersey company, and the debentures which had been purchased by the bankers and transferred to her by these bankers in exchange for sixty-two of her shares. The debentures came to her, not from the New Jersey company but from the bankers who were the owners of them. In these circumstances the legacy of the stock of the Standard Oil Company of New Jersey was adeemed. The legacy of the specific thing had been disposed of by the testatrix before her death. The case cannot be distinguished from Moffatt v. Heon, 242 Mass. 201, where it was held that the specific legacy of a mortgage which was paid before the death of the testator had been adeemed. In that case the authorities are reviewed and this quotation from Tomlinson v. Bury, 145 Mass. 346, 348, appears at pages 203-204:

> If the testator subsequently parts with the property, even if he exchanges it for other property or purchases other property with the proceeds, the legatee has no claim on the estate for the value of his legacy. The legacy is adeemed by the act of the testator.

The legatee relies on Pope v. Hinckley, 209 Mass. 323. In that case the . . . exchange was not made during the lifetime of the testator, but was made by his executors shortly after his death. . . .

We do not think it necessary to discuss the cases from other jurisdictions, cited by the legatee. In many of them the facts are different from those in the case at bar; in so far as the decisions appear to be contrary to the conclusion we have reached, we must decline to follow them. We do not decide what would have been the rights of the legatee if the testatrix, in substitution of her stock in the New Jersey company, had received the debentures directly from that company. That question does not arise and we make no intimation regarding it. . . .

The decree is affirmed.

In re MANDELLE'S ESTATE
252 Mich. 375, 233 N.W. 230 (1930)

WIEST, C.J.

Mary S. Mandelle, possessed of a large estate, died testate, August 17, 1928. In her will, executed September 10, 1923, among many other bequests, she made the following:

> In recognition of his faithful and kindly medical services to me and his contribution to science and humanity, which I wish to facilitate, I give to Charles Jack Hunt, of Mt. Vernon, New York, his heirs and assigns forever, twelve hundred (1,200) shares, par value, of the capital stock of Parke, Davis & Company, a corporation, etc., of Detroit, Michigan.

At that time testatrix owned 3,744 shares of the stock of that company of the par value of $25 each. In February, 1927, the stockholders of Parke, Davis & Company reframed its capital structure in form only, and authorized the exchange of the $25 par value shares for no par value shares in the ratio of one par value share for five no par value shares, and in March, 1927, testatrix exchanged the mentioned par value shares, owned by her, for the no par value shares in accord with the designated ratio, and, at her death, held the no par shares only. The executors of her estate, being in doubt whether Dr. Hunt was entitled to 6,000 shares of the no par stock (the number of shares equivalent to the

1,200 shares of par value stock), or to only 1,200 shares of the no par stock, petitioned the probate court for instruction. The probate court held that the bequest to Dr. Hunt called for 6,000 shares of the no par stock, together with dividends received upon the 6,000 shares by the executors after the death of testatrix. The residuary legatees appealed to the circuit court, and, upon affirmance there of the probate order, prosecute review here.

Attorneys for the legatee contend that the legacy is specific, while attorneys for the residuary legatees say it is general, and attorneys for the executors think it demonstrative.

If the legacy is general, then the legatee takes 1,200 shares of the no par stock and may not participate in any accruals thereon during the course of administration. If the legacy is specific, then the legatee takes 6,000 shares of the no par stock, with all accruals since the death of the testatrix.

Appellants argue that the will speaks as of the date of death of testatrix. It is not expressive of the whole subject to say that a will speaks as of the date of the death of the maker. It is more accurate to say that a will is not operative until the death of the maker, and then speaks the intention of the maker at the time of its execution. It has been held that: "As to specific legacies, the will speaks as of the time of its execution."

The legacy is either specific or general. It is not a demonstrative legacy. Briefly stated, a demonstrative legacy is a pecuniary gift with a particular fund or source of means pointed out for its satisfaction. We think testatrix intended something more, in specifying the shares of stock bequeathed, than to point them out as a mere yardstick with which to measure a pecuniary gift. Upon the question of whether the legacy is specific or general, there exist certain general rules all, however, recognizing that the intention of the maker, found in any part of the will or reasonably deducible from the instrument, considered as a whole, must govern construction.

It is said, in behalf of appellants, that specific legacies are not favored. The main reasons for this is the peril of ademption, and not that the courts frown thereon. Our attention has been directed to many English and American cases. Without reviewing the cases, we will state our conclusions, together with applicable authority.

It was stated in Burnett v. Heinrichs, 95 N.J. Eq. 112 (122 A. 681):

> But the language of the bequest is not controlling. The entire instrument is to be examined, and if, upon the whole, it clearly appears that the testator intended to dispose of *his* stock, the legacy will be regarded as specific. If in the clause the testator has referred to the stock as "my" or "now in my possession" or "now owned by me," or like words of identification, the bequest would have been specific according to all accepted authority. And if similar expressions are found in the rest of the will, referable to and inclusive of the bequest, it is specific.

In the forty-second paragraph of the will testatrix declared:

> It is my express wish and desire that all of the above legacies and trust funds shall, as far as possible, be paid in stocks and bonds or other property which I may own at the time of my death. . . .

This expression of purpose is referable to every provision in the will and to the bequest to Dr. Hunt, and discloses that in making the bequest to Dr. Hunt she intended to give shares of stock then owned by her. . . .

We think the will, considered as a whole, shows it was the intention of testatrix to constitute her bequest in favor of Dr. Hunt a specific legacy. We think the provisions of the will individualized the shares of stock bequeathed to Dr. Hunt as stock then owned by testatrix. This brings us to the question of whether there was an ademption by reason of exchange of par value shares of stock for no value shares. The stock was changed in name and form only and at all times remained substantially the same thing.

There was no ademption accomplished by taking five shares of no par stock for each share of par value stock. Testatrix did not initiate the change in form of the shares of stock; the change occurred in consequence of corporate action which she could not control. Johns Hopkins University v. Uhrig, 145 Md. 114 (125 A. 606). Dividends, subsequent to death of a testator, on specific legacies of shares of stock follow the stock. Tifft v. Porter, 8 N.Y. 516; Dryden v. Owings, 49 Md. 356.

The judgment is affirmed, with costs against appellants.

Consider what the preceding cases and Problem 19-A, dealing with stock dividends and splits, suggest to the lawyer regarding the advisability of bequests of stock and about the drafting of such bequests when they are to be made. Consider especially the importance of such problems when the bequest is of shares in a closely held corporation or one in which control of the business may be involved. See generally Uniform Probate Code §2-605.

2. Satisfaction

The doctrine of satisfaction or *ademption by satisfaction,* as it is sometimes called, is analogous to the doctrine of advancement in intestate estates.

> A general or residuary legacy may be satisfied in whole or in part by testator's inter vivos gift to the legatee after the execution of the will. When the testator stands in loco parentis to the legatee, the gift is presumed to

be intended as satisfaction of the legacy. By the prevailing view the doctrine of satisfaction does not apply to devises of land.

T. Atkinson, Wills §133 (2d ed. 1953). Later in the same section Atkinson adds that when the "thing given is not of the same nature as the thing bequeathed, a presumption arises that an ademption by satisfaction was not intended." In some states statutes provide that "advancements or gifts are not to be taken as ademptions of general legacies, unless such intention is expressed by the testator in writing." Rees, American Wills Statutes, 46 Va. L. Rev. 856, 904 (1960); see also Uniform Probate Code §2-609.

MATTER OF ESTATE OF WOLFE
349 N.W.2d 33 (S.D. 1984)

WOLLMAN, J.

This is an appeal from a decree of distribution . . . which held that there had been an ademption of certain devises of land in decedent's will. We affirm.

Jacob Wolff, Sr., (decedent) accumulated approximately 2,800 acres of farm land in Perkins County in South Dakota. When decedent and his wife moved to California in 1950, his three sons, Jacob Jr., Arthur, and Erwinn, remained on the farmland. Jacob Jr., who had been farming 762 acres known as the "home place" with Erwinn, left South Dakota in 1957.

In 1971 decedent executed a will which provided that in the event his wife should predecease him, his estate should pass to his sons "equally, share and share alike." In 1972, decedent and his wife deeded 1,000.16 acres of the Perkins County land to Arthur for consideration of "one dollar and other good and valuable consideration." In 1973, decedent and his wife deeded 1,040 acres of the Perkins County land to Erwinn for the same consideration. The tracts of land deeded to Erwinn and Arthur and the remaining 762 acres were of approximately the same value.

Prior to deeding the two tracts of land to Erwinn and Arthur, decedent, who was born to immigrant parents and was not proficient in English, wrote the following to Jacob Jr. in a letter dated September 14, 1972:

> I had sent Arthur and Erwinn the Deed for their land. So from now on they did not have to send anymore rent from the land that is Deeded to them and about your land, I don't know yet. See how it is turning out. Erwinn can buy it or rent for cash, from now on. Or what did you think? I thought if Erwinn buys it I can make the Deed to him. If he rents for cash I make the Deed to you. It is 760 acres of land. All the land on the South

side of the road Sec 3 — Sec 4 — Sec 5 — Sec 9 — and Sec 10. So he buy it, I deed it to him. If he rent it, he got to rent it for cash. But if you want it to deed it to you, I will do it? Say it the [way] you like it best.

Decedent's wife died in 1974, and Erwinn moved to California to live with decedent. Arthur's son, Lynn, then took possession of the home place.

Decedent died in 1980 at the age of eighty-six. His will was admitted to probate in California, and with the exception of the land in Perkins County, South Dakota, decedent's estate was distributed in equal shares to his three sons pursuant to the California probate decree. The will was later admitted to probate in South Dakota. The circuit court concluded that decedent's delivery of the warranty deeds to Erwinn and Arthur, when considered in light of decedent's September 14, 1972, letter to Jacob Jr., constituted an ademption of their share of the South Dakota property.

"Ademption" is the term that describes either the act which makes inoperative a devise or bequest of specific property by the sale or extinction of the property during the testator's lifetime or, as is applicable to the case at hand, the satisfaction of a devise or bequest by money payment or delivery or conveyance of property to a beneficiary prior to the testator's death. . . .

The statutes regarding ademption are exclusive, and we therefore need not address common law rules and principles. . . .

Although there is authority that ademption applies only to specific legacies . . . SDCL 29-6-14 allows for ademptions of general legacies if an intention to adeem is expressed by the testator in writing.

The doctrine of ademption applies to both bequests of personalty and devises of realty. . . .

Arthur and Erwinn contend that the requirement in SDCL 29-6-14 that the testator express his intention to adeem was not satisfied by decedent's September 14, 1972, letter. In interpreting a statute similar to SDCL 29-6-14, the Supreme Court of California held:

> It is the established rule that no special form, nor even the signature of the decedent, is required to constitute a charge of the advancement in writing as prescribed by such statutes. It will be sufficient if it appears that the writing was done by the decedent and shows the intent to charge the money or property given as an advancement rather than as a gift or loan. Unsigned statements in the form of a charge entered in a book or on leaves inserted at the back of a book of miscellaneous accounts, the circumstances being such as to exclude the idea that it was charged as a debt, have been held sufficient.

In re Estate of Hayne, 165 Cal. 568, 573, 133 P. 277, 279 (1913). . . .

In the letter to Jacob Jr., decedent writes of sending Arthur and Erwinn the deed for "their land," and then refers to the remaining property as "your land." The land deeded to Arthur and Erwinn is contiguous with the respective tracts already owned by them. Moreover, after taking into account the disparity in the per acre value assigned to the several tracts, the land deeded to Arthur and Erwinn had a value closely approximating the value of the remaining 760 acres claimed by Jacob Jr. Given these facts, we conclude that the circuit court did not err in determining that the letter satisfied the writing requirement contained in SDCL 29-6-14. . . .

Decedent provided in his will that should a beneficiary contest the validity of the will, such beneficiary would forfeit his share of the estate. Arthur and Erwinn maintain that by opposing their petition for the sale of the 762 acres of South Dakota land and by raising the issue of ademption, Jacob Jr. was disputing the validity of decedent's will. We disagree. Jacob Jr. was not claiming the will was invalid, but rather was correctly asserting that a portion of the devise under the will had been satisfied.

Any issues or sub-issues not discussed in this opinion have been considered and have been found to be without merit.

The decree is affirmed. . . .

MATTER OF LUTZ
201 Misc. 539, 107 N.Y.S.2d 388 (Surr. Ct. 1951)

FRANKENTHALER, S.

Objections have been raised to the action of the executor in crediting the sum of $9,802.73 against the legacy given respondent. . . . To sustain these deductions, the accountant contends that the principal sum represents advances made by decedent to the objectant in anticipation of her legacy. . . .

At the time of his death in 1948, testator was sixty-seven years old and his closest living relative was a married son. He had first met the objectant and her husband at his son's wedding in 1942. From that time, a very warm friendship sprang up between testator and objectant; they had frequent social contacts and testator made it a point to spend his leisure time with the objectant and her husband. Testator frequently referred to objectant as his niece, being addressed as "Uncle Fred," and their relationship has been characterized by objectant as that of guardian-ward. In 1946, decedent sought to adopt the objectant but as objectant's parents were then living, the plan was abandoned. On October 1, 1946, testator executed his last will and testament in which the objectant, referred to as "my friend," was given certain household effects and $50,000 in cash. The residue, after two minor bequests, was given to decedent's son who was also appointed executor without bond. On December 4, 1947, testator executed a codicil in which he nominated the Guardian Trust Company as executor in place of his son and added an in terrorem clause. In all other respects, the codicil ratified, confirmed and republished his will.

The first payment recorded by the accountant was made on June 6, 1946, and from that date until his death, decedent made many gifts to the objectant. The amounts of the gifts varied, ranging from as little as $2.50 to as high as $2,000. The purposes for which these gifts were given can be summarized in five categories: (a) payments for the purchase and maintenance of an automobile; (b) payments for several trips taken by objectant, on two of which the decedent accompanied her; (c) payments for jewelry, clothing and household furnishings, together with the payment of insurance on certain of these articles; (d) payments related to the maintenance of objectant's art studio; and (e) miscellaneous payments and unexplained checks drawn to or for the order of objectant. The accountant does not and upon the proof cannot claim that testator expressed an intention that these gifts were to be treated as advancements. Instead, its position is that there is a presumed intent arising from the filial relationship between the parties and the nature of the gifts.

The rule in this State has been stated as follows:

> Whenever a parent gives a legacy to a child, without stating any particular object for which it is given, such legacy is regarded as a portion. And if the testator afterwards during his own lifetime, makes a settlement upon the child by way of a portion, or pays to him a sum of money by way of a portion, or makes an advancement to him, or gives him a sum of money as an advancement, such payment, portion, or advancement amounts to a satisfaction — or, as is often said, an ademption of the legacy, either pro tanto or in full. . . . This rule is based upon a presumption against double portions; that is, a presumption adopted by courts of equity that a parent, owning a common duty to all his children, could not have intended to distribute his estate unequally among them and to favor one at the expense of the others.

(Matter of Weiss, 39 Misc. 71, 72. See, also, 4 Page on Wills, §1540, and 2 Davids on New York Law of Wills, §1127.) The presumption can, of course, be rebutted (Matter of Scott, [1903] 1 Ch. 1; Matter of Lacon, [1891] 2 Ch. 482).

Hence, the elements necessary to raise the presumption are: (1) a bequest in the nature of a portion; (2) the parent-child relationship; and (3) an advancement in the nature of a portion which would cause inequality. The term "portion" has been defined as "something which is given by the parent to establish the child in life or to make what is called provision for him" (2 Jarman on Wills 1123 [7th ed., Sanger, 1930]), and it may reasonably be assumed that a legacy of $50,000 to a "child" constitutes a "portion" within the rule (Matter of Weiss, supra).

The second requisite — the parent-child relationship — is fundamental (see Matter of Cramer, 43 Misc. 494, 496). However, a blood relationship is not necessary; it is sufficient if the testator stands in loco parentis to the legatee.

> A person in loco parentis has been defined as one "who *means* to put himself in the situation of the lawful father of the child, with reference to the father's office and duty of making a provision for the child." (2 Williams Executors [7th ed.], p. 652.) . . . The primary obligation of a parent is to care for, support, educate and provide for his child. There must be proof of the assumption and performance of these obligations.

(Matter of Bernhardi, 151 Misc. 480, 482.) . . . Moreover, the relationship must be shown to have existed at the time the will was executed (Watson v. Watson, 33 Beav. 574, 55 Eng. Rep. 491).

The accountant claims that the filial relationship between the parties, characterized by objectant as that of guardian-ward, the oft-expressed love and affection of the testator for the objectant and the support rendered objectant indicate that testator was in loco parentis to objectant. The latter, on the other hand, maintains that the relationship did not exist since she was at all times supported by her husband and not dependent upon the testator.

The court has found no case in this State involving the problem here presented where the relationship claimed was found between persons not related by blood. . . . English courts have found the relationship to have existed between grandfather and granddaughter (Watson v. Watson, 33 Beav. 574, 55 Eng. Rep. 491, supra), uncle and niece (Powys v. Mansfield, 3 Myl. & Craig 359, 40 Eng. Rep. 964), and cousins (Booker v. Allen, 2 Russ. & Myl. 270, 39 Eng. Rep. 397). In all of these cases there was evidence that the "parent" had supported the child during her early years, either directly or indirectly, and had dealt with her in all matters as his daughter. In no case, was the testator found in loco parentis when the relationship had commenced during the adult life of the child. . . .

While there is evidence of decedent's intention to treat the objectant as his child, it is unquestioned that objectant was at all times supported and cared for by her husband. The gratuities rendered her were not in the discharge of parental obligations of care and support, as the gifts were for the most part luxuries, but rather resulted from decedent's affection for objectant.

It is thus evident that the requirements set forth in the *Bernhardi* case have not been satisfied and the court accordingly holds that testator was not in loco parentis to the objectant.

However, assuming that the alleged relationship is shown to have existed, the court is further of the opinion that none of the gifts constitute advancements within the rule as hereinbefore discussed. In the first place, there is no evidence that testator intended that the gifts be treated as advancements (Hine v. Hine, 39 Barb. 507; 4 Page on Wills, §1536).

Therefore, his intent must be presumed from the nature of the relation-ship, the nature of the gifts and the theory that equality among children was intended.

There have been few decisions in this State dealing with the problem of advancements, and most of them are inapplicable to the facts in this case. This is not a case where testator has included a "hotchpot" provi-sion in his will or codicil, nor one where the legatee receipted for the gift as an advancement, nor one where the legacy was for a certain purpose which was discharged during testator's lifetime, nor one where the leg-acy and the gifts were ejusdem generis.

In the cases not falling within the aforementioned categories, the courts have treated gifts as advancements when they were either the full amount of the legacy or were for such purposes as establishing a child in business, and as a settlement upon marriage, both of which are deemed "portions" within the meaning of the rule. Where the gifts were small in sum the courts have almost without exception held that they could not be deemed advancements.

While the total of the claimed advancements exceed 18% of the legacy the largest single gift is but 4% thereof. Moreover, none of the gifts has been shown to be for the purposes hereinbefore stated. Accountant's general position is that testator wanted the objectant to enjoy the benefit of the legacy during his lifetime; that the legacy was intended to afford her luxuries and that he wished the pleasure of watching her enjoyment of them. No evidence has been adduced in support of this argument and the inference that testator wished to confer additional gratuities upon the objectant is as consistent with the facts. These occasional and varying gifts can in no sense be deemed "portions" within the meaning of the rule since they were not given with a view to "establishing [objectant] in life." (Matter of Lacon [1891], 2 Ch. 482, 498, supra.) Hence, it is evi-dent that the gifts in controversy were not intended to be advancements against objectant's legacy nor are they such as a matter of law.

This conclusion is further reinforced by reference to the codicil exe-cuted December 4, 1947. It is well settled that the execution of a codicil, subsequent to the making of advancements, which merely republishes the will does not revive the adeemed legacy. However, it has also been held that if the codicil treats the legacy as extant, there has been no ademption (De Groff v. Terpenning, 14 Hun 301), and that the codicil may be viewed as evidence of testator's intention with respect to the gift (Matter of Scott [1903], 1 Ch. 1, supra).

Testator here changed his will in two respects — he replaced his son as executor by a trust company and he incorporated an in terrorem clause. Inasmuch as the latter could not be directed against any of the nonresiduary legatees, none of them having status to contest or chal-lenge, it would seem that the clause was directed against testator's son. Moreover, it could be only for the protection of objectant since the two other minor legacies were unassailable. Hence, the codicil indicates the testator's intent to assure objectant's legacy of the greatest possible protection. It also indicates that there was no intent to treat objectant and his son equally, but rather to accord objectant a preferred position.

In these circumstances, it can hardly be said that testator intended his gifts to adeem objectant's legacy, and the credits are therefore disallowed. . . .

WEST v. COOGLER

427 So. 2d 813 (Fla. App. 5 1983)

COWART, Judge.

This case involves an "advancement" to one beneficiary of a trust.

On July 30, 1962, Margaret F. Coogler, as settlor, conveyed 160 acres to her daughter, appellant Jane West, in trust for the use and benefit of the settlor during her lifetime with remainder in trust for the use and benefit of her four children: [Jane, Vivian, William, and Theodore]. The deed of trust provided that the trust expired 20 years from its date and that if any of the four children died prior to the expiration of the trust that child's interest would pass in equal shares to the surviving beneficiaries. Upon termination the corpus was to be distributed equally to the surviving beneficiaries. This was a spendthrift trust precluding any alienation of any interest therein by any beneficiary. This deed of trust was not recorded until March 3, 1964, and between the date of its execution and its recording . . . Margaret F. Coogler deeded her son Vivian . . . and his wife Clara, a quarter (40 acres) of the property included in the trust deed. On January 4, 1967, Vivian V. Coogler, Jr., deeded the forty acre tract he obtained from his mother to a third party. . . . In 1968 one of the four children, Theodore . . . , died and in 1969 the mother died. . . .

In 1979 Vivian V. Coogler, Jr., brought this action for declaratory decree and accounting, claiming a one-third interest in the corpus of the trust, being the 120 acres remaining of the 160 acres. . . .

In a strict technical sense, the legal definition of an "advancement" is an inter vivos gift made by a parent to a child with intent that such gift represents a part or the whole of the donor's estate that the donee would inherit on the death of the donor. However, the concept of an advancement rests on an ancient equitable doctrine that applies with equal force and logic to the inter vivos trust in this case . . . the assumed desire of a parent to equalize his estate among his heirs, not only as to property owned at death but as to all property that went from him to his children, so that one child will not be preferred to another in the final settlement of his estate. . . . [T]here is no apparent reason why it should not be applied to advances made by a settlor in the unusual case, as here. . . . Whether a particular transfer is an advancement or not is one of intent and the relevant intent is that of the person making the gift. . . . Therefore, whether or not Vivian . . . knew of the trust at the time he received the 40 acres from his mother is irrelevant and immaterial. . . . [He] admitted that he paid his mother nothing for the 40 acres. In addition to a presumption, the testimony of Jane . . . as to her mother's intent was made without objection and is uncontradicted. As to why the mother gave the 1964 deed of 40 acres to Vivian . . . , in her deposition Jane [reported that the settlor had said that Vivian] "was pressuring her and she felt he needed it at that time instead of later." . . .

Therefore we hold that the conveyance of 40 acres by the settlor to Vivian . . . constituted an advancement and that for the purposes of distribution the 40 acres should be grouped, hotchpot, with the remaining trust corpus and treated as an advancement and, in this case, charged, not by valuation but in kind as 40 acres against the interest of Vivian . . . in the trust corpus. The effect of this is that Vivian . . . will share with Jane . . . and William . . . the share that their brother Theodore . . . would have received had he survived. . . .

3. Abatement

Any time a testator's property, after payment of claims against the estate, is insufficient to satisfy all bequests and devises, it is obvious that the shares of some or all beneficiaries under the will must be reduced or abated. In addition to losses in asset values and payment of debts, expenses of administration, and taxes, the testator's estate may be diminished by the assertion of statutory rights in contravention of the will by a surviving spouse or a pretermitted heir. These latter sources of abatement are normally unanticipated and particularly drastic in their impact on a testator's scheme. Consequently they pose special problems and may suggest departure from the usual rules for abatement. In the case of a spouse's election against a will, there may also be questions of sequestration or of acceleration of remainders or both caused by renunciation of a testate interest. These problems are raised and considered briefly in Chapter 3.

Although it is clear that questions of abatement are controlled by the "testator's intent," typically nothing appears or may be inferred from the will regarding an actual intention. For cases in which no intention is discoverable, a presumed order of abatement for payment of debts is prescribed by decisional law or by statute. Property that would pass intestate is first taken for payment of debts before any testamentary gifts will be reduced. Generally, however, there will be no intestate property, unless there is no residuary clause or unless all or a part of the residuary provision fails for some reason. When there is no intestate property, it is apparent from the very nature of a residuary bequest that it should abate before general or specific bequests in the absence of manifestation of contrary intent or an inconsistent plan in the will. Beyond this, the order of abatement, whether prescribed by statute or common law rule, is more or less arbitrary but purportedly based on the probable intent of testators. "Modern" views on abatement are typified by the provisions of Uniform Probate Code §3-902 (except as to abatement caused by the share of a pretermitted heir, for which the statutory trend favors ratable abatement of all testate interests, essentially in the manner provided in UPC §2-207(b) for a spouse's election).

UNIFORM PROBATE CODE

§3-902. *Order in Which Assets Appropriated; Abatement.*

(a) Except as provided in subsection (b) and except as provided in connection with the share of the surviving spouse who elects to take an elective share, shares of distributees abate, without any preference or priority as between real and personal property, in the following order: (1) property not disposed of by the will; (2) residuary devises [which term in the Code includes "bequests"]; (3) general devises; (4) specific devises. For purposes of abatement, a general devise charged on any specific property or fund is a specific devise to the extent of the value of the property on which it is charged, and upon the failure or insufficiency of the property on which it is charged, a general devise to the extent of the failure or insufficiency. Abatement within each classification is in proportion to the amounts of property each of the beneficiaries would have received if full distribution of the property had been made in accordance with the terms of the will.

(b) If the will expresses an order of abatement, or if the testamentary plan or the express or implied purpose of the devise would be defeated by the order of abatement stated in subsection (a), the shares of the distributees abate as may be found necessary to give effect to the intention of the testator.

(c) If the subject of a preferred devise is sold or used incident to administration, abatement shall be achieved by appropriate adjustments in, or contribution from, other interests in the remaining assets.

Some statutes have eliminated the typical priority of specific gifts over general.

The older view, still prevailing in a few states, is that all bequests abate before devises. In some states the effects of this position are often avoided in particular cases by finding that legacies were intended to be charges on lands not specifically devised, if the legacies exceeded the testator's personal estate at the time the will was executed.

Whatever the order of abatement, within a given class of equal priority the gifts generally abate ratably. By statute or decision in some states, however, within a given class, relatives may be preferred over strangers, and testamentary provisions for near relatives may be given a priority on the basis of probable intent. Some cases recognize a priority for a spouse who is deemed to take a testamentary share as a "purchaser" by relinquishing statutory rights. This rule has even been applied to give a spouse's residuary interest priority over all other bequests. Nolte v. Nolte, 247 Iowa 868, 76 N.W.2d 881 (1956).

An interesting case dealing with a significant modern problem is Osborn v. Osborn, 334 S.W.2d 48 (Mo. 1960). In that case the testator made various specific and general bequests to his son and others and then provided that his wife should receive the amount required to take the maximum marital deduction allowable under the federal estate tax law, with the residue to the testator's son. When the estate proved inadequate to pay the marital deduction bequest and all of the other specific and general bequests, the court held that the widow's share was to be paid in full and that only the other bequests were to be abated, whether "characterized as 'specific' or not," since the testator's intent to take advantage of the maximum marital deduction rendered inoperative the normal order of abatement.

4. Miscellaneous Matters

a. Exoneration

T. Atkinson, Wills §137 (2d ed. 1953), summarizes exoneration as follows:

> In absence of statute or of testamentary directions to the contrary, mortgages and other liens upon the decedent's realty and upon the subject-matter of his specific bequests must be exonerated out of the general personal assets of the estate.

The rule varies from state to state and hardly justifies further discussion here other than to note (1) that the intent to require or not to require exoneration of encumbered property is a matter to be taken up with a client in the planning of a will, and (2) that the modern judicial and statutory tendency has been to narrow the application of the inferred right of exoneration.

A number of modern statutes, based on Model Probate Code §189, or more recently on Uniform Probate Code §2-607, abolish this right unless the will provides otherwise, and the Uniform Probate Code makes it clear that a general directive to pay debts does not create a right of exoneration. The comment to the Model Code section observes that the basis of the common law rule — that the personal estate has been benefited by the creation of the debt — generally "has no foundation in fact." See generally Estate of Brown, 240 Cal. App. 2d 818, 820, 50 Cal. Rptr. 78, 80 (1966).

b.   Right of Retainer

Uniform Probate Court §3-903 provides:

> The amount of a noncontingent indebtedness of a successor to the estate if due, or its present value if not due, shall be offset against the successor's interest; but the successor has the benefit of any defense which would be available to him in a direct proceeding for recovery of the debt.

Contrary to the last clause of the above section, at common law some of the decisions hold that the right of retainer applies even to debts barred by a statute of limitations or discharged in bankruptcy.

B.   Determination of Beneficiaries

1.   Class Gifts: Limits on Increasing Membership

As a general rule, for purposes of a testamentary gift to persons designated as a class, membership in that class includes afterborn persons satisfying the class description. Thus, a bequest to the testator's children will normally include all of the children, even those born after the will is executed. Unlike this bequest to the testator's own children (all of whom, in the conventional sense, will necessarily be born, or at least conceived, within his lifetime), some class gifts pose the question of how long this increase in class membership will be allowed to continue. The problem is illustrated by a bequest of "$100,000 to be divided among the children of my brother, B," who is still living at the testator's death. Certainly children of B born after execution of the will but before the testator's death are included, but it now becomes necessary to decide whether a child born to B after the testator's death would qualify to share in the bequest. The so-called rule of convenience provides that, for purposes of this outright and immediate class gift, the class closes and its maximum membership is determined at the death of the testator, provided at least one member of the class is then living. Class members born (or, more accurately, conceived) thereafter are excluded so that the number of B's children and amount of their shares can be finally determined at the testator's death, permitting distribution of the fund to the class. Even if $10,000 is given to each child of B, so that each class member's share would be determinable without knowing the total number of children, the class closes at the testator's death in order to determine the amount of the residuary estate and to permit final distribution of it. The operation of the rule of convenience varies with the terms and the character of the interest given to the class. The purpose of this brief summary of its application to outright bequests and devises is merely to introduce the student to this range of problems. Thorough understanding of the class-closing doctrine and critical appraisal of it depend upon a study of its application to future interests and are thus beyond the scope of this chapter. For further examination of the subject, see E. Halbach and E. Scoles, Materials on Future Interests 132-138 (1977); 5 American Law of Property §§22.39-22.46 (J. Casner ed. 1952).[1]

2. Lapse

When a legatee or devisee dies between the execution of a will and the death of the testator,[2] the bequest or devise *lapses* — that is, it fails — in the absence of testamentary or statutory provision to the contrary. If the named beneficiary is dead when a will is executed, the provision for him is *void* at common law. Void or lapsed gifts generally pass under the residuary provision, unless, of course, it is the residuary gift or a part thereof that fails, in which case the property usually is intestate. The distinction between void and lapsed gifts is of no consequence in most cases. Occasionally, however, an antilapse statute has been held not to apply to void gifts when the statute does not cover the point.

1. If this subject is to be pursued further at this point, Re Wernher's Settlement Trusts, 1 All Eng. Rep. 184 (1961), is an interesting case that provides a useful vehicle for discussion of the doctrine, including its application to future interests, and of the reasons underlying its general acceptance.
2. Lapse is a rule of law and, as noted in the text above, relates to the date of the testator's death. It is thus to be distinguished from the *constructional* question of whether a future interest beneficiary is required to be alive at a date *later than the effective date of the transfer* — that is, whether the remainder beneficiary, C, must be alive at the date of distribution (the death of the life beneficiary, B) where A bequeaths to T in trust for B for life, remainder to C. The standard answer here would be no. C's remainder is subject to no implied condition of survivorship; it thus takes effect on B's death and belongs, if C is dead, to C's successors in interest (usually C's will beneficiaries, or C's heirs at law if C leaves no will). The reluctance to imply conditions of survival carries over to most class gift situations in most states. For example, in the case of a remainder to someone's "children," the presumption is that a child's interest is not defeated by failure to survive the life beneficiary; but this reluctance does not carry over to all class gifts, such as a remainder to "issue," for which there is generally a presumption that survival is required. See generally E. Halbach and E. Scoles, Materials on Future Interests 85-130 (1977).
Where a beneficiary of a revocable trust predeceases the settlor but was alive when the trust was established and the trust makes no provisions for the beneficiary's death, in most states the beneficiary's future interest is not subject to an implied condition of survival to the date the trust becomes irrevocable. If, however, it is the view of the particular court that this is a "lapse" situation and that a beneficiary who predeceases the settlor of a revocable trust cannot take, the court may decide that the state's antilapse statute for wills also applies here. See Estate of Button, 79 Wash. 2d 849, 490 P.2d 731 (1971).

Nearly all states have enacted antilapse statutes, intended to give effect to what legislatures have thought to be the probable intention of the average testator. The terms of most current statutes (often without the UPC's 120-hour survival requirement) are illustrated by original UPC §2-605, which (before the 1990 comprehensive revision, below) provided: "If a devisee who is a grandparent or a lineal descendant of a grandparent of the testator is dead at the time of execution of the will, fails to survive the testator, or is treated as if he predeceased the testator, the issue of the deceased devisee who survive the testator by 120 hours take in place of the deceased devisee and if they are all of the same degree of kinship to the devisee they take equally, but if of unequal degree then those of more remote degree take by representation. One who would have been a devisee under a class gift if he had survived the testator is treated as a devisee for purposes of this section whether his death occurred before or after the execution of the will."

UNIFORM PROBATE CODE

§2-603. *Antilapse; Deceased Devisee; Class Gifts.*

(a) [Definitions.] In this section:

(1) "Alternative devise" means a devise that is expressly created by the will and, under the terms of the will, can take effect instead of another devise on the happening of one or more events, including survival of the testator or failure to survive the testator, whether an event is expressed in condition-precedent, condition-subsequent, or any other form. A residuary clause constitutes an alternative devise with respect to a nonresiduary devise only if the will specifically provides that, upon lapse or failure, the nonresiduary devise, or nonresiduary devises in general, pass under the residuary clause.

(2) "Class member" includes an individual who fails to survive the testator but who would have taken under a devise in the form of a class gift had he [or she] survived the testator.

(3) "Devise" includes an alternative devise, a devise in the form of a class gift, and an exercise of a power of appointment.

(4) "Devisee" includes (i) a class member if the devise is in the form of a class gift, (ii) an individual or class member who was deceased at the time the testator executed his [or her] will as well as an individual or class member who was then living but who failed to survive the testator, and (iii) an appointee under a power of appointment exercised by the testator's will.

(5) "Stepchild" means a child of the surviving, deceased, or former spouse of the testator or of the donor of a power of appointment, and not of the testator or donor.

(6) "Surviving devisee" or "surviving descendant" means a devisee or a descendant who neither predeceased the testator nor is deemed to have predeceased the testator under Section 2-702.

(7) "Testator" includes the donee of a power of appointment if the power is exercised in the testator's will.

(b) [Substitute Gift.] If a devisee fails to survive the testator and is a grandparent, a descendant of a grandparent, or a stepchild of either the testator or the donor of a power of appointment exercised by the testator's will, the following apply:

(1) Except as provided in paragraph (4), if the devise is not in the form of a class gift and the deceased devisee leaves surviving descendants, a substitute gift is created in the devisee's surviving descendants. They take by representation the property to which the devisee would have been entitled had the devisee survived the testator.

(2) Except as provided in paragraph (4), if the devise is in the form of a class gift, other than a devise to "issue," "descendants," "heirs of the body," "heirs," "next of kin," "relatives," or "family," or a class described by language of similar import, a substitute gift is created in the deceased devisee or devisee's surviving descendants. The property to which the devisees would have been entitled had all of them survived the testator passes to the surviving devisees and the surviving descendants of the deceased devisees. Each surviving devisee takes the share to which he [or she] would have been entitled had the deceased devisees survived the testator. Each deceased devisees's surviving descendants who are substituted for the deceased devisee take by representation the share to which the deceased devisee would have been entitled had the deceased devisee survived the testator. For the purposes of this paragraph, "deceased devisee" means a class member who failed to survive the testator and left one or more surviving descendants.

(3) For the purposes of Section 2-601, words of survivorship, such as in a devise to an individual "if he survives me," or in a devise to "my surviving children," are not, in the absence of additional evidence, a sufficient indication of an intent contrary to the application of this section.

(4) If the will creates an alternative devise with respect to a devise for which a substitute gift is created by paragraph (1) or (2), the substitute gift is superseded by the alternative devise only if an expressly designated devisee of the alternative devise is entitled to take under the will.

(5) Unless the language creating a power of appointment expressly excludes the substitution of the descendants of an appointee for the appointee, a surviving descendant of a deceased appointee of a power of appointment can be substituted for the appointee under this section, whether or not the descendant is an object of the power.

(c) [More Than One Substitute Gift; Which One Takes.] If, under sub-section (b), substitute gifts are created and not superseded with respect to more than one devise and the devises are alternative devises, one to the other, the determination of which of the substitute gifts takes effect is resolved as follows:

(1) Except as provided in paragraph (2), the devised property passes under the primary substitute gift.

(2) If there is a younger-generation devise, the devised property passes under the younger-generation substitute gift and not under the primary substitute gift.

(3) In this subsection:

(i) "Primary devise" means the devise that would have taken effect had all the deceased devisees of the alternative devises who left surviving descendants survived the testator.

(ii) "Primary substitute gift" means the substitute gift created with respect to the primary devise.

(iii) "Younger-generation devise" means a devise that (A) is to a descendant of a devisee of the primary devise, (B) is an alternative devise with respect to the primary devise, (C) is a devise for which a substitute gift is created, and (D) would have taken effect had all the deceased devisees who left surviving descendants survived the tes-tator except the deceased devisee or devisees of the primary devise.

(iv) "Younger-generation substitute gift" means the substitute gift created with respect to the younger-generation devise.

The statutes vary regarding the legatees and devisees to whom they can apply. A few statutes limit their coverage to descendants of the testator, while several are so broad as to include all legatees and devisees. Most of the statutes extend coverage to certain described relatives or to all per-sons described as *kindred* or *relations* of the testator. These latter terms are held not to include a spouse. Would you expect the word "relative" to include a stepchild? See the typical, negative answer in Kimball v. Story, 108 Mass. 382 (1871); cf. Oliver v. Bank One, 60 Ohio St. 3d 32, 573 N.E.2d 55 (1991) (bequest to brother-in-law). A few statutes, how-ever, now expressly extend their protection to issue of a spouse, and at least one recent statute applies to bequests and devises to "kindred of a surviving, deceased, or former spouse of the testator." Cal. Prob. Code §6147.

Nearly all antilapse statutes apply to the share of the described lega-tees and devisees only if they leave issue alive at the testator's death. Absent some manifestation of contrary intention, the issue are then sub-stituted for the named beneficiary. In one state the share of a deceased legatee or devisee passes to his "heirs." Iowa Code Ann. §633.273 (1991). In another it passes as if the "legatee had died . . . owning the property." Md. Ann. Est. & Tr. Code §4-403 (1991).

See generally French, Antilapse Statutes Are Blunt Instruments: A Blueprint for Reform, 37 Hast. L.J. 335 (1985).

PROBLEMS

20-D.   *T* has recently died. His will left $50,000 to his son, *S*, and the residue to his daughter, *D*. *S* predeceased *T*, leaving a wife, *W*, a child, *C*, and several unpaid creditors. *W* and *C* come to consult you. They inform you that some time prior to *S*'s death *T* had given *S* $25,000, either as a gift or a loan. They ask you what their rights are in *T*'s estate under the law of your state. What would you tell them? What additional information would you want to obtain?

20-E.   *T*'s will leaves her entire estate "equally to my brothers, *A* and *B*, or to the survivor." Under the laws of your state, what would the result be if *A* predeceased *T*, and *T* then died survived by *B* and by *A*'s child, *C*? Would it matter if *A* and *B* had been *T*'s children? See Estate of Burruss, 152 Mich. App. 660, 394 N.W.2d 466 (1986); Shalkhauser v. Beach, 14 Ohio Misc. 1, 233 N.E.2d 527 (1968) ("Words of survivorship are usually sufficient to indicate an intent that the statute shall not apply"); In re Estate of Price, 454 P.2d 411 (Wash. 1969) ("then surviving children" bars statute, but dissent would find the language insufficiently clear to avoid statutorily favored result). Cf. Cal. Prob. Code §6147(c). But see In re Estate of Bulger, 586 N.E.2d 673 (Ill. App. 1991) ("to my children . . . or to the survivor or survivors of them" insufficient to overcome antilapse statute provision for issue of child who predeceased testator); Estate of Fitzpatrick, 159 Mich. App. 120, 406 N.W.2d 483 (1987); and cf. UPC §2-603(b)(3) and (4), supra.[3]

20-F.   *D*, a widow, died intestate, leaving a modest estate. She did, however, have two large life insurance policies each payable primarily to her husband, if he survived her (which he did not); alternatively one policy was payable "to my children equally" and the other was payable "in equal shares to my children who survive me." Many years after this "estate planning" was completed by her life insurance agent, *D*'s two grandchildren were born to son, *S*, who died some years later in an automobile accident. *D* has just died, survived by two daughters and the grandchildren. On behalf of the grandchildren and at the suggestion of *D*'s insurance agent,

3. Compare Estate of Taylor, 6 Cal. 2d 855, 428 P.2d 301, 59 Cal. Rptr. 437 (1967), in which the will left decedent's residuary estate to a named beneficiary but provided that if she "predeceases the distribution of my estate" the residue was to go to others. The named beneficiary died during administration, and the trial court found that the executor was aware of her illness and unduly delayed administration of the estate. The California Supreme Court affirmed the lower court's ruling that "vesting cannot be postponed by unreasonable delay in preparing an estate for distribution" and that the beneficiary's interest "vest[ed] at the time distribution should have been made," noting that the decision was in accord with the rule in England and other states, protects testator intentions, and promotes prompt distribution of estates, while finding no merit in the contention that the holding will lead to undesirable uncertainty in the settlement of estates.

S's widow has come to you in the hope that the grandchildren are entitled not only to one-third of *D*'s probate estate but also to a third of the insurance proceeds.

(a) How would you advise her under the antilapse statute of your state? Under the Uniform Probate Code? Cf. Dollar Sav. & Trust Co. v. Turner, 39 Ohio St. 3d 182, 529 N.E.2d 1261 (1988), and In re Button's Estate, 79 Wash. 2d 849, 400 P.2d 731 (unusual extensions of antilapse statutes to revocable inter vivos trusts).

(b) Alternatively, might a claim by the grandchildren have a better chance under the pretermitted heir statute of your state or one like UPC §2-302?

Cf. West v. Coogler, supra this chapter; Miller v. First Natl. Bank & Trust Co., 637 P.2d 75 (Okla. 1981) (pour-over will incorporated receptacle trust by reference, subjecting it to statute invalidating *will* provisions in favor of an ex-spouse following divorce); and Clymer v. Mayo, 473 N.E.2d 1084 (Mass. 1985) (like *Miller*, applied statute revoking will provision for ex-spouse to inter vivos trust). More common is the view expressed in Williams v. Gatling, 542 N.E.2d 121 (Ill. App. 1989), in which the administrator of a divorced man's estate sought to recover life insurance and employee stock ownership plan proceeds, of which the decedent's former wife was named beneficiary. The administrator had urged the court to rule "that divorce automatically revokes the designation of beneficiary" in a manner similar to an Illinois statute applicable to devises to a former spouse in a will executed before the divorce. The court responded: "[W]e are not persuaded by any argument that we should extend . . . the Probate Act to . . . a contract," adding that "[s]uch an argument is properly directed, instead, to the legislature."

20-G.   *T*'s will bequeathed "the residue of my estate in equal shares to *A*, *B*, and *C*." After execution of the will but before *T*'s death, *C* died leaving no issue. *A*, *B*, and *C* were all nephews of *T* but are not his next of kin. What happens to the share that would have been *C*'s had he survived *T*? Consider the cases that follow.

Would your answer be affected: (a) if *T*'s residuary bequest had read "one-third to *A*, one-third to *B*, and one-third to *C*"? (b) if the bequest had been "to my nephews, *A*, *B*, and *C*, in equal shares"? (c) if the bequest had been simply "to my nephews equally"?

In re MURPHY'S ESTATE
157 Cal. 63, 106 P. 230 (1910)

[Denis Murphy's will provided for the residue of his estate to be "equally divided among the four children of my late sister Catherine C. Flynn, deceased; that is to say: I give [the residue] to Timothy J. Flynn, William D. Flynn, Mary Jane Logan and Kate I. Prendergast." William

D. Flynn died without issue before the testator's death. In petitioning for distribution of the estate, the executors alleged that the residue was left to the sister's children as members of a class and that the whole residue should be divided among the three remaining children as the sole surviving members of the class. Certain other nieces and nephews of the testator, claiming to be among his heirs at law, answered that the testator died intestate as to the portion of his estate left to William D. Flynn and that they were entitled to participate in the distribution thereof. The court found that the intention was to devise the residue to the children of the sister as a class, and the contesting heirs appealed.]

LORIGAN, J. . . .

It must be conceded upon this appeal that under the testamentary clause in question the devise to William D. Flynn lapsed upon his death without leaving lineal descendants, before the testator (Civ. Code, §1343), and that as to the portion of the estate devised to him the testator died intestate, unless from the clause in the will creating the devise in which he was to participate, considered by itself, it is apparent that the testator intended the devise of the residue of his estate to go to the children of his sister Catherine as a class, or that such intention appears from extraneous evidence properly admissible to disclose it. While the lower court reached the conclusion that the devise in question was to a class consisting of the children of the deceased sister of testator who might survive him, we are of the opinion, in the light of the established rules of construction and authorities, that this conclusion was not justified either from the express terms of the devise itself or aided by extrinsic evidence. . . .

It is not contended by the respondents that the clause . . . [creates a] joint tenancy, nor do they predicate their right to take the whole devise as survivors by reason of any expressly created joint tenancy. They base their claim solely on the ground that the devise, while not in terms creating a joint tenancy, still is a devise to a class — the children of the deceased sister of testator — and that under a well-recognized rule of law, where a devise is made to a class, the death of one of the class prior to the death of the testator does not have the effect of causing the legacy to lapse, but those of the class who survive the testator take the whole devise. The rule contended for by respondents is correct, but we cannot agree with them, or the trial court, in the conclusion that either the terms of the devise disclose an intention on the part of the testator to devise to a class, or that, accepting the extraneous testimony admitted as bearing on his intention, it discloses any such intention. As to a gift to a class, the rule is stated as follows: "In legal contemplation a gift to a class is a gift of an aggregate sum to a body of persons uncertain in number at the time of the gift, to be ascertained at a future time, who are all to take in equal or some other definite proportions, the share of each being dependent for its amount upon the ultimate number." Jarman on Wills

(6th Ed.) §232. . . . Tested under this rule, there is nothing in the devise which would indicate that the intention of the testator was that the devisees should take as a class, or in any other way than as individuals, and under our Code provision as tenants in common. There is nothing on the face of the devise indicating any uncertainty in the number of persons who were to take the property, or that they were to be ascertained at a future time, or that the share of the residuary estate which the devisees were ultimately to have was to be determined as to the amount by the number of those who would survive the testator. All the persons who are to take were specifically named and the share of each was designated. In fact, it is not only quite apparent that under the rule relied on this devise cannot be said to contain any of the elements which should characterize a gift to a class, but the plain impression which one would receive by reading the clause is that the testator intended to give to each individual an equal portion of his estate. It is true that the testator uses language in the clause of his will which would, if it stood alone, amount to a devise to a class. This would be the result if the devise had been to "the four children of my late sister Catherine" without further words. But here the terms of the bequest — the designation of the number of the children, followed by a repeated and express devise to them by name and in an equal share — cannot be ignored so as to make the other words in the will constitute a class.

And in determining whether a devise is to a class or to individuals great importance is attached in the solution of the question to the fact that the gift is to the devisees nominatim and that the particular share they shall each receive is mentioned, and, when this appears, the bequest is held to constitute a gift and devise individually as tenants in common, and not as a devise to a class. . . . But, assuming, however, that the language used in the clause in question is capable of two different legal meanings resulting from the testator devising his estate to the four children of his late sister, followed by other words of express devise to each of the children by name and in equal proportions, still this mention of them by name and a devise to them in equal shares will control the description of them as children of his deceased sister. If words, which, standing alone, would be effectual to create a class, are followed by equally operative words of devise to devisees by name and in definite proportions, the law infers from the designation by name and mention of the share each is to take that the devisees are to take individually and as tenants in common, and that the descriptive portion of the clause (children of a deceased sister) is intended merely as matter of identification. . . .

It is not pretended that there are any other provisions of the will bearing on the subject, and the only circumstances appearing from the extrinsic evidence are that the testator had lived with his sister . . . ; that he had a deep affection for these four children and took great interest in them and in their welfare; also, that he had other nieces and nephews not mentioned in his will. . . . All that this evidence discloses is just what the clause of the will does. It furnishes a reason generally why the testator devised his estate to these four devisees in preference to his other nieces and nephews. . . . Giving this evidence the greatest force that can be claimed for it, it discloses at most that the intention of the testator was just as compatible with the devise to these children individually as to them as a class. [Therefore] we are still remitted to the application of the general rule that when in a devise a class and individuals are both mentioned, and nothing appears from other clauses of the will or extraneous evidence requiring a different construction, the devise will be construed as one to devisees individually and not to them collectively — to them as tenants in common and not to them as survivors of a class.

Nor is the claim of respondents that the devise should be held to be one to a class strengthened by invoking the canon of construction that such an interpretation should be given to a will as will prevent intestacy as to any portion of the testator's estate. . . . [A] canon of interpretation applicable to prevent intestacy cannot be invoked to set aside plain rules of law declaring the legal meaning and effect to be given to language used in such a devise as is here under consideration. . . .

Under the law, that clause must be construed as a devise to the devisees individually and as tenants in common. By it each devisee was given one-fourth of the residue of the testator's estate, and, had all lived, each would have been entitled to that proportion on distribution. One of the devisees, William D. Flynn, having died prior to the testator, the devise of one-fourth of the residue of the estate to him lapsed. No provision being made in the will otherwise disposing of this portion of his estate, the testator died intestate as to it and it vested in his heirs at law, and should have been distributed to them and not to the surviving devisees as a class.

The decree of distribution is reversed.

In the *Murphy* case, assume that the property of the testator minus other bequests and devises amounted to $100,000 before debts and expenses. Assume further that the debts of the estate were $5,000 and that the expense of administration (including such of the costs of litigating the above case as were charged to the estate) were $15,000. How much would each of the three surviving residuary legatees be entitled to take under the will and how much would actually pass intestate?

Similar to *Murphy* is Brown v. Leadley, 81 Ill. App. 3d 504, 401 N.E.2d 599 (1980) ("to my children, to wit: [four names], in equal shares" held not a class gift). Contrast with *Murphy* (which is now superseded by Cal. Prob. Code §6148) the opinion and note case that follow; in particular, note the judicial method involved in these two opinions.

In re SLACK TRUST
126 Vt. 37, 220 A.2d 472 (1966)

BARNEY, J.

A residuary legatee predeceased the testator, John T. Slack, without issue. On distribution of the estate the share of the deceased residuary legatee, Ruth Merritt Waite, was decreed to the remaining residuary legatees, or their representatives or estates, as part of the residue of the estate. The widow and certain heirs challenged this distribution, asserting that a lapsed residual legacy should pass as intestate property.

Almost every jurisdiction that has dealt with the problem has announced its allegiance to the rule declaring that a lapsed legacy of part of the residue shall pass as intestate property. Other than its large numerical following, this rule admittedly has little to recommend it. Indeed, some of the more devastating criticisms of the rule have come from courts who declare "stare decisis" to be their only ground for following it. In Oliver v. Wells, 254 N.Y. 451, 457-458, 176 N.E. 676, Justice Cardozo characterized it "[as] a technical rule, reluctantly enforced by courts when tokens are not at hand to suggest an opposite intention." . . . In re Dunster, (1909) 1 Ch. 103, suggests that the rule defeats the testator's intent in almost every case in which it is applied. As might be expected, the rule has been generally criticized in law reviews and treatises. . . .

The policy supporting the rule is not easy to determine. . . . How [a contrary rule would be] substantially different from increasing the share [of residuary legatees] by allowing lapsed specific bequests to pass under the residuary clause is difficult to see. Yet, this is an accepted rule. . . . And to say that because a lapsed legacy is already in the residue it cannot "fall into" the residue but must "fall out" of the will is confusing simile for substance. . . .

This approach is supported by a cardinal principle reiterated in our own cases that intestacy will not be presumed. . . . The majority rule overrides this major consideration. As a consequence, courts that operate under this rule constantly strain to supply exceptions in order that its application will be unnecessary. This certainly suggests that, as a rule, it is founded on a very shaky premise. It seems far sounder to operate under a rule which is acceptable according to its terms, rather than its exceptions. . . .

It should be borne in mind that this is a rule of construction only, adopted because it appears to comport most closely with the presumed intent of the testator in the usual case. It is at all times subject to contrary expressions of intent in the instrument by a testator. . . . Until this case, this court had not ruled on the issue. . . . However, by this case, we do now adopt the rule that lapsed residuary legacies become part of the residue and pass with the balance of it, being content to let a general residuary clause perform its "dragnet" function unless a contrary disposition is demonstrably applicable, which is not this case.

In fact, not only is there no contrary intent on the part of this testator discoverable, but the presumption against intestacy is reinforced by the provisions of his will. One provision specifically excludes a particular relative who would be entitled to take under intestate succession, and the language establishing the trust of the residue broadly defines it as "all the residue of my estate of every kind and nature." Although such "tokens" are unnecessary to the application of the rule as we adopt it, they confirm the presumption that here, as in the usual case, this rule in fact truly carries out the testator's intent.

Since the adoption of this rule fully confirms the judgment and decree rendered below, other questions need not be considered.

Judgment affirmed. Let the result be certified.

See also Corbett v. Skaggs, 11 Kan. 380, 382-384, 207 P. 819, 820-822 (1922). In holding that the lapsed portion of the residue passes to the other residuary legatees, the court stated:

> It is a rule of the English common law . . . that, on the death before the testator, of one of several residuary legatees (who do not take . . . as members of a class) his share goes, not to the others, but to whoever would have inherited the property in case no will had been made. . . . In one state the court has held to the contrary [and in] two states the rule has been abrogated by statute. . . . The rule has been severely criticized even by judges and textwriters, who have felt constrained to follow it. . . .
>
> > The rule thus established does not commend itself to sound reasoning, and is a sacrifice of the settled presumption that a testator does not mean to die intestate as to a portion of his estate, and also of his plain actual intent. . . . If the question were new in this state, speaking for myself I should not hesitate to reject the English rule as wrong in principle and subversive of the great canon of construction, the carrying out of the intent of the testator.

Gray's Estate, 146 Pa. 67, 74, 75, 23 A. 205, 206.

[Although there are facts from which an intention contrary to the usual rule can be inferred, we] prefer to rest our decision on the general principle [rather] than upon exceptional features of the particular case.

We regard the rule that lapsed shares of deceased residuary legatees shall be treated as intestate property as in direct conflict with the one . . . that the actual purpose of the testator . . . must be given effect. . . . The statement sometimes made in support of the [usual rule in other states] — that the share of a deceased residuary legatee cannot fall into the residue, because it is itself a part of the residue — appears rather to play upon words than to point out any real difficulty.

UNIFORM PROBATE CODE

§2-604.   *Failure of Testamentary Provision.*

(a) Except as provided in Section 2-603, a devise, other than a residuary devise, that fails for any reason becomes a part of the residue.

(b) Except as provided in Section 2-603, if the residue is devised to two or more persons, the share of a residuary devisee that fails for any reason passes to the other residuary devisee, or to other residuary devisees in proportion to the interest of each in the remaining part of the residue.

PROBLEM

20-H.   S bequeathed the residue of her estate "to my brothers equally." S had four brothers: B, who survived her; X, who was dead when S's will was executed; and Y and Z, both of whom died after S made her will but before her death. Z left no issue. The entire residuary estate is claimed by B, while a nephew (the only descendant of X) and a niece (Y's only issue) claim, respectively, one-third and one-half of the estate.

(a) Explain the basis for each of these claims under the applicable statute, which provides:

> If a devisee or legatee dies during the lifetime of the testator, the testamentary disposition to him lapses, unless an intention appears from the will to substitute another in his place; but, when property is devised or bequeathed to blood kindred of the testator and when such devisee or legatee dies before the testator, leaving lineal descendants, or is dead at the time the will is executed, leaving lineal descendants who survive the testator, such legacy or devise does not lapse but such descendants take the property in the same manner as the devisee or legatee would have done had he survived the testator.

(b) How would you argue on behalf of each of the claimants in an appeal before the highest court of your state if the excerpt below is the opinion of the intermediate appellate court?

> At common law if a testamentary gift is to a class and a member of the class dies before the death of the testator, his interest goes to the surviving members of the class unless the testator has expressed a contrary intention. Unquestionably our statute applies to testamentary gifts to named beneficiaries. However, the question is whether it applies to testamentary gifts to a class as well. A majority of states hold that a non-lapse statute does not apply to a member of a class who was dead at the execution of the will, based upon the common-law principle that a gift to a beneficiary who is dead when the will is executed is void, and no question of lapse arises. On the other hand, a majority of states hold that, in the absence of express provision on the point, non-lapse statutes apply to class members who die after the execution of the will but prior to the death of the testa-

tor, on the premise that the gift will pass to those the testator would most likely have wished substituted for the deceased class member. States which hold to a contrary view do so on the basis that a gift to members of a class cannot lapse so long as any member of the class survives the testator.

In this jurisdiction, statutes in derogation of the common law must be strictly construed. But even strictly construing our antilapse statute [above], it seems to us that the legislature intended that statute to be applied to class gifts to blood relatives, at least those alive when the will was executed.

A more difficult question is whether the statute should be applied to one who was deceased when the will was executed — a gift which, at common law, was void, and hence no question of lapse was presented. The antilapse statute, being directly in derogation of this principle of the common law, must be strictly construed. There is nothing in the will to suggest that the testatrix wanted to provide for her then-deceased brother or his descendants. It would be more logical to infer, when a testator provides for a class of his relatives, that he intends to include only his living relatives. We therefore align ourselves with the courts which have held that antilapse statutes do not apply in favor of members of a class who died before the execution of the will in question.

For the foregoing reasons we affirm the Chancellor's holding excluding the child of the testatrix's brother (X) who was deceased at the time of the execution of her will; but we reverse the holding excluding the child of her brother (Y) who died before her but after she executed her will.

Adapted from Drafts v. Drafts, 114 So. 2d 473 (Fla. App. 1959).

A dissenting opinion (also adapted from *Drafts*) states:

Non-lapse statutes are enacted solely to prevent lapse of testamentary gifts, but a gift to a class is legally incapable of lapsing so long as any member of the class survives the testator. It is for this reason that non-lapse statutes have been held not to apply to class gifts unless made so by clear and unambiguous statutory language. A testator is free to amend his will to include descendants of a deceased class member if he cares to do so. Failure to do so should be construed as evidencing a testamentary intent to confine class gifts to those who survive the testator. To hold otherwise would require that we read into the statute language which cannot be found there. To do this would constitute judicial legislation of the rankest sort, a practice in which I am not willing to indulge.

GIANOLI v. GABACCIA
82 Nev. 108, 412 P.2d 439 (1966)

[John Data's will bequeathed $5,000 "to each of my brothers and sisters" and left the residue of his estate "to my nephews and nieces, share and share alike." At the time the will was executed, one brother and one sister were dead; subsequently but prior to Data's death, two other brothers and another sister died. Only one sister survived Data. In petitioning for distribution, the personal representative proposed distributing $5,000 to the sister and $5,000 to the issue of each of the two brothers and one sister who were alive when Data executed his will, based on NRS 133.200 providing: "When any estate shall be devised or bequeathed to any child or other relation of the testator and the devisee or legatee shall die before the testator, leaving lineal descendants, such descendants, in the absence of a provision in the will to the contrary, shall take the estate so given by the will in the same manner as the devisee or legatee would have done if he had survived the testator."]

ZENOFF, D.J. . . .

The lower court [found that] the will was ambiguous and that NRS 133.200 did not apply. We disagree. . . .

There is nothing in either [the $5,000 bequests or the residuary clause] of Data's will which creates . . . an ambiguity. We therefore are restricted to the writing alone. . . .

We first consider the two brothers and sister of Data who were alive at the time of the will's execution but predeceased Data. At common law, their bequests would be said to "lapse" and thereby fail. Presuming this result contrary to a testator's intent, Nevada, as almost all other states, enacted an "anti-lapse statute." . . . Data's brothers and sisters come within this protection "in the absence of a provision in the will to the contrary." NRS 133.200.

It is argued that the second paragraph refers to the brothers and sisters as a "class" and our anti-lapse statute should not apply to "class" gifts. We agree with the overwhelming weight of authority that an antilapse statute does apply to class gifts. . . .

Next, it is argued that Data intended for the anti-lapse statute not to apply. Such intent, of course, would control, "but to render the statute inoperative a contrary intent on the part of the testator must be plainly indicated." Nowhere is such a "plain intent" expressed within Data's will; nor did he even state "I give . . . to each of my *surviving* brothers and sisters. . . ." The fact that in the third paragraph he bequeathed his residue to his nieces and nephews "share and share alike" does not influence who takes "through an entirely separate channel, . . . an entirely different right" under the second paragraph.

Finally, we consider the status of the brother and sister who predeceased the execution of Data's will. At common law, their bequest would fail as "void." Our anti-lapse statute only speaks of a testamentary beneficiary who "shall die before the testator;" there is no specification as to how *long* "before," nor is there any express reference within the statute to "lapse" or "void" bequests or their distinction. However, "[i]t seems obvious that the [anti-lapse statute] was motivated by the purpose to protect the kindred of the testator and by a belief that a more fair and equitable result would be assured if a defeated legacy were disposed of by law to the lineal descendants of the legatees or devisees selected by the testator." Accepting this rationale, as have the majority of courts, we see little reason to not equally apply it to void as well as lapsed bequests and devises. . . .

Reversed. . . .

PROBLEM

20-I. *D* had four children, one of whom (*C*) died two months before the execution of *D*'s will, leaving a son, *G*, who survived *D*. *G* seeks a construction of *D*'s will and claims the right to participate in the distribution of her estate. *D*'s will provides in relevant part:

> I hereby give, devise and bequeath all the rest, remainder, and residue of my estate and hereby direct that the same be divided into as many equal parts as I shall have children surviving me; and I hereby give one of such equal parts to each of my children me surviving, share and share alike; with the exception that, in apportioning the share that would go to my beloved child *J*, the sum of $40,000 be deducted therefrom, my reason being that both he and his family are well provided for.
>
> In the event that any child or children of mine shall predecease me, then it is my wish and I hereby direct that the share or shares that he or they would have become entitled to, had they survived me, shall go to the child or children of such deceased child or children, per stirpes and not per capita.

How would you argue in support of *G*'s claim to a share of the residue or of $40,000? How would you expect his claim to be resisted by *D*'s three surviving children? What result would you expect? Why? Cf. In re Eisner's Estate, 34 Misc. 2d 662, 228 N.Y.S.2d 29 (1962).

Table of Cases

Index

Note: Where page references are not in numerical sequence, first references are to material most directly in point.

Abatement
  in general, 969–971
  for share of spouse or pretermitted heir, 97, 105
Acceleration and sequestration. *See also* Spouse
  by spouse's election, 105–107
Accounting. *See also* Fiduciaries; Principal and income
  effect of, 745–748
  in court, 739–742, 746
  nonjudicial, 745–746
Acknowledgment. *See* Execution of wills
Ademption
  by extinction, 953–961
  by satisfaction, 961–969
Administration of decedents' estates. *See also* Fiduciaries
  ancillary, 613–615, 40
  devices to avoid (will substitutes), 236–302, 317–319, 379–422
  function and necessity, 558–581
  notice, 604–612
  opening of, 582–584, 616–617, 140
  procedural matters, 584–612
Administration of trusts. *See also* Fiduciaries
  notice, 597–604
  supervision of courts, 417–418, 583, 415–417
Administrators and executors. *See also* Fiduciaries
  procedural matters, 584–612
  purposes and functions, 559, 314–319
Adopted children
  inheritance by, from, and through, 62–68
  virtual adoption, 66–68
Advancements, 84–87
Alienation. *See* Modification and termination of trusts; Transfer of beneficiary's interest
Alimony. *See* Support
Ambiguities. *See* Interpretation and construction
Apportionment of taxes. *See* Principal and income; Taxes

Assignment of expectancy, 87–89. *See also* Transfer of beneficiary's interest
Attestation. *See* Execution of wills

Beneficiaries. *See also* Bequests and devises; Charitable gifts and trusts; Discretionary trusts and powers; Fiduciaries; Modification and termination of trusts; Transfer of beneficiary's interest
  acceptance and renunciation by, 437–446
  animal as (honorary trusts), 333–334, 523–524
  charity as, 118–119, 328–329, 513–557
  class as, 334–339
  definiteness and necessity of, 326–329
  nature of interest, 423–471
  power to terminate or modify trust, 478–493
  who can be, 327–328
Bequests and devises *See also* Abatement; Ademption; Assignment of expectancy; Charitable gifts and trusts; Interpretation and construction; Transfer of beneficiary's interest
  after-acquired property, 159–160
  class gift
    anti-lapse statute, 974–977
    closing of class, 972–973
    lapse, 973–987
  classification (specific, general, demonstrative, residual), 951–952, 863
  exoneration, 971–972
  income, increase and interest, 863–873, 884, 874–879
  lapse, 973–987
  renunciation (disclaimer), 438–446
  retainer, 972
  tax apportionment. *See* Taxes

997